NINTH EDITION

STRATEGIC MANAGEMENT

CONCEPTS & CASES

FRED R. DAVID

Francis Marion University

Prentice
Hall

Upper Saddle River, New Jersey 07458

To Joy, Forest, Byron, and Meredith—my wife and children—
for their encouragement and love.

Strategic management: concepts and cases / Fred R. David.—9th ed.
    p. cm.
Includes bibliographical references and indexes.
ISBN 0-13-047912-8
1. Strategic planning—Case studies. 2. Strategic planning. I. Title.
HD30.28.D385 2002
658.4'012—dc21   2002031173

Acquisitions Editor: Michael Ablassmeir
Editor-in-Chief: Jeff Shelstad
Managing Editor (Editorial): Jennifer Glennon
Assistant Editor: Melanie Olsen
Senior Marketing Manager: Shannon Moore
Media Project Manager: Michele Faranda
Managing Editor (Production): Judy Leale
Production Editor: Marcela Maslanczuk
Production Assistant: Joseph DeProspero
Permissions Coordinator: Suzanne Grappi
Associate Director, Manufacturing: Vincent Scelta
Production Manager: Arnold Vila
Design Manager: Maria Lange
Designer: Steven Frim
Interior Design: Steven Frim/Donna Wickes
Cover Design: Steven Frim
Cover Illustration: Roger Allyn Lee/Superstock
Manager, Print Production: Christy Mahon
Composition: Black Dot Group
Cover Printer: Phoenix
Printer/Binder: R.R. Donnelley – Willard

Credits and acknowledgments borrowed from other sources and reproduced, with permission, in
this textbook appear on appropriate page within text.

Pearson Education LTD.
Pearson Education Australia PTY, Limited
Pearson Education Singapore, Pte. Ltd
Pearson Education North Asia Ltd
Pearson Education, Canada, Ltd
Pearson Educación de Mexico, S.A. de C.V.
Pearson Education–Japan
Pearson Education Malaysia, Pte. Ltd

10 9 8 7 6 5 4 3 2 1
ISBN 0-13-047912-8

BRIEF CONTENTS

CONTENTS

PART 2 ▶
Strategy Formulation 54

CHAPTER 2
THE BUSINESS MISSION 54

CHAPTER 3
THE EXTERNAL ASSESSMENT 78

CHAPTER 4
THE INTERNAL ASSESSMENT 118

STRATEGIC MANAGEMENT CASES

PREFACE

The global recession and war on terrorism has ushered in a radically different and more complex business world than it was just two years ago, when the previous edition of this text was published. E-commerce has changed the nature of business to its core. Thousands of strategic alliances and partnerships were formed in 2000–2002. Hundreds of companies declared bankruptcy, and interest rates fell to their lowest level in fifty years. Downsizing, rightsizing, reengineering, and countless divestitures, acquisitions, and liquidations permanently altered the corporate landscape. Thousands of firms globalized, and thousands more merged in the last two years. Thousands prospered, and yet thousands more failed. Many manufacturers became e-commerce suppliers, and many rival firms became partners. Long-held competitive advantages eroded, and new ones formed. Both the challenges and opportunities facing organizations of all sizes today are greater than ever.

Changes made in this ninth edition are aimed squarely at illustrating the effect of this new world order on strategic-management theory and practice. Changes in this edition are substantial. To survive and prosper in the new millennium, organizations must build and sustain a competitive advantage. This new edition provides up-to-date, state-of-the-art coverage of strategic-management concepts and techniques for achieving a competitive advantage.

Our mission in preparing the ninth edition of *Strategic Management* was "to create the most current, well-written business policy textbook on the market—a book that is exciting and valuable to both students and professors." To achieve this mission, every page has been revamped, updated, and improved. New strategic-management research and practice are incorporated throughout the chapters, and hundreds of new examples abound. There is a new Cohesion Case on American Airlines—2002. A wonderful selection of new cases include such companies as Royal Caribbean, Winn-Dixie, Coors, Hewlett-Packard Corporation, and Best Buy Company. The time basis for all cases included in this edition is 2002, representing the most up-to-date compilation of cases ever assembled in a business policy text.

I believe, along with scores of reviewers, that you will find this edition to be the best ever—and now the best business policy textbook available for communicating both the excitement and value of strategic management. The text is concise and exceptionally well organized. Now published in six different languages—English, Chinese, Spanish; Arabic, Indonesian, and Japanese—this text is the most widely used strategic-planning book in the world.

SPECIAL NOTE TO PROFESSORS

This textbook meets all AACSB guidelines for the business policy and strategic management course at both the graduate and undergraduate levels. Previous editions of this text have been used at more than five hundred colleges and universities. Prentice Hall maintains a separate Web site for this text at **www.prenhall.com/david**. The author maintains the Strategic Management Club Online Web site at **www.strategyclub.com**. Membership is now free to both professors and students.

Although the structure of this edition parallels the last, dramatic improvements have been made in readability, currentness, and coverage. In keeping with the mission "to become the most current, well-written business policy textbook on the market," every page has undergone rethinking and rewriting to streamline, update, and improve the caliber of presentation. A net result of this activity is that every chapter is shorter in length. New concepts and practices in strategic management are presented in a style that is clear, focused, and relevant.

CHAPTER THEMES

Three themes permeate all chapters in this edition and contribute significantly to making this text timely, informative, exciting, and valuable. A new boxed insert for each theme and substantial new narrative appear in each chapter. The three themes follow.

1. Global Factors Affect Virtually All Strategic Decisions

The global theme is greatly enhanced in this edition because doing business globally has become a necessity, rather than a luxury, in most industries. Nearly all strategic decisions today are affected by global issues and concerns. There is substantial new global coverage in each chapter due to growing interdependence among countries and companies worldwide. The dynamics of political, economic, and cultural differences across countries directly affect strategic management decisions. Doing business globally is more risky and complex than ever before. The global theme is targeted at illustrating how organizations today can effectively do business in the new millennium.

2. E-Commerce Is a Vital Strategic Management Tool

The e-commerce theme is deeply integrated throughout the chapters in response to immense e-commerce opportunities and threats facing organizations today. Almost all products can now be purchased over the Internet. Business-to-business e-commerce is ten times greater even than business-to-consumer e-commerce. The accelerating use of the Internet to gather, analyze, send, and receive information has changed the way strategic decisions are made. Since the last edition, literally millions of companies have established World Wide Web sites and are conducting e-commerce internationally.

3. Preserving the Natural Environment Is a Vital Strategic Issue

Unique to strategic-management texts, the natural environment theme is strengthened in this edition in order to promote and encourage firms to conduct operations in an environmentally sound manner. Countries worldwide have enacted laws to curtail firms from polluting streams, rivers, the air, land, and sea. Environmental concerns are a new point of contention in World Trade Organization (WTO) policies and practices. The strategic efforts of both companies and countries to preserve the natural environment are described in this edition. Respect for the natural environment has become an important concern for consumers, companies, society, and the AACSB.

TIME-TESTED FEATURES—CHAPTERS

This edition continues many of the time-tested chapter features and content that have made this text so successful over the last two decades. Trademarks of this text strengthened in this edition are as follows:

Chapters: Time-Tested Features

- The text meets AACSB guidelines which support a practitioner orientation rather than a theory/research approach. This text supports that effort by taking a skills-oriented approach to developing a mission statement, performing an external audit, conducting an internal assessment, and formulating, implementing, and evaluating strategies.
- The global theme permeating all chapters couches strategic-management concepts in a global perspective.
- A simple, integrative strategic-management model appears in all chapters and on the inside front cover of the text.
- A Cohesion Case (American Airlines—2002) appears after Chapter 1 and is revisited at the end of each chapter. This case allows students to apply strategic-management concepts and techniques to a real organization as chapter material is covered. This integrative (cohesive) approach readies students for case analysis.
- End-of-chapter Experiential Exercises effectively apply concepts and techniques in a challenging, meaningful, and enjoyable manner. Eighteen exercises apply text material to the Cohesion Case; ten apply textual material to a college or university; another ten send students into the business world to explore important strategy topics. The exercises are relevant, interesting, and contemporary.
- Excellent pedagogy, including Notable Quotes and Objectives to open each chapter, and Key Terms, Current Readings, Discussion Questions, and Experiential Exercises to close each chapter.
- Excellent coverage of business ethics aimed at more than meeting AACSB standards.
- Excellent coverage of strategy implementation issues such as corporate culture, organizational structure, marketing concepts, and financial tools and techniques.
- A systematic, analytical approach presented in Chapter 6, including matrices such as the TOWS, BCG, IE, GRAND, SPACE, and QSPM.
- The chapter material is again published in four-color.
- The Web site **www.prenhall.com/david** provides chapter and case updates, an online study guide, and support materials.

KEY CHAPTER IMPROVEMENTS

- Dramatically improved coverage of global issues and concerns has been woven into every chapter.
- Mostly new E-Commerce Perspective boxed inserts appear in each chapter to portray the increasing reliance upon e-commerce by both large and small firms.

- Mostly new Global Perspective boxed inserts are provided in each chapter to support the expanded global theme.
- Mostly new Natural Environment Perspective boxed inserts appear in each chapter to show strategic relevance of this issue to business.
- All new examples are provided in every chapter.
- New research is integrated into every chapter, with new current readings at the end of each chapter.
- More than one hundred new Web site addresses are provided throughout the chapters in a new Visit the Net feature.

 ## TIME-TESTED FEATURES—CASES

This edition continues many of the time-tested case features and content that have made this text so successful over the last two decades. Trademarks of this text strengthened in this edition are as follows:

- The 2002 timeframe for cases offers the most current set in any business policy text on the market.
- The cases focus on well-known firms in the news making strategic changes. All cases are undisguised and most are exclusively written for this text to reflect current strategic-management problems and practices.
- The cases feature a great mix of small business, international, and not-for-profit firms organized conveniently by industry.
- All cases have been class tested to ensure that they are interesting, challenging, and effective for illustrating strategic-management concepts.
- Almost all cases provide complete financial information about the firm and an organizational chart.
- Customized inclusion of cases to comprise a tailored text is available to meet the special needs of some professors.
- A split-paperback version including only cases is available.
- An outstanding ancillary package, including a comprehensive *Instructor's Manual* and an elaborate *Case Instructor's Manual*. An extensive transparency package, color case videos, PowerPoint diskettes, and computerized test bank come free with adoption.

Changes in the Cases

- Nine brand-new, yearend 2001 cases focusing on companies in the news appear exclusively for the first time in this text. The cases are:

American Airline—The New Cohesion Case	Best Buy Company
Winn-Dixie	Hewlett-Packard
Coors	First State Bank of Roans Prairie
Royal Caribbean	US Airways
Strictly Roots Natural Hair Salon	

- Thirty-two fully updated cases from the last edition are included as follows:

Reader's Digest Association	Lockheed Martin Corporation
Reebok International	Dell Computer Corporation
E*Trade	Limited Brands
eBay	Wal-Mart Stores
Amazon.com	Target Corporation

Mandalay Resort Group
Harrah's Entertainment
The Audubon Institute
Riverbanks Zoological Park and Botanical
    Garden
The Classic Car Club of America
Carnival Corporation
Southwest Airlines Co.
Central United Methodist Church
Elkins Lake Baptist Church
Harley-Davidson
Winnebago Industries

Avon Products
Revlon
UST
Pilgrim's Pride Corporation
H.J. Heinz Company
Hershey Foods Corporation
The Boeing Company
Stryker Corporation
Biomet
Playboy Enterprises
Nike

- The new mix of forty-one cases includes a nice balance of twenty-one service companies and twenty manufacturing companies
- The new mix of cases includes three purely e-commerce cases to support the new e-commerce theme. The cases are E*Trade, eBay, and Amazon.
- The new mix of cases includes eight small-business cases and six not-for-profit cases.
- The new mix of cases include thirty-two "international" companies.

ANCILLARY MATERIALS

- *Instructor's Resource CD-ROM.* Includes improved PowerPoint slides for both cases and concepts, offering professors easy lecture outlines for in-class presentations. Chapter headings and topics are highlighted on up to thirty PowerPoint slides per chapter. The *Instructor's Manual* and *Test Manager Software* are also included.
- *Case Instructor's Manual.* Provides a comprehensive teacher's note for all forty-one cases. The teachers' notes feature detailed analyses, classroom discussion questions with answers, an external and internal assessment, specific recommendations, strategy implementation material, and an epilogue for each case. Each teachers' note is also provided on a PowerPoint slide for convenience to the professor.
- *Instructor's Manual with Test Item File.* Provides lecture notes, teaching tips, answers to all end-of-chapter Experiential Exercises and Review Questions, additional Experiential Exercises not in the text, sample course syllabi, and a Test Item file with multiple-choice, true/false, and essay questions.
- *Twenty Color Case Video Segments.* To accompany the Cohesion Case, a color video prepared by American Airlines is available to adopters free of charge. Shown near the beginning of the course, the American Airlines video can arouse students' interest in studying the Cohesion Case and completing Experiential Exercises that apply chapter material to this case. In addition, a collection of nineteen other color case video segments is available free of charge. The segments average fifteen minutes each and were professionally prepared by firms used in cases in this text.
- *The Prentice Hall Companion Website.* **www.prenhall.com/david** features an interactive and exciting online student study guide. Students can access multiple-choice, true/false, and Internet-based essay questions that accompany each chapter in the text. Objective questions are scored online, and incorrect answers are keyed to the text for student review. Supplements are available for faculty download on the password–protected side of the Web site.
- *Standard Web CT–Free to Adoptors.* Standard Web CT, an online course from Prentice Hall, features Companion Website and *Test Manager Software* content in an easy-to-use system. Developed by educators for educators and their students,

the online content and tools feature the most advanced educational technology and instructional design available today. The rich set of materials, communication tools, and course management resources can be easily customized either to enhance a traditional course or to create the entire course online.

- *Printed and Computerized Test Bank.* The test bank for this text includes true/false questions, multiple-choice questions, and essay questions for the text chapters. Answers to all objective questions are provided. The test questions given in the *Instructor's Manual* are also available on computerized text software to facilitate preparing and grading tests.

- *Blackboard.* Easy to use, Blackboard's single template and tools make it easy to create, manage, and use online course materials. Instructors can create online courses using the Blackboard tools, which include design, communication, testing, and course management tools. For more information, please visit our Web site located at **http://www.prenhall.com/blackboard**.

- *CourseCompass.* This customizable, interactive online course management tool powered by Blackboard provides the most intuitive teaching and learning environment available. Instructor's can communicate with students, distribute course material, and access student progress online. For further information, please visit our Web site located at **http://www.prenhall.com/coursecompass**.

 ## SPECIAL NOTE TO STUDENTS

Welcome to business policy. This is a challenging and exciting course that will allow you to function as the owner or chief executive officer of different organizations. Your major task in this course will be to make strategic decisions and to justify those decisions through oral and written communication. Strategic decisions determine the future direction and competitive position of an enterprise for a long time. Decisions to expand geographically or to diversify are examples of strategic decisions.

Strategic decision making occurs in all types and sizes of organizations, from General Motors to a small hardware store. Many people's lives and jobs are affected by strategic decisions, so the stakes are very high. An organization's very survival is often at stake. The overall importance of strategic decisions makes this course especially exciting and challenging. You will be called on in business policy to demonstrate how your strategic decisions could be successfully implemented.

In this course, you can look forward to making strategic decisions both as an individual and as a member of a team. No matter how hard employees work, an organization is in real trouble if strategic decisions are not made effectively. Doing the right things (effectiveness) is more important than doing things right (efficiency). For example, Lucent Technologies was prosperous during the 1990s but ineffective strategies in the years 2000–2002 led to massive losses, the ouster of chief executive Richard McGinn, an SEC investigation, a debt-rating one notch above junk, and a battle to raise any turnaround capital. The number of bankruptcies increased 30 percent in 2001, including such well know companies as AMF Bowling, Polaroid cameras, Converse sneakers, Schwinn bicycles, Vlasic pickles, Coleman camping supplies, Chiquita bananas, Sunbeam appliances, Enron, and Burlington Industries. The Houston-based energy firm Enron is the largest U.S. company ever to file for Chapter 11 bankruptcy.

You will have the opportunity in this course to make actual strategic decisions, perhaps for the first time in your academic career. Do not hesitate to take a stand and defend specific strategies that you determine to be the best. The rationale for your strategic decisions will be more important than any actual decision, because no one knows for sure what the best strategy is for a particular organization at a given point in time. This fact accents the subjective, contingency nature of the strategic-management process.

Use the concepts and tools presented in this text, coupled with your own intuition, to recommend strategies that you can defend as being most appropriate for the organizations that you study. You will also need to integrate knowledge acquired in previous business courses. For this reason, business policy is often called a capstone course; you may want to keep this book for your personal library.

This text is practitioner-oriented and applications-oriented. It presents strategic-management concepts that will enable you to formulate, implement, and evaluate strategies in all kinds of profit and nonprofit organizations. The end-of-chapter Experiential Exercises allow you to apply what you've read in each chapter to the American Cohesion Case and to your own university.

Be sure to visit the Strategic Management Club Online Web site at **www.strategy club.com**. The templates and links there will save you time in performing analyses and will make your work look professional. Work hard in policy this semester and have fun. Good luck!

 ## ACKNOWLEDGMENTS

Many persons have contributed time, energy, ideas, and suggestions for improving this text over nine editions. The strength of this text is largely attributed to the collective wisdom, work, and experiences of business policy professors, strategic-management researchers, students, and practitioners. Names of particular individuals whose published research is referenced in the nine edition of this text are listed alphabetically in the Name Index. To all individuals involved in making this text so popular and successful, I am indebted and thankful.

Many special persons and reviewers contributed valuable material and suggestions for this edition. I would like to thank my colleagues and friends at Auburn University, Mississippi State University, East Carolina University, and Francis Marion University. These are universities where I have served on the management faculty. Scores of students and professors at these schools shaped the development of this text. I would like to thank the following reviewers who contributed valuable suggestions for this and earlier editions of this text:

Anthony F. Chelte, Western New England
  College
Leyland M. Lucas, Rutgers University
Joshua D. Martin, Temple University
Bob D. Cutler, Cleveland State University

Cathleen Folker, University of
  Nebraska–Lincoln
Jeffrey J. Bailey, University of Idaho
David Dawley, Florida State University
J. Michael Geringer, California State University

Individuals who develop cases for the North American Case Research Association Meeting, the Midwest Society for Case Research Meeting, the Eastern Casewriters Association Meeting, the European Case Research Association Meeting, and Harvard Case Services are vitally important for continued progress in the field of strategic management. From a research perspective, writing business policy cases represents a valuable scholarly activity among faculty. Extensive research is required to structure business policy cases in a way that exposes strategic issues, decisions, and behavior. Pedagogically, business policy cases are essential for students in learning how to apply concepts, evaluate situations, formulate strategies, and resolve implementation problems. Without a continuous stream of updated business policy cases, the strategic-management course and discipline would lose much of their energy and excitement.

The following individuals wrote cases that were selected for inclusion with this text. These persons helped develop the most current compilation of cases ever assembled with a business policy text:

M. Jill Austin, Middle Tennessee State University

Robert Barrett, Francis Marion University

Alen Badal, The Union Institute

Henry Beam, Western Michigan University

Eugene Bland, Francis Marion University

Donald Bumpass, Sam Houston State University

Jim Camerius, Northern Michigan University

Maria Cruz-Batista, Francis Marion University

Forest David, Mississippi State University

Satish Deshpande, Western Michigan University

Mary Dittman, Francis Marion University

Ronald Earl, Sam Houston State University

Todd Ellison, Francis Marion University

Sandy Durant, Francis Marion University

Will Eskridge, Francis Marion University

Caroline Fisher, Loyola University, New Orleans

Jason Gooch, Sam Houston State University

Margie Goodson, Francis Marion University

Christie Haney, Sam Houston State University

James Harbin, East Texas State University

Lenessa Hawkins, Francis Marion University

Marilyn Helms, Dalton State College

Brian Kinard, Mississippi State University

Gerald Kohers, Sam Houston State University

Kay Lawrimore-Belanger, Francis Marion University

John Marcis, Coastal Carolina University

Bill Middlebrook, Southwest Texas State University

Valerie Muehsam, Sam Houston State University

Paul Reed, Sam Houston State University

John Ross, Southwest Texas State University

Carlisle Sampson, Francis Marion University

Nicole Seminario, Francis Marion University

Amit Shah, Frostburg State University

Robert Shane, Francis Marion University

Matthew Sonfield, Hofstra University

Charles Sterrett, Frostburg State University

Carolyn Stokes, Francis Marion University

John Urbanski, Francis Marion University

Stephanie Wilhelm, Francis Marion University

Anthony Williams, Sam Houston State University

Scores of Prentice Hall employees and salespersons have worked diligently behind the scenes to make this text a leader in the business policy market. I appreciate the continued hard work of all those persons.

I especially appreciate the wonderful work completed by the ninth edition ancillary authors as follows:

Bruce Barringer, *Instructor's Manual*
University of Central Florida

Forest David, *Case Instructor's Manual*
Missippippi State University

Amit Shah, *Test Manager Software and Companion Website Content*

Frostburg State University

Tony Chelte, *PowerPoint Electronic*
Western New England College

Forest David, *Case PowerPoints*
Mississippi State University

I also want to thank you, the reader, for investing the time and effort it took you to read and study this text. As we have entered the new millennium, this book will help you formulate, implement, and evaluate strategies for organizations with which you become associated. I hope you come to share my enthusiasm for the rich subject area of strategic management and for the systematic learning approach taken in this text.

Finally, I want to welcome and invite your suggestions, ideas, thoughts, and comments and questions regarding any part of this text or the ancillary materials. Please call me at 843-661-1431, fax me at 843-661-1432, e-mail me at Fdavid@Fmarion.edu, or write me at the School of Business, Francis Marion University, Florence, South Carolina 29501. I sincerely appreciate and need your input to continually improve this text in future editions. Drawing my attention to specific errors or deficiencies in coverage or exposition will especially be appreciated.

Thank you for using this text.

Fred R. David

	STOCK SYMBOL	STOCK EXCHANGE	TELEPHONE NUMBER	HEADQUARTERS ADDRESS	WEB PAGE ADDRESS
COHESION CASE					
American Airlines	AMR	NY	817-963-1234	4333 Amon Carter Blvd Fort Worth, TX 76155	www.amrcorp.com
NINTH EDITION SERVICE COMPANY CASES					
AIRLINES					
1. Southwest Airlines	LUV	NY	214-792-4908	2702 Love Field Dallas, TX 75235	www.iflyswa.com www.southwest.com
2. US Airways	U	NY	703-872-5009	2345 Crystal Drive Arlington, VA 22227	www.usairways.com
INTERNET COMPANIES					
3. E*Trade	ET	NY	650-331-6000 888-772-3477	4500 Bohannon Dr. Menlo Park, CA 94025	www.etrade.com
4. eBay	EBAY	NASD	408-558-7400	2005 Hamilton Ave. San Jose, CA 95125	www.ebay.com
5. Amazon	AMZN	NASD	206-622-2335	1516 2nd Avenue Seattle, WA 98101	www.amazon.com
RETAILERS					
6. Limited Brands	LTD	NY	614-415-7000	3 Limited Parkway Columbus, Ohio 43216	www.limited.com
7. Wal-Mart Stores, Inc.	WMT	NY	501-273-4000 501-277-6921	702 SW Eighth St. Bentonville, Arkansas 72716-8611	www.wal-mart.com
8. Target Corporation	TGT	NY	612-370-6948	777 Nicollet Mall Minneapolis, Minnesota 55402-2055	www.target.com
9. Best Buy Company	BBY	NY	952-947-2422	Eden Prairie, Minnesota	www.bestbuy.com
HOTEL AND GAMING					
10. Mandalay Resort Group	MBG	NY	702-734-0410 702-632-7777	3950 Las Vegas Blv Las Vegas, NV 89119	www.mandalay resortgroup.com
11. Harrah's Entertainment	HET	NY	901-762-8600 702-407-6000	1023 Cherry Road Memphis, TN 38117	www.harrahs.com
BANKS					
12. Wachovia	WB	NY	704-374-6565	1 Wachovia Center Charlotte, NC 28288-0570	www.wachovia.com
13. First State Bank of Roans Prairie	N/A	N/A	936-395-2141	Roans Prairie, TX	N/A
ZOOS					
14. Audubon Nature Institute	N/A	N/A	504-861-2537	6500 Magazine Street New Orleans, LA 70118	www.audubon institute.org
15. Riverbanks Zoo	N/A	N/A	803-779-8717	Riverbanks Society PO Box 1060 Columbia, SC 29202	www.riverbanks.org

Continued

	STOCK SYMBOL	STOCK EXCHANGE	TELEPHONE NUMBER	HEADQUARTERS ADDRESS	WEB PAGE ADDRESS
CRUISE LINES					
16. Carnival Corp.	CCL	NY	800-438-6744 305-599-2600	3655 N.W. 87th Ave. Miami, FL 33178	www.carnivalcorp.com
17. Royal Caribbean	RCL	NY	305-539-6000	1050 Caribbean Way Miami, FL 33132	www.royal caribbean.com
CHURCHES					
18. Central United Methodist Church	N/A	N/A	843-662-3218	225 W. Cheves St. Florence, SC 29501	www.centralumcsc. web.com
19. Elkins Lake Baptist Church	N/A	N/A	409-295-7694	Huntsville, Texas 77340	www.elbc.org
GROCERY CHAIN					
20. Winn-Dixie	WIN	NY	904-783-5000	P.O. Box B Jacksonville, FL 32203	www.winndixie.com
MOM AND POP BUSINESS					
21. Strictly Roots Natural Hair Salon	N/A	N/A	713-529-5017	Houston, Texas	www.strictly-roots. com
NONPROFIT ORGANIZATION					
22. Classic Car Club of America	N/A	N/A	847-390-0443	1645 Des Plaines River Rd. Suite 7 Des Plaines, IL 60018	www.classiccarclub. org/

NINTH EDITION MANUFACTURING COMPANY CASES

	STOCK SYMBOL	STOCK EXCHANGE	TELEPHONE NUMBER	HEADQUARTERS ADDRESS	WEB PAGE ADDRESS
TRANSPORTATION					
23. Harley-Davidson	HDI	NY	414-342-4680	3700 W. Juneau Ave. Milwaukee, WI 53208	www.harley-davidson.com
24. Winnebago Industries	WGO	NY	641-585-3535	605 W. Crystal Lake Rd. Forest City, Iowa 50436	www.winnebagoind. com
COSMETICS					
25. Avon Products Inc.	AVP	NY	212-282-5000	Avenue of the Americas New York, NY 10105-0196	www.avon.com
26. Revlon Inc.	REV	NY	212-527-4000	625 Madison Ave. New York, NY 10022	www.revlon.com
FOOD					
27. Pilgrim's Pride Corp.	CHX	NY	903-855-1000	110 South Texas St. Pittsburg, Texas 75686	www.pilgrimspride. com
28. H.J. Heinz Co.	HNZ	NY	412-456-5700	600 Grant Street Pittsburg, PA 15219	www.heinz.com
29. Hershey Foods	HSY	NY	717-534-6799	100 Crystal Drive Hershey, PA 17033	www.hersheys.com

Continued

	STOCK SYMBOL	STOCK EXCHANGE	TELEPHONE NUMBER	HEADQUARTERS ADDRESS	WEB PAGE ADDRESS
AEROSPACE					
30. Boeing	BA	NY	206-655-2121	7755 E. Marginal Way S. Seattle, WA 98108	**www.boeing.com**
31. Lockheed Martin	LMT	NY	800-934-3566 301-897-6000	6801 Rockledge Drive Bethesda, MD 20817	**www.lockheed martin.com**
COMPUTERS					
32. Dell Computer	DELL	NASD	512-338-4400	1 Dell Way Round Rock, TX 78682	**www.dell.com**
33. Hewlett-Packard	HPQ	NY	650-857-1501	3000 Hanover Street Palo Alto, CA 94304	**www.hewlett-packrd. com**
MEDICAL					
34. Stryker Corp.	SYK	NY	616-385-2600	2775 Fairfield Rd. Kalamazoo, MI 49002	**www.strykercorp.com**
35. Biomet Inc.	BMET	NASD	219-267-6639	Airport Industrial Pk. Warsaw, Indiana 46581	**www.biomet.com**
MAGAZINES					
36. Playboy Enterprises	PLA	NY	312-751-8000	680 N. Lake Shore Dr. Chicago, IL 60611	**www.playboy.com**
37. Reader's Digest Association	RDA	NY	914-238-1000	Reader's Digest Road Pleasantville, NY 10570-7000	**www.readersdigest. com**
FOOTWEAR					
38. Nike Inc.	NKE	NY	503-671-6453 800-640-8007	1 Bowerman Dr. Beaverton, OR 97005	**www.nike.com**
39. Reebok	RBK	NY	781-401-5000	100 Technology Center Dr. Stroughton, MA 02072	**www.reebok.com**
TOBACCO					
40. UST Inc.	UST	NY	203-661-1100	100 W. Putnam Ave. Greenwich, CT 06830	**www.ustshareholder. com**
BREWERY					
41. Coors	RKY	NY	800-642-6116	310 North 10th St. Golden, CO 80401	**www.coors.com**

INTRODUCTION

HOW TO ANALYZE A BUSINESS POLICY CASE

OBJECTIVES

After studying this chapter, you should be able to do the following:

1. Describe the case method for learning strategic-management concepts.
2. Identify the steps in preparing a comprehensive written case analysis.
3. Describe how to give an effective oral case analysis presentation.
4. Discuss fifty tips for doing case analysis.

NOTABLE QUOTES

The essential fact that makes the case method an educational experience of the greatest power is that it makes the student an active rather than a passive participant.

WALLACE B. DONHAM

Two heads are better than one.

UNKNOWN AUTHOR

Good writers do not turn in their first drafts. Ask someone else to read your written case analysis, and read it out loud to yourself. That way, you can find rough areas to clear up.

LAWRENCE JAUCH

One reaction frequently heard is, "I don't have enough information." In reality, strategists never have enough information because some information is not available and some is too costly.

WILLIAM GLUECK

I keep six honest serving men. They taught me all I know. Their names are What, Why, When, How, Where, and Who.

RUDYARD KIPLING

Don't recommend anything you would not be prepared to do yourself if you were in the decision maker's shoes.

A. J. STRICKLAND III

A picture is worth a thousand words.

UNKNOWN AUTHOR

The purpose of this section is to help you analyze business policy cases. Guidelines for preparing written and oral case analyses are given, and suggestions for preparing cases for class discussion are presented. Steps to follow in preparing case analyses are provided. Guidelines for making an oral presentation are described.

WHAT IS A BUSINESS POLICY CASE?

A *business policy case* describes an organization's external and internal condition and raises issues concerning the firm's mission, strategies, objectives, and policies. Most of the information in a business policy case is established fact, but some information may be opinions, judgments, and beliefs. Business policy cases are more comprehensive than those you may have studied in other courses. They generally include a description of related management, marketing, finance/accounting, production/operations, R&D, computer information systems, and natural environment issues. A business policy case puts the reader on the scene of the action by describing a firm's situation at some point in time. Business policy cases are written to give you practice applying strategic-management concepts. The case method for studying strategic management is often called *learning by doing*.

GUIDELINES FOR PREPARING CASE ANALYSES

The Need for Practicality

There is no such thing as a complete case, and no case ever gives you all the information you need to conduct analyses and make recommendations. Likewise, in the business world, strategists never have all the information they need to make decisions: information may be unavailable or too costly to obtain, or it may take too much time to obtain. So in preparing business policy cases, do what strategists do every day—make reasonable assumptions about unknowns, state assumptions clearly, perform appropriate analyses, and make decisions. *Be practical*. For example, in performing a pro forma financial analysis, make reasonable assumptions, state them appropriately, and proceed to show what impact your recommendations are expected to have on the organization's financial position. Avoid saying, "I don't have enough information." You can always supplement the information provided in a case with Internet and library research.

The Need for Justification

The most important part of analyzing cases is not what strategies you recommend, but rather how you support your decisions and how you propose that they be implemented. There is no single best solution or one right answer to a case, so give ample justification for your recommendations. This is important. In the business world, strategists usually do not know if their decisions are right until resources have been allocated and consumed. Then it is often too late to reverse a decision. This cold fact accents the need for careful integration of intuition and analysis in preparing business policy case analyses.

The Need for Realism

Avoid recommending a course of action beyond an organization's means. *Be realistic*. No organization can possibly pursue all the strategies that could potentially benefit the firm. Estimate how much capital will be required to implement what you recommended.

Determine whether debt, stock, or a combination of debt and stock could be used to obtain the capital. Make sure your recommendations are feasible. Do not prepare a case analysis that omits all arguments and information not supportive of your recommendations. Rather, present the major advantages and disadvantages of several feasible alternatives. Try not to exaggerate, stereotype, prejudge, or overdramatize. Strive to demonstrate that your interpretation of the evidence is reasonable and objective.

The Need for Specificity

Do not make broad generalizations such as "The company should pursue a market penetration strategy." *Be specific* by telling *what, why, when, how, where,* and *who.* Failure to use specifics is the single major shortcoming of most oral and written case analyses. For example, in an internal audit say, "The firm's current ratio fell from 2.2 in 2002 to 1.3 in 2003, and this is considered to be a major weakness," instead of, "The firm's financial condition is bad." Rather than concluding from a Strategic Position and Action Evaluation (SPACE) Matrix that a firm should be defensive, be more specific, saying, "The firm should consider closing three plants, laying off 280 employees, and divesting itself of its chemical division, for a net savings of $20.2 million in 2003." Use ratios, percentages, numbers, and dollar estimates. Businesspeople dislike generalities and vagueness.

The Need for Originality

Do not necessarily recommend the course of action that the firm plans to take or actually undertook, even if those actions resulted in improved revenues and earnings. The aim of case analysis is for you to consider all the facts and information relevant to the organization at the time, to generate feasible alternative strategies, to choose among those alternatives, and to defend your recommendations. Put yourself back in time to the point when strategic decisions were being made by the firm's strategists. Based on the information available then, what would you have done? Support your position with charts, graphs, ratios, analyses, and the like—not a revelation from the library. You can become a good strategist by thinking through situations, making management assessments, and proposing plans yourself. *Be original.* Compare and contrast what you recommend versus what the company plans to do or did.

The Need to Contribute

Strategy formulation, implementation, and evaluation decisions are commonly made by a group of individuals rather than by a single person. Therefore, your professor may divide the class into three- or four-person teams and ask you to prepare written or oral case analyses. Members of a strategic-management team, in class or in the business world, differ on their aversion to risk, their concern for short-run versus long-run benefits, their attitudes toward social responsibility, and their views concerning globalization. There are no perfect people, so there are no perfect strategies. Be open-minded to others' views. *Be a good listener and a good contributor.*

 ## PREPARING A CASE FOR CLASS DISCUSSION

Your professor may ask you to prepare a case for class discussion. Preparing a case for class discussion means that you need to read the case before class, make notes regarding the organization's external opportunities/threats and internal strengths/weaknesses, perform appropriate analyses, and come to class prepared to offer and defend some specific recommendations.

The Case Method Versus Lecture Approach

The case method of teaching is radically different from the traditional lecture approach, in which little or no preparation is needed by students before class. The *case method* involves a classroom situation in which students do most of the talking; your professor facilitates discussion by asking questions and encouraging student interaction regarding ideas, analyses, and recommendations. Be prepared for a discussion along the lines of "What would you do, why would you do it, when would you do it, and how would you do it?" Prepare answers to the following types of questions:

- What are the firm's most important external opportunities and threats?
- What are the organization's major strengths and weaknesses?
- How would you describe the organization's financial condition?
- What are the firm's existing strategies and objectives?
- Who are the firm's competitors, and what are their strategies?
- What objectives and strategies do you recommend for this organization? Explain your reasoning. How does what you recommend compare to what the company plans?
- How could the organization best implement what you recommend? What implementation problems do you envision? How could the firm avoid or solve those problems?

The Cross-Examination

Do not hesitate to take a stand on the issues and to support your position with objective analyses and outside research. Strive to apply strategic-management concepts and tools in preparing your case for class discussion. Seek defensible arguments and positions. Support opinions and judgments with facts, reasons, and evidence. Crunch the numbers before class! Be willing to describe your recommendations to the class without fear of disapproval. Respect the ideas of others, but be willing to go against the majority opinion when you can justify a better position.

Business policy case analysis gives you the opportunity to learn more about yourself, your colleagues, strategic management, and the decision-making process in organizations. The rewards of this experience will depend on the effort you put forth, so do a good job. Discussing business policy cases in class is exciting and challenging. Expect views counter to those you present. Different students will place emphasis on different aspects of an organization's situation and submit different recommendations for scrutiny and rebuttal. Cross-examination discussions commonly arise, just as they occur in a real business organization. Avoid being a silent observer.

 ## PREPARING A WRITTEN CASE ANALYSIS

In addition to asking you to prepare a case for class discussion, your professor may ask you to prepare a written case analysis. Preparing a written case analysis is similar to preparing a case for class discussion, except written reports are generally more structured and more detailed. There is no ironclad procedure for preparing a written case analysis because cases differ in focus; the type, size, and complexity of the organizations being analyzed also vary.

When writing a strategic-management report or case analysis, avoid using jargon, vague or redundant words, acronyms, abbreviations, sexist language, and ethnic or racial slurs. And watch your spelling! Use short sentences and paragraphs and simple words and phrases. Use quite a few subheadings. Arrange issues and ideas from the most important to the least important. Arrange recommendations from the least controversial to the most controversial. Use the active voice rather than the passive voice for all verbs; for example, say, "Our team recommends that the company diversify," rather than, "It is recommended by our team to diversify." Use many examples to add specificity and clarity. Tables, figures, pie charts, bar charts, time lines, and other kinds of exhibits help communicate important points and ideas. Sometimes a picture *is* worth a thousand words.

The Executive Summary

Your professor may ask you to focus the written case analysis on a particular aspect of the strategic-management process, such as (1) to identify and evaluate the organization's existing mission, objectives, and strategies; or (2) to propose and defend specific recommendations for the company; or (3) to develop an industry analysis by describing the competitors, products, selling techniques, and market conditions in a given industry. These types of written reports are sometimes called *executive summaries*. An executive summary usually ranges from three to five pages of text in length, plus exhibits.

The Comprehensive Written Analysis

Your professor may ask you to prepare a *comprehensive written analysis*. This assignment requires you to apply the entire strategic-management process to the particular organization. When preparing a comprehensive written analysis, picture yourself as a consultant who has been asked by a company to conduct a study of its external and internal environment and to make specific recommendations for its future. Prepare exhibits to support your recommendations. Highlight exhibits with some discussion in the paper. Comprehensive written analyses are usually about ten pages in length, plus exhibits.

Steps in Preparing a Comprehensive Written Analysis

In preparing a comprehensive written analysis, you could follow the steps outlined here, which correlate to the stages in the strategic-management process and the chapters in this text.

Step	1	Identify the firm's existing vision, mission, objectives, and strategies.
Step	2	Develop vision and mission statements for the organization.
Step	3	Identify the organization's external opportunities and threats.
Step	4	Construct a Competitive Profile Matrix (CPM).
Step	5	Construct an External Factor Evaluation (EFE) Matrix.
Step	6	Identify the organization's internal strengths and weaknesses.
Step	7	Construct an Internal Factor Evaluation (IFE) Matrix.
Step	8	Prepare a Threats-Opportunities-Weaknesses-Strengths (TOWS) Matrix, Strategic Position and Action Evaluation (SPACE) Matrix, Boston Consulting Group (BCG) Matrix, Internal-External (IE) Matrix, Grand Strategy Matrix, and Quantitative Strategic Planning Matrix (QSPM) as appropriate. Give advantages and disadvantages of alternative strategies.
Step	9	Recommend specific strategies and long-term objectives. Show how much your recommendations will cost. Itemize these costs clearly for each projected year. Compare your recommendations to actual strategies planned by the company.
Step	10	Specify how your recommendations can be implemented and what results you can expect. Prepare forecasted ratios and pro forma financial statements. Present a timetable or agenda for action.

Step 11   Recommend specific annual objectives and policies.

Step 12   Recommend procedures for strategy review and evaluation.

MAKING AN ORAL PRESENTATION

Your professor may ask you to prepare a business policy case analysis, individually or as a group, and present your analysis to the class. Oral presentations are usually graded on two parts: content and delivery. *Content* refers to the quality, quantity, correctness, and appropriateness of analyses presented, including such dimensions as logical flow through the presentation, coverage of major issues, use of specifics, avoidance of generalities, absence of mistakes, and feasibility of recommendations. *Delivery* includes such dimensions as audience attentiveness, clarity of visual aids, appropriate dress, persuasiveness of arguments, tone of voice, eye contact, and posture. Great ideas are of no value unless others can be convinced of their merit through clear communication. The guidelines presented here can help you make an effective oral presentation.

Organizing the Presentation

Begin your presentation by introducing yourself and giving a clear outline of topics to be covered. If a team is presenting, specify the sequence of speakers and the areas each person will address. At the beginning of an oral presentation, try to capture your audience's interest and attention. You could do this by displaying some products made by the company, telling an interesting short story about the company, or sharing an experience you had that is related to the company, its products, or its services. You could develop or obtain a video to show at the beginning of class; you could visit a local distributor of the firm's products and tape a personal interview with the business owner or manager. A light or humorous introduction can be effective at the beginning of a presentation.

Be sure the setting of your presentation is well organized, with chairs, flip charts, a transparency projector, and whatever else you plan to use. Arrive at least fifteen minutes early at the classroom to organize the setting, and be sure your materials are ready to go. Make sure everyone can see your visual aids well.

Controlling Your Voice

An effective rate of speaking ranges from 100 to 125 words per minute. Practice your presentation out loud to determine if you are going too fast. Individuals commonly speak too fast when nervous. Breathe deeply before and during the presentation to help yourself slow down. Have a cup of water available; pausing to take a drink will wet your throat, give you time to collect your thoughts, control your nervousness, slow you down, and signal to the audience a change in topic.

Avoid a monotone by placing emphasis on different words or sentences. Speak loudly and clearly, but don't shout. Silence can be used effectively to break a monotone voice. Stop at the end of each sentence, rather than running sentences together with *and* or *ub*.

Managing Body Language

Be sure not to fold your arms, lean on the podium, put your hands in your pockets, or put your hands behind you. Keep a straight posture, with one foot slightly in front of the other. Do not turn your back to the audience; doing so is not only rude, but it also prevents your voice from projecting well. Avoid using too many hand gestures. On occasion, leave the podium or table and walk toward your audience, but do not walk around too much. Never block the audience's view of your visual aids.

Maintain good eye contact throughout the presentation. This is the best way to persuade your audience. There is nothing more reassuring to a speaker than to see members of the audience nod in agreement or smile. Try to look everyone in the eye at least once during your presentation, but focus more on individuals who look interested than on those who seem bored. Use humor and smiles as appropriate throughout your presentation to stay in touch with your audience. A presentation should never be dull!

Speaking from Notes

Be sure not to read to your audience, because reading puts people to sleep. Perhaps worse than reading is memorizing. Do not try to memorize anything. Rather, practice using notes unobtrusively. Make sure your notes are written clearly so you will not flounder when trying to read your own writing. Include only main ideas on your note cards. Keep note cards on a podium or table if possible so that you won't drop them or get them out of order; walking with note cards tends to be distracting.

Constructing Visual Aids

Make sure your visual aids are legible to individuals in the back of the room. Use color to highlight special items. Avoid putting complete sentences on visual aids; rather, use short phrases and then elaborate on issues orally as you make your presentation. Generally, there should be no more than four to six lines of text on each visual aid. Use clear headings and subheadings. Be careful about spelling and grammar; use a consistent style of lettering. Use masking tape or an easel for posters—do not hold posters in your hand. Transparencies and handouts are excellent aids; however, be careful not to use too many handouts or your audience may concentrate on them instead of you during the presentation.

Answering Questions

It is best to field questions at the end of your presentation, rather than during the presentation itself. Encourage questions, and take your time to respond to each one. Answering questions can be persuasive because it involves you with the audience. If a team is giving the presentation, the audience should direct questions to a specific person. During the question-and-answer period, be polite, confident, and courteous. Avoid verbose responses. Do not get defensive with your answers, even if a hostile or confrontational question is asked. Staying calm during potentially disruptive situations, such as a cross-examination, reflects self-confidence, maturity, poise, and command of the particular company and its industry. Stand up throughout the question-and-answer period.

 ## FIFTY TIPS FOR SUCCESS IN CASE ANALYSIS

Business policy students who have used this text over eight editions offer you the following fifty tips for success in doing case analysis:

1. View your case analysis and presentation as a product that must have some competitive factor to differentiate it favorably from the case analyses of other students.
2. Prepare your case analysis far enough in advance of the due date to allow time for reflection and practice. Do not procrastinate.

3. Develop a mind-set of *why,* continually questioning your own and others' assumptions and assertions.

4. The best ideas are lost if not communicated to the reader, so as ideas develop, think of their most appropriate presentation.

5. Maintain a positive attitude about the class, working *with* problems rather than against them.

6. Keep in tune with your professor, and understand his or her values and expectations.

7. Since business policy is a capstone course, seek the help of professors in other specialty areas when necessary.

8. Other students will have strengths in functional areas that will complement your weaknesses, so develop a cooperative spirit that moderates competitiveness in group work.

9. Read your case frequently as work progresses so you don't overlook details.

10. When preparing a case analysis as a group, divide into separate teams to work on the external analysis and internal analysis. Each team should write its section as if it were to go into the paper; then give each group member a copy.

11. At the end of each group session, assign each member of the group a task to be completed for the next meeting.

12. Have a good sense of humor.

13. Capitalize on the strengths of each member of the group; volunteer your services in your areas of strength.

14. Set goals for yourself and your team; budget your time to attain them.

15. Become friends with the library.

16. Foster attitudes that encourage group participation and interaction. Do not be hasty to judge group members.

17. Be creative and innovative throughout the case analysis process.

18. Be prepared to work. There will be times when you will have to do more than your share. Accept it, and do what you have to do to move the team forward.

19. Think of your case analysis as if it were really happening; do not reduce case analysis to a mechanical process.

20. To uncover flaws in your analysis and to prepare the group for questions during an oral presentation, assign one person in the group to actively play the devil's advocate.

21. Do not schedule excessively long group meetings; two-hour sessions are about right.

22. A goal of case analysis is to improve your ability to think clearly in ambiguous and confusing situations; do not get frustrated that there is no single best answer.

23. Push your ideas hard enough to get them listened to, but then let up; listen to others and try to follow their lines of thinking; follow the flow of group discussion, recognizing when you need to get back on track; do not repeat yourself or others unless clarity or progress demands repetition.

24. Do not confuse symptoms with causes; do not develop conclusions and solutions prematurely; recognize that information may be misleading, conflicting, or wrong.

25. Work hard to develop the ability to formulate reasonable, consistent, and creative plans; put yourself in the strategist's position.

26. Develop confidence in using quantitative tools for analysis. They are not inherently difficult; it is just practice and familiarity you need.

27. Develop a case-writing style that is direct, assertive, and convincing; be concise, precise, fluent, and correct.

28. Have fun when at all possible. It is frustrating at times, but enjoy it while you can; it may be several years before you are playing CEO again.

29. Acquire a professional typist and proofreader. Do not perform either task alone.

30. Strive for excellence in writing and in the technical preparation of your case. Prepare nice charts, tables, diagrams, and graphs. Use color and unique pictures. No messy exhibits!

31. In group cases, do not allow personality differences to interfere. When they occur, they must be understood for what they are—and then put aside.

32. Do not forget that the objective is to learn; explore areas with which you are not familiar.

33. Pay attention to detail.

34. Think through alternative implications fully and realistically. The consequences of decisions are not always apparent. They often affect many different aspects of a firm's operations.

35. Get things written down (drafts) as soon as possible.

36. Read everything that other group members write, and comment on it in writing. This allows group input into all aspects of case preparation.

37. Provide answers to such fundamental questions as *what, when, where, why, who,* and *how.*

38. Adaptation and flexibility are keys to success; be creative and innovative.

39. Do not merely recite ratios or present figures. Rather, develop ideas and conclusions concerning the possible trends. Show the importance of these figures to the corporation.

40. Support reasoning and judgment with factual data whenever possible.

41. Neatness is a real plus; your case analysis should look professional.

42. Your analysis should be as detailed and specific as possible.

43. A picture speaks a thousand words, and a creative picture gets you an A in many classes.

44. Let someone else read and critique your paper several days before you turn it in.

45. Emphasize the Strategy Selection and Strategy Implementation sections. A common mistake is to spend too much time on the external or internal analysis parts of your paper. Always remember that the meat of the paper or presentation is the strategy selection and implementation sections.

46. Make special efforts to get to know your group members. This leads to more openness in the group and allows for more interchange of ideas. Put in the time and effort necessary to develop these relationships.

47. Be constructively critical of your group members' work. Do not dominate group discussions. Be a good listener and contributor.

48. Learn from past mistakes and deficiencies. Improve upon weak aspects of other case presentations.

49. Learn from the positive approaches and accomplishments of classmates.

50. Use the Strategic Management Club Online at **www.strategyclub.com.**

MASTERING STRATEGY

Mastering Strategy is the first product in the *Mastering Business* series. It offers students an interactive, multimedia experience as they follow the people and issues of Cango, Inc., a small Internet startup. The text, video, and interactive exercises provide students an opportunity to simulate the strategic planning experience and to chart the future activities for Cango.

> Strategy has an impact across an entire organization, and the behaviors involved are often very subtle. Using this material really provides an opportunity to give an experiential approach to strategic concepts as applied in the business world. The videos and exercises demonstrate actual theories, practices and assumptions in daily operations. These are practical applications as faced in the real world, with real language, problems and relevant issues faced by modern companies.
>
> Students are drawn into a living, breathing, dynamic company and immediately get a feeling for strategy in operation, rather than in retrospect. This helps students assimilate their learning in a systemic manner as they move from watching the events unfold for the company to applying their own intuition about the problems and solutions. When they are on the mark, they see the results in the company's performance. If they are off the mark, they learn what they don't know and where they need to go back for a deeper understanding.
>
> —Helen Rothberg, Professor at the Marist College School
> of Management and co-author of the Strategy series

THE MASTERING STRATEGY ENVIRONMENT

Students will learn strategy concepts within the context of Cango, Inc., a fictitious Internet company that focuses its efforts in the entertainment arena of the e-commerce world. The company began by retailing books on the Internet and has branched out to offer CDs, videos, MP3 files, and customized players. Cango employs mostly recent college graduates who are enthusiastic about working with an online business and its possibilities for expansion. Currently, Cango is experiencing great growth, but little profit.

Thus, Cango employees are always on the lookout for new ventures. The company is considering hosting streaming video, e-books and e-book readers, and partnerships with other firms. One example would be a film studio so that Cango can serve the needs of independent filmmakers and tap into the growing popularity of home video hardware and software.

The company's goals are to get bigger and better, and to someday make a significant profit. In *Mastering Strategy,* the firm transforms from a small, independent company to one listed on the NASDAQ through the Initial Public Offering (IPO) process. The firm's founder and the management team must deal with all the implications of this change, both within the company and in the context of the external world of investors, the board of directors, and potential competitors. Visit **www.prenhall.com/masteringbusiness** to find out more.

STRATEGIC
MANAGEMENT
CONCEPTS

■ PART 1

Overview of Strategic Management

1 THE NATURE OF STRATEGIC MANAGEMENT

CHAPTER OUTLINE

- What Is Strategic Management?
- Key Terms in Strategic Management
- The Strategic-Management Model
- Benefits of Strategic Management
- Why Some Firms Do No Strategic Planning
- Pitfalls in Strategic Planning
- Guidelines for Effective Strategic Management
- Business Ethics and Strategic Management
- Comparing Business and Military Strategy
- The Nature of Global Competition
- Cohesion Case: American Airlines (AMR)—2002

EXPERIENTIAL EXERCISE 1A
Strategy Analysis for American Airlines (AMR)

EXPERIENTIAL EXERCISE 1B
Developing a Code of Business Ethics for American Airlines (AMR)

EXPERIENTIAL EXERCISE 1C
The Ethics of Spying on Competitors

EXPERIENTIAL EXERCISE 1D
Strategic Planning for My University

EXPERIENTIAL EXERCISE 1E
Strategic Planning at a Local Company

EXPERIENTIAL EXERCISE 1F
Does My University Recruit in Foreign Countries?

EXPERIENTIAL EXERCISE 1G
Getting Familiar with SMCO

CHAPTER OBJECTIVES

After studying this chapter, you should be able to do the following:

1. Describe the strategic-management process.
2. Explain the need for integrating analysis and intuition in strategic management.
3. Define and give examples of key terms in strategic management.
4. Discuss the nature of strategy formulation, implementation, and evaluation activities.
5. Describe the benefits of good strategic management.
6. Explain why good ethics is good business in strategic management.
7. Explain the advantages and disadvantages of entering global markets.
8. Discuss the relevance of Sun Tzu's *The Art of War* to strategic management.

NOTABLE QUOTES

If we know where we are and something about how we got there, we might see where we are trending—and if the outcomes which lie naturally in our course are unacceptable, to make timely change.

ABRAHAM LINCOLN

Without a strategy, an organization is like a ship without a rudder, going around in circles. It's like a tramp; it has no place to go.

JOEL ROSS AND MICHAEL KAMI

Plans are less important than planning.

DALE McCONKEY

The formulation of strategy can develop competitive advantage only to the extent that the process can give meaning to workers in the trenches.

DAVID HURST

Most of us fear change. Even when our minds say change is normal, our stomachs quiver at the prospect. But for strategists and managers today, there is no choice but to change.

ROBERT WATERMAN, JR.

If business is not based on ethical grounds, it is of no benefit to society and will, like all other unethical combinations, pass into oblivion.

C. MAX KILLAN

If a man take no thought about what is distant, he will find sorrow near at hand. He who will not worry about what is far off will soon find something worse than worry.

CONFUCIUS

It is human nature to make decisions based on emotion, rather than on fact. But nothing could be more illogical.

TOSHIBA CORPORATION

No business can do everything. Even if it has the money, it will never have enough good people. It has to set priorities. The worst thing to do is a little bit of everything. This makes sure that nothing is being accomplished. It is better to pick the wrong priority than none at all.

PETER DRUCKER

Executives, consultants, and B-school professors all agree that strategic planning is now the single most important management issue and will remain so for the next five years. Strategy has become a part of the main agenda at lots of organizations today. Strategic planning is back with a vengeance.

JOHN BYRNE

Planners should not plan, but serve as facilitators, catalysts, inquirers, educators, and synthesizers to guide the planning process effectively.

A. HAX AND N. MAJLUF

This chapter provides an overview of strategic management. It introduces a practical, integrative model of the strategic-management process; it defines basic activities and terms in strategic management; and it discusses the importance of business ethics.

This chapter initiates several themes that permeate all the chapters of this text. First, *global considerations impact virtually all strategic decisions!* The boundaries of countries no longer can define the limits of our imaginations. To see and appreciate the world from the perspective of others has become a matter of survival for businesses. The underpinnings of strategic management hinge upon managers' gaining an understanding of competitors, markets, prices, suppliers, distributors, governments, creditors, shareholders, and customers worldwide. The price and quality of a firm's products and services must be competitive on a worldwide basis, not just on a local basis. A "Global Perspective" box is provided in all chapters of this text to emphasize the importance of global factors in strategic management.

A second theme is that *electronic commerce (e-commerce) has become a vital strategic-management tool.* An increasing number of companies are gaining a competitive advantage by using the Internet for direct selling and for communication with suppliers, customers, creditors, partners, shareholders, clients, and competitors who may be dispersed globally. E-commerce allows firms to sell products, advertise, purchase supplies, bypass intermediaries, track inventory, eliminate paperwork, and share information. In total, e-commerce is minimizing the expense and cumbersomeness of time, distance, and space in doing business, thus yielding better customer service, greater efficiency, improved products, and higher profitability.

The Internet and personal computers are changing the way we organize our lives; inhabit our homes; and relate to and interact with family, friends, neighbors, and even ourselves. The Internet promotes endless comparison shopping, which thus enables consumers worldwide to band together to demand discounts. The Internet has transferred power from business to individuals so swiftly that in another decade there may be "regulations" imposed on groups of consumers. Politicians may one day debate the need for "regulation on consumers" rather than "regulation on big business" because of the Internet's empowerment of individuals. Buyers used to face big obstacles when attempting to get the best price and service, such as limited time and data to compare, but now consumers can quickly scan hundreds of vendor offerings. Or they can go to Web sites, such as CompareNet.com, that offer detailed information on more than 100,000 consumer products.

The Internet has changed the very nature and core of buying and selling in nearly all industries. It has fundamentally changed the economics of business in every single industry worldwide. Slogans and companies such as broadband, e-Bay, e-Trade, e-commerce, e-mail, and e-Toys have become an integral part of everyday life worldwide. Business-to-business e-commerce is five times greater than consumer e-commerce. Fully 74 percent of Americans think the Internet will change society more than the telephone and television combined.[1] An "E-commerce Perspective" box is included in each chapter to illustrate how electronic commerce impacts the strategic-management process.

A third theme is that *the natural environment has become an important strategic issue.* Global warming, bioterrorism, and increased pollution suggest that perhaps there is now no greater threat to business and society than the continuous exploitation and decimation of our natural environment. Mark Starik at George Washington University says, "Halting and reversing worldwide ecological destruction and deterioration . . . is a strategic issue that needs immediate and substantive attention by all businesses and managers." A "Natural Environment Perspective" box is provided in all chapters to illustrate how firms are addressing natural environment and bioterrorism concerns.

VISIT THE NET

Designed by the author, Fred David, especially for this textbook, this Web site provides strategic planning tools, templates, links, and information that will directly help strategic-management students analyze cases. Strategic Management Club Online-
www.strategyclub.com

WHAT IS STRATEGIC MANAGEMENT?

Once there were two company presidents who competed in the same industry. These two presidents decided to go on a camping trip to discuss a possible merger. They hiked deep into the woods. Suddenly, they came upon a grizzly bear that rose up on its hind legs and snarled. Instantly, the first president took off his knapsack and got out a pair of jogging shoes. The second president said, "Hey, you can't outrun that bear." The first president responded, "Maybe I can't outrun that bear, but I surely can outrun you!" This story captures the notion of strategic management, which is to achieve and maintain competitive advantage.

Defining Strategic Management

Strategic management can be defined as the art and science of formulating, implementing, and evaluating cross-functional decisions that enable an organization to achieve its objectives. As this definition implies, strategic management focuses on integrating management, marketing, finance/accounting, production/operations, research and development, and computer information systems to achieve organizational success. The term *strategic management* in this text is used synonymously with the term *strategic planning*. The latter term is more often used in the business world, whereas the former is often used in academia. Sometimes the term *strategic management* is used to refer to strategy formulation, implementation, and evaluation, with *strategic planning* referring only to strategy formulation. The purpose of strategic management is to exploit and create new and different opportunities for tomorrow; *long-range planning,* in contrast, tries to optimize for tomorrow the trends of today.

The term *strategic planning* originated in the 1950s and was very popular between the mid-1960s to mid-1970s. During these years, strategic planning was widely believed to be the answer for all problems. At the time, much of corporate America was "obsessed" with strategic planning. Following that "boom," however, strategic planning was cast aside during the 1980s as various planning models did not yield higher returns. The 1990s, however, brought the revival of strategic planning, and the process is widely practiced today in the business world.

The term *strategic management* is used at many colleges and universities as the subtitle for the capstone course in business administration, Business Policy, which integrates material from all business courses. The Strategic Management Club Online at **www.strategyclub.com** offers many benefits for business policy students.

Stages of Strategic Management

The *strategic-management process* consists of three stages: strategy formulation, strategy implementation, and strategy evaluation. *Strategy formulation* includes developing a vision and mission, identifying an organization's external opportunities and threats, determining internal strengths and weaknesses, establishing long-term objectives, generating alternative strategies, and choosing particular strategies to pursue. Strategy-formulation issues include deciding what new businesses to enter, what businesses to abandon, how to allocate resources, whether to expand operations or diversify, whether to enter international markets, whether to merge or form a joint venture, and how to avoid a hostile takeover.

Because no organization has unlimited resources, strategists must decide which alternative strategies will benefit the firm most. Strategy-formulation decisions commit an organization to specific products, markets, resources, and technologies over an extended period of time. Strategies determine long-term competitive advantages. For better or worse, strategic decisions have major multifunctional consequences and enduring effects on an organization. Top managers have the best perspective to understand fully the ramifications of strategy-formulation decisions; they have the authority to commit the resources necessary for implementation.

Strategy implementation requires a firm to establish annual objectives, devise policies, motivate employees, and allocate resources so that formulated strategies can be executed. Strategy implementation includes developing a strategy-supportive culture, creating an effective organizational structure, redirecting marketing efforts, preparing budgets, developing and utilizing information systems, and linking employee compensation to organizational performance.

Strategy implementation often is called the action stage of strategic management. Implementing strategy means mobilizing employees and managers to put formulated strategies into action. Often considered to be the most difficult stage in strategic management, strategy implementation requires personal discipline, commitment, and sacrifice. Successful strategy implementation hinges upon managers' ability to motivate employees, which is more an art than a science. Strategies formulated but not implemented serve no useful purpose.

Interpersonal skills are especially critical for successful strategy implementation. Strategy-implementation activities affect all employees and managers in an organization. Every division and department must decide on answers to questions, such as "What must we do to implement our part of the organization's strategy?" and "How best can we get the job done?" The challenge of implementation is to stimulate managers and employees throughout an organization to work with pride and enthusiasm toward achieving stated objectives.

Strategy evaluation is the final stage in strategic management. Managers desperately need to know when particular strategies are not working well; strategy evaluation is the primary means for obtaining this information. All strategies are subject to future modification because external and internal factors are constantly changing. Three fundamental strategy-evaluation activities are (1) reviewing external and internal factors that are the bases for current strategies, (2) measuring performance, and (3) taking corrective actions. Strategy evaluation is needed because success today is no guarantee of success tomorrow! Success always creates new and different problems; complacent organizations experience demise.

Strategy formulation, implementation, and evaluation activities occur at three hierarchical levels in a large organization: corporate, divisional or strategic business unit, and functional. By fostering communication and interaction among managers and employees across hierarchical levels, strategic management helps a firm function as a competitive team. Most small businesses and some large businesses do not have divisions or strategic business units; they have only the corporate and functional levels. Nevertheless, managers and employees at these two levels should be actively involved in strategic-management activities.

Peter Drucker says the prime task of strategic management is thinking through the overall mission of a business:

> . . . that is, of asking the question, "What is our Business?" This leads to the setting of objectives, the development of strategies, and the making of today's decisions for tomorrow's results. This clearly must be done by a part of the organization that can see the entire business; that can balance objectives and the needs of today against the needs of tomorrow; and that can allocate resources of men and money to key results.[2]

VISIT THE NET

Provides a nice narrative regarding strategy formulation and implementation at Southern Polytechnic State University. http://www.spsu.edu/ planassess/strategic.htm.

Integrating Intuition and Analysis

The strategic-management process can be described as an objective, logical, systematic approach for making major decisions in an organization. It attempts to organize qualitative and quantitative information in a way that allows effective decisions to be made under conditions of uncertainty. Yet strategic management is not a pure science that lends itself to a nice, neat, one-two-three approach.

Based on past experiences, judgment, and feelings, most people recognize that *intuition* is essential to making good strategic decisions. Intuition is particularly useful for making decisions in situations of great uncertainty or little precedent. It is also helpful when highly interrelated variables exist or when it is necessary to choose from several plausible alternatives. Some managers and owners of businesses profess to have extraordinary abilities for using intuition alone in devising brilliant strategies. For example, Will Durant, who organized General Motors Corporation, was described by Alfred Sloan as "a man who would proceed on a course of action guided solely, as far as I could tell, by some intuitive flash of brilliance. He never felt obliged to make an engineering hunt for the facts. Yet at times, he was astoundingly correct in his judgment."[3] Albert Einstein acknowledged the importance of intuition when he said, "I believe in intuition and inspiration. At times I feel certain that I am right while not knowing the reason. Imagination is more important than knowledge, because knowledge is limited, whereas imagination embraces the entire world."[4]

Although some organizations today may survive and prosper because they have intuitive geniuses managing them, most are not so fortunate. Most organizations can benefit from strategic management, which is based upon integrating intuition and analysis in decision making. Choosing an intuitive or analytic approach to decision making is not an either-or proposition. Managers at all levels in an organization inject their intuition and judgment into strategic-management analyses. Analytical thinking and intuitive thinking complement each other.

Operating from the I've-already-made-up-my-mind-don't-bother-me-with-the-facts mode is not management by intuition; it is management by ignorance.[5] Drucker says, "I believe in intuition only if you discipline it. 'Hunch' artists, who make a diagnosis but don't check it out with the facts, are the ones in medicine who kill people, and in management kill businesses."[6] As Henderson notes:

> The accelerating rate of change today is producing a business world in which customary managerial habits in organizations are increasingly inadequate. Experience alone was an adequate guide when changes could be made in small increments. But intuitive and experience-based management philosophies are grossly inadequate when decisions are strategic and have major, irreversible consequences.[7]

In a sense, the strategic-management process is an attempt both to duplicate what goes on in the mind of a brilliant, intuitive person who knows the business and to couple it with analysis.

Adapting to Change

The strategic-management process is based on the belief that organizations should continually monitor internal and external events and trends so that timely changes can be made as needed. The rate and magnitude of changes that affect organizations are increasing dramatically. Consider, for example, e-commerce, laser surgery, the war on terrorism, economic recession, the aging population, the Enron scandal, and merger mania. To survive, all organizations must be capable of astutely identifying and adapting to change.

VISIT THE NET

Provides titles and brief descriptions of many books relating to strategic planning. www.ccp.ca/ information/management/ planning/mgmtplan.html

VISIT THE NET

Reveals that strategies may need to be constantly changed. http://www. csuchico.edu/mgmt/ strategy/module1/ sld041.htm

The strategic-management process is aimed at allowing organizations to adapt effectively to change over the long run. As Waterman has noted:

> In today's business environment, more than in any preceding era, the only constant is change. Successful organizations effectively manage change, continuously adapting their bureaucracies, strategies, systems, products, and cultures to survive the shocks and prosper from the forces that decimate the competition.[8]

E-commerce and globalization are external changes that are transforming business and society today. On a political map, the boundaries between countries may be clear, but on a competitive map showing the real flow of financial and industrial activity, the boundaries have largely disappeared. The speedy flow of information has eaten away at national boundaries so that people worldwide readily see for themselves how other people live. People are traveling abroad more: ten million Japanese travel abroad annually. People are emigrating more: Germans to England and Mexicans to the United States are examples. As the Global Perspective indicates, U.S. firms are challenged by competitors in many industries. We are becoming a borderless world with global citizens, global competitors, global customers, global suppliers, and global distributors!

The need to adapt to change leads organizations to key strategic-management questions, such as "What kind of business should we become?" "Are we in the right field(s)?" "Should we reshape our business?" "What new competitors are entering our industry?" "What strategies should we pursue?" "How are our customers changing?" "Are new technologies being developed that could put us out of business?"

VISIT THE NET

Reveals that actual strategy results from planned strategy coupled with reactive changes.
http://www.csuchico.edu/
mgmt/strategy/module1/
sld032.htm

KEY TERMS IN STRATEGIC MANAGEMENT

Before we further discuss strategic management, we should define eight key terms: strategists, vision and mission statements, external opportunities and threats, internal strengths and weaknesses, long-term objectives, strategies, annual objectives, and policies.

Strategists

Strategists are the individuals who are most responsible for the success or failure of an organization. Strategists have various job titles, such as chief executive officer, president, owner, chair of the board, executive director, chancellor, dean, or entrepreneur. Jay Conger, professor of organizational behavior at the London Business School and author of *Building Leaders,* says, "All strategists have to be chief learning officers. We are in an extended period of change. If our leaders aren't highly adaptive and great models during this period, then our companies won't adapt either, because ultimately leadership is about being a role model." In 2001 and 2002, quite a few CEOs were fired or resigned, including Jacques Nasser of Ford Motor Company, Peter Bonfield of British Telecom, Lars Ramqvist of Ericsson, James Goodwin of UAL, and Shailesh Mehta of Providian.

Strategists help an organization gather, analyze, and organize information. They track industry and competitive trends, develop forecasting models and scenario analyses, evaluate corporate and divisional performance, spot emerging market opportunities, identify business threats, and develop creative action plans. Strategic planners usually serve in a support or staff role. Usually found in higher levels of management, they typically have considerable authority for decision making in the firm. The CEO is the most visible and critical strategic manager. Any manager who has responsibility for a unit or

GLOBAL PERSPECTIVE

Do U.S. Firms Dominate All Industries?

The Wall Street Journal's annual ranking of the world's largest companies reveals that U.S. firms are being challenged in many industries. The world's ten largest insurance companies and banks are listed below in rank order. Note that U.S. firms do not dominate these two industries.

Insurance Firms	Banks
Axa Group, France	Deutsche Bank, Germany
Allianz Group, Germany	UBS, Switzerland
Nippon Life, Japan	Bank of Tokyo-Mitsubishi, Japan
Zenkyoren & Prefectural Ins. Federations, Japan	Bank of America, U.S.
Dai-ichi Mutual Life, Japan	Fuji Bank, Japan
American International Group, U.S.	ABN Amro, Netherlands
Metropolitan Life Insurance, U.S.	HSBC Holdings, United Kingdom
Sumitomo Life, Japan	Credit Suisse Group, Switzerland
Zurich Financial Services Group, Switzerland	Bayerische Hypotheken & Vereinsbank, Germany
Prudential Corporation, United Kingdom	Sumitomo Bank, Japan

Source: Adapted from "See World Business" section, *The Wall Street Journal* (September 27, 1999): R30.

division, responsibility for profit and loss outcomes, or direct authority over a major piece of the business is a strategic manager (strategist).

Strategists differ as much as organizations themselves, and these differences must be considered in the formulation, implementation, and evaluation of strategies. Some strategists will not consider some types of strategies because of their personal philosophies. Strategists differ in their attitudes, values, ethics, willingness to take risks, concern for social responsibility, concern for profitability, concern for short-run versus long-run aims, and management style. The founder of Hershey Foods, Milton Hershey, built the company to manage an orphanage. From corporate profits, Hershey Foods today cares for over one thousand boys and girls in its School for Orphans.

Some strategists agree with Ralph Nader, who proclaims that organizations have tremendous social obligations. Others agree with Milton Friedman, the economist, who maintains that organizations have no obligation to do any more for society than is legally required. Most strategists agree that the first social responsibility of any business must be to make enough profit to cover the costs of the future, because if this is not achieved, no other social responsibility can be met. Strategists should examine social problems in terms of potential costs and benefits to the firm, and they should address social issues that could benefit the firm most.

Vision and Mission Statements

Many organizations today develop a *vision statement* that answers the question, "What do we want to become?" Developing a vision statement is often considered the first step in strategic planning, preceding even development of a mission statement. Many vision statements are a single sentence. For example, the vision statement of Stokes Eye Clinic in Florence, South Carolina, is "Our vision is to take care of your vision." The vision of the Institute of Management Accountants is "Global leadership in education, certification, and practice of management accounting and financial management."

Mission statements are "enduring statements of purpose that distinguish one business from other similar firms. A mission statement identifies the scope of a firm's operations in product and market terms."[9] It addresses the basic question that faces all strategists: "What is our business?" A clear mission statement describes the values and priorities of an organization. Developing a mission statement compels strategists to think about the nature and scope of present operations and to assess the potential attractiveness of future markets and activities. A mission statement broadly charts the future direction of an organization. An example of a mission statement is provided below for Microsoft.

> Microsoft's mission is to create software for the personal computer that empowers and enriches people in the workplace, at school and at home. Microsoft's early vision of a computer on every desk and in every home is coupled today with a strong commitment to Internet-related technologies that expand the power and reach of the PC and its users. As the world's leading software provider, Microsoft strives to produce innovative products that meet our customers' evolving needs. At the same time, we understand that long-term success is about more than just making great products. Find out what we mean when we talk about Living Our Values (**www.microsoft.com/mscorp/**).

External Opportunities and Threats

External opportunities and *external threats* refer to economic, social, cultural, demographic, environmental, political, legal, governmental, technological, and competitive trends and events that could significantly benefit or harm an organization in the future. Opportunities and threats are largely beyond the control of a single organization—thus the word *external*. The wireless revolution, biotechnology, population shifts, changing work values and attitudes, space exploration, recyclable packages, and increased competition from foreign companies are examples of opportunities or threats for companies. These types of changes are creating a different type of consumer and consequently a need for different types of products, services, and strategies. Many companies in many industries face the severe external threat of online sales capturing increasing market share in their industry. For example, online grocery shopping is expected to surge to $10.8 billion by 2003—to the dismay of traditional grocers.[10]

Other opportunities and threats may include the passage of a law, the introduction of a new product by a competitor, a national catastrophe, or the declining value of the dollar. A competitor's strength could be a threat. Unrest in the Middle East, rising energy costs, or the war against terrorism could represent an opportunity or a threat. The World Trade Center attack resulted in a sharp decline in travel and thus represented an external threat to airline, cruise line, and hotel companies. To mitigate the effect of this threat, Starwood Hotels & Resorts froze all capital expenses over $3 million, including the development of the upscale St. Regis Hotel and Towers in San Francisco. Many other hotel chains, including Motel 6, Red Roof Inn, Park Place, Caesars Palace, and Omni Hotels, also ceased expansion and retrenched.

A basic tenet of strategic management is that firms need to formulate strategies to take advantage of external opportunities and to avoid or reduce the impact of external threats. For this reason, identifying, monitoring, and evaluating external opportunities and threats is essential for success. This process of conducting research and gathering and assimilating external information is sometimes called *environmental scanning* or industry analysis. Lobbying is one activity that some organizations utilize to influence external opportunities and threats.

Internal Strengths and Weaknesses

Internal strengths and *internal weaknesses* are an organization's controllable activities that are performed especially well or poorly. They arise in the management, marketing, finance/accounting, production/operations, research and development, and management information systems activities of a business. Identifying and evaluating organizational strengths and weaknesses in the functional areas of a business is an essential strategic-management activity. Organizations strive to pursue strategies that capitalize on internal strengths and eliminate internal weaknesses.

Strengths and weaknesses are determined relative to competitors. *Relative* deficiency or superiority is important information. Also, strengths and weaknesses can be determined by elements of being rather than performance. For example, a strength may involve ownership of natural resources or a historic reputation for quality. Strengths and weaknesses may be determined relative to a firm's own objectives. For example, high levels of inventory turnover may not be a strength to a firm that seeks never to stock-out.

Internal factors can be determined in a number of ways, including computing ratios, measuring performance, and comparing to past periods and industry averages. Various types of surveys also can be developed and administered to examine internal factors such as employee morale, production efficiency, advertising effectiveness, and customer loyalty.

Long-Term Objectives

Objectives can be defined as specific results that an organization seeks to achieve in pursuing its basic mission. *Long-term* means more than one year. Objectives are essential for organizational success because they state direction; aid in evaluation; create synergy; reveal priorities; focus coordination; and provide a basis for effective planning, organizing, motivating, and controlling activities. Objectives should be challenging, measurable, consistent, reasonable, and clear. In a multidimensional firm, objectives should be established for the overall company and for each division. Minnesota Power's long-term objectives are to achieve a 13 percent return on equity (ROE) in its core electric utility, 14 percent ROE on water resource operations, and 15 percent ROE on support businesses. Minnesota Power also strives to stay in the top 25 percent of electric utilities in the United States in terms of common stock's market-to-book ratio and to maintain an annual growth in earnings per share of 5 percent.

Strategies

Strategies are the means by which long-term objectives will be achieved. Business strategies may include geographic expansion, diversification, acquisition, product development, market penetration, retrenchment, divestiture, liquidation, and joint ventures. Strategies currently being pursued by Barnes & Noble, SunTrust Banks, and Yahoo! are described in Table 1–1.

Strategies are potential actions that require top management decisions and large amounts of the firm's resources. In addition, strategies affect an organization's long-term prosperity, typically for at least five years, and thus are future-oriented. Strategies have multifunctional or multidivisional consequences and require consideration of both the external and internal factors facing the firm. Boston Market and KFC battle each other these days with similar strategies for selling fast-food chicken. Boston Market is remodeling all of its 680 stores to provide booths, padded chairs, and an expanded menu. The company is adding 40 new restaurants in 2002. In late 2001, KFC launched a $200 million television advertising campaign that featured *Seinfeld* star Jason Alexander, with a new tag line: "There's fast food. Then there's KFC." KFC is eliminating paper boxes and is beginning to serve food on black plastic plates; this is similar to what Boston Market

TABLE 1.1   Three Organizations' Strategies in 2002

BARNES & NOBLE

Barnes & Noble, the large bookseller, hesitated with an online strategy, while upstart
Amazon.com captured a huge market share in online bookselling. Despite huge capital
expenditures and massive advertising in recent years, Barnes & Noble still remains barely
more than one-tenth Amazon's size online. Barnes & Noble initially did not want to "can-
nibalize" its own core franchise. The lesson for other businesses may be that the Internet
does not tolerate caution and hesitation. Many brick-and-mortar companies today "hesitate" with an online strategy because of perceived "cannibalism" with existing walk-in
sales. Caution could spell disaster.

SUNTRUST BANKS

SunTrust Banks is aggressively pursuing a horizontal integration strategy by acquiring
other banks. SunTrust acquired all the Florida business of Huntington Bancshares in late
2001 after losing out in efforts to acquire Wachovia earlier that year. Instead, First Union
acquired Wachovia. The Huntington acquisition boosts SunTrust's market share in
Florida from 10 percent to 12 percent, placing it third in Florida behind Bank of America
(22 percent) and Wachovia (15 percent). Based in Atlanta, SunTrust obtained 143
Huntington branches in Florida with the acquisition to complement its 400 existing
branches in that state.

YAHOO!

Yahoo!'s strategy is to shift from obtaining 80 percent of its revenue from advertising to
obtaining more revenue from customers who pay for services. Yahoo! has devised a new
strategy to offer services such as personalized Web pages, audio subscriptions, and music
videos for a fee. Historically, Yahoo! provided free services to get customers and obtained
revenue from company advertisers. Analysts, who are skeptical that Yahoo!'s new strategy
can succeed, drove down the company stock price from a high of $88.75 in late 2000 to a
low of $9.90 in late 2001. Yahoo! laid off 20 percent of its staff—or roughly one thousand
employees—in 2001. Yahoo! also is forming strategic alliances, such as its new agreement
with SBC Communications to jointly offer high-speed Internet access over SBC's phone
lines using Yahoo!'s brand name and Web service. Strategic-alliance formation is a major
new strategic management thrust in the 2000s (to be discussed fully in Chapter 5).

does. KFC is also renovating all of its 5,300 stores in the United States by providing
track lighting and café-style tables. Employees of the two companies depend on the
respective top management teams to pursue effective strategies; otherwise, demise could
be in the offing due to fierce competition.[11] (Alternative types of strategies are discussed
fully in Chapter 5).

Annual Objectives

Annual objectives are short-term milestones that organizations must achieve to reach long-
term objectives. Like long-term objectives, annual objectives should be measurable,
quantitative, challenging, realistic, consistent, and prioritized. They should be established at the corporate, divisional, and functional levels in a large organization. Annual
objectives should be stated in terms of management, marketing, finance/accounting,
production/operations, research and development, and management information systems
(MIS) accomplishments. A set of annual objectives is needed for each long-term objective. Annual objectives are especially important in strategy implementation, whereas

long-term objectives are particularly important in strategy formulation. Annual objectives represent the basis for allocating resources.

Campbell Soup Corporation has an annual objective to achieve 20 percent growth in earnings, a 20 percent ROE, and a 20 percent return on invested cash. The company calls this ERC, for earnings, returns, and cash.

Policies

Policies are the means by which annual objectives will be achieved. Policies include guidelines, rules, and procedures established to support efforts to achieve stated objectives. Policies are guides to decision making and address repetitive or recurring situations.

Policies are most often stated in terms of management, marketing, finance/accounting, production/operations, research and development, and computer information systems activities. Policies can be established at the corporate level and apply to an entire organization at the divisional level and apply to a single division, or at the functional level and apply to particular operational activities or departments. Policies, like annual objectives, are especially important in strategy implementation because they outline an organization's expectations of its employees and managers. Policies allow consistency and coordination within and between organizational departments.

Substantial research suggests that a healthier workforce can more effectively and efficiently implement strategies. The National Center for Health Promotion estimates that more than 80 percent of all American corporations have No Smoking policies. No Smoking policies are usually derived from annual objectives that seek to reduce corporate medical costs associated with absenteeism and to provide a healthy workplace.

THE STRATEGIC-MANAGEMENT MODEL

The strategic-management process can best be studied and applied using a model. Every model represents some kind of process. The framework illustrated in Figure 1–1 is a widely accepted, comprehensive model of the strategic-management process.[12] This model does not guarantee success, but it does represent a clear and practical approach for formulating, implementing, and evaluating strategies. Relationships among major components of the strategic-management process are shown in the model, which appears in all subsequent chapters with appropriate areas shaped to show the particular focus of each chapter.

Identifying an organization's existing vision, mission, objectives, and strategies is the logical starting point for strategic management because a firm's present situation and condition may preclude certain strategies and may even dictate a particular course of action. Every organization has a vision, mission, objectives, and strategy, even if these elements are not consciously designed, written, or communicated. The answer to where an organization is going can be determined largely by where the organization has been!

The strategic-management process is dynamic and continuous. A change in any one of the major components in the model can necessitate a change in any or all of the other components. For instance, a shift in the economy could represent a major opportunity and require a change in long-term objectives and strategies; a failure to accomplish annual objectives could require a change in policy; or a major competitor's change in strategy could require a change in the firm's mission. Therefore, strategy formulation, implementation, and evaluation activities should be performed on a continual basis, not

FIGURE 1–1

A Comprehensive Strategic-Management Model

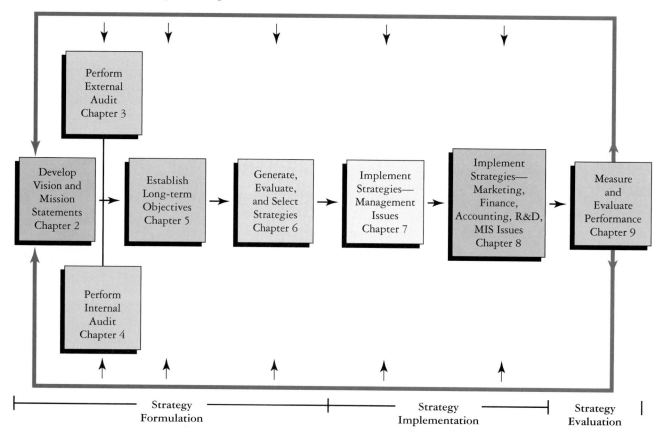

Source: Fred R. David, "How Companies Define Their Mission," *Long Range Planning* 22, no. 3 (June 1988): 40.

just at the end of the year or semi-annually. The strategic-management process never really ends.

The strategic-management process is not as cleanly divided and neatly performed in practice as the strategic-management model suggests. Strategists do not go through the process in lockstep fashion. Generally, there is give-and-take among hierarchical levels of an organization. Many organizations conduct formal meetings semiannually to discuss and update the firm's vision/mission, opportunities/threats, strengths/weaknesses, strategies, objectives, policies, and performance. These meetings are commonly held off-premises and are called *retreats*. The rationale for periodically conducting strategic-management meetings away from the work site is to encourage more creativity and candor from participants. Good communication and feedback are needed throughout the strategic-management process.

Application of the strategic-management process is typically more formal in larger and well-established organizations. Formality refers to the extent that participants, responsibilities, authority, duties, and approach are specified. Smaller businesses tend to be less formal. Firms that compete in complex, rapidly changing environments, such as technology companies, tend to be more formal in strategic planning. Firms that have many divisions, products, markets, and technologies also tend to be more formal in applying strategic-management concepts. Greater formality in applying the strategic-management process is usually positively associated with the cost, comprehensiveness, accuracy, and success of planning across all types and sizes of organizations.[13]

 ## BENEFITS OF STRATEGIC MANAGEMENT

Strategic management allows an organization to be more proactive than reactive in shaping its own future; it allows an organization to initiate and influence (rather than just respond to) activities—and thus to exert control over its own destiny. Small business owners, chief executive officers, presidents, and managers of many for-profit and non-profit organizations have recognized and realized the benefits of strategic management.

Historically, the principal benefit of strategic management has been to help organizations formulate better strategies through the use of a more systematic, logical, and rational approach to strategic choice. This certainly continues to be a major benefit of strategic management, but research studies now indicate that the process, rather than the decision or document, is the more important contribution of strategic management.[14] *Communication is a key to successful strategic management.* Through involvement in the process, managers and employees become committed to supporting the organization. Dialogue and participation are essential ingredients. The chief executive officer of Rockwell International explains, "We believe that fundamental to effective strategic management is fully informed employees at all organizational levels. We expect every business segment to inform every employee about the business objectives, the direction of the business, the progress towards achieving objectives, and our customers, competitors and product plans."

The manner in which strategic management is carried out is thus exceptionally important. A major aim of the process is to achieve the understanding of and commitment from all managers and employees. Understanding may be the most important benefit of strategic management, followed by commitment. When managers and employees understand what the organization is doing and why, they often feel that they are a part of the firm and become committed to assisting it. This is especially true when employees also understand linkages between their own compensation and organizational performance. Managers and employees become surprisingly creative and innovative when they understand and support the firm's mission, objectives, and strategies. A great benefit of strategic management, then, is the opportunity that the process provides to empower individuals. *Empowerment* is the act of strengthening employees' sense of effectiveness by encouraging and rewarding them to participate in decision making and to exercise initiative and imagination.

More and more organizations are decentralizing the strategic-management process, recognizing that planning must involve lower-level managers and employees. The notion of centralized staff planning is being replaced in organizations by decentralized line-manager planning. The process is a learning, helping, educating, and supporting activity, not merely a paper-shuffling activity among top executives. Strategic-management dialogue is more important than a nicely bound strategic-management document.[15] The worst thing strategists can do is develop strategic plans themselves and then present them to operating managers to execute. Though involvement in the process, line managers become "owners" of the strategy. Ownership of strategies by the people who have to execute them is a key to success!

Although making good strategic decisions is the major responsibility of an organization's owner or chief executive officer, both managers and employees must also be

VISIT THE NET

Explains in detail how to develop a strategic plan and compares this document to a business plan. http://www.planware.org/strategy.htm#1

involved in strategy formulation, implementation, and evaluation activities. Participation is a key to gaining commitment for needed changes.

An increasing number of corporations and institutions are using strategic management to make effective decisions. But strategic management is not a guarantee for success; it can be dysfunctional if conducted haphazardly.

Financial Benefits

Research indicates that organizations using strategic-management concepts are more profitable and successful than those that do not.[16] Businesses using strategic-management concepts show significant improvement in sales, profitability, and productivity compared to firms without systematic planning activities. High-performing firms tend to do systematic planning to prepare for future fluctuations in their external and internal environments. Firms with planning systems more closely resembling strategic-management theory generally exhibit superior long-term financial performance relative to their industry.

VISIT THE NET

Provides excellent narrative on the "Benefits of Strategic Planning," "Pitfalls of Strategic Planning," and the "Steps in Doing Strategic Planning." http://www.entarga.com/ stratplan/index.htm

High-performing firms seem to make more informed decisions with good anticipation of both short- and long-term consequences. On the other hand, firms that perform poorly often engage in activities that are shortsighted and do not reflect good forecasting of future conditions. Strategists of low-performing organizations are often preoccupied with solving internal problems and meeting paperwork deadlines. They typically underestimate their competitors' strengths and overestimate their own firm's strengths. They often attribute weak performance to uncontrollable factors such as a poor economy, technological change, or foreign competition.

Dun & Bradstreet reports that more than 100,000 businesses in the United States fail annually. Business failures include bankruptcies, foreclosures, liquidations, and court-mandated receiverships. Although many factors besides a lack of effective strategic management can lead to business failure, the planning concepts and tools described in this text can yield substantial financial benefits for any organization. An excellent Web site for businesses engaged in strategic planning is **www.checkmateplan.com**.

Nonfinancial Benefits

Besides helping firms avoid financial demise, strategic management offers other tangible benefits, such as an enhanced awareness of external threats, an improved understanding of competitors' strategies, increased employee productivity, reduced resistance to change, and a clearer understanding of performance-reward relationships. Strategic management enhances the problem-prevention capabilities of organizations because it promotes interaction among managers at all divisional and functional levels. Firms that have nurtured their managers and employees, shared organizational objectives with them, empowered them to help improve the product or service, and recognized their contributions can turn to them for help in a pinch because of this interaction.

In addition to empowering managers and employees, strategic management often brings order and discipline to an otherwise floundering firm. It can be the beginning of an efficient and effective managerial system. Strategic management may renew confidence in the current business strategy or point to the need for corrective actions. The strategic-management process provides a basis for identifying and rationalizing the need for change to all managers and employees of a firm; it helps them view change as an opportunity rather than as a threat.

Greenley stated that strategic management offers the following benefits:

1. It allows for identification, prioritization, and exploitation of opportunities.
2. It provides an objective view of management problems.

3. It represents a framework for improved coordination and control of activities.

4. It minimizes the effects of adverse conditions and changes.

5. It allows major decisions to better support established objectives.

6. It allows more effective allocation of time and resources to identified opportunities.

7. It allows fewer resources and less time to be devoted to correcting erroneous or ad hoc decisions.

8. It creates a framework for internal communication among personnel.

9. It helps integrate the behavior of individuals into a total effort.

10. It provides a basis for clarifying individual responsibilities.

11. It encourages forward thinking.

12. It provides a cooperative, integrated, and enthusiastic approach to tackling problems and opportunities.

13. It encourages a favorable attitude toward change.

14. It gives a degree of discipline and formality to the management of a business.[17]

WHY SOME FIRMS DO NO STRATEGIC PLANNING

Some firms do not engage in strategic planning, and some firms do strategic planning but receive no support from managers and employees. Some reasons for poor or no strategic planning are as follows:

- *Poor Reward Structures*—When an organization assumes success, it often fails to reward success. When failure occurs, then the firm may punish. In this situation, it is better for an individual to do nothing (and not draw attention) than to risk trying to achieve something, fail, and be punished.

- *Fire-Fighting*—An organization can be so deeply embroiled in crisis management and fire-fighting that it does not have time to plan.

- *Waste of Time*—Some firms see planning as a waste of time since no marketable product is produced. Time spent on planning is an investment.

- *Too Expensive*—Some organizations are culturally opposed to spending resources.

- *Laziness*—People may not want to put forth the effort needed to formulate a plan.

- *Content with Success*—Particularly if a firm is successful, individuals may feel there is no need to plan because things are fine as they stand. But success today does not guarantee success tomorrow.

- *Fear of Failure*—By not taking action, there is little risk of failure unless a problem is urgent and pressing. Whenever something worthwhile is attempted, there is some risk of failure.

- *Overconfidence*—As individuals amass experience, they may rely less on formalized planning. Rarely, however, is this appropriate. Being overconfident or overestimating experience can bring demise. Forethought is rarely wasted and is often the mark of professionalism.

- *Prior Bad Experience*—People may have had a previous bad experience with planning, that is, cases in which plans have been long, cumbersome, impractical, or inflexible. Planning, like anything else, can be done badly.

VISIT THE NET

Gives reasons why some organizations avoid strategic planning.
http://www.mindtools.com/plfailpl.html

- *Self-Interest*—When someone has achieved status, privilege, or self-esteem through effectively using an old system, he or she often sees a new plan as a threat.
- *Fear of the Unknown*—People may be uncertain of their abilities to learn new skills, of their aptitude with new systems, or of their ability to take on new roles.
- *Honest Difference of Opinion*—People may sincerely believe the plan is wrong. They may view the situation from a different viewpoint, or they may have aspirations for themselves or the organization that are different from the plan. Different people in different jobs have different perceptions of a situation.
- *Suspicion*—Employees may not trust management.[18]

PITFALLS IN STRATEGIC PLANNING

Strategic planning is an involved, intricate, and complex process that takes an organization into unchartered territory. It does not provide a ready-to-use prescription for success; instead, it takes the organization through a journey and offers a framework for addressing questions and solving problems. Being aware of potential pitfalls and being prepared to address them is essential to success.

Some pitfalls to watch for and avoid in strategic planning are provided below:

- Using strategic planning to gain control over decisions and resources
- Doing strategic planning only to satisfy accreditation or regulatory requirements
- Too hastily moving from mission development to strategy formulation
- Failing to communicate the plan to employees, who continue working in the dark
- Top managers making many intuitive decisions that conflict with the formal plan
- Top managers not actively supporting the strategic-planning process
- Failing to use plans as a standard for measuring performance
- Delegating planning to a "planner" rather than involving all managers
- Failing to involve key employees in all phases of planning
- Failing to create a collaborative climate supportive of change
- Viewing planning to be unnecessary or unimportant
- Becoming so engrossed in current problems that insufficient or no planning is done
- Being so formal in planning that flexibility and creativity are stifled[19]

GUIDELINES FOR EFFECTIVE STRATEGIC MANAGEMENT

Failing to follow certain guidelines in conducting strategic management can foster criticisms of the process and create problems for the organization. An integral part of strategy evaluation must be to evaluate the quality of the strategic-management process. Issues such as "Is strategic management in our firm a people process or a paper process?" should be addressed.

Even the most technically perfect strategic plan will serve little purpose if it is not implemented. Many organizations tend to spend an inordinate amount of time, money, and effort on developing the strategic plan, treating the means

VISIT THE NET

Provides nice discussion of the limitations of strategic planning process within an organization. http://www.des.calstate.edu/limitations.html

and circumstances under which it will be implemented as afterthoughts! Change comes through implementation and evaluation, not through the plan. A technically imperfect plan that is implemented well will achieve more than the perfect plan that never gets off the paper on which it is typed.[20]

Strategic management must not become a self-perpetuating bureaucratic mechanism. Rather, it must be a self-reflective learning process that familiarizes managers and employees in the organization with key strategic issues and feasible alternatives for resolving those issues. Strategic management must not become ritualistic, stilted, orchestrated, or too formal, predictable, and rigid. Words supported by numbers, rather than numbers supported by words, should represent the medium for explaining strategic issues and organizational responses. A key role of strategists is to facilitate continuous organizational learning and change.

R. T. Lenz offered some important guidelines for effective strategic management:

Keep the strategic-management process as simple and nonroutine as possible. Eliminate jargon and arcane planning language. Remember, strategic management is a process for fostering learning and action, not merely a formal system for control. To avoid routinized behavior, vary assignments, team membership, meeting formats, and the planning calendar. The process should not be totally predictable, and settings must be changed to stimulate creativity. Emphasize word-oriented plans with numbers as back-up material. If managers cannot express their strategy in a paragraph or so, they either do not have one or do not understand it. Stimulate thinking and action that challenge the assumptions underlying current corporate strategy. Welcome bad news. If strategy is not working, managers desperately need to know it. Further, no pertinent information should be classified as inadmissible merely because it cannot be quantified. Build a corporate culture in which the role of strategic management and its essential purposes are understood. Do not permit "technicians" to co-opt the process. It is ultimately a process for learning and action. Speak of it in these terms. Attend to psychological, social, and political dimensions, as well as the information infrastructure and administrative procedures supporting it.[21]

An important guideline for effective strategic management is open-mindedness. A willingness and eagerness to consider new information, new viewpoints, new ideas, and new possibilities is essential; all organizational members must share a spirit of inquiry and learning. Strategists such as chief executive officers, presidents, owners of small businesses, and heads of government agencies must commit themselves to listen to and understand managers' positions well enough to be able to restate those positions to the managers' satisfaction. In addition, managers and employees throughout the firm should be able to describe the strategists' positions to the satisfaction of the strategists. This degree of discipline will promote understanding and learning.

No organization has unlimited resources. No firm can take on an unlimited amount of debt or issue an unlimited amount of stock to raise capital. Therefore, no organization can pursue all the strategies that potentially could benefit the firm. Strategic decisions thus always have to be made to eliminate some courses of action and to allocate organizational resources among others. Most organizations can afford to pursue only a few corporate-level strategies at any given time. It is a critical mistake for managers to pursue too many strategies at the same time, thereby spreading the firm's resources so thin that all strategies are jeopardized. Joseph Charyk, CEO of the Communication Satellite Corporation (Comsat), said, "We have to face the cold fact that Comsat may not be able to do all it wants. We must make hard choices on which ventures to keep and which to fold."

Strategic decisions require trade-offs such as long-range versus short-range considerations or maximizing profits versus increasing shareholders' wealth. There are ethics issues too. Strategy trade-offs require subjective judgments and preferences. In many cases, a lack of objectivity in formulating strategy results in a loss of competitive posture and profitability. Most organizations today recognize that strategic-management concepts and techniques can enhance the effectiveness of decisions. Subjective factors such as attitudes toward risk, concern for social responsibility, and organizational culture will always affect strategy-formulation decisions, but organizations need to be as objective as possible in considering qualitative factors.

BUSINESS ETHICS AND STRATEGIC MANAGEMENT

VISIT THE NET

Describes "Why Have a Code of Ethics" and gives "Guidelines on Writing a Code of Ethics."
www.ethicsweb.ca/codes

Business ethics can be defined as principles of conduct within organizations that guide decision making and behavior. Good business ethics is a prerequisite for good strategic management; good ethics is just good business!

A rising tide of consciousness about the importance of business ethics is sweeping America and the world. Strategists are the individuals primarily responsible for ensuring that high ethical principles are espoused and practiced in an organization. All strategy formulation, implementation, and evaluation decisions have ethical ramifications.

Newspapers and business magazines daily report legal and moral breaches of ethical conduct by both public and private organizations. Managers and employees of firms must be careful not to become scapegoats blamed for company environmental wrongdoings. Harming the natural environment is unethical, illegal, and costly. When organizations today face criminal charges for polluting the environment, firms increasingly are turning on their managers and employees to win leniency for themselves. Employee firings and demotions are becoming common in pollution-related legal suits. Managers being fired at Darling International, Inc. and Niagara Mohawk Power Corporation for being indirectly responsible for their firms' polluting water exemplifies this corporate trend. Therefore, managers and employees today must be careful not to ignore, conceal, or disregard a pollution problem, or they may find themselves personally liable.

VISIT THE NET

Gives example codes of business ethics for companies such as Halliburton and Johnson & Johnson. http://www.ethics.ubc.ca/resources/business/codes.html

A new wave of ethics issues related to product safety, employee health, sexual harassment, AIDS in the workplace, smoking, acid rain, affirmative action, waste disposal, foreign business practices, cover-ups, takeover tactics, conflicts of interest, employee privacy, inappropriate gifts, security of company records, and layoffs has accented the need for strategists to develop a clear code of business ethics. United Technologies Corporation has issued a twenty-one-page Code of Ethics and named a new vice president of business ethics. Baxter Travenol Laboratories, IBM, Caterpillar Tractor, Chemical Bank, Exxon/Mobil, Dow Corning, and Celanese are firms that have formal codes of business ethics. A *code of business ethics* can provide a basis on which policies can be devised to guide daily behavior and decisions at the work site.

The explosion of the Internet into the workplace has raised many new ethical questions in organizations today. For example, United Parcel Service (UPS) caught an employee actually running a personal business from his computer. A Lockheed Martin employee recently sent a religious e-mail to sixty thousand fellow employees that disabled company networks for more than six hours. Boeing is an example of a company that seemingly has accepted the inevitable by instituting a policy specifically allowing employees to use company faxes, e-mail, and the Internet for personal reasons for "reasonable duration and frequency without embarrassment to the company." In contrast, Ameritech has a policy that says "computers and other company equipment are to be used only to provide service to customers and for other business purposes."

E-COMMERCE PERSPECTIVE

e-biz

Business Ethics and the Internet

May employees use the Internet at work to conduct day-trading of personal stocks? May employees send e-mail to personal friends and relatives from the workplace? Is it ethical for employees to shop online while at work? May employees hunt for a new job while online at work? May employees play games online while at work? Before answering these questions, consider the following facts:

- Employee productivity can suffer immensely when many workers surf the Web at work.

- Unlike phone calls, e-mail can often be retrieved months or years later and can be used against the company in litigation.

- When employees surf the Web at work, they drag the company's name along with them everywhere. This could be harmful to the company if employees visit certain sites such as racist chat rooms or pornographic material.

- Software packages are now available to companies that report Web site visits by individual employees. Companies such as Telemate.Net Software Inc. in Atlanta produce software that tells managers who went to what sites at what times and for how long.

- Some 27 percent of large U.S. firms have begun checking employee e-mail, up from 15 percent in 1997. BellSouth employees must regularly click OK to a message warning them against misuse of e-mail and the Internet, and alerting them that their actions can be monitored.

- Many companies such as Boeing grant Internet usage to employees as a perk, but many of those firms are finding that this "fringe benefit" must be managed.

Lockheed Martin now directs its employees onto the Internet for extensive training sessions on topics that include business ethics, legal compliance, sexual harassment, and day-trading. Lockheed even has an Internet ethics game, Ethics Challenge, which every single employee and manager must play once a year. During a recent six-month period, Lockheed discharged 25 employees for ethics violations, suspended 14 others, gave a written reprimand to 51 persons, and an oral reprimand to 146 employees.

Soon after installing the Telemate software, Wolverton & Associates learned that broadcast.com was the company's third-most visited site; people download music from that site. And E*TRADE was the company's eighth-most visited site; people day-trade stocks at that site.

Recent research reveals that 38 percent of companies today choose to store and review employees' e-mail messages; this represents a rise of 15 percent since 1997. In addition, 54 percent of companies also monitor employees' Internet connections, with 29 percent blocking access to unauthorized or inappropriate Web sites.[22]

Sources: Adapted from Michael McCarthy, "Virtual Morality: A New Workplace Quandary," *The Wall Street Journal* (October 21, 1999): B1; Michael McCarthy. "Now the Boss Knows Where You're Clicking," *The Wall Street Journal* (October 21, 1999); and Michael McCarthy, "How One Firm Tracks Ethics Electronically," *The Wall Street Journal* (October 21, 1999): B1.

The E-Commerce Perspective focuses on business ethics issues related to the Internet. Merely having a code of ethics, however, is not sufficient to ensure ethical business behavior. A code of ethics can be viewed as a public relations gimmick, a set of platitudes, or window dressing. To ensure that the code is read, understood, believed, and remembered, organizations need to conduct periodic ethics workshops to sensitize people to workplace circumstances in which ethics issues may arise.[23] If employees see examples of punishment for violating the code and rewards for upholding the code, this helps reinforce the importance of a firm's code of ethics.

Internet privacy is an ethical issue of immense proportions. There is a national push for industry assurances that children have parental permission before giving out their names, ages, and other private details to companies that run Web sites. Privacy

VISIT THE NET

An excellent Web site to obtain additional information regarding business ethics is www.ethicsweb.ca/codes; *it describes "Why Have a Code of Ethics" and gives "Guidelines on Writing a Code of Ethics."*

advocates increasingly argue for new government regulations to enforce protection of young users.

Millions of computer users are worried about privacy on the Internet and want the U.S. government to pass laws about how data can be collected and used. Advertisers, marketers, companies, and people with various reasons to snoop on other people now can discover easily on the Internet others' buying preferences, hobbies, incomes, medical data, social security numbers, addresses, previous addresses, sexual preferences, credit card purchases, traffic tickets, divorce settlements, and much more. Many Internet users are ready for what they call "some law and order" in cyberspace.

NATURAL ENVIRONMENT PERSPECTIVE

Combating Terrorism

In light of the World Trade Center, Pentagon, and anthrax attacks, there is much that businesses can and should do to help in the global war to combat terrorism. As part of their ongoing concern for natural environment issues, businesses should include decision and expense consideration for combating biological or chemical terrorism because it may impact their corporations. After anthrax-tainted mail began arriving at government and business offices, firms began to implement security measures such as wearing gloves in mailrooms, securing air ducts in buildings, and establishing hotlines for obtaining antibiotics. Post offices and corporate mailrooms are the first line of defense against bioterrorism.

According to the Centers for Disease Control, the biggest terrorist threat that could impact business operations comes from the following seven agents: anthrax, smallpox, pneumonic plague, botulinum toxin, tularemia, filoviruses such as ebola, and arenaviruses such as Lassa fever. Pathogens or toxins could be sprayed from an airplane or placed in air-conditioning or water systems of buildings or manufacturing plants. Methods for dispensing deadly biological agents are almost unlimited. Viruses considered to be hazardous agents under the Antiterrorism and Effective Death Penalty Act include equine morbillvirus, Venezuelan equine encephalitis virus, marburg virus, Rift Valley fever virus, and yellow fever virus. The act also includes the following bacteria: Yersinia pestis (plague), anthrax, burkholderia pseudomallei, and Clostridium botulinum.

There are also numerous chemical weapons that also could destroy the natural environment and life, including mustard gas, nitrogen dioxide, and nerve toxins such as sarin. Some companies are more vulnerable than others, and these businesses need to be much more proactive in taking steps to safeguard themselves and their operations against natural environment terrorism. No industry or company is immune to this threat, but the following two industries are especially vulnerable:

- Transportation: Airlines, Railroads, Trucks, and Cruise Lines—Airport security has quadrupled due to the special vulnerability of this mode of transportation, and passengers are again becoming comfortable with the idea of flying. Railroads have stepped up the inspection of tracks, equipment, tunnels, and telecommunications centers. Transportation-oriented firms have increased their communication with federal agencies regarding security and intelligence. Trucking companies have tightened security at terminals. Truck drivers now stay with their trucks as much as possible. Closer screening of drivers and employees among trucking companies and cruise operators is common practice.

- Chemical: Pharmaceutical and Agricultural—Terrorists could target chemical-oriented facilities and operations, especially those that deal with deadly agents, such as pharmaceutical and agricultural companies. Enhanced security on, near, and above particular operations is necessary. Firms should reevaluate the amount of chemical information they provide on their Web sites. Closer screening of all employees is warranted.

Sources: Adapted from Laura Johannes and Marilyn Chase, "Experts Say Bioterrorism Threat Is Real, Yet Likelihood Is Uncertain," *Wall Street Journal* (September 28, 2001): B1, B6; Ted Bridis, "State of the Union: America the Vulnerable?" *Wall Street Journal* (September 28, 2001): B1 and B4.

Given the global nature of e-commerce, any U.S. government regulations to inhibit the free flow of information will not carry much weight in places such as Moldova, home of a phone-porn scam. But perhaps the United States at least should set a standard for e-commerce rules and regulations that other countries could consider adopting.

An ethics "culture" needs to permeate organizations! To help create an ethics culture, Citicorp developed a business ethics board game that is played by forty thousand employees in forty-five countries. Called The Work Ethic, this game asks players business ethics questions, such as, how do you deal with a customer who offers you football tickets in exchange for a new, backdated IRA? Diana Robertson at The Wharton School of business believes the game is effective because it is interactive. Many organizations, such as Prime Computer and Kmart, have developed a code-of-conduct manual outlining ethical expectations and giving examples of situations that commonly arise in their businesses. Harris Corporation's managers and employees are warned that failing to report an ethical violation by others could bring discharge.

One reason strategists' salaries are high compared to those of other individuals in an organization is that strategists must take the moral risks of the firm. Strategists are responsible for developing, communicating, and enforcing the code of business ethics for their organizations. Although primary responsibility for ensuring ethical behavior rests with a firm's strategists, an integral part of the responsibility of all managers is to provide ethics leadership by constant example and demonstration. Managers hold positions that enable them to influence and educate many people. This makes managers responsible for developing and implementing ethical decision making. Gellerman and Drucker, respectively, offer some good advice for managers:

> All managers risk giving too much because of what their companies demand from them. But the same superiors, who keep pressing you to do more, or to do it better, or faster, or less expensively, will turn on you should you cross that fuzzy line between right and wrong. They will blame you for exceeding instructions or for ignoring their warnings. The smartest managers already know that the best answer to the question "How far is too far?" is don't try to find out.[24]
>
> A man (or woman) might know too little, perform poorly, lack judgment and ability, and yet not do too much damage as a manager. But if that person lacks character and integrity—no matter how knowledgeable, how brilliant, how successful—he destroys. He destroys people, the most valuable resource of the enterprise. He destroys spirit. And he destroys performance. This is particularly true of the people at the head of an enterprise. For the spirit of an organization is created from the top. If an organization is great in spirit, it is because the spirit of its top people is great. If it decays, it does so because the top rots. As the proverb has it, "Trees die from the top." No one should ever become a strategist unless he or she is willing to have his or her character serve as the model for subordinates.[25]

No society anywhere in the world can compete very long or successfully with people stealing from one another or not trusting one another, with every bit of information requiring notarized confirmation, with every disagreement ending up in litigation, or with government having to regulate businesses to keep them honest. Being unethical is a recipe for headaches, inefficiency, and waste. History has proven that the greater the trust and confidence of people in the ethics of an institution or society, the greater its economic strength. Business relationships are built mostly on mutual trust and reputation. Short-term decisions based on greed and questionable ethics will preclude the necessary self-respect to gain the trust of others. More and more firms believe that ethics training and an ethics culture create strategic advantage.

VISIT THE NET

The Web site http://www.ethics.ubc.ca/resources/business/codes.html *gives example codes of business ethics for companies such as Halliburton and Johnson & Johnson.*

Some business actions considered to be unethical include misleading advertising or labeling, causing environmental harm, poor product or service safety, padding expense accounts, insider trading, dumping banned or flawed products in foreign markets, lack of equal opportunities for women and minorities, overpricing, hostile takeovers, moving jobs overseas, and using nonunion labor in a union shop.[26]

Internet fraud, including hacking into company computers and spreading viruses, has become a major unethical activity that plagues every sector of online commerce from banking to shopping sites. More than three hundred Web sites now show individuals how to hack into computers; this problem has become endemic nationwide and around the world.

Ethics training programs should include messages from the CEO emphasizing ethical business practices, the development and discussion of codes of ethics, and procedures for discussing and reporting unethical behavior. Firms can align ethical and strategic decision making by incorporating ethical considerations into long-term planning, by integrating ethical decision making into the performance appraisal process, by encouraging whistle-blowing or the reporting of unethical practices, and by monitoring departmental and corporate performance regarding ethical issues.

In a final analysis, ethical standards come out of history and heritage. Our fathers, mothers, brothers, and sisters of the past left us with an ethical foundation to build upon. Even the legendary football coach Vince Lombardi knew that some things were worth more than winning, and he required his players to have three kinds of loyalty: to God, to their families, and to the Green Bay Packers, "in that order."

COMPARING BUSINESS AND MILITARY STRATEGY

A strong military heritage underlies the study of strategic management. Terms such as *objectives, mission, strengths*, and *weaknesses* first were formulated to address problems on the battlefield. According to *Webster's New World Dictionary,* strategy is "the science of planning and directing large-scale military operations, of maneuvering forces into the most advantageous position prior to actual engagement with the enemy." The word *strategy* comes from the Greek *strategos*, which refers to a military general and combines *stratos* (the army) and *ago* (to lead). The history of strategic planning began in the military. A key aim of both business and military strategy is "to gain competitive advantage." In many respects, business strategy is like military strategy, and military strategists have learned much over the centuries that can benefit business strategists today. Both business and military organizations try to use their own strengths to exploit competitor's weaknesses. If an organization's overall strategy is wrong (ineffective), then all the efficiency in the world may not be enough to allow success. Business or military success is generally not the happy result of accidental strategies. Rather, success is the product of both continuous attention to changing external and internal conditions and the formulation and implementation of insightful adaptations to those conditions. The element of surprise provides great competitive advantages in both military and business strategy; information systems that provide data on opponents' or competitors' strategies and resources are also vitally important.

Of course, a fundamental difference between military and business strategy is that business strategy is formulated, implemented, and evaluated with an assumption of *competition,* whereas military strategy is based on an assumption of *conflict*. Nonetheless, military conflict and business competition are so similar that many strategic-management techniques apply equally to both. Business strategists have access to valuable insights that military thinkers have refined over time. Superior strategy formulation and implementation can overcome an opponent's superiority in numbers and resources.

Both business and military organizations must adapt to change and constantly improve to be successful. Too often, firms do not change their strategies when their environment and competitive conditions dictate the need to change. Gluck offered a classic military example of this:

> When Napoleon won, it was because his opponents were committed to the strategy, tactics, and organization of earlier wars. When he lost—against Wellington, the Russians, and the Spaniards—it was because he, in turn, used tried-and-true strategies against enemies who thought afresh, who were developing the strategies not of the last war but of the next.[27]

Similarities can be construed from Sun Tzu writings to the practice of formulating and implementing strategies among businesses today. Table 1–2 provides narrative excerpts from *The Art of War*. As you read through Table 1–2, consider which of the principles of war apply to business strategy as companies today compete aggressively to survive and grow.

THE NATURE OF GLOBAL COMPETITION

VISIT THE NET

Provides a nice account of strategic planning, tracing history back to the military. http://www.des.calstate.edu/history.html

VISIT THE NET

An excellent Web site that describes Sun Tzu's famous The Art of War *writings is provided at* http://www.ccs.neu.edu/home/thigpen/html/art_of_war.html

For centuries before Columbus discovered America and surely for centuries to come, businesses have searched and will continue to search for new opportunities beyond their national boundaries. There has never been a more internationalized and economically competitive society than today's. Some American industries, such as textiles, steel, and consumer electronics, are in complete disarray as a result of the international challenge.

Organizations that conduct business operations across national borders are called *international firms* or *multinational corporations*. The term *parent company* refers to a firm investing in international operations, while *host country* is the country where that business is conducted. The strategic-management process is conceptually the same for multinational firms as for purely domestic firms; however, the process is more complex for international firms because of the presence of more variables and relationships. The social, cultural, demographic, environmental, political, governmental, legal, technological, and competitive opportunities and threats that face a multinational corporation are almost limitless, and the number and complexity of these factors increase dramatically with the number of products produced and the number of geographic areas served.

More time and effort are required to identify and evaluate external trends and events in multinational corporations, than in domestic corporations. Geographical distance, cultural and national differences, and variations in business practices often make communication between domestic headquarters and overseas operations difficult. Strategy implementation can be more difficult because different cultures have different norms, values, and work ethics.

The global war on terrorism and advancements in telecommunications are drawing countries, cultures, and organizations worldwide closer together. Foreign revenue as a percent of total company revenues already exceeds 50 percent in hundreds of U.S. firms, including Exxon/Mobil, Gillette, Dow Chemical, Citicorp, Colgate-Palmolive, and Texaco. Joint ventures and partnerships between domestic and foreign firms are becoming the rule rather than the exception!

Fully 95 percent of the world's population lives outside the United States, and this group is growing 70 percent faster than the American population! The lineup of competitors in virtually all industries today is global. Global competition is more than a management fad. General Motors, Ford, and Chrysler compete with Toyota and Hyundai. General Electric and Westinghouse battle Siemens and Mitsubishi. Caterpillar

TABLE 1-2   **Excerpts from Sun Tzu's *The Art of War* Writings**
(Note: Substitute the words *strategy* or *strategic planning* for *war* or *warfare*)

- War is a matter of vital importance to the state; a matter of life or death, the road either to survival or ruin. Hence, it is imperative that it be studied thoroughly.

- Warfare is based on deception. When near the enemy, make it seem that you are far away; when far away, make it seem that you are near. Hold out baits to lure the enemy. Strike the enemy when he is in disorder. Avoid the enemy when he is stronger. If your opponent is of choleric temper, try to irritate him. If he is arrogant, try to encourage his egotism. If enemy troops are well prepared after reorganization, try to wear them down. If they are united, try to sow dissension among them. Attack the enemy where he is unprepared, and appear where you are not expected. These are the keys to victory for a strategist. It is not possible to formulate them in detail beforehand.

- A speedy victory is the main object in war. If this is long in coming, weapons are blunted and morale depressed. When the army engages in protracted campaigns, the resources of the state will fall short. Thus, while we have heard of stupid haste in war, we have not yet seen a clever operation that was prolonged.

- Generally, in war the best policy is to take a state intact; to ruin it is inferior to this. To capture the enemy's entire army is better than to destroy it; to take intact a regiment, a company, or a squad is better than to destroy it. For to win one hundred victories in one hundred battles is not the acme of skill. To subdue the enemy without fighting is the supreme excellence. Those skilled in war subdue the enemy's army without battle.

- The art of using troops is this—When ten to the enemy's one, surround him. When five times his strength, attack him. If double his strength, divide him. If equally matched, you may engage him with some good plan. If weaker, be capable of withdrawing. And if in all respects unequal, be capable of eluding him.

- Know your enemy and know yourself, and in a hundred battles you will never be defeated. When you are ignorant of the enemy but know yourself, your chances of winning or losing are equal. If ignorant both of your enemy and of yourself, you are sure to be defeated in every battle.

- He who occupies the field of battle first and awaits his enemy is at ease, and he who comes later to the scene and rushes into the fight is weary. And therefore, those skilled in war bring the enemy to the field of battle and are not brought there by him. Thus, when the enemy is at ease, be able to tire him; when well fed, be able to starve him; when at rest, be able to make him move.

- Analyze the enemy's plans so that you will know his shortcomings as well as his strong points. Agitate him in order to ascertain the pattern of his movement. Lure him out to reveal his dispositions and to ascertain his position. Launch a probing attack in order to learn where his strength is abundant and where deficient. It is according to the situation that plans are laid for victory, but the multitude does not comprehend this.

- An army may be likened to water, for just as flowing water avoids the heights and hastens to the lowlands, so an army should avoid strength and strike weakness. And as water shapes its flow in accordance with the ground, so an army manages its victory in accordance with the situation of the enemy. And as water has no constant form, there are in warfare no constant conditions. Thus, one able to win the victory by modifying his tactics in accordance with the enemy situation may be said to be divine.

- If you decide to go into battle, do not announce your intentions or plans. Project "business as usual."

- Unskilled leaders work out their conflicts in courtrooms and an battlefields. Brilliant strategists rarely go to battle or to court; they generally achieve their objectives through tactical positioning well in advance of any confrontation.

- When you do decide to challenge another company (or army), much calculating, estimating, analyzing, and positioning brings triumph. Little computation brings defeat.

- Skillful leaders do not let a strategy inhibit creative counter-movement. Nor should commands from those at a distance interfere with spontaneous maneuvering in the immediate situation.

- When a decisive advantage is gained over a rival, skillful leaders do not press on. They hold their position and give their rivals the opportunity to surrender or merge. They do not allow their forces to be damaged by those who have nothing to lose.

- Brilliant strategists forge ahead with illusion, obscuring the area(s) of major confrontation, so that opponents divide their forces in an attempt to defend many areas. Create the appearance of confusion, fear, or vulnerability so the opponent is helplessly drawn toward this illusion of advantage.

Source: Adapted from *The Art of War* and from the Web site **www.ccs.neu.edu/home/thigpen/html/art_of_war.html.**

and John Deere compete with Komatsu. Goodyear battles Michelin, Bridgestone/ Firestone, and Pirelli. Boeing competes with Airbus. Only a few U.S. industries, such as furniture, printing, retailing, consumer packaged goods, and retail banking, are not yet greatly challenged by foreign competitors. But many products and components in these industries too are now manufactured in foreign countries.

International operations can be as simple as exporting a product to a single foreign country, or as complex as operating manufacturing, distribution, and marketing facilities in many countries. U.S. firms are acquiring foreign companies and forming joint ventures with foreign firms, and foreign firms are acquiring U.S. companies and forming joint ventures with U.S. firms. This trend is accelerating dramatically. AT&T's former Chief Executive Officer, Robert Allen, said, "The phrase *global markets* is not empty rhetoric. Foreign competitors are here. And we must be there." Many U.S. firms have been spoiled by the breadth and number of home markets and remain ignorant of foreign languages and culture. For example, Hershey Foods, the leading chocolate producer in the United States, derives less than 15 percent of its total revenues from outside the United States.

Advantages and Disadvantages of International Operations

Firms have numerous reasons for formulating and implementing strategies that initiate, continue, or expand involvement in business operations across national borders. Perhaps the greatest advantage is that firms can gain new customers for their products and services, thus increasing revenues. Growth in revenues and profits is a common organizational objective and often an expectation of shareholders because it is a measure of organizational success.

In addition to seeking growth, firms have the following potentially advantageous reasons to initiate, continue, and expand international operations:

1. Foreign operations can absorb excess capacity, reduce unit costs, and spread economic risks over a wider number of markets.
2. Foreign operations can allow firms to establish low-cost production facilities in locations close to raw materials and/or cheap labor.
3. Competitors in foreign markets may not exist, or competition may be less intense than in domestic markets.
4. Foreign operations may result in reduced tariffs, lower taxes, and favorable political treatment in other countries.
5. Joint ventures can enable firms to learn the technology, culture, and business practices of other people and to make contacts with potential customers, suppliers, creditors, and distributors in foreign countries.
6. Many foreign governments and countries offer varied incentives to encourage foreign investment in specific locations.
7. Economies of scale can be achieved from operation in global rather than solely domestic markets. Larger-scale production and better efficiencies allow higher sales volumes and lower price offerings.

A firm's power and prestige in domestic markets may be significantly enhanced with various stakeholder groups if the firm competes globally. Enhanced prestige can translate into improved negotiating power among creditors, suppliers, distributors, and other important groups.

There are also numerous potential disadvantages of initiating, continuing, or expanding business across national borders. One risk is that foreign operations could be seized by nationalistic factions. Other disadvantages include the following:

1. Firms confront different and often little-understood social, cultural, demographic, environmental, political, governmental, legal, technological, economic, and competitive forces when doing business internationally. These forces can make communication difficult between the parent firm and subsidiaries.

2. Weaknesses of competitors in foreign lands are often overestimated, and strengths are often underestimated. Keeping informed about the number and nature of competitors is more difficult when doing business internationally.

3. Language, culture, and value systems differ among countries, and this can create barriers to communication and problems managing people.

4. Gaining an understanding of regional organizations such as the European Economic Community, the Latin American Free Trade Area, the International Bank for Reconstruction and Development, and the International Finance Corporation is difficult but is often required in doing business internationally.

5. Dealing with two or more monetary systems can complicate international business operations.

6. The availability, depth, and reliability of economic and marketing information in different countries vary extensively, as do industrial structures, business practices, and the number and nature of regional organizations.

CONCLUSION

All firms have a strategy, even if it is informal, unstructured, and sporadic. All organizations are heading somewhere, but unfortunately some organizations do not know where they are going. The old saying "If you do not know where you are going, then any road will lead you there!" accents the need for organizations to use strategic-management concepts and techniques. The strategic-management process is becoming more widely used by small firms, large companies, nonprofit institutions, governmental organizations, and multinational conglomerates alike. The process of empowering managers and employees has almost limitless benefits.

Organizations should take a proactive rather than a reactive approach in their industry, and they should strive to influence, anticipate, and initiate rather than just respond to events. The strategic-management process embodies this approach to decision making. It represents a logical, systematic, and objective approach for determining an enterprise's future direction. The stakes are generally too high for strategists to use intuition alone in choosing among alternative courses of action. Successful strategists take the time to think about their businesses, where they are with the businesses, and what they want to be as organizations—and then to implement programs and policies to get from where they are to where they want to be in a reasonable period of time.

It is a known and accepted fact that people and organizations that plan ahead are much more likely to become what they want to become than those that do not plan at all. A good strategist plans and controls his or her plans, while a bad strategist never plans and then tries to control people! This textbook is devoted to providing you with the tools necessary to be a good strategist.

Success in business increasingly depends upon offering products and services that are competitive on a world basis, not just on a local basis. If the price and quality of a firm's products and services are not competitive with those available elsewhere in the world, the firm may soon face extinction. Global markets have become a reality in all but the most remote areas of the world. Certainly throughout the United States, even in small towns, firms feel the pressure of world competitors. Nearly half of all the automobiles sold in the United States, for example, are made in Japan and Germany.

We invite you to visit the David page on the Prentice Hall Companion Website at www.prenhall.com/david for this chapter's World Wide Web exercises.

KEY TERMS AND CONCEPTS

Annual Objectives (p. 12)

Business Ethics (p. 20)

Code of Business Ethics (p. 20)

Empowerment (p. 15)

Environmental Scanning (p. 10)

External Opportunities (p. 10)

External Threats (p. 10xx)

Host Country (p. 25)

Internal Strengths (p. 11)

Internal Weaknesses (p. 11)

International Firms (p. 25)

Intuition (p. 7)

Long-Range Planning (p. 5)

Long-Term Objectives (p. 11)

Mission Statements (p. 10)

Multinational Corporations (p. 25)

Policies (p. 13)

Strategic Management (p. 5)

Strategic-Management Model (p. 13)

Strategic-Management Proces (p. 5)

Strategies (p. 5)

Strategists (p. 5)

Strategy Evaluation (p. 6)

Strategy Formulation (p. 5)

Strategy Implementation (p. 6)

Vision Statement (p. 9)

ISSUES FOR REVIEW AND DISCUSSION

1. Explain why Business Policy often is called a "capstone course."
2. Read one of the suggested readings at the end of this chapter. Prepare a one-page written summary that includes your personal thoughts on the subject.
3. What aspect of strategy formulation do you think requires the most time? Why?
4. Why is strategy implementation often considered the most difficult stage in the strategic-management process?
5. Why is it so important to integrate intuition and analysis in strategic management?
6. Explain the importance of a vision and mission statement.
7. Discuss relationships among objectives, strategies, and policies.
8. Why do you think some chief executive officers fail to use a strategic-management approach to decision making?
9. Discuss the importance of feedback in the strategic-management model.
10. How can strategists best ensure that strategies will be effectively implemented?
11. Give an example of a recent political development that changed the overall strategy of an organization.
12. Who are the major competitors of your college or university? What are their strengths and weaknesses? What are their strategies? How successful are these institutions compared to your college?

13. If you owned a small business, would you develop a code of business conduct? If yes, what variables would you include? If no, how would you ensure that ethical business standards were being followed by your employees?
14. Would strategic-management concepts and techniques benefit foreign businesses as much as domestic firms? Justify your answer.
15. What do you believe are some potential pitfalls or risks in using a strategic-management approach to decision making?
16. In your opinion, what is the single major benefit of using a strategic-management approach to decision making? Justify your answer.
17. Compare business strategy and military strategy.
18. What do you feel is the relationship between personal ethics and business ethics? Are they—or should they be—the same?
19. Why is it important for all business majors to study strategic management since most students will never become a chief executive officer nor even a top manager in a large company?
20. Explain why consumption patterns are becoming similar worldwide. What are the strategic implications of this trend?
21. What are the advantages and disadvantages of beginning export operations in a foreign country?

NOTES

1. KEVIN MANEY, "The Net Effect: Evolution or Revolution?" *USA Today* (August 9, 1999): B1.

2. PETER DRUCKER, *Management: Tasks, Responsibilities, and Practices* (New York: Harper & Row, 1974): 611.

3. ALFRED SLOAN, JR., *Adventures of the White Collar Man* (New York: Doubleday, 1941): 104.

4. Quoted in Eugene Raudsepp, "Can You Trust Your Hunches?" *Management Review* 49, no. 4 (April 1960): 7.

5. STEPHEN HARPER, "Intuition: What Separates Executives from Managers," *Business Horizons* 31, no. 5 (September–October 1988): 16.

6. RON NELSON, "How to Be a Manager," *Success* (July–August 1985): 69.

7. BRUCE HENDERSON, *Henderson on Corporate Strategy* (Boston: Abt Books, 1979): 6.

8. ROBERT WATERMAN, JR., *The Renewal Factor: How the Best Get and Keep the Competitive Edge* (New York: Bantam, 1987). See also *Business Week* (September 14, 1987): 100. Also, see *Academy of Management Executive* 3, no. 2 (May 1989): 115.

9. JOHN PEARCE II and FRED DAVID, "The Bottom Line on Corporate Mission Statements," *Academy of Management Executive* 1, no. 2 (May 1987): 109.

10. LORRIE GRANT, "Grocery Chore No More," *USA Today* (July 21, 1999): p. B1.

11. SHIRLEY LEUNG, "Competition Heats Up Between Boston Market and KFC," *Wall Street Journal* (November 6, 2001): p. B4.

12. FRED R. DAVID, "How Companies Define Their Mission," *Long Range Planning* 22, no. 1 (February 1989): 91.

13. JACK PEARCE and RICHARD ROBINSON, *Strategic Management,* 7th ed. (New York: McGraw-Hill, 2000): p. 8.

14. ANN LANGLEY, "The Roles of Formal Strategic Planning," *Long Range Planning* 21, no. 3 (June 1988): 40.

15. BERNARD REIMANN, "Getting Value from Strategic Planning," *Planning Review* 16, no. 3 (May–June 1988): 42.

16. G. L. SCHWENK and K. SCHRADER, "Effects of Formal Strategic Planning in Financial Performance in Small Firms: A Meta-Analysis," *Entrepreneurship and Practice* 3, no. 17 (1993): 53–64. Also, C. C. Miller and L. B. Cardinal, "Strategic Planning and Firm Performance: A Synthesis of More than Two Decades of Research," *Academy of Management Journal* 6, no. 27 (1994): 1649–1665. Also, Michael Peel and John Bridge, "How Planning and Capital Budgeting Improve SME Performance," *Long Range Planning* 31, no. 6 (October 1998): 848–856. Also, Julia Smith, "Strategies for Start-Ups," *Long Range Planning* 31, no. 6 (October 1998): 857–872.

17. GORDON GREENLEY, "Does Strategic Planning Improve Company Performance?" *Long Range Planning* 19, no. 2 (April 1986): 106.

18. Adapted from: **www.mindtools.com/plreschn.html**.

19. Adapted from the Web sites: **www.des.calstate.edu/limitations.html** and **www.entarga.com/stratplan/purposes.html**.

20. DALE MCCONKEY, "Planning in a Changing Environment," *Business Horizons* (September–October 1988): 66.

21. R. T. LENZ, "Managing the Evolution of the Strategic Planning Process," *Business Horizons* 30, no. 1 (January–February 1987): 39.

22. SAUL GELLERMAN, "Managing Ethics from the Top Down," *Sloan Management Review* (Winter 1989): 77.

23. JOANN GRECO, "Privacy—Whose Right Is It Anyhow?" *Journal of Business Strategy* (January/February 2001): 32.

24. SAUL GELLERMAN, "Why 'Good' Managers Make Bad Ethical Choices," *Harvard Business Review* 64, no. 4 (July–August 1986): 88.

25. DRUCKER, 462, 463.

26. GENE LACZNIAK, MARVIN BERKOWITZ, RUSSELL BROOKER, and JAMES HALE, "The Ethics of Business: Improving or Deteriorating?" *Business Horizons* 38, no. 1 (January–February 1995): 43.

27. FREDERICK GLUCK, "Taking the Mystique Out of Planning," *Across the Board* (July–August 1985): 59.

CURRENT READINGS

AHLSTROM, DAVID, GARRY D. BRUTON, and STEVEN S. Y. LUI. "Navigating China's Changing Economy: Strategies for Private Firms." *Business Horizons* 43, no. 1 (January–February 2000): 5.

ALVAREZ, SHARON A., and JAY B. BARNEY. "How Entrepreneurial Firms Can Benefit from Alliances with Large Partners." *Academy of Management Executive* 15, no. 1 (February 2001): 139.

AMIT, R., and C. ZOTT. "Value Creation in E-Business." *Strategic Management Journal* 22, no. 6–7 (June–July 2001): 493.

BARNEY, JAY B. "Is the Resource-Based 'View' a Useful Perspective for Strategic Management Research? Yes." *Academy of Management Journal* 26, no. 1 (January 2001): 41.

BOSSIDY, LARRY. "The Job No CEO Should Delegate." *Harvard Business Review* (March 2001): 46.

BOWMAN, E. H., and C. E. HELFAT. "Does Corporate Strategy Matter?" *Strategic Management Journal* 22, no. 1 (January 2001): 1.

BRUSH, CANDIDA G., PATRICIA G. GREENE, and MYRA M. HART. "From Initial Idea to Unique Advantage: The Entrepreneurial Challenge of Constructing a Resource

Base." *Academy of Management Executive* 15, no. 1 (February 2001): 64.

CANNELLA, ALBERT, A., JR., and KENNETH STARKEY. "Donald Hambrick on Executives and Strategy." *Academy of Management Executive* 15, no. 3 (August 2001): 36.

CARPENTER, MASON A., and JAMES W. FREDICKSON. "Top Management Teams, Global Strategic Posture, and the Moderating Role of Uncertainty." *Academy of Management Journal* 44, no. 3 (June 2001): 533.

CHAN, RICKY Y. K. "An Emerging Green Market in China: Myth or Reality?" *Business Horizons* 43, no. 2 (Mar.–April 2000): 55.

CHANG, S. J., and P. M. ROSENZWEIG. "The Choice of Entry Mode in Sequential Foreign Direct Investment." *Strategic Management Journal* 22, no. 8 (August 2001): 747.

CLEMONS, ERIC K., and JASON A. SANTAMARIA. "Maneuver Warfare: Can Modern Military Strategy Lead You to Victory?" *Harvard Business Review* (April 2002): 56.

DRUCKER, PETER F. "They're Not Employees, They're People." *Harvard Business Review* (February 2002): 70.

FORD, CAMERON M., and DENNIS GIOIA. "Factors Influencing Creativity in the Domain of Managerial Decision Making." *Journal of Management* 26, no. 4 (2000): 685.

GIBSON, KEVIN. "Excuses, Excuses: Moral Slippage in the Workplace." *Business Horizons* 43, no. 6 (November–December 2000): 65.

HARPER, STEPHEN C. "Timing—The Bedrock of Anticipatory Management." *Business Horizons* 43, no. 1 (January–February 2000): 75.

HAYASHI, ALDEN M. "When to Trust Your Gut." *Harvard Business Review* (February 2001): 59.

IRELAND, R. DUANE, MICHAEL A. HITT, S. MICHAEL CAMP, and DONALD L. SEXTON. "Integrating Entrepreneurship and Strategic Management Actions to Create Firm Wealth." *Academy of Management Executive* 15, no. 1 (February 2001): 49.

KELLY, EILEEN P., and HUGH C. ROWLAND. "Ethical and Online Privacy Issues in Electronic Commerce." *Business Horizons* 43, no. 3 (May–June 2000): 3.

KOVACH, KENNETH A., SANDRA J. CONNER, TAMAR LIVNEH, KEVIN M. SCALLAN, and ROY L. SCHWARTZ. "Electronic Communication in the Workplace—Something's Got to Give." *Business Horizons* 43, no. 4 (July–August 2000): 59.

KRAATZ, MATTHEW S., and JAMES H. MOORE. "Executive Migration and Institutional Change." *Academy of Management Journal* 45, no. 1 (February 2002): 120.

LI, ZHAN G., and NURIT GERY. "E-tailing—For All Products?" *Business Horizons* 43, no. 6 (November–December 2000): 49.

LYON, DOUGLAS W., G. T. LUMPKIN, and GREGORY G. DESS. "Enhancing Entrepreneurial Orientation Research: Operationalizing and Measuring a Key Strategic Decision Making Process." *Journal of Management* 26, no. 5 (2000): 1055.

MINTZBERG, HENRY, and CONSTANTINOS MARKIDES. "Henry Mintzberg and Constantinos Markides on Strategy and Management." *Academy of Management Journal* 14, no. 3 (August 2000): 31.

MOULSON, TOM, and GEORGE SPROLES. "Styling Strategy." *Business Horizons* 43, no. 5 (September–October 2000): 45.

PORTER, MICHAEL E. "Strategy and the Internet." *Harvard Business Review* (March 2001): 62.

PRIEM, RICHARD L., and JOHN E. BUTLER. "Is the Resource-Based 'View' a Useful Perspective for Strategic Management Research?" *Academy of Management Journal* 26, no. 1 (January 2001): 22.

ROSEN, CHRISTINE MEISNER. "Environmental Strategy and Competitive Advantage: An Introduction." *California Management Review* 43, no. 3 (Spring 2001): 8.

ROWE, W. GLENN. "Creating Wealth in Organizations: The Role of Strategic Leadership." *Academy of Management Executive* 15, no. 1 (February 2001): 81.

SORCHER, MELVIN, and JAME BRANT. "Are You Picking the Right Leaders?" *Harvard Business Review* (February 2002): 78.

SOULE, EDWARD. "Managerial Moral Strategies—In Search of a Few Good Principles." *Academy of Management Review* 27, no. 1 (January 2002): 114.

WALDMAN, DAVID A., GABRIEL G. RAMIREZ, ROBERT J. HOUSE, and PHANISH PURANAM. "Does Leadership Matter? CEO Leadership Attributes and Profitability Under Conditions of Perceived Environmental Uncertainty." *Academy of Management Journal* 44, no. 1 (February 2001): 134.

WEAVER, GARY R., and BRADLEY R. AGLE. "Religiosity and Ethical Behavior in Organizations: A Symbolic Interactionist Perspective." *Academy of Management Review* 27, no. 1 (January 2002): 77.

YOFFIE, DAVID B., and MARY KWAK. "Playing by the Rules: How Intel Avoids Antitrust Litigation." *Harvard Business Review* (June 2001): 119.

COHESION CASE

AMERICAN AIRLINES—2002
Fred R. David
Francis Marion University
AMR
www.AA.com
www.amrcorp.com

OVERVIEW

The largest airline in the world, American Airlines (AMR), makes forty-one hundred flights daily to forty-one countries, but it is in trouble. As the first quarter of 2002 ends, AMR continues to be adversely affected by the September 11, 2001, terrorist attacks. The parent company of AMR Investments, American Cargo, AMR Training Group, American Eagle, and American Airlines, AMR's first quarter 2002 revenues showed a $624 million (13.1 percent) decline from the prior year's first quarter, while net income for this period was a negative $575 million compared to a negative $43 million the prior year.

In addition to the threat of terrorism, AMR's poor performance is also due to a weak economy, the decline in both business and vacation air travel, and increased airfare price competition. American is reportedly losing $10 to $15 million per day. CEO Don Carty calls this "the worst financial crisis in the history of the company." After September 11, 2001, and through early 2002, AMR has:

- Reduced the number of flights by 20 percent
- Grounded and accelerated the retirement of some airplanes
- Cut 2001 and 2002 capital spending by $2.5 billion, partly by delaying the delivery of 29 airplanes on order from Boeing
- Closed 105 travel centers, six Admiral's Clubs, and five Platinum Centers
- Cut in-flight food and beverages
- Laid off twenty thousand employees
- Asked for voluntary pay cuts (the Board of Directors and the CEO volunteered to work without pay)
- Requested and received government assistance
- Borrowed approximately $800 million in cash from American's credit line
- Borrowed an additional $200 million on Wall Street using aircraft as collateral[1]

Founded in 1982, AMR acquired Trans World Airlines (TWA) in 2001, and today it provides jet service to more than 161 destinations throughout North America, Latin America, the Caribbean, Canada, Europe, and the Pacific. American is one of the largest freight and mail-service carriers in the world. AMR's operating revenues from foreign operations were approximately 28 percent, 30 percent, and 29 percent of the firm's total operating revenues in 2001, 2000, and 1999, respectively.

INTERNAL ISSUES

Airplanes

American Airline's average aircraft age is 9.9 years, down from 10.8 years on March 31, 2001. American Eagle's average aircraft age is 6.6 years, up from 6.5 years last year. AMR's operating aircraft as of March 31, 2002, are as follows:

AMERICAN AIRLINES

Aircraft	Number of Aircrafts
Airbus A300-600R	34
Boeing 717-200	11
Boeing 727-200	15
Boeing 737-800	77
Boeing 757-200	150
Boeing 767-200	8
Boeing 767-200 Extended Range	21
Boeing 767-300 Extended Range	58
Boeing 777-200 Extended Range	42
Fokker 100	74
McDonnell Douglas MD-11	4
McDonnell Douglas MD-80	362
Total	717

AMERICAN EAGLE

Aircraft	Number of Aircraft
ATR 42	29
Embraer 135	40
Embraer 140	22
Embraer 145	56
Super ATR	42
Saab 340	66
Saab 340B Plus	25
Bombardier CRJ-700	3
Total	283

Hub and Spoke

All of the major airlines have what is known as a hub-and-spoke operation, which allows an airline to route most of its passengers through one or more centralized locations in order to reduce costs. American Airlines operates five hubs: Dallas/Fort Worth, Chicago O'Hare, Miami, St. Louis, and San Juan, Puerto Rico. AMR's two largest competitors, Delta Air Lines and United, have hub operations at Dallas/Fort Worth and Chicago O'Hare, respectively. American Eagle serves smaller markets in the United States and feeds customers to American's hubs. American has contracts with three other regional airlines called American Connection to provide connecting service through its St. Louis hub.

Global Alliances and Code Sharing

Airports outside the United States are subject to widely varying government regulations, which often change depending on the relationship between the U.S. government and the foreign government. One way to limit an airline's global expansion is to place restrictions on slots. Slots are takeoff and landing authorizations. In most nondomestic airports, slots are needed before a carrier can begin to offer services. Since a carrier cannot be assured that it will be able to obtain slots, it may be locked out of certain markets. Slots may be purchased or traded in some countries, but some foreign governments restrict slot availability.

To gain access to different international airports, AMR has entered into alliances with other airlines to utilize each other's facilities and marketing efforts. As indicated in Exhibit 1, there are currently five major global airline alliances: Star Alliance, anchored by United Airlines and Lufthansa; Oneworld, with American Airlines and British Airways; Qualiflyer Group, with 11 foreign airlines as members; the SkyTeam alliance that unites Delta and Air France; and Wings, which comprises Continental, KLM, and Northwest. Each alliance involves several secondary carriers. SkyTeam is shaping up to be a stronger-than-anticipated alliance. Although Delta lost Austrian Airlines, Sabena, and Swissair, it has won AeroMexico and Korean Airlines. Star Alliance, which had fifteen members in early 2002, is perhaps the strongest of the lot.

AMR has entered into code-sharing programs with many foreign and domestic airlines. Code-sharing is an agreement which allows an airline to put its identification code on the flights of another airline. Airlines that share codes also coordinate other aspects of travel, like connection times and baggage checking. These alliances and code-sharing programs have greatly expanded American's network in areas where it would be prohibitively expensive or impossible to expand by merger or purchase. American Airlines currently has code-sharing programs with Aer Lingus, Air Pacific, Alaska Airlines, Asiana Airlines, China Eastern Airlines, EVA Air, Finnair, Gulf Air, Hawaiian Airlines, Iberia, Japan Airlines, LanChile, LOT Polish Airlines, Qantas Airways, SNCF, TACA Group, the TAM Group, TAP Air Portugal, Thalys, and Turkish Airlines. American Eagle also has code-sharing programs with Continental, Delta, Midwest Express, and Northwest; in addition, it has code-sharing arrangements with some of American's code-share partners. Certain of these relationships also include reciprocity between American and the other airlines' frequent flyer programs. In addition, AMR expects to implement code shares with Cathay Pacific Airways and Vietnam Airlines pending regulatory approval. In the coming years, AMR expects to develop these programs further and to evaluate new alliances with other carriers. AMR's most recent code-sharing agreement is with Swissair.

EXHIBIT 1   Airline Alliances

Star Alliance	Oneworld	Qualiflyer Group	SkyTeam	Wings
http://www.star-alliance.com	http://www.oneworldallance.com	http://www.qualiflyergroup.com	http://www.skyteam.com	
Air Canada	Aer Lingus	Air Europe	AeroMexico	KLM
Air New Zeland	**American Airlines**	Air Liberte	Air France	Northwest
All Nippon Airways	British Airways	Air Littoral	Alitalia	Continental
Ansett Australia	Cathay Pacific Airways	Crossair	Czech Airlines	
Austrian Airlines	Finnair	**LOT Polish Airlines**	Delta Airlines	
British Midland	Iberia	Portugalia	Korean Air	
Lauda Air	LANChile	Sabena		
Lufthansa	Quantas Airways	Swissair		
Mexicana		TAP Air Portugal		
Scandinavian		Turkish Airlines		
Singapore Airlines		Volare Airlines		
Thai				
Tyrolean				
United Airlines				

Source: **www.AA.com.**

American Airlines and British Airways (BA), the largest airline in Europe, seek antitrust immunity for an alliance that would enable them to cooperate more fully with each other and give them the ability to better serve their customers. American Airlines and British Airways have not been allowed to code-share or integrate their networks beyond a rudimentary marketing level. Not surprisingly, all of the major competitors in the market have opposed the alliance. American and BA have insisted that such an alliance would lead to an "open skies" arrangement between the two countries, which would lead to reduced regulations on their operations. Their opponents make the claim that the agreement would be strongly anticompetitive and would dominate the market for air service between the United States and the United Kingdom. Government regulators in the United States and the United Kingdom in mid-2002 are on the verge of approving the AMR/BA alliance.

Operating Statistics

Revenue passenger-miles (RPMs) is an indicator that measures the total number of passengers carried by the industry's airlines, multiplied by the number of miles flown. The RPM numbers are available on a monthly basis from the Air Transport Association (ATA), an industry trade group. For the industry as a whole, RPMs declined 7.7 percent in 2001, to 561.3 billion. This is in contrast to the industry's ten-year growth rate of about 4 percent.

Available seats per mile (ASM) is an indicator that measures the total number of seats in the active fleet, multiplied by the number of miles flown, for either an individual airline or the entire industry. The ATA compiles an industrywide figure on a monthly basis. Changes in ASMs are influenced by the net addition of aircraft to the industry's fleet, the seating mix of aircraft, seat pitch (or spacing), as well as by how quickly the industry turns around its aircraft between flights. ASMs for the major airlines totaled 795.2 billion in 2001, a decline of 4.4 percent from 2000's total. The decline reflects the large number of flights taken out of service after the September 11, 2001, terrorist attacks as well as actions by American and United to remove seats to provide more legroom.

AMR's domestic revenue per available seat mile (RASM) decreased 15.4 percent in the first quarter of 2002. The company's overall international RASM declined 10.6 percent due to a 14.1 percent RASM decline in travel to Europe, an 11.9 percent decrease in Latin America travel, and a 9 percent increase in travel to the Pacific Far East. AMR Eagle's passenger revenues declined 13.8 percent, while American Cargo revenues declined 23.9 percent in the first quarter of 2002. However, due to labor union problems, AMR's outlays for wages, salaries, and benefits increased 19.1 percent for the quarter.

Load factor is an indicator, compiled monthly by the ATA, that measures the percentage of available seating capacity that is filled with passengers. It may be calculated as a percentage of a single airline's seats, or of all seats in the industry. Once AMR's load factor exceeds its breakeven point, profit margins can expand dramatically as an ever-larger percentage of incremental revenue filters down to the bottom line. Load factor can also be calculated by dividing a carrier's revenue passenger-miles (RPMs) by its total available seats per mile (ASMs).

Exhibit 2 provides operating statistics for American Airlines (excluding TWA) and American Eagle for the years ending December 31, 2001, 2000, and 1999.

Exhibit 3 provides operating statistics for American Airlines (excluding TWA) and American Eagle for March 31, 2002, and March 31, 2001.

Marketing

AMR's advertising expenses were $202 million, $221 million, and $206 million for 2001, 2000, and 1999, respectively. One of the company's newer commercials promotes

EXHIBIT 2   **AMR's Annual Operating Statistics**

	2001	2000	1999
AMERICAN AIRLINES			
Revenue passenger miles (RPM) (in millions)	106,224	116,594	112,067
Available seats per mile (in millions)	153,035	161,030	161,211
Cargo ton miles (in millions)	2,058	2,280	2,068
Passenger load factor	69.4%	72.4%	69.5%
Breakeven load factor	78.1%	65.9%	63.8%
Passenger revenue yield per passenger mile (cents)	13.28	14.06	3.14
Passenger revenue per available seat mile (cents)	9.22	10.18	9.13
Cargo revenue yield per ton mile (cents)	0.24	31.31	30.70
Operating expenses per available seat mile (cents)	1.14	10.48	9.50
Operating aircraft at year-end	712	717	697
AMERICAN EAGLE			
Revenue passenger miles (in millions)	3,725	3,731	3,371
Available seats per mile (in millions)	6,471	6,256	5,640
Passenger load factor	57.6%	59.6%	59.8%
Operating aircraft at year-end	276	261	268

Source: **www.AA.com**.

EXHIBIT 3   **AMR's Quarterly Operating Statistics**

	March 31, 2002	March 31, 2001
AMERICAN AIRLINES		
Revenue passenger miles (in millions)	27,817	26,452
Available seats per mile (in millions)	40,089	38,977
Cargo ton miles (in millions)	463	549
Passenger load factor	87.4%	68.2%
Breakeven load factor	87.1%	65.4%
Passenger revenue yield per passenger mile (cents)	12.52	14.88
Passenger revenue per available seat mile (cents)	8.69	10.10
Cargo revenue yield per ton mile (cents)	28.74	31.68
Operating expenses per available seat mile (cents)	11.30	11.26
Fuel consumption (gallons, in millions)	745	743
Fuel price per gallon (cents)	61.2	87.6
Fuel price per gallon, excluding fuel taxes (cents)	61.7	82.0
Operating aircraft at period-end	852	719
AMERICAN EAGLE		
Revenue passenger miles (in millions)	919	860
Available seats per mile (in millions)	1,567	1,588
Passenger load factor	58.6%	54.2%
Operating aircraft at period-end	283	267

Source: **www.AA.com**.

the new "More Room Throughout Coach" feature of AMR flights. A key AMR marketing tool, the AAdvantage frequent flyer program, was created to develop passenger loyalty by offering awards to travelers for their continued patronage. The largest such program in the United States, AAdvantage members earn mileage credits for flights on American, American Eagle, and certain other participating airlines, or by utilizing services of other program participants, including hotels, car rental companies, and bank credit card issuers. American sells mileage credits and related services to the other companies participating in the program.

American has entered into a marketing alliance with America Online to offer AOL AAdvantage miles. The miles can be earned through services that AOL owns or promotes and can also be traded for retail products through AOL. Members can also earn miles from hotel and car rental companies as well as from participating retail and financial service organizations. Awards include travel prizes, upgrades, car rentals, special services, and retail purchases.

Price competition is a key marketing weapon that airlines commonly use to win a greater share of the leisure market. Fare differentials of just a few dollars can persuade leisure travelers to select one airline over another or to make their journeys by a different mode. To attract leisure travelers, airlines advertise deeply discounted fares. Analysts expect average fares to rise modestly in 2002 over 2001 levels as both the industry and the economy improve later in the year, a development which should help to stimulate demand.

The airline industry distributes tickets primarily through travel agents. However, it also books flights directly through company clerks and via the Internet. Travel agents generate about 70 percent to 80 percent of total airline bookings. Some 135,000 travel agents and 29,000 travel agencies operate in the United States. These numbers have been declining due to a more difficult operating environment—airlines have been reducing their commissions and competition from the Internet has been growing.

The fees paid to travel agents vary from airline to airline. In late 2001, most major airlines, including AMR, cut their commission rates to 5 percent of fares, with a $20 cap on domestic roundtrip fares ($100 cap for international); previously, the commission rate was 8 percent of fares with a $50 cap. As might be expected, this change led to a sharp decline in commissions paid in the fourth quarter of the year, a development which should continue in 2002 as the cut takes its toll. Total commissions paid in 2001 accounted for about 4.0 percent of airline industry costs, down from 6.2 percent in 2000 and as much as 10.9 percent in 1993. The majority of the tickets for travel on American and American Eagle are sold by travel agents.

E-commerce

Ever on the lookout for ways to cut costs, airlines have enthusiastically embraced "ticketless travel"—the practice of issuing electronic tickets, or e-tickets, to customers. E-tickets are booked in the conventional manner, through a travel agent or directly through the airline, though no paper ticket is issued. Instead, passengers obtain boarding passes at the airport check-in counter or from an automated dispensing machine, which is activated with a credit card or frequent-flyer card. Currently, e-tickets may account for close to 50 percent of all tickets, although Southwest issues 75 percent of its tickets electronically. According to United Airlines, electronic ticketing costs just 50 cents per ticket, versus $8 for paper tickets, because it eliminates fourteen accounting and processing procedures. Much of the savings comes from not having to mail actual tickets. Travelers can get a receipt and itinerary via fax or e-mail, or they can pick them up these items at the airport.

The continued boom in Internet travel purchases, combined with the lower commissions required by Internet travel providers, has greatly reduced American's distribution costs. American has formed agreements with several travel Web sites, including Travelocity.com, Expedia.com, Hotwire.com, Priceline.com, and Orbitz. However, American's own Internet distribution system, **www.AA.com**, continues to be the foundation of AMR's e-commerce strategy. AMR continues to expand the capabilities of AA.com. Not only can you plan and book your flight online, but flight status information is also available either online or by e-mail to your phone. AA.com seeks to be the consumer's one-stop source for travel planning and sales. AMR offers online travel resources such as maps as well as assistance for those, who reserve hotels and automobiles through its Car and Hotel Wizards. The AA.com site offers travel tips, news, and other information about air travel in its Travel Information Center. AA.com received over 10 million site visits each month in 2001. In addition, over 1.5 million consumers receive American's Net SAAver e-mails each week, which offer information about American's sales, specials, and programs. The base commission for sales through Internet travel providers is lower than through traditional travel agencies.

Orbitz ranks third behind Expedia and Travelocity in online travel bookings, and it displays all airline inventories, including special discounted Internet fares. At present, not all airlines participate in all computer reservation systems (CRSs), and not all online travel agents subscribe to all CRSs. Currently, about 45 airlines have signed up for Orbitz's service, including AMR. (Southwest Airlines does not do business with Orbitz, Expedia, or Travelocity.) Orbitz offers lower fares than other online travel agents do because it undercuts their commissions, often 3.5 percent of the fare. Travelocity and Expedia have an aggregate 30 percent of the online airline booking market.

Natural Environment and Social Responsibility

AMR was the first airline to formally adopt the CERES principles (**www.ceres.org**), which require an annual self-evaluation of how well the company addresses environmental issues, such as a reduction in and the disposal of waste, conservation, environmental restoration, and management commitment. American has been identified by the EPA as a potentially responsible party (PRP) at the Operating Industries, Inc., Superfund Site in California. American has also been identified as a PRP at the Beede Waste Oil Superfund Site in New Hampshire. Both American Airlines and American Eagle have a pollution problem at Miami International Airport (MIA), which is funding the remediation costs through landing fees and various cost-recovery methods.

American and Executive Airlines, along with other tenants at Luis Munoz Marin International Airport in San Juan, have been named as PRPs for environmental claims at the airport. American Eagle Airlines, Inc., has been notified of its potential liability under New York law at an inactive hazardous waste site in Poughkeepsie, New York.

American has been the recipient of many awards for its commitment to diversity. In 2001, American received recognition and awards from *Equal Employment Magazine*, *Hispanic Magazine*, the Women's Business Enterprise National Council, Gay Financial Network, and the Gay and Lesbian Values Index.

Fuel Concerns

Airlines are energy-intensive operations; in 2001, fuel costs accounted for about 14.9 percent of total airline expenses. One of the few positives for the industry in the wake of September 11, 2001, has been declining fuel costs. Domestic jet fuel reached a high of

91.0 cents per gallon in December 2000, 45 percent higher than the year-earlier period. For 2000, it averaged 78.7 cents per gallon, a 52 percent hike from 1999. In 2001, even before the attacks, a combination of lower crude oil prices, reduced consumption, and oil cartel overproduction helped push the price down. In August 2001, jet fuel prices had fallen to 76.5 cents per gallon. After the attacks, reduced demand for jet fuel pushed the price down even farther. Domestic jet fuel hit 66.0 cents per gallon in November 2001 and continued to drop into early 2002.

AMR has a fuel hedging program in which it enters into jet fuel, heating oil, and crude swap and option contracts to protect against increases in jet fuel prices, which has had the effect of reducing the firm's average cost per gallon. During 2001 and 2000, AMR's fuel hedging program reduced the firm's fuel expense by approximately $29 million and $545 million, respectively. To reduce the impact of potential fuel price increases in 2002, AMR has hedged approximately 40 percent of its estimated 2002 fuel requirements. Based on projected fuel usage, AMR estimates that a 10 percent increase in the price per gallon of fuel would result in an increase to aircraft fuel expense of approximately $169 million in 2002. AMR's fuel costs and consumption for the years 1999 through 2001 are provided in Exhibit 4.

Finance Issues

AMR's income statements and balance sheets for 2001 and 2000 are provided in Exhibit 5 and Exhibit 6, respectively. AMR's capital expenditures in 2001 totaled $3.6 billion, compared to $3.7 billion in 2000 and $3.5 billion in 1999. In 2001, American took delivery of 26 Boeing 737-800s, 13 Boeing 777-200ERs, and 16 Boeing 757-200s. AMR Eagle took delivery of 15 Embraer 140s, 7 Embraer 135s, 6 Embraer 145s, and 1 Bombardier CRJ-700 aircraft. These expenditures were financed primarily through secured mortgage and debt agreements. Ten Boeing 737-800 aircraft were financed through sale-leaseback transactions, and as a result, AMR received approximately $352 million in cash. Proceeds from the sale of equipment and property and other investments of $401 million included the proceeds received upon the delivery of five McDonnell Douglas MD-11 aircraft to FedEx.

In late 2001, AMR reached an agreement with Boeing for aircraft delivery deferrals, substitutions, and limited additional aircraft orders. As a direct result of the agreement with Boeing, AMR's 2002 and 2003 aircraft commitment amounts have been reduced, in the aggregate, by approximately $700 million. Following this agreement, at year-end 2001, AMR had commitments to acquire the following aircraft: 47 Boeing 737-800s, 14 Boeing 777-200ERs, 9 Boeing 767-300ERs, 7 Boeing 757-200s, 124 Embraer regional jets, and 24 Bombardier CRJ-700s. Deliveries of all aircraft

EXHIBIT 4		AMR's Fuel Costs	
Year	Gallons Consumed (in millions)	Total Cost (in millions)	Average Cost per Gallon (in cents)
1999	3,084	$1,696	55.0
2000	3,197	2,495	78.1
2001	3,461	2,888	81.4

Source: www.AA.com.

EXHIBIT 5   AMR Corporation—Consolidated Statements of Operations (in millions, except per-share amounts)

| | Year Ended December 31, | | |
	2001	2000	1999
REVENUES			
Passenger—American Airlines	$15,780	$16,394	$14,724
AMR Eagle	1,378	1,452	1,294
Cargo	662	721	643
Other revenues	1,143	1,136	1,069
Total operating revenues	$18,963	$19,703	$17,730
EXPENSES			
Wages, salaries, and benefits	$8,032	$6,783	$6,120
Aircraft fuel	2,888	2,495	1,696
Depreciation and amortization	1,404	1,202	1,092
Other rentals and landing fees	1,197	999	942
Maintenance, materials, and repairs	1,165	1,095	1,003
Commissions to agents	835	1,037	1,162
Aircraft rentals	829	607	630
Food service	778	777	740
Other operating expenses	3,695	3,327	3,189
Special charges, net of U.S. government grant	610	–	–
Total operating expenses	$21,433	$18,322	$16,574
Operating income (loss)	(2,470)	1,381	1,156
OTHER INCOME (EXPENSE)			
Interest income	110	154	95
Interest expense	(538)	(467)	(393)
Interest capitalized	144	151	118
Miscellaneous—net	(2)	68	30
Total Other Income	(286)	(94)	(150)
Income (loss) from continuing operations before income taxes and extraordinary loss	(2,756)	1,287	1,006
Income tax provision (benefit)	(994)	508	350
Income (loss) from continuing operations before extraordinary loss	(1,762)	779	656
Income from discontinued operations, net of applicable income taxes and minority interest	–	43	265
Gain on sale of discontinued operations, net of applicable income taxes	–	–	64
Income (loss) before extraordinary loss	(1,762)	822	985
Extraordinary loss, net of applicable income taxes	–	(9)	–
Net earnings (loss)	$ (1,762)	$813	$985
Earnings (loss) applicable to common shares earnings (loss) per share	$ (1,762)	$813	$985
Basic			
Income (loss) from continuing operations	$ (11.43)	$5.20	$4.30
Discontinued operations	–	0.30	2.16
Extraordinary loss	–	(0.07)	–
Net earnings (loss)	$ (11.43)	$5.43	$6.46
Diluted			
Income (loss) from continuing operations	$ (11.43)	$4.81	$4.17
Discontinued operations	–	0.27	2.09
Extraordinary loss	–	(0.05)	–
Net earnings (loss)	$ (11.43)	$5.03	$6.26

Source: www.AA.com.

EXHIBIT 6	AMR Corporation—Consolidated Balance Sheets (in millions, except shares and par value)		

	December 31,	
	2001	*2000*
ASSETS		
CURRENT ASSETS		
Cash	$120	$89
Short-term investments	2,872	2,144
Receivables, less allowance for uncollectible accounts (2001—$52; 2000—$27)	1,414	1,303
Inventories, less allowance for obsolescence (2001—$383; 2000—$332)	822	757
Deferred income taxes	790	695
Other current assets	522	191
Total current assets	6,540	5,179
EQUIPMENT AND PROPERTY		
Flight equipment, at cost	21,707	20,041
Less accumulated depreciation	6,727	6,320
	14,980	13,721
Purchase deposits for flight equipment	929	1,700
Other equipment and property, at cost	4,202	3,639
Less accumulated depreciation	2,123	1,968
Subtotal	2,079	1,671
	17,988	17,092
EQUIPMENT AND PROPERTY UNDER CAPITAL LEASES		
Flight equipment	2,658	2,618
Other equipment and property	163	159
Subtotal	2,821	2,777
Less accumulated amortization	1,154	1,233
Subtotal	1,667	1,544
OTHER ASSETS		
Route acquisition costs and airport operating and gate lease rights, less accumulated amortization (2001—$556; 2000—$498)	1,325	1,143
Goodwill, less accumulated amortization (2001—$110; 2000—$83)	1,392	385
Other	3,929	870
	6,646	2,398
TOTAL ASSETS	$32,841	$26,213
LIABILITIES AND STOCKHOLDERS' EQUITY		
CURRENT LIABILITIES		
Accounts payable	$1,785	$1,267
Accrued salaries and wages	721	955
Accrued liabilities	1,471	1,276
Air traffic liability	2,763	2,696
Current maturities of long-term debt	556	569
Current obligations under capital leases	216	227
Total current liabilities	7,512	6,990
Long-term debt, less current maturities	8,310	4,151
Obligations under capital leases, less current obligations	1,524	1,323

EXHIBIT 6   **AMR Corporation—Consolidated Balance Sheets**
(in millions, except shares and par value) (*continued*)

	December 31,	
	2001	*2000*
LIABILITIES AND STOCKHOLDERS' EQUITY (*continued*)		
OTHER LIABILITIES AND CREDITS		
Deferred income taxes	1,627	2,385
Deferred gains	520	508
Postretirement benefits	2,538	1,706
Other liabilities and deferred credits	5,437	1,974
TOTAL	$10,122	$6,573
COMMITMENTS AND CONTINGENCIES		
STOCKHOLDERS' EQUITY		
Preferred stock–20,000,000 shares authorized; none issued	–	–
Common stock—$1 par value; 750,000,000 shares authorized; 182,278,766 shares issued	182	182
Additional paid-in capital	2,865	2,911
Treasury shares at cost: 2001—27,794,380; 2000—30,216,218	(1,716)	(1,865)
Accumulated other comprehensive loss	(146)	(2)
Retained earnings	4,188	5,950
TOTAL	5,373	7,176
Total liabilities and stockholders' equity	$32,841	$26,213

Source: www.AA.com.

extend through 2008. Future payments for all aircraft, including the estimated amounts for price escalation will approximate $1.3 billion in 2002, $1.7 billion in 2003, $1.2 billion in 2004 and an aggregate of approximately $1.9 billion in 2005 through 2008. AMR's financial commitments to be paid in 2002 and 2003 are as follows:

NATURE OF COMMITMENT (IN MILLIONS)

	2002	2003
Operating lease payments for aircraft and facility obligations (*)	$1,336	$1,276
Firm aircraft commitments	1,300	1,700
Long-term debt (**)	556	296
Capital lease obligations (**)	326	243
Total obligations and commitments	$3,518	$3,515

Source: AMR's 2001 *Annual Report*.

AMR has announced that it will remove from service its remaining Boeing 717-200 fleet by June 2002 and its Boeing 727-200 fleet will be removed from service by May 2003. AMR has agreed to sell its McDonnell Douglas MD-11s to FedEx Corporation (FedEx), with delivery to be completed by the third quarter of 2002. The ten McDonnell Douglas DC-10 aircraft are currently being leased to Hawaiian Airlines, Inc. (Hawaiian), but upon termination of the lease agreement with Hawaiian, AMR has agreed to sell these aircraft to FedEx also. Deliveries began in early 2002. AMR is actively marketing its remaining non-operating aircraft and does not anticipate bringing these aircraft back into its operations.

Labor Issues

In 2001, American commenced negotiations with the Allied Pilots Association (APA). The AMR/APA contract limits the number of ASMs and block hours flown by American's regional carriers when pilots from American are on furlough. American Eagle continues to accept previously ordered regional jets. This will cause the ASM cap to be reached in the first half of 2002, necessitating actions to comply with that cap. American is working with its regional partners to ensure that it is in compliance with this provision. Toward that end, American Eagle is reducing the number of ASMs flown by its carriers, including, but not limited to (1) the removal of seats from its Saab and ATR aircraft, (2) the reduction in the number of turboprop aircraft, and (3) the reduction in the frequency of flights and/or its withdrawal from several routes across its network.

The Association of Flight Attendants (AFA), which represents the flight attendants of the Eagle carriers, reached an agreement with American Eagle, effective March 2, 1998, to have all flight attendants of the American Eagle carriers covered by a single contract. The agreement became amendable on September 2, 2001. However, the parties agreed to commence negotiations over amendments to the agreement in March 2001. The parties are still engaged in direct negotiations. The other union employees at the American Eagle carriers are covered by separate agreements with the Transport Workers Union, which were effective April 28, 1998, and are amendable April 28, 2003.

EXTERNAL ISSUES

For 2001, airline industry losses were a record $11 billion, and most U.S. airlines now face a severe liquidity crisis, have large new debt burdens, and have used up their credit lines. Investors are increasingly worried about airline balance sheet stability, especially in the wake of the Enron Corporation collaspe. For example, AMR Corp. ended 2001 with total debt of $16.1 billion and a debt to total capital ratio of 76 percent, both sharply higher than at the end of 2000. US Airways also had a sharp increase in debt, which totaled $3.7 billion at the end of 2001, and pushed its debt-to-total capital ratio well over 100 percent. The most recent U.S. airline to file for bankruptcy protection was Midway Airlines, which did so on August 13, 2001. A month later, Midway announced that it would permanently cease operations (liquidate).

In emergency mode after the September 11, 2001, terrorist attacks most U.S. airlines cut both capacity (scheduled takeoffs and landings) and staffing. According to the ATA, domestic carriers reduced head count by 80,300 employees after September 11. American and United led the group by furloughing 20,000 employees each, followed by US Airways (11,000), Northwest Airlines Corp. (10,000), and Continental Airlines Inc. (8,500). Of the major carriers, only Southwest Airlines and Alaska Air Group Inc. did not announce layoffs. United ended 2001 as the industry leader in terms of revenue passenger miles, but it was significantly behind American in terms of passenger revenues.

Standard & Poor's estimates that the U.S. airline industry took in revenues of $116.5 billion in 2001, a 10 percent decline from the $129.5 billion in revenues the industry recorded in 2000. About 72 percent of this total is derived from passenger fares. The remaining revenues derived from mail and cargo transport, and in-flight sales. Income from frequent flyer programs delivered another $35.9 billion. Domestic travel accounts for about 79 percent of passenger revenues, while international travel accounts for about 21 percent.

Competitors

Airlines are subject to vigorous competition, which often leads to cutthroat pricing and razor-thin margins. The largest domestic airline in 2001, based on carrier revenues, was

American Airlines, a unit of AMR Corp. American reported 2001 operating revenues of almost $19.0 billion (including its American Eagle unit), which equaled approximately 16 percent of total industry revenues. United Airlines, a unit of UAL Corp., took second place with revenues of $16.1 billion (about 14 percent). Delta Air Lines Inc. followed with $13.9 billion (approximately 12 percent). In terms of traffic, according to DOT data, the top ten carriers logged an estimated 590.0 billion RPMs in 2001. United was number one, tallying 116.6 billion RPMs. American ranked second, with 108.4 billion RPMs, followed by Delta with 97.3 billion RPMs.

AMR faces intense competition from other airlines, including Alaska Airlines, America West Airlines, Continental Airlines, Delta, Northwest Airlines, Southwest Airlines, United, and US Airways, all as well as from of their affiliated regional carriers. Of the nine major airlines, only Southwest posted a profit in 2001. Southwest earned $511 million in 2001, a 19 percent decline from the $627 million profit the company posted in 2000. Southwest was the only carrier that kept its capacity and employee count intact after September 11, a development made possible by the airline's high efficiency levels, low-cost operating structure, and profitable route schedule. Southwest remains profitable in 2002.

AMR also competes with cargo and charter air carriers and as well as with automobiles, buses, and the Amtrak rail system. Amtrak fares are partly subsidized by the U.S. government (though Amtrak has been mandated to reach self-sufficiency by December 2, 2002). While Amtrak operates some long-distance routes, its passengers use it for an average journey length of about 280 miles. Intercity bus travel, although much more popular than railroads, rarely competes directly with air travel because the typical bus journey is just 140 miles.

Airlines compete aggressively with each other in both service and price. For business travelers, flight frequency and reliability are critical; frequent-flyer programs, cuisine, and other amenities also are influential. Small airlines that cannot obtain gate space during peak travel periods have difficulty attracting business travelers.

Security Issues

Although the U.S. government federalized all airport security screening as of February 17, 2002, airline security costs have risen dramatically in the past year. Security today ranges from the securing of all cockpit doors to the opening of extra security lanes to ease the logjam caused by stricter screening requirements. Airlines are now required either to screen all bags for explosives or to make sure each bag on a plane is matched up to a passenger seated on that flight; both of these requirements are time-consuming and expensive. By the end of 2002, all checked bags will have to pass through bomb detection machines, which cost up to $1 million each and are currently in short supply. While necessary to ensure passenger safety and to ease fears, these expenses will cut into airline profits for the foreseeable future.

Effective February 1, 2002, a $2.50 per enplanement security service fee (a $5 one-way maximum fee) is collected by all air carriers and submitted to the government to pay for enhanced security measures. Additionally, air carriers may soon be required to submit to the government an amount equal to the amount the air carriers paid for screening passengers and property in 2000. After that, this fee may be assessed based on the air carrier's market share.

Much secrecy has surrounded the Federal Air Marshal Program, which was sent into overdrive following the September 11, 2001, terrorist attacks. Operated by the Federal Aviation Administration (FAA), the program deploys specially trained, armed teams of security specialists on both domestic and international flights. While the number of total marshals in place and their itineraries remain unknown, the FAA says that it has taken steps to sharply increase the number of marshals on flights.

Regional Jet Services

Regional jet services have grown rapidly in recent years. The Regional Air Service Initiative (RASI), a Web site that tracks these operations, estimated that by the end of 2001, some 800 regional jets were in operation in the United States. In 1997, there were 137. RASI reports that 946 regional jets are on firm or conditional order, while 1,193 units are under option. This implies that future growth in regional jets should be strong. Including turboprop planes, the nation's total regional fleet was 2,300 aircraft in early 2002, a total that has remained relatively unchanged over the previous two years.

More than a dozen low-fare startup carriers currently operate, and a half-dozen others are in the planning stages. JetBlue Airways, which is the biggest threat to industry price stability since the emergence of Southwest Airlines, began flying out of New York City's Kennedy International Airport in February 2000. JetBlue is well capitalized, uses spanking new jets, and has been generating high load factors since its launch.

Regional jets can be credited with getting people out of cars, buses, and trains, and onto planes. According to Bombardier, regional jets are used to supplement existing regional service (44 percent), create new nonstop regional service (33 percent), replace mainline jet service (15 percent), and replace turboprop service (8 percent). With its low purchase and operating costs, the regional jet has made short-haul markets, previously abandoned by major airlines, into viable destinations. The regional jet also offers greater comfort and range than does the turboprop plane. It can handle routes of 1,300 miles, up to 2,300 nautical miles in some cases, while most propeller planes are confined to flights of 350 miles or less.

The regional affiliates of major airlines use regional jets to provide off-peak service when demand is insufficient to warrant a standard one-hundred-plus seat aircraft. Regional jets can be profitable for such service because their breakeven point is a 50 percent load factor, versus about 63 percent for large jets. By offering round-the-clock service in this manner, an airline will appeal to business travelers, who account for 70 percent of regional jet passengers. With regional jets gaining in passenger capacity (seventy or more seats) and range, they are increasingly being used not only to feed passengers into hub airports but also to provide point-to-point competition against carriers employing full-sized jets.

Having recognized the value of the regional carriers, the major airlines have taken steps to increase their control over such companies. Many have acquired partial or total equity positions in carriers with a strong regional jet presence. Among the majors, Delta is perhaps the most active player in the regional market. In early 2000, Delta acquired Comair, whose entire fleet consists of regional jets and Atlantic Southeast Airlines (ASA). AMR owns the largest regional carrier, American Eagle, which is the holding company for Executive Airlines, Flagship Airlines, Simmons Airlines, and Wings West Airlines. The FAA predicts that the nation's regional aircraft fleet will reach twenty-five hundred by 2006, up from twenty-three hundred in 2002.

All pilot contracts have scope clauses, which establish the definition (scope) of a pilot's jobs and stipulates who may and may not perform those jobs. Scope clauses in existing labor contracts will severely limit the ability of some airlines to participate in the regional jet market boom. American Eagle, for instance, can fly regional jets, but its scope clause limits such aircraft to forty-five seats or fewer. In April 2000, US Airways' new pilots' contract doubled the number of regional jets the airline could operate to seventy. The company, however, would like to operate four hundred. Delta Air Lines can operate as many regional jets as it likes, provided none has more than seventy seats. In March 2000, Delta ordered nearly 400 regional jet aircraft, worth $10 billion. Although this move may enable the carrier to step boldly into regional operations, Delta may also have bought itself some labor trouble, as its mainline pilots insist on limiting the carrier's use of regional jets.

The only airlines whose labor contracts carry no restrictions on aircraft use are Continental Airlines (which flies regional jets through its 100 percent-owned Continental Express affiliate), Alaska Air, America West, and Southwest. All airlines with restrictive scope clauses in their pilots' agreements are working to get relief. As pilot contracts come up for renewal, the airlines are trying to gain more flexibility with regard to flying regional jets. Many observers see the biggest emerging segment of the regional jet market in 70–100 seat aircraft, which are just now beginning to roll out of the assembly lines. However, pilots at mainline carriers, who make substantially higher salaries than those at regional operators, worry that their routes will be displaced by regional affiliates operating these larger jets.

Technology and Internet Issues

The air travel industry is capital-, labor-, and technology-intensive. Despite the Internet's considerable size and commercial potential, accurate measurements of the amount of air travel being booked online are hard to come by. Jupiter Communications, a New York-based research firm covering the consumer online industry, estimates that the percentage of airline tickets sold online will reach 11 percent by 2003, up from an estimated 7 percent in 2001. Forrester Research, a technology research firm headquartered in Cambridge, Massachusetts, estimates that total online travel bookings (which includes cruises, hotels, and car rentals as well as air travel) will reach $29 billion by 2003, up from $14.2 billion in 2001.

Southwest Airlines has for years led the industry in this area, obtaining 40 percent of its revenues from Internet sales. Southwest's secret is to offer customers one free round-trip ticket for every four round-trip tickets booked through its Web site. America West does about 12 percent of its business online, whereas Continental Airlines and United are the industry laggards at only 3 percent and 4 percent, respectively.

The Internet's appeal for airlines is apparent. A commercial Web site can be kept open for business twenty-four hours a day, seven days a week. It allows an airline to reduce the number of customer service agents, since fewer such employees are needed to field flight information questions. Southwest Airlines reported in 2002 that each Internet booking cost it about $1, whereas its cost to book with a travel agent is between $6 and $8. Tickets booked through Southwest's own agents cost several dollars. Indeed, a big incentive for airlines to distribute tickets via the Internet is the fact that such transactions allow them to eliminate travel agent commissions.

On the down side, the Internet may hurt airlines by making travelers very price-sensitive. With airfares changing at lightning speed and the Internet keeping customers apprised of such fares, airlines must respond quickly to match rivals' fare cuts. Consequently, the range of fares that competing airlines can charge on a point-to-point route will tend to be extremely compressed.

Globalization

While U.S. airlines still see international markets as an avenue for growth, a slowdown in Asia/Pacific markets has not allowed that growth to materialize in recent years. International travel, defined here as flights between the United States and a second nation, encompasses both business and leisure travel. In 2001, international travel accounted for 11.4 percent of enplanements for U.S. airlines, versus 11.0 percent in 2000, according to the ATA. Because the average stage (or flight) length is nearly four times longer for international than for domestic flights, international travel generates a disproportionately high level of revenue: 20.8 percent of the industry's total passenger revenues in 2000 (latest available) and 20.4 percent of 1999 total passenger revenues.

Many foreign nations see increased airline competition as a way to boost tourism and commerce because it lowers the cost of air travel. Nations such as China, with state-controlled airlines, have been more reluctant to enter open skies agreements than those with privately owned commercial aviation systems. By early 2002, 97 nations had signed agreements with the United States, the most recent being Sri Lanka in November 2001. Not all of these aviation pacts provide for unfettered competition, but all move strongly in that direction, providing for phased-in deregulation. These agreements provide for reduced economic regulation and unrestricted code-sharing between international carriers, the formation of alliances, and at least partial ownership rights.

The European Union (EU) objects to the piecemeal approach the United States takes to airline deregulation. Instead, if favors the negotiation of a single bilateral aviation agreement between the United States and the European Union and the elimination of individual aviation treaties between the United States and European nations. The European Court of Justice will issue a final ruling later in 2002.

Business Before Pleasure

The airline industry has turned the commercial world into one big marketplace. Many businesspeople use air travel to make sales trips, visit far-flung factories, and attend industry conventions. Because business trips are often scheduled within seven days of the flight, business travelers tend to pay full fare, whether in coach or first class. Because their firms pick up the tab, these travelers tend to be relatively price-insensitive. However, corporations have become more cost-conscious in recent years as business fares have climbed significantly faster than leisure fares.

Airlines actively solicit the business traveler. Many larger aircraft contain designated business sections with roomy seats and premium food service. Recently, airlines have expanded their business-class sections. Airlines compete for business passengers by offering priority check-in, expedited baggage handling, luxurious airport lounges, and in-flight amenities such as faxes, telephones, and power outlets for recharging laptop computers. To appeal to this class of traveler, airlines must provide frequent flights, reliable on-time performance, and top safety records.

In marked contrast to the business traveler, the leisure traveler is highly price-sensitive. The cheaper fares resulting from deregulation have allowed people from all walks of life to travel by air to visit distant friends and relatives or to take more frequent vacations. Leisure travelers can secure discount fares in two ways. First, low fares are available to individuals who book flights at least twenty-one days in advance. Second, deeply discounted fares are also available (mainly through the Internet) a few days before departure. Commonly, leisure travelers defer making any trip arrangements until a fare sale is offered. The upshot of these patterns is that over short periods, leisure travel can be erratic. Over the longer term, leisure travel is more cyclical than business travel; it waxes and wanes together with consumer sentiment and disposable income levels.

Cargo and Cocktails

All passenger aircraft also are capable of carrying cargo, but most freight tends to move on wide-body jets on long stage lengths. Major airlines carry significantly more mail and cargo in the belly space under the passenger cabin than do regional and commuter airlines. Passenger airlines view freight transport as a byproduct of their main business, and they charge discounted rates compared with those charged by specialized air freight carriers. Lacking sales forces to pursue this business, the airlines often accept freight from only a few air forwarders. Some airlines, having more cargo demand than belly space, lease freighter aircraft to their customers. Among passenger airlines, Northwest generated the most revenue from cargo in 2001—about $715 million. This represented about 7 percent of the carrier's 2001 revenues. Cargo and mail together accounted for just 3.7 percent of the industry's total revenues in 2001.

In addition to income from fares and freight, airlines generate revenues from the sale of in-flight alcoholic beverages and various amenities and services. The "other" revenue category may also include income from international code-sharing programs. On long-haul flights, most carriers provide telephone, automated teller machine (ATM), fax, and television and entertainment services for a fee. Some international flights even offer video gambling. Although such supplementary sales carry high margins, they account for a relatively small portion of industry revenues.

Labor Unions

Labor is the industry's largest single airline expense, accounting for about 48 percent of total costs in 2001, up sharply from 34.9 percent in 2000. Labor costs should decline sharply both on an absolute basis and as a percentage of revenues in 2002. More than eighty-thousand employees were laid off by the airlines in late 2001, and the airlines are negotiating concessions with most major unions to help them through the current downturn.

Employment can be divided into several broad craft positions: flight crews (pilots and engineers), flight attendants, ground service (including baggage handlers), dispatchers, maintenance, and customer service (bookings and boardings). Most airline workers belong to one of a dozen major unions. The larger unions include the Association of Flight Attendants, the Allied Pilots Association, and the International Association of Machinists and Aerospace Workers. At any given time, a half-dozen or more contracts may be in negotiation.

The downsizing of the U.S. Air Force—the main if not the sole source of experienced pilots—is reducing the number of pilots who are available to fly civilian planes. The resulting shortage of qualified pilots has led to outsized gains in recent pilot union contracts. For example, in October 2000, United's pilots won a four-year pact giving them a 23.8 percent raise retroactive to April of that year, with an additional 4.5 percent raise to come in each of the subsequent years. The contract pushed United's pilots to the top of the industry pay scale. First-year pension contributions increased from 1 percent of pay under the old contract to 11 percent in the new contract.

To lure new pilots to their ranks, major airlines are raiding lower-paid pilots at regional carriers. Airlines also hope to alleviate the shortage by getting Congress to raise the mandatory retirement age to sixty-five from sixty. Unless this happens, pilot pay will continue to experience upward pressure. In addition, because pilot contracts tend to set the pattern for other craft unions in the industry, labor unrest will increase as other workers demand comparable percentages in their own pay hikes.

Regulation

Federal regulation of domestic airline fares and markets ended with the Airline Deregulation Act of 1978. However, the DOT and its affiliated agency, the FAA, continue to regulate the industry with regard to safety, labor, operating procedures, and aircraft fitness and emission levels. The International Civil Aviation Organization (ICAO), an entity affiliated with the United Nations, proposes noise standards, although the standards aren't legally binding in a given country unless the country has formally agreed to them.

CONCLUSION

Standard & Poor's puts a low probability on future merger deals being struck between any of the nation's largest air carriers. Given the industry's overcapacity, weakened balance sheets, and high debt levels, analysts feel that the largest airlines will seek to shrink capacity, conserve cash, and restore profitability before seeking to acquire other firms. The industry's dramatic downturn after the September 11, 2001, terrorist attacks has focused management attention on restoring industry profitability rather than on mergers. However, the American/TWA merger was completed in December 2001, and there are airlines now that could be acquired at bargain prices.

The airline industry has extremely high fixed costs. When revenue declines, expenses stay close to constant. When there is a gradual decline in passenger traffic, management has time to gradually reduce costs. But after September 11, 2001, the gradual decline due to an economic slowdown was converted into a plummeting fall. AMR and other airlines are now in a very tenuous financial position. Survival of AMR itself is dependent upon an effective strategic plan.

With industry load factors far below industry breakeven load factors, it is apparent that there will be dramatic changes in the airline industry. Reductions in capacity and employee layoffs have not reversed continuing losses. Other measures must be taken. Should AMR cut more routes? How many should be cut? If AMR cuts too deeply, it will lose needed revenue. If it does not cut enough, then high fixed costs could sink the company. Route decisions are hampered by the fact that it is difficult to determine when a route will return to profitability. A route currently losing money may become profitable in the next quarter. If capacity is cut further, AMR may not have the infrastructure (planes, slots, gates, people) to provide services if demand increases.

Perhaps AMR should view the current situation as a growth opportunity and take advantage of the failure other airlines. Should AMR expand routes as others abandon routes and buy planes as others sell planes? CEO Donald Carty announced in April 2002 that AMR will recall about forty-five hundred workers by the end of the year. He announced in June 2002 that AMR is adding service from Boston to Port-au-Prince, Haiti, and to the Turks and Caicos Islands in the Caribbean; it is also adding service from New York to Grand Cayman. AMR also just added new nonstop service from New York to Tokyo.

With billion-dollar annual losses and billion-dollar debt obligations, AMR is indeed in trouble. AMR's traffic decreased another 15.9 percent in April 2002 on a capacity decrease of 13.3 percent. Without a clear strategic plan and successful implementation, AMR will perish, and thousands of people will be out of work. Then terrorists, who do not like the name American anyway, could claim another victory if AMR fails. Develop a clear strategic plan for AMR's CEO Donald Carty.

NOTES

1. AMR's 2001 *Annual Report.*
2. Parts of this section are taken from S&P Airline *Industry Surveys,* March 28, 2002. Used with permission of S&P.

EXPERIENTIAL EXERCISES

EXPERIENTIAL EXERCISE 1A ▶

Strategy Analysis for American Airlines (AMR)

PURPOSE

The purpose of this exercise is to give you experience identifying an organization's opportunities, threats, strengths, and weaknesses. This information is vital to generating and selecting among alternative strategies.

INSTRUCTIONS

Step 1 Identify what you consider to be AMR's major opportunities, threats, strengths, and weaknesses. On a separate sheet of paper, list these key factors under separate headings. Describe each factor in specific terms.

Step 2 Through class discussion, compare your lists of external and internal factors to those developed by other students. From the discussion, add to your lists of factors. Keep this information for use in later exercises.

EXPERIENTIAL EXERCISE 1B ▶

Developing a Code of Business Ethics for American Airlines (AMR)

PURPOSE

This exercise can give you practice in developing a code of business ethics. Research was conducted to examine codes of business ethics from large manufacturing and service firms in the United States. The twenty-eight variables that follow were found to be included in a sample of more than eighty codes of business ethics. The variables are presented in order of how frequently they occurred. Thus, the first variable, "conduct business in compliance with all laws," was most often included in the sample documents; "firearms at work are prohibited" was least often included.

1. Conduct business in compliance with all laws.
2. Payments for unlawful purposes are prohibited.
3. Avoid outside activities that impair duties.
4. Comply with all antitrust and trade regulations.
5. Comply with accounting rules and controls.
6. Bribes are prohibited.
7. Maintain confidentiality of records.
8. Participate in community and political activities.
9. Provide products and services of the highest quality.
10. Exhibit standards of personal integrity and conduct.
11. Do not propagate false or misleading information.
12. Perform assigned duties to the best of your ability.
13. Conserve resources and protect the environment.
14. Comply with safety, health, and security regulations.
15. Racial, ethnic, religious, and sexual harassment at work is prohibited.
16. Report unethical and illegal activities to your manager.
17. Convey true claims in product advertisements.
18. Make decisions without regard for personal gain.
19. Do not use company property for personal benefit.
20. Demonstrate courtesy, respect, honesty, and fairness.
21. Illegal drugs and alcohol at work are prohibited.

22. Manage personal finances well.
23. Employees are personally accountable for company funds.
24. Exhibit good attendance and punctuality.
25. Follow directives of supervisors.
26. Do not use abusive language.
27. Dress in businesslike attire.
28. Firearms at work are prohibited.[1]

INSTRUCTIONS

Step 1 On a separate sheet of paper, write a code of business ethics for AMR. Include as many variables listed above as you believe appropriate to AMR's business. Limit your document to one hundred words or less.

Step 2 Read your code of ethics to the class. Comment on why you did or did not include certain variables.

Step 3 Explain why having a code of ethics is not sufficient for ensuring ethical behavior in an organization. What else does it take?

NOTES

1. DONALD ROBIN, MICHAEL GIALLOURAKIS, FRED R. DAVID, and THOMAS E. MORITZ. "A Different Look at Codes of Ethics," *Business Horizons* 32, no. 1 (January–February 1989): 66–73.

EXPERIENTIAL EXERCISE 1C ▶

The Ethics of Spying on Competitors

PURPOSE

This exercise gives you an opportunity to discuss ethical and legal issues in class as related to methods being used by many companies to spy on competing firms. Gathering and using information about competitors is an area of strategic management that Japanese firms do more proficiently than American firms.

INSTRUCTIONS

On a separate sheet of paper, number from 1 to 18. For the 18 spying activities listed below, indicate whether or not you believe the activity is Ethical or Unethical and Legal or Illegal. Place either an *E* for ethical or *U* for unethical, and either an *L* for legal or an *I* for illegal for each activity. Compare your answers to your classmates', and discuss any differences.

1. Buying competitors' garbage.
2. Dissecting competitors' products.
3. Taking competitors' plant tours anonymously.
4. Counting tractor-trailer trucks leaving competitors' loading bays.
5. Studying aerial photographs of competitors' facilities.
6. Analyzing competitors' labor contracts.
7. Analyzing competitors' help-wanted ads.
8. Quizzing customers and buyers about the sales of competitors' products.
9. Infiltrating customers' and competitors' business operations.
10. Quizzing suppliers about competitors' level of manufacturing.
11. Using customers to buy out phony bids.
12. Encouraging key customers to reveal competitive information.

13. Quizzing competitors' former employees.
14. Interviewing consultants who may have worked with competitors.
15. Hiring key managers away from competitors.
16. Conducting phony job interviews to get competitors' employees to reveal information.
17. Sending engineers to trade meetings to quiz competitors' technical employees.
18. Quizzing potential employees who worked for or with competitors.

EXPERIENTIAL EXERCISE 1D ▶

Strategic Planning for My University

PURPOSE

External and internal factors are the underlying bases of strategies formulated and implemented by organizations. Your college or university faces numerous external opportunities/threats and has many internal strengths/weaknesses. The purpose of this exercise is to illustrate the process of identifying critical external and internal factors.

External influences include trends in the following areas: economic, social, cultural, demographic, environmental, technological, political, legal, governmental, and competitive. External factors could include declining numbers of high school graduates; population shifts; community relations; increased competitiveness among colleges and universities; rising numbers of adults returning to college; decreased support from local, state, and federal agencies; and increasing numbers of foreign students attending American colleges.

Internal factors of a college or university include faculty, students, staff, alumni, athletic programs, the physical plant, grounds and maintenance, student housing, administration, fundraising, academic programs, food services, parking, placement, clubs, fraternities, sororities, and public relations.

INSTRUCTIONS

Step 1 On a separate sheet of paper, make four headings: External Opportunities, External Threats, Internal Strengths, and Internal Weaknesses.

Step 2 As related to your college or university, list five factors under each of the four headings.

Step 3 Discuss the factors as a class. Write the factors on the board.

Step 4 What new things did you learn about your university from the class discussion? How could this type of discussion benefit an organization?

EXPERIENTIAL EXERCISE 1E ▶

Strategic Planning at a Local Company

PURPOSE

This activity is aimed at giving you practical knowledge about how organizations in your city or town are doing strategic planning. This exercise also will give you experience interacting on a professional basis with local business leaders.

INSTRUCTIONS

Step 1 Use the telephone to contact business owners or top managers. Find an organization that does strategic planning. Make an appointment to visit with the strategist (president, chief executive officer, or owner) of that business.

Step 2 Seek answers to the following questions during the interview:

a. How does your firm formally conduct strategic planning? Who is involved in the process?

b. Does your firm have a written mission statement? How was the statement developed? When was the statement last changed?

c. What are the benefits of engaging in strategic planning?

d. What are the major costs or problems in doing strategic planning in your business?

e. Do you anticipate making any changes in the strategic planning process at your company? If yes, please explain.

Step 3   Report your findings to the class.

EXPERIENTIAL EXERCISE 1F ▶

Does My University Recruit in Foreign Countries?

PURPOSE

A competitive climate is emerging among colleges and universities around the world. Colleges and universities in Europe and Japan are increasingly recruiting American students to offset declining enrollments. Foreign students already make up more than one-third of the student body at many American universities. The purpose of this exercise is to identify particular colleges and universities in foreign countries that represent a competitive threat to American institutions of higher learning.

INSTRUCTIONS

Step 1   Select a foreign country. Conduct research to determine the number and nature of colleges and universities in that country. What are the major educational institutions in that country? What programs are those institutions recognized for offering? What percentage of undergraduate and graduate students attending those institutions are American? Do these institutions actively recruit American students?

Step 2   Prepare a report for the class that summarizes your research findings. Present your report to the class.

EXPERIENTIAL EXERCISE 1G ▶

Getting Familiar with SMCO

PURPOSE

This exercise is designed to get you familiar with the Strategic Management Club Online (SMCO), which offers many benefits for the strategy student.

INSTRUCTIONS

Step 1   Go to the **www.strategyclub.com** Web site. Review the various sections of this site.

Step 2   Select a section of the SMCO site that you feel will be most useful to you in this class. Write a one-page summary of that section and why you feel it will benefit you most.

2

THE BUSINESS MISSION

CHAPTER OUTLINE

CHAPTER OBJECTIVES

After studying this chapter, you should be able to do the following:

1. Describe the nature and role of vision and mission statements in strategic management.
2. Discuss why the process of developing a mission statement is as important as the resulting document.
3. Identify the components of mission statements.
4. Discuss how clear vision and mission statements can benefit other strategic-management activities.
5. Evaluate mission statements of different organizations.
6. Write good vision and mission statements.

NOTABLE QUOTES

A business is not defined by its name, statutes, or articles of incorporation. It is defined by the business mission. Only a clear definition of the mission and purpose of the organization makes possible clear and realistic business objectives.

PETER DRUCKER

A corporate vision can focus, direct, motivate, unify, and even excite a business into superior performance. The job of a strategist is to identify and project a clear vision.

JOHN KEANE

Where there is no vision, the people perish.

PROVERBS 29:18

Customers are first, employees second, shareholders third, and the community fourth. That's the credo at H. B. Fuller, the century-old adhesives maker in St. Paul.

PATRICIA SELLERS

For strategists, there's a trade-off between the breadth and detail of information needed. It's a bit like an eagle hunting for a rabbit. The eagle has to be high enough to scan a wide area in order to enlarge his chances of seeing prey, but he has to be low enough to see the detail—the movement and features that will allow him to recognize his target. Continually making this trade-off is the job of a strategist—it simply can't be delegated.

FREDERICK GLUCK

The best laid schemes of mice and men often go awry.

ROBERT BURNS (paraphrased)

A strategist's job is to see the company not as it is . . . but as it can become.

JOHN W. TEETS, CHAIRMAN OF GREYHOUND, INC.

That business mission is so rarely given adequate thought is perhaps the most important single cause of business frustration.

PETER DRUCKER

Vision is the art of seeing things invisible.

JONATHAN SWIFT

The very essence of leadership is that you have to have vision. You can't blow an uncertain trumpet.

THEODORE HESBURGH

Some men see things as they are and say why. I dream of things that never were and say why not.

JOHN F. KENNEDY

55

This chapter focuses on the concepts and tools needed to evaluate and write business vision and mission statements. A practical framework for developing mission statements is provided. Actual mission statements from large and small organizations and for-profit and nonprofit enterprises are presented and critically examined. The process of creating a vision and mission statement is discussed.

We can perhaps best understand vision and mission by focusing on a business when it is first started. In the beginning, a new business is simply a collection of ideas. Starting a new business rests on a set of beliefs that the new organization can offer some product or service to some customers, in some geographic area, using some type of technology, at a profitable price. A new business owner typically believes that the management philosophy of the new enterprise will result in a favorable public image and that this concept of the business can be communicated to, and will be adopted by, important constituencies. When the set of beliefs about a business at its inception is put into writing, the resulting document mirrors the same basic ideas that underlie the vision and mission statements. As a business grows, owners or managers find it necessary to revise the founding set of beliefs, but those original ideas usually are reflected in the revised statements of vision and mission.

Vision and mission statements often can be found in the front of annual reports. They often are displayed throughout a firm's premises and are distributed with company information sent to constituencies. The statements are part of numerous internal reports, such as loan requests, supplier agreements, labor relations contracts, business plans, and customer service agreements. In a recent study, researchers concluded that 90 percent of all companies have used a mission statement sometime in the previous five years.[1]

 ## WHAT DO WE WANT TO BECOME?

It is especially important for managers and executives in any organization to agree upon the basic vision that the firm strives to achieve in the long term. A vision statement should answer the basic question, "What do we want to become?" A clear vision provides the foundation for developing a comprehensive mission statement. Many organizations have both a vision and mission statement, but the vision statement should be established first and foremost. The vision statement should be short, preferably one sentence, and as many managers as possible should have input into developing the statement.

Several example vision statements are provided below and in Table 2–1.

The Vision of the National Pawnbrokers Association is to have complete and vibrant membership that enjoys a positive public and political image and is the focal organization of all pawn associations.—National Pawnbrokers Association (http://npa.ploygon.net)

Our Vision as an independent community financial institution is to achieve superior long-term shareholder value, exercise exemplary corporate citizenship, and create an environment which promotes and rewards employee development and the consistent delivery of quality service to our customers.—First Reliance Bank of Florence, South Carolina

At CIGNA, we intend to be the best at helping our customers enhance and extend their lives and protect their financial security. Satisfying customers is the key to meeting employee needs and shareholder expectations, and will enable CIGNA to build on our reputation as a financially strong and highly respected company. (www.cigna.com)

VISIT THE NET

Gives an introduction to the vision concept. http://www.csuchico.edu/mgmt/strategy/module1/sld007.htm

TABLE 2-1   **Vision and Mission Statement Examples**

THE BELLEVUE HOSPITAL

Vision Statement

The Bellevue Hospital is the LEADER in providing resources necessary to realize the community's highest level of HEALTH throughout life.

Mission Statement

The Bellevue Hospital, with *respect, compassion, integrity, and courage*, honors the individuality and confidentiality of our patients, employees, and community, and is progressive in anticipating and providing future health care services.

U.S. POULTRY & EGG ASSOCIATION

Vision Statement

A national organization which represents its members in all aspects of poultry and eggs on both a national and an international level.

Mission Statement:

1. We will partner with our affiliated state organizations to attack common problems.
2. We are committed to the advancement of all areas of research and education in poultry technology.
3. The International Poultry Exposition must continue to grow and be beneficial to both exhibitors and attendees.
4. We must always be responsive and effective to the changing needs of our industry.
5. Our imperatives must be such that we do not duplicate the efforts of our sister organizations.
6. We will strive to constantly improve the quality and safety of poultry products.

We will continue to increase the availability of poultry products.

JOHN DEERE, INC.

Vision Statement

John Deere is committed to providing Genuine Value to the company's stakeholders, including our customers, dealers, shareholders, employees, and communities. In support of that commitment, Deere aspires to:

- Grow and pursue leadership positions in each of our businesses.
- Extend our preeminent leadership position in the agricultural equipment market worldwide.
- Create new opportunities to leverage the John Deere brand globally.

Mission Statement

John Deere has grown and prospered through a long-standing partnership with the world's most productive farmers. Today, John Deere is a global company with several equipment operations and complementary service businesses. These businesses are closely interrelated, providing the company with significant growth opportunities and other synergistic benefits.

MANLEY BAPTIST CHURCH

The Vision of Manley Baptist Church is to be the people of God, on mission with God, motivated by a love for God, and a love for others.

The Mission of Manley Baptist Church is to help people in the Lakeway area become fully developed followers of Jesus Christ.

U.S. GEOLOGICAL SURVEY (USGS)

The Vision of USGS is to be a world leader in the natural sciences through our scientific excellence and responsiveness to society's needs.

The mission of USGS is to serve the Nation by providing reliable scientific information to

Continued

TABLE 2-1   Vision and Mission Statement Examples (*continued*)

- describe and understand the Earth
- minimize loss of life and property from natural disasters
- manage water, biological, energy, and mineral resources; and enhance and protect our quality of life

MASSACHUSETTS DIVISION OF BANKS

Vision Statement

To protect the public interest, ensure competition, accessibility and fairness within the relevant financial services industries, respond innovatively to a rapidly changing environment, and foster a positive impact on the Commonwealth's economy.

Mission Statement

To maintain a safe and sound competitive banking and financial services environment throughout the Commonwealth and ensure compliance with community reinvestment and consumer protection laws by chartering, licensing and supervising state regulated financial institutions in a professional and innovative manner.

OHIO DIVISION OF HAZARDOUS WASTE MANAGEMENT

Vision Statement

Ohio's Division of Hazardous Waste Management is recognized as a leader among state hazardous waste management programs through our expertise, effectiveness, application of sound science, and delivery of quality service to out stakeholders.

Mission Statement

The Division of Hazardous Waste Management protects and improves the environment and therefore the health of Ohio's citizens by promoting pollution prevention and the proper management and cleanup of hazardous waste. We provide quality service to our stakeholders by assisting them in understanding and complying with the hazardous waste management regulations, and by implementing our program effectively.

ATLANTA WEB PRINTERS, INC.

Vision Statement

To be the first choice in the printed communications business. The first choice is the best choice, and *being the best* is what Atlanta Web *pledges* to work hard at being—*every day!*

Mission Statement

- to make our clients feel welcome, appreciated, and worthy of our best efforts in everything we do . . . each and every day
- to be recognized as an exceptional leader in our industry and community
- to conduct all our relationships with an emphasis on long-term mutual success and satisfaction, rather than short-term gain
- to earn the trust and respect of all we work with as being a Company of honesty, integrity, and responsibility
- to provide an environment of positive attitude and action to accomplish our vision, by increasing positive feedback and recognition at all levels of the Company
- to train and motivate our employees and to develop cooperation and communication at all levels
- to use our resources, knowledge, and experience to create win/win relationships for our clients, employees, suppliers, and shareholders in terms of growing compensation, service, and value

CALIFORNIA ENERGY COMMISSION

Vision Statement

It is the vision of the California Energy Commission for Californians to have energy choices that are affordable, reliable, diverse, safe, and environmentally acceptable.

Mission Statement

It is the California Energy Commission's mission to assess, advocate, and act through public/private partnerships to improve energy systems that promote a strong economy and a healthy environment.

WHAT IS OUR BUSINESS?

Current thought on mission statements is based largely on guidelines set forth in the mid-1970s by Peter Drucker, who is often called "the father of modern management" for his pioneering studies at General Motors Corporation and for his twenty-two books and hundreds of articles. *Harvard Business Review* has called Drucker, "the preeminent management thinker of our time."

Drucker says that asking the question, "What is our business?," is synonymous with asking the question, "What is our mission?" An enduring statement of purpose that distinguishes one organization from other similar enterprises, the *mission statement* is a declaration of an organization's "reason for being." It answers the pivotal question, "What is our business?" A clear mission statement is essential for effectively establishing objectives and formulating strategies.

Sometimes called a *creed statement,* a statement of purpose, a statement of philosophy, a statement of beliefs, a statement of business principles, or a statement "defining our business," a mission statement reveals what an organization wants to be and whom it wants to serve. All organizations have a reason for being, even if strategists have not consciously transformed this reason into writing. As illustrated in Figure 2–1, carefully prepared statements of vision and mission are widely recognized by both practitioners and academicians as the first step in strategic management.

> A business mission is the foundation for priorities, strategies, plans, and work assignments. It is the starting point for the design of managerial jobs and, above all, for the design of managerial structures. Nothing may seem simpler or more obvious than to know what a company's business is. A steel mill makes steel, a railroad runs trains to carry freight and passengers, an insurance company underwrites fire risks, and a bank lends money. Actually, "What is our business?" is almost always a difficult question and the right answer is usually anything but obvious. The answer to this question is the first responsibility of strategists. Only strategists can make sure that this question receives the attention it deserves and that the answer makes sense and enables the business to plot its course and set its objectives.[2]

Some strategists spend almost every moment of every day on administrative and tactical concerns, and strategists who rush quickly to establish objectives and implement strategies often overlook the development of a vision and mission statement. This problem is widespread even among large organizations. Many corporations in America have not yet developed a formal vision or mission statement, but most do have formal mission statements.[3] An increasing number of organizations are developing these statements.

Some companies develop mission statements simply because they feel it is fashionable, rather than out of any real commitment. However, as will be described in this chapter, firms that develop and systematically revisit their vision and mission statements, treat them as living documents, and consider them to be an integral part of the firm's culture realize great benefits. Johnson & Johnson (J&J) is an example firm. J&J managers meet regularly with employees to review, reword, and reaffirm the firm's vision and mission. The entire J&J workforce recognizes the value that top management places on this exercise, and these employees respond accordingly.

Vision versus Mission

Many organizations develop both a mission statement and a vision statement. Whereas the mission statement answers the question, "What is our business," the *vision statement*

VISIT THE NET

Gives an introduction to the mission concept. http://www.csuchico.edu/mgmt/strategy/module1/sld008.htm

FIGURE 2–1

A Comprehensive Strategic-Management Model

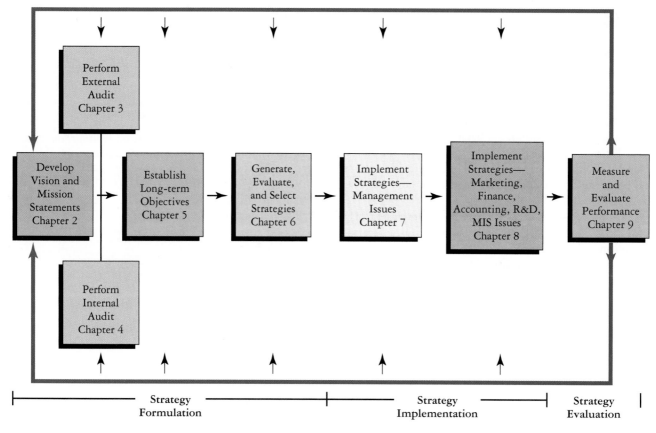

Source: Fred R. David, "How Companies Define Their Mission," *Long Range Planning* 22, no. 3 (June 1988): 40.

answers the question, "What do we want to become?" Many organizations have both a mission and vision statement. Several examples are given in Table 2–1.

It can be argued that profit, not mission or vision, is the primary corporate motivator. But profit alone is not enough to motivate people.[4] Profit is perceived negatively by some employees in companies. Employees may see profit as something that they earn and management then uses and even gives away to shareholders. Although this perception is undesired and disturbing to management, it clearly indicates that both profit and vision are needed to effectively motivate a workforce.

When employees and managers together shape or fashion the vision and mission statements for a firm, the resultant documents can reflect the personal visions that managers and employees have in their hearts and minds about their own futures. Shared vision creates a commonality of interests that can lift workers out of the monotony of daily work and put them into a new world of opportunity and challenge.

The Process of Developing a Mission Statement

As indicated in the strategic-management model, a clear mission statement is needed before alternative strategies can be formulated and implemented. It is important to involve as many managers as possible in the process of developing a mission statement, because through involvement, people become committed to an organization.

A widely used approach to developing a mission statement is first to select several articles about mission statements and ask all managers to read these as background information. Then ask managers themselves to prepare a mission statement for the organization. A facilitator, or committee of top managers, should then merge these statements into a single document and distribute this draft mission statement to all managers. A request for modifications, additions, and deletions is needed next, along with a meeting to revise the document. To the extent that all managers have input into and support the final mission statement document, organizations can more easily obtain managers' support for other strategy formulation, implementation, and evaluation activities. Thus, the process of developing a mission statement represents a great opportunity for strategists to obtain needed support from all managers in the firm.

During the process of developing a mission statement, some organizations use discussion groups of managers to develop and modify the mission statement. Some organizations hire an outside consultant or facilitator to manage the process and help draft the language. Sometimes an outside person with expertise in developing mission statements and unbiased views can manage the process more effectively than an internal group or committee of managers. Decisions on how best to communicate the mission to all managers, employees, and external constituencies of an organization are needed when the document is in final form. Some organizations even develop a videotape to explain the mission statement and how it was developed.

An article by Campbell and Yeung emphasizes that the process of developing a mission statement should create an "emotional bond" and "sense of mission" between the organization and its employees.[5] Commitment to a company's strategy and intellectual agreement on the strategies to be pursued do not necessarily translate into an emotional bond; hence, strategies that have been formulated may not be implemented. These researchers stress that an emotional bond comes when an individual personally identifies with the underlying values and behavior of a firm, thus turning intellectual agreement and commitment to strategy into a sense of mission. Campbell and Yeung also differentiate between the terms *vision* and *mission*, saying that vision is "a possible and desirable future state of an organization" that includes specific goals, whereas mission is more associated with behavior and the present.

IMPORTANCE OF VISION AND MISSION STATEMENTS

The importance of vision and mission statements to effective strategic management is well documented in the literature, although research results are mixed. Rarick and Vitton found that firms with a formalized mission statement have twice the average return on shareholders' equity than those firms without a formalized mission statement; Bart and Baetz found a positive relationship between mission statements and organizational performance; *Business Week* reports that firms using mission statements have a 30 percent higher return on certain financial measures than those without such statements; O'Gorman and Doran, however, found that having a mission statement does not directly contribute positively to financial performance.[6] The extent of manager and employee involvement in developing vision and mission statements can make a difference in business success. This chapter provides guidelines for developing these important documents. In actual practice, wide variations exist in the nature, composition, and use of both vision and mission statements. King and Cleland recommend that organizations carefully develop a written mission statement for the following reasons:

1. To ensure unanimity of purpose within the organization
2. To provide a basis, or standard, for allocating organizational resources
3. To establish a general tone or organizational climate
4. To serve as a focal point for individuals to identify with the organization's purpose and direction, and to deter those who cannot from participating further in the organization's activities
5. To facilitate the translation of objectives into a work structure involving the assignment of tasks to responsible elements within the organization
6. To specify organizational purposes and then to translate these purposes into objectives in such a way that cost, time, and performance parameters can be assessed and controlled[7]

Reuben Mark, former CEO of Colgate, maintains that a clear mission increasingly must make sense internationally. Mark's thoughts on vision are as follows:

> When it comes to rallying everyone to the corporate banner, it's essential to push one vision globally rather than trying to drive home different messages in different cultures. The trick is to keep the vision simple but elevated: "We make the world's fastest computers" or "Telephone service for everyone." You're never going to get anyone to charge the machine guns only for financial objectives. It's got to be something that makes people feel better, feel a part of something.[8]

A Resolution of Divergent Views

Developing a comprehensive mission statement is important because divergent views among managers can be revealed and resolved through the process. The question, "What is our business?," can create controversy. Raising the question often reveals differences among strategists in the organization. Individuals who have worked together for a long time and who think they know each other suddenly may realize that they are in fundamental disagreement. For example, in a college or university, divergent views regarding the relative importance of teaching, research, and service often are expressed during the mission statement development process. Negotiation, compromise, and eventual agreement on important issues are needed before people can focus on more specific strategy formulation activities.

> "What is our mission?" is a genuine decision; and a genuine decision must be based on divergent views to have a chance to be a right and effective decision. Developing a business mission is always a choice between alternatives, each of which rests on different assumptions regarding the reality of the business and its environment. It is always a high-risk decision. A change in mission always leads to changes in objectives, strategies, organization, and behavior. The mission decision is far too important to be made by acclamation. Developing a business mission is a big step toward management effectiveness. Hidden or half-understood disagreements on the definition of a business mission underlie many of the personality problems, communication problems, and irritations that tend to divide a top-management group. Establishing a mission should never be made on plausibility alone, should never be made fast, and should never be made painlessly.[9]

Considerable disagreement among an organization's strategists over vision and mission statements can cause trouble if not resolved. For example, unresolved disagreement over the business mission was one of the reasons for W. T. Grant's bankruptcy and eventual liquidation. As one executive reported:

There was a lot of dissension within the company whether we should go the Kmart route or go after the Montgomery Ward and JCPenney position. Ed Staley and Lou Lustenberger (two top executives) were at loggerheads over the issue, with the upshot being we took a position between the two and that consequently stood for nothing.[10]

Too often, strategists develop vision and business mission statements only when the organization is in trouble. Of course, it is needed then. Developing and communicating a clear mission during troubled times indeed may have spectacular results and even may reverse decline. However, to wait until an organization is in trouble to develop a vision and mission statement is a gamble that characterizes irresponsible management. According to Drucker, the most important time to ask seriously, "What do we want to become?" and "What is our business?," is when a company has been successful:

Success always obsoletes the very behavior that achieved it, always creates new realities, and always creates new and different problems. Only the fairy story ends, "They lived happily ever after." It is never popular to argue with success or to rock the boat. The ancient Greeks knew that the penalty of success can be severe. The management that does not ask, "What is our mission?," when the company is successful is, in effect, smug, lazy, and arrogant. It will not be long before success will turn into failure. Sooner or later, even the most successful answer to the question, "What is our business?," becomes obsolete.[11]

In multidivisional organizations, strategists should ensure that divisional units perform strategic-management tasks, including the development of a statement of vision and mission. Each division should involve its own managers and employees in developing a vision and mission statement that is consistent with and supportive of the corporate mission.

An organization that fails to develop a vision statement as well as a comprehensive and inspiring mission statement loses the opportunity to present itself favorably to existing and potential stakeholders. All organizations need customers, employees, and managers, and most firms need creditors, suppliers, and distributors. The vision and mission statements are effective vehicles for communicating with important internal and external stakeholders. The principal value of these statements as tools of strategic management is derived from their specification of the ultimate aims of a firm:

They provide managers with a unity of direction that transcends individual, parochial, and transitory needs. They promote a sense of shared expectations among all levels and generations of employees. They consolidate values over time and across individuals and interest groups. They project a sense of worth and intent that can be identified and assimilated by company outsiders. Finally, they affirm the company's commitment to responsible action, which is symbiotic with its need to preserve and protect the essential claims of insiders for [the] sustained survival, growth, and profitability of the firm.[12]

CHARACTERISTICS OF A MISSION STATEMENT

A Declaration of Attitude

A mission statement is more than a statement of specific details; it is a declaration of attitude and outlook. It usually is broad in scope for at least two major reasons. First, a good mission statement allows for the generation and consideration of a range of feasible alternative objectives and strategies without unduly stifling management creativity. Excess specificity would limit the potential of creative growth for the organization. On the other hand, an overly general statement that does not exclude any strategy alternatives could be dysfunctional. Apple Computer's mission statement, for example, should not open the possibility for diversification into pesticides—or Ford Motor Company's into food processing. As indicated in the Global Perspective box, French mission statements are more general than British mission statements.

Second, a mission statement needs to be broad to effectively reconcile differences among and appeal to an organization's diverse *stakeholders,* the individuals and groups of individuals who have a special stake or claim on the company. Stakeholders include employees, managers, stockholders, boards of directors, customers, suppliers, distributors, creditors, governments (local, state, federal, and foreign), unions, competitors, environmental groups, and the general public. Stakeholders affect and are affected by an organization's strategies, yet the claims and concerns of diverse constituencies vary and often conflict. For example, the general public is especially interested in social responsibility, whereas stockholders are more interested in profitability. Claims on any business

GLOBAL PERSPECTIVE

Concern About Company Mission Across Continents

Researchers recently studied the mission statements of British and French firms. The results are summarized here.

Researchers found that a highly participative (French) approach to developing a mission statement is more effective in gaining employee commitment than a less participative (British) approach. Differences between British and French statements are rooted in or attributable to different cultural, social, and economic factors in the two countries. For example, in Britain, because of the predominance of equity financing, lead companies are frequently bought and sold like commodities. In contrast, the traditions of family ownership are stronger in France, providing a sense of community and a better basis for the development of shared mission statements.

British mission statements tend to be short and specific, and they are generally developed by top managers, whereas French mission statements tend to be long and general, and they are generally developed by all managers and employees.

A large study of chief executive officers (CEOs) around the world revealed management challenges. The table below provides the percentage of CEOs in each area that consider various topics to be a management challenge. Note that 38 percent of Japanese CEOs considered "engaging employees in the company mission" to be a major management challenge.

Major Management Challenge in 2000	*United States*	*Europe*	*Japan*
Customer Loyalty	44%	28%	3%
Managing Mergers, Acquisitions, Alliances	30	42	16
Reducing Costs	29	32	41
Engaging Employees in Company's Mission	28	32	38
Competing for Talent	26	9	3
Increasing Flexibility and Speed	24	39	31

Sources: Adapted from Julienne Brabet and Mary Klemm, "Sharing the Vision: Company Mission Statements in Britain and France," *Long Range Planning* (February 1994): 84–94; adapted from Anne Carey and Alejandro Gonzalez, "What's Troubling CEOs?" *USA Today* (August 12, 1999): B1.

literally may number in the thousands, and they often include clean air, jobs, taxes, investment opportunities, career opportunities, equal employment opportunities, employee benefits, salaries, wages, clean water, and community services. All stakeholders' claims on an organization cannot be pursued with equal emphasis. A good mission statement indicates the relative attention that an organization will devote to meeting the claims of various stakeholders. Many firms are environmentally proactive in response to the concerns of stakeholders, as indicated in the Natural Environment Perspective box.

NATURAL ENVIRONMENT PERSPECTIVE

Is Your Firm Environmentally Proactive?

Conducting business in a way that preserves the natural environment is more than just good public relations; it is good business. Preserving the environment is a permanent part of doing business for the following reasons:

1. Consumer demand for environmentally safe products and packages is high.

2. Public opinion demanding that firms conduct business in ways that preserve the natural environment is strong.

3. Environmental advocacy groups now have over twenty million Americans as members.

4. Federal and state environmental regulations are changing rapidly and becoming more complex.

5. More lenders are examining the environmental liabilities of businesses seeking loans.

6. Many consumers, suppliers, distributors, and investors shun doing business with environmentally weak firms.

7. Liability suits and fines against firms having environmental problems are on the rise.

More firms are becoming environmentally proactive, which means they are taking the initiative to develop and implement strategies that preserve the environment while enhancing their efficiency and effectiveness. The old undesirable alternative is to be environmentally reactive—waiting until environmental pressures are thrust upon a firm by law or consumer pressure. A reactive environmental policy often leads to high cleanup costs, numerous liability suits, loss in market share, reduced customer loyalty, and

higher medical costs. In contrast, a proactive policy views environmental pressures as opportunities and includes such actions as developing green products and packages, conserving energy, reducing waste, recycling, and creating a corporate culture that is environmentally sensitive.

A proactive policy forces a company to innovate and upgrade process; this leads to reduced waste, improved efficiency, better quality, and greater profits. Successful firms today assess "the profit in preserving the environment" in decisions ranging from developing a mission statement to determining plant location, manufacturing technology, design, products, packaging, and consumer relations. A proactive environmental policy is simply good business. However, the *Wall Street Journal* reports that consumer interest in buying environmentally-friendly products has declined significantly since 2000. The *Journal* says "Eco-marketing is fading faster than the ozone over Antarctica." Many companies now conclude that "green" sales pitches do not sell. Consumers today "leave their conscience at the landfill when they head to the store." More than 40 percent of consumers "don't buy green products because they fear the products won't work as well." The remaining consumers focus on price and convenience. Recycling rates for plastic bottles dropped 66 percent in the United States from 1995 to 2002. Even New York City is considering elimation of all metal, glass, and plastic recycling services to save $57 million annually.

Sources: Adapted from "The Profit in Preserving America," *Forbes* (November 11, 1991): 181–189; and Forest Beinhardt, "Bringing the Environment Down to Earth," *Harvard Business Review* (July–August 1999): 149–158; Christine Rosen, "Environmental Strategy and Competitive Advantage," *California Management Review* 43, 3 (Spring 2001): 8–15; and Geoffrey Fowler, "Green Sales Pitch Isn't Moving Many Products," *Wall Street Journal* (March 6, 2002): B1 and B4.

Reaching the fine balance between specificity and generality is difficult to achieve, but it is well worth the effort. George Steiner offers the following insight on the need for a mission statement to be broad in scope:

> Most business statements of mission are expressed at high levels of abstraction. Vagueness nevertheless has its virtues. Mission statements are not designed to express concrete ends, but rather to provide motivation, general direction, an image, a tone, and a philosophy to guide the enterprise. An excess of detail could prove counterproductive since concrete specification could be the base for rallying opposition. Precision might stifle creativity in the formulation of an acceptable mission or purpose. Once an aim is cast in concrete, it creates a rigidity in an organization and resists change. Vagueness leaves room for other managers to fill in the details, perhaps even to modify general patterns. Vagueness permits more flexibility in adapting to changing environments and internal operations. It facilitates flexibility in implementation.[13]

An effective mission statement should not be too lengthy. Less than 200 words is a recommended length. An effective mission statement also arouses positive feelings and emotions about an organization; it is inspiring in the sense that it motivates readers to action. An effective mission statement generates the impression that a firm is successful, has direction, and is worthy of time, support, and investment—from all socio-economic groups of people.

It reflects judgments about future growth directions and strategies that are based upon forward-looking external and internal analyses. A business mission should provide useful criteria for selecting among alternative strategies. A clear mission statement provides a basis for generating and screening strategic options. The statement of mission should be dynamic in orientation, allowing judgments about the most promising growth directions and those considered less promising.

A Customer Orientation

A good mission statement describes an organization's purpose, customers, products or services, markets, philosophy, and basic technology. According to Vern McGinnis, a mission statement should (1) define what the organization is and what the organization aspires to be, (2) be limited enough to exclude some ventures and broad enough to allow for creative growth, (3) distinguish a given organization from all others, (4) serve as a framework for evaluating both current and prospective activities, and (5) be stated in terms sufficiently clear to be widely understood throughout the organization.[14]

A good mission statement reflects the anticipations of customers. Rather than developing a product and then trying to find a market, the operating philosophy of organizations should be to identify customers' needs and then provide a product or service to fulfill those needs. Good mission statements identify the utility of a firm's products to its customers. This is why AT&T's mission statement focuses on communication rather than on telephones; it is why Exxon/Mobil's mission statement focuses on energy rather than on oil and gas; it is why Union Pacific's mission statement focuses on transportation rather than on railroads; it is why Universal Studio's mission statement focuses on entertainment rather than on movies. The following utility statements are relevant in developing a mission statement:

> Do not offer me things.
>
> Do not offer me clothes. Offer me attractive looks.

E-COMMERCE PERSPECTIVE

Is the Internet Revolution Bypassing the Poor and Minorities?

YES. The U.S. Department of Commerce recently conducted a massive study that concluded the Internet revolution in America is largely bypassing the poor, minorities, rural areas, and inner cities. This fact is resulting in a widening gap between the rich and the poor in this country and a widening gap between the educated and uneducated.

Nearly 90 percent of all shares of common stock of American companies are held by the wealthiest 10 percent of Americans. The wealthiest 10 percent of Americans hold 73.2 percent of this country's net worth today, up from 68.2 percent in 1983. Stock ownership disparity between rich and poor Americans exemplifies growing separation between economic classes.

The *Wall Street Journal* reported in 2002 that Web usage is growing slowest among poor and minority citizens. The so-called digital divide in Internet access between the rich and poor in America is widening. President Bush opposes Democratic proposals for tax incentives for companies that bring broadband Internet access to poor and rural areas. The percentage gap between Americans making $25,000 or less per year who use the Internet versus Americans making over $75,000 annually has grown from 35 percent to 50 percent between 1997 and 2002—despite progress in both groups.

Sources: Adapted from David Lieberman, "Internet Gap Widening—Study: Revolution Bypassing Poor; Minorities," *USA Today* (July 9, 1999): 1A; Jacob Schlesinger, "Wealth Gap Grows: Why Does It Matter," *The Wall Street Journal* (September 13, 1999); A1 Alejandro Gonzalez, "Average Net Worth for U.S. Families," *USA Today* (October 12, 1999): 5A; Yochi Dreazen, "White House Takes Aim at Technology Programs," *Wall Street Journal* (February 27, 2002): A22.

Do not offer me shoes. Offer me comfort for my feet and the pleasure of walking.

Do not offer me a house. Offer me security, comfort, and a place that is clean and happy.

Do not offer me books. Offer me hours of pleasure and the benefit of knowledge.

Do not offer me records. Offer me leisure and the sound of music.

Do not offer me tools. Offer me the benefits and the pleasure that come from making beautiful things.

Do not offer me furniture. Offer me comfort and the quietness of a cozy place.

Do not offer me things. Offer me ideas, emotions, ambience, feelings, and benefits.

Please, do not offer me *things*.

A major reason for developing a business mission statement is to attract customers who give meaning to an organization. Hotel customers today want to use the Internet, so more and more hotels are providing Internet service. A classic description of the purpose of a business reveals the relative importance of customers in a statement of mission:

It is the customer who determines what a business is. It is the customer alone whose willingness to pay for a good or service converts economic resources into wealth and things into goods. What a business thinks it produces is not of first importance, especially not to the future of the business and to its success. What the customer thinks he/she is buying, what he/she considers value, is decisive— it determines what a business is, what it produces, and whether it will prosper. And what the customer buys and considers value is never a product. It is always utility, meaning what a product or service does for him or her. The customer is the foundation of a business and keeps it in existence.[15]

A Declaration of Social Policy

The term *social policy* embraces managerial philosophy and thinking at the highest levels of an organization. For this reason, social policy affects the development of a business mission statement. Social issues mandate that strategists consider not only what the organization owes its various stakeholders but also what responsibilities the firm has to consumers, environmentalists, minorities, communities, and other groups. After decades of debate on the topic of social responsibility, many firms still struggle to determine appropriate social policies. As indicated in the E-Commerce Perspective, there is a growing gap in economic well-being between the poor and the rich in America.

The issue of social responsibility arises when a company establishes its business mission. The impact of society on business and vice versa is becoming more pronounced each year. Social policies directly affect a firm's customers, products and services, markets, technology, profitability, self-concept, and public image. An organization's social policy should be integrated into all strategic-management activities, including the development of a mission statement. Corporate social policy should be designed and articulated during strategy formulation, set and administered during strategy implementation, and reaffirmed or changed during strategy evaluation.[16] The emerging view of social responsibility holds that social issues should be attended to both directly and indirectly in determining strategies. In 2002, the *Wall Street Journal* rated the top companies for social responsibility to be as follows:[17]

1. Johnson & Johnson
2. Coca-Cola
3. Wal-Mart
4. Anheuser Busch
5. Hewlett-Packard
6. Walt Disney
7. Microsoft
8. IBM
9. McDonald's
10. 3M
11. UPS
12. FedEx
13. Target
14. Home Depot
15. General Electric

VISIT THE NET

Provides example mission and vision statements that can be critiqued.

http://www.csuchico.edu/mgmt/strategy/module1/sld015.htm;
http://www.csuchico.edu/mgmt/strategy/module1/sld014.htm;
http://www.csuchico.edu/mgmt/strategy/module1/sld017.htm

Firms should strive to engage in social activities that have economic benefits. For example, Merck & Co. recently developed the drug, ivermectin, for treating river blindness, a disease caused by a fly-borne parasitic worm endemic in poor, tropical areas of Africa, the Middle East, and Latin America. In an unprecedented gesture that reflected its corporate commitment to social responsibility, Merck then made ivermectin available at no cost to medical personnel throughout the world. Merck's action highlights the dilemma of orphan drugs, which offer pharmaceutical companies no economic incentive for development and distribution.

Despite differences in approaches, most American companies try to assure outsiders that they conduct their businesses in socially responsible ways. The mission statement is an effective instrument for conveying this message.

 ## COMPONENTS OF A MISSION STATEMENT

Mission statements can and do vary in length, content, format, and specificity. Most practitioners and academicians of strategic management feel that an effective statement exhibits nine characteristics or components. Because a mission statement is often the most visible and public part of the strategic-management process, it is important that it includes all of these essential components:

1. *Customers:* Who are the firm's customers?

2. *Products or services:* What are the firm's major products or services?

3. *Markets:* Geographically, where does the firm compete?

4. *Technology:* Is the firm technologically current?

5. *Concern for survival, growth, and profitability:* Is the firm committed to growth and financial soundness?

6. *Philosophy:* What are the basic beliefs, values, aspirations, and ethical priorities of the firm?

7. *Self-concept:* What is the firm's distinctive competence or major competitive advantage?

8. *Concern for public image:* Is the firm responsive to social, community, and environmental concerns?

9. *Concern for employees:* Are employees a valuable asset of the firm?

Excerpts from the mission statements of different organizations are provided in Table 2–2 to exemplify the nine essential mission statement components.

WRITING AND EVALUATING MISSION STATEMENTS

Perhaps the best way to develop a skill for writing and evaluating mission statements is to study actual company missions. Therefore, six mission statements are presented in Table 2–3. These statements are then evaluated in Table 2–4 based on the nine criteria presented above.

There is no one best mission statement for a particular organization, so good judgment is required in evaluating mission statements. In Table 2–4, a *Yes* indicates that the given mission statement answers satisfactorily the question posed in Table 2–2 for the respective evaluative criteria. Some individuals are more demanding than others in rating mission statements in this manner. For example, if a statement includes the word *employees* or *customer,* is that alone sufficient for the respective component? Some companies answer this question in the affirmative and some in the negative. You may ask yourself this question: "If I worked for this company, would I have done better with regard to including a particular component in its mission statement." Perhaps the important issue here is that mission statements include each of the nine components in some manner.

As indicated in Table 2–4, the Dell Computer mission statement was rated to be the best among the six statements evaluated. Note, however, that the Dell Computer statement lacks inclusion of the "Philosophy" and the "Concern for Employees" components. The PepsiCo mission statement was evaluated as the worst because it included only three of the nine components. Note that only one of these six statements included the "Technology" component in their document.

VISIT THE NET

Provides the NIH Clinical Center's vision and mission statements and its overall strategic plan. http://www.cc.nih.gov/od/strategic/index.html

TABLE 2–2   **Examples of the Nine Essential Components of a Mission Statement**

---

1.   CUSTOMERS

We believe our first responsibility is to the doctors, nurses, patients, mothers, and all others who use our products and services. (Johnson & Johnson)

To earn our customers' loyalty, we listen to them, anticipate their needs, and act to create value in their eyes. (Lexmark International)

---

2.   PRODUCTS OR SERVICES

AMAX's principal products are molybdenum, coal, iron ore, copper, lead, zinc, petroleum and natural gas, potash, phosphates, nickel, tungsten, silver, gold, and magnesium. (AMAX Engineering Company)

Standard Oil Company (Indiana) is in business to find and produce crude oil, natural gas, and natural gas liquids; to manufacture high-quality products useful to society from these raw materials; and to distribute and market those products and to provide dependable related services to the consuming public at reasonable prices. (Standard Oil Company)

---

3.   MARKETS

We are dedicated to the total success of Corning Glass Works as a worldwide competitor. (Corning Glass Works)

Our emphasis is on North American markets, although global opportunities will be explored. (Blockway)

---

4.   TECHNOLOGY

Control Data is in the business of applying micro-electronics and computer technology in two general areas: computer-related hardware; and computing-enhancing services, which include computation, information, education, and finance. (Control Data)

We will continually strive to meet the preferences of adult smokers by developing technologies that have the potential to reduce the health risks associated with smoking. (RJ Reynolds)

---

5.   CONCERN FOR SURVIVAL, GROWTH, AND PROFITABILITY

In this respect, the company will conduct its operations prudently and will provide the profits and growth which will assure Hoover's ultimate success. (Hoover Universal)

To serve the worldwide need for knowledge at a fair profit by adhering, evaluating, producing, and distributing valuable information in a way that benefits our customers, employees, other investors, and our society. (McGraw-Hill)

---

6.   PHILOSOPHY

Our world-class leadership is dedicated to a management philosophy that holds people above profits. (Kellogg)

It's all part of the Mary Kay philosophy—a philosophy based on the golden rule. A spirit of sharing and caring where people give cheerfully of their time, knowledge, and experience. (Mary Kay Cosmetics)

---

7.   SELF-CONCEPT

Crown Zellerbach is committed to leapfrogging ongoing competition within 1,000 days by unleashing the constructive and creative abilities and energies of each of its employees. (Crown Zellerbach)

---

8.   CONCERN FOR PUBLIC IMAGE

To share the world's obligation for the protection of the environment. (Dow Chemical)

To contribute to the economic strength of society and function as a good corporate citizen on a local, state, and national basis in all countries in which we do business. (Pfizer)

Continued

TABLE 2-2   **Examples of the Nine Essential Components of a Mission Statement (*continued*)**

9.   CONCERN FOR EMPLOYEES

To recruit, develop, motivate, reward, and retain personnel of exceptional ability, character, and dedication by providing good working conditions, superior leadership, compensation on the basis of performance, an attractive benefit program, opportunity for growth, and a high degree of employment security. (The Wachovia Corporation)

To compensate its employees with remuneration and fringe benefits competitive with other employment opportunities in its geographical area and commensurate with their contributions toward efficient corporate operations. (Public Service Electric & Gas Company)

TABLE 2-3   **Mission Statements of Six Organizations**

PepsiCo's mission is to increase the value of our shareholders' investment. We do this through sales growth, cost controls, and wise investment resources. We believe our commercial success depends upon offering quality and value to our consumers and customers; providing products that are safe, wholesome, economically efficient, and environmentally sound; and providing a fair return to our investors while adhering to the highest standards of integrity.

Ben & Jerry's mission is to make, distribute, and sell the finest quality all-natural ice cream and related products in a wide variety of innovative flavors made from Vermont dairy products. To operate the Company on a sound financial basis of profitable growth, increasing value for our shareholders, and creating career opportunities and financial rewards for our employees. To operate the Company in a way that actively recognizes the central role that business plays in the structure of society by initiating innovative ways to improve the quality of life of a broad community—local, national, and international.

The Mission of the Institute of Management Accountants (IMA) is to provide to members personal and professional development opportunities through education, association with business professionals, and certification in management accounting and financial management skills. The IMA is globally recognized by the financial community as a respected institution influencing the concepts and ethical practices of management accounting and financial management.

The Mission of Genentech, Inc., is to be the leading biotechnology company, using human genetic information to develop, manufacture, and market pharmaceuticals that address significant unmet medical needs. We commit ourselves to high standards of integrity in contributing to the best interests of patients, the medical profession, and our employees, and to seek significant returns to our stockholders based on the continued pursuit of excellent science.

The Mission of Barrett Memorial Hospital is to operate a high-quality health care facility, providing an appropriate mix of services to the residents of Beaverhead County and surrounding areas. Service is given with ultimate concern for patients, medical staff, hospital staff, and the community. Barrett Memorial Hospital assumes a strong leadership role in the coordination and development of health-related resources within the community.

Dell Computer's mission is to be the most successful computer company in the world at delivering the best customer experience in markets we serve. In doing so, Dell will meet customer expectations of highest quality; leading technology; competitive pricing; individual and company accountability; best-in-class service and support; flexible customization capability; superior corporate citizenship; financial stability.

TABLE 2-4   **An Evaluation Matrix of Mission Statements**

COMPONENTS

Organization	Customers	Products/ Services	Markets	Technology	Concern for Survival, Growth, Profitability
PepsiCo	Yes	No	No	No	Yes
Ben & Jerry's	No	Yes	Yes	No	Yes
Institute of Management Accountants	Yes	Yes	Yes	No	No
Genentech, Inc.	Yes	Yes	No	No	Yes
Barrett Memorial Hospital	Yes	Yes	Yes	No	No
Dell Computer	Yes	Yes	Yes	Yes	Yes

Organization	Philosophy	Self-Concept	Concern for Public Image	Concern for Employees
PepsiCo	Yes	No	No	No
Ben & Jerry's	No	Yes	Yes	Yes
Institute of Management Accountants	Yes	Yes	Yes	No
Genentech, Inc.	Yes	Yes	Yes	Yes
Barrett Memorial Hospital	No	Yes	Yes	Yes
Dell Computer	No	Yes	Yes	No

CONCLUSION

VISIT THE NET

Provides the strategic plan for Kansas State University, including its vision and mission statements.
www.ksu.edu/provost/planning/

Every organization has a unique purpose and reason for being. This uniqueness should be reflected in vision and mission statements. The nature of a business vision and mission can represent either a competitive advantage or disadvantage for the firm. An organization achieves a heightened sense of purpose when strategists, managers, and employees develop and communicate a clear business vision and mission. Drucker says that developing a clear business vision and mission is the "first responsibility of strategists."

A good mission statement reveals an organization's customers; products or services; markets; technology; concern for survival, growth, and profitability; philosophy; self-concept; concern for public image; and concern for employees. These nine basic components serve as a practical framework for evaluating and writing mission statements. As the first step in strategic management, the vision and mission statements provide direction for all planning activities.

Well-designed vision and mission statements are essential for formulating, implementing, and evaluating strategy. Developing and communicating a clear business vision and mission is one of the most commonly overlooked tasks in strategic management. Without clear statements of vision and mission, a firm's short-term actions can be counterproductive to long-term interests. Vision and mission statements always should be subject to revision, but, if carefully prepared, they will require infrequent major changes. Organizations usually reexamine their vision and mission statements annually. Effective mission statements stand the test of time.

Vision and mission statements are essential tools for strategists, a fact illustrated in a short story told by Porsche former CEO Peter Schultz:

Three people were at work on a construction site. All were doing the same job, but when each was asked what his job was, the answers varied: "Breaking rocks," the first replied; "Earning a living," responded the second; "Helping to build a cathedral," said the third. Few of us can build cathedrals. But to the extent we can see the cathedral in whatever cause we are following, the job seems more worthwhile. Good strategists and a clear mission help us find those cathedrals in what otherwise could be dismal issues and empty causes.[18]

We invite you to visit the David page on the Prentice Hall Companion Website at www.prenhall.com/david for this chapter's World Wide Web exercise.

KEY TERMS AND CONCEPTS

Concern for Employees (p. 69)

Concern for Public Image (p. 69)

Concern for Survival, Growth, and Profitability (p. 69)

Creed Statement (p. 59)

Customers (p. 69)

Markets (p. 69)

Mission Statement (p. 59)

Mission Statement Components (p. 69)

Philosophy (p. 69)

Products or Services (p. 69)

Self-Concept (p. 69)

Social Policy (p. 68)

Stakeholders (p. 64)

Technology (p. 69)

Vision Statement (p. 59)

ISSUES FOR REVIEW AND DISCUSSION

1. Compare and contrast vision statements with mission statements in terms of composition and importance.

2. Do local service stations need to have written vision and mission statements? Why or why not?

3. Why do you think organizations that have a comprehensive mission tend to be high performers? Does having a comprehensive mission cause high performance?

4. Explain why a mission statement should not include strategies and objectives.

5. What is your college or university's self-concept? How would you state that in a mission statement?

6. Explain the principal value of a vision and a mission statement.

7. Why is it important for a mission statement to be reconciliatory?

8. In your opinion, what are the three most important components that should be included when writing a mission statement? Why?

9. How would the mission statements of a for-profit and a nonprofit organization differ?

10. Write a vision and mission statement for an organization of your choice.

11. Go to www.altavista.com and conduct a search with the keywords *vision statement* and *mission statement*. Find various company vision and mission statements and evaluate the documents.

12. Who are the major stakeholders of the bank that you do business with locally? What are the major claims of those stakeholders?

13. Select one of the current readings at the end of this chapter. Look up that article in your college library, and give a five-minute oral report to the class summarizing the article.

NOTES

1. BARBARA BARTKUS, MYRON GLASSMAN, and BRUCE McAFEE, "Mission Statements: Are They Smoke and Mirrors?" *Business Horizons* (November–December 2000): 23.

2. PETER DRUCKER, *Management: Tasks, Responsibilities, and Practices* (New York: Harper & Row, 1974): 61.

3. FRED DAVID, "How Companies Define Their Mission," *Long Range Planning* 22, no. 1 (February 1989): 90–92; John Pearce II and Fred David, "Corporate Mission Statements: The Bottom Line," *Academy of Management Executive* 1, no. 2 (May 1987): 110.

4. JOSEPH QUIGLEY, "Vision: How Leaders Develop It, Share It and Sustain It," *Business Horizons* (September–October 1994): 39.

5. ANDREW CAMPBELL and SALLY YEUNG, "Creating a Sense of Mission," *Long Range Planning* 24, no. 4 (August 1991): 17.

6. CHARLES RARICK and JOHN VITTON, "Mission Statements Make Cents," *Journal of Business Strategy* 16 (1995): 11. Also, Christopher Bart and Mark Baetz, "The Relationship Between Mission Statements and Firm Performance: An Exploratory Study," *Journal of Management Studies* 35 (1998): 823; "Mission Possible," *BusinessWeek* (August 1999): F12.

7. W. R. KING and D. I. CLELAND, *Strategic Planning and Policy* (New York: Van Nostrand Reinhold, 1979): 124.

8. BRIAN DUMAINE, "What the Leaders of Tomorrow See," *Fortune* (July 3, 1989): 50.

9. DRUCKER: 78, 79.

10. "How W. T. Grant Lost $175 Million Last Year," *BusinessWeek* (February 25, 1975): 75.

11. DRUCKER, 88.

12. JOHN PEARCE II, "The Company Mission as a Strategic Tool," *Sloan Management Review* 23, no. 3 (Spring 1982): 74.

13. GEORGE STEINER, *Strategic Planning: What Every Manager Must Know* (New York: The Free Press, 1979): 160.

14. VERN MCGINNIS, "The Mission Statement: A Key Step in Strategic Planning," *Business* 31, no. 6 (November–December 1981): 41.

15. DRUCKER, 61.

16. ARCHIE CARROLL and FRANK HOY, "Integrating Corporate Social Policy into Strategic Management," *Journal of Business Strategy* 4, no. 3 (Winter 1984): 57.

17. RONALD ALSOP, "Perits of Corporate Philanthropy," *Wall Street Journal* (January 16, 2002): p. 81.

18. ROBERT WATERMAN, JR., *The Renewal Factor: How the Best Get and Keep the Competitive Edge* (New York: Bantam, 1987); *Business Week* (September 14, 1987): 120.

CURRENT READINGS

BAETZ, MARK C., and CHRISTOPHER K. BART, "Developing Mission Statements Which Work." *Long Range Planning* 29, no. 4 (August 1996): 526–533.

BARTKUS, BARBARA, MYRON GLASSMAN, and R. BRUCE MCAFEE. "Mission Statements: Are They Smoke and Mirrors?" *Business Horizons* 43, no. 6 (November–December 2000): 23.

BARTLETT, CHRISTOPHER A., and SUMANTRA GHOSHAL. "Changing the Role of Top Management: Beyond Strategy to Purpose." *Harvard Business Review* (November–December 1994): 79–90.

BRABET, JULIENNE, and MARY KLEMM. "Sharing the Vision: Company Mission Statements in Britain and France." *Long Range Planning* (February 1994): 84–94.

CIULLA, JOANNE B. "The Importance of Leadership in Shaping Business Values." *International Journal of Strategic Management* 32, no. 2 (April 1999): 166–172.

COLLINS, JAMES C., and JERRY I. PORRAS. "Building a Visionary Company." *California Management Review* 37, no. 2 (Winter 1995): 80–100.

COLLINS, JAMES C., and JERRY I. PORRAS. "Building Your Company's Vision." *Harvard Business Review* (September–October 1996): 65–78.

CUMMINGS, STEPHEN, and JOHN DAVIES. "Brief Case—Mission, Vision, Fusion." *Long Range Planning* 27, no. 6 (December 1994): 147–150.

DAVIES, STUART W., and KEITH W. GLAISTER. "Business School Mission Statements—The Bland Leading the Bland?" *Long Range Planning* 30, no. 4 (August 1997): 594–604.

GRATTON, LYNDA. "Implementing a Strategic Vision—Key Factors for Success." *Long Range Planning* 29, no. 3 (June 1996): 290–303.

GRAVES, SAMUEL B., and SANDRA A. WADDOCK. "Institutional Owners and Corporate Social Performance." *Academy of Management Journal* 37, no. 4 (August 1994): 1034–1046.

HEMPHILL, THOMAS A. "Legislating Corporate Social Responsibility." *Business Horizons* 40, no. 2 (March–April 1997): 53–63.

JONES, IAN W., and MICHAEL G. POLLITT. "Putting Values into Action: Lessons from Best Practice." *International Journal of Strategic Management* 32, no. 2 (April 1999): 162–165.

LARWOOD, LAURIE, CECILIA M. FALBE, MARK P. KRIGER, and PAUL MIESING. "Structure and Meaning of Organizational Vision." *Academy of Management Journal* 38, no. 3 (June 1995): 740–769.

LISSAK, MICHAEL, and JOHAN ROOS. "Be Coherent, Not Visionary." *Long Range Planning* 34, no. 1 (February 2001): 53.

MCTAVISH, RON. "One More Time: What Business Are You In?" *Long Range Planning* 28, no. 2 (April 1995): 49–60.

MARKOCZY, L. "Consensus Formation During Strategic Change." *Strategic Management Journal* 22, no. 11 (November 2001): 1013.

MARTIN, ROGER L. "The Virtue Matrix: Calculating the Return on Corporate Responsibility." *Harvard Business Review* (March 2002): 68.

MITOFF, IAN I., and ELIZABETH A. DENTON. "A Study of Spirituality in the Workplace." *Sloan Management Review* 40, no. 4 (Summer 1999): 83–92.

NASSER, JAC "Ford Motor Company's CEO Jac Nasser on Transformational Change, E-business, and Environmental Responsibility." *Academy of Management Journal* 14, no. 3 (August 2000): 46.

OSBORNE, RICHARD L. "Strategic Values: The Corporate Performance Engine." *Business Horizons* 39, no. 5 (September–October 1996): 41–47.

OSWALD, S. L., K. W. MOSSHOLDER, and S. G. HARRIS. "Vision Salience and Strategic Involvement: Implications for Psychological Attachment to Organization and Job." *Strategic Management Journal* 15, no. 6 (July 1994): 477–490.

ROUNDTABLE DISCUSSION. "Business as a Living System: The Value of Industrial Ecology." *California Management Review* 43, no. 3 (Spring 2001): 16.

SHANKLIN, WILLIAM L. "Creatively Managing for Creative Destruction." *Business Horizons* 43, no. 6 (November–December 2000): 29.

SNYDER, NEIL H., and MICHELLE GRAVES. "The Editor's Chair/Leadership and Vision." *Business Horizons* 37, no. 1 (January–February 1994): 1–7.

SWANSON, DIANE L. "Addressing a Theoretical Problem by Reorienting the Corporate Social Performance Model." *Academy of Management Review* 20, no. 1 (January 1995): 43–64.

SWANSON, DIANE L. "Toward an Integrative Theory of Business and Society: A Research Strategy for Corporate Social Performance." *Academy of Management Review* 24, no. 3 (July 1999): 506–521.

EXPERIENTIAL EXERCISES

**EXPERIENTIAL
EXERCISE 2A** ▶

Evaluating Mission
Statements

PURPOSE

A business mission statement is an integral part of strategic management. It provides direction for formulating, implementing, and evaluating strategic activities. This exercise will give you practice evaluating mission statements, a skill that is prerequisite to writing a good mission statement.

INSTRUCTIONS

Step 1 Your instructor will select some or all of the following mission statements to evaluate. On a separate sheet of paper, construct an evaluation matrix like the one presented in Table 2–4. Evaluate the mission statements based on the nine criteria presented in the chapter.

Step 2 Record a *yes* in appropriate cells of the evaluation matrix when the respective mission statement satisfactorily meets the desired criteria. Record a *no* in appropriate cells when the respective mission statement does not meet the stated criteria.

MISSION STATEMENTS

Criterion Productions, Inc.

The mission statement of Criterion Productions, Inc., is to increase the success of all who avail themselves of our products and services by providing image enhancement and a medium that communicates our customer's corporate identity and unique message to a targeted audience. In this, our tenth year of business, Criterion Productions, Inc., pledges to offer a distinct advantage and a superior value in all of your video production needs. We will assist our customers in their endeavors to grow and prosper through celebrity associations that are "effectively appropriate" to their industry, and/or who possess the qualities and characteristics most respected by our customers.

Mid-America Plastics, Inc.

"Continuous Improvement Every Day, In Everything We Do."
In order for us to accomplish our mission, every employee must be "Committed to Excellence" in everything he or she does by performing his or her job right the first time.

Hatboro Area YMCA

To translate the principles of the YMCA's Christian heritage into programs that nurture children, strengthen families, build strong communities, and develop healthy minds, bodies, and spirits for all.

Integrated Communications, Inc.

Our mission is to be perceived by our customers as providing the highest quality of customer service and salesmanship, delivered with a sense of ownership, friendliness, individual pride, and team spirit. We will accomplish this with the quality of our Wireless Products that supply complete solutions to our customers needs. And, through unyielding loyalty to our customers and suppliers, ICI will provide opportunities and security to our employees as well as [maximize] our long-term financial growth.

American Counseling Association (ACA)

The Mission of ACA is to promote public confidence and trust in the counseling profession.

Idaho Hospital Association

The mission of the Idaho Hospital Association is to provide representation, advocacy and assistance for member hospitals, healthcare systems and the healthcare services they provide. The Association, through leadership and collaboration among healthcare providers and others, promotes quality healthcare that is adequately financed and accessible to all Idahoans.

PURPOSE

There is no one best vision or mission statement for a given organization. Analysts feel that AMR needs a clear vision and mission statement to survive. Writing a mission statement that includes desired components—and at the same time is inspiring and reconciliatory—requires careful thought. Mission statements should not be too lengthy; statements under two-hundred words are desirable.

INSTRUCTIONS

Step 1   Take 15 minutes to write vision and mission statements for AMR. Scan the case for needed details as you prepare your statements.

Step 2   Join with three other classmates to form a group of four people. Read each other's statements silently. As a group, select the best vision statement and best mission statement from your group.

Step 3   Read those best statements to the class.

PURPOSE

Most universities have a vision and mission statement. The purpose of this exercise is to give you practice writing a vision and mission statement for a nonprofit organization such as your own university.

INSTRUCTIONS

Step 1   Take 15 minutes to write a vision statement and a mission statement for your university. Your mission statement should not exceed two hundred words.

Step 2   Read your vision and mission statements to the class.

Step 3   Determine whether your institution has a vision and/or mission statement. Look in the front of the college handbook. If your institution has a written statement, contact an appropriate administrator of the institution to inquire as to how and when the statement was prepared. Share this information with the class. Analyze your college's mission statement in light of concepts presented in this chapter.

EXPERIENTIAL EXERCISE 2B ▶

Writing a Vision and Mission Statement for American Airlines (AMR)

EXPERIENTIAL EXERCISE 2C ▶

Writing a Vision and Mission Statement for My University

**EXPERIENTIAL
EXERCISE 2D ▶**

Conducting Mission
Statement Research

PURPOSE

This exercise gives you the opportunity to study the nature and role of vision and mission statements in strategic management.

INSTRUCTIONS

Step 1   Call various organizations in your city or county to identify firms that have developed a formal vision and/or mission statement. Contact nonprofit organizations and government agencies in addition to small and large businesses. Ask to speak with the director, owner, or chief executive officer of one organization. Explain that you are studying vision and mission statements in class and are conducting research as part of a class activity.

Step 2   Ask several executives the following four questions, and record their answers.

1. When did your organization first develop its vision and/or mission statement? Who was primarily responsible for its development?

2. How long have your current statements existed? When were they last modified? Why were they modified at that point in time?

3. By what process are your firm's vision and mission statements altered?

4. How are your vision and mission statements used in the firm? How do they affect the firm's strategic-planning process?

Step 3   Provide an overview of your findings to the class.

3 THE EXTERNAL ASSESSMENT

CHAPTER OUTLINE

- The Nature of an External Audit
- Economic Forces
- Social, Cultural, Demographic, and Environmental Forces.
- Political, Governmental, and Legal Forces
- Technological Forces
- Competitive Forces
- Competitive Analysis: Porter's Five-Forces Model
- Sources of External Information
- Forecasting Tools and Techniques
- The Global Challenge
- Industry Analysis: The External Factor Evaluation (EFE) Matrix
- The Competitive Profile Matrix (CPM)

EXPERIENTIAL EXERCISE 3A
Developing an EFE Matrix for American Airlines (AMR)

EXPERIENTIAL EXERCISE 3B
The Internet Search

EXPERIENTIAL EXERCISE 3C
Developing an EFE Matrix for My University

EXPERIENTIAL EXERCISE 3D
Developing a Competitive Profile Matrix for American Airlines (AMR)

EXPERIENTIAL EXERCISE 3E
Developing a Competitive Profile Matrix for My University

CHAPTER OBJECTIVES

After studying this chapter, you should be able to do the following:

1. Describe how to conduct an external strategic-management audit.
2. Discuss ten major external forces that affect organizations: economic, social, cultural, demographic, environmental, political, governmental, legal, technological, and competitive.
3. Identify key sources of external information, including the Internet.
4. Discuss important forecasting tools used in strategic management.
5. Discuss the importance of monitoring external trends and events.
6. Explain how to develop an EFE Matrix.
7. Explain how to develop a Competitive Profile Matrix.
8. Discuss the importance of gathering competitive intelligence.
9. Describe the trend toward cooperation among competitors.
10. Discuss the political environment in Russia.
11. Discuss the global challenge facing American firms.

NOTABLE QUOTES

If you're not faster than your competitor, you're in a tenuous position, and if you're only half as fast, you're terminal.

GEORGE SALK

The opportunities and threats existing in any situation always exceed the resources needed to exploit the opportunities or avoid the threats. Thus, strategy is essentially a problem of allocating resources. If strategy is to be successful, it must allocate superior resources against a decisive opportunity.

WILLIAM COHEN

Organizations pursue strategies that will disrupt the normal course of industry events and forge new industry conditions to the disadvantage of competitors.

IAN C. MACMILLAN

The idea is to concentrate our strength against our competitor's relative weakness.

BRUCE HENDERSON

There was a time in America when business was easier. We set the pace for the rest of the world. We were immune to serious foreign competition. Many of us were regulated [and] therefore protected. No longer. Today's leaders must recreate themselves and their ways of doing business in order to stay on top and stay competitive.

ROBERT H. WATERMAN, JR.

If everyone is thinking alike, then somebody isn't thinking.

GEORGE PATTON

Prediction is very difficult, especially about the future.

NEILS BOHR

The best preparation for good work tomorrow is to do good work today.

ELBERT HUBBARD

This chapter examines the tools and concepts needed to conduct an external strategic management audit (sometimes called *environmental scanning* or *industry analysis*). An *external audit* focuses on identifying and evaluating trends and events beyond the control of a single firm, such as increased foreign competition, population shifts to the Sunbelt, an aging society, consumer fear of traveling, and stock market volatility. An external audit reveals key opportunities and threats confronting an organization so that managers can formulate strategies to take advantage of the opportunities and avoid or reduce the impact of threats. This chapter presents a practical framework for gathering, assimilating, and analyzing external information.

THE NATURE OF AN EXTERNAL AUDIT

The purpose of an *external audit* is to develop a finite list of opportunities that could benefit a firm and threats that should be avoided. As the term *finite* suggests, the external audit is not aimed at developing an exhaustive list of every possible factor that could influence the business; rather, it is aimed at identifying key variables that offer actionable responses. Firms should be able to respond either offensively or defensively to the factors by formulating strategies that take advantage of external opportunities or that minimize the impact of potential threats. Figure 3–1 illustrates how the external audit fits into the strategic-management process.

VISIT THE NET

Reveals how strategic planning evolved from long-range planning and environmental scanning (external audit or assessment).
http://horizon.unc.edu/projects/seminars/futuresresearch/strategic.asp#planning

Key External Forces
External forces can be divided into five broad categories: (1) economic forces; (2) social, cultural, demographic, and environmental forces; (3) political, governmental, and legal forces; (4) technological forces; and (5) competitive forces. Relationships among these forces and an organization are depicted in Figure 3–2. External trends and events significantly affect all products, services, markets, and organizations in the world.

Changes in external forces translate into changes in consumer demand for both industrial and consumer products and services. External forces affect the types of products developed, the nature of positioning and market segmentation strategies, the types of services offered, and the choice of businesses to acquire or sell. External forces directly affect both suppliers and distributors. Identifying and evaluating external opportunities and threats enables organizations to develop a clear mission, to design strategies to achieve long-term objectives, and to develop policies to achieve annual objectives.

The increasing complexity of business today is evidenced by more countries developing the capacity and will to compete aggressively in world markets. Foreign businesses and countries are willing to learn, adapt, innovate, and invent to compete successfully in the marketplace. There are more competitive new technologies in Europe and the Far East today than ever before. American businesses can no longer beat foreign competitors with ease.

The Process of Performing an External Audit
The process of performing an external audit must involve as many managers and employees as possible. As emphasized in earlier chapters, involvement in the strategic management process can lead to understanding and commitment from organizational members. Individuals appreciate having the opportunity to contribute ideas and to gain a better understanding of their firm's industry, competitors, and markets.

FIGURE 3–1

A Comprehensive Strategic-Management Model

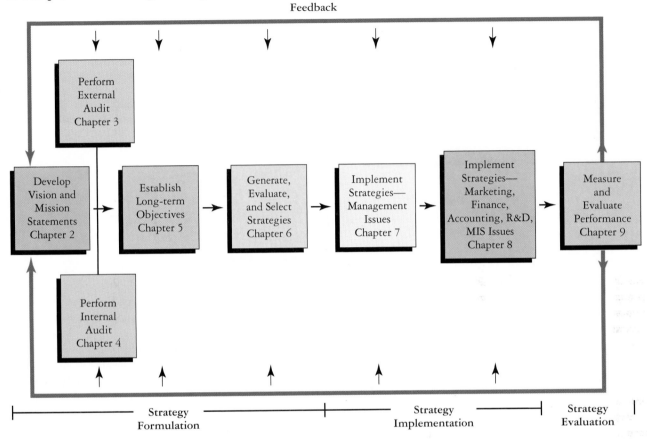

To perform an external audit, a company first must gather competitive intelligence and information about economic, social, cultural, demographic, environmental, political, governmental, legal, and technological trends. Individuals can be asked to monitor various sources of information, such as key magazines, trade journals, and newspapers. These persons can submit periodic scanning reports to a committee of managers charged with performing the external audit. This approach provides a continuous stream of timely strategic information and involves many individuals in the external-audit process. The Internet provides another source for gathering strategic information, as do corporate, university, and public libraries. Suppliers, distributors, salespersons, customers, and competitors represent other sources of vital information.

Once information is gathered, it should be assimilated and evaluated. A meeting or series of meetings of managers is needed to collectively identify the most important opportunities and threats facing the firm. These key external factors should be listed on flip charts or a blackboard. A prioritized list of these factors could be obtained by requesting that all managers rank the factors identified, from 1 for the most important opportunity/threat to 20 for the least important opportunity/threat. These key external factors can vary over time and by industry. Relationships with suppliers or distributors are often a critical success factor. Other variables commonly used include market share,

VISIT THE NET

Describes the external audit process in a university setting.
http://horizon.unc.edu/ projects/seminars/ futuresresearch/stages.asp

FIGURE 3–2

Relationships Between Key External Forces and an Organization

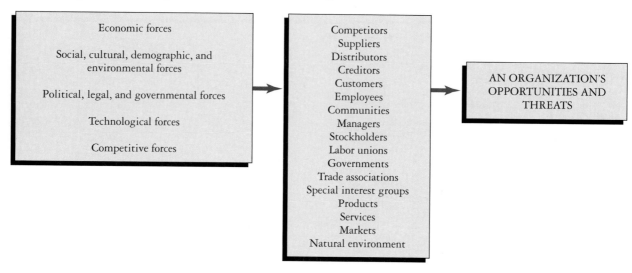

breadth of competing products, world economies, foreign affiliates, proprietary and key account advantages, price competitiveness, technological advancements, population shifts, interest rates, and pollution abatement.

Freund emphasized that these key external factors should be (1) important to achieving long-term and annual objectives, (2) measurable, (3) applicable to all competing firms, and (4) hierarchical in the sense that some will pertain to the overall company and others will be more narrowly focused on functional or divisional areas.[1] A final list of the most important key external factors should be communicated and distributed widely in the organization. Both opportunities and threats can be key external factors.

 ## ECONOMIC FORCES

As domestic and global economies slowly recover from recession, consumer confidence and disposable income are the lowest in a decade, whereas unemployment and consumer debt are the highest in a decade. Stock prices, interest rates, corporate profits, exports, and imports are all very low in the United States and abroad. Foreign direct investment among countries fell by nearly 50 percent in 2001, the sharpest decline in thirty years. The number and value of cross-country mergers in 2001 fell to less than one-third the volume of the year before, as the overall downturn in international investment worsened following the September 11, 2001, terrorist attacks.

Increasing numbers of two-income households is an economic trend in America. As affluence increases, individuals place a premium on time. Improved customer service, immediate availability, trouble-free operation of products, and dependable maintenance and repair services are becoming more important. Americans today are more willing than ever to pay for good service if it limits inconvenience.

Economic factors have a direct impact on the potential attractiveness of various strategies. For example, when interest rates rise, funds needed for capital expansion become more costly or unavailable. Also, when interest rates rise, discretionary income declines, and the demand for discretionary goods falls. When stock prices increase, the desirability of equity as a source of capital for market development increases. Also, when the market rises, consumer and business wealth expands. A summary of economic variables that often represent opportunities and threats for organizations is provided in Table 3–1.

Trends in the dollar's value have significant and unequal effects on companies in different industries and in different locations. For example, the pharmaceutical, tourism, entertainment, motor vehicle, aerospace, and forest products industries benefit greatly when the dollar falls against the yen and euro. Agricultural and petroleum industries are hurt by the dollar's rise against the currencies of Mexico, Brazil, Venezuela, and Australia. Generally, a strong or high dollar makes American goods more expensive in overseas markets. This worsens America's trade deficit. When the value of the dollar falls, tourism-oriented firms benefit because Americans do not travel abroad as much when the value of the dollar is low; rather, foreigners visit and vacation more in the United States.

A low value of the dollar means lower imports and higher exports; it helps U.S. companies' competitiveness in world markets. Recent years have seen the U.S. dollar gaining against virtually every other currency. One benefit of this trend is that consumers pay less for imported goods such as cars and computer memory chips. Domestic firms that manufacture extensively outside the United States also benefit from the rising value of the dollar. The euro lost nearly a quarter of its value against the dollar in 2000 and 2001. As the value of the dollar declines, prices of products the United States imports increase, which can result in higher inflation and interest rates domestically.

Every business day, thousands of American workers learn that they will lose their jobs. More than 500,000 annual employee layoffs by U.S. firms in the 1990s led to terms such as *downsizing, rightsizing,* and *decruiting* becoming common. European firms, too, are beginning to downsize. The U.S. and world economies face a sustained period of slow, low-inflationary expansion, global overcapacity, high unemployment, price wars, and increased competitiveness. Thousands of laid-off workers are being forced to become entrepreneurs to make a living. The United States is becoming more entrepreneurial every day.

VISIT THE NET

Provides excellent narrative on NASA's strategic-management process, especially its external assessment activities. Provides NASA's entire strategic plan with outstanding narrative and illustrations about how to do strategic planning.
http://www.hq.nasa.gov/office/nsp/toc.htm

TABLE 3–1   **Key Economic Variables to Be Monitored**

Shift to a service economy in the United States	Demand shifts for different categories of goods and services
Availability of credit	Income differences by region and consumer groups
Level of disposable income	Price fluctuations
Propensity of people to spend	Export of labor and capital from the United States
Interest rates	Monetary policies
Inflation rates	Fiscal policies
Money market rates	Tax rates
Federal government budget deficits	European Economic Community (ECC) policies
Gross domestic product trend	Organization of Petroleum Exporting Countries (OPEC) policies
Consumption patterns	Coalitions of Lesser Developed Countries (LDC) policies
Unemployment trends	
Worker productivity levels	
Value of the dollar in world markets	
Stock market trends	
Foreign countries' economic conditions	
Import/export factors	

Deregulation of industries worldwide is acting to restrain inflation worldwide. Deregulation in the utility and telecommunications industries, for example, is lowering electricity and phone prices worldwide. Energy deregulation worldwide contributes to keeping inflation in check in most industrialized countries of the world. Global cross-border mergers and alliances, too, serve to increase competitiveness within industries, thus lowering prices and also lessening inflation pressures worldwide.

The 15-nation European Union (EU) is Iran's biggest trading partner, with imports exceeding $5 billion annually. To the dismay of U.S. officials, the EU is close to signing an economic trade pact with Iran, despite the fact that the Khatami government in Iran supports some Mideast terrorist groups, such as Hezbollah and Hamas, in their fight against Israel. U.S. companies are today banned from investing in or trading with Iran, while the EU looks to further its trade ties.

The North American Free Trade Agreement (NAFTA) has spurred economic trade between the United States and Mexico. For example, since the United States signed the treaty, its exports to Mexico have increased 170 percent, far above the 68 percent gain for overall U.S. exports. In 2000, the United States ran a $25 billion trade deficit with Mexico, compared to $84 billion with China and $81 billion with Japan. More than $85 billion of investment has gone into the Mexican economy since NAFTA was born. However, in 2001, as a result of the recession that had struck the U.S. and world economies, more than 60,000 individuals were laid off from work along the Mexican border with the United States.[2]

Russia's Economy

The Russian economy is in trouble. Many companies are bankrupt and out of cash but keep operating. Many employees are not paid in cash but keep working. Many companies do not pay their electricity bills yet rarely face power cutoffs. *Business Week* magazine calls the Russian economy bizarre because real money, goods, and output play such a small role.[3] Most business between companies and individuals is done through IOUs known as *veksel* and barter. Noncash forms of payment now make up 45 percent of most companies' and cities' budget. Some companies rely totally on barter, such as Velta Company, a bicycle factory on the outskirts of the Western Russia city of Perm, which pays its employees in bicycles.

The major barriers to increased U.S. exports to Russia are a substantial value-added tax, high import duties, and onerous Russian excise levies. In addition, the government has imposed strict quality and safety standards on the majority of goods entering Russia. However, Russian standards authorities have permitted only a tightly circumscribed number of groups to perform this testing in the United States. The customs clearance process at Russian border points is frequently cumbersome and unpredictable. Local transportation problems also complicate the process of getting goods to the Russian market.

SOCIAL, CULTURAL, DEMOGRAPHIC, AND ENVIRONMENTAL FORCES

Social, cultural, demographic, and environmental changes have a major impact upon virtually all products, services, markets, and customers. Small, large, for-profit and nonprofit organizations in all industries are being staggered and challenged by the opportunities and threats arising from changes in social, cultural, demographic, and environmental variables. In every way, the United States is much different today than it was yesterday, and tomorrow promises even greater changes.

The United States is getting older and less Caucasian. The oldest members of America's 76 million baby boomers plan to retire in 2011, and this has lawmakers and younger taxpayers deeply concerned about who will pay their social security, Medicare, and Medicaid. Individuals age 65 and older in the United States as a percent of the population will rise to 18.5 percent by 2025.

By the year 2075, the United States will have no racial or ethnic majority. This forecast is aggravating tensions over issues such as immigration and affirmative action. Hawaii, California, and New Mexico already have no majority race or ethnic group.

Population of the world passed 6 billion on October 12, 1999; the United States has less than 300 million people. That leaves billions of people outside the United States who may be interested in the products and services produced through domestic firms. Remaining solely domestic is an increasingly risky strategy, especially as the world population continues to grow to estimated numbers of 7 billion in 2013, 8 billion in 2028, and 9 billion in 2054.

Social, cultural, demographic, and environmental trends are shaping the way Americans live, work, produce, and consume. New trends are creating a different type of consumer and, consequently, a need for different products, different services, and different strategies. There are now more American households with people living alone or with unrelated people than there are households consisting of married couples with children. Census data suggest that Americans are not returning to traditional lifestyles. Church membership fell substantially during the 1980s for nearly all religious denominations, except for Southern Baptists and Mormons. It is interesting to note that Protestant churches in the United States take in over $7 billion in donations annually. The eight largest U.S. church denominations are (in millions of members) Roman Catholic (60.3), Southern Baptist (15.7), National Baptist (11.7), United Methodist (8.5), Lutheran (5.2), Mormon (4.7), Presbyterian (3.7), and Episcopalian (3.5).

Significant trends for the 2000s include consumers becoming more educated, the population aging, minorities becoming more influential, people looking for local rather than federal solutions to problems, and fixation on youth decreasing. The United States Census Bureau projects that the number of Hispanics will increase to 15 percent of the population by 2021, when they will become a larger minority group than African Americans in America. The percentage of African Americans in the U.S. population is expected to increase to 14 percent by 2021. Many states currently have more than 500,000 Hispanics as registered voters, including California, New Mexico, Arizona, Texas, Florida, New York, Illinois, and New Jersey. The Hispanic population in the United States increased by over 40 percent in the 1990s. States with the largest percentage increase of Hispanics during that period were Arkansas (149%), Nevada (124%), North Carolina (110%), Georgia (103%), and Nebraska (96%).

During the 1990s, the number of individuals age fifty and over increased 18.5 percent—to 76 million. In contrast, the number of Americans under age fifty grew by just 3.5 percent. The trend toward an older America is good news for restaurants, hotels, airlines, cruise lines, tours, resorts, theme parks, luxury products and services, recreational vehicles, home builders, furniture producers, computer manufacturers, travel services, pharmaceutical firms, automakers, and funeral homes. Older Americans are especially interested in healthcare, financial services, travel, crime prevention, and leisure. The world's longest-living people are the Japanese, with Japanese women living to 86.3 years and men living to 80.1 years on average. By 2050, the Census Bureau projects that the number of Americans age one hundred and older will increase to over 834,000 from just under 100,000 centenarians in the United States in 2000. Senior citizens are also senior executives at hundreds of American companies. Examples include eighty-seven-year-old William Dillard at Dillard's Department Stores; seventy-nine-year-old Sumner Redstone, CEO of Viacom; seventy-one-year-old Ellen Gordon, president of Tootsie Roll Industries; seventy-seven-year-old Richard Jacobs, CEO of the Cleveland Indians; seventy-six-year-old Leslie Quick, CEO of Quick & Reilly; eighty-three-year-old Ralph

Roberts, chairman of Comcast; and seventy-six-year-old Alan Greenspan, chairman of the Federal Reserve. Americans age sixty-five and over will increase from 12.6 percent of the U.S. population in 2000 to 20.0 percent by the year 2050.

The aging American population affects the strategic orientation of nearly all organizations. Apartment complexes for the elderly, with one meal a day, transportation, and utilities included in the rent, have increased nationwide. Called *lifecare facilities,* these complexes now exceed two million. Some well-known companies building these facilities include Avon, Marriott, and Hyatt. By the year 2005, individuals age sixty-five and older in the United States will rise to 13 percent of the total population; Japan's elderly population ratio will rise to 17 percent, and Germany's to 19 percent.

Americans are on the move in a population shift to the South and West (Sunbelt) and away from the Northeast and Midwest (Frost Belt). The Internal Revenue Service provides the Census Bureau with massive computer files of demographic data. By comparing individual address changes from year to year, the Census Bureau publishes extensive information about population shifts across the country. For example, Nevada is the fastest-growing state. Arizona, Colorado, and Florida are close behind. States incurring the greatest loss of people are North Dakota, West Virginia, Iowa, Louisiana, and Pennsylvania. This type of information can be essential for successful strategy formulation, including where to locate new plants and distribution centers and where to focus marketing efforts.

Americans are becoming less interested in fitness and exercise. Fitness participants declined in the United States by 3.5 percent annually in the 1990s. Makers of fitness products, such as Nike, Reebok International, and CML Group—which makes NordicTrack—are experiencing declines in sales growth. American Sports Data in Hartsdale, New York, reports that "the one American in five who exercises regularly is now outnumbered by three couch potatoes."

Except for terrorism, no greater threat to business and society exists than the voracious, continuous decimation and degradation of our natural environment. The U.S. Clean Air Act went into effect in 1994. The U.S. Clean Water Act went into effect in 1984. As indicated in the Natural Environment Perspective box, air and water pollution causes great anguish worldwide. A summary of important social, cultural, demographic, and environmental variables that represent opportunities or threats for virtually all organizations is given in Table 3–2.

The U.S.–Mexican Border

Stretching 2,100 miles from the Pacific Ocean to the Gulf of Mexico, this 180-mile-wide strip of land is North America's fastest-growing region. With 11 million people and $150 billion in output, this region's economy is larger than Poland's. For the 6.1 million residents on the U.S. side, the average hourly wage plus benefits is $7.71, but for the 5.1 million residents on the Mexican side, the average is $1.36. The developed and developing nations meet along this border, which features shantytowns just down the street from luxury residential neighborhoods.

There are now over fifteen hundred *maquiladoras* (assembly plants) on the Mexican side of the border. Many analysts contend that the *maquiladoras* are a vital key to continued U.S. global competitiveness. Mexico now ranks only behind China as global investors' favorite location for establishing business in the developing world. Amid the swelter of economic activity, deep disparities and contrasts are likely to persist. But the two sides of the border are now so interdependent that they can only move forward together.

Tijuana, fifteen minutes from San Diego, is the television-manufacturing capital of the world. Plants of Sony, Samsung, Matsushita, and others produce fourteen million units annually. Per capita income in San Diego is $25,000; in Tijuana, it is $3,200.

TABLE 3-2   **Key Social, Cultural, Demographic, and Environmental Variables**

Childbearing rates	Attitudes toward retirement
Number of special interest groups	Attitudes toward leisure time
Number of marriages	Attitudes toward product quality
Number of divorces	Attitudes toward customer service
Number of births	Pollution control
Number of deaths	Attitudes toward foreign peoples
Immigration and emigration rates	Energy conservation
Social security programs	Social programs
Life expectancy rates	Number of churches
Per capita income	Number of church members
Location of retailing, manufacturing, and service businesses	Social responsibility
Attitudes toward business	Attitudes toward careers
Lifestyles	Population changes by race, age, sex, and level of affluence
Traffic congestion	Attitudes toward authority
Inner-city environments	Population changes by city, county, state, region, and country
Average disposable income	
Trust in government	Value placed on leisure time
Attitudes toward government	Regional changes in tastes and preferences
Attitudes toward work	Number of women and minority workers
Buying habits	Number of high school and college graduates by geographic area
Ethical concerns	
Attitudes toward saving	Recycling
Sex roles	Waste management
Attitudes toward investing	Air pollution
Racial equality	Water pollution
Use of birth control	Ozone depletion
Average level of education	Endangered species
Government regulation	

Cuidad Juarez, midway between the Pacific Ocean and the Gulf of Mexico and just 15 minutes from El Paso, has 235 factories employing 178,000, the largest concentration of *maquiladoras* anywhere along the border. General Motors alone has 17 auto parts plants. But explosive industrial growth and uncontrolled urban expansion have far surpassed municipal services such as sewers and street paving. Juarez and El Paso share the worst air pollution anywhere on the border.

Nuevo Laredo, fifteen minutes from Laredo, Texas, is home to the largest rail and truck crossings of the Rio Grande River from Mexico into the United States. More than 4,000 loaded trucks cross the Rio Grande daily at Nuevo Laredo, which is home to Wal-Mart's largest distribution center.

POLITICAL, GOVERNMENTAL, AND LEGAL FORCES

Federal, state, local, and foreign governments are major regulators, deregulators, subsidizers, employers, and customers of organizations. Political, governmental, and legal factors, therefore, can represent key opportunities or threats for both small and large organizations.

NATURAL ENVIRONMENT PERSPECTIVE

Is Your Business Polluting the Air or Water?

AIR

More than 1.5 billion people around the world live in urban areas with dangerous levels or air pollution. Alarmingly, cities are growing too rapidly to reverse this trend. Seven of the ten worst cities for sulfur dioxide and carbon monoxide are in developing countries. These and other pollutants cause acute and chronic lung disease, heart disease, lung cancer, and lead-induced neurological damage in children. Lung cancer alone kills over one million people annually, and more than a million new cases of lung cancer are diagnosed annually. In the European Union countries, a 33 percent increase in female lung cancer cases is predicted by 2005. There is no effective treatment for lung cancer—only 10 percent of patients are alive five years after diagnosis. Polluted air knows no city, state, country or continent boundaries.

The Environmental Protection Agency (EPA) wants to expand air pollution regulations in the United States to cover microscopic particles as tiny as 2.5 microns, down from the current standard of 10 microns. The EPA says this will cut premature deaths in the United States by 20,000; cases or aggravated asthma by 250,000; cases of acute childhood respiratory problems by 250,000; bronchitis cases by 60,000; hospital admissions by 9,000; and cases of major breathing problems by 1.5 million. The total savings of these benefits would exceed $115 billion. Critics say the proposed new regulations will cost U.S. companies and cities too much.

Source: Adapted from William Miller, "Clean-Air Contention," *Industry Week* (May 5, 1997): 14. Also, *World Health Organization Report* (1997).

WATER

Is your business polluting the water? Contaminated water is blamed for as much as 80 percent of all disease in developing countries. Well over one billion people in the world still are without safe water to drink, bathe, cook, and clean. Less than 2 percent of the domestic and industrial wastewater generated in developing countries receives any kind of treatment; it just runs into rivers and groundwater resources, thus poisoning populations, the environment, and the planet. Unsafe drinking water is a prime cause of diarrhea, malaria, cancer, infant deformities, and infant mortality. A few statistics reveal the severity, harshness, and effect of water pollution.

- More than five million babies born in developing countries die annually in the first month of life, mainly because of polluted water.
- About four million babies are born with deformities annually.
- Diarrhea and dysentery kill 2.5 million people annually.
- Malaria kills 2.1 million people annually.

Industrial discharge, a major water problem even in the United States, contributes significantly to the dramatic rise in cancer both here and abroad. More than 10 million new cases of cancer are diagnosed annually, and about 6.5 million people die of cancer annually. More than 1.2 billion of these deaths are caused by stomach and colon cancer, two types often associated with poor water and eating habits. Besides deaths, the anguish, sickness, suffering, and expense inflicted upon people directly or indirectly because of contaminated water is immeasurably high even in the United States. Dangerous industrial chemicals are used here as fertilizers, pesticides, solvents, food additives, fuels, medicines, cosmetics, and in a wide range of manufacturing processes.

The EPA's most recent proposal for the Great Lakes would reduce by 91 percent the twenty-two toxic chemicals comprising about ninety thousand pounds being dumped each year into those waters. The chemicals include mercury, dioxin, chlordane, DDT, and mirex.

Source: Adapted from *World Health Organization Report* (1997). John Jones, "EPA Proposes to Limit PCBs In Great Lakes," *The Wall Street Journal* (September 27, 1999): B19G.

E-COMMERCE PERSPECTIVE

Should Internet Sales Remain Tax Free?

Currently, nobody pays sales taxes when they buy books, clothing, cars, or anything else on the Internet. The average sales tax nationwide is 6.3 percent, so the absence of any tax on Internet sales means that state and local governments are giving e-business a huge subsidy. Currently about 49 percent of all state tax revenues are from sales taxes, more than individual and corporate taxes combined. Those revenues are used for schools, law enforcement, highway repair and other work of governments. Traditional retail stores argue that it will soon be impossible for them to compete with e-tailers if Internet sales remain tax free.

A thorny question thus looms on the horizon in terms of whether to tax Internet sales. With online sales rising 300 percent a year and topping $1 trillion in 2003, advocates pro and con debate whether those sales taxes should go uncollected. The national moratorium on new Internet taxes was renewed for three years in October 2001. Grover Norquist, president of Americans for Tax Reform says, "Any business guy stupid enough to participate in leading the charge to tax the Internet is going to find that tax named after him or his company." And surely no state or federal legislator wants an Internet tax named for him or her.

Some considerations and contentions regarding taxing Internet sales are as follows:

- Keeping Internet sales tax-free will help the economy grow faster.

- Traditional merchants contend that online shopping with no sales tax robs them of customers.

- Local and state governments contend those sales tax dollars are needed for schools and public safety.

- Americans may buy from foreign companies if sales taxes are imposed on Internet shopping.

- Consumers in other countries may bypass U.S. products if sales taxes are imposed.

- Imposing a sales tax on Internet shopping will slow the growth of Internet shopping, thus hutting online businesses.

- Neither state nor federal legislators want to be responsible for tax increases.

- Currently there are over sixty-six hundred sales tax jurisdictions in the United States; taxing Internet sales could logistically be a nightmare for interstate retailers who would have to calculate these rates.

- Research concludes that online spending would drop by 30 percent or more if taxes were suddenly imposed. This would cripple many marginal Internet businesses.

Source: Adapted from: Mike France, "A Web Sales Tax: Not If, But When," *Business Week* (June 21, 1999): 104–106. Also, Richard Wolf, "Taxes on Internet Sales Opposed," *USA Today* (September 14, 1999): 6A.

Mexican companies laid off almost half a million employees during the first ten months of 2001; these companies included ADC Telecommunications (4,300 in Chihuahua), Goodyear (1,559 in Tultitlán), Selectron (2,000 in Guadalajara), General Motors (600 in Ramos Arizpe), and Vtech (3,000 in Guadalajara). Mexico has very strict regulations that penalize employers with expensive severance packages who lay off employees. For example, when Goodyear Tire & Rubber fired nearly 1,600 workers from a factory outside Mexico City recently, the company paid more that $48 million in severance pay—an average of $31,000 per worker. Federal government decisions regarding taxation of Internet sales is an important factor, as indicated in the E-Commerce Perspective box.

For industries and firms that depend heavily on government contracts or subsidies, political forecasts can be the most important part of an external audit. Changes in patent laws, antitrust legislation, tax rates, and lobbying activities can affect firms significantly. The U.S. Justice Department offers excellent information at its Web site (**www.usdoj. gov**) on such topics.

In the world of biopolitics, Americans are still deeply divided over issues such as assisted suicide, genetic testing, genetic engineering, cloning, stem-cell research, and abortion. Such political issues have great ramifications for companies in many industries, ranging from pharmaceuticals to computers.

The increasing global interdependence among economies, markets, governments, and organizations makes it imperative that firms consider the possible impact of political variables on the formulation and implementation of competitive strategies. A number of nationally known firms forecast political, governmental, and legal variables. Some of the best Web sites for finding legal help on the Internet are listed below:[4]

www.findlaw.com

www.lawguru.com

www.freeadvice.com

www.nolo.com

www.lectlaw.com

www.abanet.org

Political forecasting can be especially critical and complex for multinational firms that depend on foreign countries for natural resources, facilities, the distribution of products, special assistance, or customers. Strategists today must possess skills that enable them to deal more legalistically and politically than previous strategists, whose attention was directed more toward economic and technical affairs of the firm. Strategists today are spending more time anticipating and influencing public policy actions. They spend more time meeting with government officials, attending hearings and government-sponsored conferences, giving public speeches, and meeting with trade groups, industry associations, and government agency directors. Before entering or expanding international operations, strategists need a good understanding of the political and decision-making processes in countries where their firms may conduct business. For example, republics that made up the former Soviet Union differ greatly in wealth, resources, language, and lifestyle.

Increasing global competition accents the need for accurate political, governmental, and legal forecasts. Many strategists will have to become familiar with political systems in Europe, Africa, and Asia and with trading currency futures. East Asian countries already have become world leaders in labor-intensive industries. A world market has emerged from what previously was a multitude of distinct national markets, and the climate for international business today is much more favorable than yesterday. Mass communication and high technology are creating similar patterns of consumption in diverse cultures worldwide. This means that many companies may find it difficult to survive by relying solely on domestic markets.

> It is no exaggeration that in an industry that is, or is rapidly becoming, global, the riskiest possible posture is to remain a domestic competitor. The domestic competitor will watch as more aggressive companies use this growth to capture economies of scale and learning. The domestic competitor will then be faced with an attack on domestic markets using different (and possibly superior) technology, product design, manufacturing, marketing approaches, and economies of scale. A few examples suggest how extensive the phenomenon of world markets has already become. Hewlett-Packard's manufacturing chain reaches halfway around the globe, from well-paid, skilled engineers in California to low-wage assembly workers in Malaysia. General Electric has survived as a manufacturer of inexpensive audio products by centralizing its world production in Singapore.[5]

Local, state, and federal laws, regulatory agencies, and special interest groups can have a major impact on the strategies of small, large, for-profit, and nonprofit organizations. Many companies have altered or abandoned strategies in the past because of political or governmental actions. Other federal regulatory agencies include the Food and Drug Administration (FDA), the National Highway Traffic and Safety Administration (NHTSA), the Occupational Safety and Health Administration (OSHA), the Consumer Product Safety Commission (CPSC), the Federal Trade Commission (FTC), the Securities and Exchange Commission (SEC), the Equal Employment Opportunity Commission (EEOC), the Federal Communications Commission (FCC), the Federal Maritime Commission (FMC), the Interstate Commerce Commission (ICC), the Federal Energy Regulatory Commission (FERC), the National Labor Relations Board (NLRB), and the Civil Aeronautics Board (CAB). A summary of political, governmental, and legal variables that can represent key opportunities or threats to organizations is provided in Table 3–3.

Russia

Russia's gross domestic product grew 8.3 percent in 2000 and another 5 percent in 2001 due partly to high world commodity prices. Despite economic growth in Russia, the country's debt payments as a proportion of GDP are growing—to 5.4 percent in 2003 from 4.7 percent in 2001. Russia has announced it cannot repay upcoming loans on international capital markets.

However Russia is the last large country outside of the World Trade Organization and is prepared to make big concessions to join the WTO. Russia has agreed to open its markets in banking, insurance, and agriculture, but not in the automobile and aircraft industries. The Russian parliament is currenting passing legislation to pave the way for WTO rules and policies.

The Russian government has failed at one of its primary responsibilities—collecting taxes. The government has no money to send to regional governments for social services or the military, or to pay government employees. It has no money to run the judicial system or to enforce federal laws. Many Russian people have lost trust in their government, their banking system, their legal system, and their currency. Law and order itself is in jeopardy in Russia as a result of a crippled economy. Mismanagement of the economy and corruption have so severely discredited democracy in the eyes of ordinary Russian people that communist and organized-crime approaches to government are the rule rather than the exception. President Putin promises to crack down on organized crime, revamp the Russian tax code, strengthen the judiciary, and maintain democratic freedoms.

The climate for business in Russia is poor because of the continued devaluation of the ruble, high unemployment, organized crime, high inflation, and skyrocketing taxes.

TABLE 3-3   Some Political, Governmental, and Legal Variables

Government regulations or deregulations	Sino-American relationships
Changes in tax laws	Russian-American relationships
Special tariffs	European-American relationships
Political action committees	African-American relationships
Voter participation rates	Import-export regulations
Number, severity, and location of government protests	Government fiscal and monetary policy changes
Number of patents	Political conditions in foreign countries
Changes in patent laws	Special local, state, and federal laws
Environmental protection laws	Lobbying activities
Level of defense expenditures	Size of government budgets
Legislation on equal employment	World oil, currency, and labor markets
Level of government subsidies	Location and severity of terrorist activities
Antitrust legislation	Local, state, and national elections

Russian tax laws are among the world's most punitive and confusing, so firms keep business off the books to avoid paying out about 90 percent of their profits to the government. Tax receipts by the Russian government are far lower than expected or needed to run the country.

It is almost impossible today to run a business in Russia legally. Racketeering, money laundering, financial scams, and organized criminal activity plague businesses. Russian organized crime operations have been so successful within the country that they now aggressively infiltrate governments and businesses worldwide.

The risk of business investments in Russia decreases from south to north and west to east. Thus, investments in Siberia and along the Pacific coast are more stable and much less corrupt than those near Moscow or the Russian areas bordering Europe. Because the ruble is virtually of no value in Russia, companies need to pay their workers with something besides money, such as apartments, healthcare, and medical and food products. Bartering is an excellent way to motivate Russian workers.

Since the war on terrorism began in late 2001, Russia and the United States have become much better friends, and implications suggest that trade and cooperation between the two countries are improving rapidly. President Bush and President Putin realize that they and their countries need each other, and rapport between the two leaders is excellent. *Business Week* says, "As the United States and Russia become allies determined to defeat the same foe, their political and economic interests are starting to converge. Putin has recently pushed through the Duma a broad array of reform legislation that makes U.S. investments in Russia much more attractive."[6] In contrast to the early 1990s and earlier, more and more Russian businesses are succeeding today through good management and high quality products rather than through bribery and crime. Russia's gross national product grew 8.4 percent in 2000 and 5.5 percent in 2001, making it one of the world's fastest growing economies.

 ## TECHNOLOGICAL FORCES

Revolutionary technological changes and discoveries are having a dramatic impact on organizations. Superconductivity advancements alone, which increase the power of electrical products by lowering resistance to current, are revolutionizing business operations, especially in the transportation, utility, healthcare, electrical, and computer industries.

The *Internet* is acting as a national and even global economic engine that is spurring productivity, a critical factor in a country's ability to improve living standards. The Internet is saving companies billions of dollars in distribution and transaction costs from direct sales to self-service systems. For example, the familiar Hypertext Markup Language (HTML) is being replaced by Extensible Markup Language (XML). XML is a programming language based on "tags," whereby a number represents a price, an invoice, a date, a zip code, or whatever. XML is forcing companies to make a major strategic decision in terms of whether to open their information to the world in the form of catalogs, inventories, prices and specifications, or to attempt to withhold their data to preserve some perceived advantage.[7] XML is reshaping industries, reducing prices, accelerating global trade, and revolutionizing all commerce. Microsoft and other software companies reoriented most of its software development around XML, replacing HTML.

The Internet is changing the very nature of opportunities and threats by altering the life cycles of products, increasing the speed of distribution, creating new products and services, erasing limitations of traditional geographic markets, and changing the historical trade-off between production standardization and flexibility. The Internet is altering economies of scale, changing entry barriers, and redefining the relationship between industries and various suppliers, creditors, customers, and competitors.

To effectively capitalize on e-commerce, a number of organizations are establishing two new positions in their firms: *chief information officer (CIO)* and *chief technology officer (CTO)*. This trend reflects the growing importance of *information technology (IT)* in strategic management. A CIO and CTO work together to ensure that information needed to formulate, implement, and evaluate strategies is available where and when it is needed. These individuals are responsible for developing, maintaining, and updating a company's information database. The CIO is more a manager, managing the overall external-audit process; the CTO is more a technician, focusing on technical issues such as data acquisition, data processing, decision-support systems, and software and hardware acquisition.

Technological forces represent major opportunities and threats that must be considered in formulating strategies. Technological advancements can dramatically affect organizations' products, services, markets, suppliers, distributors, competitors, customers, manufacturing processes, marketing practices, and competitive position. Technological advancements can create new markets, result in a proliferation of new and improved products, change the relative competitive cost positions in an industry, and render existing products and services obsolete. Technological changes can reduce or eliminate cost barriers between businesses, create shorter production runs, create shortages in technical skills, and result in changing values and expectations of employees, managers, and customers. Technological advancements can create new *competitive advantages* that are more powerful than existing advantages. No company or industry today is insulated against emerging technological developments. In high-tech industries, identification and evaluation of key technological opportunities and threats can be the most important part of the external strategic-management audit.

Organizations that traditionally have limited technology expenditures to what they can fund after meeting marketing and financial requirements urgently need a reversal in thinking. The pace of technological change is increasing and literally wiping out businesses every day. An emerging consensus holds that technology management is one of the key responsibilities of strategists. Firms should pursue strategies that take advantage of technological opportunities to achieve sustainable, competitive advantages in the marketplace.

> Technology-based issues will underlie nearly every important decision that strategists make. Crucial to those decisions will be the ability to approach technology planning analytically and strategically. . . . technology can be planned and managed using formal techniques similar to those used in business and capital investment planning. An effective technology strategy is built on a penetrating analysis of technology opportunities and threats, and an assessment of the relative importance of these factors to overall corporate strategy.[8]

In practice, critical decisions about technology too often are delegated to lower organizational levels or are made without an understanding of their strategic implications. Many strategists spend countless hours determining market share, positioning products in terms of features and price, forecasting sales and market size, and monitoring distributors; yet too often, technology does not receive the same respect.

Not all sectors of the economy are affected equally by technological developments. The communications, electronics, aeronautics, and pharmaceutical industries are much more volatile than the textile, forestry, and metals industries. For strategists in industries affected by rapid technological change, identifying and evaluating technological opportunities and threats can represent the most important part of an external audit.

For example, in the office supply industry, business customers find that purchasing supplies over the Internet to be more convenient than shopping in a store. Office Depot was the first office supply company to establish a Web site for this purpose and remains the largest Internet office supply retailer, with close to $1 billion in sales. Staples, Inc., has recently also entered the Internet office supply business with its **staples.com** Web site, but it has yet to make a profit on these operations, although revenue growth from the site is growing dramatically.

 ## COMPETITIVE FORCES

VISIT THE NET

Provides information regarding the importance of gathering information about competitors. This Web site offers audio answers to key questions about intelligence systems.
www.fuld.com

The top five U.S. competitors in four different industries are identified in Table 3–4. An important part of an external audit is identifying rival firms and determining their strengths, weaknesses, capabilities, opportunities, threats, objectives, and strategies.

Collecting and evaluating information on competitors is essential for successful strategy formulation. Identifying major competitors is not always easy because many firms have divisions that compete in different industries. Most multidivisional firms generally do not provide sales and profit information on a divisional basis for competitive reasons. Also, privately held firms do not publish any financial or marketing information.

However, many businesses use the Internet to obtain most of their information on competitors. The Internet is fast, thorough, accurate, and increasingly indispensable in this regard. Addressing questions about competitors such as those presented in Table 3–5 is important in performing an external audit.

Competition in virtually all industries can be described as intense—and sometimes as cutthroat. For example, when United Parcel Service (UPS) employees were on strike in 1997, competitors such as FedEx, Greyhound, Roadway, and United Airlines lowered prices, doubled advertising efforts, and locked new customers into annual contracts in efforts to leave UPS customer-less when the strike ended. If a firm detects weakness in a competitor, no mercy at all is shown in capitalizing on its problems.

Seven characteristics describe the most competitive companies in America: (1) Market share matters; the 90th share point isn't as important as the 91st, and nothing is more dangerous than falling to 89; (2) Understand and remember precisely what business you are in; (3) Whether it's broke or not, fix it—make it better; not just products, but the whole company, if necessary; (4) Innovate or evaporate; particularly in technology-driven businesses, nothing quite recedes like success; (5) Acquisition is essential to growth; the most successful purchases are in niches that add a technology or a related market; (6) People make a difference; tired of hearing it? Too bad; (7) There is no substitute for quality and no greater threat than failing to be cost-competitive on a global basis; these are complementary concepts, not mutually exclusive ones.[9]

Competitive Intelligence Programs

What is competitive intelligence? *Competitive intelligence,* as formally defined by the Society of Competitive Intelligence Professionals (SCIP), is a systematic and ethical process for gathering and analyzing information about the competition's activities and general business trends to further a business' own goals (SCIP Web site).

Good competitive intelligence in business, as in the military, is one of the keys to success. The more information and knowledge a firm can obtain about its competitors,

TABLE 3-4   The Top Five U.S. Competitors in Four Different Industries in 2002

	2001 SALES (IN $ MILLIONS)	PERCENTAGE CHANGE (FROM 2000)	2001 PROFITS (IN $ MILLIONS)	PERCENTAGE CHANGE FROM 2000
AEROSPACE				
Boeing	58,198	+13	2,826	+33
United Technologies	27,897	+5	1,938	+7
Lockheed Martin	23,990	−2	79	NM
Northrop Grumman	13,558	+78	427	−32
General Dynamics	12,163	+17	943	+5
FOREST PRODUCTS				
International Paper	26,363	−6	−1,142	NM
Georgia-Pacific	25,016	13	−255	NM
Weyerhaeuser	14,545	−9	354	−58
Boise Cascade	7,422	−5	−42	NM
Loussiana-Pacific	2,359	−20	−171	NM
COMPUTERS				
IBM	85,866	−3	7,723	−5
Hewlett-Packard	44,211	−11	712	−77
Compaq Computer	33,554	−21	−563	NM
Dell Computer	31,168	−2	1,246	−44
Xerox	19,228	−1	1,424	+143
PUBLISHING & BROADCASTING				
AOL Time Warner	38,234	NM	−4,921	NM
Walt Disney	24,884	−4	316	−63
Viacom	23,222	+16	−219	NM
Comcast	9,674	+18	226	−89
Gannett	6,344	+2	831	−14

Source: Adapted from Industry Rankings of the S&P 500, *Business Week* (Spring 2002): 87–113.
NM: Not Measurable.

the more likely it is that it can formulate and implement effective strategies. Major competitors' weaknesses can represent external opportunities; major competitors' strengths may represent key threats.

According to *Business Week*, there are more than five thousand corporate spies now actively engaged in intelligence activities, and nine out of ten large companies have employees dedicated solely to gathering competitive intelligence.[10] The article contends that many large U.S. companies spend more than $1 million annually tracking their competitors. Evidence suggests that the benefits of corporate spying include increased revenues, lower costs, and better decision making.

The global war on terrorism has even led countries to place more emphasis on gathering and sharing intelligence. Even former foes—such as the United States, Russia, China, and even Iran—share intelligence to reach common goals. Do you feel that intelligence sharing among countries will spur increased intelligence sharing among rival companies?

TABLE 3-5   Key Questions About Competitors

1. What are the major competitors' strengths?
2. What are the major competitors' weaknesses?
3. What are the major competitors' objectives and strategies?
4. How will the major competitors most likely respond to current economic, social, cultural, demographic, environmental, political, governmental, legal, technological, and competitive trends affecting our industry?
5. How vulnerable are the major competitors to our alternative company strategies?
6. How vulnerable are our alternative strategies to successful counterattack by our major competitors?
7. How are our products or services positioned relative to major competitors?
8. To what extent are new firms entering and old firms leaving this industry?
9. What key factors have resulted in our present competitive position in this industry?
10. How have the sales and profit rankings of major competitors in the industry changed over recent years? Why have these rankings changed that way?
11. What is the nature of supplier and distributor relationships in this industry?
12. To what extent could substitute products or services be a threat to competitors in this industry?

Unfortunately, the majority of U.S. executives grew up in times when American firms dominated foreign competitors so much that gathering competitive intelligence seemed not worth the effort. Too many of these executives still cling to these attitudes—to the detriment of their organizations today. Even most MBA programs do not offer a course in competitive and business intelligence, thus reinforcing this attitude. As a consequence, three strong misperceptions about business intelligence prevail among American executives today:

1. Running an intelligence program requires lots of people, computers, and other resources.
2. Collecting intelligence about competitors violates antitrust laws; business intelligence equals espionage.
3. Intelligence gathering is an unethical business practice.[11]

VISIT THE NET

Provides the strategic plan for the University of Hawaii, including its Planning Assumptions.
www2.hawaii.edu/uhhilo/strategic

All three of these perceptions are totally misguided. Any discussions with a competitor about price, market, or geography intentions could violate antitrust statutes, but this fact must not lure a firm into underestimating the need for and benefits of systematically collecting information about competitors for the purpose of enhancing a firm's effectiveness. The Internet has become an excellent medium for gathering competitive intelligence. Information gathering from employees, managers, suppliers, distributors, customers, creditors, and consultants also can make the difference between having superior or just average intelligence and overall competitiveness.

Firms need an effective competitive intelligence *(CI)* program. The three basic missions of a CI program are (1) to provide a general understanding of an industry and its competitors, (2) to identify areas in which competitors are vulnerable and to assess the impact strategic actions would have on competitors, and (3) to identify potential moves that a competitor might make that would endanger a firm's position in the market.[12] Competitive information is equally applicable for strategy formulation, implementation, and evaluation decisions. An effective CI program allows all areas of a firm to access consistent and verifiable information in making decisions. All members of an organization—from the chief executive officer to custodians—are valuable intelligence agents and should feel themselves to be a part of the CI process. Special characteristics of a successful CI program include flexibility, usefulness, timeliness, and cross-functional cooperation.

The increasing emphasis on *competitive analysis* in the United States is evidenced by corporations putting this function on their organizational charts under job titles such as Director of Competitive Analysis, Competitive Strategy Manager, Director of Information Services, or Associate Director of Competitive Assessment. The responsibilities of a *director of competitive analysis* include planning, collecting data, analyzing data, facilitating the process of gathering and analyzing data, disseminating intelligence on a timely basis, researching special issues, and recognizing what information is important and who needs to know. Competitive intelligence is not corporate espionage because 95 percent of the information a company needs in order to make strategic decisions is available and accessible to the public. Sources of competitive information include trade journals, want ads, newspaper articles, and government filings, as well as customers, suppliers, distributors, competitors themselves, and the Internet.

Unethical tactics such as bribery, wiretapping, and computer break-ins should never be used to obtain information. Marriott and Motorola—two American companies that do a particularly good job of gathering competitive intelligence—agree that all the information you could wish for can be collected without resorting to unethical tactics. They keep their intelligence staffs small, usually under five people, and spend less than $200,000 per year on gathering competitive intelligence.

Unilever recently sued Procter & Gamble (P&G) over that company's corporate-espionage activities to obtain the secrets of its Unilever hair-care business. After spending $3 million to establish a team to find out about competitors in the domestic hair-care industry, P&G allegedly took roughly eighty documents from garbage bins outside Unilever's Chicago offices. P&G produces Pantene and Head & Shoulders shampoos, while Unilver has hair-care brands such as ThermaSilk, Suave, Salon Selectives, and Finesse. Similarly, Oracle Corp. recently admitted that detectives it hired paid janitors to go through Microsoft Corp.'s garbage, looking for evidence to use in court.

The security software company McAfee estimates that cybertheft and cybervandalism cost U.S. companies $20 billion annually. More and more companies are, therefore, using new weapons to compbat cyber-attacks, including "honey pots" and tracers. A honey pot is a fake server set up to trap the unwitting intruder and to monitor the hacker's every keystroke and method of entry. Tracers are surveillance algorithms powerful enough to trace a hacker's entry back to its origin. The Nimda computer virus in late 2001 crippled more than one million computers in the United States, Europe, and Asia, and it cost firms more than the earlier Code Red virus. The Code Red virus cost firms an estimated $2.4 billion in cleanup expenses.[13]

Cooperation Among Competitors

Strategies that stress cooperation among competitors are being used more. For example, Lockheed teamed up with British Aerospace PLC to compete against Boeing Company to develop the next-generation U.S. fighter jet. Lockheed's cooperative strategy with a profitable partner in the Airbus Industrie consortium encourages broader Lockheed-European collaboration as Europe's defense industry consolidates. The British firm offers Lockheed special expertise in the areas of short takeoff and vertical landing technologies, systems integration, and low-cost design and manufacturing.

Cooperative agreements between competitors are even becoming popular. For example, Boeing and Lockheed are working together to modernize the United States' overburdened air-traffic-control system. Northrop Grumman, also a competitor in the defense industry, may join the cooperative agreement too. For collaboration between

VISIT THE NET

Gives the National Oceanic and Atmospheric Administration (NOAA) Strategic Plan, including its external assessment.
http://www.strategic.noaa.gov/

competitors to succeed, both firms must contribute something distinctive, such as technology, distribution, basic research, or manufacturing capacity. But a major risk is that unintended transfers of important skills or technology may occur at organizational levels below where the deal was signed.[14] Information not covered in the formal agreement often gets traded in the day-to-day interactions and dealings of engineers, marketers, and product developers. Firms often give away too much information to rival firms when operating under cooperative agreements! Tighter formal agreements are needed.

Renault SA and Nissan Motor Company are forming a joint venture company solely to develop joint strategies whereby the two rival firms can cooperate more effectively. Renault already owns 36.8 percent of Nissan, and under the new company, Nissan may take part ownership of Renault. When cooperation among rival firms reaches high levels, part ownership between involved companies can be an effective strategy.

Two other fierce competitors, ABC and CBS, have formed a strategic alliance to share satellite-uplink facilities in Pakistan and another alliance with Fox News to share raw news footage. Satellite-uplink equipment costs up to $500,000, so sharing this expense benefits both firms. However, the two companies will not share stories or producers, and they remain fierce rivals; yet they desire to become "permanent partners" in mutually beneficial areas.

The idea of joining forces with a competitor is not easily accepted by Americans, who often view cooperation and partnerships with skepticism and suspicion. Indeed, joint ventures and cooperative arrangements among competitors demand a certain amount of trust if companies are to combat paranoia about whether one firm will injure the other. However, multinational firms are becoming more globally cooperative, and increasing numbers of domestic firms are joining forces with competitive foreign firms to reap mutual benefits. Kathryn Harrigan at Columbia University says, "Within a decade, most companies will be members of teams that compete against each other."

American companies often enter alliances primarily to avoid investments, being more interested in reducing the costs and risks of entering new businesses or markets than in acquiring new skills. In contrast, *learning from the partner* is a major reason why Asian and European firms enter into cooperative agreements. American firms, too, should place learning high on the list of reasons to cooperative with competitors. American companies often form alliances with Asian firms to gain an understanding of their manufacturing excellence, but Asian competence in this area is not easily transferable. Manufacturing excellence is a complex system that includes employee training and involvement, integration with suppliers, statistical process controls, value engineering, and design. In contrast, American know-how in technology and related areas more easily can be imitated. American firms thus need to be careful not to give away more intelligence than they receive in cooperative agreements with rival Asian firms.

COMPETITIVE ANALYSIS: PORTER'S FIVE-FORCES MODEL

As illustrated in Figure 3–3, *Porter's Five-Forces Model* of competitive analysis is a widely used approach for developing strategies in many industries. The intensity of competition among firms varies widely across industries. Table 3–6 reveals the average return on equity for firms in twenty-four different industries in 2001. Intensity of competition is highest in lower-return industries. According to Porter, the nature of competitiveness in a given industry can be viewed as a composite of five forces:

FIGURE 3–3

The Five-Forces Model of Competition

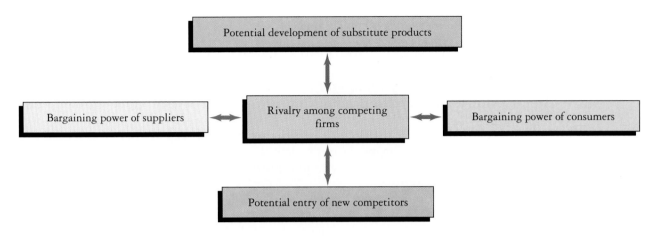

TABLE 3-6   **Intensity of Competition Among Firms in Different Industries—2001 Results Provided**

RANK	INDUSTRY	2001 AVERAGE RETURN ON EQUITY/ AVERAGE EARNINGS PER SHARE
1	Consumer Products	26.7/1.91
2	Healthcare	22.5/1.34
3	Conglomerates	18.1/1.45
4	Fuel	16.4/2.40
5	Food	15.2/1.21
6	Aerospace and Defense	13.0/2.31
7	Housing and Real Estate	12.6/2.17
8	Nonbank Financial	12.4/2.11
9	Discount and Fashion Retailing	12.2/0.98
10	Utilities and Power	11.7/2.10
11	Banks	11.4/1.84
12	Manufacturing	10.9/1.36
13	Chemicals	9.3/1.13
14	Leisure Time Industries	8.0/0.74
15	Containers and Packaging	7.4/0.90
16	Service Industries	6.0/0.46
17	Publishing and Broadcasting	2.6/0.33
18	Office Equipment and Computers	−1.0/−0.10
19	Paper and Forest Products	−2.6/−0.62
20	Transportation	−2.7/−0.43
21	Metals and Mining	−7.6/−0.83
22	Automotive	−9.1/−1.20
23	Telecommunications	−9.3/−0.91
24	Electrical and Electronics	−44.6/−3.14

Source: Adapted from "Corporate Scoreboard," *Business Week* (February 25, 2002): 63–102.

1. Rivalry among competing firms
2. Potential entry of new competitors
3. Potential development of substitute products
4. Bargaining power of suppliers
5. Bargaining power of consumers

Rivalry Among Competing Firms

Rivalry among competing firms is usually the most powerful of the five competitive forces. The strategies pursued by one firm can be successful only to the extent that they provide competitive advantage over the strategies pursued by rival firms. Changes in strategy by one firm may be met with retaliatory countermoves, such as lowering prices, enhancing quality, adding features, providing services, extending warranties, and increasing advertising.

In the Internet world, competitiveness is fierce. Amazon.com watches in dismay as customers use its site's easy-to-use format, in-depth reviews, expert recommendations—and then bypass the cash register as they click their way over to deep-discounted sites such as Buy.com to make their purchases. Buy.com's CEO says, "The Internet is going to shrink retailers' margins to the point where they will not survive." Price-comparison Web sites allow consumers to efficiently find the lowest-priced seller on the Internet. Kate Delhagen of Forrester Research says, "If you're a consumer and you're thinking about any kind of researched purchase, you're leaving thousands of dollars on the table if you don't at least look online."[15] The costs of setting up a great e-commerce site are nothing compared to the cost of acquiring real estate for building retail stores—or even printing and mailing catalogs.

Free-flowing information on the Internet is driving down prices and inflation worldwide. The Internet, coupled with the common currency in Europe, enables consumers to easily make price comparisons across countries. Just for a moment, consider the implications for car dealers who used to know everything about a new car's pricing, while you, the consumer, knew very little. You could bargain, but being in the dark, you rarely could win. Now you can go to Web sites such as CarPoint or Edmunds.com and know more about new car prices than the car salesperson, and you can even shop online in a few hours at every dealership within five hundred miles to find the best price and terms. So you, the consumer, can win. This is true in many, if not most, business-to-consumer and business-to-business sales transactions today.

The intensity of rivalry among competing firms tends to increase as the number of competitors increases, as competitors become more equal in size and capability, as demand for the industry's products declines, and as price cutting becomes common. Rivalry also increases when consumers can switch brands easily; when barriers to leaving the market are high; when fixed costs are high; when the product is perishable; when rival firms are diverse in strategies, origins, and culture; and when mergers and acquisitions are common in the industry. As rivalry among competing firms intensifies, industry profits decline, in some cases to the point where an industry becomes inherently unattractive.

Potential Entry of New Competitors

Whenever new firms can easily enter a particular industry, the intensity of competitiveness among firms increases. Barriers to entry, however, can include the need to gain economies of scale quickly, the need to gain technology and specialized know-how, the lack of experience, strong customer loyalty, strong brand preferences, large capital requirements, lack of adequate distribution channels, government regulatory policies, tariffs, lack of access to raw materials, possession of patents, undesirable locations, counterattack by entrenched firms, and potential saturation of the market.

Despite numerous barriers to entry, new firms sometimes enter industries with higher-quality products, lower prices, and substantial marketing resources. The strategist's job, therefore, is to identify potential new firms entering the market, to monitor the new rival firms' strategies, to counterattack as needed, and to capitalize on existing strengths and opportunities.

Potential Development of Substitute Products

In many industries, firms are in close competition with producers of substitute products in other industries. Examples are plastic container producers competing with glass, paperboard, and aluminum can producers, and acetaminophen manufacturers competing with other manufacturers of pain and headache remedies. The presence of substitute products puts a ceiling on the price that can be charged before consumers will switch to the substitute product.

Competitive pressures arising from substitute products increase as the relative price of substitute products declines and as consumers' switching costs decrease. The competitive strength of substitute products is best measured by the inroads into the marketshare those products obtain, as well as those firms' plans for increased capacity and market penetration.

Bargaining Power of Suppliers

The bargaining power of suppliers affects the intensity of competition in an industry, especially when there is a large number of suppliers, when there are only a few good substitute raw materials, or when the cost of switching raw materials is especially costly. It is often in the best interest of both suppliers and producers to assist each other with reasonable prices, improved quality, development of new services, just-in-time deliveries, and reduced inventory costs, thus enhancing long-term profitability for all concerned.

Firms may pursue a backward integration strategy to gain control or ownership of suppliers. This strategy is especially effective when suppliers are unreliable, too costly, or not capable of meeting a firm's needs on a consistent basis. Firms generally can negotiate more favorable terms with suppliers when backward integration is a commonly used strategy among rival firms in an industry.

Bargaining Power of Consumers

When customers are concentrated or large, or buy in volume, their bargaining power represents a major force affecting the intensity of competition in an industry. Rival firms may offer extended warranties or special services to gain customer loyalty whenever the bargaining power of consumers is substantial. Bargaining power of consumers also is higher when the products being purchased are standard or undifferentiated. When this is the case, consumers often can negotiate selling price, warranty coverage, and accessory packages to a greater extent. Even for a huge company such as Wal-Mart, the drastic increase in bargaining power of consumers caused by Internet usage is a major external threat.

SOURCES OF EXTERNAL INFORMATION

A wealth of strategic information is available to organizations from both published and unpublished sources. Unpublished sources include customer surveys, market research, speeches at professional and shareholders' meetings, television programs, interviews, and

TABLE 3–7   **Excellent Internet Sources of Information**

I. INVESTMENT RESEARCH

Strategic Management Club Online → **www.strategyclub.com**
American Stock Exchange → **www.amex.com**
DBC Online → **www.esignal.com**
Hoover's Online → **www.hoovers.com**
InvestorGuide → **www.investorguide.com**
Wall Street Research Net → **www.wsrn.com**
Market Guide → **www.marketguide.com**
Money Search—Find It! → **www.moneysearch.com**
NASDAQ → **www.nasdaq.com**
New York Stock Exchange → **www.nyse.com/public/home.html**
PC Financial Network → **www.csfbdirect.com**
Quote.Com → **www.quote.com**
Stock Smart → **www.stocksmart.com**
Wright Investors' Service on the World Wide Web → **www.wisi.com**
Zacks Investment Research → **www.zacks.com**

II. SEARCH ENGINES

Alta Vista → **www.altavista.com**
Deja News → **www.dejanews.com**
DogPile → **www.dogpile.com**
Excite → **www.excite.com**
HotBot → **www.hotbot.com**
InfoSeek → **www.go.com**
Lycos → **www.lycos.com**
Metacrawler → **www.metacrawler.com**
WebCrawler → **www.webcrawler.com**
Yahoo! → **www.yahoo.com**

III. DIRECTORIES

Argus Clearinghouse → **www.clearinghouse.net**
BigBook → **www.bigbook.com**
ComFind → **www.allbusiness.com**
Thomas Publishing Co. → **www.thomaspublishing.com**
Competitive Intelligence Guide → **www.fuld.com**

IV. NEWS, MAGAZINES, AND NEWSPAPERS

PR Newswire → **www.prnewswire.com**
American Demographics → **www.marketingtools.com**
Barron's Magazine → **www.barrons.com**
Business Week → **www.businessweek.com**
CNNfn → **www.cnnfn.com/search**
Financial Times → **www.ft.com**
Forbes Magazine On-line → **www.forbes.com**
Fortune Magazine → **www.fortune.com**
USA Today → **www.usatoday.com**
Wall Street Journal → **www.wsj.com**
Washington Post Online → **www.washingtonpost.com**

V. U.S. GOVERNMENT

Better Business Bureau → **www.bbb.org**
Census Bureau → **www.census.gov**

Continued

TABLE 3-7   **Excellent Internet Sources of Information (*continued*)**

Federal Trade Commission → **www.ftc.gov**
FreeEDGAR → **www.freeedgar.com**
Edgar-Online → **www.edgar-online.com**
General Printing Office → **www.gpo.gov**
Internal Revenue Service → **www.irs.ustreas.gov**
Library of Congress → **www.loc.gov**
SEC's Edgar Database → **www.sec.gov/edgarhp.htm**
Small Business Administration → **www.sba.gov**
U.S. Department of Commerce → **www.doc.gov**
U.S. Department of the Treasury → **www.ustreas.gov**
Environmental Protection Agency → **www.epa.gov**
National Aeronautics and Space Administration → **www.hq.nasa.gov**

conversations with stakeholders. Published sources of strategic information include periodicals, journals, reports, government documents, abstracts, books, directories, newspapers, and manuals. Computerization and the Internet have made it easier today for firms to gather, assimilate, and evaluate information.

Internet

Millions of people today use other online services for both business and personal purposes. *America Online* and other leading commercial online services are expanding their menus of available services to include everything from online access to most major television networks, newspapers, and magazines to online interviews with celebrities, and they offer access to the furthermost boundaries of the Internet. These companies harness the power of multimedia, combining sound, video, and graphics with text. Excellent sources of strategic management and case research information on the *World Wide Web* are provided in Table 3–7. Table 3–8 provides selected academic and consulting strategic planning Web sites.

The Internet offers consumers and businesses a widening range of services and information resources from all over the world. Interactive services offer users not only access to information worldwide but also the ability to communicate with the person or company that created the information. Historical barriers to personal and business success—time zones and diverse cultures—are being eliminated. The Internet has become as important to our society as television and newspapers.

VISIT THE NET

Dr. Porter today heads the Institute for Strategy and Competitiveness at Harvard Business School in Boston, Massachusetts. Michael Porter's home Web page can be found at http://www.people.hbs.edu/oporter/

FORECASTING TOOLS AND TECHNIQUES

Forecasts are educated assumptions about future trends and events. Forecasting is a complex activity because of factors such as technological innovation, cultural changes, new products, improved services, stronger competitors, shifts in government priorities, changing social values, unstable economic conditions, and unforeseen events. Managers often must rely upon published forecasts to identify key external opportunities and threats effectively.

A sense of the future permeates all action and underlies every decision a person makes. People eat expecting to be satisfied and nourished—in the future. People sleep assuming that in the future they will feel rested. They invest energy, money, and time because they believe their efforts will be rewarded in the future. They build highways

TABLE 3-8   **Important Strategic Planning Web Sites**

I. ACADEMIC

1. *STRATEGIC MANAGEMENT SOCIETY*—**www.virtual-indiana.com/sms/**
   This is a non-profit, professional society composed of nearly two thousand academic, business, and consulting members from forty-five countries. This group publishes the *Strategic Management Journal* and offers annual meetings and conferences. The Web site is well designed and outlines the society's services and resources.

2. *AMERICAN MANAGEMENT ASSOCIATION*—**www.amanet.org**
   AMA provides educational forums worldwide for business to learn practical business skills. This Web site is comprehensive in providing access to all AMA seminars, videos, and courses worldwide, including strategic planning products. AMA publishes *Management Review*.

3. *ACADEMY OF MANAGEMENT ONLINE*—**www.aom.pace.edu**
   This non-profit organization is the leading professional association for management research and education in the United States. Almost ten thousand members from businesses and universities around the world participate. About twenty-five hundred of these members specify business policy and strategy as their primary interest. This site provides a search engine to locate and contact all these members. Many links and personal Web pages are provided. This organization publishes *Academy of Management Executive, Academy of Management Review*, and *Academy of Management Journal*.

4. *STRATEGIC LEADERSHIP FORUM*—**www.slfnet.org**
   This is an international organization of executives focusing on strategic management and planning. The Web site is outstanding. Many excellent strategic planning links are provided. The Forum publishes *Strategy and Leadership* (formerly *Planning Review*).

II. CONSULTANTS

1. *STRATEGIC PLANNING SYSTEMS*—**www.checkmateplan.com**
   This site provides *CheckMATE*, the industry leader in strategic planning software worldwide. This software is Windows-based and easy to use. The new version released in mid-2002 is improved ten-fold over prior versions.

2. *MIND TOOLS*—**www.mindtools.com/planpage.html**
   This is an excellent Web site for providing strategic planning information. More than thirty pages of narrative about how and why to do strategic planning are provided. Planning templates are provided.

3. *PALO ALTO SOFTWARE*—**www.bizplans.com**
   This Web site offers a model of the business planning process with excellent narrative as well as seven example business plans from real firms. This is one of the two best sites available for business planning information. (The other is the Small Business Administration Web site.)

4. *CENTER FOR STRATEGIC MANAGEMENT*—**www.csmweb.com**
   This Web site describes strategic management training, seminars, and facilitation services. The site also provides excellent links to other strategic planning academic and government sites.

5. *BOSTON CONSULTING GROUP (BCG)*—**www.bcg.com**
   This is perhaps the best-known strategic planning consulting firm. The Web site offers some nice discussion of strategic planning but focuses mostly on getting a job with BCG rather than on strategic planning information.

Continued

TABLE 3-8   **Important Strategic Planning Web Sites (*continued*)**

6. *FULD & COMPANY*—**www.fuld.com**
   This Web site specializes in competitive intelligence. Nice links are provided regarding the importance of gathering information about competitors. This site offers audio answers to key questions about intelligence systems.

assuming that automobiles and trucks will need them in the future. Parents educate children on the basis of forecasts that they will need certain skills, attitudes, and knowledge when they grow up. The truth is we all make implicit forecasts throughout our daily lives. The question, therefore, is not whether we should forecast but rather how we can best forecast to enable us to move beyond our ordinarily unarticulated assumptions about the future. Can we obtain information and then make educated assumptions (forecasts) to better guide our current decisions to achieve a more desirable future state of affairs. We should go into the future with our eyes and our minds open, rather than stumbling into the future with our eyes closed.[16]

Many publications and sources on the Internet forecast external variables. Several published examples include *Industry Week*'s "Trends and Forecasts," *Business Week*'s "Investment Outlook," and Standard & Poor's *Industry Survey*. The reputation and continued success of these publications depend partly on accurate forecasts, so published sources of information can offer excellent projections.

Sometimes organizations must develop their own projections. Most organizations forecast (project) their own revenues and profits annually. Organizations sometimes forecast market share or customer loyalty in local areas. Because forecasting is so important in strategic management and because the ability to forecast (in contrast to the ability to use a forecast) is essential, selected forecasting tools are examined further here.

Forecasting tools can be broadly categorized into two groups: quantitative techniques and qualitative techniques. Quantitative forecasts are most appropriate when historical data are available and when the relationships among key variables are expected to remain the same in the future. *Linear regression*, for example, is based on the assumption that the future will be just like the past—which, of course, it never is. As historical relationships become less stable, quantitative forecasts becomes less accurate.

No forecast is perfect, and some forecasts are even wildly inaccurate. This fact accents the need for strategists to devote sufficient time and effort to study the underlying bases for published forecasts and to develop internal forecasts of their own. Key external opportunities and threats can be effectively identified only through good forecasts. Accurate forecasts can provide major competitive advantages for organizations. Forecasts are vital to the strategic-management process and to the success of organizations.

Making Assumptions

Planning would be impossible without assumptions. McConkey defines assumptions as the "best present estimates of the impact of major external factors, over which the manager has little if any control, but which may exert a significant impact on performance or the ability to achieve desired results.[17] Strategists are faced with countless variables and imponderables that can be neither controlled nor predicted with 100 percent accuracy.

By identifying future occurrences that could have a major effect on the firm and by making reasonable assumptions about those factors, strategists can carry the strategic-management process forward. Assumptions are needed only for future trends and events that are most likely to have a significant effect on the company's business. Based on the best information at the time, assumptions serve as checkpoints on the validity of strategies. If future occurrences deviate significantly from assumptions, strategists know that corrective actions may be needed. Without reasonable assumptions, the strategy-formulation process could not proceed effectively. Firms that have the best information generally make the most accurate assumptions, which can lead to major competitive advantages.

THE GLOBAL CHALLENGE

Foreign competitors are battering U.S. firms in many industries. In its simplest sense, the international challenge faced by U.S. business is twofold: (1) how to gain and maintain exports to other nations and (2) how to defend domestic markets against imported goods. Few companies can afford to ignore the presence of international competition. Firms that seem insulated and comfortable today may be vulnerable tomorrow; for example, foreign banks do not yet compete or operate in most of the United States.

America's economy is becoming much less American. A world economy and monetary system is emerging. Corporations in every corner of the globe are taking advantage of the opportunity to share in the benefits of worldwide economic development. Markets are shifting rapidly and in many cases converging in tastes, trends, and prices. Innovative transport systems are accelerating the transfer of technology, and shifts in the nature and location of production systems are reducing the response time to changing market conditions.

More and more countries around the world are welcoming foreign investment and capital. As a result, labor markets have steadily become more international. East Asian countries have become market leaders in labor-intensive industries, Brazil offers abundant natural resources and rapidly developing markets, and Germany offers skilled labor and technology. The drive to improve the efficiency of global business operations is leading to greater functional specialization. This is not limited to a search for the familiar low-cost labor in Latin America or Asia. Other considerations include the cost of energy, availability of resources, inflation rates, existing tax rates, and the nature of trade regulations.

Multinational Corporations

Multinational corporations (MNCs) face unique and diverse risks, such as expropriation of assets, currency losses through exchange rate fluctuations, unfavorable foreign court interpretations of contracts and agreements, social/political disturbances, import/export restrictions, tariffs, and trade barriers. Strategists in MNCs are often confronted with the need to be globally competitive and nationally responsive at the same time. With the rise in world commerce, government and regulatory bodies are more closely monitoring foreign business practices. The United States Foreign Corrupt Practices Act, for example, defines corrupt practices in many areas of business. A sensitive issue is that some MNCs sometimes violate legal and ethical standards of the home country, but not of the host country.

Before entering international markets, firms should scan relevant journals and patent reports, seek the advice of academic and research organizations, participate in international trade fairs, form partnerships, and conduct extensive research to broaden their contacts and diminish the risk of doing business in new markets. Firms can also reduce the risks of doing business internationally by obtaining insurance from the U.S. government's Overseas Private Investment Corporation (OPIC). Note in the Global Perspective that U.S. firms are doing more extensive research today before entering particular global markets.

Globalization

Globalization is a process of worldwide integration of strategy formulation, implementation, and evaluation activities. Strategic decisions are made based on their impact upon global profitability of the firm, rather than on just domestic or other individual country

GLOBAL PERSPECTIVE

The Old Way versus the New Way to Take a Company Global

The old way to take a company global was to get in fast, do minimal research, strike deals with top officials, make quick acquisitions, focus on upscale consumers, and watch local customers begin buying up the company's products. That approach, however, failed more often that it succeeded.

The new, more effective approach to taking a company global is to do extensive homework regarding culture, distributors, suppliers, and customers before placing operations in a foreign land. Successful globalization today requires investing time and energy to understand the nature of business in those countries and to methodically build a presence from the ground up. Companies successfully going global today work closely with bureaucrats, entrepreneurs, social groups, and other potential customers at the grassroots level. These companies are also targeting individuals in countries where the average income is low yet whose numbers far exceed those of the richest 10 percent of countries and customers. These companies have come to realize that developing nations are growing much faster than the industrial nations. Fully four billion people who earn the equivalent of

$1,500 or less annually live in developing nations, and this group is growing more rapidly than well-to-do citizens and countries.

A number of companies are using this new approach to be successful globally. Hewlett-Packard is presently marketing its products heavily in Central America and Africa. Citibank also is following this new approach by persuading its corporate customers in developing countries to set up retail bank accounts for their entire staffs—from janitors to top managers. Kodak also is following this new approach for being successful globally. Kodak has struggled in the United States recently, but the company's sales in Asia are up nicely. The company has increased its number of Kodak Express photo supply shops in China from 6,000 in early 2001 to 10,000 in 2002. A final example of a company using this new approach to be successful globally is Whirlpool, which invested fourteen months of research in the effort before rolling out what has become the leading brand of washing machines in India.

Source: Adapted from "Smart Globalization," *Business Week* (August 27, 2001): 132–137.

---

considerations. A global strategy seeks to meet the needs of customers worldwide, with the highest value at the lowest cost. This may mean locating production in countries with the lowest labor costs or abundant natural resources, locating research and complex engineering centers where skilled scientists and engineers can be found, and locating marketing activities close to the markets to be served. A global strategy includes designing, producing, and marketing products with global needs in mind, instead of considering individual countries alone. A global strategy integrates actions against competitors into a worldwide plan.

Globalization of industries is occurring for many reasons, including a worldwide trend toward similar consumption patterns, the emergence of global buyers and sellers, and e-commerce and the instant transmission of money and information across continents. The European Economic Community (EEC), religions, the Olympics, the World Bank, world trade centers, the Red Cross, the Internet, environmental conferences, telecommunications, and economic summits all contribute to global interdependencies and the emerging global marketplace.

It is clear that different industries become global for different reasons. The need to amortize massive R&D investments over many markets is a major reason why the aircraft manufacturing industry became global. Monitoring globalization in one's industry is an important strategic-management activity. Knowing how to use that information for one's competitive advantage is even more important. For example, firms may look around the world for the best technology and select one that has the most promise for the largest number of markets. When firms design a product, they design it to be marketable in as many countries as possible. When firms manufacture a product, they select the lowest cost source, which may be Japan for semiconductors, Sri Lanka for textiles, Malaysia for simple electronics, and Europe for precision machinery. MNCs design manufacturing systems to accommodate world markets. One of the riskiest strategies for a domestic firm is to remain solely a domestic firm in an industry that is rapidly becoming global.

China: Opportunities and Threats

U.S. firms increasingly are doing business in China as market reforms create a more businesslike arena daily. Foreign direct investment in China is about $50 billion annually. This places China second behind the United States. Motorola is investing $6.6 billion in China between 2002–2006, even as the firm cuts its workforce elsewhere. Hitachi Ltd. and Intel are doubling their investment in Shanghai during this same time.

Risks that still restrain firms from initiating business with China include the following:

- Poor infrastructure
- Disregard for the natural environment
- Absence of a legal system
- Rampant corruption
- Lack of freedom of press, speech, and religion
- Severe human-rights violations
- Little respect for parents, copyrights, brands, and logos
- Counterfeiting, fraud, and pirating of products
- Little respect for legal contracts
- No generally accepted accounting principles

The minimum wage in China is twelve cents per hour, but many firms pay even less. Chinese workers usually have no healthcare and no compensation for injury. Few factories have fire extinguishers. Bribes are often paid to officials to avoid fines and shutdowns. Labor unions are illegal and nonexistent in China. Child labor is commonplace. Political and religious oppression and imprisonment occur. Levi Strauss has pulled all its business operations out of China to protest its human rights violations.

Business Week offers the following formula for success in doing business with China:

Pick partners wisely. Avoid forming ventures with inefficient state-owned enterprises. Search for entrepreneurial companies owned by local governments—or go it alone. Insist on management control.

Focus on fundamentals. Capitalize on China rapidly becoming a market economy by executing the basics, such as marketing, distribution, and service.

Guard know-how. Do not hand over state-of-the-art technology just to get an agreement. Aggressively fight theft of intellectual property because China wants to shed its bad reputation in this regard.

Fly low. Begin with a series of small ventures rather than big, costly, high-profile projects that often get snarled in bureaucratic red tape and politics.[18]

Hong Kong is the centerpiece of China's efforts to reform, privatize, and expand imports and exports worldwide. The map in Figure 3–4 illustrates Hong Kong's strategic location for China. With its 6.3 million people, magnificent harbor, financial wealth, 500 banks from 43 countries, the world's eighth-largest stock market, and minimum taxation, Hong Kong serves as the gateway to a fast-growing China. U.S. companies alone have 178 regional headquarters in Hong Kong and $10.5 billion in direct investment.

Much of Hong Kong's economic base is shifting north thirty miles to Shenzhen on mainland China. Shenzhen has a vast new shipping port and offers greatly reduced prices for retail goods and home ownership. China is actually melding Hong Kong and Shenzhen into one economic region under Chinese rules and regulations, such as arbitrary arrests and few legal protections. The people of Hong Kong had previously enjoyed freedom for decades prior to this slow unification with Shenzhen.[19]

Both the European community and the United States have approved China's membership in the World Trade Organization. This action integrates the world's most populated country into the global trading order. Some key changes in China resulting from this action are as follows:

1. Foreign companies can take increased stakes in mobile phone companies.
2. Tariffs on high-tech products will be phased out and eliminated by 2005.
3. Import tariffs on automobiles will drop to 25 percent by mid-2006 from 90 percent today.
4. Foreign banks may conduct domestic currency business with Chinese firms.
5. Foreign banks may do business anywhere in China by 2006.
6. Foreign firms will be allowed a 49 percent stake in securities joint ventures by 2004.
7. Foreign insurance firms may own operations in China.
8. Retail oil distribution will open in China by 2004.[20]

However, entry into the World Trade Organization may not be enough to revive China's worsening economy. China exports 20 percent of its products to the United States, and these sales declined greatly in late 2001 and early 2002. The United States is second behind Japan in buying Chinese products, which mostly are cheap consumer goods such as televisions, toys, and textiles.

As the twenty-first century begins, Hong Kong is still an attractive city to establish business operations, but China is moving Hong Kong more toward regulation, government control, and a China-like culture. For example, schools now must adopt Chinese as the main language of instruction, whereas English proficiency previously was required

FIGURE 3–4

Hong Kong's Strategic Location

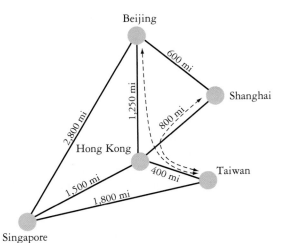

at schools. The Hong Kong government awarded various companies rights to develop government land without public bids, which previously was the accepted democratic way to do business. The government previously was a regulator of the Hong Kong stock market but now is its biggest investor and controller. The government is making decisions that trample longstanding principles of free markets and consistent rule of law. The Heritage Foundation has lowered Hong Kong's rating as a free economy to one notch below that of Singapore "unless it sees the error of its ways and reverses course."[21]

However, Taiwan and mainland China are cooperating more and more on economic issues, which is good for the region and indeed the world. Companies in the two separate countries recently agreed to jointly explore the Taiwan Strait for oil and gas under the Taiwan Basin. This unprecedented contract marks the first major commercial agreement between state-owned companies from the two countries. The involved companies are China National Offshore Oil, which is China's No. 3 oil producer, and Taiwan's China Petroleum, which has excellent refining capabilities.

Fifty years of separation between China and Taiwan has pushed the two countries so far apart politically, socially, and culturally that it is hard to even imagine them ever being part of the same whole. Further indication that commercial relations between Taipei and Beijing are improving is that China Airlines of Taiwan has signed an agreement to invest in China's first all-cargo airline, China Cargo Airlines. China Airlines soon expects to feed traffic from China Cargo into Taipei. Taiwan and China thus are beginning to engage in direct trade and transportation, something Taiwan has banned since the two sides separated in 1949 after a civil war. China's civil aviation authority is now holding technical talks with Taiwan's air-traffic controllers. The global economic recession has been the spark to help normalize relations between these two countries, which actually have much to offer each other in trade and travel. Taiwanese companies, such as Microtek, now view China as a primary market for their products, rather than viewing the mainland as simply a base for its manufacturing operations.

INDUSTRY ANALYSIS: THE EXTERNAL FACTOR EVALUATION (EFE) MATRIX

An *External Factor Evaluation (EFE) Matrix* allows strategists to summarize and evaluate economic, social, cultural, demographic, environmental, political, governmental, legal, technological, and competitive information. Illustrated in Table 3–9, the EFE Matrix can be developed in five steps:

1. List key external factors as identified in the external-audit process. Include a total of from ten to twenty factors, including both opportunities and threats, that affect the firm and its industry. List the opportunities first and then the threats. Be as specific as possible, using percentages, ratios, and comparative numbers whenever possible.

2. Assign to each factor a weight that ranges from 0.0 (not important) to 1.0 (very important). The weight indicates the relative importance of that factor to being successful in the firm's industry. Opportunities often receive higher weights than threats, but threats too can receive high weights if they are especially severe or threatening. Appropriate weights can be determined by comparing successful with unsuccessful competitors or by discussing the factor and reaching a group consensus. The sum of all weights assigned to the factors must equal 1.0.

3. Assign a 1-to-4 rating to each key external factor to indicate how effectively the firm's current strategies respond to the factor, where 4 = *the response is superior,*

TABLE 3-9   An Example External Factor Evaluation Matrix for UST, Inc.

KEY EXTERNAL FACTORS	WEIGHT	RATING	WEIGHTED SCORE
Opportunities			
1. Global markets are practically untapped by smokeless tobacco market	.15	1	.15
2. Increased demand caused by public banning of smoking	.05	3	.15
3. Astronomical Internet advertising growth	.05	1	.05
4. Pinkerton is leader in discount tobacco market	.15	4	.60
5. More social pressure to quit smoking, thus leading users to switch to alternatives	.10	3	.30
Threats			
1. Legislation against the tobacco industry	.10	2	.20
2. Production limits on tobacco increases competition for production	.05	3	.15
3. Smokeless tobacco market is concentrated in southeast region of United States	.05	2	.10
4. Bad media exposure from the FDA	.10	2	.20
5. Clinton administration	.20	1	.20
TOTAL	1.00		2.10

3 = *the response is above average*, 2 = *the response is average*, and 1 = *the response is poor*. Ratings are based on effectiveness of the firm's strategies. Ratings are thus company-based, whereas the weights in Step 2 are industry-based. It is important to note that both threats and opportunities can receive a 1, 2, 3, or 4.

4. Multiply each factor's weight by its rating to determine a weighted score.

5. Sum the weighted scores for each variable to determine the total weighted score for the organization.

Regardless of the number of key opportunities and threats included in an EFE Matrix, the highest possible total weighted score for an organizations is 4.0 and the lowest possible total weighted score is 1.0. The average total weighted score is 2.5. A total weighted score of 4.0 indicates that an organization is responding in an outstanding way to existing opportunities and threats in its industry. In other words, the firm's strategies effectively take advantage of existing opportunities and minimize the potential adverse effects of external threats. A total score of 1.0 indicates that the firm's strategies are not capitalizing on opportunities or avoiding external threats.

An example of an EFE Matrix is provided in Table 3–9 for UST, Inc., the manufacturer of Skoal and Copenhagen smokeless tobacco. Note that the Clinton administration was considered to be the most important factor affecting this industry, as indicated by the weight of 0.20. UST was not pursuing strategies that effectively capitalize on this opportunity, as indicated by the rating of 1.0. The total weighted score of 2.10 indicates that UST is below average in its effort to pursue strategies that capitalize on external opportunities and avoid threats. It is important to note here that a thorough understanding of the factors being used in the EFE Matrix is more important than the actual weights and ratings assigned.

THE COMPETITIVE PROFILE MATRIX (CPM)

The *Competitive Profile Matrix (CPM)* identifies a firm's major competitors and its particular strengths and weaknesses in relation to a sample firm's strategic position. The weights and total weighted scores in both a CPM and EFE have the same meaning. However, *critical success* factors in a CPM include both internal and external issues; therefore, the ratings refer to strengths and weaknesses, where 4 = major strength, 3 = minor strength, 2 = minor weakness, and 1 = major weakness. There are some important differences between the EFE and CPM. First of all, the critical success factors in a CPM are broader, they do not include specific or factual data and even may focus on internal issues. The critical success factors in a CPM also are not grouped into opportunities and threats as they are in an EFE. In a CPM, the ratings and total weighted scores for rival firms can be compared to the sample firm. This comparative analysis provides important internal strategic information.

A sample Competitive Profile Matrix is provided in Table 3–10. In this example, advertising and global expansion are the most important critical success factors, as indicated by a weight of 0.20. Avon's and L'Oreal's product quality is superior, as evidenced by a rating of 4; L'Oreal's "financial position" is good, as indicated by a rating of 3; Procter & Gamble is the weakest firm overall, as indicated by a total weighted score of 2.80.

Other than the critical success factors listed in the example CPM, factors often included in this analysis include breadth of product line, effectiveness of sales distribution, proprietary or patent advantages, location of facilities, production capacity and efficiency, experience, union relations, technological advantages, and e-commerce expertise.

A word on interpretation: Just because one firm receives a 3.2 rating and another receives a 2.8 rating in a Competitive Profile Matrix, it does not follow that the first firm is 20 percent better than the second. Numbers reveal the relative strengths of firms, but their implied precision is an illusion. Numbers are not magic. The aim is not to arrive at a single number, but rather to assimilate and evaluate information in a meaningful way that aids in decision making.

TABLE 3–10   An Example Competitive Profile Matrix

CRITICAL SUCCESS FACTORS	WEIGHT	AVON RATING	AVON SCORE	L'OREAL RATING	L'OREAL SCORE	PROCTER & GAMBLE RATING	PROCTER & GAMBLE SCORE
Advertising	0.20	1	0.20	4	0.80	3	0.60
Product Quality	0.10	4	0.40	4	0.40	3	0.30
Price Competitiveness	0.10	3	0.30	3	0.30	4	0.40
Management	0.10	4	0.40	3	0.30	3	0.30
Financial Position	0.15	4	0.60	3	0.45	3	0.45
Customer Loyalty	0.10	4	0.40	4	0.40	2	0.20
Global Expansion	0.20	4	0.80	2	0.40	2	0.40
Market Share	0.05	1	0.05	4	0.20	3	0.15
TOTAL	1.00		3.15		3.25		2.80

Note: (1) The ratings values are as follows: 1 = major weakness, 2 = minor weakness, 3 = minor strength, 4 = major strength. (2) As indicated by the total weighted score of 2.8, Competitor 3 is weakest. (3) Only eight critical success factors are included for simplicity; this is too few in actuality.

CONCLUSION

Increasing turbulence in markets and industries around the world means the external audit has become an explicit and vital part of the strategic-management process. This chapter provides a framework for collecting and evaluating economic, social, cultural, demographic, environmental, political, governmental, legal, technological, and competitive information. Firms that do not mobilize and empower their managers and employees to identify, monitor, forecast, and evaluate key external forces may fail to anticipate emerging opportunities and threats and, consequently, may pursue ineffective strategies, miss opportunities, and invite organizational demise. Firms not taking advantage of the Internet are falling behind technologically.

A major responsibility of strategists is to ensure development of an effective external-audit system. This includes using information technology to devise a competitive intelligence system that works. The external-audit approach described in this chapter can be used effectively by any size or type of organization. Typically, the external-audit process is more informal in small firms, but the need to understand key trends and events is no less important for these firms. The EFE Matrix and Porter's Five-Forces Model can help strategists evaluate the market and industry, but these tools must be accompanied by good intuitive judgment. Multinational firms especially need a systematic and effective external-audit system because external forces among foreign countries vary so greatly.

We invite you to visit the David page on the Prentice Hall Companion Website at **www.prenhall.com/david** for this chapter's World Wide Web exercises.

KEY TERMS AND CONCEPTS

America Online (p. 103)

Chief Information Officer (CIO) (p. 93)

Chief Technology Officer (CTO) (p. 93)

Competitive Advantages (p. 93)

Competitive Analysis (p. 97)

Competitive Intelligence (CI) (p. 94)

Competitive Profile Matrix (CPM) (p. 112)

Decruiting (p. 83)

Director of Competitive Analysis (p. 97)

Downsizing (p. 83)

Environmental Scanning (p. 80)

External Audit (p. 80)

External Factor Evaluation (EFE) Matrix (p. 110)

External Forces (p. 80)

Industry Analysis (p. 80)

Information Technology (IT) (p. 93)

Internet (p. 92)

Learning from the Partner (p. 98)

Linear Regression (p. 105)

Lifecare Facilities (p. 86)

Porter's Five-Forces Model (p. 98)

Rightsizing (p. 83)

World Wide Web (p. 103)

ISSUES FOR REVIEW AND DISCUSSION

1. Explain how to conduct an external strategic-management audit.
2. Identify a recent economic, social, political, or technological trend that significantly affects financial institutions.
3. Discuss the following statement: Major opportunities and threats usually result from an interaction among key environmental trends rather than from a single external event or factor.
4. Identify two industries experiencing rapid technological changes and three industries that are experiencing little technological change. How does the need for technological forecasting differ in these industries? Why?
5. Use Porter's Five-Forces Model to evaluate competitiveness within the U.S. banking industry.
6. What major forecasting techniques would you use to identify (1) economic opportunities and threats

and (2) demographic opportunities and threats? Why are these techniques most appropriate?

7. How does the external audit affect other components of the strategic-management process?

8. As the owner of a small business, explain how you would organize a strategic-information scanning system. How would you organize such a system in a large organization?

9. Construct an EFE Matrix for an organization of your choice.

10. Make an appointment with a librarian at your university to learn how to use online databases. Report your findings in class.

11. Give some advantages and disadvantages of cooperative versus competitive strategies.

12. As strategist for a local bank, explain when you would use qualitative versus quantitative forecasts.

13. What is your forecast for interest rates and the stock market in the next several months? As the stock market moves up, do interest rates always move down? Why? What are the strategic implications of these trends?

14. Explain how information technology affects strategies of the organization where you worked most recently.

15. Let's say your boss develops an EFE Matrix that includes sixty-two factors. How would you suggest reducing the number of factors to twenty?

16. Select one of the current readings at the end of this chapter. Prepare a one-page written summary that includes your personal opinion of the article.

17. Discuss the ethics of gathering competitive intelligence.

18. Discuss the ethics of cooperating with rival firms.

19. Visit the SEC Web site at **www.sec.gov**, and discuss the benefits of using information provided there.

20. What are the major differences between U.S. and multinational operations that affect strategic management?

21. Why is globalization of industries a common factor today?

22. Discuss the opportunities and threats a firm faces in doing business in China.

NOTES

1. YORK FREUND, "Critical Success Factors," *Planning Review* 16, no. 4 (July–August 1988): 20.

2. CHARLES WHALEN "NAFTA's Scorecard: So Far, So Good." *Business Week* (July 9, 2001): 54–55.

3. EMILY THORTON, "Russia—What Happens When Markets Fail," *Business Week* (April 26, 1999): 50–52.

4. SUSAN DECKER, "Where to Find Legal Help On the Net," *USA Today* (October 18, 1999): 8B.

5. FREDERICK GLUCK, "Global Competition in the 1990s," *Journal of Business Strategy* (Spring 1983): 22, 24.

6. STAN CROCK, "From Evil Empire to Strategic Ally," *Business Week* (November 12, 2001): 76.

7. DAVID BANK, "Internet Learns New Lingo, XML, and the Hype Is On," *The Wall Street Journal* (September 16, 1999): A10.

8. JOHN HARRIS, ROBERT SHAW, JR., and WILLIAM SOMMERS, "The Strategic Management of Technology," *Planning Review* 11, no. 11 (January–February 1983): 28, 35.

9. BILL SAPORITO, "Companies That Compete Best," *Fortune* (May 22, 1989): 36.

10. LOUIS LAVELLE, "The Case of the Corporate Spy," *Business Week* (November 26, 2001): 56–57.

11. KENNETH SAWKA, "Demystifying Business Intelligence," *Management Review* (October 1996): 49.

12. JOHN PRESCOTT and DANIEL SMITH, "The Largest Survey of 'Leading-Edge' Competitor Intelligence Managers," *Planning Review* 17, no. 3 (May–June 1989): 6–13.

13. JON SWARTZ, "Nimda Called Most Serious Internet Attack on Business," *USA Today* (September 26, 2001): 5B. See also Srikumar Rao, "Counterspy," *Forbes* (February 5, 2001): 130.

14. GARY HAMEL, YVES DOZ, and C. K. PRAHALAD, "Collaborate with Your Competitors—and Win," *Harvard Business Review* 67, no. 1 (January–February 1989): 133.

15. DAVID BANK, "A Site-Eat-Site World," *The Wall Street Journal* (July 12, 1999): R8.

16. **http://horizon.unc.edu/projects/seminars/futures research/rationale.asp.**

17. DALE MCCONKEY, "Planning in a Changing Environment," *Business Horizons* 31, no. 5 (September–October 1988): 67.

18. "How Can You Win in China?" *Business Week* (May 26, 1997): 65.

19. GEORGE MELLOAN, "Hong Kong Is Gradually Melding with the Mainland," *Wall Street Journal* (September 11, 2001): A27.

20. GEOFF WINESTOCK and KARBY LEGGETT, "China to Enter WTO: Dispute on Insurance to Be First Test," *Wall Street Journal* (September 18, 2001): A14.

21. ERIK GUYOT, "Reined In: For Years, Hong Kong was the Poster Child for Laissez-faire Economics. No Longer," *The Wall Street Journal* (September 27, 1999): R20.

CURRENT READINGS

BERGH, D. D. and J. F. FAIRBANK. "Measuring and Testing Change in Strategic Management Research." *Strategic Management Journal* 23, no. 4 (April 2002): 359.

BIRKINSHAW, JULIAN and NEIL HOOD. "Unleash Innovation in Foreign Subsidiaries." *Harvard Business Review* (March 2001): 131.

BONABEAU, ERIC. "Predicting the Unpredictable." *Harvard Business Review* (March 2002): 109.

BONABEAU, ERIC and CHRISTOPHER MEYER. "Swarm Intelligence: A Whole New Way to Think About Business." *Harvard Business Review* (May 2001): 106.

CHATTOPADHYAY, PRITHVIRAJ, WILLIAM H. GLICK, and GEORGE P. HUBER. "Organizational Actions in Response to Threats and Opportunities." *Academy of Management Journal* 44, no. 5 (October 2001): 937.

CLAMPITT, PHILLIP G., ROBERT J. DEKOCH, and THOMAS CASHMAN. "A Strategy for Communicating About Uncertainty." *Academy of Management Executive* 14, no. 4 (November 2000): 41.

FERRIER, WALTER J. "Navigating the Competitive Landscape: The Drivers and Consequences of Competitive Aggressiveness." *Academy of Management Journal* 44, no. 4 (August 2001): 858.

GHEMAWAT, PANKAJ. "Distance Still Matters: The Hard Reality of Global Expansion." *Harvard Business Review* (September 2001): 137.

MICHAILOVA, SNEJINA. "Contrasts in Culture: Russian and Western Perspectives on Organizational Change." *Academy of Management Executive* 14, no. 4 (November 2000): 99.

PITT, LEYLAND F., MICHAEL T. EWING, and PIERRE BERTHON. "Turning Competitive Advantage into Customer Equity." *Business Horizons* 43, no. 5 (September–October 2000): 11.

POWELL, T. C. "Competitive Advantage: Logical and Philosophical Considerations." *Strategic Management Journal* 22, no. 9 (September 2001): 875.

PRESTON, LYNELLE. "Sustainability at Hewlett-Packard: From Theory to Practice." *California Management Review* 43, no. 3 (Spring 2001): 26.

RAMAMURTI, RAVI and DEVESH KAPUR. "India's Emerging Competitive Advantages in Services." *Academy of Management Executive* 15, no. 2 (May 2001): 20.

SHAMA, AVRAHAM. "After the Meltdown: A Survey of International Firms in Russia." *Business Horizons* 43, no. 4 (July–August 2000): 73.

SLATER, STANLEY F. and ERIC M. OLSON. "A Fresh Look at Industry and Market Analysis." *Business Horizons* 45, no. 1 (January-February 2002): 15.

VIBERT, CONOR. "Secrets of Online Sleuthing." *Journal of Business Strategy* 22, no. 3 (May/June 2001): 39.

EXPERIENTIAL EXERCISES

Developing an EFE Matrix for American Airlines (AMR)

PURPOSE

This exercise will give you practice developing an EFE Matrix. An EFE Matrix summarizes the results of an external audit. This is an important tool widely used by strategists.

INSTRUCTIONS

Step 1 Join with two other students in class, and jointly prepare an EFE Matrix for American Airlines. Refer back to the Cohesion Case and to Experiential Exercise 1A, if necessary, to identify external opportunities and threats.

Step 2 All three-person teams participating in this exercise should record their EFE total weighted scores on the board. Put your initials after your score to identify it as your team's.

Step 3 Compare the total weighted scores. Which team's score came closest to the instructor's answer? Discuss reasons for variation in the scores reported on the board.

The Internet Search

PURPOSE

This exercise will help you become familiar with important sources of external information available in your college library. A key part of preparing an external audit is searching the Internet and examining published sources of information for relevant economic, social, cultural, demographic, environmental, political, governmental, legal, technological, and competitive trends and events. External opportunities and threats must be identified and evaluated before strategies can be formulated effectively.

INSTRUCTIONS

Step 1 Select a company or business. Conduct an external audit for this company. Find opportunities and threats in recent issues of newspapers and magazines. Search for information using the Internet.

Step 2 On a separate sheet of paper, list ten opportunities and ten threats that face this company. Be specific in stating each factor.

Step 3 Include a bibliography to reveal where you found the information.

Step 4 Share your information with a manager of that company. Ask for his or her comments and additions.

Step 5 Write a three-page summary of your findings, and submit it to your teacher.

Developing an EFE Matrix for My University

PURPOSE

More colleges and universities are embarking upon the strategic-management process. Institutions are consciously and systematically identifying and evaluating external opportunities and threats facing higher education in your state, the nation, and the world.

INSTRUCTIONS

Step 1 Join with two other individuals in class, and jointly prepare an EFE Matrix for your institution.

Step 2 Go to the board and record your total weighted score in a column that includes the scores of all three-person teams participating. Put your initials after your score to identify it as your team's.

Step 3 Which team viewed your college's strategies most positively? Which team viewed your college's strategies most negatively? Discuss the nature of the differences.

EXPERIENTIAL EXERCISE 3D ▶

Developing a Competitive Profile Matrix for American Airlines (AMR)

PURPOSE

Monitoring competitors' performance and strategies is a key aspect of an external audit. This exercise is designed to give you practice evaluating the competitive position of organizations in a given industry and assimilating that information in the form of a Competitive Profile Matrix.

INSTRUCTIONS

Step 1 Turn back to the Cohesion Case and review the section on competitors.

Step 2 On a separate sheet of paper, prepare a Competitive Profile Matrix that includes American Airlines (AMR) and United Airlines (UAL).

Step 3 Turn in your Competitive Profile Matrix for a classwork grade.

EXPERIENTIAL EXERCISE 3E ▶

Developing a Competitive Profile Matrix for My University

PURPOSE

Your college or university competes with all other educational institutions in the world, especially those in your own state. State funds, students, faculty, staff, endowments, gifts, and federal funds are areas of competitiveness. The purpose of this exercise is to give you practice thinking competitively about the business of education in your state.

INSTRUCTIONS

Step 1 Identify two colleges or universities in your state that compete directly with your institution for students. Interview several persons who are aware of particular strengths and weaknesses of those universities. Record information about the two competing universities.

Step 2 Prepare a Competitive Profile Matrix that includes your institution and the two competing institutions. Include the following factors in your analysis:

1. Tuition costs
2. Quality of faculty
3. Academic reputation
4. Average class size
5. Campus landscaping
6. Athletic programs
7. Quality of students
8. Graduate programs
9. Location of campus
10. Campus culture

Step 3 Submit your Competitive Profile Matrix to your instructor for evaluation.

4

THE INTERNAL ASSESSMENT

CHAPTER OUTLINE

- The Nature of an Internal Audit
- Integrating Strategy and Culture
- Management
- Marketing
- Opportunity Analysis
- Finance/Accounting
- Production/Operations
- Research and Development
- Management Information Systems
- The Internal Factor Evaluation (IFE) Matrix

EXPERIENTIAL EXERCISE 4A
Performing a Financial Ratio Analysis for American Airlines (AMR)

EXPERIENTIAL EXERCISE 4B
Constructing an IFE Matrix for American Airlines (AMR)

EXPERIENTIAL EXERCISE 4C
Constructing an IFE Matrix for My University

CHAPTER OBJECTIVES

After studying this chapter, you should be able to do the following:

1. Describe how to perform an internal strategic-management audit.
2. Discuss key interrelationships among the functional areas of business.
3. Compare and contrast culture in America with other countries.
4. Identify the basic functions or activities that make up management, marketing, finance/accounting, production/operations, research and development, and management information systems.
5. Explain how to determine and prioritize a firm's internal strengths and weaknesses.
6. Explain the importance of financial ratio analysis.
7. Discuss the nature and role of management information systems in strategic management.
8. Develop an Internal Factor Evaluation (IFE) Matrix.

NOTABLE QUOTES

Like a product or service, the planning process itself must be managed and shaped, if it is to serve executives as a vehicle for strategic decision-making.

ROBERT LENZ

The difference between now and five years ago is that information systems had limited function. You weren't betting your company on it. Now you are.

WILLIAM GRUBER

Weak leadership can wreck the soundest strategy.

SUN ZI

A firm that continues to employ a previously successful strategy eventually and inevitably falls victim to a competitor.

WILLIAM COHEN

An organization should approach all tasks with the idea that they can be accomplished in a superior fashion.

THOMAS WATSON, JR.

By 2010, managers will have to handle greater cultural diversity. Managers will have to understand that employees don't think alike about such basics as "handling confrontation" or even what it means "to do a good day's work."

JEFFREY SONNENFELD

Sad but true, U.S. businesspeople have the lowest foreign language proficiency of any major trading nation. U.S. business schools do not emphasize foreign languages, and students traditionally avoid them.

RONALD DULEK

Great spirits have always encountered violent opposition from mediocre minds.

ALBERT EINSTEIN

This chapter focuses on identifying and evaluating a firm's strengths and weaknesses in the functional areas of business, including management, marketing, finance/accounting, production/operations, research and development, and management information systems. Relationships among these areas of business are examined. Strategic implications of important functional area concepts are examined. The process of performing an internal audit is described.

THE NATURE OF AN INTERNAL AUDIT

VISIT THE NET

Excellent strategic planning quotes. http://www. planware.org/quotes.htm#3

All organizations have strengths and weaknesses in the functional areas of business. No enterprise is equally strong or weak in all areas. Maytag, for example, is known for excellent production and product design, whereas Procter & Gamble is known for superb marketing. Internal strengths/weaknesses, coupled with external opportunities/threats and a clear statement of mission, provide the basis for establishing objectives and strategies. Objectives and strategies are established with the intention of capitalizing upon internal strengths and overcoming weaknesses. The internal-audit part of the strategic-management process is illustrated in Figure 4–1.

Key Internal Forces

It is not possible in a business policy text to review in depth all the material presented in courses such as marketing, finance, accounting, management, management information systems, and production/operations; there are many subareas within these functions, such as customer service, warranties, advertising, packaging, and pricing under marketing.

For different types of organizations, such as hospitals, universities, and government agencies, the functional business areas, of course, differ. In a hospital, for example, functional areas may include cardiology, hematology, nursing, maintenance, physician support, and receivables. Functional areas of a university can include athletic programs, placement services, housing, fundraising, academic research, counseling, and intramural-programs. Within large organizations, each division has certain strengths and weaknesses.

VISIT THE NET

Gives excellent information about the need for planning. http://www. mindtools.com/plintro.html

A firm's strengths that cannot be easily marched or imitated by competitors are called *distinctive competencies*. Building competitive advantages involves taking advantage of distinctive competencies. For example, 3M exploits its distinctive competence in research and development by producing a wide range of innovative products. Strategies are designed in part to improve on a firm's weaknesses, turning them into strengths—and maybe even into distinctive competencies.

Some researchers emphasize the importance of the internal audit part of the strategic-management process by comparing it to the external audit. Robert Grant concluded that the internal audit is more important, saying:

> In a world where customer preferences are volatile, the identity of customers is changing, and the technologies for serving customer requirements are continually evolving; an externally focused orientation does not provide a secure foundation for formulating long-term strategy. When the external environment is in a state of flux, the firm's own resources and capabilities may be a much more stable basis on which to define its identity. Hence, a definition of a business in terms of what it is capable of doing may offer a more durable basis for strategy than a definition based upon the needs which the business seeks to satisfy.[1]

FIGURE 4–1

A Comprehensive Strategic-Management Model

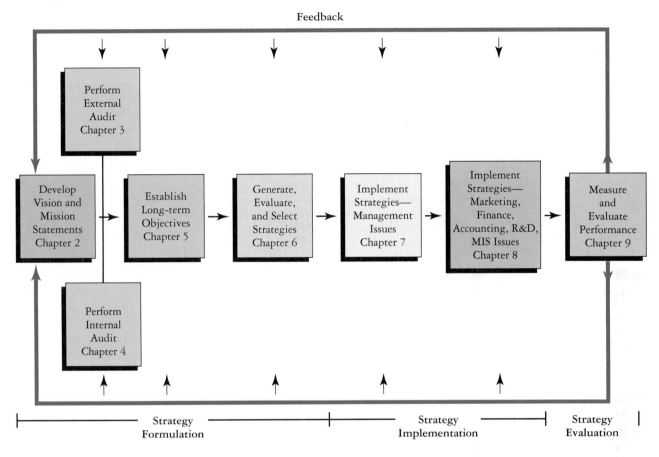

The Process of Performing an Internal Audit

The process of performing an *internal audit* closely parallels the process of performing an external audit. Representative managers and employees from throughout the firm need to be involved in determining a firm's strengths and weaknesses. The internal audit requires gathering and assimilating information about the firm's management, marketing, finance/accounting, production/operations, research and development (R&D), and management information systems operations. Key factors should be prioritized as described in Chapter 3 so that the firm's most important strengths and weaknesses can be determined collectively.

Compared to the external audit, the process of performing an internal audit provides more opportunity for participants to understand how their jobs, departments, and divisions fit into the whole organization. This is a great benefit because managers and employees perform better when they understand how their work affects other areas and activities of the firm. For example, when marketing and manufacturing managers jointly discuss issues related to internal strengths and weaknesses, they gain a better appreciation of the issues, problems, concerns, and needs of all the functional areas. In organizations that do not use strategic management, marketing, finance, and manufacturing managers often do not interact with each other in significant ways. Performing an internal audit thus is an excellent vehicle or forum for improving the process of communication in the organization. Communication may be the most important word in management.

Performing an internal audit requires gathering, assimilating, and evaluating information about the firm's operations. Critical success factors, consisting of both strengths and weaknesses, can be identified and prioritized in the manner discussed in Chapter 3. According to William King, a task force of managers from different units of the organization, supported by staff, should be charged with determining the ten to twenty most important strengths and weaknesses that should influence the future of the organization. He says:

> The development of conclusions on the 10 to 20 most important organizational strengths and weaknesses can be, as any experienced manager knows, a difficult task, when it involves managers representing various organizational interests and points of view. Developing a 20-page list of strengths and weaknesses could be accomplished relatively easily, but a list of the 10 to 15 most important ones involves significant analysis and negotiation. This is true because of the judgments that are required and the impact which such a list will inevitably have as it is used in the formulation, implementation, and evaluation of strategies.[2]

VISIT THE NET

Provides the complete strategic plan for the Wyoming Insurance Department Agency, including its list of strengths and weaknesses.
http://www.state.wy.us/state/strategy/insurance.html

Strategic management is a highly interactive process that requires effective coordination among management, marketing, finance/accounting, production/operations, R&D, and management information systems managers. Although the strategic-management process is overseen by strategists, success requires that managers and employees from all functional areas work together to provide ideas and information. Financial managers, for example, may need to restrict the number of feasible options available to operations managers, or R&D managers may develop products that marketing managers need to set higher objectives. A key to organizational success is effective coordination and understanding among managers from all functional business areas. Through involvement in performing an internal strategic-management audit, managers from different departments and divisions of the firm come to understand the nature and effect of decisions in other functional business areas in their firm. Knowledge of these relationships is critical for effectively establishing objectives and strategies.

A failure to recognize and understand relationships among the functional areas of business can be detrimental to strategic management, and the number of those relationships that must be managed increases dramatically with a firm's size, diversity, geographic dispersion, and the number of products or services offered. Governmental and nonprofit enterprises traditionally have not placed sufficient emphasis on relationships among the business functions. Some firms place too great an emphasis on one function at the expense of others. Ansoff explained:

> During the first fifty years, successful firms focused their energies on optimizing the performance of one of the principal functions: production/operations, R&D, or marketing. Today, due to the growing complexity and dynamism of the environment, success increasingly depends on a judicious combination of several functional influences. This transition from a single function focus to a multifunction focus is essential for successful strategic management.[3]

Financial ratio analysis exemplifies the complexity of relationships among the functional areas of business. A declining return on investment or profit margin ratio could be the result of ineffective marketing, poor management policies, research and development errors, or a weak management information system. The effectiveness of strategy formulation, implementation, and evaluation activities hinges upon a clear understanding of how major business functions affect one another. For strategies to succeed, a coordinated effort among all the functional areas of business is needed. In the case of planning, George wrote:

> We may conceptually separate planning for the purpose of theoretical discussion and analysis, but in practice, neither is it a distinct entity nor is it capable of being separated. The planning function is mixed with all other business functions and, like ink once mixed with water, it cannot be set apart. It is spread throughout and is a part of the whole of managing an organization.[4]

INTEGRATING STRATEGY AND CULTURE

Relationships among a firm's functional business activities perhaps can be exemplified best by focusing on organizational culture, an internal phenomenon that permeates all departments and divisions of an organization. *Organizational culture* can be defined as "a pattern of behavior [that has been] developed by an organization as it learns to cope with its problem of external adaptation and internal integration, [and] that has worked well enough to be considered valid and to be taught to new members as the correct way to perceive, think, and feel."[5] This definition emphasizes the importance of matching external with internal factors in making strategic decisions.

Organizational culture captures the subtle, elusive, and largely unconscious forces that shape a workplace. Remarkably resistant to change, culture can represent a major strength or weakness for the firm. It can be an underlying reason for strengths or weaknesses in any of the major business functions.

Defined in Table 4–1, *cultural products* include values, beliefs, rites, rituals, ceremonies, myths, stories, legends, sagas, language, metaphors, symbols, heroes, and heroines. These products or dimensions are levers that strategists can use to influence and direct strategy formulation, implementation, and evaluation activities. An organization's culture compares to an individual's personality in the sense that no two organizations have the same culture and no two individuals have the same personality. Both culture and personality are fairly enduring and can be warm, aggressive, friendly, open, innovative, conservative, liberal, harsh, or likable.

Dimensions of organizational culture permeate all the functional areas of business. It is something of an art to uncover the basic values and beliefs that are deeply buried in an organization's rich collection of stories, language, heroes, and rituals, but cultural products can represent both important strengths and weaknesses. Culture is an aspect of an organization that can no longer be taken for granted in performing an internal strategic-management audit because culture and strategy must work together.

The strategic-management process takes place largely within a particular organization's culture. Lorsch found that executives in successful companies are emotionally committed to the firm's culture, but he concluded that culture can inhibit strategic management in two basic ways. First, managers frequently miss the significance of changing external conditions-because they are blinded by strongly held beliefs. Second, when a particular culture has been effective in the past, the natural response is to stick with it in the future, even during times of major strategic change.[6] An organization's culture must support the collective commitment of its people to a common purpose. It must foster competence and enthusiasm among managers and employees.

Organizational culture significantly affects business decisions and thus must be evaluated during an internal strategic-management audit. If strategies can capitalize on

VISIT THE NET

Provides excellent narrative on how the state of Missouri does strategic planning, including its internal assessment.
http://www.mri.state.mo.us/SP/model.htm

TABLE 4-1   **Cultural Products and Associated Definitions**

Rites	Relatively elaborate, dramatic, planned sets of activities that consolidate various forms of cultural expressions into one event, carried out through social interactions, usually for the benefit of an audience
Ceremonial	A system of several rites connected with a single occasion or event
Ritual	A standardized, detailed set of techniques and behaviors that manage anxieties, but seldom produce intended, technical consequences of practical importance
Myth	A dramatic narrative of imagined events, usually used to explain origins or transformations of something. Also, an unquestioned belief about the practical benefits of certain techniques and behaviors that is not supported by facts
Saga	A historical narrative describing the unique accomplishments of a group and its leaders, usually in heroic terms
Legend	A handed-down narrative of some wonderful event that is based on history but has been embellished with fictional details
Story	A narrative based on true events, sometimes a combination of truth and fiction
Folktale	A completely fictional narrative
Symbol	Any object, act, event, quality, or relation that serves as a vehicle for conveying meaning, usually by representing another thing
Language	A particular form or manner in which members of a group use sounds and written signs to convey meanings to each other
Metaphors	Shorthand words used to capture a vision or to reinforce old or new values
Values	Life-directing attitudes that serve as behavioral guidelines
Belief	An understanding of a particular phenomenon
Heroes/Heroines	Individuals whom the organization has legitimized to model behavior for others

Source: Adapted from H. M. Trice and J. M. Beyer, "Studying Organizational Cultures through Rites and Ceremonials," *Academy of Management Review* 9, no. 4 (October 1984): 655.

cultural strengths, such as a strong work ethic or highly ethical beliefs, then management often can implement changes swiftly and easily. However, if the firm's culture is not supportive, strategic changes may be ineffective or even counterproductive. A firm's culture can become antagonistic to new strategies, with the result being confusion and disorientation. An organization's culture should infuse individuals with enthusiasm for implementing strategies. Allarie and Firsirotu emphasized the need to understand culture:

> Culture provides an explanation for the insuperable difficulties a firm encounters when it attempts to shift its strategic direction. Not only has the "right" culture become the essence and foundation of corporate excellence, it is also claimed that success or failure of reforms hinges on management's sagacity and ability to change the firm's driving culture in time and in time with required changes in strategies.[7]

The potential value of organizational culture has not been realized fully in the study of strategic management. Ignoring the effect that culture can have on relationships among the functional areas of business can result in barriers to communication, lack of coordination, and an inability to adapt to changing conditions. Some tension between culture and a firm's strategy is inevitable, but the tension should be monitored so that it does not reach a point at which relationships are severed and the culture becomes antagonistic. The resulting disarray among members of the organization would disrupt strategy formulation, implementation, and evaluation. On the other hand, a supportive organizational culture can make managing much easier.

Internal strengths and weaknesses associated with a firm's culture sometimes are overlooked because of the interfunctional nature of this phenomenon. It is important, therefore, for strategists to understand their firm as a sociocultural system. Success is often determined by linkages between a firm's culture and strategies. The challenge of strategic management today is to bring about the changes in organizational culture and individual mind-sets that are needed to support the formulation, implementation, and evaluation of strategies.

American versus Foreign Cultures

To successfully compete in world markets, U.S. managers must obtain a better knowledge of historical, cultural, and religious forces that motivate and drive people in other countries. In Japan, for example, business relations operate within the context of *Wa*, which stresses group harmony and social cohesion. In China, business behavior revolves around *guanxi*, or personal relations. In Korea, activities involve concern for *inhwa*, or harmony based on respect of hierarchical relationships, including obedience to authority.[8] Note in the Global Perspective box that it is important to be sensitive to foreign business cultures.

In Europe, it is generally true that the farther north on the continent, the more participatory the management style. Most European workers are unionized and enjoy

GLOBAL PERSPECTIVE

American versus Foreign Communication Differences

As Americans increasingly interact with managers in other countries, it is important to be sensitive to foreign business cultures. Americans too often come across as intrusive, manipulative, and garrulous, and this impression reduces their effectiveness in communication. *Forbes* recently provided the following cultural hints from Charis Intercultural Training:

1. Italians, Germans, and French generally do not soften up executives with praise before they criticize. Americans do soften up folks, and this practice seems manipulative to Europeans.
2. Israelis are accustomed to fast-paced meetings and have little patience for American informality and small talk.
3. British executives often complain that American executives chatter too much. Informality, egalitarianism, and spontaneity from Americans in business settings jolt many foreigners.

4. Europeans feel they are being treated like children when asked to wear name tags by Americans.
5. Executives in India are used to interrupting one another. Thus, when American executives listen without asking for clarification or posing questions, they are viewed by Indians as not paying attention.
6. When negotiating orally with Malaysian or Japanese executives, periodically allow for a time of silence. However, do not pause when negotiating in Israel.

Refrain from asking foreign managers questions such as "How was your weekend?" That is intrusive to foreigners, who tend to regard their business and private lives as totally separate.

Source: Adapted from Lalita Khosla, "You Say Tomato," *Forbes* (May 21, 2001): 36.

more frequent vacations and holidays than U.S. workers. A ninety-minute lunch break plus twenty-minute morning and afternoon breaks are common in European firms. Guaranteed permanent employment is commonly a part of employment contracts in Europe. In socialist countries such as France, Belgium, and the United Kingdom, the only ground for immediate dismissal from work is a criminal offense. A six-month trial period at the beginning of employment is usually part of the contract with a European firm. Many Europeans resent pay-for-performance, commission salaries, and objective measurement and reward systems. This is true especially of workers in southern Europe. Many Europeans also find the notion of team spirit difficult to grasp because the unionized environment has dichotomized worker-management relations throughout Europe.

A weakness that U.S. firms have in competing with Pacific Rim firms is a lack of understanding of Far Eastern cultures, including how Asians think and behave. Spoken Chinese, for example, has more in common with spoken English than with spoken Japanese or Korean. Managers around the world face the responsibility of having to exert authority while at the same time trying to be liked by subordinates. U.S. managers consistently put more weight on being friendly and liked, whereas Asian and European managers exercise authority often without this concern. Americans tend to use first names instantly in business dealings with foreigners, but foreigners find this presumptuous. In Japan, for example, first names are used only among family members and intimate friends; even long-time business associates and coworkers shy away from the use of first names. Other cultural differences or pitfalls that U.S. managers need to know about are given in Table 4–2.

U.S. managers have a low tolerance for silence, whereas Asian managers view extended periods of silence as important for organizing and evaluating one's thoughts. U.S. managers are much more action-oriented than their counterparts around the world; they rush to appointments, conferences, and meetings—and then feel the day has been

TABLE 4–2   Cultural Pitfalls That You Need to Know

Waving is a serious insult in Greece and Nigeria, particularly if the hand is near someone's face.

Making a "good-bye" wave in Europe can mean "no," but it means "come here" in Peru.

In China, last names are written first.

A man named Carlos Lopez-Garcia should be addressed as Mr. Lopez in Latin America, but as Mr. Garcia in Brazil.

Breakfast meetings are considered uncivilized in most foreign countries.

Latin Americans average being twenty minutes late to business appointments.

Direct eye contact is impolite in Japan.

Don't cross your legs in Arab or many Asian countries—it's rude to show the sole of your shoe.

In Brazil, touching your thumb and first finger—an American "OK" sign—is the equivalent of raising your middle finger.

Nodding or tossing your head back in southern Italy, Malta, Greece, and Tunisia means "no." In India, this body motions means "yes."

Snapping your fingers is vulgar in France and Belgium.

Folding your arms across your chest is a sign of annoyance in Finland.

In China, leave some food on your plate to show that your host was so generous that you couldn't finish.

Do not eat with your left hand when dining with clients from Malaysia or India.

One form of communication works the same worldwide. It's the smile—so take that along wherever you go.

productive. But for foreign managers, resting, listening, meditating, and thinking is considered productive. Sitting through a conference without talking is unproductive in the United States, but it is viewed as positive in Japan if one's silence helps preserve unity.

U.S. managers also put greater emphasis on short-term results than foreign managers do. In marketing, for example, Japanese managers strive to achieve "everlasting customers," whereas many Americans strive to make a one-time sale. Marketing managers in Japan see making a sale as the beginning, not the end, of the selling process. This is an important distinction. Japanese managers often criticize U.S. managers for worrying more about shareholders, whom they do not know, than employees, whom they do know. Americans refer to "hourly employees," whereas many Japanese companies still refer to "lifetime employees."

Rose Knotts recently summarized some important cultural differences between U.S. and foreign managers:[9]

1. Americans place an exceptionally high priority on time, viewing time as an asset. Many foreigners place more worth on relationships. This difference results in foreign managers often viewing U.S. managers as "more interested in business than people."

2. Personal touching and distance norms differ around the world. Americans generally stand about three feet from each other when carrying on business conversations, but Arabs and Africans stand about one foot apart. Touching another person with the left hand in business dealings is taboo in some countries. American managers need to learn the personal space rules of foreign managers with whom they interact in business.

3. People in some cultures do not place the same significance on material wealth as American managers often do. Lists of the "largest corporations" and "highest-paid" executives abound in the United States. "More is better" and "bigger is better" in the United States, but not everywhere. This can be a consideration in trying to motivate individuals in other countries.

4. Family roles and relationships vary in different countries. For example, males are valued more than females in some cultures, and peer pressure, work situations, and business interactions reinforce this phenomenon.

5. Language differs dramatically across countries, even in countries where people speak the same language. Words and expressions commonly used in one country may be disrespectful in another.

6. Business and daily life in some societies is governed by religious factors. Prayer times, holidays, daily events, and dietary restrictions, for example, need to be respected by American managers not familiar with these practices in some countries.

7. Time spent with the family and the quality of relationships are more important in some cultures than the personal achievement and accomplishments espoused by the traditional American manager. For example, where a person stands in the hierarchy of a firm's organizational structure, how large the firm is, and where the firm is located are much more important factors to American managers than to many foreign managers.

8. Many cultures around the world value modesty, team spirit, collectivity, and patience much more than the competitiveness and individualism that are so important in America.

9. Punctuality is a valued personal trait when conducting business in America, but it is not revered in many of the world's societies. Eating habits also differ dramatically across cultures. For example, belching is acceptable in many countries as evidence of satisfaction with the food that has been prepared. Chinese culture considers it good manners to sample a portion of each food served.

10. To prevent social blunders when meeting with managers from other lands, one must learn and respect the rules of etiquette of others. Sitting on a toilet seat is viewed as unsanitary in most countries, but not in the United States. Leaving food or drink after dining is considered impolite in some countries, but not in China. Bowing instead of shaking hands is customary in many countries. Many cultures view Americans as unsanitary for locating toilet and bathing facilities in the same area, whereas Americans view people of some cultures as unsanitary for not taking a bath or shower every day.

11. Americans often do business with individuals they do not know, but this practice is not accepted in many other cultures. In Mexico and Japan, for example, an amicable relationship is often mandatory before conducting business.

In many countries, effective managers are those who are best at negotiating with government bureaucrats rather than those who inspire workers. Many U.S. managers are uncomfortable with nepotism and bribery, which are common in many countries. In almost every country except the United States, bribery is tax-deductible.

The United States has gained a reputation for defending women from sexual harassment and minorities from discrimination, but not all countries embrace the same values. For example, in the Czech Republic, it is considered a compliment when the boss openly flirts with his female secretary and invites her to dinner. U.S. managers in the Czech Republic who do not flirt seem cold and uncaring to some employees.

American managers in China have to be careful about how they arrange office furniture because Chinese workers believe in *feng shui,* the practice of harnessing natural forces. American managers in Japan have to be careful about *nemaswashio,* whereby Japanese workers expect supervisors to alert them privately of changes rather than informing them in a meeting. Japanese managers have little appreciation for versatility, expecting all managers to be the same. In Japan, "If a nail sticks out, you hit it into the wall," says Brad Lashbrook, an international consultant for Wilson Learning.

Probably the biggest obstacle to the effectiveness of U.S. managers—or managers from any country working in another—is the fact that it is almost impossible to change the attitude of a foreign workforce. "The system drives you; you cannot fight the system or culture," says Bill Parker, president of Phillips Petroleum in Norway.

MANAGEMENT

The *functions of management* consist of five basic activities: planning, organizing, motivating, staffing, and controlling. An overview of these activities is provided in Table 4–3.

Planning
The only thing certain about the future of any organization is change, and *planning* is the essential bridge between the present and the future that increases the likelihood of achieving desired results. Planning is the process by which one determines whether to attempt a task, works out the most effective way of reaching desired objectives, and prepares to overcome unexpected difficulties with adequate resources. Planning is the start

TABLE 4-3   **The Basic Functions of Management**

FUNCTION	DESCRIPTION	STAGE OF STRATEGIC-MANAGEMENT PROCESS WHEN MOST IMPORTANT
Planning	Planning consists of all those managerial activities related to preparing for the future. Specific tasks include forecasting, establishing objectives, devising strategies, developing policies, and setting goals.	Strategy Formulation
Organizing	Organizing includes all those managerial activities that result in a structure of task and authority relationships. Specific areas include organizational design, job specialization, job descriptions, job specifications, span of the control, unity of command, coordination, job design, and job analysis.	Strategy Implementation
Motivating	Motivating involves efforts directed toward shaping human behavior. Specific topics include leadership, communication, work groups, behavior modification, delegation of authority, job enrichment, job satisfaction, needs fulfillment, organizational change, employee morale, and managerial morale.	Strategy Implementation
Staffing	Staffing activities are centered on personnel or human resource management. Included are wage and salary administration, employee benefits, interviewing, hiring, firing, training, management development, employee safety, affirmative action, equal employment opportunity, union relations, career development, personnel research, discipline policies, grievance procedures, and public relations.	Strategy Implementation
Controlling	Controlling refers to all those managerial activities directed toward ensuring that actual results are consistent with planned results. Key areas of concern include quality control, financial control, sales control, inventory control, expense control, analysis of variances, rewards, and sanctions.	Strategy Evaluation

of the process by which an individual or business may turn empty dreams into achievements. Planning enables one to avoid the trap of working extremely hard but achieving little.

Planning is an up-front investment in success. Planning helps a firm achieve maximum effect from a given effort. Planning enables a firm to take into account relevant factors and focus on the critical ones. Planning helps ensure that the firm can be prepared for all reasonable eventualities and for all changes that will be needed. Planning enables a firm to gather the resources needed and carry out tasks in the most efficient way possible. Planning enables a firm to conserve its own resources, avoid wasting ecological resources, make a fair profit, and be seen as an effective, useful firm. Planning enables a firm to identify precisely what is to be achieved and to detail precisely the who, what, when, where, why, and how needed to achieve desired objectives. Planning enables a firm to assess whether the effort, costs, and implications associated with achieving desired objectives are warranted.[10] Planning is the cornerstone of effective strategy formulation. But even though it is considered the foundation of management, it is commonly the task that managers neglect most. Planning is essential for successful strategy implementation and strategy evaluation, largely because organizing, motivating, staffing, and controlling activities depend upon good planning.

The process of planning must involve managers and employees throughout an organization. The time horizon for planning decreases from two to five years for top-level to less than six months for lower-level managers. The important point is that all managers do planning and should involve subordinates in the process to facilitate employee understanding and commitment.

Planning can have a positive impact on organizational and individual performance. Planning allows an organization to identify and take advantage of external opportunities as well as minimize the impact of external threats. Planning is more than extrapolating from the past and present into the future. It also includes developing a mission, forecasting future events and trends, establishing objectives, and choosing strategies to pursue.

An organization can develop synergy through planning. *Synergy* exists when everyone pulls together as a team that knows what it wants to achieve; synergy is the 2 + 2 = 5 effect. By establishing and communicating clear objectives, employees and managers can work together toward desired results. Synergy can result in powerful competitive advantages. The strategic-management process itself is aimed at creating synergy in an organization.

Planning allows a firm to adapt to changing markets and thus to shape its own destiny. Strategic management can be viewed as a formal planning process that allows an organization to pursue proactive rather than reactive strategies. Successful organizations strive to control their own futures rather than merely react to external forces and events as they occur. Historically, organisms and organizations that have not adapted to changing conditions have become extinct. Swift adaptation is needed today more than ever before because changes in markets, economies, and competitors worldwide are accelerating.

Organizing

The purpose of *organizing* is to achieve coordinated effort by defining task and authority relationships. Organizing means determining who does what and who reports to whom. There are countless examples in history of well-organized enterprises successfully competing against—and in some cases defeating—much stronger but less-organized firms. A well-organized firm generally has motivated managers and employees who are committed to seeing the organization succeed. Resources are allocated more effectively and used more efficiently in a well-organized firm than in a disorganized firm.

The organizing function of management can be viewed as consisting of three sequential activities: breaking tasks down into jobs (work specialization), combining jobs to form departments (departmentalization), and delegating authority. Breaking tasks down into jobs requires the development of job descriptions and job specifications. These tools clarify for both managers and employees what particular jobs entail. In *Wealth of Nations,* published in 1776, Adam Smith cited the advantages of work specialization in the manufacture of pins:

> One man draws the wire, another straightens it, a third cuts it, a fourth points it, a fifth grinds it at the top for receiving the head. Ten men working in this manner can produce 48,000 pins in a single day, but if they had all wrought separately and independently, each might at best produce twenty pins in a day.[11]

Combining jobs to form departments results in an organizational structure, span of control, and a chain of command. Changes in strategy often require changes in structure because positions may be created, deleted, or merged. Organizational structure dictates how resources are allocated and how objectives are established in a firm. Allocating resources and establishing objectives geographically, for example, is much different from doing so by product or customer.

The most common forms of departmentalization are functional, divisional, strategic business unit, and matrix. These types of structure are discussed further in Chapter 7.

Delegating authority is an important organizing activity, as evidenced in the old saying "You can tell how good a manager is by observing how his or her department functions when he or she isn't there." Employees today are more educated and more capable of participating in organizational decision making than ever before. In most cases, they expect to be delegated authority and responsibility, and to be held accountable for results. Delegation of authority is embedded in the strategic-management process.

Motivating

Motivating can be defined as the process of influencing people to accomplish specific objectives.[12] Motivation explains why some people work hard and others do not. Objectives, strategies, and policies have little chance of succeeding if employees and managers are not motivated to implement strategies once they are formulated. The motivating function of management includes at least four major components: leadership, group dynamics, communication, and organizational change.

When managers and employees of a firm strive to achieve high levels of productivity, this indicates that the firm's strategists are good leaders. Good leaders establish rapport with subordinates, empathize with their needs and concerns, set a good example, and are trustworthy and fair. Leadership includes developing a vision of the firm's future and inspiring people to work hard to achieve that vision. Kirkpatrick and Locke reported that certain traits also characterize effective leaders: knowledge of the business, cognitive ability, self-confidence, honesty, integrity, and drive.[13]

Research suggests that democratic behavior on the part of leaders results in more positive attitudes toward change and higher productivity than does autocratic behavior. Drucker said:

> Leadership is not a magnetic personality. That can just as well be demagoguery. It is not "making friends and influencing people." That is flattery. Leadership is the lifting of a person's vision to higher sights, the raising of a person's performance to a higher standard, the building of a person's personality beyond its normal limitations.[14]

Group dynamics play a major role in employee morale and satisfaction. Informal groups or coalitions form in every organization. The norms of coalitions can range from being very positive to very negative toward management. It is important, therefore, that strategists identify the composition and nature of informal groups in an organization to facilitate strategy formulation, implementation, and evaluation. Leaders of informal groups are especially important in formulating and implementing strategy changes.

Communication, perhaps the most important word in management, is a major component in motivation. An organization's system of communication determines whether strategies can be implemented successfully. Good two-way communication is vital for gaining support for departmental and divisional objectives and policies. Top-down communication can encourage bottom-up communication. The strategic-management process becomes a lot easier when subordinates are encouraged to discuss their concerns, reveal their problems, provide recommendations, and give suggestions. A primary reason for instituting strategic management is to build and support effective communication networks throughout the firm.

> The manager of tomorrow must be able to get his people to commit themselves to the business, whether they are machine operators or junior vice-presidents. Ah, you say, participative management. Have a cigar. But just because most managers tug a forelock at the P word doesn't mean they know how to make it

work. Today, throwing together a few quality circles won't suffice. The key issue will be empowerment, a term whose strength suggests the need to get beyond merely sharing a little information and a bit of decision making.[15]

Staffing

The management function of *staffing*, also called *personnel management* or *human resource management*, includes activities such as recruiting, interviewing, testing, selecting, orienting, training, developing, caring for, evaluating, rewarding, disciplining, promoting, transferring, demoting, and dismissing employees, as well as managing union relations.

Staffing activities play a major role in strategy-implementation efforts, and for this reason, human resource managers are becoming more actively involved in the strategic-management process. It is important to identify strengths and weaknesses in the staffing area.

The complexity and importance of human resource activities have increased to such a degree that all but the smallest organizations now need a full-time human resource manager. Numerous court cases that directly affect staffing activities are decided each day. Organizations and individuals can be penalized severely for not following federal, state, and local laws and guidelines related to staffing. Line managers simply cannot stay abreast of all the legal developments and requirements regarding staffing. The human resources department coordinates staffing decisions in the firm so that an organization as a whole meets legal requirements. This department also provides needed consistency in administering company rules, wages, and policies.

Human resources management is particularly challenging for international companies. For example, the inability of spouses and children to adapt to new surroundings has become a major staffing problem in overseas transfers. The problems include premature returns, job performance slumps, resignations, discharges, low morale, marital discord, and general discontent. Firms such as Ford Motor and Exxon/Mobil have begun screening and interviewing spouses and children before assigning persons to overseas positions. 3M Corporation introduces children to peers in the target country and offers spouses educational benefits.

Strategists are becoming increasingly aware of how important human resources are to effective strategic management. Human resource managers are becoming more involved and more proactive in formulating and implementing strategies. They provide leadership for organizations that are restructuring, or they allow employees to work at home.

Controlling

The *controlling* function of management includes all of those activities undertaken to ensure that actual operations conform to planned operations. All managers in an organization have controlling responsibilities, such as conducting performance evaluations and taking necessary action to minimize inefficiencies. The controlling function of management is particularly important for effective strategy evaluation. Controlling consists of four basic steps:

1. Establishing performance standards
2. Measuring individual and organizational performance
3. Comparing actual performance to planned performance standards
4. Taking corrective actions

Measuring individual performance is often conducted ineffectively or not at all in organizations. Some reasons for this shortcoming are that evaluations can create confrontations that most managers prefer to avoid, can take more time than most managers are willing to give, and can require skills that many managers lack. No single approach to measuring individual performance is without limitations. For this reason, an organization should examine various methods, such as the graphic rating scale, the behaviorally anchored rating scale, and the critical incident method, and then develop or select a performance appraisal approach that best suits the firm's needs. Increasingly, firms are striving to link organizational performance with managers' and employees' pay. This topic is discussed further in Chapter 7.

Management Audit Checklist of Questions

The checklists of questions provided below can help determine specific strengths and weaknesses in the functional area of business. An answer of *no* to any question could indicate a potential weakness, although the strategic significance and implications of negative answers, of course, will vary by organization, industry, and severity of the weakness. Positive or *yes* answers to the checklist questions suggest potential areas of strength.

1. Does the firm use strategic-management concepts?
2. Are company objectives and goals measurable and well communicated?
3. Do managers at all hierarchical levels plan effectively?
4. Do managers delegate authority well?
5. Is the organization's structure appropriate?
6. Are job descriptions and job specifications clear?
7. Is employee morale high?
8. Are employee turnover and absenteeism low?
9. Are organizational reward and control mechanisms effective?

 ## MARKETING

Marketing can be described as the process of defining, anticipating, creating, and fulfilling customers' needs and wants for products and services. There are seven basic *functions of marketing:* (1) customer analysis, (2) selling products/services, (3) product and service planning (4) pricing, (5) distribution, (6) marketing research, and (7) opportunity analysis.[16] Understanding these functions helps strategists identify and evaluate marketing strengths and weaknesses.

Customer Analysis

Customer analysis—the examination and evaluation of consumer needs, desires, and wants—involves administering customer surveys, analyzing consumer information, evaluating market positioning strategies, developing customer profiles, and determining optimal market segmentation strategies. The information generated by customer analysis can be essential in developing an effective mission statement. Customer profiles can reveal the demographic characteristics of an organization's customers. Buyers, sellers, distributors, salespeople, managers, wholesalers, retailers, suppliers, and creditors can all participate in gathering information to identify customers' needs and wants successfully. Successful organizations continually monitor present and potential customers' buying patterns.

Selling Products/Services

Successful strategy implementation generally rests upon the ability of an organization to sell some product or service. *Selling* includes many marketing activities, such as advertising, sales promotion, publicity, personal selling, sales force management, customer relations, and dealer relations. These activities are especially critical when a firm pursues a market penetration strategy. The effectiveness of various selling tools for consumer and industrial products varies. Personal selling is most important for industrial goods companies, and advertising is most important for consumer goods companies. Determining organizational strengths and weaknesses in the selling function of marketing is an important part of performing an internal strategic-management audit.

With regard to advertising products and services on the Internet, a new trend is to base advertising rates exclusively on sales rates. This new accountability contrasts sharply with traditional broadcast and print advertising, which bases rates on the number of persons expected to see a given advertisement. The new cost-per-sale online advertising rates are possible because any Web site can monitor which user clicks on which advertisement and then can record whether that consumer actually buys the product. If there are no sales, then the advertisement is free.

Due to weakening consumer confidence, falling demand, and increased layoffs, total corporate advertising expenditures declined 4 percent in 2001. Company expenditures on advertising in traditional media such as television, newspapers, and magazines declined more rapidly than nontraditional junk mail and direct mail. Newspaper advertising declined 5.9 percent in 2001, television ad spending fell 3.5 percent, and magazines advertising fell 8 percent. Ad spending on television fell another 4 percent in 2002.[17]

Product and Service Planning

Product and service planning includes activities such as test marketing; product and brand positioning; devising warranties; packaging; determining product options, product features, product style, and product quality; deleting old products; and providing for customer service. Product and service planning is particularly important when a company is pursuing product development or diversification.

One of the most effective product and service planning techniques is *test marketing*. Test markets allow an organization to test alternative marketing plans and to forecast future sales of new products. In conducting a test market project, an organization must decide how many cities to include, which cities to include, how long to run the test, what information to collect during the test, and what action to take after the test has been completed. Test marketing is used more frequently by consumer goods companies than by industrial goods companies. Test marketing can allow an organization to avoid substantial losses by revealing weak products and ineffective marketing approaches before large-scale production begins.

Pricing

Five major stakeholders affect *pricing* decisions: consumers, governments, suppliers, distributors, and competitors. Sometimes an organization will pursue a forward integration strategy primarily to gain better control over prices charged to consumers. Governments can impose constraints on price fixing, price discrimination, minimum prices, unit pricing, price advertising, and price controls. For example, the Robinson-Patman Act prohibits manufacturers and wholesalers from discriminating in price among channel member purchasers (suppliers and distributors) if competition is injured.

Competing organizations must be careful not to coordinate discounts, credit terms, or condition of sale; not to discuss prices, markups, and costs at trade association meetings; and not to arrange to issue new price lists on the same date, to rotate low bids on contracts, or to uniformly restrict production to maintain high prices. Strategists should view price from both a short-run and a long-run perspective, because competitors can copy price changes with relative ease. Often a dominant firm will aggressively match all price cuts by competitors.

With regard to pricing, as the value of the dollar increases, U.S. multinational companies have a choice. They can raise prices in the local currency of a foreign country or risk losing sales and market share. Alternatively, multinational firms can keep prices steady and face reduced profit when their export revenue is reported in the United States in dollars.

The largest operator of pay telephones in the United States, Verizon Communications, increased the price of local pay-phone calls to 50 cents because of declining pay-phone revenue and increased competition from cellphones. Previously, the cost was 35 cents for local calls. Verizon operates 430,000 pay phones in 33 states.

Prices on handheld computers are falling dramatically because distributors have excess inventory due to slowing consumer demand. Analysts contend that handheld computers will soon become as inexpensive as cellphones—and eventually may be given away when a consumer purchases the company's wireless Internet service. Palm is the largest handheld-computer maker, but other competitors include Casio, Handspring, and Hewlett-Packard. While the current economic downturn has wreaked havoc for companies on Wall Street, it has benefited consumers on Main Street, who have seen lower prices almost everywhere they shop.

Distribution

Distribution includes warehousing, distribution channels, distribution coverage, retail site locations, sales territories, inventory levels and location, transportation carriers, wholesaling, and retailing. Most producers today do not sell their goods directly to consumers. Various marketing entities act as intermediaries; they bear a variety of names such as wholesalers, retailers, brokers, facilitators, agents, vendors—or simply distributors.

Distribution becomes especially important when a firm is striving to implement a market development or forward integration strategy. Some of the most complex and challenging decisions facing a firm concern product distribution. Intermediaries flourish in our economy because many producers lack the financial resources and expertise to carry out direct marketing. Manufacturers who could afford to sell directly to the public often can gain greater returns by expanding and improving their manufacturing operations. Even General Motors would find it very difficult to buy out its more than eighteen thousand independent dealers.

Successful organizations identify and evaluate alternative ways to reach their ultimate market. Possible approaches vary from direct selling to using just one or many wholesalers and retailers. Strengths and weaknesses of each channel alternative should be determined according to economic, control, and adaptive criteria. Organizations should consider the costs and benefits of various wholesaling and retailing options. They must consider the need to motivate and control channel members and the need to adapt to changes in the future. Once a marketing channel is chosen, an organization usually must adhere to it for an extended period of time.

But as indicated in the E-Commerce Perspective, furniture manufacturers are now selling direct to consumers to the dismay of their brick-and-mortar distributors. However, Federated Stores is one of many brick-and-mortar firms pulling back from Internet operations. Federated is substantially reducing its macys.com and its bloomingdales.com Internet catalog operations. Federated has found that customers shopping online are most comfortable buying hard goods, such as jewelry and gifts, than apparel. These two Federated Web sites have never been profitable, but they still remain in operation, primarily as marketing sites. Other traditional retailers are scaling back their Internet operations, including Kmart with **bluelight.com** and Wal-Mart with **walmart.com**, as well as Toys R Us and Saks Fifth Avenue.

Marketing Research

Marketing research is the systematic gathering, recording, and analyzing of data about problems relating to the marketing of goods and services. Marketing research can uncover critical strengths and weaknesses, and marketing researchers employ numerous scales, instruments, procedures, concepts, and techniques to gather information. Marketing research activities support all of the major business functions of an organization. Organizations that possess excellent marketing research skills have a definite strength in pursuing generic strategies.

> The President of PepsiCo [said], "Looking at the competition is the company's best form of market research. The majority of our strategic successes are ideas that we borrow from the marketplace, usually from a small regional or local competitor. In each case, we spot a promising new idea, improve on it, and then out-execute our competitor."[18]

E-COMMERCE PERSPECTIVE

E-Stores Replacing Brick Stores

Like many industries, retail furniture stores nationwide are intensely debating whether the Internet will destroy their business or simply add another small sales channel. Furniture retailers nationwide are demanding assurance from furniture suppliers (manufacturers) that discount Internet retailers will not be supplied with their same furniture brands. The furniture industry is crazed over this subject. Some analysts contend that all furniture stores in the United States will disappear and some say Internet furniture sales will actually spur retail furniture sales. The furniture manufacturer, Stanley Furniture Company in Stanleytown, Virginia, decided to sell its products on the Internet, but after a month of loud protests from its retail distributors, Stanley banned all online sales of its products. But two other big furniture makers, Ethan Allan Interiors in Danbury, Connecticut, and La-Z-Boy Inc. in Monroe, Michigan, both plan to distribute their products online in "cooperation" with their retailers. The nation's largest furniture manufacturer with 9 percent of the market, Furniture Brands, in St. Louis, contends that people will want to "see and touch" before purchasing furniture. However, an increasing number of discount online furniture companies, such as Benchmark Industries in Olathe,

Kansas, and JCPenney of Plano, Texas, now offer furniture online. Online furniture sales are expected to increase to nearly $4 billion by 2004 from $0.5 billion in 2000, representing a market share increase from 0.75 to 5.0.

Gone are the days when furniture stores had a geographically captive customer, when merchants had the advantage of being the only store within driving distance, and when only the merchants knew the actual costs of their brands being sold. Using the Internet, the next furniture store is only seconds away for customers. and it is open twenty-four hours a day. Cybershoppers research furniture brands and prices from any computer, anywhere, and make their purchase(s) with the click of a mouse. Various Web sites now do the furniture research for the customer. This approach is garnering an ever-increasing number of furniture customers. Traditional brick-and-mortar furniture stores must offer superior customer service, low prices, and more to have a chance to compete in this market.

Source: Adapted from James, Hagerty, "Furniture Brands May Have to Rethink Its Web Policy," *The Wall Street Journal* September 14, 1999: B4.

About twenty thousand new products are introduced by U.S. companies annually, but 85 percent of these fail within three years. Many CEOs continue to trust their own best judgment over market research; this mindset can be detrimental to a business. For example, the Greyhound Bus Company first pursued the African American market by advertising on African American radio stations. However, instead of creating a new commercial, Greyhound used its popular country & western music ad, which later was considered to have failed in that market.

OPPORTUNITY ANALYSIS

The eighth function of marketing is *opportunity analysis,* which involves assessing the costs, benefits, and risks associated with marketing decisions. Three steps are required to perform a *cost/benefit analysis:* (1) compute the total costs associated with a decision, (2) estimate the total benefits from the decision, and (3) compare the total costs with the total benefits. When expected benefits exceed total costs, an opportunity becomes more attractive. Sometimes the variables included in a cost/benefit analysis cannot be quantified or even measured, but usually reasonable estimates can be made to allow the analysis to be performed. One key factor to be considered is risk. Cost/benefit analyses should also be performed when a company is evaluating alternative ways to be socially responsible.

Marketing Audit Checklist of Questions

The following questions about marketing, much like the earlier questions for management, are pertinent:

1. Are markets segmented effectively?
2. Is the organization positioned well among competitors?
3. Has the firm's market share been increasing?
4. Are present channels of distribution reliable and cost-effective?
5. Does the firm have an effective sales organization?
6. Does the firm conduct market research?
7. Are product quality and customer service good?
8. Are the firm's products and services priced appropriately?
9. Does the firm have an effective promotion, advertising, and publicity strategy?
10. Are marketing, planning, and budgeting effective?
11. Do the firm's marketing managers have adequate experience and training?

FINANCE/ACCOUNTING

Financial condition is often considered the single best measure of a firm's competitive position and overall attractiveness to investors. Determining an organization's financial strengths and weaknesses is essential to formulating strategies effectively. A firm's liquidity, leverage, working capital, profitability, asset utilization, cash flow, and equity can eliminate some strategies as being feasible alternatives. Financial factors often alter existing strategies and change implementation plans.

An especially good Web site to obtain financial information about a company is **www.quicken.com**, which provides excellent financial ratio, stock, and valuation information on all publicly held companies. Simply insert the company's stock symbol when the screen first loads and a wealth of information follows. Another nice site for obtaining financial information is **www.forbes.com**. Be sure to access the Manufacturing and Service section of **www.strategy club.com** for excellent financial-related Web sites.

Finance/Accounting Functions

According to James Van Horne, the *functions of finance/accounting* comprise three decisions: the investment decision, the financing decision, and the dividend decision.[19] Financial ratio analysis is the most widely used method for determining an organization's strengths and weaknesses in the investment, financing, and dividend areas. Because the functional areas of business are so closely related, financial ratios can signal strengths or weaknesses in management, marketing, production, research and development, and management information systems activities.

The *investment decision*, also called *capital budgeting*, is the allocation and reallocation of capital and resources to projects, products, assets, and divisions of an organization. Once strategies are formulated, capital budgeting decisions are required to implement strategies successfully. The *financing decision* determines the best capital structure for the firm and includes examining various methods by which the firm can raise capital (for example, by issuing stock, increasing debt, selling assets, or using a combination of these approaches). The financing decision must consider both short-term and long-term needs for working capital. Two key financial ratios that indicate whether a firm's financing decisions have been effective are the debt-to-equity ratio and the debt-to-total-assets ratio.

Dividend decisions concern issues such as the percentage of earnings paid to stockholders, the stability of dividends paid over time, and the repurchase or issuance of stock. Dividend decisions determine the amount of funds that are retained in a firm compared to the amount paid out to stockholders. Three financial ratios that are helpful in evaluating a firm's dividend decisions are the earnings-per-share ratio, the dividends-per-share ratio, and the price-earnings ratio. The benefits of paying dividends to investors must be balanced against the benefits of retaining funds internally, and there is no set formula on how to balance this trade-off. For the reasons listed here, dividends are sometimes paid out even when funds could be better reinvested in the business or when the firm has to obtain outside sources of capital:

1. Paying cash dividends is customary. Failure to do so could be thought of as a stigma. A dividend change is considered a signal about the future.
2. Dividends represent a sales point for investment bankers. Some institutional investors can buy only dividend-paying stocks.
3. Shareholders often demand dividends, even in companies with great opportunities for reinvesting all available funds.
4. A myth exists that paying dividends will result in a higher stock price.

Many companies, such as Xerox, have recently suspended paying dividends due to consistently falling revenues and earnings.

Basic Types of Financial Ratios

Financial ratios are computed from an organization's income statement and balance sheet. Computing financial ratios is like taking a picture because the results reflect a situation at just one point in time. Comparing ratios over time and to industry averages is

FIGURE 4–2

A Financial Ratio Trend Analysis

Current ratio

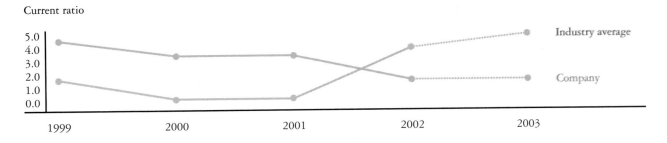

Profit margin
(percent)

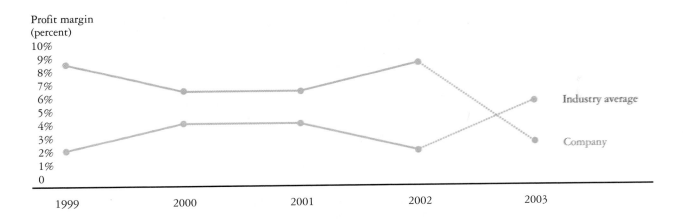

more likely to result in meaningful statistics that can be used to identify and evaluate strengths and weaknesses. Trend analysis, illustrated in Figure 4–2, is a useful technique that incorporates both the time and industry average dimensions of financial ratios. Note that the dotted lines reveal projected ratios. Some Web sites, such as Wall Street Research Net at **www.wsrn.com**, calculate financial ratios and provide data with charts. Four major sources of industry-average financial ratios follow:

1. Dun & Bradstreet's *Industry Norms and Key Business Ratios*—Fourteen different ratios are calculated in an industry-average format for eight hundred different types of businesses. The ratios are presented by Standard Industrial Classification (SIC) number and are grouped by annual sales into three size categories.

2. Robert Morris Associates' *Annual Statement Studies*—Sixteen different ratios are calculated in an industry-average format. Industries are referenced by SIC numbers published by the Bureau of the Census. The ratios are presented in four size categories by annual sales for all firms in the industry.

3. *Almanac of Business & Industrial Financial Ratios*—Twenty-two financial ratios and percentages are provided in an industry-average format for all major industries. The ratios and percentages are given for twelve different company-size categories for all firms in a given industry.

VISIT THE NET

Click on the showcase site at bottom, then enter your stock symbol in upper right, and then scroll down left column to the financial ratio comparison and click.
http://www.stockpoint.com

4. *Federal Trade Commission Reports*—The FTC publishes quarterly financial data, including ratios on manufacturing companies. FTC reports include analyses by industry group and asset size.

Table 4–4 provides a summary of key financial ratios showing how each ratio is calculated and what each ratio measures. However, all the ratios are not significant for all industries and companies. For example, accounts receivable turnover and average collection period are not very meaningful to a company that primarily does a cash receipts business. Key financial ratios can be classified into the following five types:

1. *Liquidity ratios* measure a firm's ability to meet maturing short-term obligations.

    Current ratio
    Quick (or acid-test) ratio

2. *Leverage ratios* measure the extent to which a firm has been financed by debt.
    Debt-to-total-assets ratio
    Debt-to-equity ratio
    Long-term debt-to-equity ratio
    Times-interest-earned (or coverage) ratio

3. *Activity ratios* measure how effectively a firm is using its resources.
    Inventory-turnover
    Fixed assets turnover
    Total assets turnover
    Accounts receivable turnover
    Average collection period

4. *Profitability ratios* measure management's overall effectiveness as shown by the returns generated on sales and investment.
    Gross profit margin
    Operating profit margin
    Net profit margin
    Return on total assets (ROA)
    Return on stockholders' equity (ROE)
    Earnings per share (EPS)
    Price-earnings ratio

5. *Growth ratios* measure the firm's ability to maintain its economic position in the growth of the economy and industry.
    Sales
    Net income
    Earnings per share
    Dividends per share

Financial ratio analysis is not without some limitations. First of all, financial ratios are based on accounting data, and firms differ in their treatment of such items as depreciation, inventory valuation, research and development expenditures, pension plan costs, mergers, and taxes. Also, seasonal factors can influence comparative ratios. Therefore, conformity to industry composite ratios does not establish with certainty that a firm is performing normally or that it is well managed. Likewise, departures from industry averages do not always indicate that a firm is doing especially well or badly. For example, a high inventory turnover ratio could indicate efficient inventory management and a strong working capital position, but it also could indicate a serious inventory shortage and a weak working capital position.

TABLE 4-4   A Summary of Key Financial Ratios

RATIO	HOW CALCULATED	WHAT IT MEASURES
Liquidity Ratios		
Current Ratio	$\dfrac{\text{Current assets}}{\text{Current liabilities}}$	The extent to which a firm can meet its short-term obligations
Quick Ratio	$\dfrac{\text{Current assets minus inventory}}{\text{Current liabilities}}$	The extent to which a firm can meet its short-term obligations without relying upon the sale of its inventories
Leverage Ratios		
Debt-to-Total-Assets Ratio	$\dfrac{\text{Total debt}}{\text{Total assets}}$	The percentage of total funds that are provided by creditors
Debt-to-Equity Ratio	$\dfrac{\text{Total debt}}{\text{Total stockholders' equity}}$	The percentage of total funds provided by creditors versus by owners
Long-Term Debt-to-Equity Ratio	$\dfrac{\text{Long-term debt}}{\text{Total stockholders' equity}}$	The balance between debt and equity in a firm's long-term capital structure
Times-Interest-Earned Ratio	$\dfrac{\text{Profits before interest and taxes}}{\text{Total interest charges}}$	The extent to which earnings can decline without the firm becoming unable to meet its annual interest costs
Activity Ratios		
Inventory Turnover	$\dfrac{\text{Sales}}{\text{Inventory of finished goods}}$	Whether a firm holds excessive stocks of inventories and whether a firm is selling its inventories slowly compared to the industry average
Fixed Assets Turnover	$\dfrac{\text{Sales}}{\text{Fixed assets}}$	Sales productivity and plant and equipment utilization
Total Assets Turnover	$\dfrac{\text{Sales}}{\text{Total assets}}$	Whether a firm is generating a sufficient volume of business for the size of its asset investment
Accounts Receivable Turnover	$\dfrac{\text{Annual credit sales}}{\text{Accounts receivable}}$	The average length of time it takes a firm to collect credit sales (in percentage terms)
Average Collection Period	$\dfrac{\text{Accounts receivable}}{\text{Total credit sales/365 days}}$	The average length of time it takes a firm to collect on credit sales (in days)
Profitability Ratios		
Gross Profit Margin	$\dfrac{\text{Sales minus cost of goods sold}}{\text{Sales}}$	The total margin available to cover operating expenses and yield a profit
Operating Profit Margin	$\dfrac{\text{Earnings before interest and taxes (EBIT)}}{\text{Sales}}$	Profitability without concern for taxes and interest
Net Profit Margin	$\dfrac{\text{Net income}}{\text{Sales}}$	After-tax profits per dollar of sales
Return on Total Assets (ROA)	$\dfrac{\text{Net income}}{\text{Total assets}}$	After-tax profits per dollar of assets; this ratio is also called return on investment (ROI)
Return on Stockholders' Equity (ROE)	$\dfrac{\text{Net income}}{\text{Total stockholders' equity}}$	After-tax profits per dollar of stockholders' investment in the firm
Earnings Per Share (EPS)	$\dfrac{\text{Net income}}{\text{Number of shares of common stock outstanding}}$	Earnings available to the owners of common stock
Price-earnings Ratio	$\dfrac{\text{Market price per share}}{\text{Earnings per share}}$	Attractiveness of firm on equity markets
Growth Ratios		
Sales	Annual percentage growth in total sales	Firm's growth rate in sales
Net Income	Annual percentage growth in profits	Firm's growth rate in profits
Earnings Per Share	Annual percentage growth in EPS	Firm's growth rate in EPS
Dividends Per Share	Annual percentage growth in dividends per share	Firm's growth rate in dividends per share

It is important to recognize that a firm's financial condition depends not only on the functions of finance, but also on many other factors that include (1) management, marketing, management production/operations, research and development, and management information systems decisions; (2) actions by competitors, suppliers, distributors, creditors, customers, and shareholders; and (3) economic, social, cultural, demographic, environmental, political, governmental, legal, and technological trends. Even natural environment liabilities can affect financial ratios, as indicated in the Natural Environment Perspective. So financial ratio analysis, like all other analytical tools, should be used wisely.

Finance/Accounting Audit Checklist of Questions

The following finance/accounting questions, like the similar questions about marketing and management earlier, should be examined:

1. Where is the firm financially strong and weak as indicated by financial ratio analyses?
2. Can the firm raise needed short-term capital?
3. Can the firm raise needed long-term capital through debt and/or equity?
4. Does the firm have sufficient working capital?
5. Are capital budgeting procedures effective?
6. Are dividend payout policies reasonable?

NATURAL ENVIRONMENT PERSPECTIVE

Environmental Liability on the Balance Sheet

Environmental liability may be the largest recognized or unrecognized liability on a company's balance sheet. More American firms are finding themselves liable for cleanup costs and damages stemming from waste disposal practices of the past—in some cases going back 100 years. Environmental liabilities associated with air and water pollution, habitat destruction, deforestation, and medical problems can be immense. For this reason, many financial institutions now inquire about environmental liabilities as part of their commercial lending procedures. Firms such as American Insurance Company specialize in providing environmental liability insurance to companies.

Environmental Protection Agency (EPA) regulations take up more than 11,000 pages; they vary with location and size of firm and are added to daily. The complexity of these regulations can translate into liabilities for the environmentally reactive firm. Proactive firms, on the other hand, are adding a "green executive" and department to oversee management of environmental policies and practices of the

firm. The responsibility of green executives includes thinking through environmental regulations, marketing needs, public attitudes, consumer demands, and potential problems. Ideally, green executives should promote development of a corporate culture in which all managers and employees become "green," or environmentally sensitive. Such a culture would represent an internal strength to the firm.

The September 11, 2001, terrorist attacks and the global war on terrorism accents the need for companies to include antibiological and antichemical terrorism expenses on the firm's financial statements. Thousands of businesses today are upgrading security measures to safeguard their operations, employees, and customers from possible terrorist attacks on the natural environment.

Source: Adapted from Laura Johannes and Marilyn Chase, "Experts Say Bioterrorism Threat Is Real, Yet Likelihood Is Uncertain," *Wall Street Journal* (September 28, 2001): B1 and B6. See also Ted Bridis, "State of the Union: America the Vulnerable?" *Wall Street Journal* (September 28, 2001): B1 and B4.

7. Does the firm have good relations with its investors and stockholders?

8. Are the firm's financial managers experienced and well trained?

PRODUCTION/OPERATIONS

The *production/operations function* of a business consists of all those activities that transform inputs into goods and services. Production/operations management deals with inputs, transformations, and outputs that vary across industries and markets. A manufacturing operation transforms or converts inputs such as raw materials, labor, capital, machines, and facilities into finished goods and services. As indicated in Table 4–5, Roger Schroeder suggested that production/operations management comprises five functions or decision areas: process, capacity, inventory, workforce, and quality.

Most automakers require a thirty-day notice to build vehicles, but Toyota Motor fills a buyer's new car order in just five days. Honda Motor was considered the industry's fastest producer, filling orders in fifteen days. Automakers have for years operated under just-in-time inventory systems, but Toyota's 360 suppliers are linked to the company via computers on a virtual assembly line. The new Toyota production system was developed in the company's Cambridge, Ontario, plant and now applies to its Solara, Camry, Corolla, and Tacoma vehicles.

Capacity utilization for light trucks in the automobile industry has dropped from 107 percent in 2000 to an expected 75 percent in 2005, due to oversupply and falling demand. Light trucks, which include SUVs, minivans, and pickups, accounted for nearly all the profits for Ford, DaimlerChrysler, and General Motors in 2000 and 2001. These American automobile producers have been slow to upgrade their car models, and consequently, foreign makes of cars now comprise more than half of the market share for all

TABLE 4–5   The Basic Functions of Production Management

FUNCTION	DESCRIPTION
1. Process	Process decisions concern the design of the physical production system. Specific decisions include choice of technology, facility layout, process flow analysis, facility location, line balancing, process control, and transportation analysis.
2. Capacity	Capacity decisions concern determination of optimal output levels for the organization—not too much and not too little. Specific decisions include forecasting, facilities planning, aggregate planning, scheduling, capacity planning, and queuing analysis.
3. Inventory	Inventory decisions involve managing the level of raw materials, work-in-process, and finished goods. Specific decisions include what to order, when to order, how much to order, and materials handling.
4. Workforce	Workforce decisions are concerned with managing the skilled, unskilled, clerical, and managerial employees. Specific decisions include job design, work measurement, job enrichment, work standards, and motivation techniques.
5. Quality	Quality decisions are aimed at ensuring that high-quality goods and services are produced. Specific decisions include quality control, sampling, testing, quality assurance, and cost control.

Source: Adapted from R. Schroeder, *Operations Management* (New York: McGraw-Hill Book Co., 1981): 12.

cars sold in the United States. For example, General Motors is selling Saturns with an eleven-year-old design and Chevrolet Cavaliers with a seven-year-old one—and complaining that they're unprofitable.[20] In contrast, Volkswagen, Toyota, and Honda all have redesigned Beetles, Corollas, and Civics, respectively, and all of these models are profitable.

All domestic automobile makers are closing plants due to slowing consumer demand for most models of cars and trucks. The movement of supplies and parts needed for automobile manufacturing has slowed dramatically as some analysts even question whether just-in-time inventory control will ever again be the norm given shipment delays along the United States-Mexican border.

Production/operations activities often represent the largest part of an organization's human and capital assets. In most industries, the major costs of producing a product or service are incurred within operations, so production/operations can have great value as a competitive weapon in a company's overall strategy. Strengths and weaknesses in the five functions of production can mean the success or failure of an enterprise.

Many production/operations managers are finding that cross-training of employees can help their firms respond to changing markets faster. Cross-training of workers can increase efficiency, quality, productivity, and job satisfaction. For example, at General Motors's Detroit gear & axle plant, costs related to product defects were reduced 400 percent in two years as a result of cross-training workers. A shortage of qualified labor in America is another reason cross-training is becoming a common management practice.

Singapore rivals Hong Kong as an attractive site for locating production facilities in Southeast Asia. Singapore is a city-state near Malaysia. An island nation of about four million, Singapore is changing from an economy built on trade and services to one built upon information technology. A large-scale program in computer education for older (over twenty-six-year-old) residents is very popular. Singapore children receive outstanding computer training in schools. All government services are computerized nicely. Singapore lures multinational businesses with great tax breaks, world-class infrastructure, excellent courts that handle business disputes efficiently, exceptionally low tariffs, large land giveaways, impressive industrial parks, excellent port facilities, and a government very receptive to and cooperative with foreign businesses. Foreign firms now account for 70 percent of manufacturing output in Singapore.

There is much reason for concern that many organizations have not taken sufficient account of the capabilities and limitations of the production/operations function in formulating strategies. Scholars contend that this neglect has had unfavorable consequences on corporate performance in America. As shown in Table 4–6, James Dilworth outlined several types of strategic decisions that a company might make with production/operations implications of those decisions. Production capabilities and policies can also greatly affect strategies.

Production/Operations Audit
Checklist of Questions

Questions such as the following should be examined:

1. Are supplies of raw materials, parts, and subassemblies reliable and reasonable?
2. Are facilities, equipment, machinery, and offices in good condition?
3. Are inventory-control policies and procedures effective?
4. Are quality-control policies and procedures effective?
5. Are facilities, resources, and markets strategically located?
6. Does the firm have technological competencies?

TABLE 4-6   **Impact of Strategy Elements on Production Management**

POSSIBLE ELEMENTS OF STRATEGY	CONCOMITANT CONDITIONS THAT MAY AFFECT THE OPERATIONS FUNCTION AND ADVANTAGES AND DISADVANTAGES
1. Compete as low-cost provider of goods or services	Discourages competition Broadens market Requires longer production runs and fewer product changes Requires special-purpose equipment and facilities
2. Compete as high-quality provider	Often possible to obtain more total profit from a smaller volume of sales Requires more quality-assurance effort and higher operating cost Requires more precise equipment, which is more expensive Requires highly skilled workers, necessitating higher wages and greater training efforts
3. Stress customer service	Requires broader development of servicepeople and service parts and equipment Requires rapid response to customer needs or changes in customer tastes, rapid and accurate information system, careful coordination Requires a higher inventory investment
4. Provide rapid and frequent introduction of new products	Requires versatile equipment and people Has higher research and development costs Has high retraining costs and high tooling and changeover in manufacturing Provides lower volumes for each product and fewer opportunities for improvements due to the learning curve
5. Strive for absolute growth	Requires accepting some projects or products with lower marginal value, which reduces ROI Diverts talents to areas of weakness instead of concentrating on strengths
6. Seek vertical integration	Enables company to control more of the process May not have economies of scale at some stages of process May require high capital investment as well as technology and skills beyond those currently available within the organization
7. Maintain reserve capacity for flexibility	Provides ability to meet peak demands and quickly implement some contingency plans if forecasts are too low Requires capital investment in idle capacity Provides capability to grow during the lead time normally required for expansion
8. Consolidate processing (Centralize)	Can result in economies of scale Can locate near one major customer or supplier Vulnerability: one strike, fire, or flood can halt the entire operation
9. Disperse processing of service (Decentralize)	Can be near several market territories Requires more complex coordination network: perhaps expensive data transmission and duplication of some personnel and equipment at each location If each location produces one product in the line, then other products still must be transported to be available at all locations If each location specializes in a type of component for all products, the company is vulnerable to strike, fire, flood, etc. If each location provides total product line, then economies of scale may not be realized
10. Stress the use of mechanization, automation, robots	Requires high capital investment Reduces flexibility May affect labor relations Makes maintenance more crucial
11. Stress stability of employment	Serves the security needs of employees and may develop employee loyalty Helps to attract and retain highly skilled employees May require revisions of make-or-buy decisions, use of idle time, inventory, and subcontractors as demand fluctuates

RESEARCH AND DEVELOPMENT

The fifth major area of internal operations that should be examined for specific strengths and weaknesses is *research and development* (R&D). Many firms today conduct no R&D, and yet many other companies depend on successful R&D activities for survival. Firms pursuing a product development strategy especially need to have a strong R&D orientation.

Organizations invest in R&D because they believe that such an investment will lead to a superior product or services and will give them competitive advantages. Research and development expenditures are directed at developing new products before competitors do at improving product quality, or at improving manufacturing processes to reduce costs.

Effective management of the R&D function requires a strategic and operational partnership between R&D and the other vital business functions. A spirit of partnership and mutual trust between general and R&D managers is evident in the best-managed firms today. Managers in these firms jointly explore; assess; and decide the what, when, where, why, and how much of R&D. Priorities, costs, benefits, risks, and rewards associated with R&D activities are discussed openly and shared. The overall mission of R&D thus has become broad-based, including supporting existing businesses, helping launch new businesses, developing new products, improving product quality, improving manufacturing efficiency, and deepening or broadening the company's technological capabilities.[21]

The best-managed firms today seek to organize R&D activities in a way that breaks the isolation of R&D from the rest of the company and promotes a spirit of partnership between R&D managers and other managers in the firm. R&D decisions and plans must be integrated and coordinated across departments and divisions by having the departments share experiences and information. The strategic-management process facilitates this cross-functional approach to managing the R&D function.

Internal and External R&D

Cost distributions among R&D activities vary by company and industry, but total R&D costs generally do not exceed manufacturing and marketing startup costs. Four approaches to determining R&D budget allocations commonly are used: (1) financing as many project proposals as possible, (2) using a percentage-of-sales method, (3) budgeting about the same amount that competitors spend for R&D, or (4) deciding how many successful new products are needed and working backward to estimate the required R&D investment.

R&D in organizations can take two basic forms: (1) internal R&D, in which an organization operates its own R&D department, and/or (2) contract R&D, in which a firm hires independent researchers or independent agencies to develop specific products. Many companies use both approaches to develop new products. A widely used approach for obtaining outside R&D assistance is to pursue a joint venture with another firm. R&D strengths (capabilities) and weaknesses (limitations) play a major role in strategy formulation and strategy implementation.

Most firms have no choice but to continually develop new and improved products because of changing consumer needs and tastes, new technologies, shortened product life cycles, and increased domestic and foreign competition. A shortage of ideas for new products, increased global competition, increased market segmentation, strong special-interest groups, and increased government regulation are several factors making the successful development of new products more and more difficult, costly, and risky. In the pharmaceutical industry, for example, only one out of every few thousand drugs created in the laboratory ends up on pharmacists' shelves. Scarpello, Boulton, and Hofer emphasized that different strategies require different R&D capabilities:

> The focus of R&D efforts can vary greatly depending on a firm's competitive strategy. Some corporations attempt to be market leaders and innovators of new products, while others are satisfied to be market followers and developers of currently available products. The basic skills required to support these strategies will vary, depending on whether R&D becomes the driving force behind competitive strategy. In cases where new product introduction is the driving force for strategy, R&D activities must be extensive. The R&D unit must then be able to advance scientific and technological knowledge, exploit that knowledge, and manage the risks associated with ideas, products, services, and production requirements.[22]

Motorola recently announced that it had figured out how to combine silicon and gallium arsenide in one semiconductor chip. The company said this discovery will greatly reduce manufacturing process costs and result in smaller, faster products. The discovery is expected to yield products by the end of 2003 and may lead to cellphones as small as shirt buttons.

Intel and Microsoft are continuing to increase their expenditures on research and development. Intel spent just over $4 billion on R&D in 2001, nearly 15 percent of sales, while Microsoft spent $4.8 billion, up 37 percent from two years earlier. Both companies expect to increase R&D spending an additional $500 million in 2002. Intel is developing more powerful and smaller chips to power computers, while Microsoft is improving its Windows XP operating system.

Research and Development Audit Checklist of Questions

Questions such as the following should be asked in performing an R&D audit:

1. Does the firm have R&D facilities? Are they adequate?
2. If outside R&D firms are used, are they cost-effective?
3. Are the organization's R&D personnel well qualified?
4. Are R&D resources allocated effectively?
5. Are management information and computer systems adequate?
6. Is communication between R&D and other organizational units effective?
7. Are present products technologically competitive?

MANAGEMENT INFORMATION SYSTEMS

Information ties all business functions together and provides the basis for all managerial decisions. It is the cornerstone of all organizations. Information represents a major source of competitive management advantage or disadvantage. Assessing a firm's internal strengths and weaknesses in information systems is a critical dimension of performing an internal audit. The company motto of Mitsui, a large Japanese trading company, is "Information is the lifeblood of the company." A satellite network connects Mitsui's 200 worldwide offices.

A management information system's purpose is to improve the performance of an enterprise by improving the quality of managerial decisions. An effective information system thus collects, codes, stores, synthesizes, and presents information in such a manner that it answers important operating and strategic questions. The heart of an information system is a database containing the kinds of records and data important to managers.

A *management information system* receives raw material from both the external and internal evaluation of an organization. It gathers data about marketing, finance, production, and personnel matters internally, and social, cultural, demographic, environmental, economic, political, governmental legal, technological, and competitive factors externally. Data are integrated in ways needed to support managerial decision making.

There is a logical flow of material in a computer information system, whereby data is input to the system and transformed into output. Outputs include computer printouts, written reports, tables, chairs, graphs, checks, purchase orders, invoices, inventory records, payroll accounts, and a variety of other documents. Payoffs from alternative strategies can be calculated and estimated. *Data* become *information* only when they are evaluated, filtered, condensed, analyzed, and organized for a specific purpose, problem, individual, or time.

An effective management information system utilizes computer hardware, software, models for analysis, and a database. Some people equate information systems with the advent of the computer, but historians have traced recordkeeping and noncomputer data processing to Babylonian merchants living in 3500 B.C. Benefits of an effective information system include an improved understanding of business functions, improved communications, more informed decision making, a better analysis of problems, and improved control.

Because organizations are becoming more complex, decentralized, and globally dispersed, the function of information systems is growing in importance. Spurring this advance is the falling cost and increasing power of computers. There are costs and benefits associated with obtaining and evaluating information, just as with equipment and land. Like equipment, information can become obsolete and may need to be purged from the system. An effective information system is like a library, collecting, categorizing, and filing data for use by managers throughout the organization. Information systems are a major strategic resource, monitoring environmental changes, identifying competitive threats, and assisting in the implementation, evaluation, and control of strategy.

We are truly in an information age. Firms whose information-system skills are weak are at a competitive disadvantage. On the other hand, strengths in information systems allow firms to establish distinctive competencies in other areas. Low-cost manufacturing and good customer service, for example, can depend on a good information system.

A good executive information system provides graphic, tabulate, and textual information. Graphic capabilities are needed so current conditions and trends can be examined quickly; tables provide greater detail and enable variance analyses; textual information adds insight and interpretation to data.

Most companies today use the Internet to connect with their employees, their customers, and their suppliers. Now companies are using technology to drive better customer relationships, create new revenue streams, offer innovative services, and generate greater efficiencies.

Strategic Planning Software

Some strategic decision support systems, however, are too sophisticated, expensive, or restrictive to be used easily by managers in a firm. This is unfortunate because the strategic-management process must be a people process to be successful. People make the difference! Strategic planning software should thus be simple and unsophisticated. Simplicity allows wide participation among managers in a firm and participation is essential for effective strategy implementation.

One strategic-planning software product that parallels this text and offers managers and executives a simple yet effective approach for developing organizational strategies is *CheckMATE*. This personal computer software performs planning analyses and generates strategies a firm could pursue. *CheckMATE* incorporates the most modern strategic planning techniques. No previous experience with computers or knowledge of strategic planning is required of the user. *CheckMATE* thus promotes communication, understanding, creativity, and forward thinking among users.

CheckMATE is not a spreadsheet program or database; it is an expert system that carries a firm through strategy formulation and implementation. A major strength of the new 2002 version of *CheckMATE* strategic-planning software is its simplicity and participative approach. The user is asked appropriate questions, responses are recorded, information is assimilated, and results are printed. Individuals can work through the software independently and then the program will develop joint recommendations for the firm.

Specific analytical procedures included in the *CheckMATE* program are Strategic Position and Action Evaluation (SPACE) analysis, Threats-Opportunities-Weaknesses-Strengths (TOWS) analysis, Internal-External (IE) analysis, and Grand Strategy Matrix analysis. These widely used strategic-planning analyses are described in Chapter 6.

An individual license for *CheckMATE* costs $995. More information about *CheckMATE* can be obtained at **www.checkmateplan.com** or 843-669-6960 (phone).

Management Information Systems Audit
Checklist of Questions

Questions such as the following should be asked when conducting this audit:

1. Do all managers in the firm use the information system to make decisions?
2. Is there a chief information officer or director of information systems position in the firm?
3. Are data in the information system updated regularly?
4. Do managers from all functional areas of the firm contribute input to the information system?
5. Are there effective passwords for entry into the firm's information system?
6. Are strategists of the firm familiar with the information systems of rival firms?
7. Is the information system user-friendly?
8. Do all users of the information system understand the competitive advantages that information can provide firms?
9. Are computer training workshops provided for users of the information system?
10. Is the firm's information system continually being improved in content and user-friendliness?

THE INTERNAL FACTOR EVALUATION (IFE) MATRIX

A summary step in conducting an internal strategic-management audit is to construct an *Internal Factor Evaluation (IFE) Matrix*. This strategy-formulation tool summarizes and evaluates the major strengths and weaknesses in the functional areas of a business, and it also provides a basis for identifying and evaluating relationships among those areas. Intuitive judgments are required in developing an IFE Matrix, so the appearance of a scientific approach should not be interpreted to mean this is an all-powerful technique. A thorough understanding of the factors included is more important than the actual numbers. Similar to the EFE Matrix and Competitive Profile Matrix described in Chapter 3, an IFE Matrix can be developed in five steps:

1. List key internal factors as identified in the internal-audit process. Use a total of from ten to twenty internal factors, including both strengths and weaknesses. List strengths first and then weakness. Be as specific as possible, using percentages, ratios, and comparative numbers.

2. Assign a weight that ranges from 0.0 (not important) to 1.0 (all-important) to each factor. The weight assigned to a given factor indicates the relative importance of the factor to being successful in the firm's industry. Regardless of whether a key factor is an internal strength or weakness, factors considered to have the greatest effect on organizational performance should be assigned the highest weights. The sum of all weights must equal 1.0.

3. Assign a 1-to-4 rating to each factor to indicate whether that factor represents a major weakness (rating = 1), a minor weakness (rating = 2), a minor strength (rating = 3), or a major strength (rating = 4). Note that strengths must receive a 4 or 3 rating and weaknesses must receive a 1 or 2 rating. Ratings are thus company-based, whereas the weights in Step 2 are industry-based.

4. Multiply each factor's weight by its rating to determine a weighted score for each variable.

5. Sum the weighted scores for each variable to determine the total weighted score for the organization.

Regardless of how many factors are included in an IFE Matrix, the total weighted score can range from a low of 1.0 to a high of 4.0, with the average score being 2.5. Total weighted scores well below 2.5 characterize organizations that are weak internally, whereas scores significantly above 2.5 indicate a strong internal position. Like the EFE Matrix, an IFE Matrix should include from 10 to 20 key factors. The number of factors has no effect upon the range of total weighted scores because the weights always sum to 1.0.

When a key internal factor is both a strength and a weakness, the factor should be included twice in the IFE Matrix, and a weight and rating should be assigned to each statement. For example, the Playboy logo both helps and hurts Playboy Enterprises; the logo attracts customers *Playboy* magazine, but it keeps the Playboy cable channel out of many markets.

An example of an IFE Matrix for Mandalay Bay is provided in Table 4–7. Note that the firm's major strengths are its size, occupancy rates, property, and long-range planning as indicated by the rating of 4. The major weaknesses are locations and recent joint venture. The total weighted score of 2.75 indicates that this large gaming corporation is above average in its overall internal strength.

In multidivisional firms, each autonomous division or strategic business unit should construct an IFE Matrix. Divisional matrices then can be integrated to develop an overall corporate IFE Matrix.

CONCLUSION

Management, marketing, finance/accounting, production/operations, research and development, and management information systems represent the core operations of most businesses. A strategic-management audit of a firm's internal operations is vital to organizational health. Many companies still prefer to be judged solely on their bottom-line performance. However, an increasing number of successful organizations are using the internal audit to gain competitive advantages over rival firms.

Systematic methodologies for performing strength-weakness assessments are not well developed in the strategic-management literature, but it is clear that strategists

TABLE 4-7   A Sample Internal Factor Evaluation Matrix for Mandalay Bay

KEY INTERNAL FACTORS	WEIGHT	RATING	WEIGHTED SCORE
Internal Strengths			
1. Largest casino company in the United States	.05	4	.20
2. Room occupancy rates over 95% in Las Vegas	.10	4	.40
3. Increasing free cash flows	.05	3	.15
4. Owns one mile on Las Vegas Strip	.15	4	.60
5. Strong management team	.05	3	.15
6. Buffets at most facilities	.05	3	.15
7. Minimal comps provided	.05	3	.15
8. Long-range planning	.05	4	.20
9. Reputation as family-friendly	.05	3	.15
10. Financial ratios	.05	3	.15
Internal Weaknesses			
1. Most properties are located in Las Vegas	.05	1	.05
2. Little diversification	.05	2	.10
3. Family reputation, not high rollers	.05	2	.10
4. Laughlin properties	.10	1	.10
5. Recent loss of joint ventures	.10	1	.10
TOTAL	1.00		2.75

must identify and evaluate internal strengths and weaknesses in order to formulate and choose among alternative strategies effectively. The EFE Matrix, Competitive Profile Matrix, IFE Matrix, and clear statements of vision and mission provide the basic information needed to formulate competitive strategies successfully. The process of performing an internal audit represents an opportunity for managers and employees throughout the organization to participate in determining the future of the firm. Involvement in the process can energize and mobilize managers and employees.

We invite you to visit the David page on the Prentice Hall Companion Website at **www.prenhall.com/david** for this chapter's World Wide Web exercises.

KEY TERMS AND CONCEPTS

Activity Ratios (p. 140)

Capital Budgeting (p. 138)

Communication (p. 131)

Controlling (p. 132)

Cost/Benefit Analysis (p. 137)

Cultural Products (p. 123)

Customer Analysis (p. 133)

Distinctive Competencies (p. 120)

Distribution (p. 135)

Dividend Decision (p. 138)

Financial Ratio Analysis (p. 122)

Financing Decision (p. 138)

Functions of Finance/Accounting (p. 138)

Functions of Management (p. 128)

Functions of Marketing (p. 133)

Functions of Production/Operations (p. 143)

Growth Ratios (p. 140)

Human Resource Management (p. 132)

Internal Audit (p. 121)

Internal Factor Evaluation (IFE) Matrix (p. 149)

Investment Decision (p. 138)

Leverage Ratios (p. 140)

Liquidity Ratios (p. 140)

Management Information Systems (p. 148)

Marketing Research (p. 136)

Motivating (p. 131)

Opportunity Analysis (p. 137)

Organizational Culture (p. 123)

ISSUES FOR REVIEW AND DISCUSSION

1. Explain why prioritizing the relative importance of strengths and weaknesses in an IFE Matrix is an important strategic-management activity.

2. How can delegation of authority contribute to effective strategic management?

3. Diagram a formal organizational chart that reflects the following positions: a president, two executive officers, four middle managers, and eighteen lower-level managers. Now, diagram three overlapping and hypothetical informal group structures. How can this information be helpful to a strategist in formulating and implementing strategy?

4. How could a strategist's attitude toward social responsibility affect a firm's strategy? What is your attitude toward social responsibility?

5. Which of the three basic functions of finance/accounting do you feel is most important in a small electronics manufacturing concern? Justify your position.

6. Do you think aggregate R&D expenditures for American firms will increase or decrease next year? Why?

7. Explain how you would motivate managers and employees to implement a major new strategy.

8. Why do you think production/operations managers often are not directly involved in strategy-formulation activities? Why can this be a major organizational weakness?

9. Give two examples of staffing strengths and two examples of staffing weaknesses of an organization with which you are familiar.

10. Would you ever pay out dividends when your firm's annual net profit is negative? Why? What effect could this have on a firm's strategies?

11. If a firm has zero debt in its capital structure, is that always an organizational strength? Why or why not?

12. Describe the production/operations system in a police department.

13. After conducting an internal audit, a firm discovers a total of 100 strengths and 100 weaknesses. What procedures then could be used to determine the most important of these? Why is it important to reduce the total number of key factors?

14. Select one of the suggested readings at the end of this chapter. Look up that article, and give a five-minute oral report to the class that summarizes the article and your views on the topic.

15. Why do you believe cultural products affect all the functions of business?

16. Do you think cultural products affect strategy formulation, implementation, or evaluation the most? Why?

17. Identify cultural products at your college or university. Do these products, viewed collectively or separately, represent a strength or weakness for the organization?

18. Describe the management information system at your college or university.

19. Explain the difference between data and information in terms of each being useful to strategists.

20. What are the most important characteristics of an effective management information system?

NOTES

1. ROBERT GRANT, "The Resource-Based Theory of Competitive Advantage: Implications for Strategy Formulation," *California Management Review* (Spring 1991): 116.

2. Reprinted by permission of the publisher from "Integrating Strength-Weakness Analysis into Strategic Planning," by WILLIAM KING, *Journal of Business Research 2*, no. 4: p. 481. Copyright 1983 by Elsevier Science Publishing Co., Inc.

3. IGOR ANSOFF, "Strategic Management of Technology," *Journal of Business Strategy* 7, no. 3 (Winter 1987): 38.

4. CLAUDE GEORGE, JR., *The History of Management Thought*, 2nd ed. (Englewood Cliffs, N.J.: Prentice-Hall, 1972): 174.

5. EDGAR SCHEIN, *Organizational Culture and Leadership* (San Francisco: Jossey-Bass, 1985): 9.

6. JOHN LORSCH, "Managing Culture: The Invisible Barrier to Strategic Change," *California Management Review* 28, no. 2 (1986): 95–109.

7. Y. ALLARIE and M. FIRSIROTU, "How to Implement Radical Strategies in Large Organizations," *Sloan Management Review* (Spring 1985): 19.

8. JON ALSTON, "Wa, Guanxi, and Inhwa: Managerial Principles in Japan, China and Korea," *Business Horizons* 32, no. 2 (March–April 1989): 26.

9. ROSE KNOTTS, "Cross-Cultural Management: Transformations and Adaptations," *Business Horizons* (January–February 1989): 29–33.

10. http://www.mindtools.com/plfailpl.html

11. ADAM SMITH, *Wealth of Nations* (New York: Modern Library, 1937): 3–4.

12. RICHARD DAFT, *Management*, 3rd ed. (Orlando, FL: Dryden Press, 1993): 512.

13. SHELLEY KIRKPATRICK and EDWIN LOCKE, "Leadership: Do Traits Matter?" *Academy of Management Executive* 5, no. 2 (May 1991): 48.

14. PETER DRUCKER, *Management Tasks, Responsibilities, and Practice* (New York: Harper & Row, 1973): 463.

15. BRIAN DUMAINE, "What the Leaders of Tomorrow See," *Fortune* (July 3, 1989): 51.

16. J. EVANS and B. BERGMAN, *Marketing* (New York: Macmillan, 1982): 17.

17. Venessa O'Connell, "Ad-Spending Outlook Is Worsening," *Wall Street Journal* (September 4, 2001): B4.

18. Quoted in ROBERT WATERMAN, JR., "The Renewal Factor," *Business Week* (September 14, 1987): 108.

19. J. VAN HORNE, *Financial Management and Policy* (Englewood Cliffs, N.J.: Prentice-Hall, 1974): 10.

20. Robyn Meredith, "Paradise Lost," *Forbes* (May 28, 2001): 56.

21. PHILIP ROUSEBL, KAMAL SAAD, and TAMARA ERICKSON, "The Evolution of Third Generation R&D," *Planning Review* 19, no. 2 (March–April 1991): 18–26.

22. VIDA SCARPELLO, WILLIAM BOULTON, and CHARLES HOFER, "Reintegrating R&D into Business Strategy," *Journal of Business Strategy* 6, no. 4 (Spring 1986): 50, 51.

CURRENT READINGS

BAKER, WALTER, MIKE MARN, and CRAIG ZAWANDA. "Price Smarter on the Net." *Harvard Business Review* (February 2001): 122.

BEAL, REGINALD and MASOUD YASAI-ARDEKANI. "Performance Implications of Aligning CEO Functional Experiences with Competitive Strategies." *Journal of Management* 26, no. 4 (2000): 733.

BERNICK, CAROL LAVIN. "When Your Culture Needs a Makeover." *Harvard Business Review* (June 2001): 53.

DENIS, JEAN-LOUIS, LISE LAMOTHE, and ANN LANGLEY. "The Dynamics of Collective Leadership and Strategic Change in Pluralistic Organizations." *Academy of Management Journal* 44, no. 4 (August 2001): 809.

FAGENSON-ELAND, ELLEN. "The National Football League's Bill Parcells on Winning, Leading, and Turning Around Teams." *Academy of Management Executive* 15, no. 3 (August 2001): 48.

FORRESTER, RUSS. "Empowerment: Rejuvenating a Potent Idea." *Academy of Management Executive* 14, no. 3 (August 2000): 67.

GILBERT, JACQUELINE A. and JOHN M. IVANCEVICH. "Valuing Diversity: A Tale of Two Organizations." *Academy of Management Executive* 14, no. 1 (February 2000): 93.

GUPTA, ANIL K. and VIJAY GOVINDARAJAN. "Converting Global Presence into Global Competitive Advantage." *Academy of Management Executive* 15, no. 2 (May 2001): 45.

HEMPHILL, THOMAS A. "Airline Marketing Alliances and U.S. Competition Policy: Does the Consumer Benefit?" *Business Horizons* 43, no. 2 (March–April 2000): 17.

KING, ADELAIDE, SALLY FOWLER, and CARL ZEITHAML. "Managing Organizational Competencies for Competitive Advantage: The Middle-Management Edge." *Academy of Management Executive* 15, no. 2 (May 2001): 95.

KIRKMAN, BRADLEY L. and DEBRA L. SHAPIRO. "The Impact of Cultural Values on Job Satisfaction and Organizational Commitment in Self-Managing Work Teams: The Mediating Role of Employee Resistance." *Academy of Management Journal* 44, no. 3 (June 2001): 557.

LUO, Y. and S. H. PARK. "Strategic Alignment and Performance of Market-Seeking MNC's in China." *Strategic Management Journal* 22, no. 2 (February 2001): 141.

PARK, S. H. and Y. LUO. "Guanxi and Organizational Dynamics: Organizational Networking in Chinese Firms." *Strategic Management Journal* 22, no. 5 (May 2001): 455.

PITT, LEYLAND F., PIERRE BERTHON, RICHARD T. WATSON, and MICHAEL EWING. "Pricing Strategy and the Net." *Business Horizons* 44, no. 2 (March–April 2001): 45.

PRATT, D. JANE. "Corporations, Communities, and Conservation: The Mountain Institute and Antamina Mining Company." *California Management Review* 43, no. 3 (Spring 2001): 38.

SCHRAGE, MICHAEL. "Playing Around with Brainstorming." *Harvard Business Review* (March 2001): 149.

YOUNG, DAVID W. "The Six Levers for Managing Organizational Culture." *Business Horizons* 43, no. 5 (September–October 2000): 19.

EXPERIENTIAL EXERCISES

EXPERIENTIAL EXERCISE 4A ▶

Performing a Financial Ratio Analysis for American Airlines (AMR)

PURPOSE

Financial ratio analysis is one of the best techniques for identifying and evaluating internal strengths and weaknesses. Potential investors and current shareholders look closely at firms' financial ratios, making detailed comparisons to industry averages and to previous periods of time. Financial ratio analyses provide vital input information for developing an IFE Matrix.

INSTRUCTIONS

Step 1   On a separate sheet of paper, number from 1 to 20. Referring to American Airline's statement of operations and balance sheet (pp. 40–42), calculate twenty financial ratios for 2001 for the company. Use Table 4–4 as a reference.

Step 2   Go to www.investor.stockpoint.com and find industry average financial ratios for the airline industry. Record the industry average values in a second column on your paper.

Step 3   In a third column, indicate whether you consider each ratio to be a strength, a weakness, or a neutral factor for AMR.

EXPERIENTIAL EXERCISE 4B ▶

Constructing an IFE Matrix for American Airlines (AMR)

PURPOSE

This exercise will give you experience in developing an IFE Matrix. Identifying and prioritizing factors to include in an IFE Matrix fosters communication among functional and divisional managers. Preparing an IFE Matrix allows human resource, marketing, production/operations, finance/accounting, R&D, and management information systems managers to articulate their concerns and thoughts regarding the business condition of the firm. This results in an improved collective understanding of the business.

INSTRUCTIONS

Step 1   Join with two other individuals to form a three-person team. Develop a team IFE Matrix for AMR.

Step 2   Compare your team's IFE Matrix to other teams' IFE Matrices. Discuss any major differences.

Step 3   What strategies do you think would allow AMR to capitalize on its major strengths? What strategies would allow AMR to improve upon its major weaknesses?

EXPERIENTIAL EXERCISE 4C ▶

Constructing an IFE Matrix for My University

PURPOSE

This exercise gives you the opportunity to evaluate your university's major strengths and weaknesses. As will become clearer in the next chapter, an organization's strategies are largely based upon striving to take advantage of strengths and improving upon weaknesses.

INSTRUCTIONS

Step 1 Join with two other individuals to form a three-person team. Develop a team IFE Matrix for your university. You may use the strengths/weaknesses determined in Experimential Exercise 1D.

Step 2 Go to the board and diagram your team's IFE Matrix.

Step 3 Compare your team's IFE Matrix to other teams' IFE Matrices. Discuss any major differences.

Step 4 What strategies do you think would allow your university to capitalize on its major strengths? What strategies would allow your university to improve upon its major weaknesses?

5

STRATEGIES IN ACTION

CHAPTER OUTLINE

- Long-Term Objectives
- Types of Strategies
- Integration Strategies
- Intensive Strategies
- Diversification Strategies
- Defensive Strategies
- Michael Porter's Generic Strategies
- Means for Achieving Strategies
- Merger/Acquisition
- Strategic Management in Nonprofit and Governmental Organizations
- Strategic Management in Small Firms

EXPERIENTIAL EXERCISE 5A
What Happened at American Airlines (AMR) in the Year 2002?

EXPERIENTIAL EXERCISE 5B
Examining Strategy Articles

EXPERIENTIAL EXERCISE 5C
Classifying Some Year 2002 Strategies

EXPERIENTIAL EXERCISE 5D
How Risky Are Various Alternative Strategies?

EXPERIENTIAL EXERCISE 5E
Developing Alternative Strategies for My University

EXPERIENTIAL EXERCISE 5F
Lessons in Doing Business Globally

CHAPTER OBJECTIVES

After studying this chapter, you should be able to do the following:

1. Discuss the value of establishing long-term objectives.
2. Identify sixteen types of business strategies.
3. Identify numerous examples of organizations pursuing different types of strategies.
4. Discuss guidelines when particular strategies are most appropriate to pursue.
5. Discuss Porter's generic strategies.
6. Describe strategic management in nonprofit, governmental, and small organizations.
7. Discuss joint ventures as a way to enter the Russian market.

NOTABLE QUOTES

Alice said, "Would you please tell me which way to go from here?" The cat said, "That depends on where you want to get to."

LEWIS CARROLL

Tomorrow always arrives. It is always different. And even the mightiest company is in trouble if it has not worked on the future. Being surprised by what happens is a risk that even the largest and richest company cannot afford, and even the smallest business need not run.

PETER DRUCKER

Planning. Doing things today to make us better tomorrow. Because the future belongs to those who make the hard decisions today.

EATON CORPORATION

One big problem with American business is that when it gets into trouble, it redoubles its effort. It's like digging for gold. If you dig down twenty feet and haven't found it, one of the strategies you could use is to dig twice as deep. But if the gold is twenty feet to the side, you could dig a long time and not find it.

EDWARD DE BONO

If you don't invest for the long term, there is no short term.

GEORGE DAVID

Even if you're on the right track, you'll get run over if you just sit there.

WILL ROGERS

We always plan too much and always think too little.

JOSHEP SCHUMPER

Behold the turtle, he makes progress only when he sticks his neck out.

BRUCE LEVIN

157

Hundreds of companies today, including Sears, IBM, Searle, and Hewlett-Packard, have embraced strategic planning fully in their quest for higher revenues and profits. Kent Nelson, former chair of UPS, explains why his company has created a new strategic planning department: "Because we're making bigger bets on investments in technology, we can't afford to spend a whole lot of money in one direction and then find out five years later it was the wrong direction."[1]

This chapter brings strategic management to life with many contemporary examples. Sixteen types of strategies are defined and exemplified, including Michael Porter's generic strategies: cost leadership, differentiation, and focus. Guidelines are presented for determining when it is most appropriate to pursue different types of strategies. An overview of strategic management in nonprofit organizations, governmental agencies, and small firms is provided.

 # LONG-TERM OBJECTIVES

Long-term objectives represent the results expected from pursuing certain strategies. Strategies represent the actions to be taken to accomplish long-term objectives. The time frame for objectives and strategies should be consistent, usually from two to five years.

The Nature of Long-Term Objectives

VISIT THE NET

Gives the basic principles of strategic planning.
http://www.
eaglepointconsulting.com/
sp_principles.html

Objectives should be quantitative, measurable, realistic, understandable, challenging, hierarchical, obtainable, and congruent among organizational units. Each objective should also be associated with a time line. Objectives are commonly stated in terms such as growth in assets, growth in sales, profitability, market share, degree and nature of diversification, degree and nature of vertical integration, earnings per share, and social responsibility. Clearly established objectives offer many benefits. They provide direction, allow synergy, aid in evaluation, establish priorities, reduce uncertainty, minimize conflicts, stimulate exertion, and aid in both the allocation of resources and the design of jobs.

Long-term objectives are needed at the corporate, divisional, and functional levels of an organization. They are an important measure of managerial performance. Many practitioners and academicians attribute a significant part of U.S. industry's competitive decline to the short-term, rather than long-term, strategy orientation of managers in the United States. Arthur D. Little argues that bonuses or merit pay for managers today must be based to a greater extent on long-term objectives and strategies. A general framework for relating objectives to performance evaluation is provided in Table 5–1. A particular organization could tailor these guidelines to meet its own needs, but incentives should be attached to both long-term and annual objectives.

TABLE 5–1   **Varying Performance Measures by Organizational Level**

ORGANIZATIONAL LEVEL	BASIS FOR ANNUAL BONUS OR MERIT PAY
Corporate	75% based on long-term objectives
	25% based on annual objectives
Division	50% based on long-term objectives
	50% based on annual objectives
Function	25% based on long-term objectives
	75% based on annual objectives

Clearly stated and communicated objectives are vital to success for many reasons. First, objectives help stakeholders understand their role in an organization's future. They also provide a basis for consistent decision making by managers whose values and attitudes differ. By reaching a consensus on objectives during strategy-formulation activities, an organization can minimize potential conflicts later during implementation. Objectives set forth organizational priorities and stimulate exertion and accomplishment. They serve as standards by which individuals, groups, departments, divisions, and entire organizations can be evaluated. Objectives provide the basis for designing jobs and organizing activities to be performed in an organization. They also provide direction and allow for organizational synergy.

Without long-term objectives, an organization would drift aimlessly toward some unknown end. It is hard to imagine an organization or individual being successful without clear objectives. Success only rarely occurs by accident; rather, it is the result of hard work directed toward achieving certain objectives.

Not Managing by Objectives

An unknown educator once said, "If you think education is expensive, try ignorance." The idea behind this saying also applies to establishing objectives. Strategists should avoid the following alternative ways to "not managing by objectives."

VISIT THE NET

Provides good narrative on why to do strategic planning.
http://www.orggrow.co.uk/gap/plan.html

- Managing by Extrapolation—adheres to the principle "If it ain't broke, don't fix it." The idea is to keep on doing about the same things in the same ways because things are going well.

- Managing by Crisis—based on the belief that the true measure of a really good strategist is the ability to solve problems. Because there are plenty of crises and problems to go around for every person and every organization, strategists ought to bring their time and creative energy to bear on solving the most pressing problems of the day. Managing by crisis is actually a form of reacting rather than acting and of letting events dictate the whats and when of management decisions.

- Managing by Subjectives—built on the idea that there is no general plan for which way to go and what to do; just do the best you can to accomplish what you think should be done. In short, "Do your own thing, the best way you know how" (sometimes referred to as *the mystery approach to decision making* because subordinates are left to figure out what is happening and why).

- Managing by Hope—based on the fact that the future is laden with great uncertainty, and that if we try and do not succeed, then we hope our second (or third) attempt will succeed. Decisions are predicted on the hope that they will work and the good times are just around the corner, especially if luck and good fortune are on our side![2]

 ## TYPES OF STRATEGIES

The model illustrated in Figure 5–1 provides a conceptual basis for applying strategic management. Defined and exemplified in Table 5–2, alternative strategies that an enterprise could pursue can be categorized into thirteen actions—forward integration, backward integration, horizontal integration, market penetration, market development, product development, concentric diversification, conglomerate diversification, horizontal diversification, joint venture/partnering, retrenchment, divestiture, and liquidation. Each alternative strategy has countless variations. For example, market penetration can

FIGURE 5–1

A Comprehensive Strategic-Management Model

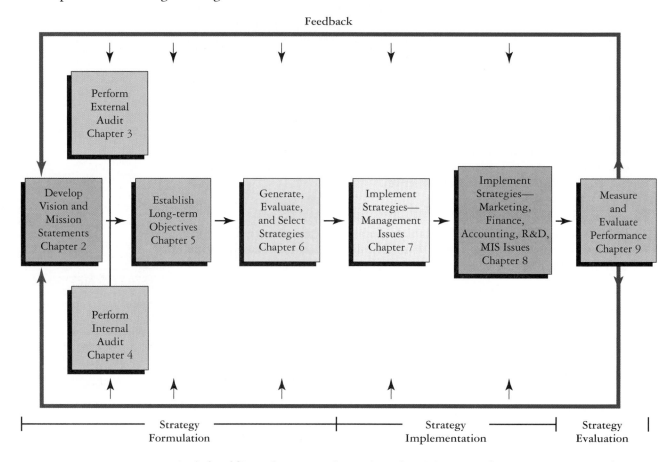

Feedback

| Perform External Audit Chapter 3 |
| Develop Vision and Mission Statements Chapter 2 |
| Establish Long-term Objectives Chapter 5 |
| Generate, Evaluate, and Select Strategies Chapter 6 |
| Implement Strategies— Management Issues Chapter 7 |
| Implement Strategies— Marketing, Finance, Accounting, R&D, MIS Issues Chapter 8 |
| Measure and Evaluate Performance Chapter 9 |
| Perform Internal Audit Chapter 4 |

Strategy Formulation   Strategy Implementation   Strategy Evaluation

include adding salespersons, increasing advertising expenditures, couponing, and using similar actions to increase market share in a given geographic area.

Many, if not most, organizations pursue a combination of two or more strategies simultaneously, but a *combination strategy* can be exceptionally risky if carried too far. No organization can afford to pursue all the strategies that might benefit the firm. Difficult decisions must be made. Priority must be established. Organizations, like individuals, have limited resources. Both organizations and individuals must choose among alternative strategies and avoid excessive indebtedness.

Organizations cannot do too many things well because resources and talents get spread thin and competitors gain advantage. In large diversified companies, a combination strategy is commonly employed when different divisions pursue different strategies. Also, organizations struggling to survive may employ a combination of several defensive strategies, such as divestiture, liquidation, and retrenchment, simultaneously.

 ## INTEGRATION STRATEGIES

Forward integration, backward integration, and horizontal integration are sometimes collectively referred to as *vertical integration* strategies. Vertical integration strategies allow a firm to gain control over distributors, suppliers, and/or competitors.

TABLE 5-2   **Alternative Strategies Defined and Exemplified**

STRATEGY	DEFINITION	EXAMPLE
Forward Integration	Gaining ownership or increased control over distributors or retailers	Gateway Computer Company opening its own chain of retail computer stores.
Backward Integration	Seeking ownership or increased control of a firm's suppliers	Financial firms such as J.P. Morgan are outsourcing their technology operations to firms such as EDS and IBM.
Horizontal Integration	Seeking ownership or increased control over competitors	Reader's Digest Association acquired Reiman Publications LLC.
Market Penetration	Seeking increased market share for present products or services in present markets through greater marketing efforts	American Express launched a $100 million+ advertising campaign in 2002 to boost its lead over Citigroup in the credit card industry.
Market Development	Introducing present products or services into new geographic area	South African Breweries PLC is trying to acquire Miller Brewing Company for about $5 billion.
Product Development	Seeking increased sales by improving present products or services or developing new ones	Miller Brewing developed the new Skyy Blue citrus and "vodka-flavored" malt beverage.
Concentric Diversification	Adding new but related products or services	Hilton Hotels is now selling time shares to fill rooms. The Hilton in New York City is selling off the two top floors of rooms.
Horizontal Diversification	Adding new, unrelated products or services for present customers	The New York Yankees baseball team is merging business operations with the New Jersey Nets basketball team.
Retrenchment	Regrouping through cost and asset reduction to reverse declining sales and profit	Net2Phone in 2002 cut 110 jobs, or 28 percent of its workforce, as part of its restructuring plan.
Divestiture	Selling a division or part of an organization	Tyco International is selling off its plastics division, which accounts for about 4 percent of Tyco's sales.
Liquidation	Selling all of a company's assets, in parts, for their tangible worth	Service Merchandise liquidated in 2002, closing all of its 216 stores in 32 states. The firm had been operating for three years under Chapter 11 bankruptcy.

Forward Integration

Forward integration involves gaining ownership or increased control over distributors or retailers. Increasing numbers of manufacturers (suppliers) today are pursuing a forward integration strategy by establishing Web sites to sell products directly to consumers. This strategy is causing turmoil in some industries. For example, Home Depot warned its suppliers not to compete with them in selling products online. Many manufacturers are reluctant to offend their distributors (retailers) by selling online, but low relative costs in selling online versus retail stores makes forward integration a very tempting strategy for many suppliers. Manufacturer Joe Boxer sells underwear on Macy's Web site, but this degree of cooperation between supplier and distributor is the exception rather than the rule.

The external threat of online sales, perhaps from suppliers eroding its catalog market share, is a primary reason why L.L. Bean opened its first full-line retail store in eighty-seven years. The store is located in McLean, Virginia. L.L. Bean is pursuing forward integration out of concern that online stores will further erode catalog sales, which are slowing. Other catalog retailers such as Delia's and J. Jill have opened retail stores for the first time in their history.

Brick-and-mortar retailers such as Wal-Mart, Sharper Image, and The Right Start are rapidly combating the purely online retailers by mobilizing a multichannel attack selling via stores and the Internet. Many traditional retailers are adding catalogs too and offering auctions to further enhance their distribution network. **Wal-Mart.com** is aimed at becoming the leading Internet discounter. Even Amway has a new online division named Quixtar to sell its and other companies' products. "We're looking at the biggest change in forty years," said Amway executive Ken McDonald. Amway's sales force continues to sell products to friends and family but now also has the option to sell products online for Quixtar.

Both Sears and Home Depot are employing forward integration to battle for American homeowners' decorating dollars. The two retailers are rushing to open their own freestanding home-décor stores. As part of its effort to expand beyond its do-it-yourself warehouses, Home Depot plans to have 200 Expo Design Center stores by 2005, while Sears is opening 150 The Great Indoors stores by 2003.

Oakland, California-based Dreyers Ice Cream has used forward integration to gain 18 percent of the U.S. market share for ice cream, followed by its major competitor Breyers with 15 percent. Dreyers' competitive advantage in this industry is its outstanding distribution system, led by a new fleet of 1,100 trucks and a new computerized form of delivery and ordering. Dreyers' distribution system is so efficient that competitors such as Ben & Jerry's, Häagen-Dazs, and Godiva all use Dreyers for distribution. Breyers, however, does not use Dreyers, even though both Breyers and Ben & Jerry's are divisions of Unilever.[3]

Toronto-Dominion (TD) Bank of Canada is pursuing forward integration by beginning to offer banking services at 100 Wal-Mart supercenter stores beginning in 2002. This strategy enables the Toronto-based bank to build a retail-banking presence without investing in its own distribution or branch network. While Wal-Mart already offers banking services, no single bank has operations in as many Wal-Mart stores as TD will have. Wal-Mart had tried to diversify into the banking business in 1999 by acquiring a small savings bank, but that move was blocked by Congress. Wal-Mart will not own or operate the TD operations in its stores. Congress is determined to see that banking and commerce in the United States should stay separate.

An effective means of implementing forward integration is *franchising*. Approximately two thousand companies in about fifty different industries in the United States use franchising to distribute their products or services. Businesses can expand rapidly by franchising because costs and opportunities are spread across many individuals. Total sales by franchises in the United States are about $1 trillion annually.

Six guidelines when forward integration may be an especially effective strategy are:[4]

- When an organization's present distributors are especially expensive, or unreliable, or incapable of meeting the firm's distribution needs.
- When the availability of quality distributors is so limited as to offer a competitive advantage to those firms that integrate forward.
- When an organization competes in an industry that is growing and is expected to continue to grow markedly; this is a factor because forward integration reduces an organization's ability to diversify if its basic industry falters.
- When an organization has both the capital and human resources needed to manage the new business of distributing its own products.

- When the advantages of stable production are particularly high; this is a consideration because an organization can increase the predictability of the demand for its output through forward integration.

- When present distributors or retailers have high profit margins; this situation suggests that a company profitably could distribute its own products and price them more competitively by integrating forward.

Backward Integration

Both manufacturers and retailers purchase needed materials from suppliers. *Backward integration* is a strategy of seeking ownership or increased control of a firm's suppliers. This strategy can be especially appropriate when a firm's current suppliers are unreliable, too costly, or cannot meet the firm's needs.

When you buy a box of Pampers diapers at Wal-Mart, a scanner at the store's checkout counter instantly zaps an order to Procter & Gamble Company. In contrast, in most hospitals, reordering supplies is a logistical nightmare. Inefficiency caused by lack of control of suppliers in the healthcare industry is, however, rapidly changing as many giant health-care purchasers, such as the U.S. Defense Department and Columbia/HCA Healthcare Corporation, move to require electronic bar codes on every supply item purchased. This allows instant tracking and recording without invoices and paperwork. Of the estimated $83 billion spent annually on hospital supplies, industry reports indicate that $11 billion can be eliminated through more effective backward integration.

Some industries in the United States (such as the automotive and aluminum industries) are reducing their historical pursuit of backward integration. Instead of owning their suppliers, companies negotiate with several outside suppliers. Ford and Daimler-Chrysler buy over half of their components parts from outside suppliers such as TRW, Eaton, General Electric, and Johnson Controls. Deintegration makes sense in industries that have global sources of supply. *Outsourcing,* whereby companies use outside suppliers, shop around, play one seller against another, and go with the best deal, is becoming widely practiced. Small steel manufacturers such as Arrowhead Steel Company and Worthington Steel Company are pursuing backward integration today through the use of the Internet. Owners of most small steel firms now click on Web sites such as MetalSite LP, based in Pittsburgh, or e-Steel Corporation, based in New York, to find the lowest-priced supplier of scrap steel that they need. These two sites give buyers and sellers of steel the opportunity to trade, buy, and sell metal from a variety of companies. Many steel companies now have Web sites to capitalize on backward integration opportunities in the industry.

Global competition is also spurring firms to reduce their number of suppliers and to demand higher levels of service and quality from those they keep. Although traditionally relying on many suppliers to ensure uninterrupted supplies and low prices, American firms now are following the lead of Japanese firms, which have far fewer suppliers and closer, long-term relationships with those few. "Keeping track of so many suppliers is onerous," says Mark Shimelonis, formerly of Xerox.

Seven guidelines when backward integration may be an especially effective strategy are:[5]

- When an organization's present suppliers are especially expensive, or unreliable, or incapable of meeting the firm's needs for parts, components, assemblies, or raw materials.

- When the number of suppliers is small and the number of competitors is large.

- When an organization competes in an industry that is growing rapidly; this is a factor because integrative-type strategies (forward, backward, and horizontal) reduce an organization's ability to diversify in a declining industry.

VISIT THE NET

Read about the Immigration and Naturalization Strategic Management Process.
www.ins.usdoj.gov/text/aboutins/insmission/dojplan.htm

- When an organization has both capital and human resources to manage the new business of supplying its own raw materials.
- When the advantages of stable prices are particularly important; this is a factor because an organization can stabilize the cost of its raw materials and the associated price of its product(s) through backward integration.
- When present supplies have high profit margins, which suggests that the business of supplying products or services in the given industry is a worthwhile venture.
- When an organization needs to acquire a needed resource quickly.

Horizontal Integration

Horizontal integration refers to a strategy of seeking ownership of or increased control over a firm's competitors. One of the most significant trends in strategic management today is the increased use of horizontal integration as a growth strategy. Mergers, acquisitions, and takeovers among competitors allow for increased economies of scale and enhanced transfer of resources and competencies. Kenneth Davidson makes the following observation about horizontal integration:

> The trend towards horizontal integration seems to reflect strategists' misgivings about their ability to operate many unrelated businesses. Mergers between direct competitors are more likely to create efficiencies than mergers between unrelated businesses, both because there is a greater potential for eliminating duplicate facilities and because the management of the acquiring firm is more likely to understand the business of the target.[6]

Horizontal integration has become the most favored growth strategy in many industries. For example, explosive growth in e-commerce has telecommunications firms worldwide frantically merging and pursuing horizontal integration to gain competitiveness. Telecommunications mergers occur almost weekly.

Oklahoma City-based Devon Energy recently purchased Calgary, Alberta-based Anderson Exploration to become the largest independent producer of oil and gas in North America. With the acquisition, Devon increased its oil and gas reserves in Canada from 11 percent to 32 percent. The Anderson acquisition came on the heels of Devon's purchase of Woodlands, Texas-based Mitchell Energy & Development. For another horizontal integration example in the energy field, consider Santa Fe International's recent acquisition of Global Marine, which makes it one of the world's largest contract oil drilling firms. The new firm is named GlobalSantaFe Corporation.

In the largest horizontal integration merger ever recorded in the computer industry, Hewlett-Packard (HP) purchased Compaq to become the largest computer company in the world. Previously, HP was number three and Compaq was number two, while Dell was number one. The combined company now holds a 19 percent share of the global personal computer business, leapfrogging leader Dell, which has about 13 percent of the market share.

In one of the most depressed forest products and paper markets in a decade, Westvaco and Mead—two midsize paper companies—recently integrated horizontally to form MeadWestvaco, based in Stamford, Connecticut. The merged company is the nation's second-largest producer of coated papers and one of the largest packaging companies. Westvaco was a large producer of bleached paperboard, which is used in packaging, whereas Mead was a large producer of coated natural kraft, which is used in packaging. The merged company is divesting nonstrategic assets—operations not involved in paper or packaging.

Canadian laser eye-surgery provider TLC Laser Eye Centers recently acquired rival Laser Vision Centers in St. Louis for almost $100 million, creating the largest operator of laser eye-surgery clinics in North America. The deal brings together TLC's strength in

VISIT THE NET

Provides Federal Emergency Management Agency's (FEMA) strategic plan. www.fema.gov/library/spln_7.htm

urban areas and Laser Vision's strong presence in small towns and rural areas of the United States.

Five guidelines when horizontal integration may be an especially effective strategy are:[7]

- When an organization can gain monopolistic characteristics in a particular area or region without being challenged by the federal government for "tending substantially" to reduce competition.
- When an organization competes in a growing industry.
- When increased economies of scale provide major competitive advantages.
- When an organization has both the capital and human talent needed to successfully manage an expanded organization.
- When competitors are faltering due to a lack of managerial expertise or a need for particular resources that an organization possesses; note that horizontal integration would not be appropriate if competitors are doing poorly, because in that case overall industry sales are declining.

 ## INTENSIVE STRATEGIES

Market penetration, market development, and product development are sometimes referred to as *intensive strategies* because they require intensive efforts if a firm's competitive position with existing products is to improve.

Market Penetration

A *market-penetration* strategy seeks to increase market share for present products or services in present markets through greater marketing efforts. This strategy is widely used alone and in combination with other strategies. Market penetration includes increasing the number of salespersons, increasing advertising expenditures, offering extensive sales promotion items, or increasing publicity efforts. Japan's Canon, Inc., has crushed its rival Xerox with an effective market penetration strategy in recent years. Canon established an excellent direct-sales force and a customer service operation; at the same time, it maintains great relations with its dealers. Nearly 75 percent of Canon's business comes from countries other than Japan. Canon has doubled its market share in the fast-growing digital camera industry to about 20 percent of the United States market, thus moving ahead of Kodak.

Five guidelines when market penetration may be an especially effective strategy are:[8]

- When current markets are not saturated with a particular product or service.
- When the usage rate of present customers could be increased significantly.
- When the market shares of major competitors have been declining while total industry sales have been increasing.
- When the correlation between dollar sales and dollar marketing expenditures historically has been high.
- When increased economies of scale provide major competitive advantages.

Market Development

Market development involves introducing present products or services into new geographic areas. The climate for international market development is becoming more favorable. In many industries, such as Internet service providers, it is going to be hard to maintain a competitive edge by staying close to home. For example, AOL is expanding its services aggressively worldwide. In Latin and South America, AOL still trails Terra Lycos and Universo Online, and it is number three or number four in Brazil, Mexico, and Argentina. But AOL is the fastest-growing Internet service provider in Latin and South America, and it expects its operations there to become profitable by 2003. AOL is also expanding into China, even though it is technically illegal today for Chinese individuals to receive foreign satellite programs. AOL now claims to reach more than 10 million mainland households in China through its majority stake in China Entertainment Television Broadcast. AOL is in talks with Beijing to allow the company to set up a separate broadcast channel in the southern Chinese province of Guangdong.

Wal-Mart has used a global-market development strategy to become the largest retailer not only in the United States but also in Canada and Mexico. Wal-Mart's revenues outside the United States now comprise 17 percent of its total, with more than eleven hundred stores in nine countries. Wal-Mart added another 120 stores outside the United States in 2001.

Coca-Cola Company recently launched its new sports-drink, Powerade, into seven European countries, challenging PepsiCo's Gatorade. The number three and four sports drinks in Europe are Aquarius, already produced by Coke, and Lucozade, which is made by Novartis AG's Isostar. Coke believes Europeans age thirteen to twenty-nine, the target market for Powerade, are increasingly making sports a bigger part of their lives. Coke says Powerade increases one's endurance and energy during exercise.

Gap, the large specialty retail store chain, has used a global market development strategy for years, but the company reduced its international store growth to 20 percent in 2001 from 41 percent in 2000. Gap's corporate operating profit margin is about 16 percent, but its margin from international operations is less than 10 percent. According to Forbes, "Gap's failing may be in believing that it can apply uniform merchandising and marketing around the world. In Japan, the tags on Gap clothing are in English. Gap employees cheerfully greet customers with the casual Japanese version of 'hi,' an unaccustomed informality for the mannerly Japanese. Despite all the Americanizing, the Japanese seem to mostly want bargains. Uniqlo, a 480-store Gap rival in Japan, undercuts the Gap on prices by 50 percent."[9]

Six guidelines when market development may be an especially effective strategy are:[10]

- When new channels of distribution are available that are reliable, inexpensive, and of good quality.
- When an organization is very successful at what it does.
- When new untapped or unsaturated markets exist.
- When an organization has the needed capital and human resources to manage expanded operations.
- When an organization has excess production capacity.
- When an organization's basic industry is becoming rapidly global in scope.

Product Development

Product development is a strategy that seeks increased sales by improving or modifying present products or services. Product development usually entails large research and development expenditures.

Microsoft constantly pursues product development. The company recently introduced its Pocket PC 2002 to compete against Palm, Inc., as the leading provider of handheld-device software. Microsoft has several key computer hardware partners, such as Compaq, who are committed to marketing the PC 2002 software on their products.

Catalogs are considered by marketers to be the cheapest way to launch a new retail line of clothes, manage the risk, and test a new market.

Talbots, a retailer of classic women's apparel, recently entered the men's clothing market. Talbots is targeting men in a move that is consistent with its current women's demographic—career-oriented, age 35 and older. If Talbot's new men's line of clothes does well in its 2002 catalogs, then the company plans to open freestanding menswear retail outlets in 2003. Talbots has 762 stores nationwide.

Hampton Inn is pursuing product development by opening 500 small-room, small hotels in small towns, with populations of 10,000 to 30,000. Hampton's 1,100 properties to date are mostly large, with large rooms, and they are located off interstates and in suburban locations. These smaller units will not include restaurants or bellhops, but they will offer swimming pools and business services. Fortunately—or perhaps unfortunately—for Hampton, other competitors have been pursuing the same strategy—including Sleep Inns, La Quinta, Holiday Inn Express, Howard Johnson Express, and Super 8.

Abercrombie & Fitch is employing product development to segment its customers by age. The company finds that high-school-age teenagers have different buying habits than college-age students. For example, college students shun logo-laden clothes, while high-school students love logos. High-school-age students tend to desire more graphics and sparkles on clothes. The two groups do not mix that well in stores either. Thus, Abercrombie recently developed its Hollister stores that cater to the 14-to-18 year olds. By 2003, there will be 80 Hollister stores, each designed to evoke a California-surfing atmosphere. This strategy is designed to allow traditional Abercrombie stores to focus on the older young people.

Five guidelines when product development may be an especially effective strategy to pursue are:[11]

- When an organization has successful products that are in the maturity stage of the product life cycle; the idea here is to attract satisfied customers to try new (improved) products as a result of their positive experience with the organization's present products or services.
- When an organization competes in an industry that is characterized by rapid technological developments.
- When major competitors offer better-quality products at comparable prices.
- When an organization competes in a high-growth industry.
- When an organization has especially strong research and development capabilities.

DIVERSIFICATION STRATEGIES

There are three general types of *diversification strategies:* concentric, horizontal, and conglomerate. Overall, diversification strategies are becoming less popular as organizations are finding it more difficult to manage diverse business activities. In the 1960s and 1970s, the trend was to diversify so as not to be dependent on any single industry, but the 1980s saw a general reversal of that thinking. Diversification is now on the retreat. Michael Porter of the Harvard Business School says, "Management found [it] couldn't manage the beast." Hence, businesses are selling, or closing, less profitable divisions in order to focus on core businesses.

There are, however, a few companies today that pride themselves on being conglomerates, from small firms such as Pentair Inc. and Blount International to huge companies

NATURAL ENVIRONMENT PERSPECTIVE

Songbirds and Coral Reefs in Trouble

SONGBIRDS

Bluebirds are one of seventy-six songbird species in the United States that have dramatically declined in numbers in the last two decades. Not all birds are considered songbirds, and why birds sing is not clear. Some scientists say they sing when calling for mates or warning of danger, but many scientists now contend that birds sing for sheer pleasure. Songbirds include chickadees, orioles, swallows, mockingbirds, warblers, sparrows, vireos, and the wood thrush. "These birds are telling us there's a problem, something's out of balance in our environment," says Jeff Wells, bird conservation director for the National Audubon Society. Songbirds may be telling us that their air or water is too dirty or that we are destroying too much of their habitat. People collect Picasso paintings and save historic buildings. "Songbirds are part of our natural heritage. Why should we be willing to watch songbirds destroyed anymore than allowing a great work of art be destroyed?" asks Wells. Whatever message songbirds are singing to us today about their natural environment, the message is becoming less and less heard nationwide. Listen when you go outside today. Each of us as individuals, companies, states, and countries should do what we reasonably can to help improve the natural environment for songbirds.

CORAL REEFS

The ocean covers more than 71 percent of the Earth. The destructive effect of commercial fishing on ocean habitats coupled with increasing pollution runoff into the ocean and global warming of the ocean have decimated fisheries, marine life, and coral reefs around the world. The unfortunate consequence of fishing over the last century has been *overfishing*—with the principal reasons being politics and greed. Trawl fishing with nets destroys coral reefs and has been compared to catching squirrels by cutting down forests, since bottom nets scour and destroy vast areas of the ocean. The great proportion of marine life caught in a trawl is "by-catch" juvenile fish and other life that are killed and discarded. Warming of the ocean due to CO_2 emissions also kills thousands of acres of coral reefs annually. The total area of fully protected marine habitats in the United States is only about 50 square miles, compared to some 93 million acres of national wildlife refuges and national parks on the nation's land. Ocean ecosystems and a healthy ocean is vital to the economic and social future of the nation—and, indeed, all countries of the world. Everything we do on land ends up in the ocean, so we all must become better stewards of this last frontier on Earth in order to sustain human survival and the quality of life.

Source: Adapted from Tom Brook, "Declining Numbers Mute Many Birds' Songs," *USA Today* (September 11, 2001): 4A. Also, adapted from John Ogden, "Maintaining Diversity in the Oceans," *Environment* (April 2001): 29–36.

such as Textron, Allied Signal, Emerson Electric, General Electric, and Viacom. Viacom's acquisition of CBS for $36 billion turned Viacom into an $80 billion company with diverse assets in broadcast and cable television, movies, radio, theme parks, Internet sites, home video, publishing, and billboards. Similarly, Textron, through numerous diverse acquisitions, now produces and sells Cessna airplanes, Bell helicopters, Jacobsen lawn mowers, golf products, transmissions, consumer loans, and telescopic machinery. Conglomerates prove that focus and diversity are not always mutually exclusive.

Peters and Waterman's advice to firms is to "stick to the knitting" and not to stray too far from the firm's basic areas of competence. However, diversification is still an appropriate and successful strategy sometimes. Hamish Maxwell, Philip Morris's former CEO, says, "We want to become a consumer-products company." Diversification makes sense for Philip Morris because cigarette consumption is declining, product liability suits are a risk, and some investors reject tobacco stocks on principle. In a diversification move, Philip Morris spent $12.9 billion in a hostile takeover of Kraft General Foods, the world's second-largest food producer behind Nestlé.

Concentric Diversification

Adding new, but related, products or services is widely called *concentric diversification*. An example of this strategy is Amazon.com Inc.'s recent move to sell personal computers through its online store. Rather than keeping the computers in its warehouses, however, Amazon will simply transmit orders for computers to wholesaler Ingram Micro, based in Santa Ana, California. Ingram will package and send the computers to customers, so Amazon is minimizing its own risk in this diversification initiative.

The largest African-American-owned business in America, Active Transportation and Automotive Carrier Services (ATACS), based in Louisville, Kentucky, is considering concentric diversification to reverse its falling profitability.[12] The business hauls everything from steel and turbines to heavy trucks, but orders for heavy hauling have lately been down 40 percent, ATACS would like to diversify into hauling lighter cargo.

Six guidelines when concentric diversification may be an effective strategy are provided below.[13]

- When an organization competes in a no-growth or a slow-growth industry.
- When adding new, but related, products would significantly enhance the sales of current products.
- When new, but related, products could be offered at highly competitive prices.
- When new, but related, products have seasonal sales levels that counterbalance an organization's existing peaks and valleys.
- When an organization's products are currently in the declining stage of the product's life cycle.
- When an organization has a strong management team.

Horizontal Diversification

Adding new, unrelated products or services for present customers is called *horizontal diversification*. This strategy is not as risky as conglomerate diversification because a firm already should be familiar with its present customers. For example, consider the increasing number of hospitals that are creating miniature malls by offering banks, bookstores, coffee shops, restaurants, drugstores, and other retail stores within its buildings. Many hospitals previously had only cafeterias, gift shops, and maybe a pharmacy, but the movement into malls and retail stores is aimed at improving the ambiance for patients and their visitors. The new University Pointe Hospital in West Chester, Ohio, has 75,000 square feet of retail space. The CEO says, "Unless we diversify our revenue, we won't be able to fulfill our mission of providing healthcare. We want our hospital to be a place that people want to go to."[14]

Four guidelines when horizontal diversification may be an especially effective strategy are:[15]

- When revenues derived from an organization's current products or services would increase significantly by adding the new, unrelated products.
- When an organization competes in a highly competitive and/or a no-growth industry, as indicated by low industry profit margins and returns.
- When an organization's present channels of distribution can be used to market the new products to current customers.
- When the new products have countercyclical sales patterns compared to an organization's present products.

Conglomerate Diversification

Adding new, unrelated products or services is called *conglomerate diversification*. For example, ESPN is diversifying from sports programming into movies and ministries with the creation of a new division called ESPN Original Entertainment. ESPN's first movie is about basketball coach Bobby Knight called "A Season on the Brink." ESPN is part of the Walt Disney Company. ESPN's ratings dropped 22 percent from 1997 to 2002.[16]

Six guidelines when conglomerate diversification may be an especially effective strategy to pursue are listed below.[17]

- When an organization's basic industry is experiencing declining annual sales and profits
- When an organization has the capital and managerial talent needed to compete successfully in a new industry
- When an organization has the opportunity to purchase an unrelated business that is an attractive investment opportunity
- When there exists financial synergy between the acquired and acquiring firm (note that a key difference between concentric and conglomerate diversification is that the former should be based on some commonality in markets, products, or technology, whereas the latter should be based more on profit considerations)
- When existing markets for an organization's present products are saturated
- When antitrust action could be charged against an organization that historically has concentrated on a single industry

General Electric is a classic firm that is highly diversified. GE makes locomotives, lightbulbs, power plants, and refrigerators; GE manages more credit cards than American Express; GE owns more commercial aircraft than American Airlines.

 ## DEFENSIVE STRATEGIES

In addition to integrative, intensive, and diversification strategies, organizations also could pursue retrenchment, divestiture, or liquidation.

Retrenchment

Retrenchment occurs when an organization regroups through cost and asset reduction to reverse declining sales and profits. Sometimes called a turnaround or reorganizational strategy, retrenchment is designed to fortify an organization's basic distinctive competence. During retrenchment, strategists work with limited resources and face pressure from shareholders, employees, and the media. Retrenchment can entail selling off land and buildings to raise needed cash, pruning product lines, closing marginal businesses, closing obsolete factories, automating processes, reducing the number of employees, and instituting expense control systems.

Michelin North America recently announced that it will cut two thousand jobs—or 7 percent of its workforce—by the end of 2002 due to weak demand for tires. Based in Greenville, South Carolina, Michelin says the job cuts will be made in every location and will involve every job type within the company.

Advanced Micro Devices (AMD) is closing two plants and laying off 2,300 employees—or nearly 15 percent of its workforce—as the chip maker struggles from slowing sales. AMD's major competitor, Intel, is slashing computer chip prices in efforts to keep its market share and to stimulate demand. Gateway in late 2001 switched from AMD to Intel as the primary supplier for its computer chips.

Gateway is undergoing major retrenchment as domestic and worldwide personal computer sales continue to decline. The company recently announced a 25 percent cut in its worldwide staff, and it is closing its operations in Europe, Asia, and Australia. Based in San Diego, Gateway is also closing its manufacturing plant in Salt Lake City and its sales and support centers in California, South Dakota, Utah, and Virginia. CEO Ted Watt says, "We don't have to be a global business to succeed. Outside the United States, we don't have the brand awareness, or the local presence and solutions capability."

The terrorist events of September 11, 2001, and the anthrax scares thereafter resulted in many firms rethinking their efforts to globalize, and many firms are actually pulling back from global operations. For example, Merrill Lynch is scaling back its operations in Japan, using retrenchment, after stumbling in its advertising and marketing efforts there. Toshiba Corp. recently discontinued its manufacturing and marketing of desktop PCs in the United States, focusing instead on Asia and Europe. Toshiba cut 12 percent of its U.S. employees with the announcement.

The office supplies market has slowed to a no-growth situation, and many competing firms are using a retrenchment strategy. Office Depot, for example, is shutting down seventy stores and cutting sixteen hundred jobs, while Office Max is shutting fifty stores and cutting twelve hundred jobs. However, Staples, Inc., at the same time is opening 160 new stores and expanding its catalog and Internet sales. Staples currently has nearly fifteen hundred stores worldwide.

For another retrenchment example, consider that Club Med is closing fifteen of its 120 resorts worldwide. Bookings at Club Med resorts are off from 15 to 50 percent due to the war on terrorism and the reluctance of travelers to travel. Along with the closings, Club Med announced a new $20 million advertising campaign—"Wanna Play"—that emphasizes skiing and sports instead of sensuality.

The U.S. Postal Service expects to close many of its thirty-eight thousand post offices nationwide or reduce hours over the next decade as online transactions for sending and paying bills is expected to reduce first class mail dramatically beginning in 2003.[18] First-class mail volume will peak in 2002 and then decline at an annual rate of 2.5 percent from 2003 to 2008. Advertisers shifting their business to the Internet from bulk mailings also contributes to the Postal Service considering a retrenchment strategy for the future.

In some cases, *bankruptcy* can be an effective type of retrenchment strategy. Bankruptcy can allow a firm to avoid major debt obligations and to void union contracts. There are five major types of bankruptcy: Chapter 7, Chapter 9, Chapter 11, Chapter 12, and Chapter 13.

Chapter 7 bankruptcy is a liquidation procedure used only when a corporation sees no hope of being able to operate successfully or to obtain the necessary creditor agreement. All the organization's assets are sold in parts for their tangible worth.

Chapter 9 bankruptcy applies to municipalities. A municipality successfully declaring bankruptcy is Camden, New Jersey, the state's poorest city and the fifth-poorest city in the United States. A crime-ridden city of eighty-seven thousand, Camden received $62.5 million in state aid and has withdrawn its bankruptcy petition. Between 1980 and 2000, only eighteen U.S. cities declared bankruptcy. Some states do not allow municipalities to declare bankruptcy.

Chapter 11 bankruptcy allows organizations to reorganize and come back after filing a petition for protection. Bankruptcy filings surged 19 percent in 2001 to a record 1.5 million; filings by publicly-traded companies soared 46 percent in 2001 to 257.[19]

Midway Airlines Corporation recently filed for Chapter 11 bankruptcy and fired half of its fourteen hundred employees. With rare exception, Chapter 11 of the U.S. Bankruptcy Code makes no provision for parties other than debtors, creditors, and shareholders. For example, when Enron and Pacific Gas & Electric in California declared bankruptcy in 2001, customers sued for benefits but were denied consideration. Employees and customers of Midway are now in court seeking compensation from Midway.

Also declaring bankruptcy recently was McCrory Corporation, a New York–based discount store operator with 175 stores in the Northeast as well as Arizona, California, New Mexico, Oregon, Texas, and Washington. Founded in 1882, the McCrory retail stores operate under the names Dollar Zone, G.C. Murphy, McCrory, J.J. Newberry, and T.G, & Y.

One of Japan's largest retailers, Mycal Corporation, recently declared bankruptcy after it had amassed 1.55 trillion yen ($13 billion) in debt. Mycal operates hundreds of supermarkets and shopping centers. Historically, Japanese banks have stepped in to aid and save ailing companies, but this trend is changing as banks themselves are struggling to survive, much less prosper.

In the cruise industry, Renaissance Cruises filed for Chapter 11 bankruptcy in late 2001 as the United States officially entered an economic recession. Analysts expect an industrywide shakeout among cruise-line companies. Larger cruise lines, such as Carnival and Royal Caribbean, are launching heavily discounted prices to lure passengers, while smaller cruise companies, such as Disney, Norwegian, and P&O Princess, struggle to compete.

Bethlehem Steel Corporation, the nation's third largest steel company, declared bankruptcy in late 2001. Based in Bethlehem, 50 miles from Philadelphia, the company was once a symbol of American industrial and military might, having produced more than one thousand ships during World War II and girders for the Golden Gate Bridge and Empire State Building.

Polaroid Corporation also declared bankruptcy recently and notified potential acquirers that the company is for sale. Based in Cambridge, Massachusetts, Polaroid had been struggling to turn around its fading instant-photography business and could not meet its debt obligations.

Burlington Industries declared bankruptcy at the end of fiscal 2001 after reporting a loss of $91.1 million. Burlington's CEO George Henderson cited as the primary reason for the company's demise the volume of imported apparel into the United States, which is growing at five times the rate of consumption; he also reported that four out of five garments sold in the United States today are imported. Based in Greensboro, North Carolina, Burlington is a $1.4 billion per year textile maker.

Chiquita Brands International, the banana producer, declared bankruptcy in late 2001 due in part to a worldwide glut in bananas and a drop in prices. The U.S.–European Union eight-year trade battle over EU banana-import quotas ended in late 2001, but it cost Chiquita millions of dollars.

According to the Administrative Office of the U.S. Courts, there were 9,527 Chapter 11 bankruptcies declared for the twelve-month period ending June 30, 2001. During this time period, there were also 206 and 5,422 Chapter 12 and Chapter 13 bankruptcies, respectively. Bankruptcies in 2001 were up almost 30 percent over 2000 according to **bankruptcydata.com**, a Boston-based Web site that tracks such filings.

Chapter 12 bankruptcy was created by the Family Farmer Bankruptcy Act of 1986. This law became effective in 1987 and provides special relief to family farmers with debt equal to or less than $1.5 million.

Chapter 13 bankruptcy is a reorganization plan similar to Chapter 11, but it is available only to small businesses owned by individuals with unsecured debts of less than $100,000 and secured debts of less than $350,000. The Chapter 13 debtor is allowed to operate the business while a plan is being developed to provide for the successful operation of the business in the future.

Five guidelines when retrenchment may be an especially effective strategy to pursue are as follows.[20]

- When an organization has a clearly distinctive competence but has failed to meet its objectives and goals consistently over time
- When an organization is one of the weaker competitors in a given industry
- When an organization is plagued by inefficiency, low profitability, poor employee morale, and pressure from stockholders to improve performance
- When an organization has failed to capitalize on external opportunities, minimize external threats, take advantage of internal strengths, and overcome internal weaknesses over time; that is, when the organization's strategic managers have failed (and possibly will be replaced by more competent individuals)
- When an organization has grown so large so quickly that major internal reorganization is needed

Divestiture

Selling a division or part of an organization is called *divestiture*. Divestiture often is used to raise capital for further strategic acquisitions or investments. Divestiture can be part of an overall retrenchment strategy to rid an organization of businesses that are unprofitable, that require too much capital, or that do not fit well with the firm's other activities. An example company using divestiture as a primary strategy is Lucent Technologies, which is currently trying to divest itself of its Octel division, a manufacturer of equipment and software used for voice-messaging systems. A possible acquirer would be Converse Technology based in Woodbury, New York. Converse controls nearly 60 percent of the $2 billion voice-messaging industry. Octel had sales of about $325 million in 2001.

The nation's largest maker of peanut butter, Procter & Gamble, recently divested itself of its Jif peanut butter and Crisco shortening operations, turning them over to J.M. Smucker, the nation's largest maker of jelly. Smucker nows has a 41 percent market share in jelly, 38 percent in peanut butter, and 24 percent in cooking oils in the United States, making it the leader in all three categories.

Divestiture has become a very popular strategy as firms try to focus on their core strengths, lessening their level of diversification. For example, a few divestitures consummated in 2001 are given in Table 5–3.

Six guidelines when divestiture may be an especially effective strategy to pursue are listed below.[21]

- When an organization has pursued a retrenchment strategy and failed to accomplish needed improvements
- When a division needs more resources to be competitive than the company can provide
- When a division is responsible for an organization's overall poor performance
- When a division is a misfit with the rest of an organization; this can result from radically different markets, customers, managers, employees, values, or needs
- When a large amount of cash is needed quickly and cannot be obtained reasonably from other sources
- When government antitrust action threatens an organization

Liquidation

Selling all of a company's assets, in parts, for their tangible worth is called *liquidation*. Liquidation is a recognition of defeat and consequently can be an emotionally difficult

TABLE 5-3   **Recent Divestitures**

PARENT COMPANY	PART BEING DIVESTED	ACQUIRING COMPANY
Dell Computer	Web-hosting division	FON Group
Citigroup	Citi Capital	GE Capital Fleet Services
Maytag	Blodgett	Middleby Corporation
Westcoast Energy	British Columbia Gas	BC Gas
Westcoast Energy	Union Energy	Epcor Utilities
Westcoast Energy	Westcoast Capital	Epcor Utilities
Credit Suisse	CSFBdirect	Bank of Montreal
Emerson Electric	Chromalox	JPMorgan Partners
General Motors	Hughes Electronics	EchoStar Communications
DuPont	drug division	Bristol-Myers Squibb
Gaylord Entertainment	Word Entertainment	AOL Time Warner

strategy. However, it may be better to cease operating than to continue losing large sums of money.

Thousands of small businesses in the United States liquidate annually without ever making the news. It is tough to start and successfully operate a small business. In China and Russia, thousands of government-owned businesses liquidate annually as those countries try to privatize and consolidate industries.

Two cybercurrency companies, Flooz.com.Inc., in New York, and Beenz Company Ltd., in Britain, recently liquidated. These two companies provided their own currency to customers, who could redeem the "money" as gift certificates at retailers such as Barnes & Noble and J. Crew. Each company cited the worldwide economic recession and credit card fraud as the reasons for the liquidation.

General Motors terminated production of its Chevrolet Camaro and Pontiac Firebird in 2002 and closed the Canadian factory where they were made. Sales of Camaro and Firebird were down 25 percent in 2001, following a decade of slumping market share due largely to competition from imported rivals and sport-utility vehicles.

For the twelve months ended June 30, 2001, there were 21,935 liquidations in the United States according to the Administrative Office of the U.S. Courts, up dramatically from the same period the year before.

Three guidelines when liquidation may be an especially effective strategy to pursue are:[22]

- When an organization has pursued both a retrenchment strategy and a divestitute strategy, and neither has been successful.
- When an organization's only alternative is bankruptcy; liquidation represents an orderly and planned means of obtaining the greatest possible cash for an organization's assets. A company can legally declare bankruptcy first and then liquidate various divisions to raise needed capital.
- When the stockholders of a firm can minimize their losses by selling the organization's assets.

MICHAEL PORTER'S GENERIC STRATEGIES

Probably the three most widely read books on competitive analysis in the 1980s were Michael Porter's (**www.hbs.edu/bios/mporter**) *Competitive Strategy* (Free Press, 1980),

Competitive Advantage (Free Press, 1985), and *Competitive Advantage of Nations* (Free Press, 1989). According to Porter, strategies allow organizations to gain competitive advantage from three different bases: cost leadership, differentiation, and focus. Porter calls these bases *generic strategies*. *Cost leadership* emphasizes producing standardized products at a very low per-unit cost for consumers who are price-sensitive. *Differentiation* is a strategy aimed at producing products and services considered unique industrywide and directed at consumers who are relatively price-insensitive. *Focus* means producing products and services that fulfill the needs of small groups of consumers.

Porter's strategies imply different organizational arrangements, control procedures, and incentive systems. Larger firms with greater access to resources typically compete on a cost leadership and/or differentiation basis, whereas smaller firms often compete on a focus basis.

Porter stresses the need for strategists to perform cost-benefit analyses to evaluate "sharing opportunities" among a firm's existing and potential business units. Sharing activities and resources enhances competitive advantage by lowering costs or raising differentiation. In addition to prompting sharing, Porter stresses the need for firms to "transfer" skills and expertise among autonomous business units effectively in order to gain competitive advantage. Depending upon factors such as type of industry, size of firm, and nature of competition, various strategies could yield advantages in cost leadership, differentiation, and focus.

Cost Leadership Strategies

A primary reason for pursuing forward, backward, and horizontal integration strategies is to gain cost leadership benefits. But cost leadership generally must be pursued in conjunction with differentiation. A number of cost elements affect the relative attractiveness of generic strategies, including economies or diseconomies of scale achieved, learning and experience curve effects, the percentage of capacity utilization achieved, and linkages with suppliers and distributors. Other cost elements to consider in choosing among alternative strategies include the potential for sharing costs and knowledge within the organization, R&D costs associated with new product development or modification of existing products, labor costs, tax rates, energy costs, and shipping costs.

Striving to be the low-cost producer in an industry can be especially effective when the market is composed of many price-sensitive buyers, when there are few ways to achieve product differentiation, when buyers do not care much about differences from brand to brand, or when there are a large number of buyers with significant bargaining power. The basic idea is to underprice competitors and thereby gain market share and sales, driving some competitors out of the market entirely.

A successful cost leadership strategy usually permeates the entire firm, as evidenced by high efficiency, low overhead, limited perks, intolerance of waste, intensive screening of budget requests, wide spans of control, rewards linked to cost containment, and broad employee participation in cost control efforts. Some risks of pursuing cost leadership are that competitors may imitate the strategy, thus driving overall industry profits down; that technological breakthroughs in the industry may make the strategy ineffective; or that buyer interest may swing to other differentiating features besides price. Several example firms that are well known for their low-cost leadership strategies are Wal-Mart, BIC, McDonald's, Black and Decker, Lincoln Electric, and Briggs and Stratton.

Differentiation Strategies

Different strategies offer different degrees of differentiation. Differentiation does not guarantee competitive advantage, especially if standard products sufficiently meet customer needs or if rapid imitation by competitors is possible. Durable products protected by barriers to quick copying by competitors are best. Successful differentiation can mean greater product flexibility, greater compatibility, lower costs, improved service, less maintenance, greater convenience, or more features. Product development is an example of a strategy that offers the advantages of differentiation.

A differentiation strategy should be pursued only after a careful study of buyers' needs and preferences to determine the feasibility of incorporating one or more differentiating features into a unique product that features the desired attributes. A successful differentiation strategy allows a firm to charge a higher price for its product and to gain customer loyalty because consumers may become strongly attached to the differentiation features. Special features that differentiate one's product can include superior service, spare parts availability, engineering design, product performance, useful life, gas mileage, or ease of use.

A risk of pursuing a differentiation strategy is that the unique product may not be valued highly enough by customers to justify the higher price. When this happens, a cost leadership strategy easily will defeat a differentiation strategy. Another risk of pursuing a differentiation strategy is that competitors may develop ways to copy the differentiating features quickly. Firms thus must find durable sources of uniqueness that cannot be imitated quickly or cheaply by rival firms.

Common organizational requirements for a successful differentiation strategy include strong coordination among the R&D and marketing functions and substantial amenities to attract scientists and creative people. Firms pursuing a differentiation strategy include Dr. Pepper, Jenn-Air, The Limited, BMW, Grady-White, Ralph Lauren, Maytag, and Cross.

Focus Strategies

A successful focus strategy depends on an industry segment that is of sufficient size, has good growth potential, and is not crucial to the success of other major competitors. Strategies such as market penetration and market development offer substantial focusing advantages. Midsize and large firms can effectively pursue focus-based strategies only in conjunction with differentiation or cost leadership–based strategies. All firms in essence follow a differentiated strategy. Because only one firm can differentiate itself with the lowest cost, the remaining firms in the industry must find other ways to differentiate their products.

Focus strategies are most effective when consumers have distinctive preferences or requirements and when rival firms are not attempting to specialize in the same target segment. Firms pursuing a focus strategy include San Antonio-based Clear Channel, the nation's largest radio chain, billboard owner, and concert promoter. Clear Channel has used a focus strategy for a decade to achieve $5.3 billion in annual revenues from operations in sixty-three countries, including twelve hundred radio stations, nineteen television stations, and 770,000 outdoor advertising displays. The next largest radio company in the nation is Infinity Broadcasting Corp., which owns only 183 radio stations. Clear Channel owns eight radio stations in each of the following cities: Los Angeles, Houston, Denver, and Washington, D.C.

Bally Total Fitness Holding Corporation, the nation's leader in health clubs, recently acquired Crunch, a large health-club company. Bally is allowing New York-based Crunch to keep its name and to expand from nineteen clubs to forty clubs before 2004. Bally operates about four hundred clubs with four million members. Obviously pursuing a focus strategy, Bally had just purchased the Sports Clubs of Canada.

Another excellent example of a focus strategy is the fact that Germany's Bayerische Motoren Werke AG (BMW) focuses exclusively on premium, luxury cars. The BMW strategy bucks conventional wisdom in the anto industry to produce for the mass market too.

Risks of pursuing a focus strategy include the possibility that numerous competitors will recognize the successful focus strategy and copy it, or that consumer preferences will drift toward the product attributes desired by the market as a whole. An organization using a focus strategy may concentrate on a particular group of customers, geographic markets, or on particular product-line segments in order to serve a well-defined but narrow market better than competitors who serve a broader market.

The Value Chain

According to Porter, the business of a firm can best be described as a *value chain,* in which total revenues minus total costs of all activities undertaken to develop and market a product or service yields value. All firms in a given industry have a similar value chain, which includes activities such as obtaining raw materials, designing products, building manufacturing facilities, developing cooperative agreements, and providing customer service. A firm will be profitable as long as total revenues exceed the total costs incurred in creating and delivering the product or service. Firms should strive to understand not only their own value chain operations, but also their competitors', suppliers', and distributors' value chains.

MEANS FOR ACHIEVING STRATEGIES

Joint Venture/Partnering

Joint venture is a popular strategy that occurs when two or more companies form a temporary partnership or consortium for the purpose of capitalizing on some opportunity. Often, the two or more sponsoring firms form a separate organization and have shared equity ownership in the new entity. Other types of *cooperative arrangements* include research and development partnerships, cross-distribution agreements, cross-licensing agreements, cross-manufacturing agreements, and joint-bidding consortia.

Joint ventures and cooperative arrangements are being used increasingly because they allow companies to improve communications and networking, to globalize operations, and to minimize risk. Kathryn Rudie Harrigan, professor of strategic management at Columbia University, summarizes the trend toward increased joint venturing:

> In today's global business environment of scarce resources, rapid rates of technological change, and rising capital requirements, the important question is no longer "Shall we form a joint venture?" Now the question is "Which joint ventures and cooperative arrangements are most appropriate for our needs and expectations?" followed by "How do we manage these ventures most effectively?"[23]

In a global market tied together by the Internet, joint ventures, partnerships, and alliances are proving to be a more effective way to enhance corporate growth than mergers and acquisitions.[24] Strategic partnering takes many forms, including outsourcing, information sharing, joint marketing, and joint research and development. Many companies such as Eli Lilly even now host partnership training classes for their managers and partners. There are today more than ten thousand joint ventures formed annually, more than all mergers and acquisitions. There are countless examples of successful strategic alliances, such as Kmart's recent $4.5 billion supply-chain alliance with grocery wholesaler Fleming, which is integrating Kmart's buying, inventory control, and logistics with its own high tech system.

A major reason why firms are using partnering as a means to achieve strategies is globalization. Wal-Mart's successful joint venture with Mexico's Cifra is indicative of how a domestic firm can benefit immensely by partnering with a foreign company to gain substantial presence in that new country. Technology also is a major reason behind the need to form strategic alliances, with the Internet linking widely dispersed partners. The Internet paved the way and legitimized the need for alliances to serve as the primary means for corporate growth. IBM in 2001 doubled its strategic software alliances to more than one hundred by year-end.[25]

Evidence is mounting that firms should use partnering as a means for achieving strategies. However, the sad fact is that most American firms in many industries, such as financial services, forest products, and metals and retailing, still operate in a merger or acquire mode to obtain growth. Partnering is not yet taught at most business schools and is often viewed within companies as a financial issue rather than a strategic issue. However, partnering has become a core competency, a strategic issue of such importance that top management involvement initially and throughout the life of an alliance is vital.[26]

Dell Computer, based in Austin, Texas, and its fierce rival, EMC Corporation, based in Hopkinton, Massachusetts, announced a sales and development alliance in late 2001, one in which Dell will resell and cooperate on the development of EMC's Clarion storage systems. It is interesting that just a year earlier, Dell Chairman Michael Dell had joked that the initials of EMC stood for "Excess Margin Corporation" and insisted that Dell would undercut those margins with lower-cost products.[27]

Cingular Wireless and VoiceStream Wireless recently formed a 50–50 joint venture to share their mobile infrastructure in major U.S. markets. These two companies are saving "hundreds of millions of dollars" in capital expenditures and operating expenses by cooperating in this manner. Another benefit of this venture and others like it is that such agreements do not require approval from the Federal Communications Commission; this is in contrast to a merger or acquisition, which would require approval.

General Motors in the early 2000s weaved together a large number of alliances and joint ventures throughout Asia to enhance its operations. GM's share of the Asian market is now about 16 percent, second only to Toyota. GM attributes its success in Asia to its new partnerships and cooperative arrangements. GM has alliances with the bankrupt Korean automaker Daewoo Motor as well as Japan's Suzuki Motor, Isuzu Motor, Fuji Heavy Industries, and many other rival and supplier firms. GM acknowledges that alliances with non-American firms are more difficult to manage, but it insists that the many Asian partnerships benefit the company immensely and "avoid much of the pain, tension, and risk of a merger."[28]

IBM and the German company Lion Bioscience AG in 2001 established an alliance in which the firms will develop and market their computer technologies and data-mining software as a package to major drug makers and to other research laboratories trying to assimilate research data being generated in human gene research. The companies say their alliance will shorten the discovery and development time for new medicines. The market for genomics equipment should double to $43 billion from 2001 to 2003. IBM formed a new life-sciences division in August 2000.

Burger King Corp. and AOL Time Warner recently formed a strategic alliance that allows the number two hamburger chain's twelve million daily customers to obtain AOL software at the restaurants. This is among the first ventures of its kind in the fast-food industry, which to date has not focused on the Internet revolution. AOL in return is marketing Burger King online.

Sprint and AOL in late 2001 formed a new strategic alliance, one in which AOL will promote Sprint's long-distance phone service while AOL members receive a variety of Sprint long-distance plans. Sprint is the third-ranked long-distance business, but it faces increasing competition from regional bells.

Although ventures and partnerships are preferred over mergers as a means for achieving strategies, certainly they are not all successful. The good news is that joint ventures and partnerships are less risky for companies than mergers, but the bad news is that many alliances fail. Forbes recently reported that about 30 percent of all joint ventures and partnership alliances are outright failures, while another 17 percent have limited success and then dissipate due to problems.[29] There are countless examples of failed joint ventures. A few common problems that cause joint ventures to fail are as follows:

1. Managers who must collaborate daily in operating the venture are not involved in forming or shaping the venture.
2. The venture may benefit the partnering companies but may not benefit customers who then complain about poorer service or criticize the companies in other ways.
3. The venture may not be supported equally by both partners. If supported unequally, problems arise.
4. The venture may begin to compete more with one of the partners than the other.[30]

Swedish telecommunications-equipment maker Telefon L. M. Ericsson currently has nine joint ventures in China and is one of that country's largest suppliers of telecommunications network equipment and mobile phones. Ericsson plans to increase its investment in China to $5.1 billion by 2005 from $2.4 billion in 2001.

Six guidelines when a joint venture may be an especially effective strategy to purse are:[31]

- When a privately owned organization is forming a joint venture with a publicly owned organization; there are some advantages to being privately held, such as closed ownership; there are some advantages of being publicly held, such as access to stock issuances as a source of capital. Sometimes, the unique advantages of being privately and publicly held can be synergistically combined in a joint venture.
- When a domestic organization is forming a joint venture with a foreign company; a joint venture can provide a domestic company with the opportunity for obtaining local management in a foreign country, thereby reducing risks such as expropriation and harassment by host country officials.
- When the distinct competencies of two or more firms complement each other especially well.
- When some project is potentially very profitable but requires overwhelming resources and risks; the Alaskan pipeline is an example.
- When two or more smaller firms have trouble competing with a large firm.
- When there exists a need to introduce a new technology quickly.

Joint Ventures in Russia

A joint venture strategy offers a possible way to enter the Russian market. Joint ventures create a mechanism to generate hard currency, which is important because of problems valuing the ruble. Russia's joint venture law has been revised to allow foreigners to own up to 99 percent of the venture and to allow a foreigner to serve as chief executive officer.

The following guidelines are appropriate when considering a joint venture in Russia. First, avoid regions with ethnic conflicts and violence. Also, make sure the potential partner has a proper charter that has been amended to permit joint venture participation. Be aware that businesspeople in these lands have little knowledge of marketing, contract law, corporate law, fax machines, voice mail, and other business practices that Westerners take for granted.

Business contracts with Russian firms should address natural-environment issues because Westerners often get the blame for air and water pollution problems and habitat destruction. Work out a clear means of converting rubles to dollars before entering a proposed joint venture, because neither Russian banks nor authorities can be counted on to facilitate foreign firms' getting dollar profits out of a business. Recognize that chronic shortages of raw materials hamper business in Russia, so make sure an adequate supply of competitively priced, good-quality raw materials is reliably available. Finally, make sure the business contract limits the circumstances in which expropriation would be legal. Specify a lump sum in dollars if expropriation should occur unexpectedly, and obtain expropriation insurance before signing the agreement.

 # MERGER/ACQUISITION

Merger and acquisition are two commonly used ways to pursue strategies. A *merger* occurs when two organizations of about equal size unite to form one enterprise. An *acquisition* occurs when a large organization purchases (acquires) a smaller firm, or vice versa. When a merger or acquisition is not desired by both parties, it can be called a *takeover* or *hostile takeover*. For example, when Clorox recently acquired First Brands, Clorox made it clear from the start that the union was a takeover, not a merger of equals. Clorox excluded First Brands' executives from the conference call announcing the deal and soon thereafter fired 255 employees at First Brands' headquarters. Perhaps because of the unhealthy takeover climate, Clorox has had trouble with First Brands' products ever since the merger, especially the Glad bag product line. For example, Northrup Grumman Corp. in 2002 launched a hostile takeover attempt of TRW Inc. There are numerous and powerful forces driving once-fierce rivals to merge around the world. Some of these forces are deregulation, technological change, excess capacity, inability to boost profits through price increases, a depressed stock market, and the need to gain economies of scale.

In addition, there are bargains available as companies struggle and while stock prices are low. For example, Palm, the leading handheld computer maker, recently purchased software maker Be for $11 million in stock in late 2001, whereas three years earlier Apple Computer sought to acquire Be for about $300 million. In this recession, cash-starved economy, large firms that do have cash are prowling for opportunistic purchases: SBC Communications acquired Prodigy and Cisco Systems acquired ten small firms in 2002.

Not all mergers are effective and successful. Pricewaterhouse Coopers LLP recently researched mergers and found that the average acquirer's stock was 3.7 percent lower than its industry peer group a year later. *Business Week* and *The Wall Street Journal* studied mergers and concluded that about half produced negative returns to shareholders. Warren Buffett once said in a speech that "too-high purchase price for the stock of an excellent company can undo the effects of a subsequent decade of favorable business developments." So a merger between two firms can yield great benefits, but the price and reasoning must be right.

Within three business days following the Hewlett-Packard proposed acquisition of Compaq, the stock price of each company fell nearly 20 percent. The stock decline cut more than $6 billion off the value of the all-stock deal as analysts and consumers were skeptical of the future success of the merged firm. Recent research indicates that 73 percent of all mergers between domestic and foreign companies fail to prosper or deliver value. For companies acquired between 1998 and 2001 in deals of $15 billion or more, the stocks of the acquirers have underperformed the S&P 500 stock index by 14 percent.[32] A reason why companies still merge—even in the face of odds against success—is the fact that investors and shareholders greatly reward increased market share and geographic expansion, yet they also mercilessly punish firms with flat sales. Future growth expectations account for more than 60 percent of an average company's market value today, up from about 40 percent a decade ago.[33]

Among mergers, acquisitions, and takeovers in recent years, same-industry combinations have predominated. A general market consolidation is occurring in many industries, especially banking, insurance, defense, and healthcare, but also in pharmaceuticals, food, airlines, accounting, publishing, computers, retailing, financial services, and biotechnology. For example, United Airlines and US Airways are still interested in merging, but the Department of Justice is concerned that the merger would not be good for competition. Delta and Continental are also talking about a merger just in case the United/US Air merger is approved. On the global front, Japan's top airline, Japan Airlines, recently acquired the country's number three airline, Japan Air System. The new company controls nearly half of Japan's domestic market, followed by All Nippon Airways, and it is also now the number three global carrier behind United Airlines and American Airlines.

Procter & Gamble (P&G) recently acquired Clairol from Bristol-Myers Squibb. The acquisition gave P&G such brands as Herbal Essences, Aussie, and Clairol to go with its other hair-care products, such as Pantene, Head & Shoulders, Pert, Physique, and Vidal Sassoon. The acquisition marks P&G's first entry into the $1.5 billion hair-coloring business, an area that is growing faster than the shampoo market.

Table 5–4 shows some mergers and acquisitions completed in 2001. There are many reasons for mergers and acquisitions, including the following:

- To provide improved capacity utilization
- To make better use of the existing sales force
- To reduce managerial staff
- To gain economies of scale
- To smooth out seasonal trends in sales
- To gain access to new suppliers, distributors, customers, products, and creditors
- To gain new technology
- To reduce tax obligations

TABLE 5-4   **Some Recent Example Mergers**

ACQUIRING FIRM	ACQUIRED FIRM
Hewlett-Packard	Compaq Computer
SouthTrust Corp.	Bank of Tidewater
eBay	HomesDirect
PepsiCo	Quaker Oats
Sara Lee	Earthgrains Company
Amerada Hess	Triton Energy
Westvaco Corporation	Mead Corporation
Devon	Anderson Exploration
Santa Fe International	Global Marine
Dominion Resources	Louis Dreyfus Natural
AMR	TWA
TLC Laser Eye Centers	Laser Vision Centers
Tyco International Ltd.	Paragon Trade Brands, Inc.
Tellabs	Ocular Networks
Philips Petroleum	Conoco
Royal Caribbean Cruises	Princess Cruises
Barrick Gold Corp.	Homestake Mining Co.
Newport Mining Corp.	Normandy Mining Ltd.
BB&T Corp.	Mid-America Bancorp
BB&T Corp.	Area Bancshares
Northrop Grumman	Newport News Shipbuildung
Medtronic Inc.	VidaMed Inc.
Millennium Pharmaceuticals	Cor Therapeutics Inc.

The volume of mergers completed annually worldwide is growing dramatically and exceeds $1 trillion annually. There are more than ten thousand mergers annually in the United States that total more than $700 billion.

The proliferation of mergers is fueled by companies' drive for market share, efficiency, and pricing power as well as by globalization, the need for greater economies of scale, reduced regulation and antitrust concerns, the Internet, and e-commerce.

A *leveraged buyout* (LBO) occurs when a corporation's shareholders are bought (hence *buyout*) by the company's management and other private investors using borrowed funds (hence *leverage*).[34] Besides trying to avoid a hostile takeover, other reasons for initiating an LBO are senior management decisions that particular divisions do not fit into an overall corporate strategy or must be sold to raise cash, or receipt of an attractive offering price. An LBO takes a corporation private.

STRATEGIC MANAGEMENT IN NONPROFIT AND GOVERNMENTAL ORGANIZATIONS

The strategic-management process is being used effectively by countless nonprofit and governmental organizations, such as the Girl Scouts and Boy Scouts, the Red Cross, chambers of commerce, educational institutions, medical institutions, public utilities, libraries, government agencies, and churches. The nonprofit sector, surprisingly, is by far

America's largest employer. Many nonprofit and governmental organizations outperform private firms and corporations on innovativeness, motivation, productivity, and strategic management. For many nonprofit examples of strategic planning in practice, click on Strategic Planning Links found at the **www.strategyclub.com** Web site.

Compared to for-profit firms, nonprofit and governmental organizations often function as a monopoly, produce a product or service that offers little or no measurability of performance, and are totally dependent on outside financing. Especially for these organizations, strategic management provides an excellent vehicle for developing and justifying requests for needed financial support.

Educational Institutions

Educational institutions are using strategic-management techniques and concepts more frequently. Richard Cyert, president of Carnegic-Mellon University, says, "I believe we do a far better job of strategic management than any company I know." Population shifts nationally from the Northeast and Midwest to the Southeast and West are but one factor causing trauma for educational institutions that have not planned for changing enrollments. Ivy League schools in the Northeast are recruiting more heavily in the Southeast and West. This trend represents a significant change in the competitive climate for attracting the best high school graduates each year.

The first all-Internet law school, Concord University School of Law, boasts nearly two hundred students who can access lectures anytime and chat at fixed times with professors. Online college degrees are becoming common and represent a threat to traditional colleges and universities. "You can put the kids to bed and go to law school," says Andrew Rosen, chief operating officer of Kaplan Education Centers, a subsidiary of the Washington Post Company, that owns Concord. Concord is not accredited by the American Bar Association, which prohibits study by correspondence and requires more than one thousand hours of classroom time.

For a list of college strategic plans, click on strategic-planning links found at the **www.strategyclub.com** Web site, and scroll down through the academic sites.

Medical Organizations

The $200 billion American hospital industry is experiencing declining margins, excess capacity, bureaucratic overburdening, poorly planned and executed diversification strategies, soaring healthcare costs, reduced federal support, and high administrator turnover. The seriousness of this problem is accented by a 20 percent annual decline in inpatient use nationwide. Declining occupancy rates, deregulation, and accelerating growth of health maintenance organizations, preferred provider organizations, urgent care centers, outpatient surgery centers, diagnostic centers, specialized clinics, and group practices are other major threats facing hospitals today. Many private and state-supported medical institutions are in financial trouble as a result of traditionally taking a reactive rather than a proactive approach in dealing with their industry.

Hospitals—originally intended to be warehouses for people dying of tuberculosis, smallpox, cancer, pneumonia, and infectious diseases—are creating new strategies today as advances in the diagnosis and treatment of chronic diseases are undercutting that earlier mission. Hospitals are beginning to bring services to the patient as much as bringing the patient to the hospital; health care is more and more being concentrated in the home and in the residential community, not on the hospital campus. Chronic care will require day-treatment facilities, electronic monitoring at home, user-friendly ambulatory services, decentralized service networks, and laboratory testing. A successful hospital

E-COMMERCE PERSPECTIVE

e-Universities, e-Courses, and e-Learning

Although dot-com companies nationwide are in retreat and failing, educational institutions harnessing the Internet are growing dramatically. For example, the University of Maryland's enrollment in Internet courses grew 50 percent in 2001 to sixty-three thousand, and the institution now offers more than seventy degrees and certificates entirely online (**www.umuc.edu**). The largest online for-profit university, the University of Phoenix Online, enjoyed a 76 percent increase in revenues in 2001 (**http://onl.uophx.edu**). Even the U.S. Army has a rapidly growing e-learning program with more than ten thousand soldiers currently taking courses and earning degrees online from twenty-four participating colleges. The eArmyU Program offers a free laptop and printer and 100 percent of its students' tuition and expects enrollment to hit eighty thousand by 2005 (**www.eArmyu.com**). Indeed, more than 4,000 major colleges and universities in the United States now offer courses over the Internet or use the Web to enhance classes on campus.

More than two million students take courses today from institutions of higher learning in the United States, and that number is expected to increase to over five million by 2006. Since about 50 percent of all higher education students today are over age twenty-five and working, the e-learning approach offers the flexibility such students need to advance their careers through education. At Duke's Fuqua School of Business, 65 percent of an MBA student's work is now done over the Internet and just 35 percent is done in class (**www.fuqua.duke.edu**). Revenues from this e-learning approach are allowing Fuqua to double its faculty. The nation's largest online law school, Concord Law School, has eight hundred students, and graduates can take the California bar exam, although Concord is not accredited by the American Bar Association (**www.concordlawschool.com**).

Corporate spending on e-learning is expected to more than quadruple by 2005 to $18 billion. For example, at IBM, more than 200,000 employees receive education or training online annually, and 75 percent of the firm's Basic Blue course for new managers is online. The new Web approach to the Basic Blue course cut IBM's travel expenses by $350 million in 2001 alone.

Perhaps one of the greatest benefits of the e-learning movement is that it is getting more adults to study throughout their working lives. More adults today view education as a lifelong learning experience, and this is good.

Source: Adapted from William Symonds, "Giving It the Old Online Try," *Business Week* (December 3, 2001): 76–80.

---

strategy for the future will require renewed and deepened collaboration with physicians, who are central to hospitals' well-being, and a reallocation of resources from acute to chronic care in home and community settings.

Current strategies being pursued by many hospitals include creating home health services, establishing nursing homes, and forming rehabilitation centers. Backward integration strategies that some hospitals are pursuing include acquiring ambulance services, waste disposal services, and diagnostic services. Millions of persons annually research medical ailments online, which is causing a dramatic shift in the balance of power between doctor, patient, and hospitals.[35] The number of persons using the Internet to obtain medical information is skyrocketing. A motivated patient using the Internet can gain knowledge on a particular subject far beyond his or her doctor's knowledge, because no person can keep up with the results and implications of billions of dollars of medical research reported weekly. Patients today often walk into the doctor's office with a file folder of the latest articles detailing research and treatment options for their ailments. On Web sites such as America's Doctor (**www.americasdoctor.com**), consumers can consult with a physician in an online chat room twenty-four hours a day. Excellent consumer health Web sites are proliferating, boosted by investments from such firms as

Microsoft, AOL, Reader's Digest, and CBS. Drug companies such as Glaxo Wellcome are getting involved, as are hospitals. The whole strategic landscape of healthcare is changing because of the Internet. Intel recently began offering a new secure medical service whereby doctors and patients can conduct sensitive business on the Internet, such as sharing results of medical tests and prescribing medicine. The ten most successful hospital strategies today are providing free-standing outpatient surgery centers, outpatient surgery and diagnostic centers, physical rehabilitation centers, home health services, cardiac rehabilitation centers, preferred provider services, industrial medicine services, women's medicine services, skilled nursing units, and psychiatric services.[36]

Governmental Agencies and Departments

Federal, state, county, and municipal agencies and departments, such as police departments, chambers of commerce, forestry associations, and health departments, are responsible for formulating, implementing, and evaluating strategies that use taxpayers' dollars in the most cost-effective way to provide services and programs. Strategic-management concepts increasingly are being used to enable governmental organizations to be more effective and efficient. For a list of government agency strategic plans, click on strategic-planning links found at the **www.strategyclub.com** Web site, and scroll down through the government sites.

But strategists in governmental organizations operate with less strategic autonomy than their counterparts in private firms. Public enterprises generally cannot diversify into unrelated businesses or merge with other firms. Governmental strategists usually enjoy little freedom in altering the organizations' missions or redirecting objectives. Legislators and politicians often have direct or indirect control over major decisions and resources. Strategic issues get discussed and debated in the media and legislatures. Issues become politicized, resulting in fewer strategic choice alternatives. There is now more predictability in the management of public sector enterprises.

Government agencies and departments are finding that their employees get excited about the opportunity to participate in the strategic-management process and thereby have an effect on the organization's mission, objectives, strategies, and policies. In addition, government agencies are using a strategic-management approach to develop and substantiate formal requests for additional funding.

STRATEGIC MANAGEMENT IN SMALL FIRMS

Strategic management is vital for large firms' success, but what about small firms? The strategic-management process is just as vital for small companies. From their inception, all organizations have a strategy, even if the strategy just evolves from day-to-day operations. Even if conducted informally or by a single owner/entrepreneur, the strategic-management process can significantly enhance small firms' growth and prosperity. Recent data clearly show that an ever-increasing number of men and women in the United States are starting their own businesses. This means that more individuals are becoming strategists. Widespread corporate layoffs have contributed to an explosion in small businesses and new ideas.

Numerous magazine and journal articles have focused on applying strategic-management concepts to small businesses.[37] A major conclusion of these articles is that a lack of strategic-management knowledge is a serious obstacle for many small business owners. Other problems often encountered in applying strategic-management concepts

VISIT THE NET

Gives the Department of Veteran's Affairs strategic plan. www.va.gov/ StrategicPlan98/html/ StratPlan98_1.html

GLOBAL PERSPECTIVE

Mexico's Lure Starting to Wane

As consumer demand falls and global economies falter, the lure of locating or even keeping business operations in Mexico has faded. Scores of companies such as General Electric, SCI Systems, Goodyear, Michelin, and Flextronics are moving their operations from the U.S.-Mexico border to China and Malaysia. What do China and Malaysia have to offer companies over Mexico? The answer: Wages as low as 60 cents an hour, tax incentives, center tariffs, and close proximity to markets that are growing instead of contracting.

Mexico has long suffered from poor schools, rampant corruption, and outmoded infrastructure, but its close proximity to the United States, its low wages, and the passage of NAFTA were appealing to companies. Mexican President Vicente Fox has promised to boost education spending from 5 percent of Gross Domestic Product (GDP) to 8 percent, but many companies feel this is too little, too late. Telephone penetration in Mexico is among the lowest in Latin America, and Mexico's judicial system is prone to corruption. Mexicans average fewer than seven years of education, compared with about 10 years for Koreans and Poles. Malaysia and Singapore charge no corporate taxes on electronics assembly, while China and Ireland tax rates are about 10 percent. In contrast, Mexico's tax rate is 34 percent. The level of spending on research and development as a percentage of GDP in Mexico is 0.25 percent, compared to 0.75 percent, 0.85 percent and 2.6 percent in China, India, and the United States, respectively.

Mexico indeed is at a crossroads. To compete more effectively with other low-wage-rate countries such as China, Singapore, Malaysia, and Brazil, Mexico must improve its education system and infrastructure, and it must fight against drug trafficking to attract companies in the twenty-first century. Low wages and hard-working employees are no longer sufficient attractors.

Source: Adapted from Geri Smith, "Is the Magic Starting to Fade?" *Business Week* (August 6, 2001): 42–43.

VISIT THE NET

Site provides sixty sample business plans for small businesses. http://www.bplans.com/sp/index.cfm?a=bc

to small businesses are a lack of both sufficient capital to exploit external opportunities and a day-to-day cognitive frame of reference. Research also indicates that strategic management in small firms is more informal than in large firms, but small firms that engage in strategic management outperform those that do not. The *CheckMATE* strategic planning software at **www.checkmateplan.com** offers a version especially for small businesses.

CONCLUSION

The main appeal of any managerial approach is the expectation that it will enhance organizational performance. This is especially true of strategic management. Through involvement in strategic-management activities, managers and employees achieve a better understanding of an organization's priorities and operations. Strategic management allows organizations to be efficient, but more important, it allows them to be effective. Although strategic management does not guarantee organizational success, the process allows proactive rather than reactive decision making. Strategic management may represent a radical change in philosophy for some organizations, so strategists must be trained to anticipate and constructively respond to questions and issues as they arise. The sixteen strategies discussed in this chapter can represent a new beginning for many firms, especially if managers and employees in the organization understand and support the plan for action.

We invite you to visit the David page on the Prentice Hall Companion Website at
www.prenhall.com/david for this chapter's World Wide Web exercise.

KEY TERMS AND CONCEPTS

Acquisition (p. 180)

Backward Integration (p. 163)

Bankruptcy (p. 171)

Combination Strategy (p. 160)

Concentric Diversification (p. 169)

Conglomerate Diversification (p. 170)

Cooperative Arrangements (p. 177)

Cost Leadership (p. 175)

Differentiation (p. 175)

Diversification Strategies (p. 167)

Divestiture (p. 173)

Focus (p. 175)

Forward Integration (p. 161)

Franchising (p. xxx)

Generic Strategies (p. 175)

Horizontal Diversification (p. 169)

Horizontal Integration (p. 164)

Hostile Takeover (p. 180)

Integration Strategies (p. 165)

Intensive Strategies (p. 165)

Joint Venture (p. 177)

Leveraged Buyout (p. 182)

Liquidation (p. 173)

Long-Term Objectives (p. 158)

Market Development (p. 165)

Market Penetration (p. 165)

Merger (p. 180)

Outsourcing (p. 163)

Product Development (p. 166)

Retrenchment (p. 170)

Takeover (p. 180)

Vertical Integration (p. 160)

ISSUES FOR REVIEW AND DISCUSSION

1. How does strategy formulation differ for a small versus a large organization? How does it differ for a for-profit versus a nonprofit organization?

2. Give recent examples of market penetration, market development, and product development.

3. Give recent examples of forward integration, backward integration, and horizontal integration.

4. Give recent examples of concentric diversification, horizontal diversification, and conglomerate diversification.

5. Give recent examples of joint venture, retrenchment, divestiture, and liquidation.

6. Do you think hostile takeovers are unethical? Why or why not?

7. What are the major advantages and disadvantages of diversification?

8. What are the major advantages and disadvantages of an integrative strategy?

9. How does strategic management differ in profit and nonprofit organizations?

10. Why is it not advisable to pursue too many strategies at once?

11. Consumers can purchase tennis shoes, food, cars, boats, and insurance on the Internet. Are there any products today than cannot be purchased online? What is the implication for traditional retailers?

12. What are the pros and cons of a firm merging with a rival firm?

13. Does the United States lead in small business start-ups globally?

14. Visit the *CheckMATE* Strategic Planning software Web site at **www.checkmateplan.com**, and discuss the benefits offered.

15. Read one of the suggested current readings at the end of this chapter. Prepare a five-minute oral report on the topic.

NOTES

1. JOHN BYRNE, "Strategic Planning—It's Back," *Business Week* (August 26, 1996): 46.

2. STEVEN C. BRANDT, *Strategic Planning in Emerging Companies* (Reading, MA: Addison-Wesley, 1981). Reprinted with permission of the publisher.

3. ROB WHERRY, "Ice Cream Wars," *Forbes* (May 28, 2001): 160.

4. Adapted from F.R. DAVID, "How Do We Choose Among Alternative Growth Strategies?" *Managerial Planning* 33, no. 4 (January–February 1985): 14–17, 22.

5. Ibid.
6. KENNETH DAVIDSON, "Do Megamergers Make Sense?" *Journal of Business Strategy* 7, no. 3 (Winter 1987): 45.
7. op. cit., DAVID.
8. Ibid.
9. KELLY BARRON, "Culture Gap," *Forbes* (March 19, 2001): 62.
10. op. cit., DAVID.
11. Ibid.
12. THOMAS KELLNER, "A Tough Haul," *Forbes* (March 19, 2001): 186.
13. SHEILA MUTO, "Seeing a Boost, Hospitals Turn to Retail Stores," *Wall Street Journal* (November 7, 2001): B1 & B8.
14. op. cit., DAVID.
15. op. cit., DAVID.
16. BRUCE ORWALL, "ESPN Adds Entertainment Shows To Its Playbook." *Wall Street Journal* (March 6, 2002): B1.
17. Ibid.
18. MIKE SNIDER, "E-mail Use May Force Postal Service Cuts," *USA Today* (October 20, 1999): 1A.
19. CHRISTINE DUGAS, "Bankruptcy filings reach record 1.5 million," *USA Today* (February 20, 2002): 1B.
20. op. cit., DAVID.
21. Ibid.
22. Ibid.
23. KATHRYN RUDIE HARRIGAN, "Joint Ventures: Linking for a Leap Forward," *Planning Review* 14, no. 4 (July–August 1986): 10.
24. MATTHEW SCHIFRIN, "Partner or Perish," *Forbes* (May 21, 2001): 26.
25. Ibid., p. 28.
26. Ibid., p. 28.
27. GARY McWILLIAMS, "Dell Computer, EMC Plan Sales Alliance," *Wall Street Journal* (September 25, 2001), B4.
28. GREGORY WHITE, "In Asia, GM Pins Hopes on a Delicate Web of Alliances," *Wall Street Journal* (October 23, 2001): A23.
29. NIKHIL HUTHEESING, "Marital Blisters," *Forbes* (May 21, 2001): 32.
30. Ibid., p. 32.
31. STEVEN RATTNER, "Mergers: Windfalls or Pitfalls?" *The Wall Street Journal* (October 11, 1999): A22. Also, NIKHIL DEOGUN, "Merger Wave Spurs More Stock Wipeouts," *The Wall Street Journal* (November 29, 1999): C1.
32. PETER KRASS, "Why Do We Do It," *Across the Board*, (May–June 2001): 23.
33. Ibid., p. 24.
34. ROBERT DAVIS, "Net Empowering Patients," *USA Today* (July 14, 1999): 1A.
35. *Hospital* (May 5, 1991): 16.
36. Some recent articles are KEITH D. BROUTHERS, FLORIS ANDRIESSEN, and IGOR NICOLAES, "Driving Blind: Strategic Decision-Making in Small Companies," *Long Range Planning* 31 (1998): 130–138; KARGAR, JAVAD, "Strategic Planning System Characteristics and Planning Effectiveness in Small Mature Firms," *Mid-Atlantic Journal of Business* 32, no. 1 (1996): 19–35; PEEL, MICHAEL J. and JOHN BRIDGE, "How Planning and Capital Budgeting Improve SME Performance," *Long Range Planning* 31, no. 6 (1998): 848–856; SMELTZER, LARRY R., GAIL L. FANN, and V. NEAL NIKOLAISEN, "Environmental Scanning Practices in Small Business," *Journal of Small Business Management* 26, no. 3 (1988): 55–63; STEINER, MICHAEL P. and OLAF SOLEM, "Factors for Success in Small Manufacturing Firms," *Journal of Small Business Management* 26, no. 1 (1988): 51–57.
37. ANNE CAREY and GRANT JERDING, "Internet's Reach on Campus," *USA Today* (August 26, 1999): A1. Also, BILL MEYERS, "It's a Small-Business World," *USA Today* (July 30, 1999): B1–2.

CURRENT READINGS

ALLEN, SANDY, and ASHOK CHANDRASHEKAR. "Outsourcing Services: The Contract Is Just the Beginning." *Business Horizons* 43, no. 2 (March–April 2000): 25.

BAUM, J. ROBERT, EDWIN A. LOCKE, and KEN G. SMITH. "A Multidimensional Model of Venture Growth." *The Academy of Management Journal* 44, no. 2 (April 2001): 292.

CAPRON, L., W. MITCHELL, and A. SWAMINATHAN. "Asset Divestiture Following Horizontal Acquisitions: A Dynamic View." *Strategic Management Journal* 22, no. 9 (September 2001): 817.

CHURCHILL, NEIL C., and JOHN W. MULLINS. "How Fast Can Your Company Afford to Grow?" *Harvard Business Review* (May 2001): 135.

DELMAS, MAGALI A., and ANN K. TERLAAK. "A Framework for Analyzing Environmental Voluntary Agreements." *California Management Review* 43, no. 3 (Spring 2001): 44.

FROST, T. S. "The Geographic Sources of Foreign Subsidiaries' Innovations." *Strategic Management Journal* 22, no. 2 (February 2001): 101.

GARVIN, DAVID A., and MICHAEL A. ROBERTO. "What You Don't Know About Making Decisions." *Harvard Business Review* (September 2001): 108.

GILLEY, K. MATTHEW, and ABDUL RASHEED. "Making More by Doing Less: An Analysis of Outsourcing and Its Effects on Firm Performance." *Journal of Management* 26, no. 4 (2000): 763.

GUPTA, ANIL K., and VIJAY GOVINDARAJAN. "Managing Global Expansion: A Conceptual Framework." *Business Horizons* 43, no. 2 (March–April 2000): 45.

GUPTA, ANIL K., and VIJAY GOVINDARAJAN. "Converting Global Presence into Global Competitive Advantage." *The Academy of Management Executive* 15, no. 2 (May 2001): 45.

HAMBRICK, D. C., J. LI, K. XIN, and A. S. TSUI. "Compositional Gaps and Downward Spirals in International Joint Venture." *Strategic Management Journal* 22, no. 11 (November 2001): 1033.

HENSMANS, MANUEL, FRANS A. J. VAN DEN BOSH, and HENK W. VOLBERDA. "Clicks vs. Bricks in the Emerging Online Financial Services Industry." *Long Range Planning* 34, no. 2 (April 2001): 231.

HOFFMAN, WERNER H., and ROMAN SCHLOSSER. "Success Factors of Strategic Alliances in Small and Medium-sized Enterprises—An Empirical Survey." *Long Range Planning* 34, no. 3 (June 2001): 357.

INSINGA, RICHARD C., and MICHAEL J. WERLE. "Linking Outsourcing to Business Strategy." *The Academy of Management Executive* 14, no. 4 (November 2000): 58.

JUDGE, WILLIAM Q., and JOEL A. RYMAN. "The Shared Leadership Challenge in Strategic Alliances: Lessons from the US Healthcare Industry." *The Academy of Management Executive* 15, no. 2 (May 2001): 71.

KERNS, CHARLES D. "Strengthen Your Business Partnership: A Framework and Application." *Business Horizons* 43, no. 4 (July–August 2000): 17.

KUEMMERLE, WALTER. "Go Global—or No?" *Harvard Business Review* (June 2001): 37.

LUO, Y. "Product Diversification in International Joint Ventures: Performances Implications in an Emerging Market." *Strategic Management Journal* 23, no. 1 (January 2002): 1.

MARKS, MITCHELL LEE, and PHILIP H. MIRVIS. "Making Mergers and Acquisitions Work: Strategic and Psychological Preparation." *The Academy of Management Executive* 15, no. 2 (May 2001): 80.

MCCARTY, WILLIAM, MARK KASOFF, and DOUG SMITH. "The Importance of International Business at the Local Level." *Business Horizons* 43, no. 3 (May–June 2000): 35.

MONTI, JOSEPH A., and GEORGE S. YIP. "Taking the High Road When Going International." *Business Horizons* 43, no. 4 (July–August 2000): 65.

PARKHE, ARVIND. "Executive Briefing/Global Business Alliances." *Business Horizons* 43, no. 5 (September–October 2000): 2.

RAMASWAMY, K. "Organizational Ownership, Competitive Intensity, and Firm Performance: An Empirical Study of the Indian Manufacturing Sector." *Strategic Management Journal* 22, no. 10 (October 2001): 989.

SCHULZE, W. S., A. MAINKAR, and R. W. COTTERILL. "Ecological Investigation of Firm-Effects in Horizontal Mergers." *Strategic Management Journal* 22, no. 4 (April 2001): 335.

SMITH, KEN G., WALTER J. FERRIER, and CURTIS M. GRIMM. "King of the Hill: Dethroning the Industry Leader." *The Academy of Management Executive* 15, no. 2 (May 2001): 59.

SONG, MICHAEL, and MITZI M. MONTOYA-WEISS. "The Effect of Perceived Technological Uncertainty on Japanese New Product Development." *The Academy of Management Journal* 44, no. 1 (February 2001): 61.

SWINK, MORGAN L., and VINCENT A. MABERT. "Product Development Partnerships: Balancing the Needs of OEMs and Suppliers." *Business Horizons* 43, no. 3 (May–June 2000): 59.

VERMEULEN, FREEK, and HARRY BARKEMA. "Learning Through Acquisitions." *Academy of Management* 44, no. 3 (June 2001): 457.

WOLFINBARGER, MARY, and MARY C. GILLY. "Shopping Online for Freedom, Control, and Fun." *California Management Review* 43, no. 2 (Winter 2001): 34.

WRIGHT, P., M. KROLL, A. LADO, and B. VAN MESS. "The Structure of Ownership and Corporate Acquisition Strategies." *Strategic Management Journal* 23, no. 1 (January 2002): 41.

EXPERIENTIAL EXERCISES

EXPERIENTIAL EXERCISE 5A ▶

What Happened at American Airlines (AMR) in the Year 2002?

PURPOSE

In performing business policy case analysis, you will need to find epilogue information about the respective companies to determine what strategies actually were employed since the time of the case. Comparing *what actually happened* with *what you would have recommended and expected to happen* is an important part of business policy case analysis. Do not recommend what the firm actually did, unless in-depth analysis of the situation at the time reveals those strategies to have been best among all feasible alternatives. This exercise gives you experience conducting library research to determine what strategies airlines pursued in 2002.

INSTRUCTIONS

Step 1   Look up American Airlines, US Air, and United Airlines on the Internet. Find some recent articles about firms in the airline industry. Scan Moody's, Dun & Bradstreet, and Standard & Poor's publications for information. Check the **www.investor.stockpoint.com** Web site.

Step 2   Summarize your findings in a three-page report entitled "Strategies of American Airlines in 2002." Also include your personal reaction to American Airlines strategies in terms of their attractiveness.

EXPERIENTIAL EXERCISE 5B ▶

Examining Strategy Articles

PURPOSE

Strategy articles can be found weekly in journals, magazines, and newspapers. By reading and studying strategy articles, you can gain a better understanding of the strategic-management process. Several of the best journals in which to find corporate strategy articles are *Planning Review, Long Range Planning, Journal of Business Strategy*, and *Strategic Management Journal*. These journals are devoted to reporting the results of empirical research in strategic management. They apply strategic-management concepts to specific organizations and industries. They introduce new strategic-management techniques and provide short case studies on selected firms.

Other good journals in which to find strategic-management articles are *Harvard Business Review, Sloan Management Review, Business Horizons, California Management Review, Academy of Management Review, Academy of Management Journal, Academy of Management Executive, Journal of Management*, and *Journal of Small Business Management*.

In addition to journals, many magazines regularly publish articles that focus on business strategies. Several of the best magazines in which to find applied strategy articles are *Dun's Business Month, Fortune, Forbes, Business Week, Inc.,* and *Industry Week.* Newspapers such as *USA Today, The Wall Street Journal, The New York Times,* and *Barrons* cover strategy events when they occur—for example, a joint venture announcement, a bankruptcy declaration, a new advertising campaign start, acquisition of a company, divestiture of a division, a chief executive officer's hiring or firing, or a hostile takeover attempt.

In combination, journal, magazine, and newspaper articles can make the business policy course more exciting. They allow current strategies of profit and nonprofit organizations to be identified and studied.

INSTRUCTIONS

Step 1 Go to your college library and find a recent journal article that focuses on a strategic-management topic. Select your article from one of the journals listed earlier, not from a magazine. Copy the article and bring it to class.

Step 2 Give a three-minute oral report summarizing the most important information in your article. Include comments giving your personal reaction to the article. Pass your article around in class.

PURPOSE

This exercise can improve your understanding of various strategies by giving you experience classifying strategies. This skill will help you use the strategy-formulation tools presented later. Consider the following ten year 2002 strategies by various firms:

1. Swedish phone company Telia AB acquired Finland's phone company, Sonera Corp. in 2002. This was the first merger of two national phone companies in Europe.
2. eBay shut down its Internet auction operations in Japan in March 2002, conceding its market share there to Yahoo! and Japan's Softbank Corp.
3. General Electric announced it would sell off its property-and-casualty insurance operations.
4. Japan's top pharmaceutical company, Takeda Chemical Industries, is increasing its outsourcing of drug manufacturing operations from 30 percent in 2002 to 70 percent in 2006.
5. Ford is totally redesigning its Ford Expedition and Lincoln Navigator sport-utility-vehicles (SUVs) to reverse falling sales and profits.
6. Travelocity.com acquired Site59.com, a "last-minute" travel company.
7. Dell Computer signed a $5 billion contract to have Philips Electronics NV supply its computer tubes, monitors, and peripherals.
8. Merck & Co., the large drug company, is selling off its pharmacy-benefits division, Medco.
9. Adolph Coors Co. of Colorado acquired Carling Brewers of the United Kingdom.
10. eBay acquired NeoCom of Taiwan in bid to expand into that country.

INSTRUCTIONS

Step 1 On a separate sheet of paper, number from 1 to 10. These numbers correspond to the strategies described above.

Step 2 What type of strategy best describes the 10 actions cited above? Indicate your answers.

Step 3 Exchange papers with a classmate, and grade each other's paper as your instructor gives the right answers.

PURPOSE

This exercise focuses on how risky various alternative strategies are for organizations to pursue. Different degrees of risk are based largely on varying degrees of *externality*, defined as movement away from present business into new markets and products. In general, the greater the degree of externality, the greater the probability of loss result-

EXPERIENTIAL EXERCISE 5C ►
Classifying Some Year 2002 Strategies

EXPERIENTIAL EXERCISE 5D ►
How Risky Are Various Alternative Strategies?

ing from unexpected events. High-risk strategies generally are less attractive than low-risk strategies.

INSTRUCTIONS

Step 1   On a separate sheet of paper, number vertically from 1 to 10. Think of 1 as "most risky," 2 as "next most risky," and so forth to 10, "least risky."

Step 2   Write the following strategies beside the appropriate number to indicate how risky you believe the strategy is to pursue: horizontal integration, horizontal diversification, liquidation, forward integration, backward integration, product development, market development, market penetration, joint venture/partnering, and conglomerate diversification.

Step 3   Grade your paper as your teacher gives you the right answers and supporting rationale. Each correct answer is worth 10 points.

EXPERIENTIAL EXERCISE 5E ▶

Developing Alternative Strategies for My University

PURPOSE

It is important for representatives from all areas of a college or university to identify and discuss alternative strategies that could benefit faculty, students, alumni, staff, and other constituencies. As you complete this exercise, notice the learning and understanding that occurs as people express differences of opinions. Recall that *the process of planning is more important than the document.*

INSTRUCTIONS

Step 1   Recall or locate the external opportunity/threat and internal strength/weakness factors that you identified as part of Experiential Exercise 1D. If you did not do that exercise, discuss now as a class important external and internal factors facing your college or university.

Step 2   Identify and put on the chalkboard alternative strategies that you feel could benefit your college or university. Your proposed actions should allow the institution to capitalize on particular strengths, improve upon certain weaknesses, avoid external threats, and/or take advantage of particular external opportunities. List at least twenty possible strategies on the board. Number the strategies as they are written on the board.

Step 3   On a separate sheet of paper, number from 1 to the total number of strategies listed on the board. Everyone in class individually should rate the strategies identified, using a 1 to 3 scale, where 1 = *I do not support implementation*, 2 = *I am neutral about implementation*, and 3 = *I strongly support implementation*. In rating the strategies, recognize that your institution cannot do everything desired or potentially beneficial.

Step 4   Go to the board and record your ratings in a row beside the respective strategies. Everyone in class should do this, going to the board perhaps by rows in the class.

Step 5   Sum the ratings for each strategy so that a prioritized list of recommended strategies is obtained. This prioritized list reflects the collective wisdom of your class. Strategies with the highest score are deemed best.

Step 6   Discuss how this process could enable organizations to achieve understanding and commitment from individuals.

Step 7   Share your class results with a university administrator, and ask for comments regarding the process and top strategies recommended.

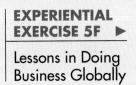

EXPERIENTIAL EXERCISE 5F ▶

Lessons in Doing Business Globally

PURPOSE

The purpose of this exercise is to discover some important lessons learned by local businesses that do businesses internationally.

INSTRUCTIONS

Contact several local business leaders by phone. Find at least three firms that engage in international or export operations. Ask the businessperson to give you several important lessons that his or her firm has learned in doing business globally. Record the lessons on paper, and report your findings to the class.

6 STRATEGY ANALYSIS AND CHOICE

1. Describe a three-stage framework for choosing among alternative strategies.
2. Explain how to develop a TOWS Matrix, SPACE Matrix, BCG Matrix, IE Matrix, and QSPM.
3. Identify important behavioral, political, ethical, and social responsibility considerations in strategy analysis and choice.
4. Discuss the role of intuition in strategic analysis and choice.
5. Discuss the role of organizational culture in strategic analysis and choice.
6. Discuss the role of a board of directors in choosing among alternative strategies.

NOTABLE QUOTES

Strategic management is not a box of tricks or a bundle of techniques. It is analytical thinking and commitment of resources to action. But quantification alone is not planning. Some of the most important issues in strategic management cannot be quantified at all.

PETER DRUCKER

Objectives are not commands; they are commitments. They do not determine the future; they are the means to mobilize resources and energies of an organization for the making of the future.

PETER DRUCKER

Life is full of lousy options.

GENERAL P. X. KELLEY

When a crisis forces choosing among alternatives, most people will choose the worst possible one.

RUDIN'S LAW

Strategy isn't something you can nail together in slapdash fashion by sitting around a conference table.

TERRY HALLER

Planning is often doomed before it ever starts, either because too much is expected of it or because not enough is put into it.

T. J. CARTWRIGHT

To acquire or not to acquire, that is the question.

ROBERT J. TERRY

Corporate boards need to work to stay away from the traps that force every member to go along with the majority. Devil's advocates represent one easy-to-implement solution.

CHARLES SCHWENK

Whether it's broke or not, fix it—make it better. Not just products, but the whole company if necessary.

BILL SAPORITO

Strategy analysis and choice largely involve making subjective decisions based on objective information. This chapter introduces important concepts that can help strategists generate feasible alternatives, evaluate those alternatives, and choose a specific course of action. Behavioral aspects of strategy formulation are described, including politics, culture, ethics, and social responsibility considerations. Modern tools for formulating strategies are described, and the appropriate role of a board of directors is discussed.

THE NATURE OF STRATEGY ANALYSIS AND CHOICE

As indicated by Figure 6–1, this chapter focuses on generating and evaluating alternative strategies, as well as an selecting strategies to pursue. Strategy analysis and choice seeks to determine alternative courses of action that could best enable the firm to achieve its mission and objectives. The firm's present strategies, objectives, and mission, coupled with the external and internal audit information, provide a basis for generating and evaluating feasible alternative strategies.

FIGURE 6–1

A Comprehensive Strategic-Management Model

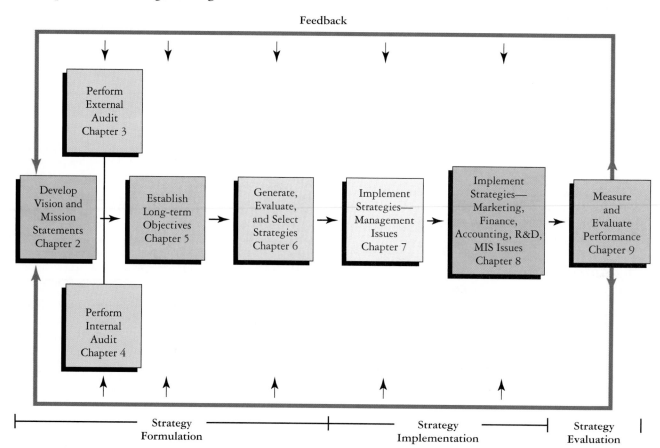

Unless a desperate situation confronts the firm, alternative strategies will likely represent incremental steps that move the firm from its present position to a desired future position. Alternative strategies do not come out of the wild blue yonder, they are derived from the firm's vision, mission, objectives, external audit, and internal audit; they are consistent with, or build on, past strategies that have worked well. Note from the Natural Environment Perspective box that natural environment attitudes of people can be an important factor in deciding among alternative strategies.

The Process of Generating and Selecting Strategies

Strategists never consider all feasible alternatives that could benefit the firm, because there are an infinite number of possible actions and an infinite number of ways to implement those actions. Therefore, a manageable set of the most attractive alternative strategies must be developed. The advantages, disadvantages, trade-offs, costs, and benefits of these strategies should be determined. This section discusses the process that many firms use to determine an appropriate set of alternative strategies.

VISIT THE NET

Cautions that planners must not usurp the responsibility of line managers in strategic planning.
http://www.csuchico.edu/mgmt/strategy/module1/sld050.htm

NATURAL ENVIRONMENT PERSPECTIVE

Formulating Strategies Based on Environmental Attitudes

Americans can be grouped into categories based on their attitudes, actions, and concern toward natural environment deterioration and preservation, Those individuals most concerned about the natural environment tend to be female, have higher household income, and live in the Midwest or Northeast. These individuals especially engage in activities such as not purchasing products from companies that are environmentally irresponsible, avoiding purchasing aerosol products, recycling paper and bottles, using biodegradable products, and contributing money to environmental groups. This information can be helpful to companies in formulating strategies such as market development (where to locate new facilities), product development (manufacturing new equipment or developing green products), and market penetration (whom to focus advertising efforts upon).

Individuals with a high concern rather than a low concern for the natural environment are relatively young, with a mean age of thirty-nine. They also are relatively smart: A full 69 percent have had some college or are college graduates. Individuals with a high concern for the natural environment have household incomes over $50,000, tend to be Internet savvy (62 percent own a personal computer), and tend to be female.

Web sites offering environmentally friendly products are **EthicalShopper.com**, **GreenHome.com**, and **EcoMall.com**, as well as **DolphinBlue.com**, which sells recycled paper and office supplies, and **EcoBaby. com**, which sells environmentally safe baby products. The Internet has made it easier for those who might not normally go out of their way to buy environmentally friendly products to find those products easily. Analysts expect the demand for green products to decline in the short run due to the economy and the fixation on terrorism; but in the long run, this demand should increase as young people grow into positions of power as heads of both households and businesses. Today's young people constitute the first generation to have been taught in school about the consequence of human actions on the earth's health.

Source: Adapted from the Roper Organization, 205 East 42nd Street, New York, NY 10017. Also from Joe Schwartz and Thomas Miller, "The Earth's Best Friends," *American Demographics* (February 1991): 28. Also adapted from Rebecca Gardyn, "Saving the Earth, One Click at a Time," *American Demographics* (January 2001): 30–33.

Identifying and evaluating alternative strategies should involve many of the managers and employees who earlier assembled the organizational vision and mission statements, performed the external audit, and conducted the internal audit. Representatives from each department and division of the firm should be included in this process, as was the case in previous strategy-formulation activities. Recall that involvement provides the best opportunity for managers and employees to gain an understanding of what the firm is doing and why, and to become committed to helping the firm accomplish its objectives.

All participants in the strategy analysis and choice activity should have the firm's external and internal audit information by their sides. This information, coupled with the firm's mission statement, will help participants crystallize in their own minds particular strategies that they believe could benefit the firm most. Creativity should be encouraged in this thought process.

Alternative strategies proposed by participants should be considered and discussed in a meeting or series of meetings. Proposed strategies should be listed in writing. When all feasible strategies identified by participants are given and understood, the strategies should be ranked in order of attractiveness by all participants, with 1 = should not be implemented, 2 = possibly should be implemented, 3 = probably should be implemented, and 4 = definitely should be implemented. This process will result in a prioritized list of best strategies that reflects the collective wisdom of the group.

A COMPREHENSIVE STRATEGY-FORMULATION FRAMEWORK

Important strategy-formulation techniques can be integrated into a three-stage decision-making framework, as shown in Figure 6–2. The tools presented in this framework are applicable to all sizes and types of organizations and can help strategists identify, evaluate, and select strategies.

Stage 1 of the formulation framework consists of the EFE Matrix, the IFE Matrix, and the Competitive Profile Matrix (CPM). Called the *Input Stage,* Stage 1 summarizes the basic input information needed to formulate strategies. Stage 2, called the *Matching*

FIGURE 6–2

The Strategy-Formulation Analytical Framework

STAGE 1: THE INPUT STAGE		
External Factor Evaluation (EFE) Matrix	Competitive Profile Matrix (CPM)	Internal Factor Evaluation (IFE) Matrix

STAGE 2: THE MATCHING STAGE				
Threats-Opportunities-Weaknesses-Strengths (TOWS) Matrix	Strategic Position and Action Evaluation (SPACE) Matrix	Boston Consulting Group (BCG) Matrix	Internal-External (IE) Matrix	Grand Strategy Matrix

STAGE 3: THE DECISION STAGE
Quantitative Strategic Planning Matrix (QSPM)

Stage, focuses upon generating feasible alternative strategies by aligning key external and internal factors. Stage 2 techniques include the Threats-Opportunities-Weaknesses-Strengths (TOWS) Matrix, the Strategic Position and Action Evaluation (SPACE) Matrix, the Boston Consulting Group (BCG) Matrix, the Internal-External (IE) Matrix, and the Grand Strategy Matrix. Stage 3, called the *Decision Stage,* involves a single technique, the Quantitative Strategic Planning Matrix (QSPM). A QSPM uses input information from Stage 1 to objectively evaluate feasible alternative strategies identified in Stage 2. A QSPM reveals the relative attractiveness of alternative strategies and thus provides an objective basis for selecting specific strategies.

All nine techniques included in the *strategy-formulation framework* require the integration of intuition and analysis. Autonomous divisions in an organization commonly use strategy-formulation techniques to develop strategies and objectives. Divisional analyses provide a basis for identifying, evaluating, and selecting among alternative corporate-level strategies.

Strategists themselves, not analytic tools, are always responsible and accountable for strategic decisions. Lenz emphasized that the shift from a words-oriented to a numbers-oriented planning process can give rise to a false sense of certainty; it can reduce dialogue, discussion, and argument as a means for exploring understandings, testing assumptions, and fostering organizational learning.[1] Strategists therefore must be wary of this possibility and use analytical tools to facilitate, rather than to diminish, communication. Without objective information and analysis, personal biases, politics, emotions, personalities, and *halo error* (the tendency to put too much weight on a single factor) unfortunately may play a dominant role in the strategy-formulation process.

THE INPUT STAGE

Procedures for developing an EFE Matrix, an IFE Matrix, and a CPM were presented in the previous two chapters. The information derived from these three matrices provides basic input information for the matching and decision stage matrices described later in this chapter.

The input tools require strategists to quantify subjectivity during early stages of the strategy-formulation process. Making small decisions in the input matrices regarding the relative importance of external and internal factors allows strategists to generate and evaluate alternative strategies more effectively. Good intuitive judgment is always needed in determining appropriate weights and ratings.

THE MATCHING STAGE

Strategy is sometimes defined as the match an organization makes between its internal resources and skills and the opportunities and risks created by its external factors.[2] The matching stage of the strategy-formulation framework consists of five techniques that can be used in any sequence: the TOWS Matrix, the SPACE Matrix, the BCG Matrix, the IE Matrix, and the Grand Strategy Matrix. These tools rely upon information derived from the input stage to match external opportunities and threats with internal strengths and weaknesses. *Matching* external and internal critical success factors is the key to effectively generating feasible alternative strategies. For example, a firm with excess working capital (an internal strength) could take advantage of the cell phone industry's 20 percent annual growth

VISIT THE NET

Gives purpose and characteristics of objectives. http://www.csuchico.edu/mgmt/strategy/module1/sld022.htm

VISIT THE NET

Gives example objectives. http://www.csuchico.edu/mgmt/strategy/module1/sld024.htm

TABLE 6-1   **Matching Key External and Internal Factors to Formulate Alternative Strategies**

KEY INTERNAL FACTOR		KEY EXTERNAL FACTOR		RESULTANT STRATEGY
Excess working capacity (an internal strength)	+	20% annual growth in the cell phone industry (an external opportunity)	=	Acquire Cellfone, Inc.
Insufficient capacity (an internal weakness)	+	Exit of two major foreign competitors from the industry (an external opportunity)	=	Pursue horizontal integration by buying competitors' facilities
Strong R&D expertise (an internal strength)	+	Decreasing numbers of younger adults (an external threat)	=	Develop new products for older adults
Poor employee morale (an internal weakness)	+	Strong union activity (an external threat)	=	Develop a new employee benefits package

rate (an external opportunity) by acquiring Cellfone, Inc., a firm in the cell phone industry. This example portrays simple one-to-one matching. In most situations, external and internal relationships are more complex, and the matching requires multiple alignments for each strategy generated. The basic concept of matching is illustrated in Table 6–1.

Any organization, whether military, product-oriented, service-oriented, governmental, or even athletic, must develop and execute good strategies to win. A good offense without a good defense, or vice versa, usually leads to defeat. Developing strategies that use strengths to capitalize on opportunities could be considered an offense, whereas strategies designed to improve upon weaknesses while avoiding threats could be termed defensive. Every organization has some external opportunities and threats and internal strengths and weaknesses that can be aligned to formulate feasible alternative strategies.

The Threats-Opportunities-Weaknesses-Strengths (TOWS) Matrix

The *Threats-Opportunities-Weaknesses-Strengths (TOWS) Matrix* is an important matching tool that helps managers develop four types of strategies: SO (strengths-opportunities) Strategies, WO (weaknesses-opportunities) Strategies, ST (strengths-threats) Strategies, and WT (weaknesses-threats) Strategies.[3] Matching key external and internal factors is the most difficult part of developing a TOWS Matrix and requires good judgment—and there is no one best set of matches. Note in Table 6-1 that the first, second, third, and fourth strategies are SO, WO, ST, and WT strategies, respectively.

SO Strategies use a firm's internal strengths to take advantage of external opportunities. All managers would like their organizations to be in a position in which internal strengths can be used to take advantage of external trends and events. Organizations generally will pursue WO, ST, or WT strategies in order to get into a situation in which they can apply SO Strategies. When a firm has major weaknesses, it will strive to overcome them and make them strengths. When an organization faces major threats, it will seek to avoid them in order to concentrate on opportunities.

WO Strategies aim at improving internal weaknesses by taking advantage of external opportunities. Sometimes key external opportunities exist, but a firm has internal weaknesses that prevent it from exploiting those opportunities. For example, there may be a high demand for electronic devices to control the amount and timing of fuel injection in automobile engines (opportunity), but a certain auto parts manufacturer may lack the technology required for producing these devices (weakness). One possible WO Strategy would be to acquire this technology by forming a joint venture with a firm having competency in this area. An alternative WO Strategy would be to hire and train people with the required technical capabilities.

VISIT THE NET

Gives a nice sample strategic plan, including the bases for developing a TOWS Matrix.
http://www.planware.org/ strategicsample.htm

ST Strategies use a firm's strengths to avoid or reduce the impact of external threats. This does not mean that a strong organization should always meet threats in the external environment head-on. An example of ST Strategy occurred when Texas Instruments used an excellent legal department (a strength) to collect nearly $700 million in damages and royalties from nine Japanese and Korean firms that infringed on patents for semi-conductor memory chips (threat). Rival firms that copy ideas, innovations, and patented products are a major threat in many industries. This is still a major problem for U.S. firms selling products in China.

WT Strategies are defensive tactics directed at reducing internal weakness and avoid-ing external threats. An organization faced with numerous external threats and internal weaknesses may indeed be in a precarious position. In fact, such a firm may have to fight for its survival, merge, retrench, declare bankruptcy, or choose liquidation.

A schematic representation of the TOWS Matrix is provided in Figure 6–3. Note that a TOWS Matrix is composed of nine cells. As shown, there are four key factor cells, four strategy cells, and one cell that is always left blank (the upper-left cell). The four strat-

E-COMMERCE PERSPECTIVE

Most U.S. Servicepersons May Soon Carry Pocket Computers

The USS *McFaul,* a U.S. destroyer stationed offshore near Afghanistan, is a designated "test platform" for handheld computers. Tests are proving to be very suc-cessful. Sailors on board download their e-mail and access the ship's Plan of the Day by plugging into infrared ports located throughout the ship. In Afghanistan, the handheld computers are being used by commandos on the ground as logistical and tactical weapons to gain a competitive advantage. Programs are available to map enemy locations, track personnel, and conduct heat-stress surveys. The U.S. Army says, "We are trying to provide our soldiers with information dominance." The U.S. Army now uses handheld com-puters to expedite such tasks as keeping track of equip-ment and food supplies. In 2001, Palm, Inc., sold between 30,000 and 50,000 Palms to the Navy and 25,000 to 30,000 units to the Army. The devices are mostly being used for data collection and information dissemination, but their uses are being expanded daily.

Soldiers and sailors carry the devices into action because the devices can track enemy and friendly troop and equipment movements. Handheld computers can interact with laser binoculars. Commander Sutherland of the U.S. Atlantic Fleet says, "Handheld computers are a tremendous morale booster among serviceper-sons." They can send and receive e-mail messages as well as manage military operations more efficiently and effectively with these devices. Companies produc-ing these products today include Palm, Inc.; Symbol Technologies, Inc.; Paravant Computer Systems; and Microsoft. Mobile phones also are increasingly being used in the military. The following table gives world-wide mobile-phone market leaders.

Source: Adapted from Pui-Wing Tam, "U.S. Forces Pack Pocket Computers in Afghanistan," *The Wall Street Journal* (October 23, 2001): B1. Also, adapted from David Pringle, "Motorola Hopes Early Push in 3G Market Yields Gains," *Wall Street Journal* (March 28, 2002): B4.

COMPANY	—SHIPMENTS, IN MILLIONS OF UNITS—			—MARKET SHARE—	
	2001	2000	% CHANGE	2001	2000
Nokia	139.67	126.37	+10.5%	35.0%	30.6%
Motorola	59.09	60.09	− 1.7	14.8	14.6
Siemens	29.75	26.99	+10.2	7.4	6.5
Samsung	28.23	20.64	+36.8	7.1	5.0
Ericsson	26.96	41.47	−35.0	6.7	10.0
Others	115.88	137.17	−15.5	29.0	33.2
Total	399.58	412.73	− 3.2	—	—

FIGURE 6–3

The TOWS Matrix

	STRENGTHS—S	WEAKNESSES—W
Always leave blank	1. 2. 3. 4. 5. 6. 7. 8. 9. 10. List strengths	1. 2. 3. 4. 5. 6. 7. 8. 9. 10. List weaknesses
OPPORTUNITIES—O 1. 2. 3. 4. 5. 6. 7. 8. 9. 10. List opportunities	SO STRATEGIES 1. 2. 3. 4. 5. 6. 7. 8. 9. 10. Use strengths to take advantage of opportunities	WO STRATEGIES 1. 2. 3. 4. 5. 6. 7. 8. 9. 10. Overcome weaknesses by taking advantage of opportunities
THREATS—T 1. 2. 3. 4. 5. 6. 7. 8. 9. 10. List threats	ST STRATEGIES 1. 2. 3. 4. 5. 6. 7. 8. 9. 10. Use strengths to avoid threats	WT STRATEGIES 1. 2. 3. 4. 5. 6. 7. 8. 9. 10. Minimize weaknesses and avoid threats

egy cells, labeled *SO, WO, ST,* and *WT,* are developed after completing four key factor cells, labeled *S, W, O,* and *T.* There are eight steps involved in constructing a TOWS Matrix:

1. List the firm's key external opportunities.
2. List the firm's key external threats.
3. List the firm's key internal strengths.
4. List the firm's key internal weaknesses.
5. Match internal strengths with external opportunities, and record the resultant SO Strategies in the appropriate cell.
6. Match internal weaknesses with external opportunities, and record the resultant WO Strategies.
7. Match internal strengths with external threats, and record the resultant ST Strategies.

FIGURE 6–4

TOWS Matrix for Carnival Cruise Lines in 2002

	STRENGTHS—S	WEAKNESSES—W
	1. Holds 34% market share 2. Largest fleet of ships 3. Six different cruise lines 4. Innovator in cruise travel industry 5. Largest variety of ships 6. Building largest cruise ship 7. High brand recognition 8. Headquartered in Miami 9. Internet friendly with online booking	1. Major loss in affiliated operations 2. Increased debt from building new ships 3. Not serving Asian market
OPPORTUNITIES—O 1. Air travel has decreased (9/11) 2. Asian market not being served 3. Possible acquisition of Princess Cruise Lines 4. New weather forecasting systems available 5. Rising demand for all-inclusive vacation packages 6. Families have increased disposable incomes 7. Marriage rates are up—more honeymoons	**SO STRATEGIES** 1. Increase capacity of ships to obtain travelers from air industry (S6, O1, O3) 2. Display the weather of vacation locations on Web site (S9, O4) 3. Offer Trans-Atlantic cruises (S6, O4) 4. Acquire P & O Princess (S1, O3)	**WO STRATEGIES** 1. Begin serving Japan and Pacific Islands (W3, O2, O3, O4) 2. Use weather forecasting to alert customers of potential storm during their vacation (W1, O4)
THREATS—T 1. Decrease in travel since 9/11 2. Terrorism 3. Competition within industry 4. Competition among other types of vacations 5. Economic recession 6. Chance of natural disasters 7. Increasing fuel prices 8. Changing government regulations	**ST STRATEGIES** 1. Advertising Carnival's ship variety, brand recognition, and safety policies (S3, S7, T1, T2, T5) 2. Advertise alternate vacations that are not affected by hurricane season (S3, T5, T7) 3. Offer discounts on Carnival Web site (S9, T6)	**WT STRATEGIES** 1. Lower prices of cruises during hurricane season (W1, T6) 2. Research viability of entering other foreign markets (W2, W3, T8, T9)

8. Match internal weaknesses with external threats, and record the resultant WT Strategies.

The purpose of each Stage 2 matching tool is to generate feasible alternative strategies, not to select or determine which strategies are best. Not all of the strategies developed in the TOWS Matrix, therefore, will be selected for implementation. A sample TOWS Matrix for Carnival Cruise Lines, is provided in Figure 6–4.

The strategy-formulation guidelines provided in Chapter 5 can enhance the process of matching key external and internal factors. For example, when an organization has both the capital and human resources needed to distribute its own products (internal strength) and distributors are unreliable, costly, or incapable of meeting the firm's needs (external threat), then forward integration can be an attractive ST Strategy. When a firm has excess production capacity (internal weakness) and its basic industry is experiencing declining annual sales and profits (external threat), then concentric diversification can be an effective WT Strategy. It is important to use specific, rather than general, strategy terms when developing a TOWS Matrix. In addition, it is important to include the "S1, O2"-type notation after each strategy in the TOWS Matrix. This notation reveals the rationale for each alternative strategy.

The Strategic Position and Action Evaluation (SPACE) Matrix

The *Strategic Position and Action Evaluation (SPACE) Matrix*, another important Stage 2 matching tool, is illustrated in Figure 6–5. Its four-quadrant framework indicates whether aggressive, conservative, defensive, or competitive strategies are most appropriate for a given organization. The axes of the SPACE Matrix represent two internal dimensions (*financial strength* [FS] and *competitive advantage* [CA]) and two external dimensions (*environmental stability* [ES] and *industry strength* [IS]). These four factors are the most important determinants of an organization's overall strategic position.[4]

Depending upon the type of organization, numerous variables could make up each of the dimensions represented on the taxes of the SPACE Matrix. Factors that were included earlier in the firm's EFE and IFE matrices should be considered in developing a SPACE Matrix. Other variables commonly included are given in Table 6–2 on page 206. For example, return on investment, leverage liquidity, working capital, and cash flow are commonly considered to be determining factors of an organization's financial strength. Like the TOWS Matrix, the SPACE Matrix should both be tailored to the particular organization being studied and based on factual information as much as possible.

The steps required to develop a SPACE Matrix are as follows:

1. Select a set of variables to define financial strength (FS), competitive advantage (CA), environmental stability (ES), and industry strength (IS).

2. Assign a numerical value ranging from +1 (worst) to +6 (best) to each of the variables that make up the FS and IS dimensions. Assign a numerical value ranging from −1 (best) to −6 (worst) to each of the variables that make up the ES and CA dimensions.

3. Compute an average score for FS, CA, IS, and ES by summing the values given to the variables of each dimension and then by dividing by the number of variables included in the respective dimension.

4. Plot the average scores for FS, IS, ES, and CA on the appropriate axis in the SPACE Matrix.

5. Add the two scores on the *x*-axis and plot the resultant point on X. Add the two scores on the *y*-axis and plot the resultant point on Y. Plot the intersection of the new *xy* point.

6. Draw a *directional vector* from the origin of the SPACE Matrix through the new intersection point. This vector reveals the type of strategies recommended for the organization: aggressive, competitive, defensive, or conservative.

Some examples of strategy profiles that can emerge from a SPACE analysis are shown in Figure 6–6 on page 207. The directional vector associated with each profile suggests the type of strategies to pursue: aggressive, conservative, defensive, or competi-

FIGURE 6–5

The SPACE Matrix

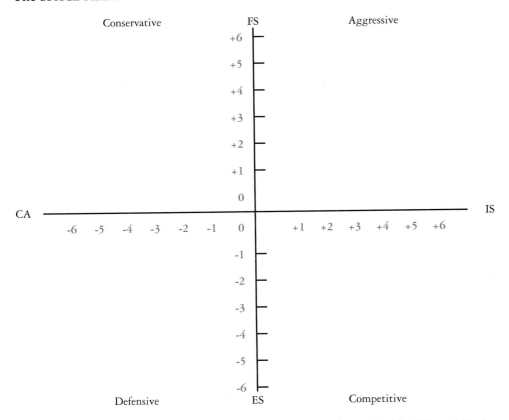

Source: H. Rowe, R. Mason, and K. Dickel, *Strategic Management and Business Policy: A Methodological Approach* (Reading, MA: Addison-Wesley Publishing Co. Inc., © 1982): 155. Reprinted with permission of the publisher.

tive. When a firm's directional vector is located in the *aggressive quadrant* (upper-right quadrant) of the SPACE Matrix, an organization is in an excellent position to use its internal strengths to (1) take advantage of external opportunities, (2) overcome internal weaknesses, and (3) avoid external threats. Therefore, market penetration, market development, product development, backward integration, forward integration, horizontal integration, conglomerate diversification, concentric diversification, horizontal diversification, or a combination strategy all can be feasible, depending on the specific circumstances that face the firm.

The directional vector may appear in the *conservative quadrant* (upper-left quadrant) of the SPACE Matrix, which implies staying close to the firm's basic competencies and not taking excessive risks. Conservative strategies most often include market penetration, market development, product development, and concentric diversification. The directional vector may be located in the lower-left or *defensive quadrant* of the SPACE Matrix, which suggests that the firm should focus on rectifying internal weaknesses and avoiding external threats. Defensive strategies include retrenchment, divestiture, liquidation, and concentric diversification. Finally, the directional vector may be located in the lower-right or *competitive quadrant* of the SPACE Matrix, indicating competitive strategies. Competitive strategies include backward, forward, and horizontal integration; market penetration; market development; product development; and joint ventures.

TABLE 6-2   **Example Factors that Make Up the SPACE Matrix Axes**

INTERNAL STRATEGIC POSITION	EXTERNAL STRATEGIC POSITION
Financial Strength (FS)	***Environmental Stability (ES)***
Return on investment	Technological changes
Leverage	Rate of inflation
Liquidity	Demand variability
Working capital	Price range of competing products
Cash flow	Barriers to entry into market
Ease of exit from market	Competitive pressure
Risk involved in business	Price elasticity of demand
Competitive Advantage (CA)	***Industry Strength (IS)***
Market share	Growth potential
Product quality	Profit potential
Product life cycle	Financial stability
Customer loyalty	Technological know-how
Competition's capacity utilization	Resource utilization
Technological know-how	Capital intensity
Control over suppliers and distributors	Ease of entry into market
	Productivity, capacity utilization

Source: H. Rowe, R. Mason, and K. Dickel, *Strategic Management and Business Policy: A Methodological Approach* (Reading, MA: Addison-Wesley Publishing Co. Inc., © 1982): 155–156. Reprinted with permission of the publisher.

A SPACE Matrix analysis for a bank is provided in Table 6–3 on page 208. Note that the competitive strategies are recommended.

The Boston Consulting Group (BCG) Matrix

Autonomous divisions (or profit centers) of an organization make up what is called a *business portfolio*. When a firm's divisions compete in different industries, a separate strategy often must be developed for each business. The *Boston Consulting Group (BCG) Matrix* and the Internal-External (IE) Matrix are designed specifically to enhance a multidivisional firm's efforts to formulate strategies. (BCG is a private management consulting firm based in Boston. BCG employs about 1,400 consultants worldwide but is cutting its workforce by 12 percent in 2002.)

The BCG Matrix graphically portrays differences among divisions in terms of relative market share position and industry growth rare. The BCG Matrix allows a multidivisional organization to manage its portfolio of businesses by examining the relative market share position and the industry growth rate of each division relative to all other divisions in the organization. *Relative market share position* is defined as the ratio of a division's own market share in a particular industry to the market share held by the largest rival firm in that industry. For example, in Table 6–4 on page 209, the relative market share of the *Wall Street Journal* is 1.78/2.24, which is 79 percent.

Relative market share position is given on the *x*-axis of the BCG Matrix. The midpoint on the *x*-axis usually is set at .50, corresponding to a division that has half the market share of the leading firm in the industry. The *y*-axis represents the industry growth rate in sales, measured in percentage terms. The growth rate percentages on the *y*-axis could range from −20 to +20 percent, with 0.0 being the midpoint. These numerical

FIGURE 6–6

Example Strategy Profiles

Aggressive Profiles

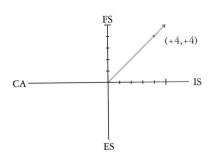

A financially strong firm that has achieved major competitive advantages in a growing and stable industry

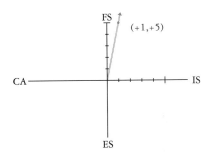

A firm whose financial strength is a dominating factor in the industry

Conservative Profiles

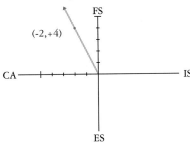

A firm that has achieved financial strength in a stable industry that is not growing; the firm has no major competitive advantages

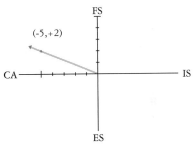

A firm that suffers from major competitive disadvantages in an industry that is technologically stable but declining in sales

Competitive Profiles

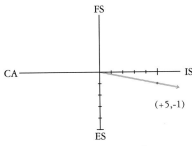

A firm with major competitive advantages in a high-growth industry

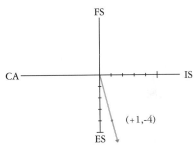

An organization that is competing fairly well in an unstable industry

Defensive Profiles

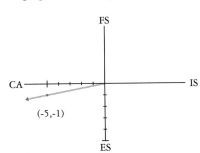

A firm that has a very weak competitive position in a negative growth, stable industry

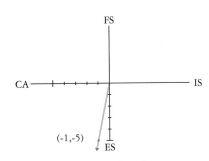

A financially troubled firm in a very unstable industry

Source: H. Rowe, R. Mason, and K. Dickel, *Strategic Management and Business Policy: A Methodological Approach* (Reading, MA: Addison-Wesley Publishing Co. Inc., © 1982): 155. Reprinted with permission of the publisher.

TABLE 6-3   **A SPACE Matrix for a Bank**

FINANCIAL STRENGTH	RATINGS
The bank's primary capital ratio is 7.23 percent, which is 1.23 percentage points over the generally required ratio of 6 percent.	1.0
The bank's return on assets is negative 0.77, compared to a bank industry average ratio of positive 0.70.	1.0
The bank's net income was $183 million, down 9 percent from a year earlier.	3.0
The bank's revenues increased 7 percent to $3.46 billion.	4.0
	9.0

INDUSTRY STRENGTH	
Deregulation provides geographic and product freedom.	4.0
Deregulation increases competition in the banking industry.	2.0
Pennsylvania's interstate banking law allows the bank to acquire other banks in New Jersey, Ohio, Kentucky, the District of Columbia, and West Virginia.	4.0
	10.0

ENVIRONMENTAL STABILITY	
Less-developed countries are experiencing high inflation and political instability.	−4.0
Headquartered in Pittsburgh, the bank historically has been heavily dependent on the steel, oil, and gas industries. These industries are depressed.	−5.0
Banking deregulation has created instability throughout the industry.	−4.0
	−13.0

COMPETITIVE ADVANTAGE	
The bank provides data processing services for more than 450 institutions in 38 states.	−2.0
Superregional banks, international banks, and nonbanks are becoming increasingly competitive.	−5.0
The bank has a large customer base.	−2.0
	−9.0

CONCLUSION

ES Average is −13.0 ÷ 3 = −4.33   IS Average is + 10.0 ÷ 3 = 3.33
CA Average is −9.0 ÷ 3 = −3.00   FS Average is + 9.0 ÷ 4 = 2.25
Directional Vector Coordinates: x-axis: −3.00 + (+3.33) = +0.33
                                                        y-axis: −4.33 + (+2.25) = −2.08
The bank should pursue Competitive Strategies.

ranges on the x- and y-axes are often used, but other numerical values could be established as deemed appropriate for particular organizations.

An example of a BCG Matrix appears in Figure 6–7 on page 210. Each circle represents a separate division. The size of the circle corresponds to the proportion of corporate revenue generated by that business unit, and the pie slice indicates the proportion of corporate profits generated by that division. Divisions located in Quadrant I of the BCG Matrix are called Question Marks, those located in Quadrant II are called Stars, those located in Quadrant III are called Cash Cows, and those divisions located in Quadrant IV are called Dogs. As indicated in the Global Perspective box on page 211, more Japanese firms are becoming Stars by changing policies that previously discouraged women from becoming managers.

- Question Marks—Divisions in Quadrant I have a low relative market share position, yet they compete in a high-growth industry. Generally these firms' cash needs are high and their cash generation is low. These businesses are called *Question*

TABLE 6-4
A. Market Share of the Ten Largest Banks in Central Europe

COMPANY	MARKET SHARE %
KBC NV of Belgium	11.7
Hypo Vereinsbank AG of Germany	9.9
Unicredito Italiano SpA of Italy	7.7
Societe Generale	7.7
Citibank of the USA	7.6
Erste Bank	7.4
BCI/Intesa	5.4
ING	4.4
RZB	4.0
Commerzbank	3.8
Other Banks	69.6%

B. Sales of the Ten Largest U.S. Newspapers

COMPANY	AVERAGE DAILY CIRCULATION (IN MILLIONS)
USA Today	2.24
The Wall Street Journal	1.78
The New York Times	1.11
The Los Angeles Times	0.97
The Washington Post	0.76
The New York Daily News	0.73
The Chicago Tribune	0.62
Newsday	0.58
Houston Chronicle	0.55
The New York Post	0.53

C. Market Share of the Leading U.S. Rental Car Companies

COMPANY	MARKET SHARE (%)
Hertz	29.1
Avis	22.6
National	15.4
Budget	12.0
Alamo	09.8
Dollar	08.9
Other	02.2

Source: Adapted from Matthew Karnitschnig, "Western Banks Quickly Expand Share of Market in Central and Eastern Europe," *The Wall Street Journal* (September 11, 2001): A21. Also, Matthew Rose and Patricia Callahan, "Can Newspapers Hold On to Postattack Readers?" *The Wall Street Journal* (October 30, 2001): B4. Also, Kortney Stringer, "Reservations Grow Over Rental-Car Industry's Weak Links," *Wall Street Journal* (November 14, 2001): B4.

Marks because the organization must decide whether to strengthen them by pursuing an intensive strategy (market penetration, market development, or product development) or to sell them.

- Stars—Quadrant II businesses (often called *Stars*) represent the organization's best long-run opportunities for growth and profitability. Divisions with a high relative market share and a high industry growth rate should receive substantial investment to maintain or strengthen their dominant positions. Forward, back-

FIGURE 6–7

The BCG Matrix

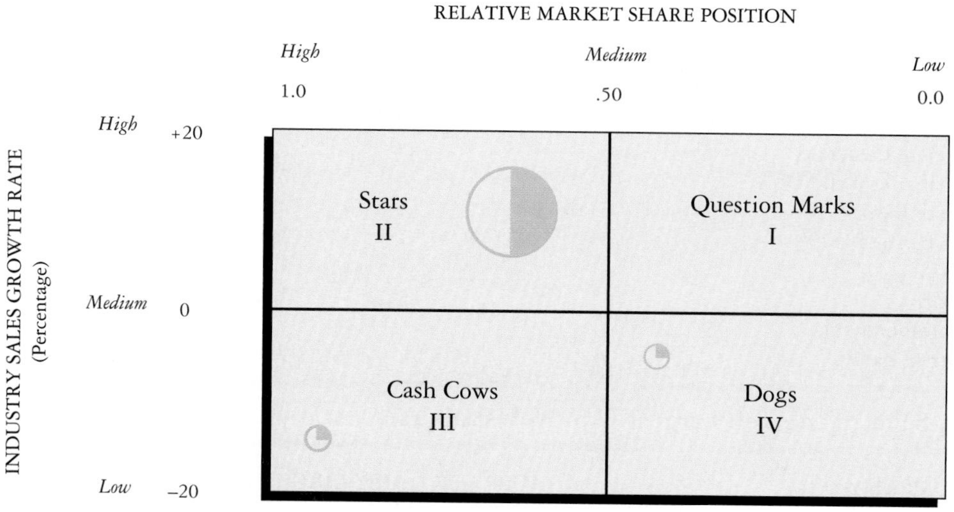

RELATIVE MARKET SHARE POSITION

| | High
1.0 | Medium
.50 | Low
0.0 |

INDUSTRY SALES GROWTH RATE (Percentage)

High +20 / Medium 0 / Low −20

Stars II

Question Marks I

Cash Cows III

Dogs IV

Source: Adapted from Boston Consulting Group, *Perspectives on Experience* (Boston: The Boston Consulting Group, 1974).

ward, and horizontal integration; market penetration; market development; product development; and joint ventures are appropriate strategies for these divisions to consider.

- Cash Cows—Divisions positioned in Quadrant III have a high relative market share position but compete in a low-growth industry. Called *Cash Cows* because they generate cash in excess of their needs, they are often milked. Many of today's Cash Cows were yesterday's Stars. Cash Cow divisions should be managed to maintain their strong position for as long as possible. Product development or concentric diversification may be attractive strategies for strong Cash Cows. However, as a Cash Cow division becomes weak, retrenchment or divestiture can become more appropriate.

- Dogs—Quadrant IV divisions of the organization have a low relative market share position and compete in a slow- or no-market-growth industry; they are *Dogs* in the firm's portfolio. Because of their weak internal and external position, these businesses are often liquidated, divested, or trimmed down through retrenchment. When a division first becomes a Dog, retrenchment can be the best strategy to pursue because many Dogs have bounced back, after strenuous asset and cost reduction, to become viable, profitable divisions.

The major benefit of the BCG Matrix is that it draws attention to the cash flow, investment characteristics, and needs of an organization's various divisions. The divisions of many firms evolve over time: Dogs become Question Marks, Question Marks become Stars, Stars become Cash Cows, and Cash Cows become Dogs in an ongoing counterclockwise motion. Less frequently, Stars become Question Marks, Question Marks become Dogs, Dogs become Cash Cows, and Cash Cows become Stars (in a clockwise motion). In some organizations, no cyclical motion is apparent. Over time, organizations should strive to achieve a portfolio of divisions that are Stars.

One example of a BCG Matrix is provided in Figure 6–8 on page 212, which illustrates an organization composed of five divisions with annual sales ranging from $5,000 to $60,000. Division 1 has the greatest sales volume, so the circle representing that division is the largest one in the matrix. The circle corresponding to Division 5 is the smallest because its sales volume ($5,000) is least among all the divisions. The pie slices within the circles reveal the percent of corporate profits contributed by each division. As shown, Division 1 contributes the highest profit percentage, 39 percent. Notice in the diagram that Division 1 is considered a Star, Division 2 is a Question Mark, Division 3 is also a Question Mark, Division 4 is a Cash Cow, and Division 5 is a Dog.

The BCG Matrix, like all analytical techniques, has some limitations. For example, viewing every business as either a Star, Cash Cow, Dog, or Question Mark is an oversimplification; many businesses fall right in the middle of the BCG Matrix and thus are not easily classified. Furthermore, the BCG Matrix does not reflect whether or not various divisions or their industries are growing over time; that is, the matrix has no temporal qualities, but rather it is a snapshot of an organization at a given point in time. Finally, other variables besides relative market share position and industry growth rate in sales, such as size of the market and competitive advantages, are important in making strategic decisions about various divisions.

The Internal-External (IE) Matrix

The *Internal-External (IE) Matrix* positions an organization's various divisions in a nine-cell display, illustrated in Figure 6–9 on page 213. The IE Matrix is similar to the BCG Matrix in that both tools involve plotting organization divisions in a schematic diagram; this is why they are both called portfolio matrices. Also, the size of each circle represents the percentage sales contribution of each division, and pie slices reveal the percentage profit contribution of each division in both the BCG and IE Matrix.

GLOBAL PERSPECTIVE

Changing Role of Women in Japan

Japan's population is projected to decline by nearly half by the end of the twenty-first century, while the aging population puts a huge burden on working people. Consequently, the conservative and male-dominated Japanese legislature is reconsidering gender equality. In 1999, the Japanese legislature passed a sweeping "basic law" to promote equal participation in society by men and women. This law covers everything from equal hiring and promotion in business and government to common practices such as listing boys' names ahead of girls' names on class rosters in public schools. Also in 1999, the legislature passed a new law that bans sexual discrimination in the workplace. The law also bans child pornography and sex with minors. Further in 1999, Japan became the last member of the United Nations to approve relatively safe, low-dose birth control pills. These are all legislative victories for Japanese women who now feel more comfortable having children or joining the workforce if they desire. New Japanese law also encourages men to join in helping women in child rearing and housework. Currently Japanese men do only 6 percent of the housework and 11 percent of the work caring for children or elders.

Any national culture that prohibits or discourages women from working outside the home disadvantages firms in that particular country as they strive to compete with firms in other countries that capitalize on the proven capability of women to perform equally with men in nearly all jobs. Certainly it will take years to change this type of business culture, but Japan got started in 1999. This business culture shift should enhance Japan's business competitiveness worldwide.

Source: Adapted from Steven Butler, "In Japan, Finally the Women Catch a Break," *U.S. News & World Report* (July 5, 1999): 41.

FIGURE 6–8

An Example BCG Matrix

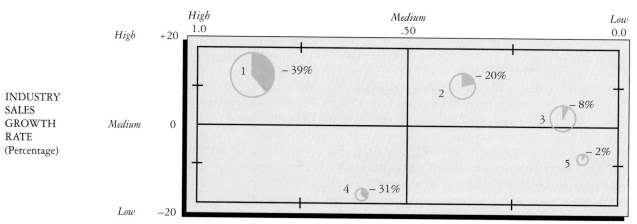

RELATIVE MARKET SHARE POSITION IN THE INDUSTRY

Division	Revenues	Percent Revenues	Profits	Percent Profits	Percent Market Share	Percent Growth Rate
1	$60,000	37	$10,000	39	80	+15
2	40,000	24	5,000	20	40	+10
3	40,000	24	2,000	8	10	1
4	20,000	12	8,000	31	60	−20
5	5,000	3	500	2	5	−10
Total	$165,000	100	$25,500	100		

But there are some important differences between the BCG Matrix and the IE Matrix. First, the axes are different. Also, the IE Matrix requires more information about the divisions than the BCG Matrix. Furthermore, the strategic implications of each matrix are different. For these reasons, strategists in multidivisional firms often develop both the BCG Matrix and the IE Matrix in formulating alternative strategies. A common practice is to develop a BCG Matrix and an IE Matrix for the present and then develop projected matrices to reflect expectations of the future. This before-and-after analysis forecasts the expected effect of strategic decisions on an organization's portfolio of divisions.

The IE Matrix is based on two key dimensions: the IFE total weighted scores on the *x*-axis and the EFE total weighted scores on the *y*-axis. Recall that each division of an organization should construct an IFE Matrix and an EFE Matrix for its part of the organization. The total weighted scores derived from the divisions allow construction of the corporate-level IE Matrix. On the *x*-axis of the IE Matrix, an IFE total weighted score of 1.0 to 1.99 represents a weak internal position; a score of 2.0 to 2.99 is considered average; and a score of 3.0 to 4.0 is strong. Similarly, on the *y*-axis, an EFE total weighted score of 1.0 to 1.99 is considered low; a score of 2.0 to 2.99 is medium; and a score of 3.0 to 4.0 is high.

The IE Matrix can be divided into three major regions that have different strategy implications. First, the prescription for divisions that fall into cells I, II, or IV can be described as *grow and build*. Intensive (market penetration, market development, and product development) or integrative (backward integration, forward integration, and horizontal integration) strategies can be most appropriate for these divisions. Second, divisions that fall into cells III, V, or VII can be managed best with *hold and maintain* strategies; market penetration and product development are two commonly employed

FIGURE 6–9

The Internal-External (IE) Matrix

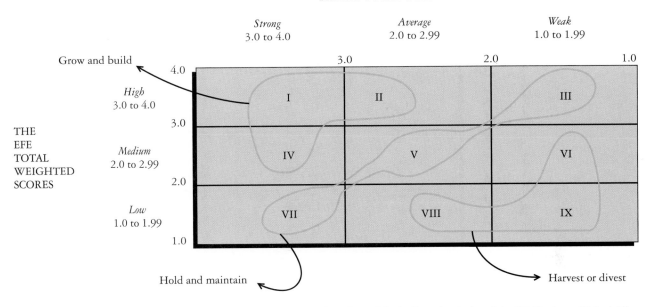

Source: The IE Matrix was developed from the General Electric (GE) Business Screen Matrix. For a description of the GE Matrix see Michael Allen, "Diagramming GE's Planning for What's WATT," in R. Allio and M. Pennington, eds., *Corporate Planning: Techniques and Applications*. (New York: AMACOM, 1979).

strategies for these types of divisions. Third, a common prescription for divisions that fall into cells VI, VIII, or IX is *harvest or divest*. Successful organizations are able to achieve a portfolio of businesses positioned in or around cell I in the IE Matrix.

An example of a completed IE Matrix is given in Figure 6–10 on page 214, which depicts an organization composed of four divisions. As indicated by the positioning of the circles, *grow and build* strategies are appropriate for Division 1, Division 2, and Division 3. Division 4 is a candidate for *harvest or divest*. Division 2 contributes the greatest percentage of company sales and thus is represented by the largest circle. Division 1 contributes the greatest proportion of total profits; it has the largest-percentage pie slice.

The Grand Strategy Matrix

In addition to the TOWS Matrix, SPACE Matrix, BCG Matrix, and IE Matrix, the *Grand Strategy Matrix* has become a popular tool for formulating alternative strategies. All organizations can be positioned in one of the Grand Strategy Matrix's four strategy quadrants. A firm's divisions likewise could be positioned. As illustrated in Figure 6–11 on page 215, the Grand Strategy Matrix is based on two evaluative dimensions: competitive position and market growth. Appropriate strategies for an organization to consider are listed in sequential order of attractiveness in each quadrant of the matrix.

Firms located in Quadrant I of the Grand Strategy Matrix are in an excellent strategic position. For these firms, continued concentration on current markets (market penetration and market development) and products (product development) is an appropriate strategy. It is unwise for a Quadrant I firm to shift notably from its established competitive advantages. When a Quadrant I organization has excessive resources, then

FIGURE 6–10

An Example IE Matrix

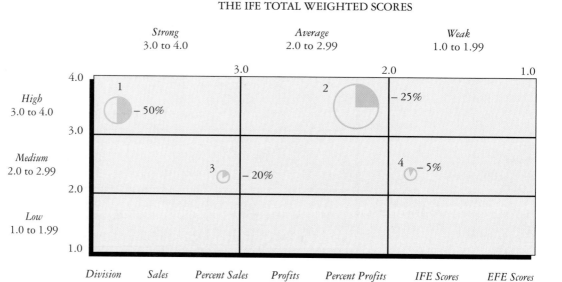

THE IFE TOTAL WEIGHTED SCORES

Division	Sales	Percent Sales	Profits	Percent Profits	IFE Scores	EFE Scores
1	$100	25.0	10	50	3.6	3.2
2	200	50.0	5	25	2.1	3.5
3	50	12.5	4	20	3.1	2.1
4	50	12.5	1	5	1.8	2.5
Total	400	100.0	20	100		

backward, forward, or horizontal integration may be effective strategies. When a Quadrant I firm is too heavily committed to a single product, then concentric diversification may reduce the risks associated with a narrow product line. Quadrant I firms can afford to take advantage of external opportunities in several areas: They can take risks aggressively when necessary.

Firms positioned in Quadrant II need to evaluate their present approach to the marketplace seriously. Although their industry is growing, they are unable to compete effectively, and they need to determine why the firm's current approach is ineffective and how the company can best change to improve its competitiveness. Because Quadrant II firms are in a rapid-market-growth industry, an intensive strategy (as opposed to integrative or diversification) is usually the first option that should be considered. However, if the firm is lacking a distinctive competence or competitive advantage, then horizontal integration is often a desirable alternative. As a last resort, divestiture or liquidation should be considered. Divestiture can provide funds needed to acquire other businesses or buy back shares of stock.

Quadrant III organizations compete in slow-growth industries and have weak competitive positions. These firms must make some drastic changes quickly to avoid further decline and possible liquidation. Extensive cost and asset reduction (retrenchment) should be pursued first. An alternative strategy is to shift resources away from the current business into different areas (diversify). If all else fails, the final options for Quadrant III businesses are divestiture or liquidation.

Finally, Quadrant IV businesses have a strong competitive position but are in a slow-growth industry. These firms have the strength to launch diversified programs into more

FIGURE 6–11

The Grand Strategy Matrix

RAPID MARKET GROWTH

Quadrant II	*Quadrant I*
1. Market development	1. Market development
2. Market penetration	2. Market penetration
3. Product development	3. Product development
4. Horizontal integration	4. Forward integration
5. Divestiture	5. Backward integration
6. Liquidation	6. Horizontal integration
	7. Concentric diversification

WEAK COMPETITIVE POSITION — STRONG COMPETITIVE POSITION

Quadrant III	*Quadrant IV*
1. Retrenchment	1. Concentric diversification
2. Concentric diversification	2. Horizontal diversification
3. Horizontal diversification	3. Conglomerate diversification
4. Conglomerate diversification	4. Joint ventures
5. Divestiture	
6. Liquidation	

SLOW MARKET GROWTH

Source: Adapted from Roland Christensen, Norman Berg, and Malcolm Salter, *Policy Formulation and Administration* (Homewood, IL): Richard D. Irwin, 1976): 16–18.

promising growth areas: Quadrant IV firms have characteristically high cash-flow levels and limited internal growth needs and often can pursue concentric, horizontal, or conglomerate diversification successfully. Quadrant IV firms also may pursue joint ventures.

THE DECISION STAGE

Analysis and intuition provide a basis for making strategy-formulation decisions. The matching techniques just discussed reveal feasible alternative strategies. Many of these strategies will likely have been proposed by managers and employees participating in the strategy analysis and choice activity. Any additional strategies resulting from the matching analyses could be discussed and added to the list of feasible alternative options. As indicated earlier in this chapter, participants could rate these strategies on a 1 to 4 scale so that a prioritized list of the best strategies could be achieved.

The Quantitative Strategic Planning Matrix (QSPM)

Other than ranking strategies to achieve the prioritized list, there is only one analytical technique in the literature designed to determine the relative attractiveness of feasible alternative actions. This technique is the *Quantitative Strategic Planning Matrix (QSPM)*, which comprises Stage 3 of the strategy-formulation analytical framework.[5] This technique objectively indicates which alternative strategies are best. The QSPM uses input from Stage 1 analyses and matching results from Stage 2 analyses to decide objectively among alternative strategies. That is, the EFE Matrix, IFE Matrix, and Competitive Profile Matrix that make up Stage 1, coupled with the TOWS Matrix, SPACE Matrix, BCG Matrix, IE Matrix, and Grand Strategy Matrix that make up Stage 2, provide the needed information for setting up the QSPM (Stage 3). The QSPM is a tool that allows strategists to evaluate alternative strategies objectively, based on previously identified external and internal critical success factors. Like other strategy-formulation analytical tools, the QSPM requires good intuitive judgment.

The basic format of the QSPM is illustrated in Table 6–5. Note that the left column of a QSPM consists of key external and internal factors (from Stage 1), and the top row consists of feasible alternative strategies (from Stage 2). Specifically, the left column of a QSPM consists of information obtained directly from the EFE Matrix and IFE Matrix. In a column adjacent to the critical success factors, the respective weights received by each factor in the EFE Matrix and the IFE Matrix are recorded.

The top row of a QSPM consists of alternative strategies derived from the TOWS Matrix, SPACE Matrix, BCG Matrix, IE Matrix, and Grand Strategy Matrix. These matching tools usually generate similar feasible alternatives. However, not every strategy suggested by the matching techniques has to be evaluated in a QSPM. Strategists should use good intuitive judgment in selecting strategies to include in a QSPM.

Conceptually, the QSPM determines the relative attractiveness of various strategies based on the extent to which key external and internal critical success factors are capitalized upon or improved. The relative attractiveness of each strategy within a set of alternatives is computed by determining the cumulative impact of each external and internal critical success factor. Any number of sets of alternative strategies can be included in the QSPM, and any number of strategies can make up a given set, but only strategies within a given set are evaluated relative to each other. For example, one set of strategies may include concentric, horizontal, and conglomerate diversification, whereas another set may include issuing stock and selling a division to raise needed capital. These two sets of strategies are totally different, and the QSPM evaluates strategies only within sets. Note in Table 6–6 that three strategies are included, and they make up just one set.

TABLE 6-5   The Quantitative Strategic Planning Matrix—QSPM

		STRATEGIC ALTERNATIVES		
Key Factors	*Weight*	*Strategy 1*	*Strategy 2*	*Strategy 3*
Key External Factors				
Economy				
Political/Legal/Governmental				
Social/Cultural/Demographic/Environmental				
Technological				
Competitive				
Key Internal Factors				
Management				
Marketing				
Finance/Accounting				
Production/Operations				
Research and Development				
Management Information Systems				

TABLE 6-6   **A QSPM for Campbell Soup Company**

		STRATEGIC ALTERNATIVES			
		Joint Venture in Europe		Joint Venture in Asia	
Key Factors	*Weight*	*AS*	*TAS*	*AS*	*TAS*
Opportunities					
1. One European currency—Euro	.10	4	.40	2	.20
2. Rising health consciousness in selecting foods	.15	4	.60	3	.45
3. Free market economies arising in Asia	.10	2	.20	4	.40
4. Demand for soups increasing 10% annually	.15	3	.45	4	.60
5. NAFTA	.05	—	—	—	—
Threats					
1. Food revenues increasing only 1% annually	.10	3	.30	4	.40
2. ConAgra's Banquet TV Dinners lead market with 27.4 percent share	.05	—	—	—	—
3. Unstable economies in Asia	.10	4	.40	1	.10
4. Tin cans are not biodegradable	.05	—	—	—	—
5. Low value of the dollar	.15	4	.60	2	.30
	1.0				
Strengths					
1. Profits rose 30%	.10	4	.40	2	.20
2. New North American division	.10	—	—	—	—
3. New health-conscious soups are successful	.10	4	.40	2	.20
4. Swanson TV dinners' market share has increased to 25.1%	.05	4	.20	3	.15
5. One-fifth of all managers' bonuses is based on overall corporate performance	.05	—	—	—	—
6. Capacity utilization increased from 60% to 80%	.15	3	.45	4	.60
Weaknesses					
1. Pepperidge Farm sales have declined 7%	.05	—	—	—	—
2. Restructuring cost $302 million	.05	—	—	—	—
3. The company's European operation is losing money	.15	2	.30	4	.60
4. The company is slow in globalizing	.15	4	.60	3	.45
5. Pretax profit margin of 8.4% is only one-half industry average	.05	—	—	—	—
Sum Total Attractiveness Score	1.0		5.30		4.65

AS = Attractiveness Score; TAS = Total Attractiveness Score
Attractiveness Score: 1 = not attractive; 2 = somewhat attractive; 3 = reasonably attractive; 4 = highly attractive.

A QSPM for a food company is provided in Table 6-6. This example illustrates all the components of the QSPM: Strategic Alternatives, Key Factors, Weights, Attractiveness Scores (AS), Total Attractiveness Scores (TAS), and the Sum Total Attractiveness Score. The three new terms just introduced—(1) Attractiveness Scores, (2) Total Attractiveness Scores, and (3) the Sum Total Attractiveness Score—are defined and explained below as the six steps required to develop a QSPM are discussed.

Step 1   **Make a list of the firm's key external opportunities/threats and internal strengths/weaknesses in the left column of the QSPM.** This information should be taken directly from the EFE Matrix and IFE Matrix. A minimum of ten external critical success factors and ten internal critical success factors should be included in the QSPM.

Step 2   **Assign weights to each key external and internal factor.** These weights are identical to those in the EFE Matrix and the IFE Matrix. The weights are presented in a straight column just to the right of the external and internal critical success factors.

Step 3   **Examine the Stage 2 (matching) matrices, and identify alternative strategies that the organization should consider implementing.** Record these strategies in the top row of the QSPM. Group the strategies into mutually exclusive sets if possible.

Step 4   **Determine the Attractiveness Scores (AS)** defined as numerical values that indicate the relative attractiveness of each strategy in a given set of alternatives. *Attractiveness Scores* are determined by examining each key external or internal factor, one at a time, and asking the question, "Does this factor affect the choice of strategies being made?" If the answer to this question is *yes*, then the strategies should be compared relative to that key factor. Specifically, Attractiveness Scores should be assigned to each strategy to indicate the relative attractiveness of one strategy over others, considering the particular factor. The range for Attractiveness Scores is 1 = not attractive, 2 = somewhat attractive, 3 = reasonably attractive, and 4 = highly attractive. If the answer to the above question is *no*, indicating that the respective key factor has no effect upon the specific choice being made, then do not assign Attractiveness Scores to the strategies in that set. Use a dash to indicate that the key factor does not affect the choice being made. Note: If you assign an AS score to one strategy, then assign AS score(s) to the other. In other words, if one strategy receives a dash, then all others must receive a dash in a given row.

Step 5   **Compute the Total Attractiveness Scores.** *Total Attractiveness Scores (TAS)* are defined as the product of multiplying the weights (Step 2) by the Attractiveness Scores (Step 4) in each row. The Total Attractiveness Scores indicate the relative attractiveness of each alternative strategy, considering only the impact of the adjacent external or internal critical success factor. The higher the Total Attractiveness Score, the more attractive the strategic alternative (considering only the adjacent critical success factor).

Step 6   **Compute the Sum Total Attractiveness Score.** Add Total Attractiveness Scores in each strategy column of the QSPM. The *Sum Total Attractiveness Scores (STAS)* reveal which strategy is most attractive in each set of alternatives. Higher scores indicate more attractive strategies, considering all the relevant external and internal factors that could affect the strategic decisions. The magnitude of the difference between the Sum Total Attractiveness Scores in a given set of strategic alternatives indicates the relative desirability of one strategy over another.

In Table 6-6, two alternative strategies—establishing a joint venture in Europe and establishing a joint venture in Asia—are being considered by Campbell Soup.

Note that NAFTA has no impact on the choice being made between the two strategies, so a dash (–) appears several times across that row. Several other factors also have no effect on the choice being made, so dashes are recorded in those rows as well. If a particular factor affects one strategy but not the other, it affects the choice being made, so attractiveness scores should be recorded. The sum total attractiveness score of 5.30 in Table 6-6 indicates that the joint venture in Europe is a more attractive strategy when compared to the joint venture in Asia.

You should have a rationale for each AS score assigned. In Table 6-6, the rationale for the AS scores in the first row is that the unification of Western Europe creates more stable business conditions in Europe than in Asia. The AS score of 4 for the joint venture in Europe and 2 for the joint venture in Asia indicates that the European venture is highly attractive and the Asian venture is somewhat attractive, considering only the first critical success factor. AS scores, therefore, are not mere guesses; they should be rational, defensible, and reasonable. Avoid giving each strategy the same AS score. Note in Table 6-6 that dashes are inserted all the way across the row when used. Also note that double 4s, or double 3s, or double 2s, or double 1s are never in a given row. These are important guidelines to follow in constructing a QSPM.

Positive Features and Limitations of the QSPM

A positive feature of the QSPM is that sets of strategies can be examined sequentially or simultaneously. For example, corporate-level strategies could be evaluated first, followed by division-level strategies, and then function-level strategies. There is no limit to the number of strategies that can be evaluated or the number of sets of strategies that can be examined at once using the QSPM.

Another positive feature of the QSPM is that it requires strategists to integrate pertinent external and internal factors into the decision process. Developing a QSPM makes it less likely that key factors will be overlooked or weighted inappropriately. A QSPM draws attention to important relationships that affect strategy decisions. Although developing a QSPM requires a number of subjective decisions, making small decisions along the way enhances the probability that the final strategic decisions will be best for the organization. A QSPM can be adapted for use by small and large for-profit and nonprofit organizations and can be applied to virtually any type of organization. A QSPM can especially enhance strategic choice in multinational firms because many key factors and strategies can be considered at once. It also has been applied successfully by a number of small businesses.[6]

The QSPM is not without some limitations. First, it always requires intuitive judgments and educated assumptions. The ratings and attractiveness scores require judgmental decisions, even though they should be based on objective information. Discussion among strategists, managers, and employees throughout the strategy-formulation process, including development of a QSPM, is constructive and improves strategic decisions. Constructive discussion during strategy analysis and choice may arise because of genuine differences of interpretation of information and varying opinions. Another limitation of the QSPM is that it can be only as good as the prerequisite information and matching analyses upon which it is based.

CULTURAL ASPECTS OF STRATEGY CHOICE

All organizations have a culture. *Culture* includes the set of shared values, beliefs, attitudes, customs, norms, personalities, heroes, and heroines that describe a firm. Culture is the unique way an organization does business. It is the human dimension that creates solidarity and meaning, and it inspires commitment and productivity in an organization when strategy changes are made. All human beings have a basic need to make sense of the world, to feel in control, and to make meaning. When events threaten meaning, individuals react defensively. Managers and employees may even sabotage new strategies in an effort to recapture the status quo.

It is beneficial to view strategic management from a cultural perspective because success often rests upon the degree of support that strategies receive from a firm's culture. If a firm's strategies are supported by cultural products such as values, beliefs, rites, rituals, ceremonies, stories, symbols, language, heroes, and heroines, then managers often can implement changes swiftly and easily. However, if a supportive culture does not exist and is not cultivated, then strategy changes may be ineffective or even counter-productive. A firm's culture can become antagonistic to new strategies, and the result of that antagonism may be confusion and disarray.

Strategies that require fewer cultural changes may be more attractive because extensive changes can take considerable time and effort. Whenever two firms merge, it becomes especially important to evaluate and consider culture-strategy linkages. For example, Hewlett-Packard (HP) and Compaq completed their merger in May 2002, but their company cultures are quite different. Compaq's culture is top-down oriented, whereas the HP culture, called the HP Way, is based on "management by walking around." Compaq is a marketer that spends only 3.5 percent of revenues on R&D, whereas HP is an inventor that spends 6 percent of its revenues annually on R&D. Compaq focuses on a few major products, whereas HP boasts a wide array of products in many categories. Compaq's management style can be described as outgoing, whereas HP's is introspective and analytical.[7] Compaq's workforce is highly competitive, aggressive, and takes risks, whereas the HP Way is to base decisions more on experience, professionalism, and careful analysis.

Culture provides an explanation for the difficulties a firm encounters when it attempts to shift its strategic direction, as the following statement explains:

> Not only has the "right" corporate culture become the essence and foundation of corporate excellence, but success or failure of needed corporate reforms hinges on management's sagacity and ability to change the firm's driving culture in time and in tune with required changes in strategies.[8]

THE POLITICS OF STRATEGY CHOICE

All organizations are political. Unless managed, political maneuvering consumes valuable time, subverts organizational objectives, diverts human energy, and results in the loss of some valuable employees. Sometimes political biases and personal preferences get unduly embedded in strategy choice decisions. Internal politics affect the choice of strategies in all organizations. The hierarchy of command in an organization, combined with the career aspirations of different people and the need to allocate scarce resources, guarantees the formation of coalitions of individuals who strive to take care of themselves first and the organization second, third, or fourth. Coalitions of individuals often form around key strategy issues that face an enterprise. A major responsibility of strategists is to guide the development of coalitions, to nurture an overall team concept, and to gain the support of key individuals and groups of individuals.

In the absence of objective analyses, strategy decisions too often are based on the politics of the moment. With development of improved strategy-formation tools, political factors become less important in making strategic decisions. In the absence of objectivity, political factors sometimes dictate strategies, and this is unfortunate. Managing political relationships is an integral part of building enthusiasm and esprit de corps in an organization.

A classic study of strategic management in nine large corporations examined the political tactics of successful and unsuccessful strategists.[9] Successful strategists were found to let weakly supported ideas and proposals die through inaction and to establish additional hurdles or tests for strongly supported ideas considered unacceptable but not openly opposed. Successful strategists kept a low political profile on unacceptable proposals and strived to let most negative decisions come from subordinates or a group consensus, thereby reserving their personal vetoes for big issues and crucial moments. Successful strategists did a lot of chatting and informal questioning to stay abreast of how things were progressing and to know when to intervene. They led strategy but did not dictate it. They gave few orders, announced few decisions, depended heavily on informal questioning, and sought to probe and clarify until a consensus emerged.

Successful strategists generously and visibly rewarded key thrusts that succeeded. They assigned responsibility for major new thrusts to *champions,* the individuals most strongly identified with the idea or product and whose futures were linked to its success. They stayed alert to the symbolic impact of their own actions and statements so as not to send false signals that could stimulate movements in unwanted directions.

Successful strategists ensured that all major power bases within an organization were represented in, or had access to, top management. They interjected new faces and new views into considerations of major changes. (This is important because new employees and managers generally have more enthusiasm and drive than employees who have been with the firm a long time. New employees do not see the world the same old way; nor do they act as screens against changes.) Successful strategists minimized their own political exposure on highly controversial issues and in circumstances in which major opposition from key power centers was likely. In combination, these findings provide a basis for managing political relationships in an organization.

Because strategies must be effective in the marketplace and capable of gaining internal commitment, the following tactics used by politicians for centuries can aid strategists:

- *Equifinality:* It is often possible to achieve similar results using different means or paths. Strategists should recognize that achieving a successful outcome is more important than imposing the method of achieving it. It may be possible to generate new alternatives that give equal results but with far greater potential for gaining commitment.
- *Satisfying:* Achieving satisfactory results with an acceptable strategy is far better than failing to achieve optimal results with an unpopular strategy.
- *Generalization:* Shifting focus from specific issues to more general ones may increase strategists' options for gaining organizational commitment.
- *Focus on Higher-Order Issues:* By raising an issue to a higher level, many short-term interests can be postponed in favor of long-term interests. For instance, by focusing on issues of survival, the auto and steel industries were able to persuade unions to make concessions on wage increases.
- *Provide Political Access on Important Issues:* Strategy and policy decisions with significant negative consequences for middle managers will motivate intervention behavior from them. If middle managers do not have an opportunity to take a position on such decisions in appropriate political forums, they are capable of successfully resisting the decisions after they are made. Providing such political access provides strategists with information that otherwise might not be available and that could be useful in managing intervention behavior.[10]

THE ROLE OF A BOARD OF DIRECTORS

A "director" according to *Webster's Dictionary* is "one of a group of persons entrusted with the overall direction of a corporate enterprise." A *board of directors* is a group of individuals who are elected by the ownership of a corporation to have oversight and guidance over management and who look out for shareholders' interests. The act of oversight and direction is referred to as *governance*. The National Association of Corporate Directors defines governance as "the characteristic of ensuring that long-term strategic objectives and plans are established and that the proper management structure is in place to achieve those objectives, while at the same time making sure that the structure functions to maintain the corporation's integrity, reputation, and responsibility to its various constituencies." This broad scope of responsibility for the board shows how boards are being held accountable for the entire performance of the firm. In the recent Enron Corporation bankruptcy and scandal, the firm's board of directors is being sued by shareholders for mismanaging their interests. New accounting rules in the United States and Europe are being passed to enhance corporate-governance codes and to require much more extensive financial disclosure among publicly held firms. The roles and duties of a board of directors can be divided into four broad categories, as indicated in Table 6–7.

The widespread lack of involvement by boards of directors in the strategic-management process is changing in America, especially since the Enron Corporation failure.[11] Historically, boards of directors mostly have been insiders who would not second-guess top executives on strategic issues. It generally has been understood that strategists are responsible and accountable for implementing strategy, so they, not board members, should formulate strategy. Consequently, chief executive officers usually avoided discussions of overall strategy with directors because the results of those discussions often restricted their freedom of action. The judgments of board members seldom were used on acquisitions, divestitures, large capital investments, and other strategic matters. Often, the board would meet only annually to fulfill its minimum legal requirements; in many organizations, boards served merely a traditional legitimizing role.

Today, boards of directors are composed mostly of outsiders who are becoming more involved in organizations' strategic management. The trend in America is toward much greater board member accountability with smaller boards, now averaging twelve members rather than eighteen as they did a few years ago. Smaller boards can discuss issues more easily; individuals in small groups take responsibility more personally.

Just as directors are beginning to place more emphasis on staying informed about an organization's health and operations, they are also taking a more active role in ensuring that publicly issued documents are accurate representations of a firm's status. It is becoming widely recognized that a board of directors has legal responsibilities to stockholders and society for all company activities, for corporate performance, and for ensuring that a firm has an effective strategy. Failure to accept responsibility for auditing or evaluating a firm's strategy is considered a serious breach of a director's duties. Stockholders, government agencies, and customers are filing legal suits against directors for fraud, omissions, inaccurate disclosures, lack of due diligence, and culpable ignorance about a firm's operations with increasing frequency. Liability insurance for directors has become exceptionally expensive and has caused numerous directors to resign.

Boards of directors in corporate America today are seriously evaluating strategic plans, evaluating the top management team, and assuming responsibility for management succession. TIAA-CREF, the nation's largest pension fund, now regularly evaluates governance practices at more than fifteen hundred companies in which it owns a stake. *Business Week*'s annual board of director's evaluation posited that good boards of directors actively perform the following responsibilities:[12]

Table 6–7   **Board of Director Duties and Responsibilities**

1. CONTROL AND OVERSIGHT OVER MANAGEMENT
   a. Select the Chief Executive Officer
   b. Sanction the CEO's team
   c. Provide the CEO with a forum
   d. Assure managerial competency
   e. Evaluate management's performance
   f. Set management's salary levels, including fringe benefits
   g. Guarantee managerial integrity through continuous auditing
   h. Chart the corporate course
   i. Devise and revise policies to be implemented by management

2. ADHERENCE TO LEGAL PRESCRIPTIONS
   a. Keep abreast of new laws
   b. Ensure the entire organization fulfills legal prescriptions
   c. Pass bylaws and related resolutions
   d. Select new directors
   e. Approve capital budgets
   f. Authorize borrowing, new stock issues, bonds, and so on

3. CONSIDERATION OF STAKEHOLDERS' INTERESTS
   a. Monitor product quality
   b. Facilitate upward progression in employee quality of work life
   c. Review labor policies and practices
   d. Improve the customer climate
   e. Keep community relations at the highest level
   f. Use influence to better governmental, professional association, and educational contacts
   g. Maintain good public image

4. ADVANCEMENT OF STOCKHOLDERS' RIGHTS
   a. Preserve stockholders' equity
   b. Stimulate corporate growth so that the firm will survive and flourish
   c. Guard against equity dilution
   d. Assure equitable stockholder representation
   e. Inform stockholders through letters, reports, and meetings
   f. Declare proper dividends
   g. Guarantee corporate survival

VISIT THE NET

Elaborates on role of a board of directors.
http://www.csuchico.edu/
mgmt/strategy/module1/
sld054.htm

- Evaluate the CEO annually.
- Link the CEO's pay to specific goals.
- Evaluate long-range strategy.
- Evaluate board members' performance through a governance committee.
- Compensate board members only in company stock.
- Require each director to own a large amount of company stock.
- Ensure that no more than two board members are insiders (work for the company).
- Require directors to retire at age seventy.
- Place the entire board up for election every year.

- Limit the number of other boards a member can serve on.
- Ban directors who draw consulting fees or other monies from the company.
- Ban interlocking directorships.

Two rulings particularly affected the role of boards of directors in the strategy-formulation process. First, the Supreme Court of Delaware ruled that the directors of the Trans Union Corporation violated the interests of shareholders when they hastily accepted a takeover bid from the Marmon Group; that ruling eroded the so-called business judgment rule, which protects directors from liability as long as their decisions represent a good-faith effort to serve the best interests of the corporation. One clear signal from the Trans Union case is that haste can be costly for board members.

In another landmark ruling that illustrates how boards of directors increasingly are being held responsible for the overall performance of organizations, the Federal Deposit Insurance Corporation forced Continental Illinois to accept the resignations of ten of the troubled bank's outside directors. The impact of increasing legal pressures on board members is that directors are demanding greater and more regular access to financial performance information.

Some boardroom reforms that are lessening the likelihood of lawsuits today include increasing the percentage of outsiders on the board, separating the positions of CEO and chairperson, requiring directors to hold substantial amounts of stock in the firm, and decreasing the board size. Outsiders now outnumber insiders at 90 percent of all American firms' boards, and the average number of outsiders is three times that of insiders.

A direct response of increased pressure on directors to stay informed and execute their responsibilities is that audit committees are becoming commonplace. A board of directors should conduct an annual strategy audit in much the same fashion that it reviews the annual financial audit. In performing such an audit, a board could work jointly with operating management and/or seek outside counsel.

The trend among corporations toward decreased diversification, increased takeover activity, increased legal pressures, multidivisional structures, and multinational operations augments the problem of keeping directors informed. Boards should play a role beyond that of performing a strategic audit. They should provide greater input and advice in the strategy-formulation process to ensure that strategists are providing for the long-term needs of the firm. This is being done through the formation of three particular board committees: nominating committees to propose candidates for the board and senior officers of the firm; compensation committees to evaluate the performance of top executives and determine the terms and conditions of their employment; and public policy committees to give board-level attention to company policies and performance on subjects of concern such as business ethics, consumer affairs, and political activities.

VISIT THE NET

Provides nice details about strategic planning at a church. http://www. apeo.org/guide/

Powerful boards of directors are associated with high organizational performance. Powerful boards participate in corporate decisions more fully, share their experiences with the CEO regarding certain strategies, and are actively involved in industry analysis. Firms can develop more powerful boards by regularly reviewing board committee activities, evaluating board meetings, and involving the board more extensively in strategic issues. More companies are paying board members partly or totally in stock, which gives outside directors more reason to identify with the shareholders they represent rather than with the CEO they oversee.

Church boards have historically been made up of parishioners only, but an increasing number of churches are placing outsiders (nonmembers) on their boards.[13] These outsiders include influential persons in the community who have financial planning, fundraising, trust management, and other desired skills. Churches want to create endowments and capitalize on older members' growing estates.

CONCLUSION

The essence of strategy formulation is an assessment of whether an organization is doing the right things and how it can be more effective in what it does. Every organization should be wary of becoming a prisoner of its own strategy, because even the best strategies become obsolete sooner or later. Regular reappraisal of strategy helps management avoid complacency. Objectives and strategies should be consciously developed and coordinated and should not merely evolve out of day-to-day operating decisions.

An organization with no sense of direction and no coherent strategy precipitates its own demise. When an organization does not know where it wants to go, it usually ends up some place it does not want to be. Every organization needs to consciously establish and communicate clear objectives and strategies.

Modern strategy-formulation tools and concepts are described in this chapter and integrated into a practical three-stage framework. Tools such as the TOWS Matrix, SPACE Matrix, BCG Matrix, IE Matrix, and QSPM can significantly enhance the quality of strategic decisions, but they should never be used to dictate the choice of strategies. Behavioral, cultural, and political aspects of strategy generation and selection are always important to consider and manage. Because of increased legal pressure from outside groups, boards of directors are assuming a more active role in strategy analysis and choice. This is a positive trend for organizations.

VISIT THE NET

Gives the strategic plans of numerous government agencies. http://www.financenet.gov/financenet/fed/docs/strat.htm

We invite you to visit the David page on the Prentice Hall Companion Website at **www.prenhall.com/david** for this chapter's World Wide Web exercise.

KEY TERMS AND CONCEPTS

Aggressive Quadrant (p. 205)

Attractiveness Scores (AS) (p. 218)

Boards of Directors (p. 221)

Boston Consulting Group (BCG) Matrix (p. 206)

Business Portfolio (p. 206)

Cash Cows (p. 210)

Champions (p. 221)

Competitive Advantage (CA) (p. 203)

Competitive Quadrant (p. 205)

Conservative Quadrant (p. 205)

Culture (p. 219)

Decision Stage (p. 198)

Defensive Quadrant (p. 205)

Directional Vector (p. 204)

Dogs (p. 210)

Environmental Stability (ES) (p. 203)

Financial Strength (FS) (p. 203)

Governance (p. 222)

Grand Strategy Matrix (p. 213)

Halo Error (p. 198)

Industry Strength (IS) (p. 203)

Input Stage (p. 197)

Internal-External (IE) Matrix (p. 211)

Long-Term Objectives (p. xxx)

Matching (p. 199)

Matching Stage (p. 197)

Quantitative Strategic Planning Matrix (QSPM) (p. 215)

Question Marks (p. 208)

Relative Market Share Position (p. 206)

SO Strategies (p. 200)

ST Strategies (p. 201)

Stars (p. 209)

Strategic Position and Action Evaluation (SPACE) Matrix (p. 203)

Strategy-Formulation Framework (p. 198)

Sum Total Attractiveness Scores (STAS) (p. 218)

Threats-Opportunities-Weaknesses-Strengths (TOWS) Matrix (p. 200)

Total Attractiveness Scores (TAS) (p. 218)

WO Strategies (p. 200)

WT Strategies (p. 201)

ISSUES FOR REVIEW AND DISCUSSION

1. How would application of the strategy-formulation framework differ from a small to a large organization?

2. What types of strategies would you recommend for an organization that achieves total weighted scores of 3.6 on the IFE and 1.2 on the EFE Matrix?

3. Given the following information, develop a SPACE Matrix for the XYZ Corporation:
FS = +2; ES = −6; CA = −2; IS = +4.

4. Given the information in the table below, develop a BCG Matrix and an IE Matrix:

Divisions	1	2	3
Profits	$10	$15	$25
Sales	$100	$50	$100
Relative Market Share	0.2	0.5	0.8
Industry Growth Rate	+.20	+.10	−.10
IFE Total Weighted Scores	1.6	3.1	2.2
EFE Total Weighted Scores	2.5	1.8	3.3

5. Explain the steps involved in developing a QSPM.

6. How would you develop a set of objectives for your school or business?

7. What do you think is the appropriate role of a board of directors in strategic management? Why?

8. Discuss the limitations of various strategy-formulation analytical techniques.

9. Explain why cultural factors should be an important consideration in analyzing and choosing among alternative strategies.

10. How are the TOWS Matrix, SPACE Matrix, BCG Matrix, IE Matrix, and Grand Strategy Matrix similar? How are they different?

11. How would for-profit and nonprofit organizations differ in their applications of the strategy-formulation framework?

12. Select an article from the suggested readings at the end of this chapter, and prepare a report on that article for your class.

13. Calculate the Relative Market Share Position of the Budget rental car company based on section C of Table 6-4 data.

NOTES

1. R. T. LENZ, "Managing the Evolution of the Strategic Planning Process," *Business Horizons* 30, no. 1 (January–February 1987): 37.

2. ROBERT GRANT, "The Resource-Based Theory of Competitive Advantage: Implications for Strategy Formulation," *California Management Review* (Spring 1991): 114.

3. HEINZ WEIHRICH, "The TOWS Matrix: A Tool for Situational Analysis," *Long Range Planning* 15, no. 2 (April 1982): 61.

4. H. ROWE, R. MASON, and K. DICKEL, *Strategic Management and Business Policy: A Methodological Approach* (Reading, MA: Addison-Wesley Publishing Co. Inc., 1982): 155–156. Reprinted with permission of the publisher.

5. FRED DAVID, "The Strategic Planning Matrix—A Quantitative Approach," *Long Range Planning* 19, no. 5 (October 1986): 102. ANDRE GIB and ROBERT MARGULIES, "Making Competitive Intelligence Relevant to the User," *Planning Review* 19, no. 3 (May–June 1991): 21.

6. FRED DAVID, "Computer-Assisted Strategic Planning in Small Businesses," *Journal of Systems Management* 36, no. 7 (July 1985): 24–34.

7. JON SWARTZ, "How Will Compaq, H-P Fit Together?" *USA Today* (September 6, 2001): 3B.

8. Y. ALLARIE and M. FIRSIROTU, "How to Implement Radical Strategies in Large Organizations," *Sloan Management Review* 26, no. 3 (Spring 1985): 19. Another excellent article is P. Shrivastava, "Integrating Strategy Formulation with Organizational Culture," *Journal of Business Strategy* 5, no. 3 (Winter 1985): 103–111.

9. JAMES BRIAN QUINN, *Strategies for Change: Logical Incrementalism* (Homewood, IL: Richard D. Irwin, 1980): 128–145. These political tactics are listed in A. Thompson and A. Strickland, *Strategic Management: Concepts and Cases* (Plano, TX: Business Publications, 1984): 261.

10. WILLIAM GUTH and IAN MACMILLAN, "Strategy Implementation Versus Middle Management Self-Interest," *Strategic Management Journal* 7, no. 4 (July–August 1986): 321.

11. CAROL HYMOWITZ, "Serving on a Board Now Means Less Talk, More Accountability," *Wall Street Journal* (January 29, 2002): p. B1.

12. "Best and Worst Corporate Boards of Directors," *Business Week* (November 25, 1996): 82–98.

13. LISA MILLER, "Seeking Cash and Connections, Churches Revamp Boards," *The Wall Street Journal* (September 23, 1999): B1.

CURRENT READINGS

BROWN, ROGER. "How We Built a Strong Company in a Weak Industry." *Harvard Business Review* (February 2001): 51.

CARPENTER, MASON A., and JAMES D. WESTPHAL. "The Strategic Context of External Network Ties: Examining the Impact of Director Appointments on Board Involvement in Strategic Decision Making." *The Academy of Management Journal* 44, no. 4 (August 2001): 639.

CLAPHAM, MARIA. "Employee Creativity: The Role of Leadership." *The Academy of Management Executive* 14, no. 3 (August 2000): 138.

COLES, JERILYN W., VICTORIA B. WILLIAMS, and NILANJAN SEN. "An Examination of the Relationship of Governance Mechanisms to Performance." *Journal of Management* 27, no. 1 (January–February 2001): 23.

DAVENPORT, THOMAS H., JEANNE G. HARIS, DAVID W. DE LONG, and ALVIN L. JACOBSON. "Data to Knowledge to Results: Building an Analytic Capability." *California Management Review* 43, no. 2 (Winter 2001): 117.

DEHAENE, ALEXANDER, VEERLE DE VUYST, and HUBERT OOGHE. "Corporate Performance and Board Structure in Belgian Companies." *Long Range Planning* 34, no. 3 (June 2001): 383.

EISENHARDT, KATHLEEN M., and DONALD N. SULL. "Strategy as Simple Rules." *Harvard Business Review* (January 2001): 106.

FERNANDO, MARIO. "Are Popular Management Techniques a Waste of Time?" *The Academy of Management Executive* 15, no. 3 (August 2001): 138.

FLORIDA, RICHARD, and DEREK DAVIDSON. "Gaining from Green Management: Environmental Management Systems Inside and Outside the Factory." *California Management Review* 43, no. 3 (Spring 2001): 64.

JUDGE, WILLIAM Q., and JOEL A. RYMAN. "The Shared Leadership Challenge in Strategic Alliances: Lessons from the U.S. Healthcare Industry." *The Academy of Management Executive* 15, no. 2 (May 2001): 71.

RANFT, ANNETTE L., and HUGH M. O'NEILL. "Board Composition and High-Flying Founders: Hints of Trouble to Come?" *The Academy of Management Executive* 15, no. 1 (February 2001): 126.

RIGBY, DARRELL. "Management Tools and Techniques: A Survey." *California Management Review* 43, no. 2 (Winter 2001): 139.

SIDERS, MARK A., GERARD GEORGE, and RAVI DHARWADKAR. "The Relationship of Internal and External Commitment Foci to Objective Job Performance Measures." *The Academy of Management Journal* 44, no. 3 (June 2001): 570.

UNSWORTH, KERRIE. "Unpacking Creativity." *The Academy of Management Review* 26, no. 2 (April 2001): 289.

ZAHRA, SHAKER A., DONALD NEUBAUM, and MORTEN HUSE. "Entrepreneurship in Medium-Sized Companies: Exploring the Effects of Ownership and Governance Systems." *Journal of Management* 26, no. 5 (September–October 2000): 947.

EXPERIENTIAL EXERCISES

EXPERIENTIAL EXERCISE 6A ▶

Developing a TOWS Matrix for American Airlines (AMR)

PURPOSE

The most widely used strategy-formulation technique among American firms is the TOWS Matrix. This exercise requires the development of a TOWS Matrix for American Airlines (AMR). Matching key external and internal factors in a TOWS Matrix requires good intuitive and conceptual skills. You will improve with practice in developing a TOWS Matrix.

INSTRUCTIONS

Recall from Experiential Exercise 1A that you already may have determined AMR's external opportunities/threats and internal strengths/weaknesses. This information could be used to complete this exercise. Follow the steps outlined below:

Step 1   On a separate sheet of paper, construct a large nine-cell diagram that will represent your TOWS Matrix. Label the cells appropriately.

Step 2   Record AMR's opportunities/threats and strengths/weaknesses appropriately in your diagram.

Step 3   Match external and internal factors to generate feasible alternative strategies for AMR. Record SO, WO, ST, and WT strategies in the appropriate cells of the TOWS Matrix. Use the proper notation to indicate the rationale for the strategies. You do not necessarily have to have strategies in all four strategy cells.

Step 4   Compare your TOWS Matrix to another student's TOWS Matrix. Discuss any major differences.

EXPERIENTIAL EXERCISE 6B ▶

Developing a SPACE Matrix for American Airlines (AMR)

PURPOSE

Should AMR pursue aggressive, conservative, competitive, or defensive strategies? Develop a SPACE Matrix for AMR to answer this question. Elaborate on the strategic implications of your directional vector. Be specific in terms of strategies that could benefit AMR.

INSTRUCTIONS

Step 1   Join with two other people in class, and develop a joint SPACE Matrix for AMR.

Step 2   Diagram your SPACE Matrix on the board. Compare your matrix with other team's matrices.

Step 3   Discuss the implications of your SPACE Matrix.

EXPERIENTIAL EXERCISE 6C ▶

Developing a BCG Matrix for American Airlines (AMR)

PURPOSE

Portfolio matrices are widely used by multidivisional organizations to help identify and select strategies to pursue. A BCG analysis identifies particular divisions that should receive fewer resources than others. It may identify some divisions that need to be divested. This exercise can give you practice developing a BCG Matrix.

INSTRUCTIONS

Step 1   Place the following five column headings at the top of a separate sheet of paper: Divisions, Revenues, Profits, Relative Market Share Position, Industry Growth Rate.

Step 2   Complete a BCG Matrix for AMR.

Step 3   Compare your BCG Matrix to other students' matrices. Discuss any major differences.

PURPOSE

This exercise can give you practice developing a Quantitative Strategic Planning Matrix to determine the relative attractiveness of various strategic alternatives.

INSTRUCTIONS

Step 1   Join with two other students in class to develop a joint QSPM for AMR.

Step 2   Go to the blackboard and record your strategies and their Sum Total Attractiveness Score. Compare your team's strategies and sum total attractiveness score to those of other teams. Be sure not to assign the same AS score in a given row. Recall that dashes should be inserted all the way across a given row when used.

Step 3   Discuss any major differences.

PURPOSE

Individuals and organizations are alike in many ways. Each has competitors and each should plan for the future. Every individual and organization faces some external opportunities and threats and has some internal strengths and weaknesses. Both individuals and organizations establish objectives and allocate resources. These and other similarities make it possible for individuals to use many strategic-management concepts and tools. This exercise is designed to demonstrate how the TOWS Matrix can be used by individuals to plan their futures. As one nears completion of a college degree and begins interviewing for jobs, planning can be particularly important.

INSTRUCTIONS

On a separate sheet of paper, construct a TOWS Matrix. Include what you consider to be your major external opportunities, your major external threats, your major strengths, and your major weaknesses. An internal weakness may be a low grade point average. An external opportunity may be that your university offers a graduate program that interests you. Match key external and internal factors by recording in the appropriate cell of the matrix alternative strategies or actions that would allow you to capitalize upon your strengths, overcome your weaknesses, take advantage of your external opportunities, and minimize the impact of external threats. Be sure to use the appropriate matching notation in the strategy cells of the matrix. Because every individual (and organization) is unique, there is no one right answer to this exercise.

PURPOSE

The purpose of this exercise is to enhance your understanding and awareness of the impact that behavioral and political factors can have on strategy analysis and choice.

EXPERIENTIAL EXERCISE 6D ▶

Developing a QSPM for American Airlines (AMR)

EXPERIENTIAL EXERCISE 6E ▶

Formulating Individual Strategies

EXPERIENTIAL EXERCISE 6F ▶

The Mach Test

INSTRUCTIONS

Step 1   On a separate sheet of paper, number from 1 to 10. For each of the ten statements given below, record a *1, 2, 3, 4,* or *5* to indicate your attitude, where
1 = I disagree a lot.
2 = I disagree a little.
3 = My attitude is neutral.
4 = I agree a little.
5 = I agree a lot.

1. The best way to handle people is to tell them what they want to hear.
2. When you ask someone to do something for you, it is best to give the real reason for wanting it, rather than a reason that might carry more weight.
3. Anyone who completely trusts anyone else is asking for trouble.
4. It is hard to get ahead without cutting corners here and there.
5. It is safest to assume that all people have a vicious streak, and it will come out when they are given a chance.
6. One should take action only when it is morally right.
7. Most people are basically good and kind.
8. There is no excuse for lying to someone else.
9. Most people forget more easily the death of their father than the loss of their property.
10. Generally speaking, people won't work hard unless they're forced to do so.

Step 2   Add up the numbers you recorded beside statements 1, 3, 4, 5, 9, and 10. This sum is Subtotal One. For the other four statements, reverse the numbers you recorded, so a *5* becomes a *1, 4* becomes *2, 2* becomes *4, 1* becomes *5,* and *3* remains *3.* Then add those four numbers to get Subtotal Two. Finally, add Subtotal One and Subtotal Two to get your Final Score.

YOUR FINAL SCORE

Your Final Score is your Machiavellian Score. Machiavellian principles are defined in a dictionary as "manipulative, dishonest, deceiving, and favoring political expediency over morality." These tactics are not desirable, are not ethical, and are not recommended in the strategic-management process! You may, however, encounter some highly Machiavellian individuals in your career, so beware. It is important for strategists not to manipulate others in the pursuit of organizational objectives. Individuals today recognize and resent manipulative tactics more than ever before. J. R. Ewing (on a television show in the 1980s, *Dallas*) was a good example of someone who was a high Mach (score over 30). The National Opinion Research Center used this short quiz in a random sample of American adults and found the national average Final Score to be 25.[1] The higher your score, the more Machiavellian (manipulative) you rend to be. The following scale is descriptive of individual scores on this test:

- Below 16:   Never uses manipulation as a tool.
- 16 to 20:   Rarely uses manipulation as a tool.
- 21 to 25:   Sometimes uses manipulation as a tool.
- 26 to 30:   Often uses manipulation as a tool.
- Over 30:   Always uses manipulation as a tool.

TEST DEVELOPMENT

The Mach (Machiavellian) test was developed by Dr. Richard Christie, whose research suggests the following tendencies:

1. Men generally are more Machiavellian than women.
2. There is no significant difference between high Machs and low Machs on measures of intelligence or ability.
3. Although high Machs are detached from others, they are detached in a pathological sense.
4. Machiavellian Scores are not statistically related to authoritarian values.
5. High Machs tend to be in professions that emphasize the control and manipulation of individuals—for example, law, psychiatry, and behavioral science.
6. Machiavellianism is not significantly related to major demographic characteristics such as educational level or marital status.
7. High Machs tend to come from a city or have urban backgrounds.
8. Older adults tend to have lower Mach scores than younger adults.[2]

A classic book on power relationships, *The Prince*, was written by Niccolo Machiavelli. Several excerpts from *The Prince* are given below.

> Men must either be cajoled or crushed, for they will revenge themselves for slight wrongs, while for grave ones they cannot. The injury therefore that you do to a man should be such that you need not fear his revenge.
>
> We must bear in mind . . . that there is nothing more difficult and dangerous, or more doubtful of success, than an attempt to introduce a new order of things in any state. The innovator has for enemies all those who derived advantages from the old order of things, while those who expect to be benefitted by the new institution will be but lukewarm defenders.
>
> A wise prince, therefore, will steadily pursue such a course that the citizens of his state will always and under all circumstances feel the need for his authority, and will therefore always prove faithful to him.
>
> A prince should seem to be merciful, faithful, humane, religious, and upright, and should even be so in reality, but he should have his mind so trained that, when occasion requires it, he may know how to change to the opposite.[3]

NOTES

1. RICHARD CHRISTIE and FLORENCE GEIS, *Studies in Machiavellianism* (Orlando, FL: Academic Press, 1970). Material in this exercise adapted with permission of the authors and the Academic Press.
2. Ibid., 82–83.
3. NICCOLO MACHIAVELLI, *The Prince* (New York: The Washington Press, 1963).

EXPERIENTIAL EXERCISE 6G ▶

Developing a BCG Matrix for My University

PURPOSE

Developing a BCG Matrix for many nonprofit organizations, including colleges and universities, is a useful exercise. Of course, there are no profits for each division or department—and in some cases no revenues. However, you can be creative in performing a BCG Matrix. For example, the pie slice in the circles can represent the number of majors receiving jobs upon graduation, or the number of faculty teaching in that area, or some other variable that you believe is important to consider. The size of the circles can represent the number of students majoring in particular departments or areas.

INSTRUCTIONS

Step 1   On a separate sheet of paper, develop a BCG Matrix for your university. Include all academic schools, departments, or colleges.

Step 2   Diagram your BCG Matrix on the blackboard.

Step 3   Discuss differences among the BCG Matrices on the board.

<table>
<tr><td>EXPERIENTIAL EXERCISE 6H ▶

The Role of Boards of Directors</td></tr>
</table>

PURPOSE

This exercise will give you a better understanding of the role of boards of directors in formulating, implementing, and evaluating strategies.

INSTRUCTIONS

Identify a person in your community who serves on a board of directors. Make an appointment to interview that person, and seek answers to the questions given below. Summarize your findings in a five-minute oral report to the class.

On what board are you a member?

How often does the board meet?

How long have you served on the board?

What role does the board play in this company?

How has the role of the board changed in recent years?

What changes would you like to see in the role of the board?

To what extent do you prepare for the board meeting?

To what extent are you involved in strategic management of the firm?

<table>
<tr><td>EXPERIENTIAL EXERCISE 6I ▶

Locating Companies in a Grand Strategy Matrix</td></tr>
</table>

PURPOSE

The Grand Strategy Matrix is a popular tool for formulating alternative strategies. All organizations can be positioned in one of the Grand Strategy Matrix's four strategy quadrants. The divisions of a firm likewise could be positioned. The Grand Strategy Matrix is based on two evaluative dimensions: competitive position and market growth. Appropriate strategies for an organization to consider are listed in sequential order of attractiveness in each quadrant of the matrix. This exercise gives you experience using a Grand Strategy Matrix.

INSTRUCTIONS

Using the year-end 2001 financial information provided, prepare a Grand Strategy Matrix on a separate sheet of paper. Write the respective company names in the appropriate quadrant of the matrix. Based on this analysis, what strategies are recommended for each company?

COMPANY	COMPANY SALES/PROFIT GROWTH (%)	INDUSTRY	INDUSTRY SALES/PROFITS GROWTH (%)
Apple Computer	−14/−47	Computers	−1/−77
PeopleSoft	+19/+31	Computers	−1/−77
Kroger	+7/+42	Food	+5/+10
Supervalue	−6/−68	Food	+5/+10
MBNA	+27/+29	Banks	−8/−15
Bank of America	−9/−10	Banks	−8/−15
General Motors	−4/−87	Automotive	−6/0
Eaton Corporation	−12/−53	Automotive	−6/0

Business Week (Spring 2002): 87–114.

7 IMPLEMENTING STRATEGIES: MANAGEMENT ISSUES

CHAPTER OUTLINE

- The Nature of Strategy Implementation
- Annual Objectives
- Policies
- Resource Allocation
- Managing Conflict
- Matching Structure with Strategy
- Restructuring, Reengineering, and E-Engineering
- Linking Performance and Pay to Strategies
- Managing Resistance to Change
- Managing the Natural Environment
- Creating a Strategy-Supportive Culture
- Production/Operations Concerns When Implementing Strategies
- Human Resource Concerns When Implementing Strategies

EXPERIENTIAL EXERCISE 7A
Revising American Airline's (AMR's) Organizational Chart

EXPERIENTIAL EXERCISE 7B
Do Organizations Really Establish Objectives?

EXPERIENTIAL EXERCISE 7C
Understanding My University's Culture

CHAPTER OBJECTIVES

After studying this chapter, you should be able to do the following:

1. Explain why strategy implementation is more difficult than strategy formulation.
2. Discuss the importance of annual objectives and policies in achieving organizational commitment for strategies to be implemented.
3. Explain why organizational structure is so important in strategy implementation.
4. Compare and contrast restructuring and reengineering.
5. Describe the relationships between production/operations and strategy implementation.
6. Explain how a firm can effectively link performance and pay to strategies.
7. Discuss employee stock ownership plans (ESOPs) as a strategic-management concept.
8. Describe how to modify an organizational culture to support new strategies.
9. Discuss the culture in Mexico, Russia, and Japan.
10. Describe the glass ceiling in the United States.

NOTABLE QUOTES

You want your people to run the business as if it were their own.

WILLIAM FULMER

The ideal organizational structure is a place where ideas filter up as well as down, where the merit of ideas carries more weight than their source, and where participation and shared objectives are valued more than executive orders.

EDSON SPENCER

A management truism says structure follows strategy. However, this truism is often ignored. Too many organizations attempt to carry out a new strategy with an old structure.

DALE McCONKEY

Poor Ike; when he was a general, he gave an order and it was carried out. Now, he's going to sit in that office and give an order and not a damn thing is going to happen.

HARRY TRUMAN

Changing your pay plan is a big risk, but not changing it could be a bigger one.

NANCY PERRY

Objectives can be compared to a compass bearing by which a ship navigates. A compass bearing is firm, but in actual navigation, a ship may veer off its course for many miles. Without a compass bearing, a ship would neither find its port nor be able to estimate the time required to get there.

PETER DRUCKER

The best game plan in the world never blocked or tackled anybody.

VINCE LOMBARDI

In most organizations, the top performers are paid too little and the worst performers too much.

CASS BETTINGER

Pretend that every single person you meet has a sign around his or her neck that says, "Make me feel important."

MARY KAY ASH, CEO OF MARY KAY, INC.

The best executive has . . . sense enough to pick good men, and the self-restraint enough to keep from meddling.

THEODORE ROOSEVELT

The strategic-management process does not end when the firm decides what strategy or strategies to pursue. There must be a translation of strategic thought into strategic action. This translation is much easier if managers and employees of the firm understand the business, feel a part of the company, and through involvement in strategy-formulation activities have become committed to helping the organization succeed. Without understanding and commitment, strategy-implementation efforts face major problems.

Implementing strategy affects an organization from top to bottom; it affects all the functional and divisional areas of a business. It is beyond the purpose and scope of this text to examine all of the business administration concepts and tools important in strategy implementation. This chapter focuses on management issues most central to implementing strategies in the year 2003, and Chapter 8 focuses on marketing, finance/accounting, R&D, and management information systems issues.

> Even the most technically perfect strategic plan will serve little purpose if it is not implemented. Many organizations tend to spend an inordinate amount of time, money, and effort on developing the strategic plan, treating the means and circumstances under which it will be implemented as afterthoughts! Change comes through implementation and evaluation, not through the plan. A technically imperfect plan that is implemented well will achieve more than the perfect plan that never gets off the paper on which it is typed.[1]

THE NATURE OF STRATEGY IMPLEMENTATION

The strategy-implementation stage of strategic management is revealed in Figure 7–1. Successful strategy formulation does not guarantee successful strategy implementation. It is always more difficult to do something (strategy implementation) than to say you are going to do it (strategy formulation)! Although inextricably linked, strategy implementation is fundamentally different from strategy formulation. Strategy formulation and implementation can be contrasted in the following ways:

- Strategy formulation is positioning forces before the action.
- Strategy implementation is managing forces during the action.
- Strategy formulation focuses on effectiveness.
- Strategy implementation focuses on efficiency.
- Strategy formulation is primarily an intellectual process.
- Strategy implementation is primarily an operational process.
- Strategy formulation requires good intuitive and analytical skills.
- Strategy implementation requires special motivation and leadership skills.
- Strategy formulation requires coordination among a few individuals.
- Strategy implementation requires coordination among many individuals.

Strategy-formulation concepts and tools do not differ greatly for small, large, for-profit, or nonprofit organizations. However, strategy implementation varies substantially among different types and sizes of organizations. Implementing strategies requires such actions as altering sales territories, adding new departments, closing facilities, hiring new employees, changing an organization's pricing strategy, developing financial budgets, developing new employee benefits, establishing cost-control procedures,

FIGURE 7–1

A Comprehensive Strategic-Management Model

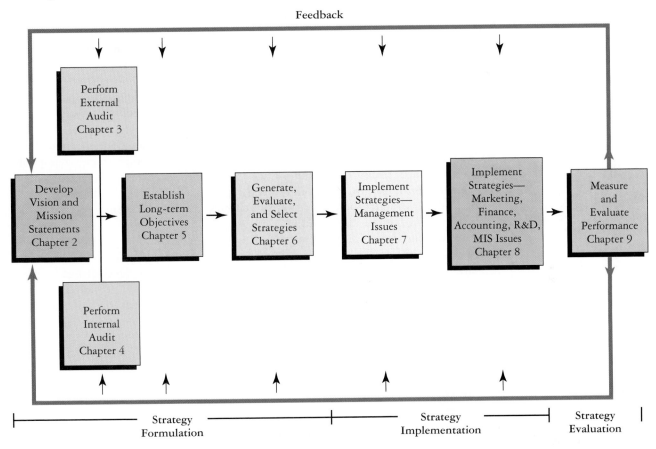

changing advertising strategies, building new facilities, training new employees, transferring managers among divisions, and building a better management information system. These types of activities obviously differ greatly between manufacturing, service, and governmental organizations.

Management Perspectives

In all but the smallest organizations, the transition from strategy formulation to strategy implementation requires a shift in responsibility from strategists to divisional and functional managers. Implementation problems can arise because of this shift in responsibility, especially if strategy-formulation decisions come as a surprise to middle- and lower-level managers. Managers and employees are motivated more by perceived self-interests than by organizational interests, unless the two coincide. Therefore, it is essential that divisional and functional managers be involved as much as possible in strategy-formulation activities. Of equal importance, strategists should be involved as much as possible in strategy-implementation activities.

Management issues central to strategy implementation include establishing annual objectives, devising policies, allocating resources, altering an existing organizational structure, restructuring and reengineering, revising reward and incentive plans, minimizing resistance to change, matching managers with strategy, developing a strategy-supportive culture, adapting production/operations processes, developing an effective human resource function and, if necessary, downsizing. Management changes are necessarily more extensive when strategies to be implemented move a firm in a major new direction.

Managers and employees throughout an organization should participate early and directly in strategy-implementation decisions. Their role in strategy implementation should build upon prior involvement in strategy-formulation activities. Strategists' genuine personal commitment to implementation is a necessary and powerful motivational force for managers and employees. Too often, strategists are too busy to actively support strategy-implementation efforts, and their lack of interest can be detrimental to organizational success. The rationale for objectives and strategies should be understood and clearly communicated throughout an organization. Major competitors' accomplishments, products, plans, actions, and performance should be apparent to all organizational members. Major external opportunities and threats should be clear, and managers' and employees' questions should be answered. Top-down flow of communication is essential for developing bottom-up support.

Firms need to develop a competitor focus at all hierarchical levels by gathering and widely distributing competitive intelligence; every employee should be able to benchmark her or his efforts against best-in-class competitors so that the challenge becomes personal. This is a challenge for strategists of the firm. Firms should provide training for both managers and employees to ensure that they have and maintain the skills necessary to be world-class performers.

 ## ANNUAL OBJECTIVES

Establishing annual objectives is a decentralized activity that directly involves all managers in an organization. Active participation in establishing annual objectives can lead to acceptance and commitment. *Annual objectives* are essential for strategy implementation because they (1) represent the basis for allocating resources; (2) are a primary mechanism for evaluating managers; (3) are the major instrument for monitoring progress toward achieving long-term objectives; and (4) establish organizational, divisional, and departmental priorities. Considerable time and effort should be devoted to ensuring that annual objectives are well conceived, consistent with long-term objectives, and supportive of strategies to be implemented. Approving, revising, or rejecting annual objectives is much more than a rubber-stamp activity. The purpose of annual objectives can be summarized as follows:

> Annual objectives serve as guidelines for action, directing and channeling efforts and activities of organization members. They provide a source of legitimacy in an enterprise by justifying activities to stakeholders. They serve as standards of performance. They serve as an important source of employee motivation and identification. They give incentives for managers and employees to perform. They provide a basis for organizational design.[2]

Clearly stated and communicated objectives are critical to success in all types and sizes of firms. Annual objectives, stated in terms of profitability, growth, and market share by business segment, geographic area, customer groups, and product are common

FIGURE 7–2

The Stamus Company's Hierarchy of Aims

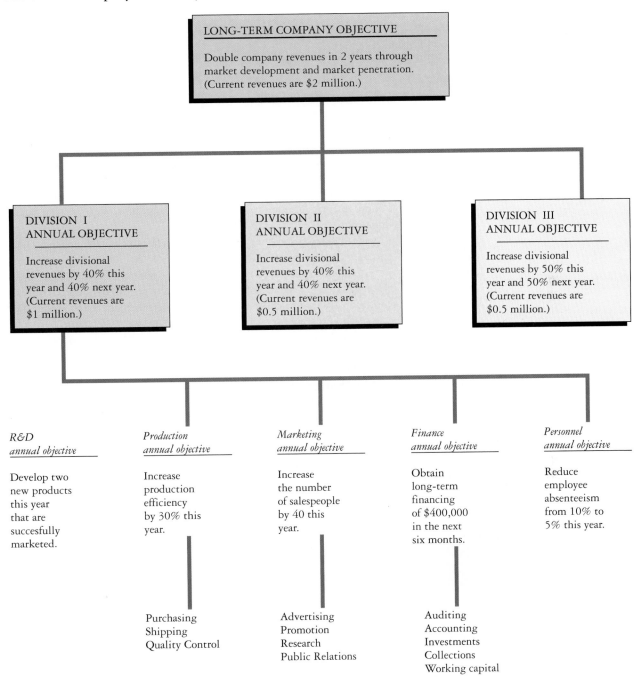

in organizations. Figure 7–2 illustrates how the Stamus Company could establish annual objectives based on long-term objectives. Table 7–1 reveals associated revenue figures that correspond to the objectives outlined in Figure 7–2. Note that, according to plan, the Stamus Company will slightly exceed its long-term objective of doubling company revenues between 2003 and the year 2005.

TABLE 7–1   The Stamus Company's Revenue Expectations (in millions of dollars)

	2003	2004	2005
Division I Revenues	1.0	1.400	1.960
Division II Revenues	0.5	0.700	0.980
Division III Revenues	0.5	0.750	1.125
Total Company Revenues	2.0	2.850	4.065

Figure 7–2 also reflects how a hierarchy of annual objectives can be established based on an organization's structure. Objectives should be consistent across hierarchical levels and form a network of supportive aims. *Horizontal consistency of objectives* is as important as *vertical consistency of objectives*. For instance, it would not be effective for manufacturing to achieve more than its annual objective of units produced if marketing could not sell the additional units.

Annual objectives should be measurable, consistent, reasonable, challenging, clear, communicated throughout the organization, characterized by an appropriate time dimension, and accompanied by commensurate rewards and sanctions. Too often, objectives are stated in generalities, with little operational usefulness. Annual objectives such as "to improve communication" or "to improve performance" are not clear, specific, or measurable. Objectives should state quantity, quality, cost, and time—and also be verifiable. Terms and phrases such as *maximize*, *minimize*, *as soon as possible*, and *adequate* should be avoided.

Annual objectives should be compatible with employees' and managers' values and should be supported by clearly stated policies. More of something is not always better! Improved quality or reduced cost may, for example, be more important than quantity. It is important to tie rewards and sanctions to annual objectives so that employees and managers understand that achieving objectives is critical to successful strategy implementation. Clear annual objectives do not guarantee successful strategy implementation, but they do increase the likelihood that personal and organizational aims can be accomplished. Overemphasis on achieving objectives can result in undesirable conduct, such as faking the numbers, distorting the records, and letting objectives become ends in themselves. Managers must be alert to these potential problems.

 POLICIES

Changes in a firm's strategic direction do not occur automatically. On a day-to-day basis, policies are needed to make a strategy work. Policies facilitate solving recurring problems and guide the implementation of strategy. Broadly defined, *policy* refers to specific guidelines, methods, procedures, rules, forms, and administrative practices established to support and encourage work toward stated goals. Policies are instruments for strategy implementation. Policies set boundaries, constraints, and limits on the kinds of administrative actions that can be taken to reward and sanction behavior; they clarify what can and cannot be done in pursuit of an organization's objectives. For example, Carnival's *Paradise* ship has a no-smoking policy anywhere, anytime aboard ship. It is the first cruise ship to comprehensively ban smoking. Another example of corporate policy relates to surfing the Web while at work. About 40 percent of companies today do not have a formal policy preventing employees from surfing the Internet, but software is being marketed now that allows firms to monitor how, when, where, and how long various employees use the Internet at work.

Policies let both employees and managers know what is expected of them, thereby increasing the likelihood that strategies will be implemented successfully. They provide a basis for management control, allow coordination across organizational units, and reduce the amount of time managers spend making decisions. Policies also clarify what work is to be done and by whom. They promote delegation of decision making to appropriate managerial levels where various problems usually arise. Many organizations have a policy manual that serves to guide and direct behavior.

Policies can apply to all divisions and departments (for example, "We are an equal opportunity employer"). Some policies apply to a single department ("Employees in this department must take at least one training and development course each year"). Whatever their scope and form, policies serve as a mechanism for implementing strategies and obtaining objectives. Policies should be stated in writing whenever possible. They represent the means for carrying out strategic decisions. Examples of policies that support a company strategy, a divisional objective, and a departmental objective are given in Table 7–2 on page 242.

Some example issues that may require a management policy are as follows:

- To offer extensive or limited management development workshops and seminars
- To centralize or decentralize employee-training activities
- To recruit through employment agencies, college campuses, and/or newspapers
- To promote from within or to hire from the outside
- To promote on the basis of merit or on the basis of seniority
- To tie executive compensation to long-term and/or annual objectives
- To offer numerous or few employee benefits
- To negotiate directly or indirectly with labor unions
- To delegate authority for large expenditures or to retain this authority centrally
- To allow much, some, or no overtime work
- To establish a high- or low-safety stock of inventory
- To use one or more suppliers
- To buy, lease, or rent new production equipment
- To stress quality control greatly or not
- To establish many or only a few production standards
- To operate one, two, or three shifts
- To discourage using insider information for personal gain
- To discourage sexual harassment
- To discourage smoking at work
- To discourage insider trading
- To discourage moonlighting

RESOURCE ALLOCATION

Resource allocation is a central management activity that allows for strategy execution. In organizations that do not use a strategic-management approach to decision making, resource allocation is often based on political or personal factors. Strategic management enables resources to be allocated according to priorities established by annual objectives.

TABLE 7-2   **A Hierarchy of Policies**

Company Strategy: Acquire a chain of retail stores to meet our sales growth and profitability objectives.
Supporting policies:

1. "All stores will be open from 8 A.M. to 8 P.M.. Monday through Saturday." (This policy could increase retail sales if stores currently are open only 40 hours a week.)
2. "All stores must submit a Monthly Control Data Report." (This policy could reduce expense-to-sales ratios.)
3. "All stores must support company advertising by contributing 5 percent of their total monthly revenues for this purpose." (This policy could allow the company to establish a national reputation.)
4. "All stores must adhere to the uniform pricing guidelines set forth in the Company Handbook." (This policy could help assure customers that the company offers a consistent product in terms of price and quality in all its stores.)

Divisional Objective: Increase the division's revenues from $10 million in 2002 to $15 million in 2004.
Supporting policies:

1. "Beginning in January 2003 each one of this division's salespersons must file a weekly activity report that includes the number of calls made, the number of miles traveled, the number of units sold, the dollar volume sold, and the number of new accounts opened." (This policy could ensure that salespersons do not place too great an emphasis in certain areas.)
2. "Beginning in January 2003, this division will return to its employees 5 percent of its gross revenues in the form of a Christmas bonus." (This policy could increase employee productivity.)
3. "Beginning in January 2003, inventory levels carried in warehouses will be decreased by 30 percent in accordance with a Just-in-Time (JIT) manufacturing approach." (This policy could reduce production expenses and thus free funds for increased marketing efforts.)

Production Department Objective: Increase production from 20,000 units in 2002 to 30,000 units in 2004.
Supporting policies:

1. "Beginning in January 2003, employees will have the option of working up to 20 hours of overtime per week." (This policy could minimize the need to hire additional employees.)
2. "Beginning in January 2003, perfect attendance awards in the amount of $100 will be given to all employees who do not miss a workday in a given year." (This policy could decrease absenteeism and increase productivity.)
3. "Beginning in January 2003, new equipment must be leased rather than purchased." (This policy could reduce tax liabilities and thus allow more funds to be invested in modernizing production processes.)

Nothing could be more detrimental to strategic management and to organizational success than for resources to be allocated in ways not consistent with priorities indicated by approved annual objectives.

All organizations have at least four types of resources that can be used to achieve desired objectives: financial resources, physical resources, human resources, and technological resources. Allocating resources to particular divisions and departments does not mean that strategies will be successfully implemented. A number of factors commonly prohibit effective resource allocation, including an overprotection of resources, too great an emphasis on short-run financial criteria, organizational politics, vague strategy targets, a reluctance to take risks, and a lack of sufficient knowledge.

Below the corporate level, there often exists an absence of systematic thinking about resources allocated and strategies of the firm. Yavitz and Newman explained why:

> Managers normally have many more tasks than they can do. Managers must allocate time and resources among these tasks. Pressure builds up. Expenses are

too high. The CEO wants a good financial report for the third quarter. Strategy formulation and implementation activities often get deferred. Today's problems soak up available energies and resources. Scrambled accounts and budgets fail to reveal the shift in allocation away from strategic needs to currently squeaking wheels.[3]

The real value of any resource allocation program lies in the resulting accomplishment of an organization's objectives. Effective resource allocation does not guarantee successful strategy implementation because programs, personnel, controls, and commitment must breathe life into the resources provided. Strategic management itself is sometimes referred to as a "resource allocation process."

MANAGING CONFLICT

Interdependency of objectives and competition for limited resources often leads to conflict. *Conflict* can be defined as a disagreement between two or more parties on one or more issues. Establishing annual objectives can lead to conflict because individuals have different expectations and perceptions, schedules create pressure, personalities are incompatible, and misunderstandings between line managers (such as production supervisors) and staff managers (such as human resource specialists) occur. For example, a collection manager's objective of reducing bad debts by 50 percent in a given year may conflict with a divisional objective to increase sales by 20 percent.

Establishing objectives can lead to conflict because managers and strategists must make trade-offs, such as whether to emphasize short-term profits or long-term growth, profit margin or market share, market penetration or market development, growth or stability, high risk or low risk, and social responsiveness or profit maximization. Conflict is unavoidable in organizations, so it is important that conflict be managed and resolved before dysfunctional consequences affect organizational performance. Conflict is not always bad. An absence of conflict can signal indifference and apathy. Conflict can serve to energize opposing groups into action and may help managers identify problems.

Various approaches for managing and resolving conflict can be classified into three categories: avoidance, defusion, and confrontation. *Avoidance* includes such actions as ignoring the problem in hopes that the conflict will resolve itself or physically separating the conflicting individuals (or groups). *Defusion* can include playing down differences between conflicting parties while accentuating similarities and common interests, compromising so that there is neither a clear winner not loser, resorting to majority rule, appealing to a higher authority, or redesigning present positions. *Confrontation* is exemplified by exchanging members of conflicting parties so that each can gain an appreciation of the other's point of view, or holding a meeting at which conflicting parties present their views and work through their differences.

MATCHING STRUCTURE
WITH STRATEGY

Changes in strategy often require changes in the way an organization is structured for two major reasons. First, structure largely dictates how objectives and policies will be established. For example, objectives and policies established under a geographic organizational structure are couched in geographic terms. Objectives and policies are stated largely in terms of products in an organization whose structure is based on product groups. The structural format for developing objectives and policies can significantly impact all other strategy-implementation activities.

The second major reason why changes in strategy often require changes in structure is that structure dictates how resources will be allocated. If an organization's structure is based on customer groups, then resources will be allocated in that manner. Similarly, if an organization's structure is set up along functional business lines, then resources are allocated by functional areas. Unless new or revised strategies place emphasis in the same areas as old strategies, structural reorientation commonly becomes a part of strategy implementation.

Changes in strategy lead to changes in organizational structure. Structure should be designed to facilitate the strategic pursuit of a firm and, therefore, follows strategy. Without a strategy or reasons for being (mission), companies find it difficult to design an effective structure. Chandler found a particular structure sequence to be often repeated as organizations grow and change strategy over time; this sequence is depicted in Figure 7–3.

There is no one optimal organizational design or structure for a given strategy or type of organization. What is appropriate for one organization may not be appropriate for a similar firm, although successful firms in a given industry do tend to organize themselves in a similar way. For example, consumer goods companies tend to emulate the divisional structure-by-product form of organization. Small firms tend to be functionally structured (centralized). Medium-size firms tend to be divisionally structured (decentralized). Large firms tend to use an SBU (strategic business unit) or matrix structure. As organizations grow, their structures generally change from simple to complex as a result of concatenation, or the linking together of several basic strategies.

Numerous external and internal forces affect an organization; no firm could change its structure in response to every one of these forces, because to do so would lead to chaos. However, when a firm changes its strategy, the existing organizational structure may become ineffective. Symptoms of an ineffective organizational structure include too many levels of management, too many meetings attended by too many people, too much attention being directed toward solving interdepartmental conflicts, too large a span of

VISIT THE NET

Provides software to draw organizational charts easily.

www.smartdraw.com
You may download the SmartDraw software and use it free for thirty days.

FIGURE 7–3

Chandler's Strategy-Structure Relationship

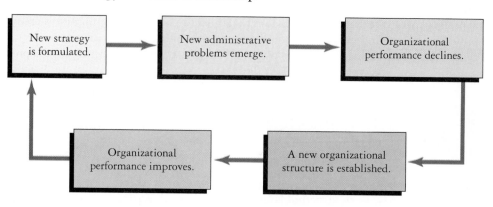

Source: Adapted from Alfred Chandler, *Strategy and Structure* (Cambridge, MA: MIT Press, 1962).

control, and too many unachieved objectives. Changes in structure can facilitate strategy-implementation efforts, but changes in structure should not be expected to make a bad strategy good, to make bad managers good, or to make bad products sell.

Structure undeniably can and does influence strategy. Strategies formulated must be workable, so if a certain new strategy required massive structural changes it would not be an attractive choice. In this way, structure can shape the choice of strategies. But a more important concern is determining what types of structural changes are needed to implement new strategies and how these changes can best be accomplished. We examine this issue by focusing on seven basic types of organizational structure: functional, divisional by geographic area, divisional by product, divisional by customer, divisional process, strategic business unit (SBU), and matrix.

VISIT THE NET

Lists some items that strategy implementation must include.
http://www.csuchico.edu/ mgmt/strategy/module1/ sld045.htm

The Functional Structure

The most widely used structure is the functional or centralized type because this structure is the simplest and least expensive of the seven alternatives. A *functional structure* groups tasks and activities by business function, such as production/operations, marketing, finance/accounting, research and development, and management information systems. A university may structure its activities by major functions that include academic affairs, student services, alumni relations, athletics, maintenance, and accounting. Besides being simple and inexpensive, a functional structure also promotes specialization of labor, encourages efficiency, minimizes the need for an elaborate control system, and allows rapid decision making. Some disadvantages of a functional structure are that it forces accountability to the top, minimizes career development opportunities, and is sometimes times characterized by low employee morale, line/staff conflicts, poor delegation of authority, and inadequate planning for products and markets. Most large companies abandoned the functional structure in favor of decentralization and improved accountability.

The Divisional Structure

The *divisional* or *decentralized structure* is the second-most common type used by American businesses. As a small organization grows, it has more difficulty managing different products and services in different markets. Some form of divisional structure generally becomes necessary to motivate employees, control operations, and compete successfully in diverse locations. The divisional structure can be organized in one of four ways: by geographic area, by product or service, by customer, or by process. With a divisional structure, functional activities are performed both centrally and in each separate division.

Cisco Systems recently discarded its divisional structure by customer and reorganized into a functional structure. CEO John Chambers replaced the three-customer structure based on big businesses, small business, and telecoms, and now the company has centralized its engineering and marketing units so that they focus on technologies such as wireless networks. Chambers says the goal was to eliminate duplication, but the change should not be viewed as a shift in strategy. Chambers' span of control in the new structure is reduced to 12 managers reporting directly to him from 15. He continues to operate Cisco without a chief operating officer or a number 2 executive.

Kodak recently reduced its number of business units from seven by-customer divisions to five by-product divisions. As consumption patterns become increasingly similar worldwide, a by-product structure is becoming more effective than a by-customer or a by-geographic type divisional structure. In the restructuring, Kodak eliminated its global operations division and distributed those responsibilities across the new by-product divisions.

A divisional structure has some clear advantages. First and perhaps foremost, accountability is clear. That is, divisional managers can be held responsible for sales and profit levels. Because a divisional structure is based on extensive delegation of authority, managers and employees can easily see the results of their good or bad performances. As a result, employee morale is generally higher in a divisional structure than it is in centralized structure. Other advantages of the divisional design are that it creates career development opportunities for managers, allows local control of local situations, leads to a competitive climate within an organization, and allows new businesses and products to be added easily.

Bank One recently created a new division named Wingspan, a new bank that is accessible only on the Internet at **wingspanbank.com**. Wingspan competes directly with Bank One and all other banks, offers higher certificate of deposit interest rates than Bank One, and thus is a break from Bank One's traditional strategy of offering the same products through numerous divisions. Bank One CEO John McCoy says, "All of the sudden now, there are ways you can go and get customers without having the full brick and mortar. I'm not about . . . to sit here and let somebody else take my business."[4]

Visa USA Inc., the largest credit card association in the United States, recently formed a separate Internet division named e-Visa. This new division employs thirty-five people and is headed by Michael Beindoff. BellSouth Corporation is reorganizing into five divisions in order to flatten its organizational structure. The new divisions are customer markets, network services, wireless services, international, and advertising and publishing.

The world's largest restaurant company, McDonald's, reorganized its operations in 2001, going from thirty-seven geographic regions in the United States to twenty-one divisions. This streamlining eliminated seven hundred managerial jobs.

The divisional design is not without some limitations, however. Perhaps the most important limitation is that a divisional structure is costly, for a number of reasons. First, each division requires functional specialists who must be paid. Second, there exists some duplication of staff services, facilities, and personnel; for instance, functional specialists are also needed centrally (at headquarters) to coordinate divisional activities. Third, managers must be well qualified because the divisional design forces delegation of authority; better-qualified individuals require higher salaries. A divisional structure can also be costly because it requires an elaborate, headquarters-driven control system. Finally, certain regions, products, or customers may sometimes receive special treatment, and it may be difficult to maintain consistent, companywide practices. Nonetheless, for most large organizations and many small firms, the advantages of a divisional structure more than offset the potential limitations.

A *divisional structure by geographic area* is appropriate for organizations whose strategies need to be tailored to fit the particular needs and characteristics of customers in different geographic areas. This type of structure can be most appropriate for organizations that have similar branch facilities located in widely dispersed areas. A divisional structure by geographic area allows local participation in decision making and improved coordination within a region.

The *divisional structure by product (or services)* is most effective for implementing strategies when specific products or services need special emphasis. Also, this type of structure is widely used when an organization offers only a few products or services, or when an organization's products or services differ substantially. The divisional structure allows strict control over and attention to product lines, but it may also require a more skilled management force and reduced top management control. General Motors, DuPont, and Procter & Gamble use a divisional structure by product to implement strategies. Huffy, the largest bicycle company in the world, is another firm that is highly decentralized based on a divisional-by-product structure. Based in Ohio, Huffy's divisions are the Bicycle division, the Gerry Baby Products division, the Huffy Sports division, YLC Enterprises, and Washington Inventory Service. Harry Shaw, Huffy's chairman, believes decentralization is one of the keys to Huffy's success.

When a few major customers are of paramount importance and many different services are provided to these customers, then a *divisional structure by customer* can be the most effective way to implement strategies. This structure allows an organization to cater effectively to the requirements of clearly defined customer groups. For example, book publishing companies often organize their activities around customer groups such as colleges, secondary schools, and private commercial schools. Some airline companies have two major customer divisions: passengers and freight or cargo services. Merrill Lynch is organized into separate divisions that cater to different groups of customers, including wealthy individuals, institutional investors, and small corporations.

A *divisional structure by process* is similar to a functional structure, because activities are organized according to the way work is actually performed. However, a key difference between these two designs is that functional departments are not accountable for profits or revenues, whereas divisional process departments are evaluated on these criteria. An example of a divisional structure by process is a manufacturing business organized into six divisions: electrical work, glass cutting, welding, grinding, painting, and foundry work. In this case, all operations related to these specific processes would be grouped under the separate divisions. Each process (division) would be responsible for generating revenues and profits. The divisional structure by process can be particularly effective in achieving objectives when distinct production processes represent the thrust of competitiveness in an industry.

The Strategic Business Unit (SBU) Structure

As the number, size, and diversity of divisions in an organization increase, controlling and evaluating divisional operations become increasingly difficult for strategists. Increases in sales often are not accompanied by similar increases in profitability. The span of control becomes too large at top levels of the firm. For example, in a large conglomerate organization composed of 90 divisions, the chief executive officer could have difficulty even remembering the first names of divisional presidents. In multidivisional organizations, an SBU structure can greatly facilitate strategy-implementation efforts.

The *SBU structure* groups similar divisions into strategic business units and delegates authority and responsibility for each unit to a senior executive who reports directly to the chief executive officer. This change in structure can facilitate strategy implementation by improving coordination between similar divisions and channeling accountability to distinct business units. In the ninety-division conglomerate just mentioned, the ninety divisions could perhaps be regrouped into ten SBUs according to certain common characteristics, such as competing in the same industry, being located in the same area, or having the same customers.

Two disadvantages of an SBU structure are that it requires an additional layer of management, which increases salary expenses, and the role of the group vice president is often ambiguous. However, these limitations often do not outweigh the advantages of improved coordination and accountability. Atlantic Richfield and Fairchild Industries are examples of firms that successfully use an SBU-type structure.

The Matrix Structure

A *matrix structure* is the most complex of all designs because it depends upon both vertical and horizontal flows of authority and communication (hence the term *matrix*). In contrast, functional and divisional structures depend primarily on vertical flows of authority and communication. A matrix structure can result in higher overhead because it creates more management positions. Other characteristics of a matrix structure that contribute to overall complexity include dual lines of budget authority (a violation of the unity-of-command principle), dual sources of reward and punishment, shared authority, dual reporting channels, and a need for an extensive and effective communication system.

Despite its complexity, the matrix structure is widely used in many industries, including construction, healthcare, research, and defense. Some advantages of a matrix structure are that project objectives are clear, there are many channels of communication, workers can see the visible results of their work, and shutting down a project can be accomplished relatively easily.

In order for a matrix structure to be effective, organizations need participative planning, training, clear mutual understanding of roles and responsibilities, excellent internal communication, and mutual trust and confidence. The matrix structure is being used more frequently by American businesses because firms are pursuing strategies that add new products, customer groups, and technology to their range of activities. Out of these changes are coming product managers, functional managers, and geographic-area managers, all of whom have important strategic responsibilities. When several variables, such as product, customer, technology, geography, functional area, and line of business, have roughly equal strategic priorities, a matrix organization can be an effective structural form.

RESTRUCTURING, REENGINEERING AND E-ENGINEERING

VISIT THE NET

Provides a PowerPoint presentation on downsizing (restructuring).
http://www.cl.uh.edu/bpa/ hadm/HADM_5731/ ppt_presentations/7down/ index.htm

Restructuring and reengineering are becoming commonplace on the corporate landscape across the United States and Europe. *Restructuring*—also called *downsizing, rightsizing,* or *delayering*—involves reducing the size of the firm in terms of number of employees, number of divisions or units, and number of hierarchical levels in the firm's organizational structure. This reduction in size is intended to improve both efficiency and effectiveness. Restructuring is concerned primarily with shareholder well-being rather than employee well-being.

Recessionary economic conditions are forcing many European companies to downsize, laying off managers and employees. This was almost unheard of prior to the mid-1990s because European labor unions and laws required lengthy negotiations or huge severance checks before workers could be terminated. In contrast to the United States, labor union executives sit on most boards of directors of large European firms.

VISIT THE NET

Provides a PowerPoint presentation on reengineering.
http://www.cl.uh.edu/bpa/ hadm/HADM_5731/ ppt_presentations/ 6reengin/index.htm

Job security in European companies is slowly moving toward a U.S. scenario, in which firms lay off almost at will. From banks in Milan to factories in Mannhelm, European employers are starting to show people the door in an effort to streamline operations, increase efficiency, and compete against already slim and trim U.S. firms. Massive U.S.-style layoffs are still rare in Europe, but unemployment rates throughout the continent are rising quite rapidly. European firms still prefer to downsize by attrition and retirement rather than by blanket layoffs because of culture, laws, and unions. As indicated in the Global Perspective box, at first Nissan and now hundreds of other Japanese companies are restructured in a manner untraditional to accepted business practices in that nation.

In contrast, *reengineering* is concerned more with employee and customer well-being than shareholder well-being. Reengineering—also called process management, process innovation, or process redesign—involves reconfiguring or redesigning work, jobs, and processes for the purpose of improving cost, quality, service, and speed.

Reengineering does not usually affect the organizational structure or chart, nor does it imply job lost or employee layoffs. Whereas restructuring is concerned with eliminating or establishing, shrinking or enlarging, and moving organizational departments and divisions, the focus of reengineering is changing the way work is actually carried out.

Reengineering is characterized by many tactical (short-term, business-function–specific) decisions, whereas restructuring is characterized by strategic (long-term, affecting all business functions) decisions.

The Internet is ushering in a new wave of business transformation. No longer is it enough for companies to put up simple Web sites for customers and employees. To take full advantage of the Internet, companies need to change the way they distribute goods, deal with suppliers, attract customers, and serve customers. The Internet eliminates the geographic protection/monopoly of local businesses. Basically, companies need to reinvent the way they do business to take full advantage of the Internet. This whole process

GLOBAL PERSPECTIVE

Restructuring at Nissan and Economic Recession Have Changed a Country

Japan Nikkei 225 Stock Index fell another 25 percent in 2001 to new seventeen-year lows as the country's economy shrank another 3.2 percent. Japan's unemployment rate has climbed above 5 percent, and demand for consumer goods has fallen to recession levels. Greater reluctance to downsize and restructure is one reason Japanese companies on average make 5 percent on assets; in contrast, their U.S. counterparts average a 15 percent return on assets.

Nissan is using American-style restructuring to reverse four years of dismal performance. Nissan recently closed five plants, laid off 14 percent of the company workforce, eliminated 21,500 jobs, reduced debt from 1.4 trillion yen to less than half that amount, reduced the number of suppliers from 1,145 to 600, and reduced manufacturing capacity from 2.4 million cars to 1.65 million annually. Called the Nissan Revival Plan, this strategy runs fully against many long-time Japanese business traditions—as noted below. Following Nissan, many other Japanese companies now employ restructuring to become more competitive.

- By laying off thousands of workers, the Nissan Revival Plan disregards the "lifetime employment practice" for which Japanese firms are well-known.

- The Nissan Revival Plan violates *keiretsu*, the Japanese business custom that links manufacturers to suppliers through shareholdings, exchanges of key managers, and long-term relationships.

- The Nissan Revival Plan changes the pay and promotion of managers from seniority to performance. This ends the widespread Japanese custom at Nissan whereby managers are promoted up the corporate ladder merely by stricking around.

- The Nissan Revival Plan dissolves the company's shareholding stake in most of its 1,394 affiliated companies. This Japanese system marries business interests when divorce might be healthier.

- The Nissan Revival Plan calls for a single worldwide advertising agency to keep the company message consistent worldwide.

Following Nissan's lead, hundreds of Japanese companies have recently laid off thousands of employees. Toshiba recently announced twenty thousand job cuts, almost half in Japan. Hitachi closed operations in Singapore and Malaysia, laying off forty-five hundred employees recently. Hitachi has recently axed 10,200 jobs in Japan. Mitsubishi Motors has laid off hundreds of workers. Fujitsu is laying off 16,400 employees. Most young Japanese have now abandoned the hope of landing lifetime jobs.

Source: Adapted from Norihiko Shirouzu, "Nissan Ambitious Restructuring Plan Delivers a Blow to Japan's Longstanding System of Corporate Families," *The Wall Street Journal* (October 20, 1999): A4. James Healey, "Retooling Nissan," *USA Today* (October 19, 1999): 2B.

is being called e-engineering.[5] Dow Corning Corporation and many others have recently appointed an e-commerce top executive.

Restructuring

Firms often employ restructuring when various ratios appear out of line with competitors as determined through benchmarking exercises. *Benchmarking* simply involves comparing a firm against the best firms in the industry on a wide variety of performance-related criteria. Some benchmarking ratios commonly used in rationalizing the need for restructuring are headcount-to-sales-volume, or corporate-staff-to-operating-employees, or span-of-control figures.

The primary benefit sought from restructuring is cost reduction. For some highly bureaucratic firms, restructuring can actually rescue the firm from global competition and demise. But the downside of restructuring can be reduced employee commitment, creativity, and innovation that accompanies the uncertainty and trauma associated with pending and actual employee layoffs.

Another downside of restructuring is that many people today do not aspire to become managers, and many present-day managers are trying to get off the management track.[6] Sentiment against joining management ranks is higher today than ever. About 80 percent of employees say they want nothing to do with management, a major shift from just a decade ago when 60 to 70 percent hoped to become managers. Managing others historically led to enhanced career mobility, financial rewards, and executive perks; but in today's global, more competitive, restructured arena, managerial jobs demand more hours and headaches with fewer financial rewards. Managers today manage more people spread over different locations, travel more, manage diverse functions, and are change agents even when they have nothing to do with the creation of the plan or even disagree with its approach. Employers today are looking for people who can do things, not for people who make other people do things. Restructuring in many firms has made a manager's job an invisible, thankless role. More workers today are self-managed, entrepreneurs, interpreneurs, or team-managed. Managers today need to be counselors, motivators, financial advisors, and psychologists. They also run the risk of becoming technologically behind in their areas of expertise. "Dilbert" cartoons commonly portray managers as enemies or as morons.

Massive restructuring among companies during the economic downturn of 2001–2003 resulted in huge layoffs. An upside to restructuring, however, is that when there are layoffs, those left behind have more opportunity to advance upwards in the firm. Layoff survivors also have more opportunity to gain experience in varied areas of the firm and may be given more responsibilities.[7]

Eastman Chemical in late 2001 established a new by-product divisional organizational structure. The company's two new divisions, Eastman Company and Voridian Company, focus on chemicals and polymers, respectively. The Eastman division focuses on coatings, adhesives, inks, and plastics, whereas the Voridian division focuses on fibers, polyethylene, and other polymers.

America's oldest department store retailer, Sears, Roebuck & Company is restructuring in 2002–2004. The company is abandoning its position as a moderate-priced department store and becoming much more like a mass discount retailer with central checkouts similar to Target and Kohl's. Sears is restructuring to become neither a department store nor a discounter; it is setting itself up to be positioned exactly between the two. The Sears restructuring includes layoffs of thirty-six thousand salaried employees and thirteen hundred additional employees at its Hoffman Estates, Illinois, headquarters. Apparel, the most troubled part of Sears' business, will become more classic, casual, and moderately priced. More national brands will be on the shelf, and footwear will become self-service. Sears will strive to develop a prominent Sears line of apparel similar to its Craftsman tools and Kenmore appliances.

It is interesting to note that in France, laying off employees is almost impossible due to labor laws that require lengthy negotiations and expensive severance packages for any individuals who are laid off. French CEOs in late 2001 sent a letter to Prime Minister Lionel Jospin warning that the strict layoff policies are crippling France's economy and companies. This is true because other European countries such as Germany have recently made it much easier for companies to lay off employees in order to stay competitive—and indeed to survive. Moulinex is an example of a French company that recently tried to lay off 670 employees but was denied this option, so the firm fell into bankruptcy and possible liquidation.

Reengineering

The argument for a firm engaging in reengineering usually goes as follows: Many companies historically have been organized vertically by business function. This arrangement has led over time to managers' and employees' mindsets being defined by their particular functions rather than by overall customer service, product quality, or corporate performance. The logic is that all firms tend to bureaucratize over time. As routines become entrenched, turf becomes delineated and defended, and politics takes precedence over performance. Walls that exist in the physical workplace can be reflections of "mental" walls.

In reengineering, a firm uses information technology to break down functional barriers and create a work system based on business processes, products, or outputs rather than on functions or inputs. Cornerstones of reengineering are decentralization, reciprocal interdependence, and information sharing. A firm that exemplifies complete information sharing is Springfield Remanufacturing Corporation, which provides to all employees a weekly income statement of the firm, as well as extensive information on other companies' performances.

The *Wall Street Journal* recently noted that reengineering today must go beyond knocking down internal walls that keep parts of a company from cooperating effectively; it must also knock down the external walls that prohibit or discourage cooperation with other firms—even rival firms.[8] A maker of disposable diapers echoes this need differently when it says that to be successful "cooperation at the firm must stretch from stump to rump."

Hewlett-Packard is a good example of a company that has knocked down the external barriers to cooperation and practices modern reengineering. The HP of today shares its forecasts with all of its supply-chain partners and shares other critical information with its distributors and other stakeholders. HP does all the buying of resin for its many manufacturers, giving it a volume discount of up to 5 percent. HP has established many alliances and cooperative agreements of the kind discussed in Chapter 5.

A benefit of reengineering is that it offers employees the opportunity to see more clearly how their particular jobs affect the final product or service being marketed by the firm. However, reengineering can also raise manager and employee anxiety, which, unless calmed, can lead to corporate trauma.

LINKING PERFORMANCE AND PAY TO STRATEGIES

Most companies today are practicing some form of pay-for-performance for employees and managers other than top executives. The average employee performance bonus is 6.8 percent of pay for individual performance, 5.5 percent of pay for group productivity, and 6.4 percent of pay for companywide profitability.

Staff control of pay systems often prevents line managers from using financial compensation as a strategic tool. Flexibility regarding managerial and employee compensation is needed to allow short-term shifts in compensation that can stimulate efforts to achieve long-term objectives.

How can an organization's reward system be more closely linked to strategic performance? How can decisions on salary increases, promotions, merit pay, and bonuses be more closely aligned to support the long-term strategic objectives of the organization? There are no widely accepted answers to these questions, but a dual bonus system based on both annual objectives and long-term objectives is becoming common. The percentage of a manager's annual bonus attributable to short-term versus long-term results should vary by hierarchical level in the organization. A chief executive officer's annual bonus could, for example, be determined on a 75 percent short-term and 25 percent long-term basis. It is important that bonuses not be based solely on short-term results because such a system ignores long-term company strategies and objectives.

DuPont Canada has a 16 percent return-on-equity objective. If this objective is met, the company's four thousand employees receive a "performance sharing cash award" equal to 4 percent of pay. If return-on-equity falls below 11 percent, employees get nothing. If return-on-equity exceeds 28 percent, workers receive a 10 percent bonus.

In an effort to cut costs and increase productivity, more and more Japanese companies are switching from seniority-based pay to performance-based approaches. Toyota Motor has switched to a full merit system for twenty thousand of its seventy thousand white-collar workers. Fujitsu, Sony, Matsushita Electric Industrial, and Kao also have switched to merit pay systems. Nearly 30 percent of all Japanese companies have switched to merit pay from seniority pay.[9] This switching is hurting morale at some Japanese companies, which have trained workers for decades to cooperate rather than to compete and to work in groups rather than individually.

Richard Brown, the new CEO of Electronic Data Systems, recently removed the bottom 20 percent of EDS's sales force and said,

> You have to start with an appraisal system that gives genuine feedback and differentiates performance. Some call it ranking people. That seems a little harsh. But you can't have a manager checking a box that says you're either stupendous, magnificent, very good, good, or average. Concise, constructive feedback is the fuel workers use to get better. A company that doesn't differentiate performance risks losing its best people.[10]

Profit sharing is another widely used form of incentive compensation. More than 30 percent of American companies have profit sharing plans, but critics emphasize that too many factors affect profits for this to be a good criterion. Taxes, pricing, or an acquisition would wipe out profits, for example. Also, firms try to minimize profits in a sense to reduce taxes.

Still another criterion widely used to link performance and pay to strategies is gain sharing. *Gain sharing* requires employees or departments to establish performance targets; if actual results exceed objectives, all members get bonuses. More than 26 percent of American companies use some form of gain sharing; about 75 percent of gain sharing plans have been adopted since 1980. Carrier, a subsidiary of United Technologies, has had excellent success with gain sharing in its six plants in Syracuse, New York; Firestone's tire plant in Wilson, North Carolina, has experienced similar success with gain sharing.

Criteria such as sales, profit, production efficiency, quality, and safety could also serve as bases for an effective *bonus system*. If an organization meets certain understood, agreed-upon profit objectives, every member of the enterprise should share in the harvest. A bonus system can be an effective tool for motivating individuals to support strategy-implementation efforts. BankAmerica, for example, recently overhauled its incentive system to link pay to sales of the bank's most profitable products and services. Branch managers receive a base salary plus a bonus based both on the number of new customers and on sales of bank products. Every employee in each branch is also eligible for a bonus if the branch exceeds its goals. Thomas Peterson, a top BankAmerica executive, says, "We want to make people responsible for meeting their goals, so we pay incentives on sales, not on controlling costs or on being sure the parking lot is a swept."

Five tests are often used to determine whether a performance-pay plan will benefit an organization:

1. *Does the plan capture attention?* Are people talking more about their activities and taking pride in early successes under the plan?

2. *Do employees understand the plan?* Can participants explain how it works and what they need to do to earn the incentive?

3. *Is the plan improving communication?* Do employees know more than they used to about the company's mission, plans, and objectives?

4. *Does the plan pay out when it should?* Are incentives being paid for desired results—and being withheld when objectives are not met?

5. *Is the company or unit performing better?* Are profits up? Has market share grown? Have gains resulted in part from the incentives?[11]

In addition to a dual bonus system, a combination of reward strategy incentives such as salary raises, stock options, fringe benefits, promotions, praise, recognition, criticism, fear, increased job autonomy, and awards can be used to encourage managers and employees to push hard for successful strategic implementation. The range of options for getting people, departments, and divisions to actively support strategy-implementation activities in a particular organization is almost limitless. Merck, for example, recently gave each of its thirty-seven thousand employees a ten-year option to buy one hundred shares of Merck stock at a set price of $127. Steven Darien, Merck's vice president of human resources, says, "We needed to find ways to get everyone in the workforce on board in terms of our goals and objectives. Company executives will begin meeting with all Merck workers to explore ways in which employees can contribute more."

Increasing criticism aimed at chief executive officers for their high pay has resulted in executive compensation being linked to performance of their firms more closely than ever before. Although the linkage between CEO pay and corporate performance is getting closer, CEO pay in the United States still can be astronomical.

For 2001, the median total shareholder return among the 350 largest U.S. firms was 3.6 percent while the CEO's total direct compensation declined 0.9 percent.[12] CEO's of the best performing companies generally were rewarded much better than CEO's of poor performing firms.

MANAGING RESISTANCE TO CHANGE

No organization or individual can escape change. But the thought of change raises anxieties because people fear economic loss, inconvenience, uncertainty, and a break in normal social patterns. Almost any change in structure, technology, people, or strategies has the potential to disrupt comfortable interaction patterns. For this reason, people resist change. The strategic-management process itself can impose major changes on individuals and processes. Reorienting an organization to get people to think and act strategically is not an easy task.

Resistance to change can be considered the single greatest threat to successful strategy implementation. Resistance in the form of sabotaging production machines, absenteeism, filing unfounded grievances, and an unwillingness to cooperate regularly occurs in organizations. People often resist strategy implementation because they do not understand what is happening or why changes are taking place. In that case, employees may simply need accurate information. Successful strategy implementation hinges upon managers' ability to develop an organizational climate conducive to change. Change must be viewed as an opportunity rather than as a threat by managers and employees.

Resistance to change can emerge at any stage or level of the strategy-implementation process. Although there are various approaches for implementing changes, three commonly used strategies are a force change strategy, an educative change strategy, and a rational or self-interest change strategy. A *force change strategy* involves giving orders and enforcing those orders; this strategy has the advantage of being fast, but it is plagued by low commitment and high resistance. The *educative change strategy* is one that presents information to convince people of the need for change; the disadvantage of an educative change strategy is that implementation becomes slow and difficult. However, this type of strategy evokes greater commitment and less resistance than does the force change strategy. Finally, a *rational* or *self-interest change strategy* is one that attempts to convince individuals that the change is to their personal advantage. When this appeal is successful, strategy implementation can be relatively easy. However, implementation changes are seldom to everyone's advantage.

The rational change strategy is the most desirable, so this approach is examined a bit further. Managers can improve the likelihood of successfully implementing change by carefully designing change efforts. Jack Duncan described a rational or self-interest change strategy as consisting of four steps. First, employees are invited to participate in the process of change and in the details of transition; participation allows everyone to give opinions, to feel a part of the change process, and to identify their own self-interests regarding the recommended change. Second, some motivation or incentive to change is required; self-interest can be the most important motivator. Third, communication is needed so that people can understand the purpose for the changes. Giving and receiving feedback is the fourth step; everyone enjoys knowing how things are going and how much progress is being made.[13]

Igor Ansoff summarized the need for strategists to manage resistance to change as follows:

> Observation of the historical transitions from one orientation to another shows that, if left unmanaged, the process becomes conflict-laden, prolonged, and costly in both human and financial terms. Management of resistance involves anticipating the focus of resistance and its intensity. Second, it involves eliminating unnecessary resistance caused by misperceptions and insecurities. Third, it involves mustering the power base necessary to assure support for the change. Fourth, it involves planning the process of change. Finally, it involves monitoring and controlling resistance during the process of change . . .[14]

Because of diverse external and internal forces, change is a fact of life in organizations. The rate, speed, magnitude, and direction of changes vary over time by industry and organization. Strategists should strive to create a work environment in which change is recognized as necessary and beneficial so that individuals can adapt to change more easily. Adopting a strategic-management approach to decision making can itself require major changes in the philosophy and operations of a firm.

VISIT THE NET

Provides a PowerPoint presentation on organizational change and managing resistance to change.
http://www.cl.uh.edu/bpa/
hadm/HADM_5731/
ppt_presentations/
5orgchg/index.htm

Strategists can take a number of positive actions to minimize managers' and employees' resistance to change. For example, individuals who will be affected by a change should be involved in the decision to make the change and in decisions about how to implement the change. Strategists should anticipate changes and develop and offer training and development workshops so that managers and employees can adapt to those changes. They also need to communicate the need for changes effectively. The strategic-management process can be described as a process of managing change. Robert Waterman describes how successful organizations involve individuals to facilitate change:

> Implementation starts with, not after, the decision. When Ford Motor Company embarked on the program to build the highly successful Taurus, management gave up the usual, sequential design process. Instead [it] showed the tentative design to the workforce and asked [its] help in devising a car that would be easy to build. Team Taurus came up with no less than 1,401 items suggested by Ford employees. What a contrast from the secrecy that characterized the industry before. When people are treated as the main engine rather than interchangeable parts, motivation, creativity, quality, and commitment to implementation go up.[15]

Organizational change should be viewed today as a continuous process rather than as a project or event. The most successful organizations today continuously adapt to changes in the competitive environment, which themselves continue to change at an accelerating rate. It is not sufficient today to simply react to change. Managers need to anticipate change and ideally be the creator of change. Viewing change as a continuous process is in stark contrast to an old management doctrine regarding change, which was to unfreeze behavior, change the behavior, and then refreeze the new behavior. The new "continuous organizational change" philosophy should mirror the popular "continuous quality improvement philosophy."

VISIT THE NET

Gives good information about why employees may resist change.
http://www.mindtools.com/plreschn.html

MANAGING THE NATURAL ENVIRONMENT

All business functions are affected by natural environment considerations or by striving to make a profit. However, both employees and consumers are especially resentful of firms that take from more than give to the natural environment; likewise, people today are especially appreciative of firms that conduct operations in a way that mends rather than harms the environment.

The U.S. Justice Department recently issued new guidelines for companies to uncover environmental wrongdoing among their managers and employees without exposing themselves to potential criminal liability. The new guidelines give nine hypothetical examples to illustrate the new legal requirements. The examples include Company A, which regularly conducts a comprehensive environmental audit, goes straight to the government as soon as something wrong is turned up, disciplines the responsible people in the company, and gives their names as well as all relevant documentation to the government. The Justice Department will prosecute but be lenient in this case. The extreme example is Company K, which tries to cover up an environmental violation and does not cooperate with the government or provide names. Its audit is narrow, and its compliance program is "no more than a collection of paper." No leniency is likely for this firm.

Monsanto, a large U.S. chemical company, is an excellent example of a firm that protects the natural environment. Monsanto's motto is "Zero Spills, Zero Releases, Zero Incidents, and Zero Excuses."

The 1990s may well be remembered as the decade of the environment. Earth itself has become a stakeholder for all business firms. Consumer interests in businesses' preserving nature's ecological balance and fostering a clean, healthy environment is high. As indicated in the Natural Environment Perspective, an increasing number of businesses today are purchasing their own independent, nonpolluting power source. This strategy is in contrast to continuing to purchase electricity from large, polluting, coal-burning utilities.

The ecological challenge facing all organizations requires managers to formulate strategies that preserve and conserve natural resources and control pollution. Special natural environmental issues include ozone depletion, global warming, depletion of rain forests, destruction of animal habitats, protecting endangered species, developing biodegradable products and packages, waste management, clean air, clean water, erosion, destruction of natural resources, and pollution control. Firms increasingly are developing green product lines that are biodegradable and/or are made from recycled products. Green products sell well.

The Environmental Protection Agency recently reported that U.S. citizens and organizations spend more than about $200 billion annually on pollution abatement. Environmental concerns touch all aspects of a business's operations, including workplace risk exposures, packaging, waste reduction, energy use, alternative fuels, environmental cost accounting, and recycling practices.

Managing as if the earth matters requires an understanding of how international trade, competitiveness, and global resources are connected. Managing environmental affairs can no longer be simply a technical function performed by specialists in a firm; more emphasis must be placed on developing an environmental perspective among all employees and managers of the firm. Many companies are moving environmental affairs from the staff side of the organization to the line side, thus making the corporate environmental group report directly to the chief operating officer.

Societies have been plagued by environmental disasters to such an extent recently that firms failing to recognize the importance of environmental issues and challenges could suffer severe consequences. Managing environmental affairs can no longer be an incidental or secondary function of company operations. Product design, manufacturing, and ultimate disposal should not merely reflect environmental considerations, but also be driven by them. Firms that manage environmental affairs will enhance relations with consumers, regulators, vendors, and other industry players—substantially improving their prospects of success.

Firms should formulate and implement strategies from an environmental perspective. Environmental strategies could include developing or acquiring green businesses, divesting or altering environment-damaging businesses, striving to become a low-cost producer through waste minimization and energy conservation, and pursuing a differentiation strategy through green-product features. In addition to creating strategies, firms could include an environmental representative on the board of directors, conduct regular environmental audits, implement bonuses for favorable environmental results, become involved in environmental issues and programs, incorporate environmental values in mission statements, establish environmentally oriented objectives, acquire environmental skills, and provide environmental training programs for company employees and managers.

California reimburses companies that buy natural gas trucks rather than cheaper diesel ones because diesel exhaust from big trucks and buses account up to 70 percent of the soot in U.S. air.[16] Diesel trucks can emit 100 times more soot than cars. Researchers have found that diesel fumes pose a higher cancer risk than all other air pollution combined.

VISIT THE NET

Gives the strategic plan for a community police consortium, including a section on strategy implementation.
http://www.communitypolicing.org/outline.html

NATURAL ENVIRONMENT PERSPECTIVE

Does Your Business Generate Its Own Electricity?

If no, perhaps it should. A new era is upon us: Power production generators are rapidly selling into homes and businesses. Personal power is poised to explode into everyday life just like personal computers did in 1984—and cellular phones more recently. Even the New York City Central Park police station has pulled the plug on its public utility. Companies such as Plug Power LLC of Latham, New York, are selling dishwasher-sized fuel cells for the home for less than four thousand dollars. These new systems, which run on propane or natural gas, not diesel, are exceptionally efficient and nonpolluting. In a fossil fuel plant, only 29 percent of the original energy in the coal or oil remains when it arrives at a home or business. "The era of big central power plants is certainly over," says Chuck Linderman of Edison Electric Institute. Some businesses, such as First National Bank in Omaha, have purchased a personal power system because "being down for one hour would cost the bank about $6 million." Because of storms, big power plants often cut off power to homes and businesses, which is so costly to some businesses; as a result, personal power systems are in great demand. Some large companies leading the way in using personal power systems include McDonald's, Rogan Corporation, Heinemann Bakeries, and Citigroup. Some manufac-

turers of personal power plants include Caterpillar Inc., Ingersoll-Rand Company, and General Electric.

More than one hundred companies have already entered the personal power business, which goes by the name "distributed generation." All public utilities are worried about exponential growth in personal power. Some large utilities in the United States try to make it impossible for homes to switch to personal power, but this is a losing battle. If personal power becomes the standard business practice by 2010 as expected, then the United States can meet the stringent reductions in carbon dioxide emissions agreed to in the international global warming treaty. However, the U.S. did not sign the Kyoto Accords which aimed to reduce global warming by reducing CO_2 omissions. Global warming isn't just a fear, it's a fact—and carbon dioxide from large power plants is a major culprit. CO_2 is the most common air pollutant worldwide, and the United States emits over six million tons of it annually—by far, the most among all countries.

Source: Adapted from: Ann Keeton, "Future Generations—Small Businesses May Soon Be Producing Much of Their Own Power On-site," *The Wall Street Journal* (September 13, 1999): R8. Also, Seth Borenstein, "New Devices May Let Homes Generate Own Electricity," *Wilmington Morning Star* (July 7, 1999): 1A.

Northeast Utilities recently agreed to pay a record $10 million in penalties and to plead guilty to twenty-five felony counts for polluting water near Waterford, Connecticut, and for discharging chlorine into Long Island Sound while concealing those actions. This company previously had discharged hydrazine, a highly toxic chemical used to clean out industrial piping, into area waters without a permit.

CREATING A STRATEGY-SUPPORTIVE CULTURE

Strategists should strive to preserve, emphasize, and build upon aspects of an existing *culture* that support proposed new strategies. Aspects of an existing culture that are antagonistic to a proposed strategy should be identified and changed. Substantial research indicates that new strategies are often market-driven and dictated by competitive forces. For this reason, changing a firm's culture to fit a new strategy is usually more effective than changing a strategy to fit an existing culture. Numerous techniques are available to alter an organization's culture, including recruitment, training, transfer, promotion, restructure of an organization's design, role modeling, and positive reinforcement.

Jack Duncan described *triangulation* as an effective, multimethod technique for studying and altering a firm's culture.[17] Triangulation includes the combined use of obtrusive observation, self-administered questionnaires, and personal interviews to determine the nature of a firm's culture. The process of triangulation reveals changes that need to be made to a firm's culture in order to benefit strategy.

Schein indicated that the following elements are most useful in linking culture to strategy:

1. Formal statements of organizational philosophy, charters, creeds, materials used for recruitment and selection, and socialization
2. Designing of physical spaces, facades, buildings
3. Deliberate role modeling, teaching, and coaching by leaders
4. Explicit reward and status system, promotion criteria
5. Stories, legends, myths, and parables about key people and events
6. What leaders pay attention to, measure, and control
7. Leader reactions to critical incidents and organizational crises
8. How the organization is designed and structured
9. Organizational systems and procedures
10. Criteria used for recruitment, selection, promotion, leveling off, retirement, and "excommunication" of people[18]

In the personal and religious side of life, the impact of loss and change is easy to see.[19] Memories of loss and change often haunt individuals and organizations for years. Ibsen wrote, "Rob the average man of his life illusion and you rob him of his happiness at the same stroke."[20] When attachments to a culture are severed in an organization's attempt to change direction, employees and managers often experience deep feelings of grief. This phenomenon commonly occurs when external conditions dictate the need for a new strategy. Managers and employees often struggle to find meaning in a situation that changed many years before. Some people find comfort in memories; others find solace in the present. Weak linkages between strategic management and organizational culture can jeopardize performance and success. Deal and Kennedy emphasized that making strategic changes in an organization always threatens a culture:

> . . . people form strong attachments to heroes, legends, the rituals of daily life, the hoopla of extravaganza and ceremonies, and all the symbols of the workplace. Change strips relationships and leaves employees confused, insecure, and often angry. Unless something can be done to provide support for transitions from old to new, the force of a culture can neutralize and emasculate strategy changes.[21]

VISIT THE NET

Provides nice information on "What Is Culture" and also provides additional excellent hot links to other culture sites.
http://www.mapnp.org/library/org_thry/culture/culture.htm

The Mexican Culture

Mexico always has been and still is an authoritarian society in terms of schools, churches, businesses, and families. Employers seek workers who are agreeable, respectful, and obedient, rather than innovative, creative, and independent. Mexican workers tend to be activity-oriented rather than problem solvers. When visitors walk into a Mexican business, they are impressed by the cordial, friendly atmosphere. This is almost always true because Mexicans desire harmony rather than conflict; desire for harmony is part of the social fabric in worker-manager relations. There is a much lower tolerance for adversarial relations or friction at work in Mexico as compared to the United States.

Mexican employers are paternalistic, providing workers with more than a paycheck, but in return, they expect allegiance. Weekly food baskets, free meals, free bus service, and free daycare are often a part of compensation. The ideal working conditions for a Mexican worker is the family model, with people all working together, doing their share, according to their designated roles. Mexican workers do not expect or desire a work environment in which self-expression and initiative are encouraged. Whereas U.S. business embodies individualism, achievement, competition, curiosity, pragmatism, informality, spontaneity, and doing more than expected on the job, Mexican businesses stress collectivism, continuity, cooperation, belongingness, formality, and doing exactly what you're told.

In Mexico, business associates rarely entertain at their homes, places reserved exclusively for close friends and family. Business meetings and entertaining are nearly always done at a restaurant. Preserving one's honor, saving face, and looking important is also exceptionally important in Mexico. This is why Mexicans do not accept criticism and change easily; many find it humiliating to acknowledge having made a mistake. A meeting among employees and managers in a business located in Mexico is a forum for giving orders and directions rather than for discussing problems or participating in decision making. Mexican workers want to be closely supervised, cared for, and corrected in a civil manner. Opinions expressed by employees are often regarded as back talk in Mexico. Mexican supervisors are viewed as weak if they explain the rationale for their orders to workers.

Mexicans do not feel compelled to follow rules that are not associated with a particular person in authority they know well or work for. Thus, signs to wear earplugs or safety glasses, or attendance or seniority policies, and even one-way street signs are often ignored. Whereas Americans follow the rules, Mexicans often do not.

Life is slower in Mexico than in the United States. People do not wear watches. The first priority is often assigned to the last request, rather than to the first. Telephone systems break down. Banks may suddenly not have pesos. Phone repair can take months. Electricity for an entire plant or town can be down for hours or even days. Business and government offices open and close at different hours. Buses and taxis may be hours off schedule. Meeting times for appointments are not rigid. Tardiness is common everywhere. Doing business effectively in Mexico requires knowledge of the Mexican way of life, culture, beliefs, and customs.

The Russian Culture

In America, unsuccessful business entrepreneurs are viewed negatively as failures, whereas successful small business owners enjoy high esteem and respect. In Russia, however, there is substantial social pressure against becoming a successful entrepreneur. Being a winner in Russia makes you the object of envy and resentment, a member of the elite rather than of the masses. Although this is slowly changing, personal ambition and success in Russia are often met with vindictiveness and derision. Initiative is met with indifference at best and punishment at worst. In the face of public ridicule and organized crime, however, thousands of Russians, particularly young persons, are opening all kinds of businesses. Public scorn and their own guilt from violating the values they were raised with do not deter many. Because Russian society scorns success, publicizing achievements, material possessions, awards, or privileges earned by Russian workers is not an effective motivational tool for those workers.

The Russian people are best known for their drive, boundless energy, tenacity, hard work, and perseverance in spite of immense obstacles. This is as true today as ever. The notion that the average Russian is stupid or lazy is nonsense; Russians on average are more educated than their American counterparts and bounce up more readily from failure.

In the United States, business ethics and personal ethics are essentially the same. Deception is deception and a lie is a lie whether in business or personal affairs in America. However, in Russia, business and personal ethics are separate. To deceive someone, bribe someone, or lie to someone to promote a business transaction is ethical in Russia, but to deceive a friend or trusted colleague is unethical. There are countless examples of foreign firms being cheated by Russian business partners. The implication of this fact for American businesses is to forge strong personal relationships with their Russian business partners whenever possible; spend time with the Russians, eating, relaxing, and exercising; and in the absence of a personal relationship, be exceptionally cautious with agreements, partnerships, payments, and when granting credit.

The Russian people have great faith and confidence in as well as respect for American products and services. Russians generally have low self-confidence. American ideas, technology, and production practices are viewed by Russians as a panacea that can save them from a gloomy existence. For example, their squeaky telephone system and lack of fax machines make them feel deprived. This mindset presents great opportunity in Russia for American products of all kinds.

Russia has historically been an autocratic state. This cultural factor is evident in business; Russian managers generally exercise power without ever being challenged by subordinates. Delegation of authority and responsibility is difficult and often nonexistent in Russian businesses. The American participative management style is not well received in Russia.

A crackdown on religion is underway in Russia. The government recognizes only Russian Orthodoxy, Judaism, Islam, and Buddhism as indigenous religions. All other faiths and churches, including all other Christian denominations, have to apply each year for permission to practice in Russia. Permission may not be granted. President Putin opposes the anti-religion movement. The lower house of Russia's parliament, the State Duma, is dominated by Communists who favor antireligion and resist further economic reforms.

The Russian republic of Ingushetia recently passed a decree legalizing the practice of polygymy that allows men to have multiple wives, even a harem. The new law is a direct challenge to the Russian government, which has jurisdiction over eighty-nine republics. The Russian Constitution prohibits polygamy, but the criminal code does not provide for any penalty. Ingushetian men take more than one wife, especially when the first wife does not have a son, despite the scientific discovery in 1959 that the father's contribution alone in procreation determines a child's sex.

The Japanese Culture

The Japanese place great importance upon group loyalty and consensus, a concept called *Wa*. Nearly all corporate activities in Japan encourage *Wa* among managers and employees. *Wa* requires that all members of a group agree and cooperate; this results in constant discussion and compromise. Japanese managers evaluate the potential attractiveness of alternative business decisions in terms of the long-term effect on the group's *Wa*. This is why silence, used for pondering alternatives, can be a plus in a formal Japanese meeting. Discussions potentially disruptive to *Wa* are generally conducted in very informal settings, such as at a bar, so as to minimize harm to the group's *Wa*. Entertaining is an important business activity in Japan because it strengthens *Wa*. Formal meetings are often conducted in informal settings. When confronted with disturbing questions or opinions, Japanese managers tend to remain silent, whereas Americans tend to respond directly, defending themselves through explanation and argument.

Most Japanese managers are reserved, quiet, distant, introspective, and other-oriented, whereas most U.S. managers are talkative, insensitive, impulsive, direct, and individual-oriented. Americans often perceive Japanese managers as wasting time and carrying on pointless conversations, whereas U.S. managers often use blunt criticism, ask prying questions, and make quick decisions. These kinds of cultural differences have disrupted many potentially productive Japanese-American business endeavors. Viewing the Japanese communication style as a prototype for all Asian cultures is a stereotype that must be avoided.

Americans have more freedom in the United States to control their own fates than do the Japanese. Life in the United States and life in Japan are very different; the United States offers more upward mobility to its people. This is a great strength of the United States. Sherman explained:

> America is not like Japan and can never be. America's strength is the opposite: It opens its doors and brings the world's disorder in. It tolerates social change that would tear most other societies apart. This openness encourages Americans to adapt as individuals rather than as a group. Americans go west to California to get a new start; they move east to Manhattan to try to make the big time; they move to Vermont or to a farm to get close to the soil. They break away from their parents' religions or values or class; they rediscover their ethnicity. They go to night school; they change their names.[22]

PRODUCTION/OPERATIONS CONCERNS WHEN IMPLEMENTING STRATEGIES

Production/operations capabilities, limitations, and policies can significantly enhance or inhibit the attainment of objectives. Production processes typically constitute more than 70 percent of a firm's total assets. A major part of the strategy-implementation process takes place at the production site. Production-related decisions on plant size, plant location, product design, choice of equipment, kind of tooling, size of inventory, inventory control, quality control, cost control, use of standards, job specialization, employee training, equipment and resource utilization, shipping and packaging, and technological innovation can have a dramatic impact on the success or failure of strategy-implementation efforts.

Examples of adjustments in production systems that could be required to implement various strategies are provided in Table 7–3 for both for-profit and nonprofit organizations. For instance, note that when a bank formulates and selects a strategy to add

TABLE 7–3   **Production Management and Strategy Implementation**

TYPE OF ORGANIZATION	STRATEGY BEING IMPLEMENTED	PRODUCTION SYSTEM ADJUSTMENTS
Hospital	Adding a cancer center (Product Development)	Purchase specialized equipment and add specialized people.
Bank	Adding ten new branches (Market Development)	Perform site location analysis.
Beer brewery	Purchasing a barley farm operation (Backward Integration)	Revise the inventory control system.
Steel manufacturer	Acquiring a fast-food chain (Conglomerate Diversification)	Improve the quality control system.
Computer company	Purchasing a retail distribution chain (Forward Integration)	Alter the shipping, packaging, and transportation systems.

ten new branches, a production-related implementation concern is site location. The largest bicycle company in the United States, Huffy, recently ended its own production of bikes and now contracts out those services to Asian and Mexican manufacturers. Huffy focuses instead on the design, marketing, and distribution of bikes, but it no longer produces bikes itself. The Dayton, Ohio, company closed its plants in Ohio, Missouri, and Mississippi.

Just-in-Time (JIT) production approaches have withstood the test of time. JIT significantly reduces the costs of implementing strategies. With JIT, parts and materials are delivered to a production site just as they are needed, rather than being stockpiled as a hedge against later deliveries. Harley-Davidson reports that at one plant alone, JIT freed $22 million previously tied up in inventory and greatly reduced reorder lead time.

Factors that should be studied before locating production facilities include the availability of major resources, the prevailing wage rates in the area, transportation costs related to shipping and receiving, the location of major markets, political risks in the area or country, and the availability of trainable employees.

For high-technology companies, production costs may not be as important as production flexibility because major product changes can be needed often. Industries such as biogenetics and plastics rely on production systems that must be flexible enough to allow frequent changes and the rapid introduction of new products. An article in *Harvard Business Review* explained why some organizations get into trouble:

> They too slowly realize that a change in product strategy alters the tasks of a production system. These tasks, which can be stated in terms of requirements for cost, product flexibility, volume flexibility, product performance, and product consistency, determine which manufacturing policies are appropriate. As strategies shift over time, so must production policies covering the location and scale of manufacturing facilities, the choice of manufacturing process, the degree of vertical integration of each manufacturing facility, the use of R&D units, the control of the production system, and the licensing of technology.[23]

A common management practice, cross-training of employees, can facilitate strategy implementation and can yield many benefits. Employees gain a better understanding of the whole business and can contribute better ideas in planning sessions. Production/operations managers need to realize, however, that cross-training employees can create problems related to the following issues:

1. It can thrust managers into roles that emphasize counseling and coaching over directing and enforcing.
2. It can necessitate substantial investments in training and incentives.
3. It can be very time-consuming.
4. Skilled workers may resent unskilled workers who learn their jobs.
5. Older employees may not want to learn new skills.

HUMAN RESOURCE CONCERNS WHEN IMPLEMENTING STRATEGIES

The job of human resource manager is changing rapidly as companies continue to downsize and reorganize. Strategic responsibilities of the human resource manager include assessing the staffing needs and costs for alternative strategies proposed during strategy formulation and developing a staffing plan for effectively implementing strategies. This plan must consider how best to manage spiraling healthcare insurance costs. Employers' health coverage expenses consume an average 26 percent of firms' net profits, even though most companies now require employees to pay part of their health insurance premiums. The plan must also include how to motivate employees and managers during a time when layoffs are common and workloads are high.

The human resource department must develop performance incentives that clearly link performance and pay to strategies. The process of empowering managers and employees through their involvement in strategic-management activities yields the greatest benefits when all organizational members understand clearly how they will benefit personally if the firm does well. Linking company and personal benefits is a major new strategic responsibility of human resource managers. Other new responsibilities for human resource managers may include establishing and administering an *employee stock ownership plan (ESOP)*, instituting an effective childcare policy, and providing leadership for managers and employees in a way that allows them to balance work and family.

A well-designed strategic-management system can fail if insufficient attention is given to the human resource dimension. Human resource problems that arise when businesses implement strategies can usually be traced to one of three causes: (1) disruption of social and political structures, (2) failure to match individuals' aptitudes with implementation tasks, and (3) inadequate top management support for implementation activities.[24]

Strategy implementation poses a threat to many managers and employees in an organization. New power and status relationships are anticipated and realized. New formal and informal groups' values, beliefs, and priorities may be largely unknown. Managers and employees may become engaged in resistance behavior as their roles, prerogatives, and power in the firm change. Disruption of social and political structures that accompany strategy execution must be anticipated and considered during strategy formulation and managed during strategy implementation.

A concern in matching managers with strategy is that jobs have specific and relatively static responsibilities, although people are dynamic in their personal development. Commonly used methods that match managers with strategies to be implemented include transferring managers, developing leadership workshops, offering career development activities, promotions, job enlargement, and job enrichment.

A number of other guidelines can help ensure that human relationships facilitate rather than disrupt strategy-implementation efforts. Specifically, managers should do a lot of chatting and informal questioning to stay abreast of how things are progressing and to know when to intervene. Managers can build support for strategy-implementation efforts by giving few orders, announcing few decisions, depending heavily on informal questioning, and seeking to probe and clarify until a consensus emerges. Key thrusts that succeed should be rewarded generously and visibly.

It is surprising that so often during strategy formulation, individual values, skills, and abilities needed for successful strategy implementation are not considered. It is rare that a firm selecting new strategies or significantly altering existing strategies possesses the right line and staff personnel in the right positions for successful strategy implementation. The need to match individual aptitudes with strategy-implementation tasks should be considered in strategy choice.

Inadequate support from strategists for implementation activities often undermines organizational success. Chief executive officers, small business owners, and government agency heads must be personally committed to strategy implementation and express this commitment in highly visible ways. Strategists' formal statements about the importance of strategic management must be consistent with actual support and rewards given for activities completed and objectives reached. Otherwise, stress created by inconsistency can cause uncertainty among managers and employees at all levels.

Perhaps the best method for preventing and overcoming human resource problems in strategic management is to actively involve as many managers and employees as possible in the process. Although time-consuming, this approach builds understanding, trust, commitment, and ownership and reduces resentment and hostility. The true potential of strategy formulation and implementation resides in people.

Employee Stock Ownership Plans (ESOPs)

An *ESOP* is a tax-qualified, defined-contribution, employee-benefit plan whereby employees purchase stock of the company through borrowed money or cash contributions. ESOPs empower employees to work as owners; this is a primary reason why the number of ESOPs grew dramatically throughout the 1980s and 1990s to more than ten thousand plans covering more than fifteen million employees. ESOPs now control more than $80 billion in corporate stock in the United States.

Besides reducing worker alienation and stimulating productivity, ESOPs allow firms other benefits, such as substantial tax savings. Principal, interest, and dividend payments on ESOP-funded debt are tax-deductible. Banks lend money to ESOPs at interest rates below prime. This money can be repaid in pretax dollars, lowering the debt service as much as 30 percent in some cases.

If an ESOP owns more than 50 percent of the firm, those who lend money to the ESOP are taxed on only 50 percent of the income received on the loans. ESOPs are not for every firm, however, because the initial legal, accounting, actuarial, and appraisal fees to set up an ESOP are about $50,000 for a small or midsized firm, with annual administration expenses of about $15,000. Analysts say ESOPs also do not work well in firms that have fluctuating payrolls and profits. Human resource managers in many firms conduct preliminary research to determine the desirability of an ESOP, and then they facilitate its establishment and administration if benefits outweigh the costs.

To establish an ESOP, a firm sets up a trust fund and purchases shares of its stock, which are allocated to individual employee accounts. All full-time employees over the age of twenty-one usually participate in the plan. Allocations of stock to the trust are made on the basis of relative pay, seniority, or some other formula. When an ESOP borrows money to purchase stock, the debt is guaranteed by the company and thus appears on the firm's balance sheet. On average, ESOP employees get $1,300 worth of stock per year, but they cannot take physical possession of the shares until they quit, retire, or die. The median level of employee ownership in ESOP plans is 30 to 40 percent, although the range is from about 10 to 100 percent.

Research confirms that ESOPs can have a dramatic positive effect on employee motivation and corporate performance, especially if ownership is coupled with expanded employee participation and involvement in decision making. Market surveys indicate that customers prefer to do business with firms that are employee-owned.

Many companies are following the lead of Polaroid, which established an ESOP as a tactic for preventing a hostile takeover. Polaroid's CEO MacAllister Booth says, "Twenty years from now we'll find that employees have a sizable stake in every major American corporation." (It is interesting to note here that Polaroid is chartered in the state of Delaware, which requires corporate suitors to acquire 85 percent of a target company's shares to complete a merger; over 50 percent of all American corporations are incorporated in Delaware for this reason.) Wyatt Cafeterias, a southwestern U.S. operator of 120 cafeterias, also adopted the ESOP concept to prevent a hostile takeover. Employee productivity at Wyatt greatly increased since the ESOP began, as illustrated in the following quote:

The key employee in our entire organization is the person serving the customer on the cafeteria line. In the past, because of high employee turnover and entry-level wages for many line jobs, these employees received far less attention and recognition than managers. We now tell the tea cart server, "You own the place. Don't wait for the manager to tell you how to do your job better or how to provide better service. You take care of it." Sure, we're looking for productivity increases, but since we began pushing decisions down to the level of people who deal directly with customers, we've discovered an awesome side effect—suddenly the work crews have this "happy to be here" attitude that the customers really love.[25]

Companies such as Avis, Procter & Gamble, BellSouth, ITT, Xerox, Delta, Austin Industries, Health Trust, the Parsons Corporation, Dyncorp, and Charter Medical have established ESOPs to assist strategists in divesting divisions, going private, and consummating leveraged buyours. ESOPs can be found today in all kinds of firms, from small retailers to large manufacturers. Nearly all ESOPs are established in healthy firms, not failing firms.

Balancing Work Life and Home Life

Work/family strategies have become so popular among companies today that the strategies now represent a competitive advantage for those firms that offer such benefits as elder care assistance, flexible scheduling, job sharing, adoption benefits, an on-site summer camp, employee help lines, pet care, and even lawn service referrals. New corporate titles such as Work/Life Coordinator and Director of Diversity are becoming common.

Working Mother magazine in late 2001 published its listing of "The 100 Best Companies for Working Mothers" (**http://workingmother.com/oct_2001/100best. shtml**). Three especially important variables used in the ranking were availability of flextime, advancement opportunities, and equitable distribution of benefits among companies. *Working Mother*'s top ten best companies for working women in 2001 are listed here:

1. Bristol-Myers Squibb Company
2. Citigroup
3. Fannie Mae
4. IBM Corporation
5. Marriott International
6. Morgan Stanley
7. PricewaterhouseCoopers
8. Procter & Gamble Company
9. Prudential
10. Texas Instruments

Human resource managers need to foster a more effective balancing of professional and private lives because nearly sixty million people in the United States are now part of two-career families. A corporate objective to become more lean and mean must today include consideration for the fact that a good home life contributes immensely to a good work life.

The work/family issue is no longer just a women's issue. Some specific measures that firms are taking to address this issue are providing spouse relocation assistance as an employee benefit, providing company resources for family recreational and educational use, establishing employee country clubs such as those at IBM and Bethlehem Steel, and creating family/work interaction opportunities. A study by Joseph Pleck of Wheaton

VISIT THE NET

To see how a large company, Johnson & Johnson, is balancing "Work and Family Issues," visit the Web site www.jnj.com/who_is_jnj/ framework_index.html.

College found that in companies that do not offer paternity leave for fathers as a benefit, most men take short informal paternity leaves anyway by combining vacation time and sick days.

Some organizations have developed family days, when family members are invited into the workplace, taken on plant or office tours, dined by management, and given a chance to see exactly what other family members do each day. Family days are inexpensive and increase the employee's pride in working for the organization. Flexible working hours during the week are another human resource response to the need for individuals to balance work life and home life. The work/family topic is being made part of the agenda at meetings and thus is being discussed in many organizations.

Research indicates that employees who are dissatisfied with childcare arrangements are most likely to be absent or unproductive.[26] Lack of adequate childcare in a community can be a deterrent in recruiting and retaining good managers and employees. Some benefits of on-site childcare facilities are improved employee relations, reduced absenteeism and turnover, increased productivity, enhanced recruitment, and improved community relations.

A recent survey of women managers revealed that one-third would leave their present employer for another employer offering childcare assistance. The Conference Board recently reported that more than five hundred firms in the United States had created on-site or near-site childcare centers for their employees, including Merck, Campbell Soup, Hoffman-LaRoche, Stride-Rite, Johnson Wax, CIGNA, Champion International, Walt Disney World, and Playboy Resorts.

Other common childcare service arrangements include employer-sponsored daycare, childcare information, and referral services. IBM, Steelcase, Honeywell, Citibank, 3M, and Southland have established contracts with third-party childcare information and referral services.

Most of the sixty-four million women in the U.S. labor force are employed in what the Department of Labor calls "nontraditional occupations"—areas of employment in which women now comprise 25 percent or less of the workforce. This list includes pilots, truck drivers, funeral directors, dentists, architects, bellhops, barbers, meter readers, and construction workers. Women in the United States now head one in every four households with children under age eighteen. Women must and should therefore get their fair share of these jobs for our society to progress. More women in the United States are employed as teachers, secretaries, and cashiers than work in any other jobs. Among the jobs in which less than 5 percent of those employed are women include fishermen (4.6 percent), pest control (4.1 percent), airplane pilots and navigators (4.1 percent), firefighting and fire prevention (2.5 percent), construction (2.0 percent), and tool and die makers (0.2 percent).[27]

It is encouraging to note that more and more talented women in business are being promoted to top-level managerial positions in the United States. Carleton Fiorina is CEO of Hewlett-Packard and Andrea Jung is CEO of Avon—by far the largest companies ever run by women. Thirteen percent of Texas Instruments' top executives are women, up from only 2 percent in 1994. Fiorina is only the third woman CEO of a Fortune 500 company; the others include Barad at Mattel and Sandler at Golden West Financial. Among the Fortune 1000 companies, there are only seven female CEOs, so the *glass ceiling* in America still exists and needs to be broken. Only 11.1 percent of all company executives are female among Fortune 500 companies. In the automobile industry, only 8 percent of executives at Ford, DaimlerChrysler, and General Motors are female. However, women buy more than half the vehicles sold in the United States and take part in more than 80 percent of all purchases.[28]

Benefits of a Diverse Workforce

When Toyota was threatened with a boycott by African Americans in late 2001, the company committed almost $8 billion oven ten years to diversify its workforce and to use more minority suppliers. Hundreds of other firms, such as Ford Motor Company and Coca-Cola, are also striving to become more diversified in their workforce. TJX Companies, the parent of fifteen-hundred T.J. Maxx and Marshalls stores, has experienced great benefits of being an exemplary company in terms of diversity. A recent *Wall Street Journal* article listed, in rank order of importance, the following major benefits of having a diverse workforce:[29]

1. Improves corporate culture
2. Improves employee morale
3. Leads to a higher retention of employees
4. Leads to an easier recruitment of new employees
5. Decreases complaints and litigation
6. Increases creativity
7. Decreases interpersonal conflict between employees
8. Enables the organization to move into emerging markets
9. Improves client relations
10. Increases productivity
11. Improves the bottom line
12. Maximizes brand identity
13. Reduces training costs

An organization can perhaps be most effective when its workforce mirrors the diversity of its customers. For global companies, this goal can be optimistic, but it is a worthwhile goal. According to the 2001 census figures, African Americans comprise 13 percent of the U.S. population, followed by Hispanics at 12.5 percent, and Asian Americans at 3.6 percent. Women account for about 46.6 percent of the American workforce. Minorities and women are still scarce in top management positions in America; this problem needs immediate attention.

CONCLUSION

Successful strategy formulation does not at all guarantee successful strategy implementation. Although inextricably interdependent, strategy formulation and strategy implementation are characteristically different. In a single word, strategy implementation means *change*. It is widely agreed that "the real work begins after strategies are formulated." Successful strategy implementation requires the support of as well as discipline and hard work from motivated managers and employees. It is sometimes frightening to think that a single individual can sabotage strategy-implementation efforts irreparably.

Formulating the right strategies is not enough, because managers and employees must be motivated to implement those strategies. Management issues considered central to strategy implementation include matching organizational structure with strategy, linking performance and pay to strategies, creating an organizational climate conducive to change, managing political relationships, creating a strategy-supportive culture, adapting production/operations processes, and managing human resources. Establishing annual objectives, devising policies, and allocating resources are central strategy-implementation activities common to all organizations. Depending on the size and type of the organization, other management issues could be equally important to successful strategy implementation.

 We invite you to visit the David page on the Prentice Hall Companion Website at **www.prenhall.com/david** for this chapter's World Wide Web exercises.

KEY TERMS AND CONCEPTS

Annual Objectives (p. 238)

Avoidance (p. 243)

Benchmarking (p. 250)

Bonus System (p. 252)

Conflict (p. 243)

Confrontation (p. 243)

Culture (p. 257)

Defusion (p. 243)

Delayering (p. 248)

Decentralized Structure (p. 245)

Divisional Structure by Geographic Area, Product, Customer, or Process (pp. 245–246)

Downsizing (p. 248)

Educative Change Strategy (p. 254)

Employee Stock Ownership Plans (ESOP) (p. 264)

Establishing Annual Objectives (p. 238)

Force Change Strategy (p. 254)

Functional Structure (p. 245)

Gain Sharing (p. 252)

Glass Ceiling (p. 266)

Horizontal Consistency of Objectives (p. 240)

Just in Time (JIT) (p. 262)

Matrix Structure (p. 248)

Policy (p. 240)

Profit Sharing (p. 252)

Rational Change Strategy (p. 254)

Reengineering (p. 249)

Resistance to Change (p. 254)

Resource Allocation (p. 241)

Restructuring (p. 248)

Rightsizing (p. 248)

Self-Interest Change Strategy (p. 254)

Strategic Business Unit (SBU) Structure (p. 247)

Triangulation (p. 258)

Vertical Consistency of Objectives (p. 240)

ISSUES FOR REVIEW AND DISCUSSION

1. Allocating resources can be a political and an ad hoc activity in firms that do not use strategic management. Why is this true? Does adopting strategic management ensure easy resource allocation? Why?

2. Compare strategy formulation with strategy implementation in terms of each being an art or a science.

3. Describe the relationship between annual objectives and policies.

4. Identify a long-term objective and two supporting annual objectives for a familiar organization.

5. Identify and discuss three policies that apply to your present business policy class.

6. Explain the following statement: Horizontal consistency of goals is as important as vertical consistency.

7. Describe several reasons why conflict may occur during objective-setting activities.

8. In your opinion, what approaches to conflict resolution would be best for resolving a disagreement between a personnel manager and a sales manager over the firing of a particular salesperson? Why?

9. Describe the organizational culture of your college or university.
10. Explain why organizational structure is so important in strategy implementation.
11. In your opinion, how many separate divisions could an organization reasonably have without using an SBU-type organizational structure? Why?
12. Would you recommend a divisional structure by geographic area, product, customer, or process for a medium-sized bank in your local area? Why?
13. What are the advantages and disadvantages of decentralizing the wage and salary functions of an organization? How could this be accomplished?
14. Consider a college organization with which you are familiar. How did management issues affect strategy implementation in that organization?
15. As production manager of a local newspaper, what problems would you anticipate in implementing a strategy to increase the average number of pages in the paper by 40 percent?
16. Read an article from the suggested readings at the end of this chapter and give a summary report to the class revealing your thoughts on the topic.
17. Do you believe expenditures for childcare or fitness facilities are warranted from a cost/benefit perspective? Why or why not?
18. Explain why successful strategy implementation often hinges on whether the strategy-formulation process empowers managers and employees.
19. Compare and contrast the cultures in Mexico, Russia, and Japan.
20. Discuss the glass ceiling in the United States, giving your ideas and suggestions.

NOTES

1. DALE MCCONKEY, "Planning in a Changing Environment," *Business Horizons* (September–October 1988): 66.
2. A. G. BEDEIAN and W. F. GLUECK, *Management*, 3rd ed. (Chicago: The Dryden Press, 1983): 212.
3. BORIS YAVITZ and WILLIAM NEWMAN, *Strategy in Action: The Execution, Politics, and Payoff of Business Planning* (New York: The Free Press, 1982): 195.
4. RICK BROOKS, "Bank One's Strategy As Competition Grows: New, Online Institution," *USA Today* (August 25, 1999): A1.
5. STEVE HAMM and MARCIA STEPANEK, "From Reengineering to E-engineering," *Business Week* (March 22, 1999): EB 15.
6. "Want to Be a Manager? Many People Say No, Calling Job Miserable," *The Wall Street Journal* (April 4, 1997): 1. Also, STEPHANIE ARMOUR, "Management Loses Its Allure," *USA Today* (October 10, 1997): 1B.
7. STEPHANIE ARMOUR, "Layoff Survivors Climb Ladder Faster," *USA Today* (September 10, 2001), B1.
8. PAUL CARROLL, "No More Business as Usual, Please. Time to Try Something Different," *The Wall Street Journal* (October 23, 2001): A24.
9. JULIE SCHMIT, "Japan Shifts to Merit Pay," *USA Today* (July 23, 1999): 5B.
10. RICHARD BROWN, "Outsider CEO: Inspiring Change With Force and Grace," *USA Today* (July 19, 1999): 3B.
11. YAVITZ and NEWMAN, 58.
12. JOHN JONES, "Winners and Losers," *Wall Street Journal,* (April 11, 2002): B10.
13. JACK DUNCAN, *Management* (New York: Random House, 1983): 381–390.
14. H. IGOR ANSOFF, "Strategic Management of Technology," *Journal of Business Strategy* 7, no. 3 (Winter 1987): 38.
15. ROBERT WATERMAN, JR., "How the Best Get Better," *Business Week* (September 14, 1987): 104.
16. TRACI WATSON, "Pollution From Trucks Targeted," *USA Today* (July 7, 1999): 4A.
17. JACK DUNCAN, "Organizational Culture: Getting a Fix on an Elusive Concept," *Academy of Management Executive* 3, no. 3 (August 1989): 229.
18. E. H. SCHEIN, "The Role of the Founder in Creating Organizational Culture," *Organizational Dynamics* (Summer 1983): 13–28.
19. T. DEAL and A. KENNEDY, "Culture: A New Look Through Old Lenses," *Journal of Applied Behavioral Science* 19, no. 4 (1983): 498–504.
20. H. IBSEN, "The Wild Duck," in O. G. Brochett and L. Brochett (eds.), *Plays for the Theater* (New York: Holt, Rinehart & Winston, 1967). Also, R. Pascale, "The Paradox of 'Corporate Culture': Reconciling Ourselves to Socialization," *California Management Review* 28, 2 (1985): 26, 37–40.
21. T. DEAL and A. KENNEDY, *Corporate Cultures: The Rites and Rituals of Corporate Life* (Reading, MA: Addison-Wesley, 1982): 256.

22. STRATFORD SHERMAN, "How to Beat the Japanese," *Fortune* (April 10, 1989): 145.

23. ROBERT STOBAUGH and PIERO TELESIO, "Match Manufacturing Policies and Product Strategy," *Harvard Business Review* 61, no. 2 (March–April 1983): 113.

24. R. T. LENZ and MARJORIE LYLES, "Managing Human Resource Problems in Strategy Planning Systems," *Journal of Business Strategy* 60, no. 4 (Spring 1986): 58.

25. J. WARREN HENRY, "ESOPs with Productivity Payoffs," *Journal of Business Strategy* (July–August 1989): 33.

26. RICHARD LEVINE, "Childcare: Inching up the Corporate Agenda," *Management Review* 78, no. 1 (January 1989): 43.

27. DEWAYNE WICKHAM, "Women Still Fighting for Job Equality," *USA Today* (August 31, 1999): 15A.

28. MICHELINE MAYNARD, "Practically Alone at the Top," *USA Today* (September 7, 1999): B1.

29. JULIE BENNETT, "Corporate Downsizing Doesn't Deter Search for Diversity," *The Wall Street Journal* (October 23, 2001): B18.

CURRENT READINGS

ARTHUR, JEFFREY B., and LYNDA AIMAN-SMITH. "Gain Sharing and Organizational Learning: An Analysis of Employee Suggestions over Time." *The Academy of Management Journal* 44, no. 4 (August 2001): 737.

BARUCH, YEHUDA. "No Such Thing as a Global Manager." *Business Horizons* 45, no. 1 (January–February 2002): 36.

BEGLEY, THOMAS M., and DAVID P. BOYD. "Articulating Corporate Values Through Human Resource Policies." *Business Horizons* 43, no. 4 (July–August 2000): 8.

BLOOM, MATT, and JOHN G. MICHAEL. "The Relationships among Organizational Context, Pay Dispersion, and Managerial Turnover." *The Academy of Management Journal* 45, no. 1 (February 2002): 33.

BOYD, B. K., and A. SALAMIN. "Strategic Reward Systems: A Contingency Model of Pay System Design." *Strategic Management Journal* 22, no. 8 (August 2001): 777.

CANNELLA, JR., ALBERT A., and WEI SHEN. "So Close and Yet So Far: Promotion Versus Exit for CEO Heirs Apparent." *Academy of Management* 44, no. 2 (April 2001): 271.

CARPENTER, M. A., and W. G. SANDERS. "Top Management Team Compensation: The Missing Link Between CEO Pay and Firm Performance?" *Strategic Management Journal* 23, no. 4 (April 2002): 367.

CASE, JOHN. "When Salaries Aren't Secret." *Harvard Business Review* (May 2001): 37.

CHILTON, KENNETH W. "Reengineering U.S. Environmental Protection." *Business Horizons* 43, no. 2 (March–April 2000): 7.

DENIS, JEAN-LOUIS, LISE LAMOTHE, and ANN LANGLEY. "The Dynamics of Collective Leadership and Strategic Change in Pluralistic Organizations." *The Academy of Management Journal* 44, no. 4 (August 2001): 809.

FIOL, C. MARLENE, EDWARD J. O'CONNOR, and HERMAN AGUINIS. "All for One and One for All? The Development and Transfer of Power Across Organizational Levels." *The Academy of Management Review* 26, no. 2 (April 2001): 224.

GELETKANYCZ, M. A., B. K. BOYD, and S. FINKELSTEIN. "The Strategic Value of CEO External Directorate Networks: Implications for CEO Compensation." *Strategic Management Journal* 22, no. 9 (September 2001): 889.

GOOLD, MICHAEL, and ANDREW CAMPBELL. "Do You Have a Well-Designed Organization?" *Harvard Business Review* (March 2002): 117.

HENDERSON, DAVID A., GABRIEL G. RAMIREZ, ROBERT J. HOUSE, and PHANISH PURANAM. "Does Leadership Matter? CEO Leadership Attributes and Profitability Under Conditions of Perceived Environmental Uncertainty." *The Academy of Management Journal* 44, no. 1 (February 2001): 96.

HEWLETT, SYLVIA ANN. "Executive Women and the Myth of Having It All." *Harvard Business Review* (April 2002): 66.

HUDSON, KATHERINE M. "Transforming a Conservative Company—One Laugh at a Time." *Harvard Business Review* (July–August 2001): 45.

JEHN, KAREN A., and ELIZABETH A. MANNIX. "The Dynamic Nature of Conflict: A Longitudinal Study of Intragroup Conflict and Group Performance." *The Academy of Management Journal* 44, no. 2 (April 2001): 238.

KELLER, ROBERT T. "Cross-Functional Project Groups in Research and New Product Development: Diversity, Communications, Job Stress, and Outcomes." *The Academy of Management Journal* 44, no. 3 (June 2001): 547.

KING, ADELAIDE WILCOX, SALLY W. FOWLER, and CARL P. ZEITHAML. "Managing Organizational Competencies for Competitive Advantage: The Middle-Management Edge." *The Academy of Management Executive* 15, no. 2 (May 2001): 95.

KNIGHT, DON, CATHY C. DURHAM, and EDWIN A. LOCKE. "The Relationship of Team Goals, Incentives, and Efficacy to Strategic Risk, Tactical Implementation, and Performance." *The Academy of Management Journal* 44, no. 2 (April 2001): 326.

MARKS, MICHAEL LEE, and PHILIP H. MIRVIS. "Making Mergers and Acquisitions Work: Strategic and Psychological Preparation." *The Academy of Management Executive* 15, no. 2 (May 2001): 80.

MEZIAS, JOHN, PETER GRINYER, and WILLIAM D. GUTH. "Changing Collective Cognition: A Process Model for Strategic Change." *Long Range Planning* 34, no. 1 (February 2001): 71.

NAIR, A., and S. KOTHA. "Does Group Membership Matter? Evidence from the Japanese Steel Industry." *Strategic Management Journal* 22, no. 3 (March 2001): 221.

NELSON, DEBRA L., and RONALD J. BURKE. "Women Executives: Health, Stress, and Success." *The Academy of Management Executive* 14, no. 2 (May 2000): 107.

RAMUS, CATHERINE A. "Organizational Support for Employees: Encouraging Creative Ideas for Environmental Sustainability." *California Management Review* 43, no. 3 (Spring 2001): 85.

RAYNOR, MICHAEL E., and JOSEPH L. BOWER. "Lead from the Center: How to Manage Divisions Dynamically." *Harvard Business Review* (May 2001): 92.

SHAW, J. D., N. GUPTA, and J. E. DELERY. "Congruence Between Technology and Compensation Systems: Implications for Strategy Implementations." *Strategic Management Journal* 22, no. 4 (April 2001): 379.

TULGAN, BRUCE. "Real Pay for Performance." *Journal of Business Strategy* 22, no. 3 (May/June 2001): 19.

WOLF, J., and W. G. EGELHOFF. "A Reexamination and Extension of International Strategy-Structure Theory." *Strategic Management Journal* 23, no. 2 (February 2002): 181.

WRZESNIEWSKI, AMY, and JANE E. DUTTON. "Crafting a Job: Revisioning Employees as Active Crafters of Their Work." *The Academy of Management Review* 26, no. 2 (April 2001): 179.

EXPERIENTIAL EXERCISES

EXPERIENTIAL EXERCISE 7A ▶

Revising American Airline's (AMR's) Organizational Chart

PURPOSE

Developing and altering organizational charts is an important skill for strategists to possess. This exercise can improve your skill in altering an organization's hierarchical structure in response to new strategies being formulated.

INSTRUCTIONS

Step 1   Turn back to the American Airlines (AMR) Cohesion Case (p. 32). On a separate sheet of paper, diagram an organizational chart that you believe would best suit AMR's needs if the company decided to form a divisional structure by-product.

Step 2   Provide as much detail in your chart as possible, including the names of individuals and the titles of positions.

EXPERIENTIAL EXERCISE 7B ▶

Do Organizations Really Establish Objectives?

PURPOSE

Objectives provide direction, allow synergy, aid in evaluation, establish priorities, reduce uncertainty, minimize conflicts, stimulate exertion, and aid in both the allocation of resources and the design of jobs. This exercise will enhance your understanding of how organizations use or misuse objectives.

INSTRUCTIONS

Step 1   Join with one other person in class to form a two-person team.

Step 2   Contact by telephone the owner or manager of an organization in your city or town. Request a thirty-minute personal interview or meeting with that person for the purpose of discussing "business objectives." During your meeting, seek answers to the following questions:

1. Do you believe it is important for a business to establish and clearly communicate long-term and annual objectives? Why or why not?

2. Does your organization establish objectives? If yes, what type and how many? How are the objectives communicated to individuals? Are your firm's objectives in written form or simply communicated orally?

3. To what extent are managers and employees involved in the process of establishing objectives?

4. How often are your business objectives revised and by what process?

Step 3   Take good notes during the interview. Let one person be the note taker and one person do most of the talking. Have your notes typed up and ready to turn in to your professor.

Step 4   Prepare a five-minute oral presentation for the class, reporting the results of your interview. Turn in your typed report.

EXPERIENTIAL EXERCISE 7C ▶

Understanding My University's Culture

PURPOSE

It is something of an art to uncover the basic values and beliefs that are buried deeply in an organization's rich collection of stories, language, heroes, heroines, and rituals, yet culture can be the most important factor in implementing strategies.

INSTRUCTIONS

Step 1   On a separate sheet of paper, list the following terms: hero/heroine, belief, metaphor, language, value, symbol, story, legend, saga, folktale, myth, ceremonial, rite, and ritual.

Step 2   For your college or university, give examples of each term. If necessary, speak with faculty, staff, alumni, administration, or fellow students of the institution to identify examples of each term.

Step 3   Report your findings to the class. Tell the class how you feel regarding cultural products being consciously used to help implement strategies.

8 IMPLEMENTING STRATEGIES: MARKETING, FINANCE/ACCOUNTING, R&D, AND MIS ISSUES

CHAPTER OUTLINE

- The Nature of Strategy Implementation
- Marketing Issues
- Finance/Accounting Issues
- Research and Development (R&D) Issues
- Management Information Systems (MIS) Issues

EXPERIENTIAL EXERCISE 8A
Developing a Product-Positioning Map for American Airlines (AMR)

EXPERIENTIAL EXERCISE 8B
Performing an EPS/EBIT Analysis for American Airlines (AMR)

EXPERIENTIAL EXERCISE 8C
Preparing Pro Forma Financial Statements for American Airlines (AMR)

EXPERIENTIAL EXERCISE 8D
Determining the Cash Value of American Airlines (AMR)

EXPERIENTIAL EXERCISE 8E
Developing a Product-Positioning Map for My University

EXPERIENTIAL EXERCISE 8F
Do Banks Require Pro Forma Statements?

CHAPTER OBJECTIVES

After studying this chapter, you should be able to do the following:

1. Explain market segmentation and product positioning as strategy-implementation tools.
2. Discuss procedures for determining the worth of a business.
3. Explain why pro forma financial analysis is a central strategy-implementation tool.
4. Explain how to evaluate the attractiveness of debt versus stock as a source of capital to implement strategies.
5. Discuss the nature and role of research and development in strategy implementation.
6. Explain how management information systems can determine the success of strategy-implementation efforts.

NOTABLE QUOTES

The greatest strategy is doomed if it's implemented badly.
BERNARD REIMANN

There is no "perfect" strategic decision. One always has to pay a price. One always has to balance conflicting objectives, conflicting opinions, and conflicting priorities. The best strategic decision is only an approximation—and a risk.
PETER DRUCKER

The real question isn't how well you're doing today against your own history, but how you're doing against your competitors.

DONALD KRESS

As market windows open and close more quickly, it is important that R&D be tied more closely to corporate strategy.
WILLIAM SPENSER

Most of the time, strategists should not be formulating strategy at all; they should be getting on with implementing strategies they already have.

HENRY MINTZBERG

Strategies have no chance of being implemented successfully in organizations that do not market goods and services well, in firms that cannot raise needed working capital, in firms that produce technologically inferior products, or in firms that have a weak information system. This chapter examines marketing, finance/accounting, R&D, and management information systems (MIS) issues that are central to effective strategy implementation. Special topics include market segmentation, market positioning, evaluating the worth of a business, determining to what extent debt and/or stock should be used as a source of capital, developing pro forma financial statements, contracting R&D outside the firm, and creating an information support system. Manager and employee involvement and participation are essential for success in marketing, finance/accounting, R&D, and MIS activities.

THE NATURE OF STRATEGY IMPLEMENTATION

The quarterback can call the best play possible in the huddle, but that does not mean the play will go for a touchdown. The team may even lose yardage unless the play is executed (implemented) well. Less than 10 percent of strategies formulated are successfully implemented! There are many reasons for this low success rate, including failing to segment markets appropriately, paying too much for a new acquisition, and falling behind competitors in R&D.

Strategy implementation directly affects the lives of plant managers, division managers, department managers, sales managers, product managers, project managers, personnel managers, staff managers, supervisors, and all employees. In some situations, individuals may not have participated in the strategy-formulation process at all and may not appreciate, understand, or even accept the work and thought that went into strategy formulation. There may even be foot dragging or resistance on their part. Managers and employees who do not understand the business and are not committed to the business may attempt to sabotage strategy-implementation efforts in hopes that the organization will return to its old ways. The strategy-implementation stage of the strategic-management process is emphasized in Figure 8–1.

MARKETING ISSUES

VISIT THE NET

An excellent PowerPoint presentation on marketing issues related to strategic management.
http://www.cl.uh.edu/bpa/hadm/HADM_5731/ppt_presentations/3mktpln/index.htm

Countless marketing variables affect the success or failure of strategy implementation, and the scope of this text does not allow us to address all those issues. Some examples of marketing decisions that may require policies are as follows:

1. To use exclusive dealerships or multiple channels of distribution
2. To use heavy, light, or no TV advertising
3. To limit (or not) the share of business done with a single customer
4. To be a price leader or a price follower
5. To offer a complete or limited warranty
6. To reward salespeople based on straight salary, straight commission, or a combination salary/commission
7. To advertise online or not

FIGURE 8–1

A Comprehensive Strategic-Management Model

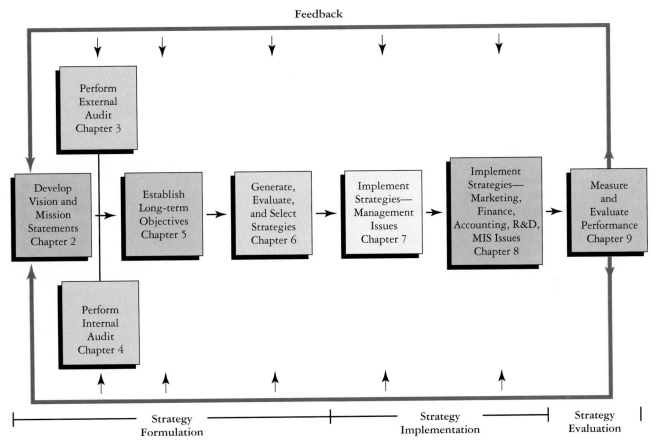

A marketing issue of increasing concern to consumers today is the extent to which companies can track individuals' movements on the Internet—and even be able to identify an individual by name and e-mail address. Individuals' wanderings on the Internet are no longer anonymous, as many persons believe. Marketing companies such as Doubleclick, Flycast, AdKnowledge, AdForce, and Real Media have sophisticated methods to identify who you are and your particular interests.[1] If you are especially concerned about being tracked, visit the **www.networkadvertising.org** Web site that gives details about how marketers today are identifying you and your buying habits.

Recently completed research reveals that Web advertising dollars spent by businesses was 27 percent of total advertising expenditures in 2002, up from 17 percent in 1999. Web advertising's market share increase will come at the expense of all other media. Newspapers, radio, magazines, television, and the Yellow Pages have long worried about online rivals siphoning off advertising dollars. This worry now totals about $600 billion in business advertising expenditures annually being diverted to online media.

Two variables are of central importance to strategy implementation: *market segmentation* and *product positioning*. Market segmentation and product positioning rank as marketing's most important contributions to strategic management.

Market Segmentation

Market segmentation is widely used in implementing strategies, especially for small and specialized firms. Market segmentation can be defined as the subdividing of a market into distinct subsets of customers according to needs and buying habits.

Market segmentation is an important variable in strategy implementation for at least three major reasons. First, strategies such as market development, product development, market penetration, and diversification require increased sales through new markets and products. To implement these strategies successfully, new or improved market-segmentation approaches are required. Second, market segmentation allows a firm to operate with limited resources because mass production, mass distribution, and mass advertising are not required. Market segmentation enables a small firm to compete successfully with a large firm by maximizing per-unit profits and per-segment sales. Finally, market segmentation decisions directly affect *marketing mix variables:* product, place, promotion, and price, as indicated in Table 8–1. For example, SnackWells, a pioneer in reduced-fat snacks, has shifted its advertising emphasis from low-fat to great taste as part of its new market-segmentation strategy.

Perhaps the most dramatic new market-segmentation strategy is the targeting of regional tastes. Firms from McDonald's to General Motors are increasingly modifying their products to meet different regional preferences within the United States. Campbell's has a spicier version of its nacho cheese soup for the Southwest, and Burger King offers breakfast burritos in New Mexico but not in South Carolina. Geographic and demographic bases for segmenting markets are the most commonly employed, as illustrated in Table 8–2. Note that gender is a popular demographic segmentation variable, and is discussed further in the E-Commerce Perspective box.

Evaluating potential market segments requires strategists to determine the characteristics and needs of consumers, to analyze consumer similarities and differences, and to develop consumer group profiles. Segmenting consumer markets is generally much simpler and easier than segmenting industrial markets, because industrial products, such as electronic circuits and forklifts, have multiple applications and appeal to diverse customer groups. Note in Figure 8–2 that customer age is used to segment automobile car purchases. Note that older buyers especially like Cadillacs and Buicks.

Segmentation is a key to matching supply and demand, which is one of the thorniest problems in customer service. Segmentation often reveals that large, random fluctuations in demand actually consist of several small, predictable, and manageable patterns.

TABLE 8–1   The Marketing Mix Component Variables

PRODUCT	PLACE	PROMOTION	PRICE
Quality	Distribution channels	Advertising	Level
Features and options	Distribution coverage	Personal selling	Discounts and
Style	Outlet location	Sales promotion	allowances
Brand name	Sales territories	Publicity	Payment terms
Packaging	Inventory levels		
Product line	and locations		
Warranty	Transportation carriers		
Service level			
Other services			

Source: E. Jerome McCarthy, *Basic Marketing: A Managerial Approach*, 9th ed. (Homewood, IL: Richard D. Irwin, Inc., 1987): 37–44.

TABLE 8-2   **Alternative Bases for Market Segmentation**

VARIABLE	TYPICAL BREAKDOWNS
GEOGRAPHIC	
Region	Pacific, Mountain, West North Central, West South Central, East North Cental, East South Central, South Atlantic, Middle Atlantic, New England
County Size	A,B,C,D
City Size	Under 5,000; 5,000–20,000; 20,000–50,000; 50,000–100,000; 100,000–250,000; 250,000–500,000; 500,000–1,000,000; 1,000,000–4,000,000; 4,000,000 or over
Density	Urban, suburban, rural
Climate	Northern, southern
DEMOGRAPHIC	
Age	Under 6, 6–11, 12–19, 20–34, 35–49, 50–64, 65+
Gender	Male, female
Family Size	1–2, 3–4, 5+
Family Life Cycle	Young, single; young, married, no children; young, married, youngest child under 6; young, married, youngest child 6 or over; older, married, with children; older, married, no children under 18; older, single; other
Income	Under $10,000; $10,001–$15,000; $15,001–$20,000; $20,001–$30,000; $30,001–$50,000; $50,001–$70,000; $70,001–$100,000; over $100,000
Occupation	Professional and technical; managers, officials, and proprietors; clerical, sales; craftsmen, foremen; operatives; farmers; retired; students; housewives; unemployed
Education	Grade school or less; some high school; high school graduate; some college; college graduate
Religion	Catholic, Protestant, Jewish, Islamic, other
Race	White, Asian, Hispanic, African American
Nationality	American, British, French, German, Scandinavian, Italian, Latin American, Middle Eastern, Japanese
PSYCHOGRAPHIC	
Social Class	Lower lowers, upper lowers, lower middles, upper middles, lower uppers, upper uppers
Personality	Compulsive, gregarious, authoritarian, ambitious
BEHAVIORAL	
Use Occasion	Regular occasion, special occasion
Benefits Sought	Quality, service, economy
User Status	Nonuser, ex-user, potential user, first-time user, regular user
Usage Rate	Light user, medium user, heavy user
Loyalty Status	None, medium, strong, absolute
Readiness Stage	Unaware, aware, informed, interested, desirous, intending to buy
Attitude Toward Product	Enthusiastic, positive, indifferent, negative, hostile

Source: Adapted from Philip Kotler, *Marketing Management: Analysis, Planning and Control*, © 1984: 256. Adapted by permission of Prentice-Hall, Inc., Englewood Cliffs, New Jersey.

Matching supply and demand allows factories to produce desirable levels without extra shifts, overtime, and subcontracting. Matching supply and demand also minimizes the number and severity of stock-outs. The demand for hotel rooms, for example, can be dependent on foreign tourists, businesspersons, and vacationers. Focusing on these three market segments separately, however, can allow hotel firms to predict overall supply and demand more effectively.

FIGURE 8–2

Average Age of Automobile Buyers, by brand

Plymouth 38	Pontiac 42	Infiniti 45
Mitsubishi 38	Acura 42	Subaru 45
Volkswagen 38	Hyundai 42	Oldsmobile 46
Honda 41	Suzuki 42	Saturn 46
Isuzu 41	Audi 42	Chrysler 47
Kia 41	Daewoo 43	Lexus 47
Land Rover 41	Chevrolet 43	Jaguar 49
Mazda 41	Porsche 43	Mercury 50
Nissan 41	Saab 43	Lincoln 51
BMW 42	GMC 44	Cadillac 53
Dodge 42	Toyota 44	Buick 57
Jeep 42	Volvo 44	
Ford 42	Mercedes-Benz 45	

Source: Adapted from Norihiko Shirouzu, "This Is Not Your Father's Toyota," *Wall Street Journal* (March 26, 2002): B1.

Banks now are segmenting markets to increase effectiveness. "You're dead in the water if you aren't segmenting the market," says Anne Moore, president of a bank consulting firm in Atlanta. As indicated in the E-Commerce Perspective box, the Internet makes market segmentation easier today because consumers naturally form "communities" on the Web.

E-COMMERCE PERSPECTIVE

Male versus Female Internet Usage Globally

Note from the table below that the U.S. and Canada are the only countries in the would where female Internet usage is higher than male usage. Note that in many countries, including Germany, Italy, and India, male usage exceeds female usage by more than 20 percent.

COUNTRY	FEMALE	MALE	COUNTRY	FEMALE	MALE
Argentina	45.4%	54.6%	Japan	42.3%	57.7%
Australia	46.9	53.1	Mexico	40.6	59.4
Austria	42.8	57.2	Netherlands	43.1	57.0
Belgium	40.5	59.5	New Zealand	49.6	50.4
Brazil	43.1	56.9	Norway	43.4	56.6
Canada	51.9	48.1	Singapore	45.0	55.0
Denmark	44.8	55.2	South Africa	43.1	56.9
Finland	47.0	53.0	South Korea	45.9	54.1
France	39.8	60.2	Spain	41.1	58.9
Germany	39.0	61.0	Sweden	44.9	55.1
Hong Kong	43.9	56.1	Switzerland	41.4	58.6
India	33.9	66.1	Taiwan	45.0	55.0
Ireland	45.2	64.8	United Kingdom	44.5	55.5
Israel	42.6	57.4	United States	51.4	48.6
Italy	36.4	63.6			

Source: Adapted from Brad Reagan, "The Great Divide," *Wall Street Journal* (April 15, 2002): R4.

Does the Internet Make Market Segmentation Easier?

Yes. The segments of people that marketers want to reach online are much more precisely defined than the segments of people reached through traditional forms of media, such as television, radio, and magazines. For example, **Quepasa.com** is widely visited by Hispanics. Marketers aiming to reach college students, who are notoriously difficult to reach via traditional media, focus on sites such as **collegeclub.com** and **studentadvantage.com**. The gay and lesbian population, which is estimated to comprise about 5 percent of the U.S. population, has always been difficult to reach via traditional media but now can be focused on sites such as **gay.com**. Marketers can reach persons interested in specific topics, such as travel or fishing, by placing banners on related Web sites.

People all over the world are congregating into virtual communities on the Web by becoming members/customers/visitors of Web sites that focus on an endless range of topics. People in essence segment themselves by nature of the Web sites that comprise their "favorite places," and many of these Web sites sell information regarding their "visitors." Businesses and groups of individuals all over the world pool their purchasing power in Web sites to get volume discounts.

Product Positioning

After markets have been segmented so that the firm can target particular customer groups, the next step is to find out what customers want and expect. This takes analysis and research. A severe mistake is to assume the firm knows what customers want and expect. Countless research studies reveal large differences between how customers define service and rank the importance of different service activities and how producers view services. Many firms have become successful by filling the gap between what customers and producers see as good service. What the customer believes is good service is paramount, not what the producer believes service should be.

Identifying target customers upon whom to focus marketing efforts sets the stage for deciding how to meet the needs and wants of particular consumer groups. Product positioning is widely used for this purpose. Positioning entails developing schematic representations that reflect how your products or services compare to competitors' on dimensions most important to success in the industry. The following steps are required in product positioning:

1. Select key criteria that effectively differentiate products or services in the industry.
2. Diagram a two-dimensional product-positioning map with specified criteria on each axis.
3. Plot major competitors' products or services in the resultant four-quadrant matrix.
4. Identify areas in the positioning map where the company's products or services could be most competitive in the given target market. Look for vacant areas (niches).
5. Develop a marketing plan to position the company's products or services appropriately.

Because just two criteria can be examined on a single product-positioning map, multiple maps are often developed to assess various approaches to strategy implementation. Multidimensional scaling could be used to examine three or more criteria simultaneously, but this technique requires computer assistance and is beyond the scope of this text. Some examples of product-positioning maps are illustrated in Figure 8–3.

FIGURE 8–3

Examples of Product-Positioning Maps

A. A PRODUCT-POSITIONING MAP
    FOR BANKS

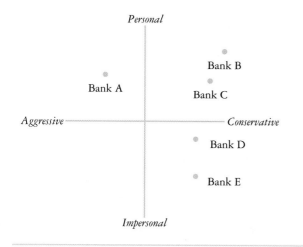

B. A PRODUCT-POSITIONING MAP
    FOR PERSONAL COMPUTERS

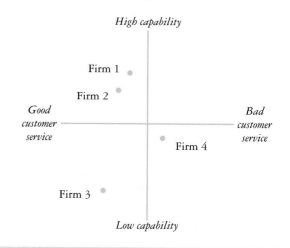

C. A PRODUCT-POSITIONING MAP FOR
    MENSWEAR RETAIL STORES

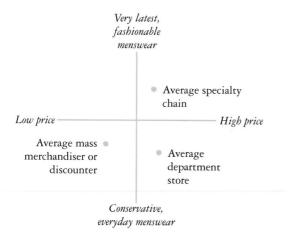

D. A PRODUCT-POSITIONING MAP
    FOR THE RENTAL CAR MARKET

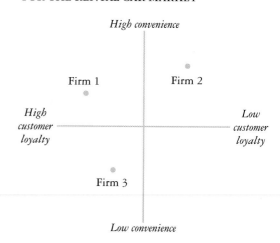

VISIT THE NET

Provides the 2000 Strategic Plan of the National Archives and Records Administration, including "What Must We Do to Get There?" (implementation) issues.
www.archives.gov/about_us/ strategic_planning_and_ reporting/strategic_ planning_and_reporting.html

Some rules for using product positioning as a strategy-implementation tool are the following:

1. Look for the hole or *vacant niche*. The best strategic opportunity might be an unserved segment.

2. Don't squat between segments. Any advantage from squatting (such as a larger target market) is offset by a failure to satisfy one segment. In decision-theory terms, the intent here is to avoid suboptimization by trying to serve more than one objective function.

3. Don't serve two segments with the same strategy. Usually, a strategy successful with one segment cannot be directly transferred to another segment.

4. Don't position yourself in the middle of the map. The middle usually means a strategy that is not clearly perceived to have any distinguishing characteristics. This rule can vary with the number of competitors. For example, when there are only two competitors, as in U.S. presidential elections, the middle becomes the preferred strategic position.[2]

An effective product-positioning strategy meets two criteria: (1) it uniquely distinguishes a company from the competition, and (2) it leads customers to expect slightly less service than a company can deliver. Firms should not create expectations that exceed the service the firm can or will deliver. Network Equipment Technology is an example of a company that keeps customer expectations slightly below perceived performance. This is a constant challenge for marketers. Firms need to inform customers about what to expect and then exceed the promise. Underpromise and then overdeliver!

 ## FINANCE/ACCOUNTING ISSUES

In this section, we examine several finance/accounting concepts considered to be central to strategy implementation: acquiring needed capital, developing pro forma financial statements, preparing financial budgets, and evaluating the worth of a business. Some examples of decisions that may require finance/accounting policies are:

1. To raise capital with short-term debt, long-term debt, preferred stock, or common stock.
2. To lease or buy fixed assets.
3. To determine an appropriate dividend payout ratio.
4. To use LIFO (Last-in, First-out), FIFO (First-in, First-out), or a market-value accounting approach.
5. To extend the time of accounts receivable.
6. To establish a certain percentage discount on accounts within a specified period of time.
7. To determine the amount of cash that should be kept on hand.

Acquiring Capital to Implement Strategies

Successful strategy implementation often requires additional capital. Besides net profit from operations and the sale of assets, two basic sources of capital for an organization are debt and equity. Determining an appropriate mix of debt and equity in a firm's capital structure can be vital to successful strategy implementation. An *Earnings Per Share/Earnings Before Interest and Taxes (EPS/EBIT) analysis* is the most widely used technique for determining whether debt, stock, or a combination of debt and stock is the best alternative for raising capital to implement strategies. This technique involves an examination of the impact that debt versus stock financing has on earnings per share under various assumptions as to EBIT.

Theoretically, an enterprise should have enough debt in its capital structure to boost its return on investment by applying debt to products and projects earning more than the cost of the debt. In low earning periods, too much debt in the capital structure of an organization can endanger stockholders' return and jeopardize company survival. Fixed debt obligations generally must be met, regardless of circumstances. This does not mean that stock issuances are always better than debt for raising capital. Some special concerns with stock issuances are dilution of ownership, effect on stock price, and the need to share future earnings with all new shareholders.

Without going into detail on other institutional and legal issues related to the debt versus stock decision, EPS/EBIT may be best explained by working through an example. Let's say the Brown Company needs to raise $1 million to finance implementation of a market-development strategy. The company's common stock currently sells for $50 per share, and 100,000 shares are outstanding. The prime interest rate is 10 percent, and the company's tax rate is 50 percent. The company's earnings before interest and taxes next year are expected to be $2 million if a recession occurs, $4 million if the economy stays as is, and $8 million if the economy significantly improves. EPS/EBIT analysis can be used to determine if all stock, all debt, or some combination of stock and debt is the best capital financing alternative. The EPS/EBIT analysis for this example is provided as shown in Table 8–3.

As indicated by the EPS values of 9.5, 19.50, and 39.50 in Table 8–3, debt is the best financing alternative for the Brown Company if a recession, boom, or normal year is expected. An EPS/EBIT chart can be constructed to determine the breakeven point, where one financing alternative becomes more attractive than another. Figure 8–4 indicates that issuing common stock is the least attractive financing alternative for the Brown Company.

EPS/EBIT analysis is a valuable tool for making the capital financing decisions needed to implement strategies, but several considerations should be made whenever using this technique. First, profit levels may be higher for stock or debt alternatives when EPS levels are lower. For example, looking only at the earnings after taxes (EAT) values in Table 8–3, you can see that the common stock option is the best alternative, regardless of economic conditions. If the Brown Company's mission includes strict profit maximization, as opposed to the maximization of stockholders' wealth or some other criterion, then stock rather than debt is the best choice of financing.

Another consideration when using EPS/EBIT analysis is flexibility. As an organization's capital structure changes, so does its flexibility for considering future capital needs. Using all debt or all stock to raise capital in the present may impose fixed obligations, restrictive covenants, or other constraints that could severely reduce a firm's ability to raise additional capital in the future. Control is also a concern. When additional

TABLE 8–3   EPS/EBIT Analysis for the Brown Company (in millions)

	COMMON STOCK FINANCING			DEBT FINANCING			COMBINATION FINANCING		
	Recession	*Normal*	*Boom*	*Recession*	*Normal*	*Boom*	*Recession*	*Normal*	*Boom*
EBIT	$2.0	$ 4.0	$ 8.0	$2.0	$ 4.0	$ 8.0	$2.0	$ 4.0	$ 8.0
Interest[a]	0	0	0	.10	.10	.10	.05	.05	.05
EBT	2.0	4.0	8.0	1.9	3.9	7.9	1.95	3.95	7.95
Taxes	1.0	2.0	4.0	.95	1.95	3.95	.975	1.975	3.975
EAT	1.0	2.0	4.0	.95	1.95	3.95	.975	1.975	3.975
#Shares[b]	.12	.12	.12	.10	.10	.10	.11	.11	.11
EPS[c]	8.33	16.66	33.33	9.5	19.50	39.50	8.86	17.95	36.14

[a]The annual interest charge on $1 million at 10% is $100,000 and on $0.5 million is $50,000. This row is in $, not %.
[b]To raise all of the needed $1 million with stock, 20,000 new shares must be issued, raising the total to 120,000 shares outstanding. To raise one-half of the needed $1 million with stock, 10,000 new shares must be issued, raising the total to 110,000 shares outstanding.
[c]EPS = Earnings After Taxes (EAT) divided by shares (number of shares outstanding).

FIGURE 8–4

An EPS/EBIT Chart for the Brown Company

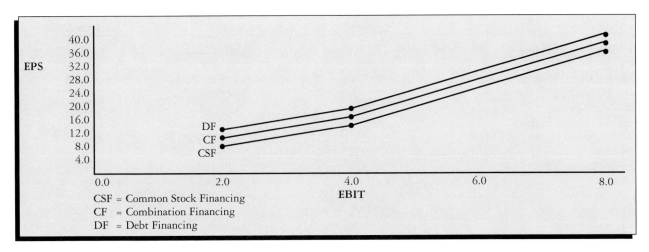

CSF = Common Stock Financing
CF = Combination Financing
DF = Debt Financing

stock is issued to finance strategy implementation, ownership and control of the enterprise are diluted. This can be a serious concern in today's business environment of hostile takeovers, mergers, and acquisitions.

Dilution of ownership can be an overriding concern in closely held corporations in which stock issuances affect the decision-making power of majority stockholders. For example, the Smucker family owns 30 percent of the stock in Smucker's, a well-known jam and jelly company. When Smucker's acquired Dickson Family, Inc., the company used mostly debt rather than stock in order not to dilute the family ownership.

When using EPS/EBIT analysis, timing in relation to movements of stock prices, interest rates, and bond prices becomes important. In times of depressed stock prices, debt may prove to be the most suitable alternative from both a cost and a demand standpoint. However, when cost of capital (interest rates) is high, stock issuances become more attractive.

Pro Forma Financial Statements

Pro forma (projected) financial statement analysis is a central strategy-implementation technique because it allows an organization to examine the expected results of various actions and approaches. This type of analysis can be used to forecast the impact of various implementation decisions (for example, to increase promotion expenditures by 50 percent to support a market-development strategy, to increase salaries by 25 percent to support a market-penetration strategy, to increase research and development expenditures by 70 percent to support product development, or to sell $1 million of common stock to raise capital for diversification). Nearly all financial institutions require at least three years of projected financial statements whenever a business seeks capital. A pro forma income statement and balance sheet allow an organization to compute projected financial ratios under various strategy-implementation scenarios. When compared to prior years and to industry averages, financial ratios provide valuable insights into the feasibility of various strategy-implementation approaches.

Primarily as a result of the Enron collapse and accounting scandal, companies today are being much more diligent in preparing pro forma financial statements to "reasonably rather than too optimistically" project future expenses and earnings. There is much more care not to mislead shareholders and other constituencies.[3]

TABLE 8-4   **A Pro Forma Income Statement and Balance Sheet for the Litten Company (in millions)**

	PRIOR YEAR 2003	PROJECTED YEAR 2004	REMARKS
PRO FORMA INCOME STATEMENT			
Sales	100	150.00	50% increase
Cost of Goods Sold	70	105.00	70% of sales
Gross Margin	30	45.00	
Selling Expense	10	15.00	10% of sales
Administrative Expense	5	7.50	5% of sales
Earnings Before Interest and Taxes	15	22.50	
Interest	3	3.00	
Earnings Before Taxes	12	19.50	
Taxes	6	9.75	50% rate
Net Income	6	9.75	
Dividends	2	5.00	
Retained Earnings	4	4.75	
PRO FORMA BALANCE SHEET			
Assets			
Cash	5	7.75	Plug figure
Accounts Receivable	2	4.00	Incr. 100%
Inventory	20	45.00	
Total Current Assets	27	56.75	
Land	15	15.00	
Plant and Equipment	50	80.00	Add 3 new plants at $10 million each
Less Depreciation	10	20.00	
Net Plant and Equipment	40	60.00	
Total Fixed Assets	55	75.00	
Total Assets	82	131.75	
Liabilities			
Accounts Payable	10	10.00	
Notes Payable	10	10.00	
Total Current Liabilities	20	20.00	
Long-term Debt	40	70.00	Borrowed $30 million
Additional Paid-in-Capital	20	35.00	Issued 100,000 shares at $150 each
Retained Earnings	2	6.75	2 + 4.75
Total Liabilities and Net Worth	82	131.75	

A 2004 pro forma income statement and balance sheet for the Litten Company are provided in Table 8–4. The pro forma statements for Litten are based on five assumptions: (1) The company needs to raise $45 million to finance expansion into foreign markets; (2) $30 million of this total will be raised through increased debt and $15 million through common stock; (3) sales are expected to increase 50 percent; (4) three new facilities, costing a total of $30 million, will be constructed in foreign markets; and (5) land for the new facilities is already owned by the company. Note in Table 8–4 that Litten's strategies and its implementation are expected to result in a sales increase from $100 million to $150 million and in a net increase in income from $6 million to $9.75 million in the forecasted year.

There are six steps in performing pro forma financial analysis:

1. Prepare the pro forma income statement before the balance sheet. Start by forecasting sales as accurately as possible.

2. Use the percentage-of-sales method to project cost of goods sold (CGS) and the expense items in the income statement. For example, if CGS is 70 percent of sales in the prior year (as it is in Table 8–4), then use that same percentage to calculate CGS in the future year—unless there is a reason to use a different percentage. Items such as interest, dividends, and taxes must be treated independently and cannot be forecasted using the percentage-of-sales method.

3. Calculate the projected net income.

4. Subtract from the net income any dividends to be paid and add the remaining net income to Retained Earnings. Reflect the Retained Earnings total on both the income statement and balance sheet because this item is the key link between the two projected statements.

5. Project the balance sheet items, beginning with retained earnings and then forecasting stockholders' equity, long-term liabilities, current liabilities, total liabilities, total assets, fixed assets, and current assets (in that order). Use the cash account as the plug figure—that is, use the cash account to make the assets total the liabilities and net worth. Then make appropriate adjustments. For example, if the cash needed to balance the statements is too small (or too large), make appropriate changes to borrow more (or less) money than planned.

6. List comments (remarks) on the projected statements. Any time a significant change is made in an item from a prior year to the projected year, an explanation (remark) should be provided. Remarks are essential because otherwise pro formas are meaningless.

The U.S. Securities and Exchange Commission (SEC) warned in late 2001 that it will launch fraud investigations if pro forma numbers are misleading or if they omit information that's important to investors.[4] Pro forma statements must conform with generally accepted accounting principles (GAAP) and must not be designed to hide poor expected results.

Financial Budgets

A *financial budget* is a document that details how funds will be obtained and spent for a specified period of time. Annual budgets are most common, although the period of time for a budget can range from one day to more than ten years. Fundamentally, financial budgeting is a method for specifying what must be done to complete strategy implementation successfully. Financial budgeting should not be thought of as a tool for limiting expenditures but rather as a method for obtaining the most productive and profitable use of an organization's resources. Financial budgets can be viewed as the planned allocation of a firm's resources based on forecasts of the future.

There are almost as many different types of financial budgets as there are types of organizations. Some common types of budgets include cash budgets, operating budgets, sales budgets, profit budgets, factory budgets, capital budgets, expense budgets, divisional budgets, variable budgets, flexible budgets, and fixed budgets. When an organization is experiencing financial difficulties, budgets are especially important in guiding strategy implementation.

Perhaps the most common type of financial budget is the *cash budget*. The Financial Accounting Standards Board (FASB) has mandated that every publicly held company in the United States must issue an annual cash-flow statement in addition to the usual financial reports. The statement includes all receipts and disbursements of cash in operations, investments, and financing. It supplements the Statement on Changes in Financial

TABLE 8–5   **A Six-Month Cash Budget for the Toddler Toy Company in 2004**

CASH BUDGET (IN THOUSANDS)	JULY	AUG.	SEPT.	OCT.	NOV.	DEC.	JAN.
Receipts							
Collections	$12,000	$21,000	$31,000	$35,000	$22,000	$18,000	$11,000
Payments							
Purchases	14,000	21,000	28,000	14,000	14,000	7,000	
Wages and Salaries	1,500	2,000	2,500	1,500	1,500	1,000	
Rent	500	500	500	500	500	500	
Other Expenses	200	300	400	200	—	100	
Taxes	—	8,000	—	—	—	—	
Payment on Machine	—	—	10,000	—	—	—	
Total Payments	$16,200	$31,800	$41,400	$16,200	$16,000	$8,600	
Net Cash Gain (Loss) During Month	−4,200	−10,800	−10,400	18,800	6,000	9,400	
Cash at Start of Month If No							
Borrowing Is Done	6,000	1,800	−9,000	−19,400	−600	5,400	
Cumulative Cash (Cash at start plus							
gains or minus losses)	1,800	−9,000	−19,400	−600	5,400	14,800	
Less Desired Level of Cash	−5,000	−5,000	−5,000	−5,000	−5,000	−5,000	
Total Loans Outstanding to							
Maintain $5,000 Cash Balance	$3,200	$14,000	$24,400	$5,600	—	—	
Surplus Cash	—	—	—	—	400	9,800	

Position formerly included in the annual reports of all publicly held companies. A cash budget for the year 2004 for the Toddler Toy Company is provided in Table 8–5. Note that Toddler is not expecting to have surplus cash until November 2004.

The severe economic downturn of 2001–2002 led many companies to deplete their cash positions. Ford Motor's cash position, for example, fell from $18 billion at the end of 2000 to less than $11 billion at the end of 2001. Thousands of "good" companies, such as Disney and Campbell Soup, have seen their debt ratings downgraded, thus raising the cost of borrowing. More than one hundred twenty U.S. companies defaulted on $74 billion of debt (bonds) in the first nine months of 2001, a domestic record.[5]

Financial budgets have some limitations. First, budgetary programs can become so detailed that they are cumbersome and overly expensive. Overbudgeting or underbudgeting can cause problems. Second, financial budgets can become a substitute for objectives. A budget is a tool and not an end in itself. Third, budgets can hide inefficiencies if based solely on precedent rather than on periodic evaluation of circumstances and standards. Finally, budgets are sometimes used as instruments of tyranny that result in frustration, resentment, absenteeism, and high turnover. To minimize the effect of this last concern, managers should increase the participation of subordinates in preparing budgets.

Evaluating the Worth of a Business

Evaluating the worth of a business is central to strategy implementation because integrative, intensive, and diversification strategies are often implemented by acquiring other firms. Other strategies, such as retrenchment and divestiture, may result in the sale of a division of an organization or of the firm itself. Thousands of transactions occur each year in which businesses are bought or sold in the United States. In all these cases, it is necessary to establish the financial worth or cash value of a business to successfully implement strategies.

All the various methods for determining a business's worth can be grouped into three main approaches: what a firm owns, what a firm earns, or what a firm will bring in the market. But it is important to realize that valuation is not an exact science. The valuation of a firm's worth is based on financial facts, but common sense and intuitive judgment must enter into the process. It is difficult to assign a monetary value to some factors—such as a loyal customer base, a history of growth, legal suits pending, dedicated employees, a favorable lease, a bad credit rating, or good patents—that may not be reflected in a firm's financial statements. Also, different valuation methods will yield different totals for a firm's worth, and no prescribed approach is best for a certain situation. Evaluating the worth of a business truly requires both qualitative and quantitative skills.

The first approach in evaluating the worth of a business is determining its net worth or stockholders' equity. Net worth represents the sum of common stock, additional paid-in capital, and retained earnings. After calculating net worth, add or subtract an appropriate amount for goodwill and overvalued or undervalued assets. This total provides a reasonable estimate of a firm's monetary value. If a firm has goodwill, it will be listed on the balance sheet, perhaps as "intangibles."

The second approach to measuring the value of a firm grows out of the belief that the worth of any business should be based largely on the future benefits its owners may derive through net profits. A conservative rule of thumb is to establish a business's worth as five times the firm's current annual profit. A five-year average profit level could also be used. When using the approach, remember that firms normally suppress earnings in their financial statements to minimize taxes.

The third approach, letting the market determine a business's worth, involves three methods. First, base the firm's worth on the selling price of a similar company. A potential problem, however, is that sometimes comparable figures are not easy to locate, even though substantial information on firms that buy or sell to other firms is available in major libraries. The second approach is called the *price-earnings ratio method*. To use this method, divide the market price of the firm's common stock by the annual earnings per share and multiply this number by the firm's average net income for the past five years. The third approach can be called the *outstanding shares method*. To use this method, simply multiply the number of shares outstanding by the market price per share and add a premium. The premium is simply a per-share dollar amount that a person or firm is willing to pay to control (acquire) the other company. As indicated in the Global Perspective, European firms aggressively are acquiring American firms, using these and perhaps other methods for evaluating the worth of their target companies.

Business evaluations are becoming routine in many situations. Businesses have many strategy-implementation reasons for determining their worth in addition to preparing to be sold or to buy other companies. Employee plans, taxes, retirement packages, mergers, acquisitions, expansion plans, banking relationships, death of a principal, divorce, partnership agreements, and IRS audits are other reasons for a periodic valuation. It is just good business to have a reasonable understanding of what your firm is worth. This knowledge protects the interests of all parties involved.

Deciding Whether to Go Public

Going public means selling off a percentage of your company to others in order to raise capital; consequently, it dilutes the owners' control of the firm. Going public is not recommended for companies with less than $10 million in sales because the initial costs can be too high for the firm to generate sufficient cash flow to make going public worthwhile. One dollar in four is the average total cost paid to lawyers, accountants, and underwriters when an initial stock issuance is under $1 million; one dollar in twenty will go to cover these costs for issuances over $20 million.

In addition to initial costs involved with a stock offering, there are costs and obligations associated with reporting and management in a publicly held firm. For firms with more than $10 million in sales, going public can provide major advantages: It can allow

GLOBAL PERSPECTIVE

September 11, 2001, Events Usher in Corporate Retreat from Global Operations

Cutbacks in foreign direct investment had begun prior to the terrorists attacks on September 11, 2001, but following that event, companies have accelerated their retreat from globalization. For example, Gateway withdrew from Asia and Europe, AT&T dissolved its joint venture with British Telecommunications, Merrill Lynch closed many offices in Asia, and Ford Motor reduced its operations in Europe. U.S. telecom and energy companies have withdrawn from expansion in South America. Where globalization used to mean openness and new opportunity, now for many companies it means more vulnerability, more government involvement, and higher security risks and costs.

Ralph Shrader, CEO of consulting firm Booze-Allen & Hamilton, recently said, "I do not know of any companies that aren't carefully reevaluating their global strategies in light of the recession and September 11." Evidence of the globalization pullback is that between 2001 and 2000 cross-border mergers declined 50 percent, and flows of direct foreign investment around the world dropped 40 percent. The decline in globalization has reduced American exports and imports dramatically, which further hampers the domestic economy.

There are major risks when firms reduce their enthusiasm for and interest in globalization. First,

these firms forfeit their ability to build a wider customer base and make it possible for foreign competitors to strengthen their own competitive hand. Former General Electric CEO Jack Welch says, "The biggest competitive threat on the horizon are those companies whose names we can't spell or pronounce." Still, 95 percent of the world's population lives outside the United States, and that group is growing much faster than the American population. Second, U.S. corporate investment abroad is vital to giving poorer nations the chance to develop and become viable members of the world economy rather than breeding grounds for terrorism and despair. Winning the war on terrorism may hinge more on the efforts of U.S. companies than on the U.S. military in the global economic sphere.

China is a notable exception to overall foreign investment curtailment as U.S. investment in that country continues to increase. For example, Motorola is investing $6.6 billion on production in China from 2002–2006, and it is the largest foreign investor in China. Motorola intends to be the leader in wireless, Internet, and broadband in China, where it already has $5 billion in annual sales and more than thirteen thousand employees.

Source: Adapted from Jeffrey Garten, "The Wrong Time for Companies to Beat a Global Retreat," *Business Week* (December 17, 2001): 22.

the firm to raise capital to develop new products, build plants, expand, grow, and market products and services more effectively.

RESEARCH AND DEVELOPMENT (R&D) ISSUES

Research and development (R&D) personnel can play an integral part in strategy implementation. These individuals are generally charged with developing new products and improving old products in a way that will allow effective strategy implementation. R&D employees and managers perform tasks that include transferring complex technology, adjusting processes to local raw materials, adapting processes to local markets, and altering products to particular tastes and specifications. Strategies such as product development, market penetration, and concentric diversification require that new products be successfully developed and that old products be significantly improved. But the level of management support for R&D is often constrained by resource availability.

Technological improvements that affect consumer and industrial products and services shorten product life cycles. Companies in virtually every industry are relying on the development of new products and services to fuel profitability and growth. However, in 2002 U.S. companies plan to boost R&D spending by only 2.2 percent, compared to increases of 5.4 percent in 2001 and 10.8 percent in 2000.[6] Some firms, such as 3M, plan to keep their R&D expenditures at 6 percent of sales despite a weak economy and lower earnings.

Surveys suggest that the most successful organizations use an R&D strategy that ties external opportunities to internal strengths and is linked with objectives. Well-formulated R&D policies match market opportunities with internal capabilities. R&D policies can enhance strategy implementation efforts to:

1. Emphasize product or process improvements.
2. Stress basic or applied research.
3. Be leaders or followers in R&D.
4. Develop robotics or manual-type processes.
5. Spend a high, average, or low amount of money on R&D.
6. Perform R&D within the firm or to contract R&D to outside firms.
7. Use university researchers or private sector researchers.

There must be effective interactions between R&D departments and other functional departments in implementing different types of generic business strategies. Conflicts between marketing, finance/accounting, R&D, and information systems departments can be minimized with clear policies and objectives. Table 8–6 gives some examples of R&D activities that could be required for successful implementation of various strategies. Many American utility, energy, and automotive companies are employing their research and development departments to determine how the firm can effectively reduce its gas emissions.

Many firms wrestle with the decision to acquire R&D expertise from external firms or to develop R&D expertise internally. The following guidelines can be used to help make this decision:

1. If the rate of technical progress is slow, the rate of market growth is moderate, and there are significant barriers to possible new entrants, then in-house R&D is the preferred solution. The reason is that R&D, if successful, will result in a temporary product or process monopoly that the company can exploit.

TABLE 8-6   Research and Development Involvement in Selected Strategy-Implementation Situations

TYPE OF ORGANIZATION	STRATEGY BEING IMPLEMENTED	R&D ACTIVITY
Pharmaceutical company	Product development	Test the effects of a new drug on different subgroups.
Boat manufacturer	Concentric diversification	Test the performance of various keel designs under various conditions.
Plastic container manufacturer	Market penetration	Develop a biodegradable container.
Electronics company	Market development	Develop a telecommunications system in a foreign country.

2. If technology is changing rapidly and the market is growing slowly, then a major effort in R&D may be very risky, because it may lead to the development of an ultimately obsolete technology or one for which there is no market.

3. If technology is changing slowly but the market is growing quickly, there generally is not enough time for in-house development. The prescribed approach is to obtain R&D expertise on an exclusive or nonexclusive basis from an outside firm.

4. If both technical progress and market growth are fast, R&D expertise should be obtained through acquisition of a well-established firm in the industry.[7]

There are at least three major R&D approaches for implementing strategies. The first strategy is to be the first firm to market new technological products. This is a glamorous and exciting strategy but also a dangerous one. Firms such as 3M and General Electric have been successful with this approach, but many other pioneering firms have fallen, with rival firms seizing the initiative.

A second R&D approach is to be an innovative imitator of successful products, thus minimizing the risks and costs of start-up. This approach entails allowing a pioneer firm to develop the first version of the new product and to demonstrate that a market exists. Then, laggard firms develop a similar product. This strategy requires excellent R&D personnel and an excellent marketing department.

A third R&D strategy is to be a low-cost producer by mass-producing products similar to but less expensive than products recently introduced. As a new product is accepted by customers, price becomes increasingly important in the buying decision. Also, mass marketing replaces personal selling as the dominant selling strategy. This R&D strategy requires substantial investment in plant and equipment, but fewer expenditures in R&D than the two approaches described earlier.

R&D activities among American firms need to be more closely aligned to business objectives. There needs to be expanded communication between R&D managers and strategists. Corporations are experimenting with various methods to achieve this improved communication climate, including different roles and reporting arrangements for managers and new methods to reduce the time it takes research ideas to become reality.

Perhaps the most current trend in R&D management has been lifting the veil of secrecy whereby firms, even major competitors, are joining forces to develop new products. Collaboration is on the rise due to new competitive pressures, rising research costs, increasing regulatory issues, and accelerated product development schedules. Companies not only are working more closely with each other on R&D, but they are also turning to consortia at universities for their R&D needs. More than 600 research consortia are now in operation in the United States. Lifting of R&D secrecy among many firms through collaboration has allowed the marketing of new technologies and products even before they are available for sale.

MANAGEMENT INFORMATION SYSTEMS (MIS) ISSUES

Firms that gather, assimilate, and evaluate external and internal information most effectively are gaining competitive advantages over other firms. Recognizing the importance of having an effective *management information system (MIS)* will not be an option in the future; it will be a requirement. Information is the basis for understanding in a firm. In many industries, information is becoming the most important factor differentiating successful

NATURAL ENVIRONMENT PERSPECTIVE

The Natural Environment Cost/Benefit Analysis

Carol Browner is former head of the Environmental Protection Agency (EPA) under President Clinton. She recently said, "If we find ourselves subjecting the health protections of our children and our most vulnerable citizens to the outcome of cost/benefit analysis, literally putting a price on their heads, we will have dishonored our past and devalued our future." Do you agree with Browner? Yes or no?

At what point do the costs of preserving the natural environment exceed the benefits? People make trade-off decisions every day that affect their health and billfold. For example, if you buy a large car instead of a small one, you will be protected better from a collision, but you may have less money for a mammogram. Similarly, more costly environmental regulations may harm people just by making them less able to afford regular doctor visits, safe cars, and good insurance. The EPA estimates that full compliance with its new smog and soot standards will cost companies and individuals almost $50 billion a year.

Can we afford these new regulations given that our weak economy has severely reduced individuals' disposable income for taking care of their own health and other needs?

After debating for a year with local city officials in Houston, Texas, the EPA signed an agreement in late 2001 which requires that city to reduce its air pollution 75 percent by 2007. Houston currently is one of the nation's most polluted cities.

All of life is full of trade-off decisions. Smog on balance is detrimental to health, but smog also blocks out ultraviolet radiation. The new EPA smog standards will make air easier to breathe, but it will also cause several thousand more cases of skin cancer and cataracts annually. We must not ignore the trade-off benefits/costs in policing pollution and caring for the natural environment.

Source: Adapted from Ira Carnahan, "Where Money Is No Object," *Forbes* (March 5, 2001): 78.

and unsuccessful firms. The process of strategic management is facilitated immensely in firms that have an effective information system. Many companies are establishing a new approach to information systems, one that blends the technical knowledge of the computer experts with the vision of senior management.

Information collection, retrieval, and storage can be used to create competitive advantages in ways such as cross-selling to customers, monitoring suppliers, keeping managers and employees informed, coordinating activities among divisions, and managing funds. Like inventory and human resources, information is now recognized as a valuable organizational asset that can be controlled and managed. Firms that implement strategies using the best information will reap competitive advantages in the twenty-first century.

A good information system can allow a firm to reduce costs. For example, online orders from salespersons to production facilities can shorten materials ordering time and reduce inventory costs. Direct communications between suppliers, manufacturers, marketers, and customers can link elements of the value chain together as though they were one organization. Improved quality and service often result from an improved information system.

Firms must increasingly be concerned about computer hackers and take specific measures to secure and safeguard corporate communications, files, orders, and business conducted over the Internet. Gap, Playboy Enterprises, Hitachi America, PeopleSoft, and Twentieth Century Fox average over thirty computer intrusion attempts daily. Thousands of companies today are plagued by computer hackers who include disgruntled employees, competitors, bored teens, sociopaths, thieves, spies, and hired agents. Computer vulnerability is a giant, expensive headache.

Dun & Bradstreet is an example of a company that has an excellent information system. Every D&B customer and client in the world has a separate nine-digit number. The database of information associated with each number has become so widely used that it is like a business social security number. D&B reaps great competitive advantages from its information system.

In many firms, information technology is doing away with the workplace and allowing employees to work at home or anywhere, anytime. The mobile concept of work allows employees to work the traditional 9-5 workday across any of the twenty-four time zones around the globe. Affordable desktop videoconferencing software developed by AT&T, Lotus, or Vivo Software allows employees to "beam in" whenever needed. Any manager or employee who travels a lot away from the office is a good candidate for working at home rather than in an office provided by the firm. Salespersons or consultants are good examples, but any person whose job largely involves talking to others or handling information could easily operate at home with the proper computer system and software. The accounting firm Ernst & Young has reduced its office space requirements by 2 million square feet over the past three years by allowing employees to work at home.

Many people see the officeless office trend as leading to a resurgence of family togetherness in American society. Even the design of homes may change from having large open areas to having more private small areas conducive to getting work done.[8]

CONCLUSION

Successful strategy implementation depends on cooperation among all functional and divisional managers in an organization. Marketing departments are commonly charged with implementing strategies that require significant increases in sales revenues in new areas and with new or improved products. Finance and accounting managers must devise effective strategy-implementation approaches at low cost and minimum risk to that firm. R&D managers have to transfer complex technologies or develop new technologies to successfully implement strategies. Information systems managers are being called upon more and more to provide leadership and training for all individuals in the firm. The nature and role of marketing, finance/accounting, R&D, and management information systems activities, coupled with the management activities described in Chapter 7, largely determine organizational success.

We invite you to visit the David page on the Prentice Hall Companion Website at **www.prenhall.com/david** for this chapter's World Wide Web exercises.

KEY TERMS AND CONCEPTS

Cash Budget (p. 287)

EPS/EBIT Analysis (p. 283)

Financial Budget (p. 287)

Management Information Systems (MIS) (p. 292)

Market Segmentation (p. 277)

Marketing Mix Variables (p. 278)

Outstanding Shares Method (p. 289)

Price-Earnings Ratio Method (p. 289)

Product Positioning (p. 277)

Pro Forma (Projected) Financial Statement Analysis (p. 285)

Research and Development (R&D) (p. 290)

Vacant Niche (p. 282)

ISSUES FOR REVIEW AND DISCUSSION

1. Suppose your company has just acquired a firm that produces battery-operated lawn mowers, and strategists want to implement a market-penetration strategy. How would you segment the market for this product? Justify your answer.

2. Explain how you would estimate the total worth of a business.

3. Diagram and label clearly a product-positioning map that includes six fast-food restaurant chains.

4. Explain why EPS/EBIT analysis is a central strategy-implementation technique.

5. How would the R&D role in strategy implementation differ in small versus large organizations?

6. Discuss the limitations of EPS/EBIT analysis.

7. Explain how marketing, finance/accounting, R&D, and management information systems managers' involvement in strategy formulation can enhance strategy implementation.

8. Consider the following statement: "Retained earnings on the balance sheet are not monies available to finance strategy implementation." Is it true or false? Explain.

9. Explain why pro forma financial statement analysis is considered both a strategy-formulation and a strategy-implementation tool.

10. Describe some marketing, finance/accounting, R&D, and management information systems activities that a small restaurant chain might undertake to expand into a neighboring state.

11. Select one of the suggested readings at the end of this chapter, find that article in your college library, and summarize it in a five-minute oral report for the class.

12. Discuss the management information system at your college or university.

13. What effect is e-commerce having on firms' efforts to segment markets?

NOTES

1. LESLIE MILLER and ELIZABETH WEISE, "E-Privacy—FTC Studies 'Profiling' by Web Sites," *USA Today* (November 8, 1999): 1A, 2A.

2. RALPH BIGGADIKE, "The Contributions of Marketing to Strategic Management," *Academy of Management Review* 6, no. 4 (October 1981): 627.

3. PHYLLIS PLITCH, "Companies in Many Sectors Give Earnings a Pro Forma Makeover, Survey Finds," *Wall Street Journal* (January 22, 2002): A4.

4. MONICA ROMAN, "When Pro Forma Is Bad Form," *Business Week* (December 17, 2001): 50.

5. MATT KRANTZ, "Debt Weighs More as Firms Gobble Cash," *USA Today* (October 10, 2001): B1.

6. AMY MERRICK, "U.S. Research Spending to Rise Only 3.2 Percent," *Wall Street Journal* (December 28, 2001): A2.

7. PIER ABETTI, "Technology: A Key Strategic Resource," *Management Review* 78, no. 2 (February 1989): 38.

8. Adapted from EDWARD BAIG, "Welcome to the Officeless Office," *Business Week* (June 26, 1995).

CURRENT READINGS

DUTTON, JANE E., SUSAN J. ASHFORD, REGINA M. O'NEILL, and KATHERINE A. LAWRENCE. "Moves That Matter: Issue Selling and Organizational Change." *The Academy of Management Journal* 44, no. 4 (August 2001): 716.

HERREMANS, IRENE M., JOHN K. RYANS, JR., and RAJ AGGARWAL. "Linking Advertising and Brand Value." *Business Horizons* 43, no. 3 (May–June 2000): 19.

MEDCOF, J. W. "Resource-Based Strategy and Managerial Power in Networks of Internationally Dispersed Technology Units." *Strategic Management Journal* 22, no. 11 (November 2001): 999.

PAGELL, MARK, STEVE MELNYK, and ROBERT HANDFIELD. "Do Trade-offs Exist in Operations Strategy? Insights from the Stamping Die Industry." *Business Horizons* 43, no. 3 (May–June 2000): 69.

POLONSKY, MICHAEL JAY, and PHILIP J. ROSENBERGER III. "Reevaluating Green Marketing: A Strategic Approach." *Business Horizons* 44, no. 5 (September–October 2001): 21.

SCHROEDER, R. G., K. A. BATES, and M. A. JUNTTILA. "A Resource-Based View of Manufacturing Strategy and the Relationship to Manufacturing Processes." *Strategic Management Journal* 23, no. 2 (February 2002): 105.

SLATER, S. F., and E. M. OLSON. "Marketing's Contribution to the Implementation of Business Strategy: An Empirical Analysis." *Strategic Management Journal* 22, no. 11 (November 2001): 1055.

SMITH, H. JEFF. "Information Privacy and Marketing: What the U.S. Should (and Shouldn't) Learn from Europe." *California Management Review* 43, no. 2 (Winter 2001): 8.

SEYBOLD, PATRICIA B. "Get Inside the Lives of Your Customers." *Harvard Business Review* (May 2001): 80.

EXPERIENTIAL EXERCISES

EXPERIENTIAL EXERCISE 8A ▶

Developing a Product-Positioning Map for American Airlines (AMR)

PURPOSE

Organizations continually monitor how their products and services are positioned relative to competitors. This information is especially useful for marketing managers, but is also used by other managers and strategists.

INSTRUCTIONS

Step 1   On a separate sheet of paper, develop a product-positioning map for American Airlines (AMR).

Step 2   Go to the blackboard and diagram your product-positioning map.

Step 3   Compare your product-positioning map with those diagrammed by other students. Discuss any major differences.

EXPERIENTIAL EXERCISE 8B ▶

Performing an EPS/EBIT Analysis For American Airlines (AMR)

PURPOSE

An EPS/EBIT analysis is one of the most widely used techniques for determining the extent that debt and/or stock should be used to finance strategies to be implemented. This exercise can give you practice performing EPS/EBIT analysis.

INSTRUCTIONS

Let's say AMR needs to raise $2 billion to begin flying to twenty new countries around the world in 2001. Determine whether AMR should have used all debt, all stock, or a 50-50 combination of debt and stock to finance this market-development strategy. Assume a 50 percent tax rate, 10 percent interest rate, AMR stock price of $70 per share, and an annual dividend of $2.00 per share of common stock. The EBIT range for 2001 is between $1 billion and $1.5 billion. A total of 90 million shares of common stock are outstanding. Develop an EPS/EBIT chart to reflect your analysis.

EXPERIENTIAL EXERCISE 8C ▶

Preparing Pro Forma Financial Statements for American Airlines (AMR)

PURPOSE

This exercise is designed to give you experience preparing pro forma financial statements. Pro forma analysis is a central strategy-implementation technique because it allows managers to anticipate and evaluate the expected results of various strategy-implementation approaches.

INSTRUCTIONS

Step 1   Work with a classmate. Develop a 2003 pro forma income statement and balance sheet for AMR. Assume that AMR plans to raise $900 million in 2002 to begin flights to ten AMR new countries and plans to obtain 50 percent financing from a bank and 50 percent financing from a stock issuance. Make other assumptions as needed, and state them clearly in written form.

Step 2   Compute AMR's current ratio, debt-to-equity ratio, and return-on-investment ratio for 1999, 2000, and 2001. How do your 2002 projected ratios compare to the 2000 and 2001 ratios? Why is it important to make this comparison?

Step 3   Bring your pro forma statements to class, and discuss any problems or questions you encountered.

Step 4 Compare your pro forma statements to the statements of other students. What major differences exist between your analysis and the work of other students?

EXPERIENTIAL EXERCISE 8D ▶

Determining the Cash Value of American Airlines (AMR)

PURPOSE

It is simply good business practice to periodically determine the financial worth or cash value of your company. This exercise gives you practice determining the total worth of a company using several methods. Use 2001 as the sample year.

INSTRUCTIONS

Step 1 Calculate the financial worth of AMR based on three methods: (1) the net worth or stockholders' equity, (2) the future value of AMR earnings, and (3) the price-earnings ratio.

Step 2 In a dollar amount, how much is AMR worth?

Step 3 Compare your analyses and conclusions with those of other students.

EXPERIENTIAL EXERCISE 8E ▶

Developing a Product-Positioning Map for My University

PURPOSE

The purpose of this exercise is to give you practice developing product-positioning maps. Nonprofit organizations, such as universities, are increasingly using product-positioning maps to determine effective ways to implement strategies.

INSTRUCTIONS

Step 1 Join with two other people in class to form a group of three.

Step 2 Jointly prepare a product-positioning map that includes your institution and four other colleges or universities in your state.

Step 3 Go to the blackboard and diagram your product-positioning map.

Step 4 Discuss differences among the maps diagrammed on the board.

EXPERIENTIAL EXERCISE 8F ▶

Do Banks Require Pro Forma Statements?

PURPOSE

The purpose of this exercise is to explore the practical importance and use of projected financial statements in the banking business.

INSTRUCTIONS

Contact two local bankers by phone and seek answers to the questions listed below. Record the answers you receive, and report your findings to the class.

1. Does your bank require projected financial statements as part of a business loan application?

2. How does your bank use projected financial statements when they are part of a business loan application?

3. What special advice do you give potential business borrowers in preparing projected financial statements?

9 STRATEGY REVIEW, EVALUATION, AND CONTROL

CHAPTER OUTLINE

- The Nature of Strategy Evaluation
- A Strategy-Evaluation Framework
- Published Sources of Strategy-Evaluation Information
- Characteristics of an Effective Evaluation System
- Contingency Planning
- Auditing
- Using Computers to Evaluate Strategies

EXPERIENTIAL EXERCISE 9A
Preparing a Strategy-Evaluation Report for American Airlines (AMR)

EXPERIENTIAL EXERCISE 9B
Evaluating My University's Strategies

EXPERIENTIAL EXERCISE 9C
Who Prepares an Environmental Audit?

CHAPTER OBJECTIVES

After studying this chapter, you should be able to do the following:

1. Describe a practical framework for evaluating strategies.
2. Explain why strategy evaluation is complex, sensitive, and yet essential for organizational success.
3. Discuss the importance of contingency planning in strategy evaluation.
4. Discuss the role of auditing in strategy evaluation.
5. Explain how computers can aid in evaluating strategies.

NOTABLE QUOTES

Complicated controls do not work. They confuse. They misdirect attention from what is to be controlled to the mechanics and methodology of the control.

SEYMOUR TILLES

Although Plan A may be selected as the most realistic . . . the other major alternatives should not be forgotten. They may well serve as contingency plans.

DALE McCONKEY

Organizations are most vulnerable when they are at the peak of their success.

R. T. LENZ

Strategy evaluation must make it as easy as possible for managers to revise their plans and reach quick agreement on the changes.

DALE McCONKEY

While strategy is a word that is usually associated with the future, its link to the past is no less central. Life is lived forward but understood backward. Managers may live strategy in the future, but they understand it through the past.

HENRY MINTZBERG

Unless strategy evaluation is performed seriously and systematically, and unless strategists are willing to act on the results, energy will be used up defending yesterday. No one will have the time, resources, or will to work on exploiting today, let alone to work on making tomorrow.

PETER DRUCKER

The best-formulated and best-implemented strategies become obsolete as a firm's external and internal environments change. It is essential, therefore, that strategists systematically review, evaluate, and control the execution of strategies. This chapter presents a framework that can guide managers' efforts to evaluate strategic-management activities, to make sure they are working, and to make timely changes. Management information systems being used to evaluate strategies are discussed. Guidelines are presented for formulating, implementing, and evaluating strategies.

THE NATURE OF STRATEGY EVALUATION

VISIT THE NET

Gives excellent additional information about evaluating strategies, including some analytical tools. http://www.mindtools.com/plevplan.html

The strategic-management process results in decision that can have significant, long-lasting consequences. Erroneous strategic decisions can inflict severe penalties and can be exceedingly difficult, if not impossible, to reverse. Most strategists agree, therefore, that strategy evaluation is vital to an organization's well-being; timely evaluations can alert management to problems or potential problems before a situation becomes critical. Strategy evaluation includes three basic activities: (1) examining the underlying bases of a firm's strategy, (2) comparing expected results with actual results, and (3) taking corrective actions to ensure that performance conforms to plans. The strategy-evaluation stage of the strategic-management process is illustrated in Figure 9–1.

Adequate and timely feedback is the cornerstone of effective strategy evaluation. Strategy evaluation can be no better than the information on which it operates. Too much pressure from top managers may result in lower managers contriving numbers they think will be satisfactory.

Strategy evaluation can be a complex and sensitive undertaking. Too much emphasis on evaluating strategies may be expensive and counterproductive. No one likes to be evaluated too closely! The more managers attempt to evaluate the behavior of others, the less control they have. Yet too little or no evaluation can create even worse problems. Strategy evaluation is essential to ensure that stated objectives are being achieved.

In many organizations, strategy evaluation is simply an appraisal of how well an organization has performed. Have the firm's assets increased? Has there been an increase in profitability? Have sales increased? Have productivity levels increased? Have profit margin, return on investment, and earnings-per-share ratios increased? Some firms argue that their strategy must have been correct if the answers to these types of questions are affirmative. Well, the strategy or strategies may have been correct, but this type of reasoning can be misleading, because strategy evaluation must have both a long-run and short-run focus. Strategies often do not affect short-term operating results until it is too late to make needed changes.

It is impossible to demonstrate conclusively that a particular strategy is optimal or even to guarantee that it will work. One can, however, evaluate it for critical flaws. Richard Rumelt offered four criteria that could be used to evaluate a strategy: consistency, consonance, feasibility, and advantage. Described in Table 9–1, *consonance* and *advantage* are mostly based on a firm's external assessment, whereas *consistency* and *feasibility* are largely based on an internal assessment.

Strategy evaluation is important because organizations face dynamic environments in which key external and internal factors often change quickly and dramatically. Success today is no guarantee of success tomorrow! An organization should never be lulled into complacency with success. Countless firms have thrived one year only to struggle for survival the following year. Organizational trouble can come swiftly, as further evidenced by the examples described in Table 9–2.

VISIT THE NET

Describes the how and why of strategy evaluation. http://www.csuchico.edu/mgmt/strategy/module1/sld046.htm

FIGURE 9–1

A Comprehensive Strategic-Management Model

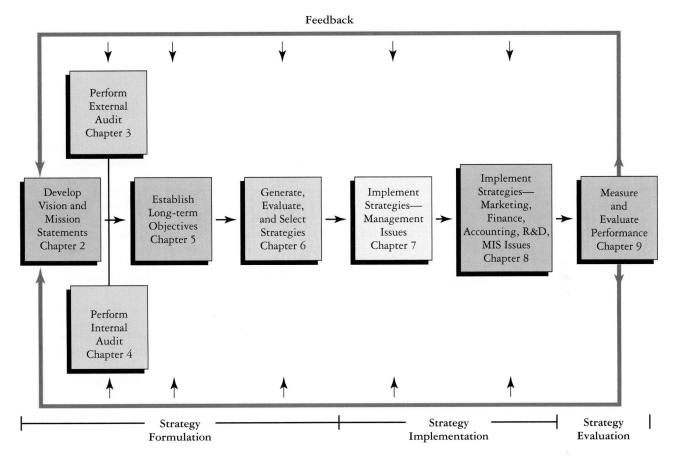

Strategy evaluation is becoming increasingly difficult with the passage of time, for many reasons. Domestic and world economies were more stable in years past, product life cycles were longer, product development cycles were longer, technological advancement was slower, change occurred less frequently, there were fewer competitors, foreign companies were weak, and there were more regulated industries. Other reasons why strategy evaluation is more difficult today include the following trends:

1. A dramatic increase in the environment's complexity
2. The increasing difficulty of predicting the future with accuracy
3. The increasing number of variables
4. The rapid rate of obsolescence of even the best plans
5. The increase in the number of both domestic and world events affecting organizations
6. The decreasing time span for which planning can be done with any degree of certainty[1]

A fundamental problem facing managers today is how to effectively control employees in light of modern organizational demands for greater flexibility, innovation,

TABLE 9-1   **Rumelt's Criteria for Evaluating Strategies**

CONSISTENCY

A strategy should not present inconsistent goals and policies. Organizational conflict and interdepartmental bickering are often symptoms of managerial disorder, but these problems may also be a sign of strategic inconsistency. There are three guidelines to help determine if organizational problems are due to inconsistencies in strategy:

- If managerial problems continue despite changes in personnel and if they tend to be issue-based rather than people-based, then strategies may be inconsistent.
- If success for one organizational department means, or is interpreted to mean, failure for another department, then strategies may be inconsistent.
- If policy problems and issues continue to be brought to the top for resolution, then strategies may be inconsistent.

CONSONANCE

Consonance refers to the need for strategists to examine *sets of trends* as well as individual trends in evaluating strategies. A strategy must represent an adaptive response to the external environment and to the critical changes occurring within it. One difficulty in matching a firm's key internal and external factors in the formulation of strategy is that most trends are the result of interactions among other trends. For example, the daycare explosion came about as a combined result of many trends that included a rise in the average level of education, increased inflation, and an increase in women in the workforce. Although single economic or demographic trends might appear steady for many years, there are waves of change going on at the interaction level.

FEASIBILITY

A strategy must neither overtax available resources nor create unsolvable subproblems. The final broad test of strategy is its feasibility; that is, can the strategy be attempted within the physical, human, and financial resources of the enterprise? The financial resources of a business are the easiest to quantify and are normally the first limitation against which strategy is evaluated. It is sometimes forgotten, however, that innovative approaches to financing are often possible. Devices such as captive subsidiaries, sale-leaseback arrangements, and tying plant mortgages to long-term contracts have all been used effectively to help win key positions in suddenly expanding industries. A less quantifiable, but actually more rigid, limitation on strategic choice is that imposed by individual and organizational capabilities. In evaluating a strategy, it is important to examine whether an organization has demonstrated in the past that it possesses the abilities, competencies, skills, and talents needed to carry out a given strategy.

ADVANTAGE

A strategy must provide for the creation and/or maintenance of a competitive advantage in a selected area of activity. Competitive advantages normally are the result of superiority in one of three areas: (1) resources, (2) skills, or (3) position. The idea that the positioning of one's resources can enhance their combined effectiveness is familiar to military theorists, chess players, and diplomats. Position can also play a crucial role in an organization's strategy. Once gained, a good position is defensible—meaning that it is so costly to capture that rivals are deterred from full-scale attacks. Positional advantage tends to be self-sustaining as long as the key internal and environmental factors that underlie it remain stable. This is why entrenched firms can be almost impossible to unseat, even if their raw skill levels are only average. Although not all positional advantages are associated with size, it is true that larger organizations tend to operate in markets and use procedures that turn their size into advantage, while smaller firms seek product/marker positions that exploit other types of advantage. The principal characteristic of good position is that it permits the firm to obtain advantage from policies that would not similarly benefit rivals without the same position. Therefore, in evaluating strategy, organizations should examine the nature of positional advantages associated with a given strategy.

Source: Adapted from Richard Rumelt, "The Evaluation of Business Strategy," in W. F. Glueck, ed., *Business Policy and Strategic Management* (New York: McGraw-Hill, 1980): 359–367.

TABLE 9-2   Examples of Organizational Trouble

A. Large Companies That Experienced More Than A 38% Decline in Revenues in 2001

	PERCENT DECREASE
KINDER MORGAN	–61%
MICRON TECHNOLOGY	–58
CONEXANT SYSTEMS	–56
PMC-SIERRA	–54
TERADYNE	–53
VITESSE SEMICONDUCTOR	–50
ADC TELECOMMUNICATIONS	–46
COMPUTER ASSOCIATES INTL.	–45
APPLIED MATERIALS	–41
ALTERA	–39

B. Large Companies That Experienced More Than an 85% Decline in Return on Equity

	PERCENT
JDS UNIPHASE	–747.6%
NORTEL NETWORKS	–503.9
PMC-SIERRA	–234.8
APPLIED MICRO CIRCUITS	–203.7
LUCENT TECHNOLOGIES	–105.0
CORNING	–101.4
CIENA	–92.7
CONEXANT SYSTEMS	–91.8
SPRINT PCS GROUP	–87.8
BROADCOM	–85.5

Source: "The Best Performers," Business Week (Spring 2002): 37–38.

creativity, and initiative from employees.[2] How can managers today ensure that empowered employees acting in an entrepreneurial manner do not put the well-being of the business at risk? Recall that Kidder, Peabody & Company lost $350 million when one of its traders allegedly booked fictitious profits; Sears, Roebuck and Company took a $60 million charge against earnings after admitting that its automobile service businesses were performing unnecessary repairs. The costs to companies such as these in terms of damaged reputations, fines, missed opportunities, and diversion of management's attention are enormous.

When empowered employees are held accountable for and pressured to achieve specific goals and are given wide latitude in their actions to achieve them, there can be dysfunctional behavior. For example, Nordstrom, the upscale fashion retailer known for outstanding customer service, was subjected to lawsuits and fines when employees underreported hours worked in order to increase their sales per hour—the company's primary performance criterion. Nordstrom's customer service and earnings were enhanced until the misconduct was reported, at which time severe penalties were levied against the firm.

The Process of Evaluating Strategies

Strategy evaluation is necessary for all sizes and kinds of organizations. Strategy evaluation should initiate managerial questioning of expectations and assumptions, should trigger a review of objectives and values, and should stimulate creativity in generating

VISIT THE NET

Elaborates on the "taking corrective actions" phase of strategy evaluation.
http://www.csuchico.edu/
mgmt/strategy/module1/
sld047.htm

alternatives and formulating criteria of evaluation.[3] Regardless of the size of the organization, a certain amount of *management by wandering around* at all levels is essential to effective strategy evaluation. Strategy-evaluation activities should be performed on a continuing basis, rather than at the end of specified periods of time or just after problems occur. Waiting until the end of the year, for example, could result in a firm closing the barn door after the horses have already escaped.

Evaluating strategies on a continuous rather than on a periodic basis allows benchmarks of progress to be established and more effectively monitored. Some strategies take years to implement; consequently, associated results may not become apparent for years. Successful strategists combine patience with a willingness to take corrective actions promptly when necessary. There always comes a time when corrective actions are needed in an organization! Centuries ago, a writer (perhaps Solomon) made the following observations about change:

> There is a time for everything,
> A time to be born and a time to die,
> A time to plant and a time to uproot,
> A time to kill and a time to heal,
> A time to tear down and a time to build,
> A time to weep and a time to laugh,
> A time to mourn and a time to dance,
> A time to scatter stones and a time to gather them,
> A time to embrace and a time to refrain,
> A time to search and a time to give up,
> A time to keep and a time to throw away,
> A time to tear and a time to mend,
> A time to be silent and a time to speak,
> A time to love and a time to hate,
> A time for war and a time for peace.[4]

Managers and employees of the firm should be continually aware of progress being made toward achieving the firm's objectives. As critical success factors change, organizational members should be involved in determining appropriate corrective actions. If assumptions and expectations deviate significantly from forecasts, then the firm should renew strategy-formulation activities, perhaps sooner than planned. In strategy evaluation, like strategy formulation and strategy implementation, people make the difference. Through involvement in the process of evaluating strategies, managers and employees become committed to keeping the firm moving steadily toward achieving objectives.

VISIT THE NET

Provides the strategic plan of Northeastern Regional Association of State Agricultural Experiment Station Directors for the years 1996 to 2000, including its "Measures of Success" (strategy evaluation criteria).
http://www.agnr.umd.edu/ users/NERA/newplan. html#strategies

A STRATEGY- EVALUATION FRAMEWORK

Table 9–3 summarizes strategy-evaluation activities in terms of key questions that should be addressed, alternative answers to those questions, and appropriate actions for an organization to take. Notice that corrective actions are almost always needed except when (1) external and internal factors have not significantly changed and (2) the firm is progressing satisfactorily toward achieving stated objectives. Relationships among strategy-evaluation activities are illustrated in Figure 9–2.

TABLE 9-3   **A Strategy-Evaluation Assessment Matrix**

HAVE MAJOR CHANGES OCCURRED IN THE FIRM'S INTERNAL STRATEGIC POSITION?	HAVE MAJOR CHANGES OCCURRED IN THE FIRM'S EXTERNAL STRATEGIC POSITION?	HAS THE FIRM PROGRESSED SATISFACTORILY TOWARD ACHIEVING ITS STATED OBJECTIVES?	RESULT
No	No	No	Take corrective actions
Yes	Yes	Yes	Take corrective actions
Yes	Yes	No	Take corrective actions
Yes	No	Yes	Take corrective actions
Yes	No	No	Take corrective actions
No	Yes	Yes	Take corrective actions
No	Yes	No	Take corrective actions
No	No	Yes	Continue present strategic course

Reviewing Bases of Strategy

As shown in Figure 9–2, *reviewing the underlying bases of an organization's strategy* could be approached by developing a revised EFE Matrix and IFE Matrix. A *revised IFE Matrix* should focus on changes in the organization's management, marketing, finance/accounting, production/operations, R&D, and management information systems strengths and weaknesses. A *revised EFE Matrix* should indicate how effective a firm's strategies have been in response to key opportunities and threats. This analysis could also address such questions as the following:

1. How have competitors reacted to our strategies?
2. How have competitors' strategies changed?
3. Have major competitors' strengths and weaknesses changed?
4. Why are competitors making certain strategic changes?
5. Why are some competitors' strategies more successful than others?
6. How satisfied are our competitors with their present market positions and profitability?
7. How far can our major competitors be pushed before retaliating?
8. How could we more effectively cooperate with our competitors?

Numerous external and internal factors can prohibit firms from achieving long-term and annual objectives. Externally, actions by competitors, changes in demand, changes in technology, economic changes, demographic shifts, and governmental actions may prohibit objectives from being accomplished. Internally, ineffective strategies may have been chosen or implementation activities may have been poor. Objectives may have been too optimistic. Thus, failure to achieve objectives may not be the result of unsatisfactory work by managers and employees. All organizational members need to know this to encourage their support for strategy-evaluation activities. Organizations desperately need to know as soon as possible when their strategies are not effective. Sometimes managers and employees on the front lines discover this well before strategists.

External opportunities and threats and internal strengths and weaknesses that represent the bases of current strategies should continually be monitored for change. It is not really a question of whether these factors will change, but rather when they will change and in what ways. Some key questions to address in evaluating strategies are given here.

VISIT THE NET

The Small Business Administration Web site provides a forty-page Business Plan Outline.
http://www.sba.gov/starting/businessplan.html

FIGURE 9–2

A Strategy-Evaluation Framework

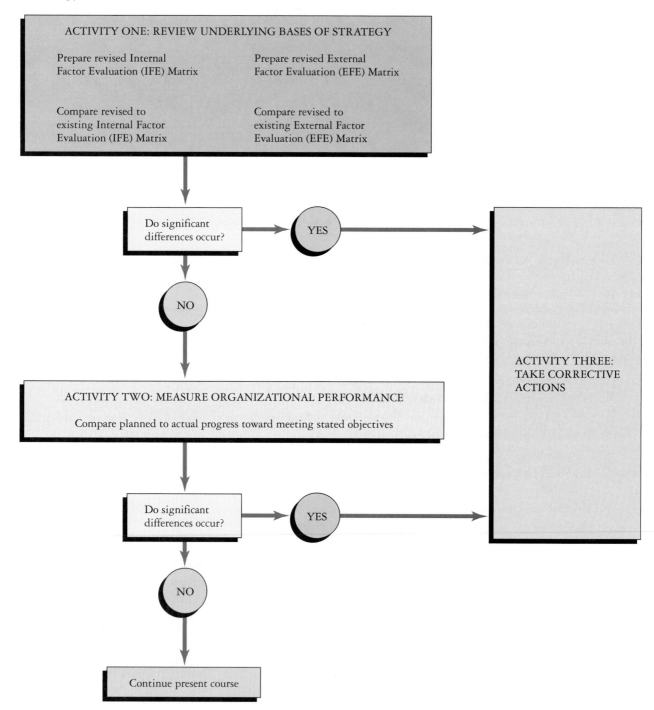

1. Are our internal strengths still strengths?
2. Have we added other internal strengths? If so, what are they?
3. Are our internal weaknesses still weaknesses?
4. Do we now have other internal weaknesses? If so, what are they?
5. Are our external opportunities still opportunities?
6. Are there now other external opportunities? If so, what are they?
7. Are our external threats still threats?
8. Are there now other external threats? If so, what are they?
9. Are we vulnerable to a hostile takeover?

Measuring Organizational Performance

Another important strategy-evaluation activity is *measuring organizational performance*. This activity includes comparing expected results to actual results, investigating deviations from plans, evaluating individual performance, and examining progress being made toward meeting stated objectives. Both long-term and annual objectives are commonly used in this process. Criteria for evaluating strategies should be measurable and easily verifiable. Criteria that predict results may be more important than those that reveal what already has happened. For example, rather than simply being informed that sales in the last quarter were 20 percent under what was expected, strategists need to know that sales in the next quarter may be 20 percent below standard unless some action is taken to counter the trend. Really effective control requires accurate forecasting.

Failure to make satisfactory progress toward accomplishing long-term or annual objectives signals a need for corrective actions. Many factors, such as unreasonable policies, unexpected turns in the economy, unreliable suppliers or distributors, or ineffective strategies, can result in unsatisfactory progress toward meeting objectives. Problems can result from ineffectiveness (not doing the right things) or inefficiency (doing the right things poorly).

Determining which objectives are most important in the evaluation of strategies can be difficult. Strategy evaluation is based on both quantitative and qualitative criteria. Selecting the exact set of criteria for evaluating strategies depends on a particular organization's size, industry, strategies, and management philosophy. An organization pursuing a retrenchment strategy, for example, could have an entirely different set of evaluative criteria from an organization pursuing a market-development strategy. Quantitative criteria commonly used to evaluate strategies are financial ratios, which strategists use to make three critical comparisons: (1) comparing the firm's performance over different time periods, (2) comparing the firm's performance to competitors', and (3) comparing the firm's performance to industry averages. Some key financial ratios that are particularly useful as criteria for strategy evaluation are as follows:

1. Return on investment (ROI)
2. Return on equity (ROE)
3. Profit margin
4. Market share
5. Debt to equity
6. Earnings per share
7. Sales growth
8. Asset growth

VISIT THE NET

Provides strategic management handbooks with detailed instructions for planning in certain U.S. states. http://www.opm.state.ct.us/mgmt/busguide/50states/guides.htm

But there are some potential problems associated with using quantitative criteria for evaluating strategies. First, most quantitative criteria are geared to annual objectives rather than long-term objectives. Also, different accounting methods can provide different results on many quantitative criteria. Third, intuitive judgments are almost always involved in deriving quantitative criteria. For these and other reasons, qualitative criteria are also important in evaluating strategies. Human factors such as high absenteeism and turnover rates, poor production quality and quantity rates, or low employee satisfaction can be underlying causes of declining performance. Marketing, finance/accounting, R&D, or management information systems factors can also cause financial problems. Seymour Tilles identified six qualitative questions that are useful in evaluating strategies:

1. Is the strategy internally consistent?
2. Is the strategy consistent with the environment?
3. Is the strategy appropriate in view of available resources?
4. Does the strategy involve an acceptable degree of risk?
5. Does the strategy have an appropriate time framework?
6. Is the strategy workable?[5]

Some additional key questions that reveal the need for qualitative or intuitive judgments in strategy evaluation are as follows:

1. How good is the firm's balance of investments between high-risk and low-risk projects?
2. How good is the firm's balance of investments between long-term and short-term projects?
3. How good is the firm's balance of investments between slow-growing markets and fast-growing markets?
4. How good is the firm's balance of investments among different divisions?
5. To what extent are the firm's alternative strategies socially responsible?
6. What are the relationships among the firm's key internal and external strategic factors?
7. How are major competitors likely to respond to particular strategies?

Taking Corrective Actions

The final strategy-evaluation activity, *taking corrective actions,* requires making changes to reposition a firm competitively for the future. Examples of changes that may be needed are altering an organization's structure, replacing one or more key individuals, selling a division, or revising a business mission. Other changes could include establishing or revising objectives, devising new policies, issuing stock to raise capital, adding additional salespersons, allocating resources differently, or developing new performance incentives. Taking corrective actions does not necessarily mean that existing strategies will be abandoned or even that new strategies must be formulated.

> The probabilities and possibilities for incorrect or inappropriate actions increase geometrically with an arithmetic increase in personnel. Any person directing an overall undertaking must check on the actions of the participants as well as the results that they have achieved. If either the actions or results do not comply with preconceived or planned achievements, then corrective actions are needed.[6]

No organization can survive as an island; no organization can escape change. Taking corrective actions is necessary to keep an organization on track toward achieving scared objectives. In his thought-provoking books, *Future Shock* and *The Third Wave,*

VISIT THE NET

Provides the U.S. Customs' Strategic Plan. www. customs.treas.gov/about/ strat/index.htm

Alvin Toffler argued that business environments are becoming so dynamic and complex that they threaten people and organizations with *future shock,* which occurs when the nature, types, and speed of changes overpower an individual's or organization's ability and capacity to adapt. Strategy evaluation enhances an organization's ability to adapt successfully to changing circumstances. Brown and Agnew referred to this notion as *corporate agility*.[7]

Taking corrective actions raises employees' and managers' anxieties. Research suggests that participation in strategy-evaluation activities is one of the best ways to overcome individuals' resistance to change. According to Erez and Kanfer, individuals accept change best when they have a cognitive understanding of the changes, a sense of control over the situation, and an awareness that necessary actions are going to be taken to implement the changes.[8]

Strategy evaluation can lead to strategy-formulation changes, strategy-implementation changes, both formulation and implementation changes, or no changes at all. Strategists cannot escape having to revise strategies and implementation approaches sooner or later. Hussey and Langham offered the following insight on taking corrective actions:

> Resistance to change is often emotionally based and not easily overcome by rational argument. Resistance may be based on such feelings as loss of status, implied criticism of present competence, fear of failure in the new situation, annoyance at not being consulted, lack of understanding of the need for change, or insecurity in changing from well-known and fixed methods. It is necessary, therefore, to overcome such resistance by creating situations of participation and [a] full explanation when changes are envisaged.[9]

Corrective actions should place an organization in a better position to capitalize upon internal strengths; to take advantage of key external opportunities; to avoid, reduce, or mitigate external threats; and to improve internal weaknesses. Corrective actions should have a proper time horizon and an appropriate amount of risk. They should be internally consistent and socially responsible. Perhaps most important, corrective actions strengthen an organization's competitive position in its basic industry. Continuous strategy evaluation keeps strategists close to the pulse of an organization and provides information needed for an effective strategic-management system. Carter Bayles described the benefits of strategy evaluation as follows:

> Evaluation activities may renew confidence in the current business strategy or point to the need for actions to correct some weaknesses, such as erosion of product superiority or technological edge. In many cases, the benefits of strategy evaluation are much more far-reaching, for the outcome of the process may be a fundamentally new strategy that will lead, even in a business that is already turning a respectable profit, to substantially increased earnings. It is this possibility that justifies strategy evaluation, for the payoff can be very large.[10]

PUBLISHED SOURCES OF STRATEGY-EVALUATION INFORMATION

A number of publications are helpful in evaluating a firm's strategies. For example, *Fortune* annually identifies and evaluates the Fortune 1,000 (the largest manufacturers) and the Fortune 50 (the largest retailers, transportation companies, utilities, banks, insurance companies, and diversified financial corporations in the United States). *Fortune* ranks the best and worst performers on various factors such as return on investment, sales volume, and profitability. In its March issue each year, *Fortune* publishes its strategy evaluation research

NATURAL ENVIRONMENT PERSPECTIVE

How Much Carbon Dioxide Is Your Firm Emitting?

To the dismay of Europeans and indeed many Americans, the U.S. federal government withdrew from the Kyoto Protocol, an international treaty to reduce the output of CO_2 emissions and five other greenhouse gases. President Bush says the treaty will hurt the nation's economy. However, recognizing the importance of this issue, numerous states within the United States are tackling the issue with passion. Seven states in particular have recently instituted effective CO_2 monitoring programs, including New Jersey, Massachusetts, New York, New Hampshire, North Carolina, Florida, and Illinois. Perhaps New Jersey best leads this effort: Fifty-six of that state's colleges and community colleges also have joined the state's environmental program, agreeing to measure and curb their own emissions.

Global warming isn't just a fear. It's a fact. Carbon dioxide is the major culprit and the most common air pollutant. Plants, of course, breathe in carbon dioxide, which is the reason why widespread cutting of trees and rain forests and the clearing of land and harvesting kelp in the oceans are so detrimental to the natural environment. The following statistics reveal annual carbon-dioxide emissions for various countries worldwide. Note that the United States is guiltiest.

	Total Tons (Millions)	Tons per Capita
United States	5,475	20.52
China	3,196	2.68
Russia	1,820	12.26
Japan	1,126	9.03
India	910	0.90
Germany	833	10.24
United Kingdom	539	9.29
Ukraine	437	8.48
Canada	433	14.83
Italy	411	7.19
South Korea	370	8.33
Mexico	359	3.93

Continents and countries relative share of harmful CO_2 emissions is given below:

Eastern Europe and former Soviet Union	27%
United States	22%
Western Europe	17%
Other Asian countries	13%
China	11%
Latin America	4%
Africa	3%

Source: Adapted from "Clear Skies Are Goal as Pollution Is Turning into a Commodity," *The Wall Street Journal* (October 3, 1997): A4. Also, "States Are Stepping in to Reduce Levels of Carbon Dioxide," *The Wall Street Journal* (September 11, 2001): A28.

in an article entitled "America's Most Admired Companies." Nine key attributes serve as evaluative criteria: quality of management; innovativeness; quality of products or services; long-term investment value; financial soundness; community and environmental responsibility; ability to attract, develop, and keep talented people; use of corporate assets; and international acumen. In October of each year, *Fortune* publishes additional strategy evaluation research in an article entitled "The World's Most Admired Companies."[11] The Global Perspective box reveals the best managed companies in Britain, France, Germany, and elsewhere in Europe. *Fortune*'s 2001 evaluation in Table 9–4 reveals the firms ranked as the top ten most admired (best managed).

Another excellent evaluation of corporations in America, "The Annual Report on American Industry," is published annually in the January issue of *Forbes*. It provides a detailed and comprehensive evaluation of hundreds of American companies in many different industries. *Business Week, Industry Week,* and *Dun's Business Month* also periodically publish detailed evaluations of American businesses and industries. Although published

TABLE 9-4   **Top Ten**

RANK	COMPANY
1	General Electric
2	Southwest Airlines
3	Wal-Mart Stores
4	Microsoft
5	Berkshire Hathaway
6	Home Depot
7	Johnson & Johnson
8	FedEx
9	Citigroup
10	Intel

Source: **http://www.fortune.com/lists/mostadmired/index.html** (from the Mar. 4, 2002 issue of *Fortune*)

sources of strategy-evaluation information focus primarily on large, publicly held businesses, the comparative ratios and related information are widely used to evaluate small businesses and privately owned firms as well.

CHARACTERISTICS OF AN EFFECTIVE EVALUATION SYSTEM

Strategy evaluation must meet several basic requirements to be effective. First, strategy-evaluation activities must be economical; too much information can be just as bad as too little information; and too many controls can do more harm than good. Strategy-evaluation activities also should be meaningful; they should specifically relate to a firm's objectives. They should provide managers with useful information about tasks over which they have control and influence. Strategy-evaluation activities should provide timely information; on occasion and in some areas, managers may need information daily. For example, when a firm has diversified by acquiring another firm, evaluative information may be needed frequently. However, in an R&D department, daily or even weekly evaluative information could be dysfunctional. Approximate information that is timely is generally more desirable as a basis for strategy evaluation than accurate information that does not depict the present. Frequent measurement and rapid reporting may frustrate control rather than give better control. The time dimension of control must coincide with the time span of the event being measured.

Strategy evaluation should be designed to provide a true picture of what is happening. For example, in a severe economic downturn, productivity and profitability ratios may drop alarmingly, although employees and managers are actually working harder. Strategy evaluations should portray this type of situation fairly. Information derived from the strategy-evaluation process should facilitate action and should be directed to those individuals in the organization who need to take action based on it. Managers commonly ignore evaluative reports that are provided for informational purposes only; not all managers need to receive all reports. Controls need to be action-oriented rather than information-oriented.

GLOBAL PERSPECTIVE

What Are the Best Companies in Britain, France, Germany, and Switzerland?

Fortune annually evaluates companies within particular countries. The evaluative criteria are management, products/services, innovativeness, long-term investment value, financial soundness, getting/keeping talent, social/environmental responsibility/wise use of assets, and international acumen. In 2001, the best companies in Britain, France, Germany, and Switzerland were ranked on these criteria and are listed below in rank order:

Company	Industry	Company	Industry
Britain		*Germany*	
Royal Dutch/Shell Group	Petroleum refining	BMW	Motor vehicles
BP	Petroleum refining	Volkswagen	Motor vehicles
Tesco	Food and drugstores	BASF	Chemicals
HSBC Holdings	Banks	Siemens	Electronics
J. Sainsbury	Food and drugstores	Bayer	Chemicals
France		*Switzerland*	
L'Oréal	Soaps, cosmetics	Nestlé	Food
Vivendi Universal	Entertainment	ABB	Electronics
Total Fina Elf	Petroleum refining	UBS	Banks
Christian Dior (LVMH)	Soaps, cosmetics	Novartis Group	Pharmaceuticals
Vinci	Engineering, Construction	Swiss Re	Insurance P&C (stock)

Source: **http://www.fortune.com/lists/globaladmired/country_list.html** (from the March 4, 2002 issue of *Fortune*)

The strategy-evaluation process should not dominate decisions; it should foster mutual understanding, trust, and common sense. No department should fail to cooperate with another in evaluating strategies. Strategy evaluations should be simple, not too cumbersome, and not too restrictive. Complex strategy-evaluation systems often confuse people and accomplish little. The test of an effective evaluation system is its usefulness, not its complexity.

Large organizations require a more elaborate and detailed strategy-evaluation system because it is more difficult to coordinate efforts among different divisions and functional areas. Managers in small companies often communicate with each other and their employees daily and do not need extensive evaluative reporting systems. Familiarity with local environments usually makes gathering and evaluating information much easier for small organizations than for large businesses. But the key to an effective strategy-evaluation system may be the ability to convince participants that failure to accomplish certain objectives within a prescribed time is not necessarily a reflection of their performance.

There is no one ideal strategy-evaluation system. The unique characteristics of an organization, including its size, management style, purpose, problems, and strengths, can determine a strategy-evaluation and control system's final design. Robert Waterman offered the following observation about successful organizations' strategy-evaluation and control systems:

> Successful companies treat facts as friends and controls as liberating. Morgan Guaranty and Wells Fargo not only survive but thrive in the troubled waters of bank deregulation, because their strategy evaluation and control systems are sound, their risk is contained, and they know themselves and the competitive situation so well. Successful companies have a voracious hunger for facts. They see information where others see only data. They love comparisons, rankings, anything that removes decision making from the realm of mere opinion. Successful companies maintain tight, accurate financial controls. Their people don't regard controls as an imposition of autocracy but as the benign checks and balances that allow them to be creative and free.[12]

 ## CONTINGENCY PLANNING

A basic premise of good strategic management is that firms plan ways to deal with unfavorable and favorable events before they occur. Too many organizations prepare contingency plans just for unfavorable events; this is a mistake, because both minimizing threats and capitalizing on opportunities can improve a firm's competitive position.

Regardless of how carefully strategies are formulated, implemented, and evaluated, unforeseen events such as strikes, boycotts, natural disasters, arrival of foreign competitors, and government actions can make a strategy obsolete. To minimize the impact of potential threats, organizations should develop contingency plans as part of their strategy-evaluation process. *Contingency plans* can be defined as alternative plans that can be put into effect if certain key events do not occur as expected. Only high-priority areas require the insurance of contingency plans. Strategists cannot and should not try to cover all bases by planning for all possible contingencies. But in any case, contingency plans should be as simple as possible.

Some contingency plans commonly established by firms include the following:

1. If a major competitor withdraws from particular markets as intelligence reports indicate, what actions should our firm take?
2. If our sales objectives are not reached, what actions should our firm take to avoid profit losses?
3. If demand for our new product exceeds plans, what actions should our firm take to meet the higher demand?
4. If certain disasters occur—such as loss of computer capabilities; a hostile takeover attempt; loss of patent protection; or destruction of manufacturing facilities because of earthquakes, tornados, or hurricanes—what actions should our firm take?
5. If a new technological advancement makes our new product obsolete sooner than expected, what actions should our firm take?

Too many organizations discard alternative strategies not selected for implementation although the work devoted to analyzing these options would render valuable information.

Alternative strategies not selected for implementation can serve as contingency plans in case the strategy or strategies selected do not work.

When strategy-evaluation activities reveal the need for a major change quickly, an appropriate contingency plan can be executed in a timely way. Contingency plans can promote a strategist's ability to respond quickly to key changes in the internal and external bases of an organization's current strategy. For example, if underlying assumptions about the economy turn out to be wrong and contingency plans are ready, then managers can make appropriate changes promptly.

In some cases, external or internal conditions present unexpected opportunities. When such opportunities occur, contingency plans could allow an organization to capitalize on them quickly. Linneman and Chandran reported that contingency planning gave users such as DuPont, Dow Chemical, Consolidated Foods, and Emerson Electric three major benefits: (1) It permitted quick response to change, (2) it prevented panic in crisis situations, and (3) it made managers more adaptable by encouraging them to appreciate just how variable the future can be. They suggested that effective contingency planning involves a seven-step process:

1. Identify both beneficial and unfavorable events that could possibly derail the strategy or strategies.
2. Specify trigger points. Calculate about when contingent events are likely to occur.
3. Assess the impact of each contingent event. Estimate the potential benefit or harm of each contingent event.
4. Develop contingency plans. Be sure that contingency plans are compatible with current strategy and are economically feasible.
5. Assess the counter impact of each contingency plan. That is, estimate how much each contingency plan will capitalize on or cancel out its associated contingent event. Doing this will quantify the potential value of each contingency plan.
6. Determine early warning signals for key contingent events. Monitor the early warning signals.
7. For contingent events with reliable early warning signals, develop advance action plans to take advantage of the available lead time.[13]

 ## AUDITING

A frequently used tool in strategy evaluation is the audit. *Auditing* is defined by the American Accounting Association (AAA) as "a systematic process of objectively obtaining and evaluating evidence regarding assertions about economic actions and events to ascertain the degree of correspondence between those assertions and established criteria, and communicating the results to interested users."[14] Since the Enron, Worldcom, and Johnson & Johnson scandals in 2002, auditing has taken on greater emphasis and care in companies. Independent auditors basically are certified public accountants (CPAs) who provide their services to organizations for a fee; they examine the financial statements of an organization to determine whether they have been prepared according to generally accepted accounting principles (GAAP) and whether they fairly represent the activities of the firm. Independent auditors use a set of standards called generally accepted audit-

TABLE 9-5   **Key Strategy-Evaluation Questions**

1. Do you feel that the strategic-management system exists to provide service to you in your day-to-day work? How has it helped you in this respect?

2. Has the strategic-management system provided the service that you feel was promised at the start of its design and implementation? In which areas has it failed and succeeded, in your opinion?

3. Do you consider that the strategic-management system has been implemented with due regard to costs and benefits? Are there any areas in which you consider the costs to be excessive?

4. Do you feel comfortable using the system? Could more attention have been paid to matching the output of the system to your needs and, if so, in what areas?

5. Is the system flexible enough in your opinion? If not, where should changes be made?

6. Do you still keep a personal store of information in a notebook or elsewhere? If so, will you share that information with the system? Do you see any benefits in so doing?

7. Is the strategic-management system still evolving? Can you influence this evolution and, if not, why not?

8. Does the system provide timely, relevant, and accurate information? Are there any areas of deficiency?

9. Do you think that the strategic-management system makes too much use of complex procedures and models? Can you suggest areas in which less complicated techniques might be used to advantage?

10. Do you consider that there has been sufficient attention paid to the confidentiality and security of the information in the system? Can you suggest areas for improvement of these aspects of its operation?

Source: Adapted from K. J. Radford, *Information Systems for Strategic Decisions,* © 1978: 220–221. Adapted by permission of Prentice-Hall, Inc., Englewood Cliffs, New Jersey. Also, Lloyd Byars, *Strategic Management* (New York: Harper & Row, 1984): 237.

ing standards (GAAS). Public accounting firms often have a consulting arm that provides strategy-evaluation services. The Arthur Andersen public accounting firm in 2001 experienced serious troubles in auditing the accounting practices of Enron Corporation.

Two government agencies—the General Accounting Office (GAO) and the Internal Revenue Service (IRS)—employ government auditors responsible for making sure that organizations comply with federal laws, statutes, and policies. GAO and IRS auditors can audit any public or private organization. The third group of auditors consists of employees within an organization who are responsible for safeguarding company assets, for assessing the efficiency of company operations, and for ensuring that generally accepted business procedures are practiced. To evaluate the effectiveness of an organization's strategic-management system, internal auditors often seek answers to the questions posed in Table 9–5.

The Environmental Audit

For an increasing number of firms, overseeing environmental affairs is no longer a technical function performed by specialists; rather, it has become an important strategic-management concern. Product design, manufacturing, transportation, customer use, packaging, product disposal, and corporate rewards and sanctions should reflect environmental considerations. Firms that effectively manage environmental affairs are benefiting from constructive relations with employees, consumers, suppliers, and distributors.

Shimell emphasized the need for organizations to conduct environmental audits of their operations and to develop a Corporate Environmental Policy (CEP).[15] Shimell contended that an environmental audit should be as rigorous as a financial audit and should include training workshops in which staff can help design and implement the policy. The CEP should be budgeted, and requisite funds should be allocated to ensure that it is not a public relations facade. A Statement of Environmental Policy should be published periodically to inform shareholders and the public of environmental actions taken by the firm.

Instituting an environmental audit can include moving environmental affairs from the staff side of the organization to the line side. Some firms are also introducing environmental criteria and objectives in their performance appraisal instruments and systems. Conoco, for example, ties compensation of all its top managers to environmental action plans. Occidental Chemical includes environmental responsibilities in all its job descriptions for positions.

 ## USING COMPUTERS TO EVALUATE STRATEGIES

When properly designed, installed, and operated, a computer network can efficiently acquire information promptly and accurately. Networks can allow diverse strategy-evaluation reports to be generated for—and responded to by—different levels and types of managers. For example, strategists will want reports concerned with whether the mission, objectives, and strategies of the enterprise are being achieved. Middle managers could require strategy-implementation information, such as whether construction of a new facility is on schedule or a product's development is proceeding as expected. Lower-level managers could need evaluation reports that focus on operational concerns, such as absenteeism and turnover rates, productivity rates, and the number and nature of grievances.

Business today has become so competitive that strategists are being forced to extend planning horizons and to make decisions under greater degrees of uncertainty. As a result, more information has to be obtained and assimilated to formulate, implement, and evaluate strategic decisions. In any competitive situation, the side with the best intelligence (information) usually wins; computers enable managers to evaluate vast amounts of information quickly and accurately. Use of the Internet, World Wide Web, e-mail, and search engines can make the difference today between a firm that is up-to-date or out-of-date in the currentness of information the firm uses to make strategic decisions.

A limitation of management-based systems when it comes to evaluating and monitoring strategy execution is that personal values, attitudes, morals, preferences, politics, personalities, and emotions are not programmable. This limitation accents the need to view computers as tools, rather than as actual decision-making devices. Computers can significantly enhance the process of effectively integrating intuition and analysis in strategy evaluation. The General Accounting Office of the U.S. government offered the following conclusions regarding the appropriate role of computers in strategy evaluation:

> The aim is to enhance and extend judgment. Computers should be looked upon not as a provider of solutions, but rather as a framework which permits science

and judgment to be brought together and made explicit. It is the explicitness of this structure, the decision-maker's ability to probe, modify, and examine "What if?" alternatives, that is of value in extending judgment.[16]

CONCLUSION

This chapter presents a strategy-evaluation framework that can facilitate accomplishment of annual and long-term objectives. Effective strategy evaluation allows an organization to capitalize on internal strengths as they develop, to exploit external opportunities as they emerge, to recognize and defend against threats, and to mitigate internal weaknesses before they become detrimental.

Strategists in successful organizations take the time to formulate, implement, and then evaluate strategies deliberately and systematically. Good strategists move their organization forward with purpose and direction, continually evaluating and improving the firm's external and internal strategic position. Strategy evaluation allows an organization to shape its own future rather than allowing it to be constantly shaped by remote forces that have little or no vested interest in the well-being of the enterprise.

Although not a guarantee for success, strategic management allows organizations to make effective long-term decisions, to execute those decisions efficiently, and to take corrective actions as needed to ensure success. Computer networks and the Internet help to coordinate strategic-management activities and to ensure that decisions are based on good information. A key to effective strategy evaluation and to successful strategic management is an integration of intuition and analysis:

> A potentially fatal problem is the tendency for analytical and intuitive issues to polarize. This polarization leads to strategy evaluation that is dominated by either analysis or intuition, or to strategy evaluation that is discontinuous, with a lack of coordination among analytical and intuitive issues.[17]

Strategists in successful organizations realize that strategic management is first and foremost a people process. It is an excellent vehicle for fostering organizational communication. People are what make the difference in organizations.

> The real key to effective strategic management is to accept the premise that the planning process is more important than the written plan, that the manager is continuously planning and does not stop planning when the written plan is finished. The written plan is only a snapshot as of the moment it is approved. If the manager is not planning on a continuous basis—planning, measuring, and revising—the written plan can become obsolete the day it is finished. This obsolescence becomes more of a certainty as the increasingly rapid rate of change makes the business environment more uncertain.[18]

We invite you to visit the David page on the Prentice Hall Companion Website at **www.prenhall.com/david** for this chapter's World Wide Web exercises.

KEY TERMS AND CONCEPTS

Advantage (p. 300)
Auditing (p. 314)
Consistency (p. 300)
Consonance (p. 300)
Contingency Plans (p. 313)
Corporate Agility (p. 309)
Feasibility (p. 300)

Future Shock (p. 309)
Management by Wandering Around (p. 304)
Measuring Organizational Performance (p. 307)

Reviewing the Underlying Bases of an Organization's Strategy (p. 305)
Revised EFE Matrix (p. 305)
Revised IFE Matrix (p. 305)
Taking Corrective Actions (p. 308)

ISSUES FOR REVIEW AND DISCUSSION

1. Why has strategy evaluation become so important in business today?
2. BellSouth Services is considering putting divisional EFE and IFE matrices online for continual updating. How would this affect strategy evaluation?
3. What types of quantitative and qualitative criteria do you think David Glass, CEO of Wal-Mart, uses to evaluate the company's strategy?
4. As owner of a local, independent supermarket, explain how you would evaluate the firm's strategy.
5. Under what conditions are corrective actions not required in the strategy-evaluation process?
6. Identify types of organizations that may need to evaluate strategy more frequently than others. Justify your choices.
7. As executive director of the state forestry commission, in what way and how frequently would you evaluate the organization's strategies?
8. Identify some key financial ratios that would be important in evaluating a bank's strategy.
9. As owner of a chain of hardware stores, describe how you would approach contingency planning.
10. Strategy evaluation allows an organization to take a proactive stance toward shaping its own future. Discuss the meaning of this statement.

NOTES

1. Dale McConkey, "Planning in a Changing Environment," *Business Horizons* (September–October 1988): 64.
2. Robert Simons, "Control in an Age of Empowerment," *Harvard Business Review* (March–April 1995): 80.
3. Dale Zand, "Reviewing the Policy Process," *California Management Review* 21, no. 1 (Fall 1978): 37.
4. Eccles. 3: 1–8.
5. Seymour Tilles, "How to Evaluate Corporate Strategy," *Harvard Business Review* 41 (July–August 1963): 111–121.
6. Claude George, Jr., *The History of Management Thought* (Englewood Cliffs, New Jersey: Prentice-Hall, 1968), 165–166.
7. John Brown and Neil Agnew, "Corporate Agility," *Business Horizons* 25, no. 2 (March–April 1982): 29.
8. M. Erez and F. Kanfer, "The Role of Goal Acceptance in Goal Setting and Task Performance," *Academy of Management Review* 8, no. 3 (July 1983): 457.
9. D. Hussey and M. Langham, *Corporate Planning: The Human Factor* (Oxford, England: Pergamon Press, 1979): 138.
10. Carter Bayles, "Strategic Control: The President's Paradox," *Business Horizons* 20, no. 4 (August 1977): 18.
11. See the March 4, 2002 issue of *Fortune*.
12. Robert Waterman, Jr., "How the Best Get Better," *Business Week* (September 14, 1987): 105.
13. Robert Linneman and Rajan Chandran, "Contingency Planning: A Key to Swift Managerial Action in the Uncertain Tomorrow," *Managerial Planning* 29, no. 4 (January–February 1981): 23–27.
14. American Accounting Association, *Report of Committee on Basic Auditing Concepts* (1971): 15–74.
15. Pamela Shimell, "Corporate Environmental Policy in Practice," *Long Range Planning* 24, no. 3 (June 1991): 10.
16. GAO *Report* PAD—80–21, 17.
17. Michael McGinnis, "The Key to Strategic Planning: Integrating Analysis and Intuition," *Sloan Management Review* 26, no. 1 (Fall 1984): 49.
18. McConkey, 72.

CURRENT READINGS

BLOUNT, SALLY, and GREGORY A. JANICIK. "When Plans Change: Examining How People Evaluate Timing Canges in Work Organizations." *The Academy of Management Review*, 26, no. 4 (October 2001): 566.

GELETKANYCZ, MARTA A., and SYLVIA SLOAN BLACK. "Bound by the Past? Experience-Based Effects on Commitment to the Strategic Status Quo." *Journal of Management* 27, no. 1 (2001): 3.

HITT, MICHAEL A., LEONARD BIERMAN, KATSUHIKO SHIMIZU, and RAHUL KOCHHAR. "Direct and Moderating Effects of Human Capital on Strategy and Performance in Professional Service Firms: A Resource-Based Perspective." *The Academy of Management Journal* 44, no. 1 (February 2001): 13.

HUY, QUY NGUYEN. "Time, Temporal Capability, and Planned Change." *The Academy of Management Review* 26, no. 4 (October 2001): 601.

PEIPERL, MAURY A. "Getting 360-Degree Feedback Right." *Harvard Business Review* (January 2001): 142.

SCHULZ, MARTIN. "The Uncertain Relevance of Newness: Organizational Learning and Knowledge Flows." *The Academy of Management Journal* 44, no. 4 (August 2001): 661.

EXPERIENTIAL EXERCISES

EXPERIENTIAL EXERCISE 9A ▶

Preparing a Strategy-Evaluation Report for American Airlines (AMR)

PURPOSE

This exercise can give you experience locating strategy-evaluation information. Use of the Internet coupled with published sources of information can significantly enhance the strategy-evaluation process. Performance information on competitors, for example, can help put into perspective a firm's own performance.

INSTRUCTIONS

Step 1   Visit **www.invester.stockpoint.com** to locate strategy-evaluation information on AMR's competitors. Read five to ten articles written in the last six months that discuss the airline industry.

Step 2   Summarize your research findings by preparing a strategy-evaluation report for your instructor. Include in your report a summary of AMR's strategies and performance in 2001 and a summary of your conclusions regarding the effectiveness of AMR's strategies.

Step 3   Based on your analysis, do you feel that AMR is pursuing effective strategies? What recommendations would you offer to AMR's chief executive officer?

EXPERIENTIAL EXERCISE 9B ▶

Evaluating My University's Strategies

PURPOSE

An important part of evaluating strategies is determining the nature and extent of changes in an organization's external opportunities/threats and internal strengths/weaknesses. Changes in these underlying critical success factors can indicate a need to change or modify the firm's strategies.

INSTRUCTIONS

As a class, discuss positive and negative changes in your university's external and internal factors during your college career. Begin by listing on the board new or emerging opportunities and threats. Then identify strengths and weaknesses that have changed significantly during your college career. In light of the external and internal changes that were identified, discuss whether your university's strategies need modifying. Are there any new strategies that you would recommend? Make a list to recommend to your department chair, dean, or chancellor.

EXPERIENTIAL EXERCISE 9C ▶

Who Prepares on Environmental Audit?

PURPOSE

The purpose of this activity is to determine the nature and prevalence of environmental audits among companies in your state.

INSTRUCTIONS

Contact by phone at least five different plant managers or owners of large businesses in your area. Seek answers to the questions listed below. Present your findings in a written report to your instructor.

1.   Does your company conduct an environmental audit? If yes, please describe the nature and scope of the audit.

2. Are environmental criteria included in the performance evaluation of managers? If yes, please specify the criteria.
3. Are environmental affairs more a technical function or a management function in your company?
4. Does your firm offer any environmental workshops for employees? If yes, please describe them.

Name Index

Note: Page numbers followed by *f* indicate figures; page numbers followed by *t* indicate tables; page numbers followed by *n* indicate notes.

SUBJECT INDEX

Note: Page numbers followed by *f* indicate figures; page numbers followed by *t* indicate tables.

Company Index

Note: Page numbers followed by *n* indicate notes. Page numbers followed by *t* indicate tables.

STRATEGIC
MANAGEMENT
CASES

SOUTHWEST AIRLINES CO.—2002

Amit Shah and Charles R. Sterrett
Frostburg State University

LUV

www.iflyswa.com

In the first week following the September 11, 2001, terrorist attacks, the shutdown of air travel, an exodus of travelers, and strict new security measures cost the airline industry close to $1 billion. Many major airlines responded by cutting their capacity by about 20 percent while tapping their lines of credit and hunting for more sources of cash. The airlines, their businesses already experiencing problems because of a sick economy, began to take desperate measures to avert disaster, and they lobbied the federal government for aid to rescue the industry. CEO Leo Mullins of Delta Air Lines stated, "The airline industry cannot be made the first (corporate) casualty of this war." A major question emerged: What would be the effect of the terrorist hijackings on the industry in both the short and long run, and, particularly, how would the "low price" companies such as Southwest Airlines be affected?

For eleven consecutive years (1991 through 2001), the Department of Transportation (DOT) *Air Travel Consumer Report* listed Southwest Airlines (tel. 214-792-4000 or 1-800-I-FLY-SWA) as among the top five of all major carriers for on-time performance, best baggage handling, and fewest customer complaints. In a highly competitive industry, all carriers continually strive to place first in any of these categories of the DOT report; Southwest is the only airline to ever hold the Triple Crown (first in all of the categories) for its annual performance. No other airline has earned the Triple Crown for even one month. In addition to this honor, Southwest is consistently among *Fortune* magazine's most admired companies (fourth in 2001), and it is also on the magazine's list of the one hundred best companies to work for. In September 1999, the *Wall Street Journal* also ranked Southwest among the top thirty companies on the basis of reputation—the only airline to make the cut. In addition to these achievements, Southwest continues to operate profitably; it made $625.2 million in net income on $5.6 billion in 2000 revenues. In an industry that historically has been awash in red ink, where airlines continually go in and out of bankruptcy or fail, Southwest has an enviable record of over twenty-eight consecutive years of operating at a profit. But, given the events of September 11 and the weeks that followed, could this record of success be sustained?

In their best-selling book *Nuts*, Kevin and Jackie Freiburg point to a company with people who are committed to working hard and having fun and who avoid following industry trends. The Freiburgs note that Southwest, based in Dallas, Texas, is a company which likes to keep prices at rock bottom; believes the customer comes second; runs recruiting ads that say, "Work at a place where wearing pants is optional"; paints its $30 million assets to look like killer whales and state flags; avoids trendy management programs; avoids formal, documented strategic planning; spends more time at planning parties than writing policies; and once settled a legal dispute by arm wrestling. Will this strategy and culture sustain the company through the rough years ahead?

(Note – If you are using the hardback *Strategic Management* textbook by Fred R. David, then refer to the External Issues part of the American Airlines Cohesion Case for additional information about Southwest Airlines.)

HISTORY AND GROWTH OF SOUTHWEST AIRLINES

According to Southwest folklore, the airline was conceived in 1967 on a napkin when Rollin King, an investment adviser, met with his lawyer, Herb Kelleher, to discuss his idea for a low-fare, no-frills airline to fly between three of the major cities in Texas. At that time, King ran an unprofitable air charter service between small Texas cities. One day, his banker, John Parker, suggested that King concentrate on flying between the three biggest cities in the state. Parker suggested that the market was open for exploitation because he could never get a seat on the airlines currently flying between those cities, and besides, the fares were too high. King knew he couldn't compete with the airlines currently serving the cities, so he decided to start a bigger one. He put together a plan and a feasibility study, and then he went to see Kelleher. In that meeting, King scribbled three lines on a cocktail napkin; labeled the points Houston, Dallas, and San Antonio; and muttered, "Herb, let's start our own airline." Kelleher loosened his tie and knitted his brow before replying. "Rollin, you're crazy," he said. "Let's do it!" Kelleher completed the necessary paperwork to create Air Southwest Co. (later renamed Southwest Airlines). Then the two filed for approval with the FAA; and on February 20, 1968, the Texas Aeronautical Commission approved their plans to fly between the three cities.

The very next day, the upstart airline ran into stiff opposition from several of the major carriers then doing business in Texas. On February 21, 1968, these carriers—Braniff, Texas International, and Continental—blocked approval with a temporary restraining order. They argued that Texas didn't need another carrier. For the next three years, Southwest was unable to proceed while it fought legal battles with these airlines over the right to offer flights between the three cities. In 1971, however, Southwest won the right to fly and began to offer service with a total of three planes and about two hundred employees. The efforts to quash the airline led to unbridled enthusiasm for the airline by King, Kelleher, and the other employees, which became an important part of Southwest's culture.

The outlook for Southwest, however, remained bleak. The legal battles left the airline flat broke and deep in debt. In its first year of operation, it lost $3.7 million, and it did not earn a profit for the next year and a half. But in 1973, it turned its first profit—and it never looked back. By 1978, it was one of the most profitable airlines in the country.

In its early years, Southwest faced other legal battles. For example, in 1974 a new airport opened to serve the greater Dallas-Fort Worth area; but it was farther from downtown Dallas than Love Field, the airport that had previously served the area. Southwest was using Love Field and wanted to continue to do so. But competitors wanted Southwest to move to the new airport to share in the costs, and they began to pressure Congress to pass a law barring flights from Love Field to any airport outside of the state of Texas. Southwest was able to negotiate a compromise, known as the Wright amendment, that allowed flights from Love Field to airports in the four states bordering on Texas. The Wright amendment forced Southwest into a key part of its strategy: to become an interstate carrier.

Southwest grew steadily and by 1975 had expanded its operations to eight more cities in Texas. By the end of the 1970s, it dominated the Texas market. Its major appeal was to passengers who wanted low prices and frequent departures. In the 1980s and 1990s, Southwest continued to expand, and by 1993, it was serving thirty-four cities in fifteen states. Southwest slowly, but methodically, moved across the Southwestern states into California, the Midwest, and the Northwest. It added new destinations in Florida and the East Coast. With its low prices and no-frills approach, it quickly dominated the markets it entered. In some markets, after Southwest entered, competitors soon withdrew, allowing the airline to expand even faster than projected. For example, when Southwest entered the California market in 1990, it quickly became the second-largest player, with over 20 percent of the intrastate market. Several competitors soon abandoned the Los Angeles-San Francisco route because they were unable to match Southwest's $59 one-way fare. Before Southwest entered this market, fares had been as high as $186 one way.

California offers a good example of the real dilemma facing competing carriers, which often referred to Southwest as a "500 pound cockroach that was too big to stamp out." While airfares were dropping, passenger traffic increased dramatically. But competitors, such as American and US Airways, were losing money on several key route segments, even though they cut service drastically. In late 1994, United began to fight back by launching a low-cost, high-frequency shuttle service on the West Coast. But it found that even a shuttle could not win against Southwest in a head-to-head battle. So United repositioned its shuttle away from Southwest's routes and even abandoned some routes altogether. According to the DOT, eight airlines surrendered West Coast routes to Southwest; at the same time, one-way fares fell by over 30 percent to an average of $60, and traffic increased by almost 60 percent. The major problem for the larger airlines was the fact that many of these West Coast routes were critical for feeding traffic into their highly profitable transcontinental and transpacific routes, and Southwest was cutting into that market.

Southwest is currently the fourth largest domestic carrier in terms of customers boarded. The airline has transformed itself from a regional carrier operating out of Dallas into a truly national carrier. At yearend 2001, the airline served 58 cities in 30 states and operated more than 2,800 flights a day with its fleet of 355 Boeing 737s. In 2001, Southwest flew 44.5 billion revenue passenger miles (RPMs) compared with 42.2 billion RPMs in 2000. But most remarkable is its twenty-ninth year in a row of profitable operations, with total operating revenue in 2001 being $5.55 billion—a decrease of 1.7 percent over 2000. Operating income in 2001 fell by 38.2 percent in 2000. Net income fell by 18.2 percent from $625.2 million in 2000 to 511.1 million in 2001. However, Southwest was the only profitable U.S. airline in 2001. Financial statements are shown in Exhibits 1 and 2.

MANAGEMENT

While Southwest was going through its traumatic beginnings, King and Kelleher realized they needed someone to run the company. King hired Lamar Muse, an executive who had airline experience, as CEO. Muse raised funding to keep the airline going and hired an experienced management team as company officers. He was able to purchase three brand new Boeing 737s at bargain-basement prices because Boeing had overproduced in a period when airlines were in a slump. Muse led the airline in its climb to profitability; but, in a dispute with the board, he was ousted in 1978. With Muse out, Kelleher moved into the top position, and he ran the airline until June 19, 2001. On that date, Mr. Kelleher was succeeded as CEO by Southwest's vice president and general counsel, James F. Parker, 54. Colleen C. Barrett, 56, who started her collaboration with Mr. Kelleher 34 years earlier as his legal secretary, would be president and chief operating officer. Mr. Kelleher is slated to remain as chairman for three years. Exhibit 3 shows the organizational chart of the company.

Mr. Parker has been the airline's top labor negotiator, making him well known to the company's employees, and, according to Mr. Kelleher, he has had a say in every important decision for a "long, long time." Ms. Barrett, the unsung hero of Southwest, has been the keeper and crusader of Southwest's culture, and she has successfully indoc-

EXHIBIT 1   Operating Statistics for Southwest Airlines

Consolidated Highlights

(in thousands except per-share amounts)	2001	2000	Change
Operating revenues	$5,555,174	$5,649,560	(1.7)%
Operating expenses	$4,924,052	$4,628,415	6.4%
Operating income	$631,122	$1,021,145	(38.2)%
Operating margin	11.4%	18.1%	(6.7)pts.
Net income	$511,147	$625,224*	(18.2)%
Net margin	9.2%	11.1%*	(1.9)pts.
Net income per share – basic	$0.67	$0.84*	(20.2)%
Net income per share – diluted	$0.63	$0.79*	(20.3)%
Stockholders' equity	$4,014,053	$3,451,320	16.3%
Return on average stockholders' equity	13.7%	19.9%	(6.2)pts.
Stockholders' equity per common share outstanding	$5.24	$4.53	15.7%
Revenue passengers carried	64,446,773	63,678,261	1.2%
Revenue passenger miles (RPMs) (000s)	44,493,916	42,215,162	5.4%
Available seat miles (ASMs) (000s)	65,295,290	59,909,965	9.0%
Passenger load factor	68.1%	70.5%	(2.4)pts.
Passenger revenue yield per RPM	12.09¢	12.95¢	(6.6)%
Operating revenue yield per ASM	8.51¢	9.43¢	(9.8)%
Operating expenses per ASM	7.54¢	7.73¢	(2.5)%
Employees at yearend	31,580	29,274	7.9%

*Excludes cumulative effect of change in accounting principle of $22.1 million ($.03 per share)
Source: 2001 Annual Report, p. 2.

trinated thousands of new workers into Southwest's ways. Parker's plan as CEO is to stay with the blueprint—keep Southwest the low-cost, low-fare, no-frills airline it has always been. "There will be no change in our core philosophy and our basic business model," he says. It's a model he helped shape as general counsel for fifteen years.

Even though the airline has grown to 31,580 employees at yearend 2001, Southwest's management team drives home the feeling that all of its people are part of one big family. Southwest's Culture Committee, formerly headed by Colleen Barrett, devised unique ways to preserve Southwest's underdog background and can-do spirit. She constantly reinforced the company's message that employees should be treated like customers and continually celebrated workers who went above and beyond the call of duty. Barrett also regularly visited each of the company's stations to reiterate the airline's history and to motivate employees. As keeper of the company's culture, Barrett commemorated all employee birthdays and special events with cards signed, "Herb and Colleen." Employees know the culture and expect others to live up to it. Donna Conover, another long-time Southwest employee, who also understands and supports the company's culture, will succeed Barrett as president and COO.

STRATEGY

Southwest's operation under Herb Kelleher has a number of characteristics that seem to contribute to its success. It has always been able to seize quickly a strategic opportunity whenever one arises. Other key factors are its conservative growth pattern, its cost-containment policy, and the commitment of its employees.

EXHIBIT 2   Southwest Airlines Co. Consolidated Statement of Income

(in thousands, except per share amounts)	Yearended December 31,		
	2001	2000	1999
OPERATING REVENUES:			
Passenger	$5,378,702	$5,467,965	$4,562,616
Freight	91,270	110,742	102,990
Other	85,202	70,853	69,981
Total operating revenues	5,555,174	5,649,560	4,735,587
OPERATING EXPENSES:			
Salaries, wages, and benefits	1,856,288	1,683,689	1,455,237
Fuel and oil	770,515	804,426	492,415
Maintenance materials and repairs	397,505	378,470	367,606
Agency commissions	103,014	159,309	156,419
Aircraft rentals	192,110	196,328	199,740
Landing fees and other rentals	311,017	265,106	242,002
Depreciation	317,831	281,276	248,660
Other operating expenses	975,772	859,811	791,932
Total operating expenses	4,924,052	4,628,415	3,954,011
OPERATING INCOME	631,122	1,021,145	781,576
OTHER EXPENSES (INCOME):			
Interest expense	69,827	69,889	54,145
Capitalized interest	(20,576)	(27,551)	(31,262)
Interest income	(42,562)	(40,072)	(25,200)
Other (gains) losses, net	(203,226)	1,515	10,282
Total other expenses (income)	(196,537)	3,781	7,965
INCOME BEFORE INCOME TAXES AND CUMULATIVE EFFECT OF CHANGE IN ACCOUNTING PRINCIPLE	827,659	1,017,364	773,611
PROVISION FOR INCOME TAXES	316,512	392,140	299,233
INCOME BEFORE CUMULATIVE EFFECT OF CHANGE IN ACCOUNTING PRINCIPLE	511,147	625,22	474,378
CUMULATIVE EFFECT OF CHANGE IN ACCOUNTING PRINCIPLE, NET OF INCOME TAXES	–	(22,131)	–
NET INCOME	$ 511,147	$ 603,093	$ 474,378
NET INCOME PER SHARE, BASIC BEFORE CUMULATIVE EFFECT OF CHANGE IN ACCOUNTING PRINCIPLE	$.67	$.84	$.63
CUMULATIVE EFFECT OF CHANGE IN ACCOUNTING PRINCIPLE	–	(.03)	–
NET INCOME PER SHARE, BASIC	$ .67	$ .81	$ .63
NET INCOME PER SHARE, DILUTED BEFORE CUMULATIVE EFFECT OF CHANGE IN ACCOUNTING PRINCIPLE	$ .63	$ .79	$ .59
CUMULATIVE EFFECT OF CHANGE IN ACCOUNTING PRINCIPLE	–	(.03)	–
NET INCOME PER SHARE, DILUTED	$ .63	$ .76	$ .59

Source: 2001 Annual Report, p. 9.

Kelleher always resisted attempts to expand too rapidly. His philosophy was to expand only when there were resources available to go into a new location with ten to twelve flights per day—not just one or two. For years, he also resisted the temptation to begin transcontinental operations or to get into a head-to-head battle with the major carriers on long-distance routes. But even with a conservative approach, Southwest expanded at a vigorous pace. Its debt has remained the lowest among U.S. carriers, and,

EXHIBIT 3   Southwest Organizational Chart

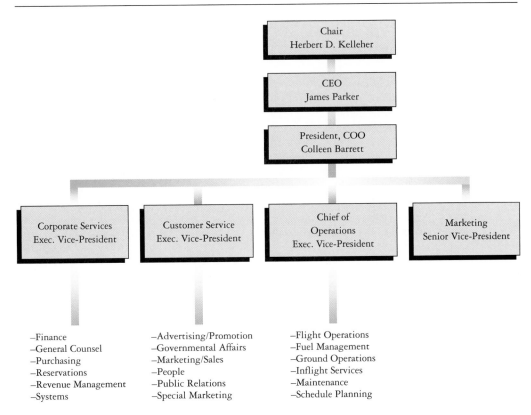

Source: Southwest Airlines Co. (February 1998).

with an A-rating, Southwest has the highest Standard & Poor's credit rating in the industry.

Southwest has made its mark by concentrating on flying large numbers of passengers on high frequency, short hops (usually one hour or less) at bargain fares. Southwest avoided the hub-and-spoke operations of its larger rivals, taking its passengers directly from city to city. Southwest also tends to avoid the more congested major airports in favor of smaller satellite fields. Kelleher revealed the niche strategy of Southwest when he noted that whereas other airlines set up hub-and-spoke systems in which passengers are shuttled to a few major hubs from which they are transferred to other planes going to their destinations, "we wound up with a unique market niche: We are the world's only short-haul, high-frequency, low-fare, point-to-point carrier. . . . We wound up with a market segment that is peculiarly ours, and everything about the airline has been adapted to serving that market segment in the most efficient and economical way possible." (See Exhibit 4.)

However, this strategy may be changing. Southwest has begun to introduce longer, nonstop trips on such routes as Baltimore, Maryland, to Las Vegas, Nevada (2,099 miles), and Austin, Texas, to Los Angeles, California (1,234 miles). Even one-stop trips are being added through central cities such as Nashville and Kansas City for coast-to-coast travel. The prospect of Southwest going long-haul on a grand scale is what "the

EXHIBIT 4   Southwest Airlines Co. Consolidated Balance Sheet

	DECEMBER 31,	
(in thousands, except per share amounts)	*2001*	*2000*
ASSETS		
Current assets:		
Cash and cash equivalents	$ 2,279,861	$ 522,995
Accounts and other receivables	71,283	138,070
Inventories of parts and supplies, at cost	70,561	80,564
Deferred income taxes	46,400	28,005
Prepaid expenses and other current assets	52,114	61,902
Total current assets	2,520,219	831,536
Property and equipment, at cost:		
Flight equipment	7,534,119	6,831,913
Ground property and equipment	899,421	800,718
Deposits on flight equipment purchase contracts	468,154	335,164
	8,901,694	7,967,795
Less allowance for depreciation	2,456,207	2,148,070
	6,445,487	5,819,725
Other assets	31,435	18,311
	$ 8,997,141	$ 6,669,572
LIABILITIES AND STOCKHOLDERS' EQUITY		
Current liabilities:		
Accounts payable	$ 504,831	$ 312,716
Accrued liabilities	547,540	499,874
Air traffic liability	450,407	377,061
Aircraft purchase obligations	221,840	—
Short-term borrowings	475,000	—
Current maturities of long-term debt	39,567	108,752
Total current liabilities	2,239,185	1,298,403
Long-term debt less current maturities	1,327,158	760,992
Deferred income taxes	1,058,143	852,865
Deferred gains from sale and leaseback of aircraft	192,342	207,522
Other deferred liabilities	166,260	98,470
Commitments and contingencies		
Stockholders' equity:		
Common stock, $1.00 par value: 2,000,000 shares authorized; 766,774 and 507,897 shares issued in 2001 and 2000, respectively	766,774	507,897
Capital in excess of par value	50,409	103,780
Retained earnings	3,228,408	2,902,007
Accumulated other comprehensive income (loss)	(31,538)	—
Treasury stock, at cost: 3,735 shares in 2000	—	(62,364)
Total stockholders' equity	4,014,053	3,451,320
	$ 8,997,141	$ 6,669,572

Source: 2001 *Annual Report,* p. 8.

genie [rivals] always hoped would not come out of the bottle," says analyst Kevin C. Murphy of Morgan Stanley Dean Witter. He believes that Southwest will continue its expansion and that it "will really rewrite the economics of the airline industry." This shifting strategy is downplayed by the fact that Southwest still flies about 80 percent of its flights on route that are shorter than 750 miles. "We're built for the short-haul markets, and we know that," says Chief Financial Officer Gary C. Kelly. Kelleher explains the jump into routes that are one-thousand-plus miles as a way to deal with the changes in the federal ticket tax in 1997 which was pushed by the bigger carriers. The incorporation of the new tax system replaced a percentage tax with a tax that included a flat, per-segment fee, which hits low-fare carriers harder.

Competitors believe that Southwest would have moved strongly into the long-haul flights market despite the altered tax requirements. "They've dug all the shallow holes," says Rona J. Dutta, senior vice president for planning at United Airlines, Inc. He also replies that the majors' low-fare units are increasing the competition in Southwest's core markets. Short-haul lines such as US Airways' MetroJet, Shuttle by United, and Delta Express may affect Southwest's profitability, but analysts say that with its lower costs and impressive balance sheet, Southwest should prevail.

Southwest continues to be the lowest-cost airline in its markets. Even when trying to match Southwest's cut-rate fares, the larger carriers could not do so without incurring substantial losses. Southwest's operating costs per available seat mile (the number of seats multiplied by the distance flown) average 15 to 25 percent below its rivals. One of the major factors in this enviable record is that all of its planes used to be of a single type—Boeing 737s—which dramatically lowered the company's cost of training, maintenance, and inventory. Because all Southwest crews know the 737 inside and out, they could substitute personnel rapidly from one flight to another in an emergency. In addition, Southwest recognized that planes only earn you money while they are in the air, so the company worked hard to achieve a faster turnaround time on the ground. Most airlines take up to one hour to unload passengers, clean and service the plane, and board new passengers. Southwest has a turnaround time for most flights of twenty minutes or less. Thorough knowledge of the 737 has helped in this achievement.

This ability to turn planes around rapidly, however, may now be jeopardized by the events after September 11. New government-mandated security procedures are expected to force airlines to spend as much as forty minutes or longer on the ground at each destination. This change will undoubtedly cause Southwest to incur added costs in its operations.

Southwest has also cut costs in the customer service area as well. Because its flights are usually one hour or less, it does not offer meals—only peanuts and drinks. Boarding passes are reusable plastic cards, and boarding time is saved since the airline has no assigned seating. The airline does not subscribe to any centralized reservation service. It will not even transfer baggage to other carriers: That is the passenger's responsibility. Even with this frugality, passengers do not seem to object, since the price is right.

Southwest has achieved a team spirit that others can only envy. One of the reasons for this team spirit is that the company truly believes that employees come first, not the customers. Southwest is known for providing its employees with tremendous amounts of information that will enable them to better understand the company, its mission, its customers, and its competition. Southwest believes that information is power. It is the resource that enables employees to do their jobs better. Armed with this knowledge, they are able to serve the customer better, and customers who deal with Southwest rarely get the runaround.

Even though unionized, Southwest has been able to negotiate flexible work rules that enabled it to meet the rapid turnaround schedules. It's not unusual for pilots to help flight attendants clean the airplanes or to help the ground crew load baggage.

Consequently, employee productivity is very high, and the airline is able to maintain a lean staff. In good times, Kelleher resisted the temptation to overhire, and he so avoided layoffs during lean times. Southwest has only laid off three people in twenty-five years—and it immediately hired them back. Even now, in the days after the attacks on September 11, 2001, as competitors announced job cuts of 20 percent, Southwest execs were scheming to cut costs in other ways. New plane deliveries were delayed, renovations to the company headquarters were scrapped—but layoffs were not considered. Said CEO Parker, "We are willing to suffer some damage, even to our stock price, to protect the jobs of our people." This employee retention policy has contributed to employees' feelings of security and a fierce sense of loyalty. The people of Southwest see themselves as crusaders whose mission is to give ordinary people the opportunity to fly.

Maximizing profitability is a major goal at Southwest. This leads to a drive to keep costs low and quality high. The airline's ideal service consists of safe, frequent, low-cost flights that get passengers to their destinations on time—and often closer to their destination than the major airlines do, because its competitors use larger airports farther from the cities. Southwest uses Dallas's Love Field, Houston Hobby airport, and Chicago's Midway, which are closer to their respective downtown areas, are less congested, and are, therefore, more convenient for the business traveler. This also helps Southwest's on-time performance.

In its marketing approach, Southwest always tries to set itself apart from the rest of the industry. It also played up its fun-loving, rebel reputation. In the early years, when the big airlines were trying to run Southwest out of business by undercutting its low fares, Southwest made its customers an unprecedented offer. In response to a Braniff ad offering a $13 fare to fly between Houston and Dallas, Southwest placed an ad that read, "Nobody's going to shoot Southwest Airlines out of the sky for a lousy $13." It then offered passengers the opportunity to purchase a ticket from Southwest for the same price, which was half the normal fare, or to buy a full-fare ticket for $26 and receive a bottle of premium whiskey along with it. The response was unprecedented. Southwest's planes were full and, for a short time, Southwest was one of the top liquor distributors in the state of Texas.

Southwest's ads always try to convince the customer that what the airline offers them is of real value to them. Southwest also believes it is in the business of making flying fun. With its ads, the company wants customers to know that when they fly Southwest, they'll have an experience unlike any other. Southwest promises safe, reliable, frequent, low-cost air transportation that is topped off with outstanding service. By keeping its promises, Southwest has earned extremely high credibility in every market it serves.

e-BUSINESS

Southwest has been aggressively marketing its services on the Internet, and it was the first airline to establish a home page on the Web. When *Fortune* magazine asked the experts which businesses have Web sites that work, the answer they got was "not many." However, Southwest was one of ten cited as a business doing it right. In the Internet travel race, many observers think Southwest has lost the battle to a subsidiary of American Airlines, Travelocity. Yet while American has been getting most of the attention, Southwest has been getting the business. According to a Nielsen/NetRatings' survey, 13.8 percent of the people who visited Southwest's site booked a flight. The company's "look-to-book" ratio is twice that of Travelocity and higher than that of any traditional retailer on the Web. Southwest, it seems, has been a success in turning browsers into buyers. Southwest reports that approximately 30 percent of its passenger revenue is generated by online bookings. Southwest's cost per booking via the Internet is about $1; in comparison, the cost per booking via a travel agent is about $10.

Southwest's Web site has also been named the top ranking Web site for customer satisfaction among major travel sites according to research conducted by Harris Interactive. The Southwest site scored a rating of 8.62 out of 10, with its Web site attracting 4 million unique visitors during March 2001. In the June 11, 2001, issue of *InternetWeek*, Southwest's Web site was named as one of the top one hundred e-businesses in the United States, as determined by the publication's survey.

COMPETITORS

Three of Southwest's major competitors are United Airlines, Delta Air Lines, and America West Airlines. Before September 11, 2001, United, with over ninety thousand employees, was one of Southwest's most formidable competitors, and it still remains so in many of Southwest's markets. United, the number two U.S. airline, flies over five hundred aircraft to about 140 locations in the United States and overseas. In addition, it operates United Express, which feeds passengers from regional carriers into the United system, and its United Shuttle provides over 450 short-haul flights between twenty cities in the western states. The latter service is one that has often put United into direct competition with Southwest.

Delta, the third largest U.S. carrier, has over sixty-three thousand employees. Delta flies to about 225 U.S. and foreign locations, and it is particularly strong throughout much of the southern tier of the United States, where two of its major hubs—Atlanta and Dallas-Fort Worth—are located. Delta has also built up a low-fare regional carrier service, Delta Express, and it has acquired a minority stake in three regional airlines which can feed passengers into its several hubs. Delta has begun to focus much of its attention on its transatlantic operations, but it remains a strong U.S. competitor and is intent on attracting more business traffic.

America West, the smallest of Southwest's competitors, has about eleven thousand employees. The airline serves 144 cities in the United States and seven foreign locations in Mexico and Canada. America West has strong positions in its hubs, Phoenix and Las Vegas. However, many of its locations put it into direct competition with Southwest. With Continental and Mesa Airlines, which have small stakes in America West, America West has formed alliances which give it access to another thirty-five destinations.

All of the competitors have come into head-to-head competition with Southwest on several occasions. Southwest always welcomed competition and firmly believes it can come out ahead in any of those situations. Kelleher, when asked about his thoughts on facing a competitor such as the United Shuttle head-on, stated, "I think its good to have some real competitive activity that gets your people stirred up and renews their vigor and their energy and their desire to win. I think that United's Shuttle assault on Southwest Airlines, which was a very direct assault, drew our people closer together and made them better as a consequence."

Long-haul success for Southwest will put pressure on the profits realized by its bigger competitors. The cost advantage for Southwest includes the rapid twenty-minute gate turnarounds; an efficient all-Boeing 737 fleet, including new 737-700s that can fly cross-country nonstop; and a more productive workforce. Even if longer flights increase the costs, Southwest still realizes a significant competitive advantage. Roberts, Roach & Associates Inc., an airline consultant in Hayward, California, says that Southwest has at least a 59 percent cost advantage over bigger rivals at flights of five hundred miles, as well as a 35 percent lead for flights at fifteen hundred miles. "It's a huge threat," says a rival airline executive. These long-haul flights will be a new focus for Southwest's higher-cost rivals. Already, according to an estimate by analyst Samuel C. Buttrick from Paine Webber, Inc., nonstop flights longer than one thousand miles account for more than 16 percent of Southwest's capacity.

But, all this may be changing, based on the events of September 11. One analyst at Atlanta-based Raymond James & Associates stated, "We're seeing a restructuring of the industry." US Airways' low-fare MetroJet service to Fort Lauderdale was shut down before Christmas 2001. Gone, too, is Delta's Delta Express low-fare service to that city. What's happening in Florida is just an example of what's happening elsewhere in the industry. AirTran CEO Joe Leonard said, "In our market, the eastern U.S., there are four thousand fewer flights today (October 25) than [on] September 10." During 2001, Southwest added service to West Palm Beach, Florida, and to Norfolk, Virginia, while discontinuing service to San Francisco.

Metrojet and Delta Express in the East and United's Shuttle in the West were launched to compete with Southwest. But they couldn't match Southwest and were thought to be marginally profitable at best. Now, MetroJet and United's Shuttle are phasing out, and Delta Express is grounding half its service, while Southwest hasn't cut it's schedule at all. Other major carriers are dropping or reducing regular flights to mid-size cities that weren't profitable enough. For passengers, the effect of schedule cutbacks will mean fewer flights to choose from and, possibly, fewer airline choices on routes they fly. This situation may open the door to low-fare carriers like Southwest that can make money in those locations.

Before the attacks on September 11, discount carriers were even beginning to make inroads with cost-conscious business travelers. The low-fare carriers were doing better because they don't rely on high business fares and don't offer the frills the major carriers offer. In 1994, revenues earned by low-fare carriers represented 5 percent of the $76 billion U.S. air travel market. By 2001, their share was 10 percent, according to Raymond James & Associates. Also, several of the nation's most important business markets are now home to successful low-fare airlines, such as JetBlue, AirTran, Frontier, and so on. Joe Leonard of AirTran says, "What's important now is staying power—the ability first of all to survive, see what happens, and act fast."

THE FUTURE

Today, Southwest provides service to only fifty-eight cities, so there are tremendous opportunities for expansion. The problem: Where to go next? Over one hundred cities have asked the airline to begin service in their communities because of the positive impact the company has had when it began operations in a new location. The introduction of Southwest's low fares and frequent flights opens up the market and gives many more people the freedom to fly. But the events of September 11, as well as economic recession, have put all expansion plans on hold for the present.

Southwest continues to forge ahead in other ways. The airline introduced a new aircraft to the fleet in October 1997: the Boeing 737–700. Southwest was the launch customer for this aircraft, which is able to fly high, fast, and far and still be fuel-efficient. Southwest has purchased ninety-two of these aircraft, which require less maintenance time than the traditional 737s, but future purchases have been delayed to save costs in the current environment.

In 1997, Southwest Airlines added a twenty-four-hour emergency medical service for its customers for in-flight medical emergencies. The airline now has emergency room physicians on call twenty-four hours a day through a service called MedLink. MedLink can put a physician in contact with Southwest's flight attendants during a medical emergency. The physician can make diagnoses, advise treatments, and issue medical recommendations, including whether or not an emergency landing should be made. Southwest is the first major airline to make the medical service accessible by in-flight telephone.

Throughout it history, Southwest consistently followed a clearly defined purpose and a well-thought-out strategy: to make a profit, achieve job security for every employee, and make flying affordable for more people. Can Southwest continue to maintain this strategy? Will its position remain unassailable by competitors—especially with the growing presence of other low-fare carriers? What are the implications of expanding to longer-haul operations? Will Southwest begin to lose the distinguishing characteristics that were the hallmarks of its success? What will be the effects of September 11 and the shakeout occurring in the industry on Southwest? How should Southwest be prepared to respond to these events? And how about international routes—especially to Canada or Mexico, our NAFTA partners, where business travel is growing as a result of this treaty? Southwest certainly has come a long way from the little company with three aircraft that began operations in 1971. What's next?

US AIRWAYS GROUP, INC.—2002

John C. Urbanski and Eugene M. Bland
Francis Marion University

U

www.usairways.com

The September 11, 2001, terrorist attacks on the United States had serious repercussions for the U.S. airline industry. Passenger traffic immediately dropped precipitously; not only did passengers cancel reservations and avoid air travel out of fear for their lives, but also the the U.S. government ordered the complete grounding of all nonmilitary aircraft for a period of several days. Additionally, the government completely shut down operations at Reagan International Airport in Washington, D.C., for an extended period of time.

A resulting major loss in revenue was experienced by all U.S. commercial passenger operations. Indeed, Midway Airlines, which had been in some significant financial difficulty for an extended period before these events, immediately and permanently ceased operations, going "belly-up." Some carriers, such as Southwest Airlines, were in a better financial position to weather this drastic revenue loss. Other carriers, in financial straits before September 11 due to a downturn in passenger travel, found themselves on the brink of disaster. US Airways was one of the most notable and vulnerable of these carriers.

HISTORY

Beginnings

US Airways began operation in western Pennsylvania in 1939 as All American Aviation, flying airmail service to smaller communities in western Pennsylvania and eastern Ohio. In 1949, the company changed its name to All American Airways and began operations as a passenger carrier with the acquisition of World War II surplus DC-3 aircraft, but it maintained regional service in Pennsylvania and Ohio. The company changed its name again in 1953 to Allegheny Airlines. For the next fifteen years, Allegheny remained a small regional carrier, but in 1968, combined with Lake Central Airlines, a small regional carrier serving Ohio, Indiana, and Missouri, the company began an expansion that would continue for the next twenty-odd years.

Large-Scale Growth

Allegheny's growth consisted primarily of a continuing series of acquisitions of and mergers with smaller regional carriers whose service areas were roughly contiguous with that of its own existing service region. In 1972, Allegheny acquired Mohawk Airlines, thus allowing Allegheny to begin servicing New York State as well as New England. This made Allegheny the world's sixth-largest airline, measured by the total number of customers boarded. In 1979, after deregulation of the airline industry by the now defunct federal Civil Aeronautics Board (CAB), Allegheny initiated new, long-distance

(Note – If you are using the hardback *Strategic Management* textbook by Fred R. David, then refer to the External Issues part of the American Airlines Cohesion Case for additional information about Southwest Airlines.)

14

routes between cities in its current network and cities in Florida, California, Texas, Arizona, and Colorado. Allegheny changed its name to USAir to reflect its new national service orientation.

In 1987, in competition for a share of the West Coast market, USAir returned to its former growth formula, acquiring Pacific Southwest Airlines, based in San Diego, California, as a wholly-owned subsidiary of USAir. In addition to increasing the size of USAir's service area, this acquisition also provided a feeder system for many of USAir's transcontinental routes. In 1987, Piedmont Airlines, a large carrier serving the U.S. Mid-Atlantic region, also became a subsidiary of USAir, a reflection of USAir's continuing expansion into contiguous markets. In 1988, Pacific Southwest Airlines was merged into USAir.

In 1989, USAir made a quantum leap in the size of its service region, as well as in the nature of the airline's service area, by completing the acquisition of Piedmont and merging it into USAir. Not only was this the largest airline merger in history at the time, but with the assumption of Piedmont's international routes, it also transformed USAir into an international carrier. It also gave USAir control of Piedmont's major airport hubs in Charlotte, North Carolina, and Baltimore, Maryland.

Expansion in the 1990s

Throughout the 1990s, USAir continued to expand. Service was instituted to Frankfurt, Germany, from USAir's major hubs in Pittsburgh and Charlotte, as well as to London, England, from Charlotte, Philadelphia, and Baltimore. USAir also initiated service to Rome, Italy, Munich, Germany, and Madrid, Spain, from its Philadelphia hub. Service area growth also continued with the expansion of shorter international routes serviced by US Airways Express to various destinations in the Caribbean basin and Canada. Caribbean expansion has continued into late 2001.

In 1992, USAir entered into a domestic marketing agreement with the then-named Trump Shuttle and purchased a minority position in that airline, which continued operations as the USAir Shuttle. The shuttle provided hourly service between New York-LaGuardia and Boston as well as between New York and Washington, D.C.-National, later renamed Reagan International. In 1998, USAir acquired the shuttle operation outright. During this period, USAir, now US Airways as a result of a name change in 1997, began the operation of MetroJet, a startup subsidiary designed to provide single-class low-fare service in the eastern United States.

Today, US Airways is the sixth-largest carrier in the United States and serves 204 locations in the United States, Europe, Canada, the Caribbean, and Mexico. In the past several years, however, the fiscal health of US Airways has been in steady decline. The company operated 472 aircraft at yearend 2001 as indicated in Exhibit 1.

The fortunes of most of the companies in the U.S. airline industry are tied closely to economic fluctuations, demand for air transportation being positively correlated to general economic conditions. With more available disposable income, people travel more. When the economy is expanding, businesses require their employees to travel more often in order to address organizational requirements. Airline operations are also sensitive to specific economic factors, such as fuel prices and labor activity, that addresses employee compensation issues. The U.S. and global economies in 2001–2002 have not done well.

Recent Setbacks

Labor unrest and the threat of a work stoppage immediately upon expiration of the pilots' union contract in March 2000 resulted in a significant decline in US Airways

EXHIBIT 1   US Airways' Aircaft at Yearend 2001

A. US Airways Aircraft

Type	Average Seat Capacity	Average Age (years)	Owned[1]	Leased[2]	Total
Airbus A330	266	1.4	9	–	9
Boeing 767-200ER	203	12.7	7	4	11
Boeing 757-200	182	11.2	23	11	34
Airbus A321	169	0.7	15	8	23
Airbus A320	145	2.1	11	13	24
Boeing 737-400	144	12.0	19	35	54
McDonnell Douglas MD-80	141	19.3	11	3	14
Boeing 737-300	126	14.8	11	74	85
Airbus A319	120	1.9	22	44	66
Fokker 100	97	11.1	21	1	22
		9.1	149	193	342

[1]Of the owned aircraft, 127 were pledged as collateral for various secured financing arrangements.
[2]The terms of the leases expire between 2002 and 2023.

B. US Airways' Regional Airline Aircraft

Type	Seat Capacity	Average Age (years)	Owned	Leased[1]	Total
de Havilland Dash 8-300	50	10.0	–	8	8
de Havilland Dash 8-100/200	37	10.4	26	73	99
Dornier 328-110	32	6.3	–	25	25
		9.6	26	106	132

[1]The terms of the leases expire between 2002 and 2009.
Source: US Airways 2001 *Form 10K,* p. 10 and 11.

ticket sales. In May 2000, a consolidation with United Airlines was proposed as a method both of reducing the operating costs of both carriers and of remaining competitive in the face of expansion into US Airways territory by other carriers. Fuel costs also continued to increase. For 2000, US Airways posted a net loss of $269 million, its first loss since 1994.

During 2001, the economy continued its cool-down. Despite a 12 percent increase in passenger traffic over the same period in 1999, rising costs caused US Airways to continue to lose money at an alarming rate. Losses for the first two quarters of 2001 totaled $196 million. To make matters worse, despite the approval of the European Union and despite the earlier acquisition of TWA by American Airlines, making it the world's largest carrier, the proposed consolidation of US Airways and United broke down in the face of likely opposition from the U.S. government. By August 2001, United had backed out of merger negotiations, and the proposed consolidation was a dead issue. Then at yearend 2001, US Airways posted a whopping $2.11 billion loss for the year. The company's yearend 2001 financial statements are provided in Exhibits 2 through 5.

EXHIBIT 2   US Airways Group, Inc., Consolidated Statements of Operations Year Ended December 31, (dollars in millions, except per share amounts)

	2001	2000	1999
Operating Revenues			
Passenger transportation	$ 7,164	$ 8,341	$ 7,685
Cargo and freight	164	164	149
Other	960	764	761
Total Operating Revenues	8,288	9,269	8,595
Operating Expenses			
Personnel costs	3,726	3,637	3,380
Aviation fuel	1,103	1,284	727
Aircraft rent	573	519	480
Other rent and landing fees	449	448	430
Aircraft maintenance	532	504	499
Other selling expenses	368	419	379
Depreciation and amortization	392	369	341
Commissions	279	371	484
Asset impairments and other special charges	958	–	45
Airline stabilization act grant	(320)	–	–
Other	1,911	1,771	1,694
Total Operating Expenses	9,971	9,322	8,459
Operating Income (Loss)	(1,683)	(53)	136
Other Income (Expense)			
Interest income	61	76	66
Interest expense	(297)	(251)	(193)
Interest capitalized	18	33	38
Merger termination fee	50	–	–
Gain on sale of investment	–	–	274
Other, net	(1)	(28)	24
Other Income (Expense), Net	(169)	(170)	209
Income (Loss) Before Income Taxes and Cumulative Effect of Accounting Change	(1,852)	(223)	345
Provision (Credit) for Income Taxes	272	(57)	148
Income (Loss) Before Cumulative Effect of Accounting Change	(2,124)	(166)	197
Cumulative Effect of Accounting Change, Net of Applicable Income Taxes of $5 Million and $63 Million, respectively	7	(103)	–
Net Income (Loss)	$ (2,117)	$ (269)	$ 197
Earnings (Loss) per Common Share			
Basic			
Before Cumulative Effect of Accounting Change	$ (31.59)	$ (2.47)	$ 2.69
Cumulative Effect of Accounting Change	$ 0.11	$ (1.55)	$ –
Net Earnings (Loss) per Common Share	$ (31.48)	$ (4.02)	$ 2.69
Diluted			
Before Cumulative Effect of Accounting Change	$ (31.59)	$ (2.47)	$ 2.64
Cumulative Effect of Accounting Change	$ 0.11	$ (1.55)	$ –
Net Earnings (Loss) per Common Share	$ (31.48)	$ (4.02)	$ 2.64
Shares Used for Computation (000)			
Basic	67,227	66,855	73,316
Diluted	67,227	66,855	74,603

Source: US Airways 2001 *Form 10K,* p. 37.

EXHIBIT 3   US Airways Group, Inc., Consolidated Balance Sheets December 31, (dollars in millions, except per share amount)

Assets	2001	2000
Current Assets		
Cash	$ 36	$ 40
Cash equivalents	557	503
Short-term investments	485	773
Receivables, net	281	331
Materials and supplies, net	209	249
Deferred income taxes	–	428
Prepaid expenses and other	207	268
Total Current Assets	1,775	2,592
Property and Equipment		
Flight equipment	7,472	6,762
Ground property and equipment	1,211	1,148
Less accumulated depreciation and amortization	(4,075)	(3,118)
	4,608	4,792
Purchase deposits for flight equipment	85	197
Total Property and Equipment	4,693	4,989
Other Assets		
Goodwill, net	531	551
Pension assets	411	401
Other intangibles, net	343	313
Other assets, net	272	281
Total Other Assets	1,557	1,546
	$ 8,025	$ 9,127

Liabilities and Stockholders' Equity (Deficit)		
Current Liabilities		
Current maturities of long-term debt	$ 159	$ 284
Accounts payable	625	538
Traffic balances payable and unused tickets	817	890
Accured aircraft rent	257	358
Accrued salaries, wages and vacation	372	324
Other accrued expenses	796	524
Total Current Liabilities	3,026	2,918
Noncurrent Liabilities		
Long-term debt, net of current maturities	3,515	2,688
Accrued aircraft rent	293	182
Deferred gains, net	589	606
Postretirement benefits other than pensions	1,474	1,407
Employee benefit liabilities and other	1,743	1,684
Total Noncurrent Liabilities	7,614	6,567
Commitments and Contingencies		
Stockholders' Equity (Deficit)		
Common Stock, par value $1 per share, issued 101,172,000 shares	101	101
Paid-in capital	2,185	2,241
Retained earnings (deficit)	(2,937)	(820)
Common Stock held in treasury, at cost, 33,584,000 shares and 34,166,000 shares, respectively	(1,749)	(1,807)
Deferred compensation	(62)	(75)
Accumulated other comprehensive income (loss), net of income tax effect	(153)	2
Total Stockholders' Equity (Deficit)	(2,615)	(358)
	$ 8,025	$ 9,127

Source: US Airways 2001 *Form 10K*, p. 38.

EXHIBIT 4   US Airways Operating Segment Information
(in millions)

	YEAR ENDED DECEMBER 31,		
	2001	*2000*	*1999*
Operating Revenues:			
US Airways external	$ 7,220	$8,295	$7,764
US Airways intersegment	70	75	67
US Airways Express external	983	893	798
US Airways Express intersegment	61	47	33
All Other	85	81	33
Intersegment elimination	(131)	(122)	(100)
	$ 8,288	$9,269	$8,595
Depreciation and amortization:			
US Airways	$ 376	$ 355	$ 327
US Airways Express	16	14	14
All Other	–	–	–
	$ 392	$ 369	$ 341
Interest income:			
US Airways	$ 77	$ 95	$ 187
US Airways Express	1	2	2
All Other	125	146	96
Intercompany elimination	(142)	(167)	(219)
	$ 61	$ 76	$ 66
Interest expense:			
US Airways	$ 319	$ 274	$ 205
US Airways Express	4	4	4
All Other	83	102	173
Intercompany elimination	(109)	(129)	(189)
	$ 297	$ 251	$ 193
Income (Loss) Before Income Taxes and Cumulative Effect of Accounting Change:	$(1,860)	$ (349)	$ 18
US Airways	(9)	94	132
US Airways Express	17	32	195
All Other	$(1,852)	$ (223)	$ 345
Capital Expenditures:			
US Airways	$ 1,104	$1,948	$1,419
US Airways Express	23	12	10
All Other	8	18	19
	$ 1,135	$1,978	$1,448
Assets:			
US Airways	$ 6,999	$7,768	
US Airways Express	169	162	
All Other	857	1,197	
	$ 8,025	$9,127	

Source: US Airways 2001 *Form 10K,* p. 63.

EXHIBIT 5   Selected US Airways Operating and Financial Statistics[1]

	2001	2000[2]	1999[2]
Revenue passengers (thousands)*	56,114	60,636	57,397
Total RPMs (millions)[3]	45,979	47,065	41,878
RPMs (millions)*	45,948	47,012	41,793
Total ASMs (millions)[4]	66,744	66,919	59,925
ASMs (millions)*	66,704	66,851	59,815
Passenger load factor*[5]	68.9%	70.3%	69.9%
Break-even load factor[6]	80.8%	73.0%	69.5%
Yield*[7]	14.32¢	16.28¢	17.15¢
Passenger revenue per ASM*[8]	9.86¢	11.45¢	11.98¢
Revenue per ASM[9]	10.92¢	12.51¢	13.02¢
Cost per ASM[10]	12.46¢	12.72¢	12.99¢
Average passenger journey (miles)*	819	775	728
Average stage length (miles)*	667	633	604
Cost of aviation fuel per gallon[11]	86.28¢	95.76¢	58.61¢
Cost of aviation fuel per gallon, excluding fuel taxes[12]	80.09¢	89.11¢	52.41¢
Gallons of aviation fuel consumed (millions)	1,208	1,267	1,170
Operating aircraft at yearend	342	417	393
Full-time equivalent employees at yearend	35,232	43,467	42,016

*Scheduled service only (excludes charter service).

[1]Operating statistics include free frequent travelers and the related miles they flew. Unusual items (see Note 13 to US Airways' Notes to Consolidated Financial Statements for additional information) and revenues and expenses associated with US Airways' capacity purchase arrangements with certain affiliated airlines have been excluded from US Airways' financial results for purposes of financial statistical calculation and to provide better comparability between periods.

[2]Includes the activity of the former Shuttle on a pro forma basis as if it was merged into US Airways as of January 1, 1999. Also, effective January 1, 2000, US Airways changed its accounting policy related to Dividend Miles revenue recognition. The 1999 amount is presented on a pro forma basis to show what US Airways would have reported if the new accounting policy had been in effect in periods prior to 2000.

[3]Revenue Passenger Miles (RPMs)—revenue passengers multiplied by the number of miles they flew.

[4]Available Seat Miles (ASMs)—seats available multiplied by the number of miles flown (a measure of capacity).

[5]Percentage of aircraft seating capacity that is actually utilized (RPMs/ASMs).

[6]Percentage of aircraft seating capacity utilized that equates to US Airways breaking-even at the pretax income level.

[7]Passenger transportation revenue divided by RPMs.

[8]Passenger transportation revenue divided by ASMs (a measure of unit revenue).

[9]Total Operating Revenues divided by ASMs (a measure of unit revenue).

[10]Total Operating Expenses divided by ASMs (a measure of unit cost).

[11]Includes fuel taxes and transportation charges.

[12]Includes transportation charges (excludes fuel taxes).

Source: US Airways, 2001 Form 10K, pp. 29–30.

STRATEGY

Hub Operations

The hub system currently used by all major carriers other than Southwest ideally allows any airline to fly passengers to any destination on the globe. Rather than fly directly from an origination point A to destination B, as was the practice before airline deregulation, passengers fly from origination point A to the airline's hub and then transfer to another aircraft, which flies them to destination B (along with passengers from origination points C, D, E, etc.). The hub system also allows airlines to feed passengers from small markets into the carrier's transcontinental and international routes, thus allowing competition in these markets as well. In essence, with a strategically placed hub, any airline can compete for passengers flying on any route as long as there is space at the hub and destination terminals.

Hub size often varies substantially among carriers. Among the major carriers, US Airways suffers from two hub-related drawbacks. First, its hubs are smaller in capacity than those of other carriers, creating a bottleneck for the transfer of passengers and limiting the number of aircraft the hub can handle at any one time. As noted earlier, US Airways began addressing this shortcoming by expanding the facilities at several of its hubs. Second, and perhaps more telling, its hubs are bunched together geographically, being limited to several cities on the East Coast of the United States, specifically Boston, New York-LaGuardia, Pittsburgh, Philadelphia, Baltimore, Washington, D.C., and Charlotte. This East Coast concentration makes its route network more difficult to defend from competition. In contrast, Delta Airlines, one of US Airways main competitors, has the world's busiest hub in Atlanta, a major hub in Dallas/Fort Worth, another in Salt Lake City, and a smaller facility in Cinncinati.

Load Factor

As a result of this hub system, the phrase *too much of a good thing* now applies to seat capacity of both individual airlines and the industry in general. There is a more than an ample supply of seats offered by numerous carriers, all of which serve a majority of the same routes. Fare prices fluctuate as with any commodity, and they affect the load factor, the percentage of filled seats on any given flight. Increase the load factor above breakeven (B/E), which is the expense required to fly the aircraft to a destination plus a portion of fixed costs, and profits result. Decrease the load factor and losses occur. Any small "twitch" in load factor, and the resultant financial effect can be critical to airlines, an industry which has traditionally operated on a 1 percent to 2 percent margin.

The primary goal of US Airways, as with most of its competitors, is to move "load factor" above the breakeven point into the profit range. This can be accomplished by raising the number of paying passengers per flight, by lowering operating costs or a portion of fixed costs and thus lowering the breakeven point, or some combination of both approaches.

Some type of fare war is the generally accepted method that is used to attempt increasing load capacity. The addition of a passenger does not have a significant effect on operating expenses, but it does significantly affect revenue. By offering the lowest priced fares to a destination, an airline hopes to lure customers from competitors—and even increase the amount of overall passenger traffic by attracting passengers who would not have considered air travel under a higher pricing structure. This allows the airline to significantly increase load capacity and to reach profitability. This also may be used to increase overall market share for any particular route, and in extreme form, it may often be used to drive the competition from the market, just as Southwest Airlines did in the West Coast market in the mid-1990s. Revenue may also be generated by increasing the service area or by increasing profitability on core routes to cover underperformance on other routes. Promotional "e-fares," available at the airline's Web site, offer significantly reduced fares for last minute travelers as a method of filling seats which would otherwise go unfilled. Airlines may also attempt to attract customers by increasing the levels of customer service significantly above that of competitors in areas such as overbooking, on-time arrivals, reductions in lost luggage, and other sensitive areas. US Airways continues to engage in fare reduction activity, both proactively and as a reaction to the fare reduction activities of its competitors. This is especially critical to US Airways due to the significantly increasing presence of its competitors in the company's regional market.

Generic Solutions

Reducing operating expenses is not easily accomplished. Unlike other commodities, supply cannot be adjusted to demand. "Production" of seating cannot be curtailed, nor can excess inventory be warehoused until needed. A Boeing 767 cannot be "sized" to meet fluctuations in demand. It costs roughly as much to operate an aircraft carrying one passenger as it does one carrying a full load. Operating costs can often be addressed only by reducing the cost of a contributing factor, such as a reduction in fuel expense or payroll expenses, or by eliminating passenger amenities, such as meals. One attempt to match demand to supply, which has had limited success, is switching aircraft type to match route demand. Thus, a route using a 203-seat 767 but averaging only 100 passengers may switch to a 737, which has a lower operating expense but a maximum capacity approaching average demand. Operating costs may also be addressed through aircraft type. The carrier may limit the type of aircraft in its fleet, lowering costs through standardization in maintenance, flexibility in crew assignments, and reduced turnaround time; or it may purchase more efficient aircraft types, reducing expenditures for fuel or other costs.

Current Restructuring

US Airways' current strategy is aimed at reducing operating expenses and increasing expansion of its international operation. Even though the company services international destinations, it is still primarily a regional carrier, albeit a larger one than it once was. Its expense structure, however, mirrors that of a large international carrier, while its revenues do not. After the collapse of the proposed merger with United and before the terrorist attacks of September 11, US Airways had already begun refocusing and restructuring activities in order to regain profitability. In an effort to match seat supply to route demand, the company reassigned regional-type aircraft to underperforming critical core routes to increase load factors. This type of aircraft offers great flexibility, since it has a smaller capacity, is significantly more efficient to operate, and has a shorter turnaround time than larger aircraft. The company's discretion in reassigning this type of aircraft is currently subject to restrictions. Under the existing labor agreement, use of this type of aircraft in the US Airways fleet was capped at seventy. As a result, many nontranscontinental-length routes are served by turboprop aircraft, which are not able to operate efficiently in routes with greater stage lengths. An increase in the use of regional jets would allow an increase in operating efficiency on these routes. At this time, US Airways has sixty regional jets in service.

As mentioned earlier, US Airways also entered into an agreement with Airbus to substantially modernize its fleet of major aircraft, ordering approximately four hundred Airbus A320 aircraft, with the first deliveries occurring in 1999. These aircraft replaced older Boeing 737s and 727s as well as variations of the DC-9 aircraft in the US Airways inventory. Compared to the aircraft being retired, the new-generation Airbus jets provide significantly increased fuel efficiency, have significantly lower maintenance costs, have longer operational ranges, and provide increased passenger amenities. This move to aircraft standardization also increased certain maintenance EOS, increased crew flexibility, and reduced crew training expenses. The company also ordered up to forty Airbus A330 wide-body aircraft for use in an expanded system of transatlantic routes. The acquisition of these aircraft offers the same advantages as the acquisition of the A320 aircraft. Both moves, however, create the paradox of increasing capacity in the face of a continued decline in demand. Due to the precarious financial position of the company, however, scheduled delivery of some A320 and A330 aircraft are being deferred from 2003–2006 until 2005–2009 in order to reduce debt and free cash.

US Airways is also addressing the reduction of overhead. Personnel costs represent the largest of US Airways expenses. To address these expenses, US Airways entered into labor contracts in 1999 and 2000 with several groups of employees. All contracts contained a parity clause, which ties employee compensation to the weighted average cost plus 1 percent of comparable positions in the four largest U.S. airlines, bringing compensation expenses to a more reasonable level. However, the company's operations and revenue structure still do not mirror that of these four airlines. In a related issue, as mentioned earlier, the company's labor contract with the Air Line Pilots Association (ALPA) capped the number of regional jets the company could use on its longer-leg regional routes. These jets are operated by several of the company's wholly-owned subsidiaries, such as US Airways Express and MetroJet. Pilots working for these subsidiaries are paid significantly less than their counterparts, who fly jet aircraft in US Airways' main fleet. The cap on the use of regional jet aircraft is an attempt to address this pay inequity issue. As business continued to decline in 2001, the company again began to address labor issues. It began attempts to gain salary concessions from several of its unions in order to further reduce labor overhead, and it began pressuring ALPA to abandon the current cap on use of regional-type jet aircraft. The terrorist attacks of September 11 resulted both in the layoff of approximately 25 percent (eleven thousand) of US Airways employees and a 23 percent cut in flight capacity. Both developments strengthened the company's negotiating position.

International Operations

To take advantage of an annual increase in foreign travel to and from the United States over the past several years, US Airways also continued its efforts to increase its presence in the international arena, specifically in its service to western Europe. Although the concentration of its various hubs along the East Coast of the United States makes US Airways vulnerable to other regional low-cost competition, it does provide an ideal jumping-off point for transAtlantic flights, since the majority of passengers traveling between Europe and the United States begin or end their travel in the eastern United States. To support international expansion, the company addressed needs in several areas. As mentioned, it began acquiring a new generation of wide-bodied aircraft to facilitate long-haul international routes. In keeping with this hub's role as US Airway's primary international gateway, it also began a major upgrade of its international terminal at its Philadelphia hub. The company has also expanded the number of international destinations served, adding Amsterdam in the Netherlands and Brussels, Belgium, in 2001. US Airways also petitioned the U.S. Department of Transportation for authority to begin service to Heathrow Airport in London. The company currently serves Gatwick, another London-area facility. US Airways also continued expanding service to the Caribbean basin, another region conveniently served from the eastern United States. Even after September 11 and a 23 percent decline in service, US Airways announced service to new Caribbean destinations. The potential payoff from international expansion remains unclear; despite an 8 percent growth in international travel in 2000, a 1.3 percent decline in the first half of 2001 mirrored the decline in domestic travel. US Airway's domestic versus foreign revenues are given in Exhibit 6.

COMPETITORS

Although US Airways is the sixth-largest airline in the United States at present, much of its competition comes from smaller regional carriers as well as from other majors. Southwest Airlines is one of the chief thorns in the side of US Airways. Southwest

EXHIBIT 6   Operating Revenues (based on revenue passenger miles and yield) in Principal Geographic Areas (in millions)

	2001	2000	1999	1998
United States	$ 7,449	$ 8,524	$ 8,006	$ 8,143
Foreign	839	745	589	545
	$ 8,288	$ 9,269	$ 8,595	$ 8,688

Source: SEC *Form 10K* for the yearend December 31, 2001, p. 63.

currently operates a fleet of 358 Boeing 737 aircraft, and it serves fifty-eight cities in various regions of the United States. In contrast to other major U.S. carriers, Southwest does not use the hub system: It prefers to fly direct routes, and it counts on its twenty-minute turnaround times to deliver high-frequency service between destinations. It is unclear, however, how drastically increased security measures at airports since the terrorist attack will affect this turnaround time.

Since 1990, when Southwest began a rapid expansion in the West Coast market, its operations have been a threat to US Airways as well as to other carriers. Using a combination of fare cuts of two-thirds or more as well as by adding flights to several major cities in northern and southern California, Southwest forced US Airways to essentially abandon its service on north-south California routes. Eventually, Southwest became the second-largest carrier in the California region, second only to United. In 1993, mistakenly believing that US Airways was about to abandon service from its Baltimore hub, Southwest aggressively entered this market. This became one of Southwest's fastest growing cities, and Southwest eventually surpassed US Airways in this market. US Airways had been cutting back service from its Baltimore hub, eliminating fifty-one of seventy-five mainline routes, including nonstop service to Florida. Since September 11, US Airways has also ceased operations of MetroJet, its express jet service. In addition to overlapping MetroJet's Baltimore operations, Southwest also overlapped MetroJet's services in New England cities such as Providence, Rhode Island. After the initial shock of the September 11 attack, most airlines reduced service on routes—or abandoned routes completely. Due to its strong financial position (its 33.3 percent debt-to-total capital ratio is the lowest in the industry), Southwest elected to maintain preattack levels of service, and it even drastically reduced ticket prices in order to attract leisure travel to make up for a decline in business travel. Expansion plans were temporarily halted, however, as Southwest delayed delivery of new aircraft. Additionally, Southwest was the only airline that was not forced to lay off employees after the attack. This strong financial position may allow Southwest to continue undercutting the fares of its more highly-leveraged competitors. Finally, although delivery has been delayed, Southwest had placed orders for Boeing 737-700 aircraft, extremely efficient versions of this type, which also have true transcontinental range. It has long been rumored that Southwest plans to inaugurate this type of service.

Delta Airlines, the third largest U.S. carrier, has two wholly owned subsidiaries, Delta Express and The Delta Connection, which consists of Comair, Atlantic Coast Airlines (ACA), and Atlantic Southeast Airlines (ASA). In 1996, Delta Express began direct competition with US Airways Shuttle, using a fleet of modern Boeing 737-800 aircraft to offer seventeen daily flights between NY-LaGuardia and Washington, D.C., and between NY-LaGuardia and Boston. The Delta Connection offers service out of

Delta hubs in Atlanta and Dallas/Fort Worth via ASA, Cincinnati and Orlando via Comair, as well as the New York and Boston hubs via ACA. These service areas considerably overlap many of the same destinations served by US Airways. Significantly, except for a few turboprop aircraft which are being phased out of ASA service, all Delta Connection subsidiaries exclusively operate some type of regional jet, a distinct advantage over the largely turboprop fleet operated over the same routes by US Airways Express. The large number of competitors in US Airways' region makes it difficult to achieve or exceed breakeven load factors on flights due to the sheer number of choices available to travelers. US Airways and Delta Airlines also compete for transcontinental passengers. Recently, Delta has increased its service to Philadelphia, US Airways' international gateway, and it has initiated international service to Brussels, a new destination for US Airways as well.

In addition to Southwest and Delta, the cumulative encroachment of other competitors into US Airways' service areas poses a substantial threat to the company's load factors, because it continues the saturation of an already crowded market with additional seats, as 82 percent of all US Airways flights are concentrated in the eastern U.S. region. Low-fare, no-frills startups such as JetBlue, Spirit Airlines, and AirTran Airways have collectively increased departures from East Coast facilities by 25 percent in the last quarter of 2000. JetBlue, backed by capital from George Soros, among others, competes for East Coast Florida service, flying between New York and several Florida destinations, all served by US Airways. JetBlue has taken a novel approach to no-frills service, exclusively operating brand new Airbus A320 aircraft, providing JetBlue with the same operating overhead that US Airways' upgraded fleet will provide. All aircraft in the JetBlue fleet are equipped with leather seating throughout the passenger cabin, and they provide seatback video screens which deliver twenty-four channels of DirecTV to all passengers. The cost includes blue corn nacho chips! JetBlue has also expanded service to a number of West Coast destinations, including cities in California and Washington, as well as several in mountain states such as Colorado and Utah. Recently, JetBlue placed an order for forty-eight more A320 aircraft, bringing its total fleet order to 131 aircraft. Interestingly, several of JetBlue's top management team had recently held similar positions with Southwest.

THE FUTURE

After the September 11 attacks, the future of US Airways was questionable at best. All commercial flights originating from or terminating in the United States were suspended for several days. Reagan International Airport, a terminus for the US Airways shuttle, which operates 45 percent of its flights from this facility, was closed for a period of several weeks. The fear of flying caused passenger traffic to nose-dive; load factors plummeted, and the resulting steep drop in revenue placed additional burdens on an airline which had already been struggling financially. This was not helped by the crash of an American Airlines Airbus in November, which resulted in the loss of 250 lives. Although found not to be terrorist-related, this tragedy further eroded travelers' confidence. In addition to losses incurred during the first half of 2001, the company suffered a staggering net loss of $766 million for the third quarter of that year. Although load factors have significantly increased, they are still not at breakeven levels, due largely to the inability of the airline industry to lure back passengers. Especially critical was the further decline in business traffic, which comprises 50 percent of airline traffic but generates 65 percent of ticket revenue. An economy in recession requires less business travel; additionally, organizations began to use alternative strategies, such as teleconferencing,

Web-based conferencing, and sometimes travel by train and automobile, to reduce exposure of employees to further possible terrorist activity.

Some short-term solutions seemed to offer some relief. US Airways, as did most other airlines, laid off 24 percent of its employees to reduce payroll expenses. This resulted in a dramatic decrease in customer service, however, which was already a consumer flashpoint. Combined with slowdowns caused by increased security measures, this may have a further deleterious effect on air travel. US Airways also cut service by 23 percent. Routes were dropped and flights on many routes were consolidated to fill aircraft, which increased load factors but resulted in a decline in overall company revenues.

Short-term cash infusions were also available. US Airways was owed $50 million by United as a condition of their failed merger. The company raised $404 million of additional operating cash in November by the sale and leaseback of some aircraft. The U.S. government had passed legislation federalizing airport security operations, a move which relieved the airlines of this expense. Immediately after the terrorist attack, the U.S. Congress passed legislation providing $14 billion in aid to the airline industry. It is unclear, however, how this will help US Airways. Some of the package permits direct grants to airlines; however, the bulk of the package is in the form of loan packages which require the participating airlines to provide assets as loan collateral. With a leverage ratio of 92 percent, the second-highest in the airline industry, the company had little unencumbered assets to offer as collateral for these loans.

On November 27, 2001, Rakesh Gangwal, US Airways CEO, abruptly and unexpectedly resigned, ostensibly to pursue opportunities in venture capital investing. Gangwal's chief strengths were his attention to detail and a mastery of the airline industry's economics, critical requirements under the current conditions. Mr. Gangwal was immediately succeeded by Stephen Wolf, chairman of the airline, who had been CEO of the company before turning control over to Gangwal in 1998. Wolf's strengths, however, seemed to lie in deal making rather than in daily operations, and since at least 1987, he has had Gangwal present as his extremely capable number two man. Whether Wolf had the acumen to pull US Airways out of the morass without the help of Gangwal was a significant question for both company employees and the industry in general. At that moment, US Airways seemed to be rudderless—and continuing to lose altitude.

In August 2002, US Airways announced that they were filing Chapter 11 bankruptcy. A federal bankruptcy judge granted US Airways $75 million to continue flying through September 2002. Operations will continue as normal, however the airline didn't rule out flight cuts. US Airways expects to submit a reorganization plan by Dec. 31, 2002. (**www.usatoday.com**, August 13, 2002)

E*TRADE GROUP, INC.—2002

Sandra H. DuRant
Francis Marion University

ET

www.etrade.com

The phrase *It's a small world after all* was coined years ago but never had quite the meaning it has today in the world of cyberspace. You can travel the world with the stroke of a key through the Internet and e-mail. The Internet can actually make money for you and let you "take it to the bank" without leaving your home if you invest wisely. This is every individual's fantasy, regardless of culture or country. E*Trade is a company that wants to make this fantasy a reality. E*Trade is a global leader in Internet online personal financial services. The company offers a full range of products that include investment and brokerage services, integrated banking, research capabilities, and educational and advisory services. E*Trade's banking service is currently the largest integrated online banking service in the world, with the largest Automated Teller Machine (ATM) network, and it offers a variety of financial services. E*Trade provides service twenty-four-hours a day, seven days a week through the Internet, direct modem access, automated telephone service, and live telephone support. E*Trade has 3,960 employees and is located in Menlo Park, California.

E*Trade has diversified significantly over the past two years and now offers extended trading hours for many exchanges around the world as well as direct international trades during trading hours. E*Trade has customers in 50 states and 119 countries. It has established branded sites in eleven countries, including South Africa, Denmark, Korea, Japan, the United Kingdom, Sweden, Australia, New Zealand, Canada, Norway, and the United States.

HISTORY

E*Trade was founded in 1983 by Bill Porter, a physicist and inventor, and it provided online quotes and trading services to Fidelity, Charles Schwab, and Quick & Reilly. These are the same companies E*Trade is now fighting for market share. Bill Porter began to wonder why, as an individual investor, he had to pay a broker hundreds of dollars for stock transactions. He had great foresight and envisioned the day when everyone would have a computer and invest through E*Trade. Bill Porter's foresight helped him fulfill his vision, and in 1992 E*Trade Securities, Inc., became one of the original all-electronic brokerage companies. E*Trade Securities, Inc., began offering online investing services through America Online and CompuServe. In 1996, Bill Porter's dream became a reality when **www.etrade.com** was launched and the demand skyrocketed.

Porter appointed Christos Cotsakos as president and CEO of the company in 1996. Cotsakos brought over twenty years of senior level management experience with him to E*Trade. Prior to working at E*Trade, Cotsakos worked at FedEx and A.C. Nielsen, where he served as the former president, co-chief executive officer, and director. In the spring of 2001, E*Trade was ranked number three overall by Gomez Advisors Internet Brokers Scorecard for top Internet brokers. The Gomez Advisors Internet Brokers Scorecard results are based on a comprehensive review of the top fifty online brokerages across the nation in ten major categories and 150 different criteria.

EXTERNAL FACTORS

The Terrorist Attacks

On September 11, 2001, global investment activities of E*Trade and the entire online investment industry were greatly altered by the World Trade Center attack. The attack intensified a yearlong economic slowdown that began in the first quarter of 2000 and continued through 2001 with decreasing prices and downturns in the securities market. The attack shook the foundation of the American economy. The attack pushed the country into economic recession that extended far beyond the borders of the United States.

The World Trade Center attack resulted in a record one-day drop on September 17, 2001, of 684 points in the Dow Jones Industrial Average. The disaster was immediately felt around the globe, as signs of economic fallout became apparent. The federal government made a historical decision to close all airports in the United States for four days. The U.S. Congress and the federal government approved a $40 billion relief package to rebuild New York City and to bail out the airline industry. Wall Street was shut down for four days, the longest period of closure since the Depression.

The terrorist attacks caused a severe deterioration in global economic activity. The economic output loss in the United States is expected to exceed $50 billion. Gross Domestic Product (GDP) growth is expected to decline by 3 percent in the third quarter of 2001, which will be the first decline in the nation's GDP since the first quarter of 1993. The Federal Reserve lowered short-term interest rates a total of ten times in 2001 to stimulate the economy. The entire online brokerage industry has suffered decreasing profits due to declining trading volumes. This trend forced major players in the online brokerage industry, including E*Trade, to restructure their companies, to lay off employees, and to turn to diversification to enhance and expand their products and services. E*Trade is developing key strategic alliances to gain competitive advantages—with such companies as Yahoo!, AOL, Microsoft, AT&T, and CompuServe. E*Trade also has alliance agreements with industry leaders in the airline industry, the hotel industry, and the credit card industry to enhance product offerings and expand its client bases.

Competitors

E*Trade and its major competitors are diversifying beyond domestic retail brokerage services by offering products and services that include initial public offerings, mutual fund offerings, banking services, global cross-border trading, institutional investing, and educational opportunities for customers. E*Trade's major competitors in the market are Charles Schwab, Fidelity Investments, TD Waterhouse, Ameritrade, Datek, and Harris Direct (formerly CSFBdirect). Charles Schwab is the largest broker in the industry, with 30 percent of the market share and revenues totaling almost $5.8 billion as of year-end 2000. Fidelity is ranked second, with a 20 percent market share. E*Trade increased its market share to 18 percent in 2000 and reported almost $2 billion in revenues, as indicated in Exhibit 1. However, by the period ending June 30, 2001, E*Trade reported a loss of $19 million. TD Waterhouse, Ameritrade, Datek, and Harris Direct collectively claim an additional 24 percent of the market share, and all other online brokerage firms represent the remaining 8 percent.

Established in 1974 and based in San Francisco, California, Charles Schwab Corporation is the largest broker in the industry. It is a full-service financial company that offers brokerage and trading services, investment planning services, a full range of financial products, and other related services. For the three months ending June 30, 2001, Charles Schwab reported a net income of $102 million and $1,071 billion in total revenues. Charles Schwab is publicly traded on the New York Stock Exchange (NYSE) under the ticker [SCH].

EXHIBIT 1   Industry Comparison of Major Competitors in 2000

Broker	Market Share	Customer Accounts	Client Assets	Revenues*	Net Income*
Charles Schwab	30%	3,700,000	$418,000,000,000	$5,787,651	$718,137
Fidelity	20%	4,220,000	$328,000,000,000	$ N/A	$ N/A
E*Trade	18%	2,443,000	$ 62,000,000,000	$1,973,200	$ 19,200
TD Waterhouse	11%	1,728,000	$118,000,000,000	$1,575,415	$210,316
Ameritrade	7%	992,000	$ 39,000,000,000	$ 654,500	$(13,600)
Datek	3%	457,000	$ 15,000,000,000	$ N/A	$ N/A
Harris Direct	3%	402,000	$ 27,000,000,000	$ 80,400	$(10,800)
Others	8%	1,318,000	$ 52,100,000,000	–	–

*Revenues and net income in thousands
Fidelity and Datek are privately held entities.
Source: "Industry Report," *Market Guide,* **www.marketguide.com**; annual reports and 10Ks of individual companies for the year 2000, **www.freeedgar.com**; *Market Research* (2000), **www.infotechtrends.com**.

Based in New York City, TD Waterhouse has operations in the United States, Canada, Australia, the United Kingdom, Hong Kong, and Australia. The company's primary markets are in Canada and the United States. TD Waterhouse has a worldwide global branch network that includes over 230 offices in Asia, Europe, and North America. TD Waterhouse is a provider of online investing and brokerage services. For the three months ending April 30, 2001, total revenues were $282 million, while net income totaled $6.5 million. TD Waterhouse is publicly traded on the New York Stock Exchange (NYSE) under the ticker of [TWE].

Located in Omaha, Nebraska, Ameritrade provides online brokerage services, an Internet-based personal financial management service, touch-tone telephone and market data, and research tools. For the month ended June 30, 2001, revenue was $120 million, and net income totaled $1 million. Ameritrade had plans to engage in an aggressive advertising and marketing campaign in 2001; however, the campaign is currently on hold. The campaign was intended to establish Ameritrade as the dominant brand in online trading. Ameritrade is publicly traded on the (NASDAQ) under the ticker [AMTD].

A comparison of commissions for the leading online brokerage firms is provided in Exhibit 2.

Industry Outlook

The online brokerage industry is facing a consolidation trend that continues into 2002. Revenues and trading are steadily declining, creating a very volatile competitive environment. The unstable economy has caused investors to significantly limit or entirely discontinue their trading activities. Limited trading activity has caused an industrywide decline in revenues and forced online brokerage firms to restructure and diversify their business models to increase efficiency and profitability. Restructuring efforts have triggered staff reductions for most competitors, including Charles Schwab (with a reduction of 3,400 employees), Harris Direct (with a 10 percent reduction), Ameritrade (with a reduction of 1,991 employees), TD Waterhouse (with a reduction of 600 employees), and E*Trade (with a reduction of 360 contract workers).

E*Trade purchased E*Trade Bank as part of the company's business strategy, and the venture has been successful, with approximately 25 percent of net revenues now

---

EXHIBIT 2   Commission Comparison of Leading Online Brokerage Firms

Company	Commission per 1,000 Shares (2001)
Ameritrade	$8.00
Datek	$10.00
TD Waterhouse	$12.00
Fidelity	$15.00
E*Trade	$15.00
HarrisDirect	$20.00
Charles Schwab	$30.00

Source: "Investment Brokerage Industry Report," Market Guide, **www.marketguide.com**.

---

coming from banking-related operations. E*Trade's diversification into banking makes the company less susceptible to stock market fluctuations.

The gross annual revenue for financial services in 2002 is projected to be $400 billion, and only 10 percent of the total will come from online offerings. As diversification and consolidation efforts intensify industrywide, the remaining $360 billion represents a financial opportunity for the online brokerage industry in the form of increased customer accounts.

Legislation passed in March 2000 allows securities firms, insurance companies, and banks more flexibility when it comes to affiliating under one holding company. E*Trade is restructuring, continuing global expansion, pursuing consolidation opportunities, and diversifying its products and services. A major threat to the online brokerage industry is large banking firms such as Citigroup, which could enter the online banking and investments business. These firms have very large revenue bases, strong brand awareness, and loyal customers who are already clients of the online brokerage business.

INTERNAL FACTORS

Organizational Structure

E*Trade has successfully completed sixteen acquisitions as part of the company's global expansion strategy, resulting in a top-heavy executive team. E*Trade made the decision in 2001 to restructure the organization, and as part of this effort, numerous senior-level job titles were changed to lower status positions. The pay levels of affected employees, however, remained the same. The number of vice presidents dropped from 170 to 85 and the number of business managers decreased from 600 to approximately 300. A large number of top managers resigned following the change, as indicated by an 11 percent decrease in employees, from 4,440 at the peak to 3,960 at the end of June 2001. The new structure improved efficiencies of the company and reduced human resource costs through attrition. The new organization structure is shown in Exhibit 3.

E*Trade ranks third in market share, third in number of customers' accounts, and third in revenue base among Internet brokerages. E*Trade has acquired E*Trade Bank, E*Trade Mortgage, and E*Trade Access, which provides ATM services.

EXHIBIT 3   E*Trade's Organization Chart

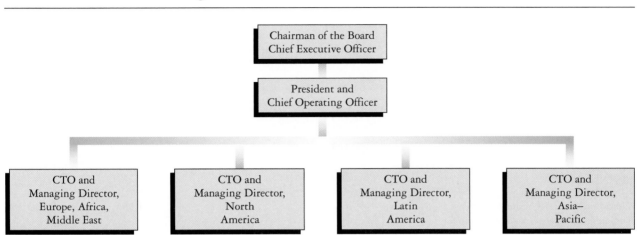

Source: E*Trade's 2001 *Annual Report.*

Financial Condition

E*Trade has separated its financial services into four major segments: domestic retail brokerage, banking, global and institutional, and asset gathering and other. The financial information for both domestic retail brokerage and asset gathering and other are aggregated by management to form three reportable segments. The domestic retail brokerage category is comprised of E*Trade Securities, which offers Internet domestic retail brokerage services.

The banking category consists of the activities of the E*Trade Bank, which include E*Trade Access, a network of 9,600 Automatic Teller Machines; E*Trade Mortgage; and E*Trade Zone service center, a brokerage and planning service center located in New York.

Global and Institutional consists of TIR Holdings Limited, a service center for institutional investors; and also VERSUS Technologies, Inc., which provides both retail and institutional services and international affiliates that provide service to nondomestic retail investors.

The asset gathering and other category includes the mutual funds operations, e-Investing, Business Solutions Group (BSG), the money management delivery service, and the activities and product offerings generated from corporate operations. This category is aggregated into the domestic retail brokerage and other section.

E*Trade has diversified the company's operations from conventional online brokerage activities to reduce the company's overall risk and to have the ability to generate revenues from more than one activity.

Exhibit 4 contains extrapolated financial information on the three reportable financial segments and reveals the effect the economy has taken on E*Trade's bottom line.

E*Trade operates in the United States and in international markets, and it established geographic regions in 2001 that include North America; Latin America; Asia-Pacific; and Europe, Africa, and the Middle East. Each region has a general manager, whose objective is to provide seamless, localized, and integrated services to existing worldwide markets.

EXHIBIT 4   E*Trade's Financial Services Segment Report (in millions)

	Domestic Retail Brokerage & Other	Banking	Global and Institutional	Total
Three Months Ended June 30, 2001:				
Interest income—net of interest expense	$ 51,920	$ 38,286	$ 2,133	$ 92,339
Noninterest revenue—net of provision for loan losses	138,185	40,576	37,079	215,840
Net revenues	$ 190,105	$ 78,862	$ 39,212	$ 308,179
Operating income (loss)	$(4,369)	$ 22,373	$ (10,547)	$7,457
Three Months Ended June 30, 2000:				
Interest income—net of interest expense	59,192	32,395	1,963	93,550
Noninterest revenue—net of provision for loan losses	195,429	6,193	43,124	244,746
Net revenues	$ 254,621	$ 38,588	$ 45,087	$ 338,296
Operating income (loss)	$ 1,511	$ 3,365	$ (6,507)	$ (1,631)
Six Months Ended June 30, 2001:				
Interest income—net of interest expense	$ 111,568	$ 74,605	$ 4,495	$ 190,668
Noninterest revenue—net of provision for loan losses	296,879	75,870	74,343	447,092
Net revenues	$ 408,447	$ 150,475	$ 78,838	$ 637,760
Operating income (loss)	$ (12,550)	$ 46,833	$ (23,900)	$ 10,383
Six Months Ended June 30, 2000:				
Interest income—net of interest expense	$ 125,577	$ 61,699	$ 3,247	$ 190,523
Noninterest revenue—net of provision for loan losses	464,509	5,621	94,343	564,473
Net revenues	$ 590,086	$ 67,320	$ 97,590	$ 754,996
Operating loss	$ (14,518)	$ (5,109)	$ (7,270)	$ (26,897)
As of June 30, 2001:				
Segment assets	$6,184,821	$12,690,075	$425,275	$19,300,171
As of September 30, 2000:				
Segment assets	$7,805,843	$ 9,027,185	$484,409	$17,317,437

No single customer accounted for more than 10% of total revenues in the three and six months ended June 30, 2001, or 2000, respectively.
Source: "Security and Exchange Commission E*Trade *Quarterly Report* for the quarter ended June 30, 2001."

E*Trade's revenues increased 241 percent in 2001. E*Trade reported a net loss for 2001 of $241.5 million. Consolidated financial statements for E*Trade are listed as Exhibit 5 and Exhibit 6.

E*Trade had no debt until year 2000; but it obtained a term loan in 2001 of $17.2 million, and it renewed a $50 million line of credit that had no outstanding balance as of June 30, 2001. E*Trade repurchased 2.2 percent of the company's outstanding stock, or

EXHIBIT 5   E*Trade's Annual Income Statements

In Millions of U.S. Dollars (except for per share items)	12 Months Ending 12/31/01	3 Months Ending 12/31/00	12 Months Ending 09/30/00
Revenue	1,891.2	536.3	1,865.5
Other Revenue	170.9	32.7	107.7
Total Revenue	**2,062.1**	**569.0**	**1,973.2**
Cost of Revenue	1,382.3	368.5	1,120.4
Gross Profit	**508.8**	**167.8**	**745.1**
Selling/General/Administrative Expenses	489.8	155.8	731.0
Research & Development	88.7	29.2	142.9
Depreciation/Amortization	43.1	7.8	22.8
Interest Expense (Income), Net Operating	–	–	–
Unusual Expense (Income)	244.1	0.8	36.4
Other Operating Expenses	–	–	–
Total Operating Expense	**2,248.1**	**562.1**	**2,053.5**
Operating Income	**(186.0)**	**6.9**	**(80.3)**
Interest Expense, Net Non-Operating	(52.9)	(11.2)	(29.5)
Interest/Investment Income, Non-Operating	22.2	7.1	17.2
Interest Income (Expense), Net Non-Operating	(30.7)	(4.2)	(12.3)
Gain (Loss) on Sale of Assets	(56.0)	3.5	199.6
Other, Net	(37.6)	(3.1)	(2.5)
Income Before Tax	**(310.3)**	**3.2**	**104.4**
Income Tax	(39.9)	1.9	85.5
Income After Tax	**(270.3)**	**1.3**	**19.0**
Minority Interest	(0.5)	0.1	0.2
Equity In Affiliates	–	–	–
Net Income Before Extra. Items	**(270.8)**	**1.4**	**19.2**
Accounting Change	0.0	(0.1)	–
Discontinued Operations	–	–	–
Extraordinary Item	29.3	–	–
Net Income	**(241.5)**	**1.4**	**19.2**
Preferred Dividends	–	–	0.0
Income Available to Common Excl. Extra. Items	**(270.8)**	**1.4**	**19.2**
Income Available to Common Incl. Extra. Items	**(241.5)**	**1.4**	**19.2**
Basic/Primary Weighted Average Shares	332.4	311.4	301.9
Basic/Primary EPS Excl. Extra. Items	**(0.815)**	**0.005**	**0.063**
Basic/Primary EPS Incl. Extra. Items	**(0.727)**	**0.004**	**0.063**
Dilution Adjustment	0.0	0.0	0.0
Diluted Weighted Average Shares	332.4	321.4	319.3
Diluted EPS Excl. Extra. Items	**(0.815)**	**0.004**	**0.060**
Diluted EPS Incl. Extra. Items	**(0.727)**	**0.004**	**0.060**
Dividends per Share – Common Stock	0.000	0.000	0.000
Gross Dividens – Common Stock	0.0	0.0	0.0
Stock Based Compensation	–	–	128.1
Pro Forma Net Income	–	–	(108.9)
Pro Forma Basic EPS	–	–	(0.360)
Pro Forma Diluted EPS	–	–	(0.360)
Depreciation/Amortization, Supplemental	52.9	11.2	29.5
Total Special Items	343.2	5.1	(140.4)
Normalized Income Before Tax	**33.0**	**8.3**	**(36.0)**
Effect of Special Charge on Income Taxes	0.0	3.0	0.0
Income Taxes Excl. Impact of Special Items	(39.9)	4.9	85.5
Normalized Income	**72.9**	**3.4**	**(121.5)**
Normalized Income Available to Common	**72.4**	**3.5**	**(121.3)**
Basic Normalized EPS	0.218	0.011	(0.402)
Diluted Normalized EPS	0.218	0.011	(0.380)

Source: http://www.investor.stockpoint.com.

EXHIBIT 6   E*Trade's Annual Balance Sheet

In Millions of U.S. Dollars (except for per share items)	As of 12/31/01	As of 12/31/00	As of 09/30/00
Cash & Equivalents	1,600.9	592.7	301.3
Short Term Investments	–	–	–
Cash and Short Term Investments	1,600.9	592.7	301.3
Trade Accounts Receivable, Net	–	–	–
Other Receivables	2,119.8	4,639.1	6,542.5
Total Receivables, Net	2,119.8	4,639.1	6,542.5
Total Inventory	–	–	–
Prepaid Expenses	–	–	–
Other Current Assets	–	–	–
Total Current Assets	–	–	–
Property/Plant/Equipment—Gross	–	–	–
Accumulated Depreciation	–	–	(135.4)
Property/Plant/Equipment, Net	331.7	368.4	334.3
Goodwill, Net	684.4	442.0	484.2
Intangibles, Net	–	–	–
Long Term Investments	4,725.2	6,151.8	5,173.8
Other Long Term Assets	–	–	–
Total Assets	18,205.9	17,741.1	17,317.4
Accounts Payable	–	–	–
Accrued Expenses	–	–	–
Notes Payable/Short Term Debt	–	–	–
Current Port. LT Debt/Capital Leases	760.3	650.0	650.0
Other Current Liabilities	2,606.1	4,226.1	6,055.5
Total Current Liabilities	–	–	–
Long Term Debt	–	–	–
Capital Lease Obligations	–	–	–
Total Long Term Debt	–	–	–
Total Debt	760.3	650.0	650.0
Deferred Income Tax	–	–	–
Minority Interest	–	–	–
Other Liabilities	12,322.8	10,410.3	8,283.4
Total Liabilities	16,627.2	15,995.1	15,460.6
Redeemable Preferred Stock	–	–	–
Preferred Stock—Non Redeemable, Net	–	–	–
Common Stock	3.5	3.1	3.1
Additional Paid-In Capital	2,072.7	1,827.4	1,814.6
Retained Earnings (Accum. Deficit)	(247.1)	(5.6)	(6.9)
Treasury Stock—Common	–	–	–
Other Equity	(250.3)	(77.5)	47.6
Total Equity	1,578.8	1,746.0	1,856.8
Total Liability & Shareholders' Equity	18,205.9	17,741.1	17,317.4
Shares Outs.—Common Stock	347.6	308.2	304.5
Total Common Shares Outstanding	347.6	308.2	304.5
Total Preferred Stock Shares Outs.	–	–	–
Employees (actual figures)	–	–	3,778.0
Number of Common Shareholders (actual figures)			2,118.0

Source: http://www.investor.stockpoint.com.

7.19 million shares of common stock, for $5.45 per share on August 20, 2001. Chairman and CEO Cotsakos personally purchased an additional two million shares on the same terms as the company. The strategic move was to increase the stock price and to restore confidence in the company's stock.

The key performance indicators used by E*Trade to measure financial performance are the increase or percentage change in new and active domestic brokerage accounts, new and active banking accounts, and new and active global and institutional accounts. Other key indicators are the cost per new account and the number of total domestic brokerage transactions, customer households, and assets in customer accounts. Instability and volatility of the market resulted in a drastic decrease of 78 percent in new domestic brokerage accounts, 21 percent in banking accounts, and 40 percent in global and institutional accounts as of June 30, 2000, when compared to the same period in June 30, 2001. Total new accounts also decreased by 71 percent, resulting in a 22 percent increase in the cost per new account during the same period.

As indicated in Exhibit 7, the decline in the number of new accounts resulted in a 38 percent decrease in domestic brokerage transactions from June 30, 2000, to June 30, 2001. The average commission per domestic brokerage transaction for new accounts also decreased, from $15.55 to $13.44, or 14 percent, primarily due to the severe decline in the value of publicly traded securities being held by E*Trade.

EXHIBIT 7   E*Trade's Key Performance Indicators (Customer Accounts and Assets)

	Three Months Ended June 30,			Six Months Ended June 30,		
	2001	2000	Percentage Change	2001	2000	Percentage Change
Net new domestic brokerage accounts	65,610	270,708	(76)%	176,646	817,881	(78)%
Net new banking accounts	30,039	51,998	(42)%	72,187	91,947	(21)%
Net new global and institutional accounts	7,840	10,854	(28)%	20,768	34,413	(40)%
Total net new accounts	103,489	333,560	(69)%	269,601	944,241	(71)%
Cost per new account	$232	$291	(20)%	$328	$269	22%
Total domestic brokerage transactions	7,148,235	10,491,288	(32)%	15,233,084	24,733,340	(38)%
Daily average domestic brokerage transactions	113,464	166,528	(32)%	121,865	196,296	(38)%
Average commission per domestic brokerage transaction	$13.23	$15.13	(13)%	$13.44	$15.55	(14)%
Rebate income per domestic brokerage transaction	$2.06	$1.79	15%	$2.36	$1.92	23%

	June 30, 2001	September 30, 2000	Percentage Change
Active domestic brokerage accounts	3,289,014	2,951,946	11%
Active banking accounts	434,804	288,073	51%
Active global and institutional accounts	104,792	75,416	39%
Total active accounts at period end	3,828,610	3,315,435	15%
Total customer households end of period	2,738,838	Not Available	N/A
Average assets per household	$19,513	Not Available	N/A
Total assets in domestic brokerage accounts	$44,553,710	$59,901,277	(26)%
Total deposits in banking accounts	7,687,006	4,630,068	66%
Total assets in global and institutional accounts	1,202,718	1,348,672	(11)%
Total assets/deposits in customer accounts at period end	$53,443,434	$65,880,017	(19)%

Source: Security and Exchange Commission E*Trade *Quarterly Report* for the quarter ended June 30, 2001.

E*Trade's total active accounts increased 15 percent, from September 30, 2000, to June 30, 2001, mainly from banking and global and institutional accounts, with an increase of 51 percent and 39 percent, respectively.

As a result of the declining number of customer accounts and the declining values of securities held by E*Trade, the company reported a net loss of $19.4 million on June 30, 2001.

Marketing

E*Trade's marketing expenditures decreased 50 percent in the six months ending June 30, 2001. The expenditures primarily supported the cost of selling products in both the global and institutional business as well as the asset gathering and other segments. E*Trade has been cross-selling banking services to its active brokerage customers in an effort to use marketing resources more effectively. E*Trade made substantial investments in marketing efforts during the 2000 fiscal year to build a strong brand identity, and the company feels the decreased marketing expenditures will not significantly affect the company's competitive position during the economic downturn.

The marketing strategy for fiscal year 2002 is to focus on cross-selling the existing customer base to generate new banking and brokerage accounts, to sustain the existing accounts, to develop current customer households, and to review statistics, such as assets per household. The major thrust of the marketing campaign is to focus on the banking segment in order to capture a significant percentage of the projected growth in online banking.

Banking was the only segment that reported an increase in net revenues— 123 percent—from June 30, 2000, to June 30, 2001. A report by Robertson Stephens Investment Bank predicted that the number of households banking online will be over 96.3 million by the year ending 2003, representing an annual growth rate of over 66 percent.

E*Trade has developed marketing partnership agreements with Delta Airlines, United Airlines, Northwest Airlines, and Trans World Airlines that allows E*Trade customers, who are also airline skymile members, to earn up to fifty thousand bonus miles each year by investing using E*Trade's online Web site. The bonus miles for the airline agreements are to be awarded based on the individual's investments. The bonus mile incentive is a tiered system and is based on the amount of an investment, ranging from a $1,000 deposit to a $50,000 deposit. E*Trade also has in place a marketing agreement with Marriott International and Hilton Hotels for similar bonus programs.

In the first six months of 2001, E*Trade acquired LoansDirect, Inc., an online mortgage originator, and WebStreet, Inc., an online brokerage firm. Also, E*Trade launched E*Trade Hong Kong and E*Trade Israel, and it opened E*Trade Center, a financial service superstore located in New York City that is designed to give consumers value-added financial services and educational content. Also in 2001, E*Trade extended an alliance with Target for twenty new E*Trade zones and over one thousand ATMs. E*Trade Mortgage was launched, and the company acquired fifteen thousand customer accounts in a transaction with Advanata National Bank, which has deposits valued at $389.7 million.

CONCLUSION

E*Trade plans to continue its global expansion strategy of purchasing sites in the international market to grow its asset base. E*Trade should perhaps aggressively acquire smaller online brokerage companies during the economic downturn, which may be easy targets due to financial difficulties. Possible target companies include Ameritrade and Datek. Consolidation will add customer assets and accounts that can result in increased revenues. By purchasing smaller companies, E*Trade may ensure that the company maintains its rent among the top five major competitors. According to Jupiter Research, total online assets are predicated to grow from $1.5 trillion today to $5.4 trillion by 2005. This growth will be targeted by E*Trade through marketing and advertising campaigns as market conditions improve.

REFERENCES

Ameritrade Inc., *Annual Report and 10K* (2000). **www.freeedgar.com**.

"Attack on America: Update on the Fallout in the U.S. Economy" (September 25, 2001). **www.economy.com**.

Charles Schwab, Inc., *Annual Report and 10K* (2000). **www.freeedgar.com**.

Datek Inc., *Annual Report and 10K* (2000). **www.freeedgar.com**.

DLJ Direct Inc., *Annual Report and 10K* (2000). **www.freeedgar.com**.

E*Trade Group Inc., *Annual Report and 10K* (2000). **www.etrade.com**.

Fidelity Inc., *Annual Report and 10K* (2000). **www.freeedgar.com**.

Forbes (October 1, 2001).

"Investment Brokerage Industry Report," *Market Guide*. **www.marketguide.com**.

"Market Research (2000)." **www.infotrends. com**.

Security and Exchange Commission E*Trade 2001 Quarterly Filing. **www.hoovers.com**.

"Reviews; Today in Reviews, Top of the Charts, The Week in Reviews" (September 21, 2001). **www.pcworld.com**.

"Scoreboard" (2001). **www.Gomez.com**.

TD Waterhouse Inc., *Annual Report and 10K* (2000). **www.freeedgar.com**.

The Wall Street Journal (October 2001).

EBAY—2002

Will Eskridge
Francis Marion University

EBAY

www.ebay.com

It is yearend 2001, and we are in the midst of a recession. The Gross Domestic Product for the third quarter shrank 1.1 percent, our first quarter of negative growth in ten years. The figure was negative again in the fourth quarter as well as the first quarter of 2002. Daily news headlines report job cuts and layoffs affecting virtually every industry. Since March 2001, the nation's workforce has shrunk by 887,000 jobs, or about 0.7 percent. The Dow Jones Industrial Average is down over 20 percent for the year to date, while the NASDAQ is down over 30 percent for the same period. The once golden tech sector, responsible for driving the stock market to heights never before seen, has not stumbled, but fallen. The irrational exuberance fueling the stock market in the 1998–1999 period has disappeared, and in its wake we find four-year-old companies, which, once upon a time, had valuations greater than bellweather companies like General Electric, but which are now wondering if they will survive. Not long ago, adding "dot-com" to the end of a corporate name and going public could turn people into multimillionaires overnight. Companies with little more than a plan and a dream were commanding some of the highest valuations on Wall Street. Today, those valuations seem like dreams, as investors are no longer willing to gamble on potential but instead are seeking companies making profits.

Nearly 1,000 Internet companies folded in 2000 and 2001. Companies such as Etoys and Pets.com no longer exist, while the vast majority of Internet companies have yet to make any profits. Amazon.com, arguably the most well-known company on the Internet, has yet to make a steady profit and has seen its market valuation decline from an unbelievably high $39 billion in December 1999 to $4.1 billion in November 2001.

The outlook for a recovery in the tech sector anytime soon seems bleak at best, and while most other dot-com companies continue to struggle, as one of the few Internet companies to make a profit, eBay seems to be the silver lining in a dark cloud. eBay owns and operates eBay.com, which, based upon the aggregate value of goods traded, is the world's largest and most popular online marketplace. eBay was the first company to bring the sale of goods via auction to the Internet, and it has proven to be a match made in new-economy heaven. eBay has established an Internet-based community of buyers and sellers who get together in an auction format to buy and sell items ranging from antiques, electronics, and collectibles to cars, boats, and real estate. Because the service is completely automated, it operates twenty-four hours a day, seven days a week.

HISTORY

The eBay service was begun in September 1995 by Pierre Omidyar. Born in France and raised in the United States, Omidyar moved to the West Coast after graduating from college as a computer programmer. The business was started in his apartment as a means for his then-girlfriend, an avid Pez dispenser collector, to contact others who shared her interest in Pez dispensers. She complained that she found it difficult to find others who were willing to buy or sell. Omidyar's creation allowed her and other individuals to use the Internet for their Pez trading needs.

In the beginning, the original site, called Auction Web, made no promises or guarantees. Individuals logged on and bid for items, and the transactions occurred. At that time, there were no fees, no registrations, no security, few items, and little business—that is, until Omidyar made one very positive marketing decision. He listed his trading site on the National Center for Supercomputing Applications' What's Cool list—and the rest is history. After the listing was posted, business started to pick up, and in March 1996 the business turned a profit.

The business continued to grow, and in 1998 the company, now renamed eBay, went public. At the end of 1999, eBay had 10 million registered users, and by the end of 2000 the number had increased 125 percent to 22 million. During this expansion, the eBay community has become more diverse than ever, featuring homemakers, major corporations, and everyone in between. Users listed more than 265 million items on the site in 2000, up 104 percent from 1999. For 2001, eBay's revenues increased 74 percent to $748 million while their net income increased 87 percent to $90.5 million.

HOW IT WORKS

Anyone can visit eBay and browse through the items listed for sale. However, if you wish to bid on items or list items for sale, you must register. The registration process is simple and quick: It takes less then five minutes, and once registered, you can immediately bid on or list items for sale. All buyers and sellers must be eighteen to bid on or list items.

Once registered, bidders can immediately search for specific items by category (there are generally more than eight thousand), and then they can click on individual items for detailed descriptions. The entire database can be queried by entering keywords that describe a desired item. eBay's search engine will locate all relevant items for sale and link the bidder to detailed descriptions. Each auction has a unique identifier that allows bidders to easily locate specific items.

eBay also provides highlights that alert bidders to certain types of auctions. For example, auctions that have started within the last twenty-four hours are highlighted with "New Today"; auctions that are ending on that day are highlighted with "Ending Today"; and those ending within three hours are highlighted under "Going Going Gone."

When the bidding on a particular auction has expired, eBay will determine if a bid exceeds the minimum asking price and the reserve price, if a reserve has been set. A seller can set a reserve price, the minimum that the seller will accept, which is usually higher than the minimum asking price. eBay will then notify both buyer and seller via e-mail, and the buyer and seller consummate the transaction independently of eBay. The buyer and seller agree upon and arrange for shipment and payment. eBay has no power to force the buyer and seller to complete the transaction, but it can ban either or both offending parties from trading on eBay in the future.

VISION AND MISSION

eBay has no formal vision; however, the company states its mission as follows: "eBay's mission is to help practically anyone trade practically anything on earth."

The eBay mission statement obviously does not encompass the desirable characteristics of a corporate mission, and, as such, eBay should develop an appropriate formal mission statement. It could use its existing mission statement as a basis for its vision statement.

Proposed eBay Mission Statement

eBay's mission is to be the world's most utilized and most profitable trading post. Hiring bright and talented employees who are dedicated to serving their customers and communities, eBay will provide the most technologically advanced, reliable, and secure trading platform available to individuals, business, and governments, while always striving to stay ahead of our competition.

As indicated in Exhibit 1, eBay appears to be functional in structure, which has worked very well thus far. Many companies are initially structured functionally, but if they experience any significant growth—and eBay certainly has—they outgrow this form of corporate structure. As eBay continues its massive global expansion, it is very possible it will need to restructure itself, possibly by geographic divisions.

REVENUE

There is no charge for buyers to shop on eBay. Bidding is free, and revenue is derived from fees that sellers are charged for listing and selling items. Sellers pay a small placement fee to list items for sale, and placement fee rates are as follows:

- Insertion fees for regular, Reserve Price, and Dutch Auction listings.

Minimum Bid, Opening Value, or Reserve Price	Insertion Fee
$0.01–$9.99	$0.30
$10.00–$24.99	$0.55
$25.00–$49.99	$1.10
$50.00–199.99	$2.20
$200.00 and up	$3.30

EXHIBIT 1   Corporate Structure

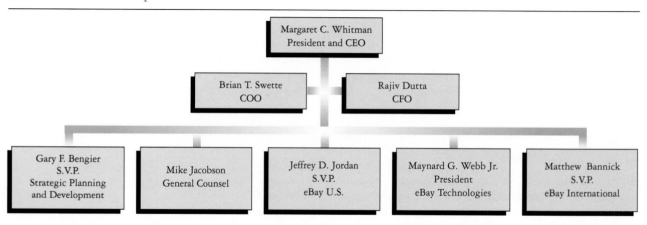

- Insertion fees for vehicles on eBay Motors:

Item Category	Insertion Fee
Vehicles (Cars, Motorcycles, Other Vehicles)	$25.00 For a breakdown of all eBay Motors fees please *click here*.

- Insertion fees for items covered by the Non-Binding Bid policy:

Item Category	Insertion Fee
Real Estate	$50.00 Real Estate may be listed for an extended period (30 days) for an additional fixed fee of $50.00.

- Additional Reserve Price Auction fee **(fully refunded if item sells)**:

Reserve Price	Reserve Price Auction Fee
$0.01–$24.99	$0.50
$25.00 and up	$1.00

Additional revenue from listings can come in a variety of ways. eBay offers sellers many ways to enhance their listings to attract bidders. Sellers can feature their auctions by paying additional incremental fees for various highlights. Available highlights and fee schedule are as follows:

Fee	Highlight
$.10	10 day auction listing (longest time available)
$.25	Sellers can have photos placed in the Gallery section
$2.00	Bold font for heading
$5.00	Highlight—eye-catching yellow band
$14.95	Featured plus, featured within an eBay category
$19.95	Feature the item in the Gallery section
$99.95	"Featured auction," which allows the item to be rotated on the eBay homepage

Finally, the seller pays eBay a commission if the seller is successful in selling his/her item(s). At the time of notification of a winning bid, eBay charges the seller a final value fee. Final value fees are shown below.

Success Fee	Purchase Price
5%	First $25.00 of the purchase price
2.5%	Portion of the purchase price from $25.01 to $1,000.00
1.25%	Portion of the purchase price over $1,000.00
$25.00	Per vehicle
No Fee	Real Estate

In the event that buyer and seller cannot complete the transaction, the seller can notify eBay to credit the fee. All invoices for placement fees, highlight fees, and successful selling fees are sent to sellers via e-mail on a monthly basis. Many sellers maintain a credit with eBay, and the account is charged shortly after an invoice is sent. At no time does eBay take possession of the merchandise or hold the receivable for the item. In contract to other Internet sites, the company does not enjoy revenue from advertisements. eBay sells no ad space on its site.

THE EBAY COMMUNITY

In providing a place for trading of various items, eBay attempts to foster a sense of community among its users. CEO and President Whitman has stated that eBay began with commerce but quickly grew into a very large community. eBay users believe that this sense of community is what separates it from other Internet auction and retail sites, and eBay invests heavily in the programs that make users feel that their transactions and information are safe from Internet thieves and fraudulent users.

One method used to establish the reputations of users is eBay's Feedback Forum, which encourages users to record comments, both favorable and unfavorable, about the trading partners. All this feedback information is recorded and creates a feedback rating for a specific person. Naturally, too many negative comments will likely cause users to avoid transactions with the individual in question.

eBay users with favorable reputations will have a star next to their user identifications. This star is color-coded and indicates the amount of positive versus negative feedback that the user has received. Users may review a person's feedback profile prior to doing business with that person.

The Feedback Forum is a self-regulating system: The users police themselves. However, some users may be tempted to manipulate the system in order to discredit other users or to enhance their own reputations. eBay has several policies in place to prevent this, and the system has several automated features in place to detect and to prevent various forms of abuse.

Dealing with unknown individuals over the Internet can be a cause for concern for some and may cause many others to shy away from eBay. In order to ease user's fears, eBay has instituted what is called its Safe Harbor program, which provides trading guidelines and rules, provides information to help resolve disputes among users, and addresses and responds to misuse of the eBay system. Safe Harbor is composed of approximately twenty-eight individuals, a group that includes regular eBay employees and contract employees. These individuals investigate possible misuse of the system and will take appropriate action, which may include suspension from buying or selling on the site. Safe Harbor provides users with information to assist both with disputes over the quality of goods and with possible fraudulent activities. If fraudulent activities occur, eBay will usually suspend the offending party or parties from further eBay activity.

Because community plays such an important part in the eBay experience, the company has focused resources on its efforts to establish a community experience. The company believes that the eBay community is one of the strongest on the Internet. eBay offers a wide array of features that support the community, and these features solidify the eBay community and ensure its continued growth and loyalty. The company uses e-mail to provide users with category-specific chatrooms, the eBay café (a chatroom for the entire community), a bulletin board for feedback on new features, and announcements that cover new features and eBay news. Customer-support bulletin boards and an "items wanted" listing where users can post their requests for specific items are also provided.

Also available is *My eBay*, which gives users a report on recent activity. Users who have their own Web pages can post links to their homepage, and those without a Web site can use *About Me* to create a homepage free of charge.

The company also offers an insurance program for users. To qualify, a user must be a buyer in good standing or a seller with a Feedback Rating of zero or above. The insurance program provides coverage on qualified transactions if a winning bidder sends money to a seller and either does not receive the item or does not receive the item described on the site.

In June 1998, eBay donated 643,500 shares of common stock and established a fund called the eBay Foundation. eBay solicits input from users for worthwhile charities. Other unique promotions are held to support worthwhile causes. After the September 11 terrorist attacks, eBay started the Auction for America; items are donated by sellers to this site and eBay charges no fees, and the proceeds then go to the families of the victims. Examples of items donated are a Harley Davidson motorcycle signed by numerous celebrities who visited the *Tonight Show*. Also of interest was a U.S. flag signed by all the members of Congress; it is believed to be the first such mass signing since the time of the signing of the Declaration of Independence.

CUSTOMER SUPPORT

eBay devotes significant resources to providing personalized, timely customer service and support. eBay offers customer support on a seven-days-a-week basis. Most customer support inquiries are handled via e-mail, with customer e-mail inquiries typically being answered within twenty-four hours after submission. In 2000, eBay continued its relationship with SatMetrix (formerly known as Customer Cast), an online customer satisfaction survey company, to help eBay understand and improve overall customer support. Overall customer satisfaction with eBay's support services has remained extremely high. eBay also offers an online tutorial for new eBay users. In 2000, eBay completed the relocation of all customer support personnel to its center in Salt Lake City, Utah.

MARKETING

Historically, eBay relied on word of mouth to promote its Web site and occasionally has utilized links and sponsorships with other Web sites. Today, eBay employs a variety of methods to promote its brand and to attract potential buyers and sellers. Currently, eBay uses strategic purchases of online advertising to place advertisements in areas in which eBay believes it can reach its target audience. eBay also engages in a number of marketing activities in traditional media such as radio, broadcast as well as national and local TV advertising, print media, trade shows, and other events.

In March 1999, eBay expanded the scope of its preexisting strategic relationship with AOL. Under the amended agreement, eBay is given a prominent presence, featuring it as the preferred provider of online trading services on AOL's proprietary services (both domestic and international), including AOL.com, Digital Cities, ICQ, CompuServe (both domestic and international), and Netscape. eBay will pay $75 million over the four-year term of the contract. eBay has developed a co-branded version of its service for each AOL property, which prominently features each party's brand. AOL is entitled to all advertising revenue from the co-branded sites. The company also uses its site for brand advertising by offering a variety of eBay-branded merchandise that can be purchased through it's own online store, eBay Store.

OPERATIONS PLATFORM

The eBay site operates on a software platform that was developed internally. This platform handles all aspects of the trading cycle, including e-mail notifications of when a bid is successful and when a bidder is outbid. The system sends daily reports to all active sellers and bidders on the status of eBay's auctions. In addition, the system also stores registration information, billing information, and credit card information for traders who use an open account balance. The software system is also the platform for all eBay chatroom and bulletin board information.

With the exception of once-a-week maintenance that takes a few hours, the system operates twenty-four hours a day, seven days a week. The eBay platform consists of Sun database servers running Oracle relational database management software. The company uses an outside load balancing system and has its own servers as back-up to reduce faults and outages. Outages do occasionally occur and are caused by a number of factors, including problems resulting from third party hardware and from software providers. eBay uses Resonate Inc.'s load balancing systems and its own redundant servers to provide for fault tolerance. The company's systems are vulnerable to attack from unauthorized persons.

The use rate of the eBay site has increased substantially during the last few years, and in fact, the increase has been not linear but exponential. As a result, the company is constantly adding to its infrastructure of software, hardware, and engineers. Because the entire eBay system operates on this platform, integrity and uptime are of the utmost importance. Any unscheduled or unanticipated downtime could severely harm current revenues and cause a ripple effect that could make users switch to competitive sites and thus affect long-term revenue.

GROWTH

Growth as measured by several factors has increased exponentially over the past three years. As measured by registered users, merchandise sales, number of items listed, number of log-ons, and number of minutes on the site per user, the company is one of the most popular sites on the Web. By all measures, eBay is one of the most active and widely visited Internet sites. For the month of September 2001, eBay was the eighth most visited site on the Web, and the time spent per person on the site (1:45:05) is the most of any Web site—it is seven times higher than time spent on rival site Amazon (0:15:12).[1]

The following table shows the growth of registered users.

Year	Number of Registered Users
1996	41,000
1999	2.1 million
2000	22 million
2001	42.4 million

Gross merchandise sales—that is, the dollar value of transactions between buyers and sellers—has increased from $5.4 billion in 2000 to $9.3 billion in 2001.

The number of items listed as available for bidding on the eBay site grew from 264.7 million in 2000 to 423.1 million in 2001. Gross revenue, gross profits, and net income all increased substantially from 2000 to 2001. Revenues have increased for twenty-eight consecutive quarters and have grown from $431.4 million in 2000 to $748.8 million in 2001. Gross profits have increased from $335.9 in 2000 to $614.0 million in 2001, while net income grew from $48.2 million at the end in 2000 to $90.4 million in 2001.

eBay is one of the few Internet companies to return a profit. Each year since eBay's IPO, it has experienced phenomenal growth in its sales, gross profits, and net profits. As a result, cash, working capital, total assets, and total stockholders' equity have all increased substantially. Acting as a facilitator and broker for individual traders keeps the company's business model a very profitable one.

COMPETITION

The Internet has emerged as a global medium enabling millions of people worldwide to share information and to communicate and conduct electronic commerce transactions. According to Nua Internet Surveys, as of November 2000, more than 400 million people worldwide had access to the Internet either at home or at work. And according to Forrester Research, the total value of global e-commerce transactions in 2001 exceeded $1.2 trillion, up from approximately $657 billion in 2000.

Depending on the category of product, eBay currently or potentially competes with a number of companies serving particular categories of goods as well as those serving broader ranges of goods. The Internet is a new, rapidly evolving and intensely competitive area. eBay expects competition to intensify in the future insofar as the barriers to entry are relatively low, and current and new competitors can launch new sites at a nominal cost using commercially available software. eBay's broad-based competitors include the vast majority of traditional department and general merchandise stores as well as emerging online retailers. They include most prominently Wal-Mart, Kmart, Target, Sears, Macy's, JCPenney, Costco, Sam's Clubs as well as Amazon.com, Buy.com, AOL.com, Yahoo!shopping, and the Microsoft Network.

At the present time, eBay dominates the online auction business, having trounced its competition. More than two-thirds of all online auction revenues go to eBay. Yahoo!, Microsoft, and Amazon.com have made high-profile attempts to gain footholds in the online auction business. However, with the current global recession, those companies have been forced to look for ways to cut costs and trim unprofitable operations; as a result, all three have taken steps away from the auction business and shifted their focus into other areas.

Yahoo! operates localized versions of its Web site in twenty-four countries and has offices in the Asia/Pacific region, Europe, Latin America, and North America. Once seen as the chief rival to eBay, Yahoo! saw its listings plummet in January 2000 after it initiated a listing fee. According to independent estimates, Yahoo!'s listings dropped from more than 2 million to about two hundred thousand. Yahoo!'s annual sales for the year 2000 were $1.11 billion, more than double that of eBay. Only a tiny fraction of Yahoo!'s sales can be attributed to its online auction services. Twelve-month revenue growth is a negative 15.6 percent, compared to eBay's positive 79.1 percent, and the net income growth is (100) percent vs. 132.60 percent, respectively. Yahoo!'s gross profit margin, 88.25 percent, is only 1.5 percent lower than eBay's; however, Yahoo! has a net profit margin of (21.67) percent, while eBay's is 13.33 percent. Yahoo!'s current market capitalization, $9.5 billion, is approximately half of eBay's, at $18.2 billion. It is rather ironic that a little more than a year and a half ago, Yahoo! was worth $100 billion or so, and it was targeting eBay as a possible acquisition. It opted instead to develop its own online auction business.

The Seattle-based Amazon.com, which was locked in a battle with eBay for the title of "King of e-Commerce," has been scaling back its efforts in light of current economic conditions and its lack of market penetration. Amazon has cut staff in its online auction department and no longer has a manager solely dedicated to running auctions. Amazon.com has customers in all fifty states and more than 150 countries, with distribution facilities in New Castle, Delaware; Coffeyville, Kansas; Campbellsville and Lexington, Kentucky; Fernley, Nevada; Grand Forks, North Dakota; and Seattle in the United States; as well as in France, Germany, and the United Kingdom. An examination of the financial comparisons shows that Amazon's annual sales for year 2000 were approximately $2.76 billion, which is about 6.4 times eBay's gross sales revenue. Amazon has a significantly lower gross margin, 28.75 percent, and its net margin is (37.15) percent; eBay's gross is 89.91 percent, and its net margin is 13.33 percent. Amazon's twelve month revenue growth of 20.80 percent is approximately one-fourth of eBay's 79.10 percent.

Microsoft has scaled back its efforts to tackle the online auction industry, deciding instead to partner with eBay. In March 2001, eBay and Microsoft agreed to an alliance that is intended to supercharge eBay's Application Program Interface (API), extending it to Microsoft's legions of developers worldwide. Microsoft will also integrate eBay's marketplace into a number of its Web properties, including select MSN sites worldwide, CarPoint, bCentral, and WebTV.

At the present time, no one denies that eBay is the undisputed king of the online auction business—and quite possibly the best performing company in e-commerce and all of technology. In 2000 and 2001, eBay branched out from its traditional auction format. With the acquisition of Half.com and its adoption of the "Buy it Now" slogan, eBay has moved into the fixed price arena, and it has done so with great success. These moves into fixed pricing will make competition from Amazon.com and Yahoo! shopping more relevant than ever before.

The principal competitive factors for eBay include its ability to attract buyers, the volume of its transactions and the selection of goods, customer service, and brand recognition. With respect to eBay's online competition, additional competitive factors are community cohesion and interaction, system reliability, the reliability of delivery and payment, Web site convenience and accessibility, level of service fees, and the quality of search tools. Some current and potential competitors have longer company operating histories, larger customer bases, greater brand recognition in other businesses, and Internet spaces than eBay does. Some of these competitors also have significantly greater financial, marketing, technical, and other resources. As a result, eBay constantly monitors the activities of all competitors and adjusts its services to counter competitive activity. While eBay's rivals have been retrenching, the company has been expanding its own operations and cementing its dominant status in auctions.

INTERNET FRAUD

Current laws regarding liability issues for online service providers remain vague and are still evolving. Although eBay only provides the platform in which individuals trade their merchandise, the company realizes that it may face potential liability for certain user conduct on its site. eBay understands that items such as alcohol, tobacco, firearms, and adult material are subject to certain local, state, and federal guidelines. The company also understands that it may be unable to prevent unlawful activity on its site and may be subject to penalties for the conduct of some of its users.

The company realizes that Internet fraud can severely damage its community atmosphere. Users will quickly abandon a community that is rife with fraud and dishonesty, and eBay has taken steps to prevent fraud and unlawful activity by implementing certain checks and balances during the registration process. The Safe Harbor program, customer service department, and Feedback Forum have been put in place to foster the sense of community that eBay holds important to successful trading. eBay is counting on the community at large to hold fraudulent and illegal activity to a minimum.

According to eBay, fewer than thirty auctions per million generate a possible fraud complaint, but the company wants to lower the number of complaints and eliminate the potential for an unhappy experience. In response to fraud concerns, the company has established a simpler escrow system, new rules preventing sellers from bidding on their own items, tougher ID checks, penalties if bidders do not complete transactions, and free buyer's insurance. The company's reputation could be severely damaged or it could be held liable for any illegal or fraudulent activity that occurs on its Web site. Even if found innocent, eBay could find that the costs of litigation might cause financial harm.

GOVERNMENT REGULATION

Because eBay does not take possession of any of the items that are sold on its site or hold any receivables for merchandise sold, the company does not collect sales taxes associated with the transactions. The individual seller must conduct any tax requirements resulting from transactions. At present, sellers are not likely to collect and administer sales taxes. In the future, federal, state, and local governments may force the issue of sales tax collection and require compensation for such taxes. At that time, because eBay provides the platform for operation, the government may press eBay into some type of assistant or administrative role. This could conceivably add costs to operations without adding revenues.

Today, very few laws govern Internet sales. However, because Internet commerce is becoming more popular, it is very likely that within a few years, laws will be enacted to address user contracts, privacy, price structures, freedom of expression, security, and other areas. Additional costs may result from compliance.

LEGAL PROCEEDINGS

Other third parties have from time to time claimed and may claim in the future that eBay is infringing on their past, current, or future intellectual property rights. eBay may become more vulnerable to such claims as laws such as the Digital Millennium Copyright Act are interpreted by the courts. eBay expects that it will increasingly be subject to infringement claims as the number of services and direct competitors grow. These claims, whether meritorious or not, could be time-consuming, result in costly litigation, cause service upgrade delays, require expensive changes in its methods of doing business, or could require eBay to enter into costly royalty or licensing agreements, if available. As a result, these claims could harm the business.

ACQUISITIONS AND IMPROVEMENTS

During 2000, a number of improvements to the eBay trading platform were introduced. It acquired Half.com, a fixed-price, person-to-person trading Web site, where buyers and sellers can trade used books, CDs, movies, and video games at fixed prices that are less than the list price. Also, the launch of eBay Motors, in association with AutoTrader.com, created the Internet's largest auction-style Web site where consumers and dealers could buy and sell used cars. Furthermore, the eBay regional sites and the API and Developers Program, which allows other companies to use eBay content to drive their own businesses, are both new. The API provides three basic benefits. First, it allows eBay to be fully integrated into independent sites across the Internet. A new site will be able to use the eBay commerce engine to power its business, eliminating time and expense from the startup process. As a second benefit, the API will allow eBay and its commercial partners to more easily and rapidly add eBay's services to new devices, such as wireless telephones and handheld computers. Finally, the new platform interface will improve the user experience by allowing more companies to provide services to eBay users. The launch of electronic checks as a new payment option provides buyers and sellers with a means for faster transactions without returned checks, with no paperwork, and no charge-back risk. For eBay buyers, electronic checks combines the convenience of paper checks with the safety, convenience, and speed of electronic payments. For eBay sellers, electronic checks is a cost-effective alternative to paper checks and credit cards, in which payment is guaranteed. The launch of eBay Anywhere, a comprehensive mobile strategy, makes eBay accessible from any Internet-enabled mobile device. From WAP mobile phones to the latest PDAs, eBay Anywhere brings together leading technology companies, mobile carriers, portals, and hardware vendors with the goal of making eBay accessible to any user with a handheld Internet device. The launch of a new category called eBay Real Estate makes property transactions on eBay easier for buyers and sellers and provides a dedicated home for eBay's emerging real estate marketplace.

INTERNATIONAL EXPANSION

To create a truly global trading platform, eBay is establishing a strong presence in countries whose populations generate the majority of the world's e-commerce revenue. In 2000, eBay entered four new markets: Japan, Canada, France, and Austria. In the first eight weeks of 2001, the company announced the launch of an Italian site and the acquisition of a controlling interest in Internet Auction, South Korea's largest auction-style Web site. eBay also announced the acquisition of iBazar, the pioneer in online auction-style trading in Europe. With the iBazar acquisition as well as the recent launches of sites in Ireland, Switzerland, New Zealand, Singapore, and its 20 percent stake in Mercado Libre (Latin America's leading auction site), eBay will have a strong leadership position in seventeen of the top twenty global markets, representing approximately 90 percent of the world's e-commerce dollars and a vast majority of the world's Internet users. In 2001, eBay's international revenues increased 294 percent to $114 million from $28.9 million the year before.

FINANCIAL STATEMENTS

Income statements and balance sheets for 2000 and 2001 are provided in Exhibits 2 and 3, as well as some select financial ratios. The statements speak for themselves; eBay has experienced remarkable growth and is financially sound. In 2001, eBay again had record bottom-line profits, which were driven by record user growth, revenues, and gross merchandise sales.

eBay has identified two primary reporting segments: online trading services and offline, traditional auction services. The online trading services segment consists of the operations of eBay, Billpoint, alando.de.ag, and Half.com. The offine, traditional auction segment consists of the current operations of Butterfields and Kruse. eBay reports 2001 net revenues of $714 million and $34 million for online and offline, respectively.

CONCLUSION

In a poor economy when virtually every Internet company is treading water or drowning, eBay is growing by leaps and bounds. eBay has managed to do what virtually no other Internet company has been able to do, and having done so under the current economic climate makes its accomplishment even more astounding. The business model is solid and eBay shows no signs of slowing down. eBay is the market leader in Internet auction

EXHIBIT 2   eBay Inc. Consolidated Statement of Income
(in thousands, except per share amounts)

	Yearended December 31,		
	1999	*2000*	*2001*
Net revenues	$224,724	$431,424	$748,821
Cost of net revenues	57,588	95,453	134,816
Gross profit	167,136	335,971	614,005
Operating expenses:			
Sales and marketing	96,239	166,767	253,474
Product development	24,847	55,863	75,288
General and administrative	43,919	73,027	105,784
Payroll expense on employee stock options	–	2,337	2,442
Amortization of acquired intangible assets	1,145	1,433	36,591
Merger related costs	4,359	1,550	–
Total operating expenses	170,509	300,977	473,579
Income (loss) from operations	(3,373)	34,994	140,426
Interest and other income, net	23,833	46,337	41,613
Interest expense	(2,319)	(3,374)	(2,851)
Impairment of certain equity investments	–	–	(16,245)
Income before income taxes and minority interests	18,141	77,957	162,943
Provision for income taxes	(8,472)	(32,725)	(80,009)
Minority interests in consolidated companies	(102)	3,062	7,514
Net income	$ 9,567	$ 48,294	$ 90,448
Net income per share:			
Basic	$ 0.04	$ 0.19	$ 0.34
Diluted	$ 0.04	$ 0.17	$ 0.32
Weighted average shares:			
Basic	217,674	251,776	268,971
Diluted	273,033	280,346	280,595

Source: eBay's 2001 *Annual Report,* p. 62.

selling, and it operates in a rapidly expanding market. Driving the company's growth is the success eBay has had in moving overseas into Germany, Australia, and other markets. The company has seen its market grow from a site at which collectibles are traded to a marketplace for practical goods and services, which is certain to attract a larger audience. The gradual move into fixed-price trading may also prove to be huge for eBay, further expanding its appeal to the mainstream and attracting customers who might never have shopped on the auction site.

eBay is in a fantastic position to develop and to grow as a company. As the market leader with tremendous financial strength, it should take advantage of the current economic situation, and while others are forced to downsize and lay off employees, eBay can afford to seek out and hire the best and brightest individuals. eBay should also leverage its current brand recognition to further enhance and develop its position as a business-to-business trading platform, since the B2B (business to business) market is expected to account for $4.3 trillion in sales by 2005. At the heart of eBay's continued growth will be its continuous improvements and upgrades to its trading platform. Using the leading technologies to keep the platform reliable and dependable while maintaining the users feelings of security and trust will help ensure eBay's success for years to come.

EXHIBIT 3   eBay Inc. Consolidated Balance Sheet
(in thousands, except per share amounts)

	December 31,	
	2000	*2001*

ASSETS

Current assets:

	2000	2001
Cash and cash equivalents	$ 201,873	$ 523,969
Short-term investments	354,166	199,450
Accounts receivable, net	67,163	101,703
Other current assets	52,262	58,683
Total current assets	675,464	883,805
Long-term investments	218,197	286,998
Restricted cash and investments	126,390	129,614
Property and equipment, net	125,161	142,349
Intangible assets, net	13,063	198,639
Deferred tax assets	13,892	21,540
Other assets	10,236	15,584
	$1,182,403	$1,678,529

LIABILITIES AND STOCKHOLDERS' EQUITY

Current liabilities:

	2000	2001
Accounts payable	$ 31,725	$ 33,235
Accrued expenses and other current liabilities	66,697	94,593
Deferred revenue and customer advances	12,656	15,583
Short-term debt	15,272	16,111
Income taxes payable	11,092	20,617
Total current liabilities	137,442	180,139
Long-term debt	11,404	12,008
Other liabilities	6,549	19,493
Minority interests	13,248	37,751
Total liabilities	168,643	249,391
Commitments and contingencies		
Stockholders' equity:		
Convertible Preferred Stock, $0.001 par value; 10,000 shares authorized; no shares issued or outstanding	–	–
Common Stock, $0.001 par value; 900,000 shares authorized; 269,250 and 277,259 shares issued and outstanding	269	277
Additional paid-in capital	941,285	1,275,240
Unearned stock-based compensation	(1,423)	(2,367)
Retained earnings	74,504	164,633
Accumulated other comprehensive loss	(875)	(8,645)
Total stockholders' equity	1,013,760	1,429,138
	$1,182,403	$1,678,529

Source: eBay's 2001 *Annual Report,* p. 61.

EXHIBIT 4   eBay Inc. Segment Information

	2000		
	Online	Offline	Consolidated
Net revenues from external customers	$ 391,952	$ 39,472	$ 431,424
Operating income (loss), as adjusted	49,767	(2,312)	47,455
Interest and other income and expense, net	45,642	695	46,337
Interest expense	(1,071)	(2,303)	(3,374)
Amortization of certain non-cash items	(11,464)	(997)	(12,461)
Income (loss) before income taxes and minority interest and equity interest in partnership income	$ 82,874	$ (4,917)	$ 77,957
Total assets	$1,084,909	$ 97,494	$1,182,403

	2001		
	Online	Offline	Consolidated
Net revenues from external customers	$ 714,405	$ 34,416	$ 748,821
Operating income (loss), as adjusted	185,298	(2,759)	182,539
Interest and other income and expense, net	42,208	(595)	41,613
Impairment of certain equity investments	(16,245)	–	(16,245)
Interest expense	(1,686)	(1,165)	(2,851)
Amortization of certain non-cash items	(41,772)	(341)	(42,113)
Income (loss) before income taxes and minority interest and equity interest in partnership income	$ 167,803	$ (4,860)	$ 162,943
Total assets	$1,588,913	$ 89,616	$1,678,529

	Yearended December 31,		
	1999	2000	2001
United States revenues	$ 222,130	$402,446	$ 634,659
International revenues	2,594	28,978	114,162
Net revenues	$ 224,724	$431,424	$ 748,821

Source: eBay's 2001 *Annual Report,* p. 77.

NOTES

[1]Nielson/Net Ratings Audience Measurement Service.

EXHIBIT 5   eBay's Percentage Analysis

The following table sets forth, for the periods presented, certain data from our consolidated statement of income as a percentage of net revenues.

	Yearended December 31,		
	1999	*2000*	*2001*
Net revenues	100.0%	100.0%	100.0%
Cost of net revenues	25.6	22.1	18.0
Gross profit	74.4	77.9	82.0
Operating expenses:			
Sales and marketing	42.8	38.7	33.8
Product development	11.1	12.9	10.1
General and administrative	19.5	16.9	14.1
Payroll expense on employee stock options	–	0.5	0.3
Amortization of acquired intangible assets	0.5	0.3	4.9
Merger related costs	1.9	0.4	–
Total operating expenses	75.8	69.7	63.2
Income (loss) from operations	(1.4)	8.2	18.8
Interest and other income, net	10.6	10.7	5.6
Interest expense	(1.0)	(0.8)	(0.4)
Impairment of certain equity investments	–	–	(2.2)
Income before income taxes and minority interests	8.2	18.1	21.8
Provision for income taxes	(3.8)	(7.6)	(10.7)
Minority interests in consolidated companies	(0.1)	0.7	1.0
Net income	4.3%	11.2%	12.1%

Source: eBay's 2001 *Annual Report,* p. 23.

EXHIBIT 6   eBay Operating Data: Net Revenues

	1999	Percent Change	2000	Percent Change	2001
			(in thousands, except percent changes)		
Online net revenues:					
Transactions	$179,895	94%	$348,174	73%	$602,671
Third-party advertising	2,030	541%	13,022	544%	83,853
End-to-end services and promotions	608	4,959%	30,756	(9)%	27,881
Total online net revenues	182,533	115%	$391,952	82%	714,405
Butterfields	31,319	(6)%	29,405	(14)%	25,251
Kruse	10,872	(7)%	10,067	(9)%	9,165
Total offline net revenues	42,191	(6)%	39,472	(13)%	34,416
Total net revenues	$224,724	92%	$431,424	74%	$748,821
U.S. net revenues	$222,130	81%	$402,446	58%	$634,659
International net revenues	2,594	1,017%	28,978	294%	114.162
Total net revenues	$224,724	92%	$431,424	74%	$748,821

	1999	Percent Change	2000	Percent Change	2001
			(in millions, except percent and per listing amounts)		
Supplemental Operating Data:					
Confirmed registered users at end of year	10.0	125%	22.5	89%	42.4
Number of items listed	129.6	104%	264.7	60%	423.1
Gross merchandise sales	$ 2,805	93%	$ 5,422	72%	$ 9,319

Source: eBay's 2001 *Annual Report,* p. 24.

AMAZON.COM, INC.—2002

Margie Goodson
Francis Marion University

AMZN

www.Amazon.com

September 11, 2001, began as just another ordinary day. There was a crispness in the air that always ushers in the fall season. No one could have predicted the events that would take place that day. The news resounded throughout the world. A plane had crashed into the World Trade Center in downtown Manhattan, New York, hitting one of the twin towers. Surely, it was a horrible accident. Then not many minutes later, another plane hit the remaining tower. Clearly, these events were no accident. Minutes later, news reports revealed that the Pentagon had also been struck by a hijacked plane. America was under attack by terrorists who had plotted against the country and had succeeded in violating a nation and a way of life. America would never be the same.

In mere seconds, thousands of lives were lost, and millions of dollars of property was damaged. Wall Street shut down for four days, the longest time ever. When the markets reopened on September 17, everyone waited to see how Wall Street would react. The first day saw a sputtering market that tried to rally only to close just above eight hundred by the session's end. The uncertainty of the market reflected the uncertainty felt by the United States—and the entire world. Could the American economy fight its way back from this destructive act? While digging among the rubble in recovery efforts and while waging a war on terrorism, could the American economy survive an almost certain recession? How long would the recession last? These are questions that all individuals as well as businesses in every sector of the economy will seek to answer in the days that lie ahead. It will be difficult for established companies that are viable and profitable to weather the rough days to come. It will be an even greater challenge for companies that are relatively new, unproven, and have not reached the realm of profitability. Amazon.com is one such company.

HISTORY

Amazon.com, Inc. (Amazon) is an Internet-based company located in Seattle, Washington. The founder of the company as well as its president, CEO, and chairman is Jeff Bezos. While working as a senior vice president for DE Shaw & Company in 1994, Bezos was given an assignment: to find good Internet companies in which to invest. While Web surfing for the first time, he discovered a site showing that the number of Internet users was growing by 2,300 percent per month. Bezos began thinking of products and services that could be sold efficiently on the Web, and he developed a list of around twenty. Within two months, Jeff and his wife Mackenzie started a trip across America. While Mackenzie drove the Chevy Blazer, Jeff constructed a business plan on a laptop and contacted potential investors by cellular phone. Selling books was chosen as the market to pursue because there was no clear powerhouse in the market. The largest competitor was Barnes & Noble, Inc. with only 15 percent of the book-selling market in 1994.

Initially, Bezos wanted to call the company Cadabra, but after an acquaintance mistakenly thought that he was naming it "Cadaver," the search for a name began anew. The company was eventually named after the mightiest river in the world, the Amazon. The company's 2000 net income was negative $1.411 billion on revenues of $2.7 billion. Amazon shares were down 75 percent from their year high of more than $40 before September 11. As of October 3, they were down another 25 percent—at $6.08. Amazon's CEO, Jeff Bezos, predicted that the company would report its first operating profit in the fourth quarter of 2001. No one could have predicted the events of September 11 and the impact they would have on consumer confidence and spending.

In 1994, Amazon.com, Inc. was incorporated in the state of Washington. It would reincorporate in 1996 in the state of Delaware. Seattle was chosen as Amazon's head-quarters because of the proximity to Ingram Book Group's warehouse and because of the population's noted computer expertise. In 1995, while operating out of a rented forty-five thousand square foot facility and using doors laid across sawhorses for desk space, Amazon started selling books exclusively online.

Amazon immediately enjoyed astounding growth rates. Sales for 1995, 1996, 1997, 1998, 1999, and 2000 were $.5, $16, $147, $610, $1,640 and $2,762.0 million, respectively. Amazon's 2001 financial statements are shown in Exhibits 1 and 2. Amazon's customer base increased from 180,000 in one hundred countries in 1996 to 20 million in 2000. The repeat purchase rate of existing customers rose from 44 percent in 1996 to 70 percent in 1999. The average spent per customer in 2000 was $134, up 19 percent over 1999.

In 1998, Amazon began expanding. Music and videos were added to the product mix. Within two months of the initial offering of these products, Amazon became the number one seller of books, music, and videos online. Further expansion followed in 1999. The company now also offers electronics and software, toys and video games, home improvements, electronic greeting cards, online auctions, DVDs, and a virtual mall called z-Shops. Amazon also operates the Internet Movie Database, a comprehensive source of information on movies and entertainment titles as well as crew and cast members. Presently, Amazon is organized into three operating segments: the U.S. books, music, and DVD/video segment; the early-stage businesses and other segment; and the international segment, consisting of sites focused in the United Kingdom, Germany, France, and Japan. Sales and Profit(Loss) information is listed in Exhibit 3.

During 2000, Amazon's Music store launched Bargain Music, Latin and Box Set stores, and a Music Accessories store. Amazon also created over thirty franchise stores for its DVD and Video stores, and it created and hosted official Web sites for a number of prominent films. In late 2000, Amazon launched a co-branded video and toy store with Toysrus.com. Amazon also has strategic partnerships with a drugstore; a deliverer of spoken audio over the Internet; an issuer of consumer credit cards; an auction site devoted to art, antiques, jewelry, and collectibles; a photography service; and an auto broker. All of these businesses operate in cyberspace. Also, Amazon has acquired businesses to produce e-commerce software and to establish a database to track customer demographic information and online buying habits. In August 2001, Amazon opened its new online computer store at a time when the PC business was at the industry's lowest point in years. In September 2001, the company introduced another new feature, a fully personalized store for every returning customer, with the launch of Your Store (**www.amazon.com/yourstore**). The site features each customer's name in a tab that contains selections from his or her favorite areas across the Amazon.com Web site. Bezos states, "At Amazon.com, we've always worked to put the customer at the center of his or her own shopping universe."

EXHIBIT 1   Amazon.com, Inc. Consolidated Balance Sheets (in thousands, except per-share data)

	December 31,	
	2001	*2000*

ASSETS

Current assets:		
Cash and cash equivalents	$ 540,282	$ 822,435
Marketable securities	456,303	278,087
Inventories	143,722	174,563
Prepaid expenses and other current assets	67,613	86,044
Total current assets	1,207,920	1,361,129
Fixed assets, net	271,751	366,416
Goodwill, net	45,367	158,990
Other intangibles, net	34,382	96,335
Investments in equity-method investees	10,387	52,073
Other equity investments	17,972	40,177
Other assets	49,768	60,049
Total assets	$ 1,637,547	$ 2,135,169

LIABILITIES AND STOCKHOLDERS' DEFICIT

Current liabilities:		
Accounts payable	$ 444,748	$ 485,383
Accrued expenses and other current liabilities	305,064	272,683
Unearned revenue	87,978	131,117
Interest payable	68,632	69,196
Current portion of long-term debt and other	14,992	16,577
Total current liabilities	921,414	974,956
Long-term debt and other	2,156,133	2,127,464
Commitments and contingencies		
Stockholders' deficit:		
Preferred stock, $0.01 par value:		
Authorized shares—500,000		
Issued and outstanding shares—none	—	—
Common stock, $0.01 par value:		
Authorized shares—5,000,000		
Issued and outstanding shares—373,218 and		
357,140 shares, respectively	3,732	3,571
Additional paid-in capital	1,462,769	1,338,303
Deferred stock-based compensation	(9,853)	(13,448)
Accumulated other comprehensive loss	(36,070)	(2,376)
Accumulated deficit	(2,860,578)	(2,293,301)
Total stockholders' deficit	(1,440,000)	(967,251)
Total liabilities and stockholders' deficit	$ 1,637,547	$ 2,135,169

Source: Amazon's 2001 *Annual Report,* p. 43.

EXTERNAL ASSESSMENT

The number of Internet users is continuing to rise. At the end of 2000, about 370.8 million users worldwide accessed the Internet at least monthly. This number is expected to soar to 1.3 billion by 2005. The number of Web pages is expected to increase from

EXHIBIT 2   Amazon.com, Inc. Consolidated Statements of Operations (in thousands, except per share data)

	Years Ended December 31,		
	2001	*2000*	*1999*
Net sales	$3,122,433	$ 2,761,983	$1,639,839
Cost of sales	2,323,875	2,106,206	1,349,194
Gross profit	798,558	655,777	290,645
Operating expenses:			
Fulfillment	374,250	414,509	237,312
Marketing	138,283	179,980	175,838
Technology and content	241,165	269,326	159,722
General and administrative	89,862	108,962	70,144
Stock-based compensation	4,637	24,797	30,618
Amortization of goodwill and other intangibles	181,033	321,772	214,694
Restructuring-related and other	181,585	200,311	8,072
Total operating expenses	1,210,815	1,519,657	896,400
Loss from operations	(412,257)	(863,880)	(605,755)
Interest income	29,103	40,821	45,451
Interest expense	(139,232)	(130,921)	(84,566)
Other income (expense), net	(1,900)	(10,058)	1,671
Other gains (losses), net	(2,141)	(142,639)	—
Net interest expense and other	(114,170)	(242,797)	(37,444)
Loss before equity in losses of equity-method investees	(526,427)	(1,106,677)	(643,199)
Equity in losses of equity-method investees, net	(30,327)	(304,596)	(76,769)
Loss before change in accounting principle	$ (556,754)	$ (1,411,273)	$ (719,968)
Cumulative effect of change in accounting principle	(10,523)	—	—
Net loss	$ (567,277)	$ (1,411,273)	$ (719,968)
Basic and diluted loss per share:			
Prior to cumulative effect of change in accounting principle	$ (1.53)	$ (4.02)	$ (2.20)
Cumulative effect of change in accounting principle	(0.03)	—	—
	$ (1.56)	$ (4.02)	$ (2.20)
Shares used in computation of basic and diluted loss per share	364,211	350,873	326,753

Source: Amazon's 2001 *Annual Report,* p. 44.

1.7 billion in 1999 to 8.0 billion in 2002. The United States accounts for more than one-half of the world's total number of Internet users; however, penetration is expected to increase in western Europe because of declines in access costs. Although 46 percent of the U.S. population is connected, there is still plenty of room for growth. Personal computer penetration in the United States rose from 42 percent in 1998 to 51 percent in 2000. A total of 98 million PCs were shipped in 1998, 114 million units were shipped in 1999 (up 23 percent), and 131 million units were shipped in 2000 (up 16 percent); and the number of units shipped rose to 139 million in 2001 (up 6 percent). The projections reflect a gradual slowing of the growth of PC shipments. While once dominated by males, Internet users are now almost equally divided between males and females. Internet users are more educated than the general population, with over 80 percent having at least some college experience. This percentage continues to fall as more people are acquiring access to the Internet using inexpensive computers and public access points, such as libraries and schools.

EXHIBIT 3   Amazon's Segment Financial Information (in billions)

	U.S. Books, Music, DVD/Videos	U.S. Electronics, Tools, and Kitchen	International	Services
NET SALES				
2001	$ 1.69	$.547	$.661	$.225
2000	1.70	.484	.381	.198
1999	1.31	.151	.168	.013
GROSS PROFIT				
2001	$.453	$.078	$.141	$.126
2000	.417	.045	.077	.116
1999	.263	−.020	.036	.012

Source: Amazon's 2001 *Annual Report,* pp. 22–24.

English is the predominant language used on Web sites. Australia, Canada, Ireland, New Zealand, South Africa, the United Kingdom, and the United States use English as a native language. The combined population and Gross Domestic Product of these countries are 322 million and $10.8 trillion, respectively.

Over 29 million people in the United States speak Spanish. That number is expected to grow to 40 million by 2010. Presently, the U.S. Hispanic market is estimated at $325 billion. Worldwide, 800 million people speak Spanish. Hispanics, both domestically and abroad, demonstrate high levels of brand loyalty.

Internet commerce, called e-commerce, is increasingly accepted. The e-commerce segment grew by over 125 percent in the year 2000. Online spending has been projected to exceed $428 billion in 2004, up from $60 billion in 2000 and just $10 billion in 1998.

E-commerce can be broken into four segments: (1) business-to-business (B2B), (2) business-to-consumer (B2C), (3) business-to-administration, and (4) customer-to-administration. The two most familiar are business-to-business and business-to-consumer commerce, during which products and services are exchanged via electronic networking systems instead of person-to-person. For example, at a checkout counter, an item is "scanned." That information is relayed to a computer system which, when the appropriate level has been sold, will order new supplies via Electronic Data Interchange (EDI). This is a form of business-to-business commerce and has been around since the 1960s. The U.S. Commerce Department projects that e-commerce will be the primary economic growth engine of the United States for the next one hundred years.

According to a study by the Boston Consulting Group, one based on a survey of European buyers, sellers, and supply-chain managers, the total volume of online transactions in Europe is expected to jump from an estimated $200 billion in 2000 to an estimated $3.1 trillion in 2004. Currently, online transactions in European countries are less than one-third of the number in the United States. Fifty-six percent of the companies surveyed expect online sales channels to enable them to increase revenues by 2004.

The B2C e-commerce segment is now experiencing rapid growth. As Internet use increases and as people grow more comfortable with ordering products online, more profit is made by businesses. Online B2C sales projected for 2004 are $428 billion, up from $60 billion in 2000 and just $10 billion in 1998. Business-to-business sales are projected to grow to $1.3 trillion by 2003, up from $251 billion in 2000.

Internet companies, including Amazon, continue to have a problem with people visiting and browsing but not buying. This is also a problem common to offline retailers. Web sites are being used to gather information about products, which is then used to purchase the product at offline locations or other Web sites. While it has been suggested that the major reason for not purchasing online is fear of the loss of private financial information, researchers have found that active online shoppers are not afraid. One of the reasons for this lack of fear is that credit card companies all but guarantee all online purchases and provide 100 percent coverage in the event that a consumer's card is misused online. Amazon also confronts this security issue by using encryption methods to encode transmitted data. In fact, the use of encryption is more secure than calling a business and giving a credit card number over an ordinary phone line.

As potential profits increase, more businesses want to come online. To paraphrase what a commercial states, "If you are not online, then you are not really in business." In today's business environment, three basic B2C structures exist: (1) traditional "brick and mortar," (2) completely online, or (3) "brick and click," a combination of the two. Amazon and E-bay, Inc. are examples of completely online businesses, while Barnes & Noble, Inc., Wal-Mart Stores, Inc., and Toys 'R' Us, Inc. are examples of the combination of "brick and mortar" and virtual. Each is offering products or services to the Internet user. Although Amazon is often considered to be the eight hundred pound gorilla of e-commerce, the Internet business market is still fragmented. It has been suggested that the "brick and click" segment of e-businesses use the Internet as another arm of their showroom to provide shoppers with product and inventory information. A retailer's Web site can be an incredibly powerful tool for driving offline sales. A lot of consumers like to research products online before purchasing them offline. Researchers have found that consumers will switch back and forth between online, offline, and a combination of the two depending upon which method serves them best for a particular purchase.

Researchers predict that sales of e-books will grow from $40 million in 2000 to $2.3 billion in 2005. People will increasingly download books from online bookstores and print them to a PC, personal digital assistant, or handheld e-book reader. E-books will not replace the traditional paper books, but they *will* provide consumers with a greater number of options. Another high growth area is that of auctions. It is predicted that consumer-to-consumer auctions will grow from $3 billion in 1999 to $6.4 billion in 2000—and to $15.1 billion in 2004. At the same time, according to predictions, B2C auction revenues will increase from $700 million in 1999 to a projected $1.1 billion in 2000—and $4.5 billion in 2004.

As the Internet becomes an increasingly essential part of people's lives, the government will begin to look at ways to evaluate and regulate online activity. The issue of Internet taxation has received much publicity. Currently, there is a ban on taxation of online purchases, and a bill was signed in November 2001 to extend the ban until Nov. 1, 2003. Losses attributed to nontaxation of the Internet have been estimated at $3.8 billion in 2000 and to be $12.4 billion in 2003. Many states are considering revising their tax codes to capture some of this potential revenue from Internet sales.

Competitors

Barnes & Noble

Amazon faces stiff and growing competition from established and growing Internet companies. Barnes & Noble, Inc. has been a classic comparative competitor for Amazon since Amazon's beginning. Barnes & Noble currently operates 908 bookstores and 978 video and entertainment software stores under several names: Barnes & Noble Booksellers, Bookstop, Bookstar, B. Dalton Booksellers, Doubleday Bookshops, and

Scribner's Bookstore. Touted as the world's largest bookseller, the company generated record sales of $4.4 billion in 2000, up 26 percent from the prior year. The company's principal business is the retail sale of trade books, mass-market paperbacks, children's books, off-price bargain books, and magazines. Sales of $2.797, $3.006, $3.486, and $4.375 billion were recorded for 1997, 1998, 1999, and 2000, respectively.

Located in high-traffic areas with convenient access to major commercial thoroughfares and ample parking, Barnes & Noble was the first bookseller to utilize the Superstore concept. The company has locations in forty-nine states and the District of Columbia as of February 3, 2001. The company has established a Web site, **http://www. barnesandnoble.com**, and is the exclusive bookseller on America Online. In November 2000, barnesandnoble.com merged with Fatbrain.com, Inc., the third largest online bookseller, which specialized in professional and technical titles for the corporate marketplace. In addition to books, B&N.com offers music, DVD/video, magazines, and related products. It also offers a large listing of rare and out-of-print books as well as an online selection of college textbooks and e-books. This segment saw a 65 percent increase in sales—to $320 million—in the fiscal year ending December 31, 2000.

Wal-Mart

Wal-Mart Stores, Inc. is a Delaware corporation with headquarters based in Bentonville, Arkansas. In fiscal 2001, the company had a growth in revenues of more than $26 billion, representing a 16 percent increase in net sales. With net sales over $137.6, $165.0, and $191.3 billion, respectively, for fiscal years ending January 31, 1999, 2000, and 2001, the company is billed as the world's largest retailer. The founder was Sam M. Walton. Wal-Mart operates 1,736 discount stores, 888 Supercenters, 475 SAM's Clubs, and 19 Neighborhood Markets domestically. The company expects to open approximately 170 to 180 new Supercenters and 40 new Wal-Mart stores in the coming year. Wal-Mart has operating units in Argentina, Brazil, Canada, Germany, Mexico, South Korea, Mexico, Puerto Rico, and the United Kingdom. Wal-Mart is principally engaged in the operation of mass merchandising stores.

General operating hours domestically range from 7:00 A.M. to 11:00 P.M., six days a week, and from 10:00 A.M. to 8:00 P.M. on Sunday for discount stores and Supercenters. However, an increasing number of Wal-Mart discount stores and almost all of the Supercenters are open twenty-four hours each day.

Wal-Mart's Web site, **http://www.wal-mart.com**, was launched in late 1999. Wal-Mart has the second largest database in the world to track and predict customer purchases. Wal-Mart continues to enjoy great success with its physical retail outlets, and it appears to be focusing more on this core competency rather than on an expansion of its Internet presence. Amazon and Wal-Mart were in negotiation earlier this year, but no strategic partnership resulted from the talks.

eBay

Ebay Inc. was formed as a sole proprietorship in 1995, and it was incorporated in California in 1996. EBay owns and operates eBay.com, which bills itself as the world's largest and most popular online marketplace. Its mission is to develop a global online trading platform that will help practically anyone buy or sell practically anything. Ebay, like Amazon, sells storefronts to businesses. The businesses pay both a fixed fee and in most cases a percentage of each item they sell. Ebay increases its sales without ever going to the expense of touching the product. The number of registered eBay users grew from approximately two million in 1998 to twenty-two million in December 2000, representing a 125 percent increase over 1999. In its attempt to establish a strong presence in countries that generate the majority of the world's e-commerce revenue, eBay entered four new markets in 2000; Japan, Canada, France, and Austria. Ebay also has introduced country-specific services for the United Kingdom, Australia, Germany, and Italy; and in February 2001, it acquired Internet Auction Company Ltd. of South Korea. The company believes its user base includes users located in over two hundred countries. For the year 2000, eBay reported net revenue of $431.4 million, a 92 percent increase over 1999. Online net revenues totaled $392 million, a 115 percent increase over 1999.

INTERNAL ASSESSMENT

Amazon is committed to customer satisfaction. Jeff Bezos claims that the key to keeping customers is to give them what they want. Amazon has designed a system that is not only easy to use but also efficient. Amazon copyrighted the One-Click approach to online shopping. A customer can now shop in several areas throughout Amazon's entire domain without having to reregister or change virtual shopping carts. In addition, the company tracks customer purchases and preferences to personalize each customer's shopping experience. Also, the customer is allowed to participate in the review of some products. Thus, in the end, customers feels as if they are more a member of a community than just another customer.

Amazon, eBay, and many other Web sites joined together to boost charitable donations after the recent terrorist attack on the World Trade Center. Within hours of the incident, Amazon had a message of condolence posted on its site and instructions on how to give for the relief efforts. The Web site collected more than $30 million, with more than 70 percent of it going to the Red Cross.

Amazon has hired several well-established businesspeople from several major companies. These new employees' expertise range from computer software development to international distribution, credit management, and brand-name building. There was no organizational chart that could be found, but the chart in Exhibit 4 was constructed using the information found in Amazon's 2000 *Annual Report*.

Amazon currently has seven U.S. distribution centers and three European centers as well as numerous customer service centers. (See Exhibit 5.) The rationale is to ship 95 percent of all orders on the same day the order is received. By having more distribution

EXHIBIT 4   Amazon.com's Organization Chart

			Jeffrey P. Bezos President Chief Executive Officer Chairman of the Board		
Mark J. Britto Senior Vice President Worldwide Services, Sales & Business Development	Rick Dalzell Sr. Vice President Chief Information Officer	Warren C. Jenson Sr. Vice President Chief Financial Officer	Diego Piacentini Sr. Vice President Worldwide Retail & Marketing	Jeff A. Wilke Sr. Vice President Worldwide Operations & Customer Service	Michelle Wilson Sr. Vice President Human Resources General Counsel

Source: Compiled from information obtained from Amazon.com's 2001 *Annual Report*.

EXHIBIT 5   *Amazon's Distribution Centers*

DISTRIBUTION (FULFILLMENT) CENTERS

1. Fernley, Nevada
2. Coffeyville, Kansas
3. Campbellsville, Kentucky
4. Lexington, Kentucky
5. New Castle, Delaware
6. Grand Forks, North Dakota
7. Seattle, Washington (seasonal)
8. United Kingdom
9. France
10. Germany
11. Japan (joint management with Nippon Express)

CUSTOMER SERVICE CENTERS

1. Tacoma, Washington
2. Huntington, West Virginia
3. Grand Forks, North Dakota
4. Slough, England
5. Regensburg, Germany
6. Sapporo, Japan
7. India (has outsourcing agreement with Daksh.com)

centers, the company can hold more accessible inventory and deliver merchandise in a reliable manner. Some criticism has been leveled against Amazon's management for not focusing on making a profit. The management response is that the focus is on the long term, not the short term, and that building a strong infrastructure is necessary to compete in today's ever-changing marketplace.

Amazon is also effective and resourceful with its promotions and advertisements. One of the first moves performed by the company was to initiate an Associates Program, allowing the company to establish exclusive contracts with owners of valuable cyberspace real estate. The program enables associated Web sites to make their products available to their respective audiences, with order fulfillment by Amazon. Amazon has currently enrolled 530,000 Web sites in the Associates Program. Amazon also has recently begun charging publishers and manufacturers to have books and other products promoted in specifically targeted e-mails to customers. This is an idea adapted from traditional retailers, which charge publishers for a special position or for a display in chain bookstores. The retailer sells the benefit of the extra attention to the publisher or manufacturer. This is a strategy that delivers a lot of cash to a business, because Amazon can track its customer's interests through its customized homepage, **www.amazon.com/yourstore**, which shows shoppers items they might want to buy based on previous visits. Consequently, Amazon can aim announcements at specific customers.

Amazon has also formed several strategic alliances that should strengthen its financial position. CEO Bezos states that Amazon has built a platform that not only allows the company to serve its customers extremely well but also allows it to serve the customers of other leading companies. Each one of its alliances is customized to make use of varying portions of Amazon's platform, which consists of its fulfillment technology, distribution centers, the customer service centers, and, of course, the customers themselves who are brought to the table. Bezos also states that many physical retailers have found that online business is a difficult business, just as physical retailing is a difficult business. They are choosing to align with an e-commerce company with a strong platform so that they can remain focused on their core competencies while providing a "best of the breed" online offering to their customers.

The partnership with Toys 'R' Us generated more than $125 million in sales of toys and video games in the fourth quarter of 2000. Amazon is eliminating a competitor to its online book selling operation by creating a site with Borders.com. This site will use Amazon's inventory, fulfillment, site content, and customer service.

In July 2001, AOL Time Warner invested $100 million in Amazon, and in exchange, Amazon's Platform Services Group agreed to develop and offer an enhanced online shopping experience for America Online users. The agreement also forbids AOL from increasing its holdings in Amazon beyond 5 percent for two years unless Amazon agrees to be acquired or if some other company attempts to take over the company. The agreement also forbids AOL from selling its 6.54 million shares for two years unless there is a material breach in certain commercial agreements. It is believed that this agreement allows Amazon to deliver technology to AOL to aid it in its battle with Microsoft.

Amazon also made a deal with Circuit City to allow in-store pickups of electronics equipment ordered at Amazon. In addition, Amazon announced a five-year alliance with Target Corp., which gives Target access to Amazon's technology and its customer base of 35 million people; in return, Amazon will receive sales commissions and annual fixed fees.

Amazon has an accumulated deficit and anticipates further losses resulting in significant indebtedness. Investors have expressed concern because of Amazon's inability to realize a steady profit. Analysts have stated that the company continues to expand its service offerings, and the company is looking for an increase in growth in its core business—the U.S. books, music, and video segment—that is barely growing. Another concern for analysts is that Amazon has to purchase some items (e.g., electronics) from distributors rather than from manufacturers. They argue that there is no positive contribution margin, and the more Amazon sells, the more it loses. One analyst went so far as to say Amazon may soon run out of money.

Amazon does not have a mission statement. The company's stated goal is "to put customer satisfaction first by using the Internet to transform product buying into the fastest, easiest, and most enjoyable shopping experience possible." Another universally accepted goal associated with Amazon is "to provide the largest selection of merchandise on Earth." These are not mission statements but instead could be considered vision statements.

CONCLUSION

Amazon is a pioneer in the emerging B2C e-commerce market. By recognizing and taking advantage of the growing number of Internet users, the company has led the way in defining B2C e-commerce. But many opportunities and threats still lie ahead.

Should Amazon scale back its costs even further by decreasing the number of fulfillment centers or by seeking to make operations more efficient at each center? Should

Amazon continue its global expansion, or should it look at reducing its global presence? Has Amazon taken full advantage of the increasing Hispanic population? Should more strategic alliances with major brick and mortar retailers be formed? Can Amazon survive in the wake of an economic downturn, or will it merge with some other company such as AOL TimeWarner? Develop a three-year strategic plan for CEO Jeff Bezos.

REFERENCES

www.amazon.com
www.thestreet.com
http://investor.stockpoint.com
http://dailynews.yahoo.com
www.forbes.com
www.marketwatch.com/news/yahoo
http://infotrac.galegroup.com/itw/
    infomamarc

www.bcg.com/new
www.thestandard.com
www.ecommercetimes.com
http://web6.infotrac.galegroup.com/itw
www.businessweek.com/reuters
www.msnbc.com/news
http://news.cnet.com/news

LIMITED BRANDS—2002

M. Jill Austin
Middle Tennessee State University

LTD

www.limited.com

Creating brands. Building value. Best talent. Best processes. Fewer, more dominant brands that understand their "best-at" and deliver it with consistency. Brands that, simply, know how to win. We'll concentrate on top stores, disciplined inventories, and tightly controlled expenses. We'll stay the course.

This is Chairman and CEO Leslie Wexner's view of Limited Brands in 2002. For over thirty-six years, Wexner's Limited stores have achieved success by "breaking the rules" in the specialty retailing industry. Instead of offering a wide variety of types of clothing, the stores offer a limited assortment of sportswear in large quantities and in a variety of colors. In the mid-1990s, The Limited, Inc., made a strategic decision to develop strong brand associations for its stores. Today, the company has a number of store-brand leaders and in May 2002, changed its name to Limited Brands. Net sales from 2001 to 2001 decreased 7 percent to $9.36 billion. Operating income was $918 million in 2001, up from $866 million in 2000. 4,614 at yearend 2001, down from 5,129 in 2000.

HISTORY

Leslie Wexner's mother and father both worked in retailing. His father worked for the Miller Wall specialty chain, and his mother was a buyer for Lazarus. When Wexner was fourteen, his parents opened their own specialty apparel store in Columbus, Ohio. After college and one year of law school, Wexner returned to work in his parents' store, where he planned to remain until he decided what he wanted to do with his life. He planned that his work in retail would be temporary, but he says he "got hooked."

In 1963, Wexner borrowed $10,000 from an aunt and a bank to open The Limited's first store. During its first year in operation, this store achieved sales of $157,000. His strategy was to provide a limited assortment of quality, fashionable sportswear at medium prices. The "limited" concept worked well, and by the late 1970s, Wexner began a twofold strategy of market development and product development. New stores were opened and acquired to appeal to women of different ages, different sizes, and different budget limits.

Throughout the 1980s, Wexner acquired a variety of businesses, including Lane Bryant, Victoria's Secret, Sizes Unlimited, Lerner, Henri Bendel, and Abercrombie & Fitch. Each of these stores was in financial trouble when acquired by Wexner. Wexner also started several store divisions during the 1980s. These included Express, Structure, Limited Too, and Cacique. Penhaligon's was acquired in 1990, and Galyan's Trading Company was acquired in 1995. Bath & Body Works was started by The Limited, Inc., in 1990. In May 1998, the company's Abercrombie & Fitch stores became an independent public company. Cacique stores closed in 1998, and Penhaligon's stores were sold in 1997.

In 1996, Wexner's Limited confronted its vulnerabilities. In response to the significant sales problems at Express, Wexner said, "We are fundamentally reinventing the business: sweeping change, greater discipline, more centralization, and a plan to build brands, not just business." This transition in thinking required each division to clearly define its fashion, advertising, price, and market position, and it required cooperation, not competition, among the division leaders. Wexner believes that retailing success in the future will be based on brand development.

PRESENT CONDITIONS

The company continues to refine its store brands, spin off successful store brands as independent companies, and sell off less successful store brands. Limited Too was established as the independent company Too, Inc. in 1999, and The Limited, Inc. sold a majority interest in Gaylan's Trading Company that same year. In August 2001, the company sold its 653 Lane Bryant stores to Charming Shoppes, Inc. for $355 million. Remaining retail store brands will be remodeled, with approximately $350 million spent in 2001. The growth of The Limited, Inc. is shown in Exhibit 1.

Limited Brands continues to be successful in spite of significant problems at some of its retail divisions. Apparel division sales in 2001 were $3.811 billion, down 5 percent from 2001, but operating income for the apparel division was down 45 percent to $64 million. The vision and mission for Limited Brands continues to include growth and dominance in specialty retailing, as indicated in Exhibit 2 on page 68.

BUSINESS STRUCTURE

Limited Brands operates as three separate business groups: Apparel, Intimate Brands, Inc. (85 percent owned by Limited Brands), and Other Retail Brands (Henri Bendel). Stores/operations included in each business group and net sales for each are shown in Exhibit 3 on page 69.

Apparel Division

Limited Stores

This is the flagship division of the organization. Originally, merchandise in these stores was targeted to women between the ages of sixteen and twenty-five, but The Limited now focuses on twenty-something women who want modern, feminine, sophisticated sportswear. These stores sell medium-priced fashion clothing and accessories. Most of the 354 Limited stores are located in regional shopping centers or malls across the United States. The number of Limited stores has been reduced significantly in recent years; there were 778 Limited stores in 1990.

Express

The Express stores are the most profitable Limited apparel brand. The company describes its Express stores as being a "modern women's brand with international runway style" for women in their late teens and early twenties. Express added a lingerie department in 1999. Express stores are currently being remodeled with a modern look that the company calls the white store design. The 682 Express stores in operation are located mostly in shopping malls.

EXHIBIT 1   Limited Brands' Stores and Selling Square Feet
(a summary of stores and selling square feet by business follows)

| | End of Year | | | Change From | |
	Plan 2002	*2001*	*2000*	*2002–2001*	*2001–2000*
Express					
Stores	682	667	667	15	–
Selling square feet	4,400,000	4,280,000	4,288,000	120,000	(8,000)
Lerner New York					
Stores	504	522	560	(18)	(38)
Selling square feet	3,751,000	3,823,000	4,163,000	(72,000)	(340,000)
Limited Stores					
Stores	354	368	389	(14)	(21)
Selling square feet	2,244,000	2,313,000	2,445,000	(69,000)	(132,000)
Structure					
Stores	409	439	469	(30)	(30)
Selling square feet	1,673,000	1,774,000	1,885,000	(101,000)	(111,000)
Total apparel businesses					
Stores	1,949	1,996	2,085	(47)	(89)
Selling square feet	12,068,000	12,190,000	12,781,000	(122,000)	(591,000)
Victoria's Secret Stores					
Stores	1,017	1,002	958	15	44
Selling square feet	4,682,000	4,458,000	4,207,000	224,000	251,000
Bath & Body Works					
Stores	1,690	1,615	1,432	75	183
Selling square feet	3,710,000	3,463,000	3,039,000	247,000	424,000
Total Intimate Brands					
Stores	2,707	2,617	2,390	90	227
Selling square feet	8,392,000	7,921,000	7,246,000	471,000	675,000
Henri Bendel					
Stores	1	1	1	–	–
Selling square feet	35,000	35,000	35,000	–	–
Lane Bryant					
Stores	–	–	653	–	(653)
Selling square feet	–	–	3,162,000	–	(3,162,000)
Total retail businesses					
Stores	4,657	4,614	5,129	43	(515)
Selling square feet	20,495,000	20,146,000	23,224,000	349,000	(3,078,000)

Source: Limited Brands' 2001 *Annual Report,* p. 34.

Lerner New York/New York & Company

This division offers "modern, city hip, and competitively priced fashion with an attitude." The store created a brand called New York & Company. In 2000, seventy-nine
Lerner New York stores were remodeled and renamed as New York & Company stores.
Presently, there are 504 Lerner/New York & Company stores in operation in malls and
shopping centers across the United States.

Structure/Express Men's

Limited Brands began testing the market for men's fashions by offering Express for Men
in Express stores beginning in 1987. Sixty-nine Structure stores were opened in 1989,
and by the end of 2001, there were 409 stores. Structure stores were merged with

---

EXHIBIT 2   Vision and Mission for Limited Brands

VISION

Create a "family of the world's best fashion brands."

MISSION

Limited Brands will focus on powerful and differentiated brands to create "sustained growth of shareholder value by focusing its time, talent, and capital on the highest return opportunities."

Source: Limited Brands, *Annual Report* (2000).

Express stores in 2001 and called Express Men's. The Express Men's stores stock good-quality, affordable clothing in the latest styles. The target customer is in his twenties and thirties and "urban, active, young, and creative." Only forty-five of the men's stores are currently side-by-side with Express stores, and a decision has not been made about whether the men's and women's stores will be combined in the same locations.

Mast Industries

The business of this division is to arrange for the manufacture and import of women's clothing from around the world, and to wholesale this merchandise to Limited Brands stores and to other companies. This division delivers more than 100 million garments to Limited Brands each year. In 2001, purchases were made from thirty-one hundred suppliers, but no more than 5 percent of the items purchased came from any single manufacturer.

Intimate Brands, Inc. (IBI)

Victoria's Secret Stores

Victoria's Secret stores are the dominant intimate apparel store in the world. The stores were redecorated in the early 1990s in a Victorian parlor style and are currently undergoing another renovation to create an "upscale, modern, and sophisticated design" and a more "residential" look. Victoria's Secret bath and fragrance products are an increasingly important portion of store sales. In 2001, a new body/skin care collection called Body by Victoria was launched. There are 1,017 Victoria's Secret stores in the United States.

Victoria's Secret Direct (Catalog/E-commerce)

Since its purchase by The Limited in 1982, the catalog has steadily increased its operations. Now the Victoria's Secret catalog is the dominant catalog for lingerie in the world. In 1996, the division established a phone center in Japan so that this market for mail order sales could be established. The company closed one of its three call centers in the United States in 2001. At the end of 1998, the company launched a Web site (**http://www.VictoriasSecret.com**) so consumers worldwide could shop online.

Bath & Body Works

In response to demand by consumers for natural personal care products, The Limited opened six Bath & Body Works stores in 1990. These stores have a natural market atmosphere and sell a variety of personal care products. There are 1,690 Bath & Body

EXHIBIT 3   Sales and Income Data (in millions)

	2001	*2000	1999	% Change 2001–2000	% Change 2000–1999
Net Sales					
Express	$ 1,542	$ 1,594	$ 1,367	(3%)	17%
Lerner New York	940	1,025	1,001	(8%)	2%
Limited Stores	618	673	704	(8%)	(4%)
Structure	502	569	607	(12%)	(6%)
Other (principally Mast)	209	158	108	32%	46%
Total apparel businesses	$ 3,811	$ 4,019	$ 3,787	(5%)	6%
Victoria's Secret Stores	2,403	2,339	2,122	3%	10%
Bath & Body Works	1,747	1,785	1,530	(2%)	17%
Victoria's Secret Direct	869	962	956	(10%)	1%
Other	2	31	24	(94%)	29%
Total Intimate Brands	$ 5,021	$ 5,117	$ 4,632	(2%)	10%
Henri Bendel	36	39	38	(8%)	3%
Lane Bryant (through August 16, 2001)	495	930	922	nm	1%
Galyan's (through August 31, 1999)	–	–	165	nm	nm
TOO (through August 23, 1999)	–	–	222	nm	nm
Total net sales	$ 9,363	$ 10,105	$ 9,766	(7%)	3%
Operating Income					
Apparel businesses	$ 64	$ 116	$ 79	(45%)	47%
Intimate Brands	667	754	794	(12%)	(5%)
Other	17	6	34	nm	nm
Subtotal	748	876	907	(15%)	(3%)
Special and nonrecurring items▪	170	(10)	24	nm	nm
Total operating income	$ 918	$ 866	$ 931	6%	(7%)

*Fifty-three week fiscal year.
▪Special and nonrecurring items:
 2001: a $170 million gain resulting from the sale of Lane Bryant, which relates to the "other" category.
 2000: a $10 million charge for Intimate Brands to close Bath & Body Works' nine stores in the United Kingdom.
 1999: (1) a $13 million charge for transaction costs related to the TOO spin-off; and (2) the reversal of a $37 million liability related to downsizing costs for Henri Bendel. These special items relate to the "Other" category.
nm = not meaningful

	2001	2000	1999
Comparable Store Sales			
Express	(2%)	15%	5%
Lerner New York	(5%)	4%	12%
Limited Stores	(2%)	5%	5%
Structure	(8%)	(4%)	4%
Total apparel businesses	(3%)	8%	7%
Victoria's Secret Stores	0%	5%	12%
Bath & Body Works	(11%)	1%	11%
Total Intimate Brands	(5%)	4%	12%
Heuri Bendel	(6%)	(1%)	7%
Lane Bryant (through August 16,2001)	3%	2%	5%
Galyan's (through August 31, 1999)	–	–	9%
TOO (through August 23, 1999)	–	–	9%
Total comparable store sales	(4%)	5%	9%

Source: Limited Brands 2001 *Annual Report,* p. 30.

Works stores. In 2000, Bath & Body Works held a 6 percent share of the $28 billion personal care market, and three of the company's fragrances were ranked among the top five U.S. fragrances. In 2001, the company closed its Bath & Body Works stores in the United Kingdom.

Other Retail Businesses

Henri Bendel

In 1985, The Limited purchased this upscale fashion store. The store offers the best in clothing and accessories from international designers. Prices are designed for "today's modern woman in her mid-thirties." This is the only upscale store owned by The Limited. The division was expanded to six stores in 1996, but the company closed five Henri Bendel stores in 1998. Currently, the New York store has high-profile parties to enhance its image, such as the party held for the *Charlie's Angels* film premiere in 2001.

Center Functions

The Limited Logistics Services

The Limited's distribution center is located in Columbus, Ohio. The center now has eight buildings and about 6.1 million square feet.

The Limited Store Planning

This division is responsible for designing store layouts and developing merchandising techniques for all of The Limited's retail store divisions.

The Limited Real Estate

This division handles store leases for the retail divisions. By the end of 1996, the total selling space of Limited Stores was 28.4 million square feet. Selling space decreased to 20.4 million square feet by the end of 2001.

The Limited Design Services

This division manages the design of apparel and merchandise for the retail stores.

The Limited Brand and Creative Services

The division works with the individual businesses and Wexner to create brands that have a distinctive character.

The Limited Technology Services

This division handles the telecommunications and computing needs for the company.

COMPETITION

The retail sale of women's clothing is a very competitive business. Competitors of Limited Brands include nationally, regionally, and locally owned department stores, specialty stores, and mail order catalog businesses. Some of Limited Brands' major competitors include Gap, American Eagle, Federated Department Stores, Dayton-Hudson, Dillard's, May Department Stores, Talbot's, Spiegel/Eddie Bauer, Nordstrom, Sears, and JCPenney.

Limited Brands is the number two apparel chain in the United States. The top fifteen apparel chains are shown in Exhibit 4. Other apparel retailers who were among the

EXHIBIT 4   Top Fifteen Apparel Chains (sales in thousands)

Company (HQ)	Sales (000)		% Change
	2000	1999	
Gap (San Francisco, Calif.)	$13,637,460	$11,635,398	+17.5%
Limited (Columbus, Ohio)	10,104,606	9,723,334	+3.5
TJX (Framingham, Mass.)	9,579,006	8,795,347	+8.9
Intimate Brands (Columbus, Ohio)	5,117,199	4,510,836	+13.4
Spiegel/Eddie Bauer (Downers Grove, Ill.)	3,724,778	3,414,703	+9.1
Ross Stores (Newark, Calif.)	2,709,039	2,468,638	+9.7
Burlington Coat (Burlington, N.J.)	2,226,183	1,988,500	+13.1
Charming Shoppes (Bensalem, Pa.)	1,617,173	1,196,529	+34.1
Talbots (Hingham, Mass.)	1,594,996	1,290,923	+21.9
Men's Wearhouse (Fremont, Calif.)	1,333,501	1,186,748	+12.4
Goody's Family Clothing (Knoxville, Tenn.)	1,250,604	1,180,930	+5.9
Abercrombie & Fitch (Reynoldsburg, Ohio)	1,237,604	1,042,056	+18.8
Ann Taylor (New York, N.Y.)	1,232,776	1,042,056	+18.3
SteinMart (Jacksonville, Fla.)	1,206,624	1,034,561	+16.6
L.L. Bean (Freeport, Maine)	1,100,000	1,050,000	+4.8

top fifteen apparel chains for sales volume include The TJX Companies, Inc., Gap Inc., and Intimate Brands, Inc.

Two of Limited Brands' major competitors are discussed below.

Gap Inc.

At the end of March 2001, Gap Inc. had 3,740 apparel stores in operation. Gap Inc. has several divisions that compete directly with Limited Brands stores. Gap Inc. (2,091 stores) sells casual sportswear items for both men and women. Banana Republic (408 stores) sells upscale casual wear. Old Navy Clothing Company, the company's fastest growing division (689 stores), sells budget-priced casual clothing. Casual and active wear for children is sold under the GapKids brand. Gap Inc. also operates 552 GapKids, Gap, and Banana Republic stores, primarily in Canada, Japan, Germany, the United Kingdom, and France. Financial information for Gap Inc. is shown in Exhibit 5.

EXHIBIT 5   Financial Information for Gap Inc.
(in millions except per-share amount)

	1999	2000
Gross revenue	$11,635	$13,673
Net income	1,127.1	877.5
Long-term debt	784.9	780.3
Net worth	$2,233.0	$2,928.2
Earnings per share	1.26	1.00

Gap Inc. is currently facing some operational challenges. In 2000, six of the company's top managers left Gap for other positions, and beginning in 2001, CEO Drexler was handling additional responsibilities because of these resignations. Old Navy recently had merchandising problems and advertising problems. As a result, sales in the division suffered in 2001. A decision was made in 2000 to stock new merchandise less often in the stores so that clothing could be sold at full price for a longer period of time. In September 2000, Banana Republic managers launched the @Yourself concept; mini-stores are set up in major companies for a day and personal shoppers assist employees in making purchases. Gap Inc. also sells its merchandise online at **http://www.gap.com.**

TJX Companies

TJX Companies is the largest off-price apparel chain in the United States. Target customers for TJX include middle-income women between the ages of twenty-five and fifty. Most TJX stores are located in strip shopping centers. At the end of July 2001, TJX Companies had 1,548 apparel stores in operation. The apparel division includes T.J. Maxx (661 stores), Marshalls (552 stores), Winners Apparel Ltd. (123 stores), Home Goods (99 stores), A.J. Wright (31 stores), and T.K. Maxx (82 stores). T.K. Maxx is an off-price apparel store located in the United Kingdom, and A.J. Wright is a Canadian off-price retailer. The company acquired Marshalls in 1995. Financial information for TJX Companies is shown in Exhibit 6.

DEMOGRAPHIC AND SOCIETAL TRENDS

Generation Y (ages 10 to 24) is an increasingly important generation for apparel retailers. There are currently 31 million people who are between the ages 12 and 19, and this number is expected to increase to 34 million teens by 2010, making it the largest teen

EXHIBIT 6   Financial Information for TJX Companies
(in millions except per-share amount)

	1999	2000
Gross revenue	$8,795.3	$9,579.0
Net income	526.8	538.1
Long-term debt	319.4	319.4
Net worth	$1,119.2	$1,218.7
Earnings per share	1.66	1.86

population in U.S. history. Another new target for retailers is the current "tween" age group of 7 to 12 years olds, who will be a part of the largest teenage population in 2010. Girls who are between the ages of 12 and 19 spent approximately $75 billion in 2000, with one-third of this spending in fashion. Gaining brand and store loyalty among these younger shoppers is essential for apparel retailers.

As women baby boomers reach their fifties, retailers and manufacturers of women's apparel have not provided for this group's needs. This large market group for women's apparel has found only youthful fashions and fads. As a result, large numbers of customers began staying away from the stores entirely or wound up purchasing fewer clothing items. In addition, many baby boomers consider retirement savings, college tuition, and mortgages to be a higher priority than spending for apparel. As more companies sell their items through the Internet, retail stores will have to learn how to contend with these competitors. Retailers in the apparel industry are likely to struggle.

Another trend affecting the apparel industry is the increasing acceptance of the casual workplace. Fewer dress work clothes are being sold, and those retailers that sell casual apparel have an easier time generating sales, especially in a slow economy. Adults are busy with work and family, so shopping is not the recreational activity it once was. More and more consumers see shopping as a chore, and retailers who make shopping easy on their customers are likely to have an advantage in the marketplace.

ECONOMIC CONDITIONS

The U.S. economy saw slow growth in 2001, but consumer confidence began to decline as early as fall 2000. After the terrorist attacks on the World Trade Center in New York City and the Pentagon in September 2001, consumer confidence continued to falter. In 2001, retailing comprised one-third of the economy, and if the economy continues to slow, consumers will likely reduce their retailing expenditures.

Household debt has continued to increase since 1994. Consumers are likely to change their purchasing habits for items such as clothing so they can pay off credit card debt. The gap between rich and poor also continues to increase. The number of downscale shoppers is increasing. Because many adults owe significant debt for cars and homes and are unable to spend much money for apparel, they often purchase clothing at outlet malls or discount stores. Occasionally, however, the downscale shopper may want to indulge him- or herself by purchasing fashion items from specialty stores. Also, many of the women in the baby boom group spend their disposable income on items for their children and not on clothing for themselves.

Apparel retailers also have economic concerns. Several major retail chains have filed for reorganization under Chapter 11 bankruptcy laws, and many others have been unprofitable for years. It is difficult for retail chains to predict consumer spending patterns. In the past fifty years, apparel retailers have seen about sixteen different economic cycles. The longest cycle was six years, while the shortest was about a year. Since these cycles corresponded with the business cycle 60 percent of the time, it appears that apparel sales are likely to stay strong when the economy is good and will be significantly reduced when the economy is not growing.

Specialty retailers may have to take more gambles to gain a competitive advantage in this volatile industry. Specialty retailers have gained a competitive advantage in the past by taking a guess at fashion trends early and purchasing inventory to provide those trends to customers. If a specialty retailer purchases inventory for a fashion trend but cannot turn over the inventory, the store loses profit and cannot afford to take more risks. However, if it does not gamble by trying to keep up with fashion trends, it is impossible for it to make a profit when the economy turns around because the merchandise will be out-of-date.

INTERNAL FACTORS FOR LIMITED BRANDS

Marketing

Wexner believes that his company is "reinventing the specialty store business." Since The Limited retail store divisions sell different price ranges and styles of clothing and related goods, Wexner has created the effect of a department store in many malls by locating the stores in close proximity to one another. Wexner considers his stores as a collection of brands rather than a group of stores. He says, "When you think of yourself as a brand, you think more broadly. You think of the efficacy of the brand, the reputation, the integrity, the channels of distribution, whether that be in a store, a catalog, on television, or overseas." Brand building includes defining each store's image, fashion, advertising, price, and market position. In the past, Limited divisions copied each other's designs so that the only difference in some divisions was the price charged for the items sold. Design teams are now assigned to each business and the fashions are designed around narrowly defined brand positions for each division. Wexner believes this is "good for now [and] even better for the long run."

The Limited spent very little money on advertising campaigns in its first twenty years. Instead, the company relied on walk-in traffic in malls to sell its products. Currently, the only brands that are advertised in a meaningful way are Intimate Brands, Inc. stores, such as Victoria's Secret. Victoria's Secret first launched its Web site in December 1998. The television announcements during the Super Bowl in January 1999, which announced a live online fashion show, generated one million hits to the Web site. In 1999, the company created Limited Brand and Creative Services, a department that serves as an in-house advertising agency for The Limited's businesses. In December 2000, as part of the promotion for the new look at Victoria's Secret stores, spokesperson Gisele Bundchen modeled a $15 million ruby and diamond studded bra at the New York store. Express used print ads in fashion and women's magazines in 2001 to appeal to young women's renewed interest in denim fabric clothing. Approximately $359 million was spent on advertising and catalogs in 2000.

Production

Limited Brands does not produce its own clothing, but it has a division that contracts for the manufacture of clothing. Mast Industries specializes in contracting for the production of high-quality, low-cost products. Much of the merchandise imported by Mast is marked with one of Limited Brands' own labels: The Limited, Victoria's Secret, Express, and NY & Co. Wexner believes that having private-label brands allows Limited Brands to keep merchandise inventory current and unique.

Limited Brands can also maintain control over its clothing supply through Mast Industries. Company managers try to maintain one-thousand-hour turnaround time between recognizing a new style and delivering the merchandise to stores. Mast can send high-resolution computer images of clothing designs by satellite to Far Eastern manufacturers. In addition, computer information that is collected from all individual stores is used to determine what needs to be produced in the Far East the next day. In a few days, the newly produced items arrive at the Columbus distribution center and are sent to the stores.

In 2000, Mast purchased merchandise from approximately thirty-one hundred different suppliers, but no more than 5 percent of Limited Brands' inventory was purchased from any single manufacturer. About half of Limited Brands' inventory is produced outside the United States. The coordination of work with so many factories made it difficult to ensure consistent quality. Two changes were made in 1995 in an effort to make sure the company's products were of consistent quality: Presidents of the store divisions have the responsibility for ensuring quality in their divisions, and individual store managers are not allowed to make significant sourcing decisions on their own.

Management

Wexner has been a guiding force for the company since its beginning. His risk-taking style has concerned some investors, but his ability to create new marketing concepts has made Limited Brands the envy of other specialty retailers. Some critics suggest that Wexner is great at starting businesses but that he has not been as effective as a day-to-day leader of established businesses; they also think that he is a micromanager. The company uses a centralized process for planning, with Wexner leading the process. This leadership approach allows Wexner to remain involved in each store division, without being involved in every detail of division operations. After the company began its approach of considering store divisions as brands, Wexner started meeting with the top managers (president, marketing director, chief financial officer, head merchant, and head designer) of each store division on a monthly basis to make sure there is "agreement and alignment around core elements of the brand."

Limited Brands' managers hope to create a "family of the world's best fashion brands." According to Wexner, Limited Brands will achieve this vision by creating "sustained growth of shareholder value by focusing its time, talent, and capital on the highest return opportunities." Wexner is aggressive regarding Limited Brands' ability to compete in the specialty apparel industry of the future. He developed a campaign called WAR (Win at Retail) to motivate workers. Wexner says, "It is a war, and in wars people really do live and people do die." The plan was later named Must Win and is designed to improve store performance by motivating workers. The Must Win approach has had mixed results, demoralizing some workers, who are seated at meetings according to their weekly performance levels, while energizing others.

Financial Condition

Note in Exhibit 7 that while Limited Brands' net sales decreased in 2001, the company's net income increased. The balance sheet (Exhibit 8) shows that the company's current assets and total assets increased in 2001 over 2000. However, the company's long-term debt decreased to $250 million in 2001.

FUTURE OUTLOOK

Wexner says he is "determined to build a company of powerful, differentiated retail brands that maintain and strengthen our position as the world's dominant specialty retailer." His standard is that if a division does not have the potential to earn at least $1 billion in sales in the United States, Limited Brands should get out of that business. If a new concept works, Wexner is aggressive. He says, "Invent the concept. Prove it. Move forward fast." Some critics suggest that Wexner has the talent to identify unserved markets and create a marketing concept around those markets, but that he has not yet demonstrated the skill at reinventing mature businesses. Wexner responds, "My view is that whether you are turning around a business—that is, reconceptualizing it—or whether you are starting from scratch, your vision of what you are driving toward is the same."

The company's plans for the future include the following:

1. All of the company's Express stores will be remodeled by 2003.
2. Selling space will increase by 349,000 square feet in 2002.
3. During 2002, the company expects to close 43 underperforming stores.
4. The company leaders will continue to refocus the company through brand building.
5. The company plans to remodel a significant number of Victoria's Secret stores by 2003.

EXHIBIT 7   Consolidated Statements of Income
(in millions except per-share amount)

	2001	2000	1999
Net sales	$ 9,363	$ 10,105	$ 9,766
Costs of goods sold, buying and occupancy	(6,110)	(6,668)	(6,443)
Gross income	3,253	3,437	3,323
General, administrative and store operating expenses	(2,505)	(2,561)	(2,416)
Special and nonrecurring items, net	170	(10)	24
Opetating income	918	866	931
Interest expense	(34)	(58)	(78)
Other income, net	22	20	41
Minority interest	(64)	(69)	(73)
Gains on sale of stock by investees	62	–	11
Income before income taxes	904	759	832
Income tax expense	385	331	371
Net income	$ 519	$ 428	$ 461
Net income per share:			
Basic	$ 1.21	$ 1.00	$ 1.05
Diluted	$ 1.19	$ 0.96	$ 1.00

The following list presents some of the concerns that Wexner—and you—might consider:

1. Will the branding concept help Limited Brands to improve its market segmentation strategies?

2. Is locating stores in close proximity in malls a good idea for Limited Brands? Should the company locate some of its stores in strip-shopping centers?

3. Is Limited Brands' strategy of spending more money on print and television advertising a good one?

4. What is the likelihood of a continued downturn in the U.S. economy that negatively affects the women's apparel industry?

5. Will Wexner be able to turn around the Structure/Express Men's and Limited stores? What approach should he take in addition to concentrating on branding?

6. How serious are the potential problems Limited Brands could face in the future?

7. Should the company continue its strategy of developing a company and splitting it off as a separate company?

REFERENCES

BARRETT, AMY. "To Reach the Unreachable Teen." *Business Week* (September 18, 2000).

BARRON, KELLY. "Limited Expectations." *Forbes* (March 5, 2001).

BERNER, ROBERT, and CHRISTOPHER PALMERI. "Just How Deep Are Those Teen Pockets?" *Business Week* (July 30, 2001).

D'INNOCENZIO, ANNE. "Turnaround at Express Attributed to Faster Pickup on Hot Trends." *Women's Wear Daily* (July 14, 1999).

EDELSON, SHARON. "Sisman: An Aggressive Plan for Advertising by Limited." *Women's Wear Daily* (June 2, 1999).

EXHIBIT 8   Consolidated Balance Sheets
(in millions excect per-share amounts)

	February 2, 2002	February 3, 2001
Assets		
Current assets		
Cash and equivalents	$ 1.375	$ 564
Accounts receivable	79	94
Inventories	966	1,157
Other	262	253
Total current assets	2,682	2,068
Property and equipment, net	1,359	1,395
Deferred income taxes	67	132
Other assets	611	493
Total assets	$ 4,719	$ 4,088
Liabilities and Shareholders' Equity		
Current liabilities		
Accounts payable	$ 245	$ 273
Current portion of long-term debt	150	–
Accrued expenses and other	648	581
Income taxes	276	146
Total current liabilities	1,319	1,000
Long-term debt	250	400
Other long-term liabilities	229	229
Minority interest	177	143
Shareholders' equity		
Preferred stock – $1.00 par value; 10 shares authorized; none issued	–	–
Common stock – $0.50 par value; 1,000 shares authorized; 432 shares issued in 2001 and 2000	216	216
Paid-in capital	53	83
Retained earnings	2,552	2,168
Less: treasury stock, at average cost; 3 shares in 2001 and 6 shares in 2000	(77)	(151)
Total shareholders' equity	2,744	2,316
Total liabilities and shareholders' equity	$ 4,719	$ 4,088

Source: Limited Brands 2001 Annual Report, p. 36.

GATLIN, GREG. "Limited, Mast Fined $500G Over Sleepwear." *The Boston Herald* (August 18, 2001).

GENTRY, CONNIE ROBBINS. "Fast Fashion." *Chain Store Age* (July 1, 2001).

GILL, PENNY. "Les Wexner: Unlimited Success Story." *Stores* (January 1993).

http://www.intimatebrands.com

http://www.limited.com

http://www.VictoriasSecret.com

MACHAN, DYAN. "Knowing Your Limits." *Forbes* (June 5, 1995).

QUICK, REBECCA. "Retail, Like War, Is Hell at the Limited." *The Wall Street Journal* (April 21, 1999).

SHEIN, ESTHER. "Intranet Logistics Goes High Fashion." *PC Week* (September 8, 1997).

THURSTON, KEN. "State of the Industry: Apparel Stores: New Merchandising and Marketing Strategies Account for Growth." *Chain Store Age State of the Industry Supplement* (August 1999).

THE LIMITED, INC. *Annual Reports* (1990, 1992, 1994, 1996, 1998).

WAL-MART STORES, INC.—2002

Amit Shah and Tyra Phipps
Frostburg State University

WMT

www.walmart.com

On September 11, 2001, the United States fell victim to a homeland tragedy heretofore unparalleled in history. U.S. retailers reported declining sales as consumers stayed at home to watch the events being broadcast on television. According to Kurt Barnard, president of Barnard's Retail Consulting Group, customer traffic has begun to pick up; however, overall retail buying has remained down as consumer confidence continues to be shaken. The tragedy of September 11 has had a decidedly negative impact on the overall U.S. economy and its retail industries, including Wal-Mart, Inc.

Headquartered in Bentonville, Arkansas, Wal-Mart's sales rose from $191.3 billion in fiscal year 2001 to $217.7 billion in 2002. Net income rose from $6.3 billion to $6.7 billion during that period. For more than a decade, Wal-Mart has been on a roller coaster ride, growing by leaps and bounds as well as rolling over large competitors such as Kmart and thousands of small businesses. Financial statements are shown in Exhibit 1 and Exhibit 2. (Note: Wal-Mart's fiscal year ends January 31.)

In 1995, Wal-Mart ended a five-year battle with local leaders of Bennington, Vermont, and opened its first store in that state, thereby laying claim to having stores in all fifty states (see Exhibit 3). The Bennington store was Wal-Mart's 2,158th store. To get approval for this store, Wal-Mart abandoned its usual 200,000 square foot store near a major highway exit and instead located in a downtown building containing just fifty thousand square feet. Environmentalists in Vermont say the rural character of the state is endangered by "sprawl-mart development." Other chains, such as Ames and Kmart, have operated in Vermont for years, so some residents are mystified by the current controversy. Wal-Mart had established four stores in Vermont by the end of fiscal 2001.

Wal-Mart does not have a formal mission statement. When asked about Wal-Mart's lack of a mission, Public Relations Coordinator Kim Ellis recently replied, "We believe that our customers are most interested in other aspects of our business, and we are focused on meeting their basic consumer needs. If, in fact, we did have a formal mission statement, it would be something like this: "To provide quality products at an everyday low price and with extended customer service . . . always.'"

HISTORY

No word better describes Wal-Mart than growth. In 1945, Sam Walton opened his first Ben Franklin franchise in Newport, Arkansas. Living in rural Bentonville, Arkansas, at the time, Walton, his wife Helen, and his brother Bud operated the nation's most successful Ben Franklin franchises. "We were a small chain," said Walton of his sixteen-store operation. "Things were running so smoothly [that] we even had time for our families." What more could a man want? A great deal, as it turned out.

Sam and Bud Walton could see that the variety store was gradually dying because supermarkets and discounters were developing. Far from being secure, Walton knew that

EXHIBIT 1   Consolidated Statements of Income

(Amounts in millions except per share data) Fiscal years ended January 31,	2002	2001	2000
Revenues			
Net sales	$217,799	$191,329	$165,013
Other income-net	2,013	1,966	1,796
	219,812	193,295	166,809
Costs and Expenses			
Cost of sales	171,562	150,255	129,664
Operating, selling and general and administrative expenses	36,173	31,550	27,040
Interest Costs			
Debt	1,052	1,095	756
Capital leases	274	279	266
	209,061	183,179	157,726
Income Before Income Taxes, Minority Interest and			
Cumulative Effect of Accounting Change	10,751	10,116	9,083
Provision for Income Taxes			
Current	3,712	3,350	3,476
Deferred	185	342	(138)
	3,897	3,692	3,338
Income Before Minority Interest and			
Cumulative Effect of Accounting Change	6,854	6,424	5,745
Minority Interest	(183)	(129)	(170)
Income Before Cumulative Effect of Accounting Change	6,671	6,295	5,575
Cumulative Effect of Accounting Change, net of tax benefit of $119	–	–	(198)
Net Income	$ 6,671	$ 6,295	$ 5,377
Net Income Per Common Share:			
Basic Net Income Per Common Share:			
Income before cumulative effect of accounting change	$ 1.49	$ 1.41	$ 1.25
Cumulative effect of accounting change, net of tax	–	–	(0.04)
Net Income Per Common Share	$ 1.49	$ 1.41	$ 1.21
Average Number of Common Shares	4,465	4,465	4,451
Diluted Net Income Per Common Share:			
Income before cumulative effect of accounting change	$ 1.49	$ 1.40	$ 1.25
Cumulative effect of accounting change, net of tax	–	–	(0.04)
Net Income Per Common Share	$ 1.49	$ 1.40	$ 1.20
Average Number of Common Shares	4,481	4,484	4,474

Source: Wal-Mart's 2002 Annual Report.

he was under siege. He decided to counterattack. He first tried to convince the people in top management of Ben Franklin to enter discounting. After their refusal, Sam Walton made a quick trip around the country in search of ideas. He then began opening his own discount stores in small Arkansas towns like Bentonville and Rogers.

The company opened its first discount department store (Wal-Mart) in November 1962. The early stores had bare tile floors and pipe racks. Wal-Mart did not begin to revamp its image significantly until the mid-1970s, and growth in the early years was slow. However, once the company went public in 1970, sales began to increase rapidly. When it initially went public, one hundred shares of Wal-Mart stock would have cost $1,650. Now, those one hundred shares are worth over $11 million. Wal-Mart's stock was up 106 percent in 1999 and was named the number one stock on the Dow.

EXHIBIT 2   Consolidated Balance Sheets

(Amounts in millions) January 31,	2002	2001
Assets		
Current Assets		
Cash and cash equivalents	$ 2,161	$ 2,054
Receivables	2,000	1,768
Inventories		
At replacement cost	22,749	21,644
Less LIFO reserve	135	202
Inventories at LIFO cost	22,614	21,442
Prepaid expenses and other	1,471	1,291
Total Current Assets	28,246	26,555
Property, Plant and Equipment, at Cost		
Land	10,241	9,433
Building and improvements	28,527	24,537
Fixtures and equipment	14,135	12,964
Transportation equipment	1,089	879
	53,992	47,813
Less accumulated depreciation	11,436	10,196
Net property, plant and equipment	42,556	37,617
Property Under Capital Lease		
Property under capital lease	4,626	4,620
Less accumulated amortization	1,432	1,303
Net property under capital leases	3,194	3,317
Other Assets and Deferred Charges		
Net goodwill and other acquired intangible assets	8,595	9,059
Other assets and deferred charges	860	1,582
Total Assets	$83,451	$78,130
Liabilities and Shareholders' Equity		
Current Liabilities		
Commercial paper	$ 743	$ 2,286
Accounts payable	15,617	15,092
Accrued liabilities	7,174	6,355
Accrued income taxes	1,343	841
Long-term debt due within one year	2,257	4,234
Obligations under capital leases due within one year	148	141
Total Current Liabilities	27,282	28,949
Long-Term Debt	15,687	12,501
Long-Term Obligations Under Capital Leases	3,045	3,154
Deferred Income Taxes and Other	1,128	1,043
Minority Interest	1,207	1,140
Shareholders' Equity		
Preferred stock ($0.10 par value; 100 shares authorized, none issued)		
Common stock ($0.10 par value; 11,000 shares authorized, 4,453 and 4,470 issued and outstanding in 2002 and 2001, respectively)	445	447
Capital in excess of par value	1,484	1,411
Retained earnings	34,441	30,169
Other accumulated comprehensive income	(1,268)	(684)
Total Shareholders' Equity	35,102	31,343
Total Liabilities and Shareholders' Equity	83,451	$78,130

Source: Wal-Mart's 2002 *Annual Report*.

EXHIBIT 3   Fiscal 2002 End-of-Year Store Count

State	Discount Stores	Supercenters	SAM'S CLUBS	Neighborhood Markets	State	Discount Stores	Supercenters	SAM'S CLUBS	Neighborhood Markets
Alabama	40	43	9	0	Nebraska	11	10	3	0
Alaska	6	0	3	0	Nevada	12	5	4	0
Arizona	26	14	9	0	New Hampshire	18	5	4	0
Arkansas	39	40	4	6	New Jersey	27	0	7	0
California	125	0	29	0	New Mexico	9	13	4	0
Colorado	20	22	12	0	New York	51	17	18	0
Connecticut	21	2	3	0	North Carolina	53	43	16	0
Delaware	3	3	1	0	North Dakota	8	0	2	0
Florida	78	69	35	0	Ohio	72	19	25	0
Georgia	44	53	18	0	Oklahoma	44	36	7	11
Hawaii	6	0	1	0	Oregon	23	3	0	0
Idaho	5	10	1	0	Pennsylvania	49	34	19	0
Ilinois	83	30	27	0	Rhade Island	8	0	1	0
Indiana	44	39	14	0	South Carolina	25	34	9	0
Iowa	32	19	7	0	South Dakota	7	2	2	0
Kansas	32	19	6	0	Tennessee	40	49	15	0
Kentucky	35	39	5	0	Texas	129	135	64	14
Louisiana	37	43	11	0	Utah	8	11	6	0
Maine	15	5	3	0	Vermont	4	0	0	0
Maryland	28	4	11	0	Virginia	24	45	12	0
Massachusetts	38	1	3	0	Washington	29	3	2	0
Michigan	51	8	21	0	West Virginia	8	20	3	0
Minnesota	34	7	11	0	Wisconsin	50	13	11	0
Mississippi	27	34	5	0	Wyoming	3	6	2	0
Missouri	61	53	14	0	U.S. Totals	1647	1066	500	31
Montana	5	6	1	0					

International/Worldwide

Country	Discount Stores	Supercenters	SAM'S CLUBS	Neighborhood Markets	Country	Discount Stores	Supercenters	SAM'S CLUBS	Neighborhood Markets
Argentina	0	11	0	0	Mexico	443†	62	46	0
Brazil	0	12	8	2*	Puerto Rico	9	1	7	0
Canada	196	0	0	0	United Kingdom	0	250‡	0	0
China	0	15	3	1	International				
Germany	0	95	0	0	Totals:	648	455	64	3
South Korea	0	9	0	0	Grand Totals	2295	1521	564	34

*Brazil includes Todo Dia
†Mexico includes 106 Bodegas, 51 Suburbias, 44 Superamas, 242 VIPS
‡United Kingdom includes 244 ASDA stores, six Supercenters

Such retailers as Target, Venture, and Kmart provided the examples that Wal-Mart sought to emulate in its growth. The old Wal-Mart store colors, dark blue and white (too harsh), were dumped in favor of a three-tone combination of light beige, soft blue, and burnt orange. Carpeting, which had long been discarded on apparel sales floors, was put back. New racks were put into use that displayed the entire garment instead of only an outer edge.

In 1987, Wal-Mart implemented two new concepts: (1) Hypermarkets, which are two-hundred-thousand-square-foot stores that sell everything, including food; and (2) Supercenters, which are scaled-down supermarkets. Also in 1987, Walton named David Glass as the new chief executive officer (CEO), while he remained chairman of the board. In 2000, H. Lee Scott was named president and CEO of Wal-Mart Stores, Inc. Exhibit 4 specifies the current organizational structure of Wal-Mart and identifies the individuals holding top management positions within the organization.

Sam Walton died in 1992. Bud Walton died in 1995. Wal-Mart's 1995 *Annual Report* is dedicated to Bud. Sam Walton once said about Bud, "Of course, my number-one retail partner has been my brother, Bud. Bud's wise counsel and guidance kept us from many a mistake. Often, Bud would advise taking a different direction or maybe changing the timing. I soon learned to listen to him because he has exceptional judgment and a great deal of common sense."

EXHIBIT 4   Wal-Mart's Organizational Chart

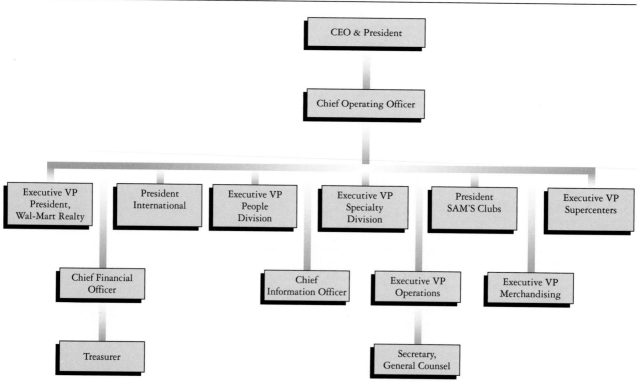

Source: **www.freeedgar.com.**

Wal-Mart's current president and CEO, H. Lee Scott, commends the past leadership and management standards set by Sam Walton. He states, "While our history is rich with success, there's no question that our best years are yet to come."

DIVISIONS

Wal-Mart Stores

Most Wal-Mart stores are located in towns of five thousand to twenty-five thousand. On occasion, smaller stores are built in communities of less than five thousand. As indicated in Exhibit 3 for fiscal 2002, Wal-Mart, Inc., currently operates domestically 1,647 Wal-Mart discount stores, 1,066 Supercenters, 500 SAM's Clubs, and 31 Neighborhood Markets. Most of Wal-Mart's $217.7 billion in fiscal 2002 sales came from Wal-Mart stores and Supercenters. Exhibit 5 provides a breakdown of net sales per division, while Exhibit 6 provides other pertinent financial data per division.

International sales accounted for approximately 28 percent of total company sales in fiscal 2002. This is up from 17 percent in fiscal 2001. For fiscal 2002, Wal-Mart operated internationally in 9 countries, with 648 discount stores, 455 Supercenters, and 64 SAM's Clubs.

Wal-Mart grouped its smaller discount stores, such as the one in Bennington, Vermont, into a new Hometown USA program. This strategy allows the company to give special attention to customers in smaller markets in rural America. Hometown USA consists of the stores that are less than 50,000 square feet and that are under one regional manager. The idea is to enable these stores to develop locally and with a different mix from the large prototypes. Although these stores represent Wal-Mart's heritage, they had become lost in the shuffle as the company opened 120,000 to 150,000 square foot stores.

Wal-Mart stores generally have thirty-six departments and offer a wide variety of merchandise, including apparel for women, girls, men, boys, and infants. Each store also carries curtains, fabrics and notions, shoes, housewares, hardware, electronics, home supplies, sporting goods, toys, cameras and supplies, health and beauty aids, pharmaceuticals, and jewelry. Nationally advertised merchandise accounts for a majority of sales of the stores. Wal-Mart has begun marketing limited lines of merchandise under the brand

---

EXHIBIT 5   Net Sales by Operating Segment

The Company and each of its operating segments had net sales (in millions) for the three fiscal years ended January 31, 2002 as follows:

Fiscal Year	Wal-Mart Stores	SAM'S CLUB	International	Other	Total Company	Total Company Increase from Prior Fiscal Year
2002	$139,131	$29,395	$35,485	$13,788	$217,799	14%
2001	121,889	26,798	32,100	10,542	191,329	16%
2000	108,721	24,801	22,728	8,763	165,013	20%

Our net sales grew by 14% in fiscal 2002 when compared with fiscal 2001. That increase resulted from our domestic and international expansion programs, and a domestic comparative store sales increase of 6% when compared with fiscal 2001. The sales increase of 16% in fiscal 2001, when compared with fiscal 2000, resulted from our domestic and international expansion programs, and a domestic comparative store sales increase of 5%. The Wal-Mart stores and SAM'S CLUB segments include domestic units only. Wal-Mart stores and SAM'S CLUBS located outside the United States are included in the International segment.

Source: Wal-Mart's 2002 *Annual Report.*

EXHIBIT 6   Wal-Mart Segment Data

A. Wal-Mart Stores Segment

Fiscal year	Segment sales increase from prior fiscal year	Segment operating income (in billions)	Segment operating income increase from prior year	Operating income as a percentage of segment sales
2002	14.1%	$ 10.3	6.0%	7.4%
2001	12.1%	9.7	11.5%	8.0%
2000	14.0%	8.7	20.2%	8.0%

The Wal-Mart Stores segment sales amounted to 63.9% of total Company sales in fiscal 2002, which compares to 63.7% and 65.9% in fiscal 2001 and 2000, respectively.

B. SAM'S CLUB Segment

Fiscal year	Segment sales increase from prior fiscal year	Segment operating income (in billions)	Segment operating income increase from prior year	Operating income as a percentage of segment sales
2002	9.7%	$ 1,028	9.1%	3.5%
2001	8.1%	942	10.8%	3.5%
2000	8.4%	850	22.7%	3.4%

The SAM'S CLUB segment net sales amounted to 13.5% of total Company net sales in fiscal 2002, which compares to 14.0% and 15.0% in fiscal 2001 and 2000, respectively.

C. International Segment

Fiscal year	Segment sales increase from prior fiscal year	Segment operating income (in billions)	Segment operating income increase from prior year	Operating income as a percentage of segment sales
2002	10.5%	$ 1,458	31.1%	4.1%
2001	41.2%	1,112	36.1%	3.5%
2000	85.6%	817	48.8%	3.6%

Our International segment is comprised of wholly-owned operations in Argentina, Canada, Germany, South Korea, Puerto Rico and the United Kingdom; operations through joint ventures in China; and operations through majority-owned subsidiaries in Brazil and Mexico. International sales accounted for approximately 16.3% of total Company sales in fiscal 2002 compared with 16.8% in fiscal 2001 and 13.8% in fiscal 2000.

D. Other

Fiscal year	Segment sales increase from prior fiscal year	Segment operating income (in billions)	Segment operating income increase from prior year	Operating income as a percentage of segment sales
2002	30.8%	($714)	(147.9%)	(5.2%)
2001	20.3%	(288)	(9.5%)	(2.7%)
2000	23.2%	(263)	37.2%	(3.0%)

Sales in the Other category comprise sales to third parties by the Company's wholly-owned subsidiary McLane Company, Inc., a wholesale distributor. McLane offers a wide variety of grocery and non-grocery products, which it sells to a variety of retailers including the Company's Wal-Mart Stores and SAM'S CLUB segments. McLane's sales to other Wal-Mart companies are not included in the total sales of the Company.

Source: Wal-Mart's 2002 *Annual Report.*

name SAM's American Choice. The merchandise is carefully selected to ensure quality and must be made in the United States. Wal-Mart has also developed new apparel lines, such as the Kathie Lee career sportswear and dress collection, Basic Equipment sportswear, and McKids children's clothing.

McLane's

McLane's is the nation's largest distributor of food and merchandise to convenience stores. McLane's offers a wide variety of grocery and nongrocery products, including perishable and nonperishable items. The nongrocery products consist primarily of tobacco products, merchandise, health and beauty aids, toys, and stationery. McLane's is a wholesale distributor that sells merchandise to a variety of retailers, including Wal-Mart stores, SAM's Clubs, and Supercenters.

SAM's Clubs

SAM's Clubs are membership only, cash-and-carry operations. A financial service credit-card program (Discover Card) is available in all clubs. Qualified members include businesses and those individuals who are members of certain qualifying organizations, such as government and state employees and credit union members. Both business and individual members have an annual membership fee of $25 for the primary membership card. In addition, two individuals of the same household who don't qualify for the previously mentioned membership can establish an Advantage membership for $35 annually, and additional names can be added to this membership for $15 each.

SAM's offers bulk displays of name-brand merchandise, some soft goods, and institutional-size grocery items. SAM's Clubs usually offer over 3,500 items, which are used most often by the consumers they serve. Each SAM's also carries jewelry, sporting goods, toys, tires, stationery, and books. Most clubs have fresh-food departments, such as bakery, meat, and produce sections.

SAM's is a $26 billion business that is starting to grow again. The clubs were never designed to sell merchandise categories, but rather items, and because the number of items is limited to about two thousand for the wholesale part of the business, which is 60 to 65 percent of sales, and to one thousand to fifteen hundred for personal and individual use, it is very important for the items to be appropriate for the location. Also, the items have to come and go seasonally, so continuity by category is not appropriate. Thus, there is a problem for buyers who are item merchants and compete for space in the clubs.

At the end of fiscal 2002, Wal-Mart had a total of 500 domestic SAM's Clubs in operation. Sales for the Wal-Mart's SAM's Clubs segment increased by 9.7 percent in fiscal 2002, compared to fiscal 2001.

Supercenters

Wal-Mart's Supercenters combine groceries with general merchandise, giving customers one-stop shopping. As evidenced by Exhibit 3, Wal-Mart operated 1,066 domestic Supercenters in fiscal 2002.

Supercenters constitute the company's fastest growing division, and management is extremely pleased with them. Currently, the limitation is distribution, and Wal-Mart is working hard to expand its food distribution capabilities. Most of the Supercenters replace Wal-Mart stores, so they had a jump-start on the general merchandise side of the store, while food has tended to build slowly. However, the company has gained market share more quickly than planned. Wal-Mart likes to locate Supercenters near the strongest food retailers so their facilities will "either get better or be run out of town."

The Wal-Mart Supercenter is one of the most important retail concepts on the landscape at this time. As with the discount stores, their real competitive impact comes not in the year they open but in the third year, because they have a maturation curve that's more like a Wal-Mart store than a food store. Also, the one-stop convenience aspect of the stores has such broad appeal that it is drawing a larger customer audience on a regular basis. Supercenters are continuing to get better in many categories and are attracting a higher-income audience, in addition to their traditional customers. Supercenters provide mart carts and are all on one floor, making the stores handicapped accessible. Wal-Mart's Supercenters average between 100,000 and 210,000 square feet of retail space. They usually employ between 200–550 associates, contingent upon store size and consumer needs. The company's broad assortments and everyday low prices are very compelling; extensive advertising is not needed. This represents an enormous saving over the competition. Furthermore, as Supercenters move more into food distribution, they gain a major cost advantage over Super Kmart and Super Target.

The Supercenters are designed with wider aisles, directory signs, departmental directories, and twenty-four-hour service. They are usually equipped with a customer service desk and scanning registers to provide more efficient checkout procedures.

Neighborhood Markets

Wal-Mart's Neighborhood Markets first began operations in 1998 and are generally located in markets with Wal-Mart Supercenters. The Neighborhood Markets offer customers groceries, pharmaceuticals, and general merchandise. These Markets range from 42,000 to 55,000 square feet and usually employ 80 to 100 associates. They provide about 28,000 items to customers, including fresh produce, meats, and dairy items; one-hour photo processing; drive-through pharmacies; pet supplies; and household chemicals.

International

As indicated in Exhibit 3, for fiscal 2002, the company had 196 Wal-Mart stores in Canada, 443 in Mexico, and 9 in Puerto Rico. Note that Wal-Mart also operated 455 Supercenters and 64 SAM's Clubs outside the United States as fiscal 2002 ended. Mexico is home to Wal-Mart's oldest and most extensive international operations. Wal-Mart de Mexico is strengthened by strong customer support, and the opening of several new stores in the near future is planned.

Wal-Mart has also reached a new market in South Korea; now there are nine Supercenters open there. Wal-Mart has recently bought the United Kingdom's number three supermarket, ASDA, for £6.7 billion ($11.19 billion) and is looking to grow ASDA in the United Kingdom and to expand further in continental Europe, including France. The United Kingdom market leader, Tesco, is trying to increase the scale of its operations internationally and recently revealed plans to have around two-hundred hypermarkets overseas by 2004, with more than £10 billion in annual sales from outside the United Kingdom.

Wal-Mart maintains a strategic competitive focus on global positioning. According to Bob L. Martin, president of the International Division, "We are a global brand name. To customers everywhere, [the name] means low cost, best value, and greatest selection of quality merchandise and highest standards of customer service. But the fact that International has grown to more than $12 billion in sales in less than seven years gives us an idea of how great the potential is."

Community involvement, responding to local needs, merchandise preferences, and buying locally are all hallmarks of the International Wal-Marts, just as they are in the United States.

Distribution Centers

Wal-Mart has forty-three distribution centers nationwide, nine of which are grocery distribution centers and two of which are import distribution centers. Wal-Mart's distribution operations are highly automated. A typical Wal-Mart Discount Store has more than seventy thousand standard items in stock; Supercenters carry more than twenty thousand additional grocery items, a lot of which are perishable. So such items have to be ordered frequently. Associates use handheld computers that are linked by radio-frequency network to area stores. To place orders, each store wires merchandise requests to warehouses, which in turn either ship immediately or reorder. Wal-Mart computers are linked directly to over two hundred vendors, so deliveries are faster. Wal-Mart has one of the world's largest private satellite communication systems that enables it to control distribution. In addition, Wal-Mart has installed point-of-sale bar code scanning in all of its stores.

Wal-Mart owns a fleet of truck-tractors that can deliver goods to any store in thirty-eight to forty-eight hours from the time the order is placed. After trucks drop off merchandise, they frequently pick up merchandise from manufacturers on the way back to the distribution center. This back-haul rate averages over 60 percent and is yet another way Wal-Mart cuts costs.

With an information systems staff of twelve hundred and system links with about five thousand manufacturers, Wal-Mart leads the industry in information technology. This means Wal-Mart is dedicated to providing its associates with the technological tools they need to work smarter everyday. "With this technology, we're getting better, quicker, and more accurate information to manage and control every aspect of our business," said Randy Mott, senior vice president and chief information officer.

WAL-MART.COM

Wal-Mart is in the retail business, which now includes Internet e-tailing. The Internet has interesting aspects and will definitely serve a growing market throughout the twenty-first century. Profits are not easily made over the Internet, and issues of cost of delivery, merchandise returns, and data security are top concerns prior to building business over the Internet. Wal-Mart moved into the Internet in 1996 with the introduction of Wal-Mart On-line, and then it relaunched the site on January 1, 2000, as **Wal-Mart.com**. Wal-Mart looks at Internet retailing as another store with possibility—but without walls.

Wal-Mart.com, with its headquarters located in the San Francisco Bay area, is a wholly owned subsidiary of Wal-Mart Stores, Inc. This location choice affords **Wal-Mart.com** access to the best pool of Internet executive and technical talent. The company was able to attract a top retail management talent in Jeanne Jackson as the CEO of **Wal-Mart.com**. This new venture combines the better of two worlds, technology and retailing, in order to provide customers easy access to more things at Wal-Mart twenty-four-hours a day and seven days a week. Its distinct purpose is to provide consumers with a convenient and rewarding online shopping experience. **Wal-Mart.com** will have a separate management team and board of directors. Ultimately, it might choose to go public; however, Wal-Mart Stores will retain a majority ownership of the new venture.

According to the information provided by the **Wal-Mart.com** Web site, Wal-Mart and AOL currently offer unlimited Internet access and e-mail to customers for a monthly charge of $9.94. This affords the global leader in retailing and the world's leading interactive services company a wide-ranging strategic alliance and a definite competitive advantage. As stated by H. Lee Scott in a December 1999 **Walmart.com** press release, "We are taking this step to benefit our customers. Millions of our customers will be enabled by this agreement to obtain affordable online offerings, and AOL's reach to more than 19 million households represents a significant opportunity for value-conscious Americans. This agreement is very consistent with our heritage. We are bringing a new form of shopping to people in small- to medium-sized communities across the country."

OPERATIONS

Wal-Mart's expense structure, measured as a percentage of sales, continues to be among the lowest in the industry. Although Walton watched expenses, he rewarded sales managers handsomely. Sales figures are available to every employee at Wal-Mart. Monthly figures for each department are ranked and made available throughout the organization. Employees who do better than average get rewarded with raises, bonuses, and a pat on the back. Poor performers are only rarely fired, although demotions are possible.

All employees (called "associates") have a stake in the financial performance of the company. Store managers earn as much as $100,000 to $150,000 per year. Even part-time clerks qualify for profit-sharing and stock-purchase plans. Millionaires among Wal-Mart's middle managers are not uncommon. Executives frequently solicit ideas for improving the organization from employees and often put them to use.

Because Wal-Mart stock sold at thirty-five to forty times earnings—an almost incredible price—Walton presided over a sizable fortune before his death. The Walton family owns 39 percent of Wal-Mart stock. Family holdings are worth nearly $16 billion.

Continuing a Walton tradition, Wal-Mart invites over one hundred analysts and institutional investors to the field house at the University of Arkansas for its annual meeting in mid-June. During the day-and-a-half session, investors meet top executives as well as Wal-Mart district managers, buyers, and two hundred thousand hourly salespeople. Investors see a give-and-take meeting between buyers and district managers.

Employee Benefits

Wal-Mart management takes pride in the ongoing development of its people. Training is seen as critical to outstanding performance, and new programs are often implemented in all areas of the company. The combination of grassroots meetings, the open-door policy, videos, printed material, classroom and home study, year-end management meetings, and on-the-job training has enabled employees to prepare themselves for advancement and added responsibilities.

Wal-Mart managers stay current with new developments and needed changes. Executives spend one week each year in hourly jobs in various stores. Walton himself once traveled at least three days per week, visiting competitors' stores and attending the opening of new stores, leading the Wal-Mart cheer, "Give me a W, give me an A. . . "

Wal-Mart encourages employee stock purchases; about 8 percent of Wal-Mart stock is owned by employees. Under the Stock Purchase Plan, stock may be bought by two different methods. First, an amount is deducted from each employee's check, with a maximum of $62.50 per check. An additional 15 percent of the amount deducted is contributed by Wal-Mart (up to $1,800 of annual stock purchases). Second, a lump-sum purchase of up to $1,500 is allowed in April, with an additional 15 percent added by the company. Wal-Mart also offers an associate Stock Ownership Plan, with approximately four thousand management associates having stock options. Over four hundred thousand associates have chosen to take part in the Stock Purchase Plan, and another two hundred thousand have enrolled in a Direct Purchase Plan.

Wal-Mart has a corporate profit-sharing plan. The purposes of the profit-sharing plan are to furnish an incentive for increased efficiency, to provide progressive recognition of service, and to encourage careers with the company by Wal-Mart associates. This is a trustee-administered plan, which means that the company's contributions are made only out of net profits and are held by a trustee. The company from time to time contributes 10 percent of net profits to the trust.

Company contributions can be withdrawn only on termination. If employment with the company is terminated because of retirement, death, or permanent disability, the company contribution is fully vested (meaning the entire amount is nonforfeitable). If termination of employment occurs for any other reason, the amount that is nonforfeitable depends on the number of years of service with the company. After completion of the third year of service with the company, 20 percent of each participant's account is nonforfeitable for each subsequent year of service. After seven years of service, a participant's account is 100-percent vested.

Predatory Pricing

Three independent pharmacies in Conway, Arkansas, recently filed a suit, claiming Wal-Mart was deliberately pricing products below cost to kill competition. Wal-Mart argued that it priced products below cost not to harm competitors but to meet or beat rivals' prices. Chancery Court Judge David L. Reynolds on October 11, 1996, found Wal-Mart guilty of predatory pricing and ordered the company to pay the pharmacies $286,407 in damages. The judge also forbade Wal-Mart from selling products below cost in Conway in the future.

Wal-Mart appealed the ruling to the Arkansas Supreme Court, which reversed and dismissed the case. It is Wal-Mart's policy that its store managers monitor the retail prices charged by competitors in their respective market areas and lower prices for highly competitive merchandise without regard to the cost of individual items. This price is frequently below Wal-Mart's cost of acquiring some of these products in highly competitive markets. The stated purpose of Wal-Mart's pricing policy is to "meet or beat" the retail prices contemporaneously charged by competitors for highly competitive, price-sensitive merchandise; to maintain "low-price leadership" in the local marketplace; and to "attract a disproportionate number of customers into a store to increase traffic."

The store's pricing practices with regard to specific articles did not violate the Arkansas Unfair Practices Act section prohibiting vendors from selling at or below their cost. The mere proof of below-cost sales was not sufficient to prove a violation of the act absent intent to destroy competition. There was no evidence showing exactly which individual items were sold below cost, the frequency of those sales, the duration of the sales, and to what extent the sales existed.

Diversity Among Employees

Sam Walton was admittedly old-fashioned in many respects. Wal-Mart store policies reflect many of his values. For example, store policies forbid employees from dating other employees without the prior approval of the executive committee. Also, women are rarely found in management positions. Annual managers meetings include sessions in which wives are allowed to speak out about the problems of living with a Wal-Mart manager. No women can be found in the ranks of Wal-Mart's top management. Walton also resisted placing women on the board of directors; however, there are two women on the board at this time. Wal-Mart is an EEO/AA employer, but it has managed to get away with certain past discriminatory policies.

Wal-Mart has instituted several initiatives to increase the recruitment and promotion of women and minorities, including:

- A mentoring program encompassing more than 750 women and minority managers,
- A women's leadership group, in partnership with Herman Miller and ServiceMaster, to develop opportunities for high-potential female managers,
- Store internships during the summer for college students between their junior and senior years, with 70 percent being women or minorities.

Philanthropy and Community Involvement

Exhibit 7 shows Wal-Mart's community involvement in fiscal 2002. Education is a primary beneficiary of Wal-Mart charitable giving. Some examples of its largesse follow.

- Each store awards a $1,000 college scholarship to a qualifying high school senior. More than $11 million in scholarships have been awarded since the program's inception.
- The company has made a major commitment to the United Negro College Fund. Wal-Mart pledged $1,000,000 to UNCF over a four-year period.
- The company sponsored the Competitive Edge Scholarship Fund. In 1993, Wal-Mart teamed up with participating vendor-partners to start the fund, which makes four-year scholarships—each worth $20,000—available to students pursuing technology-related college degrees.
- Since 1993, Wal-Mart and SAM's Clubs associates have raised more than $80 million in support of local United Way agencies.
- Wal-Mart Stores, Inc., is the number-one sponsor for the Children's Miracle Network (CMN) Telethon. Associates from all U.S. divisions of the company have helped raise more than $131 million for CMN since 1988. In 1998, Wal-Mart donated $27 million to CMN.
- In 1999, Community Matching Grants totaled more than $42 million from the Wal-Mart Foundation.

Wal-Mart's corporate citizenship extends well beyond U.S. borders and into every country in which the company operates.

Marketing

The discount retailing business is seasonal to a certain extent. Generally, the highest volume of sales and net income occurs in the fourth fiscal quarter, and the lowest volume occurs during the first fiscal quarter. Wal-Mart draws customers into the store by radio and television advertising, monthly circulars, and weekly newspaper ads. Television

EXHIBIT 7   Community Involvement 2002

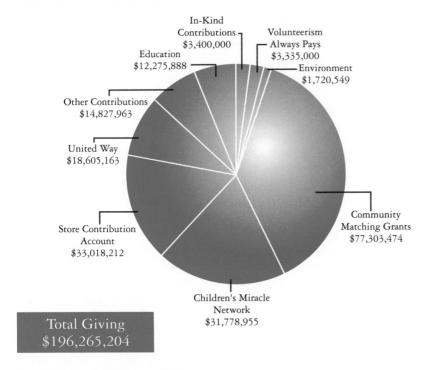

In-Kind
Contributions
$3,400,000

Volunteerism
Always Pays
$3,335,000

Education
$12,275,888

Environment
$1,720,549

Other Contributions
$14,827,963

United Way
$18,605,163

Community
Matching Grants
$77,303,474

Store Contribution
Account
$33,018,212

Children's Miracle
Network
$31,778,955

Total Giving
$196,265,204

Source: Wal-Mart's 2002 *Annual Report.*

advertising is used to convey an image of everyday low prices and quality merchandise. Radio is used to a lesser degree to promote specific products that are usually in high demand. Newspaper advertisements and monthly circulars are major contributors to the program, emphasizing deeply discounted items, and they are effective at luring customers into the stores.

Efforts are also made to discount corporate overhead. Visitors often mistake corporate headquarters for a warehouse because of its limited decor and "show." Wal-Mart executives share hotel rooms when traveling to reduce expenses. The company avoids spending money on consultants and marketing experts. Instead, decisions are made based on the intuitive judgments of managers and employees and on the assessment of strategies of other retail chains.

Wal-Mart censors some products. The company has banned recordings and removed magazines based on lyrics and graphics; it has also stopped marketing teen rock magazines. Wal-Mart advertises a "Buy American" policy in an effort to keep production at home. Consequently, Wal-Mart buyers are constantly seeking vendors in grass-roots America. In Tulsa, Zebco, the fishing equipment company, responded to Wal-Mart's challenge by bucking the trend toward overseas fishing tackle manufacturing. Zebco created more than two hundred U.S. jobs to assemble rods and to manufacture bait-and-cast reels. The company's bait-and-cast reels are the first to be manufactured in the United States in thirty years.

COMPETITORS

Kmart is one of Wal-Mart's key competitors. However, compared to Wal-Mart, the scope of Kmart's problem becomes evident. Even though each company operates roughly the same number of stores (Kmart has 2001 discount stores and 104 Supercenters), Wal-Mart's sales are roughly four times Kmart's sales (almost $37 billion). Wal-Mart's discount stores are larger than Kmart's and produce sales of about $385 per square foot, compared to $236 per square foot for Kmart.

Should Wal-Mart, the price leader in discounting, choose to sacrifice $0.10 to $0.15 of its estimated earnings per share, it virtually could ensure that Kmart would not operate above the breakeven point. Kmart is in a capital-intensive battle with Wal-Mart, whose 1999 capital expenditures were nearly four times that of Kmart's. Kmart's capital resources for this battle are limited, and if its earnings fail to improve, it cannot stay in this capital-intensive race for long. When Kmart recently cut its dividend rate in half, management took a step in the right direction toward conserving its financial resources. The CEO's recommendation regarding the dividend payout will be a litmus test of the urgency with which management intends to apply the company's assets toward turning around the Kmart discount stores.

Supercenters are revolutionizing the discount store battlefield, just as tanks redefined trench warfare. Wal-Mart started 1995 with sixty-eight Supercenters but increased this number to 1,294 in fiscal 2001. The goal of each new store is to shatter the profit potential of at least one older Kmart discount store. This is the dusk of the discount store era, and improvements in the merchandising and systems of Kmart's discount stores might do little to forestall their decline.

Kmart had slowed its rollout of its Super Kmart Centers to allow more time to develop the staff and skills needed for these stores to achieve an adequate return. As the rollout reaccelerates, Wal-Mart is operating over 1,294 Supercenters worldwide, and retailing has changed greatly.

On a positive note, Kmart's board has been strengthened by new appointments who are steering the company; new management provides a fresh perspective for the company; new strategies are being implemented; same-store sales are strong; expenses are being reduced; and earnings should rise.

JCPenney and Sears responded to the reality of retail competition several years ago by offering consumers better values than before. They have succeeded in lifting their sales in both dollars and units. Kmart planned to take market share from them but was blocked. Kmart declared bankruptcy in 2001. By December 2000, Target operations consisted of 978 Target locations, 267 Mervyn's locations, and 64 Marshall Fields' locations through out the United States.

FUTURE STRATEGIES

What strategies would you recommend to current CEO H. Lee Scott? How can Wal-Mart benefit from Internet retailing? How aggressively should Wal-Mart expand internationally and where? Should Wal-Mart get a foothold in Europe before competitors seize the initiative? Should Wal-Mart expand further in Mexico, the United States, or Canada? Should Wal-Mart make further acquisitions, like its Woolco acquisition in Canada? Is Wal-Mart's rate of growth of Supercenters too fast? What private label products should Wal-Mart consider developing? What can Wal-Mart do to improve its SAM's Clubs operations? Develop a three year strategic plan for CEO Lee Scott.

TARGET CORPORATION—2002

Henry Beam
Western Michigan University

www.target.com

Target Corporation is the country's fourth largest general merchandise retailer, behind Wal-Mart, Kmart, and Sears Roebuck. Company revenues were $39.1 billion in 2001, a 7.7 percent increase over 2000. Earnings were $1.37 billion, an increase of 0.1 percent over 2000. Headquartered in Minneapolis, Minnesota, it caters to all income groups through three operating divisions: Mervyn's, Marshall Field's, and Target. Marshall Field's department stores are strong in the upper Midwest, controlling significant shares of the market in Detroit, Chicago, and Minneapolis. Target's upscale general merchandise discount stores are spread across the country and account for nearly 80 percent of the company's sales and profits. Mervyn's, with stores primarily in California, caters to lower-to-middle income shoppers. The Target division has been so successful that the company, formerly named Dayton Hudson, changed its name to Target Corporation in 2000. In addition, all department stores named Hudson's or Dayton's were renamed Marshall Field's. Reflecting the corporate emphasis on service, all divisions refer to their customers as guests.

Sometimes, a Target store will be located near a Mervyn's and a Marshall Field's department store, or both. A mall in Kalamazoo, Michigan, has a Marshall Field's and a Mervyn's, while less than a mile away there is a Target store in a shopping center. Despite such proximity of locations, Target Corporation has made little attempt to associate the divisions with each other in the eyes of consumers, many of whom aren't aware the three divisions are part of the same company.

HISTORY

Joseph Hudson opened a men's clothing store in Detroit in 1873. Among his merchandising innovations were return privileges and price-marking in place of bargaining. By 1891, Hudson's was the largest retailer of men's clothing in America. When Hudson died in 1928, his four nephews took over and expanded the business. In 1928, Hudson's built a new building in downtown Detroit. The retailer eventually grew to twenty-five stories with forty-nine acres of floor space and exuded quality throughout. The Detroit store was closed in 1982 due to the steady economic decline which took place in downtown Detroit starting in the late 1950s. The store was demolished in 1998 to make room for a downtown Detroit redevelopment project.

In 1903, George Dayton, a former banker, opened his Dayton Dry Goods store in Minneapolis, where there was high foot traffic. Like Hudson, Dayton offered return privileges and liberal credit. His store expanded to a full-line department store that was twelve stories tall. After World War II, both companies saw that the future of retailing lay in the suburbs. In 1954, Hudson's built Northland at the northwest edge of Detroit, then the largest shopping center in the United States. Dayton's built the world's first fully enclosed shopping mall, Southdale, in Minneapolis in 1956. In an attempt to diversify, Dayton's opened its first Target discount store in 1962. After going public in 1966,

Dayton's grew through acquisitions. In 1969, it bought the family-owned Hudson's for stock, forming Dayton Hudson Corporation. In 1978, the company bought the California-based Mervyn's retail chain of forty-seven stores. Its last major acquisition came in 1990, when it bought Marshall Field's department stores, assuming $1 billion of debt in the process. Marshall Field's had grown out of a dry-goods business that was started in Chicago in 1852 by Potter Palmer. Marshall Field bought the store in 1865, the last year of the Civil War, and built it into one of Chicago's biggest retailers. His motto, "Give the lady what she wants," was a precursor of customer-oriented retailing. The original Marshall Field's store, located in downtown Chicago, was remodeled in 1992. It is the company's largest store and a major tourist attraction for visitors to Chicago. Marshall Field's 111 State Street apparel line is named for the store's Chicago street address.

Target Corporation's executive office provides leadership for all divisions and establishes the values under which those divisions operate. Each of the six operating divisions has its own CEO and president and is run like an independent business, even though the divisions are encouraged to share advances in technology and coordinate purchasing and financial management. An organization chart for the company and its operating divisions is given in Exhibit 1.

DIVISIONS

Target

At the end of 2001, the Target division consisted of 977 stores located in all forty-eight continental states as indicated in Exhibit 2. Target is an upscale discount retailer that provides good quality, family-oriented merchandise at attractive prices in a clean, spacious, and customer-friendly environment. Its motto is, "Expect more, pay less." A 1999 *Fortune* article on Target commented, "Going to Target is a cool experience, and everybody now considers it cool to save money. On the other hand, is it cool to save at Kmart, at Wal-Mart? I don't think so." Target offers innovative, well-designed merchandise at reasonable prices, such as Philips Kitchen Appliances, Calphalon cookware, Michael Graves designed small appliances, and Eddie Bauer camping gear.

Target stores, which average 125,000 square feet in size, are typically located in small, freestanding malls. Eight regional distribution centers process 90 percent of all freight for the stores. The objective of the distribution centers is to provide next-day service to all locations. Target invites evaluation from its customers on evaluation forms entitled "Be Our Guest Commentator" that are available at checkout counters.

EXHIBIT 1   Organization Chart for Target Corporation

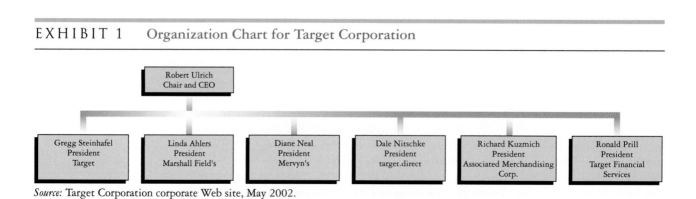

Source: Target Corporation corporate Web site, May 2002.

EXHIBIT 2   Number of Stores

	February 3, 2001	Opened	Closed	February 2, 2002
Target	977	93	17	1,053
Mervyn's	266	–	2	264
Marshall Field's	64	–	–	64
Total	1,307	93	19	1,381

Source: Target's 2001 *Annual Report,* p. 20.

Target's micromarketing program has helped improve its merchandise assortments on a store-by-store basis. Micromarketing is Target's system for tailoring merchandise assortments to customers' needs in individual stores or markets, based on regional, climatic, demographic, and ethnic factors. This permits stores as close as fifteen miles apart to offer different merchandise mixes. The typical Target customer is a married woman with children, who is part of a two-wage-earner family with an average household income of $50,000. The average household income in the United States is $39,000. Over 80 percent of its customers have attended college. Target advertises through multipage inserts placed in local newspapers and television advertisements featuring the familiar red circular bull's eye symbol.

Target plans to continue opening stores in less penetrated markets, such as Boston, New York, and Philadelphia. But increasingly, Target is building new stores in more mature markets, such as Atlanta, Denver, Indianapolis, and Phoenix. Although the cost of a store site in these more densely populated regions is generally higher, so is the sales potential. Over the past five years, Target's square footage has grown at a compound annual rate of 10 percent and is expected to continue to grow at that rate for the next few years. In 2000, comparable store sales (stores open for more than a year) increased 2.4 percent. Shortly after Montgomery Ward's declared bankruptcy in 2000, Target announced plans to buy thirty-five former Ward's stores in prime locations across the country. Most of these former Ward stores are expected to reopen as Target stores in 2002.

In 1995, Target opened its first two supercenter stores (SuperTargets) in the Plains states. The stores are about 180,000 square feet in size, with a fourth of the space devoted to grocery items, including its own line of grocery products marketed under the Archer Farms label. Certain categories, such as health and beauty aids and paper products, link the grocery and general merchandise areas and facilitate crossover shopping. The stores also feature a Starbucks Coffee Shop. The company anticipates that it will operate more than two hundred SuperTarget stores by 2010. According to CEO Robert Ulrich, Super-Targets bring "fashion to food" and offer "a store that is attractive to our guests and as differentiated from our competition as are our discount stores."

Marshall Field's

At the end of 2001, Marshall Field's operated sixty-four department stores in eight Midwestern states, as indicated in Exhibit 2. About half of the department stores are located in the major markets of Chicago, Detroit, and Minneapolis/St. Paul. Historically, they emphasized fashion leadership, quality merchandise, and superior customer service. Today, the stores offer strong national brands with competitive prices in men's and women's apparel, accessories, and home furnishings. The typical customer for the department stores is married, is female, is in her early forties, and has a median family income of $50,000. Over half have earned a college degree, and two-thirds hold white collar positions.

In 1996, Linda Ahlers became chairman and CEO of Marshall Field's, making her one of the highest ranking female executives in the United States. Under Ahlers, the division has emphasized selling more upscale merchandise, improving the look of the stores, and boosting customer service. In addition to building new stores in selected locations, such as the new two-hundred-thousand-square-foot store in the Rivertown Crossing Mall in Grand Rapids, Michigan, the division is also renovating some of its older stores. Target's 2000 *Annual Report* states, "We are committed to our department store heritage, providing superior guest service, fashion leadership and continued support of the communities we serve. Our vision to be 'The Best Store in Town' is unwavering and vital to our future success."

Mervyn's

At the end of 2001, Mervyn's consisted of 266 stores, 124 of which were in California, as indicated in Exhibit 2. The remainder were spread across the western states, with a few in Michigan and Minnesota. Mervyn's is a moderately-priced family department store chain emphasizing brand-name and private-label casual apparel and home fashions that complement the offerings of Target and Marshall Field's. Its motto is "Big brands, small prices." Mervyn's typical customer is about forty years old, female, married with children, and working outside the home. Half its stores are located in regional malls, and the rest are freestanding or in neighborhood shopping centers.

While Mervyn's showed improved sales and profitability in 2000, performance in recent years has been disappointing. In 1995, Mervyn's embarked on a new strategy that included promoting more frequently, increasing the focus on national brands sold at promotional prices, refining merchandise assortments, and using a California theme with its merchandise and advertising. Like Target, Mervyn's advertises through weekly multipage inserts in local newspapers.

Direct Marketing and target.direct

The direct merchandising and electronic retailing division of Target Corporation is called target.direct. It was formed in 2000 by combining Target's e-commerce operation with its Rivertown Trading Company direct merchandising unit to create a single organization. This division consists of two separate, wholly owned subsidiaries of Target Corporation:

- Rivertown Trading Company, acquired in 1998, is the company's catalog and e-commerce subsidiary. It produces six retail catalogs, four of which also have their own Web sites. The two largest catalogs are *Wireless,* which offers an eclectic assortment of gifts and entertainment merchandise, and *Signals,* which was originally created to appeal to the public television audience. *Signals* offers a broad selection of gifts, including videos, art prints, distinctive jewelry, and creative toys.
- target.direct LLC is the e-commerce and catalog subsidiary that supports Target Stores, Marshall Field's, and Mervyn's California, each of which has its own Web site.

All catalogs and online shopping services can be accessed through Target Corporation's corporate Web site, **www.target.com**. All merchandise purchased at target.com may be returned to any Target store location.

COMPETITION

Because its six divisions, taken together, compete across all major merchandising categories, Target Corporation faces a wide range of competitors. The largest division, Target, competes directly with "the marts": Kmart and Wal-Mart.

Kmart

Kmart traces its roots to the S.S. Kresge Company, incorporated in 1912, which was originally a Michigan-based dime store chain. By the 1950s, Kresge had become one of the largest general retailers in the nation, with stores primarily in urban locations. The first Kmart was opened in 1962 in a suburb of Detroit after an extensive study of retailing trends made in 1958 by its future CEO, Harry B. Cunningham. The Kmart large-store format was so successful that the company concentrated on it, rapidly opening Kmarts from coast to coast and closing dime stores as they became unprofitable. In 1977, the company officially changed its name to Kmart Corporation. Kmart's stores are generally perceived as older, smaller, and less attractive than those of Wal-Mart and Target. In 1996, a program was begun to redesign some of its existing stores into Big Kmarts, which featured a grocery section, brighter decor, and an expanded selection of merchandise. It featured the popular Martha Stewart line of women's apparel, home furnishings, and lawn and garden products. In December 1999, Kmart started offering an initially free internet service through its **bluelight.com** Web site. Despite these changes, Kmart declared bankruptcy in 2001.

Wal-Mart

Wal-Mart Stores is one of the best-known success stories in America. Sam Walton opened his first Wal-Mart store in Rogers, Arkansas, in 1962. Growth, slow at first, accelerated during the 1970s. Wal-Mart established highly automated distribution centers to reduce shipping time and implemented an advanced computer system to track inventory and to speed up checkout and reordering. Wal-Mart's motto is displayed on each of its stores: "We sell for less, satisfaction guaranteed."

Wal-Mart is the world's largest retailer, with sales in 2000 of $192 billion and net income of $6.3 billion. It operates 1,736 Wal-Mart stores, 888 Supercenters, and 475 SAM's Clubs in the United States. The average community served has about fifteen thousand people in it. Wal-Mart has over one thousand international stores, mostly discount stores in Canada and Mexico, where it is the largest retailer. It has also acquired or built stores in China, United Kingdom, Germany, South Korea, and South America in the past few years.

Wal-Mart plans to open about one hundred fifty new Supercenters in the United States every year for the next few years. Supercenters carry a full line of groceries as well as a moderate selection of soft and hard goods. At an average size of about one hundred eighty thousand square feet, these stores are more than twice as large as the company's traditional discount stores and significantly more profitable. Wal-Mart has overtaken Kroger to become the nation's largest seller of groceries.

In 1983, Wal-Mart entered the warehouse business with its membership-only SAM's Wholesale Clubs. Its only significant competitor in warehouse clubs is Costco Companies. SAM's Clubs-sales and net income figures are included with those of Wal-Mart. At the end of 2000, SAM's Clubs had sales of $27 billion, and Costco had sales of $32 billion.

Target, Marshall Field's, and Mervyn's also compete to some extent with large national retailers such as Penny's and Sears, as well as with regional department store chains such as Kohl's in the Midwest, Dillard Department Stores in the South, and May Department Stores in the East. Exhibit 3 gives sales and net income figures for the five largest general merchandise firms.

EXHIBIT 3   Sales and Net Income Data, Five Largest General
             Merchandise Firms, 1997–2001 (in millions)

Year		Wal-Mart	Sears	Kmart	Target	Penny (J.C.)
2001E	Sales	216,000	41,600	37,300	39,800	31,950
	Net Income	6,885	1,375	215	1,390	95
2000	Sales	191,329	40,937	37,028	36,903	31,846
	Net Income	6,295	1,540	265	1,264	78
1999	Sales	165,013	41,071	35,925	33,702	31,391
	Net Income	5,709	1,482	683	1,185	465
1998	Sales	137,634	41,322	33,674	30,662	29,656
	Net Income	4,430	1,300	581	962	654
1997	Sales	117,958	41,296	32,183	27,487	29,618
	Net Income	3,526	1,303	298	775	839

Source: Value Line Investment Survey (August 3, 2001).

FINANCIAL ASPECTS

Balance sheet and income statement data on Target Corporation are given in Exhibits 4 and 5. By-segment financial information is provided in Exhibit 6, and a percentage analysis is provided in Exhibit 7.

Financial Services

Financial services, including the credit card operation, are becoming an important part of Target's growth. Over the past five years, pretax profits from financing grew at a compound annual rate of 17 percent. Each division has its own credit card. The transactions are handled through Target Corporation's wholly-owned Retailer's National Bank, chartered in 1994. The divisions will also take other credit cards, such as VISA and MasterCard. The Target credit card, called the Target Guest Card, has been very successful. Target has over eighteen million guest card accounts and expects the number to increase by 10 percent or more each year.

Target stores now provide access to integrated banking and to brokerage and investment planing services through its alliance with E*Trade, a leading online discount brokerage service. Exhibits 8-10 provides a by-state breakdown of the company's stores.

CORPORATE SOCIAL RESPONSIBILITY

Target Corporation is considered a model corporate citizen by consumer groups. It has contributed 5 percent of its pretax profits to philanthropic purposes every year since 1946. (By contrast, most large corporations in the United States contribute about 1 percent.) In 2000, the three operating divisions and the Target Corporation Foundation (funded by the corporation) gave over $50 million to the arts, to education, and to social action causes across the United States. Major contributions were made to programs and projects that strengthen families, promote the economic independence of individuals, or help neighborhoods respond to key social and economic concerns. Target will also donate 1 percent of purchases made on the Target Guest Card to the school of the guest's choice.

EXHIBIT 4   Target's Consolidated Statements of Financial Position (in millions)

	February 2, 2002	February 3, 2001
Assets		
Cash and cash equivalents	$ 499	$ 356
Accounts receivable (net of $261 million allowance)	3,831	–
Receivable-backed securities	–	1,941
Inventory	4,449	4,248
Other	869	759
Total current assets	9,648	7,304
Property and equipment		
Land	2,833	2,467
Buildings and improvements	10,103	8,596
Fixtures and equipment	4,290	3,848
Construction-in-progress	1,216	848
Accumulated depreciation	(4,909)	(4,341)
Property and equipment, net	13,533	11,418
Other	973	768
Total assets	$24,154	$19,490
Liabilities and shareholders' investment		
Accounts payable	$ 4,160	$ 3,576
Accrued liabilities	1,566	1,507
Income taxes payable	423	361
Current portion of long-term debt and notes payable	905	857
Total current liabilities	7,054	6,301
Long-term debt	8,088	5,634
Deferred Income taxes and other	1,152	1,036
Shareholders' investment		
Common stock	75	75
Additional paid-in-capital	1,098	902
Retained earnings	6,687	5,542
Total shareholders' investment	7,860	6,519
Total liabilities and shareholders' investment	$24,154	$19,490

Source: Target's 2001 *Annual Report,* p. 25.

ROBERT ULRICH, CHAIR AND CEO

Robert Ulrich, Chair and CEO of Target Corporation since 1994, received a B.A. degree from the University of Michigan and completed the Stanford Executive Program at the Stanford University Graduate School of Business. His whole career has been with Target and its predecessor companies, starting as a merchandise trainee at Marshall Field's in 1967. Ulrich is a devotee of the arts and serves on the board of the Minneapolis Institute of Arts.

The company does not have a formal mission statement, but Mr. Ulrich's first letter to shareholders as chair set forth his vision and growth goals for Target:

We are committed to serving our guests better than the competition with trend-right, high-quality merchandise at very competitive prices. We are committed to

EXHIBIT 5   Target's Consolidated Results of Operations (millions, except per share data)

	February 2, 2002	February 3, 2001	February 2, 2000
Sales	$39,176	$36,362	$33,212
Net credit revenues	712	541	490
Total revenues	39,888	36,903	33,702
Cost of sales	27,246	25,295	23,029
Selling, general and administrative expense	8,420	7,900	7,231
Credit expense	463	290	259
Depreciation and amortization	1,079	940	854
Interest expense	464	425	393
Earnings before income taxes and extraordinary items	2,216	2,053	1,936
Provision for income taxes	842	789	751
Net earnings before extraordinary items	1,374	1,264	1,185
Extraordinary charges from purchase and redemption of debt, net of tax	(6)	–	(41)
Net earnings	$ 1,368	$ 1,264	$ 1,144
Earnings before extraordinary items	$ 1.52	$ 1.40	$ 1.32
Extraordinary items	(.01)	–	(.04)
Basic earnings per share	$ 1.52	$ 1.40	$ 1.28
Earnings before extraordinary items	$ 1.51	$ 1.38	$ 1.27
Extraordinary items	(.01)	–	(.04)
Diluted earnings per share	$ 1.50	$ 1.38	$ 1.23
Weighted average common shares outstanding:			
Basic	901.5	903.5	882.6
Diluted	909.8	913.0	931.3

Source: Target's 2001 *Annual Report,* p. 24.

being a low-cost, high-quality distributor of merchandise through "boundary-less" functioning—through leverage resources, expertise, and economies across divisions. Our primary objective is to maximize shareholder value over time. We believe we will achieve a compound annual fully diluted earnings per share growth of 15 percent over time, while maintaining a prudent and flexible capital structure.

Target Corporation has adhered closely to this management philosophy during Ulrich's tenure as CEO. Wall Street liked what it saw, since the price of Target Corporation's stock, adjusted for splits, has risen by a factor of 5 over this period of time, largely due to accelerating growth in sales and earnings at the Target division. Nevertheless, some analysts think Target Corporation's performance would be even better if it divested itself of its underperforming Marshall Field's and Mervyn's units. Yet CEO Ulrich remains as committed as ever to keeping Mervyn's, stating in the 2000 *Annual Report,*

Target Corporation reflects our core belief that our three retail segments are far more similar than they are different, and that scale matters. Though our two smaller retail divisions represent 20 percent or less of the corporation today, we believe that their combined contribution to our overall strategy and financial performance remains important. As a result, we are taking steps to leverage the power of these brands and {to} strengthen their position in the marketplace.

EXHIBIT 6   Target's Business Segment Comparisons (in millions)

	2001	2000
Revenues		
Target	$32,588	$29,278
Mervyn's	4,038	4,152
Marshall Field's	2,829	3,011
Other	433	462
Total revenues	$39,888	$36,903
Pre-tax segment profit and earnings reconciliation		
Target	$ 2,546	$ 2,223
Mervyn's	286	269
Marshall Field's	133	190
Total pre-tax segment profit	$ 2,965	$ 2,682
LIFO provision (expense)/credit	(8)	(4)
Securitization adjustments:		
Unusual items	(67)	–
Interest equivalent	(27)	(50)
Interest expense	(484)	(425)
Mainframe outsourcing	–	–
Real estate repositioning	–	–
Other	(183)	(150)
Earnings before Income taxes and extraordinary items	$ 2,216	$ 2,053
Assets		
Target	$18,515	$14,348
Mervyn's	2,379	2,270
Marshall Field's	2,284	2,114
Other	976	758
Total assets	$24,154	$19,490
Depreciation and amortization		
Target	$ 784	$ 660
Mervyn's	126	131
Marshall Field's	135	133
Other	34	16
Total depreciation and amortization	$ 1,079	$ 940
Capital expenditures		
Target	$ 2,901	$ 2,244
Mervyn's	104	106
Marshall Field's	125	143
Other	33	35
Total capital expenditures	$ 3,163	$ 2,528
Segment EBITDA		
Target	$ 3,330	$ 2,883
Mervyn's	412	400
Marshall Field's	268	323
Total segment EBITDA	$ 4,010	$ 3,606
Net assets		
Target	$13,812	$10,659
Mervyn's	1,868	1,928
Marshall Field's	1,764	1,749
Other	561	463
Total net assets	$18,005	$14,799

Source: Target's 2001 *Annual Report,* p. 35.

EXHIBIT 7   Target's Percentage Analysis

Revenues and Comparable-store Sales Growth
(52-week basis)

	2001		2000	
	Revenues	*Comparable-Store Sales*	*Revenues*	*Comparable-Store Sales*
Target	13.1%	4.1%	10.5%	3.4%
Mervyn's	(1.7)	(1.5)	0.2	0.3
Marshall Field's	(4.8)	(5.7)	(3.3)	(4.0)
Total	9.7%	2.7%	7.9%	2.4%

Revenues per Square Foot*
(52-week basis)

	2001	2000	1999
Target	$274	$268	$264
Mervyn's	188	190	189
Marshall Field's	194	210	220

*Thirteen-month average retail square feet.

Pre-tax Segment Profit and as a Percent of Revenues

	Pre-tax Segment Profit		*As a Percent of Revenues*	
(millions)	2001	2000	2001	2000
Target	$2,546	$2,223	7.8%	7.6%
Mervyn's	286	269	7.1	6.5
Marshall Field's	133	190	4.7	6.3
Total	$2,965	$2,682	7.5%	7.4%
Net earnings before extraordinary items	$1,374	$1,264		

EBITDA and as a Percent of Revenues

	EBITDA		*As a Percent of Revenues*	
(millions)	2001	2000	2001	2000
Target	$3,330	$2,883	10.2%	9.8%
Mervyn's	412	400	10.2	9.6
Marshall Field's	268	323	9.5	10.7
Total segment EBITDA	$4,010	$3,606	10.2%	9.9%

Source: Targets 2001 Annual Report, p. 17–18.

EXHIBIT 8   Target's Year-end 2001 Store Count and Square Footage by State

Density Group	Sq. Ft. per Thousand Population	No. of Stores	Retail Sq. Ft. (in thousands)	Density Group	Sq. Ft. per Thousand Population	No. of Stores	Retail Sq. Ft. (in thousands)
Minnesota	1,485	59	7,366	Ohio	391	38	4,457
Iowa	811	19	2,383	Wyoming	370	2	184
North Dakota	786	4	505	Tennessee	363	19	2,091
Anzona	744	34	3,901	Oragon	346	11	1,199
Nebraska	733	10	1,263	Delaware	337	2	267
Montana	701	6	638	**Group 3 total**	**404**	**141**	**16,393**
Nevada	692	12	1,424	North Carolina	328	24	2,677
Colorado	691	25	3,023	New Hampshire	319	3	397
Indiana	623	34	3,815	Kentucky	315	12	1,280
Wisconsin	596	28	3,218	New Jersey	311	21	2,634
Group 1 total	**801**	**231**	**27,536**	South Carolina	295	10	1,197
Utah	574	8	1,304	Oklahoma	242	8	840
Michigan	550	50	5,493	Alabama	237	7	1,064
California	543	159	18,555	Pennsylvania	236	23	2,902
Texas	539	95	11,402	Massachusetts	228	11	1,454
Washington	527	28	3,147	Connecticut	190	5	648
South Dakota	517	4	393	**Group 4 total**	**269**	**124**	**16,093**
Illinois	506	53	6,329	New York	173	25	3,294
Florida	504	69	8,177	Louisiana	125	4	563
Maryland	496	22	2,645	Rhode Island	122	1	128
Georgia	485	33	4,034	Maine	98	1	125
Group 2 total	**527**	**521**	**61,479**	Arkansas	85	2	229
Kansas	475	10	1,285	Mississippi	83	2	239
New Mexico	473	8	871	West Virginia	68	1	124
Virginia	442	26	3,157	Vermont	0	0	0
Missouri	416	20	2,346	**Group 5 total**	**139**	**35**	**4,702**
Idaho	407	5	536	**Total**	**445**	**1,053**	**125,203**

EXHIBIT 9   Mervyn's Store Count Year-end 2001

	Retail Sq. Ft. (in thousands)	No. of Stores
California	9,622	124
Texas	3,347	42
Washington	1,277	14
Arizona	1,203	15
Michigan	1,165	15
Minnesota	1,160	9
Colorado	855	11
Utah	754	8
Oregon	553	7
Louisiana	449	6
Nevada	422	6
Oklahoma	269	3
New Mexico	267	3
Idaho	82	1
Total	21,425	264

EXHIBIT 10   Marshall Field's Store Count Year-end 2001

	Retail Sq. Ft. (in thousands)	No. of Stores
Michigan	4,825	21
Illinois	4,690	17
Minnesota	3,067	12
Wisconsin	817	5
Ohio	600	3
North Dakota	295	3
Indiana	244	2
South Dakota	100	1
Total	14,638	64

Source: Target's 2001 *Annual Report,* pp. 16 and 23.

REFERENCES

BRANCH, SHELLY. "How Target Got Hot." *Fortune* (May 24, 1999): 168–174.

HELLIKER, KEVIN. "Sold on the Job: Retail Chains Offer a Lot of Opportunity, Young Managers Find." *The Wall Street Journal* (August 25, 1995): A1.

MAHONEY, TOM and LEONARD SLOANE. *The Great Merchants* (New York: Harper & Row, 1966).

BEST BUY COMPANY, INC.—2002

Alen Badal
The Union Institute

BBY

www.bestbuy.com

Best Buy Company, Inc., with its headquarters in Eden Prairie, Minnesota (952-947-2422), achieved annual sales of $15.3 million in 2001, compared to $12.4 million in 2000, and a net income of over $395 million in 2001.[1] The company has been in existence for thirty-five years and is the largest electronics specialty retailer in the United States, with 420 Best Buy stores in forty-one states.[2] Best Buy markets such commodities as home office equipment, audio/video items, cameras, appliances, and music CDs.

On October 8, 2001, Best Buy created an Internet division to sell music by way of downloading digital files.[3] The site includes such music labels as EMI Group and AOL Time Warner. The company hopes to add more such sites that allow consumers to purchase an entire CD once they have downloaded a song, because such sites should enhance Best Buy's CD sales.[4] The new Internet division provides an opportunity to increase revenues without necessarily increasing warehousing, as a result of the division's ability to sell digital files. A further advantage comes from its ability to link Web page online CD sales with digital file downloads. Best Buy recently purchased a $40 million distribution center in the state of New York, estimated to be completed in the Spring of 2003.[5]

Best Buy envisioned the following strategic objectives for fiscal 2001:

1. Acquiring Musicland, which is a retailer of music and movies, in order to reach more consumers through four outlets (Sam Goody, On Cue, Suncoast, Media Play)
2. Acquiring Magnolia Hi-Fi, a retailer of high-end electronics, which offers a broader service center, loyal customers, and pricey product lines
3. International expansion into Canada in order to broaden Best Buy operations and offer Best Buy's product lines to Canada[6]

HISTORY

One-stop electronics, CD, and appliance shopping, among others, best describes the specialty retailer Best Buy as prices are competitive and offerings comprehensive. Best Buy Company initially emerged when Richard Schulze tired of working for his father in the electronics distribution business.[7] In 1966, Schulze quit his father's business and, with a partner, founded a home/car stereo business in Minnesota which he named Sound of Music. The milestones of Best Buy Company, Inc., which emerged from Sound of Music, are displayed in Exhibit 1.

Many negative events in the United States recently have affected Best Buy in particular and the specialty retail industry in general. Such events have included the World Trade Center collapse in New York City and the cyclical employment layoffs that Silicon Valley (Northern California-Bay Area) experienced in 2001. Additionally, Montgomery Ward's, previously a direct competitor of Best Buy, has closed many locations, including locations in California, where Best Buy began emerging in the 1990s.

EXHIBIT 1   Best Buy Company, Inc. Historical Timeline

- In 1971, Schulze bought out his Sound of Music partner and expanded the business.
- In the 1980s, Schulze expanded his target customer base to an older and more affluent base by adding appliances and VCRs to his product lines.
- In 1983, Schulze changed the business name to Best Buy and expanded the business by opening larger super-stores.
- In 1985, Best Buy went public.
- As a result of the booming demands in VCRs between 1984 and 1987, Best Buy expanded from eight stores to twenty-four and, as a result, sales increased from $29 million to $240 million.
- In 1988, Best Buy opened another sixteen stores and sales increased by 84 percent; however, Best Buy began feeling pressures from rival competitors, and as a result, profits began to decline.
- In 1989, Best Buy introduced the Concept II warehouse store format, where Schulze cut payroll by reducing sales staff by 33 percent and by taking employees off commission.
- In 1994, Best Buy introduced Concept III, which was a larger-store format.
- In 1995, Best Buy opened forty-seven more stores.
- In 1997, the company's earnings plunged due to large PC inventory on hand as a result of Intel's impact on the PC market.
- Also in 1997, Best Buy began selling CDs on the Internet; however, Best Buy realized it may be growing itself out of business and decided to slow expansion and abolish its "no money down, no monthly payment, and no interest" policy.
- In 1999, Best Buy entered New England with the introduction of its Concept IV stores, which included digital products and expositions of computer software and DVD products.
- Also in 1999, Best Buy formed a separate subsidiary for online operations and invested $10 million in an etown.com site, which was closed down in February 2001.
- In 2000, Best Buy began marketing personalized computers from Micron Electronics via kiosks in its stores.
- Also in 2000, Best Buy acquired a privately held chain of Magnolia Hi-Fi high-end audio/video stores.
- In 2001, Best Buy acquired Musicland Stores, which operated more than 1,300 Sam Goody, Suncoast, On Cue, and Media Play music retailers for approximately $377 million.
- Also in August 2001, Best Buy purchased Canada's largest computer and consumer electronics retailer, Future Shop, and it also announced that it would be expanding internationally. It projected that it would open some 65 Best Buy stores in Canada over a three to four year timeframe.

Source: Dow Jones Interactive.

Product innovations, such as the transition from the VCR to DVD players and personal computer upgrades to speedier processing, have affected the electronics industry. Best Buy has been affected by both: It benefitted by capitalizing on its sale of VCRs, but it had trouble adjusting to PC changes in the market.

DIVISIONS

Best Buy Company, Inc.

Best Buy Company, Inc. stores are located throughout the United States. Best Buy historically has increased its revenues at a compound yearly growth rate of 37 percent as a

EXHIBIT 2   Consolidated Statements of Income (in millions, except per-share data)

| | FISCAL YEARS ENDED FEBRUARY 28, | | |
	2001	*2000*	*1999*
Revenues			
Net Sales	$15,326.6	$12,494.0	$10,077.9
Other Income—net	37.2	23.3	0.4
	15,363.8	12,517.3	10,078.3
Costs and Expenses			
Cost of Sales	$12,100.1	$ 9,991.1	$ 8,171.7
Selling, General, and Administrative Expenses	2,454.8	1,854.2	1,463.3
	14,554.9	11,845.3	9,635.0
Taxes			
Pretax Income	$ 641.5	$ 562.5	$ 364.9
Income Taxes	245.6	215.5	140.5
Net Income	$ 395.8	$ 347.1	$ 224.4
Net Income Earnings Per Share	$ 1.92	$ 1.70	$ 1.13

Source: Dow Jones Interactive.

result of expanding and opening new stores.[8] According to the annual letter written to shareholders and employees in 2001, the president writes, "We have an opportunity to continue our national Best Buy store growth for a number of years; we estimate that we will have blanketed the country with our yellow tag by fiscal 2005."

Best Buy has plans to open smaller stores of about thirty thousand square feet in smaller, developing markets.[9] Best Buy locations are generally much larger than these proposed smaller stores. Many of its locations are in open sections of a city, where they can be easily accessed and are visible to the general public from the highway or road. The general operating hours are Monday through Saturday from 10:00 A.M. to 9:00 P.M. and Sunday from 11:00 A.M. to 6:00 P.M. Best Buy floor plans are generally categorical, and music CDs are positioned near the checkout counters. The remaining square footage includes various departments, such as appliances, TV/VCR, and so on. As a convenience, return counters are housed near the entrance/exit doors. Stores typically include car audio installation centers, too.

Home office products continue to be the lead department in sales, followed by consumer electronics. Also, appliance sales decreased from 8 percent of total sales in 2000 to 7 percent in 2001, as noted in Exhibit 5. Moreover, while consumer electronics sales generally increased, other product sales decreased by 30 percent, falling from 10 percent to 7 percent of sales in 2001. Video sales impressively increased more than 25 percent between 2000 and 2001; the acquisitions of Musicland and Magnolia Hi-Fi may further have a positive impact on the consumer electronics categories, in general.

Best Buy and competitor Circuit City achieved nearly identical revenues in 1999. However, as Exhibit 6 indicates, Best Buy had some three hundred fewer locations in 1999 than did Circuit City. An increase in units was a result of the acquisitions Best Buy made in 2000 (Magnolia Hi-Fi) and 2001 (Musicland). Both Best Buy and Circuit City sell almost the same product lines; however, Circuit City plans to include home office products and high-profit electronics as a strategy to increase revenues.[10]

EXHIBIT 3   Consolidated Balance Sheet (in millions)

| | FEBRUARY 28, | | |
	2001	2000	1999
Current Assets			
Cash and Cash Equivalent	$ 746.9	$ 750.7	$ 785.8
Receivables	209.0	189.3	132.4
Inventories	1,766.9	1,183.7	1,046.4
Other Current Asset	205.8	114.8	98.5
Total Current Assets	2,928.7	2,238.5	2,063.1
Gross Fixed Assets	1,987.4	1,093.5	731.9
Accumulated Depreciation	543.2	395.4	308.3
Net Fixed Assets	1,444.2	698.1	423.6
Other Noncurrent Assets	81.4	58.8	25.8
Total Noncurrent Assets	1,911.0	756.9	449.4
Total Assets	4,839.6	2,995.3	2,512.5
Current Liabilities			
Accounts Payable	$1,772.7	$1,313.9	$1,011.7
Short-Term Debt	114.9	15.8	30.1
Other Current Liabilities	827.0	455.3	345.1
Total Current Liabilities	2,714.7	1,785.0	1,386.9
Long-Term Debt	181.0	14.9	30.5
Other Noncurrent Liabilities	122.0	99.4	30.9
Total Noncurrent Liabilities	303.0	114.3	61.4
Total Liabilities	3,017.6	1,899.3	1,448.3
Common Equity	1,821.9	1,096.0	1,064.1
Retained Earnings	1,224.3	828.5	511.6
Total Equity	1,821.9	1,096.0	1,064.1
Total Liabilities and Equity	4,839.5	2,995.3	2,512.4

Source: Dow Jones Interactive.

Due to Best Buy's Concept II warehouse/store strategy in 1989, some suppliers pulled their products from Best Buy because sales staff was limited and selected suppliers required more sales staff assistance in order to sell their products.[11] Otherwise, almost all brand names and products are sold by Best Buy. Even with the reduction of sales staff, it is not difficult to obtain expert assistance should a shopper need help. A majority of Best Buy products are positioned in the store next to the exhibitions/floor models, and so they are easily accessible for consumers to pick up and then proceed to the checkout counter.

Best Buy Company does run television commercials and newspaper ads as forms of advertising. The products on display can be tested in the store, and descriptive product information is included on most price tags. Best Buy plans to open approximately forty stores per year and to increase online sales, too.[12] Best Buy currently has seven distribution centers (five leased, two owned), ranging from the entertainment software center, which is 245,000 square feet, to the Findlay, Ohio, distribution center, which is 808,000 square feet.[13]

EXHIBIT 4   Corporate Officers

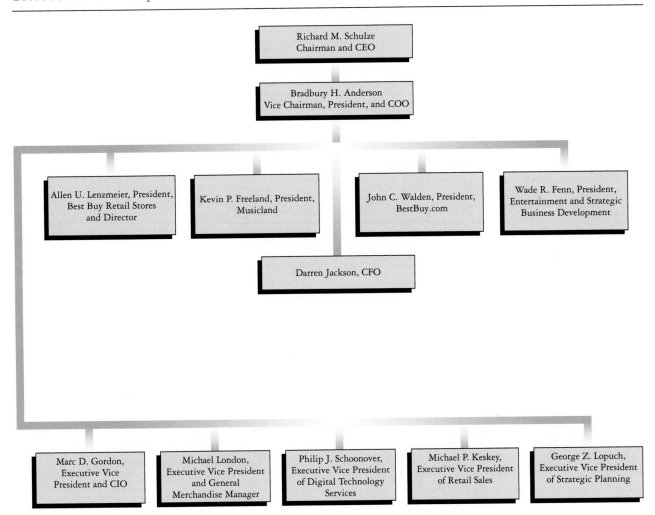

Source: Dow Jones Interactive.

Musicland

Musicland is a retailer of music and videos and is based in Minneapolis; it includes 630 Sam Goody music stores, 200 On Cue stores, four hundred mall-based Suncoast stores, and 80 Media Play superstores.[14] As noted in Exhibit 7, Musicland achieved $1,891.8 million in sales in 1999 and employed 15,900 people.[15] Best Buy acquired Musicland Stores Corporation in the fourth quarter of 2001.[16] Cumulatively, the stores are expected to generate three hundred million shopping visits annually, including more female shoppers. The outlets primarily sell music CDs (most include listening stations), tapes, books, and videos. Depending on the location, all stores hold normal business hours, seven days a week. Additionally, Best Buy Company, Inc., acquired Magnolia Hi-Fi, based in Seattle, Washington, which sells high-end audio/video products.[17]

EXHIBIT 5   Best Buy Productions/
Operations (2000/2001
Sales)

	2000	2001
	% of Total	
Home Office	35	34
Consumer Electronics		
Video	17	22
Audio	11	11
Entertainment Software	19	19
Appliances	08	07
Other	10	07
Total	100	100

Source: Hoover's Handbook of American Business 2001 (2000 Sales);
Dow Jones Interactive (2001 Sales).

EXHIBIT 6   Top Twenty Specialty Retailers (all figures in thousands)

	Revenues			No. of Units		
	2000	1999	% Change	2000	1999	% Change
Best Buy	$15,326,552	$12,494,023	22.7%	1,741	357	387.7%
Gap	13,673,460	11,635,398	17.5	3,676	3,018	21.8
Circuit City Group	12,959,028	12,614,390	2.7	636	658	−3.3
Office Depot	11,569,696	10,272,060	12.6	1,020	939	8.6
Toys 'R' Us	11,332,000	11,862,000	−4.5	1,586	1,548	2.5
Staples	10,673,671	8,936,671	19.4	1,305	1,129	15.6
Limited Brands	10,104,606	9,766,220	3.5	2,739	2,913	−6.0
TJX	9,579,006	8,795,347	8.9	1,483	1,357	9.3
CompUSA	6,150,000	6,321,391	−2.7	226	210	7.6
OfficeMax	5,156,392	4,847,022	6.4	995	946	5.2
Intimate Brands	5,117,199	4,632,029	10.5	2,390	2,110	13.3
RadioShack	4,794,700	4,126,200	16.2	7,100	7,050	0.7
AutoZone	4,482,696	4,116,392	8.9	2,915	2,711	7.5
Barnes & Noble	4,375,804	3,486,043	25.5	1,886	942	100.2
Venator Group	4,217,000	3,726,000	13.2	3,582	4,529	−20.9
Spiegel	3,724,778	3,414,703	9.1	580	560	3.6
Big Lots	3,277,088	2,933,690	11.7	1,290	2,550	−49.4
Borders Group	3,271,200	2,968,400	10.2	1,249	1,195	4.5
Payless ShoeSource	2,948,400	2,730,100	8.0	4,912	4,492	9.3
Ross Stores	2,709,039	2,468,638	9.7	409	378	8.2

Source: STORES magazine (**www.Stores.org**).

Sam Goody ("Goody got it!") competes well with music retailers when it comes to selling music. While retailers such as Wal-Mart and Target carry music CDs and tapes, Sam Goody stores market best-selling music favorites at relatively low prices, since they are a specialty music store. Shopping malls and other locations house Sam Goody stores.

On Cue stores sell music CDs, tapes, books, and movies. Suncoast stores sell music and DVDs, VHS videos, music, apparel, books, electronics, and software. Suncoast sells online, too (**www.suncoast.com**). Media Play superstores are akin to Suncoast retailers. Media Play superstores (45,000 square feet, on average) contain reading nooks and computer software and music; these stores typically draw more than 4.4 million consumers each month (**www.musicland.com/sg**).

Magnolia Hi-Fi

Magnolia Hi-Fi is a specialized retailer of high-end electronics (**www.magnoliahifi.com**). Currently, there are thirteen stores located in Washington and Oregon, and there are two in northern California, where the average size of a store is 10,200 square feet. Each store generates about $8.4 million annually.[18] This trendy outlet contains product lines, such as Bose, and offers sales experts who are available to demonstrate products or to answer any technical questions a consumer may have. Furthermore, Magnolia Hi-Fi contains a fine in-house service department. Store hours are typically Monday through Friday from 10:00 A.M. to 9:00 P.M., Saturday from 10:00 A.M. to 8:00 P.M., and Sunday from 11:00 A.M. to 6:00 P.M.

The product lines generally are the same as Best Buy's; however, Magnolia Hi-Fi, due to its larger number of sales experts, contains higher-end models/products. The stores maintain an upscale clientele, whose questions and wants are specific, which are all features of a trendy Magnolia Hi-Fi store.

In summary, the Best Buy Company, Inc. business portfolio is unique in that all of its businesses typically include the same product lines, with minor deviations. All businesses to date are within the continental United States and Puerto Rico; however, plans to go international are being developed. Best Buy locations provide one-stop shopping for electronic needs, and the company finances purchases with its own label credit card. Best Buy appears relatively stable financially.

INTERNATIONAL

Best Buy plans to expand internationally into Canada in 2003 with five stores (thirty thousand square feet, approximately), ultimately expanding to sixty to sixty-five Canadian locations.[19] The focus is to export American methods of conducting Best Buy business to Canada. To date, no other considerations to expand into other parts of the country or Mexico have been discussed; apparently, the focus is on Canadian markets. Furthermore, no plans to date have been discussed as to whether to include other businesses of Best Buy Company, Inc., such as Musicland, into Canadian markets.

EXHIBIT 7   Musicland Financials: 1997–1999

	1997	1998	1999
Sales ($ mil.)	1,768.3	1,846.9	1,891.8
Net Income ($ mil.)	14.0	38.0	58.4
Income as % of Sales	0.8%	2.1%	3.1%
Employees	16,400	15,600	15,900

Source: Hoover's Company Profile, 2001 (**web.Lexis-Nexis.com**).

OPERATIONS

Best Buy stands strong financially, with annual sales of more than $15 million in 2001.[20] Furthermore, Best Buy's revenues in 1999 of $12,494 million were generated as a result of 357 store locations, whereas Circuit City achieved only marginally higher revenues by way of 658 locations (www.Stores.org). Nonetheless, Best Buy has achieved commendable results to date as it looks into further expansion.

Best Buy and its portfolio businesses, with the exception of Magnolia Hi-Fi, focus on delivering products to all customers. However, Musicland operations focus on tailoring to mostly middle class customers, while Magnolia Hi-Fi tailors to trendier, upscale customers who prefer service centers and support.

Approximately half (52 percent) of Sam Goody's customers are between the ages of 14 and 21, whereas 42 percent are 22 to 44 year olds (www.musicland.com/sg). Media Play attracts more families (children and parents) as a core customer base, and its median incomes range from $50,000 to $60,000 a year on average (www.musicland.com/sg).

On Cue attracts and focuses on the family type of customer, too, and its locations offer a pleasant environment, where families and their children can browse through book, movie, and music sections. The locations are generally located close to main shopping hubs; as a result, they provide an opportunity for families to visit On Cue locations while spending the day shopping (www.musicland.com/sg).

Suncoast's customer base has historically been 22–44 year olds, representing 56 percent of the customers; 45+ year olds represent 17 percent (www.musicland.com/sg). Suncoast specializes in movies and videos; as a result, customers are aware of selections and availability when shopping for those items. Specialty DVD outlets such as Suncoast still remain strong. Music specialty stores such as Sam Goody and On Cue will indirectly continue to compete with the likes of Kmart and Wal-Mart insofar as both carry a sufficient selection of music CDs; however, listening stations are not available in Target, Wal-Mart and Kmart stores.

EMPLOYEES

Best Buy employees are noncommissioned hourly workers. They are not as technically proficient as Magnolia Hi-Fi employees, but they are knowledgeable enough to describe features of products to customers. Best Buy employees' level of electronic expertise ranges from novice to expert. They are generally educated on-the-job regarding products in their departments. Magnolia Hi-Fi employees are commission-based.

SPECIALTY RETAIL INDUSTRY TRENDS

Best Buy today faces new challenges, such as a lack of consumer spending as a result of the World Trade Center attack in New York City. Additionally, the Internet as a way to obtain goods has simplified shopping for consumers. Online shoppers are expected to increase exponentially; it is expected that an estimated sixty million people will make at least one online purchase every three months in 2003.[21] The process of buying online is safe and reliable; consumers can often save or obtain incentives by shopping online. Retailers are able to offer their products at a minimal discount, as opposed to facilitating the products in stores. Furthermore, shopping over the Internet is available twenty-four hours a day, seven days a week. Typically, consumers physically visit stores and test/view products and then purchase online.

Best Buy's current market share within the specialty electronics industry is attractive insofar as it offers and sells a comprehensive product line, ranging from appliances to stereos to computers. Best Buy's earnings, as compared to its competitors, are strong, considering the number of Best Buy locations currently operating. With few competitors considering or having initiated overseas expansion, testing the international markets is a potentially viable option.

The "bigger is better" theory will continue to affect smaller specialty retailers and might eventually phase them out of the arena, since one-stop-shopping offered with supercenters allows consumers to save on and purchase products at one location. On the other hand, small specialty retailers like Magnolia Hi-Fi will continue to prosper insofar as a market does exist, one consisting of upper-class consumers who are interested in personal sales, service, and a technically knowledgeable workforce.

COMPETITORS

Best Buy Company, Inc., is the number one electronics retailer in the United States, representing some 360 stores in some forty states.[22] Best Buy competes both directly and indirectly with many specialty retailers, such as Staples, Circuit City, Office Depot, CompUSA, and so on (**www.Stores.org**). Best Buy competes lean insofar as its revenues are impressive, especially considering the fact that it has fewer store locations than rival Circuit City or Office Depot.

Currently, Best Buy stands firmly as the leader, although Circuit City is attempting to capture the number one electronics specialty retailer position. Circuit City Group, which, with over 600 stores, has locations in virtually every state, is now focusing on satellite television systems and cellular telephones to make up for the PC sales deficit.[23] Also, Circuit City plans to phase out appliances and remodel stores to make space for home office products and high-profit electronics; it will also close six distribution centers.[24]

Sears store appliance departments have been successful in years past. The Good Guys Expedition stores have influenced Circuit City, causing it to revamp in much the same manner. Currently, The Good Guys does not sell appliances, which is the direction Circuit City is planning to go in. Circuit City has about 600 superstores, ranging from 9,500 to 43,000 square feet; and it has about 50 mall-based express stores, although it plans to add 30–50 more annually.[25]

Staples, Inc (locations average twenty-four thousand sq. ft.) stands as the second largest U.S. office products superstore behind Office Depot. Staples has more than eleven hundred stores in about forty states, and it internationally operates in Canada, Germany, the United Kingdom, the Netherlands, and Portugal.[26] Furthermore, Staples is looking to continue to open airport locations and superstores in suburban cities and to expand its online business services.[27] Staples primarily sells office products and furniture, which Best Buy succeeds in selling, and houses a copy center.

OfficeMax, Inc. currently has more than 950 stores in forty-nine states and has proposed to phase out computers and to market Gateway computers only.[28] OfficeMax is expanding in Japan, Mexico, and Brazil.[29] OfficeMax sells primarily office products and furniture and carries limited electronics, such as calculators; it also has a duplication center. OfficeMax competes directly with Best Buy in home office products, which, to date, is the highest achiever as a percent in sales for Best Buy.

Office Depot, Inc. currently has more than 950 stores in the United States and abroad too, which sell by way of a warehouse format and delivery system.[30] Office Depot sells via the Internet (**www.officedepot.com**). Office Depot sells computers and copying services, which primarily cater to small businesses; approximately one-third of its sales are achieved from small business sales.[31] Office Depot, Inc. plans to continue with superstore operations and to terminate smaller supply stores, office furniture businesses (Furniture at Work), and copy-printing service stores (Images).[32] This strategy will ultimately redirect revenues toward warehouse stores and possible additions abroad.

THE FUTURE

1. What strategies would you recommend to CEO Richard M. Schulze?

2. Should Best Buy Company enter other international markets? Why or why not? If so, what should the timeline be? Which countries should be targeted?

3. Is the current global strategy to enter Canada appropriate? Why or why not?

4. Should Best Buy continue to expand in the United States and/or carry or eliminate products?

5. Considering Best Buy Company's current financial situation, should it consider acquiring other businesses? If so, which ones would be appropriate, and why?

6. What relative emphasis do you think Best Buy should place on its various divisions in terms of further growth? Why?

ENDNOTES

[1] Dow Jones Interactive—available at http://ptg.djnr.com/ccroot/asp/cqs_exe_report.asp? mdnum=87128.

[2] Ibid.

[3] *The New York Times* (October 9, 2001), p. C12.

[4] Ibid.

[5] Dow Jones Interactive, op. cit.

[6] Lexis-Nexis Academic Universe-Document—available at http://web.lexis-nexis.com/universe... d5=8e5c496318500dff0b1db280bda1b20e.

[7] Dow Jones Interactive, op. cit.

[8] Lexis-Nexis Academic, op. cit.

[9] Ibid.

[10] *Hoover's Handbook of American Business* (2001).

[11] Dow Jones Interactive, op. cit.

[12] *Hoover's Handbook*, op cit.

[13] Best Buy Company, Inc., *10K Report* (web.lexis-nexis.com).

[14] Lexis-Nexis Academic, op. cit.

[15] *Hoover's 2001 Company Profile* (web.Lexis-Nexis.com).

[16] Best Buy, op. cit.

[17] Lexis-Nexis Academic, op. cit.

[18] Best Buy, op. cit.

[19] Lexis-Nexis Academic, op. cit.

[20] Dow Jones Interactive, op. cit.

[21] Standard & Poor's Industry Surveys (July 26, 2001).

[22] *Hoover's Handbook*, op. cit.

[23] Ibid.

[24] Ibid.

[25] Ibid.

[26] Ibid.

[27] Ibid.

[28] Ibid.

[29] Ibid.

[30] Ibid.

[31] Ibid.

[32] Ibid.

MANDALAY RESORT GROUP—2002

John K. Ross, III, Mike Keeffe, and Bill Middlebrook
Southwest Texas State University

MBG

www.mandalayresortgroup.com

Las Vegas, the kingdom of glitz and glamour, was no more. Where once was heard the sounds of laughter and the clink of coins falling from slot machines, now only crickets could be heard on the strip. The terrorist attacks in New York and Washington on September 11, 2001, had cast a gloomy spell on the land of make-believe. The flights to Las Vegas, the colossal hotels/casinos, the bright lights, and the large crowds now became possible terrorist targets to be avoided.

On September 17, 2001, six days after the terrorist attacks, David Strow of the *Las Vegas Sun* reported that:

> *Resorts along the Las Vegas strip are considering layoffs and some are already cutting workers' hours as business slows down in response to Tuesday's terrorist attacks. This expected downturn is already causing one company to make a big change in its plans. This morning, Park Place Entertainment Corp. announced it is delaying a $475 million expansion at Caesars Palace. "We're just going day by day," said John Marz, vice president of marketing at Mandalay Resort Group. When asked if the company was considering layoffs, he said, "not that I know of."*

"Not that I know of." Suddenly, the lives of everyone associated with Mandalay Resort Group had been affected by what happened in New York and Washington, D.C. Within days, Mandalay had donated $1 million to aid families of the victims in New York and Washington, and by the end of the month it had laid off forty-five hundred employees (about 15 percent of the workforce in Nevada). What is going to happen to the tourist/entertainment industry—and more specifically to the Las Vegas gaming industry? How long will the effects last? What does Mandalay need to do to survive? What happens after the crisis is over? These and other tough questions are the ones to which management at Mandalay Resort had to respond—and respond quickly.

MANDALAY RESORT GROUP

Mandalay Resort Group (hereafter Mandalay) describes itself as in the business of entertainment, and it has been one of the innovators in the theme resort concept that is popular in casino gaming. Its areas of operation are the extravagant vacation and convention centers of Las Vegas, Reno, and Laughlin, Nevada, as well as other locations in the United States and abroad. Historically, Mandalays' marketing of its products has been called "right out of the bargain basement" and has catered to "low rollers." Beginning with the opening of the Excalibur in 1990, Mandalay has broadened its market and now targets the middle-income gambler and family-oriented vacationer as well as the more upscale traveler and player.

Mandalay began in 1974, when partners William G. Bennett, an aggressive cost-cutter who ran furniture stores before entering the gaming industry in 1965, and William N. Pennington bought a small and unprofitable casino operation for $50,000. The partners were able to rejuvenate Circus Circus with fresh marketing, went public with a stock offering in October 1983, and experienced rapid growth and high profitability. Within the five-year period between 1993 and 1997, the average return on invested capital was 16.5 percent, and Mandalay generated over $1 billion in free cash flow. Today, Mandalay is one of the major players in the Las Vegas, Laughlin, and Reno markets in terms of both the square footage of casino space and the number of hotel rooms, and it has achieved this success despite the incredible growth in both markets. Casino gaming operations provide slightly less than one-half of total revenues, and that trend continued into 2002 (see Exhibit 1). On January 31, 2001, Mandalay reported a net income of $53.0 million on revenues of $2.46 billion.

Mission

Mandalay currently does not seem to have a formally stated mission. No publicly stated vision statement is available; however, the continued development of the Mandalay Mile continues to be the core of Mandalay's future development. The Mandalay Mile consists of three interconnected gaming resorts in Las Vegas on 230 acres.

OPERATIONS

Mandalay defines entertainment as pure play and fun, and it goes out of its way to see that customers have plenty of opportunities for both. Each Mandalay location has a distinctive personality, and the Mandalay corporate structure seems to allow each site to exploit that difference to its best advantage. Although Mandalay does not publish its organization chart, it appears that Mandalay Resort Group provides overall direction and strategic leadership as well as functional coordination in the areas of finance, accounting, human resources, legal issues, and marketing. Each resort, in turn, has its own functional structure that enables it to handle the specific activities required to successfully operate a large combined hotel, casino, and entertainment resort.

EXHIBIT 1   Mandalay's Revenues by Segment

	2001	2000	1999	1998
Casinos	48.8%	46.3%	48.0%	46.7%
Food & Beverage	16.7	16.9	16.7	15.9
Rooms	23.6	26.0	24.0	24.4
Other	13.5	12.2	11.5	10.5
Unconsolidated	4.6	4.8	5.7	7.3
Less: Complementary Allowances	7.2	6.3	5.9	4.8

Note: 2001 column is for fiscal year ending 1-31-02.
Source: Mandalay Resort Group 10K (January 31, 1996–2002).

The largest hotel/casino—and the crown jewel of the Mandalay group—is Mandalay Bay, which was completed in the first quarter of 1999 and opened on March 2 of that year at an estimated cost of $950 million (excluding land). This is the third addition to the Mandalay Mile, a contiguous mile at the southern end of the Las Vegas strip that currently contains the Mandalay Bay, Excalibur, and Luxor resorts (see Exhibit 2 for

EXHIBIT 2   The Las Vegas Strip

Las Vegas Blvd. "The Strip"

North/South Streets
2. Decatur Boulevard
3. Valley View Boulevard
4. Rancho Drive
5. Martin Luther King Boulevard
6. Koval Lane
7. Paradise Road
8. Swenson Street
9. Maryland Parkway

East/West Streets
A. Charleston Boulevard
B. Sahara Avenue
C. Desert Inn Road
D. Spring Mountain Road
E. Karen Avenue
F. Flamingo Avenue
G. Harmon Avenue
H. Tropicana Avenue
I. Russel Road

Hotels, Casinos and Landmarks

1. Stratosphere	12. Riviera	23. The Mirage	34. Jockey Club	45. Wild Wild West
2. Bonanza Gifts	13. Stardust	24. Imperial Palace	35. Paris	46. New York-New York
3. Holy Cow Brewery	14. LV Convention Center	25. O'Shea's	36. Helicopter Rides	47. MGM Grand
4. Palace Station	15. The New Frontier	26. Flamingo	37. Aladdin	48. Howard Johnson's
5. Sahara	16. Desert Inn – *Closed*	27. Gold Coast	38. Hard Rock	49. Excalibur
6. Circus Circus	17. Fashion Show Mall	28. Rio	39. Boardwalk	50. Tropicana
7. Wet 'N Wild	18. Treasure Island	29. Caesars Palace	40. Harley-Davidson Cafe	51. San Remo
8. Slots a Fun	19. Venetian	30. Barbary Coast	41. Polo Towers	52. Luxor
9. Algiers	20. Casino Royale	31. Bellagio	42. Monte Carlo	53. Mandalay Bay
10. Las Vegas Hilton	21. Sands Expo Center	32. Bally's	43. Showcase Mall	54. Four Seasons
11. Westward Ho	22. Harrah's	33. Terrible's	44. The Orleans	

Map courtesy Donrey Media Group, http://www.lasvegas.com, Copyright 2001.

a map of the Las Vegas "Strip" and the locations of the major hotel/casinos). All three themed hotels/casinos are connected by an elevated monorail system. Located next to the Luxor, Mandalay Bay aims for the upscale traveler and player and is styled as a South Seas adventure.

The Mandalay Bay hotel/casino contains a 43-story hotel/casino with over 3,700 rooms and an 11-acre aquatic environment. The aquatic environment contains a surfing beach, a swim-up shark tank, and a snorkeling reef. A Four Seasons Hotel with some 424 rooms complements the remainder of Mandalay Bay and strives for the high roller gamblers. Mandalay anticipates that the remainder of the "Masterplan Mile" will eventually consist of at least one additional casino resort, a convention center, and a number of stand-alone hotels and amusement centers. The planned convention center was placed on hold after the September 11 terrorist attacks.

Circus Circus-Las Vegas is the world of the Big Top, where live circus acts perform free every thirty minutes. Kids may cluster around video games while the adults migrate to nickel slot machines and dollar game tables. Located at the north end of the Vegas strip, Circus Circus-Las Vegas sits on 69 acres of land with 3,744 hotel rooms, shopping areas, two specialty restaurants, a buffet with seating for 1,200, fast-food shops, cocktail lounges, video arcades, and 109,000 square-feet of casino space, and it includes the Grand Slam Canyon, a five-acre glass enclosed theme park, including a four-loop roller coaster.

Luxor, an Egyptian-themed hotel and casino complex, opened on October 15, 1993, when 10,000 people entered to play the 2,245 slot and video poker games and 110 table games in the 120,000 square-foot casino in the hotel atrium (reported to be the world's largest). By the end of the opening weekend, 40,000 people per day were visiting the 30-story bronze pyramid that encases the hotel and entertainment facilities.

Luxor features a thirty-story pyramid and two new 22-story hotel towers, including 492 suites. It is connected to Excalibur by a climate-controlled skyway with moving walkways. Situated at the south end of the Las Vegas strip on a 64-acre site adjacent to Excalibur, Luxor features a food and entertainment area on three different levels beneath the hotel atrium. The pyramids' hotel rooms can be reached from the four corners of the building by state-of-the-art "inclinators" that travel at a 39-degree angle. Parking is available for nearly 3,200 vehicles, including a covered garage that contains approximately 1,800 spaces.

The Luxor underwent major renovations costing $323.3 million during fiscal 1997 and another $116.5 million in fiscal 1998. The resulting complex contains 4,425 hotel rooms, extensively renovated casino space, an additional 20,000 square-feet of convention area, an 800-seat buffet, a series of IMAX attractions, 5 theme restaurants, 7 cocktail lounges, and a variety of specialty shops. Mandalay expects to draw significant walk-in traffic to the newly refurbished Luxor, which is one of the principal components of the Masterplan Mile.

Located next to the Luxor, Excalibur is one of the first sights travelers see as they exit Interstate 15 (management was confident that the sight of a giant, colorful medieval castle would make a lasting impression on mainstream tourists and vacationing families arriving in Las Vegas). Guests cross a drawbridge that is over a moat and proceed onto a cobblestone walkway where multicolored spires, turrets, and battlements loom above. The castle walls are four 28-story hotel towers containing a total of 4,008 rooms. Inside is a medieval world complete with a Fantasy Faire inhabited by strolling jugglers, fire-eaters and acrobats, as well as a Royal Village complete with peasants, serfs, and ladies-in-waiting who wander around medieval theme shops. The 110,000 square-foot casino encompasses 2,442 slot machines, more than 89 game tables, a sports book, and a poker and keno area. There are 12 restaurants that are capable of feeding

The company's other big-top facility is Circus Circus-Reno. With the addition of Skyway Tower in 1985, this big top now offers a total of 1,605 hotel rooms, 60,600 square feet of casino, a buffet which can seat 700 people, shops, video arcades, cocktail lounges, midway games, and circus acts. Circus Circus-Reno had several marginal years, but it has become one of the leaders in the Reno market. Mandalay anticipates that recent remodeling, at a cost of $25.6 million, will increase this property's revenue-generating potential.

The Colorado Belle and The Edgewater Hotel are located in Laughlin, Nevada, on the banks of the Colorado River, a city 90 miles south of Las Vegas. The Colorado Belle, opened in 1987, features a huge paddle wheel riverboat replica, buffet, cocktail lounges, and shops. The Edgewater, acquired in 1983, has a southwestern motif, a 57,000 square-foot casino, a bowling center, a buffet, and cocktail lounges. Combined, these two properties contain 2,700 rooms and over 120,000 square-feet of casino. These two operations contributed 7 percent of the company's revenues in the year ending January 31, 2001, down from 21 percent in 1994. The extensive proliferation of casinos throughout the region, primarily on Indian land, and the development of megaresorts in Las Vegas, have seriously eroded outlying markets such as Laughlin.

Three properties purchased in 1995 and located in Jean and Henderson, Nevada, represent continuing investments by Mandalay in outlying markets. The Gold Strike and Nevada Landing service the I-15 market between Las Vegas and southern California. These properties have over 73,000 square-feet of casino space, 2,140 slot machines, and forty-two gaming tables combined. Each has limited hotel space (1,116 rooms total) and depends heavily on I-15 traffic. The Railroad Pass is considered a local casino and is dependent on Henderson residents as its market. This smaller casino contains only 395 slot machines and eleven gaming tables.

Gold Strike-Tunica (formally Circus Circus-Tunica) is a dockside casino located in Tunica, Mississippi. Opened in 1994 on twenty-four acres of land located along the Mississippi River, it lies approximately twenty miles south of Memphis.

JOINT VENTURES

In Las Vegas, Mandalay joined with Mirage Resorts to build and operate the Monte Carlo, a hotel-casino with 3,002 rooms designed along the lines of the grand casinos of the Mediterranean. It is located on 46-acres (with 600 feet on the Las Vegas strip) between the New York-New York casino and the Bellagio; all three casinos are connected by monorail. The Monte Carlo features a 90,000 square-foot casino containing 2,221 slot machines and 95 gaming tables, along with a 550-seat bingo parlor, high-tech arcade rides, restaurants and buffets, a microbrewery, approximately 15,000 square feet of meeting and convention space and a 1,200 seat theater. Opened on June 21, 1996, the Monte Carlo generated $14.6 million as Mandalay's share in operating income for the first seven months of operation.

In Elgin, Illinois, Mandalay is in a 50 percent partnership with Hyatt Development Corporation in The Grand Victoria. Styled to resemble a Victorian riverboat, this floating casino and land-based entertainment complex includes some 36,000 square-feet of casino space, containing 977 slot machines and 56 gaming tables. The adjacent land-based complex contains two movie theaters, a 240 seat buffet, restaurants, and parking for approximately 2,000 vehicles. Built for a total of $112 million, The Grand Victoria returned all of Mandalay's initial investment.

The third joint venture is a 50 percent partnership with Eldorado Limited in the Silver Legacy. Opened in 1995, this casino is located between Circus Circus-Reno and the Eldorado Hotel and Casino on two city blocks in downtown Reno, Nevada. The Silver Legacy has 1,711 hotel rooms, 85,000 square-feet of casino, 2,275 slot machines, and 89 gaming tables. Management seems to believe that the Silver Legacy holds promise; however, the Reno market is suffering, and the opening of the Silver Legacy has cannibalized the Circus Circus-Reno market.

A final current joint venture is with the Atwater Casino Group to build and operate a hotel/casino in Detroit, Michigan. A temporary 75,000 square-foot casino was built under a plan agreed to by the city of Detroit. Future plans call for the construction of an approximately 800-room hotel, expansion of the gaming areas, the addition of new restaurants, more retail space, more convention space, and other amenities. Total costs are estimated at some $600 million, with Mandalay contributing 20 percent and the remainder being funded by debt with the joint venture. However, the Detroit City Council has not yet given final approval for the completion of this project. As anticipated in the construction of new gaming facilities outside of Las Vegas, a number of lawsuits have been filed that could delay or halt new construction.

Mandalay has achieved success through an aggressive growth strategy and a renovated corporate structure designed to enhance that growth. A strong cash position, innovative ideas, and attention to cost control have allowed Mandalay to satisfy the bottom line during a period when competitors were typically taking on large debt obligations to finance new projects. Yet the market is changing. Gambling of all kinds has spread across the country; no longer does the average individual need to go to Las Vegas or Atlantic City. Instead, gambling can be found as close as the local quick market (lottery), bingo hall, many Indian reservations, the Mississippi River, and of course on the Internet. There are now almost 300 casinos in Las Vegas alone, 60 in Colorado, and 160 in California. In order to maintain a competitive edge, Mandalay has continued to invest heavily in the renovation of existing properties (a strategy common to the entertainment/amusement industry), it continues to develop new projects, and it has shifted from a strategy dependent on gaming to one focusing as well on income from hotel, food, and entertainment.

New Ventures

Mandalay owns a contiguous mile at the southern end of the Las Vegas strip, which is called the Masterplan Mile (or Mandalay Mile) and which currently contains the Excalibur, Luxor, and Mandalay Bay resorts. Located next to the Luxor, Mandalay Bay aims for the upscale traveler and player, and its presence enhances the destination resort value of all three properties. Mandalay anticipates that the remainder of the Masterplan Mile will eventually consist of at least one additional casino resort and a number of stand-alone hotels and amusement centers.

Mandalay also plans three other casino projects, provided all the necessary licenses and agreements can be obtained. In Detroit, Michigan, Mandalay has combined with the Atwater Casino Group in a joint venture to build a $600 million project. Negotiations with the city to develop the project have been completed; however, the remainder of the appropriate licenses will need to be obtained before construction begins.

Along the Mississippi Gulf, at the north end of St. Louis, Mandalay plans to construct a casino resort containing fifteen hundred rooms at an estimated cost of $225 million. Mandalay has received all of the necessary permits to begin construction; however, these approvals have been challenged in court, delaying the project.

Most of Mandalay's projects are being tailored to attract mainstream tourists and family vacationers. However, the addition of several joint ventures and the completion of the Masterplan Mile will also attract the more upscale customer.

THE GAMING INDUSTRY

By 2001, the gaming industry had captured a large amount of the vacation/leisure time dollars spent in the United States. Gamblers lost over $58.2 billion on legal wagering in 1999 (up from $29.9 billion in 1992), including wagers at racetracks, bingo parlors, lotteries, and casinos. This figure does not include dollars spent on lodging, food, transportation, and other related expenditures associated with visits to gaming facilities. Casino gambling accounts for 40.6 percent of all legal gambling expenditures, still ahead of spending on second-place lotteries at 32.2 percent and third-place Indian reservations at 15.4 percent. The popularity of casino gambling may be credited to more frequent and somewhat higher pay-outs as compared to lotteries and racetracks; however, as winnings are recycled, the multiplier effect restores a high return to casino operators.

Geographic expansion has slowed considerably since no additional states have approved casino type gambling since 1993. Growth has occurred in developed locations, with Las Vegas, Nevada, and Atlantic City, New Jersey, leading the way. However, the Internet as a gaming venue has exploded.

Las Vegas remains the largest U.S. gaming market and one of the largest convention markets with more than 124,000 hotel rooms hosting more than 35.8 million visitors in 2000. By August 2001, Las Vegas had hosted over 24.3 million visitors, up 1 percent over the previous year. However, it can be anticipated that total visitation will be down for 2001 and may be down for 2002. Prior to the September 11 terrorist attacks, casino operators had been building to take advantage of this continued growth. Recent projects have included the Monte Carlo ($350 million), New York-New York ($350 million), Bellagio ($1.4 billion), Hilton Hotels ($750 million), Mandalay Bay ($950 million), Venetian ($1.4 billion), and Paris-Las Vegas ($760 million). Las Vegas hotel and casino capacity continued to expand when some 12,300 rooms opened in 1999, another 4,219 in 2000, 3,099 in 2001, 3,070 for 2002, and 3,761 expected for 2003. According to the Las Vegas Convention and Visitor Authority, Las Vegas is a destination market, with most visitors planning their trips more than a week in advance (81 percent), arriving by car (43 percent) or airplane (46 percent), and staying in a hotel (72 percent). Gamblers are typically return visitors (79 percent), averaging 2.2 trips per year because they like playing the slots (65 percent).

For Atlantic City, besides the geographical separation, the primary differences in the two markets reflect the different types of consumers frequenting these markets. While Las Vegas attracts overnight resort-seeking vacationers, Atlantic City's clientele is predominantly day-trippers traveling by automobile or bus. Gaming revenues are expected to continue to grow, and they reached $4.2 billion in 1999, up some 2 percent over 1998, split between twelve casinos/hotels currently operating. Growth in the Atlantic City area will be concentrated in the Marina section of town, where Mirage Resorts has entered into an agreement with the city to develop 150 acres of the Marina as a destination resort. This development will include a resort wholly owned by Mirage, a casino/hotel developed by Mandalay, and a complex developed by a joint venture with Mirage and Boyd Corp. Currently in Atlantic City, Donald Trump's gaming empire holds the largest market share with Trump Marina, Trump Plaza, and the Trump Taj Mahal (total market share is 29 percent). The next closest in market share is Bally's (12.1 percent), Caesar's (11.2 percent), Tropicana (9.9 percent), and Harrah's (9.5 percent).

EXHIBIT 6   Mandalay Resort Group and Subsidiaries Consolidated Balance Sheets
(in thousands, except share data)

	January 31,	
	2002	*2001*
Assets		
Current assets		
Cash and cash equivalents	$ 105,905	$ 105,941
Accounts receivable, net of allowance	58,372	78,359
Income tax receivable	18,089	—
Inventories	30,555	31,180
Prepaid expenses	40,848	40,986
Deferred income tax	13,218	30,164
Total current assets	266,987	286,630
Property, equipment and leasehold interests, at cost, net	3,049,812	3,236,824
Other assets		
Excess of purchase price over fair market value of net assets acquired, net	45,445	65,778
Investments in unconsolidated affiliates	554,086	560,987
Other investments	35,751	27,021
Deferred charges and other assets	84,953	71,026
Total other assets	720,235	724,812
Total assets	$4,037,034	$4,248,266
Liabilities and Stockholders' Equity		
Current liabilities		
Current portion of long-term debt	$ 39,251	$ 42,262
Accounts and contracts payable		
Trade	33,473	37,275
Construction	8,284	3,920
Accrued liabilities		
Salaries, wages and vacations	52,680	51,866
Progressive jackpots	11,556	11,334
Advance room deposits	13,242	14,069
Interest	58,592	53,122
Other	92,163	82,827
Total current liabilities	309,241	296,675
Long-term debt, net of current portion	2,482,087	2,623,597
Other liabilities		
Deferred income tax	199,478	235,763
Deferred gain	28,339	—
Other long-term liabilities	80,919	41,966
Total other liabilities	308,736	277,729
Total liabilities	3,100,064	3,198,001
Commitments and contingent liabilities		
Minority interest	(3,639)	(18,675)
Stockholders' equity		
Common stock $.01 2/3 par value		
Authorized—450,000,000 shares		
Issued—113,634,013 shares	1,894	1,894
Preferred stock $.01 par value		
Authorized—75,000,000 shares	—	—
Additional paid-in capital	572,992	572,207
Retained earnings	1,374,376	1,321,332
Accumulated other comprehensive loss	(21,902)	(6,804)
Treasury stock (45,278,193 and 37,357,777 shares), at cost	(986,751)	(819,689)
Total stockholders' equity	940,609	1,068,940
Total liabilities and stockholders' equity	$4,037,034	$4,248,266

Source: Mandalay Group's 2001 *Annual Report*, p. 73.

There remain a number of smaller markets located around the United States, primarily in Mississippi, Louisiana, Illinois, Missouri, and Indiana. Each state has imposed various restrictions on the development of casino operations within the state. In Illinois, for example, where there are only ten gaming licenses available, growth opportunities and revenues have been severely restricted. In other states, such as Mississippi and Louisiana, revenues are up 7 percent and 6 percent, respectively, in riverboat operations. Native American casinos continue to be developed on federally controlled Indian land. These casinos are not publicly held but do tend to be managed by publicly held corporations. Overall, these other locations present a mix of opportunities and generally constitute only a small portion of overall gaming revenues.

MAJOR INDUSTRY PLAYERS

Over the past several years, there have been numerous changes as mergers and acquisitions have reshaped the gaming industry. As of year-end 2000, the industry was a combination of corporations ranging from those engaged solely in gaming to multinational conglomerates. The largest competitors, in terms of revenues, combined multiple industries to generate both large revenues and substantial profits (see Exhibit 8). However, those engaged primarily in gaming could also be extremely profitable.

Park Place was founded from the separation of the lodging and gaming operations of Hilton Hotels in December 1998. Park Place merged with the Mississippi gaming operations of Grand Casinos, and then it bought Caesars from Starwood. Now it consists of a total of 29 casinos, 20 of which are located in the United States. Its latest venture is the Paris Las Vegas Casino & Resort located next to Bally's in Las Vegas. The Paris features a 50-story replica of the Eiffel Tower, 85,000 square-feet of casino space, 13 restaurants, and 130,000 square feet of convention space. Park Place is the largest casino operator in the world, with approximately 2 million square-feet of gaming space, 28,000 rooms, and revenues of $4.9 billion in 2000.

Harrah's Entertainment, Inc., is primarily engaged in the gaming industry, with casinos/hotels in Reno, Lake Tahoe, Las Vegas, and Laughlin, Nevada, as well as in Atlantic City, New Jersey; riverboats in Joliet, Illinois, Vicksburg and Tunica, Mississippi, Shreveport, Louisiana, and Kansas City, Kansas; two Indian casinos; and one casino in Auckland, New Zealand. In June 1998 Harrah's purchased the assets of Showboat and its operations in Atlantic City and Las Vegas, and in January 1999 it merged with Rio Hotel and Casino, Inc. In 2000, it sold the Showboat and purchased Players International. The resulting company now has a total of over 1,258,220 square-feet of casino space; 6,858 slot machines; 1,099 table games; 11,562 hotel rooms or suites; approximately 294,844 square feet of convention space; 86 restaurants; 30 snack bars; 11 showrooms; and four cabarets. Harrah's attempts to target the experienced gambler who likes to play in multiple markets by establishing strong brand names of consistent high quality.

MGM Mirage (formally known as the MGM Grand) owns and operates eighteen hotels casinos worldwide. These properties include the MGM Hotel and Casino; MGM Grand Australia; MGM Grand Detroit; the Bellagio in Las Vegas; the Beau Rivage in Biloxi, Mississippi; the Golden Nugget-Downtown in Las Vegas; the Mirage on the strip in Las Vegas; Treasure Island; Holiday Inn-Boardwalk; and the Golden Nugget-Laughlin. Additionally, it is a 50 percent owner of the Monte Carlo with Mandalay. The MGM Las Vegas is located on approximately 116 acres at the northeast corner of Las Vegas Boulevard across the street from New York-New York Hotel and Casino. The casino is approximately 171,500 square-feet in size, and it is one of the largest

EXHIBIT 7   Mandalay Resort Group and Subsidiaries Consolidated Statements of Income (in thousands, except share data)

	Year ended January 31,		
	2002	*2001*	*2000*
Revenues			
Casino	$ 1,201,707	$ 1,221,595	$ 925,499
Rooms	581,551	611,352	534,132
Food and beverage	410,276	418,081	346,647
Other	332,253	299,753	251,509
Earnings of unconsolidated affiliates	113,287	114,645	98,627
	2,639,074	2,665,426	2,156,414
Less-complimentary allowances	(177,275)	(169,642)	(131,509)
	2,461,799	2,495,784	2,024,905
Costs and expenses			
Casino	669,719	670,243	494,054
Rooms	197,300	203,352	189,419
Food and beverage	283,864	299,726	276,261
Other	219,358	200,236	170,654
General and administrative	417,149	409,603	339,455
Corporate general and administrative	20,981	21,153	22,464
Depreciation and amortization	216,001	217,984	178,301
Operating lease rent	32,185	40,121	25,994
Preopening expenses	2,155	1,832	49,134
Impairment loss	52,027		
Abandonment loss	—	—	5,433
	2,110,739	2,064,250	1,751,169
Income from operations	351,060	431,534	273,736
Other income (expense)			
Interest, dividends and other income	(1,163)	8,339	2,369
Guarantee fees from unconsolidated affiliate	2,264	2,498	2,775
Interest expense	(221,352)	(219,940)	(164,387)
Interest expense from unconsolidated affiliates	(8,451)	(11,293)	(11,085)
	(228,702)	(220,396)	(170,328)
Minority interest	(29,352)	(16,746)	(292)
Income before provision for income taxes	93,006	194,392	103,116
Provision for income taxes	39,962	74,692	38,959
Income before cumulative effect of change in accounting principle	53,044	119,700	64,157
Cumulative effect of change in accounting for preopening expenses, net of tax benefit of $11,843	—	—	(21,994)
Net income	$ 53,044	$ 119,700	$ 42,163
Basic earnings per share:			
Income before cumulative effect of change in accounting principle	$ .73	$ 1.53	$ .71
Cumulative effect of change in accounting principle	—	—	(.24)
Net income	$ .73	$ 1.53	$ .47
Diluted earnings per share:			
Income before cumulative effect of change in accounting principle	$ .71	$ 1.50	$ .70
Cumulative effect of change in accounting principle	—	—	(.24)
Net income	$ .71	$ 1.50	$ .46
Average shares outstanding (basic)	72,798,916	78,334,735	90,607,487
Average shares outstanding (diluted)	74,459,831	79,700,614	91,896,224

Source: 2001 *Annual Report,* p. 74.

EXHIBIT 8　Competitors (in millions)

	2000	2000	1999	1999
	Revenue	*Net Income*	*Revenue*	*Net Income*
Park Place Entertainment	$4,896	$143	$3,176	$136
Harrah's Entertainment	3,471	(12.1)	3,024	208
MGM Mirage	3,232	160	1,392.2	209
Mandalay Resort Group	2,050	42	1,479	85
Trump Hotel and Casino	933	(29)	973	(149)
Aztar	848	53	800	10

Source: Individual companies annual reports and 10Ks (1999–2000).

casinos in the world, with 3,669 slot machines and 157 table games. Through a wholly owned subsidiary, MGM owns and operates the MGM Grand Diamond Beach Hotel and a hotel/casino resort in Darwin, Australia. In March 1999, MGM and Primadonna Resorts, Inc., merged, resulting in ownership of New York-New York Hotel and Casino and three hotels casinos on the California/Nevada border. MGM also intends to construct and operate a destination resort hotel/casino, entertainment, and retail facility in Atlantic City on approximately thirty-five acres of land on the Atlantic City boardwalk.

FUTURE CONSIDERATIONS

Mandalay was one of the innovators of the gaming resort concept and has continued to be a leader in that field. However, the mega-entertainment resort industry and the traditional casino gaming industry operate differently. In the past, consumers would visit a casino to experience the thrill of gambling. Now they not only gamble but also expect to be dazzled by enormous entertainment complexes that cost billions of dollars to build. The competition has continued to increase at the same time growth rates have been slowing.

For years, analysts have questioned the ability of the gaming industry to continue high growth in established markets as the industry matures. Through the 1970s and 1980s, the gaming industry experienced rapid growth. Through the 1990s, the industry began to experience a shake out of marginal competitors and a consolidation phase. Mandalay has been successful through this turmoil but now faces the task of maintaining high growth in a more mature industry severely impacted by the terrorist attacks of September 11, 2001.

BIBLIOGRAPHY

"AGA Fact Sheets," American Gaming Association, retrieved October 17, 2001 from http://www.americangaming.org/casino_entertainment/aga_facts/.

Aztar Corp. *1997, 1998, 1999, and 2000 10K,* retrieved from EDGAR Data Base, http://www.sec.gov/Archives/edgar/data/.

"Economic Impacts of Casino Gaming in the United States," by Arthur Andersen for the American Gaming Association (May 1997).

Harrah's Entertainment, Inc. *1997, 1998, 1999, and 2000 10K,* retrieved from EDGAR Data Base, http://www.sec.gov/Archives/edgar/data/.

"Harrah's Survey of Casino Entertainment," Harrah's Entertainment, Inc. (1996).

Industry Surveys—Lodging and Gaming, *Standard & Poor's Industry Surveys* (June 19, 1997).

"ITT Board Rejects Hilton's Offer as Inadequate, Reaffirms Belief That ITT's Comprehensive Plan Is in the Best Interest of ITT Shareholders," press release (August 14, 1997).

ITT Corp. *1997 10K,* retrieved from EDGAR Data Base, **http://www.sec.gov/ Archives/edgar/data/**.

Mandalay Resort Group (formally Circus Circus), *Annual Report to Shareholders*

(January 31, 1989; January 31, 1990; January 31, 1993; January 31, 1994; January 31, 1995; January 31, 1996; January 31, 1997; January 31, 1998; January 31, 1999; January 31, 2000; January 31, 2001).

MGM Mirage *1997, 1998, 1999, and 2000 10K,* retrieved from EDGAR Database, **http://www.sec.gov/Archives/ edgar/data/**.

Strow, David, "LV Casinos Look at Layoffs," *Las Vegas Sun* (September 17, 2001).

HARRAH'S ENTERTAINMENT, INC.—2002

Mary R. Dittman
Francis Marion University

HET

www.harrahs.com

Harrah's Entertainment, Inc., is a $3.7 billion per year gaming company that operates twenty-one casinos in seventeen markets, including properties in Arizona, Illinois, Indiana, Kansas, Louisiana, Mississippi, Missouri, Nevada, New Jersey, and North Carolina. Harrah's is headquartered in Las Vegas, Nevada, and is one of the gaming industry's forerunners in customer-oriented database marketing.

HISTORY

William F. Harrah founded Harrah's as a bingo parlor in Reno, Nevada, in 1937. Over the next thirty-two years, Harrah's grew into one of the nation's premier gaming establishments.

In 1973, Harrah's became the first casino to be listed on the New York Stock Exchange. In 1980, Holiday Inns, Inc., acquired Harrah's. In 1989, Holiday Inn announced the creation of a new spinoff company, The Promus Companies, Inc. In 1995, Promus spun off its Embassy Suites, Hampton Inn, and Homewood Suites brands; the remaining Harrah's brand was renamed Harrah's Entertainment, Inc., and it included Harrah's hotels and casinos, Harrah's assets, and a majority of the Promus headquarters and people.

In 1997 and 1998, Harrah's joined with the Cherokee Indians and the Prairie Band of Potawatomi Nation, respectively, to open tribal-run casinos in North Carolina and Kansas. Also in 1998, Harrah's purchased Showboat, Inc., which includes four properties in Atlantic City, East Chicago, Las Vegas, and Sydney, Australia. (Operation of this Australian property ceased in January 2000.) In 1999, Harrah's completed a merger with the Rio Hotel & Casino, a true destination resort in Las Vegas.

In March 2000, Harrah's acquired Players International, Inc., which contributed significantly to the company's 15 percent revenue growth over 1999. Players owned riverboat casinos in Missouri, Louisiana, and Illinois and a racetrack in Kentucky.

EXTERNAL FACTORS

Gaming Industry

The gaming industry reports revenues as GGR—Gross Gambling Revenue. GGR is the amount of money wagered less the winnings paid to the player. For example, a player goes to a casino intending to bet $100 in the slot machines. At the casino, he exchanges his $100 bill for one hundred $1.00 casino tokens. The player plays his tokens; he wins some bets and loses some bets. Because slot machines typically pay out $.90 for every $1.00 put into the machine, the player ends up with $90. He continues to bet each of his ninety $1.00 tokens and ends up with $81 (ninety bets with an expected value of $.90, or 90 × .90 = 81). He pockets the $81 and goes to a show at the casino's showroom. The player intended to spend $100 but actually spent only $19. The casino recognizes only $19 in revenue from the player.

In 1999, GGR for casinos was $22.6 billion. This was a 12.7 percent increase in revenues over 1998. The total gaming industry (including lotteries, bookmaking, and bingo) reported revenues of $58.2 billion in 1999 (up 6 percent from 1998).

Casinos' annual revenues from March 1999 through March 2000 are shown in Exhibit 1.

EXHIBIT 1   2000 Annual Casino Revenue by Market

Casino Market	Annual Revenues
Las Vegas Strip	$ 4.5 billion
Atlantic City, NJ	$ 4.2 billion
Chicago Area (IL, IN)	$ 1.8 billion
Connecticut Indian	$ 1.6 billion
Tunica, MS	$ 1 billion
Gulf Coast, MS	$ 1 billion
Reno, NV	$817.7 million
Las Vegas—Downtown	$665 million
Bossier City/Shreveport, LA	$659.9 million
St. Louis Area (IL, MO)	$652 million
Lake Charles, LA	$561.4 million
Laughlin, NV	$539.3 million
Kansas City, MO	$512.7 million
Cincinnati Area (OH)	$472.4 million
Black Hawk/Central City (CO)	$448.1 million
Delaware Racetracks	$432.1 million
New Orleans, LA	$399.3 million
Southern IL/IN	$356.8 million
Council Bluffs, IA	$337.4 million
South Shore Lake Tahoe, NV	$323.5 million
Vicksburg, MS	$222 million
Quad Cities Area (IL, IA)	$181.6 million
Des Moines, IA	$149.8 million
Baton Rouge, LA	$149.2 million
Cripple Creek, CO	$126.4 million
Peoria, IL	$122.1 million
Coahoma, MS	$102.7 million
Dubuque, IA	$ 78.4 million
Greenville, MS	$ 73.5 million
Deadwood, SD	$ 49.7 million
Natchez, MS	$ 32.5 million
Caruthersville, MO	$ 23.7 million
St. Joseph, MO	$ 20.8 million

Source: "Casino Markets by Annual Revenue", AGA Fact Sheet.
www.americangaming.org.

The Nevada market constitutes 30.2 percent of the gaming industry's volume, while New Jersey represents 18.6 percent of the volume. The commercial casino industry employs more than 370,000 people with wages of more than $10.9 billion, and the industry contributed more than $3.5 billion in tax revenue in 2000. The industry is an important part of the economies of the eleven states where more than 425 commercial casinos are located.[1]

Residents of communities where commercial casinos are located overwhelmingly support the gaming industry. According to the 2001 AGA Survey of Casino Entertainment, an annual survey conducted by the American Gaming Association:

> *Metropolis, Ill., is one example of a local community that has been transformed with help from the casino industry. Home to Harrah's Metropolis Casino, the town received more than $6.5 million from riverboat casino taxes in 2000. This revenue has helped the small rural community upgrade its infrastructure and city utilities, as well as expand municipal services. The city recently completed a capital improvement plan for the next five years that includes projects such as construction of a new water filtration plant, development of a new industrial park, and completion of several parks and recreation projects. More than 88 percent of the funds to fulfill the plan objectives are expected to come from riverboat casino funds.[2]*

The gaming industry is also active in bringing attention to problem gaming. Much like alcohol companies that encourage consumers to drink responsibly, most casinos post the phone number for Gamblers Anonymous at every cashier's cage; many also offer free literature with information on problem gambling and how to get help. In the same spirit of involvement, the gaming industry is active against underage gambling; casinos will not permit minors to even stand in the gaming areas.

Demographics

According to the 2000 State of the States: The AGA Survey of Casino Entertainment, the profile of the typical casino customer has remained consistent over the past several years.

The following factors seem to characterize the casino player market[3]:

- Casino players have a household income that is 19 percent higher than that of the U.S. population.
- The median age of casino players is similar to that of the U.S. population.
- Casino players are slightly less educated.
- Casino players are more likely to be white-collar workers.

Eighty-one percent of casino customers "always" or "usually" set a budget before visiting a casino. Exhibit 2 summarizes the differences between casino customers and the general population.

Competition

The gaming industry boasts five major players (in descending order by 2000 reported revenues): Park Place Entertainment Corporation, MGM Mirage, Harrah's Entertainment, Mandalay Resort Group, and Trump Hotels and Casino Resorts. Exhibit 3 at the end of this section summarizes each competitor's 2000 revenues and net income.

Park Place Entertainment Corporation is the world's largest gaming company and owns the Hilton Hotel (including the Las Vegas Hilton and Flamingo Hilton) chain, Grand Casinos, Caesar's, the Bally's brand, and the Paris Hotel & Casino.

EXHIBIT 2   2001 Profile of U.S. Casino Customers

Characteristic	U.S. Casino Customer	United States Population
Median Household Income	$50,453	$42,343
Median Age (adults 21 and older)	46%	45%
Education		
No College	45%	48%
Some College	27%	30%
Bachelor's Degree	17%	16%
Post-Graduate Degree	9%	9%
Employment		
White Collar	47%	41%
Blue Collar	25%	28%
Retired	25%	28%
Other	15%	18%

Source: Andrea Lessani, "How Much Do You Want to Bet That the Internet Gambling Prohibition Act of 1997 Is Not the Most Effective Way to Tackle the Problems of Online Gambling?" The UCLA Online Institute for Cyberspace Law and Policy (May 1998), p. 1. **http://www.gseis.ucla.edu/iclp/hp.html**.

MGM Mirage owns the MGM, Mirage, Bellagio, New York-New York, Beau Rivage, Treasure Island, and Golden Nugget brands, and it holds a 50 percent ownership in the Monte Carlo (Las Vegas) with the Mandalay Resort Group. MGM Mirage had successful simultaneous opening of two major properties (Bellagio and Beau Rivage), while a difficult undertaking, signaled MGM Mirage's ability to grow and expand; Bellagio and Beau Rivage doubled the size of MGM Mirage.

Trump Hotels and Casino Resorts owns three properties in Atlantic City: the Trump Taj Mahal Casino Resort, the Trump Plaza Hotel & Casino, and the Trump Marina Hotel Casino. A fourth property, the Trump Hotel Casino, is located in Buffington Harbor, Indiana.

Mandalay Resort Group holds the Mandalay Bay, Luxor, Excalibur, and Circus Circus brands, as well as a 50 percent ownership of the Monte Carlo with MGM Mirage. Mandalay Resort Group was founded in 1974 as Circus Circus Enterprises. It holds properties in Nevada, Mississippi, and Illinois.

These figures include revenue from room, food and beverages, casinos, and other corporate sources of income. It is important to note that casinos report revenues from all income sources, while the gaming industry reports revenues as GGR (as described earlier).

EXHIBIT 3   2000 Revenues of Major Gaming Competitors

Company	2000 Revenue	2000 Net Income
Park Place	$4,896,000,000	$143,000,000
MGM Mirage	3,232,590,000	160,744,000
Harrah's	2,852,048,000	(12,060,000)
Mandalay	2,050,898,000	42,163,000
Trump	1,245,014,000	(37,312,000)

Source: **www.americangaming.org**

Other Competition

The companies profiled make up slightly less than 50 percent of the gaming industry. There are many other, smaller competitors both domestically and internationally that make up the other half of the market. Since gaming could be considered part of the vast entertainment industry, hotels/casinos compete with the myriad of other entertainment venues: theme parks, resorts, theaters, cruise ships, and so on.

One potential source for intense gaming competition is the Internet. Both the state and federal governments have actively worked to regulate and even ban Internet gaming. Internet gaming is estimated to be a multibillion-dollar-per-year industry; however, there are four major concerns with this type of gaming:

1. The potential for fraud over the Internet
2. Children's access to gambling sites
3. State regulations that "lock out" commercial casinos from the Internet gaming industry
4. The need to preserve state revenues generated from legally enforced and state-run gambling operations.[4]

While the federal government does not yet ban Internet gaming, many states have passed laws regulating its use. For example, Nevada has become the first state to pass a law that specifically prohibits its residents from placing or accepting bets over the Internet.[5]

The commercial casino industry is one of the most heavily regulated industries in the United States. Not only do commercial casino companies have to meet strict state regulations, casinos also must adhere to numerous federal laws.

Members of the American Gaming Association have expressed concerns over Internet gambling because Internet gambling companies are not regulated for fairness and integrity, their revenues are not taxed equitably, and those who wager may not be protected or guaranteed the same quality gaming experience they might expect from a commercial casino company. The commercial casino industry does not seem to oppose Internet gambling because of a fear of competition. In fact, many casinos would like the opportunity to market their services over the Internet.

Over the past few years, many bills have been introduced into the U.S. Senate and the House of Representatives that would ban Internet gambling; however, these bills have consistently been defeated, including one in October 2001 that would have prohibited using credit cards to pay for Internet gambling. This bill was introduced as part of a bill designed to prevent money laundering by terrorists. While the anti-money laundering bill was passed, the final version of this legislation did not include provisions related to Internet gambling.

Technology

Three major developments affect the gaming industry: player cards, slot technology and linked jackpots, and the Internet. The Internet was examined in the previous section; the following discussion focuses on player cards and slot technology/linked jackpots.

Most casinos offer a player card, which is similar to an airline's frequent flyer card. The card is inserted into the slot machine prior to play, or it is run through a scanner at certain table games (usually with a $25 betting minimum). The card tracks player demographics and playing habits. Each casino's card is valid at that casino's locations.

Players can earn cash, prizes, and complementary meals, rooms, and other amenities by racking up points on their player cards.

Gaming industry suppliers (such as International Game Technology) have been developing new types of slotlike games with such themes as Wheel of Fortune, the Addams Family, the Richard Petty Driving Experience, and I Dream of Jeannie. The goal of such suppliers is to keep players excited and satisfied. Sierra Design Group introduced the Raining Diamonds slot machine in July 2001. The machine not only pays out coins but also rewards customers with genuine diamond jewelry, which is secured in vaults in each machine. Harrah's Rio All-Suites Hotel & Casino in Las Vegas will be the first casino in the industry to offer players the opportunity to play the Raining Diamonds slot machine.

Other than the traditional spinning reel slot machines, there are a variety of new games on the market: video-based games, multigame machines (where the player can select from a variety of games), and interactive games. Linked jackpots (like the Megabucks jackpot) pool revenues from around a gaming area (like Megabucks, which pools revenues from all over Nevada) and then pay out millions in winnings. It is conceivable that a player who wins a linked jackpot could win millions of dollars just by spending $1 dollar in a slot machine.

Economic and Government Concerns

Casino gambling has created thousands of jobs, a high percentage of which are held by minorities and women. The hundreds of millions of dollars in tax revenues that casinos pay to cities and states each year help lower taxes and pay for many basic civic needs. Casinos also lead to growth in other areas: retail, housing construction, restaurants, and other tourism venues.[6]

For these reasons, many states support gaming. In fact, Nevada residents pay no state income tax, and sales taxes are relatively low, thanks to the taxes paid by the gaming industry.

In the past, gaming benefited from consumers' growing recreational discretionary incomes. However, following the events of September 11, 2001, the industry may see a significant decline in revenues due to losses of jobs in many industries.

The events of September 11, 2001, will surely affect Harrah's revenues. Airline travel and destination travel has decreased both domestically and internationally since that date. Consumers may have concerns related to spending discretionary income on gaming. Many businesses are affected by the loss of jobs in the airline and travel sectors. Consumers who are still employed are also nervous about traveling and spending money "unwisely."

INTERNAL CONDITION

In 2000, Harrah's experienced a significant setback in revenues due to the bankruptcy reorganizations for Harrah's New Orleans and National Airlines, of which Harrah's owns 40 percent and 48 percent, respectively.

Divisions

The company owns twenty casinos in seventeen markets in ten states. Those markets are divided into four divisions: (1) western region, (2) central region, (3) eastern region, and (4) managed casinos and other.

Western Region

The western region includes northern Nevada (Reno and Lake Tahoe) and southern Nevada (Las Vegas and Laughlin). The significant increase in 1999 revenues is due to the acquisition of the Rio All-Suites Hotel & Casino in Las Vegas; however, all southern Nevada properties reported approximately a 10 percent increase in revenues that year.

In 2000, the Rio opened its new $32 million showroom complex which includes ten thousand feet of retail space, a hospitality center, and a state-of-the-art theater. This complex has not generated an increase in entertainment revenues and is the primary cause of the significant revenue shortfall in 2000. Lower table game revenue also contributed to the loss of revenue.

(in millions)	2001	2000	1999	Percentage Increase/(Decrease) 01 vs. 00	00 vs. 99
Casino revenues	$ 786.3	$ 726.8	$ 730.1	(8.2)%	(0.5)%
Total revenues	1,203.5	1,141.7	1,147.9	(6.5)%	(0.6)%
Operating profit	130.8	127.9	182.4	(2.3)%	(29.9)%
Operating margin	10.9%	11.2%	15.9%	(0.4) pts	(4.7) pts

Source: **www.americangaming.org**

Central Region

The central region includes properties in Chicago, Louisiana, Missouri, and Mississippi.

The significant increase in revenues in 2000 over 1999 are due to the acquisition of Players in March 2000; however, excluding this acquisition, revenues in the central region still increased approximately 14 percent in 2000 over 1999.

(in millions)	2001	2000	1999	1998	Percentage Increase/Decrease 01 vs. 00	00 vs. 99
Casino revenues	$1,698.0	$1,381.6	$ 970.9	$661.9	22.9%	42.3%
Total revenues	1,707.6	1,453.9	1,020.1	702.7	22.6%	43.0%
Operating profit	361.4	304.8	201.8	121.0	18.6%	51.0%
Operating margin	21.2	21.0%	19.8%	17.2%	(0.7) pts	1.2 pts

Source: **www.americangaming.org**

Eastern Region

The eastern region is composed of the Harrah's Atlantic City and Atlantic City Showboat properties.

(in millions)	2001	2000	1999	1998	Percentage Increase/Decrease 01 vs. 00	00 vs. 99
Casino revenues	$751.0	$743.3	$723.3	$540.8	1.0%	2.8%
Total revenues	724.0	791.8	775.6	590.8	0.1%	2.9%
Operating profit	183.0	182.3	173.8	129.2	0.4%	4.9%
Operating margin	25.3	23.0%	22.4%	21.9%	0.1 pts	0.5 pts

Source: **www.americangaming.org**

Managed Casinos and Other

This region includes Indian gaming partnerships, management fees from Harrah's New Orleans, and branding costs.

(in millions)	2001	2000	1999	1998	Percentage Increase/Decrease 01 vs 00	00 vs 99
Revenues	$69.0	$78.5	$77.9	$65.5	(12.1)%	0.8%
Operating profit	30.8	40.4	43.3	25.3	(23.8)%	(6.7)%

Vision and Mission

Harrah's has developed a comprehensive Code of Commitment that addresses customers, employees, and communities. This Code of Commitment can be found in various Harrah's publications and on the company's Web site:

A commitment to *our guests* to promote responsible gaming:

- We do not cash welfare or unemployment checks.
- We have a process to honor the requests of customers who wish to be denied access to our casinos, and [to have] their access to credit, check-cashing, and casino promotions . . . restricted.
- We display toll-free helpline numbers for problem gambling in our ads, brochures, and signs, and we provide financial support for those helplines.
- We train our employees to understand the signs of problem gambling and empower them to provide customers with information describing how to get help.
- We emphasize to our employees that casino gaming is an appropriate activity for adults only, and [we] require them to be vigilant in their efforts to prevent individuals under the legal age from playing at our casinos.

A commitment to *our employees* to treat them with respect and provide them opportunities to build satisfying careers:

- We invest in our employees by providing excellent pay and valuable benefits, including health insurance and a retirement plan.
- We are committed to sharing our financial success through tuition reimbursement, on the job training, career development, and promotion from within.
- We actively seek and respond to employee opinions on all aspects of their jobs, from the quality of their supervisors to the quality of our casinos.

A commitment to *our communities* to help make them vibrant places to live and work, and to market our casinos responsibly:

- We conduct our business with honesty and integrity, consistent with the highest moral, legal, and ethical standards, complying with all applicable laws and regulations.
- We share our financial success with our communities by donating one percent of company profits to civic and charitable causes.
- We encourage our employees to volunteer in civic and charitable causes.
- We restrict the placement and content of our advertising and marketing materials.

All commercial casinos prohibit minor children from participating in gaming; in fact, children are not even allowed on the casino floor. Children are permitted to walk through the casino if escorted by an adult; however, if the child stops—even to watch the adult drop a quarter into a slot machine—casino security will ask the two of them to leave the gaming floor.

Harrah's is vigilant about protecting minor-age children from gaming activity. The company has a comprehensive Marketing and Advertising Code, which governs all aspects of marketing and advertising. This code includes such policies as:

1. Not using any cartoons, illustrations, entertainment figures, or toy figures to promote gaming that would appeal to minors.
2. Not advertising in media in which the majority of the audience is known to be under the legal gambling age.
3. Not printing the Harrah's name, logo, or brand marks on items or apparel intended for persons under the legal gambling age.

Financial Data

Exhibits 4 and 5 contain Harrah's Income Statements and Balance Sheets, respectively.

Marketing

The Communications Act of 1934 prohibited all television ads that showed gambling activity. This act only affected commercial casinos—lotteries, horse and dog tracks, and Indian casinos were allowed to advertise freely. In June 1999, the Supreme Court struck down the Communications Act with its decision in the case *Greater New Orleans Broadcast Association* v. *United States*.

Harrah's has an incredibly strong focus on marketing. The casino industry is highly competitive; there are billions of dollars at stake. Because Harrah's competes in the entertainment industry, its customers are purchasing "a good time." Therefore, service is of the utmost importance.

It is difficult to place a price on the product offered by the casino industry. In terms of room, food, and amenity pricing, Harrah's is competitive with—and in some cases, slightly below—competitive pricing. For example, a room at Bellagio in Las Vegas starts around $300 per night; a full-size suite at the Rio is well under $200 per night. At Harrah's Las Vegas, the room rates are approximately $150 per night.

One area of price that is of interest to gaming customers is the probability of winning. Harrah's (Las Vegas and Reno) hosts annual multimillion dollar slot tournaments. These tournaments are easy to compete in, take no skill, appeal to the customer's belief that "maybe that can happen to me, too," and help to generate traffic onto the casino floor. The slot machines are the major revenue generator at a casino, so generating more slot business usually means more revenue for the casino. The reputation of having loose slots draws more people in.

Harrah's has twenty locations. There are eight land-based properties:

- Harrah's Reno
- Harrah's Lake Tahoe
- Harrah's Las Vegas
- Harrah's Atlantic City
- Atlantic City Showboat
- Harrah's Laughlin (Nevada)
- Rio All-Suites Hotel & Casino (Las Vegas)
- Metropolis (Players property located in Metropolis, Illinois)

EXHIBIT 4   Consolidated Statements of Operations

	Year Ended December 31,		
(in thousands, except per-share amounts)	*2001*	*2000*	*1999*
Revenues			
Casino	$3,235,761	$2,852,048	$2,424,237
Food and beverage	532,115	480,757	429,684
Rooms	301,846	270,313	253,629
Management fees	64,842	66,398	75,890
Other	140,234	142,072	127,527
Less: casino promotional allowances	(565,758)	(481,792)	(416,842)
Total revenues	3,709,040	3,329,796	2,894,125
Operating expenses			
Direct			
Casino	1,528,106	1,354,268	1,124,254
Food and beverage	234,938	228,002	218,580
Rooms	78,085	67,800	66,818
Depreciation and amortization	285,773	236,082	193,599
Write-downs, reserves and recoveries			
Reserves for New Orleans casino	2,322	220,000	–
Other	20,176	6,106	2,235
Project opening costs	13,136	8,258	2,276
Corporate expense	52,746	50,472	42,748
Headquarters relocation and reorganization costs	–	2,983	10,274
Equity in (income) losses of nonconsolidated affiliates	(148)	57,935	43,467
Venture restructuring costs	2,524	400	(322)
Amortization of intangible assets	25,288	21,540	17,617
Other	885,129	793,212	691,542
Total operating expenses	3,128,075	3,047,058	2,413,088
Income from operations	580,965	282,738	481,037
Interest expense, net of interest capitalized	(255,801)	(227,139)	(193,407)
(Losses) gains on interests in nonconsolidated affiliates	(5,040)	(41,626)	59,824
Other income, including interest income	28,219	3,866	12,129
Income before income taxes and minority interests	348,343	17,839	359,583
Provision for income taxes	(126,737)	(15,415)	(128,914)
Minority interests	(12,616)	(13,768)	(11,166)
Income (loss) before extraordinary losses	208,990	(11,344)	219,503
Extraordinary losses, net of tax benefit of $13, $388 and $5,990	(23)	(716)	(11,033)
Net income (loss)	$ 208,967	$ (12,060)	$ 208,470
Earnings (loss) per share–basic			
Before extraordinary losses	$ 1.84	$ (0.09)	$ 1.74
Extraordinary losses, net	–	(0.01)	(0.09)
Net income (loss)	$ 1.84	$ (0.10)	$ 1.65
Earnings (loss) per share–diluted			
Before extraordinary losses	$ 1.81	$ (0.09)	$ 1.71
Extraordinary losses, net	–	(0.01)	(0.09)
Net income (loss)	$ 1.81	$ (0.10)	$ (1.62)
Weighted average common shares outstanding	113,540	117,190	126,072
Dilutive effect of stock compensation programs	2,168	–	2,676
Weighted average common and common equivalent shares outstanding	115,708	117,190	128,748

Source: Harrah's Entertainment, Inc. *2001 Annual Report*

EXHIBIT 5   Consolidated Balance Sheets

	December 31,	
(in thousands, except per-share amounts)	*2001*	*2000*
ASSETS		
Current assets		
Cash and cash equivalents	$ 361,470	$ 299,202
Receivables, less allowance for doubtful accounts of $61,150 and $49,357	110,781	122,050
Deferred income taxes	45,319	35,126
Income tax refunds receivable	28,326	56,132
Prepayments and other	48,927	48,107
Inventories	22,875	22,816
Total current assets	617,698	583,433
Land, buildings, riverboats and equipment		
Land and land improvements	766,401	705,393
Buildings, riverboats and improvements	3,200,493	2,652,867
Furniture, fixtures and equipment	1,208,706	974,233
Construction in progress	164,294	248,760
	5,339,894	4,581,253
Less: accumulated depreciation	(1,280,564)	(1,084,884)
	4,059,330	3,496,369
Goodwill, net of accumulated amortization of $92,046 and $72,465	947,678	685,393
Investments in and advances to nonconsolidated affiliates	79,464	86,681
Deferred costs, trademarks and other	424,412	314,209
	$ 6,128,582	$ 5,166,085
LIABILITIES AND STOCKHOLDERS' EQUITY		
Current liabilities		
Accounts payable	$ 123,428	$ 89,051
Accrued expenses	412,897	343,524
Short-term debt	31,000	215,000
Current portion of long-term debt	1,583	130,928
Total current liabilities	568,908	778,503
Long-term debt	3,719,443	2,835,846
Deferred credits and other	173,677	177,654
Deferred income taxes	261,119	85,650
	4,723,147	3,877,653
Minority interests	31,322	18,714
Commitments and contingencies		
Stockholders' equity		
Common stock, $0.10 par value, authorized–360,000,000 shares, outstanding–112,322,143 and 115,952,394 shares (net of 28,977,890 and 22,030,805 shares held in treasury)	11,232	11,595
Capital surplus	1,143,125	1,075,313
Retained earnings	248,098	224,251
Accumulated other comprehensive loss	(1,449)	(1,036)
Deferred compensation related to restricted stock	(26,893)	(40,405)
	1,374,113	1,269,718
	$ 6,128,582	$ 5,166,085

Source: Harrah's Entertainment, Inc. *2001 Annual Report*

There are eight riverboats:

- Harrah's Joliet (Illinois)
- Harrah's Vicksburg (Mississippi)
- Harrah's Tunica (Mississippi)
- Harrah's Shreveport (Louisiana)
- Harrah's North Kansas City (Missouri)
- Harrah's St. Louis-Riverport (Missouri)
- Showboat Mardi Gras (East Chicago)
- Harrah's Lake Charles (formerly Players) (Louisiana)

There are three Indian gaming properties:

- Harrah's Phoenix Ak-Chin Casino (Arizona)
- Harrah's Cherokee Smoky Mountains (North Carolina)
- Harrah's Prairie Band (Kansas)

These many locations allow Harrah's to attract many different people into the casinos. This diversification also means that Harrah's is not dependent on any one region for its customers, nor is it dependent on one area's economy. Half of the U.S. population lives within a three-hour drive of a Harrah's owned or managed property. This strength is important given the events of September 11, 2001. If customers are hesitant to fly to destinations, Harrah's may benefit from having many properties within driving distance.

Following the bankruptcy proceedings of National Airlines, Harrah's has partnered with America West airlines to offer package deals to customers for airfares. Harrah's has also joined the travel agents' Global Distribution System, which makes it easier for travel agents and customers using the Internet to book hotel reservations and access information about Harrah's hotels and casinos.

Harrah's is a master of promotion. From slot tournaments to Internet Web sites, and from art exhibits (Treasures of Russia at the Rio was replaced by the Titanic exhibit, which features artifacts recovered from the famed ship's resting place) to world-class

---

EXHIBIT 6   Organizational Chart

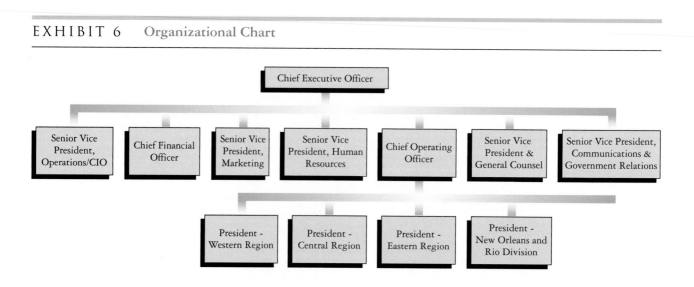

entertainers, Harrah's has a complete marketing program. Using the Total Rewards program, Harrah's has well over fifteen million customer names in its database. It uses these names and the corresponding demographic information to customize programs.

Harrah's has mastered targeted marketing. Not only does Harrah's talk to its customers, but the company also faithfully observes play patterns and conducts formal research. In fact, Harrah's surveys have formed the basis for research conducted by the Arthur Andersen Group for the American Gaming Association.

Harrah's Total Gold system, the predecessor of the Total Rewards player card, was introduced in 1997. The technology is patented, and it is the number one player card in Las Vegas and Atlantic City. In December 2000, *Information Week* and Cap Gemini Ernst & Young ranked the Total Rewards system number one among the top one hundred U.S. companies that use information technology to build customer relationships.

The customer database generated by the Total Rewards system allows Harrah's to focus on serving its market. Twenty-three percent of Harrah's Total Rewards play comes from multimarket play: from players who use their cards in more than one Harrah's casino. Harrah's can use the Total Rewards system to determine how much an Atlantic City customer plays in Las Vegas! Using this information, Harrah's placed a bank of the most popular slot machines from the Atlantic City property in the middle of Harrah's Las Vegas.

Total Rewards offers three tiers of membership: Total Gold, Total Platinum, and Total Diamond. The tiers helped generate an increase of $165 million in revenue from Platinum and Diamond level players in 2000. Also in 2000, the number of Platinum level players increased 124 percent over 1999, while the number of Diamond level players increased 118 percent.

Total Rewards allows customers to obtain discounts on shows, hotel rooms, food and beverages, as well as priority-customer status when making reservations, checking in, or making reservations for show seating.

THE FUTURE

Harrah's focuses on four main strategies to grow its business:

1. More distribution
2. Quality products
3. Patented technology
4. Great service

Harrah's has focused on acquiring and building properties in key gaming markets. The addition of the Rio allows Harrah's to compete in the Las Vegas resort market, because the Rio is classified as a full-service resort (featuring a golf course, full-service spa and salon, meeting and convention facilities, a retail promenade, and a museum).

Although none of Harrah's properties are alike, they strive for consistency in the quality of the food, service, gaming, and accommodation experiences.

In 2001, Harrah's Entertainment won 216 awards in *Strictly Slots* magazine's annual "Best Of" customer ratings issue. The company was also the only gaming company to receive *Darwin* magazine's Darwin Fittest 50 award for its management of customer relationships.

Harrah's has received numerous patents for its Total Rewards system, which allows it to keep its customer database from its competitors. Harrah's uses the database to customize marketing plans and programs and to create brand loyalty to the Harrah's, Showboat, and Rio brand names. Since the launch of the Total Rewards program,

Harrah's has seen solid same-store sales growth and increases in cross-market play. Rio and Showboat had their own player cards, which have been merged into the Harrah's system, meaning that a Rio player may use his Play Rio card at Harrah's and Showboat, with the rewards system between the three casinos being standardized and equal.

Harrah's recognizes that it is competing in a service industry. The company has a three-tiered service strategy:

1. A regular Employee Opinion Poll that measures employee attitudes and expectations
2. Spotlight on Success—a type of mystery shopper program designed to reward excellent service and correct substandard service
3. The Target Player Satisfaction Survey, which surveys the experiences of target customers

CONCLUSION

Harrah's Entertainment is focused, and it instills this focus in each employee: to become the undisputed leader in the casino entertainment industry. In the first quarter of 1998, Harrah's was the first casino to launch a national brand-image advertising campaign, with TV spots that aired during the Academy Awards. Harrah's has become one of the gaming industry's top competitors. While ranked third in revenues in 2000, the company is poised to grow its sales and increase its revenues and market share.

Harrah's faced numerous challenges in 2000, including the bankruptcy proceedings of the New Orleans casino property and National Airlines. The financial performance of the Rio property in Las Vegas also negatively affected revenues; however, Harrah's superior dedication to customer-oriented marketing and the top-notch management team's focus on healthy performance promise to help Harrah's overtake the competition.

Harrah's will likely face many financial challenges in the next five years due to the possible impending economic recession fueled by the events of September 11, 2001. Domestic consumers are reluctant to travel and to spend money on recreation, and international customers are more restricted in their travel to the United States. This potential recession may dramatically decrease Harrah's revenues.

NOTES

1. "AGA Releases First Annual Survey of Casino Entertainment," press release from American Gaming Association (September 14, 1999). **www.americangaming.org**.
2. "2001 AGA Survey of Casino Entertainment." **www.americangaming.org**.
3. "2001 AGA Survey of Casino Entertainment." **www.americangaming.org**.
4. Lessani, Andrea, "How Much Do You Want to Bet That the Internet Gambling Prohibition Act of 1997 Is Not the Most Effective Way to Tackle the Problems of Online Gambling?" The UCLA Online Institute for Cyberspace Law and Policy (May 1998), p. 1. **http://www.gseis. ucla.edu/iclp/hp.html**.
5. "Economic Impacts of Casino Gaming in the United States," in the section entitled by "Overall Conclusions," prepared by Arthur Andersen Consulting Group for the American Gaming Association (December 1996). **www.americangaming.org**.
6. "Economic Impacts of Casino Gaming in the United States," in the section entitled "Macroeconomic Impacts of the Casino Gaming Industry," prepared by Arthur Andersen Consulting Group for the American Gaming Association (December 1996). **www. americangaming.org**.

WACHOVIA CORPORATION—2002

Fred R. David
Francis Marion University

WB

www.wachovia.com

Wachovia Corporation, created through the September 1, 2001, merger of First Union and the former Wachovia, had assets of $330 billion and stockholders' equity of $28 billion at December 31, 2001. Wachovia is a leading provider of financial services to 20 million retail, brokerage, and corporate customers throughout the East Coast and the nation. Wachovia is the nation's fourth largest banking company based on assets and operates 2,800 full-service banking offices and 4,700 automated teller machines under the First Union and Wachovia names in 11 East Coast states and Washington, D.C. As the nation's fifth largest full-service retail broker dealer, based on client assets, the company offers full-service brokerage with offices in 49 states. Wachovia also provides global services through more than 30 international offices. Online banking and brokerage products and services are available through **wachovia.com** and **firstunion.com**.

HISTORY OF FIRST UNION

Born as the brainchild of H. M. Victor in 1908, then named Union Bank, First Union has evolved from a hometown bank to the nation's sixth largest financial institution. Its growth has come largely from acquisitions, with the first one taking place in 1958 and many more since then. The company's corporate headquarters is conveniently located in Charlotte, North Carolina, which is also home to its fierce rival, Bank of America (formerly NationsBank), the fifth largest U.S. financial institution.

First Union is not just a bank. The easing of the Glass-Steagall Act facilitated strategic acquisitions, thus allowing First Union to involve itself in various overlapping industries, including but not limited to:

- Banking—commericial and retail.
- Asset management.
- Brokerage and security underwriting.
- Investment banking.
- Asset leasing.

By diversifying its operations, First Union has been able to reduce the overall risk to the company's shareholders. However, the growth and diversification has not come without tremendous costs. Due to poor planning, the 1998 Corestates merger was a near disaster. After the merger, First Union realized that many of the branches that had been added to its own branch network were in close proximity to the already existing First Union branches. So at great expense, many branches were closed, and many employees were laid off. A similar situation arose in 1998 with acquisition of the high-risk lender, The Money Store. First Union planned to eliminate a portion of the high-risk lending that had enabled The Money Store to carve a profitable niche for itself over the years. Following a great deal of effort to salvage the merger, First Union in 2000 announced

143

that it would cease loan originations in that division. As the size of the acquisitions that First Union has undertaken has increased, its problems have also increased.

OPERATIONAL OVERVIEW OF FIRST UNION

At the time of its merger with Wachovia, First Union was the sixth largest financial institution in the United States, and it has the third largest branch network, with 2,200 financial centers in eleven East Coast states and Washington, D.C. The company held the largest deposit share on the East Coast and was fifth nationally. First Union also had 375 full service brokerage offices nationwide, 160 home equity loan originators in 31 states, and 3,800 automated teller machines, the nation's sixth largest network.

In 2000, First Union announced the divestiture of its credit card and mortgage servicing portfolios. According to the company press release, the reason for the divestiture was absence of any potential to be a leading competitor in the marketplace. Considering that these divisions were both profitable, analysts especially questioned the divestiture of the credit card portfolio, since credit card usage is at an all-time high and is continuing to increase.

First Union was one of the most technologically advanced organizations in the financial industry. It was the first in its industry to design and implement a standardized data processing system across all of its holdings. As firms were acquired, they were converted to First Union's common system, named Emerald, which had enabled First Union to effectively introduce new product and service offerings. First Union had the third largest and fastest growing banking Internet channel, **www.firstunion.com**. In late 2000, the company had launched its Spanish Web site (**www.firstunion.com/spanish**) in an ongoing effort to meet the needs of this rapidly growing market segment. The Spanish Web site has been very successful.

In the third quarter of 2000, First Union became the first U.S.-based bank to join the Worldwide Automated Transaction Clearing House (WATCH). WATCH is a new electronic payment system that allows cross-border/multicurrency transactions. Prior to its introduction, these types of payments were very difficult to process due to unique local methods of handling these transactions. The company believed that joining WATCH allowed another value-added service to be offered to its existing customers with international dealings and possibly garner new business.

Wachovia was an excellent merger candidate. With its corporate headquarters located in Winston-Salem, North Carolina, and $74 billion in assets, Wachovia has a very prestigious and well-respected name. Wachovia would also make First Union the fourth largest U.S. financial institution. However, Wachovia and First Union already have significant overlap in their markets, so cannibalization could be an issue, as in the case of the Corestates merger. Merger with Wachovia further increased First Union's already dominant market share on the East Coast.

With 111 million American Internet users and a projected 45 percent annual growth rate through 2005, e-commerce is causing whole industries to redefine the businesses that they are in and also the way their businesses are conducted. The major shakedown in the dot-com market has already taken place, and many shell dot-coms are gone. But the fact remains that the Internet has transformed business and life as it is known today. First Union made a significant investment in the development of its online banking services very early on, and it has continued to keep up-to-date with technology as it changes. The result is a very user-friendly Internet-based financial medium that has been widely accepted by the company's customers and led it to develop into the third largest and fastest growing banking Internet Web site.

EXHIBIT 1   Wachovia's Segment Financial Data

A. GENERAL BANK

Selected Financial Data (Dollars in millions)	2001	2000
Net interest income*	$5,151	4,382
Fee and other income	1,769	1,314
Intersegment revenue	114	100
Total revenue*	7,034	5,796
Noninterest expense	4,112	3,790
Operating earnings	1,616	1,179
Economic profit	$1,165	762
Risk adjusted return on capital	38.44%	33.01

Cash Overhead Efficieny Ratio (Percent)

64.4%   57.9%
2000   2001

Average Loans, Net (In billions)

$59.1 $75.8
2000   2001

Average Core Deposits (In billions)

$97.6 $111.1
2000   2001

*Tax equivalent.

The merger of First Union and the former Wachovia closed on September 1, 2001. Because this merger was accounted for as a purchase, prior periods have not been restated. Results in 2001 include four months of the former Wachovia.

B. CAPITAL MANAGEMENT

Selected Financial Data (Dollars in millions)	2001	2000
Net interest income*	$ 131	160
Fee and other income	2,819	2,820
Intersegment revenue	(48)	(50)
Total revenue*	2,902	2,930
Noninterest expense	2,399	2,342
Operating earnings	324	390
Economic profit	$ 222	286
Risk adjusted return on capital	37.87%	45.16

Total Assets Under Management (In billions)

$171 $226
2000   2001

Brokerage Client Assets (In billions)

$241 $274
2000   2001

Annuities Sales (In billions)

$3.5 $4.7
2000   2001

*Tax equivalent.

INTERNAL OPERATIONS OF WACHOVIA

As indicated in Exhibit 1, Wachovia is divided into four major divisions: (1) General Bank, (2) Capital Management, (3) Wealth Management, and (4) Corporate and Investment Bank. Note that the Wealth Management division and the Corporate and Investment Bank division had lower revenues in 2001 than 2000.

As indicated in Exhibit 2, Wachovia is also divided into six geographic regions. Note that Wachovia has more branches in Florida than any other state.

Wachovia's 2001 Balance Sheet and Income statement are provided in Exhibits 3 and 4, respectively. Note in Exhibit 4 that Wachovia's net income increased to $1.61 billion in 2001 from $92 million in 2000.

C. WEALTH MANAGEMENT

Selected Financial Data (Dollars in millions)	2001	2000
Net interest income*	$246	190
Fee and other income	394	319
Intersegment revenue	1	—
Total revenue*	641	509
Noninterest expense	444	317
Operating earnings	127	126
Economic profit	$ 94	102
Risk adjusted return on capital	52.27%	75.54

Assets Under Management (In billions)

2000: $53   2001: $78

Average Loans, Net (In billions)

2000: $4.2   2001: $5.7

Average Core Deposits (In billions)

2000: $5.7   2001: $7.3

*Tax equivalent.

D. CORPORATE AND INVESTMENT BANK

Selected Financial Data (Dollars in millions)	2001	2000
Net interest income*	$2,075	1,674
Fee and other income	730	1,708
Intersegment revenue	(56)	(49)
Total revenue*	2,749	3,333
Noninterest expense	1,999	1,863
Operating earnings	265	829
Economic profit	$ (320)	277
Risk adjusted return on capital	7.07%	16.73

Capital Raised for Clients (In billions)

2000: $114   2001: $222

Equity Underwriting Number of Transactions

2000: 32   2001: 61

Investment Grade Debt Number of Transactions

2000: 88   2001: 128

*Tax equivalent.

The merger of First Union and the former Wachovia closed on September 1, 2001. Because this merger was accounted for as a purchase, prior periods have not been restated. Results in 2001 include four months of the former Wachovia.

Source: Wachovia's 2001 *Annual Report*, pp. 8–9.

CONCLUSION

The name "First Union" is being phased out slowly across the United States. Wachovia is closing hundreds of branches where the two banks are located close to one another. Wachovia is adopting the First Union computer operations systems but is keeping most of the Wachovia products.

Wachovia is changing rapidly daily. Develop a three-year strategic plan for the CEO of Wachovia, Mr. Kennedy Thompson.

EXHIBIT 2   Wachovia's Geographic Regions

A. GENERAL BANKING REGIONS

Atlantic Region
New Jersey
Branches: 338
ATMs: 504

New York
Branches: 55
ATMs: 96

Connecticut
Branches: 86
ATMs: 121

Mid-Atlantic Region
Virginia
Branches: 354
ATMs: 537

Maryland
Branches: 77
ATMs: 111

Washington, D.C.
Branches: 27
ATMs: 59

Carolinas Region
North Carolina
Branches: 386
ATMs: 779

South Carolina
Branches: 171
ATMs: 331

Georgia Region
Georgia
Branches: 255
ATMs: 613

PennDel Region
Pennsylvania
Branches: 350
ATMs: 549

Delaware
Branches: 21
ATMs: 43

Florida Region
Florida
Branches: 691
ATMs: 919

B. FOREIGN BRANCHES AND REPRESENTATIVE OFFICES

International Branches
Hong Kong, China
    (Restricted License Branch)
London, England
Tokyo, Japan
Seoul, South Korea
Taipei, Taiwan

Representative Offices
Buenos Aires, Argentina
Sydney, Australia
Sao Paulo, Brazil
Santiago, Chile
Beijing, China
Guangzhou, China

Hong Kong, China
Shanghai, China
Bogota, Colombia
Guayaquil, Ecuador
Cairo, Egypt
London, England
Paris, France
Frankfurt, Germany
Hamburg, Germany
Mumbai, India
Jakarta, Indonesia
Milan, Italy
Tokyo, Japan
Kuala Lumpur, Malaysia
Mexico City, Mexico

Panama City, Panama
Manila, Philippines
Singapore
Johannesburg, South
    Africa
Seoul, South Korea
Madrid, Spain
Taipei, Taiwan
Bangkok, Thailand
Istanbul, Turkey
Dubai, United Arab
    Emirates
San Diego, California

**Embassy and
    Government Banking
    Group**
Washington, D.C.

**International
    Processing Centers**
Charlotte, North Carolina
Los Angeles, California
Miami, Florida
New York, New York
Philadelphia, Pennsylvania

Source: Wachovia's 2001 *Annual Report*, p. 15.

EXHIBIT 3   Wachovia Corporation and Subsidiaries Consolidated Balance Sheets

(in millions, except per-share data)	December 31, 2001	2000
ASSETS		
Cash and due from banks	$ 13,919	9,906
Interest-bearing bank balances	6,875	3,239
Federal funds sold and securities purchased under resale agreements		
(carrying amount of collateral held $7,207 at December 31, 2001, $2,287 repledged)	13,919	11,240
Total cash and cash equivalents	34,711	24,385
Trading account assets	25,386	21,630
Securities (amortized cost $57,776 in 2001; $47,930 in 2000)	58,467	47,603
Investment securities (market value $1,728 in 2000)	–	1,643
Loans, net of unearned income ($9,694 in 2001; $6,482 in 2000)	163,801	123,760
Allowance for loan losses	(2,995)	(1,722)
Loans, net	160,806	122,038
Premises and equipment	5,719	5,024
Due from customers on acceptances	745	874
Goodwill and other intangible assets	12,772	3,664
Other assets	31,846	27,309
Total assets	$330,452	254,170
LIABILITIES AND STOCKHOLDERS' EQUITY		
Deposits		
Noninterest-bearing deposits	43,464	30,315
Interest-bearing deposits	143,989	112,353
Total deposits	187,453	142,668
Short-term borrowings	44,385	39,446
Bank acceptances outstanding	762	880
Trading account liabilities	11,437	7,475
Other liabilities	16,227	12,545
Long-term debt	41,733	35,809
Total liabilities	301,997	238,823
STOCKHOLDERS' EQUITY		
Preferred stock, Class A, 40 million shares, no par value; 10 million shares, no par value; none issued	—	—
Dividend Equalization Preferred shares, no par value, 96 million shares issued and outstanding in 2001	17	—
Common stock, $3.33-1/3 par value; authorized 3 billion shares, outstanding 1.362 billion shares in 2001; 980 million shares in 2000	4,539	3,267
Paid-in capital	17,911	6,272
Retained earnings	5,551	6,021
Accumulated other comprehensive income, net	437	(213)
Total stockholders' equity	28,455	15,347
Total liabilities and stockholders' equity	$330,452	254,170

Source: Wachovia's 2001 Annual Report, p. 65.

EXHIBIT 4   Wachovia Corporation and Subsidiaries Consolidated Statements of Income

(in millions, except per-share data)	2001	2000	1999
INTEREST INCOME			
Interest and fees on loans	$10,537	11,246	10,629
Interest and dividends on securities	3,534	3,903	3,098
Trading account interest	760	820	600
Other interest income	1,269	1,565	824
Total interest income	16,100	17,534	15,151
INTEREST EXPENSE			
Interest on deposits	4,744	5,269	4,054
Interest on short-term borrowings	1,736	2,536	2,019
Interest on long-term debt	1,845	2,292	1,626
Total interest expense	8,325	10,097	7,699
Net interest income	7,775	7,437	7,452
Provision for loan losses	1,947	1,736	692
Net interest income after provision for loan losses	5,828	5,701	6,760
FEE AND OTHER INCOME			
Service charges and fees	2,167	1,920	1,987
Commissions	1,568	1,591	1,014
Fiduciary and asset management fees	1,643	1,511	1,238
Advisory, underwriting and other investment banking fees	836	718	702
Principal investing	(707)	395	592
Other income	789	577	1,400
Total fee and other income	6,296	6,712	6,933
NONINTEREST EXPENSE			
Salaries and employee benefits	5,810	5,659	4,716
Occupancy	730	622	546
Equipment	879	870	793
Advertising	66	114	234
Communications and supplies	480	503	481
Professional and consulting fees	359	348	287
Goodwill and other intangible amortization	523	361	391
Merger-related and restructuring charges	106	2,190	404
Sundry expense	878	1,043	1,010
Total noninterest expense	9,831	11,710	8,862
Income before income taxes and cumulative effect of a change in accounting principle	2,293	703	4,831
Income taxes	674	565	1,608
Income before cumulative effect of a change in accounting principle	1,619	138	3,223
Cumulative effect of a change in the accounting for beneficial interests, net of income taxes	—	(46)	—
Net income	1,619	92	3,223
Dividends on preferred stock	6	—	—
Net income available to common stockholders	$ 1,613	92	3,223
PER COMMON SHARE DATA			
Basic			
Income before change in accounting principle	$1.47	0.12	3.35
Net income	1.47	0.07	3.35
Diluted			
Income before change in accounting principle	1.45	0.12	3.33
Net income	1.45	0.07	3.33
Cash dividends	$ 0.96	1.92	1.88
AVERAGE SHARES			
Basic	1,096	971	959
Diluted	1,105	974	967

Source: Wachovia's 2001 *Annual Report*, p. 66.

FIRST STATE BANK OF ROANS PRAIRIE—2002

Paul Reed, Jason Gooch, and Gerald Kohers
Sam Houston State University

INTERNAL OPERATIONS

Mission Statement

The current mission statement for First State Bank of Roans Prairie, Texas, is:

> *It is the goal of management and the Board of Directors of First State Bank of Roans Prairie to prosper while adhering to the "small town" ideals which have made it successful; the banker–customer relationship must be preserved. The bank desires to serve area residents by supplying all traditional banking services. New services with profit potential will be developed and offered as the area and economy evolves.*

Operations

First State Bank of Roans Prairie (936-395-2141) is and has been since its establishment in 1903 owned and controlled by the Matthys family. Its only office is located in Roans Prairie, Texas (population less than 500). Under the leadership of the Matthys family, First State Bank of Roans Prairie pursues operational efficiencies by controlling overhead and employing technology in place of hiring additional employees. The bank currently employs ten people. This equates to one employee per $4.2 million in assets, and it compares to competitors' ratio of one employee per $2.7 million in assets (average of local competitors). This, however, is partly due to the low loan-to-deposit ratio of First State Bank.

Products

First State Bank offers most of the basic banking services, such as:

- checking, savings, money markets, CDs.
- IRAs.
- auto, real estate, commercial, agriculture, and consumer loans (most customer requests are answered the same day for loans, etc.).

The bank does not offer ATM cards, credit or debit cards, trust department services, or Internet banking. It is lagging behind the industry in offering new products (ATMs have existed in some form for nearly twenty years). This may cause a loss of customers or missed opportunities for new customers in the future. However, the bank does have an advantage over the larger metropolitan banks and mortgage companies insofar as it is able to serve the rural real estate market and agricultural lines. This may be of particular importance as more and more people look to move from the urban areas into the rural areas. Additionally, there has been an increase of "weekenders" purchasing rural land for recreational purposes. These loans do not generally fit the molds of the metropolitan banks or the mortgage companies.

Marketing

First State Bank has traditionally spent very little on advertising. Likewise, it has not solicited business in the past. Rather, it has relied on its reputation for providing superior service, low cost services, and its ability to react quickly to the needs of its customers.

This has worked well for the bank in the past. This is not to imply that the bank has not been actively involved in and supportive of the community. Furthermore, First State Bank has been successful in building and maintaining customer relationships.

Finance

First State Bank's financial statements and performance ratios for 1998 to 2000 are provided in Exhibit 1. These statements reveal increases in total assets, loans, and deposits. Additionally, a comparison of First State Bank's two primary competitors is included in the comparison report in Exhibits 2 and 3. Notice that both competitors have higher net interest margins and noninterest income. This is primarily due to First State Bank's lower loan-to-deposit ratio. Additionally, large amounts of capital and undivided profits have contributed to First State Bank's low ROE (9 percent vs. 10.6 percent for peer banks with less than $100 million in assets).

Management Style and Culture

First State Bank has created a strong culture based on customer loyalty. The employees are all very close and share a sense of companionship. This clearly is a major strength of the bank. However, it is something that has been very natural for the group and has been accomplished without coaching or training. The average length of employment for the ten employees is 9.7 years (the ranges run from five years to twenty years).

Although communication is not the greatest virtue among management people and the front lines, it does remain open. If a problem is severe enough, any employee feels that he or she can approach management to discuss such issues. Nonetheless, there is room for improvement for top-down and bottom-up communication.

The board of directors tends to resist making any changes to the organization. This explains why it has not offered some of the newer financial services. Furthermore, continuing to operate without a formal strategic plan may prevent management from having a clear vision of where the organization is and where it needs to position itself for the future.

EXTERNAL ENVIRONMENT

Industry Health

Fiscal year 2000 proved to be a record setting year for insured commercial banks. Commercial bank profits for the year were a record $71.7 billion. Full-year earnings were $9.9 billion (16.0 percent) higher than in 1999. The industry's return on assets (ROA) for 2000 was 1.31 percent, easily eclipsing the previous record of 1.23 percent set in 1998. Banks' return on equity (ROE) matched the all-time high of 15.34 percent reached in 1993. Large banks (assets greater than $100 million) experienced much of the improvement in profitability because noninterest income registered strong growth and noninterest expense growth was limited. Only 44.9 percent of banks reported higher ROAs in 2000 than in 1999. The average ROA at banks with less than $100 million in assets declined from 1.13 percent in 1999 to 1.01 percent in 2000. The decline would have been greater but for the rising proportion of banks operating as Subchapter S corporations. For the first time since 1991, more than 10 percent of commercial banks with

EXHIBIT 1   First State Bank of Roans Prairie Balance Sheet (dollar figures in thousands)

	December 31, 2000	December 31, 1999	December 31, 1998
ASSETS AND LIABILITIES			
Total employees (full-time equivalent)	10	10	10
Total assets	$42,105	$40,131	$39,029
Cash and due from depository institutions	4,861	5,344	3,555
Interest-bearing	3,102	3,693	3,198
Securities	18,843	17,125	18,784
Federal funds sold & reverse repurchase agreements	700	2,300	3,450
Net loans & leases	16,694	14,539	12,480
Loan loss allowance	179	175	180
Trading account assets	0	0	0
Bank premises and fixed assets	381	398	345
Other real estate owned	0	14	9
Goodwill and other intangibles	0	0	0
Mortgage servicing assets	0	0	0
All other assets	626	411	406
Total liabilities and capital	42,105	40,131	39,029
Total liabilities	36,627	34,655	33,173
Total deposits	36,291	34,220	32,465
Interest-bearing deposits	31,894	29,944	28,629
Deposits held in domestic offices	36,291	34,220	32,465
Percentage insured (estimated)	95.78%	95.99%	96.79%
Federal funds purchased & repurchase agreements	0	0	0
Demand notes issued to U.S. Treasury	0	0	0
Trading liabilities	0	0	0
Other borrowed funds	0	0	0
Subordinated debt	0	0	0
All other liabilities	336	435	708
Equity capital	5,478	5,476	5,856
Perpetual preferred stock	0	0	0
Common stock	321	321	500
Surplus	1,179	679	500
Undivided profits	3,978	4,476	4,856
MEMORANDA			
Noncurrent loans and leases	16	19	47
Earning assets	39,339	37,657	37,912
Long-term assets (5+ years)	11,358	5,849	7,069
Average assets, year-to-date	41,192	39,508	37,528
Average assets, quarterly	42,234	39,805	38,730
Volatile liabilities	9,814	9,836	9,215
Insider loans	125	123	137
FHLB advances (TFR filers only)	N/A	N/A	N/A
Unused loan commitments	736	575	770
Restructured loans and leases	0	0	0
Quarterly mutual fund sales	0	0	0
Off-balance-sheet derivatives	0	0	0

(continued)

EXHIBIT 1   First State Bank of Roans Prairie Balance Sheet (dollar figures in thousands) (continued)

	(Year-to-date)	(Year-to-date)	(Year-to-date)
INCOME AND EXPENSE			
Total interest income	*2,851*	*2,808*	*2,680*
Total interest expense	*1,502*	*1,473*	*1,372*
Net interest income	1,349	1,335	1,308
Provision for credit losses	31	61	22
Total noninterest income	218	191	185
Service charges on deposit accounts	196	176	162
Total noninterest expense	834	805	723
Salaries and employee benefits	471	432	406
Premises and equipment expense	121	118	71
All other noninterest expense	242	255	246
Pretax net operating income	702	660	748
Securities gains (losses)	−1	12	−8
Applicable income taxes	204	188	217
Extraordinary gains—net	0	0	0
Net income	497	484	523
Net charge-offs	26	67	51
Cash dividends	16	16	25
Net operating income	498	475	529

	(Year-to-date)	(Year-to-date)	(Year-to-date)
MEMORANDA			
Average assets	41,192	39,508	37,528
Percentage of unprofitable institutions	N/A	N/A	N/A
Percentage of institutions with earnings gains	N/A	N/A	N/A

	(Year-to-date)	(Year-to-date)	(Year-to-date)
PERFORMANCE RATIOS (%)			
Yield on earning assets	7.36%	7.45%	7.47%
Cost of funding earning assets	3.88%	3.91%	3.82%
Net interest margin	3.48%	3.54%	3.64%
Noninterest income to earning assets	0.56%	0.51%	0.52%
Noninterest expense to earning assets	2.15%	2.14%	2.01%
Net operating income to assets	1.21%	1.20%	1.41%
Return on assets	1.21%	1.23%	1.39%
Return on equity	9.05%	8.37%	9.45%
Retained earnings to average equity (YTD only)	8.76%	8.09%	8.99%
Net charge-offs to loans	*0.17%*	*0.50%*	*0.42%*
Credit loss provision to net charge-offs	114.81%	91.04%	43.14%
Earnings coverage of net loan charge-offs	28.19	10.76	15.09
Efficiency ratio	53.22%	52.75%	48.43%
Assets per employee (in millions)	4.21	4.01	3.90
Market to book value of securities held to maturity	N/A	N/A	N/A
Cash dividends to net income (ytd only)	3.21%	3.30%	4.78%

(continued)

EXHIBIT 1   First State Bank of Roans Prairie Balance Sheet (dollar figures in thousands) **(continued)**

	(Year-to-date)	(Year-to-date)	(Year-to-date)
CONDITION RATIOS (%)			
Loss allowance to loans	1.06%	1.19%	1.42%
Loss allowance to noncurrent loans	1,118.75%	921.05%	382.98%
Noncurrent assets plus other real estate owned to assets	0.04%	0.08%	0.14%
Noncurrent loans to loans	*0.09%*	*0.13%*	*0.37%*
Net loans and leases to deposits	46.00%	42.49%	38.44%
Net loans and leases to core deposits	63.05%	59.62%	53.67%
Net noncore funding to long-term assets	40.20%	38.47%	42.64%
Equity capital to assets	13.01%	13.65%	15.00%
Core capital (leverage) ratio	13.77%	13.50%	15.40%
Tier 1 risk-based capital ratio	28.12%	28.58%	34.70%
Total risk-based capital ratio	28.98%	29.51%	35.78%

less than $100 million in assets were unprofitable. Small banks were hurt by both declining net interest margins and lower contributions from noninterest income in 2000. However, the improvement in industry earnings was made possible by strong growth in noninterest income and by lower noninterest expenses, which outweighed a $1.3-billion decline in proceeds from securities sales.

Legislation

The United States recently signed into law S. 900, the Gramm-Leach-Bliley Act, the historic and wide-reaching legislation that modernizes the laws governing the financial services industry. By updating old laws that created barriers among financial service providers, the financial modernization bill allows banks, securities firms, and insurance companies to enter each other's businesses. Consumers want loans at the best rates, investment services with the most choices, and money management services from efficient providers. Consumers can take advantage of one-stop shopping for products and enjoy more flexibility and options.

Additionally, by allowing banks to offer insurance services, consumers will enjoy lower costs, convenient service, and increased availability. Insurers that use independent agents for auto insurance spend 30 percent of each premium dollar on commissions, advertising, and other costs. Those that use other methods of distribution, such as selling directly to consumers, reduce those costs up to 10 percent. Also, a majority of low-to-moderate income households are either underserved or without life insurance. Banks can reach a broader market and reduce costs through branch networks and existing household relationships. The Department of Treasury estimates U.S. firms will save $15 billion per year in gained efficiencies.

The Internet is growing and gaining acceptance at astounding rates. It has taken the Internet only four years to reach an audience of fifty million. Radio and television took thirty years and thirteen years, respectively, to accomplish the same feat.

Forward-thinking bankers recognize that the Internet provides the means of driving fundamental changes in consumer perceptions of banking. A simple example was the added convenience brought to consumers by Internet banking. For community bankers that had long relied on personal service as the basis for competitive advantage, the Internet is a natural extension of their existing business strategy.

EXHIBIT 2   Comparison Report (dollar figures in thousands)

	First State Bank Roans Prairie, TX	Anderson State Bank Anderson, TX	The National Bank of Anderson Anderson, TX
	December 31, 2000	*December 31, 2000*	*December 31, 2000*
ASSETS AND LIABILITIES			
Total employees (full-time equivalent)	10	40	23
Total assets	$42,105	$133,864	$43,071
Cash and due from depository institutions	4,861	4,146	1,866
Interest-bearing	3,102	0	0
Securities	18,843	10,723	9,437
Federal funds sold & reverse repurchase agreements	700	9,150	2,025
Net loans & leases	16,694	103,799	27,560
Loan loss allowance	179	1,939	532
Trading account assets	0	0	0
Bank premises and fixed assets	381	852	865
Other real estate owned	0	2,055	99
Goodwill and other intangibles	0	0	0
Mortgage servicing assets	0	0	0
All other assets	626	3,139	1,219
Total liabilities and capital	42,105	133,864	43,071
Total liabilities	36,627	122,813	39,443
Total deposits	36,291	121,513	39,159
Interest-bearing deposits	31,894	111,977	31,170
Deposits held in domestic offices	36,291	121,513	39,159
% insured (estimated)	95.78%	92.07%	95.88%
Federal funds purchased & repurchase agreements	0	0	0
Demand notes issued to U.S. Treasury	0	0	0
Trading liabilities	0	0	0
Other borrowed funds	0	0	0
Subordinated debt	0	0	0
All other liabilities	336	1,300	284
Equity capital	5,478	11,051	3,628
Perpetual preferred stock	0	0	300
Common stock	321	950	1,000
Surplus	1,179	9,050	1,008
Undivided profits	3,978	1,051	1,320
MEMORANDA			
Noncurrent loans and leases	16	50	883
Earning assets	39,339	123,672	39,022
Long-term assets (5+ years)	11,358	25,830	1,227
Average assets, year-to-date	41,192	127,443	44,601
Average assets, quarterly	42,234	130,632	43,878
Volatile liabilities	9,814	28,882	6,980
Insider loans	125	115	158
FHLB advances (TFR filers only)	N/A	N/A	N/A
Unused loan commitments	736	13,479	1,259
Restructured loans and leases	0	0	14
Quarterly mutual fund sales	0	0	0
Off-balance-sheet derivatives	0	0	0

EXHIBIT 3   Comparison Report

	First State Bank Roans Prairie, TX	The National Anderson State Bank Anderson, TX	Bank of Anderson Anderson, TX
	December 31, 2000	*December 31, 2000*	*December 31, 2000*
Percentage of unprofitable institutions	N/A	N/A	N/A
Percentage of institutions with earnings gains	N/A	N/A	N/A
	(Year-to-date)	*(Year-to-date)*	*(Year-to-date)*
PERFORMANCE RATIOS (%)			
Yield on earning assets	7.36%	9.58%	8.61%
Cost of funding earning assets	3.88%	4.17%	3.64%
Net interest margin	3.48%	5.42%	4.97%
Noninterest income to earning assets	0.56%	0.78%	1.58%
Noninterest expense to earning assets	2.15%	2.76%	4.66%
Net operating income to assets	1.21%	2.02%	0.67%
Return on assets	**1.21%**	**2.02%**	**0.68%**
Return on equity	9.05%	22.15%	8.59%
Retained earnings to average equity (YTD only)	8.76%	−3.72%	8.59%
Net charge-offs to loans	*0.17%*	*0.02%*	*1.79%*
Credit loss provision to net charge-offs	114.81%	0.00%	60.73%
Earnings coverage of net loan charge-offs	28.19	163.32	1.53
Efficiency ratio	53.22%	44.51%	71.26%
Assets per employee (in millions)	4.21	3.35	1.87
Market to book value of securities held to maturity	N/A	98.70%	N/A
Cash dividends to net income (YTD only)	3.21%	116.77%	0.00%
	(Year-to-date)	*(Year-to-date)*	*(Year-to-date)*
CONDITION RATIOS (%)			
Loss allowance to loans	1.06%	1.83%	1.89%
Loss allowance to noncurrent loans	1,118.75%	3,878.00%	60.25%
Noncurrent assets plus other real estate owned to assets	0.04%	1.57%	2.28%
Noncurrent loans	*0.09%*	*0.05%*	*3.14%*
Net loans and leases to deposits	46.00%	85.42%	70.38%
Net loans and leases to core deposits	63.05%	112.05%	85.64%
Net noncore funding to long-term assets	40.20%	21.61%	19.90%
Equity capital to assets	13.01%	8.26%	8.42%
Core capital (leverage) ratio	13.77%	8.31%	8.44%
Tier 1 risk-based capital ratio	28.12%	9.41%	12.73%

Multigenerational Customer Base

Today, banks are faced with both the difficult task and an enormous opportunity of serving five generational cohorts. Demographics define generational cohorts by birth ranges of twenty years. They are as follows:

- Silent generation (1925–1944): 52 million
- Baby boomers (1945–1964): 76 million

- Generation X (1965–1984): 51 million
- Nexters (1985–2004): estimated 82 million

The silent generation controls a significant part of the country's discretionary spending, and its members own billions in real estate. It is estimated that they own three-quarters of the financial assets in the United States, or $10–$12 trillion in net worth, and have personal incomes of $800 billion. Civic pride, loyalty, and respect for their country characterize this generation.

The baby boom generation marked the end of the rural, agrarian lifestyle. Its members are characterized by being highly confident, team-oriented, and egocentric. They are less loyal than the silent generation. This generation is moving into its peak earning and spending years.

Clever, resourceful, technologically savvy, comfortable with change, and a general lack of loyalty—all these qualities define Generation X. This generation represents the smallest of the five generations.

The Nexters are characterized by confidence, motivation, achievement, and optimism. Its members are the authority on technology. They are estimated to be the largest generation ever.

COMPETITION

First State Bank of Roans Prairie is located in the center of Grimes County and is only thirteen miles from Anderson. Anderson currently has three banks: (1) Anderson State Bank, (2) The National Bank of Anderson, and (3) Norwest/Wells Fargo.

Anderson State Bank

Anderson State Bank is the strongest of the three competitors. Its performance ratios indicate that it manages to control overhead while maintaining and investing in quality assets. It is are owned and managed by a bank holding company from Chicago. Management of the holding company sets the rates on loans and deposits. A substantial portion of the loan portfolio consists of participation loans in apartment complexes. These participation loans are generally for apartment complexes in Dallas, San Antonio, or Houston. Due to the large number of participation loans, Anderson State Bank has fewer assets invested in securities and a substantially higher percent loaned out. This allows the bank to pay higher rates on its deposits since it is reinvesting the money in loans that have higher returns than securities. Anderson State has traditionally led the local competition in pricing rates on deposits.

First State Bank, on the other hand, has fewer assets invested in loans and is more heavily weighted in the securities market. Thus, paying higher rates to retain deposits has reduced its net interest margin in recent years.

The National Bank of Anderson

The National Bank of Anderson also has a higher loan-to-deposit ratio than First State Bank of Roans Prairie (70 percent vs. 46 percent). However, National Bank's loans are mostly local loans. The higher loan portfolio also gives the bank a higher net interest margin than First State Bank. It appears, however, that the loan portfolio has grown at the expense of asset quality. This is indicated in the high delinquency and net charge-off to loans. This has drawn scrutiny from the board and examiners. Therefore, the bank has started turning some good business away in order to maintain liquidity (usually larger lines of credit).

Additionally, National Bank employs one employee for each $1.87 million in assets. This is a much higher ratio than First State Bank's, which is one employee per $4.2 million in assets. Likewise, National Bank's noninterest expense to earning assets is significantly higher than that of First State Bank and Anderson State Bank.

Norwest/Wells Fargo

There is no need to analyze or question the financial status of Wells Fargo. Nevertheless, the mold, which it has created for its metropolitan banks, does not work in the rural communities. For instance, one must drive fifty miles from Anderson to Bryan if he or she wants to apply for a home mortgage or real estate loan. Also, the fee schedules are much higher than those of the other local competitors. Rural customers are used to convenient, courteous, low-cost service. Wells Fargo lacks the flexibility needed to remain in Anderson. A lot of customers have migrated from Wells Fargo to the other local banks.

THE FUTURE

First State Bank of Roans Prairie wants to continue to pursue operational efficiencies through the use of technology. Management feels that by controlling overhead, it can maintain profitability in good times as well as bad. In additional, management feels that it must grow the loan portfolio in order to increase profitability. Pursuing the local rural real estate market can do this. Furthermore, management feels that it must maintain the banker–customer relationship on which it has built its reputation.

THE AUDUBON NATURE INSTITUTE—2001

Caroline M. Fisher
Loyola University, New Orleans

www.auduboninstitute.org

The tourism industry of New Orleans was devastated by the terrorist attacks of September 11, 2001. Travel to the city declined dramatically. Conferences were canceled. Hotels that usually were booked solid had such low occupancy rates that they had to lay off workers. Restaurants that depended on the tourist trade equally felt the effects of the decline. All tourism activities dwindled to a trickle.

The Audubon Nature Institute also experienced declines in usage rates—but differentially by location. The Aquarium of the Americas and the IMAX Theatre, both located in downtown New Orleans, saw dramatic declines in admissions. Admissions to the Audubon Zoo were not down as dramatically, and the Nature Center actually saw an increase in usage.

The pattern of the declines in admissions dramatized what the Audubon Nature Institute already knew—that the downtown locations are frequented by tourists to a much greater extent than the more distant zoo and nature center. But what was usually seen as a weakness—dependency on local residents for admissions—was now a strength that helped to counteract the decline in tourism. Audubon's management needed to respond to the changes in admission patterns to keep from losing money during the last part of 2001 and to keep from having to slow down development of the Audubon Insectarium and other new ventures.

HISTORY

Formed in 1988, the Audubon Nature Institute is a nonprofit "family of museums and parks dedicated to nature and unified with a purpose of celebrating life through nature." Its purpose of "celebrating the wonders of nature" guides its mission to:

1. provide a guest experience of outstanding quality.
2. exhibit the diversity of wildlife.
3. preserve native Louisiana habitats.
4. educate our diverse audience about the natural world.
5. enhance the care and survival of wildlife through research and conservation.
6. provide opportunities for recreation in natural settings.
7. operate a financially self-sufficient collection of facilities.
8. weave quality entertainment through guest experiences.

Ron Forman, Director of the Audubon Nature Institute, describes the essence of the Institute's purpose to be to "teach children, especially inner-city children, to love nature and to value living things." Another goal of the Institute is to contribute to the economic development of the New Orleans area by encouraging tourism, especially family tourism, and by creating jobs.

In 2001, the Audubon Nature Institute was in charge of (1) Audubon Zoological Garden, (2) Audubon Aquarium of the Americas, (3) Freeport-McMoRan Audubon Species Survival Center, (4) Audubon Louisiana Nature Center, (5) Entergy IMAX® Theatre, (6) Audubon Center for Research of Endangered Species, (7) Audubon Park, (8) Audubon Wilderness Park, and (9) Woldenberg Riverfront Park. It plans to open the Audubon Insectarium in 2003.

AUDUBON ZOOLOGICAL GARDEN

The Audubon Zoo was the focus of national concern in the early 1970s, because of the well-documented stories of animals kept in conditions that were termed an "animal ghetto," "the New Orleans antiquarium," and even "an animal concentration camp."

In 1971, the Bureau of Governmental Research recommended to the Audubon Park Commission and the City Council of New Orleans a $5.6 million zoo improvement plan. The Audubon Park Commission proposed a bond issue and a property tax that was earmarked for the zoo. Voters overwhelmingly approved it, and the New Orleans City Planning Commission finally approved the master plan for the Audubon Park Zoo in 1973.

The expansion of the Audubon Park Zoo took it from fourteen to fifty-eight acres. The zoo was laid out in geographic sections according to the zoo master plan developed by the Bureau of Governmental Research, and it included: the Asian Domain, the World of Primates, the World's Grasslands, Savannah, North American Prairie, South American Pampas, and Louisiana Swamp, Additional exhibits included the Wisner Discovery Zoo, the sea lion exhibit, and Flight Cage.

The main purpose of the Audubon Park Zoo is entertainment. Many of the promotional efforts of the zoo are aimed at creating an image of the zoo as an entertaining place to go. Obviously, such a campaign is necessary to attract visitors to the zoo. Behind the scenes, the zoo also preserves and breeds many animal species, conducts research, and educates the public.

The 2000 *Annual Report* states that

Ensuring the survival of endangered species becomes possible only when people learn about these animals and embrace efforts to save them. That's our goal every time visitors walk into our facilities. The more they come, the more they learn—and the more they want to help.

AUDUBON AQUARIUM OF THE AMERICAS

The Aquarium of the Americas opened in September 1990. The $40 million project, consisting of the fourteen acre Woldenberg Park and the aquarium itself, provided a logical pedestrian link between the major attractions of the Riverwalk and the Jax Brewery, two shopping centers in the French Quarter. The facility was one hundred ten thousand square feet in size and included five permanent exhibits: the Caribbean Reef, the Amazon Rainforest, the Mississippi River, the Gulf of Mexico, and Living in Water. Management of the aquarium was placed under the Audubon Nature Institute, the same organization that ran the Audubon Zoo.

Construction of Phase II of the aquarium, a $25 million project, began in 1995. It included a ten-thousand-square-foot Changing Exhibit Gallery that encompassed new tanks with 360 degree viewing, new species, and a variety of hands-on activities. The finalized aquarium was described by the *Times-Picayune,* the local newspaper, as "one of the best architecture achievements in the metro area in the past 100 years."

Besides exhibits, the aquarium has added educational shows, a summer program for students in grades seven to ten called Aquakids, and Discovery Cove, where children can see and touch aquatic species. The aquarium is also the headquarters for the Louisiana Marine Mammal and Sea Turtle Rescue program. This program is committed to the care and treatment of injured, ill, or out-of-habitat marine mammals and sea turtles.

As he championed the zoo, Forman kept the aquarium constantly changing. He initiated several temporary exhibits, including the most popular, SHARKS! The year 2000 saw the opening of a highly popular exhibit, entitled Seahorses. The Seahorse Gallery exhibit was praised by *Southern Living* as an Official Southern Travel Treasure. Summer 2001 saw the introduction of Frogs!, another exciting collection in the Changing Exhibit Gallery, which featured more than two dozen species from around the globe.

The aquarium not only has continued to attract visitors over the years with its excellent permanent and changing exhibits, but it has also received accolades for its efforts. While celebrating its tenth anniversary in 2000, the aquarium received a ranking of fourth among all U.S. zoos and aquariums in the *Places Rated Almanac*'s Family Friendly Travel Awards.

FREEPORT-MCMORAN AUDUBON SPECIES SURVIVAL CENTER

The success of the "new" zoo and the Aquarium of the Americas inspired Forman and the Audubon Nature Institute to explore future projects. The Institute sought to remain committed to preserving endangered wildlife through the development of such projects.

The Institute designated the Westbank of New Orleans (on the west bank of the Mississippi River) as the most appropriate site for its preservation projects. In December 1993, the Freeport-McMoRan Audubon Species Survival Center (FMASSC) was dedicated in conjunction with the U. S. Fish and Wildlife Service. The Center was established to provide endangered animals a refuge where they could breed in order to boost their numbers. Located on twelve-hundred acre site, the Center initially housed such animals as the Mississippi sandhill crane and the Baird's tapir, with more arriving as the Center expanded.

THE AUDUBON LOUISIANA NATURE CENTER

The Institute reaffirmed its commitment to education and entertainment with the acquisition of the Louisiana Nature and Science Center. The Audubon Nature Institute merged with the Society for Environmental Education in May 1994 and assumed control of the eighty-six-acre site. The stated purpose of the Center was to provide ecological and environmental science programs for the entire community.

The dedicated staff and volunteers of the Nature Center have received many honors for their environmental stewardship. In 2000, the Louisiana Wildlife Federation hailed the Nature Center as the Environmental Conservation Organization of the Year. The Louisiana Urban Forestry Council gave the Nature Center a Special Projects Award for its work in advancing conservation, environmental understanding, and urban forests. Newspapers across the state spotlighted the Nature Center's innovative Louisiana YES! Program. This annual Youth Environmental Summit (YES) brings together students, teachers, politicians, business people, and other professionals to brainstorm solutions to the state's environmental problems. The students then embark on projects in their home areas.

A new exhibit at the Nature Center in 2000 focused attention on the plight of the Louisiana black bear. An interactive display tracked the species' decline and the conservation efforts to save it. Also new in 2000 were special Family Saturdays at the Nature Center, with fun themes ranging from Vulture Culture to The Bear Essentials. The Nature Center also provides educational outreach programs to students.

ENTERGY IMAX® THEATRE

The Institute finished construction of the highly anticipated Entergy IMAX® Theatre in October 1995. The theatre was part of the $25 million Phase II of the aquarium and was expected to receive 650,000 visitors and to earn a profit of $700,000 in its first year. The theatre the largest of its kind in the Gulf South, included 354 seats and a nearly six-story-high screen. The Institute chose *The Living Sea,* an exotic journey through coral reefs and the depths of the Central Pacific as its initial offering, and it promised a 3-D film as its subsequent selection. The forty-minute feature cost $6.50 for adults and $4.50 for children, but a combo ticket for the theatre and aquarium was offered at a reduced price of $14.00 for adults and $9.00 for children.

The movies shown at the IMAX® Theatre are changed regularly. In 2000, the theatre presented *Dolphins, Mysteries of Egypt, Everest,* and *Michael Jordan: To the Max.* Movies for 2001 included *Galápagos, Antarctica,* and *CyberWorld 3-D.* The IMAX® Theater also participates in the New Orleans Film Festival, showcasing 3-D movies.

THE AUDUBON CENTER FOR RESEARCH OF ENDANGERED SPECIES

The Institute next constructed the Audubon Center for Research of Endangered Species (ACRES). The Research Center was to study advanced breeding techniques, animal behavior, and nutrition. The Institute opened a thirty-six-square-foot building that included labs for reproduction, molecular genetics, cryogenics, and veterinary care in the spring of 1996. Senator J. Bennett Johnston secured $19 million in federal funds for the research center, the first breeding center of its kind.

The Research Center has made an international splash with several of its research projects. First, in an unprecedented embryo transfer, a common housecat gave birth to Jazz, an African wildcat, in 1999. ACRES Director Dr. Betsy Dresser commented on the significance of this birth: "By using nonendangered species as surrogates, we can increase the number of births of endangered and rare animals." Second, the first two test-tube caracals (African wildcats) were born via in vitro fertilization using frozen sperm in 2000. The use of frozen sperm, embryos, and other genetic material of vanishing animals promises to help the scientific community preserve endangered species.

Dr. Dresser, Audubon's research head, who was responsible for the embryo transfer, earned the prestigious Chevron Conservation Award in 2000. She was praised as an internationally recognized pioneer. A local weekly newspaper, *Gambit,* named Dr. Dresser as the New Oreleanian of the Year for 2000. The Research Center was hailed in such national publications as the *Washington Post, U.S. News and World Report, Popular Science,* and *Scientific American.*

PARKS

The Audubon Nature Institute owns and operates three free public parks: (1) Audubon Park next to the zoo in uptown New Orleans, (2) Audubon Wilderness Park on the Westbank, and (3) Woldenberg Riverfront Park on the riverfront in downtown New Orleans. The Audubon Wilderness Park features an orientation center, hiking trails, and signs posting wetland facts. This park is dedicated to preserving the natural environment of Louisiana and providing opportunities for family recreation in a natural setting. Groups such as the Boy Scouts use this park for group camping outings; reservations are handled by the Audubon Nature Center. The long-term goal for the Audubon Wilderness Park is for it to serve as a major urban park. Woldenberg Riverfront Park complements the aquarium and provides an extensive area from which the public can view the river and its traffic.

Audubon Park includes many very old oak trees, a jogging path, picnic areas, riding stables, and the Audubon Golf Course. Extensive renovation of the golf course, a resurfaced jogging track, and other improvements designed to maximize opportunity for outdoor recreation at Audubon Park were begun in 2001. After some controversial feedback, the plans for the clubhouse and parking lot for the golf course were scaled back in size.

THE AUDUBON NATURE INSTITUTE

The Audubon Nature Institute has a twenty-four-member governing board. Yearly elections are held for six members of the board, who serve four-year terms. The board oversees the policies of the Audubon Nature Institute and sets guidelines for memberships, concessions, fundraising, and marketing. However, actual policy making and operations are controlled by the Audubon Commission, which sets zoo hours, admission prices, and so on.

Through its volunteer programs, the Audubon Nature Institute staffs many of the Audubon programs. The vast majority of the volunteers work at the zoo or the aquarium. Volunteers from the Audubon Nature Institute help with education, membership, public relations, graphics, clerical work, research, or even exhibits and animal care. In 2000, 900 volunteers provided 101,000 hours of service, valued at $1,554,390.

In 2001, a person could join the Audubon Nature Institute as a member of the zoo, the aquarium, the nature center, or any combination of the three. Annual fees for an individual are $45 for one facility, $65 for two, and $85 for all three. Participation in hands-on, behind-the-scenes, members-only events at the zoo, aquarium, and Nature Center, in addition to unlimited free admission and free parking, are benefits of membership. Members also receive discounts on tickets to the Entergy IMAX® Theater, discounts on selected merchandise in Institute gift shops, and a free subscription to *Audubon Up Close*, a quarterly publication for members only.

The effort to increase membership requires a special marketing approach for all of the Audubon facilities. Chip Weigand, Director of Marketing for the Zoo, stated,

> . . . {I}n marketing memberships we try to encourage repeat visitations, the feeling that one can visit as often as one wants, the idea that the zoo changes from visit to visit and that there are good reasons to make one large payment or donation for a membership card, rather than paying for each visit. . . . {T}he overwhelming factor is a good zoo that people want to visit often, so that a membership makes good economical sense.

Southern Living magazine in 2000 named Audubon Zoo among the South's favorite zoos'; *Family Fun* magazine called it one of the nation's top family-friendly zoos. *Places Rated Almanac*'s Family Friendly Travel Awards ranked the aquarium fourth among all U.S. zoos and aquariums.

The Audubon Nature Institute publishes a quarterly newsletter for members called *Audubon Up Close*. This publication received a Silver Award for design excellence from the American Institute of Graphic Arts in 2000, its first year of publication. The colorful eight-page publication is crammed full of pictures and articles about recent achievements and upcoming events at all the facilities.

PROMOTIONAL PROGRAMS

The American Association of Zoological Parks and Aquariums reported that most zoos find that the majority of their visitors live within a single population center in close proximity to the park. Thus, in order to sustain attendance over the years, zoos must attract the same visitors repeatedly. A large number of the zoo's promotional programs and special events are aimed at doing just that.

The Audubon Nature Institute conducts a multitude of very successful promotional programs. The effect is to have ongoing parties and celebrations going on, which attract a variety of people to the zoo and other facilities (and raising additional revenue). Key among these annual events are the Zoo-To-Do; the Swamp Fest, a cajun music festival held over two weekends in October; and the Boo at the Zoo Halloween. In addition to these annual promotions, the Audubon Nature Institute schedules special family weekends throughout the year.

Many educational activities are conducted all year long. These include: (1) a Junior Zookeeper program for seventh and eighth graders, (2) a Student-Intern program that enables college students to receive zookeeper training, (3) a Swamp School for third graders, (4) the Wild Science after-school program for fifth graders, and (5) AquaKids at the Audubon Aquarium.

ADMISSION POLICY

The average yearly attendance for a zoo may be estimated using projected population figures multiplied by a "visitor generating factor." The average visitor generating factor of fourteen zoos similar in size and climate to the Audubon Zoo was 1.34, with a rather wide range (from a low of .58 in the cities of Phoenix and Miami to a high of 2.80 in Jackson, Mississippi).

In 2001, the Audubon Nature Institute charged admission fees for all of its facilities, as indicated in Exhibit 1; all of the other nonzoo parks charged admissions fees from day one or when they became part of the Institute. However, admission is free for members and for children on school field trips. Nearly 300,000 students visited the nine facilities on such trips during 2000.

FINANCES

The zoo's ability to generate operating funds has been credited to the dedication of the Audubon Nature Institute, continuing increases in attendance, and creative special events and programs. A history of adequate operating funds allows the zoo to guarantee capital donors that their gifts will be used to build and maintain top-notch exhibits. A comparison of the 1998, 1999, and 2000 combined statements of income and expenses for the Audubon Nature Institute is in Exhibit 2; Exhibit 3 shows the balance sheet.

Fundraising

The Audubon Nature Institute raises funds through five major types of activities: membership, concessions, the annual fund, Adopt An Animal, Zoo-To-Do, and capital fund drives. Zoo managers from around the country come to the Audubon Park Zoo for tips on fundraising, especially to learn about the Zoo-To-Do.

EXHIBIT 1   Admission Fees

Facility	Adults	Children	Seniors
Aquarium	$13.50	$ 6.50	$10.00
IMAX	7.75	5.00	6.75
IMAX & Aquarium	17.25	10.50	14.00
Nature Center	4.75	2.50	3.75
Zoo	9.00	4.75	5.75

Source: The Audubon Nature Institute.

EXHIBIT 2   Statement of Zoo Operating Income and Expenses (in thousands)

	2000	% Change	1999	% Change	1998
OPERATING INCOME					
Admissions	$12,997	−0.44%	$13,054	−1.22%	$13,215
Concessions & Catering	6,251	0.79%	6,202	21.01%	5,125
Membership Support	2,413	13.13%	2,133	3.75%	2,056
Marketing Events & PR	211	−35.08%	325		0
Recreational & Educational Programs	1,040	6.78%	974	−21.64%	1,243
Other	601	−3.06%	620	−22.69%	802
TOTAL OPERATING INCOME	23,423	0.49%	23,308	3.86%	22,441
NON-OPERATING ITEMS*					
Debt Service Funded by Operations	−895	−4.18%	−934	−33.71%	−1,409
Dedicated Tax Millage	2,999	25.27%	2,394	4.36%	2,294
Interest/Endowment Income	804	−48.16%	1,551	1.70%	1,525
Fundraising Transfer to Operations	2,086	−99.91%	2,453	169.26%	911
TOTAL INCOME	28,417	−1.23%	28,772	11.68%	25,762
OPERATING EXPENSES					
Operations, Maintenance, & Utilities	6,792	−7.12%	7,313	39.45%	5,244
Curatorial & Research	4,888	−13.32%	5,639	−8.78%	6,182
Food Service, Catering, & Gift Shops	3,856	8.31%	3,560	27.60%	2,790
Membership	856	8.35%	790	34.13%	589
Recreational & Educational	1,200	−15.37%	1,418	7.42%	1,320
Marketing & Promotions	1,925	−15.72%	2,284	10.28%	2,071
Visitor Services & Volunteers	1,392	2.65%	1,356	11.97%	1,211
Administration, Personnel, & MIS	3,920	3.38%	3,792	5.98%	3,578
Fringe Benefits	2,265	13.99%	1,987	28.61%	1,545
TOTAL EXPENSES	27,094	−3.71%	28,139	14.70%	24,532
REVENUES—EXPENSES	1,413	123.22%	633	−48.54%	1,230
CAPITAL EXPENDITURES	11,989	20.09%	9,983		NA

*Excludes capital revenues and expenditures and depreciation associated with buildings and field exhibitry.
Source: Audubon Nature Institute *Annual Reports* (1998, 1999, 2000).

Adopt An Animal

Zoo "Parents" pay a fee to "adopt" an animal, and the fee varies with the animal chosen. Zoo Parents' names are listed on a large sign inside the zoo. They also have their own celebration, Zoo Parents Day, held at the zoo annually.

Zoo-To-Do

Zoo-To-Do is a black-tie fundraiser held annually, with live music, food and drink, and original, high-class souvenirs such as posters or ceramic necklaces. Admission tickets, limited to three thousand, are priced starting at $150 per person. A raffle is conducted in conjunction with the Zoo-To-Do, with raffle items ranging from an opportunity to be zoo curator for a day to the use of a Mercedes-Benz for a year. Despite the rather stiff price, the Zoo-To-Do is a popular sellout every year. Local restaurants and other businesses donate most of the necessary supplies, decreasing the cost of the affair. In 1985, the Zoo-To-Do raised almost $500,000 in one night, more money than any other

EXHIBIT 3   Balance Sheet for the Audubon Nature
Institute, All Units

	December 31, 2000
LIABILITIES:	
CURRENT LIABILITIES:	
Accounts payable and accrued liabilities	$ 4,255,480
Due to (or from) the Audubon Institute, Inc.	
Due to other locations/funds	2,033
Total current liabilities	4,257,513
CURRENT LIABILITIES PAYABLE FROM RA	
Accrued interest payable	174,809
Revenue bonds—current portion	840,874
Limited tax bonds—current portion	1,496,793
Construction payables	1,211,993
Due to other funds	–
Total payable from restricted assets	3,724,469
Total current liabilities	7,981,982
LONG-TERM LIABILITIES:	
Limited tax bonds	42,007,548
Revenue bonds	12,064,612
Discounts on bond issues	(1,263,428)
Other	1,001,322
Total long-term liabilites	53,810,054
TOTAL LIABILITIES	61,792,036
NET ASSETS—Operating accounts	111,293,872
TOTAL LIABILITIES & NET ASSETS	$173,085,908

(continued)

nonmedical fundraiser in the country. In 2000, the Zoo-To-Do and the Zoo-To-Do for Kids brought in more than $1 million. The Zoo-To-Do continues to sell out annually, and it remains a major fundraiser as well as a great public relations event for the Zoo.

Annual Fund

The Audubon Annual Fund, used to pay for day-to-day operations at all Audubon facilities, raised a record $266,000 in 2000.

Grants

The Institute was awarded a $112,500 operating grant in 2000 from the Institute of Museum and Library Services, a highly esteemed national grant. The horticulture department of the Audubon Park and Audubon Zoo received a $5,000 grant from the Louisiana Urban Forestry Council to inventory the site's wealth of trees.

Audubon Tea Room

In 2000, the Institute increased its revenue-generating potential by opening the Jerome S. Glazer Audubon Tea Room at the Audubon Zoo. The Tea Room provides 10,000 square feet of space, which can be rented for elegant occasions such as weddings, corporate gatherings, and other special events.

EXHIBIT 3   Balance Sheet for the Audubon Nature
Institute, All Units   (continued)

	December 31, 2000
ASSETS	
CURRENT ASSETS:	
Cash and temporary investments	$ 1,132,847
Accounts receivable—net	736,165
Accrued interest receivable	31,602
Inventories, at cost	409,462
Prepaid expenses	431,079
Total current assets	2,741,155
RESTRICTED ASSETS:	
Debt service accounts	3,201,686
Accounts receivable for capital improvements	361,828
Due from other funds for capital improvements	—
Pledges receivable	8,870,472
Endowment/funds functioning investments	22,696,487
Total restricted assets	35,130,473
PROPERTY AND EQUIPMENT:	
Land	800,000
Buildings and fixed exhibitry	137,872,539
Equipment	15,048,061
Construction in progress	9,764,776
Gross property	163,485,376
Less accumulated depreciation	(40,391,364)
Net property and equipment	123,094,012
OTHER ASSETS:	
Prepaid rent—DockBoard	9,957,820
Receivable under REDA	1,493,279
Unamortized bond issue costs	669,169
Total other assets	12,120,268
TOTAL ASSETS	$173,085,908

Source: The Audubon Nature Institute.

Expeditions

The Institute organizes and conducts several expeditions annually. In 2000, the Institute offered three different safaris to Kenya, to Zimbabwe/Zambia/South Africa, and to Botswana. In 2001, it offered an African safari to Tanzania, an expedition to Australia, and an ecotour to Ecuador and the Galápagos Islands. For 2002, a twelve-day birding and wildlife adventure in Costa Rica is already planned. This expedition will take participants from lush rainforests to an active volcano.

E-COMMERCE

The Audubon Nature Institute has not ignored the Internet and its opportunities. It has its own Web site, is listed on important informational Web sites, and has used eBay to raise funds for its work. The Institute's Web site is **www.auduboninstitute.org.** It uses its Web site to provide "outgoing" information, to provide a means for "incoming" information (through e-mail addresses for key Institute staff), and to sell admission tickets on line.

The Institute has also capitalized on the Web sites of others. It is listed on a number of Web sites that promote recreational activities in the New Orleans area to tourists and locals. Among these are **www.neworleans.net**, **www.neworleans.com**, **www.gambitno.com**, **www.louisianatravel.com**, and **www.nawlins.com**. In addition, using paintings created by the orangutans at the Audubon Zoo, the Audubon chapter of the American Association of Zookeepers sold orangutan-created paintings on eBay, raising money to support a wide range of conservation organizations, from the World Wildlife Fund to the Dian Fossey Gorilla Fund.

THE NATURAL ENVIRONMENT

The Audubon Nature Institute is "dedicated to nature and unified with a purpose of celebrating life through nature." Its purpose of "celebrating the wonders of nature" guides its mission.

An indicator of the Institute's dedication to nature is the change that was made in its name in 2000. Prior to that year, it was called Audubon Institute. The word *nature* was added to its name to emphasize the central aspect of nature to the organization. The name was paired with a new logo designed to strengthen its unity of purpose—nature—and the broad scope of the organization.

Many of the efforts of the Institute to preserve and celebrate nature were described earlier. Even the zoo, contrary to the public image of most zoos, is involved in efforts to return endangered species to the wild, not just preserve a few specimens in captivity. In 2000, the zoo staff helped release Guam rails, including four chicks born at the zoo, on the island of Rota in the Pacific Ocean. This species of birds was wiped out on the island of Guam by the brown tree snake, a species accidentally introduced to Guam. The zoo also saw the birth of three baby jaguars in 2001—an endangered species from Central and South America.

THE FUTURE

The Audubon Insectarium

This living science museum is scheduled to open in the U.S. Custom House on Canal Street in downtown New Orleans in 2003. It will become the tenth facility operated by the Audubon Nature Institute. Ron Forman sees this museum as a way to help the economic development of the city of New Orleans by bringing local people back to Canal Street in downtown New Orleans. The zoo's Bugmobile is heralding the coming opening of the Insectarium as it travels to schools and community centers to provide outreach education.

The very popular butterfly exhibit from the zoo will be moved to the Insectarium. In this exhibit, butterflies hatch from cocoons inside a large enclosed area and fly freely around the many flowers and the visitors walking through. Another exhibit will be on termites, a major problem in the New Orleans area and throughout the southern United States.

Ron Forman is tremendously optimistic about the future of the Audubon Nature Institute, especially considering the forces opposing them. The Institute faces a rather weak New Orleans economic situation. Exhibit 4 provides facts regarding the New Orleans area. The Institute operates in a city where many attractions compete for the leisure dollar of natives and tourists. It has to vie with the French Quarter, Dixieland jazz, the Superdome, casinos—and the greatest attraction of all, Mardi Gras. The decline in tourism following the terrorist attacks of September 11, 2001, adds to the challenges facing the Institute.

EXHIBIT 4   A Few Facts About New Orleans

FACTS

Population	1,337,726[1]
Per Capita Personal Income	$25,960[2]
Unemployment Rate	5.0%[3]
Average Temperature	77.42 degrees Fahrenheit[4]
Average Annual Rainfall	5.125 inches[5]
Elevation	25 feet (high)[6]
	−8 feet (low)
Area	3,401 square miles of land

MAJOR ECONOMIC ACTIVITIES

Tourism (7 million visitors per year)
Oil and Gas Industry
The Port of New Orleans (200 million tons of cargo/year)

TAXES

State Sales Tax	3.97%[7]
Parish (County) Sales Tax	4.75% (Jefferson Parish)[8]
	5.00% (Orleans Parish)[9]
State Income Tax	2.1–2.6% on first $20,000
	3.0–3.5% on next $30,000
	6.0% on $51,000 & over
Parish Property Tax	Exempt first $75,000
	$161.63/$10,000 (Orleans)[10]

[1] 2000 http://quickfacts.census.gov/qfd/states/22000.html
[2] 1999 http://www.bea.doc.gov
[3] 2000 http://data.bls.gov/cgi-bin/surveymost?la+22
[4] 2001 http://www.weather.com/weather/climatology/70118
[5] 2001 http://www.weather.com/weather/climatology/70118
[6] http://mac.usgs.gov/mac/isb/pubs/booklets/elvadist/elvadist.html#50
[7] http://www.rev.state.la.us/htmlfiles/faq/faq.asp#SalesTax
[8] http://www.rev.state.la.us/taxforms/R1003.pdf
[9] http://www.rev.state.la.us/taxforms/R1003.pdf
[10] http://www.rev.state.la.us/

One proposal that the Institute is championing is a program called "Family Freedom Days." The purpose of this program is to help Louisiana residents who sustained personal or economic loss because of the wave of attacks on the United States and to encourage residents to visit local sites. Ron Forman feels strongly that people aren't getting out and having fun as much since the September 11 terrorist attacks. Each participating organization offers free admission to its facilities on a particular Saturday. The Institute offered free admission to the zoo, aquarium, and nature center on one Saturday before the end of the year 2001. Although admission was free, donations were requested to benefit relatives of the Louisiana residents who were killed in the September 11 attacks. The last time the Audubon Zoo offered free admission (January 17, 1999), attendance exceeded 38,000 for the one day. In considering this program, the staff of the Institute needs to consider its likely impacts, both short and long term, on the Institute.

Forman believes his once weak and now overwhelmingly powerful Audubon Nature Institute possesses the necessary focus and facilities to forge successfully well into the new millennium. The Audubon Nature Institute and its facilities are well-known both locally and nationally. Exhibits 5 and 6 provide information from visitor and non-visitor surveys conducted for the Institute. The Institute has loyal membership and contributor bases. The facilities are first-class. Forman sums up the present and future of the Institute by stating, "All of our exhibits are on the leading edge of what is being done; we believe the best way to educate people is through fun."

EXHIBIT 5   Audubon Zoo Visitor Survey

	1998		1999	
	Number	*Percent*	*Number*	*Percent*
First Visit to Zoo	74	31%	136	45%
Number of Visits in Last Year				
No visits	32	22	37	23
1 visit	29	20	36	22
2 visits	20	14	27	17
3 or more visits	66	45	63	39
Average Number of Visits	6.1	–	4.7	–
When Decided to Visit				
Today or yesterday	99	41	94	31
Within the past week	77	32	144	48
Two weeks to one month ago	37	15	45	15
More than one month ago	27	11	18	6
Reasons for Visiting				
Interest in animals	145	61	109	36
Bring children	107	45	141	47
Entertainment	101	42	103	34
Sightseeing	79	33	116	39
Education	71	30	70	23
Number of Persons in Group				
Adults	2.3	–	2.1	–
Children	1.1	–	1.3	–
Adults (Adults Only)				
1	13	14	15	14
2	72	79	71	68
3 or more	6	6	19	19
Percentage of Total Groups	–	39	–	36
Average Group Size	1.9	–	2.2	–
Average Adult Age	39.6	–	40.4	–
Number of Children (Groups with Children)				
1	68	48	66	36
2	47	33	68	37
3	16	11	32	17
4 or more	11	8	17	9
Percent of Total Groups	–	61	–	64
Average Group Size				
Children	1.8	–	2.1	–
Adults	2.5	–	2.0	–
Average Child Age	6.0	–	6.5	–

(continued)

EXHIBIT 5   Audubon Zoo Visitor Survey   (continued)

	1998		1999	
	Number	*Percent*	*Number*	*Percent*
Respondent's Education				
Some high school or less	4	2	19	6
High school graduate	37	16	66	22
Some college	69	30	70	23
College degree	82	36	94	31
Graduate degree	37	16	52	17
Respondent's Household Family Income				
Less than $25,000	31	14	47	16
$25,000–39,999	47	21	68	23
$40,000–54,999	55	25	55	18
$55,000–74,999	40	18	62	21
$75,000–149,999	42	19	59	20
$150,000 or more	4	2	10	3
Respondent's Race				
Caucasian	188	82	212	71
African-American	25	11	69	23
Hispanic	8	3	7	2
Asian	2	1	10	3
Native American	4	2	0	0
Other	3	1	1	0
Respondent's Gender				
Female	137	62	179	61
Male	84	38	116	39

Source: The Audubon Nature Institute.

EXHIBIT 6   Audubon Zoo Nonvisitor Survey

Reason	Pleasure	Business
WHY RESPONDENT DID NOT VISIT THE ZOO (in %)		
No time	47%	66%
Too hot	12	15
Other plans	12	14
No interest	11	4
Been before	10	4

Source: The Audubon Nature Institute.

EXHIBIT 7   Audubon Nature Institute Mission Statements

CORE VALUES (MISSION) OF THE INSTITUTE

We believe in Quality in all we do. We believe Total Quality leads to Unprecedented Success. These beliefs are reflected in our Core Values:

- *Service.* We recognize the importance of each and every guest experience and strive to make each one memorable through genuine hospitality, an attitude of caring, and careful training to ensure exceptional customer service.
- *People.* We value the great potential of each individual within the Audubon family. We stimulate initiative and maximize talent through clearly stated goals, professional training and the job support necessary to ensure individual success that exceeds expectations.
- *Stewardship.* We adhere to the highest standards in assuring the well-being of the animals and habitats under our care, and through pace-setting research and conservation and education programs, we work to preserve nature on a local, regional, national and global scale.
- *Innovation.* We enhance and encourage creativity, aggressively seeking to set new standards in all that we do, from new exhibit development to animal breeding programs.
- *Diversity.* We believe in recruiting from a diverse talent pool to build and maintain an extraordinary workforce. Our hiring and promotion practices emphasize ability and potential, eliminating barriers based on race, age, gender, sexual orientation, physical limitations, religion, ethnic background or national origin.
- *Cooperation.* Our growth and development—our every accomplishment—is made possible through a spirit of teamwork that unites our staff, galvanizes our community and ensures attainment of our mission, from educating our diverse audience to enhancing the care and survival of wildlife.
- *Leadership.* We seek to be industry role models and civic leaders, always guided by the highest professional and ethical standards, as well as an entrepreneurial spirit that recognizes selective economic development as a vehicle for advancing environmental education.
- *Stability.* Maintaining economic stability through financial self-sufficiency is paramount as we fuel our operations and strive to fulfill our ambitious vision for the future.
- *Fun.* Our celebrations of life emphasize enjoyment of the world around us. Good humor, optimism and playfulness translate into a healthy workplace—and the ideal environment for teaching others about the wonders of life and nature.

AUDUBON PARK/AUDUBON ZOO

- *Mission Statement.* The mission of the Audubon Park/Audubon Zoo is to connect people with nature by providing superior recreational, educational, zoological and botanical experiences.

ACRES/FREEPORT-MCMORAN AUDUBON SPECIES SURVIVAL CENTER

- *Mission Statement.* The mission of the Audubon Center for Research of Endangered Species/Audubon Freeport-McMoRan Species Survival Center is to safeguard wildlife for future generations through innovative scientific programs that accelerate reproduction and preserve the Earth's genetic heritage.

AUDUBON LOUISIANA NATURE CENTER/AUDUBON WILDERNESS PARK

- *Mission Statement.* The mission of the Audubon Louisiana Nature Center/Audubon Wilderness Park is to lead and inspire a diverse audience to a better understanding and deeper appreciation of the natural world.

(continued)

EXHIBIT 7   Audubon Nature Institute Mission Statements   **(continued)**

AQUARIUM OF THE AMERICAS/AUDUBON ENTERGY IMAX® THEATER/WOLDENBERG RIVERFRONT PARK

- *Mission Statement.* The mission of the Aquarium of the Americas/Audubon Entergy IMAX® Theatre/ Woldenberg Riverfront Park is to inspire our audience to respect, conserve and enjoy the wonders of nature through an urban oasis offering unique aquatic exhibits, quality IMAX® films, excellent education programs and exceptional guest services.

AUDUBON CENTRAL ORGANIZATION

- *Mission Statement.* The mission of the Audubon Central Organization is to provide Audubon facilities with an outstanding array of shared support services that facilitate doing business while achieving the mission of the overall organization.

RIVERBANKS ZOOLOGICAL PARK AND BOTANICAL GARDEN—2002

Carolyn R. Stokes and Eugene M. Bland
Francis Marion University

http://www.riverbanks.org

The Riverbanks Zoo and Garden (803-779-8717), a 170-acre park located on the Lower Saluda River in Columbia, the capital of South Carolina, celebrated its new Lexington County entrance in 2001. The complex consists of the Zoological Park, with over two thousand animals in natural habits, and the Botanical Garden on a seventy-acre section devoted to woodlands, gardens, historic ruins, and plant collections. Riverbanks Zoo and Garden is a major attraction of the Columbia metropolitan area, of South Carolina, and of the entire Southeast.

Riverbanks, one of 185 accredited institutional members of the American Zoo and Aquarium Association (AZA), is recognized as being one of the best zoos in America because of it conservation efforts and recreational activities, and it has received numerous awards. Riverbanks is recognized as one of the top ten zoos in North America with respect to support for the AZA programs. The Zoo has received recognition for its captive breeding accomplishments. The Zoo received the prestigious Governor's Cup Award from the South Carolina Chamber of Commerce in 2002 as South Carolina's leading attraction. Riverbanks is recognized as one of the most visited zoos in America. In 2000, Riverbanks received a $112,000 grant from the prestigious Institute of Museum and Library Service. The Southeastern Tourism Society recently gave Riverbanks its Shining Example Award for Visual Excellence for its video, *The Birds of the World*. Riverbanks has been recognized as one of the twenty most visited zoos in the United States. For over ten years, it has averaged approximately 850,000 visitors annually (see Exhibit 1) with 25 percent coming from outside of the state.

Riverbanks' executive director, Palmer Krantz, continues to move Riverbanks into the future. The twenty-fifth anniversary year (1999) marked the launching of Zoo 2002, Riverbanks' largest expansion and renovation plan since its opening. This new construction effort costs in the neighborhood of $19 million. It is being funded with a $15 million bond referendum approved by the Richland and Lexington county governments and with donations from Riverbanks members and supporters, who provided the remaining $4 million. The Zoo 2002 project has received $17 million of the expected $19 million. It has provided funds for new animals, flora and fauna, habitats, and a new Lexington County entrance on the Botanical Garden side. The beautifully landscaped zoo and garden provide an educational and enjoyable experience for all families.

RIVERBANKS DEVELOPMENT

The Zoo 2002 major expansion plan that began in 1999 refurbished nearly 50 percent of the zoo's core exhibit space; it also created a new entrance into the Botanical Garden. Recently completed exhibits include the gorilla compound in the Ndoki Forest, a birdhouse, and the Bird Conservation Center (a research and breeding center that allows visitors to view the bird conservation operations). The new birdhouse replaced the 1974

EXHIBIT 1   Riverbanks Zoo Attendance Analysis

	Fiscal Year Ending		
	June 30, 2001	*June 30, 2000*	*June 30, 1999*
Paid Attendance:			
Regular	295,579	291,291	338,576
Group	95,008	112,706	115,458
Total Paid	390,587	403,997	454,034
Free Attendance			
Lexington/Richland school groups	31,016	32,065	31,631
Riverbanks Society	232,513	216,043	228,779
Prepaid and Complementary	18,751	15,554	18,445
Promotional-Free Friday's	38,077	29,729	47,855
Children under three	51,820	56,539	55,964
Total free	372,177	349,930	382,674
Total Attendance for the Year	762,764	753,927	836,708
Rain Days:			
Saturdays	5	5	11
Sundays	4	6	3
Weekdays	9	15	15

Source: Riverbanks Zoo 2001 *Annual Report.*

original birdhouse, a facility whose groundbreaking research and conservation efforts had helped to secure Riverbanks' reputation in this field. Completed in January 2002 was the Ndoki Forest elephant compound and a meerkat exhibit.

The Lexington County entrance on the botanical garden side was completed ahead of schedule in February 2001. The well-designed Lexington County entrance on the left bank of the Saluda River has a new, elaborately landscaped parking lot. This new location for the entrance is expected to increase attendance by reducing travel time for many Lexington County residents. All of these developments are in keeping with the mission (Exhibit 2) of the Riverbanks Zoological Park and Botanical Garden: "to foster an appreciation and concern for all living things."

EXHIBIT 2   Riverbanks' Mission Statement

It is our mission to foster appreciation and concern for all living things.

We are dedicated to providing:

- the highest standards of care for our animal and plant collections.
- a diverse educational and high-quality recreational experience for all Riverbanks visitors.
- all the resources at our disposal for the conservation of the earth's flora and fauna.

Source: Riverbanks Zoo 2001 *Annual Report*, p. 2.

Riverbanks is governed by the Riverbanks Parks Commission, supported by the Riverbanks Society, and managed by the Riverbanks staff under the leadership of Palmer E. Krantz, III, the executive director. Riverbanks is accredited by the American Association of Zoological Parks and Aquariums, and it is a member of the American Association of Botanical Gardens and Arboreta. Riverbanks, with approximately 160 employees, has one of the leading zoos in the country.

ZOOLOGICAL PARK

The zoo uses a modern approach to exhibit design: It houses wild animals in naturalistic settings that are preferred by both animal residents and human visitors alike. The naturalistic settings at Riverbanks enable animals to enjoy living in a setting that recreates the wild, and such settings allow visitors to see the animals in a more realistic environment rather than warehoused in cages as in earlier times. At the farm, some domesticated animals are exhibited in a barn and in related settings so that visitors can view them as they would on a working farm. The zoo is home to more than 2,000 animals including 300 birds, 300 reptiles and amphibians, and 1,300 fish and invertebrates.

Major zoo attractions include an award-winning Aquarium Reptile Complex, an African Plains section, a large mammal area, a small mammal area, a sea lion exhibit, bird exhibits, a farm, and the soon-to-be completed Ndoki Forest. The Aquarium Reptile Complex (ARC), with its 55,000 gallon aquarium, has four galleries featuring animals from South Carolina, the desert, the tropics, and the Pacific Ocean. The complex is innovative: It uniquely blend's the features of a reptile habitat with those of an aquarium. The year after the ARC opened to the public in 1989, it was named one of the top three new zoo exhibits by AZA. Attendance reached 1,000,000.

The African Plains section features giraffes, rhinoceros, zebras, and ostriches in a savanna setting complete with moats. The large mammal area features tigers and lions, and the small mammal area features monkeys, tamarins, tree kangaroos, and lemurs. The sea lion exhibit presents the animals in their habitat, swimming, playing, and feeding.

In February 2001, the new birdhouse, the first major component in the Zoo 2002 expansion plan, opened with over 12,000 square-feet of exhibit space. Visitors could walk across the boardwalk to the birdhouse, where they viewed a beach filled with colorful flamingos on one side and a koi pond filled with colorful Japanese fish on the other side. Inside the well-designed birdhouse is an Asian Trek, a Savanna Exhibit, and a Penguin Coast.

The Asian Trek, with the lush foliage of a rainforest and a simulated rainstorm, is home to rhinoceros hornbills, Bali mynas, Victoria crowned pigeons, Palawan peacock pheasants, and many other beautiful birds. The Savanna Exhibit presents the African and South American birds in a safari setting under a canvas tent complete with safari equipment. Here, visitors find the Baft crusted bustard, the African bee eater, the Tavita golden weave, and troupial and blue-crowned motmots. The Penguin Coast exhibit, with more than 1,350 square feet of space, is home to the African and rock-hopper penguins. Visitors look through a 65-foot-long glass at the penguins on their rocky coast and in the water playing and diving. The Penguin Coast is one of the finest exhibits of penguins in North America. The birdhouse is user-friendly to children and features interactive activities. Other bird exhibits include Riverbanks' new Conservation Center, which allows visitors to view zoo operations, including the raising and feeding of birds, and new outdoor aviaries, which display parrots, vultures, and other birds.

Riverbanks Farm features a barn and barnyards with animals such as goats, cows, pigs, chickens, llamas, and honey bees, as well as a backyard garden. Here, visitors can view the chickens hatching from eggs and Riverbanks staff milking a cow. Visitors can also view the feedings of many animals on the farm and in other sections of the zoo.

The Ndoki Forest is the centerpiece of ZOO 2002, a $19 million expansion plan. The forest has five acres of animal exhibits, with lush plants and visitor facilities. The Ndoki Forest provides a new natural habitat for the gorilla, elephant, and meerkat exhibits. The forest also includes an African village, a pizza restaurant, and Ndoki Lodge. The lodge overlooks the elephant exhibit, seats up to 300 dinner guests, and is available for rental.

The gorilla portion of the Ndoki Forest opened in late July 2001 to large crowds. Visitors could view the gorillas from their base camp or in the Ndoki Forest. In the first month that the gorilla exhibit was open to the public, attendance was nearly 75 percent larger than during the same period in 2000. Palmer Krantz, executive director of Riverbanks, said that 79,600 people visited the four-gorilla troop from July 28 through August 21, 2001.

The Ndoki Forest elephant exhibit houses four elephants. Riverbanks uses the recently developed form of elephant management known as "protected care." Once the elephants have had time to adjust to the new environment, Riverbanks will offer an elephant show in which visitors can watch the interaction of the elephants and their keepers.

The new meerkats exhibit in the Ndoki Forest was the most challenging to design. The U.S. Department of Interior has designated this species as Injurious Wildlife, and a permit is required to display it. The permit requires that two escape-proof barriers be maintained between the meerkats and freedom. Riverbanks' first barrier will be a stainless steel wire mesh fence to prevent them from digging out. The second barrier will be either a six-foot un-climbable wall or a wall with an impassable overhang. Riverbanks, with its zoological expertise, will provide guests the opportunity to visit meerkats, animals not often seen in captivity.

In line with the missions of Riverbanks, the zoo actively participates in the Species Survival Plans (SSP) of the AZA to ensure the survival of endangered species. Many zoos participate in the program. For example, in Texas, the Houston Zoological Gardens hatched two critically endangered species, the prairie chicken and the Hawaiian thrush. Riverbanks focuses on 24 endangered species, including the golden lion tamarin, Siberian tiger, palm cockatoo, African penguin, and Bali myna. Riverbanks has received awards for successfully breeding the back howlers and the white-faced sakis. Riverbanks had the honor of being the first zoo to breed in captivity two rare birds, the toco toucan and the crimson seedcracker, and it was the first zoo in the Western Hemisphere to breed milky eagle owls, blue-billed weavers, and cinereous vultures. Riverbanks has the only pair of cinereous vultures raising their own. Riverbanks has successfully bred the endangered pine barrens tree frog in captivity, a first for this species. In 1998, Riverbanks received the Edward H. Bean Award for its long-term success with the captive breeding of Ramphastids (i.e., toucans, toucanets, aracaris).

Riverbanks' Research Department continues to strive to fulfill its mission by leading several AZA-based conservation programs, including:

North American regional studbooks/Population Management Plans (PMPs) for the following species:

1. Rodrigues Fruit bat
2. African lion
3. Nile hippo
4. Hawk-headed parrot
5. Golden-breasted starling
6. King cobra

7. Leaf tailed gecko
8. False gharial

International Studbooks for the following species:

1. Fishing cat
2. Rare leopards
3. Black howler monkey

Species Survival Plans (SPS) for the following species:

1. Bali myna
2. Cinereous vulture

Riverbanks uses the Zoological Park for a variety of activities, such as Migratory Bird Day (with hands-on activities), Ekekeh Day, and Fiesta a la Orilla Del Rio, and if presents culture activities of the relevant countries; it also offers educational events, such as Read Between the Lions Day. On Migratory Bird Day, visitors learn about bird banding, making birdhouses and feeders, and satellite tracking. On Ekekeh Day, Africa comes alive at Riverbanks. Visitors visit an African village, listen to African music, eat African food, and listen to African story readings. At the Fiesta a la Orilla Del Rio ("party by the banks"), visitors learn about Latin America and enjoy arts and crafts; they also see performances of folkloric music and dance from Panama, Colombia, Puerto Rico, Mexico, and Argentina. On Read Between the Lions Day, children and adults listen to animal stories read at different locations in the zoo.

BOTANICAL GARDEN

The Botanical Garden provides visitors with a variety of settings to view the flora and fauna and a variety of opportunities to learn about them. The Botanical Garden includes a visitors center, a walled garden, an amphitheater, a river walk, woodlands trails, mill ruins with a log cabin, and an outdoor classroom. The Botanical Garden, with its new entrance on the Lexington side, now has two entrances for visitors. Visitors now may enter through the original gate in Richland County on the Zoological Park side or from the newly constructed entrance to the Garden on the Lexington side of the Saluda River.

On March 16, 2001, the new entrance opened ahead of schedule. Riverbanks Society members, Lexington County politicians, Riverbanks staff, and young children from the Saluda River Academy of the Arts attended the opening ceremonies. Young children in the Saluda River Singers, focusing on conservation, nature, and growth, sang about giving a tree room to grow during the special ceremonies.

The well-designed Lexington County entrance on the left bank of the Saluda River has a new, elaborately landscaped parking lot large enough for 250 cars, a landscaped entrance gate, and a boardwalk/bridge leading to the Botanical Garden. Visitors passing through the Lexington County entrance walk past the new Bog Garden in the entrance plaza. Then they walk along a short path through woodlands and over a wooden bridge about 35 feet above a brook bordered by plants and flowers and on up toward the entrance to a walled garden that is larger than a football field. Visitors entering the original gate walk or ride the tram up from the zoo to the Botanical Garden.

At the front of the walled garden is the visitors center, which provides guests with a gift shop featuring garden-related products, a gallery, and multipurpose spaces for functions. In the walled garden, guests will find cascade and pinwheel fountains as well as seasonal, exotic annuals; perennials; and bulbs that complement the permanent shrubbery and trees. Beside the walled garden is a terraced amphitheater and grass carpeted for seating as well as a large domed stage for cultural events, such as a zoo ballet and educational programs. At the rear of the garden is the entrance to the walking trail. Here, visitors enjoy scenic river views and the Saluda Factory Interpretive Center. The trail provides visitors a view of many trees, plants, flowers, and animals indigenous to the upper and lower parts of the state. The scenic trail in 1996 was featured on an episode of *Nature Scene*, a nationally broadcast series originating at the educational television station in South Carolina.

The Saluda Factory Interpretive Center is a woodland log cabin. This rough-hewn cabin located near the mill ruins features exhibits that assist in the interpretation of the mill ruins and the flora and fauna of the area. There is also an outdoor classroom for educational programs.

The Garden is a leading source of horticultural and botanical information in the area. Through a cooperative effort with Clemson Extension Service, the public can access information by talking with an extension agent or by using the Internet in the visitors center. The Garden also provides facilities for related activities. The Mid-Carolina Daylily Society holds its annual show and the South Carolina Native Plant Society holds its annual symposium in the Garden. The Community Concert Band has held its annual show in the amphitheater since 1983. Riverbanks was selected again in 2001 to host a Southern Living Gardening School.

SPECIAL ATTRACTION

In 1987, Riverbanks began an event, "Lights Before Christmas," with the lighting of about 25 percent of the zoo. Each year, except during the recent construction period, more lights were added. The 2001 "Lights Before Christmas" display lit the entire zoo for the first time since the Zoo 2002 construction began. This special attraction enhances Riverbanks in December with colorful lights along walkways, in trees, on shrubbery, and in other locations. At the entrance, visitors are greeted with lighted trees containing large stars and the sound of Christmas music. There are colorful lighted images of animals, including a bear, lion, horse, deer, frog, rhino, pig, and fox. Some of the animals appear to be in motion. For example, there is an elephant spraying water over its back, an ostrich running through the woods, and bears ice skating in the Rhino Camp. Visitors on their way to the bridge pass under an arch that is artfully decorated with colorful lights, and they view numerous decorated trees and shrubs as well as a group of frogs that appear to be playing. The bridge is decorated with images of fish and other sea life.

Riverbanks is one of a number of zoos that is presenting attractions of this kind. The Winnipeg, Canada, Assiniboine Park Zoo, for example, one of the coldest zoos in the world, features the "The Lights of the Wild" and reindeer sleigh rides. The Fort Worth Zoo presents a "Zoobilee of Lights," which increased its December attendance from only 10,000 to 12,000 visitors before its introduction to over 75,000 visitors afterward.

Attendance at Riverbanks' 2001 "Lights Before Christmas" was an all-time record: 101,825. In addition to gate receipts, this event generates revenue from concessions, from carousel rides, and from new memberships. With over a million lights designed to depict animal and garden scenes, the Riverbanks' "Lights Before Christmas" has been named one of the Top 20 Events in the Southeast by the Southeast Tourism Society and one of the Top 100 Events in North America by the American Bus Association.

RENTAL OF ZOO AND GARDEN

Riverbanks has offered members and guests the opportunity to rent various portions of the property and facilities for activities such as birthday parties and business meetings. With the completion of several new projects, Riverbanks has now increased the variety of facilities available for rental. Total revenue from all rentals has increased from approximately $74,000 in 2000 to just over $90,000 in 2001. Birthday party revenue has enjoyed a 25 percent increase in 2001 over the same time period in 2000. The revenue associated with birthday parties increased from $5,500 in 2000 to $6,900 in 2001.

The zoo offers facilities for meetings of up to 250 people during daytime hours for $500. Evening rentals can range from the bridge spanning the Lower Saluda River for $500, the entire zoo for $1,500, or the zoo and garden for $2,500. The walled garden and visitors center are available for weddings and receptions for $1,750. Rental of Riverbanks property and facilities promotes attendance by more individuals and organizations who benefit from the enjoyable and educational experience of seeing the animal exhibits and/or the flora and fauna.

RIVERBANKS EDUCATION DEPARTMENT

The Education Department, established in 1993, works to interpret animal exhibits and plants, and to assist in learning about animal and plant worlds. The primary facility of the Education Department is the Education Center, which has two classrooms, an auditorium, and a library. Other facilities available for education programs include a classroom in the Aquarium Reptile Complex, another in Riverbanks Farm, an outdoor classroom at the Saluda Factory Interpretive Center, and the amphitheater adjacent to the Botanical Garden.

During the week, Riverbanks offers classes to groups ranging from preschool through college (see Exhibit 3). On weekends and in the summer, Riverbanks offers classes and special programs for students, scouts, teachers, and family members. Special programs include the Zoo Camp for overnight guests; a one-week day camp for kindergarten; and Winter Wednesday Series, Saturday Series, and Wildlife in the Zoo for gifted classes. Annually, over 40,000 people participate in the education programs.

FINANCING

Individuals, businesses, and government have funded the original construction, major renovations, and expansions as well as the annual operating budget. The Riverbanks Zoological Park and Botanical Garden has an annual operating budget of over $5 million. Revenues (see Exhibit 4) from admissions and concession fees provide approximately 60 percent of the resources; funds from Richland and Lexington counties, the state of South Carolina, and federal and city grants provide approximately 30 percent; and the Riverbanks Society provides approximately 10 percent. Nationally, governments provide approximately 54 percent of the support for zoos.

Riverbanks, a nonprofit organization, uses fund accounting to report its financial position and the results of its operations. The balance sheet for the years ending June 30, 1998, to June 30, 2001, is shown in Exhibit 5.

Admission revenues are affected by weather conditions because most of the attractions are outdoors. Riverbanks earns admissions revenue directly from visitors who pay per visit or indirectly from Riverbanks Society members who pay per year for one of several different memberships. General admission fees are small. A single admission is $7.25 for adults and $4.75 for children ages three to twelve. Special prices of $6.00 for students and $5.75 for senior citizens are available. Discounts are available for groups,

EXHIBIT 3   Examples of Riverbanks Education Programs

Single-Grade Programs

Special Education
* Animal Encounters
Preschool and Kindergarten
* "M" Is for Mammal
* Varmint's Garments
* Ocean Odyssey
Grade 1
* Survival Senses
* Whoo's There
Grade 2
* Hedgerows to Mole Holes
* Dinosaur Detectives

Grade 3
* Trunks, Tails, Spots and Scales
* Look Out Below
Grade 4
* Herpetology
* Good Buddies
Grade 5
* Nature's Cycles and Chains
* The Living Sea
Grade 6
* Species on the Brink
* Sea of Uncertainty

Multigrade Programs

Grades 7–12
* World of Animals and Zoos
* Careers in Zoos and Botanical Gardens
* Biodiversity
* Save Our Species

College Level Programs

Contact Education Department at 803–779–8717 x1113

Source: http://www.riverbanks.org/html/s07education/p02school.

for special activities, or on special days. Free classes are provided for Lexington and Richland County schools. Charges for special activities vary.

Additional information concerning zoo and aquarium industry financing is available at the AZA Web site, **www.aza.org.**

RIVERBANKS SOCIETY

The Riverbanks Society, which started with 200 members in 1976, has grown to over 28,000 households today, making it one of the largest zoo societies per capita in the United States. The Society, which grew out of the private sector, provided much of the needed support prior to the opening of Riverbanks, and it plays a major role in the support of Riverbanks. It provides funds for operations, construction, and renovations, new exhibits, and special activities.

Many of the exhibits and portions of the gardens were provided by individual donations. For example, the Old Rose Garden established in the Botanical Garden as well as the new bird house and gorilla exhibits in the zoo were funded by private contributions as were other projects in previous years. A new endangered species carousel, funded by a local business, is a focal point of the children's play area. The carousel has 22 endangered species, which children can ride, and a scenic mural of other endangered species in their natural habitats.

EXHIBIT 4   Riverbanks Park Commission—General Fund Statement of Revenues,
Expenditures and Changes in Fund Balance
(for the fiscal year ended June 30, 2001)

	Budgeted for Year	Actual Current Month	Actual Year-to-Date Current Year	Actual Year-to-Date Last Year	Ideal Remaining Percent: 0.0%	
					Budget Remaining Amount	Percent
REVENUES:						
Earned Revenues:						
Admissions Net Revenue	$1,788,232	$217,941	$1,783,613	$1,611,621	$ 4,619	0.3%
Aramark Concession Fees	600,000	64,064	598,276	548,992	1,724	0.3%
Riverbanks Society Contribution	607,000	0	607,000	607,000	0	0.0%
Other Revenues – Page 5	610,607	88,867	599,584	563,110	11,043	1.8%
Total Earned Revenues	$3,605,839	$370,872	$3,588,453	$3,330,723	$17,386	0.5%
Governmental Support:						
Richland County	1,305,928	10,656	1,305,928	1,108,121	0	0.0%
Lexington County	699,868	13,252	699,868	666,540	0	0.0%
State of South Carolina	182,989	0	182,989	182,989	0	0.0%
Accommodations Tax Revenue	137,500	(38,500)	122,500	128,500	15,000	10.9%
Total Governmental Support	2,326,285	(14,592)	2,311,285	2,066,150	15,000	0.6%
Total Revenues	$5,932,124	$356,280	$5,899,738	$5,416,873	$32,386	0.5%
EXPENDITURES BY DIVISION:						
Administrative	1,019,797	239,728	1,058,417	922,288	(38,620)	−3.8%
Animal Care	2,216,994	272,259	2,182,747	1,924,328	34,247	1.5%
Botanical	669,584	88,834	631,979	574,678	37,605	5.6%
Facility Management/Utilities	907,518	95,674	923,417	869,411	(15,899)	−1.8%
Public Services	1,160,897	224,621	1,154,906	1,063,538	5,991	0.5%
Total Expenditures	5,974,790	898,917	5,951,465	5,354,243	23,325	0.4%
Excess (deficit) of Revenue Over Expend.	(42,666)	(542,637)	(51,727)	62,630		
Fund Balance – Beginning of Period			699,273	639,087		
Fund Balance – End of Period			$ 649,989	$ 701,717		

Source: Riverbanks Zoo 2001 *Annual Report*

The Riverbanks Society offers reasonable annual membership fees that allow admission for individuals or family members. The Society offers a variety of memberships for individuals and families, ranging from $29 to $125 for a standard membership and from $250 to $1,000 for Gold Circle memberships. Types of memberships, associated benefits, and costs are shown in Exhibit 6.

Society members enjoy benefits in addition to those in the exhibits. Riverbanks sends Society members a bimonthly newsletter and a quarterly magazine. The magazine was redesigned in 2001. Each new issue of *Riverbanks* magazine contains a feature article, timely information on zoo and garden activities, and pages devoted to younger members. Some issues of the magazine have pictures of children with their zoo art, word puzzles, and special children's programs and activities. This is especially appropriate since many children visit Riverbanks. Recent feedback indicates that the new format of the magazine is a hit with members. Riverbanks arranges tours by its staff for Society members to Africa, Australia, Peru, South America, and

EXHIBIT 5   Riverbanks Park Commission—General Fund Comparative Balance Sheets (as of June 30, 2001 and 2000)

	June 30, 2001	June 30, 2000	Changes
ASSETS			
Cash on Hand, on Deposit & Invested in REPO	$ 746,083	$ 418,259	$327,824
Accounts Receivable – General	129,600	104,460	25,139
Accounts Receivable – Local Governments	0	48,500	(48,500)
Accounts Receivable – Ticket Sales	8,515	4,852	3,863
Accounts Receivable – Riverbanks Society	118,195	556,747	(438,552)
Due from Capital Projects Fund	68,039	8,966	57,073
Inventories – General Supplies & Animal Feed	22,209	19,146	3,083
Total Assets	1,090,641	1,160,930	(70,289)
LIABILITIES AND FUND BALANCE			
Current Liabilities:			
Accounts Payable	240,234	278,046	(37,812)
Accrued Salaries Payable	55,008	41,056	13,952
Payroll Taxes Accrued and Withheld	0	339	(339)
Admissions and Use Taxes Payable	0	8,927	(8,927)
State Ret. Contrl. Payable—Employer & Employee	45,132	40,272	4,860
Due to Riverbanks/Aramark Invest. Fund	53,489	0	53,489
Deferred Revenue – Consign. Tickets/Wild Weeks	45,484	90,575	(45,091)
Total Liabilities	439,347	459,215	(19,868)
Fund Balance			
Reserved for:			
Inventories – General Supplies & Animal Feed	22,209	19,146	3,063
Operating Cushion	590,000	590,000	0
Major Repairs and Renovation	0	0	0
Endowed Funds – Phelps	33,833	32,395	1,438
Unreserved, Undesignated (Deficit)	5,252	60,175	(54,923)
Total Fund Balance	651,294	701,716	(50,422)
Total Liabilities and Fund Balance	1,090,641	1,160,931	(70,289)

Source: Riverbanks Zoo 2001 *Annual Report*

other places across the globe. The members get the opportunity to travel to each animal's country and to learn from a Riverbanks professional as they tour the natural habitats of animals.

FUTURE

The zoo and botanical garden industry always faces difficulties due to the fact that the live animals and plants are exposed to the elements; the uncertainty of the economy and competition are also concerns. The recent downturn in the economy has reduced the tax receipts of many states, including South Carolina, thus leading to budget cuts. The terrorist attacks on September 11, 2001, have resulted in greater competition for charitable donations and greater concerns about security, a development which is motivating many to seek recreation closer to home.

Many attractions in South Carolina may increase competition for the entertainment dollar and time of tourists and local residents. Myrtle Beach, a popular entertainment and

EXHIBIT 6 · Riverbanks Society Memberships

STANDARD MEMBERSHIPS

Individual—$29

FREE admission for 1 adult named on card PLUS 4 guest passes
One free admission to "Lights before Christmas,"
Free admission to 100 other zoos, *Riverbanks* magazine and newsletter, discounts in gift shops and education programs, members only events, preview of exhibits

Individual Plus—$39

Benefits of Individual Membership PLUS permanent guest option, six guest passes

Family/Grandparent—$49

Benefits of Individual Membership PLUS admission for children/grandchildren 18 years and under, six free passes

Family Plus—$64

Benefits of Family/Grandparent Membership PLUS 12 free passes, early bird enrollment in Wild Weeks Summer Camp, unlimited free admission to "Lights Before Christmas," and 4 free carousel tokens

Patron—$125

Benefits of Family Plus Membership PLUS permanent guest option, duplicate membership card, subscription to *Wildlife Conservation*

GOLD CARD MEMBERSHIPS

Curators' Circle—$250

Benefits of Patron Membership PLUS 16 free passes and private Gold Circle events

Director's Circle—$500

Same benefits as Curators' Circle PLUS escorted behind-the-scenes tours, *Satch's Scoop* newsletter, 25% discount on facility rentals

Benefactor—$1,000

Same benefits as Director's Circle PLUS VIP tours and events

Source: **http://www.riverbanks.org/html/society_membership.html**.

shopping destination, is home to Ripley's Aquarium, which is located at Broadway at the Beach, and many other forms of entertainment. Charleston, famous for its historic district, is home to the South Carolina State Aquarium, the CSS *Hunley* (the Confederate submarine credited with being the first submarine to sink a ship), and Patriot's Point (museum site of the aircraft carrier USS *Yorktown* and several other naval vessels). Columbia, the capital city, is home to the SC State Museum and other attractions.

By the end of 2002, the zoo's renovation should be complete and visitors should be enjoying the new renovations, including the new bird house, Lemur Island, Ndoki Forest (with the gorilla compound), and elephant and meerkat habitats. Riverbanks, which provides an attractive educational and recreational environment where both adults and children can enjoy and learn about our world of animals, flora, and fauna at very reasonable prices, should continue to be one of the top attractions in South Carolina.

CARNIVAL CORPORATION—2002

Mike Keeffe, John K. Ross, III, and Bill Middlebrook
Southwest Texas State University

CCL

www.carnivalcorp.com

Carnival Corporation is the largest cruise line in the world, and it is considered to be the leader and innovator in the cruise travel industry. Carnival has grown from two converted ocean liners to an organization with two cruise divisions and a chain of Alaskan hotels and tour coaches. Corporate revenues for fiscal 2001 reached $4.5 billion, with net income from operations of $962 million. Carnival has several "firsts" in the cruise industry; more than 1 million passengers carried in a single year and the first cruise line to carry 5 million total passengers by fiscal 1994. Currently, its overall market share of the cruise travel industry stands at approximately 40%.

The Carnival Corporation CEO and chairman, Micky Arison, and the Carnival Cruise Lines president and COO, Bob Dickinson, are prepared to maintain the company reputation as the leader and innovator in the industry. The two men have assembled one of the newest fleets catering to cruisers, with the introduction of several superliners built specifically for the Caribbean and Alaskan cruise markets, and they expect to invest over $3.6 billion in new ships by the year 2004.

Additionally, the company has expanded its Holland America Lines fleet to cater to more established cruisers and plans to add five of the new ships to its fleet in the premium cruise segment. Carnival also acquired 100 percent ownership of Costa Cruise Lines on September 29, 2000. Strategically, Carnival Corporation seems to have made the right moves at the right time, sometimes in direct opposition to industry analysts and cruise trends.

Cruise Lines International Association (CLIA), an industry trade group, has tracked the growth of the cruise industry for over twenty-five years. In 1970, approximately 500,000 passengers took cruises for three consecutive nights or more, reaching a peak of 6.66 million passengers in 2000, an average annual compound growth rate of approximately 9 percent. By the end of 2000, CLIA estimates that there were 164 ships with 165,000-berth capacity, which is projected to grow to 206 ships in 2004. CLIA expects the number of cruise passengers to continue to grow and the competition to intensify between cruise operators.

Carnival has exceeded the recent industry trends: Over the 1996 to 2001 period, it has achieved a growth rate of 50 percent in the number of passengers carried. The company's passenger capacity increased by 10,150 berths during 2001. Additional capacity will be added with the delivery of several new cruise ships already on order. By the summer of 2002, the company expects to have some 56,858 passenger capacity, a 44.1 percent growth over the 1998 period.

Even with the growth in the cruise industry, the company believes that cruises represent only 2 percent of the applicable North American vacation market, defined as individuals who travel for leisure purposes on trips of three nights or longer and who spend at least one night in a hotel. The Boston Consulting Group, in a 1989 study, estimated that only 5 percent of all individuals in the North American target market have taken a cruise for leisure purposes, and it estimated the market potential to be in excess of $50 billion. Carnival Corporation (in 2000) believes that only 12 percent of the North American population has ever cruised. Various cruise operators, including Carnival Corporation, have based their expansion and capital spending programs on the possibility of capturing part of the 88 percent of the North American population that has yet to take a cruise vacation.

HISTORY

In 1972, Ted Arison, backed by American Travel Services, Inc., purchased an aging ocean liner from Canadian Pacific Empress Lines for $6.5 million. The new AITS subsidiary, Carnival Cruise Line, refurbished the vessel from bow to stern and renamed it the *Mardi Gras* to capture the party spirit. (Also included in the deal was another ship later renamed the *Carnivale.*) The company start-up, however, was not promising. On the first voyage, the *Mardi Gras,* with over three hundred invited travel agents aboard, ran aground in Miami harbor. The ship was slow and guzzled expensive fuel, limiting the number of ports of call and lengthening the minimum stay of passengers on the ship to break even. Arison then bought another, older vessel from Union Castle Lines to complement the *Mardi Gras* and the *Carnivale,* and he named it the *Festivale.* To attract customers, Arison began adding diversions on board, such as planned activities, a casino, nightclubs, discos, and other forms of entertainment designed to enhance the shipboard experience.

Carnival Corporation is expanding through internally generated growth as evidenced by the number of new ships on order (see Exhibit 1). Additionally, Carnival seems to be willing to continue with its external expansion through acquisitions if the right opportunity arises.

THE CRUISE PRODUCT

Ted and Mickey Arison envisioned a product in which classical cruise elegance along with modern convenience could be had at a price comparable to land-based vacation packages sold by travel agents. Carnival's all-inclusive package, when compared to resorts or to a theme park such as Walt Disney World, is often priced below these destinations, especially when the array of activities, entertainment, and meals are considered.

A typical vacation on a Carnival cruise ship starts when the bags are tagged for the ship at the airport. Upon arriving at the port of embarkation, passengers are ferried by air-conditioned buses to the ship for boarding, and luggage is delivered by the cruise ship staff to the passenger's cabin. Waiters wander the ship, offering tropical drinks against the background sound of a Caribbean rhythm, while the cruise staff orients passengers to the various decks, cabins, and public rooms. In a few hours (most ships sail in the early evening), dinner is served in the main dining rooms, where, the wine selection rivals the finest restaurants and the variety of main dishes is designed to suit every palate. Diners can always order double portions if they decide not to save room for the variety of desserts and after-dinner specialties.

After dinner, cruisers can choose between many forms of entertainment, including live music, dancing, nightclubs, and a selection of movies; or they can sleep through the midnight buffet until breakfast. (Most ships have five or more distinct nightclubs.) During the night, a daily program of activities arrives at each passengers' cabin. The biggest decisions to be made for the duration of the vacation will be what to do (or not do), what to eat and when (there are usually eight separate serving times, not including the twenty-four-hour room service), and when to sleep. Service in all areas, from dining to housekeeping, is upscale and immediate. The service is so good that a common shipboard joke says that if you leave your bed during the night to visit the head (sea talk for

EXHIBIT 1   Carnival and Holland America Ships Under Construction

Ship	Expected Service Date (1)	Shipyard	Passenger Capacity (2)	Estimated Total Cost (3)
CARNIVAL:				
Carnival Pride (4)	12/01	Masa-Yards	2,124	$ 375
Carnival Legend	8/02	Masa-Yards	2,124	375
Carnival Conquest	12/02	Fincantieri	2,974	500
Carnival Glory	8/03	Fincantieri	2,974	500
Carnival Miracle	4/04	Masa-Yards	2,124	375
Carnival Valor	11/04	Fincantieri	2,974	500
Total Carnival			15,294	2,625
HOLLAND AMERICA:				
Zuiderdam	12/02	Fincantieri	1,848	410
Oosterdam	7/03	Fincantieri	1,848	410
Newbuild	5/04	Fincantieri	1,848	410
Newbuild	11/05	Fincantieri	1,848	410
Total Holland America			7,392	1,640
COSTA:				
Costa Mediterranea	7/03	Masa-Yards	2,114	335
Costa Fortuna	1/04	Fincantieri	2,720	390
Costa Magica	12/04	Fincantieri	2,720	390
Total Costa			7,554	1,115
CUNARD:				
Queen Mary	12/03	Chantiers de l'Atlantique	2,620	780
Newbuild	2/05	Fincantieri	1,968	410
Total Cunard			4,588	1,190
Total			34,828	$6,570

Source: Carnival's 2001 *Annual Report,* p. 81.

bathroom), your cabin steward will have made the bed and placed chocolates on the pillow by the time you return.

After the cruise, passengers are transported back to the airport in air-conditioned buses for the flight home. Representatives of the cruise line are on hand at the airport to help cruisers meet their scheduled flights. When all amenities are considered, most vacation packages would be hard-pressed to match Carnival's per diem prices which range from $112 to $250 per person/per day, depending on accommodations. (Holland America and Seabourn are higher, ranging from $157 to $624 person/per day.) Occasional specials allow for even lower prices, and special suite accommodations can be had for an additional payment.

CARNIVAL OPERATIONS

Carnival Corporation, headquartered in Miami, is composed of Carnival Cruise Lines; Holland America Lines, which includes Windstar Sail Cruises as a subsidiary; Holland America Westours; Westmark Hotels; Airtours; Costa; Seabourn; Gay Line of

Alaska and Seattle; and the newly created Cunard Line Limited. Carnival Cruise Lines, Inc., is a Panamanian corporation, and its subsidiaries are incorporated in Panama, the Antilles, the British Virgin Islands, Liberia, and the Bahamas. The ships are subject to inspection by the U.S. Coast Guard for compliance with the Convention for the Safety of Life at Sea (SOLAS), which requires specific structural requirements for the safety of passengers at sea, and by the U.S. Public Health Service for sanitary standards. The company is also regulated in some aspects by the Federal Maritime Commission.

At its helm, Carnival Corporation is led by the CEO and chairman of the board, Micky Arison, and by the Carnival Cruise Lines president and COO, Bob Dickinson. Mr. A. Kirk Lanterman is the president and CEO of the Holland America Cruise division, which includes Holland America Westours and Windstar Sail Cruises. (A listing of corporate officers is presented in Exhibit 2.)

The company's product positioning stems from its belief that the cruise market is actually comprised of three primary segments, with different passenger demographics, passenger characteristics, and growth requirements. The three segments are the contemporary, premium, and luxury segments. The contemporary segment is served by Carnival ships for cruises that are seven days or shorter in length and that feature a casual ambiance. The premium segment, served by Holland America, serves the seven-day-and-longer market and appeals to more affluent consumers. The luxury segment, while considerably smaller than the other segments, caters to experienced cruisers for seven-day-and-longer sailings and is served by Seabourn. Specialty sailing cruises are provided by Windstar Sail Cruises, a subsidiary of Holland America.

Corporate structure is built around the "profit center" concept and is updated periodically, when needed, for control and coordination purposes. The cruise subsidiaries of Carnival give the corporation a presence in most of the major cruise segments and provide for worldwide operations.

Carnival has always placed a high priority on marketing in an attempt to promote cruises as an alternative to land-based vacations. It wants customers to know that the ship itself is the destination and the ports of call are important, but secondary, to the cruise experience. Education and the creation of awareness are critical to corporate mar-

---

EXHIBIT 2   Corporate Officers of Carnival Corporation

Name	Age	Position
Richard D. Ames	54	Vice President-Audit Services
Micky Arison	52	Chairman of the Board of Directors and Chief Executive Officer
Gerald R. Cahill	50	Senior Vice President-Finance and Chief Financial Officer
Pamela C. Conover	46	President and Chief Operating Officer of Cunard Line Limited
Robert H. Dickinson	59	President and Chief Operating Officer of Carnival and Director
Kenneth D. Dubbin	48	Vice President-Corporate Development
Pier Luigi Foschi	54	Chairman and Chief Executive Officer of Costa Cruises, S.p.A.
Howard S. Frank	60	Vice Chairman of the Board of Directors and Chief Operating Officer
Ian J. Gaunt	50	Senior Vice President-International
A. Kirk Lanterman	70	Chairman of the Board of Directors, President, and Chief Executive Officer of Holland America Line-Westours Inc. and Director
Arnaldo Perez	42	Vice President, General Counsel and Secretary
Lowell Zemnick	58	Vice President and Treasurer

Source: Carnival's 2001 *Annual Report,* p. 33.

keting efforts. Carnival was the first cruise line to successfully break away from traditional print media and to use television to reach a broader market. Even though other lines have followed Carnival's lead in selecting promotional media and approximate Carnival's budget in total advertising expenditures, the organization still leads all cruise competitors in advertising and marketing expenditures.

Carnival wants to remain the leader and innovator in the cruise industry, and works to accomplish this goal with sophisticated promotional efforts and by trying to gain the loyalty of former cruisers, by refurbishing ships, by varying activities and ports of call, and by being innovative in all aspects of ship operations. Management intends to build on the theme of the ship as a destination, given its past success with this promotional effort.

FINANCIAL PERFORMANCE

The consolidated financial statements for Carnival Cruise Lines, Inc., are shown in Exhibits 3 and 4, and selected financial data are presented in Exhibit 5.

By the end of fiscal 2001, Carnival had outstanding long-term debt of $2.9 billion. According to the Internal Revenue Code of 1986, Carnival is considered a "controlled foreign corporation (CFC)" since 50 percent of its stock is held by individuals who are residents

EXHIBIT 3   Carnival Corp. Consolidated Statements of Operations (in thousands, except earnings per share)

	Years Ended November 30,		
	2001	*2000*	*1999*
REVENUES	$4,535,751	$3,778,542	3,497,470
Costs and Expenses			
Operating	2,468,730	2,058,342	1,862,636
Selling and administrative	618,664	487,403	447,235
Depreciation and amortization	372,224	287,667	243,658
Impairment charge	140,378		
	3,599,996	2,833,412	2,553,529
Operating Income Before (Loss) Income From Affiliated Operations	935,755	945,130	943,941
(Loss) Income From Affiliated Operations, Net	(44,024)	37,828	75,758
OPERATING INCOME	891,731	982,958	1,019,699
Nonoperating Income (Expense)			
Interest income	34,255	16,506	41,932
Interest expense, net of capitalized interest	(120,692)	(41,372)	(46,956)
Other income, net	108,649	8,460	29,357
Income tax benefit (expense)	12,257	(1,094)	(2,778)
Minority interest			(14,014)
	34,469	(17,500)	7,541
NET INCOME	$ 926,200	$ 965,458	$1,027,240
Earnings Per Share:			
Basic	$1.58	$1.61	$1.68
Diluted	$1.58	$1.60	$1.66

Source: Carnival's 2001 *Annual Report,* p 69.

EXHIBIT 4   Carnival Corp. Consolidated Balance Sheets (in thousands, except par value)

	November 30,	
	2001	*2000*
ASSETS		
Current Assets		
	$ 1,421,300	$ 189,282
Short-term investments	36,784	5,470
Accounts receivable, net	90,763	95,361
Inventories	91,996	100,451
Prepaid expenses and other	113,798	158,918
Fair value of hedged firm commitments	204,347	
Total current assets	1,958,988	549,482
Property and Equipment, Net	8,390,230	8,001,318
Investments in and Advances to Affiliates		437,391
Goodwill, less Accumulated Amortization of	651,814	701,385
$117,791 and $99,670		
Other Assets	188,915	141,744
Fair Value of Hedged Firm Commitments	373,605	
	$11,563,552	$9,831,320
LIABILITIES AND SHAREHOLDERS' EQUITY		
Current Liabilities		
Current portion of long-term debt	$ 21,764	$ 248,219
Accounts payable	269,467	332,694
Accrued liabilities	298,032	302,585
Customer deposits	627,698	770,425
Dividends payable	61,548	61,371
Fair value of derivative contracts	201,731	
Total current liabilities	1,480,240	1,715,294
Long-Term Debt	2,954,854	2,099,077
Deferred Income and Other Long-Term Liabilities	157,998	146,332
Fair Value of Derivative Contracts	379,683	
Commitments and Contingencies (Notes 7 and 8)		
Shareholders' Equity		
Common stock; $.01 par value; 960,000 shares authorized;		
620,019 and 617,568 shares issued	6,200	6,176
Additional paid-in capital	1,805,248	1,772,897
Retained earnings	5,556,296	4,884,023
Unearned stock compensation	(12,398)	(12,283)
Accumulated other comprehensive loss	(36,932)	(75,059)
Treasury stock; 33,848 and 33,087 shares at cost	(727,637)	(705,137)
Total shareholders' equity	6,590,777	5,870,617
	$11,563,552	$9,831,320

Source: Carnival's 2001 *Annual Report,* p. 68.

of foreign countries and its countries of incorporation exempt shipping operations of U.S. citizens from income tax. Because of its CFC status, Carnival expects that all of its income (with the exception of U.S. source income from the transportation, hotel, and tour businesses of Holland America) will be exempt from U.S. federal income taxes at the corporate level.

EXHIBIT 5   Carnival Selected Financial Data

	Revenues	Operating Income (Loss)
2001		
Cruise	$4,357,942	$ 958,273
Tour	229,483	(10,357)
Affiliated operations (d)		(44,024)
Intersegment elimination	(51,674)	
Corporate (e)		(12,161)
	$4,535,751	$ 891,731
2000		
Cruise	$3,578,372	$ 957,226
Tour	259,662	7,664
Affiliated operations		37,828
Intersegment elimination	(59,492)	
Corporate (e)		(19,760)
	$3,778,542	$ 982,958
1999		
Cruise	$3,286,701	$ 947,452
Tour	271,828	10,403
Affiliated operations		75,758
Intersegment elimination	(61,059)	
Corporate (e)		(13,914)
	$3,497,470	$1,019,699

Source: Carnival's 2001 *Annual Report,* p. 86.

The primary financial consideration of importance to Carnival management involves the control of costs, both fixed and variable, for the maintenance of a healthy profit margin. Carnival has the lowest breakeven point of any organization in the cruise industry (ships break even at approximately 60 percent of capacity) due to operational experience and economies of scale. Unfortunately, fixed costs, including depreciation, fuel, insurance, port charges, and crew costs, which represent more than 33 percent of the company's operating expenses, cannot be significantly reduced in relation to declines

EXHIBIT 6   Carnival's Revenues and Assets by Region

	2001	2000	1999
Revenues:			
United States	$ 3,489,913	$3,180,667	$2,934,492
Foreign	1,045,838	597,875	562,978
	$ 4,535,751	$3,778,542	$3,497,470
Assets:			
United States	$ 2,040,145	$ 680,897	$1,063,963
Foreign	9,523,407	9,150,423	7,222,392
	$11,563,552	$9,831,320	$8,286,355

Source: Carnival's 2001 *Annual Report,* p. 87.

in passenger loads and aggregate passenger ticket revenue. (Major expense items are air fares [25–30 percent], travel agent fees [10 percent], and labor [13–15 percent]. Increases in these costs could negatively affect the profitability of the organization.

PRINCIPLE SUBSIDIARIES

Carnival Cruise Lines

At the end of fiscal 2001, Carnival operated 16 ships, with a total berth capacity of 41,192. Carnival principally operates in the Caribbean and has an assortment of ships and ports of call serving the three, four, and seven-day cruise markets.

Each ship is a floating resort and includes a full maritime staff, shopkeepers and casino operators, entertainers, and a complete hotel staff. Approximately 14 percent of corporate revenue is generated from shipboard activities such as casino operations, liquor sales, and gift shop items. At various ports of call, passengers can also take advantage of tours, shore excursions, and duty-free shopping at their own expense.

Shipboard operations are designed to provide maximum entertainment, activities, and service. The size of the company and the similarity in design of the new cruise ships have allowed Carnival to achieve various economies of scale, and management is very cost-conscious.

Although the Carnival Cruise Lines division is increasing its presence in the shorter-cruise markets, its general marketing strategy is to use three, four, or seven-day, moderately priced cruises to fit the time and budget constraints of the middle class. Shorter cruises can cost less than $500 per person (depending on accommodations), but up to roughly $3,000 per person in a luxury suite on a seven-day cruise (costs include port charges). (Per diem rates for shorter cruises are slightly higher, on average, than per diem rates for seven-day cruises.) Average rates per day are approximately $180, excluding gambling, liquor and soft drinks, and items of a personal nature. Guests are expected to tip the cabin steward and waiter at a suggested rate of $3 per person/per day, and the busboy at $1.50 per person/per day.

Some 99 percent of all Carnival cruises are sold through travel agents, who receive a standard commission of 10 percent (15 percent in Florida). Carnival works extensively with travel agents to help promote cruises as an alternative to a Disney or European vacation. In addition to training travel agents from nonaffiliated travel/vacation firms to sell cruises, a special group of employees regularly visits travel agents posing as prospective clients. Travel agents who specify a Carnival cruise before other options receive $100 on the spot. In calendar year 2000, Carnival took reservations from about twenty-nine thousand of the approximately forty-five thousand travel agencies in the United States and Canada, and no one travel agency accounted for more than 2 percent of Carnival revenues.

On-board service is labor intensive, employing help from some fifty-one nations—mostly developing countries—with reasonable returns to employees. For example, waiters on the *Jubilee* can earn approximately $18,000 to $27,000 per year (base salary and tips), significantly greater than could be earned in their home countries for similar employment. Waiters typically work ten hours per day, with approximately one day off per week for a specified contract period (usually three to nine months). Carnival records show that employees remain with the company for approximately eight years and that applicants exceed demand for all cruise positions. Nonetheless, the American Maritime union has cited Carnival (and other cruise operators) several times for exploitation of its crew.

Holland America Lines

On January 17, 1989, Carnival acquired all of the outstanding stock of HAL Antillen N.V. from Holland America Lines N.V. for $625 million in cash. Carnival financed the purchase through $250 million in retained earnings (cash account) and borrowed the other $375 million from banks at .25 percent over the prime rate. Carnival received the assets and operations of the Holland America Lines, Westours, Westmark Hotels, and Windstar Sail Cruises. Holland America currently has ten cruise ships, with a capacity of 13,348 berths, but new ships are to be delivered in the future.

Founded in 1873, Holland America Lines is an upscale line (it charges an average of 25 percent more than similar Carnival cruises) with principal destinations in Alaska during the summer months and the Caribbean during the fall and winter, with some worldwide cruises of up to ninety-eight days. Holland America targets an older, more sophisticated cruiser and offers fewer youth-oriented activities. On Holland America ships, passengers can dance to the sounds of the Big Band era and avoid the discos of Carnival ships. Passengers on Holland America ships enjoy more service (the ships have a higher staff-to-passenger ratio than Carnival) and have more cabin and public space per person as well as a no tipping shipboard policy. Holland America has not enjoyed the spectacular growth of Carnival, but it has sustained constant growth in the 1980s and 1990s with high occupancy rates. The operation of these ships and the structure of the crew is similar to the Carnival cruise ship model, and the acquisition of the line gave the Carnival Corporation a presence in the Alaskan market, where it had none before.

Holland America Westours is the largest tour operator in Alaska and the Canadian Rockies, and it provides vacation synergy with Holland America cruises. The transportation division of Westours includes motor coaches, which consist of the Gray Line of Alaska, the Gray Line of Seattle, Westours motor coaches, the McKinley Explorer railroad coaches, and three-day boats for tours to glaciers and other points of interest. Carnival management believes that Alaskan cruises and tours should increase in the future due to a number of factors, including the fact that the aging population wants relaxing vacations with scenic beauty and the fact that Alaska is a U.S. destination.

Westmark Hotels consists of sixteen hotels in Alaska and the Yukon territories, and it also provides synergy with cruise operations and Westours. Westmark owns the largest group of hotels in the region, providing moderately priced rooms for the vacationer.

Windstar Sail Cruises was acquired by Holland America Lines in 1988 and consists of four computer-controlled sailing vessels with a berth capacity of 756. Windstar is very upscale and offers an alternative to traditional cruise liners, with a more intimate, activity-oriented cruise. The ships operate primarily in the Mediterranean and the South Pacific, visiting ports not accessible to large cruise ships. Although catering to a small segment of the cruise vacation industry, Windstar helps with Carnival's commitment to participate in all segments of the cruise industry.

Seabourn Cruise Lines

In April 1992, Carnival acquired 25 percent of the capital stock of Seabourn. As part of the transaction, the company also made a subordinated secured ten-year loan of $15 million to Seabourn and a $10 million convertible loan to Seabourn. In December 1995, the $10 million convertible loan was converted by the company into an additional 25 percent equity interest in Seabourn. In 2000, the company took full ownership of Cunard Line Limited, which owns Cunard and Seabourn.

Seabourn targets the luxury market with three vessels with a capacity of two-hundred passengers per ship; each ship provides all-suite accommodations. Seabourn is considered the Rolls Royce of the cruise industry, and in 1992 it was named the "World's Best Cruise Line" by the prestigious Condé Naste Traveler's Fifth Annual Readers Choice poll. Seabourn cruises the Americas, Europe, Scandinavia, the Mediterranean, and the Far East.

Airtours

In April 1996, Carnival acquired a 29.5 percent interest in Airtours for approximately $307 million. Airtours along with its subsidiaries is the largest air-inclusive tour operator in the world and is publicly traded on the London Stock Exchange. Airtours provides air-inclusive packaged holidays to the British, Scandinavian, and North American markets. Airtours provides holidays to approximately 5 million people per year and owns or operates thirty-two hotels, two cruise ships, and thirty-one aircraft.

Airtours operates nineteen aircraft (two additional aircraft began service in the spring of 2000) exclusively for its United Kingdom tour operators, providing a large proportion of their flying requirements. In addition, Airtours' subsidiary Premiair operates a fleet of fourteen aircraft, which provide most of the flying requirements for Airtours' Scandinavian tour operators.

Airtours owns or operates thirty-two hotels (6,500 rooms) which provide rooms to Airtours' tour operators principally in the Mediterranean and the Canary Islands. In addition, Airtours has a 50 percent interest in Tenerife Sol, a joint venture with Sol Hotels Group of Spain, which owns and operates three additional hotels in the Canary Islands that provide 1,300 rooms.

Through its subsidiary, Sun Cruises, Airtours owns and operates four cruise ships. The ships operate in the Mediterranean, the Caribbean, and around the Canary Islands, and they are booked exclusively by Airtours' tour operators.

Costa Crociere S.p.A.

In June 1997, Carnival and Airtours purchased the equity securities of Costa from the Costa family at a cost of approximately $141 million, and they completed the purchase of the remainder of the company in September 2000. Costa is headquartered in Italy and is considered to be Europe's largest cruise line, with seven ships and a 9,200 passenger capacity. Costa operates primarily in the Mediterranean, Northern Europe, the Caribbean, and South America. The major market for Costa is southern Europe, mainly Italy, Spain, and France.

FUTURE CONSIDERATIONS

Carnival's management will have to continue to monitor several strategic factors and issues for the next few years. The industry itself should see further consolidation through mergers and buyouts, and the expansion of the industry could negatively affect the profitability of various cruise operators. Another factor of concern to management is how to reach the large North American market, of which only 10 percent to 12 percent have ever taken a cruise.

With the industry maturing, cruise competitors have become more sophisticated in their marketing efforts, and price competition is the norm in most cruise segments. Royal Caribbean Cruise Lines has also instituted a major shipbuilding program and is successfully challenging Carnival Cruise Lines in the contemporary segment. The announcement that the Walt Disney Company was entering the cruise market with two eighty thousand ton cruise liners in 1998 could significantly affect the family cruise vacation segment.

The increasing industry capacity is also a source of concern to cruise operators. The slow growth in industry demand is occurring during a period when industry berth capacity continues to grow. The entry of Disney into the field and the ships already on order by current operators will increase industry berth capacity by over ten thousand per year through 2006, a significant increase. The danger lies in cruise operators using the price weapon in their marketing campaigns to fill cabins. If cruise operators cannot make a reasonable return on investment, operating costs will have to be reduced (affecting quality of services) to maintain profitability. This will increase the likelihood of further industry acquisitions, mergers, and consolidations. A worst case scenario would be the financial failure of weaker lines.

Still, Carnival's management believes that demand should increase well into the 2000s. Considering that only 12 percent of the population in the North American market has taken a cruise vacation, reaching more of the North American target market would improve industry profitability. Industry analysts state that the problem is that an assessment of market potential is only an educated guess. What if the current demand figures are not reflective of the future? The recessionary economic conditions in the United States coupled with travelers' reluctance to travel due to terrorist threats concern analysts.

ROYAL CARIBBEAN CRUISES, LTD.—2002

Lenessa E. Hawkins
Francis Marion University

RCL

www.royalcaribbean.com, www.celebrity-cruises.com, www.rclinvestor.com

"Get on board because the fate of our industry is at stake and with it the fate of our country," Air Transport Association president and CEO Carol Hallett said on October 2, 2001. She further stated that safety was the number one priority to get the public traveling again. These comments were made to delegates gathered at a Cruise Industry Conference in Florida soon after the World Trade Center and Pentagon attacks on September 11, 2001. With the economy slowing and capacity increasing every day, the cruise industry now has—and continues to have—a potentially disastrous issue with which to deal: Empty cabins.

In the aftermath of the tragic events, airports were closed. Some travelers were not able to meet their ships, some were unable to disembark, and some were able to leave their ship but had no means of getting back home. An analyst predicts that cancellations alone could result in a $2 million loss in revenue by the cruise industry. Cancellations the week following the attacks totaled nearly 1,000 for Royal Caribbean Cruises, Ltd., based in Miami, Florida. The company's share price fell 40 percent, or $8.42, from $21.18 to $12.76 in the week following the attacks, and the company lost $20 million to $25 million that week alone when bookings fell to 50 percent of the prior week's totals. Immediately following the attacks, new bookings dropped by more than 50 percent over prior-year levels. But within days, booking levels began to improve, and by the first week in October, new booking levels had almost recovered to their prior-year levels.

After the September 11, 2001, attacks, Royal Caribbean Cruises, Ltd. almost immediately redeployed ships which were docked at New York ports and several overseas ports to other North American ports such as Baltimore, New Orleans, and Galveston, Texas. Cruise lines dropped cruise prices to levels that shocked veteran travel agents. Royal Caribbean Cruises increased travel agent commissions from 10 percent to 20 percent after a five-hundred employee layoff in October 2001. These attempts to keep capacity above 90 percent have pushed the industry into a pricing war. Some cruises are being booked at $99 per day, which will make it a bargain comparable to hotel rates that average the same or higher.

Royal Caribbean launched four huge new ships in 2001, comprising 9,250 new berths. Company revenues increased 9.7 percent to $3.1 billion but net income dropped sharply to $254 million.

CRUISE INDUSTRY HISTORY

In the early 1950s, after the arrival of air transportation service between Europe and North America, large transatlantic liner companies sought an alternate use for their ships. Shipping lines renovated their large ocean liners for leisure cruising and, to appeal to the traveling public's desire for exotic travel and exploration, deployed them to more tropical climates, calmer seas, and extraordinary ports of call. The early 1970s saw the incorporation of companies such as Royal Caribbean, Norwegian Cruise Lines, Carnival Cruise Lines as well as the arrival of European-based companies such as Peninsular and Oriental (future Princess Cruises), Cunard, and Chandris (which would become Celebrity Cruises). In the next decade, the industry matured and became a solid participant in the leisure industry. As the cruise industry grew, companies built larger ships and reduced prices in order to appeal to a broader mix of passengers. In order to draw a wider audience, the companies introduced new ships that offered a variety of entertainment options such as bars, lounges, libraries, spas, workout facilities, and business centers. With the larger ships came additional capacity, which expanded the industry's passenger loads by 60 percent between 1990 and 1999.

With introduction of modern 3,000 plus passenger vessels in the Caribbean and Europe, Carnival, Royal Caribbean, and Princess Cruises have all seen an increase in their profit margins. In addition to new ship construction, better product positioning, changes in demographics, a healthy economy, and a wider range of cruise lengths and departure points also fueled swift growth in the industry. In keeping with the main marketing focus of cruise lines—namely, that the ship itself is the true destination—cruise lines offered passengers a floating resort where the amenities and conveniences rivaled that of land facilities.

Cruise passenger counts have grown in proportion to the industry's growth. The Cruise Line International Association (CLIA) predicted that North American passenger levels would surpass 7 million by year-end 2001 and these projections were indeed accurate. With the cruise industry only attracting 2 percent of the entire leisure/travel market, there is a market potential of $85 billion over the next five years.

Royal Caribbean Cruises, Ltd., like other cruise companies, is positioned for major growth in the industry. To date, only 12.3 percent of Americans have ever taken a cruise, which leaves a tremendous untapped market available for cruise lines to attract. There is an untapped market not only in the United States, but also around the world. Prior to September 11, 2001, there was a major push by leading cruise lines to expand their fleets, in order to increase capacity worldwide. Now the major cruise lines have lowered their rates in a desperate attempt to draw customers.

After the Chapter 11 bankruptcy of Renaissance Cruises and in the wake of other earnings warnings, industry analysts expect larger, financially stronger cruise companies to increase their market shares, while small, weaker companies try to survive. Occupancy rates for recent voyages of Carnival Corporation, Royal Caribbean Cruises, Ltd., and Peninsular and Oriental (P&O) Princess Cruises, PLC, were reported to be around 97.7, 97, and 92 percent, respectively, whereas the companies normally report rates of over 100 percent.

COMPANY HISTORY

Royal Caribbean Cruises, Ltd. is a foreign corporation operating in the United States that is exempt from U.S. income tax. The company was incorporated on July 23, 1985, in the Republic of Liberia under the Business Corporation Act of Liberia, but its principal executive offices are located in Miami, Florida. The original company, Royal Caribbean International, was founded in 1968, and the maiden voyage of its first ship, *Song of Norway,* occurred on November 7, 1970. In 1971, the *Nordic Prince* joined the Royal Caribbean fleet, and the *Sun Viking* followed in 1972. Royal Caribbean pioneered the concept of air/sea vacations by flying passengers to Miami from all over North America. When demand exceeded supply, management pursued an innovative strategy by slicing two of its ships apart and adding eighty-five-foot additions to each midsection. This innovation allowed the *Song of Norway* and *Nordic Prince* to emerge larger and more streamlined—and with a wider array of amenities. Introduced in 1982, the *Song of America*, the first of a new generation of large cruise ships, featured a Viking Crown Lounge that was wrapped completely around the funnel, a design soon emulated by other cruise lines. Royal Caribbean developed a long-range expansion plan when the cruise industry boomed in the 1980s. The arrival of *Sovereign of the Seas* in 1988 signaled the beginning of a growth period that saw Royal Caribbean triple in size between 1988 and 1992. In 1991, Royal Caribbean introduced CruiseMatch 2000, the travel industry's first fully automated cruise vacation reservations system. By the end of 1991, more than 25,000 travel agent CRS (Central Reservations System) users had access to this remarkable cruise booking system.

Royal Caribbean International's second expansion program occurred between 1995 and 1998 when it ordered six Vision-class vessels ranging in size from 1,804 to 2,000 berths. Royal Caribbean sold four of its original, older vessels, which were no longer consistent with its image and marketing strategy. More recently, now in the third phase of its expansion and featuring the Voyager-class and Radiance-class vessels, Royal Caribbean launched the *Voyager of the Seas* and *Explorer of the Seas* in November 1999 and October 2000, respectively. There are three additional Voyager-class vessels on order. Delivery of *Radiance of the Seas* in March 2001 marked the debut of the first of four Radiance-class vessels on order. However, the company exercised its options and delayed the purchase of additional Radiance-class vessels in December 2000 and June 2001.

Royal Caribbean Cruises, Ltd. acquired Celebrity in July 1997. Celebrity Cruises' first capital expansion program occurred between 1995 and 1997, during which period it added three Century-class vessels and disposed of one of its three original ships. Currently engaged in its second capital expansion program, Celebrity took delivery of *Millennium* and *Infinity* in June 2000 and February 2001, respectively. Two additional Millennium-class vessels are on order. In March 2000, Royal Caribbean announced the formation of a new tour company, Royal Celebrity Tours, which offers premium land tour programs in Alaska for guests traveling under the Royal Caribbean International and Celebrity Cruises brands. Royal Caribbean also entered into a strategic alliance and joint venture (to launch a European cruise line) with First Choice Holidays PLC, one of the United Kingdom's largest tour operators. Celebrity Cruises primarily serves the premium segment of the cruise vacation market. Celebrity Cruises operates seven cruise ships with 12,294 berths, and it offers various itineraries that range from five to fifteen nights. Modern vessels, gourmet dining and service, extensive and luxurious spa facilities, large staterooms, and a high staff-to-guest ratio are hallmarks of the premium cruise vacation market.

Celebrity Cruises is expanding its fleet to provide an increasing variety of itineraries and cruise lengths, and it, therefore, has deployed a higher proportion of its fleet in seasonal markets (i.e., Alaska, Bermuda, Europe, and South America) than does the Royal Caribbean International brand. Key selling points for Celebrity Cruises are its award winning gourmet cuisine; Aquaspa (SM), billed as "The Most Sophisticated Spa at Sea"; stylish, trendy clubs; spacious luxury suites; and museum-quality contemporary art.

INTERNAL OPERATIONS

Royal Caribbean is the world's second largest cruise company, with 25 cruise ships that have 45,854 berths. Both Royal Caribbean International and Celebrity Cruises offer a wide array of shipboard activities, services, and amenities, including swimming pools, sun decks, beauty salons, exercise and massage facilities, lounges, bars, showtime entertainment, retail shopping, and cinemas. Royal Caribbean ships offer a selection of destinations throughout the world: Alaska, Australia, the Bahamas, and Canada. As seen in the segmented data presented in Exhibit 1, Royal Caribbean's revenues earned from non-American consumers decreased from 82 percent in 2000 to 70 percent of total revenues in 2001.

Royal Caribbean International's volume cruise vacation market is categorized into two segments: contemporary and premium. The Royal Caribbean International brand operates 19 cruise ships with 39,182 berths, offering many itineraries that range from two to sixteen nights and include destinations worldwide. Along with varying itineraries, Royal Caribbean International also offers a variety of shore excursions at each port of call, multiple options for on-board dining, entertainment, and other on-board activities. Key selling points for Royal Caribbean International are it spectacular ships, choice itineraries, consistent quality, and on-board programs.

In 2000, Royal Caribbean Cruises, Ltd. formed sales and marketing alliances in the United Kingdom and Europe with an investment in First Choice Holidays PLC, one of the United Kingdom's largest integrated tour operators. Royal Caribbean also entered into a joint venture with First Choice Holidays to launch a European cruise line. First Choice Holidays PLC brings a large distribution base, several well-known brand outlets, and a new distribution technology to the alliance. Royal Caribbean provides special training and promotional material to assist with the distribution of both the Royal Caribbean International and Celebrity Cruises brands in the United Kingdom. The new cruise brand, called Island, is set to target the European mass market. The *Viking Serenade* has been slated to be the first ship to be operated by the new cruise line. It will be renamed and then deployed out of the Mediterranean in the summer and the Caribbean in the winter.

In 2001, Royal Caribbean also established a partnership with Abercrombie & Kent (A&K) a top-ranked tour and safari outfitter in Europe. A&K will be providing pre- and postcruise land tours for interested cruise guests. These strategies will help Royal Caribbean Cruises to gain market share in the land tour market. Land tours are vacation packages that feature travel between various destinations by tour bus, railcar, and other forms of land transportation.

After assessment and encouragement from travel partners and guests regarding a need for land-based tour opportunities, Royal Caribbean announced a new tour company in March 2000, Royal Celebrity Tours. This new company was created to enhance vacation products in Alaska by offering premium land-tour programs for guests traveling on Royal Caribbean Cruises or Celebrity Cruises brands.

According to Royal Caribbean's vision statement, the company's goal is "to empower and enable our employees to deliver the best vacation experience to our guests, thereby generating superior returns for our shareholders, and enhancing the well-being of our communities." After the resignation of Richard Sasso, former president of

EXHIBIT 1   Royal Caribbean Cruises, Ltd.—Domestic vs. Global Revenue (%)

Years	2001	2000	1999	1998
United States	70%	82%	83%	84%
All other countries	30%	18%	17%	16%

Source: Royal Caribbean's 2001 *Annual Report.*

Celebrity Cruises, Royal Caribbean's organizational structure looks like the organizational chart presented in Exhibit 2, when Jack L. Williams was named president of both Royal Caribbean International and Celebrity Cruises.

Royal Caribbean has pursued expansion in spite of taking on a high debt load to finance the purchase of both new ships and their latest acquisitions. Royal Caribbean Cruises, Ltd. is heavily leveraged, with a long-term debt of over 5.4 billion. The consolidated balance sheet in Exhibit 3 provides more information.

Natural Environment

As the result of several violations of various cruise lines, member cruise lines of the International Council of Cruise Lines (ICCL) must meet or exceed their recycling and waste discharge guidelines, beginning July 1, 2001. Alaskan legislators are considering a tax of $50 per cruise ship passenger as well. Most cruise lines have accepted the new guidelines because they have already started adopting ways to combat the problems, but all oppose the new tax by Alaskan legislators.

Royal Caribbean Cruises has significantly improved its image. In 1999, the company was fined $18 million and pled guilty to twenty-one felony counts for dumping oil and dangerous chemicals into the ocean and for illegally storing hazardous wastes. In January 2000, Royal Caribbean agreed to pay Alaska $3.5 million for dumping toxic chemicals and oil-contaminated water into the state's waters. Today, Royal Caribbean is a leader in innovative improvements in its approach to environmental concerns. Royal Caribbean Cruises is the first cruise line to invest in $32 million gas turbine engines. These engines produce almost smokeless emissions. Two Celebrity Cruises ships treat gray water using a new $1.8 million Rochem system of reverse osmosis. Royal Caribbean is *required* to discharge treated black water at least four nautical miles from shore, but it has adopted an even *stricter* discharge standard: It will not discharge wastes any closer than twelve nautical miles from shore. This "Above and Beyond Compliance" approach,

---

EXHIBIT 2   Royal Caribbean Cruises, Ltd. Organizational Chart—2001

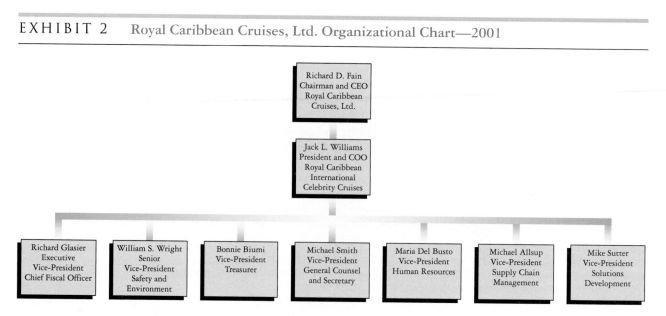

Source: Adapted from Royal Caribbean's 2001 *Annual Report,* p. 52.

EXHIBIT 3   Consolidated Balance Sheets (*in thousands, except per-share data*)

	As of December 31,	
	2001	*2000*
ASSETS		
Current Assets		
Cash and cash equivalents	$ 727,178	$ 177,810
Trade and other receivables, net	72,196	53,609
Inventories	33,493	30,115
Prepaid expenses and other assets	53,247	49,185
Total current assets	886,114	310,719
Property and Equipment—at cost less accumulated depreciation and amortization	8,605,448	6,831,809
Goodwill—less accumulated amortization of $138,606 and $128,192, respectively	278,561	288,974
Other Assets	598,659	396,963
	$10,368,782	$7,828,465
LIABILITIES AND SHAREHOLDERS' EQUITY		
Current Liabilities		
Current portion of long-term debt	$ 238,581	$ 109,926
Accounts payable	144,070	158,143
Accrued expenses and other liabilities	283,913	200,900
Customer deposits	446,085	443,411
Total current liabilities	1,112,649	912,380
Long-Term Debt	5,407,531	3,300,170
Other Long-Term Liabilities	92,018	—
Commitments and Contingencies (Note 12)		
Shareholders' Equity		
Common stock ($.01 par value; 500,000,000 shares authorized; 192,310,198 and 192,122,088 shares issued)	1,923	1,921
Paid-in capital	2,045,904	2,043,111
Retained earnings	1,731,423	1,576,921
Accumulated other comprehensive loss	(16,068)	—
Treasury stock (475,524 and 435,180 common shares at cost)	(6,598)	(6,038)
Total shareholders' equity	3,756,584	3,615,915
	$10,368,782	$7,828,465

Source: Royal Caribbean's 2001 *Annual Report,* p. 39.

among other strategies, has earned Royal Caribbean the Greater Miami Chamber of Commerce's 2001 Environmental Business Practices Award.

E-Commerce

Royal Caribbean's Web sites enable visitors to book travel, explore destinations, and view media presentations. In 2000, Royal Caribbean International was the first cruise line to install Internet centers, Royal Caribbean Online, on its fleet of ships. Celebrity Cruises will follow with Online@CelebrityCruises by the end of 2001. Royal Caribbean has introduced Web sites developed by eCompanyStore for the purchase of branded apparel and accessories. Visitors may follow links from the company's Web sites to purchase items that until now were only available on board the ships. Travel agents and other visitors may purchase items for incentives and promotions as well.

EXTERNAL AFFAIRS

The cruise industry is the fastest growing segment of the travel industry and has experienced 1,000 percent growth since 1970. Nearly 88 percent of North Americans have never been on a cruise. With 6.91 million North American cruisers in the year 2001, cruise lines offer something for everyone. Newly designed cruise ships are larger and more efficient. Higher revenues are realized by the configuration of cabins and public spaces. With 70 more cruise ships under construction or on order, with deliveries by 2006, the worldwide fleet of cruise ships could then carry 17 million passengers annually.

Royal Caribbean expects to increase its share of the market by preparing itself for the influx of supply. Several markets overseas have been studied for new cruise routes, such as France, Italy, and Germany. The United Kingdom is now the second largest cruise market in the world after North America. Europe and the Mediterranean were the fastest growing cruise regions during 2000, accounting for 15 percent of all cruises. Fifty percent of all adults dream of taking a cruise, with the highest interest exhibited by the emerging baby boomer category. The target market consists of passengers under the age of fifty-five.

Travel agencies supply the cruise industry with a distribution system. Travel agents are paid a commission on bookings by cruise lines. Cruise sales are now in second place behind air ticket sales in generation of income and profits for many agents. Travel agents sell over 95 percent of all cruises, according to the CLIA. Generating a high repeat rate, cruises are profitable to sell. Agencies that place an emphasis on selling cruises and on training personnel are the most successful and productive. Good relations with travel agencies enhance the growth of the cruise industry.

Currently, there has been an increase of bookings via the Internet. Some 60.5 million consumers are expected to use the Internet to make travel plans in 2001, up from 25 million in 1996, according to the Travel Industry Association of America. In 2002, that number is expected to increase to 71.9 million. Twenty percent of those making plans will actually make a purchase for travel online. Of those 20 percent, 44 percent are ages 18 to 34 and 48 percent are ages 35 to 54.

Public demand for travel/leisure options is directly influenced by the economic situation of travelers. With job cuts and an uncertainty regarding the recession, Americans are searching for more affordable ways to spend their vacations. Some travelers are choosing to make short day trips or to stay at home during their vacation in order to cut back on spending. The cruise lines compete with other travel alternatives, such as land-based resorts and touring destinations, for consumers' disposable spending dollars. The cruise industry is particularly cyclical as well, with peak demand during the summer months.

EXHIBIT 4   Royal Caribbean's Selected Statistical Information (unaudited)

	2001	2000	1999
Guests Carried	2,438,849	2,049,902	1,704,034
Guest Cruise Days	15,341,570	13,019,811	11,227,196
Occupancy Percentage	101.8%	104.4%	104.7%

Source: Royal Caribbean's 2001 *Annual Report,* p. 29.

EXHIBIT 5   Royal Caribbean's Fleet Expansion

Our current fleet expansion program encompasses three distinct vessel designs known as the Voyager-class, Millennium-class and Radiance-class. Since 1999, we have taken delivery of three Voyager, three Millennium and one Radiance class vessels. We currently operate 22 ships with 45,854 berths. We have six ships on order. The planned berths and expected delivery dates of the ships on order are as follows:

Vessel	Expected Delivery Date	Berths
Royal Caribbean International		
Voyager-class:		
Navigator of the Seas	1st Quarter 2003	3,114
Mariner of the Seas	1st Quarter 2004	3,114
Radiance-class:[1]		
Brilliance of the Seas	3rd Quarter 2002	2,100
Serenode of the Seas[2]	4th Quarter 2003	2,100
Jewel of the Seas[2]	2nd Quarter 2004	2,100
Celebrity Cruises		
Millennium-class:		
Constellation	2nd Quarter 2002	2,034

[1]We have two options on Radiance-class vessels with delivery dates in the third quarters of 2005 and 2006.
[2]These two ships are committed to the new southern European joint venture with P&O Princess.
Source: Royal Caribbean's 2001 *Annual Report,* p. 30.

As seen in the weeks following the World Trade Center and Pentagon attacks, terrorist attacks, war, and political uprisings directly affect the cruise industry. If consumers do not feel safe or have qualms about their travel options, they will choose to stay at home or seek alternatives as precautions.

Competitors

Carnival

Carnival is the largest and most profitable cruise company in the world. Carnival owns Carnival Cruise Lines, Holland America Line, Costa Cruises, Cunard Line, Seabourn Cruise Line, and Windstar Cruises. The company's cruise lines operate forty-four ships with voyages from two to seventeen days in length—from a variety of North American homeports to the Bahamas, the Caribbean, Mexican Riviera, Alaska, Hawaii, the Panama Canal, New England, the Canadian Maritimes, Bermuda, and Europe.

Carnival uses an exclusive marketing alliance established in October 1998, called "The World's Leading Cruise Lines" (WLCL), as a means of communicating its message regarding its highly diversified, global cruise product. This product capitalizes on the unique attributes and amenities of the company's six distinct member lines: Carnival, Holland America, Windstar, Seabourn, Cunard, and Costa. The WLCL's fleet currently consists of 43 vessels totaling more than 61,000 lower berths. The company's brands are positioned to appeal to each of the three major sectors of the vacation market—contemporary, premium, and luxury. Carnival operates fourteen cruise ships that cruise in the Caribbean and the Mexican Riviera. Holland America operates nine cruise ships that cruise in Alaska, the Caribbean, and Europe. Windstar operates four luxury, sail-powered vessels that cruise primarily in the Caribbean, Europe, and Central America. Cunard and Seabourn operate two and six luxury cruise vessels, respectively, to worldwide destinations. Holland America markets sightseeing tours both separately and as part of Holland America Westours cruise/tour packages.

During 2000, Carnival completed the acquisition of Costa Crociere S.p.A. Miami-based Carnival (the NYSE symbol is CCL) has enlisted the help of Garrigan Lyman Group (GLG) to design a new and highly interactive Web site under its multi-cruise-line brand name, World's Leading Cruise Lines **www.leaderships.com**. The site allows the company to present its six diverse cruising brands in a unique one-stop manner, giving visitors a taste of the wide range of cruising experiences that are available. Not only has Carnival expanded its online marketing strategy, but it is also one of the first cruise lines to initiate a television marketing campaign. GLG created an innovative "concierge" function for the WLCL site that automatically leads visitors through a series of questions about their cruise plans, ranging from budgets to recreation, and then recommends the cruise lines best suited to the vacation they have in mind.

Carnival is strong financially, with a debt-to-equity ratio of 0.38, a current ratio of 0.94, and a return on equity (ROE) of 16.4. Revenues were $3.779 billion in fiscal year 2000, an increase of 8 percent over 1999's $3.50 billion. Net income was $965.5 million in fiscal year 2000, a decline of 6 percent from 1999's net income of $1.03 billion. The total number of guests served increased by 12.8 percent in 2000, to 2.7 million. Carnival's shipbuilding program has been accelerated. Carnival Corporation had ordered sixteen new ships by the end of 2000, with delivery dates scheduled over the next five years at a total cost of $7 billion. Its European cruise business has been expanded to help position the company for future growth in the worldwide market.

Princess Cruises

P&O Princess Cruises, a spin-off of the Peninsular and Oriental Steam Navigation Company (NYSE: POC), is a global cruise and tour company that offers a premium-style cruise experience that appeals to a wide variety of travelers. One of the three largest cruise companies in the world, P&O Princess Cruises (the NYSE stock symbol is POC) consists of Princess Cruises in North America, P&O Cruises and Swan Hellenic in the United Kingdom, Seetours and AIDA in Germany, and P&O Cruises in Australia. P&O operates eighteen ships on 150 different itineraries, calling at nearly 260 ports around the globe, and serves more than 600,000 passengers annually. It is a leading provider of cruises to Alaska, the Caribbean, Europe, the Panama Canal, the Mexico Canal, the South Pacific, South America, Hawaii/Tahiti, Asia, India, Africa, the Holy Land, Canada/New England, and other exotic destinations. Princess Cruises owns four riverside wilderness lodges, with a fifth under construction, plus a fleet of UltraDome railcars and luxury motor coaches that take passengers through the heart of the forty-ninth state. Princess additionally operates cruise tours in China, Australia, Africa, India, Europe, the Canadian Rockies, and the eastern United States.

P&O began a major new marketing campaign in January 2001—"Princess . . . where I belong." Targeted principally at the experienced traveler and creating a sense of community, the campaign seeks to position P&O as the cruise line that focuses on individual choice and customized cruise experiences. P&O entered into an alliance with AOLTime Warner in October 2000 to enhance its direct marketing capabilities and market to approximately 27 million AOLTime Warner and CompuServe customers worldwide. P&O has revamped its Web site, **www.princesscruises.com**, to include a booking engine for travel agents, a "wedding cam," and options for choosing shore excursions when booking a cruise.

P&O Princess Cruises is moderately strong financially, with a debt-to-equity ratio of 0.52, a current ratio of 0.45, and an ROE of 10.66. Profits were $276.7 million in fiscal year 2000, compared to $310.8 million in 1999. Operating cash flow in 2000 was $532.3 million, compared to $310.8 million in 1999. In 2000, passenger cruise days increased by 22 percent to over 8.7 million. The introduction of *Golden Princess* in May 2001 marked the first of six new ships to be introduced over the next four years.

CONCLUSION

Coincidentally, Richard Fain, CEO of Royal Caribbean Cruises, Ltd., and Peter Ratcliffe, CEO of Princess Cruises, met on September 11, 2001, to discuss a merger between the two companies. In November 2001, the companies announced their intention to merge to create the world's largest cruise line, with sixty-one thousand berths and forty-one total ships. Royal Caribbean and Princess Cruises together would hold 40.2 percent of the market worldwide, based on the number of berths. There were mixed opinions on the soundness and timing of the decision given the economic recession and the 30 percent drop in U.S. cruise reservations since the start of bombings in Afghanistan. At the same time, some analysts are confident that the intended merger is a good move for both companies in spite of the uncertainty of the industry.

In spite of an uncertain future in the cruise industry, Royal Caribbean continues to pursue aggressive measures to remain competitive in the global market. Royal Caribbean has taken decisive steps to diversify and join competitors and other companies with core competitive advantages from which it can benefit. The proposed merger with Princess Cruises, if successful, will enable the company to gain market share and surpass Carnival Cruise Lines as the leader in the global cruise market. Increased capacity, global recession, and warring nations are three primary threats of the cruise industry. Will cruise lines be able to survive these threats until world conditions change? Will they be able to attract consumers to their floating paradises through competitive pricing and enticing marketing campaigns? Should Royal Caribbean Cruises, Ltd. diversify further into land-based products for uncertain travelers who are unwilling to fly but just want to get away?

REFERENCES

www.almaco.cc
http://corporate.ir.net
www.cruising.org
www.e-travelnews.com
www.finance.yahoo.com
http://FirstSearch.oclc.org
http://www.forbes.com

http://investor.stockpoint.com
www.rccl.com
The Wall Street Journal
http://web6infotrac.galegroup.com/itw/ informanarc
USA Today
http://yahoo.marketguide.com

CENTRAL UNITED METHODIST CHURCH—2002

Robert T. Barrett
Francis Marion University

www.centralmethodist.net

In the aftermath of the terrorist attack in New York City and Washington, D.C., U.S. citizens are becoming more and more aware of the need to seek out positive forces in the world. As people come to grips with the tragedy, they are frequently turning to religious organizations for support. Church attendance and memberships are swelling, in part due to this brush with reality.

Central United Methodist Church, located at the heart of downtown Florence, South Carolina, is a vibrant and growing church. This growth over the past few years has primarily resulted from the influx of young families. These young families are having babies, so the church programming thrust is increasingly centered on children and youth ministries. The church is in the final stages of a building project that has greatly increased the size of the physical facility. Focus now turns to the development and management of programs that minister to the needs of this changing congregation.

MISSION STATEMENTS

The United Methodist Church

The mission of the church is to make disciples of Jesus Christ. Local churches provide the most significant arena through which disciple-making occurs. The statement that follows was taken from the Disciplines of the United Methodist Church.

> ### Central United Methodist Church
> Central United Methodist Church exists to serve and glorify God as revealed in Jesus Christ by making disciples through worship, fellowship, education and service to the Church and the community.

CENTRAL UNITED METHODIST CHURCH—PAST AND PRESENT

Central United Methodist Church was established in the late 1800s and moved to its present site at the corner of Irby and Cheves streets in 1913. Through a variety of land and property acquisitions since 1913, Central's main campus has grown to include approximately two hundred feet of frontage on Irby Street and three hundred feet of frontage on Cheves Street. With its downtown location, a limited number of acquisition possibilities remain available to Central. In the mid-1900s, Central had the opportunity to purchase a house that was adjacent to church property for a cost of $30,000. The church turned down this opportunity, and the owner sold the property to a group which developed a hotel and cafeteria on the property. After the hotel failed, the church was able to buy the property in 1980 for $100,000. In 1984, Central purchased a building adjacent to the property that serves as both the primary facility for the youth ministry and the location of other Sunday school classes. Central continues to actively seek property for building and parking purposes.

Church Property

In addition to the main church campus in the downtown Florence location at Cheves and Irby streets, Central United Methodist Church owns a large tract of land just outside of Florence, named Camp Sexton (after the donor), and a Boy Scout hut a few miles from the main church property. Most church programs are held at the downtown location. A summer camp for children is held for several weeks at Camp Sexton. Camp Sexton hosts special programs during the year and Sunday afternoon swim sessions for church members during the summer. The church sponsors Boy Scout troop meetings weekly in the Boy Scout hut.

The church sanctuary seats approximately 400 people. Attendance averages for the two Sunday morning services are shown for the past thirteen years in Exhibit 1. The sanctuary overflows for performances of the Masterworks Choir, the Christmas Eve services, Easter and Mothers Day Sunday services, and large funerals and weddings.

New Facilities

After an extensive study of programs and facilities by a Long Range Planning committee, the church decided to embark on a building project to expand the physical plant and to enhance the programming possibilities. The efforts began in the late 1990s with a capital fundraising campaign. Pledges in excess of $2 million and collections of half of the pledges allowed the church to obtain a loan for the remainder of the $5 million project and to finalize the architectural designs and begin construction.

Central United Methodist Church is now in the final stages of this building project. Pictures of the new facility can be viewed on its Web site (**www.centralmethodist.net**). With the completion of the building project, church capacity will be increased by almost one-third. The new building provides high-quality space for infants, toddlers, and older children. One program that has taken full advantage of the new facility is the Mother's Morning Out program. This program was once cramped by space limitations, but the new building has allowed it to grow and to satisfy the needs of church families.

EXHIBIT 1   Central United Methodist Church Membership and Attendance Levels

Year	Church Membership	Average Worship Attendance	Sunday School Membership	Average Attendance
2001	1,976	637	1,992	330
2000	1,944	609	1,913	334
1999	1,901	604	1,872	333
1998	1,899	617	1,757	443
1997	1,874	593	1,399	325
1996	1,863	589	1,572	322
1995	1,866	590	1,416	380
1994	1,855	535	1,206	323
1993	1,826	535	1,111	308
1992	1,801	522	1,088	338
1991	1,797	523	1,088	338
1990	1,795	540	1,091	336
1989	1,800	534	1,048	342

Source: Central United Methodist Church.

The Davis Christian Life Center, named for the former minister who pushed the church to begin the building project and his wife, is an excellent facility for larger informal programs. The tile-floored facility has a full-length basketball court that is flanked by a raised stage for music programs, the annual talent show, and other church fellowship programs. The very popular Wednesday Night Supper program, now scheduled in the Davis Life Center, has drawn over three hundred members and averaged over two hundred attendees, up a full 33 percent over previous years when the smaller fellowship hall had seating limitations. The new Christian Life Center has truly made growth possible.

The facility expansion not only provided new space for children and the new multipurpose facility, but it also allowed existing space to be reallocated for other pressing needs. Adult groups moved into renovated classrooms that had previously housed children's Sunday school classes. A beautiful welcoming/commons area was located where members and visitors enter from a new parking lot. Many feel that this area makes the church much more open, inviting, and warm to newcomers. Handicap access to the sanctuary was greatly improved, particularly in this new commons area. The church has initiated the Igniting Ministries program, which is designed to help members reach out to visitors. Greeters meet and welcome newcomers in the commons area.

Membership Profile and Contributions

Exhibit 1 shows the membership levels for Central for twelve recent years, along with average attendance levels for the Sunday morning worship (two services) and the Sunday school. Approximately 23 percent of the members are younger than 10 years of age (note that young people on rolls prior to joining the church formally in seventh grade are only considered to be "Preparatory Members"), approximately 12 percent are in the 11-to-20 year age bracket, approximately 16 percent are in the 21-to-30 year age bracket, approximately 14 percent are in the 31-to-40 year age bracket, approximately 12 percent are in both the 41-to-50 and 51-to-60 year age brackets, and the remaining 11 percent are age 61 or older. Note that over 60 percent of the members are younger than 40, with 35 percent of this group being classified as children and youth. Another interesting breakdown of church membership shows that approximately 60 percent of the members are married, with a bulk of the remaining 40 percent being in the children and youth age brackets. This demonstrates the commitment of the membership to strong family values. In a time of declining memberships in churches across the country, Central has been able to maintain membership and participation levels.

Exhibit 2 gives information on contributions to the operating budget, to the building fund, and to the category labeled "Building Fund Extra," which is for designated project gifts. Contributions have steadily increased in recent years. Church budgets in excess of $800,000 were overpledged (and collected) in the late 1990s. However, with more and more contributions going to the building fund to pay for the new building, the operating budget has suffered. Pledges to the operating budget have been down since the startup of the capital campaign, and the church has had to scramble to meet the operating budget obligations.

Church Property and the Annual Budget

Exhibit 3 gives the value of property owned by Central and debt owed by Central over the period of twelve recent years. The value of church property has grown, while debt service has continued to decline over recent years. The annual budget for 2002 is given in Exhibit 4.

EXHIBIT 2   Central United Methodist Church Contributions

Year	Operating Budget	Building Fund	Building Fund Extra
2001	$1,174,367.00	—	—
2000	$ 997,187.00	—	—
1999	$ 968,110.00	$614,814.00	$104,133.72
1998	$ 868,987.00	$592,400.00	$ 75,108.00
1997	$ 820,610.00	$145,231.33	$ 6,464.75
1996	$ 830,009.91	$131,661.41	$ 7,251.00
1995	$ 734,799.03	$133,602.07	$ 26,527.24
1994	$ 691,713.08	$125,171.98	$ 1,589.50
1993	$ 631,750.74	$110,831.43	$ 2,204.50
1992	$ 587,278.22	$115,747.47	$ 3,810.77
1991	$ 561,148.50	$120,976.75	$ 8,635.50
1990	$ 518,341.80	$102,735.34	$ 38,221.41
1989	$ 499,069.64		

Source: Central United Methodist Church.

FLORENCE, SOUTH CAROLINA

Founded in 1850, Florence historically was and remains a railroad city. Florence is located in a region of South Carolina called the Pee Dee, named after a tribe of Indians who inhabited the area. The local Chamber of Commerce touts Florence as the trade, industrial, medical, transportation, cultural, financial, and educational center of the Pee Dee. Located where Interstate I-95 and I-20 intersect, Florence sees many travelers headed north to New York, south to Florida, east to Myrtle Beach, and west to the Appalachian Mountains.

EXHIBIT 3   Central United Methodist Church Assets and Debt

Year	Value of Church Campus Property	Parsonage & Furniture	Other Assets	Debt
2001	$14,224,880	$436,290	$ 630,931	$2,183,943
2000	$12,365,340	$495,000	$1,138,347	$ 970,000
1999	$ 9,376,600	$475,000	$2,737,150	$ 0
1998	$ 9,298,340	$457,900	$2,143,500	$ 0
1997	$ 8,880,000	$421,000	$ 918,000	$ 0
1996	$ 8,223,700	$432,700	$ 476,997	$ 103,100
1995	$ 8,223,700	$432,700	$ 476,997	$ 188,000
1994	$ 8,223,700	$432,500	$ 535,625	$ 206,105
1993	$ 6,944,000	$213,500	$ 320,000	$ 388,271
1992	$ 7,492,875	$313,000	$ 380,000	$ 458,166
1991	$ 7,492,875	$313,000	$ 380,000	$ 467,532
1990	$ 7,492,875	$313,000	$ 380,000	$ 27,348
1989	$ 6,107,068	$314,000	$ 380,000	$ 526,000

Source: Central United Methodist Church.

EXHIBIT 4   Central United Methodist Annual Budget, 2002

Accounts	Annual Budget (This Year)
EXPENSES	
SALARIES	
005001 – PASTOR	$ 70,600.00
005002 – ASSOCIATE PASTOR	$ 28,900.00
005003 – DIRECTOR CHILDREN'S MINIST	$ 35,000.00
005004 – DIRECTOR YOUTH MINISTRIES	$ 15,900.00
005005 – DIRECTOR ADULT MINISTRIES	$ 22,280.00
005006 – ADMINISTRATIVE SECRETARY	$ 20,000.00
005007 – STAFF SECRETARY	$ 16,940.00
005008 – COMMUNICATIONS DIRECTOR	$ 18,030.00
005010 – FACILITIES MANAGER	$ 26,000.00
005011 – CUSTODIAN-NIGHT	$ 13,395.00
005012 – CUSTODIAN-DAY	$ 13,395.00
005013 – CUSTODIAN/MAID	$ 15,475.00
005014 – MAINTENANCE PERSONAL	$ 17,639.00
005015 – MUSIC DIRECTOR/ORGANIST	$ 50,750.00
005016 – CHILDREN'S MUSIC DIRECTOR	$ 6,170.00
005017 – HANDBELL DIRECTOR	$ 2,429.00
005018 – CHILDREN'S ACCOMPANIST	$ 3,625.00
005019 – CAMP SEXTON DIRECTOR	$ 9,200.00
005021 – VISITOR FOR CHURCH	$ 8,000.00
005022 – DIRECTOR OF YOUNG ADULT MIN.	$ 5,100.00
005025 – BUSINESS MANAGER	$ 26,500.00
005030 – NURSERY WORKERS PAID	$ 17,160.00
005031 – CAMP SEXTON SUMMER STAFF	$ 13,500.00
005057 – FACILITY/CUSTODIAL ASSIST	$ 0.00
005070 – SALARY CONTINGENCY	$ 5,000.00
Total SALARIES	$460,988.00
ALLOWANCES	
005101 – PASTOR REIMBURSEMENT	$ 3,000.00
005102 – ASSOCIATE MINISTER REIMBU	$ 3,000.00
CONTINUING EDUCATION	
005110 – PASTOR'S CONTINUING EDUCA	$ 400.00
005111 – ASSOCIATE MINISTER CONTIN	$ 600.00
005112 – DIR CHILDREN MINIS CONTIN	$ 600.00
005113 – MUSIC DIR/ORGANIST CONTIN	$ 800.00
005114 – CHILDREN'S CHOIR DIR CONT	$ 200.00
005115 – OFFICE STAFF CONTINUING E	$ 1,200.00
005116 – HANDBELL DIR CONTIN EDUCA	$ 200.00
005117 – ADULT DIRECTOR CONT EDUCA	$ 600.00
005118 – YOUTH DIRECT CONTINU EDUC	$ 600.00
005119 – BUSINESS ADMINISTRATOR CONT EDUC	$ 600.00
Total CONTINUING EDUCATION	$ 5,800.00
SOCIAL SECURITY	
005122 – LAY EMPLOYEES SOCIAL SECU	$ 26,210.00
Total SOCIAL SECURITY	$ 26,210.00
HOSPITALIZATION	
005133 – MUSIC DIR/ORG HOSPITALIZA	$ 1,200.00
Total HOSPITALIZATION	$ 1,200.00
UTILITIES	
005140 – PASTOR UTILITIES	$ 7,500.00

Source: Central United Methodist Church.

The city of Florence has more than 33,000 residents, a total that is projected to double by the year 2010. Florence County has 122,000 residents, and it projects growth to 130,000 by 2010. Florence has churches of all denominations. Within three miles of the downtown location of Central United Methodist Church are Baptist, Presbyterian, Lutheran, Episcopal, and other Methodist churches. In the city of Florence, there are five Methodist churches. Many other churches have chosen to locate in areas on the outskirts of town. Thus, as the population of Florence grows, there is increased "competition" for parishioners.

CHURCH ORGANIZATION

Church Staff

Central United Methodist Church is served by a staff of twenty-three. The senior pastor acts as the chief administrative officer of this staff. Other primary staff members include one associate pastor, a music director, a part-time director of children's ministries, a part-time director of adult ministries, a part-time director of young adult ministries, and a part-time director of youth ministries. Clerical and custodian assistants make up most of the remaining staff positions. The church has adopted a strategy of successfully using part-time staff. The benefits of using a part-time staff are apparent in efficiencies and quality of service. This strategy allows the church to hire a person who is skilled in a particular function for the limited amount of time needed for that job. Salaries of these key personnel are presented in Exhibit 5. One change that will happen in the near future is that the half-time director-of-children's-ministries position will become a full-time position. This move will better allow the church to meet the needs of this growing sector of the congregation.

Central United Methodist Church has moved aggressively into Internet communication. The Web site (**www.centralmethodist.net**) is updated on a regular basis. The Web site has pages describing many of the church committees. The senior minister sends a weekly e-mail newsletter to church members, keeping them apprised of church programs and important church news as well as providing a weekly devotional thought. Church committees are informed of meeting schedules and agendas through e-mail. Church members contact staff members with concerns and news via the Web.

EXHIBIT 5   Central United Methodist Church,
Salary for Key Personnel

	1999 Annual Budget	*2000 Annual Budget*	*2001 Annual Budget*
Pastor	$65,156	$68,413	$69,042
Associate Pastor	$26,476	$29,132	$37,240
Director of Children's Ministries	$14,239	$15,662	$16,131
Director of Youth Ministries	$13,726	$14,137	$15,550
Director of Adult Ministries	$14,239	$15,662	$21,840
Director of Young Adult Ministries	$ 0	$ 0	$ 4,500
Business Manager	$ 0	$24,000	$25,500
Administrative Secretary	$18,211	$18,939	$19,507
Staff Secretary	$ 0	$ 0	$16,940
Financial Secretary	$21,118	$17,500	$ 0
Music Director/Organist	$41,419	$43,489	$50,000
Building/Property Superintendent	$18,287	$18,287	$25,000

Source: Central United Methodist Church.

Volunteer Structure

Like most churches, much of the church's work is carried out by volunteers. The committee structure that helps to govern and carry out church programs is headed by the Administrative Board. Under the current structure, all committees report on a bimonthly basis to the Administrative Board. The key committees are listed below along with the primary functions of each.

- *The Board of Trustees* is primarily responsible for the maintenance, upkeep, and repair of the buildings and grounds of the church property.
- *The Finance Committee* must approve all expenditures and all fundraising initiatives/ideas of groups in the church.
- *The Council on Ministries* is the key programming organization of the church, consisting of several committees that develop and implement church programs. See Exhibit 5 for a list of the committees and councils that report to the Council on Ministries, along with their annual budgets.
- *The Staff/Parish Relations Committee* handles all church personnel-related issues.

People are busy. Many want to support the ministries and missions of the church, but they want their efforts to be efficient. Some members have expressed a concern with the current church structure. A problem with the current administrative structure is that many of the church volunteers serve on multiple committees that hear the same reports several times. An example should demonstrate the extent of the problem. The chair of the Outreach Committee helps a subcommittee plan for the building of the Habitat for Humanity house sponsored by the church. This subcommittee reports the plans to the full Outreach Committee. The chair then makes this report a part of the report to the Council on Ministries. The chair finally presents this report to the Administrative Board. Thus, the chair presents this report to four groups. Members of other committees may hear the same report several times.

As the building project comes to its conclusion, the church now turns to two pressing issues. A primary reason for increasing and updating church space was that many new families with young children were joining the church. It is not unusual to baptize several babies each month of the year. As the membership mix continues to become younger, program expansion and support of that program expansion become crucial to the life of the church. Streamlining the organization that supports this program is also important. See the organizational chart in Exhibit 6.

CHARGE TO THE ADMINISTRATIVE BOARD

The senior minister would like the church to consider streamlining the program coordination structure. A resolution presented to the Administrative Board at a recent meeting follows:

> *From the Program Staff: We recommend that a committee of not more than ten be named by the Administrative Board to study the church structure which will best serve Central's Ministry and Mission needs. The study should include investigating other churches' size and a thorough examination of Central's Mission Statement so that the structure is designed to implement our mission. This committee should report {its} findings to the Administrative Board at its late spring meeting.*

The senior minister also provided the board a copy of the church standard from the *Book of Disciplines* of the United Methodist Church.

EXHIBIT 6   Organizational Chart Central United Methodist Church

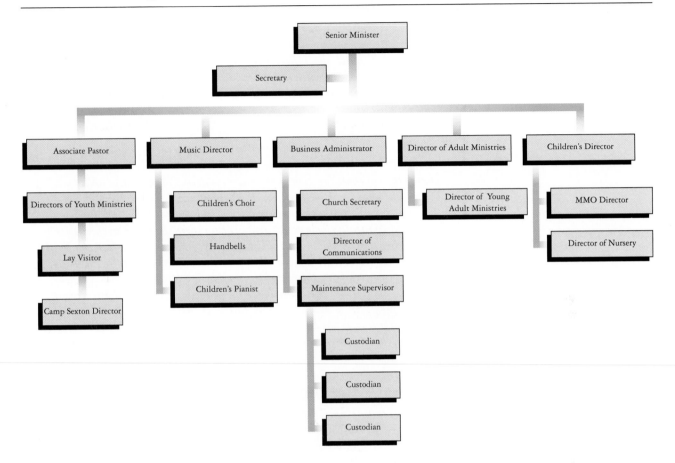

Section VI. Organization and Administration

242. *Primary Tasks*—*The local church shall be organized so that it can pursue its primary task and mission in the context of its own community— reaching out and receiving with joy all who will respond; encouraging people in their relationship with God and inviting them to commit to God's love in Jesus Christ; providing opportunities for them to seek strength and growth in spiritual formation; and supporting them to live lovingly and justly in the power of the Holy Spirit as faithful disciples.*

In carrying out its primary task, it shall be organized so that adequate provision is made for the basic responsibilities: (1) planning and implementing a program of nurture, outreach and witness for persons and families within and without the congregation; (2) providing for effective pastoral and lay leadership; (3) providing for financial support, physical facilities, and the legal obligations of the church; (4) utilizing the appropriate relationships and resources of the district and annual conferences; (5) providing for the proper creation, maintenance, and disposition of documentary record material of the local church; and (6) seeking inclusiveness in all aspects of its life.

243. *Organization*—*The basic organizational plan for the local church shall include provision for the following units: a charge conference, a church council, a committee on pastor-parish relations, a board of trustees, a committee on finance, a committee on lay leadership, and such other elected leaders, commissions councils, committees, and task forces as the charge conference may determine. Every local church shall develop a plan for organizing its administrative and programmatic responsibilities. Each local church shall provide a comprehensive program of nurture, outreach, and witness, along with leadership training, and the planning and administration of the congregation's organizational and temporal life, in accordance with the mission of The United Methodist Church.*

1. *The church council and all other administrative and programmatic structures of the local church shall be amenable to the charge conference. The church council shall function as the executive agency of the charge conference.*
2. *Alternative plans may be developed in accordance with the provisions of paragraph 246.2. Such alternatives include nurture, outreach and witness ministries; administrative council; or administrative board/council on ministries.*
3. *Members of the church council shall be persons of genuine Christian character who love the church, are morally disciplined, are committed to the mandate of inclusiveness in the life of the church, are loyal to the ethical standards of The United Methodist Church set forth in the Social Principles, and are competent to administer its affairs. It shall include youth members chosen according to the same standards as adults. All shall be members of the local church, except where central conference legislation provides otherwise. The pastor shall be the administrative officer and, as such, shall be an ex officio member of all conferences, boards, councils, commissions, committees, and tasks forces, unless otherwise restricted by the Disciplines.*

244. *Information Technology*—*Each local church, as it creates or maintains computerized information and data, is strongly encouraged to confer with its annual conference for recommendations and guidelines as it relates to information technology.*

YOUR TASK

Help the church and the senior pastor develop an administrative programming structure that best fits the mission of the church. Try to develop the structure such that volunteers are not overly taxed with duplicate meetings. Take into consideration the structures used by other churches of similar size. Also keep in mind the suggestions/recommendations of The United Methodist Church. A helpful Web site will be **www.umc.org**. (Other Web sites are **www.centralmethodist.net** and **www.umc.org**.)

ELKINS LAKE BAPTIST CHURCH—2002

Paul R. Reed, William B. Green, and Diane J. Green
Sam Houston State University

www.elbc.com

Comfortably dressed in his denim fatigues and leaning back in his captain's chair surrounded by the extensive library collection that fills his modest-sized office, Dr. Hugghins thought back to 1990 when he became pastor of Elkins Lake Baptist Church (ELBC). When he was "called" to be the ELBC pastor, the church had 487 members who were cramped into a small facility. Now, on the first of September, some eleven years later, church membership has grown to 722, and the church has moved to a new and much larger location. With this growth have come new challenges, and its pastor and members are today faced with issues that were not contemplated in 1990. Is the membership willing to accept the lifestyle and ideas of a newer, younger, and more liberal group of potential members that make up the community? Is the pastor equipped to lead the members of such a broad-based following? Will the fact that the membership is growing enable the church to fund the continued growth of the physical plant and the operating costs? Will ELBC be able to continue to function without a strategic plan? Should ELBC consider the idea of abandoning the Elkins Lake name in hopes of attracting a broader-based membership?

These and other questions seemed to multiply quickly as issues facing ELBC flowed through Dr. Hugghins' mind. No doubt, Hugghins will rely on his library and personal contacts to find some guidance or to find answers to these questions. However, it will take more than one man to deal with these issues.

EXTERNAL ENVIRONMENT

History

Elkins Lake Baptist Church was organized as a new church during a meeting in the Elkins Lake subdivisions clubhouse in 1970. For the next two years, while a sanctuary was being constructed, the new church met in a variety of locations. Initially its members met in the basement of the Elkins Lake clubhouse, where the clubhouse bar was located. Shortly thereafter, the church reached an agreement with the leadership of First Christian Church (Disciples of Christ), who allowed it to use the First Christian Church sanctuary. Churchgoers met at 8:00 on Sunday mornings and again each Sunday evening, since First Christian Church did not schedule a Sunday evening service. Because of scheduling conflicts, the new church moved into some vacant office space in the Huntsville National Bank office building for a few months. In 1972, the group was able to occupy its new building on the south side of Huntsville on State Highway 75. The facility was easily visible from Interstate 45 and from the Elkins Lake subdivision just across Interstate 45. Over the next fourteen years, the church membership grew to the point where it became necessary to build a new sanctuary on the Highway 75 site—or to search for a new location.

EXHIBIT 1   Huntsville's Southern Baptist Church Locations

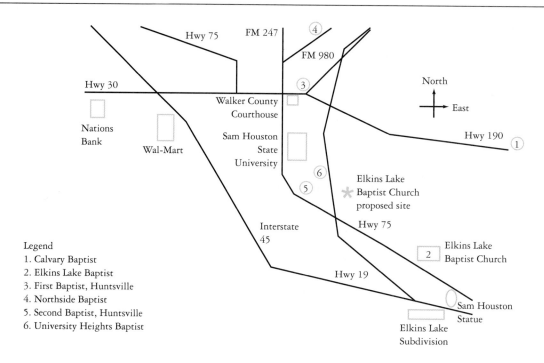

Legend
1. Calvary Baptist
2. Elkins Lake Baptist
3. First Baptist, Huntsville
4. Northside Baptist
5. Second Baptist, Huntsville
6. University Heights Baptist

In 1986, the church membership decided to relocate and voted to purchase a 9.5-acre tract located on Highway 19 on the south side of Huntsville (see Exhibit 1). This location would provide considerable room for growth, and it more centrally located the church within the city of Huntsville, Texas. The land was purchased for $225,000, and it was funded by a bank loan and the church's building fund.

In 1995, the church held a groundbreaking ceremony, and the following March, construction of the new building began. Only the trees that had to be removed were cut, and the revenue generated by the timber sales was applied toward construction costs. Additional funds came from a $620,000 bank loan, collateralized by personal guarantees from church members, and from a bond program, which raised $160,000 from its members. The bonds were repaid when the old church building and property were sold for $300,000. The remaining proceeds from the sale were used to reduce the bank note.

In March 1997, the church moved to its current location on Highway 19 and shortly thereafter acquired an additional 12.5 acres of adjoining land. The new facility included 6,527 square feet of sanctuary space; 1,890 square feet of offices and library space; 7,067 square feet of classroom space; and 2,314 square feet of kitchen, bathrooms, and miscellaneous space; as well as paved parking for 115 vehicles. Additional, spillover parking for about ten vehicles is available on an unpaved portion of the property. The sanctuary is very modern and functional. Interlocking chairs, rather than the kinds of pews that are commonly associated with Southern Baptist churches, were used. The sanctuary space is designed for use as a multifunctional space; it can be converted to nonworship space by simply taking the chairs apart and clearing the floor. Rather than the typical stained glass, the sanctuary windows provide a scenic view of the property, which overlooks a small creek. The Sunday morning service is somewhat nontraditional in that there are no altar flowers or children's sermon. Because many members of ELBC come from church communities where these features were important, these nontraditional features of the sanctuary and the service bother some parishioners. To these more traditional members, a church is just not a Southern Baptist Church without the stained glass, pews, altar flowers, and children's sermon. Conversely, a young family not steeped in Southern Baptist tradition and looking for a church home might consider Elkins Lake Baptist Church a fashionable place of worship.

Temporary buildings were moved from the old church to the present site to be utilized until additional classroom space could eventually be built. Two more temporary buildings were recently acquired to accommodate the growing religious-education space needs. Each of the new buildings has the capacity to hold two classrooms, with twenty people to a classroom. However, lack of space continues to be a problem. Classes have to be held in both the sanctuary and the regular classrooms. When questioned about the shortage of educational space and a possible date for beginning the next stage of construction, Hugghins cleverly remarked, "It is not about running an organization with a lot of amenities. It is about teaching people the word of God—and that can be done in living rooms." Hugghins would feel at home proclaiming "the word" in a large sanctuary, a small office, or in home living rooms. However, Hugghins does have individuals examining funding alternatives, and there are plans to add one more temporary building to the site soon.

Local Area

Huntsville is located along Interstate 45, approximately 70 miles north of Houston and 170 miles south of Dallas/Fort Worth. Bryan/College Station is located 54 miles to the west on Highway 30. When Interstate 45 was constructed in the 1960s, the highway was located about a mile west of Huntsville. During the ensuing 40 years, the geometric center of the town has gravitated toward the interstate. This movement of the town toward the interstate should continue since the city of Huntsville has recently begun construction of a wastewater treatment facility and a north-south arterial on the west side on Interstate 45. This additional infrastructure should stimulate development on the west side of town.

Huntsville, the county seat of Walker County (with a 2000 population of 61,758), in many respects is a typical east Texas county seat, which serves as the trade center for the county and the surrounding rural population. Huntsville, however, is also home to Sam Houston State University (SHSU) and is the headquarters for the Texas Department of Criminal Justice (TDCJ), the largest state agency and the only agency not headquartered in Austin. In addition to the administrative headquarters, five prison units are located within the Huntsville city limits, and two other prison units are located in the county about ten miles north of town. The 2000 census placed the population of Huntsville at 35,078. In addition to the local citizens, the population totals include 8,904 inmates housed in the prisons and all university students residing in Huntsville. TDCJ employs approximately 7,771 personnel to staff the system's administrative headquarters and the seven area prisons. Student enrollment at the university was 12,997 students during the fall 2001 semester, an increase of 5.2% from the fall 2000 semester. Housing data for the fall 2001 semester are not available, but for the fall 2000 semester, 43 percent of the students lived on campus or in the Huntsville/Walker County community. The remaining 57 percent of the students commuted from outside Walker County. The university employs 2,169 faculty and staff. Employment in these two institutions is quite stable. Because the prison population has grown statewide, the local TDCJ administrative staff has also grown. Additional employment is supported by the city, county, school district, Huntsville Memorial Hospital, and by the typical small service, retail, and light industry-type firms present in the community.

Criminal activity in Huntsville is similar to other college towns located in rural communities. In 2000, there were 3,336 reported offenses. Included among those offenses were 921 reported thefts, 314 cases of criminal mischief, 251 cases of public intoxication, 23 cases of disorderly conduct, and 119 cases of DWI. Many of the Sam Houston State University students come from the Houston metropolitan area and find the recreational and social activities available in Huntsville limited.

On the immediate west side of the city, there are three residential communities, the largest being the Elkins Lake subdivision. Elkins, as it commonly called, was originally developed as a retirement community for those who wished to live in a rural setting, but one with the amenities of metropolitan Houston nearby. Elkins originally contained approximately 2,200 home sites. There are about 1,100 homes in Elkins, but because some homes were built on two lots and because other lots, on account of the terrain, can't be developed, less than one-half of the home sites are available for development. During the past several years, the average age of an Elkins Lake resident has declined as more working families with children have purchased homes. Today, only half of the residents of Elkins Lake are retired. Elkins Lake Baptist Church draws a disproportionate number of its members from the Elkins area. Nearly 7 percent of the residents of Elkins are members of ELBC. So the membership has become younger as more young families from Elkins join the church. Spring Lake and Westridge, the other two residential subdivisions, have been "built out" since the late 1980s.

Competition

There are 76 churches, including 15 associated with the Southern Baptist Convention, in Walker County. The 15 Southern Baptist churches have a combined resident membership of 5,641, a Sunday school enrollment of 4,066, and average Sunday school attendance of 1,625. While the resident Baptist membership represents about 15 percent of the nonprison population, on any given Sunday less than 5 percent of the general population is in attendance in the Baptist churches in Walker County. Less than 30 percent of the residents of Huntsville are members of a local church.

ELBC, which is affiliated with the Southern Baptist Convention, faces its strongest membership competition from five other Southern Baptist churches in Huntsville. However, during the last few decades, families have become increasingly willing to select a church on the basis of factors other than "brand name." Location, youth and children's programs, activities for singles, "praise services," and other factors have become increasingly important considerations in church selection.

Dr. Hugghins has served ELBC longer than any of the other pastors. Occasionally, the Baptist preachers get together for discussions, and four of the churches come together annually for Bible study. Hugghins has an off-and-on relationship with the local Ministerial Alliance, an organization composed of all the ministers in town, not just those of the Baptist faith. The main function of the Ministerial Alliance is to organize and promote a community Thanksgiving service. The service is held in a different church each year, with the most recently employed pastor delivering the Thanksgiving message. Three of the other Southern Baptist churches are located in central Huntsville. ELBC is located on the southern perimeter, and the other two churches are on the northern and eastern perimeter of town. Assorted data from the Southern Baptist churches of Huntsville are presented in Exhibits 2 through 7.

EXHIBIT 2　Huntsville Southern Baptist Churches, Membership

Church	2000	1999	1998	1997	1996	1995	1994
Calvary Baptist	588	609	623	779	665	674	646
Elkins Lake Baptist	727	698	799	776	719	708	651
First Baptist	2,426	2,464	2,455	2,481	2,496	2,468	2,415
Northside Baptist	N/A	1,093	1,015	949	825	635	532
Second Baptist	1,028	997	1,007	NA	983	986	1,006
University Heights Baptist	1,810	N/A	1,650	1,602	1,554	1,515	1,677

Source: Tyron Evergreen Baptist Association.

EXHIBIT 3　Huntsville Southern Baptist Churches, Receipts

Church	2000	1999	1998	1997	1996	1995	1994
Calvary Baptist	$ 170,193	$171,426	$271,988	$210,151	$233,732	$248,724	$202,314
Elkins Lake Baptist	$ 433,928	$455,823	$522,869	$346,074	$357,174	$317,229	$255,922
First Baptist	$1,304,814	$885,618	$833,406	$812,551	$788,394	$776,039	$672,594
Northside Baptist	N/A	$289,440	$356,862	$301,737	$249,936	$221,000	$181,280
Second Baptist	$ 409,154	$231,766	$152,869	NA	$110,195	$159,632	$115,963
University Heights Baptist	$ 710,562	N/A	$409,942	$915,620	$660,947	$453,675	$407,454

Source: Tyron Evergreen Baptist Association.

EXHIBIT 4　Huntsville Southern Baptist Churches, A.M. Worship Service Attendance

Church	2000	1999	1998	1997	1996	1995	1994
Calvary Baptist	150	300	NA	170	132	170	300
Elkins Lake Baptist	211	203	228	207	210	278	192
First Baptist	406	245	300	384	417	464	474
Northside Baptist	N/A	350	350	375	325	275	225
Second Baptist	175	175	135	NA	84	80	95
University Heights Baptist	550	N/A	550	600	500	500	500

Source: Tyron Evergreen Baptist Association.

EXHIBIT 5　Huntsville Southern Baptist Churches, Sunday School Enrollment

Church	2000	1999	1998	1997	1996	1995	1994
Calvary Baptist	157	197	251	213	223	297	351
Elkins Lake Baptist	404	388	407	393	421	424	398
First Baptist	800	777	997	1,034	1,094	1,139	1,066
Northside Baptist	N/A	226	292	290	292	260	176
Second Baptist	144	168	80	NA	109	131	128
University Heights Baptist	1,111	N/A	979	942	940	942	1,064

Source: Tyron Evergreen Baptist Association.

EXHIBIT 6   Huntsville Southern Baptist Churches, Total Young Adult Sunday School Enrollment (Ages 18–34)

Church	2000	1999	1998	1997	1996	1995	1994
Calvary Baptist	21	35	35	34	57	47	42
Elkins Lake Baptist	96	126	126	90	77	117	51
First Baptist	126	67	229	300	292	237	156
Northside Baptist	N/A	60	34	49	57	56	12
Second Baptist	16	19	17	NA	8	0	12
University Heights Baptist	256	N/A	347	275	143	155	119

Source: Tyron Evergreen Baptist Association.

EXHIBIT 7   Huntsville Southern Baptist Churches, Value of Church Property

Church	2000	1999	1998	1997	1996	1995	1994
Calvary Baptist	$ 650,000	$ 650,000	$ 650,000	$ 650,000	$ 650,000	$ 650,000	$ 650,000
Elkins Lake Baptist	$2,085,400	$2,400,000	$1,250,000	$1,600,000	$ 800,000	$ 800,000	$ 800,000
First Baptist	$4,473,000	$4,426,700	$4,473,000	$4,472,909	$4,600,000	$4,600,000	$4,472,909
Northside Baptist	N/A	$1,500,000	$1,500,000	$1,500,000	$1,500,000	$1,500,000	$ 265,000
Second Baptist	$1,235,000	$1,235,000	$2,000,000	NA	$1,275,000	$1,275,000	$1,275,000
University Heights Baptist	N/A	N/A	$2,800,000	$2,800,000	$1,700,000	$1,700,000	$1,700,000

Source: Tyron Evergreen Baptist Association.

INTERNAL ENVIRONMENT

Elkins Lake Baptist Church is incorporated under the state laws of Texas and tends to operate under a constitution and bylaws. It follows the Southern Baptist doctrine, which tends to follow the literal descriptions and teachings of the Bible.

Personnel and Organized Committees

Besides Dr. Hugghins, ELBC has two other full-time staff members—a youth director and a financial secretary—and ten part-time employees. Three part-time employees, including a choir director, organist, and pianist, are in charge of the music program. Three interim educational directors, an education secretary, two nursery school workers, and a custodian make up the remainder of the part-time staff. The church also heavily depends on volunteers from the membership to provide services (ministries) ranging from singing in the choir, teaching classes, parenting programs, and providing nursery care to acting as a substitute pianist. The church is always looking for volunteers to undertake new ministries as new opportunities for ministry emerge.

The ELBC has for several years considered adopting a formal personnel policy manual, but this manual has remained in draft form and has never been adopted. One result of this lack of action is that there are no formal guidelines for committees. Hugghins feels that revisions need to be made to the church constitution, but he has not initiated any changes because he feels the controversy created would exceed the benefit of such changes. For example, he would prefer a constitution that makes no gender references. He also thinks that the duties of the committees should not be specifically outlined in the constitution in order to create more of a here-is-what-matters, go-and-do-it attitude.

He believes that it should be made clear to each committee what is important, and the committee, in turn, should be empowered to handle what needs to be done.

The church treasurer and the Finance and Budget Committee direct the church's financial affairs. The records are maintained and reported by the financial secretary. The annual budget is established through a process requiring the various committees and pastor to present their respective needs and anticipated expenditures for the coming year. Revenue projections are adjusted for attendance trends. When the budget is finalized, it is presented to the membership for vote. (Financial statements are shown in Exhibit 8.)

The pastor looks to a panel of deacons for general policy guidance, but he is given great latitude in exercising control over the church's affairs. There are a total of 29 deacons (and five deacon emeritis) who serve three-year terms. The pastor and his deacons use a participative management style. Normally, the pastor confers with the deacons before recommending a policy change to the membership, who then finalize the decision by majority vote.

The Pastor's Outlook

When Hugghins came to Elkins Lake Baptist Church, he assumed that it was a progressive church. Several facts had led him to this conclusion: the church's method of providing a music ministry, the fact that the education director was a woman, the fact that the preceding pastor was well-educated, and the fact that Huntsville was a university town. Within a month of his arrival, Hugghins began to see that the membership was more conservative than he anticipated. But he still believes ELBC to be the most diverse Baptist church in town.

EXHIBIT 8   ELBC Financial Statement

	As of December 31,						
	1994	*1995*	*1996*	*1997*	*1998*	*1999*	*2000*
BANK BALANCES							
Checking	$ 5,511	$ 10,766	$ 5,000	$ 30,538	$ 17,193	($ 1,408)	$ 7,787
Building Fund	36,534	28,922	94,121	56,369	29,561	17,857	3,749
Cert. of Deposit		32,500	79,709	30,000	20,378	49,003	25,000
Special/Design.					26,884	51,275	102,354
Total Receipts, Year to Date	255,922	317,229	357,174	346,074	522,869	455,823	433,928
Projected Budget Needs	270,286	227,148	278,388	320,382	422,877	454,321	460,565
Percentage of Collections Over Expenses (Under)	(94.69%)	139.66%	128.30%	108.02%	123.65%	100.3%	(94.22%)
EXPENDITURES							
100 Missions	$ 42,621	$ 55,384	$ 54,447	$ 61,200	$ 63,562	$ 77,683	$ 68,884
200 Personnel	135,252	145,417	136,255	159,583	174,808	201,226	206,878
300 Music Ministry	2,608	3,902	3,205	3,564	3,278	5,340	4,357
400 Education Ministry	8,821	11,255	8,594	10,826	18,871	11,300	24,867
500 College and Youth	2,743	3,783	1,054	2,841	1,762	15,300	7,388
600 Church Administration	14,061	15,318	15,666	20,874	19,982	22,300	23,725
700 Building and Equipment	24,599	23,856	28,110	30,313	42,956	38,900	42,238
800 Debt Retirement	18,732	18,863	17,186	18,715	82,957	82,224	82,228
900 Miscellaneous	412	431	227	458	1,402		
Total Expenditures	$249,849	$278,209	$264,744	$308,374	$409,578	$454,323	$460,565

Source: Elkins Lake Baptist Church.

Hugghins, a relatively liberal man for a Southern Baptist preacher, would like to see the church move toward a more "modern Southern Baptist atmosphere," which would include female deacons and ministers, a less literal interpretation of the Bible, and increased pastoral authority. He is well read and regularly quotes authors of other denominations, causing some members to criticize him for not quoting more Baptist authors in his sermons.

Hugghins recognizes that Huntsville is strategically located for considerable growth possibilities. Because of the availability of land and the existing community infrastructure, he is convinced that ELBC is situated to fill the church needs of those looking for a modern, progressive Baptist church. Hugghins feels that ELBC's primary growth will come from members bringing friends to church. But growth can also come from follow-up visits to visitors who just "show up."

A few members, including some large contributors, were lost to more conservative churches over the years. One former member feels not only that Hugghins is "too modern," but also that he likes to do "things his own way, and this is not particularly what the members want." Some members feel that Dr. Hugghins should consider a change in style and take a more conservative approach. For a time during the mid-1990s, Hugghins found himself the subject of a controversy between the old versus new members—as well as old versus new ideas. He feels that he has not found a common element to deal with everyone (i.e., old members, new members, Elkins residents, and non-Elkins residents), but most of the dissidents have now left and found a church that better suits their religious views.

Originally, the target market for Elkins Lake Baptist Church was a retired, upper-middle-class individual. At present, the target group is shifting toward the working middle class. Only 19 percent of the current members are retired, whereas 67 percent are families with children. One individual, who has been a member for over twenty years, feels that the target market has changed, although this person doesn't recall this ever being openly stated or even discussed.

Hugghins has found that some long-time members are resistant to new members, their ideas, and their more liberal ways. Hugghins quotes a co-worker trying to explain to a long-time member, "It's not all about you. We need to think about what is best for the member as a whole and not what makes them 'most comfortable.'"

Hugghins fears that some misperceptions may occur because of the name, Elkins Lake Baptist Church. He is afraid that non-members will feel that the church is for members of the Elkins Lake subdivision only—and for the upper-middle class of Huntsville. He has toyed with the idea of renaming the church.

One of Hugghins' concerns is how the church responds to those young adults who "dropped out of church" during their formative years, but who are now married, have families, and feel the need to have their families involved in church. "Unfortunately," says Hugghins, "these dropouts just stopped [being] religious many years ago. For some, their last meaningful religious experience was singing songs with a guitar around a campfire at church camp. Now they are adults [but] with the religious mindset of a teenager. How the church responds to their needs will be a real challenge."

Outreach Programs

ELBC has developed several outreach programs to attract new members, especially young families and children. Hugghins considers the active and visible ministries with leadership from the congregation to be a real asset for the church. A Sunday morning Bible study is conducted at the Elkins Lake clubhouse for those individuals looking for a more interactive worship session. Approximately fifteen individuals from various denominations regularly attend this Bible study.

ELBC also has a presence on the Sam Houston State University's campus. ELBC is affiliated with the Baptist Student Union (BSU) and holds lunches and services twice a year in a facility on campus. ELBC also works with the Walker County Jail and the Gulf Coast Trade Center (GCTC), a facility working for the rehabilitation of juvenile delinquents. The church regularly holds two classes at the GCTC to reach these troubled youths. In addition, the church supports various missions; for example, it is a sponsor church for the First Heritage Church in Houston. The church also makes its presence known at retirement facilities to bring the word of God to elderly individuals who are immobile. It is important to mention that all of these outreach programs are staffed by volunteers from the church.

Marketing

Dr. Hugghins is quite proud of ELBC's marketing efforts, which consist of a weekly radio broadcast of the Sunday morning service, newspaper advertisements, two thirty-second radio advertisements during each Huntsville High School home football game, and seasonal radio greetings during the Christmas season. Hugghins occasionally authors an inspirational column that the local paper eagerly publishes. The Baptist Student Union promotes the ELBC on the SHSU campus with flyers about special events and announcements concerning the activities of the church.

ELBC has two signs located near the front of the property. One is a textured concrete ground sign, parallel to Highway 19, that is four feet high and five feet wide and is located between the two entrances. The sign, which provides only the church and pastor's name, is difficult to see because of the foliage, and it is also hard to read because the lettering is small and colored in shades of gray. During the past year, the church erected a new elevated sign that is perpendicular to the highway, is much more visible, and is easy to read for southbound drivers. This sign, colored in red and blue with a white background, contains the name of the church, an arrow pointing toward its location, and times of service.

Although the church is located on busy State Highway 19, buildings are located on the reverse slope of a hill that is away from the highway. The front portion of the building site is covered with large pine trees, allowing motorists to pass by without noticing the church. During the next five years, the Texas Department of Transportation is expected to make Highway 19 a four-lane divided highway, which will make it impossible for southbound traffic to turn into the church property; but if a feeder road is constructed, as is currently planned, accessibility to the property will be enhanced.

Preparing for Future Growth

Southern Baptists have long held to the strategy of going to Sunday school from early childhood through adolescence. Therefore, great emphasis is usually placed in properly designing and utilizing educational space. Two rules of thumb are normally used: (1) to provide approximately forty-five square feet of floor space per person and (2) to maintain an average Sunday-school attendance of more than 80 percent of a church's capacity. The "80% Rule" also stands true for worship services (see Exhibit 9).

Hugghins has also utilized today's technology. He had a Web site developed that is fully operational for the church to serve as a forum that informs both members of the church and also potential members of the goings-on of the church and any special events. The pastor recognizes how fast things are changing and wants ELBC to keep up. "But is the church ready to follow?" he wonders.

EXHIBIT 9   Sunday School/Worship Attendance by Month for Elkins Lake Baptist Church

	1998		1999		2000		2001	
Month	Sunday School Attendance	Church Attendance	Sunday School Attendance	Church Attendance	Sunday School Attendance	Church Attendance	Sunday School Attendance	Church Attendance
Jan.	N/A	204	183	243	179	208	175	221
Feb.	N/A	235	188	226	182	224	186	221
March	N/A	308	170	201	169	210	172	216
April	N/A	274	161	261	164	225	171	250
May	N/A	251	158	208	168	215	148	191
June	N/A	247	158	235	163	208	156	189
July	N/A	217	151	176	171	215		
Aug.	N/A	261	171	219	185	243		
Sept.	N/A	229	184	204	175	217		
Oct.	N/A	251	180	219	173	209		
Nov.	N/A	218	160	204	173	216		
Dec.	N/A	216	172	218	148	187		

Source: Elkins Lake Baptist Church newsletter, *The Window.*

BIBLIOGRAPHY

Elkins Lake Baptist Church. *Constitution and Bylaws.*

Elkins Lake Baptist Church. *The Window* (1997, 1998, 1999, 2001).

Huntsville Police Department. *Consolidated Monthly Report* (December 2000).

Huntsville—Walker County Chamber of Commerce. *Community/Economic Profile for 2001.* <http://chamber.huntsville.tx.us/economy.html>

Judicial District Community Supervision and Corrections Department. *Fiscal Year 1998 Annual Report.* Author, no date.

Tyron Evergreen Baptist Association of Texas. Minutes of the 91st Annual Session (Conroe, Texas, 1994).

Tyron Evergreen Baptist Association of Texas. Minutes of the 92nd Annual Session (Conroe, Texas, 1995).

Tyron Evergreen Baptist Association of Texas. Minutes of the 93rd Annual Session (Conroe, Texas, 1996).

Tyron Evergreen Baptist Association of Texas. Minutes of the 94th Annual Session (Conroe, Texas, 1997).

Tyron Evergreen Baptist Association of Texas. Minutes of the 95th Annual Session (Conroe, Texas, 1998).

Tyron Evergreen Baptist Association. 1999 *Book of Reports*, 98th Annual Session (Conroe, Texas, 1999).

Tyron Evergreen Baptist Association. 2000 Book of Reports, 99th Annual Session (Conroe, Texas, 2000).

U.S. Census Bureau. State and County *Quick Facts* (Walker County, TX: <http://quickfacts.census.gov/qfd/>).

WINN-DIXIE STORES, INC.—2002

Brian Kinard
Mississippi State University

WIN

www.winn-dixie.com

> *Forty or fifty years ago, grandmother telephoned in a daily grocery order to a neighborhood market. It was delivered to her kitchen door later that same day. She was billed monthly.*
>
> *It was fairly common in those days. It was called progress.*
>
> *Cars, suburbia and "super" markets put an end to it. That was also called progress (Lind, 2000, Para. 1–2).*

Organized in Florida on December 26, 1928, Winn-Dixie Stores, Inc. is one of the nation's largest food retailers and one of the largest supermarket chains in the southeastern region of the United States. With over 1,000 stores in fourteen states, Winn-Dixie's (WD) retail stores sell groceries, meats, seafood, fresh produce, deli/bakery products, pharmaceutical products, and general merchandise items. WD also offers broad lines of merchandise and services, such as company-operated photo labs and in-store banks operated by independent third parties.

Winn-Dixie Stores, Inc. has found out recently that "winning *Dixie*" is not easy. For the past three years, the company has faced a steady decline in sales and market share. In fact, in order to fend off the new competition of mass merchandisers-turned-grocers Wal-Mart and Kmart, WD has remodeled and sometimes closed unprofitable locations. Underperforming assets were a drain on the organization, so by abandoning them, WD has lowered overall company costs. These restructuring and remodeling expenditures, costing approximately $550 million, has significantly raised WD's long-term debt. This combination of declining sales, higher debt, and the events associated with September 11, 2001, could harm WD further. In fact, to save on administrative costs, WD announced in September 2001 that there would be a shift from monthly to quarterly dividend payments. These decisions, coupled with lower than expected earnings and a plummeting stock price, have left investors skeptical about the future of the company.

HISTORY

In 1914, William M. Davis ran a small general store in Burley, Indiana. Davis' store, typical of a country town general store in that day, carried a selection of merchandise and operated on a charge and deliver basis. Then one day, another merchant came to town and opened a cash-and-carry grocery store down the street. Soon, the new merchant had the cash and Mr. Davis was left with the "carry." Quick to see the advantages of this new method of merchandising, Davis purchased a grocery store in 1925 and brought his family to Miami, Florida.

Davis died in 1934, and his four sons assumed active management of the business. Each of the brothers in his own way contributed to WD's solid growth: A. D.'s strength was in merchandising, J. E.'s was in finance and investment, Austin was a troubleshooter, and Tine had the personality for public relations and for pioneering new divisions. Following the progressive principles set by their father, his sons saw the business grow; and then in 1939, the four brothers purchased control of the 78 Winn & Lovett stores located in Florida and Georgia. In 1944, headquarters were established in Jacksonville, Florida, and the chain assumed the Winn & Lovett name.

After World War II, many retail chains in the Southeast began to join up with the Davis brothers. The company became Winn-Dixie Stores, Inc. in 1955. In 1967, eleven stores were acquired in Nassau and Freeport in the Bahamas, and in 1976, the retail assets of Kimbell, Inc. were acquired, adding Buddies and Foodway retail stores and facilities in the Southwest.

In 1995, WD acquired 25 Thriftway food and drug stores in the Greater Cincinnati, Ohio, area. The death of A. D. Davis on June 11, 1995, brought an end to WD's founding generation of Davis brothers. Chairman A. Dano Davis carries the Davis family legacy into its third generation. Winn-Dixie Stores, Inc., like many other large American businesses, has grown steadily from modest beginnings, due in large part to its strong leadership and the combined efforts of many people working together as a team (Winn-Dixie Stores, Inc., 2001).

CORPORATE MISSION STATEMENT

Winn-Dixie's mission statement states:

> *Winn-Dixie's mission is to innovate and implement a better and more efficient way of meeting the changing needs of our customers. Winn-Dixie strives to employ customer-oriented associates and provide them with the opportunity for training and promotion, while offering pay, benefits and working conditions equal to or better than those generally available in the food industry. Winn-Dixie deals fairly with customers, associates and suppliers in order to merit their continued patronage and support. The company supports civic and charitable efforts for the betterment of the communities in which we live and work. Winn-Dixie operates a financially sound business by energetically increasing sales and controlling expenses, for the purpose of earning a reasonable return for all who have an interest in the growth of our Company. By fulfilling the above commitment, we will ensure our future growth and profitability (Winn-Dixie Stores, Inc., 2001).*

CORPORATE VISION STATEMENT

Winn-Dixie's vision statement, as provided in its 2001 *Annual Report* (p. 6), states:

> *Winn-Dixie's vision is to be the best supermarket operator in the neighborhood, as well as the most efficient food operator in the industry.*

EXTERNAL ISSUES

September 11, 2001

In the wake of the September 11, 2001, terrorist attacks on the United States, the world economy has continued to decelerate, led by the U.S. economic slowdown. Asia has been weakened by the slowdown in exports to the United States, while Japan seems headed back into a recession. This is the first concerted world slowdown since the 1974–1977 period (Wyss, 2001). This slowdown in the economy could actually be good news for WD and other traditional grocers, as market share lost to restaurants and convenience stores during the economic growth period may now be regained. Consumer spending patterns are likely to change, since more individuals will be watching their budgets and will start preparing more traditional meals at home.

Food Industry Issues

During 2000, U.S. grocery sales grew by 3.4 percent, reaching $570 billion. U.S. grocery business operators are becoming much more efficient by offering better product merchandising, consolidating, and making better use of capital by relocating, renovating, and expanding existing stores ("Supermarket and Drug Store Industry," 2001).

As of June 27, 2001, Winn-Dixie had completely implemented the restructuring program that was announced in April 2000, according to the *Annual Report* (2001). In an effort to lower costs, WD closed 112 stores as well as certain manufacturing and distribution centers, all of which had been underperforming assets. WD revamped and reformatted store layouts for more than half the stores in the chain, resizing key departments to increase profitability. Not only do these renovations enhance store physical looks, but they also appeal to consumers who prefer to buy clean and well-designed products. These restructuring initiatives improve the retail stores' look and increase overall operational efficiency. In fact, WD is currently saving approximately $400 million a year, having completed the restructuring expenditures of $552.2 million by the end of fiscal 2001.

New Competition, More Acquisition

The grocery industry is now facing the new threat of supercenter and club store concepts. Wal-Mart, Kmart, and Target are learning the grocery business and are now formidable competitors in the retail grocery industry. Wal-Mart Supercenter grocery sales, 30 percent of total store sales, have reached $17.1 billion, making it the fourth largest food retailer in the U.S. (Griffith, 2001). To combat this threat, WD has acquired regional grocery chains in growing markets.

Acquiring existing chains is usually cheaper than building new units. Mergers and acquisitions substantially lower the risk involved in organizational expansion into new markets, as prior customer knowledge is readily available with little market research. Faster organizational expansion is possible through acquisitions, whereas mergers often tend to lower operating costs through shared marketing/advertising, manufacturing, and distribution facilities. Cost/benefit analyses are necessary in an industry in which pennies actually do matter. Intense competition among supermarkets for the consumer dollar is best demonstrated in profit margins that continue to be around 1 cent on each dollar of sales. That's right—one solid cent! That means that $100 in sales would produce a mere $1 in profit. According to the Food Marketing Institute, for fiscal years 1999 and 2000, the industry's after-tax net profit reached 1.18 percent, as seen in Exhibit 1. In fact, over the last decade, supermarket industry profits have averaged a mere 0.89 percent a year.

Acquisitions will play a key role in WD's strategy in 2002. Since January 2000, WD has acquired nine Gooding's supermarkets in the Orlando area, a core market that offers the potential for sales growth. Also, WD acquired 68 stores and 32 fuel centers owned by Mississippi-based Jitney-Jungle. The acquired store base, which is served by two of WD's existing distribution centers, has been easily integrated into the existing division structure. On September 5, 2001, WD changed the name of 48 Jitney-Jungle stores to Winn-Dixie, as a result of the positive customer reaction to the WD brand products and WD brand beef. Gooding's and Jitney-Jungle join a family of brands that also include Winn-Dixie, Save Rite, ThriftWay, and City Markets (Winn-Dixie Stores, Inc., 2001). Competition continually affects the grocery industry, and these measures were a necessity if WD was to stay competitive. This cutthroat competition is reflected in Exhibit 2, which shows that six companies have fallen from the top ten since 1980. This table clearly indicates how Winn-Dixie, falling from fifth in 1980 to tenth in 2000, has been affected by the impact of mass-merchandisers that have entered the market.

EXHIBIT 1 Net Profit as a Percentage of Sales

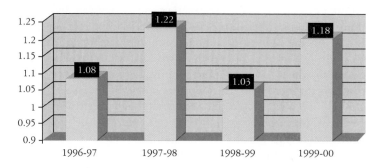

Source: *FMI Annual Financial Review* (1999–2000), p. 18.

INDUSTRY TRENDS

Online Sales

According to figures released by eMarketer, "Online grocery sales will climb to $33.6 billion by the year 2002, an increase of 3360 percent versus 1998." eMarketer also predicts that "online groceries will achieve a penetration rate of 15–20 percent of U.S. households by the year 2007." Are these numbers actually achievable? Apart from the convenience of online shopping, there is a technological factor, which puts new tools in the hands of shoppers. Online grocery shoppers can now sort and compare by price and nutritional value, making it possible to tilt previously brand-loyal consumers to cheaper options. However, it's difficult to predict the success of these Internet grocers because of the heavy capital requirements necessary to compete. Companies need to invest heavily in a delivery infrastructure to compete with traditional supermarket chains. A typical problem for these companies is same-day local delivery, which usually reflects 10 to 12 percent of the total grocery bill (**www.economy.com**). The current low volume and

EXHIBIT 2 Top Ten Supermarket Companies

1980	*1990*	*2000*
Safeway	American	Kroger
Kroger	Kroger	Wal-Mart Supercenters
A&P	Safeway	Albertson's
Lucky	A&P	Safeway
Winn-Dixie	Winn-Dixie	SUPERVALU
American	Albertson's	Ahold USA
Jewel	Penn Traffic	Fleming
Grand Union	SGC	Delhaize America
Albertson's	Publix	Loblaw
Supermarket Gen.	Ahold USA	Winn-Dixie

Source: *Supermarket News* (2001).

usage by consumers make operating these types of companies very expensive, and the current prognosis suggests that the future is bleak.

"Super" Growth

Supercenter growth is expected to continue well into the future. Exhibit 3 depicts the projected growth of supercenters through 2005. Consumers are embracing the idea of shopping for packaged grocery items at a general merchandise store such as Super Wal-Mart, Big-K, and SuperTarget. Competing on the basis of price and service, WD has been able to hold on by increasing customer service and in-store services to complement the grocery shopping experience. Grocers, including WD, are starting to place small banking centers within stores, where customers can fill out loan forms or do other banking tasks. This win-win strategy potentially increases the foot traffic for a grocery retailer, while increasing financial transactions for the bank.

Where's the Loyalty?

Supermarket chains have increased the introduction of private brand labels to compete with national brands in an effort to target price-sensitive customers. In light of the economic downturn, price-conscious consumers are more wary of overspending than previously. Purchases of store or lower-priced brands, instead of national brands, decreased one percentage point from 1999. More than half of all consumers—51 percent—are buying private brand labels "every time" or "fairly often" when they shop ("Spending and Saving Money," 2001).

WD has an opportunity to capitalize on this trend. The WD product line carries higher profit margins than the comparable national brands; at the same time, such lines promote customer loyalty. WD has one of the leading store-brand programs in the industry. WD Chek soda, for example, holds a leading position in several markets, outselling some prominent national brands (Winn-Dixie Stores, Inc., 2001).

INTERNAL ISSUES

New Look, New Ideas

A pleasant customer shopping experience heavily depends on clean, well-stocked, customer-friendly retail stores. Creating a new look for WD stores is a top priority for senior management. WD's store base has been revitalized—more than 60 percent of the stores are new or have been remodeled in the past five years. Nearly 50 percent of the stores have been improved in the past year alone. WD is already achieving increasingly accurate inventory tracking and greater purchasing leverage because of the new centralized procurement

EXHIBIT 3	Projected Number of Supercenters by 2005
Wal-Mart	1,400
Kmart	200
Meijer	180
Fred Meyer	180
SuperTarget	60
TOTAL	2,020

Source: Griffith (2001).

system. New concepts will be added, such as pet centers, soft drink and snack centers, household cleaning sections, and baby-needs centers. New growth opportunities range from pharmacy operations in stores to fuel centers, such as those acquired as part of Jitney-Jungle. Also, WD has several profitable liquor stores in operation and holds additional liquor licenses for future expansion. By aggressively building new and larger locations, remodeling and enlarging existing locations, and offering an expanded line of merchandise and services, WD seeks continued growth (Winn-Dixie Stores, Inc., 2001).

On October 3, 2001, WD unveiled a multimillion dollar ad campaign—the "Real Deal"—to communicate a new brand position. The Real Deal is a part of the company's continuous initiative to increase brand awareness and market share. The campaign addresses WD core competencies of offering real good food, to real good people, at a real good price. This effort reflects a committed approach in the transformation of the company to the new WD.

Areas of Operations

As indicated in Exhibit 4, WD currently operates supermarket and Marketplace superstores in Florida, Georgia, North and South Carolina, Alabama, Mississippi, Louisiana, Kentucky, Ohio, Tennessee, Indiana, Virginia, Texas, and Oklahoma. WD also operates twelve City Markets and Winn-Dixie Stores in the Bahamas. In addition, WD operates twenty facilities that produce or process company products as follows: coffee, tea and spices, carbonated and noncarbonated drinks, crackers, corn snacks and cookies, frozen pizza, sausage, luncheon and smoked meats, mayonnaise and salad dressings, preserves and peanut butter, and eggs and dairy products (Winn-Dixie Stores, Inc., 2001).

Financial Overview

Winn-Dixie's 1997–2001 balance sheets are provided in Exhibit 5. Note that the company took on $697 million in long-term debt in 2001.

EXHIBIT 4   Store Locations

State	Total	Winn-Dixie	Marketplace	Thriftway	Jitney-Jungle	Sack & Save	City Meat Markets	Buddies	Save Rite
Florida	436	61	372						3
Alabama	118	39	74		5				
North Carolina	109	53	56						
Georgia	94	13	81						
Louisiana	79	18	60		1				
Texas	71	14	56					1	
Mississippi	69	7	12		42	8			
South Carolina	62	24	38						
Kentucky	40	6	29	5					
Virginia	28	10	18						
Ohio	17			17					
Bahamas	12	3					9		
Tennessee	12	4	8						
Oklahoma	5	4	1						
Indiana	1		1						
Total	1,153	256	806	22	48	8	9	1	3

Source: Winn-Dixie Stores, Inc. (2001).

EXHIBIT 5   WINN-DIXIE STORES, INC. Annual Balance Sheet
(in millions, except book value per share)

	June 30,				
	2001	*2000*	*1999*	*1998*	*1997*
ASSETS					
Cash & Equivalents	121.06	29.57	24.74	23.56	14.12
Receivables	109.15	107.42	188.31	146.16	175.68
Notes Receivable	0.00	0.00	0.00	0.00	0.00
Inventories	1,198.60	1,141.40	1,425.09	1,404.91	1,249.21
Other Current Assets	170.37	193.51	159.83	161.14	148.96
Total Current Assets	**1,599.20**	**1,471.92**	**1,797.99**	**1,735.79**	**1,587.97**
Net Property & Equipment	1,146.65	1,034.49	1,222.63	1,169.84	1,128.68
Investments & Advances	0.00	0.00	128.52	38.78	88.08
Other Noncurrent Assets	0.00	0.00	0.00	0.00	0.00
Deferred Charges	106.14	166.44	0.00	22.62	22.13
Intangibles	92.87	18.79	0.00	0.00	0.00
Deposits & Other Assets	96.79	55.43	0.00	101.66	94.55
Total Assets	**3,041.67**	**2,747.09**	**3,149.14**	**3,068.71**	**2,921.41**
LIABILITIES & SHAREHOLDERS' EQUITY					
Notes Payable	0.00	235.00	465.00	420.00	380.00
Accounts Payable	599.85	575.87	662.17	660.53	604.03
Current Portion Long-Term Debt	4.29	0.00	0.00	0.00	0.00
Current Portion Capital Leases	3.27	2.84	2.75	2.90	3.02
Accrued Expenses	373.96	367.63	331.20	339.86	312.41
Income Taxes Payable	24.29	85.60	10.73	12.11	32.92
Other Current Liabilities	144.23	154.59	75.46	71.77	60.22
Total Current Liabilities	**1,149.90**	**1,421.55**	**1,547.32**	**1,507.20**	**1,392.61**
Mortgages	0.00	0.00	0.00	0.00	0.00
Deferred Taxes/Income	49.02	0.00	0.00	0.00	0.00
Convertible Debt	0.00	0.00	0.00	0.00	0.00
Long-Term Debt	697.41	0.00	0.00	0.00	0.00
Noncurrent Capital Leases	28.95	32.23	38.49	48.58	54.03
Other Noncurrent Liabilities	344.71	425.46	152.25	144.04	137.28
Minority Interest (Liabilities)	0.00	0.00	0.00	0.00	0.00
Total Liabilities	**2,270.01**	**1,879.25**	**1,738.06**	**1,699.83**	**1,583.92**
SHAREHOLDERS' EQUITY					
Preferred Stock	0.00	0.00	0.00	0.00	0.00
Common Stock (Par)	140.46	140.83	148.57	148.53	148.88
Capital Surplus	0.00	0.00	0.00	0.00	0.00
Retained Earnings	634.69	727.00	1,259.59	1,220.35	1.188.62
Other Equity	(3.50)	0.00	2.90	0.00	0.00
Treasury Stock	0.00	0.00	0.00	0.00	0.00
Total Shareholders' Equity	771.65	867.83	1,411.07	1,368.88	1,337.49
Total Liabilities & Shareholders' Equity	**3,041.67**	**2,747.09**	**3,149.14**	**3,068.71**	**2,921.41**
Total Common Equity	771.65	867.83	1,411.07	1,368.88	1,337.49
Average Shares	N/A	145.79	148.24	150.04	150.29
Book Value per Share	5.49	6.01	9.49	9.22	8.98

Source: Zack's Investment Research (2001).

The annual income statement for Winn-Dixie Stores, Inc. is depicted in Exhibit 6. Sales for fiscal 2001, a 52-week year, were $12.9 billion, compared to fiscal 2000's $13.7 billion (also a 52-week year), and fiscal 1999's $14.1 billion (a 53-week year). This reflects a decrease of 5.8 percent for fiscal 2001, a decrease of 3.1 percent for fiscal 2000, and an increase of 3.8 percent in 1999. Sales decreased largely as a result of the elimination of unprofitable sales departments, the elimination of unprofitable sales items in remaining departments, and a reduction in the number of 24-hour stores. WD has substantially completed its planned store retrofits, resulting in labor savings and other efficiencies. The store retrofits have enhanced WD's competitive position and may positively affect WD's sales during fiscal 2002.

As a percentage of sales, gross profit margins were 26.8 percent, 27.2 percent, and 27.6 percent in fiscal 2001, 2000, and 1999, respectively. Gross profit dollars have decreased in the current year partially as a result of the closing of 112 stores as part of management's restructuring plan. In addition, gross profit has been negatively affected by the elimination of high gross-profit, yet unprofitable, sales departments (Winn-Dixies Stores, Inc., 2001).

PUTTING THE CUSTOMER FIRST

Delivering what the customer wants represents the future of WD. Customer service, attractive pricing, and modern store environment play vital roles in delivering a positive

EXHIBIT 6   WINN-DIXIE STORES, INC. Annual Income Statement
(in millions except earnings per share data)

	June 30,				
	2001	*2000*	*1999*	*1998*	*1997*
Sales	12,903.37	13,697.54	14,136.50	13,617.48	13,218.71
Cost of Goods	9,449.34	10,057.70	10,335.59	9,993.56	9,902.86
Gross Profit	**3,454.02**	**3,639.84**	**3,800.91**	**3,623.91**	**3,315.85**
Selling & Admin. & Depr. & Amort. Expenses	3,180.29	3,609.24	3,593.65	3,374.90	3,093.77
Income after Depreciation & Amortization	273.74	30.60	207.26	249.02	222.09
Nonoperating Income	(147.24)	(290.38)	94.37	97.31	119.43
Interest Expense	52.84	42.62	5.15	28.53	22.08
Pretax Income	**73.64**	**(302.41)**	**296.48**	**317.79**	**319.44**
Income Taxes	28.33	(73.51)	114.14	119.17	115.00
Minority Interest	0.00	0.00	0.00	0.00	0.00
Investment Gains/Losses (+)	0.00	0.00	0.00	0.00	0.00
Other Income/Charges	0.00	0.00	0.00	0.00	0.00
Income from Continuous Operations	45.31	(228.89)	182.33	198.62	204.44
Extras & Discontinued Operations	0.00	0.00	0.00	0.00	0.00
Net Income	**45.31**	**(228.89)**	**182.33**	**198.62**	**204.44**
DEPRECIATION FOOTNOTE					
Income Before Depreciation & Amortization	457.29	287.27	499.67	579.42	513.32
Depreciation & Amortization (Cash Flow)	183.55	256.67	292.41	330.40	291.24
Income After Depreciation & Amortization	273.74	30.60	207.26	249.02	222.09
EARNINGS PER SHARE DATA					
Average Shares	N/A	145.79	148.24	150.04	150.29
Diluted EPS Before Nonrecurring Items	0.99	0.52	1.23	1.33	1.36
Diluted Net EPS	**0.33**	**(1.57)**	**1.23**	**1.33**	**1.36**

Source: Zack's Investment Research (2001).

WD shopping experience. These efforts are focused on delivering total customer satisfaction and low price leadership. In response to the customer's need for one-stop shopping, WD continues to move to larger stores in centralized locations. By increasing square footage, WD is able to surround the customer with more departments and more time-saving choices in such service center areas as seafood, floral, pharmacy, deli, bakery, international wines and cheeses, banking, ATMs, photo processing, postage stamps and money orders. WD's satellite communications system enables all locations to be networked more efficiently, thus allowing associates to spend less time on paperwork and more time assisting customers (Winn-Dixie Stores, Inc., 2001).

WD has introduced new training programs in customer service, food safety, and sanitation. New programs to measure customer satisfaction and to provide reward and recognition for top-performing employees also have been put into place. One example is the empowerment of store managers and division management, allowing them to act aggressively to meet local customer needs. The company has initiated the FIRST class customer service program, which is aimed at rewarding employees for providing exceptional customer service. Improvements in labor productivity have also been made through flex scheduling so that more associates are available to interact with customers, thus shortening waiting lines at peak hours (Winn-Dixie Stores, Inc., 2001).

Constant Community Commitment

Being a good corporate citizen and a good neighbor in the communities in which the company operates has been a part of the WD philosophy and commitment since its beginning in 1928. During the 1999 and 2000 fiscal years, the company contributed over $10 million in support of local community efforts. The following are just a few of the countless ways in which WD and its associates strive to make a difference:

Even-It-Up

WD's Even-It-Up program provides an opportunity for its customers to donate small change from their grocery orders to support nonprofit organizations. WD is currently donating these proceeds to the disaster relief fund related to the terrorist attacks in New York City and Washington, D.C.

Education

Every year, WD awards college scholarships to qualified associates and their dependents to further their education. Currently, over four hundred students are on WD scholarships. WD's Youth Management Day program demonstrates an investment in the future of the company's associates.

Natural Environment

WD is concerned about both solid waste and preserving the environment for future generations. WD's goal is to constantly find ways to reduce, reuse, and recycle solid waste. WD works within the industry and with public and private environmentally responsible institutions to promote responsible recycling. The corporate programs include the recycling of paper, plastics, and other materials; ongoing evaluation of procedures, costs, and areas for improvement is a part of these programs.

Health

The WD Hope Lodge is a $1 million commitment made by WD and its associates to establish the American Cancer Society/Winn-Dixie Hope Lodge Center in Gainesville, FL. The Lodge provides a nurturing, homelike residence where cancer patients and their families traveling away from home during treatments can stay at no charge (Winn-Dixie Stores Inc., 2001).

A Strong Foundation

WD takes great pride in the contributions that each associate makes toward keeping the company on the cutting edge. WD's strength lies in the family of more than 120,000 loyal and productive associates. Additionally, WD subscribes to a promotion-from-within policy and believes in a drug-free workplace. WD has a long history and tradition, one that that was founded on the premise that people make the difference (Winn-Dixie Stores Inc., 2001). Exhibit 7 reflects the organizational structure of the company, with focused management over geographic regions, as well as product lines.

Future Considerations

WD has opportunities to capitalize on current trends over the next few years. The economic slowdown will force many customers back into grocery stores for more traditional meals, causing more price-conscious buying behavior, which is beneficial to corporate branded products. In order to stay competitive, WD may need to continually acquire

EXHIBIT 7   Directors and Management

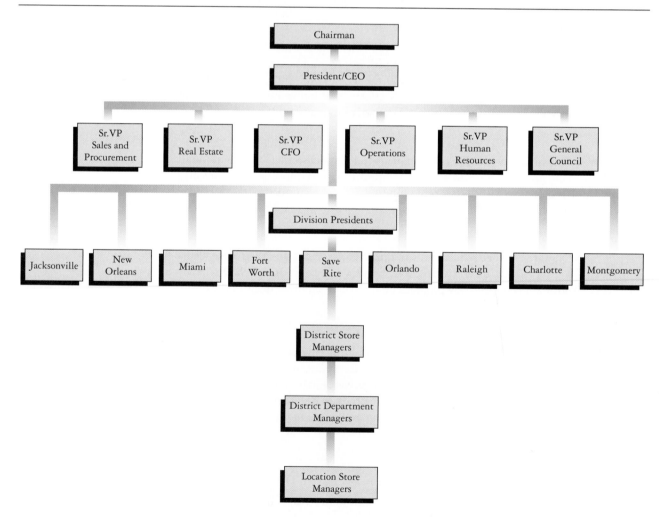

Source: Adapted from Winn-Dixie's 2001 *Annual Report.*

and expand operations of retail grocery chains in performing market areas. Mergers and acquisitions may be the only means of competing in a mass-merchandising environment.

For a future acquisition opportunity, WD could look at the Indianapolis, Indiana-based grocery retailer, Marsh Supermarkets, Inc. Marsh operates 93 supermarkets and 179 Village Pantry convenience stores in central Indiana and western Ohio. Marsh offers products and services comparable to WD's, and store locations can easily be serviced by WD's current distribution center in Louisville, Kentucky. An industry leader in technology, Marsh is currently one of the industry's best performing companies. Acquiring Marsh could enhance brand awareness and grow current market share.

Traditional grocers such as WD may find it difficult to compete merely on price with mass-merchandisers, but intangible benefits, such as exceptional customer service, should be stressed as a high priority. The institution of customer service programs, such as FIRST, should be continuously reviewed and measured to ensure that first-class customer service is maintained. Currently, such customer service in mass-merchandise locations is lacking.

Finally, WD needs to continue to improve its marketing campaigns, which seem to have been less than productive in years past, in order to induce more shopping behavior within the company's market area. These new initiatives should encompass the entire organization, not just the physical aspect of the organization. The new "Real Deal" WD campaign should be just that: a real change in products and services, which produce real measurable outcomes that make a real difference.

REFERENCES

www.economy.com
Economy.Com Network. "Retail Stores: Grocery and Drug." (2001). http://www.economy.com/research

www.fmi.org
Food Marketing Institute. "Competition and Profit." (2001). http://www.fmi.org/facts_figs/Competitionandprofit.pdf

Food Marketing Institute. "Spending and Saving Money." (2001). http://www.fmi.org/facts_figs/spendingandSavingMoney.pdf

Griffith, Tom. "The U.S. Retail Food Industry: 2001 Format Update." Willard Bishop Consulting (2001, June). http://www.bishop-consulting.com/edge_jun_01.cfm

Lind, Robin. "Online Grocery Shopping Is Growing and Ripening." WebPointers Online (2000). http://www.webpointers.com/groc99.html

"Online Grocery Sales to Increase 3360% by Year 2002." Advanced E-Commerce Home Shopping Solutions (2000). http://www.emarketer.com

"Supermarket and Drug Store Industry," U.S. Business Reporter (2001). http://www.acitivemediaguide.com/ddrugstore_industry.htm

Winn-Dixie Stores, Inc., Annual Report (2001). http://www:winn-dixie.com/company/annualreport/main.asp http://www.winn-dixie.com

Wyss, David. "U.S. Economic Forecast: The Big Engine That Could," Standard & Poor's (2001). http://www.sanp.com/Forum/MarketAnalysis/Articles/082301_bigengine.html

Zack's Investment Research, Winn-Dixie Annual Income Statement and Balance Sheet, E-Line Financials (2001). http://lada.zacks.com

STRICTLY ROOTS NATURAL HAIR CARE SALON—2002

Paul R. Reed, Anthony Williams, Valerie Muehsam, and
Donald Bumpass
Sam Houston State University

Jhamella Bolade has a hairy situation on her hands and she loves every minute of it. As she reclines in one of her hair styling stations and reflects over her recent business success, she can't help being a little anxious about her salon's future. Bolade is the owner and operator of Strictly Roots Natural Hair Care Salon (713-529-5017), which specializes in braiding and locking of the hair of African Americans in the greater Houston, Texas, area. Although her salon has been open for less than nine months, business is really booming, and Bolade wouldn't have it any other way. Bolade does not apply any permanents, nor does she apply any chemicals at her salon because this would violate her natural hair-care philosophy. Bolade even makes her own natural hair-care product, which is known as Strictly Roots Anointing Oil.

Bolade could not have secured a better location for her salon. It is located in the Third Ward area of Houston, an area that is experiencing an economic comeback and is located not very far from the downtown area. The salon is surrounded by several other businesses that attract African American customers, including a Caribbean restaurant named the Reggae Hut, the Naturally Yours Pharmacy and Health Food Store, and the D&B African Village Art Gallery. While there is limited available parking space at this location, Strictly Roots' clients and the neighboring businesses do not seem to mind.

Bolade would like to take advantage of Strictly Roots success by opening her second natural hair-care salon, which she plans to call Strictly Roots Too. Finding time to pursue this goal will be difficult since she also wants to return to college so that she can earn her bachelor's degree in business administration; she also needs time to increase the production of her anointing oil. To further complicate matters, Bolade is also the proud mother of two preschool-aged children. Finally, Bolade must always be prepared for the ever-present threat that one of her independent stylists will resign his or her post in order to open his or her own salon.

STRICTLY ROOTS' HISTORY

Bolade was born in New York City as Yvette Talley 32 years ago. She began braiding hair at the age of 13, and it was during this period in her career that she learned the Egyptian palm-rolling method of locking hair. Unlike traditional methods of locking hair, which involves tying and twisting, the Egyptian method requires stylists to lock a client's hair by rolling the hair in their palm to transform the hair into permanent locks. She eventually became a licensed master braider and loctition in the state of New York. After perfecting her natural hair sculpting techniques in New York, she left her Harlem home and worked at salons in Atlanta, Chicago, and Los Angeles. In 1987, Bolade matriculated as a college student at nearby Texas Southern University, which is located in the Third Ward area of Houston, Texas. Bolade began sculpting the hair of her classmates to earn spending money while she studied journalism, a profession in which her mother earned a living.

Formal business operations in Houston began in 1990, when Bolade decided to return to the career which she enjoyed the most. Bolade worked out of her home for several years until the birth of her first child. It was at this point that she decided that her home was no longer a good place to sculpt hair and that it was important to move her personalized consultations out of her home and into a more appropriate place of business. Shortly after making this decision, Bolade rented space at the Cut-N-Shine Barbershop, also located in the Third Ward. It was here, in the African American-friendly atmosphere which was surrounded by other business that offered services similar to Strictly Roots cultural ideals, that Bolade's business began to really take off. She began to pass out flyers to market her services and developed plans to construct her own Web site. When the news came that a Cut-N-Shine neighboring business was vacating some lease space, Bolade immediately secured the square footage and opened Strictly Roots.

STRICTLY ROOTS' SERVICES

Strictly Roots is in the business of pampering its clients' hair roots via a holistic approach to hair care. Her salon specializes in braids, dreadlocks, twists, and natural hair-care styles for African Americans. In one of her professionally designed color flyers, Bolade states that "natural hair is virgin hair, not altered by chemical or thermal services. Natural hair care, in turn, is the process by which the hair service enhances that natural state." Her holistic approach to hair care can take hours to complete and recognizes the integrated balance between the body, mind, and spirit. The services provided are gentle and wholesome, and they are corrective and nurturing to the entire body. Environmentally safe products (nontoxic) are a part of the services. Products made of plants, fruits, vegetables, herbs, or essential oils are used during these therapeutic services. The reference of these services is consistent with Bolade's anointing oil.

The service begins with a personalized consultation with the client, during which the stylist tries to ascertain the hairstyle that's desired. The stylist then assesses the client's immediate hair-care needs and recommends the most appropriate process in which these needs can be matched with a desired hairstyle. The client's hair is then washed thoroughly and slowly dried. Once dried, the client's hair is twisted, braided, or locked. If the client's hair is very short, then it will probably be twisted in a fashionable manner until it is long enough to be braided. If the client's hair does not grow much longer than its twisted length, then it will be maintained in this manner.

If the client's hair is long enough to be braided, then a more complicated hair-sculpting process takes place. If the client wants dreadlocks, then the stylist will use the Egyptian palm-rolling method and lock the hair. Unlike the temporary twisting or braiding of hair, once the client's hair is locked, it is transformed and permanent. The dreadlocks hair appears matted, somewhat unclean, cannot be combed, and must be cut if the client desires a different hairstyle.

STRICTLY ROOTS' CULTURE AND ORGANIZATIONAL STRUCTURE

Strictly Roots fosters an environment that encourages the native African experience. All of Bolade's stylists are strongly encouraged to assume a native African name which will be referred to when the stylist is sculpting hair at the salon. The salon currently accommodates up to five independent stylists at one time and has regular operating hours of 10:00 A.M. to 8:30 P.M., Tuesday through Saturday. The independent stylist must pay a $65 weekly booth fee and abide by Bolade's price listing for the various services. All income earned after the weekly booth fee is paid belongs to the stylist. Bolade currently does not have a wage-earning administrative assistant and relies on one of her long-time independent stylists to act in this capacity. This will be a problem until she develops a financial strategy to address this issue while she actively pursues other personal and professional goals.

Since the process of twisting, braiding, and locking hair is very time-consuming, independent stylists are allowed to set their own schedules: Walk-ins are routed to their stylists if they are established clients; if not, they are assigned a stylist based on the client's needs and the stylist's sculpting ability. All independent stylists must adhere to Bolade's natural hair-care philosophy if they are to continue to provide services at the salon. By enforcing this philosophy, Bolade can honestly make the claim that Strictly Roots is "Houston's Only Natural Hair-Care Salon."

The city of Houston is the fourth largest city in the United States. In 1990, Houston's 28 percent black population, or 457,990, placed it sixth among American cities in terms of the size of its black population. Preliminary 2000 U.S. Census results show that the African American population in Houston has grown approximately 45 percent to 709,432. Other reports show that approximately 15 percent of African Americans made over $30,000 annually during this period. As a result, there are more potential clients with more expendable income.

The hairstyles created at Strictly Roots are most popular among younger African Americans. Many young people idolize the many musical rappers and professional athletes who wear the hairstyles. Bolade even has some celebrity-clients who come to her for consultations, including local Houston rappers and professional NBA basketball players. Bolade would like to grow her business by capitalizing on her current celebrity clientele and by luring players on the startup Houston Texans football franchise once the team begins play.

Unfortunately, the hairstyles are not so readily accepted in the corporate environment. Many people think that individuals who wear such hairstyles may be abusing illegal drugs, may be engaging in some form of international crime, or may not be concerned about their overall appearance. The opportunity to expand the salon's base of clients still remains positive, however, since the Houston area has a large number of African American high school students as well as many college students who attend the University of Houston, Texas Southern University, Houston Baptist University, and Rice University.

STRICTLY ROOTS' ANOINTING OIL PRODUCT

Strictly Roots' Anointing Oil was designed to meet Bolade's desire to provide environmentally safe products as a part of her services. The anointing oil has the potential to bring in additional revenues if she can begin to meet her demand for the product. Bolade's current cost to produce twenty-four jars of anointing oil is approximately $50.00, or $2.08 per jar. Production time to produce the oil is approximately two hours. A jar of anointing oil sells for $9.00, yielding a net profit of $6.92. Average sales of anointing oil are only twenty-four jars per month, resulting in $166.08 profit a month—or $1,992.96 annually.

Bolade is having problems meeting the demand for the anointing oil for several reasons. She currently lacks an established schedule for producing the oil; she has no formalized production staff to produce the oil; and to have the oil produced by a contract vender may result in lost revenues for Bolade. Also, if a contract vendor produces the product, then Bolade would have to reveal her processing secrets and ingredients, which could result in a loss of her competitive edge. In addition to her own clients, there are independent businesspeople who would love to acquire the secret of Bolade's anointing oil. These people would like to make a direct profit themselves instead of paying Bolade's $9.00-per-jar price and then marking up the price of the jars in order to earn a small profit. One retailer has openly suggested that he could retain the services of a chemist to break down the compounds of the anointing oil and have the product produced under his company's name since the oil is not patented. Nonetheless, Bolade is resisting these advances and plans to increase the production of her oil internally in the near future.

STRICTLY ROOTS' COMPETITION

There are several cosmetology schools in the greater Houston area. Each graduating class has individuals who aspire to own their own salons someday. As mentioned earlier, this is a constant threat for small salons like Strictly Roots. This problem is magnified by the fact that Strictly Roots has a specific market niche that has allowed it to become an immediate success in the Houston market. Bolade experienced this threat directly on two different occasions when two of her former independent stylists left their booths at Strictly Roots so that they could open their own natural hair-care salons. The competition is intensified by the fact that both of these salons were opened within a two-block radius of Strictly Roots (see Exhibit 2). These salons are named Back to Natural, Soul Scissors, and Hyde & Jojo's. A brief summary of these salons follows.

Soul Scissors

Soul Scissors was launched in June 1997 and is owned and operated by Troy Julian. In addition to cutting hair, Soul Scissors sells acid jazz compact discs, T-shirts, African art, essential oils, and incenses. The salon provides services in a converted gasoline station approximately two blocks from Strictly Roots. The salon has a functional Web site at **www.soulscissors.com**.

The salon and African art store also has a natural hair-care specialist on-site whose name is Georgette Johnson. Johnson, a former independent stylist at Strictly Roots, is a self-proclaimed loctition who states that she specializes in dreadlocks, twists, braids, corn-rows, and other natural hair-care styles. Although Johnson originally lured some of Strictly Roots clients away from Bolade, many of these customers have since returned.

Back to Natural

There is yet another salon within a two-block radius of Strictly Roots, Back to Natural, and it is owned and operated by Keesha Eniyi. Eniyi is also a former Strictly Roots independent stylist who branched out on her own after learning the core processes of the natural hair-care philosophy. Her salon is located slightly off Almed Blvd. between Strictly Roots and Soul Scissors. However, Back to Natural has neither a functional Web site on the Internet nor any products that would rival Strictly Roots Anointing Oil. Eniyi is a relentless businesswoman who is determined to carve out her share of the natural hair-care market.

Hyde & Jojo's

This particular natural hair-care salon is located approximately twenty miles away from Strictly Roots in the Alief area of Houston, Texas, and it is owned and operated by individuals native to Jamaica. Hyde & Jojo's specializes in locking hair and has a huge following of island natives who currently reside in the Houston area. Bolade would have trouble gaining market share on these potential customers and accepts this healthy rivalry that may hold future alliances.

Strictly Roots' Finances

Strictly Roots has been quite profitable during its first few months in business. Bolade charges $65.00 to braid or lock a client's hair. Hair maintenance is also an additional $65.00 per visit. Despite the turmoil of opening the business, the anointing oil production problems, and the departure of two of her most promising independent stylists, the salon has been able to turn a respectable profit. Bolade experienced a $23,593 increase in revenues for the year 2000, but then a $6,742 decline in 2002. Although Bolade's overall cost of goods sold increased over 50 percent, most of this can be attributed to the leasing and utilities costs related to Strictly Roots versus the booth fee she paid while providing services at the Cut-N-Shine Barbershop. Likewise, her net income increased by 32 percent, from $25,351 in 1999 to $42,671 in 2000. Net income to 2002 declined to $35,929. Bolade currently has no long-term debt, nor does her company have large account receivables or payables. Strictly Roots financial summary can be found in Exhibits 1 and 2.

STRICTLY ROOTS' FUTURE

Bolade will need to decide in which direction she will move her business over the next few years. Although the business has done well over the past several months, Bolade has not experienced a full year of operations at her current location. What makes things even more interesting is the fact that Bolade may have to raise her weekly booth fee to offset lost profits resulting from a slowing economy, rising utility costs, and rising gasoline prices. It is uncertain how her independent stylists will react to such an increase, and there is still the ever-present threat that some of the stylists may depart the salon to open their own businesses.

EXHIBIT 1   Strictly Roots Consolidated Balance Sheet

	March 31, 2002	March 31, 2001	March 31, 2000
CURRENT ASSETS			
Cash and cash equivalents	$1,890.00	$2,035.00	$ 700.00
Accounts receivable	—	—	—
Inventory	$ 327.00	$ 186.00	$ 73.00
Other current assets	$ 461.00	$ 345.00	$ 94.00
Capital Assets	$4,014.00	$3,250.00	$ 467.00
Total Assets	$6,692.00	$5,816.00	$1,334.00
CURRENT LIABILITIES			
Accounts payable	$ 562.00	$ 219.00	$ 163.00
Taxes payable	$ 429.00	$ 567.00	
Notes payable	$1,073.00	—	—
Long-Term Debt	—	—	—
SHAREHOLDERS' EQUITY			
Retained Earnings	$4,628.00	$5,030.00	$1,171.00
Total liabilities and shareholders' equity	$6,692.00	$5,816.00	$1,334.00

Source: Strictly Roots' Company Report.

EXHIBIT 2   Strictly Roots' Income Statement

For the year ended	March 31, 2002	March 31, 2001	March 31, 2000
Revenues	$47,681.00	$52,393.00	$28,800.00
Cost of services	$ 7,527.00	$ 6,960.00	$ 3,120.00
Selling, marketing, and administration	$ 3,305.00	$ 2,050.00	$ 300.00
Amortization	$ 268.00	$ 145.00	$ 29.00
Income from operations	$36,581.00	$43,238.00	$25,351.00
Investment income	—	—	—
Income before taxes	$36,581.00	$43,238.00	$25,351.00
Provision for income taxes	$ 652.00	$ 567.00	—
Net Income	$35,929.00	$42,671.00	$25,351.00

Source: Strictly Roots' Company Report.

Bolade will need to secure a reliable administrative assistant who can be trusted to supervise the daily salon operations while she increases the production of Strictly Roots Anointing Oil and opens Strictly Roots Too. Pursuing either of these goals will be twice as difficult for this single mother of two, who plans to return to college for her bachelor's degree.

THE CLASSIC CAR CLUB OF AMERICA—2002

Matthew C. Sonfield
Hofstra University

www.classiccarclub.org

The Classic Car Club of America, Inc. (CCCA) was formed in 1952 by a small group of enthusiasts interested in the luxury cars of the late 1920s and 1930s. The CCCA phone number is 847-390-0443 and their e-mail address is **www.classiccarclub@aol.com** Certain high-priced, high-quality, and limited-production cars were designated as "Classic Cars," and the period of 1925 to 1942 was chosen as the "Classic Era." It was felt that cars built prior to 1925 had not yet reached technical maturity and that after World War II, the quality of most so-called luxury cars had succumbed to the economic pressures of mass production. Some pictures of Classic Cars are provided in Exhibit 1.

Over the years, the list of CCCA-recognized Classic Cars was modified and expanded, and the time period was extended to 1948 to include certain pre-WWII models that continued in production for a few years after the war. All cars included on the list were of considerably higher price and quality than the mass-production cars of this era, and most had original prices in the $2,000 to $5,000 range. (This was a considerable amount of money at that time; in 1930, a Ford Model A [*not* a Classic Car] sold new for about $450.) Some of the most luxurious Classic Cars, such as the American Duesenberg, the English Rolls-Royce, the French Hispano-Suiza, and the Italian Isotta-Fraschini, sold new in the $10,000 to $20,000 range! Exhibit 2 lists those cars recognized as Classic Cars by the CCCA in 2002.

The mission statement of the CCCA, as stated in its legal by-laws, states:

> *The purposes for which the club is founded are: for the development, publication and interchange of technical, historical and other information for and among members and other persons who own or are interested in fine or unusual foreign or domestic motor cars built between and including the years 1925 and 1948, and distinguished for their respective fine design, high engineering standards and superior workmanship, and to promote social intercourse and fellowship among its members; and to maintain references upon and encourage the maintenance, restoration and preservation of all such Classic Cars.*

THE COLLECTOR CAR HOBBY

The collector car hobby in the United States is a broad and wide-reaching activity involving a large number of Americans. Basically, a "collector car" is any automobile owned for purposes other than normal transportation. The most widely read collector car hobby magazine, *Hemmings Motor News,* had an average circulation of about 250,000 in 2001. Another magazine, *Car Collector,* estimates that nearly 1 million Americans are engaged in the old-car hobby. However, a figure of 500,000 to 750,000 would probably be a more conservative estimate of the number of Americans engaged in this hobby.

Collector car is a loose term, ranging from turn-of-the-century "horseless carriages" to currently built but limited-production cars, such as Italian super-sports cars. Naturally, owners of collector cars enjoy the company of other individuals with similar

EXHIBIT 1   Classic Cars

1926 Duesenberg (above); 1934 Rolls Royce (top right); 1941 Packard (right).
Source: The Classic Car Club of America, Inc.

interests, and thus a wide variety of car clubs exist to suit almost any particular segment of this vast hobby. The largest of these clubs, the Antique Automobile Club of America, caters to owners of virtually all cars twenty-five years old or older, and it has a membership of more than sixty thousand. In contrast, the CCCA has a much narrower collector-car focus and, thus, far fewer members.

CCCA ORGANIZATION AND ACTIVITIES

When the CCCA's 2001 fiscal year ended on December 31, 2001, the club had 5,918 members, as indicated below. (Exhibit 3 gives a comparison of membership figures for recent years.)

Active (regular membership—2002 dues @ $45/year)	4,425
Associate (for spouses, no publications—$7/year)	1,204
Life (after ten years, one-time fee of $800)	217
Life Associate (spouse of Life—$80)	69
Honorary (famous car designers, etc.)	3
	5,918

CCCA members receive a variety of benefits from their membership. A magazine, *The Classic Car*, is published four times a year. High in quality and highly respected by automotive historians, it features forty-eight pages or more of articles and photos of Classic Cars. A CCCA *Bulletin* is also published eight times a year, and it contains club and hobby news, technical columns, and members' and commercial ads for Classic Cars, parts, and related items. A further publication is the club's *Handbook and Directory*, published annually. It contains a current listing of members and the Classic Cars they own,

EXHIBIT 2　CCCA-Recognized Classic Cars

A.C.	Excelsior*	Mercer
Adler*	Farman*	M.G.*
Alfa Romeo	Fiat*	Minerva*
Alvis*	FN*	N.A.G.*
Amilcar*	Franklin*	Nash*
Armstrong-Siddeley*	Frazier-Nash*	Packard*
Aston Martin*	Georges Irat*	Peerless
Auburn*	Graham*	Peugot*
Austro-Daimler	Graham-Paige*	Pierce-Arrow
Ballot*	Hispano-Suiza*	Railton*
Bentley*	Horch	Raymond Mays*
Benz*	Hotchkiss*	Renault*
Blackhawk	Hudson*	Reo*
B.M.W.*	Humber*	Revere
Brewster*	Invicta	Roamer*
Brough Superior*	Isotta-Fraschini	Rochet Schneider*
Bucciali*	Itala	Rohr*
Bugatti	Jaguar*	Rolls-Royce
Buick*	Jensen*	Ruxton
Cadillac*	Jordan*	Squire
Chenard-Walcker*	Julian*	S.S. and S.S. Jaguar*
Chrysler*	Kissell*	Stearns-Knight
Cord	Lagonda*	Stevens-Duryea
Cunningham	Lanchester*	Steyr*
Dagmar*	Lancia*	Studebaker*
Daimler*	La Salle*	Stutz
Darracq*	Lincoln*	Sunbeam*
Delage*	Lincoln Continental	Talbot*
Delahaye*	Locomobile*	Talbot-Lago*
Delaunay Belleville*	McFarlan	Tatra*
Doble	Marmon*	Triumph*
Dorris	Maserati*	Vauxhall*
Duesenberg	Maybach	Voisin
Du Pont	Mercedes	Wills St. Claire
Elcar*	Mercedes-Benz*	Willys-Knight*

*Indicates that only certain models of this make are considered Classic. Some other 1925–1948 custom-bodied cars not listed above may be approved as Classic upon individual application.
Source: The Classic Car Club of America, Inc.

EXHIBIT 3　Selected CCCA Membership Data (at end of fiscal year)

	2001	2000	1999	1998	1997
Active Members	4,425	4,198	4,138	4,182	4,164
Associate Members	1,204	1,113	1,078	1,077	996
Life Members	217	215	213	207	205
Life Associate Members	69	69	70	69	66
Honorary Members	3	3	3	3	5
Total	5,918	5,598	5,502	5,538	5,436

Source: The Classic Car Club of America, Inc.

so that club members can locate other members who own similar cars or live nearby. Commercial car-related advertisements are solicited for this *Handbook and Directory,* and its cost is fully paid for by these advertisements. Advertisements also cover some of the costs of the magazine and bulletin.

The CCCA also sponsors three types of national events each year. The annual meeting in January includes business meetings and a car judging meet and is held in a different location in the United States each year. In the spring and summer, a series of "Grand Classic" judging meets are held simultaneously in ten to twelve locations around the country, with a total of four hundred to six hundred Classic Cars being exhibited and judged. At CCCA judging meets, cars are evaluated by a point system that takes into account the quality and authenticity of restoration and the general condition of the car, both mechanically and cosmetically. CCCA judging meets are not usually publicized to the general public, and access to view the cars is generally restricted to club members and their guests only.

Each year, the club sponsors several "Classic CARavans" in various parts of the United States and Canada. The CARavan is a tour in which members in as many as one hundred Classic Cars join together in a week-long planned itinerary. Every few years, a cross-country CARavan that lasts for several weeks is run.

The annual meeting, Grand Classics meets, and CARavans are designed to be financially self-supporting, with attending members paying fees that cover the costs of the events.

The CCCA has members who have volunteered to be technical advisers available to assist other members. Furthermore, the club makes available for sale to members certain club-related products, such as hats, ties, shirts, and umbrellas with a Classic Car design. In still another member-oriented venture, the CCCA in 1990 and 2001 commissioned the publications editor to edit two 750-page hardcover books (*The Classic Car* and *The Classic Era*), which were composed of members' photos and stories of their Classic Cars and of the time period in which they were built. These books were published by the club and sold to members and through bookstores to the general public, and they have brought in additional revenue to the CCCA.

The CCCA also maintains a World Wide Web site (**www.classiccarclub.org**). This attractive Web site provides a wide range of information about the club and about Classic Cars. At this site, one can join the club, buy the club's books, see many Classic Cars, and find much more. As of late 2001, the site had received more than one hundred thousand hits.

The club is managed by a fifteen-member board of directors, with a president, vice presidents, treasurer, secretary, and so on. All are club member volunteers (from all over the United States) who have shown a willingness and ability to help run the CCCA, and who have been elected by the total membership to three-year terms of office. They are not reimbursed for their expenses, which include attending eight board meetings each year, most of which are held at club headquarters in a club-owned office condominium in Des Plaines, Illinois (a site chosen because of its central location within the United States and its close proximity to Chicago's main airport). Another member volunteers as executive administrator and oversees the club's employees and its daily operations. The only paid employees of the club are a full-time office secretary, a part-time clerical worker, and the publications editor, who is a freelance automotive writer/editor. An organization chart of the CCCA is shown in Exhibit 4.

In addition to belonging to the national CCCA, the majority of members also pay dues and belong to a local CCCA regional chapter. In 2002, there are twenty-six regions throughout the United States (see Exhibit 5). Each region sponsors a variety of local activities for members and their Classic Cars and also publishes its own magazine or newsletter. Many of the regions also derive revenues from the sale of Classic Car replacement parts, service items, or clothing, offered to all members of the national club.

EXHIBIT 4   2002 CCCA Organization Chart

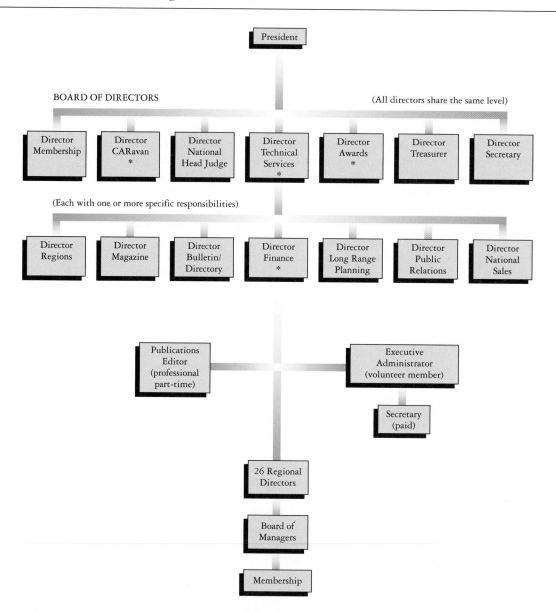

*This director chairs a committee for this functional responsibility, composed of other directors and members.
Source: The Classic Car Club of America, Inc.

Legally separate from the CCCA and its regions, a Classic Car Club of America Museum also exists. It occupies space as part of a larger old car museum in Hickory Corners, Michigan, and it displays a variety of Classic Cars that have been donated to it. The CCCA Museum, unlike the CCCA itself, is eligible to receive tax-deductible gifts of money and property (such as cars). Although the CCCA has granted the museum the right to use the CCCA name, the museum has a separate board of trustees and is run totally apart from the club. Because of this legal separation, the club's directors do not

---

EXHIBIT 5   Classic Car Club Regions

Arizona	North Texas
Chesapeake bay (MD)	Northern California
Colorado	Ohio
Delaware Valley (PA)	Oil Belt (OK)
Dixie	Oregon
Florida	Pacific Northwest (WA)
Gold Coast (So. FLorida)	Rio Grande
Greater Illinois	San Diego/Paim Springs
Indiana	Southern California
Lone Star (Texas)	Spirit of St. Louis
Metropolitan (NY, NJ, So. CT)	Upper Midwest (MN)
Michigan	Western Pennsylvania
New England (MA, ME, NH, No. CT, RI, VT)	Wisconsin

---

have the authority to make strategic decisions for the museum; nor can be museum's performance and finances directly benefit the club.

CURRENT CONCERNS THAT FACE THE CCCA

While the officers and directors of the CCCA believe the club to be strong, both financially and in its value to its members, a variety of concerns about the future exists. One concern involves the use of the word *Classic* as it refers to collector cars. While the CCCA uses this term to denote the specific listing of 1925 to 1948 luxury cars that the club has designated as "Classic Cars," many other collector car hobbyists use the term more loosely to refer to any collector car which they see as special. Thus, one can find the word *Classic* used to describe 1928 Fords and 1955 Chevrolets. While the CCCA cannot legally protect and limit the hobby's use of *Classic*, the club has legally registered the terms *Full Classic* (a CCCA-designated Classic Car with its original body and motor) and *Modified Classic* (a Classic Car chassis with a replica body or incorrect motor). In its publications and publicity, the CCCA now refers to its members' cars as "Full Classics," and it is hoped that this trademark registration and usage will help to protect the term *Classic* as used by the club.

Another concern is the continuing effect of rising costs upon the club's ability to maintain its current level of services and benefits to members. In particular, the costs of both its publications and its headquarters (i.e., the office administration) have risen considerably over the years. The board of directors has responded by both watching costs carefully and by raising annual dues several times (from $10 in the 1960s to an increase in 2001 to $45 per year), but it recognizes that certain cost increases, while unavoidable, may result in a loss of members. (Financial statements are provided in Exhibits 6 and 7.)

One way to overcome this problem is to increase the number of members and thus create greater revenues for the club. (The number of members has risen only slightly in recent years. See Exhibit 3.) The directors know that many Classic Car owners do not belong to the CCCA. While CCCA members listed about seventy-five hundred Classic Cars in the most recent *Handbook and Directory*, no one really knows how many Classic Car owners are *not* in the club. Club efforts in recent years to increase membership have been targeted at these Classic Car-owning non-CCCA members. Letters have been sent to past members who failed to renew their CCCA membership (about 5 percent to 10 percent each year), region officers have contacted local non-CCCA members known to

EXHIBIT 6   CCCA Statements of Receipts and Disbursements (Cash Flow Basis)

	FY2001	FY2000	FY1999
RECEIPTS			
Active Membership Dues (dues received for current FY)	$ 18,462	$ 25,116	$ 17,302
Prepaid Active Dues (dues received for next FY)	177,603	159,561	152,440
Associate Membership Dues	1,008	1,099	712
Prepaid Associate Dues	7,425	7,425	6,830
Life Memberships	3,600	2,500	6,400
Life Associate Memberships	180	0	240
Publications Sales	1,558	2,793	2,912
Awards Income (member registration fees for meets, etc.)	12,977	10,530	10,831
Caravan Income	27,640	27,485	14,500
National Sales Items	9,045	7,310	6,253
Insurance Income (from regions)	4,225	3,397	3,540
Book Income	67,716	128,494	988
Advertising Income—Bulletin	25,228	26,890	28,205
Advertising Income—Magazine	2,000	2,500	1,465
Advertising Income—Directory	15,750	23,100	16,550
Interest Income	7,005	9,884	11,902
Miscellaneous Income	6,182	14,794	10,852
TOTAL RECEIPTS	387,604	452,878	291,922
DISBURSEMENTS			
Membership Expense (recruitment)	6,543	6,506	13,059
Annual Meeting Expense	10,792	8,944	2,015
Awards Expense (meets, etc.)	22,933	15,032	23,085
Caravan Expense	21,474	21,969	7,895
National Sales Items	12,261	4,888	1,725
Book Expense	40,599	251,231	11,061
Bulletin Editor Fee	10,221	13,244	13,537
Bulletin Printing	43,587	49,675	35,922
Magazine Editor Fee	10,000	10,092	10,700
Magazine Printing	78,163	85,457	81,004
Directory Printing	16,325	15,586	15,045
General Administration (supplies, postage telephone, etc.)	19,252	38,438	29,755
Office (wages, condo expense)	58,021	57,009	36,106
Insurance	8,936	6,909	8,366
Professional Services	6,424	8,832	5,445
Miscellaneous Expenses	7,253	3,607	7,727
TOTAL EXPENSES	372,784	597,419	302,447
EXCESS RECEIPTS OVER DISBURSEMENTS (DEFICIT)	$ 14,820	($144,541)	($ 10,525)

Note: Certain unusual one-time receipts and disbursements omitted
Source: The Classic Car Club of America, Inc.

own Classic Cars, mailings have been sent to Classic Car-owning individuals found in directories of other old car clubs, articles about CCCA activities as well as a few paid advertisements have been placed in various old car hobby magazines, and membership ads have been placed in single-marque car clubs (such as the Packard club) in return for allowing those clubs to place their membership ads in the CCCA's publications.

Furthermore, while some CCCA members do not own Classic Cars, most do, for much of the pleasure of belonging to the club derives from participating in the various

EXHIBIT 7   CCCA Balance Sheets

	FY2001	FY2000	FY1999	FY1998	FY1997	FY1996
ASSETS						
Bank Balance	$ 20,500	$ 35,815	$ 25,550	$ 30,957	$ 8,685	$ 28,970
Investments (at cost) (money market funds, govt. notes, etc.) (includes life membership fund)	389,959	291,215	322,992	293,019	385,700	256,743
Office Condominium	166,636	148,071	151,968	154,698	84,968	84,968
TOTAL ASSETS	577,095	475,101	500,510	478,674	479,353	370,681
LIABILITIES	0	0	0	0	0	0
OWNERS' EQUITY	$577,095	$475,071	$500,510	$478,674	$479,353	$370,681

Source: The Classic Car Club of America, Inc.

activities with a Classic Car. Thus, while Classic Car enthusiasts who do not own a Classic Car might also be appropriate targets for CCCA new-membership recruitment efforts, the primary focus has been on people who currently own a Classic Car.

Currently, very few CCCA members live outside the United States. About 2 percent of all members live in Canada, and less than 2 percent live outside of North America (mainly in western Europe). While countries beyond the United States might be good targets for membership recruitment efforts, the club's directors have never been able to determine whether this is the case, and no formal attempts at international recruitment have ever been made.

The club's membership recruitment efforts have only been moderately successful. While new members have offset the annual 5 to 10 percent attrition rate, total membership has risen only slightly in recent years. Yet unless the listing of recognized Classic Cars is expanded, the number of Classic Cars in existence is fixed, and with it, by and large, so too is the number of Classic Car owners.

There are varying opinions within the CCCA with regard to expanding the current listing of Classic Cars, and there are two directions for such an expansion. One way is to add makes and/or models to the current 1925 to 1948–year limits. Another way is to add cars built before 1925 or after 1948.

Several times in recent years, the board of directors has voted to add additional models of existing Classic makes to the CCCA's 1925 to 1948 listing (for example, by adding a Packard model line slightly lower in original price to already-listed Packard model lines of the same year). Also, a few lesser-known makes of this time period have been added (such as the American Elcar and the French Georges Irat), but only a handful of these cars still exist. These additions have drawn a mixed reaction from the membership. Some members feel that such additions dilute the meaning of "Classic Car," while most other members seem to support the directors' decisions—or have no strong opinion.

More controversial is the issue of expanding the listing to before 1925 or after 1948. In a 1999 membership survey, many members supported going earlier. They argued that many luxury car models of the early 1920s were virtually identical to CCCA-recognized 1925 Classics—and, therefore, these cars should also be recognized as "Classic." Other members believe that certain high-quality pre-1925 cars should be added to the "Classic" listing, even if they are not identical to their 1925 counterparts.

In the same survey, a somewhat smaller group of members favored a post-1948 expansion, again some wanting to add only cars identical to already-recognized 1948 models and others wanting different but equally high-quality post-1948 cars. An additional argument for adding post-1948 cars is that it might add new and younger members to the CCCA. It is argued that the club is currently not attracting young members, and this is because younger people are less able to afford the cost of a Classic Car and are also unable to "identify" with a 1925 to 1948 car the way they can with a car of the 1950s or 1960s. Current prices of Classic Cars vary greatly, depending upon the make of car, its condition, and type of body. Also, it is true that many current CCCA members own Classic Cars because of nostalgia for cars of their youth.

The issue of an aging CCCA membership is supported by the numbers. In 1983, 21 percent of all members responding to a membership survey were under forty-five years of age. In 1999, only 6 percent were under forty-five. In 1983, 22 percent were sixty-five or older; in 1999, that percentage had increased to 44 percent. Clearly, the club's membership is aging. Yet the total number of club members has held fairly steady. So is an aging membership a threat to the CCCA or just a changing characteristic of the club?

The CCCA's board of directors is struggling with the issues of expanding beyond the current 1925 to 1948 "Classic Car" limits. While changes might add new (and perhaps younger) members and more dues revenues, the club's mission and focus might be diluted by any expansion. Would a broader focus and listing of accepted "Classics" reduce the attraction of the club to its existing members, who have many other old car clubs to choose from?

Beyond the board's concerns about the meaning and usage of the term *Classic Car* and the future financial strength of the club, there is also a concern about the use of members' Classic Cars and the nature of CCCA activities. As previously mentioned, the values of Classic Cars have risen significantly over the years. In 1952, when the club was founded, most people viewed Classic Cars as simply "old cars," and they could generally be bought for a few hundred to a few thousand dollars. Today, many view Classic Cars as major investment items, with professional dealers and auctions a significant factor in the marketplace. While some less exotic and unrestored Classic Car models can be found for under $15,000, most sell for $20,000 to $75,000, and the most desirable Classic Cars (convertible models with custom bodies, twelve and sixteen cylinder engines, etc.) can sell for $100,000 and more. (A very small number of especially exotic and desirable Classic Cars have sold in the $250,000 to $1,000,000 range, and a 1929 Bugatti Royale reportedly sold in 1987 for over $9.8 million!) Furthermore, judging meets have become very serious events, with awards and high scores adding significantly to a Classic Car's sales value. Thus, many highly desirable and/or top scoring Classic Cars are now hardly driven at all, and they are transported in enclosed trailers to and from judging meets. While most Classic Car owners still enjoy driving their cars—and the CCCA CARavans continue to be highly popular among club members—some members yearn for the old days when there was less emphasis on judging and on a car's value, and when CCCA members would drive and park their Classic Cars anywhere.

Still another concern of some members involves the possibility of a greater stress in future years on the conservation of gasoline in this country. If the country did focus more seriously on its high usage of gasoline, how would the public view Classic Cars and the collector-car hobby in general? Would the ownership and driving of cars for nontransportation purposes be considered unpatriotic or wasteful?

MEMBERSHIP SURVEYS

In response to these various concerns, the CCCA Board of Directors established a Long Range Planning Committee to study issues about the future of the club and to make recommendations to the board. In 1983, in 1991, and again in 1999, a membership questionnaire was sent to all members along with their membership renewal material. The response rate to each survey was excellent. Exhibit 8 presents a summary of the 1999 survey findings.

FUTURE DIRECTION OF THE CCCA

As the club's 2002 fiscal year progresses, the CCCA Board of Directors is studying these and other issues. Some issues seem more important than others and deserve more immediate attention. While the survey clarifies some of the opinions of the members, the board does not view this survey as a ballot, one that obligates the board to follow the majority preference in every question area.

Beyond the specific concerns discussed here, the officers and directors of the club simply want to do a good job. Their fellow members have elected them to keep the club strong and to improve it further. They want to be proactive as well as reactive; they want to be imaginative in their strategic management activities as well as to respond to concerns and issues already raised.

Together for their regular Board of Directors meeting in early 2002, the fifteen officers and directors of the CCCA ask themselves the following questions:

1. What are the various criteria we should consider when making strategic decisions for the club? How do we balance financial objectives and nonfinancial objectives? Which are primary and which are secondary?

2. How important are and how should we deal with rising costs to the club?

3. If we are forced to choose between raising dues or lowering the services provided to the members, which takes priority?

4. Should the club be offering more services to its members, even if this requires an increase in dues?

5. Is expansion of the listing of recognized Classic Cars desirable?

6. Which is preferable: adding cars within the 1925 to 1948 time period, or adding cars of earlier or later years? What are the pros and cons of these alternatives?

EXHIBIT 8   Classic Car Club of America 2002 Membership Survey Responses Summary

1. Thirty-two percent of the member (1,766 members) responded to the survey.
2. There is a continued aging of the membership, as well as the number of years of individuals' membership.
   Seventy-eight percent of the members are 55 years or older.
   The average age is 63.
   Seventy-eight percent of the members have been club members for 5 years or more.
   Sixty percent have been members for more than 10 years.
3. Members own an average of 3 Classic Cars.
   Members own an average of 2 other collector cars.
4. Seventy-six percent of the members belong to a CCCA Region.
5. Seventy-two percent of the members attended a national CCCA event in the past 3 years.
6. Members belonged to an average of 4 other car clubs.
7. Seventy-four percent of members rated the CCCA as "best" or "better than most" in comparison to other car clubs.
8. Sixty-six percent rated the CCCA Grand Classic judging meets "good" to "excellent." (31% had no opinion).
9. Thirty-one percent rated the annual meetings as "good" to "excellent." (64% had no opinion).
10. Eighty-one percent rated *The Classic Car* magazine as "excellent," an additional 16% rated it "good."
11. Sixty-nine percent rated the *CCCA Bulletin* as "excellent"; an additional 27% rated it "good."
12. Within the 1925–1948 time period, 44% favored keeping the listing of accepted Classic Cars as-is; 41% favored expanding the list to include additional 1925–1948 cars.
13. Regarding the possibility of expanding the 1925–1948 time period: 20% favored retaining the current 1925–1948 time period; 16% favored accepting certain pre-1925 cars but no post-1948 cars; 13% favored accepting certain post-1948 cars but no pre-1925 cars; 38% favored accepting certain pre-1925 cars *and* certain post-1948 cars; 13% gave no answer; answered "don't know," or gave inconsistent responses.

7. How important is it to increase the number of members in the club? What are some alternative ways to increase membership?

8. How serious is the aging membership of the club? How can younger people be attracted to the CCCA? How important is this? What specific strategies could be adopted to accomplish this goal?

9. Are there other possible sources of revenue to the club? What might some be?

10. How important is protecting the term *Classic Car*? What else can the CCCA do to further such protection?

11. Are there other long-range issues or concerns that the club has not yet addressed?

HARLEY-DAVIDSON, INC.—2002

Richard A. Cox
Francis Marion University

HDI

www.harley-davidson.com

There is something about the power of this brand and this company that intrigues us all. Whether you are a rider or an investor—or whether you are just interested—you have to admit that the way this company connects with its customers truly sets Harley-Davidson apart. Harley-Davidson has customers who are very passionate about their products. The name Harley-Davidson and its logo no doubt represent symbols of American individualism and even a bit of American rebelliousness. Everyone has seen at least one person with the famous Harley Bar & Shield logo tattooed on his or her arm. What is it about this company that would cause someone to want to be associated with it in such a permanent way? Is it the people and events that draw riders to Harley-Davidson? The company sponsors rides and rallies everywhere from Daytona to Houston—or even in international cities like Saint-Tropez, Sungwoo, and Lillehammer. From Mexico to Mount Fuji or from Austria to Australia, riders today can experience Harley at events in more than one hundred countries.

For some riders, however, the thrill may just be the back roads and just riding alone on a lazy Saturday afternoon. Others could have been lured in by the distinctive sound of a Harley-Davidson. Even the Harley Web site roars. No other motorcycle has the same sound as the company's legendary V-twin. The famous uneven rumble or "potato, potato, potato" sound has survived for generations and is as distinctive as the customers who ride the bikes. Whatever the reason, this type of loyalty has helped Harley-Davidson to survive against fierce international competition and maintain a strong financial performance.

In 2001, Harley-Davidson delivered record revenue and earnings for the sixteenth consecutive year. As shown in Exhibit 1, Harley's net sales for 2001 totaled $3.36 billion, a 15.7 percent increase over 2000. Net income was 437.7 million, up 25.9 percent from 2000. The company has experienced a compound annual growth rate in its stock price of over 40 percent since going public in 1986. Harley's 2001 balance sheet is provided in Exhibit 2.

HISTORY

In 1903, what was to become a legendary motorcycle company was formed in the Davidson family's backyard. The Davidson brothers, William D., Walter, Arthur, and William S. Harley, made their first motorcycle there. In 1909, Harley-Davidson introduced its first V-twin engine. This engine is still the company standard to this day.

During World War I, Harley-Davidson supplied the military with some 20,000 motorcycles. During this time, there were major advancements in the design of motorcycles, and Harley was the leader. However, a decade after the war ended, the Great Depression devastated the motorcycle industry. Only Harley-Davidson and Indian (Hendee Manufacturing) survived through the 1930s.

In 1941, World War II called, and Harley-Davidson answered with more than 90,000 motorcycles. After the war, demand for motorcycles exploded, and Harley-Davidson added

EXHIBIT 1   Consolidated Statement of Income (in thousands, except per share amounts)

Years ended December 31,	2001	2000	1999
Net sales	$3,363,414	$2,906,365	$2,452,939
Cost of goods sold	2,183,409	1,915,547	1,617,253
Gross profit	1,180,005	990,818	835,686
Financial services income	181,545	140,135	132,741
Financial services interest and operating expense	120,272	102,957	105,056
Operating income from financial services	61,273	37,178	27,685
Selling, administrative and engineering expense	(578,777)	(513,024)	(447,512)
Income from operations	662,501	514,972	415,859
Gain on sale of credit card business	—	18,915	—
Interest income, net	17,478	17,583	8,014
Other, net	(6,524)	(2,914)	(3,080)
Income before provision for income taxes	673,455	548,556	420,793
Provision for income taxes	235,709	200,843	153,592
Net income	$437,746	$ 347,713	$ 267,201
Basic earnings per common share	$1.45	$1.15	$.88
Diluted earnings per common share	$1.43	$1.13	$.86
Cash dividends per common share	$ .12	$ .10	$.09

Source: Harley's 2001 *Annual Report*, p. 55.

additional facilities in Milwaukee in 1947. That same year, the company began selling what was to become the classic black leather motorcycle jacket. After Indian closed in 1953, Harley-Davidson was the sole American motorcycle manufacturer for the next 46 years (**www.harley-davidson.com**). Harley ended family ownership in 1965 with a public offering. Only four years later, the company merged with the American Machine and Foundry Company (AMF), a longtime producer of leisure products.

By the early 1970s, the Japanese were importing huge numbers of lower-priced motorcycles into the United States. Japanese firms were able to capture a large portion of Harley's market share. Because it had expanded production so quickly, Harley was also having quality problems. In 1981, thirteen of Harley's senior executives purchased the business from AMF. The company then convinced President Ronald Reagan, by relying on a recommendation from the International Trade Commission (ITC), to impose additional tariffs on imported heavyweight Japanese motorcycles that were 700cc or larger for five years, starting in 1983. Then in 1986, Harley-Davidson, Inc. became publicly held for the first time since 1969. That same year, Harley regained its place at the top of the U.S. superheavyweight market, beating out Honda. The next year, the company asked the ITC to remove the tariffs one year early. This move made both business and American history, and President Reagan praised the company as an "American success story." Harley's U.S. market share continued to grow, and the company was listed on the New York Stock Exchange in 1987. The company had not only survived a difficult time, but some would say that it became an American icon.

CORPORATE MISSION STATEMENT

Harley's mission statement as provided in the company's 2001 *Annual Report* says, "We fulfill dreams through the experiences of motorcycling, by providing to motorcyclists and to the general public an expanding line of motorcycles, branded products and services in selected market segments."

EXHIBIT 2   Consolidated Balance Sheets (in thousands, except share amounts)

December 31,	2001	2000
ASSETS		
Current assets:		
Cash and cash equivalents	$ 439,438	$ 419,736
Marketable securities	196,011	—
Accounts receivable, net	118,843	98,311
Current portion of finance receivables, net	656,421	530,859
Inventories	181,115	191,931
Deferred income taxes	38,993	28,280
Prepaid expenses & other current assets	34,443	28,147
Total current assets	1,665,264	1,297,264
Finance receivables, net	379,335	234,091
Property, plant, and equipment, net	891,820	754,115
Goodwill, net	49,711	54,331
Other assets	132,365	96,603
	$3,118,495	$2,436,404
LIABILITIES AND SHAREHOLDERS' EQUITY		
Current liabilities:		
Accounts payable	$ 194,683	$ 169,844
Accrued expenses and other liabilities	304,376	238,390
Current portion of finance debt	217,051	89,509
Total current liabilities	716,110	497,743
Finance debt	380,000	355,000
Other long-term liabilities	158,374	81,707
Postretirement health care benefits	89,912	80,666
Deferred income taxes	17,816	15,633
Commitments and contingencies		
Shareholders' equity:		
Series A junior participating preferred stock, none issued	—	—
Common stock, 324,340,432 and 321,185, 567 shares issued in 2001 and 2000, respectively	3,242	3,210
Additional paid-in capital	359,165	285,390
Retained earnings	1,833,335	1,431,017
Accumulated other comprehensive income (loss)	(13,728)	308
	2,182,014	1,719,925
Less:		
Treasury stock (21,550,923 and 19,114,822 shares in 2001 and 2000, respectively), at cost	(425,546)	(313,994)
Unearned compensation	(185)	(276)
Total shareholders' equity	1,756,283	1,405,655
	$3,118,495	$2,436,404

Source: Harley's 2001 *Annual Report.*

CORPORATE VISION STATEMENT

Harley's vision statement is as follows:

> *Harley-Davidson is an action-oriented, international company, a leader in its commitment to continuously improve {its} mutually beneficial relationships with*

stakeholders (customers, suppliers, employees, shareholders, government, and society). Harley-Davidson believes the key to success is to balance stakeholders' interests through the empowerment of all employees to focus on value-added activities.

HARLEY DIVISIONS

Harley-Davidson is divided into two segments: (1) motorcycles and related products and (2) financial services. The motorcycles and related products segment designs, manufactures, and sells motorcycles, motorcycle parts, accessories, and general merchandise. The financial services segment consists of Harley's wholly owned subsidiary, Harley-Davidson Financial Services, Inc (HDFS). HDFS provides financial service programs to Harley and Buell dealers and consumers in the United States and Canada. Note in Exhibit 3, the organizational chart for the company, that Harley's management is centered on these two divisions.

The average purchaser of a U.S. Harley-Davidson motorcycle is a married male in his mid-forties, with a household income of approximately $77,700. Over two-thirds of the sales of Harley-Davidson motorcycles are to buyers with at least one year of higher education beyond high school, and 30 percent have college degrees. Only about 9 percent of Harley's U.S. retail motorcycle sales are to women. Repeat business is strong as about 45 percent of motorcycle purchasers owned a Harley previously.

Harley's heavyweight class of motorcycles is divided into four segments: standard, performance, touring, and custom. The standard segment emphasizes simplicity and cost, and the performance segment emphasizes handling and acceleration. The touring segment for the company focuses on comfort for long-distance travel. Harley-Davidson pioneered this segment of the heavyweight market. Harley's custom segment gives owners the opportunity to customize their bikes.

Harley-Davidson makes twenty-four models of Harley-Davidson touring and custom heavyweight motorcycles, with retail prices ranging from about $6,000 to $20,000. The prices of Harley's custom bikes on the high end can be as much as 50 percent more than its competitors' custom motorcycles. The custom segment makes up the highest number of Harley's sold and demands a higher price because of its features, styling, and high resale value.

Harley has one custom model that is priced competitively with comparable motorcycles available in the market—the 883cc Sportster. This model serves as sort of an introduction bike for new Harley-Davidson customers. The company's surveys of retail purchasers indicate that over 75 percent of the purchasers of its Sportster model have previously owned competitive-brand motorcycles, are new to the sport of motorcycling, or have been out of the sport for five or more years. The company also has research indicating that more than 92 percent of its motorcycle customers intend to repurchase. Harley is hoping that the purchasers of the lower-priced Sportster models will be tempted to purchase a higher-priced custom model the next time around.

The Buell motorcycle line serves the standard and performance segments of the market. Buell sells four heavyweight performance models, with retail prices ranging from $8,795 to $13,700. The company also introduced the Buell Blast in 2000 for the standard market, with a price tag of about $4,395. The Blast is smaller and lighter than the other motorcycles offered by Buell. The bike also has a single cylinder engine as opposed to the trademark V-engine configuration. The company's studies indicate that almost half of Buell Blast purchasers have never owned a motorcycle before, and over 50 percent are women. Harley-Davidson bought a minority interest in Buell, a sport bike company, in 1992 and finished buying the remaining interest in 1998. Production of the new Buell Firebolt XB9R began in 2001.

EXHIBIT 3   Harley Davidson's Organization Chart

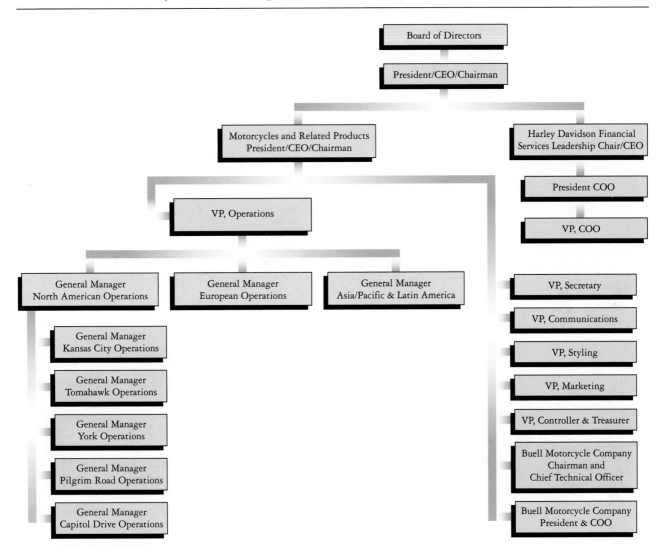

Harley-Davidson Financial Services (HDFS) has in 2001 helped over 87,000 retail buyers with the purchase of a new or used Harley. HDFS also offers wholesale financing, with services including floorplan and open account financing of motorcycles and accessories. In addition, the company often makes real estate loans, computer loans, and showroom remodeling loans to many dealers. In the United States and Canada, where these services are offered, they were used by about 97 percent of all dealers.

Note in Exhibit 4 that the financial services division had a great year during 2001; operating income increased 64.8 percent—to 61 million. The ability of HDFS to offer a package of wholesale and retail financial services is a major competitive advantage. HDFS can compete based on convenience, service, terms, and price. The financial services segment can also rely on its strong dealer relations and industry experience to compete for both the company's wholesale and retail finance businesses. HDFS finances

EXHIBIT 4   Operations Relating to the Financial Services Segment
(in thousands)

	2000	1999	1998
Interest income	$ 71,414	$ 78,502	$ 65,203
Securitization and servicing fee income	42,257	36,378	24,380
Other income	26,464	17,861	13,339
Total income	140,135	132,741	102,922
Interest expense	30,354	28,686	24,008
Provision for credit losses	9,919	17,919	10,338
Operating expenses	62,684	58,451	48,365
Total expenses	102,957	105,056	82,711
Operating income from financial services	$ 37,178	$ 27,685	$ 20,211

Source: Harley's 2001 *Annual Report*, p. 37.

about 25 percent of new Harley-Davidson motorcycles retailed in the U.S. The main competitors for the retail and wholesale businesses of HDFS are local and regional financial institutions.

MARKETING AND DISTRIBUTION

Harley-Davidson has approximately 630 independently owned full-service dealerships in the United States. The marketing efforts are divided between dealer promotions, customer events, magazine and direct mail advertising, and public relations. Harley also sponsors racing activities and special promotional events, and it participates in all major motorcycle consumer shows and rallies. The Harley Owners Group (H.O.G), which was founded in 1983, currently has approximately 660,000 members worldwide and is the industry's largest company-sponsored motorcycle enthusiast organization (**www.hog.com**). The Buell Riders' Adventure Group (BRAG) was also formed in recent years and has grown to approximately 10,000 members. Both H.O.G and BRAG sponsor events, including national rallies and rides, across the United States and around the world for motorcycle enthusiasts.

A major marketing initiative for Harley in 2003 will be the celebration of its 100th anniversary. The company plans to have a rolling birthday party lasting more than a year. The party will circle the globe with a series of traveling festivals lasting two to three days at a time. In July 2002, the Open Road Tour began in North America and then moved south to Mexico. The tour will jump continents to Australia and Japan before wrapping up with a couple of events in Europe in the summer of 2003.

Harley-Davidson is one of the most admired and recognized companies in the world today. Recently, the company has attempted to create an increased awareness of the Harley-Davidson brand name among the nonriding public and to provide a wide range of products for enthusiasts by licensing the Harley-Davidson name. The company has licensed the production and sale of T-shirts, jewelry, small leather goods, toys, and other products. The company also licenses the Harley-Davidson name to two cafes, one located in New York and one in Las Vegas. As can be seen in Exhibit 5, general merchandise sales went up 12.5 percent to $163.9 million in 2001.

Harley has also created an Academy of Motorcycling for those interested in learning to ride a motorcycle. The Academy, which is called "Rider's Edge," introduced more than one thousand aspiring motorcyclists to the sport in 2000. Those riders learned aboard the new single-cylinder Buell Blast. The participating dealers are creating new customers

EXHIBIT 5   Motorcycle Unit Shipments and Net Sales (dollars in millions)

	2001	2000	Increase (Decrease)	% Change
Motorcycle Unit Shipments				
Harley-Davidson® motorcycle units	234,461	204,592	29,869	14.6%
Buell® motorcycle units	9,925	10,189	(264)	(2.6)
Total motorcycle units	244,386	214,781	29,605	138%
Net Sales				
Harley-Davidson motorcycles	$ 2,630.1	$ 2,246.4	$ 383.7	17.1%
Buell motorcycles	61.9	58.1	38	6.6
Total motorcycles	2,692.0	2,304.5	387.5	16.8%
Motorcycle Parts and Accessories	507.3	447.9	59.4	13.3
General Merchandise	163.9	151.4	12.5	8.2
Other	.2	2.6	(2.4)	(92.3)
Total Motorcycles and Related Products	$ 3,363.4	$ 2,906.4	$ 457.0	15.7%

Source: Harley's 2001 Annual Report, p. 42.

today that could lead to lifelong relationships. Harley dealers are serious about the future success of Harley-Davidson; almost half of all U.S. dealers have opened new retail stores or completed major renovations to their existing facilities in the past three years.

Harley has an online catalog featuring its genuine motor accessories and motor-clothes. In addition to browsing and making a wish list, customers can actually purchase these products at the Web site. The orders are then distributed to local dealers who can ship the products directly or hold the items for pick-up. More than 5 million visitors surfed through the e-commerce area during the year.

INTERNATIONAL SALES

Harley-Davidson faces some unique competitive challenges in international markets. In Europe, for example, it must consider the unique tastes of many individual countries that together represent a market about the size of the U.S. market. Also, the European Union's motorcycle noise standards are lower than those of the Environmental Protection Agency (EPA). This causes research and development costs related to motorcycle noise emissions to be higher for motorcycles produced for the European market.

Another challenge for Harley is the fact that the European heavyweight motorcy-cle market is made up of 74 percent of the standard and performance segments. Harley has only recently started to compete in the performance market with the addition of its Buell motorcycles. As can be seen in Exhibit 6, the European market had 293,400 new registrations in 2000, down 4.3 percent from 306,700 in 1999. Harley ended 2001 with a 6.7 percent share of the European heavyweight market, down from 7.4 percent in 2000. The company has had difficulty growing its market share in European markets. In the European region, there are about 350 Harley-Davidson dealerships.

Harley finished 2001 with a 20.4 percent share of the Asia/Pacific heavyweight market, up from 19.5 percent in 2000. It is now easier than previously to obtain a heavy-weight motorcycle driver's license in Japan. While total market registrations in the Asia/Pacific decreased 1.0 percent in 2001, Harley registrations were up 3.7 percent over 1999. In 2001, lawmakers in Japan scrapped a widely unpopular law that restricted the speed to 48 mph (80 kph) on expressways (see **www.japanauto.com/autotrends**). The revision, the first in thirty-five years, boosts the speed to 62 mph (100 kph). The

EXHIBIT 6   Worldwide Heavyweight Motorcycle Registration Data (Engine Displacement of 651+cc) (units in thousands)

	2000	1999	1998
NORTH AMERICA[1]			
Total market new registrations	363.4	297.9	246.2
Harley-Davidson® new registrations	164.0	142.1	116.1
Buell® new registrations	4.3	4.0	3.3
Total company registrations	168.3	146.1	119.4
Total company market share %	46.3%	49.0%	48.5%
EUROPE[2]			
Total market new registrations	293.4	306.7	270.2
Harley-Davidson new registrations	19.9	17.8	15.7
Buell new registrations	1.9	2.1	1.6
Total company registrations	21.8	19.9	17.3
Total company market share %	7.4%	6.5%	6.4%
JAPAN/AUSTRALIA[3]			
Total market new registrations	62.7	63.1	69.2
Harley-Davidson new registrations	12.2	11.6	10.3
Buell new registrations	.7	.7	.5
Total company registrations	12.9	12.3	10.8
Total company market share %	20.5%	19.6%	15.6%
TOTAL			
Total new registrations	719.5	667.7	585.6
Harley-Davidson new registrations	196.1	171.5	142.1
Buell new registrations	6.9	6.8	5.4
Total company registrations	203.0	178.3	147.5
Total company market share %	28.2%	26.7%	25.2%

[1]Includes the United States and Canada. Data provided by the Motorcycle Industry Council.
[2]Includes Austria, Belgium, France, Germany, Italy, The Netherlands, Spain, Switzerland, and the United Kingdom. Data provided by Giral S.A.
[3]Data provided by JAMA and ABS.

Japanese Automobile Manufacturers Association (JAMA) reported that an American-based research firm expects motorcycle sales to rise 30 percent as a result of the changes. There are currently about 213 Harley-Davidson outlets serving eight country markets in the Asia/Pacific region (see Exhibit 7).

In 1998, the company opened a new assembly facility in Manaus, Brazil, the first such operation outside the United States. The facility imports U.S.-made components for final assembly in Brazil. This will increase the availability of Harley's motorcycles in Brazil, and it will reduce duties and taxes, making them more affordable to a larger group of Brazilian customers. In the past, only the wealthy in Brazil could afford a Harley because of the steep import tariffs. The facility currently assembles fewer than one thousand motorcycles per year.

In 2001, international sales were 597.0 million, up 20.0 percent from 2000. The motor company exported about 20.3 percent of its Harley-Davidson motorcycles in 2001, down slightly from the 22.4 percent reported in 2000.

EXHIBIT 7   Geographic Information (in thousands)

	2001	2000	1999
Net sales:			
United States	$2,766,391	$2,320,991	$1,915,631
Europe	301,729	285,372	274,737
Japan	141,181	148,684	135,589
Canada	96,928	93,352	80,271
Other foreign countries	57,185	57,966	46,711
	$3,363,414	$2,906,365	$2,452,939
Long-lived assets:			
United States	$1,021,946	$ 856,746	$ 775,764
Other foreign countries	33,234	27,844	8,948
	$1,055,180	$ 884,590	$ 784,712

Source: Harley's 2001 *Annual Report,* p. 81.

COMPETITION

The U.S. and international heavyweight (651+cc) motorcycle market is highly competitive. Some of Harley's major competitors have larger financial and marketing resources and are more diversified. For example, only about half of the sales of Yamaha Motor Company are motorcycles. Competition in the heavyweight motorcycle market is based on price, quality, reliability, styling, and customer preference. Harley-Davidson does not emphasize price in its heavyweight bikes partly because the resale prices for used Harley-Davidson motorcycles are generally higher than that of its competitors.

Since 1986, Harley has led the industry in domestic sales of heavyweight motorcycles. As shown in Exhibit 8, Harley's share of the U.S. heavyweight (651+cc) market was 47.4 percent in 2000, down from 50.2 percent in 1999. The company believes this decline was due to its ongoing capacity constraints. However, Harley's share is still significantly greater than its largest competitor in the domestic market, Honda, which had an 18.6 percent market share in 2000. During 2000, the worldwide heavyweight market grew 7.8 percent, while retail registrations for Harley-Davidson's motorcycles grew 13.8 percent. Note in Exhibit 6 that this netted the company a worldwide heavyweight market share of 28.2 percent, up from 26.7 percent in 1999.

A new potential domestic threat for Harley-Davidson in recent years is Polaris. Polaris, an American snowmobile/ATV manufacturer, started production of its Victory motorcycles on July 4, 1998. The company is planning to introduce three more models in 2002, and all are priced below the average price of a Harley (see **www.polarisindustries.com**). The company has more than three hundred dealers in the United States, and in 2000, it expanded into Canada, United Kingdom, and Australia, with plans for future expansion. While current sales volumes for Polaris motorcycles are not significant in comparison to Harley-Davidson, the threat that Polaris may gain a piece of the domestic market is very real. Polaris finished 2000 with retail sales of motorcycles up 50 percent, to about $20 million. Motorcycles currently represent only about 1 percent of overall sales at Polaris. The president of Polaris, Tom Tiller, stated in a February 2001 press release, "We are in the motorcycle business for the long-term and remain confident in Victory's ability to contribute to profitable growth for Polaris" (**www.americanmotor.com/news**).

EXHIBIT 8   Market share of U.S. Heavyweight Motorcycles[1]
(Engine Displacement of 651+cc)

	Year Ended December 31,				
	2000	*1999*	*1998*	*1997*	*1996*
NEW U.S. REGISTRATIONS (THOUSANDS OF UNITS):					
Total market new registrations	338.0	275.6	227.1	190.2	165.7
Harley-Davidson® new registrations	155.9	134.5	109.1	93.5	79.9
Buell® new registrations	4.2	3.9	3.2	1.9	1.7
Total Company new registrations	160.1	138.4	112.3	95.4	81.6
PERCENTAGE MARKET SHARE:					
Harley-Davidson motorcycles	46.1%	48.8%	48.1%	49.2%	48.2%
Buell motorcycles	1.3	1.4	1.4	1.0	1.0
Total Company	47.4	50.2	49.5	50.2	49.2
Honda	18.6	16.4	20.3	18.5	18.8
Suzuki	9.4	9.4	10.0	10.1	8.7
Kawasaki	9.1	10.3	10.1	10.4	12.2
Yamaha	8.4	7.0	4.2	5.4	5.9
Other	7.1	6.7	5.9	5.4	5.2
Total	100.0%	100.0%	100.0%	100.0%	100.0%

[1] Motorcycle registration and market share information has been derived from data published by the Motorcycle Industry Council for the years 1997-2000 and from data published by R.L. Polk & Co. for 1996.

In November 2001, Suzuki Motor Corporation and Kawasaki Heavy Industries, Ltd. formed a strategic alliance in the areas of product development, design, engineering, and manufacturing of motorcycles (see **www.suzukicycles.com**). The alliance is expected to strengthen both companies' global motorcycle businesses. Each company will continue to use its own brand insofar as marketing and sales will not be combined. Note in Exhibit 8 that when combined, the market share of Suzuki and Kawasaki rivals that of Honda, Harley's number one competitor in the United States. Harley will have to address this new competitive threat, since the alliance of these two firms will certainly strengthen their efforts to gain more of Harley's coveted domestic market for heavyweights.

STRATEGIC PLAN FOR SUSTAINABLE GROWTH

The company announced on September 19, 2001, that it plans to move the assembly operation of its "Dyna Glide" family of motorcycles to its facility in Kansas City, Missouri. This was done as part of its continuing effort to narrow the gap between supply and demand. All Dyna Glide models are currently assembled in York, Pennsylvania, and this part of its business represents around 15 percent of total production. The company also announced on July 11, 2001, that it plans to build a new $145 million, 350,000 square-foot assembly plant in York on the site of its existing manufacturing facility. The president of the motor company feels that this new facility, coupled with the movement of production between the plants, will provide strong and flexible manufacturing capabilities.

Harley plans to continue to increase its motorcycle production to be able to sustain its annual double-digit growth rate for units shipped. The company has plans to expand its operations in Tomahawk, Wisconsin, and at its product development center in

Milwaukee. Harley produced and sold 234,461 Harley-Davidson motorcycles in 2001, up 14.6 percent from the 204,592 shipped in 2000. As recently as 1999, the company had envisioned reaching an annual production target of 200,000, but not until the year 2003. Harley may have underestimated the growth in the demand for its bikes, the growth in the worldwide heavyweight market, and in its ability to increase production.

The Buell division sold 9,925 motorcycles in 2001, down 264 units from 2000. This was due in part to a shift in sales emphasis from the new Buell Blast to the heavy-weight Buell cycle.

THE FUTURE

Domestically, Harley has the kind of name recognition and brand loyalty that is the envy of the industry. Could it ever develop a similar customer relationship abroad? Recognizing that part of the Harley image was built on tradition, how can Harley stay true to the things (and people) that helped to make it what it is and still grow as it has in the past few years?

Prepare a three-year strategic plan for Harley-Davidson. Address the specific issues of international growth opportunities in European countries as well as domestic compet-itive threats from Honda and the new alliance of Suzuki and Kawasaki. Examine the strengths of the Harley-Davidson brand along with the continuing weakness of ongoing capacity constraints. Imagine you are Chairman and CEO Jeffery L. Bleustein and have the task of leading this company as it prepares to meet the growing demand for its motorcycles in the coming years. What specific actions would you take? Should your rec-ommendations be financed with debt or equity? Develop pro-forma financial statements to assess the impact of your changes.

WINNEBAGO INDUSTRIES—2002

John G. Marcis
Coastal Carolina University
Eugene M. Bland
Francis Marion University

WGO

www.winnebagoind.com

Saving money is nice, but it is not the real reason why people travel in a motor home. Motor homing is just plain fun. Motor homers are an adventurous lot—they like to go, see, and do. Florida residents have replaced Californians as the most active motor home campers. New Yorkers are third on the "most on the go" list. Recreational vehicle (RV) owners say that they not only save money when camping but also can avoid the bother of having to stop for restaurants and bathrooms.

Motor home traveling is purported to be much less expensive than traveling by car or plane and staying in a motel. Motor homers stop when there is something to see and do. They often spend summers where it is cool and winters where it is warm. In fact, industry advertisements tout the RV lifestyle with this slogan: "Wherever you go, you're always at home."

Winnebago Industries, Inc. is a leading manufacturer of motor homes. Company revenues for the fiscal year ended August 25, 2001, decreased to $681.83 million, compared to $753.38 million in 2000. Motor home shipments (Class A and Class C) during fiscal 2001 were 9,076 units, a decrease of 1,440 units, or 13.7 percent, compared to fiscal 2000. However, market share increased to 18.9 percent of the Class A and C motor home market in 2001, compared to 17.0 percent for the same period in calendar 2000. The company builds quality products with state-of-the-art computer-aided design and manufacturing systems on automotive-style assembly lines. Although Winnebago competes with Fleetwood and Coachmen, the name Winnebago is considered synonymous with the term *motor home*.

Winnebago was founded in 1958 and has always been headquartered in Forest City, Iowa (515-582-3535). The company's common stock is listed on the New York, Chicago, and Pacific Stock Exchanges, and it is traded under the symbol WGO. Options for Winnebago's common stock are traded on the Chicago Board Options Exchange. Winnebago's home page can be accessed at **http://www.winnebagoind.com**, and corporate press releases are available through Company New On-Call at **www.prnewswire.com/cnoc/exec/menu/105967**.

Winnebago Industries is financially stable. The firm owns its land, buildings, and equipment, and it has no long-term debt. The firm has an enviable cash balance, which provides the company with the opportunity for future growth. Winnebago ended fiscal 2001 as the number one motor home retail sales company for the first time in 20 years. The company improved its market share by 10 percent in 2001 from 2000.

EARLY MOTOR HOMING

The first motor home was built in 1915 to take people from the Atlantic Coast to San Francisco. It had wooden wheels and hard rubber tires. It was promoted as having all the comforts of an ocean cruiser. By the 1920s, the house car had become a fixture in the United States and a symbol of freedom. All kinds of house cars could be seen traveling across America's dirt roads. They ranged from what looked like large moving cigars to two-story houses with porches on wheels. But these house cars featured poor weight distribution, poor insulation, and poor economy. From the 1930s to the 1950s, they gave way in popularity to the trailer.

In the mid-1950s, motor homes were called motorized trailers. They were overweight, underpowered, and poorly insulated, but they were still a vast improvement over the house cars of the 1920s. In the 1960s, motor homing became much more popular, largely as a result of the innovations of Winnebago. From Forest City, Iowa, where the company was founded in 1958, Winnebago has set the pace for all new developments in motor homes. The Winnebago name became a household word. Buyers of motor homes were asked, "When will your Winnebago be delivered?"

CORPORATE PROFILE

Corporate Mission Statement

Winnebago's motto is "Quality Is a Journey—Not a Destination." From the beginning, the company recognized the critical roles played by employees, customers, and dealers in the total quality process. The significance of quality to the firm is evidenced by its Mission Statement, its Statement of Values, and its Statement of Guiding Principles, which are provided in Exhibit 1.

Production Facilities

Winnebago has major production facilities in Forest City, Iowa. Currently, over twenty buildings at this location fill more than 2 million square feet (approximately sixty acres under roof) and contain the company's manufacturing, maintenance, and service operations. There are also satellite-manufacturing facilities at Hampton and Lorimor, Iowa. These two facilities add another seven hundred thousand square feet of manufacturing space. All corporate facilities in Forest City are located on approximately 784 acres of land that is owned by Winnebago.

Winnebago has three nine-hundred-foot assembly lines for final assembly of motor homes. Statistical process control is practiced at Winnebago and has enhanced the quality of its van products. As a motor home moves down the assembly line, quality control is carefully monitored. Units are taken randomly from the line for a thorough examination. The performance of every RV is tested before it is delivered to a dealer's lot. The company makes sure that all of its motor home components meet or exceed federal and durability standards. Some of the tests routinely performed include lamination strength, appliance performance, chip resistance, vibration, drop, salt spray, and crash tests.

RESEARCH AND DEVELOPMENT

Winnebago uses computer technology to design its motor homes. The company has a state-of-the-art, computer-aided design/computer-aided manufacturing (CAD/CAM) system. This system aids in the production of low-cost sheet metal parts, new paint lines for steel and aluminum parts, and modifications of assembly equipment.

One of Winnebago's product-testing facilities at Forest City houses some of the most sophisticated technology being used in the RV industry (such as a high- and low-temperature chamber for subjecting parts to extreme temperatures and high stress).

EXHIBIT 1 Winnebago Industries, Inc. Mission Statement

MISSION STATEMENT

Winnebago Industries, Inc. is a leading manufacturer of recreation vehicles (RVs) and related products and services. Our mission is to continually improve our products and services to meet or exceed the expectations of our customers. We emphasize employee teamwork and involvement in identifying and implementing programs to save time and lower production costs while maintaining the highest quality values. These strategies allow us to prosper as a business with a high degree of integrity and to provide a reasonable return for our shareholders, the ultimate owners of our business.

VALUES

How we accomplish our mission is as important as the mission itself. Fundamental to the success of the Company are these basic values we describe as the four P's:

People—Our employees are the source of our vast strength. They provide our corporate intelligence and determine our reputation and vitality. Involvement and teamwork are our core human values.

Products—Our products are the end result of our team's efforts, and they should be the best in meeting or exceeding our customers' expectations worldwide. As our products are viewed, so are we viewed.

Plant—The Company believes its plant is the most technologically advanced in the RV industry. We continue to review facility improvements that will increase the utilization of our plant capacity and enable us to build the best quality product for the investment.

Profitability—Profitability is the ultimate measure of how efficiently we provide our customers with the best products for their needs. Profitability is required to survive and grow. As our respect and position within the marketplace grows, so will our profit.

GUIDING PRINCIPLES

Quality comes first—To achieve customer satisfaction, [we must make] the quality of our products and services . . . be our number one priority.

Customers are central to our existence—Our work must be done with our customers in mind, providing products and services that meet or exceed the expectations of our customers. We must not only satisfy our customers, we must also surprise and delight them.

Continuous improvement is essential to our success—We must strive for excellence in everything we do: in our products, in their safety and value, as well as in our services, our human relations, our competitiveness, and our profitability.

Employee involvement is our way of life—We are a team. We must treat each other with trust and respect.

Dealers and suppliers are our partners—The Company must maintain mutually beneficial relationships with dealers, suppliers, and our other business associates.

Integrity is never compromised—The Company must pursue conduct in a manner that is socially responsible and that commands respect for its integrity and for its positive contributions to society. Our doors are open to all men and women alike without discrimination and without regard to ethnic origin or personal beliefs.

Source: Winnebago Industries, 1999 *Annual Report,* p. 21.

PRODUCT LINE

In 1997, the board of directors elected Ronald D. Buckmeier to the position of vice president of product development. The new product development team implemented a process to develop new products and to maximize production efficiencies. This system involves a cross-functional approach for the design and manufacture of RVs, and it streamlines the production process. Nearly every one of the sixty product series have either been dramatically redesigned or introduced as a completely new product since the 1997 offerings.

Winnebago manufactures three principal kinds of recreational vehicles, as indicated in Exhibit 2: Class A Motor Homes, Class B Van Campers, and Class C Motor Homes (Mini). Class A motor homes are constructed on a chassis that already has the engine and drive components attached. They range in length from twenty-three to

EXHIBIT 2   Motor Home Product Classification

Class A Motor Homes

These are conventional motor homes constructed directly on medium-duty truck chassis which include the engine and drive train components. The living area of the driver's compartment is designed and produced by Winnebago Industries. Class A motor homes from Winnebago Industries include Winnebago Brave, Adventurer, Chieftain, and Journey; Itasca Sunrise, Suncruiser, Sunflyer, and Horizon; and Ultimate Advantage and Freedom.

Class B Van Campers

These are panel-type trucks to which sleeping, kitchen, and toilet facilities are added. These models also have a top extension to provide more headroom. Winnebago Industries converts the EuroVan Camper, which is distributed by Volkswagen of America and Volkswagen of Canada.

Class C Motor Homes (Mini)

These are minimotor homes built on a van-type chassis onto which Winnebago Industries constructs a living area with access to the driver's compartment. Class C motor homes from Winnebago industries include Winnebago Minnie and Minnie Winnie; Itasca Spirit and Sundancer; and Rialta.

Source: Winnebago Industries, 2001 *Annual Report,* p. 16.

thirty-seven feet and can sell for more than $250,000. Class A motor homes include the Winnebago Adventurer, Brave, Chieftain, and Journey; the Itasca Suncruiser, Sunrise, Sunflyer, and Horizon; and the Ultimate Advantage and Freedom, as indicated in Exhibit 3. Although the Winnebago Adventurer and Itasco Suncruiser are popular, the Winnebago Brave and Itasca Sunrise models are the company's top-selling vehicles. As of August 25, 2001, the backlog for orders for Class A and Class C motor homes was nearly 1,600 units (compared to only 1,355 in August of 2000, an 18 percent increase).

Winnebago's Class B van campers are actually conventional vans manufactured by Ford, General Motors, and Daimler-Chrysler that are custom tailored by Winnebago with special interiors, exteriors, windows, and vents. In many American households, van campers are replacing the family car as the vehicle of choice. These vehicles can turn a long family trip from an ordeal into a pleasant adventure. Winnebago manufactures the EuroVan Camper conversion for Volkswagen of America and Volkswagen of Canada. Class B van campers are seventeen feet in length.

Class C motor homes are constructed on a van chassis; the driver's compartment is accessible to the living area. These motor homes are compact and easy to drive. They range from twenty-one to twenty-nine feet in length and have five popular floor plans. Typical options of a Class C vehicle include six feet of headroom, shower, stove, sink, refrigerator, and two double beds. Winnebago's Minnie Winnie vehicle is the most popular Class C motor home in the country. The company's Itasca Sundancer and Itasca Spirit also are popular.

Winnebago introduced two new Class A models (the Winnebago Sightseer and the Itasca Sunova) and two new Class C models (the Winnebago Vista and the Itasca Sunstar) for the 2002 model year. The Sightseer and the Sunova are entry-level, wide-body, basement-style models with many standard features typically found as options on many competitive units in this price class. Although the Vista and Sunstar models are built in classic Class C design, they are unique in that they are fuel-efficient motor homes built on a heavy duty front-wheel-drive chassis.

EXHIBIT 3   Winnebago Family Tree

Winnebago Industries manufactures four brands of Class A and C motor homes. Listed below are the band names and model designations of the company's 2000 product line.

Winnebago	*Itasca*	*Rialta*	*Ultimate*
–Vista	–Spirit	–Rialta	–Ultimate Advantage
–Minnie	–Sundancer		–Ultimate Freedom
–Minnie Winnie	–Sunrise		
–Brave	–Suncruiser		
–Adventurer	–Sunflyer		
–Chieftain	–Horizon		
–Journey	–Sunstar		
–Journey DL			
–Sightseer	–Sunova		

OTHER RELATED PRODUCTS:

Winnebago Conversion Vehicles—Licensed truck and van conversions manufactured and marketed by Choo Choo Customs Group, Inc.
Winnebago Park Homes—Licensed products manufactured and marketed by Chariot Eagle, Inc.
Winnebago Tents—Licensed products manufactured and marketed by Avid Outdoor.

Source: Winnebago Industries, 2001 *Annual Report,* p. 16.

Marketing

Consumer research reveals that the demographics for motor home buyers are undergoing a change. Traditionally, buyers have been "woofies" ("well-off older folks" defined as people over fifty years of age with discretionary available income) with time to enjoy leisure travel and outdoor recreation. According to research, an individual in the United States is turning fifty every 7.5 seconds, thus contributing an additional 350,000 people per *month* to that prime target market. Available demographic information indicates that this trend will continue for the next thirty years.

The peak selling seasons for RVs has historically been spring and summer. Class A and Class C motor homes are marketed under the Winnebago and Itasca brand names and were sold in the United States and, to a limited extent, in Canada and other foreign countries through a network of approximately 340 dealers in 2001; this is up from 325 in 1994.

Winnebago Industries believes it has the most comprehensive service program in the RV industry. With the purchase of any new Class A or Class C motor home (except the Rialta, which has a 24-month, 24,000-mile warranty), Winnebago offers a comprehensive 12-month/15,000-mile warranty, a 3-year/36,000 mile warranty on sidewalls and slide-out room assemblies, and a 10-year fiberglass roof warranty. Winnebago features a 2-year/24,000-mile warranty on the Rialta. Winnebago also instituted a toll-free hotline at which experienced service advisers respond to inquiries from prospective customers and expedite and resolve warranty issues. Every owner of a new Winnebago motor home receives free roadside assistance for twelve months.

RECENT YEARS

Winnebago celebrated its 40th anniversary in 1998, which was a banner year for both production and revenue. Although the motor home industry had a good year overall, Winnebago outperformed the motor home industry by 12 percent during the first nine months of the calendar year. Revenues were a record $525.1 million for the fiscal year (compared with $438.1 million for the 1997 fiscal year). Income from continuing operations for the year reflected a nearly fourfold increase from the previous fiscal year. In December 1998, Winnebago had a sales order backlog of over three thousand units, the largest in the company's history.

Winnebago's good fortune continued through 2000. Unit production increased about 27.2 percent (from $525.1 million to $667.7 million) between 1998 and 1999 and an additional 12.8 percent (to $753.3 million) between 1999 and 2000. However, RV sales fell approximately 17 percent during the first six months of 2001. This decline in sales was due to a number of factors: wavering consumer confidence in the national economy, a weakening national economy, and a dramatic spike in the prices of gasoline and diesel fuel. In an attempt to sell the existing inventory, manufacturers and dealers started to offer sales incentives, which put pressure on operating margins. Consequently, Winnebago's revenues for the fiscal year ended August 25, 2001, were $681.8 million, compared with revenues of $753.4 million for the previous fiscal year. Moreover, the economic uncertainty introduced since the terrorist attacks of September 11, 2001, further cloud the fiscal picture of leisure-related activities like RVing.

WINNEBAGO'S EXTERNAL ENVIRONMENT

Winnebago's motor homes can attract a low-frills buyer who wants the most stripped-down RV, the person with expensive tastes who wants the ultimate in RV luxury—and

EXHIBIT 4   Net Revenues By Major Product Class (Unaudited)
(dollars in thousands)

	Fiscal Year Ended[1]				
	Aug. 25, 2001	Aug. 26, 2000	Aug. 28, 1999	Aug. 29, 1998	Aug. 30, 1997
Motor homes (Class A & Class C)	$630,017	$695,767	$619,171	$474,954	$387,161
	92.4%	92.4%	91.5%	89.0%	86.9%
Other recreation vehicle revenues[2]	17,808	18,813	16,620	19,222	21,159
	2.6%	2.5%	2.5%	3.6%	4.7%
Other manufactured products revenues[3]	29,768	34,894	38,225	37,133	35,881
	4.4%	4.6%	5.6%	7.0%	8.1%
Total manufactured products revenues	677,593	749,474	674,016	531,309	444,201
	99.4%	99.5%	99.6%	99.6%	99.7%
Finance revenues[4]	4,241	3,908	2,995	2,076	1,420
	.6%	.5%	.4%	.4%	.3%
Total net revenues	$681,834	$753,382	$677,011	$533,385	$445,621
	100.0%	100.0%	100.0%	100.0%	100.0%

(1) All fiscal years in the table contained 52 weeks.
(2) Primarily recreation vehicle related parts, EuroVan Campers (Class B motor homes), and recreation vehicle service revenue.
(3) Primarily sales of extruded aluminum, commercial vehicles, and component products for other manufacturers.
(4) WAC revenues from dealer financing.
Source: Winnebago Industries, 2001 Annual Report, p. 39.

EXHIBIT 5   Consolidated Statements of Income (in thousands, except per-share data)

	Year Ended		
	August 25, 2001	*August 26, 2000*	*August 28, 1999*
Revenues:			
Manufactured products	$677,593	$749,474	$674,016
Dealer financing	4,241	3,908	2,995
Total net revenues	681,834	753,382	677,011
Costs and expenses:			
Cost of manufactured products	587,330	640,488	574,603
Selling	25,423	25,118	24,321
General and administrative	13,607	17,122	14,105
Total costs and expenses	626,360	682,728	613,029
Operating income	55,474	70,654	63,982
Financial income	3,754	3,338	2,627
Income before income taxes	59,228	73,992	66,609
Provision for taxes	15,474	25,593	22,349
Income before cumulative effect of change in accounting principle	43,754	48,399	44,260
Cumulative effect of change in accounting principle, net of taxes	(1,050)	—	—
Net income	$ 42,704	$ 48,399	$ 44,260
Earnings per common share (basic):			
Income before cumulative effect of change in accounting principle	$ 2.11	$ 2.23	$ 1.99
Cumulative effect of change in accounting principle	(0.05)	—	—
Income per share (basic)	$ 2.06	$ 2.23	$ 1.99
Earnings per common share (diluted):			
Income before cumulative effect of change in accounting principle	$ 2.08	$ 2.20	$ 1.96
Cumulative effect of change in accounting principle	(.05)	—	—
Income per share (diluted)	$ 2.03	$ 2.20	$ 1.96
Weighted average shares of common stock outstanding:			
Basic	20,735	21,680	22,209
Diluted	21,040	22,011	22,537

Source: Winnebago Industries, 2001 *Annual Report,* p. 34.

everyone in between. RVs can be purchased or rented. Many families unable to buy a mobile home rent one to take on vacation. As the baby boomers age and approach retirement, many of them will consider selling their primary residences, purchasing and moving into a motor home, and traveling to any point they desire in North America.

The motel and hotel industries have been experiencing an oversupply of available rooms, which has resulted in low rates for rooms. Compared to the cost of owning/renting and operating an RV, the costs of staying in a motor home versus a motel are about the same if not a bit lower in favor of the motel. Motor home sales historically increase whenever travel, tourism, and vacationing gain in popularity. The converse is also true.

There are about 122,000 campsites in U.S. state parks, including 4,500 that are maintained by the U.S. Forest Service and 100 in the national parks system. In addition, there are more than 15,000 private campgrounds and over 1,620 county parks. Winnebagos can access nearly all of these sites.

EXHIBIT 6   Consolidated Balance Sheets (dollars in thousands)

	August 25, 2001	*August 26, 2000*
Assets		
Current assets:		
Cash and cash equivalents	$ 93,779	$ 51,443
Receivables, less allowance for doubtful accounts	20,183	32,045
($244 and $1,168, respectively)		
Dealer financing receivables, less allowance for doubtful accounts	40,263	32,696
($117 and $27, respectively)		
Inventories	79,815	85,707
Prepaid expenses	3,604	3,952
Deferred income taxes	6,723	7,675
Total current assets	244,367	213,518
Property and equipment, at cost:		
Land	1,029	1,138
Buildings	45,992	45,219
Machinery and equipment	82,182	78,099
Transportation equipment	5,482	5,414
	134,685	129,870
Less accumulated depreciation	88,149	84,415
Total property and equipment, net	46,536	45,455
Investment in life insurance	22,223	21,028
Deferred income taxes	21,495	19,044
Other assets	7,412	8,050
Total assets	$342,033	$307,095
Liabilities and Stockholders' Equity		
Current liabilities:		
Accounts payable, trade	$ 30,789	$ 26,212
Income taxes payable	4,938	8,790
Accrued expenses:		
Accrued compensation	13,730	13,924
Product warranties	8,072	8,114
Insurance	4,567	5,384
Promotional	3,181	3,145
Other	4,842	4,675
Total current liabilities	70,119	70,244
Postretirement health care and deferred compensation benefits	64,450	61,942
Contingent liabilities and commitments		
Stockholders' equity:		
Capital stock common, par value $.50; authorized 60,000,000 shares, issued 25,886,000 and 25,878,000 shares, respectively	12,943	12,939
Additional paid-in capital	22,261	21,994
Reinvested earnings	234,139	195,556
	269,343	230,489
Less treasury stock, at cost	61,879	55,580
Total stockholders' equity	207,464	174,909
Total liabilities and stockholders' equity	$342,033	$307,095

Source: Winnebago Industries, 2001 *Annual Report,* pp. 22–23.

EXHIBIT 7   Business Segment Information (dollars in thousands)

For the years ended August 25, 2001, August 26, 2000 and August 28, 1999, the Company's segment information is as follows:

	Recreation Vehicles & Other Manufactured Products	Dealer Financing	General Corporate	Total
2001				
Net revenues	$677,593	$ 4,241	$ —	$681,834
Operating income (loss)	52,120	4,102	(748)	55,474
Identifiable assets	175,343	40,856	125,834	342,033
Depreciation and amortization	7,158	5	217	7,380
Capital expenditures	8,974	19	96	9,089
2000				
Net revenues	$749,474	3,908	$ —	$753,382
Operating income (loss)	67,252	3,892	(490)	70,654
Identifiable assets	191,501	33,508	82,086	307,095
Depreciation and amortization	6,375	4	243	6,622
Capital expenditures	14,412	—	136	14,548
1999				
Net revenues	$674,016	$ 2,995	$ —	$677,011
Operating income (loss)	60,435	4,085	(538)	63,982
Identifiable assets	181,951	25,439	78,499	285,889
Depreciation and amortization	5,507	4	237	5,748
Capital expenditures	11,463	18	96	11,577

Operating income of the dealer financing segment reflects a $1,100,000 repayment of a previously fully reserved receivable.
Source: Winnebago Industries, 2001 *Annual Report,* p. 36.

COMPETITORS

Twelve firms account for 80 percent of the RV industry's volume. In addition to Winnebago Industries, some of the other major publicly held firms in the industry are Rexhall Industries, Mallard Coach, Kit Manufacturing, Harley-Davidson, and Skyline Corporation. The following is a list of major motor home competitors:

Company	Headquarters Location
Fleetwood Enterprises, Inc.	Riverside, California
Coachmen Industries, Inc.	Elkhart, Indiana
Mark III Industries, Inc.	Ocala, Florida
Jayco, Inc.	Middlebury, Indiana
Glaval Corp.	Elkhart, Indiana
Newmar Corp.	Nappanee, Indiana
Monaco Coach Corp.	Junction City, Oregon
Tiffin Motor Homes, Inc.	Red Bay, Alabama

Throughout the 1990s, Fleetwood Enterprises was first in sales, followed by Coachmen, and then Winnebago Industries. However, in early 2001, Winnebago became the industry leader in Class A and Class C retail motor home sales. It achieved the number one position in the industry with an 18.8 percent market share, compared to its 17.1 percent market share twelve months earlier.

INDUSTRY OUTLOOK

Calendar year 2000 was not a good year for the RV industry. Specifically, conventional motor home volume was down 27 percent, folding camping trailer sales declined 22 percent, and truck camper sales were down 8 percent. The poor year for the industry was due to the combined effects of a slowing national economy, faltering consumer confidence in the national economy, and relatively high gas prices nationally. Over the long term, recent demographic changes bode well for the growth of the industry. The number of people over the age of fifty is growing and should continue to grow at a similar rate.

AVON PRODUCTS, INC.—2002

James Camerius
Northern Michigan University

AVP

www.avon.com

On September 13, 2001, Andrea Jung, chairman of the board and chief executive officer of Avon Products, Inc., announced that the Avon Products Foundation would make a donation of $1 million of corporate funds to the American Red Cross in greater New York to help victims and their families recover from the September 11, 2001, terrorist attacks. She said, "There are no words that can express our sorrow for the victims and their families. As a company that touches the lives of people in many personal ways, we want to do whatever we can to aid the relief efforts and provide direct assistance to families." This contribution was later expanded to include a fund that would direct financial aid to educational institutions, after-school programs, and children's programs that provide counseling, safety education, child-care, and other related services.

The days that followed the terrorist attacks were difficult and challenging. Jung reflected on the attacks and the overall weak consumer spending trends that had developed as she sat down at her desk in her executive office in New York on the morning of September 25, 2001. Since September 11, Avon's stock had fallen 10 percent. The combined threats of additional terrorism and global economic recession were a primary concern. Economists were predicting rising unemployment, lower business profits, decreased discretionary spending, and a general retrenchment by businesses and consumers. And the firm's revenues could be hit hard insofar as many of the big overseas markets, such as Argentina and Brazil, faced economic decline. She felt encouraged when notified that Avon's business had returned quickly to near-normal levels.

Jung assumed the position of president and chief executive officer of Avon Products, Inc. on November 4, 1999. At the age of forty-one, she became the first woman to lead Avon in that position in the company's history, and she was one of the few Fortune 500 women CEOs. On September 6, 2001, she also assumed the additional post of chairman of the board of directors.

Jung had expected the appointment and was aware of the awesome responsibility of the position. Avon enjoyed a global reputation stemming largely from its formidable worldwide network of independent sales agents. But the effectiveness of the sales force had waned in the years prior to her appointment as chief executive officer as the company grappled with how best to sell cosmetics, jewelry, and apparel to an increasingly sophisticated customer and with how to compete against other mass merchandisers. Balance sheet and income statement data for Avon is shown in Exhibits 1 and 2.

AVON PRODUCTS

Avon is the world's largest direct-selling organization and merchandiser of beauty and beauty-related products. From corporate offices in New York City, Avon markets product lines to women in 143 countries through 3.5 million independent sales representatives who sold primarily on a door-to-door or direct-selling basis. Total sales in 2001 were $5.95 billion.

Avon's product line includes skin care items, makeup, perfume fragrances for men and women, and toiletries for bath, hair care, personal care, hand and body care, and sun care. It also includes an extensive line of fashion jewelry, apparel, gifts, and collectibles. Recognizable brand names such as Anew, Skin-So-Soft, Avon Color, Advance Techniques, and Avon Wellness are featured. There are approximately six hundred items in the product line. Internationally, the company's product line is marketed primarily at moderate price points. The marketing strategy emphasizes department store quality at discount store prices. Global marketing efforts resulted in a number of highly successful global "power" brands in the areas of cosmetics, skin care, and fragrance (i.e., products such as Anew, Avon Color, Avon Basics, and the recently introduced Anew Retroactive).

Avon is also the world's largest manufacturer and distributor of fashion jewelry, and it markets an extensive line of gifts and collectibles. The product line also includes watches, shoes, purses, CDs, videos, toys, and a wide array of other products from around the world. The major categories and subcategories of products are shown in Exhibit 3.

THE EARLY YEARS

In the late 1800s, David McConnell, a door-to-door book salesman, had an idea he believed would encourage women to buy his books. Following a common trade practice of the period, he gave prospective customers a gift of perfume to arouse their interest. Before long, he discovered that the perfume was more popular than the books. He formed a new firm, which he called the California Perfume Company. "I started in a space scarcely larger than an ordinary kitchen pantry," McConnell noted in 1900. "My ambition was to manufacture a line of goods superior to any other and take those goods through canvassing agents directly from the laboratory to the consumer." McConnell based his business upon several factors: (1) products sold directly to the consumer, (2) an image of the company that captured the beauty and excitement of the state of California, and (3) a national network of sales agents he had organized during his years as a bookseller.

In the early 1950s, the sales representatives' territories were reduced in size, a strategy that led to a quadrupling of the sales force and increased sales sixfold over the next twelve years. Avon advertisements appeared on television for the first time during this period. The famous slogan "Ding Dong, Avon Calling" was first used in 1954.

In 1960, total sales were $1.5 million, international sales were $8.2 million, and the company consisted of 6,800 employees and 125,000 sales representatives. Sales continued to grow dramatically throughout the 1960s. By 1969, total sales had grown to $558.6 million, international sales were $193.1 million, and the firm had 20,800 employees and over 400,000 sales representatives. Manufacturing plants, distribution centers, and sales branches were opened throughout the world as part of an expansion program.

In 2000, Avon increased its research and development budget 46 percent to get the newly developed "blockbuster" products to market faster. Normally, Avon spends at least three years developing new products, but Janice Teal, head of R&D, recalls Jung saying to her, "You've got two years. I need a breakthrough, and that's the goal."

Avon's strategy also includes making the direct-selling system more relevant to the contemporary woman. This strategy meant providing more meaningful career opportunities as well as harnessing technology to make Avon more user friendly for the sales representatives. "If Avon stops adding numbers of active representatives, the fuel and the lifeblood of the business slows down," Jung suggested. A new motivation and recruiting program was implemented as part of the strategic plan.

EXHIBIT 1   Consolidated Balance Sheets (in millions, except share data)

	December 31,	
	2001	2000
ASSETS		
Current assets		
Cash, including cash equivalents of $381.8 and $23.9	$ 508.5	$ 122.7
Accounts receivable (less allowance for doubtful accounts of $45.1 and $39.2)	519.5	499.0
Income tax receivable	—	95.2
Inventories	612.5	610.6
Prepaid expenses and other	248.6	218.2
Total current assets	1,889.1	1,545.7
Property, plant and equipment, at cost		
Land	49.4	53.0
Buildings and improvements	664.0	659.5
Equipment	841.2	810.6
	1,554.6	1,523.1
Less accumulated depreciation	779.7	754.7
	774.9	768.4
Other assets	529.1	512.3
Total assets	$3,193.1	$2,826.4
LIABILITIES AND SHAREHOLDERS' (DEFICIT) EQUITY		
Current liabilities		
Debt maturing within one year	$ 88.8	$ 105.4
Accounts payable	404.1	391.3
Accrued compensation	145.2	138.2
Other accrued liabilities	338.2	251.7
Sales and taxes other than income	108.8	101.1
Income taxes	375.9	371.6
Total current liabilities	1,461.0	1,359.3
Long-term debt	1,236.3	1,108.2
Employee benefit plans	436.6	397.2
Deferred income taxes	30.6	31.3
Other liabilities (including minority interest of $29.0 and $30.7)	103.2	95.2
Commitments and Contingencies		
Share repurchase commitments	—	51.0
SHAREHOLDERS' (DEFICIT) EQUITY		
Common stock, par value $.25—authorized:		
800,000,000 shares; issued 356,312,680 and 354,535,840 shares	89.1	88.6
Additional paid-in capital	938.0	824.1
Retained earnings	1,389.9	1,139.8
Accumulated other comprehensive loss	(489.5)	(399.1)
Treasury stock, at cost—119,631,574 and 116,373,394 shares	(2,002.1)	(1,869.2)
Total shareholders' (deficit) equity	(74.6)	(215.8)
Total liabilities and shareholders' (deficit) equity	$3,193.1	$2,826.4

Source: Avon's 2001 *Annual Report,* p. 39.

EXHIBIT 2   Consolidated Statements of Income (in millions, except per-share data)

| | Years ended December 31, | | |
	2001	2000	1999
Net sales	$5,952.0	$5,673.7	$5,289.1
Other revenue	42.5	40.9	38.8
Total revenue	5,994.5	5,714.6	5,327.9
Costs, expenses and other:			
Cost of sales	2,220.1	2,122.7	2,031.5
Marketing, distribution and administrative expenses	2,932.1	2,803.2	2,641.8
Contract settlement gain, net of related expenses	(25.9)	—	—
Asset impairment charge	23.9	—	—
Special charge	94.9	—	105.2
Operating profit	749.4	788.7	549.4
Interest expense	71.1	84.7	43.2
Interest income	(14.4)	(8.5)	(11.1)
Other expense, net	27.0	21.5	10.7
Total other expenses	83.7	97.7	42.8
Income from continuing operations before taxes, minority interest and cumulative effect of accounting changes	665.7	691.0	506.6
Income taxes	230.9	201.7	204.2
Income before minority interest and cumulative effect of accounting changes	434.8	489.3	302.4
Minority interest	(4.5)	(4.2)	—
Income from continuing operations before cumulative effect of accounting changes	430.3	485.1	302.4
Cumulative effect of accounting changes, net of tax	(0.3)	(6.7)	—
Net income	$ 430.0	$ 478.4	$ 302.4
Basic earnings per share:			
Continuing operations	$ 1.82	$ 2.04	$ 1.18
Cumulative effect of accounting changes	—	(.03)	—
	$ 1.82	$ 2.01	$ 1.18
Diluted earnings per share:			
Continuing operations	$ 1.79	$ 2.02	$ 1.17
Cumulative effect of accounting changes	—	(.03)	—
	$ 1.79	$ 1.99	$ 1.17

Source: Avon's 2001 Annual Report, p. 38.

COMPETITION

Competition in the direct-selling industry consists of a few large, well-established firms and many small organizations that sell about every product imaginable, including toys, animal food, collectibles, plant care products, clothing, computer software, and financial services. In addition to Avon, the dominant companies include Mary Kay (cosmetics), Amway (home maintenance products), Shaklee Corporation (vitamins and health foods), Encyclopaedia Britannica (reference books and learning systems), Tupperware (plastic dishes and food containers), Electrolux (vacuum cleaners), and Fuller (brushes and household products). Avon is substantially larger in terms of sales representatives, sales volume, and resources than Mary Kay Cosmetics, Inc., its nearest competitor in direct sales.

Headquartered in Dallas, Texas, Mary Kay's product line includes more than two hundred products in eight categories: facial skin care, color cosmetics, nail care, body

EXHIBIT 3   Avon Product Line

SKIN CARE PRODUCTS

Anew: Age management skin care
Avon Skin Care: Specific skin care concerns
Basics: Affordable, easy to use skin care
Clearskin: Acne-fighting products
Moisture Therapy: Dry skin care products

MAKEUP

Avon Color: Basic global cosmetics brand
Beyond Color: Anti-aging line
Hydra Finish: Sheer and natural cosmetics
Perfect Wear: Transfer-proof, long-wearing products
Color Trend: Global, trendy, chic colors at low prices

HAIR CARE

Advance Techniques: Alternative hair-care products
Herbal Care: Natural global botanical products

FRAGRANCES (includes one new product introduction each year)

BATH

Skin-So-Soft: Bath oil, bug repellent, and sunscreen
Naturals: Moisturizing cleansers
Aromatherapy: Candles, creams, lotions, bath products
Footworks: Foot care line
Avon Bubble Bath: In assorted fragrances
Milk Made: Vitamin enriched items for bath and body

JEWELRY (fashion, classic, and seasonal)

APPAREL (watches, shoes, and purses)

GIFT LINE (collectibles, toys, and unique gifts)

Source: Company records

care, sun protection, fragrances, men's skin care, and dietary supplements. Mary Kay is a privately held company whose wholesale sales for 2000 were approximately $1.2 billion; this translates to more than $2.5 billion in sales at the retail level. Since opening its first international venture in Australia in 1971, Mary Kay, Inc. has expanded and is now sold in thirty-seven countries worldwide.

Several other firms, such as Procter & Gamble Co., Unilever NV, Revlon, Inc., Estee Lauder, and France's L'Oreal sell cosmetics and personal care products primarily through department stores and mass merchandisers, and they are considered important competitors in the marketplace. Revlon, whose image varies by product line, had built a multibillion dollar business by buying out old established lines like Max Factor, Charles of the Ritz, Germain Monte, Diane Von Furstenberg, and Almay. Some international firms, such as Shiseido, Japan's biggest cosmetics maker, are experimenting with beauty service centers in the United States and other countries. The centers offer free lessons on massage techniques and information on how to apply makeup. Shiseido found that many customers who visited such centers soon made a purchase in the department stores where Shiseido products were sold.

INTERNATIONAL EXPANSION

For the three years ended 2001, 2000, and 1999, the company derived approximately 60 percent of both its consolidated net sales and consolidated pretax income from the operations of its international subsidiaries (see Exhibit 4). Total international sales in 2001 were $3.68 billion, compared to Avon North America sales of $2.27 billion. Total international operating profit in 2001 was $707.1 million, compared to Avon North American profit of $380.2 million. The international operations of the company are divided into four geographic regions: (1) North America region, which includes Canada, Puerto Rico, and the United States; (2) Latin American region, which includes Brazil, Mexico, Argentina, and Venezuela; (3) Pacific region, which includes the Philippines, Thailand, Japan, New Zealand, Australia, and China; and (4) the European region, which comprises the United Kingdom, Central Europe, and Russia.

Avon management feels that it is time to reevaluate and map out the long-term future of the firm's beauty businesses on a global level. Senior management realizes that the traditional Avon system of door-to-door house calls worked wonderfully in developing nations. The company has direct investments in fifty-three markets and through distributorships, specially appointed representatives, and licensees in 143 countries, including a significant presence in Egypt, Greece, and Saudi Arabia.

Enormous growth opportunities exist in countries with huge populations such as China, Indonesia and India. In Eastern Europe, management is excited about the potential in Poland, Czech Republic, Slovakia, and Hungary. In the Pacific Rim area, countries like Vietnam, Cambodia, and Laos are targeted as market opportunities.

The second area of potential growth is to continue to emphasize direct selling in the emerging and developing markets of Latin America, the Pacific Rim, and other areas. In those markets, the retail infrastructure is undeveloped, especially in the interiors of those countries. The Avon representative provides consumers with an opportunity to buy a wide range of quality products at acceptable prices. In some developing markets, where access to quality goods has been particularly prized, Avon's direct selling method opened up unprecedented prospects for women. In China, for example, women are so eager for Avon products that a projected six-month inventory of lotion sold out in only two weeks.

Growth in the markets of Central and Eastern Europe are considered Avon's primary opportunities for growth by management in the new millennium. Avon Russia rebounded in 2000, reversing a downturn in 1999 that followed the 1998 Russian economic crisis. Local sales nearly doubled, driven by a more than 60 percent growth in units and a nearly 30 percent rise in the number of active sales representatives. Russia also returned to profitability following an operating loss in 1999. Several new initiatives, such as a drive to improve operating efficiency, the introduction of several new products, and revised marketing management structures, were introduced in 2000.

The number of people buying from Avon in markets like the United States had been dwindling by 2 to 3 percent per year for about twelve years. "We applied all the tried-and-true stimuli to our direct-selling system: changes in recruiting, incentives, commissions, brochures, and more," suggested Preston when he was CEO. "We had some success. But we didn't stop the decline of customer purchasing activity." Management felt growth would come if it were to update the direct-selling channel.

EXHIBIT 4   Avon's Segment Financial Data

| | \multicolumn{6}{c}{Years ended December 31,} | | | | | |
| | 2001 | | 2000 | | 1999 | |
	Net Sales	Operating Profit (Loss)	Net Sales	Operating Profit (Loss)	Net Sales	Operating Profit (Loss)
A.						
North America						
U.S.	$2,016.7	$ 373.4	$1,894.9	$ 343.5	$1,809.3	$329.3
U.S. Retail*	13.9	(25.9)	8.5	(4.5)	3.4	(2.7)
Other†	242.6	32.7	244.5	29.2	237.6	34.5
Total	2,273.2	380.2	2,147.9	368.2	2,050.3	361.1
International						
Latin America North‡	966.3	251.6	848.8	215.2	731.7	181.6
Latin America South‡	933.3	175.9	992.0	200.3	909.0	184.9
Latin America	1,899.6	427.5	1,840.8	415.5	1,640.7	366.5
Europe	1,009.6	167.0	885.6	129.5	878.0	126.2
Pacific	771.4	112.6	799.4	117.8	720.1	102.1
Total	3,680.6	707.1	3,525.8	662.8	3,238.8	594.8
Total from operations	5,953.8	1,087.3	5,673.7	1,031.0	5,289.1	955.9
Global expenses	(1.8)	(242.5)	—	(242.3)	—	(255.3)
Contact settlement gain, net of related expenses	—	25.9	—	—	—	—
Asset impairment charge	—	(23.9)	—	—	—	—
Special and non-recurring charges§	—	(97.4)	—	—	—	(151.2)
Total	$5,952.0	$ 749.4	$5,673.7	$ 788.7	$5,289.1	$549.4

*Includes U.S. Retail and Avon Center.
†Includes operating information for Canada and Puerto Rico.
‡Latin America North primarily includes the markets of Mexico, Venezuela, and Central America. Latin America South primarily includes the markets of Brazil, Argentina, Chile, and Peru. Avon's operations in Mexico reported net sales for 2001, 2000, and 1999 of $620.7, $555.6 and $471.6, respectively. Avon's operations in Mexico reported operating profit for 2001, 2000, and 1999 of $154.8, $136.0, and $115.1, respectively.
§The $97.4 is included in the Consolidated Statements of Income as a Special charge ($94.9) and as inventory write downs in Cost of sales ($2.5).
Source: Avon's 2001 *Annual Report,* p. 24.

For a number of years, Avon management considered Japan to be one of the most significant trouble spots for the firm. The sluggish Japanese economy, combined with intense pricing pressure as well as operating issues, contributed to Avon Japan's disappointing performance. However, at the end of 2000, growth was driven by a 10 percent increase in orders and units. Japan's operating profit climbed 24 percent for the year. Contributing to Japan's results were several highly successful promotions, including the distribution of over 30 million flyers supported by newspaper ads. New initiatives, such as Japan's Avon Lady retail shops and the use of the Internet consumer Web site, resulted in significant new customer growth.

GLOBAL MARKETING

Satisfying the subtleties and intricacies of customer demand around the world means that a firm's business varies from country to country and market to market. In the United States, for example, Avon tested Avon Select, an early direct marketing program, to enable customers to buy Avon products in various settings. Customers could order

B.

Sales	2001	2000	1999
Beauty*	$3,730.5	$3,533.9	$3,220.8
Beauty Plus†	1,233.7	1,174.6	1,061.6
Beyond Beauty‡	987.8	965.2	1,006.7
Total net sales	$5,952.0	$5,673.7	$5,289.1

*Beauty includes cosmetics, fragrances, and toiletries.
†Beauty Plus includes fashion jewelry, watches and apparel and accessories.
‡Beyond Beauty includes home products, gift and decorative and candles.

C.

Total Assets	2001	2000	1999
North America			
U.S.	$ 638.9	$ 640.0	$ 536.9
U.S. Retail*	29.2	12.0	13.3
Other†	119.1	116.2	101.2
Total	787.2	768.2	651.4
International			
Latin America North‡	334.6	292.9	248.9
Latin America South	277.8	310.7	294.1
Latin America	612.4	603.6	543.0
Europe	512.3	451.3	415.4
Pacific	393.9	399.8	411.2
Total	1,518.6	1,454.7	1,369.6
Corporate and other	887.3	603.5	507.6
Total assets	$3,193.1	$2,826.4	$2,528.6

*Includes U.S. Retail and Avon Centre.
†Includes Canada and Puerto Rico.
‡Avon's operations in Mexico reported total assets at December 31, 2001, 2000, and 1999 of $211.0, $189.9, and $157.4, respectively.

D.

Capital Expenditures	2001	2000	1999
North America			
U.S.	$ 26.4	$ 67.6	$ 39.2
U.S. Retail*	7.5	.1	.4
Other†	6.4	8.6	8.7
Total	40.3	76.3	48.3
International			
Latin America North‡	20.5	17.5	37.6
Latin America South	15.4	24.6	15.8
Latin America	35.9	42.1	53.4
Europe	42.0	47.1	39.6
Pacific	11.9	13.4	33.6
Total	89.8	102.6	126.6
Corporate and other	25.2	14.6	28.5
Total capital expenditures	$155.3	$193.5	$203.4

‡Avon's operations in Mexico reported capital expenditures for 2001, 2000, and 1999 of $13.9, $11.7, and $32.1, respectively.
Source: Avon's 2001 Annual Report, pp. 55–57.

products via any one of four methods: (1) through an Avon representative, (2) by mail though special select catalogs, (3) by the 1-800-FOR-AVON telephone number, or (4) by fax.

The traditional door-to-door method, with the Avon lady as the homemakers' friend and beauty consultant, made the company the world's largest cosmetics firms and the number-one direct seller. The approach was viewed as expensive (the salesperson got a 20 to 50 percent commission), and there were the problems associated with hiring, training, managing, and motivating the sales force. Avon recently strengthened its traditional direct-selling channel through a program called Sales Leadership, a business model designed to attract and retain sales representatives through initiatives focused on business and beauty training. Each representative who signs up for the leadership program gets a percentage of the sales of every representative she recruits and every representative that the recruit herself recruits—and so on down through three "generations" of Avon representatives.

In September 2001, Avon announced that it had reached an agreement with the JCPenney Co. to set up shops called Becoming within retail stores operated by the firm. The shops would be built around an an assisted open-selling concept, which allows customers to browse racks that feature the Becoming brand. Each shop has six areas featuring color cosmetics, skin care, fragrance, aromatherapy, mother-and-baby beauty products, and nutritional products for active lifestyles. Becoming was designed specifically with one thought in mind: to avoid cannibalizing core Avon lines and the business done by traditional Avon sales representatives. It is priced and designed to target shoppers in mass department and specialty stores. The line is priced between mass marketed lines such as L'Oreal Paris and 10 percent to 15 percent below the entry-level department store brands. Avon had also initially planned to launch Becoming at Sears, Roebuck & Company stores, but Sears announced in July that it would stop selling cosmetics, claiming that it was a drain on profits. The in-store concept is "not without risk, but with great opportunity," said Jung. "It's a giant step." The firm used panels of sales representatives as a sounding board to design the centers and to determine the products the center will stock.

In addition to retail stores, Avon is continuing to test a direct-mail catalog, which would allow customers to bypass the Avon representative and place orders themselves. The success of a mail order catalog will depend greatly upon Avon's ability to manage its mailing and customer lists, to control inventory carefully, to offer quality merchandise, and to project a distinctive customer-benefiting image. In a limited test of a catalog, Avon has reached a more upscale customer who placed an average order of $40, more than double that of orders placed through the regular Avon sales brochure.

GROWTH STRATEGIES

Upgrading the Avon global image is considered by management to be extremely important. One important element of the image upgrade was the announcement of a global advertising strategy. By consolidating worldwide advertising, Avon management feels it can expand its global presence and communicate a more unified brand image throughout its international markets (to view a recent organizational chart, see Exhibit 5). In 2000, management increased advertising expenditures by 50 percent to more than $90 million, and it created Let's Talk, the company's first-ever global advertising campaign. Let's Talk television and print advertisements featured young sports professionals who serve as role models. A new global product line of women's health and well-being products called Avon Wellness was part of this image program. It was aimed at expanding the definition of beauty to encompass inner health as well as outward appearance, and it featured vitamins and nutritional supplements as well as various exercise, fitness, and stress relief items. The image campaign also featured the corporate line, "The Company for Women."

In September 2000, Avon revolutionized its direct sales approach by plugging its U.S. representatives into a marketing tool called youravon.com that empowered them with the technology of the World Wide Web. As e-representatives, they had a global reach and the technological advantage of the Internet that enabled them to direct sales and establish customer relationships. The company also opened kiosks, called Avon Centers, in about forty high-traffic shopping malls. The centers were designed to display an upscale beauty image, showcase the company's beauty brands, and encourage customer trials of products. The centers were modeled after similar initiatives in Malaysia, the Philippines, Taiwan, Spain, Chile, Venezuela, and Mexico. They were small but attractive 400- to 600-square-foot environments that added significantly to the company's retail presence in locations where retail and direct selling had a history of being able to coexist.

EXHIBIT 5   Avon Products, Inc., Organization Chart (2002)

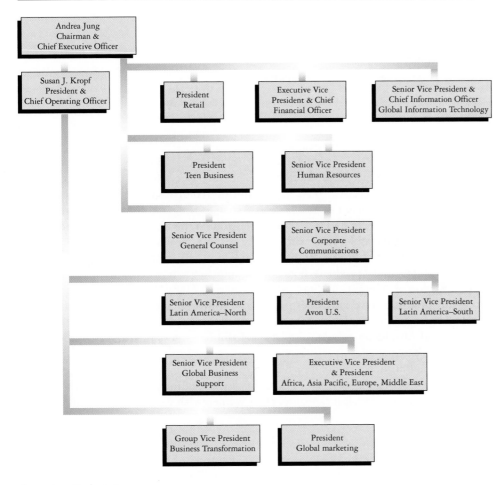

Source: Avon Products, Inc.

CONCLUSION

Avon is part of a fiercely competitive industry. The company experienced 2001 operating profit declines in a number of countries including Poland, South Africa, and the entire Pacific region.

CEO Jung needs to put in place a solid strategy for the 2002–2004 time period, including clear recommendations and support of pro forma financial statements. Let's say she asks you, as an outside management consultant, to perform this work for Avon. Do the best job that you can to explain what your strategy would be.

REVLON, INC.—2002

M. Jill Austin
Middle Tennessee State University

REV

www.revlon.com

The vision of Revlon is to "provide glamour, excitement and innovation to consumers through high-quality products at affordable prices." Net sales for 2001 decreased by $126.3 million (8.7 percent) to $1,321.5 million (compared to $1,447.8 million in 2000), and operating income in 2001 was $16.1 million, up from $15.9 million in 2000. Revlon products are sold in 175 countries around the world, with sales outside the United States accounting for approximately 41 percent of sales in 2000.

Product categories for the company include skin care, cosmetics, personal care, fragrance, and professional products. Some of the company's most recognized brand names include Revlon, Ultima, ColorStay, Almay, Charlie, Flex, Mitchum, and Jean Naté. Successful products developed recently by the company include Revlon Skinlights, Revlon High Dimension Haircolor, Almay Kinetin Skincare Advanced Anti-Aging products, and Absolutely Fabulous Lipcream. Exhibit 1 shows the company products in each business category.

It is the long-term mission of Revlon to emerge as the dominant cosmetics and personal care firm in the twenty-first century by appealing to young/trendy women, health conscious women (skin care), and older women with its variety of brands.

HISTORY

Revlon, Inc. was formed in 1932 with a $300 investment by two brothers, Charles and Joseph Revson, and by Charles Lachmann. Charles Lachmann was a nail polish supplier who is most notably remembered for his contribution of the "l" in the Revlon name. Charles Revson was the primary force behind the success of Revlon until his death in 1968. In the early years, Revson developed a near monopoly on beauty parlor sales by selling his nail polish door-to-door at salons. He expanded into the lipstick market with the slogan "Matching Lips and Fingertips." Some of the landmark advertising campaigns directed by Revson included "Fatal Apple" and "Fire & Ice." Revson was a hard taskmaster, expecting the same whole-life devotion of his workers that he gave to Revlon. He sometimes held meetings until two in the morning, called employees at home to discuss business, cursed out employees, and pretended to fall asleep during some presentations.

The company started with only one product—nail enamel. Revlon nail enamel was manufactured with pigments instead of the dyes typically used in this type of manufacturing. This approach allowed Revlon to market a large number of color options to consumers relatively quickly. It took the three company founders just six years to transform their small nail enamel company into a multimillion-dollar organization. This successful collaboration launched one of the most recognizable brands and companies in the world.

Originally, Revlon offered its nail enamels through a limited distribution system in which professional salons carried the products. However, as the 1930s progressed, the products were distributed widely in select drugstores and department stores. As the

EXHIBIT 1   Revlon, Inc. Products and Business Categories

BRAND	COSMETICS	SKIN CARE	FRAGRANCES	PERSONAL CARE PRODUCTS
Revlon	Revlon, ColorStay, Revlon Age Defying, Super Lustrous, Absolutley Fabulous, Moon Drops, Skinlights, Line & Shine, Shine Control Mattifying, New Complexion, High Dimension, Super Top Speed, Illuminance, Wet/Dry, EveryLash, StreetWear	Vitamin C Absolutes, Revlon Absolutes, Eterna 27	Charlie, Ciara, Fire & Ice, Absolutely Fabulous	Flex, Outrageous, Aquamarine, Mitchum, Lady Mitchum, ColorStay, Colorsilk, Frost & Glow, Jean Naté, Revlon Beauty Tools, High Dimension, Almay
Almay	Almay, Time-Off, Amazing, One Coat, Organic Fluoride Plus Beyond Powder, Skin Stays Clean	Almay Kinetin, Almay MilkPlus		
Ultima	Ultima, Beautiful, Nutrient, Wonderwear, Pucker & Pout Ultimate Edition, Full Moisture, Glowtion	Glowtion, Vital Radiance, CHR, Light Captor-C		
Significant Regional Brands	Jeanne Gatineau, Cutex	Jeanne Gatineau		Bozzano, Juvena

Source: Revlon's 2001 Annual Report, p. 3.

world entered WWII, Revlon contributed to the war effort by providing first aid kits and dye markers for the U.S. Navy. After the war, Revlon expanded its product lines with the introduction of manicure and pedicure instruments (a natural complement to the nail enamel products). Revlon management recognized global demand potential and began offering company products in a number of new markets. Stock was first offered in the company in 1955. The 1960s were associated with the American Look campaign designed to introduce the All-American girl to the world cosmetics market via well-known U.S. models. Further identifying with the changing role of women in the market and society, the Charlie fragrance line was introduced in the early 1970s. Sales for this extremely popular line surpassed $1 billion by 1977.

After the death of Charles Revson, Michel Bergerac took control of the company. He built up the pharmaceutical side of the business. By 1985, two-thirds of Revlon's sales were health care products such as Tums and Oxy acne medications, and the company was losing ground in cosmetics. Millionaire Ronald Perelman made five offers to purchase Revlon and eventually took over the company for $1.8 billion in a leveraged buyout. Perelman returned the company to its roots and sold off the health care product lines. He refocused the company to make it an internationally known manufacturer and seller of cosmetics and fragrances. Perelman took the company private in 1987 by buying the stock from all of the public shareholders. A subsidiary of MacAndrews & Forbes stills holds 83 percent of the outstanding shares of Revlon, and Perelman is chairman and chief executive officer of MacAndrews & Forbes Holdings, Inc. The company was taken public in 1996 and is traded on the New York Stock Exchange (NYSE).

In September 1996, Revlon was given approval to manufacture, distribute, and market Revlon products in China, and the first manufactured goods rolled off the production line in December 1996. The company acquired Bionature S.A., a South American manufacturer of hair and personal care products in 1997. The completion of acquisitions in South America increased distribution and manufacturing capabilities in these markets.

PRESENT CONDITIONS

The company has struggled in recent years and has debt of nearly $2 billion. Since October 1998, sales have fallen significantly in the United States and in countries such as Russia and Brazil, causing declines in total sales in 1998, 1999, 2000, and 2001. In an effort to reduce expenses, the company's worldwide professional products line was sold for $315 million in March 2000, and two months later, the Argentina brand Plusbelle was sold for $46 million. In November 2000 the company closed three manufacturing plants and reduced its workforce by 1,115 employees (14 percent of the workforce) in an effort to improve efficiency. A review of net sales by geographic area and product type indicates that sales in both areas have suffered in recent years (see Exhibit 2).

Even with these financial difficulties, Revlon is the number one brand in the U.S. mass market for color cosmetics. The company continues to launch new products and reintroduce some of its mature brands. The thirty-three-year-old Ultima II brand was reintroduced in 2001, and Charlie perfume was reintroduced in 2002. The new product Skinlights was launched in the United Kingdom in 2001, and in 2002 the company's Charlie perfume will be marketed to United Kingdom teenagers. Revlon spent $12.5 million advertising its new Absolutely Fabulous lip cream in 2001.

DEMOGRAPHIC AND SOCIAL TRENDS

The cosmetics and personal care industry is affected by two major changes in the demographic composition of the United States: the aging population and the change in proportions of racial and ethnic populations. Aging baby boomers make up a sig-

EXHIBIT 2   Net Sales by Geographic Area and Product Category (in millions)

	1999	2000	2001
GEOGRAPHIC AREA			
United States	$ 908.4	$ 842.8	$ 852.2
Canada	$ 46.4	$ 53.0	$ 48.8
International Ongoing Operations	815.1	$ 443.6	$ 404.1
A. Europe and Africa	—	$ 175.7	$ 160.2
B. Latin America	—	142.4	131.9
C. Far East	—	125.6	112.0
PRODUCT CATEGORY			
Cosmetics, Skin Care, and Fragrances	881.2	908.2	$ 859.4
Personal Care and Professional	828.7	539.6	462.1
TOTAL Net Sales	$1,709.9	$1,447.8	$1,321.5

Source: Revlon, Inc. 2001 *Form 10K,* p. 88.

nificant proportion of the adult U.S. population. The seventy-five million Americans born between 1946 and 1964 are a significant market for the cosmetics/personal care industry. The aging of the population has been coupled with a mini-baby boom. Many baby boomers have high levels of disposable income and are brand loyal consumers. In addition, it appears that baby boomers' consumption patterns and rates have not necessarily changed as they have aged. The number of people in the mature market (fifty-five and older) also continues to increase in number. Many of these consumers are wealthier and more willing to spend than ever before. Additionally, women in the mature age group remain active in the workforce for longer periods of time than in the past. Another market segment of interest to cosmetics companies is the U.S. teen market (ages twelve to nineteen) since this group was estimated to number 15.2 million in 2001.

The ethnic/racial makeup of the American population is shifting. While African Americans represents the largest minority segment (36 million in 2000), the Hispanic American segment is the fastest growing segment and is projected to be the largest minority segment in the United States by the year 2010, with approximately 40.5 million individuals. The result is that the non-Hispanic white share of the U.S. population is expected to decline to 68 percent by the year 2010. The Asian American population is also growing rapidly. International sales of cosmetics/skin care products are also affect by ethnic/racial issues. There are significant opportunities for companies in Asian countries (60 percent of the world's population). The youthful, increasingly affluent Latin American countries also represent a growth opportunity. Since the majority of personal care products are currently sold in the United States, Japan, and Canada, as well as in the European countries (less than 20 percent of the world's population), the potential for sales of personal care products around the world is excellent.

Other social and demographic issues that may affect the industry include consumers' concerns about product safety and animal testing by cosmetics companies. Increasingly, cosmetics/personal care is not an industry for women only; men purchase personal care products such as skin creams and hair care products/dyes, and many men are trying cosmetics in an effort to improve their appearance. The market for hair coloring has expanded because teenagers and adults want more vibrant coloring options.

ECONOMICS ISSUES

U.S. economic growth began to slow in 2001, and consumer confidence declined beginning in the fall of 2000. After the terrorist attacks on the World Trade Center in New York City and the Pentagon on September 11, 2001, consumer confidence continued to falter. In addition, American consumers now have significant credit card debt. Because of this debt, consumers may elect not to purchase some expensive or nonessential products. In addition, many baby boomers are saving for their children's college or caring for older parents and may be unwilling to spend significant dollars on items such as expensive cosmetics.

International economics provides unique challenges for companies in the cosmetics/skin-care industry. Many emerging economies in Asia and Eastern Europe are eager to have mass marketers situate operations in their countries, but operating situations are generally uncertain. Countries such as Brazil and Mexico have experienced hyperinflation for several years. The economies in Japan, Latin America, and many European countries have also slowed in recent years. High inflation, the strength of the dollar in international markets, and the fluctuation of foreign currency exchange rates all pose difficulties for companies operating in international markets.

COMPETITION

Competition is intense in the cosmetics/skin care industry. In the past, the retail cosmetics industry was dominated by sales of cosmetics in specialty stores and department stores, with beauty consultants providing service. Today, large numbers of women prefer purchasing these items at drugstores, supermarkets, mass volume retailers such as Kmart and Wal-Mart; from door-to-door sellers such as Avon; and on the Internet. Revlon's major competitors include Procter & Gamble; Avon Products; Estee Lauder Companies, Inc.; L'Oreal; and Unilever. Recent entrants into the color cosmetics market include Oil of Olay (Procter & Gamble) and Neutrogena (Johnson & Johnson). The cosmetics and skin care industry is expected to be a $200 billion business worldwide by 2003.

Other competitors include small companies, such as Urban Decay; specialty stores, such as Bath and Body Works, Body Shop, and H$_2$O; and retailers selling their own brands, such as Benneton, Banana Republic, and Victoria's Secret. Competition for the African American market is also increasing, with brands such as Fashion Flair and cosmetics lines launched by Iman and Patti LaBelle. A discussion of major competitors of Revlon, Inc. follows.

PROCTER & GAMBLE

Procter & Gamble (P&G) is a multinational company offering products in a wide range of categories, including personal care, cosmetics, fragrances, hair care, and skin care. Some of the P&G products not in the cosmetics/skin care industry include diapers, baking mixes, bleach, dish care products, juice, laundry products, oral care products, and peanut butter. The company operates in more than seventy countries.

Revlon faces competition from P&G in a number of product categories. P&G offers hair care products through its Pantene, Vidal Sassoon, and Ivory brands. P&G skin care lines include Oil of Olay, Noxzema, and Clearasil. Fragrance lines sold by P&G include Giorgio, Hugo Boss, Old Spice, Venezia, and Wings. The P&G cosmetics line includes Cover Girl, Max Factor, and Oil of Olay. In 2001, beauty care products contributed $7.3 billion to revenue and $972 million to profit for P&G.

In 1999, the singer Brandy was hired to promote Cover Girl products, and the company spent $100 million to introduce new Cover Girl products. Currently, Faith Hill and Queen Latifah promote Cover Girl products. Selected financial information for Procter & Gamble is shown in Exhibit 3.

L'Oreal

L'Oreal is the world's largest cosmetics firm. During the 1990s, the company enjoyed double-digit growth. L'Oreal acquired Maybelline, one of its leading competitors, in

EXHIBIT 3   Financial Information for Procter & Gamble (in millions)

	2000	2001
Net Sales	$39,951	$39,244
Operating Income	5,954	4,736
Net Earnings	3,542	2,922
Total Debt	22,079	22,377
Long-Term Debt	9,012	9,797

Source: www.pg.com

1996 for $758 million. This move was an attempt to strengthen its position in the U.S. market. L'Oreal previously held only a 7.5 percent share of the market, but the acquisition of Maybelline made L'Oreal the number two cosmetics firm in the United States. L'Oreal competes with Revlon in the area of cosmetics (L'Oreal, Maybelline, and Helena Rubenstein), hair care (L'Oreal and Redken), and fragrances (Vanderbilt and Ralph Lauren Perfumes). In 1998, L'Oreal acquired Soft Sheen, an ethnic hair care business and introduced a quick dry nail polish called Jet-Set. From 1997 to 1999, Maybelline sales almost doubled ($320 million to $600 million), and sales outside the United States during these years accounted for 50 percent of total sales. Some of the advertising spokespersons for the company are Milla Jovovich, Jessica Alba, and Sarah Michelle Gellar. Financial information for L'Oreal is shown in Exhibit 4.

Unilever

Unilever is an Anglo-Dutch firm that until recently has been noted as a manufacturer of soap/detergent products and food products. The company also manufactures personal care products. Some of the Unilever brands include mass skin care (Ponds, Vaseline, Pears, Hazeline), hair care (Organics, Sunsilk, Clinic, Gloria), mass perfume (Brute, Impulse, Denim, Axe/Lynx, Rexoral/Reward), and prestige fragrance lines (Elizabeth Arden, Calvin Klein, Elizabeth Taylor, Karl Lagerfeld, and Chloe). Unilever now markets seven of the top ten fragrance products in the United States, including Obsession, White Diamonds, Passion, Black Pearls, and Eternity.

The company is a world leader in prestige fragrances and leads the hair care market in Africa, the Middle East, Latin America, and Asia/Pacific. Its skin care products lead the market in North America, Africa, Latin America, Asia/Pacific, and the Middle East. Financial results for Unilever are shown in Exhibit 5.

Avon Products, Inc.

Avon is the number one direct seller of cosmetics and beauty products in the world. Its direct sales force number 3 million people in 139 countries. Some brand names for Avon products include Avon Color, Avon Skin Care, Anew, and Skin-So-Soft. In 2001, Avon began selling vitamins and nutritional supplements. Avon also sells jewelry, gift items, lingerie, and casual clothing. Venus and Serena Williams were hired in February 2001 to promote Avon products in the "Dream big . . . let's talk Avon" advertising campaign.

The company's products can be purchased through its Internet site **www.avon.com**, but 98 percent of Avon revenue is generated by sales representatives. In an attempt to address the concerns of sales representatives that Internet sales would

EXHIBIT 4   Financial Information for L'Oréal
(converted to U.S. $ in millions)

	1998	1999	2000
Revenue	$13,417.4	$10,824.8	$11,931.2
Operating Income	1,688.5	1,315.3	1,450.8
Net Income	838.6	701.5	967.8
Total Assets	12,298.5	10,719.5	12,838.2
Long-Term Debt	682.6	523.1	784.0

Source: **www.hoovers.com**

EXHIBIT 5   Financial Information for Unilever
             (converted to U.S. $ in millions)

	1999	2000
Revenue	$43,635.8	$44,813.0
Operating Profit	4,582.8	3,110.0
Net Income	3,165.1	1,041.0
Total Assets	28,023.6	54,285.0
Long-Term Debt	2,845.0	12,306.0

Source: www.hoovers.com

take away their livelihood, Avon is allowing sales representatives to have their own Web sites. Avon posted sales of $5.7 billion in 2000. Selected financial information is provided in Exhibit 6.

Estée Lauder

The Estée Lauder Companies, Inc. manufactures and markets cosmetics, fragrances, and skin care products. Some of the company's cosmetics/skin care brands include Estee Lauder and Clinique. Fragrances are sold under the brands Beautiful and White Linen. In addition, Estee Lauder holds the worldwide license for fragrances and cosmetics with the brand names Tommy Hilfiger and Donna Karan (DKNY). In 1998, the company acquired jane, a color cosmetics line targeted toward young women, and Aveda, a prestige brand of products for hair care. The company also has an investment in MAC (Make-Up Art Cosmetics, Limited). Stila Cosmetics, Inc., a Los Angeles-based company known for ecofriendly packaging, was acquired in 1999. Other Estée Lauder brands include Bobbi Brown Essentials, Aramia, Prescriptives, and Origins. Estée Lauder has sales in more than one hundred countries. In 1999, the company rehired model Karen Graham, known as the face of Estée Lauder, to be in advertisements for Resilience Lift products, which are targeted to mature women. Selected financial information for Estée Lauder is shown in Exhibit 7.

INTERNAL FACTORS FOR REVLON, INC.

Organization/Management

About 1990, then-Chairman Levin led the company in recruiting a strong team of experienced managers who would work to achieve leadership in the cosmetics/skin care industry. It was about this same time that Revlon developed its vision to "provide glam-

EXHIBIT 6   Financial Information for Avon Products (in millions)

	1998	1999	2000
Net Sales	$5,212.7	$5,289.1	$5,714.6
Gross Profit	3,159.7	3,257.6	3,591.9
Net Income	270.0	302.4	478.4
Total Assets	2,433.5	2,528.6	2,826.4
Long-Term Debt	201.0	701.4	1,108.2

Source: www.avon.com and http://www.hoovers.com

EXHIBIT 7   Financial Information for Estée Lauder Companies, Inc.
(in millions)

	1999	2000	2001
Net Sales	$3,961.5	$4,366.8	$4,608.1
Gross Profit	3,061.6	3,394.7	3,635.8
Net Income	272.9	314.1	305.2
Total Assets	2,746.7	3,043.3	3,218.8
Long-Term Debt	422.5	418.4	410.9

Source: **www.hoovers.com**

our, excitement, and innovation to consumers through high-quality products at afford-able prices." The company set up the Revlon Learning Center and developed training programs to communicate its strategic principles to employees. Training provided a means for ensuring that the company's teamwork approach remained effective. In 1994, Revlon established the Charlie Awards to recognize the efforts of employees whose accomplishments significantly affected Revlon. A number of these awards are given to deserving employees each year.

At the core of the Revlon organization is its belief in individual values and the integrity of the firm and its actions. Revlon and its employees are active in supporting women's health programs and other community efforts. In the last decade, Revlon has spent $25 million on services and research that help women. One of the events that Revlon sponsors is the Revlon Run/Walk in Los Angeles. This event has raised millions of dollars for the Revlon/UCLA Women's Cancer Research Center. In 1998, the company established a partnership with the National Council of Negro Women to help support wellness programs for African American women.

Marketing

The primary customers for Revlon products are large mass merchandisers and chain drug stores. Some of the major retail customers are Walgreens, Wal-Mart, Target, Kmart, CVS, Drug Emporium, Eckerds, Rite Aid, and JC Penney. Revlon provides point-of-sale displays and samples for these stores. In addition, the *Revlon Report* is distributed with the merchandise worldwide (and in magazines). The *Report* provides information about the company's products and the rebates/coupons that are offered. Revlon's products are also sold through its Web site (**www.revlon.com**).

Advertising continues to be one of the primary areas of promotion spending by Revlon. The company made a strategic decision in 2001 to hire outside advertising agencies to handle promotional efforts for Revlon. Revlon managers hired two firms—Kirshenbaum, Bond & Partners and Deutsch—to develop marketing ideas for the company's products. Longtime Revlon spokesperson Cindy Crawford, one of the most recognizable faces in the cosmetics world, promoted Revlon products for eighteen years. In 2001, however, the company decided to discontinue Crawford's contract, and it hired four relatively unknown models to promote the company's brands. Some of the company's recent promotions include the "Capture the Glow" and "It's fabulous being a woman" campaigns. In the summer of 2001, Revlon teamed with Absolut Vodka and W Hotels to promote its Absolutely Fabulous products. Parties for models and celebrities were held in Los Angeles, New York, Chicago, and Atlanta and were used to promote Absolutely Fabulous on Revlon's Web site. Revlon's advertising and promotion expenses were $272.9, $268.7, and $352.2 million in 2001, 2000, and 1999, respectively.

New product development continues to be a primary objective of Revlon even in bad financial times. Revlon spent $24 million and $27 million on research and development efforts for new products in 2000 and 2001, respectively, and employed 160–200 people respectively in this effort. In addition to development efforts, Revlon has plans to revitalize some of its long-established products. Revlon is updating the Charlie perfume for the company's 70th anniversary in 2002. Charlie will be available in three bottle designs and will be sold in gift boxes in Wal-Mart, CVS, and Target stores.

Manufacturing/Distribution

Globalization of the company's manufacturing and distribution efforts has enabled the company to consolidate its production facilities. This consolidation and coordination between markets has provided increased operating efficiency and better use of capital assets. The number of production facilities has been reduced and centralized to cover core regions. Currently, the company has production facilities in Oxford, North Carolina, and Irvington, New Jersey. Production facilities are also located in Venezuela and South Africa. Several of the company's plants have ISO-9002 certification, thus signifying the company's commitment to quality-manufacturing standards. Planning for long-term growth includes a focus on and utilization of top-notch production facilities and distribution systems.

Financial Conditions

Significant financial issues affect the company's operations. Long-term debt at the end of 2001 was almost $2 billion. This debt represents several years of debt problems for Revlon. Jobs lost to restructuring in 1999, 2000, and 2001, respectively, were 1,213, 403, and 1,697. Costs associated with these restructurings include employee severance, personnel benefits, and factory/warehouse/office costs.

Ron Perelman sold a large amount of his Golden State Bancorp stock in October 2001 to provide cash so Revlon could pay off junk bonds that were due. Note in Exhibit 8 (statements of operations) that sales decreased in the 1999–2001 period and that the company had net losses all three years. According to the balance sheet information in Exhibit 9, current assets, total assets, and current liabilities decreased from 2000 to 2001.

FUTURE OUTLOOK

As Revlon, Inc. deals with its debt problems and tries to continue its strategy of innovation, product development, and globalization, several issues must be considered:

1. Should Revlon concentrate its efforts on international markets?
2. Should Revlon diversify its operations or develop joint ventures with other cosmetics companies?
3. What role does innovation play in the strategic planning of Revlon, Inc.? Which specific types of innovation might Revlon use?
4. What role should branding play in the future growth strategies of Revlon?
5. How will competitive reactions affect Revlon's future plans?
6. What is the impact of social trends and economic trends on companies in the cosmetics/skin care industry?
7. What plans should Revlon, Inc. develop to pay off long-term debt?

EXHIBIT 8   Revlon, Inc. and Subsidiaries Consolidated Statements of Operations
(dollars in millions, except per-share data)

	Year Ended December 31,		
	2001	*2000*	*1999*
Net sales	$ 1,321.5	$ 1,447.8	$ 1,709.9
Cost of sales	544.2	574.3	726.3
Gross profit	777.3	873.5	983.6
Selling, general and administrative expenses	723.1	803.5	1,155.4
Restructuring costs and other, net	38.1	54.1	40.2
Operating income (loss)	16.1	15.9	(212.0)
Other expenses (income):			
Interest expense	140.5	144.5	147.9
Interest income	(3.9)	(2.1)	(2.8)
Amortization of debt issuance costs	6.2	5.6	4.3
Foreign currency losses (gains), net	2.2	1.6	(0.5)
Loss (gain) on sale of product line, brands and facilities, net	14.4	(10.8)	0.9
Miscellaneous, net	2.7	(1.8)	—
Other expenses, net	162.1	137.0	149.8
Loss before income taxes and extraordinary item	(146.0)	(121.1)	(361.8)
Provision for income taxes	4.1	8.6	9.1
Loss before extraordinary item	(150.1)	(129.7)	(370.9)
Extraordinary item – early extinguishment of debt, net of tax	(3.6)	—	—
Net loss	$ (153.7)	$ (129.7)	$ (370.9)
Basic and diluted loss per common share:			
Loss before extraordinary item	$ (2.87)	$ (2.49)	$ (7.12)
Extraordinary items	(0.07)	—	—
Net loss per common share	$ (2.94)	$ (2.49)	$ (7.12)
Weighted average number of common shares outstanding:			
Basic and diluted	52,199,349	52,166,980	52,073,558

Source: Revlon's 2001 *Annual Report*, p. 37.

EXHIBIT 9   Revlon, Inc. and Subsidiaries Consolidated Balance Sheets
(dollars in millions, except per share data)

	December 31, 2001	December 31, 2000
ASSETS		
Current assets:		
Cash and cash equivalents	$ 103.3	$ 56.3
Marketable securities	2.2	—
Trade receivables, less allowances of $15.4 and $16.1, respectively	203.9	220.5
Inventories	157.9	184.8
Prepaid expenses and other	45.6	66.1
Total current assets	512.9	527.7
Property, plant and equipment, net	142.8	221.7
Other assets	143.4	146.3
Intangible assets, net	198.5	206.1
Total assets	$ 997.6	$1,101.8

(continued)

EXHIBIT 9   Revlon, Inc. and Subsidiaries Consolidated Balance Sheets
(dollars in millions, except per share data)   (continued)

	December 31, 2001	December 31, 2000
LIABILITIES AND STOCKHOLDERS' DEFICIENCY		
Current liabilities:		
Short-term borrowings – third parties	$ 17.5	$ 30.7
Accounts payable	87.0	86.3
Accrued expenses and other	281.3	310.7
Total current liabilities	385.8	427.7
Long-term debt – third parties	1,619.5	1,539.0
Long-term debt – affiliates	24.1	24.1
Other long-term liabilities	250.9	217.7
Stockholders' deficiency:		
Preferred stock, par value $.01 per share; 20,000,000 shares authorized, 546 shares of Series A Preferred Stock issued and outstanding	54.6	54.6
Preferred stock, par value $.01 per share; 20,000,000 shares authorized, 4,333 shares of Series B Convertible Preferred Stock issued and outstanding	—	—
Class B Common Stock, par value $.01 per share; 200,000,000 shares authorized, 31,250,000 issued and outstanding	0.3	0.3
Class A Common Stock, par value $.01 per share; 350,000,000 shares authorized, 20,516,135 and 20,115,935 issued and outstanding, respectively	0.2	0.2
Capital deficiency	(201.3)	(210.3)
Accumulated deficit since June 24, 1992	(1,075.4)	(921.7)
Accumulated other comprehensive loss	(61.1)	(29.8)
Total stockholders' deficiency	(1,282.7)	(1,106.7)
Total liabilities and stockholders' deficiency	$ 997.6	$1,101.8

Source: Revlon's 2001 Annual Report, p. 36.

REFERENCES

Byrnes, Nanette. "Avon—The New Calling," Business Week (September 18, 2000): 136.

Davis, Riccardo. "Revlon to Shut Plant, Ax 900 Jobs in Valley," The Arizona Republic (November 2, 2000): A1.

Edmondson, Gail. "The Beauty of Global Branding," Business Week (June 28, 1999): 70.

Fairclough, Gordon. "Revlon Takes Down 'For Sale' Sign, As Shares Sink 34%," The Wall Street Journal (October 4, 1999): B6.

Grossman, Andrea. "Teens, Males Boost Color Sales," Drug Store News (November 23, 1998): 53.

Klepacki, Laura. "Revlon Builds Brand Foundation," Brandmarketing (March 1999): 6.

Klepacki, Laura. "Ultima Plans a Makeover," Women's Wear Daily (December 15, 2000): 10.

Mack, Ann. "Casting Call," Adweek Southwest (April 9, 2001): 16.

"Market Undergoes Sea Change," MMR (June 25, 2001): 9.

Revlon, Inc. 1996 and 1998 Annual Reports.

"Revlon Resorts to Cuts," Cosmetic Insider's Report (November 8, 1999): 2.

Sandler, Linda and Yumiko Ono. "Revlon's Makeup Fails to Hide Some Frowns as Investors Wonder if Perelman Will Pay Debt," The Wall Street Journal (December 2, 1997).

Spears, John. "Revlon to Shed 120 Jobs in Shift to U.S.," The Toronto Star (October 25, 2000).

Tode, Chantal. "Beauty Advertising Puts on a New Face," Brandmarketing (May 1999): 66.

www.avon.com

www.pg.com

www.revlon.com

www.unilever.com

PILGRIM'S PRIDE CORPORATION—2002

James L. Harbin
Texas A & M University—Texarkana

CHX

www.pilgrimspride.com

Headquartered in Pittsburg, Texas, Pilgrim's Pride Corporation (903-855-1000) is engaged in the production, processing, and marketing of fresh chicken and further processed and prepared chicken products. It is the second-largest further processing chicken company in the United States and the third-largest domestic chicken producer and fourth-largest turkey producer. In Mexico, it is the second-largest chicken company. Its prepared foods are sold throughout the United States; and its fresh chickens are sold regionally in the central, southwestern, and western United States and Northern and Central Mexico. Additionally, the company exports approximately 12 percent of its product line to overseas markets such as Russia and eastern Europe.

Among the many companies that Pilgrim's serves are Wal-Mart, KFC, PepsiCo., Kraft, Nestlé, Wendy's, Grandy's, Burger King, Church's, Chili's, and Long John Silver. At year-end 2001, Pilgrim's employed nearly 22,500 people and processed more than 2.5 billion pounds of chicken. Pilgrim's net income declined annually from $65, to $52, to $41 million in 1999 to 2000 to 2001.

Lonnie "Bo" Pilgrim, one of a family of seven children raised during the Great Depression, took his concern from a small farm-supply store fifty years ago to a corporation producing more than $2.2 billion in 2001 sales.

Pilgrim's remarkable growth has taken place in a commodity industry in which, every year for the past fifty years, economists have been predicting doom and gloom. Citing industry sales as an indicator, experts have also deduced that the chicken industry has finally matured. The big question facing Pilgrim's today is whether it can continue to grow in an industry undergoing increased consolidation through additional marketing techniques, further cost curtailment, increased integration (gaining control over supplies and distribution), improved genetics and growing techniques.

BO PILGRIM'S BACKGROUND AND PHILOSOPHY

Bo Pilgrim's story is a classic one of deprivation and determination and then success. Born in northwest Texas in 1928, he was the fourth of seven children. His father died when Bo was nine, and he left home at twelve to live with his grandmother.

His entrepreneurial spirit had early roots. One of his first goals in life, he says, was "to be able to buy a soda when I wanted it. My father would, on occasion, give me money for a cold drink, but only after I had finished some work he wanted done for it." He learned at an early age that he could buy his own soft drinks. He bought sodas from his father's general merchandise store and sold them at a profit to the local factory workers. He later peddled newspapers, raised chickens and hogs, hauled gravel, picked peas and cotton, and sacked groceries—all before he turned eighteen.

He likens business to "a game, even a war." Commenting on how he spends his time, he says, "I spend one-third of my working days dealing with the government, one-third with lawyers, and the remaining one-third of my time is spent constructively."

He commented, "Today, we don't appreciate how much we have and how easy it is to get things. I'm definitely hooked on the free enterprise system." He added, "In fact, when I visited with President Reagan, I reminded him that the chicken and the egg industry has never had any kind of subsidy. I also shared my belief that the government should not be in the business of protecting the inefficient."

On entrepreneurship, Pilgrim said, "It is more than just shooting from the hip. A company has four resources—people, dollars, time, and facilities. Our company's objective is to gain optimum use of these four through planning, building pride, and rewarding your employees."

When asked about his secret of success, Bo responded, "Take your abilities, season them with experience on the job, and combine that with drive and motivation, and you will be successful. The way to make a difference in your life is to make that mind-boggling decision not to be average."

Most Texans know Bo as the chicken king who wears a Pilgrim's hat in his television commercials. Visitors to corporate headquarters get parking spaces marked with a picture of a chicken and the words "Pullet her in." The first-floor lobby walls are festooned with more than three hundred samples of memorabilia of Pilgrim and his company—wooden thank-you plaques, framed newspaper clippings, and photographs of him with prominent politicians. In the second-floor executive office suite, representations of chickens are everywhere—there are ceramic chickens, oil paintings of chickens, photographs of chickens, and stuffed chickens.

HISTORY

Because commodity chicken down cycles had almost bankrupted Pilgrim's twice over the years, the company has increasingly emphasized value-added and branded products, including its chill-pack and further processed and prepared food lines. In the late 1980s, Pilgrim's spent $25 million on a facility for preparing chickens. Such products generate higher prices per pound, exhibit lower price volatility, and result in higher and more consistent profit margins than non-value-added products, such as whole ice-pack chicken.

In order to crack the food service business with processed and prepared chicken, Pilgrim's had to price its products below Tyson Foods, Inc. (its chief competitor) at a loss. The company also had to spend approximately $6 million to $8 million a year on advertising, promotion, and supermarket-slotting allowances to entice this business.

Pilgrim's Pride lost about $50 million over three years trying to enter the prepared chicken market. In fiscal 1988, the company lost a net $8 million on $506 million in sales. "I never envisioned how difficult it would be," Bo said. "It was like getting on the wrong ski lift, you might wish you hadn't done it, but there was no other way to get back down." Disgruntled investors dumped the stock, which had just had an initial public offering in January 1987. The value of Bo Pilgrim's stake shrank by 76 percent to $61 million.

Pilgrim's finally turned the corner with a strategic retreat from the supermarkets and a major advance into the food service market. Retail products now account for a mere 2 percent of Pilgrim's prepared chicken sales. In food service, Pilgrim's positioned itself as an alternative to Tyson, aiming at those customers who are leery of being too dependent on one supplier. "A lot of buyers gave us information to help us duplicate the products they were buying from Tyson," Pilgrim says. With over forty of the country's largest restaurant chains as customers, the company now has been able to raise its prices to be in line with Tyson.

MISSION

A large group of Pilgrim's employees representing all areas of the company recently met to brainstorm the company's direction, vision, and mission. Many in the group were afraid that rather than developing a mission, they might end up with a mission statement. The difference, according to Monty Henderson, then president and CEO, was "that a mission statement becomes very wordy and usually winds up as a long paragraph or two that no one—not even the authors—can remember and usually winds up in a file somewhere. A mission, by contrast, is known by everyone, practiced daily by everyone, and becomes a way of life."

After much discussion about the business, the customers, and the competition, the group came to a consensus that Pilgrim's vision is "to achieve and maintain leadership in each product and service that we provide." To achieve this goal, the group felt that its mission was summed up as follows: "Our job is customer satisfaction . . . every day." Because of the increased emphasis on the international market, Pilgrim's later amended its vision: "To be a world class chicken company—better than the best."

COMPETITION

Pilgrim's competes with other integrated chicken companies and to a lesser extent with local and regional poultry companies that are not fully integrated. The primary competitive factors in the chicken industry include price, product line, and customer service. Although its products are competitively priced and generally supported with in-store promotions and discount programs, the company believes that product quality, brand awareness, and customer service are the primary methods through which it competes. Pilgrim's believes that it has only one competitor (Tyson) with a more complete line of value-added products.

Tyson, the number-one poultry processor (with 2000 sales of about $8 billion), generates 24 percent of the U.S. poultry production. Gold Kist has 10 percent, Perdue Farms has 8 percent, and Pilgrim's and Conagra Poultry each have approximately 6 percent.

Tyson's strategy has been one of many acquisitions over the past decade. It acquired Hudson Foods, Inc. for $682 million in 1997. At that time, Hudson had 5 percent of the market. In 1988, *The Wall Street Journal* reported that Tyson would acquire Pilgrim's for approximately $162 million, but the deal fell through. In 2001, Tyson acquired IBP Inc., the world's largest producer of fresh beef and pork, in an approximate $3 billion-plus deal. IBP had $16.9 billion in 2000 sales. Tyson, with the IBP acquisition, has about 28 percent of the U.S. beef market, 24 percent of the chicken market, and 18 percent of the pork market.

"Our marketing strategy for success is simple—segment, concentrate, dominate. We identify a promising market segment, concentrate our resources in it, and ultimately gain for Tyson Foods a dominate share of that segment," stated a recent Tyson annual report. "Our customers include all of the nation's top 50 food service distributors, 88 of the top 100 restaurant chains, 100 of the top retail supermarket chains, and every major wholesale club."

MEXICO

Pilgrim's plants are geographically located to serve over 75 percent of the Mexican market. Its business strategy for Mexico calls for using its U.S. management expertise to solidify its position as the most efficient operator in Mexico and, at the same time, to develop a strong consumer and trade franchise for the Pilgrim's Pride brand. With the Mexican market maturing at an accelerated rate and customers increasingly selecting value-added products, it appears that Pilgrim's entry is particularly timely. Pilgrim's sales in Mexico rose to $323 million in 2001, an increase from its 1996 sales of $228 million to $323 million in 2000.

THE BROILER INDUSTRY

Before the 1950s, farmers were reluctant to undertake chicken farming because investments in buildings, equipment, feed, chicks, and other inputs could easily be lost due to disease or natural calamities. Chicken feed suppliers recognized that they could increase their own sales by extending credit to farmers, enabling them to remain in business while they paid off their debts. This risk-sharing arrangement spurred chicken production and eventually evolved into the kind of grower-contracting arrangements that are now common to all poultry production. Meanwhile, the feed suppliers integrated further into slaughter and processing operations, which are the integrated chicken firms of today.

Through contracting arrangements, integrated chicken firms accept much of the risk of chicken growing in exchange for greater control over both the quality and quantity of the birds. Usually, the firm provides company-owned chicks and feed, while the contract farmer provides the housing and labor and then returns the fully grown chickens to the firm for processing. The firm, typically, pays a pre-established fee per pound for live broilers plus a bonus or penalty for performance relative to other chicken farmers.

Vertical integration in the poultry industry was listed as one of top ten events having the greatest impact on the meat industry during the twentieth century. Other top ten events pertinent to the poultry industry were the passage of the Federal Meat Inspection Act (1906), the development of refrigerated rail cars and trucks and the national interstate highway system, the growth of fast-food chains, and the passage of both the Humane Slaughter Act (1958) and the Poultry Products Inspection Act (1957).

Profitability

Industry profitability is primarily a function of the consumption of chicken and competing meats and the costs of feed grains. Historically, the broiler industry operated on a fairly predictable cycle of about three years: a year of good profits, followed by a year of expanded output and declining profits, followed by a year of losses and production cuts.

The chicken companies have spent much of their energy trying to escape the commodity cycle through marketing and further processing. Frank Perdue, with his classic commercials, was the first to demonstrate that a company could charge a premium for a brand name bird. Today, the biggest producers all play the brand-loyalty game. This leaves the chicken producers in an odd situation: They are commodity concerns trying to behave like consumer-products companies. As Prudential-Bache's John McMillin foretold in the 1980s, "The 1990s chicken industry will be better capitalized, more competitive—and less profitable." That prediction came true.

Industry profitability can be significantly influenced by feed costs, which are influenced by a number of factors unrelated to the broiler industry, including legislation that provides discretion to the federal government to set price and income supports for grain. Historically, feed costs have averaged approximately 50 percent of total production costs of non-value-added products and have fluctuated substantially with the price of corn, milo, and soybean meal. By comparison, feed costs typically average approximately 25 percent of total production costs of further processed and prepared chicken products such as nuggets, fillets, and deli products; as a result, increased emphasis on sales of such products by chicken producers reduces the sensitivity of earnings to feed cost movements.

Although feed costs may vary dramatically, the production costs of chicken are not as severely affected by changing feed ingredient prices as are the production costs of beef and pork. Chickens require approximately two pounds of dry feed to produce one pound of meat, compared to cattle and hogs, which require approximately seven and three pounds, respectively, of feed.

Problems

Across the southeastern United States, where 85 percent of the country's chickens are processed, the poultry industry often suffers from bad publicity. Chicken processing plants are said to be dirty, rotten meat is reaching the market; salmonella-tainted chickens are poisoning people, and the chicken growers who contract with the processors are being ripped off. Ross Perot publicly lambasted Bill Cinton's gubernatorial record by saying that the Arkansas poultry business is "not an industry of tomorrow."

The industry's biggest worry may be microscopic in physical size. Chickens in battery farms (and those in farmyards) often live in their own dung, which in turn encourages the growth of bacteria such as salmonella which in turn contaminate the meat during processing. About 6 million Americans are made ill by such bacteria every year, and about 1,300 die. Scientists at the Centers for Disease Control say chickens may be the cause of up to half of those cases.

The industry's high-tech, fast-paced production lines, which can process some 200,000 birds a day at a single plant, heighten fecal contamination. Bacteria often spread among birds as they speed along conveyors from hot collective baths through wet mechanical feather pickers to tanks of cold water. Partly to hold down the price of poultry, the industry has not tried to produce cleaner chickens, but it relies instead on consumers to cook the meat thoroughly.

The trend toward larger plant sizes raises several public policy issues. The volume of animal waste is but one concern. Critics contend that the need to reduce production costs comes at the expense of worker safety. Conditions on the production line can be tough. Repetitive motion from such tasks as pulling out chicken guts can cause disabling injuries. Employees frequently spend shifts in either a freezing cooler or 95-degree heat. "The industry has one foot in the twenty-first century when it comes to chickens, but [it] left one foot back in the nineteenth century when it comes to people," stated Bob Hall, research director for the Institute for Southern Studies, a labor-funded advocacy group in Durham, North Carolina. Poultry is a highly labor intensive industry.

Consolidation has resulted in a highly centralized and vertically integrated industry in which the five top players control 55 percent of American production. As a result, the country has been carved up into regional buying monopolies, and each region's dominant processor can dictate terms to the growers. The vast majority of growers receive only short-term contracts from the processors, with no formal assurances of long-term business relationships. Farmers are at a distinct disadvantage when negotiating contract terms since they are financially unable to risk falling into disfavor with the processors.

A report from the Texas Commissioner of Agriculture concluded that although "the grower makes a substantial capital investment and takes most of the risk, he or she is not sharing in the success of the industry." In some cases, growers have received as little as $579 in annual income per 20,000-bird-capacity chicken house.

The processors defend their practices. Industry spokespeople point out that growers are guaranteed a price for adult chickens, typically about 3.5 cents to 4 cents a pound. Thus, the processors contend, growers are sheltered from much of the risk of the volatile chicken market. Bill Roenigk, spokesperson for the National Broiler Council, a processor trade group, says studies have shown that chicken farmers' average return on investment is 5 percent, which is higher than the return in many other agriculture operations.

CHANGING DEMAND AND SUPPLY

Before 1970, most poultry bought by consumers was whole chickens and turkeys, and the export business was almost nonexistent. It would have been difficult to find a restaurant or fast-food outlet selling chicken sandwiches or nuggets. Deboned chicken breasts did not exist. Today, exports account for almost one-sixth of U.S. poultry production, and consumers are confronted with an endless variety of chicken products.

Per capita poultry consumption jumped from 34 pounds in 1960 (a level that was about 50 percent of the beef total) to 96 pounds in 1999—nearly 40 percent higher than beef consumption. The USDA estimates that chicken consumption will increase at a 3 percent compounded annual growth rate into the future. Consumption in Mexico is 38 pounds per capita, and it is projected to grow by 10 percent per year.

The major factors influencing this growth are consumer awareness of the health and nutritional characteristics of chicken, the price advantage of chicken relative to red meat, and the convenience of further processed and prepared chicken products. This growth has been enhanced by new product forms and packaging that increase convenience and product versatility. A larger, more affluent, mobile population has created a demand for more convenient foods. People are willing to trade dollars for time, and the industry has cashed in by providing value-added products.

Chicken firms have further segmented the market by observing that Americans are willing to pay much higher prices for white meat breasts than for dark meat thighs and drumsticks. They have also learned—and benefited—from the fact that overseas countries provide a market for low-value parts (chicken feet, tails, wingtips, gizzards) at a higher price than Americans are willing to pay.

The poultry sector isn't solely chicken; it also includes turkey, duck, goose, and quail. But the poultry industry in America is chicken-driven. Chicken nuggets account for about 10 percent of total U.S. broiler output and showed chicken companies what could happen if they went beyond selling what are called, in the trade, "feathers-off, guts-out birds."

Chicken, priced pound-per-pound, is one-third the cost of beef and one-half the cost of pork. Non-value-added chickens are selling for less than they did in 1923, when Mrs. Wilmer Steele of Ocean View, Delaware, sold what chicken historians say was the nation's first flock of commercial broilers for 62 cents a pound. Why is chicken cheaper than the competition? The answer has to do with the fact that a chicken is highly efficient at converting feed to flesh. As noted, to produce a pound of meat, a chicken consumes less than two pounds of feed, compared with six or seven pounds for a cow and three for a pig.

Also, a chicken doesn't live long. The shorter a creature's life cycle, the quicker its generations can be manipulated genetically. Chicken breeders have steadily developed birds that grow bigger on less feed in less time. Breeders may be approaching the limits of practicality on this score; modern chickens have "put on so much weight that they have some real problems mating," said Walter Becker, professor emeritus of genetics and cell biology at Washington State University.

Furthermore, chickens don't graze. Raising cattle requires an investment in land; raising chickens doesn't. Chickens used to need to run around in the sun; otherwise, they would develop a vitamin D deficiency and rickets. But in the 1920s, poultry producers solved the vitamin D problem by adding cod-liver oil to chicken feed. Since then, they have been able to raise thousands of chickens in confinement, allowing about 0.7 square foot per bird.

THE FUTURE

During the next few years, per capita consumption of chicken could more than double throughout the world.

In the domestic market; fewer and fewer meals consumed at home are made from scratch. In 1999, Americans spent approximately $970 million a day eating out. With 70 percent of mothers working outside of the home and 40 percent of consumers not knowing what they will eat as late as four o'clock in the afternoon, meal planning and preparation take a back seat to convenience and eating out.

Concern for healthy food may be slackening. Some say nutrition is on the back burner, with taste the big thing. One analyst recently commented, "A few years back, when everyone was concerned about health and diet, the fast-food restaurants started wringing fat from hamburgers, but sales dropped because they had less and less flavor. So restaurants took bacon and slapped slices of that on the sandwiches, and sales took off like gangbusters." The increasing size of meals served in restaurants is but another sign that fat may be back.

Pilgrim's acquired WLR Foods, Inc. on January 27, 2001, expanding into the Mid-Atlantic region. WLR Foods was the seventh-largest poultry company in the United States. One analyst described the WLR deal as pricey (Pilgrim's paid about twice per share what WLR stock was trading at when the deal was announced). Another described WLR as a company "going nowhere fast" that will benefit from being absorbed by a bigger and more competitive player. He went on to say "that the last thing this industry needs is more capacity, so you have to congratulate (Pilgrim's) management for choosing this route to grow, which doesn't add to the industry's overcapacity problems."

Although the acquisition created synergistic opportunities and a chance to establish a presence in the nation's Mid-Atlantic region, Pilgrim's is faced with integration challenges combined with a more leveraged situation. There has long been pressure on management to improve margins and stock performance (see Exhibits 1–3 for details).

EXHIBIT 1   Pilgrim's Pride Corporation and Subsidiaries September 29, 2001
(in thousands)

	Fiscal Year Ended		
	September 29, 2001 (52 weeks)	September 30, 2000 (52 weeks)	October 2, 1999 (53 weeks)
Net Sales to Customers:			
Chicken and Other Products:			
United States	$1,652,199	$1,192,077	$1,102,903
Mexico	323,678	307,362	254,500
Sub-total	1,975,877	1,499,439	1,357,403
Turkey	238,835	—	—
Total	$2,214,712	$1,499,439	$1,357,403
Operating Income:			
Chicken and Other Products:			
United States	$ 78,096	$ 45,928	$ 88,177
Mexico	12,157	34,560	21,327
Sub-total	90,253	80,488	109,504
Turkey	4,289	—	—
Total	$ 94,542	$ 80,488	$ 109,504
Depreciation and Amortization:[b]			
Chicken and Other Products:			
United States	$ 38,155	$ 24,444	$ 23,185
Mexico	11,962	11,583	11,351
Sub-total	50,117	36,027	34,536
Turkey	5,273	—	—
Total	$ 55,390	$ 36,027	$ 34,536
Total Assets:			
Chicken and Other Products:			
United States	$ 764,073	$ 496,173	
Mexico	247,681	209,247	
Sub-total	1,011,754	705,420	
Turkey	203,941	—	
Total	$1,215,695	$ 705,420	
Capital Expenditures:[a]			
Chicken and Other Products			
United States	$ 80,173	$ 69,712	
Mexico	29,425	22,417	
Sub-total	109,598	92,129	
Turkey	3,034	—	
Total	$ 112,632	92,129	

(a) Excludes business acquisition cost of $239,539, incurred in connection with the acquisition of WLR Foods on January 27, 2001.

(b) Includes amortization of capitalized financing costs of approximately $0.9 million, $1.2 million, and $1.1 million in fiscal years 2001, 2000, and 1999, respectively.

Source: Pilgrim's Pride, 2001 *Annual Report,* p. 65.

EXHIBIT 2   Consolidated Statements of Income Pilgrim's Pride Corporation
(in thousands, except per-share data)

	Three Years Ended September 29		
	2001	2000	1999
Net Sales	$2,214,712	$1,499,439	$1,357,403
Cost and Expenses:			
Cost of sales	2,000,762	1,333,611	1,171,695
Selling, general and administrative	119,408	85,340	76,204
	2,120,170	1,418,951	1,247,899
Operating Income	94,542	80,488	109,504
Other Expenses (Income):			
Interest expense, net	30,775	17,779	17,666
Foreign exchange (gain) loss	122	(152)	(50)
Miscellaneous, net	351	75	984
	31,248	17,702	18,600
Income Before Income Taxes and Extraordinary Charge	63,294	62,786	90,904
Income Tax Expense	21,263	10,442	25,651
Income Before Extraordinary Charge	42,031	52,344	65,253
Extraordinary Charge, Net of Tax	894	—	—
Net Income	$41,137	$52,344	$65,253
Income per Common Share Before Extraordinary Charge—Basic and Diluted	$1.02	$1.27	$1.58
Extraordinary Charge, Net of Tax	(.02)	—	—
Net Income per Common Share-Basic and Diluted	$1.00	$1.27	1.58

See Notes to Consolidated Financial Statements.
Source: Pilgrim's Pride, *Annual Report,* p. 5.

EXHIBIT 3   Consolidated Balance Sheets Pilgrim's Pride Corporation
(in thousands, except share and per-share data)

	September 29, 2001	September 30, 2000
ASSETS		
Current Assets:		
Cash and cash equivalents	$ 20,916	$ 28,060
Trade accounts and other receivables, less allowance for doubtful accounts	95,022	50,286
Inventories	314,400	181,237
Other current assets	12,934	9,387
Total Current Assets	443,272	268,970
OTHER ASSETS	20,067	18,576
Property, Plant and Equipment:		
Land	36,350	26,137
Buildings, machinery and equipment	929,922	565,034
Autos and trucks	53,264	48,187
Construction-in-progress	71,427	68,743
	1,090,963	708,101
Less accumulated depreciation	338,607	290,227
	752,356	417,874
	$1,215,695	$705,420
LIABILITIES AND STOCKHOLDERS' EQUITY		
Current Liabilities:		
Accounts payable	$ 151,265	$105,078
Accrued expenses	83,558	34,704
Current maturities of long-term debt	5,099	4,657
Total Current Liabilities	239,922	144,439
LONG-TERM DEBT, LESS CURRENT MATURITIES	467,242	165,037
Deferred Income Taxes	126,710	52,496
Minority Interest in Subsidiary	889	889
Commitments and Contingencies	—	—
STOCKHOLDERS' EQUITY:		
Preferred stock, $.01 par value, authorized 5,000,000 shares; none issued	—	—
Common stock–Class A, $.01 par value, authorized 100,000,000 shares; and 13,794,529 shares issued and outstanding in 2001 and 2000, respectively;	138	138
Common stock – Class B, $.01 par value, authorized 60,000,000 shares; 27,589,250 issued and outstanding in 2001 and 2000	276	276
Additional paid-in capital	79,625	79,625
Retained earnings	302,758	264,088
Accumulated other comprehensive income (loss)	(297)	—
Less treasury stock, 271,100 shares	(1,568)	(1,568)
Total Stockholders' Equity	380,932	342,559
	$1,215,695	$705,420

Source: Pilgrim's Pride, 2001 *Annual Report,* p. 50.

H.J. HEINZ COMPANY—2002

Henry Beam
Western Michigan University

HNZ

www.heinz.com

H.J. Heinz Company is a worldwide provider of processed food products and nutritional services. Headquartered in Pittsburgh, Pennsylvania, it has 45,000 employees, and markets more than 5,700 varieties of food products in more than 200 countries. It has manufacturing facilities in 21 countries. Heinz reported sales of $9.43 billion and net income of $478 million in the fiscal year ending May 2, 2001. In addition to ketchup, its original and best-known product, Heinz's product mix includes steak sauces, pet food, baby food, frozen potatoes, snacks, pasta, tuna, nutrition drinks, and soup. While the company's diversified product line makes it difficult for Heinz to have a succinct mission statement, its CEO, William R. Johnson, says, "Our mission is to have a bottle of ketchup on every table, everywhere."

HISTORY

In 1869, Henry J. Heinz formed a partnership with his friend, L.C. Noble, to sell grated horseradish fresh from his family's garden in western Pennsylvania. The firm soon moved to Pittsburgh and continued to grow until the overextended enterprise was forced into bankruptcy by the banking panic of 1875. Heinz paid all related debts before founding a new business, F. & J. Heinz, with his cousin and brother that same year. In its first year, the company produced pickles, horseradish, and what would become a world-renowned product—bottled ketchup. By 1888, Heinz gained financial control of the company as well, changing the name to H.J. Heinz.

Heinz put his ketchup in the familiar narrow-necked bottle to make it easier to pour and to reduce the amount of contact with air, which darkened the sauce. In 1895, a 17-ounce "Imperial Bottle" of ketchup was introduced with a delicately embossed symmetrical shape to appeal to higher-end hotels, restaurants, and upper-income families. A succession of prepared products followed. Heinz had discovered that most people were willing to let someone else take over a share of their kitchen operations and that a pure product of superior quality would find a ready market if properly packaged and promoted.

While traveling on a New York City elevated train in 1896, Heinz saw a shoe store sign advertising "21 styles." He liked the phrase and came up with the slogan "57 varieties" to describe what his company produced. The H.J. Heinz Company already produced more than 57 varieties, but Heinz stuck with the phrase because he liked the sound of the number 57. Heinz then drew a streetcar ad featuring the slogan. The public latched onto the slogan, which is displayed on the Heinz label to this day. In 1910, Heinz printed a small dark-green pickle on the bottom of the keystone label to further product recognition. The pickle remains a key element of the Heinz label today.

When Henry Heinz died in 1919, he was succeeded by his son Howard, who continued to grow the business internally. The company was run by H.J. Heinz II from 1941 to 1966. By the end of the 1940s, Heinz and ketchup went together naturally. As stated in a 1949 issue of the *Saturday Evening Post*, "Heinz ketchup, although not the first commercial ketchup, has led the American market for so long that it has determined the shape of almost all ketchup bottles because the public just naturally recognizes that shape as ketchup." The H.J. Heinz Company went public in 1946 after 77 years as a privately held firm.

In 1958, Heinz began to grow through acquisitions in Europe and Mexico as well in the United States. In the 1980s, Heinz became a leader in the nutrition and wellness field with the purchase of Weight Watchers and as a result of its development, into a global brand. The company also built major production bases in Spain, Portugal, and New Zealand. In 1998, William R. Johnson assumed the position of president and CEO from Dr. O'Reilly, becoming only the sixth CEO in the firm's long history. Today, H.J. Heinz Company is one of the largest publicly held food companies in the United States, as shown in Exhibit 1. Its major competitors are Campbell Soup, ConAgra, and Nestlé.

PRODUCT CATEGORIES

Heinz has organized its products into six core categories in which it seeks global leadership. Products with the leading market share position in their respective markets generate about two-thirds of the company's sales.

Ketchup, Condiments, and Sauces

Ketchup, condiments, and sauces, Heinz's largest segment, saw sales increase 4 percent in 2001 to $2.54 billion.

Ketchup

Heinz ketchup has always been the company's flagship brand. The company is the world's largest buyer of tomatoes, a key ingredient for its ketchup and related products, such as steak and barbecue sauce. Each year, the company processes more than 2 million tons of tomatoes and sells over $1 billion of ketchup worldwide. In the United States, it holds market-share highs of 57 percent in dollars and 51 percent in volume.

EXHIBIT 1   The Top Ten Publicly Held Food Companies in 2000 (in millions)

Company	Sales	Net Income	Major Brands/Products
Archer Daniels	14,283	281	Agricultural commodities and products
Bestfoods[1]	8,637	717	Mazola, Hellman's, Skippy, Thomas
Campbell Soup	6,424	766	Campbell's, Pepperidge Farm, Godiva, Healthy Request
ConAgra Foods	24,594	696	Grocery products, Healthy Choice, agricultural products
Diageo plc[2,3]	18,246	618	Pillsbury, Green Giant, Burger King, Smirnoff, Guinness
General Mills[3]	6,246	567	Wheaties, Betty Crocker, Bisquick, Hamburger Helper
Group Danone	13,415	688	Dannon, Lee & Perrins sauces, Evian, Galbani cheese
H.J. Heinz	9,300	882	Heinz ketchup, Star-Kist, Ore-Ida, Ken-L Ration
Hershey	3,971	333	Hershey's, Reese's, Cadbury's, Kit-Kat
Kellogg	6,984	549	Corn Flakes, Rice Krispies, Special K, Pop Tarts

[1]Formerly CPC International; acquired by Unilever in October 2000.
[2]Created in the December 1997 merger of Grand Metropolitan plc and Guinness plc.
[3]General Mills acquired the Pillsbury unit of Diageo in July 2000.
Sources: Value Line Investment Survey and **www.hoovers.com**.

In its 2000 *Annual Report,* Heinz stated that it would focus on making ketchup its primary growth vehicle in the United States and abroad. Heinz is focusing its global advertising campaign on increasing the consumption of ketchup by teenagers. Children ages six to twelve are the largest consumers of ketchup, followed closely by twelve to eighteen year olds. Households with children consume over twice as much ketchup as households without children. In 2001, Heinz introduced its colorful EZ Squirt kids' ketchup that comes in green and purple colors as well as the traditional tomato red. The squeezable bottle has a narrow opening that allows children to draw and write on their food.

Ketchup is used in many different ways around the world. It is eaten with pasta in Sweden, with rice in Venezuela, and with fish and chips in the United Kingdom. Heinz built a ketchup factory in China to supply its emerging market there for prepared foods. Annual per capita ketchup consumption in selected countries is shown in Exhibit 2. Heinz has set a goal "to make Heinz ketchup as ubiquitous as Coca-Cola. Everywhere fast-food is sold—whether in Asia, Africa, Europe, or the Americas—Heinz ketchup will be there, too." Global ketchup consumption is expected to increase about 6 percent annually.

Heinz's ketchup faces challenges from salsa and private ketchup brands. Introduced to American consumers over fifty years ago, salsa includes an array of sauces that include picante, enchilada, taco, and other chili-based sauces that appeal particularly to younger consumers. Salsa now outsells ketchup in some retail stores, indicating the changing nature of American tastes. Large food retailers such as A&P, Jewel, and Kroger offer lower cost, private label ketchup which competes directly with Heinz ketchup. Private label brands can be sold for less because there are no promotion or advertising costs associated with them.

EXHIBIT 2   Annual per capita Ketchup Consumption in Selected Countries, All Brands (in U.S. dollars)

Country	Ketchup Consumption
Sweden	$4.00
Australia	2.50
United States	2.20
Canada	2.20
Germany	1.70
United Kingdom	1.60
Poland	1.40
Japan	1.40
France	1.20
Russia	0.90
Thailand	0.70
Malaysia	0.60
Brazil	0.40
Indonesia	0.40

Source: Heinz's 1999 *Annual Report,* p. 7.

In 2001, Heinz acquired Vlasic pickles from Vlasic Foods International, which was in bankruptcy proceedings. Vlasic has about 25 percent of the $1.1 billion pickle, pepper, and relish categories, compared to about 3 percent for Heinz prior to the acquisition. A Heinz news release commented, "The addition of Vlasic pickles, a venerable brand with a history of excellence, quality and market innovation, will provide another condiment category with a number one brand for Heinz."

Food Service

Heinz's food service segment is the largest supplier of prepared foods to restaurants, diners, cafeterias, and other away-from-home eating places. Products include packets of ketchup and salad dressing and frozen soup concentrate. U.S. families spend about 50 cents of every food dollar on meals outside the home, up from about 33 cents twenty-five years ago. Sales of this segment, over $1 billion annually, were severely affected by the events of September 11, 2001, as people cut back on travel and were reluctant to dine in public places.

Sauces

Heinz has expanded its offering of sauces by acquiring such brand names as Open Pit barbeque sauce, Mr. Yoshida's Fine Sauces, and Boston Market HomeStyle Gravies. Heinz also has a licensing agreement to market Jack Daniel's Grilling Sauces. Sauces are typically sold in the same aisle of the store as ketchup.

Frozen Meals/Snacks

This segment includes Weight Watchers Smart Ones frozen entrees; Boston Market frozen meals; Bagel Bites frozen snacks, pasta, and potatoes; and Alden Merrell premium priced frozen desserts. Sales of this category increased 26 percent to $1.96 billion in 2001. The introduction of Boston Market HomeStyle Meals was very successful, as sales reached $130 million in the first full year of national distribution.

The Ore-Ida unit, with sales of $1 billion in 2001, includes retail and specialty frozen foods. Its principal product is frozen potatoes that are sold to fast-food chains, but it also sells a wide variety of frozen potato products in supermarkets. Ore-Ida has over half of the frozen potato market. It also makes the popular Tater Tots, which are formed from the slivers of potato that remain when a square section is sliced out to be made into French fried potatoes. A successful new Ore-Ida product is Bagel Bites pizza-topped snacks.

Tuna and Seafood

Heinz's Star-Kist division is the world's largest processor of canned tuna, a high-quality, low-cost, low-fat source of protein. Star-Kist's global sales of tuna and seafood were $1.04 billion in 2001, little changed from the previous year. It introduced a single-serving pouch of tuna in the spring of 2001 as an alternative to canned tuna. The vacuum sealed pouch, available in three and seven ounce sizes, provides firmer, fresher-tasting tuna. Star-Kist advertising features icons Charlie the Tuna and Morris the Cat.

Heinz operates modern, automated canneries in the Pacific and Indian Oceans, in Africa, and in Europe. Tuna prices fell to record low levels in 2001, and Heinz closed its tuna and fishing operations in Puerto Rico.

Quick-Serve Meals/Soups

Heinz's Quick-Serve meal segment, which includes soup, beans, and pasta, had sales of $1.22 billion in 2001. Heinz is the leading soup brand in the United Kingdom, Canada, Australia, and New Zealand. Heinz U.K. launched Fridge Door Soup, which is packaged in one-liter plastic bottles that are designed for storage on refrigerator doors. In Europe, Heinz introduced fast and convenient microwavable soup and baked beans products.

Heinz is the country's largest producer of private-label soup, with a nearly 90 percent share of the private-label market. Overall, Heinz has less than a 10 percent share of the total U.S. soup market. Campbell Soup Company is by far the largest producer of brand name canned soups in the United States, with a market share of nearly 75 percent of the $2.5 billion U.S. canned soup market. Heinz made a major attempt to enter the brand-name soup business in 1970 but failed because it wasn't able to adequately fund national media advertising. Instead, it decided to withdraw from the brand-name soup market in United States and concentrate on its private-label business.

Pet Products

Pet products had sales of $1.15 billion in 2001 and offers a broad range of cat and dog foods. Heinz's 9-Lives cat food is the market leader. Its dog food brands include Kibbles'n Bits, Gravy Train, Cycle, Ken-L Ration, and Jerky Treats. Heinz, Ralcorp, and Nestlé-Alpo each have about 20 percent of the domestic pet food business. Heinz recently introduced several pet food products, including Pup-Peroni Nawsomes, soft and chewy treats that are packed in a tennis ball container and Meaty Bone Savory Bites, crunchy treats with soft centers flavored with beef, chicken, or peanut butter. Heinz has about a third of the high-margin pet treats market.

Infant Feeding

Sales of Heinz's jarred baby foods, cereals, formulas, juices, and biscuits were $971 million in 2001. Heinz's market share in the United States is significantly behind that of industry leader Gerber (a division of Novartis, a Swiss firm) but ahead of Beechnut (a division of Ralcorp Holdings). However, Heinz is the market leader outside the United States. It has over half of the infant food market in Australia, Canada, Italy, New Zealand, and the United Kingdom, and it is working to expand its infant feeding business in eastern Europe, Russia, India, and China.

FINANCE

Highlights of H.J. Heinz Company's performance for the last two years are given in Exhibit 3. Heinz has increased its dividend every year since 1967. Heinz's financial statements are given in Exhibits 4 and 5. Heinz's net income was unusually high in 2000 because of the $465 million gain it recorded for the sale of its Weight Watchers storefront business. Business segment information is given in Exhibits 6 and 7. Advertising costs for fiscal years 2001, 2000, and 1999 were $404 million, $374 million, and $374 million, respectively. Like many other multinational companies, Heinz has been adversely affected by the strength of the dollar. In recent years, exchange rates have reduced Heinz sales by about $1.1 billion when international sales are translated into U.S. dollars for reporting purposes.

EXHIBIT 3   H.J. Heinz Company and Subsidiaries Consolidated Balance Sheets (in thousands)

	May 2, 2001	May 3, 2000
ASSETS		
CURRENT ASSETS:		
Cash and cash equivalents	$ 138,849	$ 137,617
Short-term investments, at cost which approximates market	5,371	16,512
Receivables (net of allowances: 2001—$15,075 and 2000—$18,697)	1,383,550	1,237,804
Inventories:		
Finished goods and work-in-process	1,095,954	1,270,329
Packaging material and ingredients	312,007	329,577
	1,407,961	1,599,906
Prepaid expenses	157,801	171,599
Other current assets	23,282	6,511
Total current assets	3,116,814	3,169,949
PROPERTY, PLANT, AND EQUIPMENT:		
Land	54,774	45,959
Buildings and leasehold improvements	878,028	860,873
Equipment, furniture and other	2,947,978	3,440,915
	3,880,780	4,347,747
Less accumulated depreciation	1,712,400	1,988,994
Total property, plant, and equipment, net	2,168,380	2,358,753
OTHER NONCURRENT ASSETS:		
Goodwill (net of amortization: 2001—$334,907 and 2000—$312,433)	2,077,451	1,609,672
Trademarks (net of amortization: 2001—$118,254 and 2000—$104,125)	567,692	674,279
Other intangibles (net of amortization: 2001—$157,678 and 2000—$147,343)	120,749	127,779
Other noncurrent assets	984,064	910,225
Total other noncurrent assets	3,749,956	3,321,955
Total assets	$9,035,150	$8,850,657
LIABILITIES AND SHAREHOLDERS' EQUITY		
CURRENT LIABILITIES:		
Short-term debt	$1,555,869	$ 151,168
Portion of long-term debt due within one year	314,965	25,407
Accounts payable	962,497	1,026,960
Salaries and wages	54,036	48,646
Accrued marketing	146,138	200,775
Accrued restructuring costs	134,550	125,704
Other accrued liabilities	388,582	358,738
Income taxes	98,460	188,672
Total current liabilities	3,655,097	2,126,070
LONG-TERM DEBT AND OTHER LIABILITIES:		
Long-term debt	3,014,853	3,935,826
Deferred income taxes	253,690	271,831
Nonpension postretirement benefits	207,104	208,958
Other	530,679	712,116
Total long-term debt and other liabilities	4,006,326	5,128,731

(continued)

EXHIBIT 3   H.J. Heinz Company and Subsidiaries Consolidated Balance Sheets
(in thousands)   **(continued)**

	May 2, 2001	May 3, 2000
SHAREHOLDERS' EQUITY:		
Capital stock:		
Third cumulative preferred, $1.70 first series, $10 par value	126	139
Common stock, 431,096,485 shares issued, $0.25 par value	107,774	107,774
	107,900	107,913
Additional capital	331,633	304,318
Retained earnings	4,697,213	4,756,513
	5,136,746	5,168,744
Less:		
Treasury shares, at cost (82,147,565 shares at May 2, 2001 and 83,653,233 shares at May 3,2000)	2,922,630	2,920,471
Unearned compensation relating to the ESOP	3,101	7,652
Accumulated other comprehensive loss	837,288	644,765
Total shareholders' equity	1,373,727	1,595,856
Total liabilities and shareholders' equity	$9,035,150	$8,850,657

Source: Heinz's 2001 *Annual Report,* pp. 44–45.

EXHIBIT 4   H.J. Heinz Company and Subsidiaries Consolidated Statements of Income
(in thousands, except per-share amounts)

	Fiscal year ended		
	May 2, 2001 (52 Weeks)	May 3, 2000 (53 Weeks)	April 28, 1999 (52 Weeks)
Sales	$ 9,430,422	$ 9,407,949	$ 9,299,610
Cost of products sold	5,883,618	5,788,525	5,944,867
Gross profit	3,546,804	3,619,424	3,354,743
Selling, general and administrative expenses	2,564,450	2,350,942	2,245,431
Gain on sale of Weight Watchers	–	464,617	–
Operating income	982,354	1,733,099	1,109,312
Interest income	22,692	25,330	25,082
Interest expense	332,957	269,748	258,813
Other (income)/expense, net	(969)	25,005	40,450
Income before income taxes and cumulative effect of accounting changes	673,058	1,463,676	835,131
Provision for income taxes	178,140	573,123	360,790
Income before cumulative effect of accounting changes	494,918	890,553	474,341
Cumulative effect of accounting changes	(16,906)	–	–
Net income	$ 478,012	$ 890,553	$ 474,341
PER COMMON SHARE AMOUNTS:			
Income before cumulative effect of accounting changes—diluted	$ 1.41	$ 2.47	$ 1.29
Income before cumulative effect of accounting changes—basic	$ 1.42	$ 2.51	$ 1.31
Net income—diluted	$ 1.36	$ 2.47	$ 1.29
Net income—basic	$ 1.37	$ 2.51	$ 1.31
Cash dividends	$ 1.545	$ 1.445	$ 1.3425
Average common shares outstanding—diluted	$351,041,321	$360,095,455	$367,830,419
Average common shares outstanding—basic	$347,758,281	$355,272,696	$361,203,539

Source: Heinz's 2001 *Annual Report,* p.43.

EXHIBIT 5   Heinz's International vs. Domestic Income Before Taxes (in thousands)

	2001	2000	1999
Domestic	$116,126	$ 805,464	$427,089
Foreign	556,932	658,212	408,042
Total Income Before Taxes	$673,058	$1,463,676	$835,131

Source: Heinz's 2001 *Annual Report,* p. 57.

GROWTH THROUGH ACQUISITIONS AND LICENSING

The food industry is mature, and most of Heinz's major brands date back to before World War II. Heinz has had little success developing new products with large sales potential. While cost cutting can increase earnings, it does not add to sales. Thus, Heinz has sought to increase sales and earnings by making acquisitions or divesting units with low margins.

In the 1990s, Heinz made major acquisitions or entered into licensing agreements that complemented its pet food business (from Quaker Oats in 1995), its food service business (from Borden in 1994), its seafood business (John West Foods U.K. in 1997), and its frozen entrees business (Boston Market licensing arrangement, 1999). Heinz has also divested itself of peripheral businesses, such as its Hubinger corn milling unit (1991), its Italian confectionery business (1994), its Near East specialty rice business (1994), its bakery products unit (1998), and its storefront Weight Watchers business (1999).

Acquisitions are an ongoing part of Heinz's strategy. Here are some of Heinz's acquisitions in 2001:

- Poland: acquired several popular ready-meal brands
- France: acquired Comexo, a leading maker of high quality sauces sold to French restaurants and caterers
- Northern Europe: acquired the CSM Food Division of CSM Nederland NV, a leading food company in the Netherlands, Belgium, and Luxembourg
- South Africa: acquired John West Foods South Africa, a maker of branded seafood and canned and bottled spices and fruit
- United States: acquired Borden Food Company's pasta sauces and dry bouillon and soup businesses, including the Classico and Wyler's brands, Alden Merrell frozen desserts, Vlasic pickles, and Open Pit and Jack Daniel's barbeque sauces.

Heinz sold its All American Gourmet and Budget Gourmet brands of frozen foods to focus on its faster growing frozen entree brands.

CEO WILLIAM R. JOHNSON

In November 1998, William R. Johnson, then forty-eight, became president and COO while his predecessor as president and COO, Dr. Anthony O'Reilly, retained his position as chairman of the Board of Directors. Bill Johnson joined Heinz in 1982 after working for two other food processing firms, Ralston Purina and Anderson Clayton. He made his mark at Heinz by successfully cutting costs in the tuna and pet food businesses. He instituted "price-based costing," whereby he determined first what consumers were willing to pay and then drove costs down to provide adequate margins at that selling price.

EXHIBIT 6   Heinz's By-Segment Financial Data (in thousands)

	Fiscal year ended			
	May 2, 2001 (52 Weeks)	May 3, 2000 (53 Weeks)	May 2, 2001 (52 Weeks)	May 3, 2000 (53 Weeks)
	Net External Sales		Intersegment Sales	
North American Grocery & Food Service	$4,146,538	$4,124,060	$ 38,198	$ 37,987
North American Frozen	1,125,396	1,023,915	12,660	12,782
Europe	2,746,870	2,583,684	3,657	2,687
Asia/Pacific	1,087,330	1,196,049	3,376	2,853
Other Operating Entities	324,288	480,241	–	2,526
Nonoperating	–	–	(57,891)	(58,835)
Consolidated Totals	$9,430,422	$9,407,949	$ –	$ –
	Operating Income (Loss)		Operating Income (Loss) Excluding Special Items	
North American Grocery & Food Service	$ 487,013	$ 694,449	$ 876,205	$ 875,268
North American Frozen	83,964	152,018	202,012	181,511
Europe	388,647	364,207	518,009	502,302
Asia/Pacific	96,123	124,125	147,599	177,454
Other Operating Entities	49,284	540,155	37,958	32,255
Nonoperating	(122,677)	(141,855)	(99,060)	(102,337)
Consolidated Totals	$ 982,354	$1,733,099	$1,682,723	$1,666,453
	Depreciation and Amortization Expense		Capital Expenditures	
North American Grocery & Food Service	$ 127,123	$ 133,471	$ 190,254	$ 171,295
North American Frozen	37,589	36,480	20,768	79,575
Europe	90,106	81,802	140,780	127,595
Asia/Pacific	26,288	28,871	46,166	60,795
Other Operating Entities	8,117	13,066	4,716	8,495
Nonoperating	9,943	12,793	8,615	4,689
Consolidated Totals	$ 299,166	$ 306,483	$ 411,299	$ 452,444
	Identifiable Assets			
North American Grocery & Food Service	$3,775,052	$3,711,691		
North American Frozen	797,943	882,225		
Europe	3,130,680	2,781,238		
Asia/Pacific	912,515	1,085,491		
Other Operating Entities	208,267	187,684		
Nonoperating	210,693	202,328		
Consolidated Totals	$9,035,150	$8,850,657		

Source: Heinz's 2001 *Annual Report*, p. 67.

EXHIBIT 7   Heinz's Revenues By Product (in thousands)

(Unaudited)	Fiscal year ended	
	May 2, 2001 (52 Weeks)	May 3, 2000 (53 Weeks)
Ketchup, condiments, and source	$2,537,294	$2,439,109
Frozen foods	1,961,267	1,561,488
Tuna	1,035,302	1,059,317
Soups, beans, and pasta meals	1,220,348	1,197,466
Infant/nutritional foods	973,004	1,041,401
Pet products	1,151,011	1,237,671
Other	552,196	871,497
Total	$9,430,422	$9,407,949

Fiscal year ended	Net External Sales	
	May 2, 2001 (52 Weeks)	May 3, 2000 (53 Weeks)
United States	$4,911,689	$4,848,125
United Kingdom	1,459,492	1,314,550
Other	3,059,241	3,245,274
Total	$9,430,422	$9,407,949

Source: Heinz's 2001 Annual Report, p. 68.

When Johnson took office, Heinz had been criticized by stock market analysts for several years for not doing as much as it could to increase earnings in an environment of low inflation and virtually no growth. Sensitive to such criticisms, Johnson quickly took steps to improve Heinz's competitive position. He created the Frozen Foods division by merging Ore-Ida frozen potato products with Weight Watchers Gourmet Foods, created a unified headquarters in Pittsburgh for Heinz's $5-billion North American food business, and entered into a licensing agreement with Boston Market to market its frozen meals. Under the agreement, Heinz would make and sell packaged food products, including frozen dinner entrees, bearing the Boston Market name.

One of Johnson's most significant decisions was to sell the Weight Watchers International weight control business that O'Reilly had acquired in 1977 and built into the world's largest weight control system. The Weight Watchers storefront business was sold because it did "not fit strategically with Heinz. The skills required to manage this retail business are not synergistic with our core competencies." Heinz retained its Weight Watchers Smart Ones line of frozen meals, desserts, and breakfast items. An organization chart for Heinz is given in Exhibit 8.

THE FUTURE

Under CEO Johnson, Heinz has made acquisitions to fill out its product lines, streamlined its organizational structure, and invested heavily in new plants and automated equipment. Looking to the future, Johnson wants Heinz to focus on increasing sales, which have been stalled at just over the $9 billion mark since 1997. It will attempt to do this by aligning its product offerings with consumer trends, such as the demands for more convenient ways to eat food on the go and organic foods.

EXHIBIT 8   Organization Chart for H.J. Heinz Company

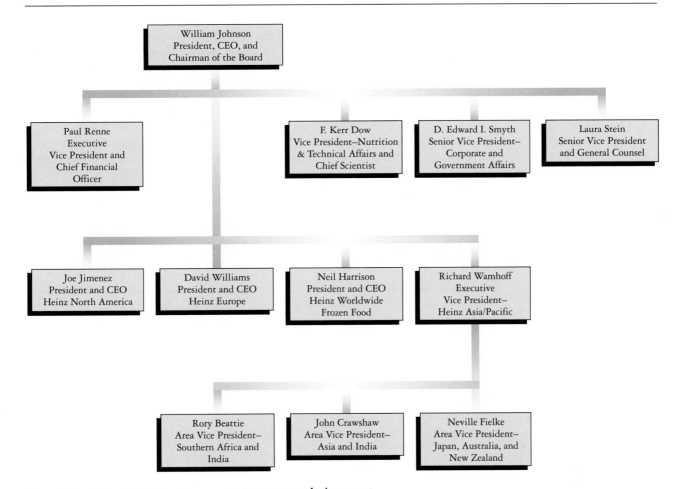

Source: Adapted from H.J. Heinz Company Web site (**www.heinz.com**).

The son of a former professional head football coach, Johnson stresses the importance of sports marketing in Heinz's future. Heinz Frozen Food has obtained endorsements from such eminent athletes as skateboarder Tony Hawk (Bagel Bites), former NBA star Larry Bird (Boston Market), and figure skater Kristi Yamaguchi (Smart Ones). Heinz acquired the naming rights for the new Pittsburgh Steeler's football stadium and called it Heinz Field. NFL football is the most popular sport in the United States, attracting over 100 million television viewers each week. Heinz Field will generate millions of media impressions for the Heinz brand, at a cost of less than $3 million per year, or about the price of a single Super Bowl television spot.

Heinz set up a new category, organic and functional foods, to run parallel to its six core food product categories. It will emphasize the development of organic and functional foods to take advantage of consumers' increasing interest in nutritional food. According to Johnson, "The category is growing at a 15 to 20 percent rate in the United States and is expected to expand in Europe at 25 percent annually over the next four years."

Johnson closed his remarks in the 2001 Heinz *Annual Report* as follows:

Heinz remains a fundamentally sound business with great brands, strong cash flow, good dividend yield and extensive global reach. People will always have to eat, and our premium brands, innovative marketing and aggressive strategies for profitable growth should position us well over the next three to five years. The tech-stock fervor and megamerger mania have cooled, leaving a stock market hungry for value, which we are committed to delivering to our loyal shareholders.

While Johnson has made major changes at Heinz, the board of directors is not entirely satisfied with his performance insofar as the price of Heinz stock has fallen about 25 percent since he became CEO. In August 2001, the board of directors increased his salary by $70,000, to $976,000, to keep it competitive with the pay of other food industry CEOs, but it decreased his bonus from $1,776,864 to $724,857.

REFERENCES

Creswell, Julie. "Bottled Up." *Fortune* (September 18, 2000): 195–196, 200, 202, 204, 206.

Dienstag, Eleanor Foa. *In Good Company: 125 Years at the Heinz Table* (Warner Books, 1994).

"Heinz CEO Takes It in the Bonus." CBS Market Watch (August 3, 2001).

"Heinz Puts Its Money Where the Young Mouths Are." *The New York Times* (September 12, 2001).

Morrow, Matt and Rekha Balu. "Corporate Icons Are a Hard Act to Follow, As Successors Discover." *The Wall Street Journal* (April 29, 1999).

HERSHEY FOODS CORPORATION—2002

Forest David
Mississippi State University

HSY

www.hersheys.com

Have you ever been to Hershey, Pennsylvania, the home of Hershey Foods Corporation? Known as Chocolate Town, USA, the air in this city actually smells like chocolate. There you can walk down Chocolate Avenue, see sidewalks lit with lights in the shape of Hershey Kisses, visit the Hershey Zoo, and see the chocolate kiss tower in Hershey Park. Hershey's Chocolate World is America's most popular corporate visitor's center.

Hershey has grown from a one-product, one-plant operation in 1894 to a $4.2 billion company producing an array of quality chocolate, nonchocolate, and grocery products. The company markets confectionery and grocery products in over ninety countries worldwide. Hershey's prominent products are chocolate and nonchocolate confectionery products consisting of bar goods, bagged items, and boxed items. Hershey grocery products include baking ingredients, peanut butter, chocolate drink mixes, dessert toppings, and beverages. Hershey markets these products under more than fifty different brands, such as Hershey Bar, Mr. Good Bar, Reese's, Kit Kat, Kisses, and Mounds. Hershey introduced no new products in the year 2000.

In 2002, Hershey remains behind M&M Mars in the confectionery market. Previously the largest candy maker, Hershey has slipped below Mars in market share. Almost 90 percent of Hershey's sales are generated in domestic markets. Hershey remains inexperienced in, ineffective in, and uncommitted to markets outside the United States, Mexico, and Canada, even though the candy industry has globalized. Mars, Borden, Nestlé, and other competitors all have a growing and effective presence in international markets. Analysts question whether Hershey can continue to survive as a domestic producer of candy while its competitors gain economies of scale and learn how to sell in world markets. Shareholders are becoming concerned too. Net income in 2001 decreased $127.4 million, or 38 percent, from 2000.

Sales to Wal-Mart stores are about 12 percent of Hershey's total revenues amounting to $819, $710, and $685 million in 2001, 2000, and 1999, respectively. Hershey needs a clear strategic plan to guide future operations and decisions. Company sales overall were up 8 percent in 2001 over 2000, and the company increased its dividend payout for the twenty-sixth seventh consecutive year.

According to its mission statement, Hershey is "to be a focused food company in North America and selected international markets and a leader in every aspect of [the] business."

HISTORY

Milton Hershey's love for candy-making began with a childhood apprenticeship under candy maker Joe Royer of Lancaster, Pennsylvania. Hershey was eager to own a candy-making business. After numerous attempts and even bankruptcy, he finally gained success in the caramel business. Upon seeing the first chocolate-making equipment at the Chicago Exhibition in 1893, Hershey envisioned endless opportunities for the chocolate industry.

By 1901, the chocolate industry in America was growing rapidly. Hershey's sales reached $662,000 that year, creating the need for a new factory. Mr. Hershey moved his company to Derry Church, Pennsylvania, a town that was renamed Hershey in 1906. The new Hershey factory provided a means of mass-producing a single chocolate product. In 1909, the Milton Hershey School for Orphans was founded. Mr. and Mrs. Hershey could not have children, so for many years the Hershey Chocolate Company operated mainly to provide funds for the orphanage. Hershey's sales reached $5 million in 1911.

In 1927, the Hershey Chocolate Company was incorporated under the laws of the state of Delaware and listed on the New York Stock Exchange. That same year, 20 percent of Hershey's stock was sold to the public. Between 1930 and 1960, Hershey went through rapid growth; the name Hershey became a household word. The legendary Milton Hershey died in 1945.

In the 1960s, Hershey acquired the H.B. Reese Candy Company, which makes Reese's Peanut Butter Cups, Reese's Pieces, and Reese's Peanut Butter Chips. Hershey also acquired San Giorgio Macaroni and Delmonico Foods, both pasta manufacturers. In 1968, Hershey Chocolate Corporation changed its name to Hershey Foods Corporation. Between 1976 and 1984, William Dearden served as Hershey's chief executive officer. An orphan who grew up in the Milton Hershey School for Orphans, Mr. Dearden diversified the company to reduce its dependence on fluctuating cocoa and sugar prices.

In the 1970s, Hershey acquired Y&S Candy Corporation, a manufacturer of licorice-type products such as Y&S Twizzlers, Nibs, and Bassett's Allsorts. The company also purchased Procino-Rossi, a pasta company, and Skinner Macaroni Company. During the 1980s, Hershey acquired A. B. Marabou of Sweden as well as the Dietrich Corporation, maker of Luden's Throat Drops, Luden's Mellomints, Queen Anne chocolate covered cherries, and 5th Avenue candy bars. It also acquired the Canadian confectionery (chocolate and nonchocolate candy) and snack nut operations of Nabisco Brands Ltd. Hershey acquired Peter Paul/Cadbury's U.S. candy operations, which gave it new products, such as Mounds, Almond Joy, York Peppermint Pattie, Cadbury Dairy Milk, Cadbury Fruit & Nut, Cadbury Caramello, and Cadbury Creme Eggs. Hershey received the rights to market the Peter Paul products worldwide.

Hershey purchased Nacional de Dulces (NDD) and renamed it Hershey Mexico, which today produces, imports, and markets chocolate products for the Mexican market under the Hershey brand name. In 1996, Hershey acquired Leaf North America in order to achieve market share leadership in North America in nonchocolate confectionery candies. In December 2000, Hershey purchased the breath freshener mints and gum businesses of Nabisco to obtain such products as Ice Breakers, Breath Savers, Bubble Yum and Fruit Stripe gum. On March 12, 2001, R.H. Lenny was elected president and chief executive officer of Hershey after previously serving as a division president with Nabisco. Hershey divested its Ludens throat drops business in 2001.

INTERNAL AFFAIRS

North American Operations

Hershey does not make public an organizational chart, but titles of executives suggest that Hershey operates from a centralized, functional structure with no divisional presidents. This type of structure would be somewhat unusual for an organization of Hershey's size, since it is more common for large companies to be decentralized in some manner. Another indication of the functional structure is that Hershey does not provide for its shareholders' financial data by segment, such as geographic region or product, again implying centralized control and accountability. In the late 1990s, Hershey operated with two divisions: Hershey North America and Hershey International.

Hershey's Mexico, Canadian, and U.S. operations generate about 90 percent of total company sales. Hershey's North American manufacturing operations are located in the following cities: Hershey, Pennsylvania; Oakdale, California; Stuarts Draft, Virginia; Lancaster, Pennsylvania; Robinson, Illinois; Smith Falls, Ontario, Canada; and Guadalajara, Mexico.

Hershey's North American operations produce an extensive line of chocolate and nonchocolate products that are sold in the form of single bars, bagged goods, and boxed items. These products are marketed under more than fifty brand names, and they are sold in over 2 million retail outlets in the United States, including grocery wholesalers, chain stores, mass merchandisers, drugstores, vending companies, wholesale clubs, convenience stores, and food distributors.

The U.S. confectionery market is growing only 2 percent annually in sales volume. The nonchocolate segment, which accounts for about one-third of the overall sweets market, is growing 5 percent annually, whereas the chocolate segment is growing at 1 percent. Hershey has only 4 percent of the nonchocolate confectionery market, while the leader is RJR Nabisco with 18 percent. RJR's Life Savers and Gummy Life Savers compete with Hershey's Amazin' Fruit Gummy Bears. Confectionery is the largest segment of the $52 billion U.S. snack market. Candy and gum represent 31 percent of this market.

Hershey recently established a new eastern distribution center near Hershey, Pennsylvania, to go with its refurbished southeastern distribution center near Atlanta, Georgia.

International Operations

Hershey's international operations have been a trouble spot, and they contributed zero profits to the company's 2000 bottom line. It is not clear what the profit contribution was in 2001. Hershey exports confectionery and grocery products worldwide. Europeans have the highest per-capita chocolate consumption rates in the world, but Hershey has no plans to overtake or even threaten Nestlé or Mars in Europe. In the Far East, Hershey has signed licensing agreements both with Selecta Dairy Products (to manufacture Hershey's ice cream products in the Philippines) and with Kuang Chuan Dairy in Taiwan (to manufacture Hershey's beverages). Hershey has introduced its products into Russia, the Philippines, and Taiwan. Overall in the Far East, however, Hershey is not planning a sustained effort due to the perceived high political and economic risks coupled with its own lack of experience in that area.

Social Responsibility

Hershey Foods Corporation is committed to the values of its founder, Milton S. Hershey, a man possessing the highest standard of quality, honesty, fairness, integrity, and respect. The firm makes annual contributions of cash, products, and services to a variety of national and local charitable organizations. Hershey is the sole sponsor of the Hershey National Track and Field Youth Program. Hershey also makes contributions to the Children's Miracle Network, a national program benefiting children's hospitals across the United States.

The corporation operates the Milton Hershey School, whose mission is to provide full-time care and education (including all costs) for disadvantaged children, mainly orphans. The school currently cares for over one thousand boys and girls in grades kindergarten through twelve. The Hershey School Trust owns over 75 percent of all Hershey Corporation's common stock.

Research and Development

Hershey engages in research and development activities in order to develop new products, improve the quality of existing products, and improve and modernize production processes. As shown here, the company has steadily decreased its research and development expenditures:

Year	Research and Development
1998	$28.6 million
1999	$26.7 million
2000	$25.4 million
2001	$26.5 million

Finance

Hershey's 2001 financial statements are given in Exhibits 1 and 2. Note that Hershey's long-term debt is $876 million and net income has declined annually since 1999.

Marketing

Hershey's marketing strategy is focused on maintaining the consistently superior quality of its products; mass distribution and the best possible consumer value in terms of price and weight are also features of its strategy. The company devotes considerable resources to the identification, development, testing, manufacturing, and marketing of new products. Hershey has developed a distribution network from its manufacturing plants; distribution centers and field warehouses are strategically located throughout the United States, Canada, and Mexico.

EXHIBIT 1   Hershey Foods Corporation Consolidated Statements of Income
(In thousands except per-share amounts)

For the years ended December 31,	2001	2000	1999
Net Sales	$4,557,241	$4,220,976	$3,970,924
Costs and Expenses:			
Cost of sales	2,665,566	2,471,151	2,354,724
Selling, marketing and administrative	1,269,964	1,127,175	1,057,840
Business realignment and asset impairments	228,314	—	—
Gain on sale of business	(19,237)	—	(243,785)
Total costs and expenses	4,144,607	3,598,326	3,168,779
Income before Interest and Income Taxes	412,634	622,650	802,145
Interest expense, net	69,093	76,011	74,271
Income before Income Taxes	343,541	546,639	727,874
Provision for income taxes	136,385	212,096	267,564
Net Income	$ 207,156	$ 334,543	$ 460,310
Net Income Per Share—Basic	$1.52	$ 2.44	$ 3.29
Net Income Per Share—Diluted	$ 1.50	$ 2.42	$ 3.26
Cash Dividends Paid Per Share:			
Common Stock	$ 1.165	$ 1.08	$ 1.00
Class B Common Stock	1.050	.975	.905

Source: Hershey's 2001 *Annual Report,* p. 16.

EXHIBIT 2   Hershey Foods Corporation Consolidated Balance Sheets
(in thousands)

December 31,	2001	2000
ASSETS		
Current Assets:		
Cash and cash equivalents	$ 134,147	$ 31,969
Accounts receivable—trade	361,726	379,680
Inventories	512,134	605,173
Deferred income taxes	96,939	76,136
Prepaid expenses and other	62,595	202,390
Total current assets	1,167,541	1,295,348
Property, Plant and Equipment, Net	1,534,901	1,585,388
Intangibles Resulting from Business Acquisitions, Net	429,128	474,448
Other Assets	115,860	92,580
Total assets	$3,247,430	$3,447,764
LIABILITIES AND STOCKHOLDERS' EQUITY		
Current Liabilities:		
Accounts payable	$ 133,049	$ 149,232
Accrued liabilities	462,901	358,067
Accrued income taxes	2,568	1,479
Short-term debt	7,005	257,594
Current portion of long-term debt	921	529
Total current liabilities	606,444	766,901
Long-term Debt	876,972	877,654
Other Long-term Liabilities	361,041	327,674
Deferred Income Taxes	255,769	300,499
Total liabilities	2,100,226	2,272,728
Stockholders' Equity:		
Preferred Stock, shares issued: none in 2001 and 2000	—	—
Common Stock, shares issued: 149,517,064 in 2001 and 149,509,014 in 2000	149,516	149,508
Class B Common Stock, shares issued: 30,433,808 in 2001 and 30,441,858 in 2000	30,434	30,442
Additional paid-in capital	3,263	13,124
Unearned ESOP compensation	(15,967)	(19,161)
Retained earnings	2,755,333	2,702,927
Treasury—Common Stock shares, at cost: 44,311,870 in 2001 and 43,669,284 in 2000	(1,689,243)	(1,645,088)
Accumulated other comprehensive loss	(86,132)	(56,716)
Total stockholders' equity	1,147,204	1,175,036
Total liabilities and stockholders' equity	$3,247,430	$3,447,764

Source: Hershey's 2001 *Annual Reports,* p. 17.

Hershey has steadily increased its advertising expenses, which were $193.3 million, $161.6 million, $164.9 million, and $187.5 million in 2001, 2000, 1999, and 1998, respectively. Hershey changes the prices and weights of its products to accommodate changes in manufacturing costs, the competitive environment, and profit objectives, while at the same time maintaining consumer value. The last standard candy bar price increase was implemented in December 1995, resulting in a wholesale price increase of approximately 11 percent on its standard and king-size candy bars, which are sold in the United States.

Per-capita candy sales in the United States have increased by 7.1 percent from 1997–2002. Americans spend over $21 billion a year on sweets. Upscale candy items such as Mars' Dove Promises are selling well. People are eating more ethnic foods today than ten years ago, which means more garlic and flavor. Breath-freshener–type candies are selling well in response to this eating trend.

Conventional wisdom in the candy industry is that a person rarely selects the same candy bar twice in a row; consequently, product variety is crucial to success. Marketing issues relative to health, nutrition, and weight consciousness are important. The media Hershey uses most often for advertising are network television, followed by syndicated television, spot television, magazines, and network and spot radio.

Confectionery sales are generally lowest during the second quarter of the year and highest during the third and fourth quarters, due largely to the holiday seasons. Hershey generates about 20 percent of its annual sales during the second quarter and 30 percent of its annual sales during the fourth quarter.

GLOBAL ISSUES

The most significant raw material used in the production of Hershey's chocolate products is cocoa beans. This commodity is imported principally from West African, South American, and Far Eastern equatorial regions. West Africa accounts for approximately 65 percent of the world's crop. Cocoa beans are not uniform, and the various grades and varieties reflect the diverse agricultural practices and natural conditions found in the many growing areas. Hershey buys a mix of cocoa beans to meet its manufacturing requirements. Because demand remained low worldwide, due partly to worsening economic conditions, cocoa prices in 2000 and 2001 remained near historic lows.

Hershey's second most important commodity for its domestic chocolate and confectionery products is sugar. Due to import quotas and duties that are imposed to support the price of sugar, sugar prices paid by U.S. users are currently substantially higher than prices on the world sugar market. Hershey also uses a large amount of peanuts, almonds, and dairy products.

The chocolate/cocoa products industry is SIC 2066, while candy/confectionery is SIC 2064. The main distribution channels for chocolate are grocery, drug, and department stores as well as vending machine operators. Almost all of these distributors are local, regional, or national; only a few are multinational. Although chocolate producers have not yet developed globally uniform marketing programs, the situation is changing. European unification extended grocery and department store channels of distribution. For example, Safeway, a U.S. grocer chain, now operates stores in Canada, the United Kingdom, Germany, and Saudi Arabia. As global channels of distribution become more available for chocolate manufacturers, global marketing uniformity will become more prevalent in the industry. Global cultural convergence is accelerating the need for more global marketing uniformity in the confectionery industry. Hershey's competitors are taking advantage of this globalization trend.

The confectionery industry is characterized by high manufacturing economies of scale. Hershey's main chocolate factory, for example, occupies more than 2 million square feet, is highly automated, and contains heavy equipment, vats, and containers. It is the largest chocolate plant in the world. High manufacturing costs in any industry encourage global market expansion, globally standardized products, and globally centralized production.

The confectionery industry is also characterized by high transportation costs for moving milk and sugar, the primary raw materials. This fact motivates companies such as Hershey to locate near their sources of supply. Since milk can be obtained in large volumes in many countries, chocolate producers have many options when locating plants. Also, producing chocolate is not labor-intensive; nor does it require highly skilled labor.

Industry analysts expect the candy industry to continue to grow. Consumption of chocolate, according to industry analysts, is closely related to national income, although the Far East is an exception to this rule. Candy consumption varies in the major markets of the developed nations. Americans consume about 22 pounds of candy annually per person, and Europeans consume about 27 pounds of candy per person.

Chocolate accounts for about 54 percent of all candy consumed. Northern Europeans consume almost twice as much chocolate per capita as Americans. In the European countries, the citizens of Switzerland, Norway, and the United Kingdom consume the most chocolate, while those of Finland and Italy consume the least. The Japanese also consume very little chocolate—about 1.4 kilos per capita. Throughout Asia and southern Europe, there is a preference for types of sweets other than chocolate, partly because of the high incidence of lactose intolerance (difficulty in digesting dairy products).

COMPETITORS

The $10-billion U.S. confectionery industry is composed of six major competitors that control nearly 70 percent of the market: Hershey, M&M Mars, Brach & Brock, Nestlé of Switzerland, RJR Nabisco, and Leaf Inc. The remaining 30 percent is divided among many local and regional candy manufacturers. Nabisco recently introduced a line of SnackWell's low-, no-, and fat-free candies in three flavors—raisin dips, chocolate chews, and caramel nut clusters.

Based in Switzerland, Nestlé clearly has an edge internationally, insofar as it is the world leader in many food categories, including candy. Almost 98 percent of Nestlé's revenues come from international sales. Hershey's other competitors also do much of their business outside North America. For example, Cadbury-Schweppes obtains 50 percent of its revenues from international sales, and Mars 50 percent, whereas Hershey obtains the least with 10 percent. Hershey's two major candy competitors are Mars and Nestlé.

Mars

Mars has a stronger presence than Hershey in Europe, Asia, Mexico, and Japan. Only one year after entering Mexico, Mars had gained 12 percent of that market. Analysts estimate Mars' worldwide sales and profits to be over $7 billion and $1 billion, respectively. Mars was successful introducing its Bounty chocolate candy into the United States without prior test marketing. Bounty was originally a European candy. Mars, unlike Hershey, uses uniform marketing globally. For example, the company's M&M candies slogan, "It melts in your mouth, not in your hands," is used worldwide. In contrast, Hershey's successful BarNone candy is named Temptation in Canada.

Mars is controlled by the Mars family through two brothers, John and Forrest, Jr. Mars is one of the world's largest, private, closely held companies. It is a secretive company, unwilling to divulge financial information and corporate strategies. Unlike Hershey, Mars has historically relied upon extensive marketing and advertising expenditures, rather than on product innovation, to gain market share. Mars has been repackaging, restyling, and reformulating its leading brands, including Snickers, M&M's, Milky Way, and 3 Musketeers, but that strategy is now being supplemented with extensive product development. New Mars products include Bounty, Balisto, and PB Max. The company also successfully developed and marketed frozen Snickers ice cream bars. The product was so successful that it dislodged Eskimo Pie and Original Klondike from the number-one ice cream snack slot without any assistance from promotional advertising. Mars has world-class production facilities in Hackettstown, New Jersey; from that plant, it ships products worldwide. In addition, it has manufacturing plants in Mexico and in several European locations.

Mars entered the Russian market in 1992 and today virtually owns the chocolate market there. Hershey is trying to gain a presence in Russia and China, but so far, it is struggling.

Nestlé

With annual sales of $7.3 billion in the United States and having recently acquired Carnation, Nestlé is the largest food company in the world. Nestlé's U.S. operations are headquartered in Glendale, California (818-549-6000). With corporate headquarters in Vevey, Switzerland (021-924-2111), Nestlé is a major competitor in Europe, the Far East, and South America. Nestlé sells products in over 360 countries on five continents, many in the developing nations. It is the world's largest instant coffee manufacturer, with Nescafe the dominant product. Nestlé also produces and markets chocolate and malt drinks, and it is the world's largest producer of milk powder and condensed milk.

Nestlé's chocolate and confectionery products carry some popular brand names, including Callier, Crunch, and Yes. With the acquisition of Rowntree, additional notable brands were added to the product line, including Smarties, After Eight, and Quality Street. The Perugina division produces Baci. Through the RJR Nabisco acquisition, Nestlé acquired Curtiss Brands, a U.S. confectionery producer of such products as Baby Ruth and Butterfinger. Nestlé manufactures chocolate in twenty-three countries, particularly in Switzerland and Latin America. Each factory is highly automated, employing an average of 250 people.

Another major product concentration for Nestlé is frozen foods and other refrigerated products. Findus in Europe and Stouffer in the United States represent the bulk of the group's frozen food sales, with well-known brands such as Lean Cuisine. Nestlé also manufactures a fast-developing range of fresh pasta and sauces in Europe and the United States under the name Contadina.

CONCLUSION

Hershey's global market share in the chocolate confectionery industry is only 10 percent, lowest among its competitors. A major strategic issue facing Hershey today is where, when, and how to best expand geographically. Perhaps Hershey should expand into the Far East, since the economies of those countries are growing so rapidly. China and India are huge untapped markets. Malaysia, Indonesia, Vietnam, and Thailand also are untapped. Should Hershey wait for Mars and Nestlé to gain a foothold in those countries?

Firms are becoming more and more environmentally proactive in their manufacturing and service delivery processes. Environmentally responsible firms market themselves and their products as being "green-sensitive." Concern for the natural environment is an issue Hershey should address before competitors seize the initiative. Developing environmentally safe products and packages, reducing industrial waste, recycling, and establishing an environmental audit process are strategies that could benefit Hershey.

Some analysts contend that Hershey's functional structure is an ineffective design. Would a divisional structure by product be more effective? The product divisions could be chocolate, nonchocolate, and grocery. Or would a divisional structure by geographic region be more effective? Can you recommend an improved organizational design that could enhance Hershey's lackluster international operations?

Should Hershey acquire firms in other foreign countries? Analysis is needed to identify and place a value on specific acquisition candidates. In developing an overall strategic plan, what recommendations would you present to CEO Kenneth Wolfe? Should Hershey diversify more into nonchocolate candies, since that segment is growing most rapidly? Should a new manufacturing plant be built in Asia or in Europe?

Design a global marketing strategy that could enable Hershey to boost its exports of chocolate. Should Hershey increase its debt further or dilute ownership of its stock further to raise the capital needed to implement your recommended strategies? Develop pro forma financial statements to fully assess and evaluate the impact of your proposed strategies.

BOEING—2002

Carolyn R. Stokes and Arthur S. Boyett
Francis Marion University

BA

www.boeing.com

The Boeing Company (312-544-2000), newly headquartered in Chicago, Illinois, is the largest aerospace firm in world, as measured by total sales, and the world's leading manufacturer of commercial aircraft, having cornered, on average, more than 60 percent of the market for the last twenty years. It is the world's leader in military aircraft, and the largest contractor for NASA. Boeing is one of the largest U.S. exporters, with about $18 billion in sales to foreign countries in 2000 (see Exhibit 1). Boeing has four major segments: (1) commercial aircraft, (2) military aircraft and missiles, (3) space and communications, and (4) customer and commercial Financing. Jetliners currently in production include the families of the Boeing 717, 737, 747, 757, 767, and 777 models. Boeing manufactures helicopters, military aircraft, electronic systems, and missiles; and it provides communication services for aerospace related activities and is a major contractor in the space station.

The aerospace industry was greatly affected by the events of September 11, 2001, when the United States was attacked by terrorists who had highjacked four commercial airliners. Two of the aircraft were flown into the Twin Towers of the World Trade Center in New York City, one aircraft was flown into the Pentagon in Washington, D.C., and the other crashed in Pennsylvania. For the first time in U.S. history, all air traffic was grounded. With new high-security measures in place, airports gradually reopened but with fewer flights and fewer passengers. Airlines, the major customer of Boeing's commercial jets, are laying off workers and ordering fewer aircraft. The U.S. president and Congress declared war on the terrorists, and the United States and its allies went to Afghanistan to hunt down the terrorist networks that had killed thousands of U.S. citizens. In this war of "Enduring Freedom," the military is depreciating its aircraft and is using up its arsenal of weapons. The U.S. intelligence community is using state of the art technological equipment, such as the satellites that Boeing produces.

Boeing, led by Chairman and CEO Philip M. Condit and President and COO Harry C. Stonecipher (see Exhibit 2), had revenues of $58.1 billion in 2001, compared to revenues of $51.3 billion in 2000. In the Military Aircraft and Missile Systems segment, Boeing recorded net earnings of $1.34 billion on sales of $12.4 billion in 2001. Growth in world air traffic is still projected to average 4.7 percent annually over the next twenty years, with much of the increase coming from Asian markets. With improved cost management and well-designed aircraft, Boeing should remain a major competitor in the aerospace industry. Boeing is in an aerospace environment that will be facing declining demand for some commercial aircraft in the near future and possible increasing demand for additional defense and space contracts due to the replacement needs for aircraft and missiles that are being used in the "Enduring Freedom" effort. Boeing's three fundamental goals are to run healthy core businesses, leverage strengths into new products, and service and open new frontiers. The company needs a clear strategic plan for the future.

EXHIBIT 1   The Boeing Company and Subsidiaries Sales by
Geographic Area (in millions)

	Year ended December 31,		
	2000	1999	1998
Asia, other than China	$ 5,568	$10,776	$14,065
China	1,026	1,231	1,572
Europe	9,038	9,678	8,646
Oceania	887	942	844
Africa	542	386	702
Non-U.S. Western Hemisphere	559	461	701
United States	33,701	34,519	29,624
Total Sales	$51,321	$57,993	$56,154

Source: www.boeing.com.

COMMERCIAL AIRCRAFT

With the attack on the United States on September 11, airline demand for new aircraft is uncertain. Boeing recognized that demand had been softening even before the September 11 attack and had already reduced the amount of time required to produce a Boeing 737 from thirty thousand labor hours to under ten thousand labor hours. Boeing's backlog of orders dropped from $86.9 billion in 1998 to $73.0 billion in 1999, before rising to $89.8 in 2000. Backlogs have averaged about $85.7 billion over the past five years. Boeing worked to solve any possible delays in production by rapidly ramping up the production process. The increased production rate helped to keep the backlog of orders under $90.0 billion. For two decades, Boeing has averaged over a 60 percent share of the world market for commercial jets. In 2000, customers announced orders for 611 jetcraft, as compared to 391 in 1999. However, by the middle of November 2001, Boeing had received only 284 gross orders. Even with the decline in orders from Asian

EXHIBIT 2   The Boeing Leadership

TOP MANAGEMENT

Philip M. Condit, Chairman of the Board and Chief Executive Officer
Harry C. Stonecipher, President and Chief Operation Officer

Source: www.boeing.com.

OPERATING MANAGEMENT

Alan R. Mulally, Senior VP of Boeing and President, Commercial Airplanes Group
Gerald E. Daniels, Senior VP of Boeing and President, Military Aircraft and Missile Systems Group
James F. Albaugh, Senior VP of Boeing and President, Space and Communications Group
James F. Palmer, Senior VP of Boeing and President, Boeing Capital Corporation
Scott Carson, Senior VP of Boeing and President, Connexion by Boeing^SM
John B. Hayhurst, Senior VP of Boeing and President, Air Traffic Management
Laurette T. Koeller, Senior VP of Boeing and President, Shared Services Group
David O. Swain, Senior VP of Engineering & Technology and President, Phantom Works

Source: www.boeing.com.

markets, approximately 34 percent of Boeing's 2000 airline sales were from non-U.S. carriers, down from 40 percent in 1999 and 47 percent in 1998.

As of December 2000, Boeing's expected number of commercial jet transport deliveries for 2000 was approximately 489, down from the 620 aircraft delivered in 1999. However, Boeing's production has greatly increased from the 274 jetcraft in 1997 and 269 in 1996. The backlogs, possible increases in military orders for aircraft, and possible returns to normal passenger demand following the September 11 attack may push production levels upward in 2002.

In March 2001, Boeing unveiled its new Sonic Cruiser, a high-speed aircraft expected to cost $10 billion to develop. The new plane, designed to fly just below the sound barrier and cut airtime by 20 percent, marks the emergence of a high-speed family that is directly derived from a supersonic transport design. The Sonic Cruiser family will replace the 767 family. Boeing expects the Sonic Cruiser to be completed in either 2006 or 2008. Boeing could use a new aircraft to compete with Airbus's new model.

Boeing's commercial airjet segment currently produces the new 717 family, together with the 737, 747, 757, 767, and 777 families. The MD-95 was redesigned as the new Boeing 717, and the other MD aircraft were phased out of production by the end of 2001. Boeing's commercial airjet development has focused on the 717, 777, and the 737 families, as well as on the long-range derivatives of the 767, 747, and 777. The new 717, originally the MD-95, was originally delivered in 1999. This 717-200 responds to the need for a one-hundred seat regional jet. Boeing had received a total of 151 orders by the end of 2000 and had delivered 44 aircraft by the end of 2000. However, Boeing had a net loss of 14 orders for the first three quarters of 2001.

Boeing is pleased with the response to the Boeing 777 family that was originally put into service in 1995. The 777 was developed to meet the need for a more efficient, comfortable, and high-capacity capacity jet. The 777-200 and 777-300 series along with their recently launched extended range derivatives can seat from 305 to 550 passengers, and the two aircraft have ranges from 5,925 to 8,861 miles. According to the results of a Boeing survey, three out of four passengers preferred the Boeing 777. Boeing had received a total of 563 orders and had delivered 316 aircraft by the end of 2000.

The smallest member of the Boeing jetliner family is the 737; it is the best-selling aircraft of all time, with 4,783 orders and 3,857 deliveries by the end of 2000. The 737 family, developed for short-to-medium range flights, is designed for greater range and speed, and it complies with new noise and emission standards. The 600, 700, 800, and 900 members of the 737 family have outsold all aircraft in their market. The 737 family includes two Boeing business jets, both derivatives of the 737-700 and 737-800 members. Boeing received 117 orders for all 737s in 2000.

The Boeing 757 and 767 are medium-capacity, fuel-efficient twinjets that meet FAA requirements for extended-range operations. The 757 can carry 194 passengers as far as 4,500 nautical miles. In 1999, Boeing introduced the 757-300, which has 20 percent more seating and 10 percent lower per-seat operating costs than the 757-200. The 757-300 can carry 289 passengers up to 3,990 nautical miles. Boeing received 1,027 orders and had delivered a total of 948 by the end of 2000.

The 767 is larger, carrying about 260 passengers in mixed-class configurations, and the range of some versions exceeds 6,000 nautical miles. The 767-200 can carry 181 to 224 passengers, and its range is 7,618 miles; the 767-300, which comes in an extended-range version, can carry 20 percent more passengers than the 200 version. The first deliveries of the extended-range version of the 767 were to Delta and Continental in August 2000. The 767-400ER can carry 304-375 passengers up to

6,501 miles. In 2000, Boeing committed to production of a longer-range version of the 767-400ER.

The flagship of the Boeing aircraft family, the 747-400, can carry 568 passengers more than eight thousand nautical miles, and it offers airline customers the lowest seat-mile costs of any twin-aisle commercial jetcraft in the world. The new extended-range version has a range of 8,850 miles. The 747-400 has both an all-cargo as well as a Combi model for passengers and freight. The Boeing 747 freight aircraft is in great demand at Narita, Tokyo's international airport, which handles more than 1.5 million tons of freight per year, more than any other airport in the world. Almost 80 percent of the jets using Narita are Boeing 747s. The 747-400F gives Boeing's airline customers the ability to carry twenty tons more payload on the routes they fly than the 747-200 freighters, or its customers can carry the same payload eight hundred nautical miles farther. Boeing had received orders for 1,338 and it had delivered a total of 1,261 by the end of 2000.

The company reported the following key financial information for the commercial aircraft segment for the most recent three years (numbers are all in millions of dollars):

	2001	2000	1999	1998
Revenues	$ 35,056	$ 31,171	$ 38,475	$ 36,998
Operating income	2,632	2,736	2,082	(148)
Assets	11,479	9,800	8,075	11,003
Liabilities	7,579	7,972	6,135	6,907
Research & Development costs	858	574	585	1,021
Contractual backlog of orders	75,850	89,780	72,972	86,057

Source: **www.boeing.com**.

Competition in Commercial Aircraft

The European Aeronautic Defense and Space Co. (EADS), which was formed in 2000 from aerospace groups in Germany, France, and Spain, remains Boeing's most formidable competitor in the commercial aircraft industry. Daniel Michaels in his November 14, 2001, *Wall Street Journal* article, "Airbus Faces Adjustment in Output as Demand Falls," states that EADS's revenue over the last nine months of 2001 was 30 percent higher than the total that was recorded in the same period a year earlier. Airbus originally planned to deliver 320 planes in 2001. Some analysts expect Airbus deliveries to outpace Boeing deliveries by the end of the decade. However, many industry analysts expect that Airbus will have to cut production to as low as 290 planes—and possibly as low as 250 planes.

Customer Service

Boeing provides regional world centers for proactive, value-added maintenance, parts, and training. Boeing acquired Continental Graphics, a specialist in airline information systems, and Jeppensen Sanderson, Inc., the leader in in-flight information services, to better support customers. The maintenance and modification market is about $90 billion annually, and Boeing is working to increase its 4 percent share. Boeing is providing ready access to parts and training programs using the Web and ED-ROM technologies. Customers can access parts information on the Web site **MyBoeingFleet.com**. Information on the availability of parts, maintenance, engineering, and operational data are provided on this Web site for customers.

BOEING FRONTIERS

Connexion by Boeing^{SM}

Connexion by Boeing^{SM} is a dynamic breakthrough consumer and commercial airline service that will provide air travelers an unparalleled array of high-speed data communication services via a space-based network. The venture's strategic focus is on providing television and high-speed real-time Internet services to commercial airlines, business jets, and government customers. Boeing, leading the airborne broadband communications frontier, has excelled at blending creative innovation with large-scale integration. Boeing's competency in satellite systems, commercial aircraft construction, and high-speed critical data transfer methodology gives it a competitive advantage that no narrow-band provider can match. Currently, a prototype of the service is available on some Boeing business jets. According to a June 14, 2001, article in the *Wall Street Journal* by J. Lynn Lunsford, Boeing has signed a letter of intent to enter into a joint venture with Delta Air, United, and American for the Connexion by Boeing^{SM} service. Boeing, the major shareholder, will share the revenue with the airlines, and it will be responsible for the overall management of the operation. Connexion by Boeing^{SM} is an example of a new frontier that was developed by using the company's core strengths.

Air Traffic Management

Boeing is developing an Air Traffic Management (ATM) system to replace the current ground-based program. The proposed ATM would integrate today's separate control, communications, navigation, surveillance, and weather services into a single, seamless Common Information Network (CIN). The new ATM will rely primarily on Global Positioning Satellites (GPSs). The system should be relatively inexpensive and easy to install on older aircraft, both those of Boeing and Airbus. Boeing's new planes already come equipped with the technology that allows them to fly from place to place without ground control. According to a May 17, 2001, *Wall Street Journal* article by J. Lynn Lunsford, United Parcel Service Inc.'s UPS Airlines and FedEx Corp.'s Federal Express have already been using an early satellite version to improve operations at large hubs. According to Bois and Sweatman in an October 2001 article in *Interavia Business & Technology*, the ATM is designed to supplement, expand, and eventually supersede the FAA's Operational Evolution Plan, which should be ready by 2010. Boeing projects that its ATM could be ready within eight years. As the air travel and air freight business increases, the current ground-based system becomes more overloaded. The proposed new Boeing ATM program may be the answer. However, the new program will require the cooperation of all stakeholders in the airline industry to be successful.

Aircraft and Missile Systems

Boeing is a major player in the field of military aircraft and missiles whose biggest customer is the U.S. Department of Defense. Boeing also sells to foreign governments under licenses granted by the U.S. government to its allies.

This segment of the company produces tactical fighters, trainers, helicopters, military transports, tankers, strike missiles, and special purpose planes. It also provides aerospace support products and services. The biggest programs in this industry segment are the C-17 Globemaster transport program and the F/A-18E/F Super Hornet fighter program. The segment also includes the F/A-18C/D Hornet, AH-64 Apache, F-22 Raptor, F-15 Eagle, V-22 Osprey, and CH-47 Chinook programs.

The company reported the following key financial information for the military aircraft and missile systems segment for the most recent years (numbers are all in millions of dollars):

	2001	2000	1999	1998
Revenues	$12,451	$12,197	$12,220	$12,990
Operating income	1,346	1,271	1,193	1,283
Assets	2,477	3,321	3,206	3,506
Liabilities	1,612	1,189	1,080	743
Research and development cost	258	257	264	304
Contractual backlog of orders	17,630	17,113	15,691	17,007

Source: **www.boeing.com.**

The company states that "The basic strategy of the . . . segment is to provide competitive products and services in every selected market . . . [and] to provide integrated product and service solutions that best meet customer needs."

The U.S. Department of Defense has pledged to examine its weapon systems and to modernize many of them, which would appear to mean that 2001 and future years continue to be bright for this segment of the company. One such innovation is the use of unmanned, reusable aircraft to fly bombing missions. These craft combine some of the best features of missiles with those of manned aircraft: (1) the aircraft loses no people if shot down and (2) the aircraft delivers its payload and returns the delivery system for reuse, unlike missiles, which destroy the delivery system with the payload.

Two major events in late 2001 may have a significant impact on this segment:

1. The September 11 destruction of the World Trade Center and part of the Pentagon, which triggered the U.S. military attacks on Afghanistan, seem to indicate that the government will be procuring additional military hardware and services in the years to come. Discussions are reported to be taking place both in Congress and in the Defense Department that could result in additional purchases of transport planes and tankers that are built from converted 767 commercial aircraft. Boeing's military aircraft and missiles segment is poised to benefit from those additional purchases.

2. The Department of Defense announced on October 26, 2001, that it had chosen Lockheed-Martin as the prime contractor to produce the Joint Strike Fighter, which is being designed to replace aging aircraft in several U.S. and U.K. military services—as well as in the arsenals of several NATO allies. Analysts project that the contract will be worth at least $200 billion in revenues—and may be worth up to $1 trillion—for Lockheed-Martin. Boeing was in the final stage of the competition, and it had expected to obtain at least a part of the final award, but the contract was granted as a "winner take all" award to Lockheed-Martin. Boeing may still benefit by subcontracting some of the components of the project from Lockheed-Martin. It is not uncommon for the winner of such a contract to subcontract various components of such a large program. It is being reported that some members of Congress are discussing legislation to require splitting the contract between Lockheed and Boeing.

SPACE AND COMMUNICATIONS

The space and communications segment, which is the newest and smallest of the significant segments, seems to be the fastest growing. The four major areas of operations in this segment are launch services, information and communication, human space flight and exploration, and missile defense and space control.

The 767 AWACS is a flying, all-weather surveillance, command, communications, and control system installed in a 767 commercial aircraft. The system is used by the military to monitor and control attack aircraft in offensive engagements and to warn those aircraft of enemy response by either airplanes or missiles. AWACS systems were also used, following the September 11 attack on the World Trade Center and the Pentagon, to enforce the order that all flights over U.S. territory be grounded. The Pentagon is reported to be considering modernizing its fleet of AWACS craft, in part due to the terrorist attacks of September 11.

Boeing's president recently set a goal of making Boeing "number 1 in space." Boeing has Delta programs that produce rocket boosters used by NASA and some private satellite-launch groups to put satellites into orbit and to launch other space-related activities. The Delta III is still undergoing tests. Some of the tests have resulted in spectacular failures, but the company is not likely to lose money on the program because its government contracts are "cost-plus" contracts.

The company reported the following key financial information for the space and communications segment for the most recent years (numbers are all in millions of dollars):

	2001	2000	1999	1998
Revenues	$10,364	$ 8,039	$ 6,831	$ 6,889
Operating income	619	(323)	415	248
Assets	10,299	9,629	4,245	3,149
Liabilities	3,123	2,903	1,350	1,452
Research and development costs	526	526	492	570
Contractual backlog of orders	13,111	13,707	10,585	9,832

Source: www.boeing.com.

The prospects for this segment are quite varied. The launch services sector is dependent on NASA and on the commercial satellite launch market. This is a highly competitive area. The information and communication services sector is positioned to experience rapid growth. For its governmental customers, Boeing offers airborne mission systems, space systems, and satellite systems; and for commercial customers, the company offers satellite manufacturing, hybrid network systems, and telecommunications. The human space flight sector expects relatively flat growth over the next ten years. Boeing's activities will include completing existing contracts for the International Space Station and operations and maintenance on the space shuttle program.

Financing

Customer and commercial financing segment revenues are made up primarily of interest from the financing of receivables and lease income from equipment leased to others under operating leases. A major expense of the segment is depreciation on the equipment leased. No interest expense on debt incurred by the company is included in the calculation of segment income. (The interest and debt expense for the company is reported as a single amount on the income statement. It is not allocated to the segments.)

The revenues from the segment were $863 million, $758 million, $771 million, and $612 million for the years 2001, 2000, 1999, and 1998, respectively. Comparable net earnings were $596 million, $494 million, $426 million, and $249 million for the same four years. The segment employed assets of $9.646 billion, $6.959 billion, $6.004 billion, and $5.751 billion; and it had liabilities of $351 million, $240 million, $228 million, and $301 million in 2001, 2000, 1999, and 1998, respectively.

This segment is likely to continue to grow as long as airline companies and others need additional airplanes. Because of the high cost of purchasing a commercial aircraft, many of Boeing's customers will opt for either financing the purchase or leasing the aircraft from the company. This should provide a steady source of revenue for this segment. As long as interest rates are low, the segment can make a good profit.

CONCLUSION

In 2001, Boeing's net income increased to $2,827 million (see Exhibits 3 and 4). Even following the attack on the United States on September 11, in each of the four major segments of the company, there were still some favorable factors. The war effort, "Enduring Freedom," has reduced our nation's supply of aircraft, missiles, and other aerospace products, thereby requiring repletion of these products by Boeing and other manufacturers. The airline passenger business is expected to increase over the next twenty years at an

EXHIBIT 3   The Boeing Company Consolidated Statements of Operations (in millions except per-share data)

	Year ended December 31,	
	2001	*2000*
Sales and other operating revenues	$58,198	$51,321
Cost of products and services	48,778	43,712
	9,420	7,609
Equity in income from joint ventures	93	64
General and administrative expense	2,389	2,335
Research and development expense	1,936	1,441
In-process research and development expense		557
Gain on dispositions, net	21	34
Share-based plans expense	378	316
Special charges due to events of September 11, 2001	935	
Earnings from operations	3,896	3,058
Other income, principally interest	318	386
Interest and debt expense	(650)	(445)
Earnings before income taxes	3,564	2,999
Income taxes	738	871
Net earnings before cumulative effect of accounting change	2,826	2,128
Cumulative effect of accounting change, net	1	
Net earnings	$ 2,827	$ 2,128
Basic earnings per share	$ 3.46	$ 2.48
Diluted earnings per share	$ 3.41	$ 2.44
Cash dividends paid per share	$ 0.68	$ 0.56

Source: www.boeing.com.

EXHIBIT 4   Boeing Company Annual Balance Sheet
(in millions except for per-share items)

	2001	2000	1999
Cash & Equivalents	633.0	1,010.0	3,354.0
Short Term Investments	—	—	100.0
Cash and Short Term Investments	633.0	1,010.0	3,454.0
Trade Accounts Receivable, Net	5,156.0	5,519.0	3,453.0
Other Receivables	—	—	—
Total Receivables, Net	5,156.0	5,519.0	3,453.0
Total Inventory	6,920.0	6,852.0	6,539.0
Prepaid Expenses	—	—	—
Other Current Assets	3,497.0	3,132.0	2,266.0
Total Current Assets	16,206.0	16,513.0	15,712.0
Property/Plant/Equipment–Gross	—	—	—
Accumulated Depreciation	(12,369.0)	(12,156.0)	(11,874.0)
Property/Plant/Equipment, Net	8,459.0	8,814.0	8,245.0
Goodwill, Net	6,443.0	5,214.0	2,233.0
Intangibles, Net	—	—	—
Long Term Investments	—	—	—
Other Long Term Assets	17,235.0	12,136.0	9,957.0
Total Assets	48,343.0	42,677.0	36,147.0
Accounts Payable	13,872.0	12,312.0	11,269.0
Accrued Expenses	—	—	—
Notes Payable/Short Term Debt	—	—	200.0
Current Port. LT Debt/Capital Leases	1,399.0	1,232.0	552.0
Other Current Liabilities	5,215.0	5,383.0	1,635.0
Total Current Liabilities	20,486.0	18,927.0	13,656.0
Long Term Debt	10,866.0	7,567.0	5,980.0
Capital Lease Obligations	—	—	—
Total Long Term Debt	10,866.0	7,567.0	5,980.0
Total Debt	12,265.0	8,799.0	6,732.0
Deferred Income Tax	177.0	0.0	172.0
Minority Interest	—	—	—
Other Liabilities	5,989.0	5,163.0	4,877.0
Total Liabilities	37,518.0	31,657.0	24,685.0
Redeemable Preferred Stock	—	—	—
Preferred Stock–Non Redeemable, Net	—	—	—
Common Stock	5,059.0	5,059.0	5,059.0
Additional Paid-In Capital	1,975.0	2,693.0	1,684.0
Retained Earnings (Accum. Deficit)	14,340.0	12,090.0	10,487.0
Treasury Stock–Common	(8,509.0)	(6,221.0)	(4,161.0)
Other Equity	(2,040.0)	(2,601.0)	(1,607.0)
Total Equity	10,825.0	11,020.0	11,462.0
Total Liability & Shareholders' Equity	48,343.0	42,677.0	36,147.0
Shares Outs.–Common Stock	837.6	875.5	909.5
Total Common Shares Outstanding	837.6	875.5	909.5
Total Preferred Stock Shares Outs.	—	—	—
Employees (actual figures)	186,900.0	198,000.0	197,000.0
Number of Common Shareholders (actual figures)	—	—	—

Source: **http://investor.stockpoint.com.**

EXHIBIT 5   The Boeing Company Segment Information

A. Sales and Other Operating Revenues

Year ended December 31,	2001	2000
Commercial Airplanes	$35,056	$31,171
Military Aircraft and Missile Systems	12,451	11,924
Space and Communications	10,364	8,039
Customer and Commercial Financing	863	728
Other	365	303
Accounting differences/eliminations	(901)	(844)
	$58,198	$51,321

B. Net Earnings (Loss) Before Cumulative Effect of Accounting Change

Year ended December 31,	2001	2000
Commercial Airplanes	$ 2,632	$ 2,736
Military Aircraft and Missile Systems	1,346	1,245
Space and Communications	619	(243)
Customer and Commercial Financing	596	516
Other	(388)	(76)
Accounting difference/eliminations	(368)	(442)
Share-based plans expense	(378)	(316)
Unallocated expense	(163)	(362)
Earnings from operations	3,896	3,058
Other income, principally interest	318	386
Interest and debt expense	(650)	(445)
Earnings before taxes	3,564	2,999
Income taxes	738	871
	$ 2,826	$ 2,128

C. Research and Development

Year ended December 31,	2001	2000
Commercial Airplanes	$ 858	$ 574
Military Aircraft and Missile Systems	258	257
Space and Communications	526	526
Other	294	84
	$ 1,936	$ 1,441

(continued)

average annual rate of 4.7 percent, with the air cargo business expected to double over the same period. The space and communications market is looking forward to significant increases in the commercial market.

In the face of the expected business environment, prepare a strategic plan for CEO Philip M. Condit and COO Harry C. Stonecipher. Keep in mind that according to the 2000 *Annual Report,* Boeing's plan for the near, medium, and long-term future is to "create converging and ever-increasing streams of value—for customers and shareholders."

EXHIBIT 5   The Boeing Company Segment Information   (**continued**)

D. Assets at December 31,

	2001	2000
Commercial Airplanes	$11,479	$ 9,800
Military Aircraft and Missile Systems	2,477	3,035
Space and Communications	10,299	9,629
Customer and Commercial Financing	9,646	6,856
Other	1,290	389
Unallocated	13,152	12,968
	$48,343	$42,677

E. Capital Expenditures, Net

	2001	2000
Commercial Airplanes	$ 207	$ 237
Military Aircraft and Missile Systems	99	25
Space and Communications	362	438
Customer and Commercial Financing	1	7
Other	32	40
Unallocated	367	185
	$ 1,068	$ 932

Source: **http://www.boeing.com.**

REFERENCES

Bois, and Sweatman. *Intervaia Business and Technology* (October 2001).

Lunsford, J. Lynn. *Wall Street Journal* (June 14, 2001).

Lunsford, J. Lynn. *Wall Street Journal* (May 17, 2001).

Michaels, Daniel. "Airbus Faces Adjustment in Output as Demand Falls." *Wall Street Journal* (November 14, 2001).

LOCKHEED MARTIN CORPORATION—2002

K. Todd Ellison
Francis Marion University

LMT

www.lockheedmartin.com

On September 11, 2001, the United States suffered a tremendous loss when terrorists viciously attacked the mainland of the United States using hijacked commercial aircraft. As the second largest company in the defense, intelligence, and aerospace industry, Lockheed Martin Corporation, previously suffering from government defense funding cuts, now faced (and continues to face) tremendous new opportunities. As the builder of many of the best-known military aircraft and rocket systems, such as the C-5A, C-130, F-16, F-22, F-117 aircraft and the Atlas, Titan, and Trident rocket systems, Lockheed Martin products are leading the war on terrorism. Lockheed Martin also produces many lower visibility high-tech products and services that possess intelligence-gathering capabilities. Lockheed Martin handles the operation of many federal and state government data processing and communications systems, including many post office, air traffic control, and social services systems. Lockheed Martin's stated vision is "to be the world's best advanced technology systems integrator."

HISTORY

Lockheed Aircraft Company was formed in 1926 by Allan Loughead, Malcolm Loughead, and Fred Keeler after the Loughead (name was later changed to Lockheed) brothers had previously experienced several unsuccessful forays into the aircraft manufacturing business. The company's first aircraft, the Vega, was designed by the future founder of the Northrup Corporation, John Northrup. Amelia Earhart was flying a Vega when she became the first woman to fly solo across the Atlantic. Wiley Post flew a Lockheed Vega during his around-the-world solo flight.

Robert Gross, Carl Squier, and Lloyd Stearman purchased Lockheed Aircraft Corporation in 1932. The Lockheed Electra, the first successful pressurized commercial aircraft, was developed in the 1930s. Lockheed continued to produce many famous aircraft, including the P-38 Lightning of WWII fame, the P-80 Shooting Star, and the F-104 Starfighter, as well as spy planes such as the U-2 (1955) and the SR-71 Blackbird (1964). The C5-A Galaxy, C-130 Hercules, and C-141 Starlifter military cargo aircraft as well as the L-1011 Tristar passenger airliner were also produced by Lockheed.

In the 1960s and 1970s, Lockheed suffered many financial setbacks, including C-5A cost overruns, cancellation of the Cheyenne helicopter program, and cost problems associated with the L-1011 passenger jet. Additional problems arose in the 1970s when Lockheed became involved in a corporate bribery scandal, which led to revisions in antibribery laws. Government loans were required in 1971 to save the company from bankruptcy. In 1992, Lockheed entered an agreement to provide satellites for Motorola's Iridium phone project.

Glenn Martin founded the Glenn L. Martin Aircraft Company in 1912 and in 1916 merged with the company founded by the Wright Brothers. The twin-engine Martin MB-2 was used by General Billy Mitchell to demonstrate the potential of air bombardment. In the 1930s, Martin built the M-130 Clipper flying boat, which became famous as the Pan Am Clipper. Martin produced the B-26 bomber during World War II.

Martin produced missiles, electronics, and nuclear systems during the 1950s. In an attempt to diversify in 1961, Martin merged with the chemical and construction material company American-Marietta Company to become Martin Marietta. Martin Marietta developed the Titan II rocket in the 1960s. Other Martin Marietta projects included the Viking Mars lander, the MX missile, and the external fuel tanks for the space shuttle. Martin Marietta was forced to sell off many of its businesses in 1982 after it acquired $1 million of debt fending off a takeover attempt from Bendix Corporation. In 1992, Martin Marietta purchased the aerospace operations of General Electric.

Lockheed Martin was formed in 1995 when Lockheed acquired Martin Marietta. These two companies seemed to be an ideal match since Lockheed was a major builder of military aircraft while Martin Marietta was a strong force in defense electronics. Lockheed Martin paid $7.6 billion in 1996 to acquire the majority of the electronics giant Loral Corporation. The merger of Lockheed and Martin Marietta and many of Lockheed Martin's early acquisitions allowed Lockheed Martin to achieve a high degree of vertical integration in many of its businesses. This development could be seen in the way the electronics and systems integration business that was acquired with the purchase of Loral complemented the defense electronics business of Martin Marietta.

In 1996, Lockheed Martin sold its defense systems and armament systems businesses to General Dynamics. L-3 Communications was formed in 1997 when Lockheed Martin spun off portions of ten technology units not deemed to be part of the core business. Lockheed Martin offered to buy Northrop Grumman for $11.6 billion in 1997, but the deal collapsed in 1998 when the U.S. government indicated it had antitrust problems with the deal.

By 1998, acquisitions and mergers had resulted in a 185 percent increase in the number of core competencies in Lockheed Martin's technology profile, with only 15 percent of the competencies being duplicated as a result of acquisitions. Lockheed Martin has achieved a high degree of vertical integration in military aircraft, avionics, airframes, and space vehicles.[1]

INTERNAL CONDITION

In 2000, Lockheed Martin completed the purchase of 49 percent of the satellite network company COMSAT for $1.7 billion. The remainder of COMSAT cannot be purchased without government approval. COMSAT is an entity that acts as an interface between U.S. communications companies and INTELSAT, an international agency that controls the majority of the world's communications satellites.

Lockheed Martin now operates approximately 440 facilities, most of which are located in the United States. The company has used its own information technology to generate internal networks to facilitate the sharing of information and technology. In this respect, Lockheed Martin operates as a virtual enterprise. Although some economies of scale could be achieved by combining divisions, Lockheed Martin believes innovation may be better promoted by small organizations working independently while remaining electronically interconnected to the rest of the organization.

Lockheed Martin has made several attempts to lower costs and improve profitability. Lockheed Martin Aeronautical Systems (LMAS) embraced the "lean" or Toyota production system in 1997. Lockheed's goal is to have the Toyota system fully in place in four years. This appears to be a rather ambitious goal since GE required twelve years to accomplish the same task.[2]

Lockheed Martin is organized into four principal sectors: systems integration, space systems, aeronautics, and technology services. Lockheed Martin's financial statements are shown in Exhibits 1–4. The company's earnings have been in decline in recent years.

Systems Integration

This segment is engaged in the design, development, and integration of complex systems for global defense, civil government, and commercial markets. Core businesses include undersea warfare, surface warfare, and land surveillance systems; tactical

EXHIBIT 1   Lockheed Martin Corporation Consolidated Statement of Operations
(In millions, except per-share data)

	Year ended December 31,		
	2001	2000	1999
Net sales	$23,990	$24,541	$24,999
Cost of sales	22,447	22,881	23,346
Earnings from operations	1,543	1,660	1,653
Other income and expenses, net	(655)	(409)	344
	888	1,251	1,997
Interest expense	700	919	809
Earnings from continuing operations before income taxes, extraordinary items and cumulative effect of change in accounting	188	332	1,188
Income tax expense	109	714	459
Earnings (loss) from continuing operations before extraordinary items and cumulative effect of change in accounting	79	(382)	729
Discontinued operations	(1,089)	(42)	8
Extraordinary loss on early extinguishments of debt	(36)	(95)	—
Cumulative effect of change in accounting	—	—	(335)
Net (loss) earnings	$ (1,046)	$ (519)	$ 382
Earnings (loss) per common share:			
Basic:			
Continuing operations before extraordinary items and cumulative effect of change in accounting	$ 0.18	$ (0.95)	$ 1.91
Discontinued operations	(2.55)	(0.10)	0.02
Extraordinary loss on early extinguishments of debt	(0.08)	(0.24)	—
Cumulative effect of change in accounting	—	—	(0.93)
	$ (2.45)	$ (1.29)	$ 1.00
Diluted:			
Continuing operations before extraordinary items and cumulative effect of change in accounting	$ 0.18	$ (0.95)	$ 1.90
Discontinued operations	(2.52)	(0.10)	0.02
Extraordinary loss on early extinguishments of debt	(0.08)	(0.24)	—
Cumulative effect of change in accounting	—	—	(0.93)
	$ (2.42)	$ (1.29)	$ 0.99

Source: Lockheed's 2001 *Annual Report*, p. 51.

EXHIBIT 2   Lockheed Martin Corporation
Consolidated Balance Sheet (in millions)

	December 31,	
	2001	*2000*
ASSETS		
Current assets:		
Cash and cash equivalents	$ 912	$ 1,505
Receivables	4,049	3,986
Inventories	3,140	3,805
Deferred income taxes	1,566	1,213
Assets of businesses held for sale	638	2,332
Other current assets	473	498
Total current assets	10,778	13,339
Property, plant and equipment, net	2,991	2,941
Investments in equity securities	1,884	2,433
Intangible assets related to contracts and programs acquired	939	1,073
Goodwill	7,371	7,479
Prepaid pension cost	2,081	1,794
Other assets	1,610	1,367
Total Assets	$27,654	$30,426
LIABILITIES AND STOCKHOLDERS' EQUITY		
Current liabilities:		
Accounts payable	$ 1,419	$ 1,106
Customer advances and amounts in excess of costs incurred	5,002	4,697
Salaries, benefits and payroll taxes	1,100	978
Income taxes	63	519
Current maturities of long-term debt	89	882
Liabilities of businesses held for sale	387	467
Other current liabilities	1,629	1,653
Total current liabilities	9,689	10,302
Long-term debt	7,422	9,065
Post-retirement benefit liabilities	1,565	1,647
Deferred income taxes	992	790
Other liabilities	1,543	1,462
Total Liabilities	21,211	23,266
Stockholders' equity:		
Common stock, $1 par value per share	441	431
Additional paid-in capital	2,142	1,789
Retained earnings	3,961	5,199
Unearned ESOP shares	(84)	(115)
Accumulated other comprehensive loss	(17)	(144)
Total stockholders' equity	6,443	7,160
Total Liabilities and Stockholders' Equity	$27,654	$30,426

Source: Lockheed's 2001 *Annual Report,* p. 53.

EXHIBIT 3   Lockheed's Financial Data by Business Segment
(in millions)

	2001	2000	1999
Net sales			
Systems Integration	$ 9,014	$ 9,647	$ 9,570
Space Systems	6,836	7,339	7,285
Aeronautics	5,355	4,885	5,499
Technology Services	2,763	2,649	2,574
Corporate and Other	22	21	71
	$23,990	$24,541	$24,999
Operating profit (loss)			
Systems Integration	$ 836	$ 583	$ 880
Space Systems	405	401	506
Aeronautics	416	343	247
Technology Services	130	82	137
Corporate and Other	(899)	(158)	227
	$ 888	$ 1,251	$ 1,997

Source: Lockheed's 2001 *Annual Report,* p. 72.

missiles, air defense systems, and fire control and sensor systems; information superiority systems; simulation and training systems; air traffic management systems; aerospace systems and platform integration; business system solutions; and distribution technologies, which includes automated material handling solutions for postal systems and commercial customers.

The total for 2000's net sales of the systems integration segment showed an increase of 1 percent over 1999's figure, and it increased 3 percent between 1998 and 1999. The increases are a result of volume increases in the segment's naval electronic and surveillance systems product line and in its electronic platform integration activities. Net sales also increased in the segment's missiles and air defense product line, primarily as a result of the Theater High Altitude Area Defense (THAAD) program's movement into the engineering, manufacturing and development (EMD) phase. These increases were partially offset by a reduction in net sales related to the AES and control systems businesses, reductions that were primarily due to the divestiture of these businesses in 2000.

Operating profit for the systems integration segment increased by 2 percent both in 2000 (compared to 1999) and in 1999 (compared to 1998). In 2000, the previously mentioned volume increases in the segment's naval electronic and surveillance systems product line and in its electronic platform integration activities contributed to the increase in operating profit from 1999. This increase was partially offset by a decline in operating profit related to the AES and control systems businesses, declines that were due to their divestiture in 2000.

Space Systems

This segment is engaged in the design, development, engineering and production of civil, commercial, and military space systems. Major product lines include spacecraft, space launch vehicles, and human space systems; their supporting ground systems and

EXHIBIT 4   Lockheed's Net Sales by Customer Category (in millions)

	2001	2000	1999
U.S. Government			
Systems Integration	$ 6,952	$ 6,855	$ 7,017
Space Systems	5,956	5,932	6,069
Aeronautics	3,437	2,784	2,979
Technology Services	2,269	2,120	2,033
Corporate and Other	—	—	—
	$18,614	$17,691	$18,098
Foreign governments [a] [b]			
Systems Integration	$ 1,790	$ 2,231	$ 2,125
Space Systems	94	79	188
Aeronautics	1,899	2,061	2,501
Technology Services	104	116	106
Corporate and Other	—	1	—
	$ 3,887	$ 4,488	$ 4,920
Commercial(b)			
Systems Integration	$ 272	$ 561	$ 428
Space Systems	786	1,328	1,028
Aeronautics	19	40	19
Technology Services	390	413	435
Corporate and Other	22	20	71
	$ 1,489	$ 2,362	$ 1,981

[a] Sales made to foreign governments through the U.S. Government are included in the foreign governments category above.

[b] Export sales, included in the foreign governments and commercial categories above, were approximately $4.1 billion, $5.2 billion and $5.7 billion in 2001, 2000 and 1999, respectively.

Source: Lockheeds' 2001 *Annual Report,* p. 74.

services; and strategic fleet ballistic missiles. In addition to its consolidated business units, this segment has investments in joint ventures that are principally engaged in businesses which complement and enhance other activities of the segment.

Net sales of the space systems segment declined by 1 percent in 2000 (compared to 1999), and by 16 percent in 1999 (compared to 1998). In 2000, net sales declined due to both volume declines in military, civil, and classified satellite activities, and to decreased ground systems activities. There was also an additional decline related to reduced volume in government launch vehicle programs. These declines were partially offset by increased volume on commercial space activities as well as by an increase in various other space system activities.

Operating profit for the segment declined by 28 percent in 2000 (compared to 1999), and it declined by 48 percent in 1999 (compared to 1998). Continued market and pricing pressures on commercial space programs, increased investment in certain launch vehicle programs, and reduced margins on commercial satellites reduced 2000 operating profit by approximately $180 million (compared to 1999).

Aeronautics

This segment is engaged in the design, research and development, and production of combat and air mobility aircraft, surveillance/command systems, reconnaissance systems, platform systems integration, and advanced development programs. Major products and programs include the F-16 multirole fighter; the F-22 air-superiority fighter; the C-130J tactical airlift aircraft; support for the C-5, F-117 and U-2 aircraft; and the Joint Strike Fighter concept demonstration program.

Net sales of the aeronautics segment declined by 11 percent in 2000 (compared to 1999), after having increased by 1 percent in 1999 (compared to 1998). Approximately 95 percent of the decline in 2000 net sales is attributable to declines in F-16 fighter aircraft and C-130J airlift aircraft sales and deliveries. These declines more than offset increases in net sales related to the F-22 fighter aircraft program. The 1999 increase consisted of $715 million in increased sales related to C-130J program activities but was offset by a $717 million decline in F-16 sales and deliveries. The remaining increase was attributable to increased sales on various other aircraft programs.

Operating profit for the segment increased by 39 percent in 2000 (compared to 1999), after having decreased by 62 percent in 1999 (compared to 1998).

Technology Services

This segment provides a wide array of management, engineering, scientific, logistic, and information services to federal agencies and other customers. Major product lines include e-commerce, enterprise information services, software modernization and data center management for the Department of Defense and for civil government agencies; engineering, science, and information services for NASA; aircraft and engine maintenance and modification services; operation, maintenance, training, and logistics support for military and civilian systems; launch, mission, and analysis services for military, classified, and commercial satellites; and research, development, engineering, and science in support of nuclear weapons stewardship and naval reactor programs.

Net sales of the technology services segment increased by 3 percent in 2000 (compared to 1999), and by 17 percent in 1999 (compared to 1998). The increases in 2000 net sales consist of increases in various federal technology services programs, including the Consolidated Space Operations contract and the Rapid Response contract. These increases were partially offset by a decline in volume on aircraft maintenance and logistics contracts and on certain defense and science energy services contracts due to program completions.

Operating profit for the segment increased by 17 percent in 2000 (compared to 1999), and by 1 percent in 1999 (compared to 1998). The increase in 2000 was primarily attributable to various federal technology services programs, including the impact of the volume increases discussed earlier, and to the increased profitability of certain information services contracts, as well as to the improved performance on certain aircraft maintenance and logistics contracts.

COMPETITORS AND EXTERNAL FACTORS

Boeing leads the industry and had 2001 revenues of $58,198 million. Lockheed Martin was second in revenues in 2001 with $23,990 million. Other industry leaders include United Technologies, Raytheon, Allied Signal, and British Aerospace. All of the industry leaders are diversified and have employed various strategies to enhance the survivability of their companies in the tenuous environment that defense contractors have operated in since the end of the Cold War.

According to *Aviation Week & Space Technology*'s "Best Managed Aerospace Performance" rankings, British Aerospace is ranked first, United Technologies is ranked third, Allied Signal is ranked eighth, Boeing is ranked fourteenth, Raytheon is ranked seventeenth, and Lockheed Martin is ranked eighteenth. This ranking compares aerospace companies' performances based on 25 financial ratios and allocates scores based on asset utilization, productivity, and financial stability.[3]

Boeing, since acquiring McDonald Douglas, has a very strong diversified position in both civil and military aerospace. The civilian aircraft portion of Boeing's business, despite European competition from Airbus, helps to add international sales revenues to Boeing's revenue stream. International sales for Boeing accounted for 47 percent of its sales in 2000, while U.S. government sales accounted for 70 percent of Lockheed Martin's sales in 2000. Additionally, while commercial aircraft sales accounted for 63 percent of Boeing's sales, foreign and domestic government sales accounted for 89 percent of Lockheed Martin's sales. Boeing is a strong competitor of Lockheed Martin in the satellite systems market.

United Technologies is noted for building Pratt and Whitney jet engines and Sikorsky helicopters. United Technologies adopted a diversification strategy in the 1970s when it acquired Otis Elevator and Carrier. As a result of this diversification strategy, the bulk of United Technologies sales are split between Carrier (27 percent), Otis (22 percent), and Pratt & Whitney (30 percent); flight systems, such as Sikorsky and Hamilton Sunstrand (10 percent), and automotive parts (11 percent), add to the mix. Also, approximately 44 percent of United Technologies' income is derived from international operations.

British Aerospace, another strong competitor of Lockheed Martin, is similar to Lockheed Martin in that 72 percent of its sales come from its defense unit. However, British Aerospace owns 20 percent of Airbus Industries, which produces commercial aircraft and generates the remaining 28 percent of British Aerospace sales. With the acquisition of Marconi Electronic Systems, British Aerospace will become a stronger competitor. In contrast to Lockheed Martin, British Aerospace derives only 11 percent of its sales from its home country, the United Kingdom. The bulk of the balance of British Aerospace sales are generated in the Middle East (38 percent), Europe (23 percent), the United States and Canada (13 percent), and the Far East, including Australia (14 percent). It has one advantage over Lockheed Martin in military sales in that it can sell military equipment to current and former Commonwealth nations without the government scrutiny that Lockheed Martin faces when it attempts to sell military products outside the United States. An additional aid to foreign military sales comes from the subsidiaries and affiliates in which British Aerospace participates in other countries. These include (in addition to Airbus) such companies as Eurofighter Jagdflugzeug of Germany (33 percent ownership), Matra Bae Dynamics of France (50 percent), Panavia Aircraft of Germany (43 percent), Saab-BAe Grippen of Sweden (50 percent), and Asia Pacific Training and Simulation in Singapore (63 percent). Additionally, British Aerospace is a primary member of Lockheed Martin's Joint Strike Fighter development team.

Late in 1999, the aerospace division of DaimlerChrysler combined with Aerospatiale Matra to form the aforementioned European Aeronautic, Defense, and Space (EADS). EADS will have combined revenues of approximately $23 billion and will become the third largest aircraft and defense business behind Boeing and Lockheed. EADS will also have an 80 percent stake in Airbus Industries. This merger will cause renewed Pentagon concerns that the major European and American defense contractors will become competitors instead of partners in the worldwide arms sales business. These concerns include worries about the interoperability of NATO weapons systems developed separately as competitive systems by U.S. and European defense companies. Another concern involves mergers that increase the probability that U.S and European defense agencies will limit purchases to those items produced by their own countries' companies.[4]

One of the observations about Lockheed Martin's competitors is that most of them have in some way managed to avoid becoming dependent on a single market (i.e., Lockheed Martin's dependence on the U.S. government) for survival. Lockheed Martin's competitors have achieved this independence from a single market by either diversification of products or diversification of customer base. Lockheed Martin's alliance with the U.S. military has enabled Lockheed Martin to develop cutting edge technologies, but the same alliance fosters government restrictions that prohibit Lockheed Martin from taking full advantage of the technologies in the worldwide marketplace. This same issue keeps Lockheed Martin from exploiting many of the advantages it has in the satellite and command, control, communications, and intelligence (C^3I) arenas. Lockheed Martin has acquired saleable skills in C^3I, which are desired for many domestic and foreign civilian business applications, but sales have been mainly to the military, to the FAA, to the Postal Service, to social services, and to other government agencies.

It should be noted that most current aerospace products are developed and constructed from products produced by numerous defense and aerospace companies. As an example, an Apache helicopter has a Boeing airframe, Lockheed Martin electro-optics, a Lockheed Martin and Northrop Grumman radar system, and General Electric engines. Military and civilian aerospace products employ this systems approach to the design and construction of most products. This translates into a situation in which most products are produced by a lead contractor who has multiple system and subsystem partners.[5]

As a lead contractor, Lockheed competes primarily against U.S. companies for U.S. defense sales, while it competes against international and U.S. companies for defense sales in foreign countries. In the commercial satellite launching and operation business, commercial aviation business, and software business, Lockheed must compete with international companies. As an additional constraint, Lockheed faces government scrutiny to ensure that it does not transfer technology to a customer who will wittingly or unwittingly use it for military purposes against the United States or one of its allies.

RECENT DEVELOPMENTS

Until late 2001, Lockheed Martin's outlook for the future was gloomy at best. With a failing economy, government defense budget cuts, elimination of the X-33 (space shuttle replacement) project, and satellite failures, Lockheed Martin was struggling. However, every cloud has a silver lining. The September 11, 2001, attacks that propelled the United States into a sustained war effort has substantially changed the Lockheed Martin outlook. Lockheed Martin's stock price soared following the attack due to the proposed increases in national security spending. As a result of the war on terrorism, Lockheed is projecting 2002 earnings to increase by 20 percent. As if the war on terrorism were not enough to give Lockheed Martin the boost it was looking for, it has also been awarded the largest defense contract ever. On October 26, 2001, Lockheed Martin was awarded a contract potentially amounting to over $200 million over the next century. The contract is to build the supersonic, stealth aircraft dubbed the Joint Strike Fighter, now also known as the F-35. The F-35 will replace thousands of aging aircraft flown by the United States, the United Kingdom, and allied countries. Although the competition for the contract was fierce, Lockheed Martin emerged on top and will be adding over 9,000 jobs as a result. Lockheed has full control over the project and may subcontract portions as desired.

CONCLUSION

Before September 11, 2001, Lockheed Martin was a company struggling with its identity and facing a challenging future. After surviving the defense industry consolidation of the 1990s, Lockheed Martin seemed to be not only having trouble maintaining its core defense business, but also seemed to be unable to take advantage of the civilian technologies it had acquired in an attempt to diversify. Lockheed Martin had had little success growing revenues and income, was holding $12 billion in debt that had been acquired during takeover activity, and had sales and revenue problems due to quality and cost control problems associated with many of its products. The terrorist attacks on the United States, the current war on terrorism, and the receipt of the largest defense contract ever awarded for the F-35, seem to nearly eliminate Lockheed Martin's problems and certainly give the firm a much needed breath of fresh air. Lockheed Martin must take advantage of these opportunities by continuing to focus on fixing its weaknesses and capitalizing on its strengths.

REFERENCES

ADVANI, R.N., M. ANDERSON, S. BOWLING, D. DOANE, and E.B. ROBERTS "Technology Strategy in Defense Industry Acquisitions: A Comparative Assessment of Two Giants." *International Journal of Technology Management,* 15 no. 8 (1998): 781–804.

BOYLE, ALAN. "Lockheed Wins Huge Fighter Contract" (October 26, 2001). **www.msnbc.com/news646985**

COLE, J. "CEO at Lockheed Martin Is Only Top Official Still Remaining." *The Wall Street Journal* (November 1, 1999): A4.

COLE, J. "Lockheed Plans to Streamline Operations." *The Wall Street Journal* (September 28, 1999): A3, A8.

COLE, J., A.M. SQUEO, and T.E. RICKS. "Specter of F-22 Funding Cut Skews Lockheed's Recovery Plans." *The Wall Street Journal* (July 26, 1999): A4.

"Daimler and Aerospatiale Matra Agree to Combine Their Aerospace Businesses— European Firms' Accord Will Create No. 3 Firm in Aircraft and Defense." *The Wall Street Journal* (October 15, 1999): A3, A4.

Lockheed Martin Corporation, 2000 *Annual Report.*

NEWMAN, R.J. "The Air Up There—If You Build Them, Will They Fly?" *U.S. News and World Report* (November 8, 1999): 38.

POPE, H. "Turks Vow to Spend Heavily as Military Expands—Arms Fair Popular as U. S. Firms See Major Opportunities." *The Wall Street Journal* (October 5, 1999): A21.

RICKS, T.E. and A.M. SQUEO. "Air Force Says F-22 Funding Cut May Hurt Programs, Contractors." *The Wall Street Journal* (July 27 1999): A4.

SQUEO, A.M. "Boeing Is Awarded Contract to Make Imagery Satellites." *The Wall Street Journal* (September 8, 1999): B14.

SQUEO, A.M. "Review of Lockheed Unit's Woes Cites Poor Oversight and Quality Control." *The Wall Street Journal* (September 9, 1999): A16.

VELOCCI, A.L. "U.K. Industry Rewarded by Focusing on 'Basics'." *Aviation Week and Space Technology* (May 31, 1999): 45–55.

VELOCCI, A.L. "Lockheed Martin Faces Long, Painful Recovery." *Aviation Week and Space Technology* (November 8, 1999): 30–33.

NOTES

1. R.N. ADVANI, M. ANDERSON, S. BOWLING, D. DOANE, and E.B. ROBERTS, "Technology Strategy in Defense Industry Acquisitions: A Comparative Assessment of Two Giants," *International Journal of Technology Management* 15, no. 8 (1998): 781–804.

2. ALAN BOYLE, "Lockheed Wins Huge Fighter Contract" (October 26, 2001). **www.msnbc.com/news646985.**

3. A.L. VELOCCI, "U.K. Industry Rewarded by Focusing on 'Basics,'" *Aviation Week and Space Technology* (May 31, 1999): 45–55.

4. "Daimler and Aerospatiale Matra Agree to Combine Their Aerospace Businesses—European Firms' Accord Will Create No. 3 Firm in Aircraft and Defense," *The Wall Street Journal* (October 15, 1999): A3, A4.

5. H. POPE, "Turks Vow to Spend Heavily as Military Expands—Arms Fair Popular as U.S. Firms See Major Opportunities," *The Wall Street Journal* (October 5, 1999): A21.

DELL COMPUTER CORPORATION—2002

Nicole Seminario
Francis Marion University

DELL

www.dell.com

The events of September 11, 2001, thrust the United States and the global economy into recession. The full impact of this tragedy arises from at least three factors:

1. Consumer confidence could plummet, dragging down consumer spending, which represents two-thirds of the gross domestic product (GDP). Just a 3 percent drop in consumption during the last quarter of 2001 would cause growth to contract at an 8 percent annual rate.

2. The war on terrorism could raise prices and weaken the economy, a development that occurred during the Persian Gulf War. Political moves and economic stimulus options that could be provided by the Federal Reserve and the government are unclear. Demand for goods, technology, and stocks have already tumbled.

3. Corporate failures in leading industries, such as finance and transportation, could further impair the economy. These industries are critical because they facilitate trade and investment in other sectors.

Just six hours after the terrorist attacks, a securities firm crippled by the attacks ordered 200 new PCs from Dell Computer. A surge of orders soon turned into a flood, and Dell immediately stepped up production at its plant in Austin, Texas. Dell has been running its factories day and night since the attacks to satisfy increased demand. A week after the attacks, Dell reported selling more than 24,000 servers, laptops, and desktop computers to replace equipment lost in the attacks. The company sent hundreds of technicians to Manhattan and Washington, D.C., converted three 18-wheel trucks into mobile technology support-and-installation facilities, and chartered an airliner to fly parts from Taiwan to its Texas factory.

Dell positioned itself to fill requests from the Pentagon, from businesses affected by the Trade Center attacks, and from disaster-management groups in Washington and New York City. Computer industry analysts agreed that Dell would probably benefit most immediately because of its flexible and quick manufacturing. Further declines in aggregate demand for computers are, however, likely to overshadow repair-related demand.

Dell Computer produces desktop computers, notebook computers, enterprise systems, refurbished systems, and third-party peripherals and software; its services include consulting, installation, Internet access, and systems integration. Dell's customers include large corporations, the government, healthcare and educational institutions, as well as individuals and small-to-medium sized businesses.

Dell competes with Compaq Computer, which has been acquired by Hewlett-Packard, to be the leading PC maker worldwide. Dell has achieved a competitive advantage over its rivals with a build-to-order approach, a direct sales approach, and an attractive price. Dell's built-to-order boxes allow for lower inventories, lower costs, and higher profit margins, all of which allow the company to compete in price wars that characterize the computer sector.

Dell's revenue for fiscal year 2002 was $31.1 billion, down from $31.9 billion in 2001, based on global market share estimates. At the end of the third quarter of 2001, figures showed that worldwide sales of PCs were down by more than 11 percent, but Dell was the bright spot in the computer sector, insofar as it was the only company to improve sales. Dell's sales increased $4.23 million and its market share increased to 13.8 percent. However, after enjoying average annual sales increases of almost 60 percent during the 1990s, Dell's revenue growth has slowed considerably, and for the first time in the company's history, employees are being laid off. Dell has approximately 40,000 regular employees; 27,000 are located in the United States, and 13,000 are located in other countries.

HISTORY

Michael Dell founded Dell Computer in 1984, at the age of twenty-one, in his dorm room at the University of Texas in Austin with a simple vision and business concept. He believed that personal computers could be built to order and sold directly to customers. When Dell started operations, it used the direct-to-consumer strategy because of Compaq's dominance in the PC retail channel. Initially, Dell started with a mail order and phone order system.

Michael Dell believed that his approach to the PC business had two advantages. First, bypassing distributors and retailers let him eliminate the markups of resellers. Second, built-to-order machines greatly reduced the costs and risks associated with carrying large stocks of parts, components, and finished goods. While Dell sometimes struggled during its early years as it tried to refine its strategy, build an adequate infrastructure, and establish market credibility against better-known rivals, its build-to-order and direct-sale approach proved appealing to growing numbers of customers in the mid-1990s as global PC sales rose to record levels. Dell's strategy gave the company a substantial cost and profit margin advantage over rivals that manufactured PCs in volume and that kept their distributors and retailers stocked with ample inventories.

Dell's approach of selling personal computer systems directly to customers demonstrates that the company has a better understanding of its customers' needs, and it thus strives to make it easier for customers to choose, purchase, and support their computing environments. Today, Dell is enhancing and broadening the fundamental competitive advantages of its direct model by increasingly applying the efficiencies of the Internet to its entire business. Approximately half of Dell's sales are Web-based, approximately half of the technical support activities occur online, and approximately three-quarters of its order-status transactions occur online. Dell pioneered direct telephone sales of computers after noticing the increased sophistication of the consumer, who was buying computers sight unseen. Dell exemplifies leadership and vision with a keen eye on execution. Dell has set up systems that are the envy of other computer manufacturers. Warehousing, supply chain integration, and build-to-order manufacturing with quick customer fulfillment give Dell the edge in what has turned into a commodity business.

Yet Dell lacks the product line and service breadth of Hewlett-Packard, or IBM, and it has no in-house repair capabilities. Also, Dell can see that its performance is affected by the global economic recession. Worldwide sales of PCs fell for the first time in fifteen years in the second quarter 2001 and were down another 11 percent in the third quarter. Dell is striving to avoid other threats too, such as the continuously changing consumer demands, rapid technological advancement, aggressive pricing wars, and the strong brand name of competitors such as IBM.

INTERNAL ISSUES

Vision and Mission Statements

Dell's current vision statement stresses its strength:

> *It's the way we do business. It's the way we interact with the community. It's the way we interpret the world around us—our customers' needs, the future of technology, and the global business climate. Whatever changes the future may bring, our vision—Dell Vision—will be our guiding force.*

Dell's current mission statement is as follows:

> *Dell's mission is to be the most successful Computer Company in the world at delivering the best customer experience in markets we serve. In doing so, Dell will meet customer expectations of:*

- *Highest quality.*
- *Leading technology.*
- *Competitive pricing.*
- *Individual and company accountability.*
- *Best-in-class service and support.*
- *Flexible customization capability.*
- *Superior corporate citizenship.*
- *Financial stability.*

Organizational Structure

Headquartered in Round Rock, Texas, Dell Computer is managed on a geographic basis. The three geographic segments are the Americas; Europe, the Middle East, and Africa; and Asia-Pacific as illustrated in Exhibit 1. The Americas segment, based in Round Rock, covers the United States, Canada, South America, and Latin America, and it represented 71 percent of the company's revenue and 81 percent of its profits in fiscal year 2001. The European segment, based in Bracknell, the United Kingdom, covers the European countries and also some countries in the Middle East and Africa. This segment represented 21 percent of the company's revenue and 13 percent of the company's profit in fiscal 2001. The Asia-Pacific segment covers the Pacific Rim, including Japan, Australia, and New Zealand, and it is based in Singapore. This segment represented 8 percent of Dell's revenue and 6 percent of the total profits.

Dell has offices in more than 30 countries, with manufacturing facilities located in or around Austin, Texas; Nashville, Tennessee; El Dorado do Sul, Brazil; Limerick, Ireland; Penang, Malaysia; and Xiamen, China.

Natural Environment

Dell provides information on environmental programs and accomplishments through annual environmental reports. Product-specific environmental attributes are available through environmental data sheets provided to customers upon request. Dell has implemented environmental management systems (EMS) at eleven manufacturing sites around the world. These systems help Dell to identify the environmental impact of its products and processes and to set achievable targets for improving environmental performance. The objective of Dell's EMS is to integrate environmental performance into overall business management so that environmental goals are seen to be as important as quality or financial

EXHIBIT 1   Dell Computer Corporation's Organizational Chart
(Probable)

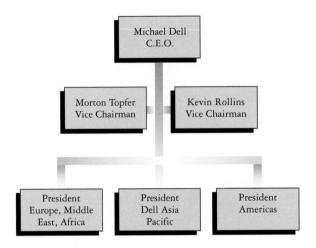

Source: Dell Computer Internal Report.

goals. Elements of the EMS include an environmental policy, planning, implementation and operation, checking and corrective action, and management review. These elements complement the ISO 9002 quality systems already established at Dell's manufacturing sites. The EMS allows all employees to participate in improving Dell's environmental performance. Dell has a corporate policy that guides the company and its employees in their handling of environmental issues. Dell's environmental policy has the following objectives:

- Comply with the law.
- Prevent waste and pollution.
- Design products with the environment in mind.
- Continually improve and communicate our performance.
- Be a responsible neighbor.

E-commerce

Dell runs one of the world's leading Internet sites at **www.dell.com:** during the second quarter of year 2001, this site trafficked 500 million page-views. Dell sells more than $50 million worth of products a day, which translates into annual sales of goods and services over the Internet of $18.3 billion. Dell's $1.2 billion in earnings 2002 were largely attributed to e-business. The Web gives Dell the following benefits:

- It increases its margins and revenues. The Web has replaced Dell's customer call center, thus eliminating the need for many sales representatives and technical support staff. Phone and material costs are lower and the sales process is faster.
- Via the Web, customers choose computers and price them without sending faxes. This makes it easier to price and compare configurations.
- Web demographics show that a high percentage of users are young professionals who already are computer literate and are comfortable with a computer, as demonstrated by the fact that they use it to link up with the Web.

- Dell provides internal virtual Web stores within large corporate Intranets to aid in the purchasing process.

Finance

Dell's financial statements are presented in Exhibits 2, 3, and 4.

Note that Dell has managed to achieve impressive net income growth, increasing 14 percent from 1999 to 2000 and 30 percent in the 2000–2001 period. These gains have come at the direct expense of its rivals. Because Dell is the low-cost producer, it has led the way in an industry price-war, increasing its market share at the expense of competitors. However Dell's net income in 2002 declined almost 50 percent.

EXHIBIT 2   Dell Computer Corporation (DELL) Annual Income Statement
(in millions except for per-share items)

	52 Weeks Ending 02/01/02	52 Weeks Ending 02/02/01	52 Weeks Ending 01/28/00
Revenue	31,168.0	31,888.0	25,265.0
Other Revenue	—	—	—
Total Revenue	**31,168.0**	**31,888.0**	**25,265.0**
Cost of Revenue	25,661.0	25,445.0	20,047.0
Gross Profit	**5,507.0**	**6,443.0**	**5,218.0**
Selling/General/Administrative Expenses	2,784.0	3,193.0	2,387.0
Research & Development	452.0	482.0	374.0
Depreciation/Amortization	—	—	—
Interest Expense (Income), Net Operating	—	—	—
Unusual Expense (Income)	482.0	105.0	194.0
Other Operating Expenses	—	—	—
Total Operating Expense	**29,379.0**	**29,225.0**	**23,002.0**
Operating Income	**1,789.0**	**2,663.0**	**2,263.0**
Interest Expense, Net Non-Operating	—	—	—
Interest/Investment Income, Non-Operating	—	—	—
Interest Income (Expense), Net Non-Operating	(58.0)	531.0	188.0
Gain (Loss) on Sale of Assets	—	—	—
Other, Net	—	—	—
Income Before Tax	1,731.0	3,194.0	2,451.0
Income Tax	485.0	958.0	785.0
Income After Tax	1,246.0	2,236.0	1,666.0
Minority Interest	—	—	—
Equity In Affiliates	—	—	—
Net Income Before Extra. Items	1,246.0	2,236.0	1,666.0
Accounting Change	0.0	(59.0)	—
Discontinued Operations	—	—	—
Extraordinary Item	—	0.0	0.0
Net Income	1,246.0	2,177.0	1,666.0
Preferred Dividends	—	—	—
Income Available to Common Excl. Extra. Items	**1,246.0**	**2,236.0**	**1,666.0**
Income Available to Common Incl. Extra. Items	**1,246.0**	**2,177.0**	**1,666.0**
Basic/Primary Weighted Average Shares	2,602.0	2,582.0	2,536.0
Basic/Primary EPS Excl. Extra. Items	**0.479**	**0.866**	**0.657**

Source: http://investor.stockpoint.com

EXHIBIT 3   Dell Computer Corporation (DELL) Annual Balance Sheet
(in millions except for per-share items)

	As of 02/01/02	As of 02/02/01	As of 01/28/00
Cash & Equivalents	3,641.0	4,910.0	3,809.0
Short Term Investments	273.0	525.0	323.0
Cash and Short Term Investments	3,914.0	5,435.0	4,132.0
Trade Accounts Receivable, Net	2,636.0	2,895.0	2,608.0
Other Receivables	—	—	—
Total Receivables, Net	2,636.0	2,895.0	2,608.0
Total Inventory	278.0	400.0	391.0
Prepaid Expenses	—	—	—
Other Current Assets	1,049.0	996.0	550.0
Total Current Assets	7,877.0	9,726.0	7,681.0
Property/ Plant/ Equipment – Gross	—	—	—
Accumulated Depreciation	—	(538.0)	(375.0)
Property/ Plant/ Equipment, Net	826.0	996.0	765.0
Goodwill, Net	—	0.0	0.0
Intangibles, Net	—	—	—
Long Term Investments	4,373.0	2,418.0	2,721.0
Other Long Term Assets	459.0	530.0	304.0
Total Assets	13,535.0	13,670.0	11,471.0
Accounts Payable	5,075.0	4,286.0	3,538.0
Accrued Expenses	2,444.0	2,492.0	1,654.0
Notes Payable/ Short Term Debt	—	—	—
Current Port. LT Debt/ Capital Leases	—	—	—
Other Current Liabilities	—	—	—
Total Current Liabilities	7,519.0	6,778.0	5,192.0
Long Term Debt	520.0	509.0	508.0
Capital Lease Obligations	—	—	—
Total Long Term Debt	520.0	509.0	508.0
Total Debt	520.0	509.0	508.0
Deferred Income Tax	—	—	—
Minority Interest	—	—	—
Other Liabilities	802.0	761.0	463.0
Total Liabilities	8,841.0	8,048.0	6,163.0
Redeemable Preferred Stock	—	—	—
Preferred Stock – Non Redeemable, Net	—	—	—
Common Stock	—	4,795.0	3,583.0
Additional Paid-In Capital	—	—	—
Retained Earnings (Accum. Deficit)	—	839.0	1,260.0
Treasury Stock – Common	—	—	—
Other Equity	4,694.0	(12.0)	465.0
Total Equity	4,694.0	5,622.0	5,308.0
Total Liability & Shareholders' Equity	13,535.0	13,670.0	11,471.0
Shares Outs. – Common Stock	2,599.0	2,601.0	2,575.0
Total Common Shares Outstanding	2,599.0	2,601.0	2,575.0
Total Preferred Stock Shares Outs.	—	—	—
Employees (actual figures)	34,600.0	40,000.0	36,500.0
Number of Common Shareholders (actual figures)	—	34,830.0	34,781.0

Source: http://investor.stockpoint.com

EXHIBIT 4   Dell Computer Corporation Financial Segment Data
(in millions)

	Fiscal Year Ended		
	February 2, 2001	January 28, 2000	January 29, 1999
GEOGRAPHIC SEGMENTS			
New Revenue			
Americas	$22,871	$17,879	$12,420
Europe	6,399	5,590	4,674
Asia-Pacific and Japan	2,618	1,796	1,149
Consolidated New Revenue	$31,888	$25,265	$18,243
PRODUCT GROUPS			
Net Revenue			
Desktop Computers	$15,452	$13,568	$10,979
Notebook Computers	8,572	5,847	3,859
Enterprise Systems	5,511	3,828	2,193
Other	2,353	2,022	1,212
Totals	$31,888	$25,265	$18,243

Source: Dell's 2001 *Annual Report.*

Marketing

Dell's customers include large corporations, government agencies, healthcare and educational institutions, small businesses, and individuals. Dell uses comparable sales and marketing approaches across its customer groups. Within each region, the sales and marketing forces are divided among the various customer groups in order to meet each customer group's specific needs.

Dell divides its customers into three groups: relationship, transactional, and Internet.

- *Relationship Customers*—This segment includes Dell's large corporate customers, as well as governmental, healthcare and educational institutions, and small-to-medium businesses. Dell maintains a field sales force throughout the world to call on its Relationship Customers and prospects.
- *Transactional Customers*—Dell has many customers among individuals and small-to-medium sized businesses. Dell markets its products and services to these customers by advertising on the Internet and television, in trade and general business publications, and by mailing a broad range of direct marketing publications, such as promotional pieces, catalogs, and customer newsletters.
- *Internet Customers*—Through Dell's World Wide Web site at **www.dell.com**, customers can access a wide range of information about Dell product and service offerings, configure and purchase systems online, and access volumes of support and technical information.

Manufacturing

Dell manufactures its computer systems in six locations: Austin, Texas; Nashville, Tennessee; El Dorado do Sul, Brazil (Americas); Limerick, Ireland (Europe, Middle East, and Africa); Penang, Malaysia (Asia-Pacific and Japan); and Xiamen, China (China). The manufacturing process at Dell's worldwide manufacturing facilities comprises the assembly, testing, and quality control of its computer systems. Parts, components, and subassemblies purchased from suppliers are tested and held to quality standards. Because of its build-to-order manufacturing process, Dell quickly produces customized computer systems, achieves rapid inventory turnover, and reduced inventory levels. These attributes lessen Dell's exposure to the risk of declining inventory values. Another advantage of this flexible manufacturing process is that Dell can incorporate new technologies or components into its product offerings quickly. To ensure a defect-free product, Dell performs tests along the process and on the final products.

EXTERNAL ISSUES

Competition

The level of competition facing Dell is formidable; Hewlett-Packard and IBM are its chief rivals. Gateway and Apple Computer also compete with Dell for their place in the PC market. Analysts expect that in the short-term, in the wake of the HP-Compaq merger, Dell will benefit because those firms will struggle to integrate their operations. Dell is already claiming to have gained new customers who have switched from the Compaq label due to uncertainty about the brand's future. Longer term, however, Compaq and HP together will have strengths that Dell does not have, especially on the service side, and IBM is already very powerful.

The combined HP-Compaq Company is now the market-share leader, with 16.8 percent. Dell presently leads the industry in market share with 13.8 percent, and it is also leading the way in an industry price war, taking market share from its competitors in the process. For the second quarter of 2001, Dell increased its market share by 20.2 percent; during the same period, one-time market leader Compaq saw its market share decline by 14.4 percent, which left with a current market share of 10.4 percent. HP lost 8.5 percent, leaving it with 6.4 percent of the market; and IBM lost 6.9 percent, which left it with a current market share of 6.6 percent.

Among the factors that make Dell an appealing choice for PC buyers, are the following factors:

- Its build-to-order approach
- Its attractive price
- Its strong understanding of customer preferences and requirements
- The close working relationships it has forged with customers
- Its ability to save customers money
- Its direct sales approach

Dell encounters aggressive competition in all aspects of its business. Competing on the basis of price, technology availability, performance, quality, reliability, service, and support, Dell could maintain profitability by reducing operating expenses and by continuing to leverage its lean inventory model to rapidly realize the benefit of component price declines.

EXHIBIT 5   Dell Computer Corporation Top Competitors

	As of September 10, 2001			
	Dell Computer	Compaq	Hewlett-Packard	IBM
Key Numbers				
Annual Sales ($ in millions)	31,888	42,383	48,782	88,396
Employees	40,000	94,600	88,500	316,303
Market Value ($ in millions)	58,772.30	17,532.90	34,770.00	167,535.6

	Dell Computer	Compaq	Hewlett-Packard	IBM	Industry	Market
Profitability						
Gross Profit Margin	20.25%	26.55%	27.68%	42.31%	20.87%	45.29%
Pretax Profit Margin	9.49%	(1.14%)	6.19%	13.31%	5.14%	6.70%
Net Profit Margin	4.51%	(0.79%)	2.95%	9.36%	3.29%	3.75%
Return on Equity	26.70%	–	9.80%	37.70%	13.70%	8.30%
Return on Assets	11.10%	(1.3%)	4.10%	10.00%	6.90%	1.60%
Return on Invested Capital	24.40%	(2.5%)	8.20%	20.40%	12.50%	4.30%

	Dell Computer	Compaq	Hewlett-Packard	IBM	Industry	Market
Valuation						
Price/Sales Ratio	1.8	0.43	0.74	1.86	1.38	2.42
Price/Earnings Ratio	40.3	–	25.93	20.61	54.08	60.49
Price/Book Ratio	10.7	1.49	2.47	7.5	5.73	5.37
Price/Cash Flow Ratio	24.27	15.92	9.52	12.53	29.5	25.05

	Dell Computer	Compaq	Hewlett-Packard	IBM	Industry	Market
Operations						
Inventory Turnover	65.7	14.5	6.4	10.8	63.7	8.9
Days Cost of Goods Sold in Inventory	–	–	57	33	6	40
Asset Turnover	2.6	1.6	1.4	1.1	2	0.5
Net Receivables Turnover Flow	12.1	5.6	6.1	3.4	11.7	7.7
Effective Tax Rate	29.70%	–	20.50%	29.70%	35.90%	43.40%

Source: www.hoovers.com.

Global Issues

Economies around the globe are in recession. The U.S. economy, which has a tremendous impact on the rest of the world, was growing at the slowest rate in ten years prior to the September 11 attacks on the World Trade Center, and it has since been thrust into a recession.

The PC market is in trouble. Worldwide shipments of personal computers fell in the second quarter of 2001, the first year-on-year decline since 1986 according to reports published by International Data Corp and Gartner Dataquest (July 2001). International sales fell 2 percent, to approximately 30 million units. Of great concern was an unanticipated slowdown of sales in Japan, a market with strong growth potential because PC penetration is relatively low there. The Japanese market had seen 30 percent growth in 2000, but it had a largely flat second quarter of 2001. The world PC market is likely to continue to be flat to negative into 2002. Dell Computer is the only PC maker managing to increase sales while the rest of the top five companies all suffered declines. Gateway announced the closing of its UK operations in September 2001.

CONCLUSION

Dell Computer is a strong company; it is the PC industry leader. Dell has also positioned itself as the industry low-cost producer, placing it in the position to weather the current decline in the market demand for PCs. Dell is using its low-cost advantage to engage the industry in a price war that is squeezing the profits out of the competition and at the same time growing its own market share in a shrinking market.

A recent strategy that should help Dell continue to grow and outperform the rest of the industry is the introduction of a standardized low-price PC. The low-price PC should help Dell continue to take market share from the competition.

HEWLETT-PACKARD COMPANY—2002

Fred David
Francis Marion University

HPQ

www.hewlett-packard.com

Hewlett-Packard (HP) was incorporated in 1947 as the successor to a partnership founded in 1939 by William Hewlett and David Packard. In May 1998, HP changed its state of incorporation from California to Delaware. In late 2001, HP acquired Compaq Computer Company to become the largest computer company in the world. HP today has approximately 145,000 employees worldwide, and business presence and services capability in more than 160 countries. The HP mission statement pre- and post merger remains unchanged as follows:

> *To invent technologies and services that drive business value, create social benefit and improve the lives of customers—with a focus on affecting the greatest number of people possible.*

In fiscal year 2001 (ended October 31, 2001), HP reported revenues of $45.2 billion, while in fiscal year 2001 (ended December 31, 2001), Compaq reported revenues of $33.6 billion. Special synergies created by this huge computer industry merger are as follows:

- Number 1 globally in Windows and UNIX servers
- Number 1 globally in enterprise storage
- Number 1 globally in imaging and printing
- Number 1 globally in personal computers
- Number 1 globally in management software
- Number 3 IT services provider in the industry

Headquartered in Palo Alto, California, HP's chief executives are Carleton S. (Carly) Fiorina, Chairman and CEO and Michael Capellas, President.

ORGANIZATIONAL STRUCTURE

Prior to the Compaq merger, HP operated in three basic segments: Imaging and Printing Systems, Computing Systems, and Information Technology (IT) Services. Exhibit 1 reveals HP's revenues and earnings by segment for 2001, 2000, and 1999. Note that only the IT segment had increasing revenues for 2001 while all three divisions had declining earnings. HP's revenues broken down by geographic area are provided in Exhibit 2. Note that HP revenues declined both in the United States and outside the U.S. in 2001. Exhibit 3 provides HP's various headquarter locations around the world. Note that Geneva, Switzerland and Hong Kong, China are important cities for HP.

The new post-merger HP operates in the following four segments described as follows:

EXHIBIT 1   Hewlett-Packard Company Segment Financial Data (in millions)

The following table presents financial information for each reportable segment as of and for the years ended October 31:

	Imaging and Printing Systems	Computing Systems	IT Services	All Other	Total Segments
2001:					
Net revenue from external customers	$19,447	$17,482	$7,599	$1,010	$45,538
Intersegment net revenue	—	289	—	—	289
Total net revenue	$19,447	$17,771	$7,599	$1,010	$45,827
Earnings (loss) from operations	$ 1,987	$ (450)	$ 342	$ (321)	$ 1,558
Depreciation expense	$ 227	$ 82	$ 508	$ 14	$ 831
Inventory	$ 3,495	$ 1,337	$ 337	$ 35	$ 5,204
2000:					
Net revenue from external customers	$20,462	$20,329	$7,139	$1,511	$49,441
Intersegment net revenue	6	324	11	45	386
Total net revenue	$20,468	$20,653	$7,150	$1,556	$49,827
Earnings (loss) from operations	$ 2,666	$ 1,007	$ 474	$ (92)	$ 4,055
Depreciation expense	$ 298	$ 76	$ 445	$ 7	$ 826
Inventory	$ 3,475	$ 1,665	$ 377	$ 182	$ 5,699
1999:					
Net revenue from external customers	$18,512	$16,837	$6,240	$1,250	$42,839
Intersegment net revenue	38	558	64	6	666
Total net revenue	$18,550	$17,395	$6,304	$1,256	$43,505
Earnings (loss) from operations	$ 2,364	$ 988	$ 494	$ (112)	$ 3,734
Depreciation expense	$ 479	$ 73	$ 408	$ 4	$ 964
Inventory	$ 2,810	$ 1,539	$ 336	$ 178	$ 4,863

Source: HP's 2001 *Annual Report,* p. 81.

- **Enterprise Systems Group (ESG),** led by Peter Blackmore, executive vice president. ESG focuses on providing the key technology components of enterprise IT infrastructure to enhance business agility—including enterprise storage, servers, management software and a variety of solutions.

EXHIBIT 2   Hewlett-Packard Company Geographic Financial Data (in millions)

GEOGRAPHIC INFORMATION

Net revenue and net property, plant and equipment, classified by major geographic areas in which HP operates, were as follows:

	Years ended October 31,		
	2001	2000	1999
Net revenue:			
U.S.	$18,833	$21,528	$18,883
Non-U.S.	26,393	27,342	23,488
Total	$45,226	$48,870	$42,371

Source: HP's 2001 *Annual Report,* p. 83.

EXHIBIT 3   HP Locations Around the World

HEADQUARTERS OF GEOGRAPHIC OPERATIONS

Latin America	Europe, Africa, Middle East	Asia Pacific
Miami, Florida	Geneva, Switzerland	Hong Kong

PRODUCT DEVELOPMENT AND MANUFACTURING

Americas	Europe	Asia Pacific
Cupertino, Costa Mesa, Mountain View, Palo Alto, Roseville, San Diego, Santa Clara, Santa Monica, Sunnyvale and Woodland, California	Grenoble and Isle D'Abeau, France	Melbourne, Australia
Fort Collins and Greeley, Colorado	Boeblingen, Germany	Shanghai, China
Boise, Idaho	Dublin, Ireland	Bangalore, India
Mt. Laurel, New Jersey	Amsterdam and Amersfoort, The Netherlands	Komiya, Japan
Corvallis, Oregon	Barcelona, Spain	Singapore
Memphis and Nashville, Tennessee	Bristol, United Kingdom	Taiwan
Austin, Texas		
Chester, Richmond and Sandston, Virginia		
Vancouver, Washington		
Aguadilla, Puerto Rico		
Sao Paulo, Brazil		
Guadalajara, Mexico		

HEWLETT-PACKARD LABORATORIES
Palo Alto, California
Grenoble, France
Bangalore, India
Haifa, Israel
Tokyo, Japan
Bristol, United Kingdom

Source: HP's 2001 *Annual Report,* p. 12.

- **Imaging and Printing Group (IPG),** led by Vyomesh Joshi ("VJ"), executive vice president. HP is the leading provider of printing and imaging solutions for both business and consumers. IPG includes printer hardware, all-in-ones, digital imaging devices such as cameras and scanners, and associated supplies and accessories. It is also expanding into the commercial printing market.

- **HP Services (HPS),** led by Ann Livermore, executive vice president. HP Services is a premier IT services team with 65,000 professionals around the globe. HPS offers guidance, know-how and a comprehensive portfolio of services to help customers realize measurable business value from their IT investment.

- **Personal Systems Group (PSG),** led by Duane Zitzner, executive vice president. PSG focuses on providing simple, reliable and affordable personal computing solutions and devices for home and business use, including desktop and notebook PCs, workstations, thin clients, smart handhelds and personal devices.

- In addition to the four business groups, **HP Labs**, led by Dick Lampman, senior vice president, provides a central research function for the company. HP Labs is focused on inventing new technologies that change markets and create business opportunities. (**www.hewlett-packard.com**)

Financial Matters

HP's net revenue for 2001 declined 7 percent to $45.2 billion. U.S. revenue in 2001 declined 13 percent to $18.8 billion, while international revenue decreased just 3 percent to $26.4 billion. HP's 2001 income statements and balance sheets are provided in Exhibits 4 and 5 respectively.

HP's research and development expense as a percentage of net revenue was 5.9 percent in 2001 compared to 5.4 percent in 2000 and 5.8 percent in 1999. On advertising, HP spent $1.0 billion, $1.1 billion, and $1.3 billion in 2001, 2000, and 1999 respectively.

CONCLUSION

CEO Fiorina needs a clear strategic plan for the coming three years. Major competitors such as IBM, Dell Computer, Apple Computer, and Gateway are looking for weakness in the new HP. These competitors are using relentless price cutting, shortened product life cycles, mass advertising, and promotions to cripple HP to the extent possible. Develop a proposed three-year strategic plan for HP.

EXHIBIT 4   Hewlett-Packard Company Consolidated Statement of Earnings

For the years ended October 31 In millions, except per share amounts	2001	2000	1999
Net revenue:			
Products	$37,498	$41,653	$36,113
Services	7,325	6,848	5,960
Financing income	403	369	298
Total net revenue	45,226	48,870	42,371
Cost of sales:			
Products	28,370	30,343	25,436
Services	4,870	4,470	4,284
Financing interest	234	233	168
Total cost of sales	33,474	35,046	29,888
Gross margin	11,752	13,824	12,483
Operating expenses:			
Research and development	2,670	2,634	2,440
Selling, general and administrative	7,259	7,063	6,225
Restructuring charges	384	102	—
Total operating expenses	10,313	9,799	8,665
Earnings from operations	1,439	4,025	3,818
Interest and other, net	171	356	345
Net investment (losses) gains	(455)	41	31
Litigation settlement	(400)	—	—
(Losses) gains on divestitures	(53)	203	—
Earnings from continuing operations before extraordinary item, cumulative effect of change in accounting principle and taxes	702	4,625	4,194
Provision for taxes	78	1,064	1,090
Net earnings from continuing operations before extraordinary item and cumulative effect of change in accounting principle	624	3,561	3,104
Net earnings from discontinued operations	—	136	387
Extraordinary item—gain on early extinguishment of debt, net of taxes	56	—	—
Cumulative effect of change in accounting principle, net of taxes	(272)	—	—
Net earnings	$ 408	$ 3,697	$ 3,491
Basic net earnings per share:			
Net earnings from continuing operations before extraordinary item and cumulative effect of change in accounting principle	$ 0.32	$ 1.80	$ 1.54
Net earnings from discontinued operations	—	0.07	0.19
Extraordinary item—gain on early extinguishment of debt, net of taxes	0.03	—	—
Cumulative effect of change in accounting principle, net of taxes	(0.14)	—	—
Net earnings	$ 0.21	$ 1.87	$ 1.73
Diluted net earnings per share:			
Net earnings from continuing operations before extraordinary item and cumulative effect of change in accounting principle	$ 0.32	$ 1.73	$ 1.49
Net earnings from discontinued operations	—	0.07	0.18
Extraordinary item—gain on early extinguishment of debt, net of taxes	0.03	—	—
Cumulative effect of change in accounting principle, net of taxes	(0.14)	—	—
Net earnings	$ 0.21	$ 1.80	$ 1.67
Weighted average shares used to compute net earnings per share:			
Basic	1,936	1,979	2,018
Diluted	1,974	2,077	2,105

Source: HP's 2001 *Annual Report*, p. 45.

EXHIBIT 5   Hewlett-Packard Company Consolidated Balance Sheet

October 31 *In millions, except par value*	*2001*	*2000*
ASSETS		
Current assets:		
Cash and Cash equivalents	$ 4,197	$ 3,415
Short-term investments	139	592
Accounts receivable, net	4,488	6,394
Financing receivables, net	2,183	2,174
Inventory	5,204	5,699
Other current assets	5,094	4,970
Total current assets	21,305	23,244
Property, plant and equipment, net	4,397	4,500
Long-term investments and other assets	6,882	6,265
Total assets	$32,584	$34,009
LIABILITIES AND STOCKHOLDERS' EQUITY		
Current liabilities:		
Notes payable and short-term borrowings	$ 1,722	$ 1,555
Accounts payable	3,791	5,049
Employee compensation and benefits	1,477	1,584
Taxes on earnings	1,818	2,046
Deferred revenue	1,867	1,759
Other accrued liabilities	3,289	3,204
Total current liabilities	13,964	15,197
Long-term debt	3,729	3,402
Other liabilities	938	1,201
Commitments and contingencies		
Stockholders' equity:		
Preferred stock, $0.01 par value (300 shares authorized; none issued)	—	—
Common stock, $0.01 par value (9,600 and 4,800 shares authorized at October 31, 2001 and 2000, respectively; 1,939 and 1,947 shares issued and outstanding at October 31, 2001 and 2000, respectively)	19	19
Additional paid-in capital	200	—
Retained earnings	13,693	14,097
Accumulated other comprehensive income	41	93
Total stockholders' equity	13,953	14,209
Total liabilities and stockholders' equity	$32,584	$34,009

Source: HP's 2001 *Annual Report*, p. 46.

STRYKER CORPORATION—2002

Henry H. Beam
Western Michigan University

SYK

www.strykercorp.com

Stryker Corporation is a leading maker of specialty surgical and medical products based in Kalamazoo, Michigan. Although not yet a household name, Stryker is one of America's most consistently profitable growth companies. In 2001, Stryker posted record sales of $2.6 billion and net income of $267 million. After John Brown became chairman in 1977, Stryker achieved 20 percent or more annual earnings-per-share growth every year until 1998, a remarkable record. In December 1998, Stryker took a strategic detour to take advantage of a unique opportunity to acquire Howmedica, the orthopedic division of Pfizer, which enabled the company to nearly double its size. CEO Brown commented, "When we acquired Howmedica, we announced our intention to get to be back at 20 percent or better net earnings growth. Not only did the company get back on the 20 percent track in 2000, but we did so with profit growth that makes up for the strategic detour of 1998 and 1999. With this return to the Stryker "Gold Standard," we have delivered the equivalent of 24 years of growth at the rate of 20 percent or higher." Stryker's consistent success has not gone unnoticed by Wall Street, where its stock is increasingly on the recommended list of leading brokerage firms.

All this growth comes from making products that people hope they never have to use—but are glad to have available when they need them. Stryker develops, manufactures, and markets a wide variety of surgical products and specialty hospital beds that are sold primarily to physicians and hospitals throughout the world. Stryker also provides outpatient physical therapy services in the United States.

In the 1950s and 1960s, Stryker's reputation was enhanced by good publicity about some of its unique products. Roy Campanella, the Brooklyn Dodger baseball star who had been paralyzed from injuries received in an automobile accident in 1958, was cared for on Stryker equipment. *Life* magazine did a story about the Tennessee American Legion buying a Circ-O-Lectric Hospital Bed for Sergeant Alvin York, the World War I Medal of Honor winner who had become an invalid by the early 1960s. When Senator Edward Kennedy suffered a back injury in a plane crash in 1964, he was cared for on a Stryker turning frame and was later moved to a Circ-O-Lectric Hospital Bed, both of which were pictured in national magazines during his recovery. More recently, former First Lady Barbara Bush has had Osteonics hip replacements. Such favorable publicity has enhanced the image of the company in the public's eye.

HISTORY

The Stryker corporation takes it name from its founder, Dr. Homer Stryker, a remarkable man in many respects. After serving briefly in World War I, Stryker earned his medical degree from the University of Michigan in 1925, chose orthopedics as his specialty, and located his medical practice in Kalamazoo, Michigan. Throughout his life, he liked to fiddle with gadgets. During the early years of his medical practice, Stryker invented a mobile hospital bed and a cast-cutting saw. The mobile bed had a frame that pivoted from side to side so physicians could position injured patients for treatment while keeping them immobile. He won a contract to supply the army with his beds during World War II and was soon running a small business as well as a medical practice. The contract was terminated when the war ended in 1945, but the business continued.

Dr. Stryker wrote about how he invented the cast-cutting saw:

> In 1943, the removal of a large cast was a tedious process for me and an unpleasant one at best for the patient. In search of a better way, I observed that if a small circular blade with sharp teeth was pressed firmly against the skin, or the soft cast padding used to protect the skin, and then moved back and forth, no more than an eighth of an inch of skin would move with the saw teeth and neither the skin or the padding and skin would be cut.
>
> However, if I took the same blade and pressed against a plaster cast and moved it back and forth with the same stroke and pressure, it would cut the plaster. I took a 1/20th horsepower electric grinder, replaced the grinding stone with a two-inch diameter saw blade and designed and attached a mechanism which would convert the rotation of the saw to oscillation, with the teeth oscillating about an eight of an inch at about 18,000 oscillations per minute. When completed, the instrument was tested by removing a cast at the hospital. I was able to remove the cast without disturbing the patient, in about one-fourth the time previously required.

This is typical of how Stryker used his creativity to improve the products that physicians used to treat their patients. The rapid acceptance of the cast cutter by physicians and hospital beds by the army convinced Stryker that he had more than a part-time business on his hands. In 1946, the Orthopedic Frame Company was incorporated, with Dr. Stryker as its sole shareholder. Stryker continued with his medical practice, where he continued to develop pioneering surgical techniques. His business grew rapidly. His son Lee joined him in the business in 1955 after earning a bachelor's degree in business administration from Syracuse University. Lee's business sense balanced his father's desire to use the company as an outlet for his inventive talents.

In 1964, the company changed its name to the Stryker Corporation. New products came regularly, and sales reached $4.7 million in 1966. Although Stryker's medical equipment manufacturing business would make him wealthy, he gave away hundreds of ideas and techniques free of charge to other physicians, who passed them on to their patients. Stryker retired from his company in 1969. The company continued to grow under the guidance of Lee Stryker until his tragic death in an airplane crash in Wyoming in July 1976. Later that year, John Brown became president of Stryker.

Brown graduated from Auburn University in 1957 with a bachelor of science degree in chemical engineering. Prior to becoming president of Stryker, Brown held management positions with Ormet Corporation, Thiokol, and Bristol-Myers Squibb, where he was president of a subsidiary. Brown took charge of a firm with sales of $23 million and net income of $1.5 million. He swiftly took steps to decentralize the company, creating the autonomous divisional structure it has today. When he realized that salespeople were quitting because the compensation system had been changed from commissions to salaries and bonuses only, he restored commissions as the dominant form of compensation for salespeople. He also established goals of 20 percent growth in sales and earnings per share a year, every year. At the time, nearly 70 percent of Stryker's sales were coming from hospital beds. Building on the strength of the Stryker name with hospitals, Brown added hip implants and medical video cameras, and he strengthened the line of power surgical tools.

Acquisitions have played an important part in Stryker's growth. In 1996, Stryker purchased Osteo Holdings AG for $45.5 million. Osteo, based in Switzerland, produces a broad variety of high-quality trauma products. Stryker saw the acquisition of Osteo as a way to enter the $1 billion global trauma market. In December 1998, Stryker acquired Howmedica, the orthopedic unit of Pfizer, for $1.65 billion in cash. Howmedica makes a wide variety of innovative products for the orthopedic market, including craniofacial trauma products through Leibenger, a German company it had purchased in 1996. At the time of its acquisition, Howmedica had sales of $850 million. At Stryker's 1999 annual meeting, a smiling John Brown gave his rationale for the Howmedica acquisition. "We did it to gain a better position in the marketplace. Bigger is better. We decided a boutique player would have a hard time in this marketplace in the years ahead."

Stryker continues to make niche acquisitions, such as the Neptune fluid and smoke waste management system used in operating rooms; Colorado Biomedical, which makes the Colorado Micro Needle used in precision electrosurgery; and Image Guided Technologies, which makes three-dimensional optical measurement devices used in image-guided surgery.

Although located mainly in Kalamazoo, Michigan, Stryker also leases facilities in other U.S. cities, France, Germany, Ireland, Switzerland, Canada, and Puerto Rico. Officers, directors, and the Stryker family trust own about a third of the shares. Stryker's financial statements are shown in Exhibits 1 through 2.

THE U.S. HEALTHCARE INDUSTRY

The U.S. healthcare system is highly diverse. Healthcare providers deliver many different kinds of services in a wide variety of settings: acute-care, inpatient general hospitals; specialty hospitals; free-standing ambulatory clinics and surgical centers; nursing homes; and patients' homes (via home healthcare services). Despite a growing proportion of elderly people in the U.S. population, hospital admission rates have declined for the past decade and are expected to continue to decline in the future. In contrast, outpatient volume has increased due to restricted reimbursement policies for inpatient care and the development of diagnostic and therapeutic procedures that do not require inpatient settings. According to the American Hospital Association, over half of all surgeries performed at community hospitals are done on an outpatient basis, up from about 20 percent ten years ago.

The United States is the global leader in the production of medical equipment and supplies, accounting for about half of the $140 billion worldwide medical device industry. Export growth in recent years has benefited from the demand for sophisticated diagnostic equipment and from the growing emphasis on the provision of quality healthcare services in countries worldwide.

Business conditions throughout the hospital industry are becoming tougher as a result of the expanding influence of managed-care plans such as health maintenance organizations (HMOs) and as a result of the constraints on reimbursement from both the federal government and insurance companies. Moreover, the number of hospitals in the United States has been declining for nearly two decades. With about a third of all hospital beds in the United States considered to be excess capacity, the fast pace of industry consolidations is likely to continue. As purchasing decisions in the 1980s and 1990s shifted away from physicians to hospitals and buying alliances, producers of medical equipment were increasingly forced to demonstrate the cost effectiveness of their products. About 60 percent of all medical device purchases in the United States are now made by managed-care buyers, and that figure is expected to increase to 80 percent in five years.

EXHIBIT 1   Consolidated Statements of Earnings
Stryker Corporation and Subsidiaries
(in millions, except per share amounts)

	Years ended December 31		
	2001	*2000*	*1999*
Net sales	$2,602.3	$2,289.4	$2,103.7
Cost of sales	963.8	815.2	989.7
Gross profit	1,638.5	1,474.2	1,114.0
Research, development and engineering expenses	142.1	122.2	105.2
Selling, general and administrative expenses	985.4	885.6	808.4
Acquisition-related and restructuring charges (credits)	0.6	(1.0)	18.9
	1,128.1	1,006.8	932.5
Other expense (income):			
Interest expense	67.9	96.6	122.6
Intangibles amortization	38.4	34.7	33.9
Other	(1.6)	1.2	(4.8)
	104.7	132.5	151.7
Earnings before income taxes and extraordinary item	405.7	334.9	29.8
Income taxes	133.9	113.9	10.4
Earnings before extraordinary item	271.8	221.0	19.4
Extraordinary loss, net of income taxes	(4.8)	—	—
Net earnings	$ 267.0	$ 221.0	$ 19.4
Basic earnings per share of common stock:			
Before extraordinary item	$ 1.38	$ 1.13	$ .10
Extraordinary loss	($.02)	—	—
Net earnings	$ 1.36	$ 1.13	$ .10
Diluted earnings per share of common stock:			
Before extraordinary item	$ 1.34	$ 1.10	$ .10
Extraordinary loss	($.02)	—	—
Net earnings	$ 1.32	$ 1.10	$ .10

Source: Stryker's 2001 *Annual Report,* pp. 36–37.

STRYKER'S ORGANIZATION

Following the Howmedica acquisition, Stryker has organized itself into five major product divisions: Howmedica Osteonics, MedSurg Equipment, Physiotherapy, International, and BioTech/Spine/Trauma. An approximate organization chart is given in Exhibit 3.

Howmedica Osteonics

The Howmedica Osteonics division produces a variety of both total and partial hip and knee implants. It is a combination of the former Stryker Osteonics division and the Howmedica acquisition and is now the company's largest division. With sales of $1.44 billion in 2001, it is Stryker's largest unit, accounting for 55 percent of its sales.

Every year, about five hundred thousand people in the United States and a comparable number abroad, most of them elderly, undergo joint replacement surgery to regain some of their previous mobility. Most hip and knee replacements result from osteoarthritis (a condition affecting the aged in which joints become painful and mobility is

EXHIBIT 2   Consolidated Balance Sheets Stryker Corporation and Subsidiaries (in millions, except per-share amounts)

	December 31	
	2001	*2000*
ASSETS		
Current Assets		
Cash and cash equivalents	$ 50.1	$ 54.0
Accounts receivable, less allowance of $36.3 ($28.8 in 2000)	332.1	343.7
Inventories	399.8	392.1
Deferred income taxes	171.5	168.7
Prepaid expenses and other current assets	39.6	38.5
Total current assets	993.1	997.0
Property, Plant and Equipment		
Land, buildings and improvements	287.6	211.9
Machinery and equipment	469.3	444.0
	756.9	655.9
Less allowance for depreciation	312.9	277.8
	444.0	378.1
Other Assets		
Goodwill, less accumulated amortization of $58.5 ($40.3 in 2000)	434.3	470.6
Other intangibles, less accumulated amortization of $74.5 ($53.2 in 2000)	368.0	368.7
Deferred charges, less accumulated amortization of $205.5 ($154.1 in 2000)	102.1	99.3
Deferred income taxes	60.4	84.0
Other	21.7	33.1
	986.5	1,055.7
	$2,423.6	$2,430.8
LIABILITIES AND STOCKHOLDERS' EQUITY		
Current Liabilities		
Accounts payable	$ 108.5	$ 94.1
Accrued compensation	128.5	115.2
Acquisition-related reorganization reserves and liabilities	9.5	56.8
Income taxes	75.1	33.6
Accrued expenses and other liabilities	210.1	181.7
Current maturities of long-term debt	1.7	136.0
Total current liabilities	533.4	617.4
Long-Term Debt, Excluding Current Maturities	720.9	876.5
Other Liabilities	113.1	82.0
Stockholders' Equity		
Common stock, $.10 par value:		
Authorized—500.0 shares		
Outstanding—196.7 shares (195.9 in 2000)	19.7	19.6
Additional paid-in capital	83.2	64.3
Retained earnings	1,120.7	873.4
Accumulated other comprehensive loss	(167.4)	(102.4)
Total stockholders' equity	1,056.2	854.9
	$2,423.6	$2,430.8

Source: Stryker's 2001 *Annual Report,* p 35.

EXHIBIT 3   Approximate Organization Chart for Stryker Corporation

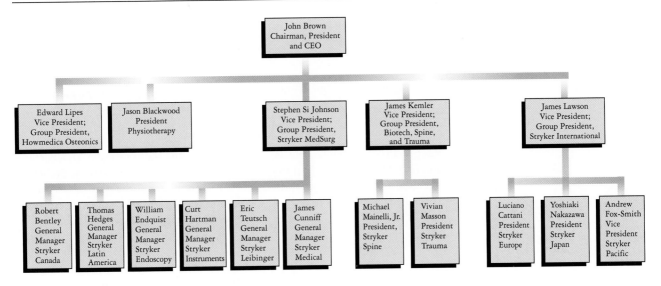

Source: Adapted from Stryker Corporation, 2001 *Annual Report.*

impaired) and rheumatoid arthritis (a disease that destroys cartilage at the joint's surface). Orthopedic research has led to the development of a broad array of prosthetic equipment and related devices, including digital cameras. Recent innovations include porous hip and knee replacements, which allow bone to grow directly into the metal implant.

MedSurg Equipment

The MedSurg (medical and surgical) division has four major components: Stryker Endoscopy, Stryker Instruments, Stryker Leibenger, and Stryker Medical. With sales of $978 million in 2001, this division accounted for 39 percent of Stryker's sales. Each MedSurg unit competes against medical equipment subsidiaries of large firms (e.g., DePuy of Johnson & Johnson, Hill-Rom of Hillenbrand Industries) as well as independent firms, such as Biomet, Midas Rex, U.S. Surgical, and Zimmer.

Stryker Endoscopy

This division makes a broad range of medical video imaging equipment and instruments for arthroscopy and general surgery. In an endoscopic (less invasive) surgical procedure, the surgeon removes or repairs damaged tissue through several small punctures rather than through an open incision. Patients experience reduced trauma and pain, less time in the hospital, and a quicker return to health. Less invasive removal of the gallbladder requires a single day in the hospital, followed by a week of convalescence. Traditional gallbladder surgery, by contrast, meant four to eight days in the hospital and a month's convalescence.

Imaging technology plays a crucial role in endoscopic procedures. Stryker is a leader in medical video imaging systems. Through pioneering engineering work, Stryker miniaturized a three-chip video camera (with a separate computer chip for each primary color) and became the first company to offer the surgeon a broadcast-quality image. This division also makes digital cameras to assist with endoscopic procedures.

Stryker Instruments

This division produces a wide range of operating room equipment that is utilized primarily in orthopedic procedures, such as bone saws and drills. It is a market leader for battery-powered heavy-duty surgical instruments. Its Stryker 940 cast removal system is the newest version of Dr. Stryker's original cast cutter.

Stryker Leibenger

Stryker Leibenger is a leading maker of surgical instruments and products primarily used for head, neck, and hand surgery. Its headquarters are in Germany.

Stryker Medical

It produces specialty stretchers and beds, which facilitate the transportation, transfer, and treatment of patients within the hospital. It has designed a line of innovative stretchers as a result of a close analysis of hospital needs, focusing on reducing the number of patient transfers (from bed to stretcher to operating table and back again) that must be performed in a hospital. It also produces accessories such as bedside stands and overbed tables.

Physiotherapy Associates

The Physiotherapy Associates division operates outpatient rehabilitation centers in over twenty states and the District of Columbia. Following orthopedic or neurological injury, the centers provide physical, occupational, and speech therapy to help speed a patient's return to work or full activity. With sales of $147 million in 2000, this division accounted for 6 percent of Stryker's sales. In the outpatient physical therapy market, Stryker's principal competitors are independent practices and hospital-based services. Competition is also provided by national rehabilitation companies such as HealthSouth, NovaCare/RCI, and Rehability.

Stryker Spine

Stryker Spine is a new division that provides both implants and instruments to assist in the repair of the human spine. An estimated ten thousand spinal injuries occur each year in the United States, nearly half of which are related to automobile and motorcycle accidents. About one-third of all spine procedures are fusions, in which surgeons seek to stop painful motion in the back by fusing unstable vertebrae. The spinal market is estimated to be in excess of $1 billion, and it is growing at a rate of 20 percent per year.

INTERNATIONAL OPERATIONS

In the early 1990s, Stryker sought to improve the distribution of its products internationally by investing in Matsumoto, the largest Japanese distributor of orthopedic, general surgery, and emergency care products. In addition to Stryker products, Matsumoto also distributed devices from other leading American and European medical device makers. Shortly after Stryker took a majority ownership position in Matsumoto in 1995, several medical instrument companies stopped distributing through Matsumoto because they felt uncomfortable with Stryker's majority stake. As a result, Matusmoto saw sales of non-Stryker products fall by over 50 percent from 1995 to 1996. In 1999, Stryker purchased the remaining shares of Matsumoto stock, bringing its direct ownership to 100 percent. Matsumoto is now called Stryker Japan and accounts for about 13 percent of Stryker's sales. Its major competitor in Japan is Zimmer Holdings, a former Bristol Myers-Squibb unit that had sales of $1.04 billion and net income of $176 million in 2000. Zimmer designs and markets orthopedic products such as reconstructive implants and fracture management devices. Products include the NexGen knee implant series and the Versys system for hips. International sales are about 40 percent of Zimmer's total sales, with Japan accounting for about half of that market.

Stryker Europe and Stryker Pacific (all except Japan) comprise Stryker's other international operations. Segment data on Stryker's international sales is given in Exhibits 4 and 5.

MANUFACTURING AND R&D

Stryker's manufacturing processes consist primarily of precision machining, metal fabrication, assembly operations, and the investment (precision) casting of cobalt chrome and finishing of cobalt chrome and titanium. The principal raw materials used by the company are stainless steel, aluminum, cobalt chrome, and titanium alloys. In all, purchases from outside sources are about half of the company's total cost of sales.

Many of the company's products and product improvements have been developed internally. The company maintains close working relationships with physicians and medical personnel in hospitals and universities who assist in product research and development. Research and development is under the direct control of the operating divisions, where it can be focused on specific markets. Stryker seeks to obtain patent protection on its products whenever possible. It currently holds over 1,500 patents worldwide on products it has developed.

Twice in the last three years, a Stryker manufacturing facility has been named one of America's best manufacturing plants. In 1998, *Industry Week* named Howmedica Osteonics, located in Allendale, New Jersey, as one of the top ten manufacturing plants in the United States. Then in 2000, the Stryker Instruments manufacturing facility in Kalamazoo, Michigan, was similarly honored by *Industry Week*. All of the plant's workforce participates in self-directed work teams. More than 99 percent of all finished products meet quality requirements at initial inspection, and 98 percent of all deliveries are made on time. Business segment sales are given in Exhibit 6.

STRYKER'S CORPORATE CULTURE

Since John Brown became CEO, Stryker has developed a distinctive corporate culture that is sometimes described as "a lot like being in the Marine Corps," although senior executives try to downplay that image. Sayings representing Stryker's core beliefs are prominently written on walls in lobbies and cafeterias. One of the most common, "First

EXHIBIT 4   Stryker's Domestic/International and Product Line Sales Information

	Net Sales (in millions)			Percentage Change	
	2001	*2000*	*1999*	*2001/00*	*2000/99*
Domestic/international sales					
Domestic	$1,688.4	$1,408.2	$1,228.4	20%	15%
International	913.9	881.2	875.3	4	1
Total net sales	$2,602.3	$2,289.4	$2,103.7	14	9
Product line sales					
Orthopedic Implants	$1,442.5	$1,313.0	$1,248.2	10	5
MedSurg Equipment	978.9	829.1	733.5	18	13
Physical Therapy Services	180.9	147.3	122.0	23	21
Total net sales	$2,602.3	$2,289.4	$2,103.7	14	9

Source: Stryker's 2001 *Annual Report,* p. 27.

EXHIBIT 5   Stryker's Geographic Data

The Company's areas of operation outside of the United States, Japan and Europe principally include the Pacific, Canada, Latin America and the Middle East.

	Net Sales	Long-Lived Assets
Year ended December 31, 2001		
United States	$1,688.4	$ 780.7
Europe	414.5	455.6
Japan	266.5	94.1
Other foreign countries	232.9	39.7
	$2,602.3	$1,370.1
Year ended December 31, 2000		
United States	$1,408.2	$ 715.4
Europe	380.5	472.9
Japan	280.1	119.3
Other foreign countries	220.6	42.2
	$2,289.4	$1,349.8
Year ended December 31, 1999		
United States	$1,228.4	$ 746.7
Europe	416.8	498.5
Japan	266.7	143.1
Other foreign countries	191.8	39.1
	$2,103.7	$1,427.4

Source: Stryker's 2001 *Annual Report,* p. 57.

be best, then be first," refers to the competitive corporate philosophy established by Dr. Stryker that Stryker should first make the best products and then seek market leadership for those products.

Although there are no time clocks visible in Stryker facilities, employees wear scanning ID cards that keep track of when they arrive for work and when they leave. Lunch time is restricted to thirty minutes, just enough time to eat in the company cafeteria. Given the pressure of the 20 percent annual increase in earnings-per-share goal, the workweek for white collar workers is typically between fifty and sixty hours. It is common for executives to work evenings or on weekends. In return for their hard work ethic, employees are encouraged to share in the company's prosperity through a generous stock purchase plan. Employees can contribute up to 14 percent of their earnings to purchase Stryker stock. The company will match the first 8 percent contributed by the employees. None of the company's employees are covered by collective bargaining agreements.

Most of the company's products are marketed in the United States directly to more than 7,500 hospitals and to doctors and other healthcare facilities. The company maintains dedicated sales forces for each of its principal product lines to provide focus and a high level of expertise to each medical speciality served. The domestic sales force is compensated in large part by commissions. According to CEO Brown, "The beauty of commissions is there's no cap. The more the individual sells, the more he makes. The most ambitious and driven salespeople thrive in a commission environment." Stryker has been referred to as a "salesperson's paradise," where top performers can earn $200,000 or more a year. Hourly workers can earn pay increases or bonuses for meeting quality objectives. Nevertheless, some employees find Stryker's growth-oriented culture to be too demanding and leave to work for other companies.

EXHIBIT 6   Stryker's Sales and Other Financial Information by Business Segment

	Orthopedic Implants	MedSurg Equipment	Other	Total
Year ended December 31, 2001				
Net sales	$1,442.5	$978.9	$180.9	$2,602.3
Interest income	—	—	2.2	2.2
Interest expense	—	—	67.9	67.9
Depreciation and amortization expense	129.6	34.6	7.8	172.0
Acquisition-related and restructuring charges (credits)	0.8	(0.2)	–	0.6
Income taxes (credit)	111.1	54.5	(31.7)	133.9
Segment earnings (loss) before extraordinary item	197.7	115.5	(41.4)	271.8
Extraordinary loss, net of income taxes	—	–	(4.8)	(4.8)
Segment net earnings (loss)	197.7	115.5	(46.2)	267.0
Total assets	1,737.6	574.6	111.4	2,423.6
Capital expenditures	133.5	21.6	6.8	161.9
Year ended December 31, 2000				
Net sales	1,313.0	829.1	147.3	2,289.4
Interest income	—	—	4.1	4.1
Interest expense	—	—	96.6	96.6
Depreciation and amortization expense	132.8	29.6	6.2	168.6
Acquisition-related and restructuring charges (credits)	(1.8)	0.5	0.3	(1.0)
Income taxes (credit)	112.7	50.5	(49.3)	113.9
Segment net earnings (loss)	174.1	103.4	(56.5)	221.0
Total assets	1,739.1	588.2	103.5	2,430.8
Capital expenditures	56.5	19.1	5.1	80.7
Year ended December 31, 1999				
Net sales	1,248.2	733.5	122.0	2,103.7
Interest income	—	—	4.2	4.2
Interest expense	—	—	122.6	122.6
Depreciation and amortization expense	128.2	29.1	5.5	162.8
Additional cost of sales for inventory stepped-up to fair value	170.6	27.6	—	198.2
Acquisition-related and restructuring charges	9.5	9.4	—	18.9
Income taxes (credit)	43.9	21.8	(55.3)	10.4
Segment net earnings (loss)	30.8	68.0	(79.4)	19.4
Total assets	1,916.5	559.1	104.9	2,580.5
Capital expenditures	48.3	23.5	4.6	76.4

Source: Stryker's 2001 *Annual Report,* p. 56.

A manager at Stryker Instruments made the following connection between Stryker's culture and its success: "There is nothing particularly special about what we do from a manufacturing standpoint, in comparison to our competitors. The difference is in our culture. We aren't the only smart guys out there, but we do have the most highly defined, tangibly strong culture. And that is what, above all, we need to protect."

THE FUTURE

Stryker has prospered for more than twenty years under the direction of John Brown. Despite its past success, Stryker may find it increasingly difficult to make its target of 20 percent earnings growth every year. First, most of Stryker's major markets have shown annual growth rates of 5 percent or less over the last few years. This means Stryker's divisions need to grow more rapidly than the market segments in which they compete in order to meet the 20-percent-per-year growth goal. Second, mergers and acquisitions within the healthcare sector will probably continue at a rapid pace. This could lead to the emergence of larger and more powerful buying groups, such as Novation, that could put increased pressure on the suppliers of medical equipment, such as Stryker, to reduce the cost of their products. Third, Stryker faces a nimble new competitor in Zimmer, recently spun off from Bristol-Myers Squibb. Zimmer competes directly with Stryker in many of its product lines in the United States and abroad. Finally, employees may tire of the high-pressure Stryker culture and look for less stressful jobs with other companies.

Stryker does have some opportunities available to it to help make its growth goals. One opportunity is to use its strong financial position to continue making selected acquisitions to enter new markets, as it did when it entered the trauma business in 1996 with its acquisition of Osteo Holdings; or it can increase its share of existing markets, as it did with its 1998 acquisition of Howmedica. A second opportunity for growth is to add centers to its Physical Therapy Services division. Each center averages $400,000 in revenue per year. A third opportunity would be to place increased emphasis on Stryker Biotech, its corporate research and development laboratory. One of its promising products is Stryker's OP-1 bone growth protein, designed to help with difficult-to-heal fractures and spinal fusions. OP-1 has been under development for several years and is awaiting Food and Drug Administration (FDA) approval.

Stryker has seen many changes as it has grown from a $23 million company when John Brown became CEO to over $2.6 billion in sales today. It will probably see as many more in the next twenty years. However, as long as John Brown is CEO, one aspect of the Stryker culture that isn't likely to change is the expectation that every employee will do his or her best to help earnings increase 20 percent a year, every year.

QUESTIONS

- How much longer can John Brown realistically expect its sales and earnings per share to continue to grow at 20 percent every year now that Stryker's sales are more than $2 billion?
- Should salary be a component of the compensation system for the sales force?
- Should Stryker soften the no nonsense corporate culture it has developed under John Brown?
- Are adequate steps being taken to identify a successor for John Brown when he retires?
- Would a merger with Zimmer be in Stryker's best interests?

REFERENCES

Brewer, Geoffrey. "20 Percent—Or Else!" *Sales and Marketing Management* (November 1994): 67–72.

Purdum, Traci. "Employee Involvement Contributes to Rapid Productivity Gains at Surgical-Tool Maker," *Industry Week* (October 16, 2000): 109–110.

Royal, Weld. "America's Best Plants: Stryker Corporation, Allendale, N.J.," *Industry Week* (October 19, 1998): 72–74.

Willis, Clint. "Super Chiefs: Six CEOs Who Consistently Make Companies Great and Investors Wealthy," *Worth* (September 1997): 60.

BIOMET, INC.—2002[1]

Satish P. Deshpande
Western Michigan University

On September 11, 2001, the world witnessed one perhaps the most devastating attacks ever on the United States. The terrorist attacks in New York and Washington, D.C., delivered a stunning blow to an already deteriorating U.S. economy. Equities lost $1.2 trillion in value in the immediate aftermath of the tragedy. One of the sectors that many investors are looking at as a safe haven to invest their money is the healthcare sector, an industry relatively impervious to a slowing economy.

Biomet, Inc. operates in the musculoskeletal products business segment of the healthcare sector which is a $6.445 billion product market in the United States (see Exhibit 1). The company is a specialty manufacturer, designer, and marketer of orthopedic products, including reconstructive and fixation devices, electrical bone growth stimulators, orthopedic support devices, operating room supplies, general surgical instruments, and arthroscopy products. Biomet has its corporate headquarters in Warsaw, Indiana, and manufacturing facilities in eighteen worldwide locations. The company and its subsidiaries distribute products primarily aimed at musculoskeletal medical specialists who work in the fields of both surgical and nonsurgical therapy in over one hundred countries, and it employs over forty-four hundred people worldwide.

Biomet reported record sales for its fiscal year ending May 31, 2001. For the fiscal year 2001, sales increased 12 percent to $1.03 billion. This includes the impact of foreign currency fluctuations and discontinued products, which reduced sales by $31.4 million and $9.3 million respectively. Net income increased 14 percent to $197.5 million. Revenues reflect the continued market penetration of the reconstructive, fixation, spinal, and other product lines of the company. The fourth quarter of fiscal year 2001 was Biomet's sixteenth consecutive quarter of 15 percent or greater growth in earnings.

Orthopedic implant manufacturers have faced increasing pressure to contain their costs as hospitals seek various ways to limit expensive inventories. Burdensome regulations, expensive product liability, and managed care have led many manufacturers to develop and manufacture their products abroad. On the other hand, the Food and Drug Administration (FDA) has come under increasing public and political pressure to speed up the approvals of drugs and medical devices. In Senate hearings, the FDA has been attacked for failing to provide timely access to new medical technology. Congressional leaders in the past have called for privatization of the governmental agency. The federal government in response has announced a number of steps to ease restrictions. These are positive signals for Biomet.

HISTORY

Biomet, Inc. was incorporated in 1977 in Indiana by Dane A. Miller, Niles L. Noblitt, Jerry Ferguson, and Ray Harroff. Miller is president and chief executive officer of Biomet, and Mr. Noblitt is board chairman. Miller, as well as several other key managers, worked at the Zimmer Division of Bristol-Myers before forming their own company.

The company initially sold orthopedic support products through ten distributors. Biomet entered the reconstructive device market in the early 1980s when it introduced a titanium alloy-based hip system. Biomet further enhanced its reputation with a number of technological advances in hip replacement systems as well as in a total knee replacement. Biomet was founded on the premise that major orthopedic companies, which were primarily divisions of large pharmaceutical companies, had neglected a service orientation approach to orthopedic surgeons' needs. Through a dedication to high levels of service and a variety of innovative products, Biomet has rapidly penetrated the growing market for orthopedic products.

In 1992, Biomet purchased Walter Lorenz Surgical Instruments, Inc. (Lorenz Surgical) for $19 million. Lorenz Surgical, based in Jacksonville, Florida, was a leading marketer of oral-maxillofacial products used by oral surgeons. Its product offerings include orthognathic instruments (used for jaw alignment), craniofacial instruments (used to treat severe skull deformities), rigid fixation systems, TMJ instruments, exodontial instruments, and a transmandibular implant system. These products were principally used to correct deformities, to assist in the repair of trauma fractures, and for cosmetic applications.

In 1994, Biomet purchased Kirschner Medical Corporation of Maryland for $38.9 million ($13.3 million over the fair value). Kirschner, as does Biomet, produced joint replacements for hips, knees, and shoulders, along with fracture fixation products. Kirschner was a market leader in shoulder implants. Kirschner also produced braces, supports, splints, and cast materials. It had four manufacturing plants in the United States and one in Spain. During fiscal year 1996, Kirschner's orthopedic operations were consolidated into Biomet, eliminating duplicative administrative and overhead expenses. During the same period, Biomet Europe was established to coordinate manufacturing, development, and sales activities in Europe. In early 1998, Biomet entered into a joint venture agreement with Merck KgaA, a pharmaceutical and chemical company located in Darmstadt, Germany. Under this agreement, both companies joined their European orthopedic and biomaterials business operations to form Biomet Merck. Biomet also formed an alliance with Selective Genetics, Inc. during the fourth quarter of fiscal year 1999 to develop gene therapy products for the musculoskeletal market.

In late 1999, Biomet acquired Implant Innovation Inc ("3i"), a worldwide leader in the dental reconstructive implant market in a stock-for-stock exchange in which 7.8 million shares were issued for all issued and outstanding shares of 3i. Subsequently in late 2000, Biomet, through its subsidiary EBI, acquired Biolectron, Inc. for $90 million in cash. Biolectron's products are aimed at the spinal fusion, fracture healing, and arthroscopy markets.

Today, 60 percent of the company's business is in reconstructive devices, and almost 75 percent of the company's business is domestic. Biomet consists of six different strategic business units, encompassing over fifteen hundred sales representatives worldwide. They are:

- **Biomet-Warsaw**, which is the principal strategic business unit in the United States. The product line includes a comprehensive line of reconstructive devices and internal fixation devices. Products are sold through a 451-person, distributor-based sales network.

- **Arthrotek**, which is the company's sports medicine division. Arthrotek offers a complete line of arthroscopy products, including resorbable arthroscopic fixation products. These products are primarily distributed through two hundred Biomet/Arthrotek sales outlets representing sixty-four independent distributorships.

- **Electro-Biology, Inc.** (EBI), which is the market leader in the electrical stimulation and external fixation market segments. EBI also offers products in the spinal and orthopedic support market segments. Its products are sold through the division's direct 422-person sales force.

- **Lorenz Surgical**, which is a pioneer in the craniomaxillofacial market segment. The Lorenz product line includes the industry's first resorbable craniomaxillofacial fixation system. Its products are sold through its own distributor network, which encompasses ninety independent sales representatives in the United States.

- **Implant Innovations, Inc.**, which is the second largest manufacturer in the $250 million domestic market and the third largest competitor in the $740 million worldwide market for dental reconstructive implants. Its products in the United States are sold through 52 direct sales representatives. In international markets, 3i distributes its products through approximately 50 direct sales representatives and 24 independent distributors.

- **BioMer C.V.**, which is a 50/50 joint venture between Biomet, Inc. and Merck KGaA, a German chemical and pharmaceutical company. The partnership significantly expands Biomet's presence in the European marketplace while providing the company with worldwide access to key biomaterials technologies. A direct sales force of 396 sales representatives and 56 service agencies throughout Europe sells the joint product lines.

COMPETITORS

Two major changes took place in the orthopedic industry at the end of 1998. In November 1998, Johnson & Johnson acquired DePuy, Inc., and in December 1998, Stryker Corp. acquired Howmedica, Inc. As shown in Exhibit 1, the 2001 musculoskeletal products market in the United States is estimated to be nearly $6.445 billion. Reconstructive devices make up nearly 40 percent of the orthopedic market. Exhibit 2 provides detailed information on the reconstructive market in the United States. This $2.52 billion market segment includes total hip, knee, and shoulder replacements. The hip market is estimated to be $1.08 billion and is growing 10 to 12 percent annually. The $1.34 billion knee market is estimated to be growing at an annual rate of 12 to 14 percent. The shoulder market is estimated around $70 million, with an 8 percent annual growth rate.

According to Exhibit 3, Johnson & Johnson/DePuy and Stryker/Howmedica are the leaders in the reconstructive field, with each controlling around 23 percent of the market. Zimmer is the third-largest and Biomet is the fourth-largest participant, with a share of 14 percent of the market. Growth in the reconstructive market has been attributed to better products and techniques that improve surgical outcomes, cost-effective techniques, and demographics. Recent products last longer and require less surgical time in the operating room, thereby lowering costs. People today are living longer, which accounts for the expanded patient pool. Life expectancies have increased by approximately 5 percent over the past two decades. Male life expectancy has increased to 71 years, while female life expectancy has increased to 78 years. Of the estimated 37 million Americans who suffer from arthritis, approximately 14 million of them (38 percent) are between the ages of 45 and 64. A more active lifestyle, according to Biomet officials, has led to joint replacement at younger ages. Likewise, the pool of people 75 and over is increasing. Clearly, demographics are favorable for Biomet.

The general population growth rate from 1989 to 2010 is projected to be only 14 percent. But the 55–74 year sector is expected to grow 40 percent between 1997 and 2010, an increase of 16 million people. The over-75 population is expected to

EXHIBIT 1   2001 U.S. Musculoskeletal Products Market $6.445 billion
(Biomet estimates in millions)

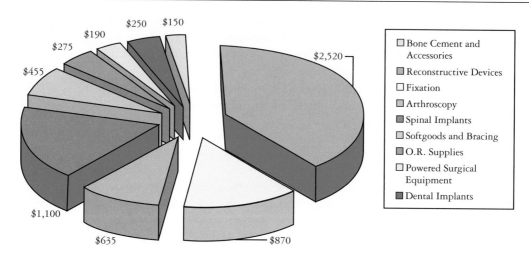

Source: Biomet 2001 *Annual Report.*

grow by 16 percent to 18 million people over the same period. The over 65 population segment accounts for more than two-thirds of total healthcare expenditures. Competition in the implant market is based primarily on service and product design, while competition in the sale of generic internal fixation devices tends to be based more on price. Purchasing decisions for hospitals are being made increasingly through buying groups that are able to negotiate price discounts from the manufacturers.

Two additional factors squeezing profits are (1) the higher utilization of lower-priced implants for the elderly, who require less functionality and longevity of implants; and (2) the fact that surgeons are becoming more cooperative with hospital administrators and are narrowing their choices of products, thereby allowing hospitals to deal with fewer manufacturers.

EXHIBIT 2   2001 U.S. Orthopedic Reconstructive Products Market
$2.52 billion (Biomet estimates in millions)

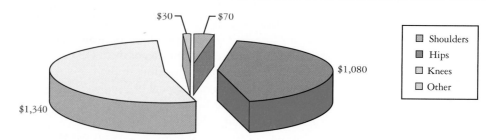

Source: Biomet 2001 *Annual Report.*

EXHIBIT 3   2001 U.S. Reconstructive Device Market Shares $2.52 billion

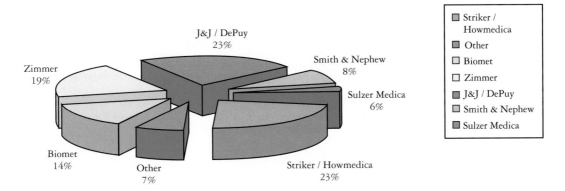

Source: Biomet 2001 *Annual Report.*

PRODUCTS

Biomet's products are divided into four groups: Reconstructive Products, Fixation Products, Spinal Products, and Other Products. Exhibit 4 gives sales by product group for three fiscal years ended May 31: 1999, 2000, and 2001.

Reconstructive Products

Biomet's net sales of reconstructive devices worldwide increased around 6 percent during fiscal year 2001 to more than $614 million. These devices replace joints that have deteriorated either from diseases such as arthritis or through injury. Reconstructive joint surgery involves modification of the area surrounding the affected joint and insertion of one or more manufactured joint components. Biomet's primary reconstructive products concern the hip, knee, and shoulder, although the company can produce peripheral joints for the wrist, elbow, finger, or large toe. A hip prosthesis consists of a femoral head, neck, and stem manufactured in a variety of head sizes, neck lengths, stem lengths, and configurations. Hip sales are expected to increase by 20 percent in the United States and 12 percent worldwide in first quarter of 2002 (fiscal year 2002). The M^2a Taper Metal-on-Metal Articulation System, specially designed for young active patients, continues to experience increased market acceptance in the United States. The minimally invasive Repicci II Unicondylar Knee and the Ascent Total Knee System drive Biomet's market-leading knee performance in the United States. In addition, the AGC Total Knee System was introduced in 1983 and has shown excellent long-term clinical results. The product features left and right femoral components, matching tibial components, and appropriately sized patella components for resurfacing. Biomet's various major knee systems, with their variety of options, are one of the most versatile and comprehensive available in the orthopedic market. Knee sales are expected to increase by 18 percent in the United States and 19 percent worldwide in the first quarter of 2002. Biomet has also a Patient-Matched-Implant (PMI) services group, which designs, manufactures, and delivers one-of-a-kind reconstructive and trauma devices for orthopedic surgeons. The company acquired a patent in 1990 that allows a physician to create, prior to surgery (through the use of CT or MRI data), electronic 3-D models that are then translated into a PMI design for manufacture.

EXHIBIT 4   Biomet's Sales of Reconstructive Devices
Years Ended May 31 (dollar amounts in thousands)

	2001		2000		1999	
	Net Sales	Percent of Net Sales	Net Sales	Percent of Net Sales	Net Sales	Percent of Net Sales
Reconstructive Products	614,308	60%	580,239	63%	521,365	63%
Fixation Products	202,152	20%	180,336	20%	162,825	20%
Spinal Products	91,103	9%	54,119	6%	45,125	5%
Other Products	123,100	12%	108,857	12%	101,520	12%
Total	1,030,663	100%	923,551	100%	830,835	100%

Source: Biomet 2001 *Annual Report.*

Fixation Products

Every year, around 7 million fractures occur in the United States. The 2001 fixation market was estimated to be $870 million, and it is growing at an estimated 7 percent per year. It includes products used to stabilize broken bones and to promote healing. Biomet's net sales in this market increased by around 12 percent to $202 million. EBI is a market leader in both the $140 million external fixation market segment (30 percent of the U.S. market) and the $135 million electrical stimulation market (70 percent of the U.S. market).

External fixation is typically used to immobilize fractured bones when traditional casting is not an option. The company introduced several new products recently, including the OptiROM Elbow Fixator, the Vision System Components, the prepackaged sterile Wristfix Distal Radius Fixator, and deformity clamps for the DynaFix Rail System.

The EBI Model Bone Healing System continues to be a market leader in the domestic electrical simulation market. This product is used on fractured bones that do not heal using normal methods. A coil connected to a battery-operated treatment unit is placed on the fracture. The system produces a pulsating electromagnetic field (PEMF) which affects the cells. Since the system is noninvasive, it poses no surgical risks and has no known side effects. The company introduced a compact version of the system during fiscal year 1998 and a lighter, more patient-friendly model in 2000. The acquisition of Biolectron, Inc. helped EBI broaden and improve its already strong product line.

With a nearly 22 percent share of the U.S. market, the company's Lorenz Surgical subsidiary is a market leader in the $130 million craniomaxillofacial fixation market. The LactoSorb Craniomaxillofacial Fixation System consists of a copolymer comparable in strength to existing titanium systems, but it is completely resorbed within nine to twelve months. This system is especially beneficial for pediatric surgical procedures, since it eliminates the need for a second surgery to remove plates and screws. During fiscal 2001, Lorenz Surgical introduced eight new products and three product enhancements to the resorbable product lines. But Biomet only has a small share of the $390 million internal fixation market.

Until 1995, Biomet held the exclusive right with Orthofix of Italy to distribute the Orthofix External Fixation System (OEFS) in the United States, which is used in trauma situations in which the bone has been fractured or crushed in many places. This system essentially allows the physician to hold in place complicated fractures of long bones when casts, rods, or plates are inappropriate. This exclusive distribution right expired in 1995. In early fiscal 1996, Biomet successfully launched the Dynafix external fixation system. On June 2, 1997, Biomet announced that it would appeal a jury verdict that was entered against it in U.S. District Court for the District of New Jersey in an action brought by Orthofix SRL against EBI and Biomet concerning events related to the expiration of the distribution agreement. The jury found that in spite of Orthofix's refusal to renew the agreement, EBI's development of the Dynafix system prior to the expiration of the contract constituted a breach of the distribution agreement. The jury awarded Orthofix $49 million in compensatory damages and $100 million in punitive damages. The jury also ruled that Orthofix breached the distribution agreement and tortiously interfered with EBI's economic relations. But only nominal damages were awarded to EBI. On June 30, 1999, Biomet announced that the appellate court virtually eliminated $50 million in punitive damages assessed against the company, which thus reduced the judgment to $49.9 million plus interest. Accordingly, Biomet recorded a $55 million special charge against pretax earnings for the quarter and year ended May 31, 1999. In 2000, the company recorded a $9 million charge to reflect the final determination of the interest element of the case.

In 2001, the company took a special charge of $26.1 million due to an appellate court's decision in the Tronzo case. The underlying dispute between Dr. Tronzo and Biomet had to do with a medical device, called an "acetabular cup," that forms the upper portion of a hip implant. Dr. Tronzo alleged that he had established a confidential relationship with Biomet for the purpose of bringing his acetabular cup design to market and that Biomet was to pay him for his invention if he could successfully obtain a patent on his invention. Dr. Tronzo claimed that Biomet failed to compensate him and, instead, took his ideas and incorporated them into its highly successful Mallory/Head cup design.

Spinal Products

The U.S. spinal implant market is estimated to be $1.1 billion (see Exhibit 1). This fastest growing segment of the musculoskeletal products market is growing at least at 20 percent annually. Back injuries cost the society nearly $16 billion every year. Over 2 million spinal procedures were performed worldwide in 2000. Nearly half of the more than three hundred thousand vertebral fusion procedures performed in the United States every year utilize some type of instrumentation. Spinal sales increased 70 percent to $91 million during 2001. This included a 55 percent increase in spinal implant sales and a 90 percent increase in spinal stimulation sales. Currently, EBI is the fourth largest participant, with nearly 9 percent of the spinal implant market in the United States. EBI is a major player in the $155 million electrical segment of the spinal market. It also has a growing presence in the $475 million plates, screws, and rods segment. Its leading product is the SpF Spinal Fusion Stimulation System. This system uses cathodes to deliver small electrical currents to facilitate successful spinal fusions. The Biolectron acquisition provided EBI with the SpinalPak noninvasive simulation system, which offers surgeons a patient-friendly device for noninvasive stimulation.

Other Products

Biomet's "other product" sales during fiscal 2001 were approximately $123 million. This was a 13 percent increase in the United States over the previous fiscal year. This was in great part due to Arthrotek's arthroscopy products, EBI's line of soft goods and bracing products, and the introduction of the CurvTek Bone Tunneling System.

OPERATIONS

Research and Development

Biomet has spent nearly $122 million on research and development from 1999–2001. A number of biomaterials projects are in progress, and they address issues like designing better implants for various applications and bone substitute materials and cements. The company is placing more emphasis on finding ways to help the body heal itself naturally. In addition, its alliance with Selective Genetics, Inc., a gene therapy company, will give it access to its technology for orthopedic indications such as spinal fusions, fracture repair, bone void filling, and tendon and ligament repair. Preclinical studies have been promising.

International Operations

Biomet manages its business segments primarily on a geographic basis. These segments are comprised of the United States, Europe, and the category labeled "Others" (Canada, South America, Mexico, Japan, and the Pacific Rim). Biomet evaluates performance based on the operating income of each geographic unit. Exhibit 5 shows the performance of each segment. The U.S. net sales in Exhibit 5 include U.S. export sales of $37 million in 2001, $50 million in 2000, and $49 million in 1999. The decline in U.S. exports in 2001 has been attributed by the company to its acquisition of foreign distributors and a changeover to direct representation in various countries like Japan and Korea. Net sales to customers in Europe and in the "Others" category in 2001 increased 4 percent to $271 million from the previous level of $261 million in 2000.

Biomet Merck provides Biomet with the exclusive rights to Merck KGaA's current and future biomaterials-based products. Currently, with a local presence in all the major markets, it is the fourth largest orthopedic company in Europe, with 9 percent of Europe's $3.03 billion musculoskeletal market. This is partly due to the successful integration of Biomet's and Merck KGaA's operations. Currently, the joint venture has a revenue of nearly $270 million and 1,360 employees.

Management Philosophy

Biomet prides, itself on having "the responsiveness and innovation of a small company, with the resources and market presence of a large company." In the absence of a formal vision statement, the phrase "The most responsive company in orthopedics" could be seen as an informal vision statement. On its Web site (**www.biomet.com/investors/faq.cfm**), Biomet explicitly states that it has no written mission statement. But the following statement, based on information in its annual report, may act as a mission statement:

> *The Biomet team is committed to the compassionate care of patients throughout the world. We do this by connecting, building, and nurturing long-term relationships with our customers and patients that allows us to deliver technologically advanced quality products with unsurpassed service. We are also committed to ensure that our team members have the best technology, educational tools, resources, and work environment in the industry. We believe that by connecting people, ideas, technology, products, and service, we provide a network that is critical to our patients and customers; and ultimately to the future success of the company.*

Team Biomet

According to CEO Dane Miller, who ranks fourth out of 278 Forbes 500 CEOs in Forbes.com's First Annual Best Value Bosses list (**www.forbes.com/2001/04/26/ceoindex.html**), the major reasons for the success of Biomet are: "(1) We remain close to the market and listen to the needs of our customers, (2) We function as a team to get the job done, and (3) Our team has creative and innovative members in place to succeed." The team concept started at Biomet in 1977 and is today an integral part of the firm's philosophy. One characteristic of the concept is that Biomet has decentralized decision making so that decisions can be made at the appropriate level. Teams are composed of employees from several functional areas (e.g., design, manufacturing, quality, and

EXHIBIT 5   Biomet's Sales by Geographic Area (in thousands)

	2001	2000	1999
NET SALES:			
United States	$ 759,465	$662,146	$597,336
Europe	239,136	236,047	215,913
Other	32,062	25,358	17,586
	$1,030,663	$923,551	$830,835
OPERATING INCOME:			
United States	$ 251,927	$224,385	$159,716
Europe	34,772	34,841	22,910
Other	3,988	4,448	3,276
	$ 290,687	$263,674	$185,902
LONG-LIVED ASSETS:			
United States	$ 204,231	$129,978	$121,363
Europe	109,758	121,350	113,719
Other	17,640	5,635	4,723
	$ 331,629	$256,963	$239,805

Source: Biomet, Inc., *Biomet Inc., and Subsidiaries Notes to Consolidated Financial Statements,* 2001 *Annual Report.*

production planning). Physically, employees are located by functional areas within the facility where routine decisions are handled. Only those decisions related to large commitments of capital expenditures or changes in strategic policies require presidential or vice presidential signatures.

Communications between subsidiaries and departments is frequent and open. Members of management interact with the workers on a daily basis, in addition, there are many corporate events that foster camaraderie. When Dane Miller and his colleagues started the company, his goal was to "create an organization that could grow unencumbered by the bureaucratic structures and conservatism that [we believed] stifle initiative and creativity at many large firms." Although Miller and his colleagues keep an open door for employees, they are constantly on the shop floor talking to employees in their work setting. The team concept is stressed in company brochures and meetings. There are a Biomet Team Appreciation Day and company picnics, Christmas parties, and other special events. The quarterly in-house publication *Bio Briefs* serves as an effective communication tool to keep employees informed of corporate and product information, as well as to recognize special events such as promotions, birthdays, births, anniversaries, and so on.

Biomet's team concept offers every employee financial incentives including cash bonuses, company shares, and stock options. Insiders own approximately 17 percent of the outstanding stock. The team concept also extends to the medical profession. When patients face unusual circumstances, Biomet officials are often called upon to design specialty products. Biomet enjoys a healthy reputation in the medical profession for its "team effort." This concept, first announced in 1989, is reinforced in daily operations. In the absence of a formal organization chart, Exhibit 6 recommends an organizational chart based on titles of the officers of Biomet, Inc., which are reported in the company's Web page.

Financial Information

Consolidated financial information is given in Exhibits 7 and 8.

EXHIBIT 6   Organizational Chart

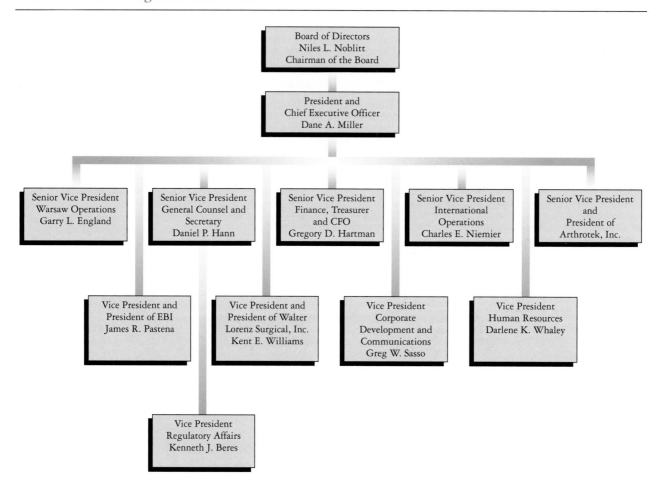

Source: Adapted from Information in Biomet's 2001 *Annual Report.*

FUTURE

Prices of orthopedic devices in the United States in 2002 are expected to be up 5 percent to 6 percent. In addition, Biomet is expected to benefit from Sulzer Medica's legal problems, all of them related to hip replacement recalls. Biomet will have to continue its strategy of finding a niche such as spinal implants and stimulators and then of dominating it. With $463 million in cash and investments, the company is well positioned to make further business acquisitions. On the other hand, Biomet itself could be a target of a pharmaceutical company such as Novartis or American Home Products that wants to get into the musculoskeletal products market. The company has a Shareholders Rights Plan expiring in 2009 that protects it against any hostile takeover. In the international arena, a strong dollar could hurt U.S. exports. In addition, the company has to come up with initiatives to make an impact in the Japanese market.

NOTES

1. The author thanks Tarkesh Veecumsee for research assistance.

EXHIBIT 7   Consolidated Financial Information (in thousands)

ANNUAL INCOME STATEMENT

| | Period Ending May 31, | | | |
	2001	2000	1999	1998
Total Revenue	$1,030,663	$ 920,582	$ 757,414	$651,405
Cost of Revenue	$ 296,063	$ 278,382	$ 229,727	$202,235
Gross Profit	$ 734,600	$ 642,200	$ 527,687	$449,170
Operating Expenses				
Research and Development	$ 43,020	$ 40,208	$ 35,472	$ 36,120
Sales, General and Administration	$ 374,793	$ 326,618	$ 265,565	$232,944
Nonrecurring Items	($26,100)	($11,700)	($55,000)	$ 0
Operating Income	$ 290,687	$ 263,674	$ 171,650	$180,106
Additional income/expense items	$ 24,099	$ 20,211	$ 15,810	$ 24,032
Earnings Before Interest and Tax	$ 314,786	$ 283,885	$ 187,460	$204,138
Interest Expense	$ 4,110	$ 3,193	$ 1,114	$ 341
Earnings Before Tax	$ 310,676	$ 280,692	$ 186,346	$203,797
Income Tax	$ 105,906	$ 99,738	$ 62,527	$ 79,071
Minority Interest	($7,224)	($7,183)	($7,458)	$ 0
Net Income—Continuing Operations	$ 197,546	$ 173,771	$ 116,361	$124,726
Net Income	$ 197,546	$ 173,771	$ 116,361	$124,726
Net Income Applicable to Common Shareholders	$ 197,546	$ 173,771	$ 116,361	$124,726

ANNUAL BALANCE SHEET

| | Period Ending May 31, | | | |
	2001	2000	1999	1998
Total Current Assets	$ 968,379	$ 789,628	$ 681,708	$570,792
Total Assets	$1,489,311	$1,218,448	$1,067,956	$848,739
Total Liabilities	$ 343,125	$ 275,125	$ 292,009	$181,321
Total Equity	$1,146,186	$ 943,323	$ 775,947	$667,418

Source: **www.biomet.com**

EXHIBIT 8   Biomet, Inc. & Subsidiaries Consolidated Balance Sheets
(in thousands, except per-share data)

	At May 31,	
	2001	*2000*
ASSETS		
Current assets:		
Cash and cash equivalents	$ 235,091	$ 213,606
Investments	52,627	34,129
Accounts and notes receivable less allowance for doubtful receivables (2001—$13,420 and 2000—$8,241)	324,848	249,792
Inventories	277,601	240,162
Deferred and refundable income taxes	48,982	25,811
Prepaid expenses and other	29,230	26,128
Total current assets	968,379	789,628
Property, plant, and equipment:		
Land and improvements	13,877	14,572
Buildings and improvements	92,459	88,103
Machinery and equipment	219,554	196,619
	325,890	299,294
Less, accumulated depreciation	140,139	116,037
Property, plant, and equipment, net	185,751	183,257
Investments	175,430	159,533
Intangible assets, net of accumulated amortization (2001—$23,183 and 2000—$20,580)	8,848	9,100
Excess acquisition costs over fair value of acquired net assets, net of accumulated amortization (2001—$32,952 and 2000—$22,869)	134,835	60,654
Other assets	16,068	16,276
Total assets	$1,489,311	$1,218,448
LIABILITIES & SHAREHOLDERS' EQUITY		
Current liabilities:		
Short-term borrowings and current maturities of long-term obligations	$ 62,734	$ 70,546
Accounts payable	21,008	25,612
Accrued income taxes	31,085	17,288
Accrued wages and commissions	33,030	24,224
Accrued litigation	26,100	–
Other accrued expenses	67,865	43,773
Total current liabilities	241,822	181,443
Deferred federal income taxes	5,783	5,386
Other liabilities	423	423
Total liabilities	248,028	187,252
Minority interest	95,097	87,873
Commitments and contingencies		
Shareholders' equity:		
Preferred shares, $100 par value: Authorized 5 shares; none issued	–	–
Common shares, without par value: Authorized 500,000 shares; issued and outstanding 2001–269,124 shares and 2000—266,480 shares	108,918	85,086
Additional paid-in capital	48,732	41,451
Retained earnings	1,044,564	866,011
Accumulated other comprehensive loss	(56,028)	(49,225)
Total shareholders' equity	1,146,186	943,323
Total liabilities and shareholders' equity	$1,489,311	$1,218,448

Source: www.biomet.com

PLAYBOY ENTERPRISES, INC.—2002

Kay Lawrimore-Belanger
Francis Marion University

PLA

www.playboyenterprises.com

Hugh M. Hefner created the first edition of *Playboy* magazine at his family's kitchen table in 1953, launched the magazine with $600 of his own cash, and created an organization which reported $307.7, $347.8, and $241.2 million in revenue in 1999, 2000, and 2001—in a disturbing downward trend. Headquartered in Chicago, Illinois, Playboy Enterprises, Inc. (PEI), (312-751-8000) is an international multimedia entertainment company that publishes editions of *Playboy* magazine around the globe; operates *Playboy* TV and the *Spice* networks; distributes programming via home video and DVD globally; licenses the *Playboy* and *Spice* trademarks internationally for consumer products; and operates Playboy.com. *This is not your father's Playboy!*

Playboy's current mission statement states:

> Playboy *is a preeminent international media and entertainment company with a worldwide recognized brand and many windows of opportunity to expand the* Playboy *franchise and develop other related entertainment franchises globally by leveraging* Playboy's *strengths of publishing, brand management, and marketing.*

COMPANY STRATEGY

Christie Hefner, Playboy's CEO, has consistently described the company's strategy as being one of leveraging the magazine brand into the higher-growth, higher-margin electronic entertainment businesses. In 1998, the CEO announced the goal of having a $1 billion market capitalization by 2003, up from the 1998 $423 million.

MANAGEMENT

In 1971, HMH Publishing Company, Inc. was consolidated under the name Playboy Enterprises, Inc. (PEI) and made its initial public offering at $23.50 per share. Since the beginning, Hugh Hefner has maintained control by holding 70 percent of the voting shares. Christie Hefner, Hugh Hefner's daughter, was named chair of the board and CEO in 1988 at the age of 29. As stated in the September 1999 issue of *Chief Executive*, "Christie didn't have CEO experience when she started, and she tried doing some things that didn't work in terms of bringing in the wrong people and putting people in the wrong places. As she got experience, she also got good at bringing people in who know what they're doing and then letting them alone to do their jobs." Corporate officers included Hugh Hefner as the founder and editor-in-chief; Christie Hefner as the chairman of the board and chief executive officer; Carr as president of the Publishing Group and publisher; English as president of Entertainment Group; Saunders as president of the Casino Gaming Group; Vaickus as president of the Product Marketing Group; and nine others. The executive group officers included the Publishing Group, the Entertainment Group, Playboy Online, the Product Marketing Group, the Casino

Gaming Group, and the Playboy Foundation. None of the approximately 650 employees in its Chicago, New York, and Los Angeles office locations are represented by collective bargaining agreements.

FINANCIAL STATUS

When Playboy Enterprises, Inc. first went public on the New York Stock Exchange in 1971, its stock certificate featured a reclining nude. Some 20,000 people purchased a single share of PEI stock just to get a copy of the certificate. In June 1990, recapitalization created two classes of stock: PLA, the common nonvoting stock, and PLAA, the voting stock. Both are traded on the New York Stock Exchange and the Pacific Stock Exchange. Although the company's certificates no longer feature a nude female, there were 19.4 million PLA shares and 4.9 million PLAA shares outstanding as of December 31, 2000.

PEI's net revenues in 2001 fell to $291.2 million, and the company posted a net loss of $33.5 million, compared with a $47.6 million loss in 2000.

ORGANIZATION

The financial statements in Exhibit 1 for PEI indicate five divisions: Publishing, Entertainment, Playboy Online, Catalog, and Licensing Businesses.

Publishing

The Publishing group includes the publication of *Playboy* magazine, other domestic publishing businesses (including specials, calendars, books, and new media), and the licensing of international editions of *Playboy* magazine. PEI considers *Playboy* magazine to be the "heart and soul" of the company.

The magazine's editorial vitality, diversity, and cultural connection are evident in the fiction, articles, investigative reporting, interviews, celebrity profiles, and entertainment and service features that are monthly staples of the publication. Regular columns on politics, books, movies, music, style, men, women, and relationships reflect contemporary social and cultural issues and further the magazine's ongoing dialogue with its readers. With a paid circulation of about 3.15 million in the United States and about 5 million worldwide, the magazine has maintained its position as the world's leading monthly magazine for men, with a circulation greater than the combined circulations of *Rolling Stone*, *GQ*, and *Esquire*. However, this 3.15 million circulation is about half of what it was in the 1970s. The magazine's revenues were $105 million in the fiscal year ending in June 1997; $105.3 million in June 1996; and $104.4 million in June 1995. The magazine's revenues for the fiscal year ending in December were $106.8 million in 1998, $107.8 million in 1999, and $110.5 million in 2000; and $102.7 million in 2001.

During the 1960s, the magazine relied upon newsstand sales, but now about 70 percent of its total sales are from subscriptions. Direct mail campaigns, online promotions and television advertising campaigns are used to attract new subscribers. The price of a one-year subscription depends on the source of the subscription and the length of time the subscription has been sold. Subscription copies are distributed by second-class mail. Presorting and other methods lower the cost. During October 2001, the online promotion for subscribing was $1 per issue.

EXHIBIT 1   PEI's Results of Operations

	Fiscal Year Ended 12/31/01
Net revenues	
Entertainment	
Domestic TV networks	$ 86.6
International TV	17.0
Worldwide home video	9.6
Movies and other	0.6
Total Entertainment	113.8
Publishing	
Playboy magazine	102.7
Other domestic publishing	15.5
International publishing	9.9
Total Publishing	128.1
Playboy Online	27.5
Catalog	11.0
Licensing Businesses	10.8
Total net revenues	$291.2
Net loss	
Entertainment	
Before programming expense	$ 67.3
Programming expense	(37.4)
Total Entertainment	29.9
Publishing	1.8
Playboy Online	(21.7)
Catalog	(0.4)
Licensing Businesses	2.6
Corporate Administration and Promotion	(19.7)
Total segment income (loss)	(7.5)
Restructuring expenses	(3.8)
Gain (loss) on disposals	(0.9)
Operating income (loss)	(12.2)
Nonoperating income (expense)	
Investment income	0.8
Interest expense	(14.0)
Minority interest	(0.7)
Equity in operations of PTVI and other	(0.7)
Playboy.com registration statement expenses	—
Legal settlement	—
Other, net	(1.5)
Total nonoperating expense	(16.1)
Loss from continuing operations before income taxes and cumulative effect of change in accounting principle	(28.3)
Income tax benefit (expense)	(1.0)
Loss from continuing operations before cumulative effect of change in accounting principle	(29.3)
Gain on disposal of discontinued operations (net of tax)	—
Loss before cumulative effect of change in accounting principle	(29.3)
Cumulative effect of change in accounting principle (net of tax)	(4.2)
Net loss	$ (33.5)

(continued)

EXHIBIT 1	PEI's Results of Operations	(continued)

	Fiscal Year Ended 12/31/01
Basic and diluted income (loss) per common share	
Income (loss) before cumulative effect of change in accounting principle	
From continuing operations	$(1.20)
From discontinued operations (net of tax)	—
Total	(1.20)
Cumulative effect of change in accounting principle (net of tax)	(0.17)
Net loss	$(1.37)

Source: PEI's 2001 *Annual Report,* pp. 15–17.

The number of issues sold in retail outlets varies from month to month, depending on the cover, the pictorials, and the editorial features. As each issue goes on sale, PEI receives a cash advance based on estimated sales. Retail outlets return unsold issues to wholesalers, who shred the returned magazines and report the returns via affidavit. The national distributor settles with PEI based upon the actual number sold compared to the forecasted number. The 1995 sales were affected by the December issue which featured Farrah Fawcett and set a six-year sales record. Fiscal 1997 did not have a blockbuster issue, and sales fell 10 percent. In 1998, the two top-selling issues featured Cindy Crawford and Olympic gold medal figure skater Katarina Witt. Extraordinary sales for the April 1999 issue were due to its feature on Rena Mero, the World Wrestling Federation champion. The November 2000 issue featured World Wrestling Federation star Chyna, and it was the strongest seller in more than ten years. According to *Crain's New York Business,* PEI is considering launching a Spanish-language version of the magazine for the growing Hispanic market in the United States in 2002.

According to Publishers Information Bureau, total magazine ad revenue for the first half of 2001 dropped 2.9 percent, to $8.0 billion. Over the same period, ad pages for all magazines slipped 11 percent, to 121,772. Five of the twelve major ad categories—technology; retail; media and advertising; financial, insurance, and real estate; and automotive are spending less on advertising. Advertising expenditures declined about 40 percent during 2001 in all media platforms. *Mediaweek Magazine Monitor* reported that for the first eight months of 2001, ads for *Playboy* magazine slipped 6.3 percent, to 340 pages, from the prior year. PEI relies on advertising for less than 10 percent of its revenue; hence, it is less affected by the ad decline than most other magazines in the publishing industry.

To attract advertisers, the U.S. version of *Playboy* magazine is published in fifteen advertising editions: eight regional, two state, four metro, and one upper-income zip-coded edition. Advertising pages peaked at 1,434 in 1988 and declined to 660 in 1993, 595 in 1994 and 1995, and 569 in 1996. (In those years, the fiscal year ended in June.) After 1997, the fiscal year ended on December 31, and the advertising pages were 601 in 1998, 640 in 1999, and 674 in 2000. During 2000, for the top three hundred U.S. magazines, ad pages grew 7.9 percent, and there was a 13 percent growth in ad revenue. *Playboy* magazine reported a 13 percent gain in advertising revenue during 2000. The magazine attracted forty-one new advertisers in 2000, including Datek, ESPN, MGM Samsung, Showtime, THQ, and Toshiba. A significant portion of the advertising revenue comes from companies selling tobacco products. In 1996, the U.S. Food and Drug Administration announced a regulation restricting publication of tobacco advertisements. PEI contends that *Playboy* qualifies as an "adult publication" and is therefore exempt from the regulation.

Net advertising revenues of the U.S. edition of *Playboy* magazine for the fiscal year ended June 30 in 1997, 1996, 1995, 1994, and 1993, respectively, were $28.4 million, $27.4 million, $27.6 million, $28.0 million, and $30.4 million. Advertising revenue for the fiscal year ended December 1998, 1999, and 2000, respectively, was $30.8 million, $33.9 million, and $38.4 million.

International Publishing

In partnership with other publishing companies, international editions of *Playboy* are produced worldwide. Overseas editions retain the distinctive style, look, and tone of the U.S. edition, and they include the work of the specific nation's writers and artists. During 2000, PEI published these international editions (dates represent the year *Playboy* was first published for these markets): Brazil (1975), Croatia (1997), Czech Republic (1991), France (1973), Germany (1972), Greece (1985), Hungary (1999), Italy (1972), Japan (1975), The Netherlands (1983), Norway (1997), Poland (1992), Romania (1999), Russia (1995), Slovakia (1997), Spain (1978), and Taiwan (1990). PEI has equity interest in only one country, Poland, in which PEI owns a majority interest. Argentina, Australia, Mexico, South Africa, Sweden, and Turkey had been licensed at one time. The terms of licensing vary but typically are for three or five years, have a guaranteed minimum royalty, and apply a formula for computing additional royalty based upon circulation and advertising revenue. Brazil, Germany, and Japan have typically accounted for 55 percent of the licensing revenues from overseas editions.

Christie Hefner says, "There is no cookie cutter for doing business overseas. In some countries, we've found the best way to get in is with small partners who are entrepreneurial." In Russia, the partner is a woman who established the first functional periodical distribution system in Russia and used the distribution system to start a daily paper, a woman's magazine, and then *Playboy*.

Entertainment—Domestic TV Networks

PEI considers the Entertainment Group to be the company's earnings driver. PEI's growth strategy consists of taking the brand value of *Playboy* and investing in higher-margin, higher-growth electronic businesses. This strategy resulted in an operating loss of $7.3 million in the fiscal year ending June 1995; a profit of $9.2 million in the fiscal year ended in June 1996; a profit of $18.3 million in the fiscal year ending in June 1997; and profits of $26.1 million, $44.37 million, and $25.3 million in the fiscal years ending in December 1998, 1999, and 2000, respectively. PEI's TV network reaches approximately 32 million U.S. and Canadian cable and direct-to-home satellite households. The CEO and chairman of PEI often says that Playboy Enterprises is about being sexy, not primarily about sex. However, the launching of three XXX-edited, digital pay-per-view networks under the *Spice* brand in 2001 and the purchase of three XX-rated pay-per-view video networks for $70 million in July 2001 may indicate that the attitude is shifting to hardcore-porn play.

In 2001, the company acquired the television assets of Califa Entertainment Group, including the explicit Hot Network and the cable-edited adult service, the Hot Zone, for $70 million. Note that investors seemed to like the move because on the day after the announcement, PEI's stock price rose 13 percent to close at $19.75, up $2.25 from the previous close. New Frontier Media, a competitor, rose 3 cents to $2.64. Showtime Event Television reports that the adult pay-per-view market generated about $409 million in 2000, surpassing the $394 million generated by other pay-per-view events.

In 1982, PEI introduced Playboy Television, available only by monthly subscription. The Playboy Networks Worldwide president, Jim English, reported in 2001 that the company had no plans to change the programming or rate card for the networks. PEI is encouraging operators to market a full range of options to consumers: VOD, pay-per-view and subscriptions. In 1999, a twenty-four-hour Spanish-language network was launched within the United States that reaches about 3 million homes on the EchoStar service. Exhibit 2 provides select data concerning cable households.

EXHIBIT 2   PEI's Consolidated Statements of Operations
(in thousands, except per-share amounts)

	Fiscal Year Ended 12/31/01	Fiscal Year Ended 12/31/00	Fiscal Year Ended 12/31/99
Net revenues	291,226	$307,722	$347,817
Costs and expenses			
Cost of sales	(240,691)	(265,369)	(277,448)
Selling and administrative expenses	(58,050)	(55,385)	(56,390)
Restructuring expenses	(3,776)	(3,908)	(1,091)
Gain (loss) on disposals	(955)	(2,924)	1,728
Total costs and expenses	(303,472)	(327,586)	(333,201)
Operating income (loss)	(12,246)	(19,864)	14,616
Nonoperating income (expense)			
Investment income	786	1,519	1,798
Interest expense	(13,970)	(9,148)	(7,977)
Minority interest	(704)	(125)	(92)
Equity in operations of PTVI and other	(746)	(375)	(13,871)
Playboy.com registration statement expenses	—	(1,582)	—
Legal settlement	—	(622)	—
Other, net	(1,447)	(1,202)	(904)
Total nonoperating expense	(16,081)	(11,535)	(21,046)
Loss from continuing operations before income taxes and cumulative effect of change in accounting principle	(28,327)	(31,399)	(6,430)
Income tax benefit (expense)	(996)	(16,227)	862
Loss from continuing operations before cumulative effect of change in accounting principle	(29,323)	(47,626)	(5,568)
Gain on disposal of discontinued operations (net of tax)	—	—	233
Loss before cumulative effect of change in accounting principle	(29,323)	(47,626)	(5,335)
Cumulative effect of change in accounting principle (net of tax)	(4,218)	—	—
Net loss	(33,541)	(47,626)	$ (5,335)
Basic and diluted weighted average number of common shares outstanding	24,411	24,240	22,872
Basic and diluted income (loss) per common share			
Income (loss) before cumulative effect of change in accounting principle			
From continuing operations	(1.20)	$ (1.96)	$ (0.24)
From discontinued operations (net of tax)	—	—	0.01
Total	(1.20)	$ (1.96)	(0.23)
Cumulative effect of change in accounting principle (net of tax)	(0.17)	—	—
Net loss	(1.37)	$ (1.96)	$ (0.23)

Source: PEI's 2001 *Annual Report*, pp. 28–29.

In May 2000, PEI won a major battle when the U.S. Supreme Court struck down a law that enabled cable operators to block signals from sexually explicit channels during the day. Section 505 had prohibited broadcast of adult-oriented networks from 6 A.M. until 10 P.M. daily, unless expensive blocking equipment was installed in cable homes. Christie Hefner estimated that the $5 million annual revenue decline in 1999 was the result of Section 505. The court ruling provides PEI with an opportunity to increase its subscriber base, because more viewers have easier access to the programming.

Digital cable television offers more channels and provides a secure, fully scrambled signal. Christie Hefner estimates that PEI reaches 12 million analong and 4.5 million U.S. cable digital households. During 2001, many operators were slow to accept the ultra-explicit content due to concerns about the community's reaction. AT&T said that the MSO was not interested in the *Spice Platinum* services.

During the fall of 2001, PEI completed a deal with Directrix, Inc. that makes PEI an anchor tenant in Directrix's West Coast Digital Operations and Studio Center for a fifteen-year term. This reduces technical costs and increases capacity to produce original programming.

International TV

In 1995, PEI entered into its first international television programming agreement when it established a joint-venture with Flextech plc to offer *Playboy Television* to the United Kingdom. In 1998, PEI introduced Playboy TV and AdulTVision networks in Spain and Portugal. Playboy TV Latin America was the fastest-growing international network in 1998. In early 1999 Playboy TV-Gmbtt Germany received a license for cable and DTH carriage in Germany. During 2000, PEI programming was available in 26.3 million households in 46 countries and 13 languages.

In 1999 the Entertainment group and the Cisneros Television Group formed Playboy TV International (PTVI). PEI owns 20 percent of PTVI. This joint venture provided a significant amount of capital and a management team that was knowledgeable about the global TV industry. PTVI owns and operates existing *Playboy* and *Spice* networks worldwide, excluding the United States and Canada, and creates additional international networks.

Recognizing that the international markets differ in the restrictions of pornography (for instance, the United Kingdom and Ireland have stricter restrictions than Germany, Portugal, and Russia), PTVI varies its programs within the different countries. In February 2001, PTVI announced that the company and Venevision International, a subsidiary of the Cisneros Group, would coproduce its first Spanish-language erotic telenovela. The plan is to subdistribute the telenovela in Europe, except for Spain and Portugal. During August 2001, PTVI announced the exclusive agreement with film production company Solar Entertainment to launch a network in the Philippines that expands PTVI's presence in the Asian market.

PEI expands its international network by entering into exclusive multiyear multiproduct output agreements with overseas pay television distributors. Licenses differ, but typically PEI receives license fees for programming and for the use of the logo and trademark. PEI has equity agreements with channels in the United Kingdom, Japan, and Latin America. Separate distribution agreements allow for U.S. home video products, with dubbing or subtitling into local languages, to be sold in countries in South America, Europe, Australia, Asia, and Africa. High sales in South Korea contributed to higher revenue and profit contribution.

Worldwide Home Video, Movies, and Other

Following the style, quality, and focus of *Playboy* magazine, Playboy home videos are distributed via video (including Blockbuster Video), music, and other retail stores. In 2000, working with Image Entertainment, Inc., the company also released all 21 new home video titles on DVD, and 16 reached Billboard's top 40 video sales chart. PEI's videos are sold in more than 55 countries and territories. In 1998, the Entertainment Group created Alta Loma Productions to produce programming for broadcast by other networks. About 150 to 200 hours of programming and about 80 movies are produced each year. During the fall of 2001, a deal with Image Entertainment Inc. to distribute DVDs and videos in the United States and Canada was announced.

Playboy Online

Christie Hefner reports that the company's profit centers will shift from print and publishing into the electronic area. With plans to be profitable in 2002, the online division has experienced three years of losses—$6.5 million in 1998, $9.06 million in 1999 and $25.2 million in 2000. The first three quarters of 2001 indicate another year of no profit. Hefner recently stated, "We are working on growing the online business and running it as efficiently as possible. Our strategic focus is to convert more of our visitors to purchasers via Playboy Cyber Club, e-commerce and gaming." The company said that to achieve its goal of converting visitors to subscribers at a faster rate, it is moving more of its content to the pay site, launching a new look for the homepage, and hiring a new head of marketing. PEI recently announced that it had entered into a five-year relationship with ACTV Inc. to support its Web- and TV-based interactive content. Hefner believes that online opportunities offer the same advantage of leveraging as the television business. As fixed costs are spread across a larger consumer base to generate higher revenue, operating margins rise. PEI think that most of the cost structure for the e-commerce business has occurred and that with revenues expected to grow, the e-commerce division will become the most valuable.

The e-division for PEI includes Playboy.com, PlayboyStore.com, CyberSpice.com, Rouze.com, Auctions.Playboy.com, SpiceTV.com, and Cyber Club. PEI's homepages on the World Wide Web provide four sources of revenue: advertising, shopping, subscriptions, and pay-per-view. Playboy.com was launched in 1994 and attracted ten thousand visitors on the first day. In 2001, when it had visitors from 163 countries, it attracted 1,490,000 visitors in January 2001 alone. During 1998, traffic on the site was more than 75 million page-views a month. In September 1999, the traffic on the site increased to 90 million page-views per month. During January 2000, the site had 1,157,000 visitors and in January 2001 it has 1,490,000 visitors. The majority of online visitors are in the 18–34 age group and do not read the magazine.

Cyber Club members (who belong to the online subscription site) pay as much as $60 a year for access to photo archives, chat sessions, and live Webcasts from the Hefner mansion. The number of subscribers increased to 88,500 during the third quarter of 2001. PlayboyStore.com provided the fastest-growing revenue stream in 2000 by offering thirty-one hundred items. The top-selling product categories included apparel, lingerie, jewelry, and collectibles.

During 2001, an Internet gaming division was established. During 2001, PEI joined the $3 billion online gambling industry by partnering with other companies. Christie Hefner said that PEI wants to partner with companies that are leaders and have the expertise in their fields and that also possess a gaming license in a favorable tax environment. With Ladbrokes eGaming Limited, it now has a site that offers a full range of sports wagering, allowing international consumers to bet on U.S. and international sports. With Penn National Gaming Inc., it now has a site that allows online wagering for parimutuel horseracing. Additionally, it has a site that offers a virtual casino, with more than fifty games; and it also has a site that offers free games, including fantasy sports leagues. PEI expects online gaming to account for 5 to 10 perent of the Web site's revenue. Note that News Corp., Viacom/CBS, software giant Microsoft, and the Virgin Group have been exploring ways to enter the e-gaming industry.

In November 2001, PEI announced a two-year licensing agreement to host the Web site with Korea Telecom Hitel Co. Ltd. to publish a Korean edition of *Playboy*. PEI chose Korea for an international Web site because of its Internet-savvy population. Earlier in 2001, the first international site was announced for Germany.

Catalog

PEI's catalog business includes Collector's Choice Music, *Spice* and *Playboy*. PEI's catalog revenues were $75.4 million for the fiscal year ending on June 30, 1997, $71.1 million in 1996, and $61.4 million in 1995. Revenues were $74.4 million for the fiscal year ending in December 1998, $60.3 million in 1999, and $32.4 million in 2000. During 2001, the company was seeking a buyer for Collector's Choice Music.

The Playboy catalog offers fashions and accessories, home videos, gifts, calendars, art products, back issues of the magazine, and newsstand specials. Introduced in 1994, the music catalog Collector's Choice Music features more than 8,000 titles in CD and cassette formats from a wide assortment of music categories: classical, pop, rock, rhythm and blues, jazz, and country. It also offers an extensive library of hard-to-find recordings. The first *Spice* brand-extension effort was introduced in 1999 with a catalog offering more than seventeen hundred video, CD-ROM, and DVD titles.

Product Marketing/Licensing

The consumer products division reported sales of $235 million in 2000. The company considers licensed products to be a key growth area. The name *Playboy* and the rabbit head design are among the most recognized trademarks in the world. The company leverages the power of its brand recognition, design expertise, art collection, and loyal customer base to develop and market apparel, accessories, and other products to consumers worldwide. Merchandise is sold in approximately 2,500 U.S. specialty stores and hundreds of international retail outlets, and it is available online. In total, more than 5,000 Playboy-branded products are sold in approximately 100 countries and territories worldwide. PEI is one of the top-selling fashion brands in China, with more than 400 retail outlets and shops-in-shops.

In 1997, to capture the cigar craze, PEI formed an agreement with a world's top cigar producer, Consolidated Cigar Corporation. The cigar line is sold in restaurants, cigar bars, golf course shops, nightclubs, and wine and liquor stores. Single tubed cigars were introduced in 1998. During 1998, PEI licensed Titan Motorcycle Co. of America to produce 102 motorcycles, licensed Zippo to produce lighters, and licensed Los Angeles-based California Sunshine Activeware, Inc. to produce apparel. In 1999, PEI signed a master license agreement with Mitsui & Company, Ltd. to produce and sell products and establish a freestanding Japanese *Playboy* boutique. A trend-forward fashion licensing program was introduced in the United States during the summer of 1999. In early 2000, a master license was signed with Sario Far East Company to establish a Femlin line in Japan. Early in 2001, the mail order specialist Damart and PEI signed a cross-marketing agreement to attract a younger market. PEI and Cedco Publishing signed a licensing agreement in February 2001 to produce stationery products, content-driven lifestyle books, and calendars. During the summer of 2001, PEI announced a licensing agreement with Twelve-Twenty Productions LLC to create, produce, and market a line of limited-edition fine art prints under the banner "Uniquely Playmates." Between six and nine editions a year are planned to be released. PEI plans to target department stores in the United States (but *not* Sears) and sign a master licensing agreement for Italy or Europe with Fiorucci during 2002. In October 2001, Bally Gaming and Systems entered into a licensing agreement with PEI for a series of interactive casino gaming devices featuring the trademarks, art, and images of the PEI brand. The games are scheduled for release and installation in casinos in 2002.

Products are marketed in North America, Europe, Asia, Australia, and South America, primarily through mass merchants and other retail outlets, by licensees under exclusive license agreements that authorize the manufacture, sale, and distribution of products in a designated territory. Royalties are based on a fixed or variable percentage of the licensee's total new sales, in some cases against a guaranteed minimum. Asia has contributed the majority of the royalties earned from licensing PEI's trademarks.

Other Business: Casinos

The Playboy Casino at Hotel des Roses on the Greek island of Rhodes was opened in the spring of 1999. Christie planned to establish similar partnerships with as many as ten casinos in resorts such as Las Vegas and overseas by 2004. In 2002, the company was still seeking partners.

IMAGE

The popularity of the Playboy name stems from its association with fun, sexiness, and quality. The words *aspiration, adventurous,* and *romantic* are a few of the many characteristics that define the Playboy customer. Overseas, the Playboy logo benefits from its strong identification with Western freedoms, American lifestyle, and a desire for "the good life." However, many investors argue that PEI is involved in peddling pornography and will thus not invest. Christie Hefner replies to the pornography concern with the following statement: "For those people who enjoy reading *Playboy*, there's no dichotomy in the fact the magazine has an erotic component and an intellectual, humorous, and celebrity component; that is the world that we live in." It has been said by industry observers that she agreed to the purchase of the hardcore-porn operation with great reluctance.

PUBLIC AFFAIRS

PEI established the Playboy Foundation in 1965 to provide financial support for organizations that were dedicated to the protection of civil rights and civil liberties, that promoted First Amendment rights and freedom of expression, and also supported research and education on human sexuality and reproductive rights. Since 1965, the foundation has contributed more than $12 million. *Playboy* magazine provides free advertising space to nonprofit groups such as the Nature Conservancy, The National Veterans Legal Services Program, and the Special Olympics. A basic tenet of the Playboy Philosophy is that the First Amendment is the keystone to all other rights. Playboy established the Hugh M. Hefner First Amendment Awards in 1979 to honor individuals who have championed freedom of expression.

EXHIBIT 3   PEI's Consolidated Balance Sheets (in thousands, except share data)

	Dec. 31, 2001	Dec. 31, 2000
ASSETS		
Cash and cash equivalents	$ 4,610	$ 2,534
Marketable securities	3,182	3,443
Receivables, net of allowance for doubtful accounts of $6,406 and $5,994, respectively	41,846	45,075
Receivables from related parties	12,417	7,575
Inventories, net	13,962	20,700
Deferred subscription acquisition costs	12,111	12,514
Other current assets	7,857	9,568
Total current assets	95,985	101,409
Receivables from related parties	50,000	57,500
Property and equipment, net	10,749	11,532
Programming costs	56,213	55,454
Goodwill, net of accumulated amortization of $7,349 and $4,761, respectively	112,338	87,260
Trademarks, net of accumulated amortization of $17,726 and $14,701, respectively	52,185	52,585
Distribution agreements acquired, net of accumulated amortization of $2,199	26,301	—
Other noncurrent assets	22,469	22,748
Total assets	$426,240	$388,488
LIABILITIES		
Financing obligations	$ 8,561	$ 3,922
Financing obligations to related parties	15,000	5,000
Acquisition liability	21,023	—
Accounts payable	19,293	25,295
Accounts payable to related parties	169	718
Accrued salaries, wages and employee benefits	8,717	8,915
Deferred revenues	47,913	41,898
Deferred revenues from related parties	8,382	4,397
Other liabilities and accrued expenses	18,453	16,861
Total current liabilities	147,511	107,006
Financing obligations	73,017	89,328
Financing obligations to related parties	5,000	5,000
Acquisition liability	41,079	—
Deferred revenues from related parties	44,350	50,875
Net deferred tax liabilities	5,313	4,679
Other noncurrent liabilities	28,445	17,415
Total liabilities	344,715	274,303
SHAREHOLDERS' EQUITY		
Common stock, $0.01 par value		
Class A voting – 7,500,000 shares authorized; 4,864,102 and 4,859,102 issued, respectively	49	49
Class B nonvoting – 30,000,000 shares authorized; 19,930,142 and 19,647,048 issued, respectively	199	196
Capital in excess of par value	123,090	120,519
Accumulated deficit	(36,925)	(3,384)
Unearned compensation restricted stock	(3,019)	(2,713)
Accumulated other comprehensive loss	(1,869)	(482)
Total shareholders' equity	81,525	114,185
Total liabilities and shareholders' equity	$426,240	$388,488

Source: PEI's 2001 *Annual Report,* pp. 30–31.

EXHIBIT 4   PEI's Selected Financial Data (in thousands, except per share amounts, number of employees and ad pages)

	Fiscal Year Ended 12/31/01	Fiscal Year Ended 12/31/00
Long-term financing obligations as a percentage of total capitalization	49%	45%
Number of common shares outstanding		
Class A voting	4,864	4,859
Class B nonvoting	19,666	19,407
Number of full-time employees	610	686
Selected operating data		
Playboy magazine ad pages	618	674
Cash investments in Company-produced and licensed entertainment programming	$37,254	$33,061
Amortization of investments in Company-produced and licensed entertainment programming	$37,395	$33,253
Playboy TV networks household units (at period end)		
DTH	18,100	15,400
Cable digital	10,300	3,200
Cable analog addressable	7,800	11,000
Movie networks household units (at period end)		
DTH	35,300	–
Cable digital	25,300	8,400
Cable analog addressable	17,000	16,200

Source: PEI's 2001 *Annual Report,* p. 15.

EXHIBIT 5   PEI's Networks Available to Household Units (in millions)

Revenues from domestic TV networks for 2001 increased $12.2 million, or 16%, and profit contribution increased $9.8 million. These increases were primarily due to the Califa acquisition described above and an increase in Playboy TV revenues.

	Dec. 31, 2001	Dec. 31, 2000
Playboy TV (1)		
DTH	18.1	15.4
Cable digital	10.3	3.2
Cable analog addressable	7.8	11.0
Movie Networks (1) (2)		
DTH	35.3	–
Cable digital	25.3	8.4
Cable analog addressable	17.0	16.2

(1) Each household unit is defined as one household carrying one given network per carriage platform. A single household can represent multiple household units if two or more of the Company's networks and/or multiple platforms (i.e., analog and digital) are available to that household.
(2) Includes additional networks in connection with the Califa acquisition in July 2001.
Source: PEI's 2001 *Annual Report,* p. 18.

EXHIBIT 6   PEI's Financial Information by Reportable Segment (in thousands)

	Fiscal Year Ended 12/31/01	*Fiscal Year Ended 12/31/00*
Net revenues (1)		
Entertainment	$113,833	$100,955
Publishing	128,139	139,870
Playboy Online	27,499	25,291
Catalog	10,986	32,360
Licensing Businesses	10,769	9,246
Total	**$291,226**	**$307,722**
Loss from continuing operations before income taxes and cumulative effect of change in accounting principle		
Entertainment	$29,921	$25,287
Publishing	1,776	6,881
Playboy Online	(21,673)	(25,199)
Catalog	(453)	54
Licensing Businesses	2,614	887
Corporate Administration and Promotion	(19,700)	(20,942)
Restructuring expenses	(3,776)	(3,908)
Gain (loss) on disposals	(955)	(2,924)
Investment income	786	1,519
Interest expense	(13,970)	(9,148)
Minority interest	(704)	(125)
Equity in operations of PTVI and other	(746)	(375)
Playboy.com registration statement expenses	–	(1,582)
Legal settlement	–	(622)
Other, net	(1,447)	(1,202)
Total	**$ (28,327)**	**$(31,399)**
EBITDA		
Entertainment	$ 75,506	$ 64,307
Publishing	2,336	7,498
Playboy Online	(19,693)	(23,497)
Catalog	(427)	180
Licensing Businesses	2,823	1,084
Corporate Administration and Promotion	(16,616)	(18,865)
Restructuring expenses	(3,776)	(3,908)
Gain (loss) on disposals	(955)	(2,924)
Total	**$ 39,198**	**$ 23,875**
Depreciation and amortization		
Entertainment	$ 45,585	$ 39,020
Publishing	560	617
Playboy Online	1,980	1,702
Catalog	26	126
Licensing Businesses	209	197
Corporate Administration and Promotion	3,544	3,249
Total	**$ 51,904**	**$ 44,911**

(continued)

EXHIBIT 6   PEI's Financial Information by Reportable Segment
(in thousands)   (continued)

	Fiscal Year Ended 12/31/01	Fiscal Year Ended 12/31/00
Identifiable assets		
Entertainment	$ 317,848	$ 267,142
Publishing	49,219	56,191
Playboy Online	4,463	7,675
Catalog	1,244	3,797
Licensing Businesses	4,732	5,003
Corporate Administration and Promotion	48,734	48,680
Total	$ 426,240	$ 388,488

(1) Net revenues include revenues attributable to foreign countries of approximately $48,522, $50,165, and $71,495 in 2001, 2000, and 1999, respectively. Revenues from individual foreign countries were not material. Revenues are generally attributed to countries based on the location of customers, except product licensing royalties where revenues are attributed based upon the location of licensees. In 1999, revenues from PTVI exceeded 10% of the Company's total net revenues. See Note (C) Playboy TV International, LIC Joint Venture.
Source: PEI's 2001 *Annual Report*, pp. 51–52.

CONCLUSION

Consider the following:

- Which of PEI's divisions should receive the greatest emphasis and resources?
- How can PEI improves its corporate image among critics who contend that its business is obscene, pornographic, and unethical?
- Should PEI continue its international expansion? If yes, which new countries should be targeted?
- Should PEI make a major acquisition in the near future to begin publishing other magazines, such as *Cosmopolitan*, *Woman's Day*, *Ladies' Home Journal*, *Gentlemen's Quarterly*, or *Esquire?*
- Should PEI continue its e-commerce expansion? If yes, develop a strategy for expansion.
- How much is the company worth today?
- Develop a three-year strategic plan for PEI.

THE READER'S DIGEST ASSOCIATION, INC.—2002

Robert Shane
Francis Marion University

RDA, RDB, RDT

www.readersdigest.com

Who has the largest single subscription magazine on the planet? Reader's Digest! Respected for its editorial creativity and direct marketing expertise, Reader's Digest Association (RDA) is heralded as the global leader in magazine publishing, direct marketing, books, recorded music collections, and home videos. The editorial mission is concentrated in the areas "home, family, health, finance and faith," the areas that "inform, enrich, entertain and inspire" customers. The flagship *Reader's Digest* magazine is published in 48 editions and 19 languages and reaches more than 100 million readers each month in virtually every area of the globe. The company's global operations include the publication of special interest magazines, do-it-yourself books, and home entertainment audio and video products. Likewise, the company actively uses the Internet, strategic alliances, and its global data centers to implement its product offerings. This vast distribution network generated revenues of $2,518 million in fiscal year 2001, an increase from $2,485 million in fiscal year 2000 and $2,459 million in 1999. Net income for 2001 was $132.1 million, a decrease from 2000's $144.7 million and 1999's $151.9 million.

Since 1998, Reader's Digest has been implementing a strategic plan to reverse previously declining revenues. These strategies have included:

- Expanding its presence in five areas of intense consumer interest—health, home, family, finance, and faith.
- Selling nonpublishing products and services in those areas.
- Continued geographic expansion.
- Developing new marketing channels.
- Broadening the customer base to include younger customers.
- Producing more products for older customers, focusing on the growing 50+ age demographic.
- Integrating the Internet into all of its businesses.

These strategic plans have resulted in an expanded international presence, increased numbers of strategic alliances, and a corporate realignment of operating segments.

HISTORY

In 1922, DeWitt and Lila Wallace published the first five thousand copies of *Reader's Digest* from their Greenwich Village apartment. These copies were sold exclusively by mail for 25 cents. The first publication contained thirty-one carefully selected articles, including "The Future of Poison Gas," "Wanted: Motives for Motherhood," and "Advice from a President's Physician." Today, substantial portions of the selections in *Reader's*

Digest are original articles written by staff writers or freelance writers. The remaining articles are selected from existing published sources.

In 1929, *Reader's Digest* appeared on newsstands for the first time, and despite the Depression, sixty-two thousand copies were sold. Six years later, circulation passed the 1 million mark. In 1938, the magazine published its first international edition in the United Kingdom. Since that time, magazine publication has expanded to other countries and areas, including Latin America, Sweden, Australia, Belgium, Canada, Denmark, Finland, France, Germany, Italy, Norway, South Africa, and Switzerland.

In the 1950s, Reader's Digest launched its *Condensed Books* series, today known as *Select Editions,* in the United States and Canada. This series of books consists of previously published works which are pared down into a "condensed" version for quicker reading. During this period of the company's development, paid advertising would also appear for the first time in the magazines. In 1958, the company purchased its first computer. Today, it operates two Global Data Centers and has expanded its use of the Internet.

In the 1960s, Reader's Digest revolutionized direct marketing by introducing its easy-to-enter sweepstakes. The Quality School Program (QSP) was founded and is one of the largest fundraising organizations of its kind. This organization helps over twenty five thousand schools and youth groups in the United States and Canada. The company also has an alliance with The World's Finest Chocolate company, which has been combined with QSP to expand this program by combining the like operations.

DeWitt Wallace died in 1981 at the age of 91, and three years later, Lila Wallace, his wife and the other co-founder of *Reader's Digest,* died at the age of 94. Several years later, Reader's Digest entered the video business with *Why We Fight.* The company also acquired its first special interest magazine. Today's magazine lineup includes *The Family Handyman, American Woodworker, New Choices: Living Even Better After 50, Moneywise, Walking,* and *Benchmark*. In 1988, *Household Hints and Handy Tips* sold more than 1.2 million copies within thirty days in the United States.

Reader's Digest stock was first publicly traded on the New York Stock Exchange as RDA, a nonvoting stock in 1990; RDB was listed in 1992 as a voting stock. The fortieth international edition was launched in Russia and increased the publication to sixteen languages. The Reader's Digest Video, *Great National Parks, II,* won the first of five Emmy Awards. A direct response television commercial was launched for *The Family Handyman's Helpful Hints*. One hundred twenty-five thousand paid orders were received as a result of the advertisement. In 1996, Reader's Digest established a Web site; a Thai edition was published; and later, Australia, Hong Kong, India, Korea, Malaysia, New Zealand, the Philippines, Singapore, and Taiwan editions were launched.

In 1998, Thomas O. Ryder was appointed chairman and chief executive officer, and he "initiated a four-phase strategy, including global reengineering and growth initiatives to build on [the company's] fundamental strengths and create long-term opportunities." During this time, a public hybrid equity offering of 11.8 million shares of Trust Automatic Common Exchange Securities was completed. This offering enabled six charitable organizations to combine a portion of their Reader' Digest Class A nonvoting common stock. The new issues trade under the ticker symbol RDT. The U.S. Postal Service honored DeWitt and Lila Wallace for their philanthropic and cultural contributions with a postage stamp as part of the Great American series. In 1999, the company acquired Books Are Fun, Ltd., a leading display marketer of books and gifts. In 2000 and 2001, Reader's Digest continued the strategic plan cited earlier.

INTERNAL ISSUES

The world economy had been in decline since early 2001. However, most of the company's strategic planning goals had been surpassed. *Reader's Digest* magazine is published in 48 distinct editions and 19 languages. The company has more than 30 Web sites worldwide. Computerized technology has enabled the company to maintain a list of prospective customers. This list consists of over 57 million households and has been recognized as one of the largest direct response lists in the United States.

Reader's Digest has formed alliances to leverage the Internet business with WebMD for health advice, Merk-MedCo for online discount prescription services, and Vanguard for investment services. Elizabeth G. Chambers, who heads Reader's Digest's business development efforts, said, "This alliance is an important part of a corporate growth strategy to leverage our brand, direct marketing expertise, and consumer databases to bring high quality financial services to customers around the world."[1] The company's other alliances in the United States include arrangements with GE Capital Assurance, Torchmark Corporation, Pethealth Inc., Physicians Mutual Insurance Company, and First USA. Internationally, the growing partner list includes AIG, AXA, GE Sovac, ING, Manulife Financial, and SCI International.

Organizational Structure

In the fourth quarter of 2001, the company began reporting financial information under a new structure to reflect new segment operations. The four segments are North American Books and Home Entertainment (BHE), U.S. magazines, International Businesses, and New Business Development. Exhibit 1 reflects a proposed organizational chart for this structure.

Mission Statement

Reader's Digest does not have a prescribed mission statement. However, the company's fundamental values are outlined in its written Code of Conduct. This code serves as a guide to the employees of Reader's Digest, who are quite diverse. The code addresses business ethics, employee relations, and environmental protection. A proposed mission statement for Reader's Digest might state:

> *Reader's Digest is a global leader in the publishing industry. We publish magazines, books, home entertainment products and provide various product offerings through our strategic partners to inform, enrich, inspire, and entertain people of all ages and cultures. We are dedicated to the success of* Reader's Digest *as a worldwide competitor and operate under a strong code of ethics. Our philosophy is to produce a quality product at a fair price. We are making and will continue to make significant investments*

EXHIBIT 1   Proposed Organizational Chart

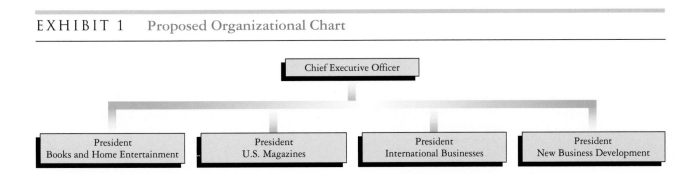

in management information systems and the Internet in order to improve our operating efficiencies and increase the level of customer services. We have established quality relationships and believe that our name, image, and reputation provide us a significant competitive advantage. We are committed to contributing to the economic strengths of the countries in which we conduct business. We will continue our efforts of recruiting, developing, rewarding, and retaining personnel who are dedicated and highly skilled professionals.

Operating Segments

During the fourth quarter of fiscal 2001, reporting segments began to reflect a new internal management organization. These segments include North American Books and Home Entertainment, U.S. Magazines, International Businesses, and New Business Development. A summary of operating segment results is provided in Exhibit 2.

North American Books and Home Entertainment

North American Books and Home Entertainment products consist of *Reader's Digest Select Editions*, series books, general books, recorded music collections and series, home video products and series, and Reader's Digest Young Families and Reader's Digest Children's Publishing products. These products are mostly sold by direct mail. Books and gifts are also sold through the Books Are Fun subsidiary. These products are displayed at schools and businesses. RDA has a direct marketing policy that allows a customer to return any book or home entertainment product for a refund, either before or after payment. Sales of Books and Home Entertainment products are seasonal, with most occurring in the fall and winter, especially during the Christmas season. The books in the category Digest Select Editions, formerly known as "Condensed Books," consist of a series of condensed versions of current popular fiction. Select

---

EXHIBIT 2   Summary of Operating Segment Results

	Years ended June 30,		
	2001	*2000*	*1999*
Revenues			
North American Books and Home Entertainment	$ 719	$ 704	$ 584
U.S. Magazines	652	580	603
International Businesses	1,093	1,146	1,239
New Business Development	54	55	33
Total revenues	$2,518	$2,485	$2,459
Operating profit (loss)			
North American Books and Home Entertainment	$ 71	$ 90	$ 39
U.S. Magazines	77	89	105
International Businesses	116	118	28
New Business Development	(17)	(40)	(5)
Segment operating profit	247	257	167
Other operating items	(18)	(3)	(38)
Total operating profit	$ 229	$ 254	$ 129

Editions books are published in 15 languages and are marketed in the United States, Canada, and 28 other countries. Up to six volumes are printed in the United States and Canada each a year, while some versions are published in four or five volumes a year. Select Editions generated revenues for North American Books and Home Entertainment of $97.7 million in fiscal 2001, $102.5 million in fiscal 2000, and $99.6 million in fiscal 1999.

Two types of series books are published—reading series and illustrated series. The reading series books are printed in four languages and are marketed in the United States, Canada, and nine other countries. These series include The World's Best Reading selections, which consists of full-length editions of classic works of literature. The illustrated series are printed in eight languages and are marketed in the United States, Canada, and 14 other countries. Series books generated revenues for North American Books and Home Entertainment of $30.1 million in fiscal 2001, $28.8 million in fiscal 2000, and $29.2 million in fiscal 1999.

The General Books category consists primarily of reference books, cookbooks, how-to and do-it-yourself books, and children's books. Books handle subjects such as history, travel, religion, health, nature, and the home, and they are published in 19 languages and marketed in the United States, Canada, and 35 other countries. General books generated revenues for North American Books and Home Entertainment of $85.4 million in fiscal 2001, $103.7 million in fiscal 2000, and $148.2 million in fiscal 1999. Most copies of a general book are sold through initial bulk promotional mailings, but they are also sold through subsequent promotions, through catalog sales, and through sales inserts in mailings for other Reader's Digest products. General books are also distributed for retail sale in stores through independent distributors.

Reader's Digest music collections are sold on compact disks and cassettes in the United States, Canada, and 29 other countries. Music includes various styles, such as classical, pop, jazz, and local folk. Approximately 20,000 selections are available. These products are also licensed to third parties for retail sales or for movie synchronization. The company is a member of the Recording Industry Association of America in the United States, and it has received 51 gold, platinum, and multiplatinum certificates. In several other countries, the company is a member of the International Federation of the Phonographic Industry. Music products generated revenues for North American Books and Home Entertainment of $79.9 million in fiscal 2001, $80.4 million in fiscal 2000, and $105.2 million in fiscal 1999.

Video products are marketed through direct response channels in the United States, Canada, and 22 other countries. In some countries, they are also sold through retail outlets. Several original programs have won awards of excellence, including five Emmy awards and, in 2001, four Crystal Awards of Excellence and a Cine Golden Eagle Award. Reader's Digest entered into a multiyear agreement with CBS Productions to develop television movies and miniseries based on the personal dramas chronicled in Reader's Digest; four scripts are currently in production. Strategic initiatives include growth into Latin America and Eastern Europe. Home video products generated revenues for North American Books and Home Entertainment of $56.1 million in fiscal 2001, $77.5 million in fiscal 2000, and $96.6 million in fiscal 1999.

Additional products are offered through Books Are Fun, Ltd., a wholly owned subsidiary which sells premium-quality books and gift items at discount prices by display marketing those products on-site at schools and businesses in all 50 states of the United States and Canada using book fairs and similar displays. Book categories include best-selling novels, cookbooks, children's books, education, sports, hobby, nature, travel, and self-help titles. Nonbook categories include music, videos, and gift items, such as jewelry and art. Reader's Digest Young Families subsidiary sells products, primarily in the United States, for children up to age eight and primarily through direct mail and telemarketing. Products include interactive books, such as *Sesame Street ABCs* and *Elmo's Neighborhood,* and videos, such as *The Country Mouse* and *The City Mouse.* The Children's Publishing subsidiary produces books, games, and other products for children up to age twelve for retail sale as well as through direct marketing through *Reader's Digest* (mail, telemarketing, display marketing, company catalogs, etc.) and the Internet. Products include Barbie, Disney (Winnie the Pooh and classic Disney characters), Hasbro (Tonka and Play-Doh), and Fisher-Price (Little People), and they have been translated into 28 languages and are marketed in the United States, Canada, Europe, South America, Australia, and Asia.

Total revenues for North American Books and Home Entertainment increased 2 percent in 2001 to $719 million, compared with $704 million in 2000 and $584 million in 1999. Operating profits for North American Books and Home Entertainment decreased 21 percent in 2001 to $71 million, compared with $90 million in 2000 and $39 million in 1999.

U.S. Magazines

The U.S. Magazines group publishes and markets, primarily through direct marketing, *Reader's Digest* magazine and several special interest magazines in the United States. In addition, U.S. Magazines sells its magazines and other magazines and products through youth fundraising campaigns of QSP, Inc. *Reader's Digest* magazine is sold in the United States and Canada and in 45 editions and 19 languages outside the United States and Canada. The U.S.-English edition of *Reader's Digest* has the largest paid circulation of any U.S. magazine, other than those automatically distributed to all members of the American Association of Retired Persons. This is based upon an audit report issued by the Audit Bureau of Circulation, Inc. *Reader's Digest* editions in the United States include an English-language edition and a Spanish-language edition entitled *Selecciones*. Large print and braille editions are available for the sight impaired and the blind.

Approximately 69 percent of total U.S. fiscal 2001 revenues for *Reader's Digest* were generated by circulation revenues and 31 percent by advertising revenues. Approximately 66 percent of total U.S. fiscal 2001 revenues for the special interest magazines were generated by circulation revenues and 34 percent by advertising revenues. Approximately 95 percent of the U.S. paid circulation of *Reader's Digest* consists of subscriptions. The balance consists of single-copy sales. Special interest magazines are sold by subscription and at newsstands. Independent contractors are licensed to publish *Reader's Digest* in India, Italy, Korea, South Africa, and Turkey, thus creating a broad global presence. These magazines are sold primarily through direct marketing. Independent contractors publish each edition in the United States.

Reader's Digest publishes several special interest magazines: *The Family Handyman, New Choices: The Magazine for Your Health, Money and Travel*™, and *American Woodworker*. Reader's Digest ceased publication of *Walking* magazine after the September/October 2001 issue. Other magazines include *Moneywise*, a magazine devoted to helping families manage their finances, in the United Kingdom; *Receptar,* a leading Czech do-it-yourself and gardening monthly magazine, and *Krizovky,* a Czech entertainment puzzle magazine. Special interest magazines are promoted in *Reader's Digest* through foreign contractor customer lists. Exhibit 3 shows circulation and advertising information for magazines for fiscal 2001 and 2000.

EXHIBIT 3   Summary of Circulation Rate Bases and Advertising for Reader's Digest

Magazine Title	Circulation Rate Base		# of Advertising Pages Carried	
	2001	2000	2001	2000
Reader's Digest—U.S.: English edition	12,500,000	12,500,000	1,155	1,131
Reader's Digest—Canada: English and French	1,255,300	Note 1	1,651	Note 1
Reader's Digest—Other: international	9,415,757	11,225,633	9,103	12,460
Reader's Digest Large Edition for Easier Reading	500,000	463,000	169	153
American Woodworker	325,000	325,000	397	324
The Family Handyman	1,100,000	1,100,000	599	131
New Choices: The Magazine for Your Health, Money and Travel™	600,000	600,000	431	494
Selecciones	250,000	210,000	262	247
Walking	650,000	650,000	388	435
Moneywise	97,182	104,000	760	712
Receptar	97,182	Note 1	30	Note 1
Krizovky	50,000	Note 1	289	Note 1

Note 1—Not specifically reported for 2000.
Source: Information obtained from Reader's Digest 2001 and 2000, 10K Report filings.

Reader's Digest and the special interest magazines are also sold in the United States and Canada through Quality Service Programs (QSP) and QSP, Inc., respectively. QSP helps schools and youth groups prepare fundraising campaigns in which magazine subscriptions, music and video products, books, and food and gifts are sold. QSP derives its revenues from the sale of products through fundraising organizations. World's Finest Chocolate, Inc. (a company and a product) is also offered through QSP via a long-term licensing agreement. In March 2000, QSP entered into an alliance agreement with Schoolpop, Inc., an online fundraiser that enables online shoppers to contribute funds to schools. Revenues for QSP products increased 53 percent in 2001, compared with the prior year, primarily due to higher sales of food and gift items from the integration of the products and sales force of World's Finest Chocolate. In June 2001, Quality Service Programs acquired **eFundraising.com**, which uses the Internet to enhance fundraising activities. The company **eFundraising.com** uses proprietary software that enables students to send e-mail messages about their schools or youth groups' fundraising activities to family and friends. The e-mail directs the recipients to the school or youth group's Web site, where they may purchase magazine subscriptions and a variety of gift and food products.

The Web site, **rd.com**, and some thirty other sites tie the company and its strategic partners to the Internet. Web sites offer various formats, such as audio, graphic, text and video enhancements, interactive discussions and reader involvement, and additional content relating to *Reader's Digest*.

Total revenues for U.S. Magazines increased 12 percent in 2001 to $652 million, compared with $580 million in 2000 and $603 million in 1999. The operating profit for U.S. Magazines declined 14 percent in 2001 to $77 million, compared with $89 million in 2000 and $105 million in 1999, with the majority of the operating profit continuing to be provided by QSP. Declining revenues and profits have been attributed to the increased testing of new subscription sources, the planned reductions in subscription rate bases, the higher costs associated with the fulfillment of a major outsourcing project, and the lower profits for the special interest magazines due to industrywide softness in certain advertising sectors particular to these magazines.

International Businesses

International Businesses operates outside of the United States and Canada (see Exhibit 4). Many of the products discussed in the other two operating segments are marketed and sold globally. Product offerings are adjusted to reflect the specific languages, cultures, and beliefs.

Many international editions of *Reader's Digest* have the largest paid circulation for monthly magazines both in the individual countries and in the regions in which they are published. For most international editions of *Reader's Digest,* subscriptions comprise almost 90 percent of the circulation. The balance is attributable to newsstand and other retail sales. Approximately 83 percent of total international fiscal 2001 revenues for *Reader's Digest* were generated by circulation revenues and 17 percent by advertising revenues. Revenues for the five International Businesses segments Select Editions, Series Books, General Books, Music Products, and Home Videos are as follows:

- Select Editions—$161.0 million in 2001, $163.5 million in 2000, and $154.4 million in 1999
- Series Books—$96.8 million in 2001, $92.7 million in 2000, and $96.3 million in 1999
- General Books—$330.8 million in 2001, $340.3 million in 2000, and $359.2 million in 1999
- Music Products—$186.4 million in 2001, $197.1 million in 2000, and $240.4 million in 1999
- Home Video Products—$79.5 million in 2001, $81.4 million in 2000, and $96.4 million in 1999

Total revenues for International Businesses segment declined 5 percent in 2001 to $1,093 million, compared with $1,146 million in 2000 and $1,239 million in 1999. However, excluding the adverse effect of foreign currency translation, revenues actually increased 4 percent in 2001. Operating profit for International Businesses declined 2 percent in 2001 to $116 million, compared with $118 million in 2000 and $28 million in 1999. Excluding the adverse effect of foreign currency translation, operating profit increased 14 percent in 2001. This segment generated approximately 43 percent of 2001 revenues and 47 percent of the operating profits.

EXHIBIT 4   Global Subsidiaries of the International Business

Argentina	Hong Kong
Australia	Japan
Austria	Mexico
Belgium	Netherlands
Brazil	New Zealand
Chile	Norway
Colombia	Peru
Czech Republic	Philippines
Denmark	Poland
England	Portugal
Finland	Russia
France	Spain
Germany	Sweden
Hungary	Switzerland
Italy	Thailand

New Business Development

New Business Development has been formed with several leading insurance companies to offer insurance products to customers globally. Partners include American International Group, Inc., Torchmark Corporation, GE Capital Assurance Company, Physicians Mutual Insurance Company, Pethealth Inc., Allianz, AXA, ING Direct, and Manulife Financial. These products include life, health, homeowners, long-term care, and pet insurance as well as hospital indemnity products. They are marketed and sold through a combination of direct mail, telemarketing, advertising in magazines, the Internet, and other marketing channels. The insurer underwrites and administers the products, provides customers and claims services, and covers marketing costs. Reader's Digest provides expertise in research and test design, database management and targeting, and promotion creation and production. Credit Products include an agreement with First USA, a subsidiary of Bank One Corporation, to market a Reader's Digest-branded credit card to customers in the United States. Under the agreement, First USA launched a Reader's Digest Platinum MasterCard in April 2000. First USA administers the credit cards. GE Capital Assurance Company and its subsidiaries market loan products internationally in France and Germany and with the Bank of Scotland in the United Kingdom. In June 2001, an alliance was formed with The Vanguard Group under which Vanguard will offer its mutual funds and other financial services, such as brokerage, financial planning, asset management, and trust services, to customers in the United States.

Other new international business developments include the publication of *Moneywise* magazine, the **Moneywise.co.uk** Web site, and Benchmark, Ltd., a publisher of quarterly investment guides distributed in Hong Kong, Taiwan, and Singapore in English and Chinese. Benchmark publishes twelve issues per year, with a fiscal 2001 annual circulation of approximately 20,000, and it operates the Web site **asiafunds.com**.

Health-services marketing involves an alliance with Twinlab Corporation, a leading U.S.-based vitamin manufacturer and marketer, to market vitamins, minerals, and supplements to *Reader's Digest* customers in the United States and Europe. Products are marketed principally through direct mail, through advertising in *Reader's Digest* and on both companies' Web sites. Twinlab is responsible for manufacturing and fulfilling the products. The arrangement includes both revenue and cost sharing. Similar alliances exist with Vitahealth in Canada. Several vitamin catalogs are also promoted in Germany. These businesses are managed by North American Books and Home Entertainment, and their results are reported in that segment. Likewise, an agreement with McMurry Publishing, Inc., a leading independent custom publisher in the health category in the United States, delivers custom publishing services to clients in North America. Several experimental pilot programs are being tested, such as the Books Are Fun efforts in Mexico and France, a QSP pilot in the United Kingdom, a test of an Australian version of *The Family Handyman*, and the testing of Reader's Digest Young Families products in several international markets. More financial information is provided in Exhibits 4 and 5.

Gifts.com, Inc. is a subsidiary of the Good Catalog Company division, a catalog marketer of home, garden, and gift-related products, and the **Gifts.com** division, an online and catalog gift shopping service. Reader's Digest owns an 80.1 percent interest in Gifts.com, Inc., and Domain.com, Inc., an affiliate of StarTek, Inc., owns a 19.9 percent interest. The **Gifts.com** Web site and catalogs feature over 500 different products. Good Catalog Company offers over 2,000 different products through five different catalog titles, which have a total circulation of over 15 million, and through its Web site, **goodcatalog.com**. Merchandise ranges from home furnishing and decorative accents to garden, health, fitness, sports, and electronic goods, as well as children's toys, games, and crafts.

EXHIBIT 5   Reader's Digest Association, Inc. Income Statement
(in millions except per-share data)

| | Year ending June 30, | | |
	2001	*2000*	*1999*
Revenues	$2,518.2	$2,484.5	$2458.5
Product, distribution, and editorial expenses	(971.2)	(907.1)	(962.6)
Promotional, marketing, and administrative expenses	(1299.6)	(1320.2)	(1328.9)
Other operating items	(18.4)	(3.4)	(37.9)
Operating profit	229.0	253.8	129.1
Other (expenses) income, net	(41.2)	(19.1)	(82.6)
Income before provisions for income taxes	187.8	234.7	211.7
Income taxes	(55.7)	(90.0)	(85.1)
Income before cumulative effect of change in accounting principles	132.1	144.7	126.6
Cumulative effect of change in accounting principles for pension assets, net of tax provision of $(15.2)	0.0	0.0	25.3
Net Income	132.1	144.7	151.9
Basic EPS from Total Operations	$1.27	$1.35	$1.40
Diluted EPS from Total Operations	$1.26	$1.34	$1.39

Source: **www.readersdigest.com**

Revenues from New Business Development segment declined 2 percent for 2001 to $54 million, compared with $55 million in 2000 and $33 million in 1999. Operating losses declined in 2001 to $(17) million, compared with $(40) million in 2000 and $(5) million in 1999. Revenues were lower for Gifts.com, Inc. as a result of the Good Catalog Company division's reduction in merchandise catalog promotions. This decline was partially offset by higher sales generated by the **Gifts.com** Web site and financial services alliances. Operating losses for 2001 were lower, primarily as a result of the planned reductions in marketing and development costs related to the **Gifts.com** Web site. Losses for 2000 were from marketing and startup costs for a number of ventures, primarily Gifts.com, Inc.

EXTERNAL ISSUES

Standard & Poor's provides an interesting monthly outlook for the publishing industry. S&P indicates a number of positive occurrences within the group, including mergers and alliances involving some of the major names such as Harcourt General, Bertelsmann, Reader's Digest, Pearson plc, Scholastic Inc., and Houghton Mifflin. The industry is experiencing sharp drops in advertising. Magazine advertising declined about 8.5 percent in 2001, following a 14 percent advance for 2000. Circulation revenues should gain slowly due to higher cover prices. Single-copy sales have been trending lower for more than ten years, while the growth in the number of subscriptions has been sluggish to boot. While paper prices are stable and coming down for most grades of coated paper, postage costs for mailed subscriptions will be rising over the course of the year in response to rate hikes that went into effect in the first quarter of 2001. S&P projects consumer expenditures to reach $38.1 billion by 2003, up from $30.5 billion in 1999 and

EXHIBIT 6   Reader's Digest Association, Inc. Balance Sheet
(in millions except per-share data)

	Year ending June 30,	
	2001	*2000*
ASSETS		
Cash and cash equivalents	$35.4	$49.7
Receivables, net	305.1	285.3
Inventories, net	161.6	120.3
Prepaid and deferred promotion costs	106.7	115.5
Prepaid expenses and other current costs	161.8	185.8
Total current assets	770.6	756.6
Marketable securities	10.8	173.5
Property, plant, & equipment, net	160.2	152.4
Intangible assets, net	409.8	438.8
Other noncurrent assets	323.7	208.4
Total Assets	**$1,675.1**	**$1,729.7**
LIABILITIES AND STOCKHOLDERS' EQUITY		
Loans and notes payable	$160.3	$89.4
Accounts payable	86.4	104.8
Short-term debt	160.3	89.4
Accrued expenses	251.1	351.2
Income taxes payable	41.2	38.7
Unearned revenues	291.6	289.4
Other current liabilities	28.9	30.9
Total current liabilities	859.5	904.4
Postretirement and postemployment benefits other than pensions	138.7	142.3
Unearned revenue	54.1	63.8
Other noncurrent liabilities	166.6	144.0
Total Liabilities	**$1,218.9**	**$1,254.5**
STOCKHOLDERS' EQUITY		
Capital stock	$29.6	$28.9
Paid-in capital	226.1	223.1
Retained earnings	1187.7	1077.5
Total equity	456.2	504.3
Accumulated other comprehensive (loss) income	(84.6)	31.0
Treasury stock	(902.6)	(885.3)
Total Liabilities & Stockholders' Equity	**$1,675.1**	**$1,758.8**
Total common shares outstanding (in millions)	102.7	106.0

Source: www.readersdigest.com

$32.2 billion in 2000; it also expects a 5.7 percent average annual growth rate, with net book sales likely to grow at a 5.3 percent average annual rate in the five years through 2003. Children's books have benefited from the Harry Potter series, as well as from the sale of TV show and movie tie-ins. Adult trade books will be characterized in 2001 by sluggish unit sales and greater discounting. College and professional sales are benefiting from demographics, online purchases, effective marketing, and other factors.

Two of Reader's Digest major competitors are Thomas Nelson Publishers and Time Warner, Inc. Thomas Nelson revenues increased by 12 percent in 2001 to $297.9 million. Time Inc. is part of AOL-Time Warner and is the leading US consumer magazine publisher, with more than sixty magazines in its collection. Among its well-known magazine titles are *Entertainment Weekly, People, Southern Living, Sports Illustrated, Time, People en Español, Time for Kids, Teen People, Field & Stream, Golf, Skiing,* and *Yachting.* AOL-Time Warner total revenues for 2001 were $9,202 million.

CONCLUSION

Reader's Digest's has completed many strategic initiatives, including a number of strategic alliances which capitalize on the company's marketing capabilities. RDA has been expanding and contracting its businesses as needed in order to become a more global competitor. The company has experienced rapid growth in non-U.S. markets, while revenues suffer within the United States. The effects of the September 11, 2001, attacks on economic conditions have undoubtedly been felt by numerous businesses. Likewise, in 2002, the Euro was implemented in Europe. The Reader's Digest Web site has been improved significantly. The company is a leader in publishing and direct marketing but has experienced a flattening of revenues. A clear strategic plan is needed for the future.

NOTES

1. Standard & Poor's 2001 Industry Report.

REFERENCES

Comtex News Network.
Hoover's Online.
www.msnbc.com.
Reader's Digest, 2001 *Annual Report.*

www.readersdigest.com.
Standard & Poor's 2001 Industry Report.
Strategy Club Web site. Available at
    www.strategyclub.com.

NIKE, INC.—2002

M. Jill Austin
Middle Tennessee State University

NKE

www.nike.com

Nike is about play. It's in everything we do and everything we make. Play is the root of every sport—and of countless other activities we undertake for the same purpose: to find joy in the arc of a ball, the swing of a club, the power of a wave . . . the simple joy of our own bodies in motion.

These perspectives on play from the company Web site, **www.nikebiz.com**, indicate a shift in the company focus. Nike has always been a company about sports. However, the traditional definition of sport is confining, and since Nike now sells yoga, snowboarding, and outdoor gear, it seems natural for the company to broaden its definition of sport. As part of the change in focus, Nike announced a new goal in 2000: to increase the women's apparel business from 22 percent of company apparel sales to 30 percent by 2003. The company's vision and mission are shown in Exhibit 1.

CEO Phil Knight believes that for 2001 the company was more "gutsy than great." Net income in 2001 for Nike, Inc. ($589.7 million) increased by only 1.8 percent over 2000. Increases in net income from 1999 to 2000 were a much more significant 28.3 percent ($579.1 million). For fiscal year 2001, revenues at Nike increased by 5.5 percent over 2000 to $9.489 billion. Since 1997, the company's successes include maintaining the number two position in soccer (the world's number one sport), becoming a major player in the golf market, increasing its market share in Europe, and becoming known as an apparel company.

HISTORY

Philip Knight, a dedicated long-distance runner, developed a plan to make low-cost running shoes in Japan and to sell them in the United States as part of his work toward an MBA degree at Stanford University. After graduation, Knight teamed up with Bill

---

EXHIBIT 1   Nike, Inc. Vision and Mission

Vision—"To bring inspiration and innovation to every athlete* in the world"
Mission—Nike, Inc. is the "largest seller of athletic footwear and athletic apparel in the world. Performance and reliability of shoes, apparel, and equipment, new product development, price, product identity through marketing and promotion, and customer support and service are important aspects of competition in the athletic footwear, apparel, and equipment industry . . . We believe we are competitive in all of these areas." The company aims to "lead in corporate citizenship through proactive programs that reflect caring for the world family of Nike, our teammates, our consumers, and those who provide services to Nike."

*Nike co-founder Bill Bowerman defined an athlete by saying, "If you have a body, you're an athlete."
Source: **http://nikebiz.com** and Nike, Inc. Form 10-K, 2001.

Bowerman, his former track coach at the University of Oregon, to make his plan a reality. Since Bowerman's hobby was making handcrafted lightweight running shoes, his expertise was very valuable to entrepreneur Knight. In 1964, Bowerman and Knight each contributed $500 and started Blue Ribbon Sports. Knight negotiated with a Japanese athletic shoe manufacturer, Onitsuka Tiger Co., to manufacture the shoes that Bowerman had designed. Blue Ribbon Sports shoes gained a cult following among serious runners because Knight distributed the shoes, called Tigers, at track meets.

In 1971, Blue Ribbon Sports received a trademark on its Swoosh logo, and it introduced the brand name Nike that same year. Blue Ribbon Sports parted ways with Onitsuka Tiger in 1972 and contracted with other Asian manufacturers to produce the company's shoes. Blue Ribbon Sports officially changed its name to Nike in 1978. During the late 1970s and early 1980s, Nike researchers used their technological expertise to develop several types of athletic shoes that revolutionized the industry. The company became more and more successful every year, with profits increasing steadily during this time.

In 1984, after five years of 44 percent annual growth, Nike missed the emerging market for aerobic shoes. The company had concentrated its efforts on an unsuccessful line of casual shoes. Reebok took the lead in the athletic shoe industry when it began selling large numbers of its fashion-oriented aerobic shoes to women. Nike stock prices decreased by 60 percent in 1984.

In 1990, Nike opened its first retail store, called Nike Town, in Portland, Oregon. Nike acquired Tetra Plastics (now called Nike, IHM, Inc.), the manufacturer of the plastic film in Nike's air sole shoes, in 1991 for $37.5 million. Nike purchased a cap-making company called Sports Specialties (now called Nike Team Sports, Inc.) in 1993. In 1994, the outdoor division added a new shoe called "Air Mada," and the Nike sport sandal became the top seller in the market. In 1995, Nike acquired Canstar Sports, Inc. (the world's largest hockey equipment maker) for $409 million. Canstar, now called Bauer Nike Hockey, Inc., manufactures in-line roller skates, ice skates and blades, protective gear, hockey sticks, and hockey jerseys.

PRESENT CONDITIONS

Nike sells athletic shoes, accessories, sports equipment, and clothing for men, women, and children. The company's products are sold to approximately seventeen thousands retail accounts in the United States, including department stores, footwear stores, and sporting goods stores. Nike also sells its products through independent distributors, licensees, and subsidiaries in 140 countries around the world. Approximately thirty thousand international retail outlets sell Nike products. Nike operates a total of nineteen distribution centers in several different international markets: Asia, Canada, Latin America, Europe, and Australia. Two Nike Goddess stores, geared to women's clothing and footwear, were opened in Los Angeles in 2001. Nike purchased Impact Golf Technologies and, in 2002, will begin marketing golf clubs.

The Nike name and logo have such high consumer awareness that the company no longer includes the Nike name on its products; the "swoosh" logo is all that is needed.

Nike, Inc. operates 157 retail stores in the United States, including 81 factory outlets, 2 Nike stores, 57 Cole Haan stores, 4 employee-only stores, and 13 Nike Town stores. The company's Nike Town stores are located in major U.S. cities such as Portland, Chicago, Atlanta, New York City, Seattle, Boston, Los Angeles, and San Francisco. In 1999, Nike Town stores opened in London, England, and Berlin, Germany. Nike Town stores contain sports memorabilia, educational exhibits, basketball nets for use by customers, and Nike products. There are currently 111 Nike retail outlets outside the United States.

Almost 45 percent of total revenue in 2001 came from international sales. Non-U.S. countries that have the largest Nike business include the United Kingdom, Japan, France, Italy, Spain, Germany, and Canada. Revenues increased in all geographic categories (the United States, Europe, Asia-Pacific and the Americas) in 2001, with only the U.S. footwear segment showing a decline in sales from the previous year. Critics suggest that Nike lost ground in the U.S. footwear market because the company neglected the $60 to $90 shoe that makes up most of the industry's U.S. sales. Domestic and international revenues for Nike are shown in Exhibit 2.

The company has several recent additions to its line of businesses. The Michael Jordan collection of basketball clothing was launched in 1998. In 1999, clothing designed for young men who want the "urban look" was added to the Michael Jordan collection, and sports stars Randy Moss and Derek Jeter were hired to promote the Jordan brand. A new line called ACG (all Conditions Gear), which sells gear for snowboarding, skateboarding, surfing, and mountain biking, was launched in 1999. In 2001, the company launched **www.nikegoddess.com**, a Web site that celebrates women in sports. The company began distributing *Nike Goddess* magazines in NikeTown, Nordstrom, The Finish Line, and other retailers and as an insert in magazines such as *Sports Illustrated for Women*. Beginning in the spring of 2002, the company began selling three brands of apparel: Nike Performance (for athletes), Nike Active (gym-to-street wear), and Nike Fusion (stylish clothing made of high performance fabrics).

EXHIBIT 2   Domestic and International Revenues for Nike (in millions)

	1999	2000	2001
USA Region			
Footwear	$3,244.6	$3,351.2	$3,208.9
Apparel	1,385.3	1,154.4	1,260.3
Equipment and Other	93.8	226.5	349.8
Total USA	$4,723.7	$4,732.1	$4,819.0
Europe Region			
Footwear	$1,182.7	$1,309.4	$1,422.8
Apparel	1,005.1	933.9	976.3
Equipment and Other	68.0	163.7	185.7
Total Europe	$2,255.8	$2,407.0	$2,584.8
Asia-Pacific Region			
Footwear	$455.3	$557.0	$632.4
Apparel	366.0	321.0	374.8
Equipment and Other	23.2	77.1	102.8
Total Asia Pacific	$844.5	$955.1	$1,110.0
Americas Region			
Footwear	$3,35.8	$343.9	$359.6
Apparel	12.9	137.7	152.2
Equipment and Other	12.9	12.5	27.3
Total Americas	$507.1	$494.1	$539.1
Total Nike Brand	$8,331.1	$8,588.3	$9,052.9
Other Brands	$445.8	$406.8	$435.9
Total Revenues	$8,776.9	$8,995.1	$9,488.8

Source: Nike, Inc., *Form 10-K* (1999, 2001).

COMPETITION

The athletic shoe industry has changed tremendously since sneakers were invented. In 1873, the sneaker was developed from India rubber and canvas material. Dunlop became the dominant seller of sneakers in 1938. Keds and PF Fliers dominated the children's market in the 1960s. Adult standard brands such as Adidas and Converse were well accepted by sports enthusiasts for years. When Nike entered the market in the late 1960s, the industry changed forever. In addition to new competition, lifestyles began to change, and companies began to contract manufacturing rather than invest in plant and equipment to manufacture their own products.

The major competitors in the industry are Nike and Reebok, who hold 37 percent and 15 percent percent market shares, respectively. Some of the other two dozen competitors in the industry include Adidas-Salomon AG, New Balance, K-Swiss, Fila, Asics, Keds, and Converse. Designer brands such as Tommy Hilfiger and Nautica have entered the athletic shoe market and provide shoes for fashion-minded young people. Fashion shoe brands, such as Vans and Skechers, that appeal to teenagers and young adults are taking some market share from the major competitors. Vans, a California company specializing in skateboarding shoes, earned $15.5 million in 2001. Skechers is endorsed by Britney Spears, and the company exceeded $1 billion in sales in 2001. The most intense competition continues to be among the two industry leaders, Nike and Reebok. The secret to success for these two competitors is that they contract out the manufacture of shoes to low-wage factories in Far East countries. This strategy allows each company to concentrate on marketing, image, and research and development.

Reebok International, Ltd.

Reebok designs and develops athletic shoes and clothing worldwide. The company sells athletic shoes in different color combinations for aerobics, cycling, volleyball, tennis, fitness, running, basketball, soccer, walking, and children's footwear. The company diversified its offerings recently to include more types of casual shoes, sports clothing, other types of athletic shoes, and sports-related equipment. There are currently 204 Reebok stores in the United States. The company's four product divisions include Reebok, the Greg Norman Collection, Rockport, and Ralph Lauren footwear.

In the early 1980s, Reebok sold aerobic shoes primarily to women, but by the mid-1980s, large numbers of men were buying Reebok shoes too. Men now account for about half of Reebok's sales. The company's shoes are designed to make a fashion statement and are marketed to build on this image. Reebok CEO Paul Fireman believes that "Reebok is basically about freedom of expression." Reebok took the lead in revenues from Nike in 1987, but Nike regained its lead over Reebok in 1990. Despite Reebok's marketing efforts, the company continued to lose ground to Nike in the 1990s.

Reebok developed a series of marketing campaigns around sports stars in an effort to increase its market share. Some of the sports personalities who signed marketing contracts with Reebok include Julie Foudy, Venus Williams, Allen Iverson, Michael Chang, Greg Norman, and the Harlem Globetrotters. Reebok was also an early sponsor of the TV show *Survivor*. In August 2001, Reebok signed a ten-year contract with the National Basketball Association to provide all court apparel beginning with the 2004–2005 season. Sales of National Football League apparel is was greater than $125 million in 2001 and should reach $200 million in 2002. NBA Star Allen Iverson currently has a five-year, $48-million endorsement contract that is expected to be renewed by Reebok with a significant increase for the basketball star. Selected financial information for Reebok is shown in Exhibit 3.

EXHIBIT 3   Selected Financial Information for Reebok
(in millions except per-share amount)

	1999	2000
Gross Revenue	$2,899.9	$2,865.2
Net Income	50.8	80.9
Long-term Debt	370.3	345.0
Net Worth	528.8	607.9
Net Profit Margin (%)	1.8	2.8
Earnings Per Share	.89	1.40

Source: Value Line.

International Competition

Competition is increasing in Europe. Adidas-Salomon AG, a German company, is the number one seller of athletic shoes in Europe and number two worldwide. Analysts believe that doing well in the European market is crucial to the continued success of companies in the athletic shoe industry. Nike sales in Europe, Asia, Canada, and Latin America increased to almost $3.8 billion in 2000 and to $4.2 billion in 2001. Reebok's total international sales were about $1.2 billion in 2000. Both Nike and Reebok hope to continue increasing their presence in the international retail market.

Adidas, the top European-owned competitor, will be fighting to maintain its 13 percent worldwide share of the competitive market for athletic shoes. Founded in 1948, Adidas outfitted such sports stars as Al Oerter (1956 Olympics) and Kareem Abdul-Jabbar (NBA). Family disputes in this family-owned company threatened its success after it gained a 70 percent market share in the United States. One brother became so angry he founded the rival company Puma. During this time, the company's U.S. market share dropped from 70 percent to 2 percent. The company was sold in 1989 for $320 million. The new owner became involved in other issues and neglected the company. By the time the current CEO took over in 1993, Adidas was losing about $100 million per year. When asked what he knew about the athletic shoe industry, CEO Robert Louis-Dreyfus replied, "All I did was borrow what Nike and Reebok were doing. It was there for everybody to see."

Adidas-Salomon AG brands include Adidas (footwear, balls, bags, and apparel), Erima (swimwear and team sport apparel), Salomon (ski equipment and apparel, hiking boots, and inline skates), Taylor Made (golf equipment), Mavic (cycle components), and Bonfire (winter sports clothing). Some of the sports stars who currently have endorsement contracts with Adidas include Kobe Bryant, Martina Hingis, Anna Kournikova, Donovan Bailey, and Peyton Manning. Selected financial information for Adidas is shown in Exhibit 4.

ECONOMIC CONDITIONS

The U.S. athletic footwear market is growing again after slowing in the late 1990s. Sales in 1998 and 1999 were lower than previous years, but by the second half of 2000, sales levels were improving over previous years. U.S. sales rose 3.6 percent in 2000 over 1999 sales. Beginning in the fall of 2000, consumer confidence began to decline, and slow general economic growth continued through 2001. After the terrorist attack on the World Trade Center and Pentagon on September 11, 2001, the U.S. economy continued

EXHIBIT 4   Selected Financial Information for Adidas
(in millions except per-share amount)

	1999	2000
Gross Revenue	$5,391.7	$5,494.1
Net Income	229.3	171.1
Long-Term Debt	1,494.9	1,522.9
Total Assets	3,612.7	3,783.8
Total Equity	684.8	767.7
Net Profit Margin (%)	4.3	3.1
Earnings Per Share	–	3.78

Source: www.hoovers.com.

to falter. Athletic shoe manufacturers have also experienced economic crises in some international markets. In 1999, for example, there were economic problems in Asia, but that economy recovered by the end of the year. In addition, the impact of foreign currency fluctuations and interest rate changes has the potential to create financial problems for athletic shoe manufacturers. The transition toward the Euro has also created some economic pressures in the European Union countries that recently converted their currencies to the Euro.

Most athletic shoe companies contract with manufacturing companies in the Far East to produce their shoes. Some of the countries that manufacture shoes for Nike, Reebok, and other companies include South Korea, Taiwan, China, Thailand, Malaysia, and Indonesia. The athletic shoe companies develop design specifications and new technology for the shoes in the United States and then send them to the factory to be produced. The primary advantage of foreign contract manufacturing is that no capital investment is required and the athletic shoe companies can operate with very little long-term debt. There are also several disadvantages to contract manufacturing. Some countries, such as Korea, that have produced large numbers of athletic shoes in the past are developing the expertise and contacts to begin producing more sophisticated electronics products and do not have available capacity to continue producing athletic shoes. Some additional disadvantages of overseas production include labor unrest, political unrest, delays caused by shipping, and unreliability of quota systems (embargoes).

SOCIAL FACTORS

Beginning in the late 1970s, athletic shoe buyers became brand conscious, and the major competitors relied on their well-known brand names to sell their products. In recent years, consumers have changed their view of athletic footwear/clothing as fashion accessories. The ages of potential consumers present some unique challenges for athletic shoe/apparel companies. Generation Y children (born from 1979–1994) rival the size of the baby boom generation, are 60 million strong, and will be a significant market in the future. Generation Y consumers prefer fashion-oriented sportswear rather than athletic brand clothing. The Generation Y population responds differently to advertising than other generations did; this group is not swayed by glossy national advertising campaigns. It responds to truth in advertising and is more cynical and practical than other generations. Typically, Generation Y members prefer to use the Internet as a source of product information. Generation Y is an important target market for athletic shoe companies. Members of the large baby boom generation are interested in staying fit and healthy. In the 1980s, adults became obsessed with fitness, and by 1991 sales in the fitness equipment industry exceeded $30 billion. Currently, exercise is not as popular a pastime for baby boomers as it was in the early 1990s, but demand for clothing/footwear for leisure activities continues to increase for this group.

Changes in the lifestyles of girls/women will likely affect the industry. Since the mid-1990s, women have purchased more athletic shoes than men have. In addition, more girls are involved in sports today than ever before. There are currently more than 13 million women and girls who play basketball and approximately 7 million who play soccer.

NIKE INTERNAL FACTORS

Nike Research and Development

Nike is able to stay on the cutting edge in technology because research and development in the athletic shoe industry is largely design innovation and does not require a large investment in equipment. In 1980, the company formed the Nike Sport Research Laboratory (NSRL), which uses video cameras and traction testing devices and researches several types of concerns including children's foot morphology, "turf toe," and apparel aerodynamics. In addition, NSRL evaluates ideas that have been developed by the Advanced Product Engineering (APE) group. APE is involved in long-term product development. Shoes are created for five years in the future. This group developed cross-training shoes, the Nike Footbridge stability device, inflatable fit systems, and the Nike 180 air cushioning system. The company also uses its knowledge of technology to improve sports clothing. In June 2000, Nike introduced the Swift Suit, a full-length body suit designed to help runners keep muscles warm and reduce drag. One of the newest footwear developments is a spring-loaded shoe called Nike Shox that was introduced after sixteen years of research and development.

In addition to its laboratory work, Nike gets its designers to visit athletes to learn more about shoe technology. In 1996, the Nike staff worked with the Philadelphia 76ers to test a variety of shoes, and Nike's 1999 Air Seismic cross-trainer was the result. In 1997, Nike designers visited Mia Hamm to learn about what she expected of women's soccer shoes, and the company designed a lightweight shoe with a fiber cushion and foam. Nike continues to rely on superior technological developments to differentiate its products from competitors. Exhibit 5 indicates the major developments of Nike technology from 1990 to the present.

Marketing

Since Nike does not actually produce shoes, the main focus of the company is creating and marketing its products. Nike positions its products as high-performance shoes designed with high-technology features. The general target market for Nike athletic shoes is males and females between the ages of eighteen and thirty-four. Nike, which recently decided to target women more aggressively, created Nike Goddess stores and began marketing more toward women who have an active lifestyle. Currently, 20 percent of Nike's sales are to women, while the industry average is 50 percent.

EXHIBIT 5   Recent Nike Technological Developments

Date	Development	Purpose
1990	Air 180	Air cushioning in the heel and front of the shoe; heel cushion is 50 percent larger than previous models (consumer has a 180 degree view of the heel air bag)
1991	Huarache Fit Technology	Combination of neoprene and lycra spandex that provides runners with a form-fitting, supportive, and lightweight shoe
1993	Air Max Cushioning technology	Provides 30 percent more cushioning
1996	Zoom Air Cushioning	Material that is used in midsole to absorb pounding without taking away stability or speed
1997	Foamposite	Material that ensures no rough spots in the shoe
1997	Air Flightposite shoe	Dual-pigmented material with metallic hues that can be molded into a shoe
2000	Air Presto	Fashion shoes made almost entirely of stretch mesh

Nike advertises its products in a variety of ways and targets its ads to specific groups or types of people. Advertising expenditures were $1 billion in 2001. The company continues to spend advertising dollars on TV ads during professional and college sports events, prime time programs, and late night programs. Prime-time ads are intended to reach a broad range of adults, and late night TV advertising is geared toward younger adults. Print is also a very important way to advertise Nike products. Print media such as *Sports Illustrated, People, Runner's World, Glamour, Self, Tennis, Money, Bicycling*, and *Weight Watchers* are also very important media for advertising Nike products. The company sponsored the U.S. Women's soccer team that won the 1999 World Cup and has significant sponsorships for the 2002 World Cup in Japan and Korea.

Nike sells its products online through **www.nike.com**, and Phil Knight meets with the Internet team daily. The online store sells a variety of products, including shoes, equipment, and apparel. In November 1999, the company began offering NIKEiD to its online customers. Customers can personalize their athletic shoes by selecting shoe colors and a personal ID or nickname. Nike adds a $10 fee for customization and will accept up to four hundred personalized orders each day. The company believes its online business will be an important component of its future sales. According to Phil Knight, "We absolutely believe it (Internet) is creating an entire business revolution and we truly intend to be a part of that revolution."

Some of the celebrity spokespersons for Nike include Michael Jordan, Andre Agassi, Monica Seles, Mia Hamm, Charles Barkley, Pete Sampras, Cheryl Swoopes, Marion Jones, Brandi Chastain, and Tiger Woods. Michael Jordan's Nike contract has, to date, been the most lucrative endorsement contract of all time for a professional sports player. Tiger Woods signed a reported $90 million deal in 1999 to promote Nike golf wear. In September 2000, Woods signed a five-year extension on his endorsement contract that was worth an estimated $100 million. Woods plans to begin playing with Nike clubs in 2002. Michael Jordan earned approximately $500 million in his playing career promoting products for twelve companies. In the three years after his retirement, his total endorsements have been worth $40 million. It remains to be seen whether Jordan's return to professional play will be as lucrative for Nike as it was in the past. Exhibit 6 shows some of Nike's advertising campaigns.

International marketing efforts continue. Nike has operations in 140 countries on six continents. Phil Knight says, "There's a pretty strong recognition that we'll be bigger in a couple of years outside the U.S. than inside." Nike is already number one in the overall footwear market in Spain, France, Belgium, Holland, Luxembourg, Finland, Italy, and the United Kingdom. Some of the new markets that are now being pursued include Chile, Peru, Bolivia, India, Mexico, South Africa, and several Eastern European countries. Wieden and Kennedy, the advertising agency responsible for most of Nike's ads, has opened offices in London, Tokyo, and Amsterdam so that advertising can be developed by local people to fit with local cultures.

EXHIBIT 6　　Selected Nike Advertisements

Theme	Visual Image
"Hangtime"	An Air Jordan basketball shoe promotion features Michael Jordan and Spike Lee.
"Revolution"	The Beatles song "Revolution" is played, and images of sports stars were shown.
"Bo Knows"	The ad illustrates the range of Nike shoes (20 different sport categories).
"Just Do It"	The ad shows people from many walks of life exercising in Nike shoes.
"Multiple Bo's"	Bo Jackson meets Sonny Bono and fourteen other Bo Jacksons who represent different sports.
"Rock 'n' Roll Tennis"	Andre Agassi shows his tennis skills in rock video format.
"I am not a role model"	Charles Barkley says sports stars are not role models, but parents should be role models.
"Aerospace Jordan"	Cartoon characters Bugs Bunny, Looney Tunes bad guy Marvin Martin, and Michael Jordan travel to Mars. (Super Bowl XXVII)
"Air Swoopes"	An ad with Sheryl Swoopes introduces the Air Swoopes basketball shoe and announcing Nike sponsorship of the women's U.S. Olympic basketball team.
"Broad-Minded"	In an advertisement with Tiger Woods, the statement made is "We're not just canvas and leather shoes. We're big—and broad-minded."
"Date"	The U.S. Women's Soccer Team says, "We will take on the world as a team," and everyone on the team goes on a date with one person
"Two Fillings"	The U.S. Women's Soccer Team all want fillings when Brandi Chastain said she had two fillings. Each woman stands and says, "I will have two fillings."
"Chicks Dig the Long Ball"	Pitchers Tom Glavine and Greg Maddox try to get Heather Locklear's attention from Mark McGwire.
"Overjoyed"	Several Jordan-brand athletes are shown in slow motion: Randy Moss in a crowded hotel lobby and Derek Jeter surrounded by media in a locker room.
"Freestyle"	A group of basketball players plays to a musical soundtrack; this was part of Nike's sponsorship of the NBA All Star game.
"Much Respect"	A basketball music video is shown on BET and MTV2 television and **www.nba.com**.
"Why Sport? You'll Live Longer"	Suzy Hamilton (track runner) is shown sprinting away from a person wielding a chainsaw.

Distribution

Nike opened a 630,000-square-foot apparel distribution center in Memphis in 1992 that is called Nike Next Day. Footwear is distributed from centers in Greenland, New Hampshire; Beaverton, Oregon; Wilsonville, Oregon; and Memphis, Tennessee. Nike apparel is shipped from the Memphis distribution center. Sports specialty products are distributed from Irvine, California, and Cole Haan and Bauer products are distributed from Greenland, New Hampshire. The company operates a "Futures" ordering program that allows retailers to order up to six months in advance and be guaranteed to receive their orders within a certain time period and at a certain price.

However, retailers can receive apparel orders the next day if they place their orders by 7 P.M. the day before. Nike's automatic replenishment system provides automatic shipments to high-volume merchandisers in an effort to ensure a constant supply for retailers. Approximately $100 million in annual sales comes through the automatic replenishment system.

Knight worries that the brand will lose its image as a technically superior sports shoe if international marketing is not monitored carefully. Nike has purchased the distribution operations of many of its worldwide distributors in an attempt to control the marketing of Nike products. Some of these countries with "Nike owned" distributors include Singapore, Taiwan, Hong Kong, New Zealand, Korea, Japan, and Malaysia.

Social Responsibility

Nike has been criticized in the past few years for employment practices at its international manufacturing sites. Some consumers are concerned about the exploitive practices of managers in some Asian countries. In 2001, for example, Indonesian factory managers making Nike products were charged with sexual harassment, physical and verbal abuse, restrictions in health services, and forced overtime. In addition, some of these managers were charged with requiring employees who misbehave or are late for work to run laps or clean toilets. Nike promises to investigate and improve inappropriate conditions wherever they exist.

The company first set up a labor practices department in 1996, and in 1998 the position vice president of social responsibility was created. In 1998, Nike joined the Fair Labor Association (FLA), a sweatshop-monitoring organization founded by a presidential task force made up of apparel manufacturers and human rights organizations. The company also belongs to the Global Alliance for Workforce and Communities (GAWC), a business group whose objective is to improve factory employees' work lives. Nike's leadership on labor initiatives in factories producing its products is shown in Exhibit 7.

In addition to its membership in FLA and GAWC, Nike has developed a process for ensuring that its factories comply with the company's code of conduct. The Nike Code of Conduct can be seen in Exhibit 8.

Nike has developed several programs that show the company's concern about social responsibility issues, and the company provides contributions to several charitable and nonprofit organizations. Some of the organizations Nike supports include the September 11 Fund, 100 Black Men of America, INROADS, Boys and Girls Clubs of America, the National Head Start Association, Habitat for Humanity, the YWCA of the United States, and the Jackie Robinson Foundation. Howard White, vice president of Marketing for the Jordan brand, conducts seminars called "Believe to Achieve" for at-risk youths. The seminars include a variety of local and national celebrity speakers from entertainment, sports, and business, and the seminars provide encouragement for youths to work toward success through vision, self-esteem, and commitment.

EXHIBIT 7   Recent Nike Labor Initiatives

- 1997—Ambassador Andrew Young conducted an independent assessment of Nike labor practices. In response to Young's recommendations, Nike adopted a termination policy for contractors who violate the code of conduct, developed penalties for violations of the code of conduct, implemented training for managers, and established training programs for U.S. managers who will work in international markets.
- 1997—Eight weeks of training in 16 Asian cities was completed to reinforce the Nike code of conduct.
- 1997—Comprehension of the code was added to the corporate audit manual as a criterion for judgment.
- 1998—Nike joined the Fair Labor Association (FLA), a sweatshop monitoring organization founded by a presidential task force made up of apparel manufacturers and human rights organizations. Companies involved include Nike, Reebok, Liz Claiborne, and Phillips Van Heusen. Efforts to recruit other businesses to the FLA have been unsuccessful. Most of the apparel manufacturers and some retailers are joining an effort that has less stringent requirements than FLA and that has been spearheaded by the American Apparel Manufacturing Association. The group United Students Against Sweatshops (students from 100 universities) has demanded that universities withdraw support from the FLA and create a more rigorous plan for monitoring sweatshops. The student group wants companies to publicly disclose the locations of their foreign factories so that independent investigations of labor practices can occur.
- 1999—Nike joined the Global Alliance for Workers and Communities, a labor monitoring project.
- 2001—Nike began revealing the results of monitoring on its Web site on a quarterly basis.

Source: "Nike Puts Its Code of Conduct in the Pocket of Workers," *PR Newswire* (September 17, 1997) "Sweatshop Reform: How to Solve the Standoff," *Business Week* (May 3, 1999), and **www.nikebiz.com**.

N.E.A.T. (Nike Environmental Action Team) was formed in 1993. The purpose of this group is to pursue environmental initiatives and to recycle old athletic shoes and reuse them in new products. Nike recovers one hundred thousand pairs of shoes each month in its Reuse-A-Shoe program for recycling. Nike demonstrates its concern for the environment by using the recycled materials in the soles of its new shoes and by providing recycled material for sports fields/tracks. Every year, Nike recycles 5 million pounds of solid wastes. Exhibit 9 shows the life of a Nike product and Nike's environmental impact.

Management Style/Culture

Phil Knight has created a strong culture at Nike, Inc. that is based on company loyalty and locker room camaraderie. Most corporate employees are health conscious young people and are in their thirties or younger. Knight trusts these employees to "Just Do It." In

EXHIBIT 8   Nike, Inc. Code of Conduct

Nike, Inc. is committed to the promotion of best practices and continuous improvement in:
- Occupational health and safety, compensation, hours of work, and benefits.
- Minimizing our impact on the environment.
- Management practices that recognize the dignity of the individual, the rights of free association and collective bargaining, and the right to a workplace free of harassment, abuse, and/or corporal punishment.
- The principle that decisions on hiring, salary, benefits, advancement, termination and retirement are based solely on the ability of an individual to do his/her job.

Source: **www.nikebiz.com**.

EXHIBIT 9   The Life of a Nike Product—Natural Environmental Issues

---

1. **Research and Development**—Nike evaluates raw materials to reduce environmental impact (recycled materials, durable materials).
2. **Manufacturing**—The goal is to maximize product quality and minimize waste. The company does not dump the overflow of rubber from molds; instead [it grates] it into powder and [mixes] it with new rubber so it can be used. Dangerous chemicals used in the production process have been replaced with cleaner, water-based products.
3. **Retail**—Packaging has been reduced, no glues are used in the boxes, and box content includes recycled materials.
4. **Consumers**—Nike collects used shoes through its Reuse-A-Shoe program. This reduces the number of shoes in landfills.
5. **Down-Cycling**—Old athletic shoes are ground up into three materials: lights, foam, and rubber. These materials are made into new products such as carpet padding, equestrian trails, basketball courts, running tracks, and tennis courts.

Source: Nike, Inc., Consumer Affairs (1997).

the past, he often dropped out of sight for months at a time and then reemerged with some new approach for the company. His philosophy is "Play by the rules, but be ferocious. . . . It's all right to be Goliath, but always act like David." The seventy-four-acre corporate campus of Nike, Inc. provides a sense of the culture: It has wooded areas, running trails, a lake, and a fitness center. Knight believes that people should find a "sense of peace at work." Nike's organizational chart is shown in Exhibit 10.

EXHIBIT 10   Nike, Inc. Organization Chart

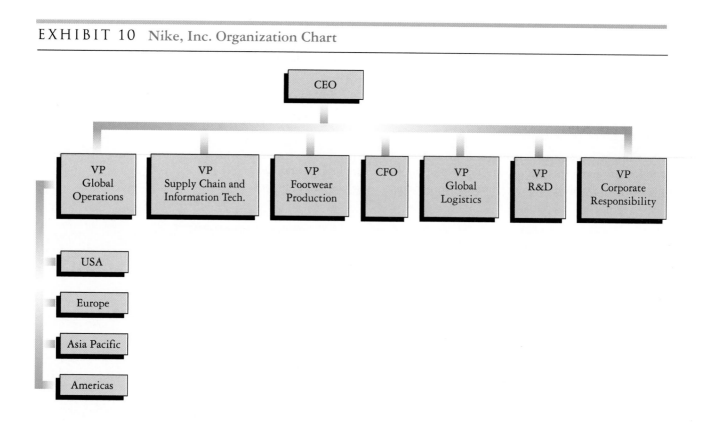

Some critics suggest that the Nike culture may be so strong that "entrenched" Nike employees' ideas are heard while new employees' ideas are dismissed quickly without consideration. Currently, 40 percent of the company's vice presidents have been with Nike, Inc. for less than five years. These new vice presidents have been asked to solve some serious dilemmas for Nike such as "How can the manufacturing and logistics system can be improved?" and "How can the company gain market share for its extreme sports products?"

Finance/Accounting

During its years of rapid growth, Nike, Inc. managers encouraged free spending to develop and market company products. After cost-cutting layoffs and a search for efficiency that began in 1998, vice presidents began to spend more time making employees aware of the need for financial accountability. Each geographic region manager began receiving a profit-and-loss statement in 1998, and now compensation is partly tied to performance. Note in the income statement in Exhibit 11 that revenues for 2001 increased by 5 percent over 2000 while net income increased only 2 percent. The balance sheet (see Exhibit 12) provides information on assets and liabilities for 2000 and 2001.

FUTURE OUTLOOK

Even with limited growth and intense competition in the athletic shoe/athletic apparel markets, Nike managers expect that the company will perform well in the future.

EXHIBIT 11   Nike Consolidated Statement of Income
(in millions except per-share data)

	Year-To-Date Ending		
	5/31/01	*5/31/00*	*%Chg*
Revenues	$9,488.8	$8,995.1	5%
Cost of Sales	5,784.9	5,403.8	7%
Gross Profit	3,703.9	3,591.3	3%
	39.0%	39.9%	
SG&A	2,689.7	2,606.4	3%
	28.3%	29.0%	
Interest Expense	58.7	45.0	30%
Other	34.1	20.7	65%
Pretax Income	921.4	919.2	0%
Income Taxes	331.7	340.1	−2%
	36.0%	37.0%	
Net Income	$589.7	$579.1	2%
Diluted EPS	$2.16	$2.07	4%
Basic EPS	$2.18	$2.10	4%
Weighted Average Common Shares Outstanding:			
Diluted	273.3	279.4	
Basic	270.0	275.7	
Dividend	$0.48	$0.48	

Source: Nike, Inc., 2001 *Annual Report.*

EXHIBIT 12   Nike Consolidated Balance Sheet (in millions)

	May 31, 2001	May 31, 2000
Assets		
Cash & Investments	$304.0	$254.3
Accounts Receivable	1,621.4	1,567.2
Inventory	1,424.1	1,446.0
Deferred Taxes	113.3	111.5
Income Taxes Receivable	0.0	2.2
Prepaid Expenses	162.5	215.2
Current Assets	**3,625.3**	**3,596.4**
Fixed Assets	2,552.8	2,393.8
Depreciation	934.0	810.4
Net Fixed Assets	1,618.8	1,583.4
Identifiable Intangible		
Assets and Goodwill	397.3	410.9
Other Assets	178.2	266.2
Total Assets	**$5,819.6**	**$5,856.9**
Liabilities and Equity		
Current Long-Term Debt	$0	$50.1
Payable to Banks	855.3	924.2
Accounts Payable	432.0	543.8
Accrued Liabilities	472.1	621.9
Income Taxes Payable	21.9	0.0
Current Liabilities	**1,781.3**	**2,140.0**
Long-Term Debt	441.3	470.3
Deferred Income Taxes & Other Liabilities	102.2	110.3
Preferred Stock	0.3	0.3
Common Equity	3,494.5	3,136.0
Total Liabilities & Equity	**$5,819.6**	**$5,856.9**

Source: Nike, Inc., 2001 *Annual Report.*

According to Phil Knight, "This is the fourth downturn in 18 years as a public company. I said going into the 1990s that if we can get through it with only two downturns, we'll have a great decade. And I'll look forward to 2000 through 2010 coming up with the same statement." The company analyzed its 2001 activities by dividing them into "successes" and "sweat." It is likely that in the future, Phil Knight will continue to "sweat" while trying to build "successes" at Nike, Inc.

Consider the following questions regarding Nike's future:

1. Is Nike trying to supply products for too many sports? Should Nike narrow its product line in athletic shoes?
2. What types of acquisitions for Nike would you suggest to Philip Knight?
3. Should Nike begin producing some of its own products?
4. Is Nike taking the correct approach in marketing its shoes internationally?
5. What changes in product and advertising should the company pursue to appeal to the aging baby boomers? To Generation Y?
6. How can Nike maintain a competitive advantage over Reebok?

7. Is Nike responding correctly to concerns about the treatment of employees in international manufacturing facilities?

8. How can the company revitalize its U.S. footwear business?

9. Has Nike chosen the appropriate targets for new marketing efforts? Can the company be successful in gaining market share among women? Can the company be successful in the extreme sports segment of the market?

REFERENCES

BERNSTEIN, AARON. "Sweatshop Reform: How to Solve the Standoff." *Business Week* (May 3, 1999): 186.

CHANDRASEKARAN, RAJIV. "Indonesian Workers in Nike Plants List Abuses." *The Washington Post* (February 23, 2001): E1.

"Core Passion Displaces Emotion-Added Brands." *Marketing Week* (September 2, 1999): 26.

DAWSON, ANGELA. "Swing for the Fences." *AdWeek* (May 3, 1999): 40.

ELLIOTT, STUART. "The Media Business: Advertising." *The New York Times* (April 10, 2001): C8.

GRANT, LORRIE. "Reebok Goes Toe to Toe with Nike." *USA Today* (September 4, 2001): B1.

HAMILTON, JOAN. "A Show of One's Own." *Business Week* (May 24, 1999): 62.

HIMELSTEIN, LINDA. "The Swoosh Heard 'Round the World." *Business Week* (May 12, 1997): 76.

"Insider: If the Shoe Fits, Will Nike Let You Wear It?" *Bangkok Post* (February 28, 2001).

KELLY, JANE. "Stranger than Fiction." *AdWeek* (January 4, 1999): 25.

LEE, LOUISE. "Can Nike Still Do It?" *Business Week* (February 21, 2000): 121.

NEUBRONE, ELLEN, and KATHLEEN KERWIN. "Generation Y." *Business Week* (February 15, 1999): 80.

Nike *Annual Reports* (1993, 1995, 1997, 1999, 2001).

"Team Mia." *AdWeek* (June 21, 1999): 42.

"There're Running as Fast as They Can." *Business Week* (July 12, 1999): 106.

WANG, EDWARD. "Nike Trying New Strategies for Women; Company Seeks Merger of Athletics and Fashion." *The New York Times* (June 19, 2001): C1.

WALLACE, CHARLES. "Adidas Back in the Game." *Fortune* (August 18, 1997): 176.

REEBOK INTERNATIONAL, LTD.—2002

Carlisle P. Sampson
Francis Marion University

RBK

www.reebok.com

"Reebok, a company which strives to do what's right!" Reebok was one of the first companies to leave South Africa early in the apartheid era. On May 1, 2001, former U.S. President Carter met with Reebok Chairman Paul Fireman and Reebok's Board of Directors, to discuss the company's continuing efforts to promote human rights worldwide. Carter has served on Reebok's Human Rights Award Board of Advisors since 1989.

A possible vision statement for Reebok might define the company's goal like this: "to become the largest and most profitable athletic footwear and apparel company in the world."

A possible mission statement for Reebok might state:

> *"If you don't stand for something, you'll fall for anything." We stand for human rights everywhere, equal respect and fair treatment for all people—including our employees around the globe, while providing for the athletic apparel needs of all people. We offer athletic apparel in multiple brand availability through Reebok Brand, Rockport, the Greg Norman Collection and the Ralph Lauren-Polo sport line. Through the latest technology, we are able to offer the "Defy Convention" sensation in footwear, at competitive pricing. Also, through advanced computer systems, we are consistently able to communicate the changing needs of our customers to our global divisions. Our goal is to be the leading provider of footwear and apparel at the best price and profit-level for our customer and shareholder.*

Headquartered in Stoughton, Massachusetts, Reebok is a global company engaged primarily in the design and marketing of sports and fitness products, including footwear, apparel, and products for nonathletic use. Reebok launched a new "It's a Woman's World" campaign in October 2001 to attract young women. Beginning with the 2002 season, all 32 football teams in the NFL will exclusively wear the Reebok brand. The company operates in 201 retail stores and has about 6,700 employees. Reebok's sales for 2001 increased 4.5 percent to $2,993 billion.

HISTORY

Reebok's ancestor company, based in the United Kingdom, was founded to enable athletes to run faster. In the 1890s, the first running shoes with spikes were made by Joseph William Foster. In 1895, J.W. Foster and Sons provided shoes to international athletes. By 1958, a companion company, today recognized as Reebok, was started by two of the founder's grandsons. The company was named after an African gazelle.

In 1979, Reebok introduced three running shoes into the United States. By 1981, Reebok's sales exceeded $1.5 million. In the following year, the company introduced the first athletic shoe designed especially for women. The birth of this shoe coincided with a new fitness exercise called aerobic dance. Called the Freestyle, the shoe transformed the athletic footwear industry by encouraging aerobic exercise movement and the influx of women into sports. Products are now available in over 140 countries.

In 1992, Reebok began a transformation from a company identified principally with fitness and exercise to one equally involved in many sports. The company created a host of new footwear and apparel products for football, baseball, soccer, track and field, and numerous other sports. Reebok signed numerous professional athletes, teams, and federations to sponsorship contracts. After 20 years of spectacular growth globally, Reebok is now focused on greater accomplishments and continued innovation.

One of Reebok's most recent developments is the DMX technology, which provides superb cushioning, utilizing an active airflow system. The company's apparel products include the HYDROMOVE moisture-management system, which helps to keep athletes dry and thereby facilitates regulation of the wearer's body temperature. Reebok recently made licensing deals with the National Basketball Association (NBA). Mr. Paul Fireman, Reebok's chairman, president, and CEO, and his wife own about 20 percent of the company.

INTERNAL FACTORS

Organizational Structure

Although Reebok does not actually provide an organizational chart, a possible organizational structure is illustrated in Exhibit 1. Reebok is organized into six strategic business units, which include Classic Footwear (focus on lifestyle footwear); Performance Footwear (responsible for football, running, outdoor footwear, tennis, basketball, baseball, golf, cross-training, adventure and outdoor footwear); Global Apparel (responsible for fitness and sports apparel worldwide); Retail Operations (responsible for retail stores as well as for developing retail merchandise and promotional concepts); Kid's Products (focusing on children's products sold under the Reebok and Weebok brands); and Fitness (responsible for men's and women's fitness products).

Reebok operates 204 stores in the United States and consists of three subsidiaries; Rockport Company, the Ralph Lauren Footwear, and the Greg Norman Collection. The Rockport Company produces and distributes specially engineered comfort footwear for men and women worldwide. This division's product lines include performance, casual, and dress shoes that are designed to address the different aspects of consumers' lives. Rockport continues to use technologies to enhance comfort in its expanding product line, the men's Prowalker DMX. The Ralph Lauren Footwear products include the RLX collection and the Lauren collection for women. The Greg Norman Collection produces a range of men's apparel and accessories, all marketed and endorsed by golfer Greg Norman. This collection includes men's sportswear, with products ranging from leather jackets and sweaters to active wear and swimwear.

The executive officers of Reebok International can be observed from Exhibit 1.

Reebok places a strong emphasis on technology and focuses on cushioning, stability, and lightweight features. Reebok's most significant advancement is its DMX technology, which provides superb cushioning by utilizing a heel-to-foot, active airflow system that delivers cushioning when and where it is needed. In late 2000, Reebok introduced the latest iteration of its DMX technology with Viz-DMX. Reebok also introduced an enhanced version of its Traxtar shoe for children. This new "smart" technology measures a wearer's athletic performance and provides interactive feedback through a sound and light display unit in the shoe's tongue.

EXHIBIT 1   Reebok's Probable Organizational Structure

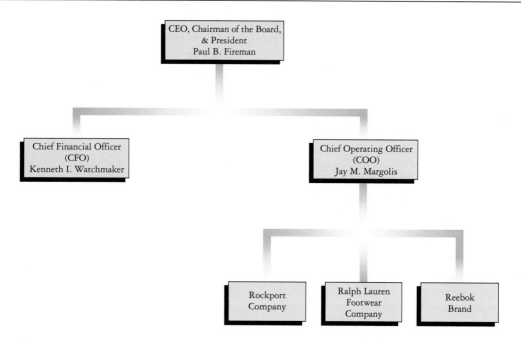

Source: Adapted from information in Reebok's 2001 *Annual Report.*

Marketing

Reebok advertises through television, radio, print, and other media and utilizes its relationship with internationally recognized sport figures to maintain and enhance visibility for the Reebok brand. In early 2000, Reebok implemented product segmentation for its Classic products, which included certain new product introductions. To support this new Classic introduction, Reebok later launched a new advertising campaign featuring black and white photographs depicting both celebrities and noncelebrities wearing Classic footwear. The portraits appeared in *Vogue* and *Vanity Fair.* In addition, new relationships with two fashion boutiques, Fred Segal in Los Angeles and Gimme Shoes in San Francisco, were established. Reebok sponsored the highly successful CBS television show *Survivor,* which aired in the summer of 2000. As the exclusive title sponsor of all footwear and apparel to the show, Reebok gained significant brand exposure. Reebok also sponsored *Survivor II*, which began airing in early 2001.

Reebok continues to rely on athletic endorsements and sport sponsorships involving key athletes. In December 2000, Reebok resigned Venus Williams, winner of Wimbledon (2000), the Olympic gold medalist in both singles and doubles, and winner of both the 2000 and 2001 U.S. Open championships. This endorsement relationship reaffirms Reebok's heritage of commitment to women's sports and fitness. In its advertising campaign ("Defy Convention"), Reebok plans to showcase Venus as an icon. Other Reebok endorsements to promote the sale of its shoes are with NBA star Alan Iverson, NFL star Edgerin James, and Major League Baseball player Roger

Clemens. In soccer, Ryan Giggs, currently playing for the English league champion Manchester United, also sports Reebok boots. To gain further visibility for the Reebok brand, the company fitted 2,500 coaches, athletes, and officials in training apparel and footwear at the 2000 Summer Olympic Games in Sydney. Reebok sponsored several Olympic committees, including South Africa. Additional endorsements and sponsorships include professional tennis players Patrick Rafter and Andy Roddick.

Finance

As indicated in Exhibit 2, for 2001 net income was $102.7 million, as opposed to net income of $80.8 million for 2000. Net sales as reported in U.S. dollars for 2001 were $2.99 billion, an increase from 2000 sales of $2.865 billion. Sales comparisons continue to be adversely affected by the weaker exchange rates of foreign currencies against the U.S. dollar.

As can be observed from Exhibit 3, footwear sales for 2001 decreased to $2.081 billion. Apparel sales in 2001 were $911.4 million, an increase from $767.2 million in 2000. Reebok's international sales of Reebok Branded products amounted to $346.1, $511, $467, and $292 million to the United Kingdom, Europe, and other countries respectively.

Rockport's sales decreased to $399.6 million in 2001 from $422.4 million in 2000, a decline of 5.4 percent. In 2001, Rockport's international revenues increased 5.2 percent. Net sales of Ralph Lauren Footwear decreased 8.8 percent to $97.3 million in 2001 from $106.7 million in 2000.

EXHIBIT 2   Reebok International Ltd. Consolidated Statements of Income
(Amounts in thousands, except per-share data)

	Year ended December 31		
	2001	*2000*	*1999*
Net sales	$2,992,878	$2,865,240	$2,899,872
Costs and expenses			
Cost of sales	1,894,497	1,779,686	1,783,914
Selling, general and administrative expenses	913,941	915,387	971,945
Special charges	(532)	3,289	61,625
Interest expense, net	17,630	22,126	40,532
Other expenses, net	11,536	8,947	13,818
	2,837,072	2,729,435	2,871,834
Income before income taxes and minority interest	155,806	135,805	28,038
Income taxes	48,300	49,000	10,093
Income before minority interest	107,506	86,805	17,945
Minority interest	4,780	5,927	6,900
Net income	$ 102,726	$ 80,878	$ 11,045
Basic earnings per share	$ 1.75	$ 1.42	$ .20
Diluted earnings per share	$ 1.66	$ 1.40	$ .20

Source: Reebok's 2001 *Annual Report,* p. 39.

EXHIBIT 3   Reebok International Ltd. Net Sales

Net sales by product type are summarized below and include all brands.

	2001	2000	1999
Net sales:			
Footwear	$2,081,393	$2,098,028	$2,071,768
Apparel	911,485	767,212	828,104
	$2,992,878	$2,865,240	$2,899,872

Net sales to unaffiliated customers and long-lived assets by geographic area are summarized below:

	2001	2000	1999
Net sales:			
United States	$1,721,834	$1,599,406	$1,609,697
United Kingdom	511,426	514,772	545,562
Europe	467,207	462,342	476,695
Other countries	292,411	288,770	267,918
	$2,992,878	$2,865,240	$2,899,872
Long-lived assets:			
United States	$ 152,383	$ 142,577	$ 167,068
United Kingdom	16,550	18,269	28,149
Europe	32,807	35,890	40,737
Other countries	8,898	9,387	11,049
	$ 210,638	$ 206,123	$ 247,003

Source: Reebok's 2001 *Annual Report,* p. 61–62.

EXTERNAL FACTORS

Research & Development

In 2001, Reebok spent $41.7 million on product research and development, compared to $49.8 million in 2000 and $55.4 million in 1999.

E-Commerce

Use of the Internet as a distribution channel has become prominent in the apparel and footwear business. Online apparel sales exceeded $7 billion in 2001 and accounted for 3.2 percent of total apparel sales, having more than doubled since 1999.

More than 50 percent of online fashion buyers are 35 years or older, and two-thirds earn $60,000 or more annually. Reebok allows select retailers to sell Reebok and Greg Norman products to consumers through the Internet. Such e-commerce arrangements are expected to continue.

Global Issues

The principal materials used in Reebok's footwear products are leather, nylon, and rubber. A loss of supply could temporarily disrupt production. In Europe and Great Britain, the supply of hides was recently reduced due to mad cow and foot-and-mouth diseases. This problem resulted in cost increases for the leather used in some of Reebok's footwear.

EXHIBIT 4   Reebok International Ltd Consolidated Balance Sheets
(Amount in thousands, except per-share data)

	December 31	
	2001	*2000*
ASSETS		
Current assets:		
Cash and cash equivalents	$ 413,281	$ 268,665
Accounts receivable, net of allowance for doubtful accounts (2001, $55,240; 2000, $48,016)	383,372	423,830
Inventory	362,927	393,599
Deferred income taxes	104,280	101,715
Prepaid expenses and other current assets	30,835	37,396
Total current assets	1,294,695	1,225,205
Property and equipment, net	133,952	141,835
Other non-current assets:		
Intangibles, net of amortization	76,686	64,288
Deferred income taxes	16,094	18,110
Other	21,746	13,608
Total Assets	$1,543,173	$1,463,046
LIABILITIES AND STOCKHOLDERS' EQUITY		
Current liabilities:		
Notes payable to banks	$ 11,779	$ 8,878
Current portion of long-term debt	97	13,813
Accounts payable	127,286	172,035
Accrued expenses	269,738	272,076
Income taxes payable	40,506	21,337
Total current liabilities	449,406	488,139
Long-term debt, net of current portion	351,210	345,015
Minority interest and other long-term liabilities	22,619	22,029
Commitments and contingencies		
Stockholders' equity:		
Common stock, par value $.01; authorized 250,000,000 shares; issued shares:		
98,049,605 in 2001; 96,208,558 in 2000	981	962
Retained earnings	1,453,348	1,301,269
Less 39,010,827 shares in 2001 and 38,716,227 shares in 2000 in treasury at cost	(660,422)	(653,370)
Unearned compensation	(2,736)	(1,402)
Accumulated other comprehensive income (expense)	(71,233)	(39,596)
Total Stockholders' Equity	719,938	607,863
Total Liabilities and Stockholders' Equity	$1,543,173	$1,463,046

Source: Reebok's 2001 *Annual Report*, p. 38.

Reebok's main suppliers are located in China and Indonesia—and thus are subject to U.S. customs duties. Duties on the footwear products range from 51 percent to 66 percent. An increase in customs duties would have a negative impact on Reebok's finances. If events should prevent Reebok from acquiring products from its suppliers in China, Indonesia, or Thailand, its operations could be disrupted until alternative suppliers could be found, and this development could have a negative financial impact. Nearly a third of Reebok's shoes are made in Indonesia. Reebok has relocated most of its non-Indonesian employees out of Indonesia because of safety concerns. If factories in Indonesia were not able to operate, it could take 30–45 days to replace a full set of molds for the bottoms of shoes that are needed to keep factories operating. Potential production slowdowns concern investors, because if prolonged, they could affect Reebok's ability to fill orders and get merchandise to retail stores. If it has to, Reebok has contingency plans it can institute, including securing excess production in China.

The European Union (EU) imposes quotas on footwear from China. If quotas are limited further, Reebok's product lines could be affected adversely, requiring sourcing from countries other than China. In addition to the quotas on China-sourced footwear, the EU has imposed antidumping duties against certain textile footwear from China and Indonesia. If the athletic footwear exemption remains in its current form, Rockport products would be subject to these duties. Reebok believes that its Reebok and Rockport trademarks and its rights to use the Greg Norman and Ralph Lauren names and logos are of great value. The company is vigilant in protecting its trademarks from counterfeiting. Loss of Reebok, Rockport, Ralph Lauren, or Greg Norman trademark rights could have a serious impact on Reebok's business.

Sales of athletic and casual footwear tend to be seasonal in nature, with the strongest sales occurring in the first and third quarters. Apparel sales also generally vary during the course of the year, with the greatest demand occurring during the spring and fall seasons.

Competitors

Footwear competitors include Nike, Adidas, Fila, and New Balance. Apparel competitors include Nike, Adidas, Fubu, Mecca, and 2NYCE. The casual footwear market into which the Rockport product lines fall includes competitors such as Timberland, Clarks, Merrell, and Gabor. The Greg Norman line competes with Tommy Hilfiger and Nautica. The Ralph Lauren Footwear brand competes with Timberland, Tommy Hilfiger, and Gucci. Reebok International's four major competitors include Adidas-Salomon, New Balance, Fila, and Nike. Reebok currently holds the number two position behind Nike in total revenues. According to analyst John Stanley, "This industry has been as flat as a pancake for the last 9 years." From 1997–2001, Nike's market share has declined from 47 percent to 37 percent, while in the last year, Reebok's market share has increased from 12 to 15 percent.

The footwear and apparel industry is subject to rapid changes in consumer preferences. A major technological breakthrough or promotional success by one of Reebok's competitors could adversely affect its competitive position, as could a shift in consumer preferences. The athletic footwear and apparel industry has recently seen a shift away from athletic footwear to "casual" product offerings. This change of preference has adversely affected Reebok's business as well as that of some of its competitors.

In countries in which the athletic footwear market is mature, sales growth may be dependent in part on Reebok increasing its market share at the expense of its competitors. Competition for Reebok's products occurs in a variety of areas, including price, quality, product designs, brand image, marketing and promotion, and ability to meet delivery commitments to retailers. Rapid changes in consumer preference and technology in the footwear and apparel markets constitute significant risk factors for Reebok's operations.

Reebok's business is subject to changing economic conditions, including recession, inflation, general weakness in retail markets, and changes in consumer purchasing power and preferences. Adverse changes have a negative effect on Reebok. Retail sales of apparel rose by 1.5 percent in 2000. The U.S. economy slowed during the first six months of 2001. Real gross domestic product (GDP) rose 5.7 percent in the second quarter of 2000 and then slowed to a 1.3 percent increase in the third quarter and a 1.9 percent increase in the fourth. After rising 1.3 percent in the first quarter of 2001, GDP increased only 0.2 percent in the second. Prior to the terrorist attacks, the economy appeared to be hitting bottom. Since then, the economy has worsened.

CONCLUSION

Reebok strives to "make a difference," and one official motto of Reebok has been that the company strives to become "the best, most innovative and exciting sporting goods company in the world." Reebok is currently undertaking various global restructuring activities designed to enable it to achieve operating efficiencies, improve logistics, and reduce expenses. There can be no assurance that Reebok will be able to effectively execute on its restructuring plans or that such benefits will be achieved. In the short-term, Reebok could experience difficulties in product delivery or with some of its other logistical operations as a result of its restructuring activities, and it could be subject to increased expenditures and charges due to inefficiencies resulting from such restructuring activities. Possible strategies that Reebok could embark on include streamlining its workforce and divesting operations in countries where it is most at risk. To survive in the future, Reebok needs a clear strategic plan.

REFERENCES

www.cbs.com.

www.cnn.com.

"Economic Slowdown Takes a Toll." *Standard & Poor's Apparel and Footwear Industry Survey* (October 11, 2001): 1, 13, 20.

Jeffrey Edelman. "Reebok Gets a Boost." *Fortune* 134, no. 7 (2001): 63.

www.fortune500.com.

www.freeedgar.com.

www.msnbc.com.

www.quicken.com.

www.reebok.com.

www.strategyclub.com.

www.valueline.com.

www.wsj.com.

www.wsrn.com.

www.zacks.com.

UST, INC.—2002

Marilyn M. Helms
Dalton State College

UST

www.ustshareholder.com

Vincent A. Gierer, Jr., CEO and chairman of the board for UST, Inc., examined the third quarter 2001 results and was pleased that the company's net earnings had increased 10.4 percent to $124.2 million, with a 7.2 percent sales increase to $417.8 million. The first nine months of 2001 saw sales increase 6.3 percent and earnings increase 8.3 percent. He reread his quote in the e-mail to the shareholders: "We experienced a strong quarter, exceeding our internal forecast and first call earnings estimates. In line with our strategic plan, all business segments have improved, and fundamentals continue to be strong for smokeless tobacco and wine. I remain confident that we will achieve our 10 percent EPS (earnings per share) growth forecast for the year." Yet with the September 11, 2001, terrorist attacks on the United States and the subsequent prolonged war and signs of a deepening recession, Gierer wondered if the external issues would hinder the firm's projected future growth. He also pondered future earnings potential given the number of pending lawsuits, increasing excise taxes in states like California, and the antitrust litigation appeal involving rival Conwood. Yet the third quarter numbers were strong, and investors remained happy and were quick to note that the company has paid cash dividends without interruption since 1912.

Favorable news came with the August 28, 2001, report that Standard & Poor's had raised UST Inc.'s long-term corporate credit and senior secured debt ratings from A− to A, as well as its senior unsecured debt from BBB+ to A− and short-term corporate credit ratings from A−2 to A−1. S & P felt that the ratings "reflect the company's moderate financial policies, solid profitability levels, and strong cash flow." Even with the S & P ratings and the strong third quarter, Gierer wondered about the company's plans for the winter of 2001. UST was planning to appeal the $1.05 billion verdict against the company in an antitrust lawsuit that had been won by its major competitor, Conwood. Could he and the company win the appeal, continue implementing their company's five-year plan, and provide superior returns to shareholders? He still remembered the initial verdict and its input on Wall Street; the company's share price had plunged $2.9375, or 15 percent, to $16.4375, a 52-week low. If the company lost the appeal, it would be a serious blow to UST and would drain the company's cash flow and possibly put its future dividends at risk.

COMPANY PRODUCTS AND SCOPE

UST, Inc. has a company history dating to 1822, and the name U.S. Tobacco Company itself dates back to 1922. Copenhagen, UST's flagship brand, was introduced in 1822 and represents one of America's oldest trademarks; it also remains the best-selling moist, smokeless tobacco in the world. The company, based in Greenwich, Connecticut, is a holding company for four wholly owned subsidiaries: (1) United States Tobacco Company; (2) International Wine & Spirits Ltd; (3) UST Enterprises Inc.; and (4) UST

International Inc. The four groups combined employ approximately 4,800 employees. UST, through its subsidiary, U.S. Smokeless Tobacco Company (USSTC), is a leading producer and marketer of moist, smokeless tobacco products, including Copenhagen, Copenhagen Long Cut, Skoal, Skoal Long Cut, Skoal Bandits, Red Seal, and Rooster. Internationally, UST markets its products primarily in Canada, and sales have been both profitable and stable there for a number of years.

Other consumer products marketed by the company include premium wines sold nationally through the Chateau Ste. Michelle, Columbia Crest, and Villa Mt. Eden wineries as well as sparkling wine produced under the Domaine Ste. Michelle label. Other consumer products marketed by UST subsidiaries include Don Tomas and Astral premium cigars.

COMPANY HISTORY

George Weyman, who invented Copenhagen snuff, opened a tobacco shop in Pittsburgh in 1822. Following his death in 1870, his sons took over the shop, renaming it Weyman & Bro. American Tobacco Company. A tobacco monopoly acquired Weyman & Bro. in 1905. When a Supreme Court ruling dissolved the monopoly in 1911 (finding it in violation of the Sherman Antitrust Act), the company was reorganized as Weyman-Bruton. After acquiring the United States Tobacco Company in 1921, the company took the name of the acquisition the following year. The firm introduced Skoal, a wintergreen-flavored tobacco, in 1934.

In 1965, United States Tobacco purchased the W. H. Snyder & Sons Cigar Company and later, after merging it into Wolf Brothers Cigar, renamed it House of Windsor (1981); Then it sold the company to its employees (1987). United States Tobacco entered the pipe business with the 1969 purchase of Henry, Leonard & Thomas, Inc., maker of the Dr. Grabow brand of presmoked pipes. In 1974, it added Mastercraft Pipes and bought its first winery (now called Chateau Ste. Michelle). Under Louis Bantle, who became chairman in 1973, sales of the company's snuff climbed 10 percent annually between 1974 and 1979, and by using rodeo and sports personalities as endorsers, the company expanded beyond its traditional northern markets into the Southeast and Southwest.

In the 1970s and the 1980s, the market structure of the industry began to change. Swisher International Group, Inc. and Conwood entered the market in the late 1970s. By 1980, three manufacturers sold five brands of moist snuff. Output was 26 million pounds, up from 17 million pounds in 1972. By the 1990s four manufacturers sold 28 brands. UST's share declined to 87 percent and industry output grew to 44 million pounds.

In 1983, United States Tobacco introduced Skoal Bandits, a teabag-like premeasured "dip" aimed at beginning consumers; at the time, the company denied targeting minors. Three years later, it acquired the Villa Mt. Eden and Conn Creek wineries and was incorporated as UST, a holding company for United States Tobacco.

UST's fortune fizzled in the late 1980s. Although previously excluded from the regulations imposed on cigarette makers, a $147 million case filed against the company in 1986 (Betty Ann Marsee claimed her son died of oral cancer caused by dipping Copenhagen) led to restrictions on smokeless tobacco. The suit was concluded in UST's favor in 1989, but the negative publicity led to mandatory warning notices on packaging, a ban on radio and TV advertising, and the imposition of an excise tax. Today, UST voluntarily displays the Age of Purchase Icon on print and point-of-sale ads for its products as well as on direct mailings; the message it proclaims states UST's policy of "not [being] for sale to minors." Despite the growing controversy, smokeless tobacco was the only growing segment of the industry in the early 1990s, and UST had more than 80 percent of the U.S. market. Vincent Gierer became CEO of UST in 1990.

Market growth in the industry accelerated throughout the 1990s. By 1999, there were approximately 40 brands, 24 of which were from UST's competitors. UST's share dropped to 76 percent, and total output exceeded 60 million pounds, an increase of 36 percent over 1990. By contrast, industry sales for all other tobacco products fell in the 1990s.

Allegations of nicotine manipulation in its products led the company to testify before Congress in 1994. In 1997, UST joined four other tobacco companies and paid $11.3 billion as part of Florida's settlement against the tobacco industry. It also launched discount dip Red Seal the same year. In 1998, following the tobacco industry's $206 billion settlement in several states, the company entered into a separate agreement to pay $100–$200 million over ten years for youth-targeted antismoking programs. In 1999, 34 Native American tribes filed suit in New Mexico against UST and other major tobacco companies for $1 billion of the $206 billion judgment.

In March 2000, a federal jury ordered UST to pay $1.05 billion (more than twice its 1999 profits) to competitor Conwood as a result of a 1998 antitrust lawsuit accusing UST of using unethical tactics to keep Conwood's products out of stores. UST is appealing the decision (*Hoover's Handbook of American Business, 2001*).

Today, UST is the largest U.S. manufacturer and distributor of moist chewing tobacco and snuff. CEO Gierer has an annual salary of $2,755,000. The company ranks number eight among top Republican donors, contributing some $1,927,200 from January 1990 to June 1999, as reported by Democracy Now (**http://democracynow.org/companies/ust.html**). Wine yields about 11 percent of UST's sales. The firm also makes cigars and owns Bert Grant's Ale microbrewery in Washington State. The McLane Company (a distributor owned by Wal-Mart) sells about 20 percent of UST's products. UST's profit margins (over 30 percent) are as good as Microsoft's. Its impressive returns rank among the highest of any public company, with a return on sales of 29 percent, a return on assets of 24 percent, and a return on equity of 84 percent (all in 2001).

Its tobacco division features both moist smokeless tobacco made from 100 percent American tobacco (Copenhagen, Red Seal, Rooster, Skoal, and Skoal Bandits) as well as premium cigars (Astral, Don Tomas, Habano Primero). The beverages products include craft beer (Bert Grant's Ale), premium wine (Conn Creek, Villa Mt. Eden), premium varietal wine (Chateau Ste. Michelle, Columbia Crest, Snoqualmie), and sparking wines (Domaine Ste. Michelle).

MARKET SHARE

Of UST's $1.67 billion in total sales for 2001, $1.45 billion of this was from the smokeless tobacco segment. This was an 8 percent increase over 2000. The tobacco segment accounts for 87.5 percent of consolidated UST's sales. The wine segment had net sales of $188 million in 2001, while all other UST sales were $30.7 million. It is the leader in the smokeless tobacco market, having captured about 77 percent. This figure is down from a near 85 percent market share high in 1993. This loss shows that UST has not escaped the industry's problems. The drop also represents a 3 percent slide from 1997, when UST had a near 80 percent share of the market. Mr Gierer indicated that net volume only grew at 0.2 percent, citing slowing category growth as the reason why. The company lost one point in market share attributed to the discontinuance of some UST products.

According to the *Tobacco Report: 1998–1999*, which was issued in 2001 by the Federal Trade Commission in a report to Congress, of the five major domestic manufacturers of smokeless tobacco, UST continued to lead the industry in 1999, with 75 percent of the moist snuff market in terms of pounds sold; its closest competitor, Conwood, reportedly had 13 percent of that market. Swedish Match reportedly controlled

39 percent of the loose-leaf market in 1999; Conwood controlled 34 percent, National controlled 19 percent, and Swisher controlled 8 percent.

SALES TRENDS BY PRODUCT SEGMENT 2001

2001

Smokeless Tobacco

For 2001, net sales of smokeless tobacco increased 8 percent to $1.451 billion, and gross profit increased 8.5 percent. Moist, smokeless tobacco net can sales increased 2.5 percent to 648.7 million cans in 2001. During 2001, UST introduced three new products, Copenhagen Black, Rooster Wild Berry, and Red Seal Long Cut Straight. Premium promotional can sales in 2001 were reduced by 10.4 million, or 33.6 percent for the nine-month period ending September 30, 2001; moist, smokeless tobacco net can sales increased 0.6 percent to 480.1 million cans.

Wine Segment

2001 wine segment revenue increased 8.2 percent to $188.9 million. Premium case sales advanced 8.8 percent, while nonpremium case sales declined. Case sales for the segment's best selling wines—Columbia Crest and Chateau Ste. Michelle—increased 13.7 and 9.3 percent respectively. Operating profit increased 22.1 percent to $21.2 million.

UST is the only wine company in the world to place five wines on *Wine Spectator*'s "Top 100 Wines of the World." In 2001, UST's Chateau Ste. Michelle Cold Creek Chardonnay was the highest ranked white wine on this prestigious list. Strong demand for premium wine in 2001 is encouraging for the company; the installation of a new president is likewise an encouraging development. Instead of expanding by acquisition, Stimson Lane will shift its focus to improving operating results by reducing costs of goods sold,

EXHIBIT 1   UST Consolidated Statement of Earnings
(in thousands, except per-share amounts)

Year ended December 31	2001	2000	1999
Net Sales	$1,670,315	$1,547,644	$1,512,331
Costs and Expenses			
Cost of products sold	312,304	294,802	276,358
Excise taxes	37,277	35,277	27,917
Selling, advertising and administrative	487,706	464,842	431,578
Total Costs and Expenses	837,287	794,921	735,853
Operating Income	833,028	752,723	776,478
Interest, net	33,760	34,288	13,535
Earnings Before Income Taxes	799,268	718,435	762,943
Income Taxes	307,666	276,549	293,650
Net Earnings	$ 491,602	$ 441,886	$ 469,293
Net Earnings Per Share			
Basic	$ 2.99	$ 2.71	$ 2.69
Diluted	$ 2.97	$ 2.70	$ 2.68
Average Number of Shares			
Basic	164,250	163,181	174,355
Diluted	165,682	163,506	175,114

Source: UST's 2001 *Annual Report*, p. 24.

improving top-end quality wines, and eliminating underperforming assets. By refocusing on existing operations, the wine business is expected to deliver operating profit increases in excess of 20 percent in each of the next several years, according to the 2000 Annual Report.

MISSION AND VISION

According to U.S. Smokeless Tobacco Company's vision statement, "Our smoke-free products will be recognized by adults as the preferred way to experience tobacco satisfaction. The four key strategies to attaining this vision are breaking down barriers, improving the value equation, effectively allocating resources, and developing next-generation products." Stimson Lane's vision statement says that the company strives—"To be the leader in the ultra-premium wine segment, to elevate Washington State wines to the quality and prestige of the top wine regions of the world, and to be known for superior products, innovation, and customer focus. To realize its vision, Stimson Lane will continue to build on the significant critical acclaim it achieved in 2000."

EXHIBIT 2   UST Consolidated Segment Information (in thousands)

Year ended December 31	2001	2000	1999
Net Sales to Unaffiliated Customers			
Smokeless Tobacco	$1,450,714	$1,343,779	$1,309,566
Wine	188,858	174,472	174,272
All other	30,743	29,393	28,493
Net sales	$1,670,315	$1,547,644	$1,512,331
Operating Profit (Loss)			
Smokeless Tobacco	$833,185	$768,786	$777,122
Wine	21,212	17,377	20,234
All other	(8,907)	(15,772)	(10,240)
Operating profit	845,490	770,391	787,116
Corporate expenses	(12,462)	(17,668)	(10,638)
Interest, net	(33,760)	(34,288)	(13,535)
Earnings before income taxes	$799,268	$718,435	$762,943
Identifiable Assets at December 31			
Smokeless Tobacco	$1,268,065	$1,120,377	$529,518
Wine	389,243	342,447	305,447
All other	60,180	68,776	87,678
Corporate	294,214	114,799	93,005
Assets	$2,011,702	$1,646,339	$1,015,648
Capital Expenditures			
Smokeless Tabacco	$27,364	$28,743	$26,830
Wine	19,336	20,720	31,182
All other	246	522	939
Corporate	284	1,090	338
Capital expenditures	$47,230	$51,075	$59,289
Depreciation			
Smokeless Tobacco	$20,298	$19,573	$17,279
Wine	12,842	13,869	13,279
All other	914	1,395	1,534
Corporate	951	1,677	1,645
Depreciation	$35,005	$36,514	$33,737

Source: UST's 2001 *Annual Report*, p. 23.

EXHIBIT 3   UST Consolidated Statement of Financial Position
(In thousands)

December 31	2001	2000
Assets		
Current assets		
Cash and cash equivalents	$ 271,969	$ 96,034
Accounts receivable	85,423	82,698
Inventories	493,820	449,284
Deferred income taxes	16,855	9,907
Income taxes receivable	—	28,915
Prepaid expenses and other current assets	23,892	24,567
Total current assets	891,959	691,405
Property, plant and equipment, net	369,568	358,586
Restricted deposits	659,897	505,755
Other assets	90,278	90,653
Total assets	$2,011,702	$1,646,399
Liabilities and Stockholders' Equity		
Current liabilities		
Short-term debt	$ 3,300	$ 3,300
Accounts payable and accrued expenses	171,610	155,179
Income taxes payable	47,552	14,393
Total current liabilities	222,462	172,872
Long-term debt	862,575	865,875
Postretirement benefits other than pensions	81,679	81,677
Deferred income taxes	183,524	186,559
Other liabilities	80,400	68,844
Contingencies [see note]		
Total liabilities	1,430,640	1,375,827
Stockholders' equity		
Capital stock	101,710	102,372
Additional paid-in capital	635,380	526,996
Retained earnings	915,990	885,074
Accumulated other comprehensive loss	(18,256)	(13,606)
	1,634,824	1,500,836
Less treasury stock	1,053,762	1,230,264
Total stockholder's equity	581,062	270,572
Total liabilities and stockholders' equity	$2,011,702	$1,646,399

Source: UST's 2001 Annual Report, p. 25.

PRODUCT/MARKET SHIFTS

UST Inc. seems to be benefiting from higher cigarette prices. As a maker of moist, smokeless tobacco products, UST isn't necessarily luring new consumers who don't want to pay more for cigarettes, but the company is actually winning over its own customers, who incidentally don't want to pay more for cigarettes. About 25 percent of UST's consumers also smoke cigarettes, so instead of using both, many tobacco users are moving away from higher-priced cigarettes and buying more snuff. While growth in moist snuff volume has increased, the Tobacco Merchants Association indicates that the chewing tobacco industry has been plummeting since 1988.

PRODUCT AND FLAVOR TRENDS

Snuff is a finely ground or shredded form of tobacco, most commonly sold in small tin cans or pouches. Users put a pinch between their lower lip or cheek and gum. Snuff contains nicotine and a variety of cancer-causing chemicals that are absorbed into the blood. Because snuff is held in the mouth for minutes at a time, some argue that more of the chemicals enter the body than they would from cigarette smoking.

One of the growing trends in smokeless tobacco, besides the type of cut that is preferred (fine cut or long cut), is the preponderance toward added flavors. Mint or ice seems to be the favorite among the younger adult consumers. Changes in the smokeless tobacco market are consumer driven, and the entire smokeless market is striving to meet the changing trend. Other smokeless products that are appearing on the scene are tobacco and nicotine-free chews. These herbal snuffs are a substitute for the standard product and smokeless tobacco in general, as well as a substitute for many smokers. In mid-1995, when UST introduced its new product, the Skoal Flavor Packs, the product was marketed to "smokers who can't smoke." Skoal Bandits, a moist snuff that is packaged in portion packs similar to small tea bags, along with other smokeless products are aiding profits. In contrast to the increase in moist snuff, chewing tobacco, a longer cut tobacco sold in foil packages, has been continually losing ground.

Most competitors in the smokeless category have added a discount brand. Companies such as Conwood and Swedish Match have launched Durango, Cougar, and Southern Pride, to meet this market, which is continuing to grow. Coupled with this bargain trend, companies such as Smokey Mountain Snuff and Conwood are linking their products to sporting events as a promotional strategy.

Another factor that helps to boost the trend toward increasing sales of moist snuff is its availability within the market. This product can be purchased in locations such as supermarkets, smoke shops, mass merchandisers, and discount and convenience stores. The products can even be purchased online at retailers such as **www.freshnuff.com/orderonline.htm**. Additionally, as the number of places that people can smoke are further restricted, moist snuff sales will grow because it is easy to use anywhere. Driving the trend further is aggressive advertising, which is directed at the moist snuff segment of the market. According to the *Maxwell Report,* smokeless tobacco use in 2000 edged up 10.5 percent to 116.5 per cent million pounds versus 1999. The moist snuff category slipped 2 percent to 64.8 million pounds.

UST's newest product, Revel, was introduced in the fall of 2001 in two test markets—in Topeka, Kansas, and Youngstown, Ohio—for six months. Supporting the product launch was print advertising; direct marketing, adult sampling, and point-of-sale and retail promotions. Revel is marketed as an "Anytime, Anywhere"™ product for adults to use when they can't smoke cigarettes—for example, on airplanes, in meetings, on the factory floor, or in a shopping mall. The product is a blend of tobacco and mint flavor in a packet. Offered in both regular and mild, it differs from previous smokeless tobacco products insofar as adults who have tried it report that they feel no need to expectorate. Offered in a plastic push and flip container, each has 20 packs and is priced competitively with a pack of premium cigarettes.

Rooster has been promoted to college students in college newspapers since 2000. UST had waited one year before ending its 35-year self-imposed ban on advertising in college newspapers in 1999. Its break with the past has also generated discussions in newsrooms and on colleges campuses as students and professors have debated whether campus papers would be breaching tobacco's First Amendment rights by rejecting ads for a legal product. The campaign has had little negative response, according to advertising managers at various campus newspapers.

MARKETING

UST is in the next phase of its "A pinch better" campaign, having launched a nearly $3 million Skoal Heavy Chevy Camero Sweepstakes effort in August 2001, which ran to the end of the year. Consumers can win a 2002 Chevrolet Camaro SS and a trip to Frank Hawley's Drag Racing School or Cobra two-way radios. Ads were placed in magazines, including *Playboy, Hot Rod,* and *Drag Race.* POP (point-of-purchase) and direct mail to 525,000 moist, smokeless tobacco users supported the campaign. Skoal recently switched from passive outdoor images after consumers requested masculine and active images more befitting the brand, said Rich Fasanelli, USSTC's VP of Marketing. The new initiative focuses on motorcycle riders, firefighters, and rugby players. Skoal also sponsors the Don Prudhomme NHRA racing team. Other marketing strategies includes special packaging to stress "outdoor adventures," mail-in sweeps for boats and trips or cash or personal navigation systems, and a "lids for gear" program that allows consumers to redeem Skoal lids for prizes such as fishing gear, knives, Cobra handheld radios, and other discounts.

CURRENT LITIGATION

Approximately 35 cases have been filed against UST (and other tobacco manufacturers) since 1954. Only one case has been tried to a verdict, and it resulted in a unanimous jury decision in favor of UST. Most of the litigation has focused on cigarettes, and UST continues to stress the difference between cigarettes and smokeless tobacco.

UST was ordered to pay $1.05 billion to rival Conwood after a federal jury ruled that the company violated antitrust laws. After a month-long trial, the jury awarded damages, which were automatically tripled under antitrust laws. Both companies accused each other of removing display racks from stores, making under-the-table cash rebates to win retailers, and holding strategy sessions to plot ways to eliminate the other competitor from the lucrative retail-checkout market. Jurors found that UST monopolized the market by controlling prices or excluding competition or both. Conwood attorneys accused UST of spreading rumors that Conwood's snuff contained stems and was stale. Conwood also alleged that UST controlled point-of-sale advertising and often inserted its ads over Conwood's own sales displays in stores. UST hopes to have the jury's award for Conwood overturned or reversed on appeal.

UST has not escaped the class-action litigation aimed at the major domestic cigarette companies. These legal cases are geared toward the reimbursement of healthcare costs in addition to damages and other relief for smokers. While the predominance of the cases relate specifically to cigarettes, there are a few that relate directly to smokeless tobacco products like those manufactured and sold by UST.

Litigation continues to plague the smokeless tobacco industry. West Virginia has legislation pending to impose the state's first smokeless tobacco tax. The bill (SB116) would impose a 7 percent excise (or sin) tax on smokeless tobacco products. This is down from the original 25 percent tax Governor Bob Wise had proposed. Monies from the tax would be distributed to the countries. The *Charleston Daily Mail* (March 31, 2001) reported results of a study that indicated nearly half of West Virginia's teenage boys who use smokeless tobacco would quit if the price increased, but some lawmakers doubt whether a smokeless tobacco tax would help lower the relatively high percentage of West Virginian teens who use the tobacco. In males, the state ranks third in the country in smokeless tobacco use, and a 1999 Youth Risk Behavior Survey showed that West Virginian teens were twice as likely to use smokeless tobacco as other U.S. teens. Opponents of the tax want to maximize profits, while supporters of the tax want to prevent addiction and save lives. Health advocates cite scientific studies indicating that price increases are the most effective deterrent to tobacco use by youths. Retailers and wholesalers do not believe this to be true, yet they clearly believe the tax increase will hurt sales. Estimates are that approximately 12 million people in the United States use smokeless tobacco, and 3 million of these users are under 21. An estimated 2,200 young people age 11–19 try smokeless tobacco every day, and 830 become regular users. Vast regional differences are apparent, and tobacco use is highest in the South.

West Virginia could join California, which recently passed a new tax on smokeless tobacco to attempt to slash at least a third of the 100 million ounces of smokeless tobacco sold in California every year. Supporters feel the tax will deliver an extra $67 million annually to the state. Some say the tax will lead to a thriving underground racket in snuff and chewing tobacco and cheat the state of tax revenue. Moist snuff in California now costs around $8 for a can, up from about $3.

THE SMOKELESS TOBACCO INDUSTRY

Today, the U.S. tobacco industry is an approximately $53 billion industry, with cigarettes accounting for nearly 94 percent of the total. The remaining 6 percent of usage is for cigars, moist smokeless tobacco, chewing tobacco, and snuff. The cigarette industry is quite mature and consolidated, with the top four producers accounting for approximately 72 percent of industry sales (Standard & Poor's Industry Surveys).

The smokeless tobacco industry (NAICS 312229), divided into two major areas—chewing tobacco and snuff—consists of different products. The chewing tobacco area consists of loose-leaf, moist, firm plug, and twist/roll products. The snuff group consists of dry and moist, depending on the amount of moisture added to the tobacco during manufacturing. Despite the fact that consumption patterns have shifted from loose leaf to moist snuff, there is still a large number of consumers who use both products.

Consumers of moist smokeless tobacco products are extremely brand loyal and demand product freshness. Research shows that consumers looking for a particular brand will go elsewhere if they don't find it rather than purchase another brand. Out-of-stock sales can hurt sales performance, but carrying excess inventory can result in stale products. Retailers work with suppliers to develop selections to maintain stock and to preserve product freshness.

The aggregate tobacco industry is classed with oligopolistic industries. Firms face high capital costs, hazardous antitrust and legal action, futile price-cutting, and charges of monopolistic practices if firms should try to join in a concerted action. The U.S. tobacco products industry has undergone substantial consolidation over the years. Prompted mainly by the combined challenges of declining U.S. consumption trends in a highly developed marketplace and the steady rise in legal and regulatory burdens, many manufacturers have either joined forces with competitors or perished. The increased scale needed to compete in the industry has erected very high barriers to entry.

The smokeless tobacco industry is highly concentrated in the tobacco-producing region of the United States. The five states that have the greatest number of workers in the industry are Kentucky, Tennessee, Georgia, North Carolina, and Illinois. Georgia and Illinois have replaced Virginia and Pennsylvania as leading employers of smokeless tobacco workers. Over one-half of the employment in the industry is concentrated in Kentucky. The reasons for this geographic concentration are obvious, the first being a desire to locate factories close to raw materials. Another reason is that the industry is concentrated in the area of the country that has traditionally been considered the prime market for the smokeless industry—the South.

The cigarette industry dwarfs the smokeless industry, and cigar consumption has increased among men over the age of eighteen. Magazines such as *Cigar Aficionadom, Cigar*

Insider, and *Smoke,* all of which are smoking lifestyle magazines, are capitalizing on the stogie's neo-cool image and drawing in luxury-goods advertisers. While its cigar operations are small, UST markets many recognized brands. This area of its business has been affected by a substantial oversupply in the marketplace, a development that has resulted from the fact that many companies flood the market in an effort to meet this neo-cool trend. UST is currently evaluating the situation to determine its prospects and alternatives.

RETAIL DISTRIBUTION OF MOIST SNUFF

Manufacturers typically sell moist snuff to independent wholesalers that resell to retailers. By 1999, approximately 300,000 retail stores in the United States sold moist snuff, but sales volume was dominated by large chains, including mass merchandisers (e.g., Wal-Mart, 2,300 stores; Kmart, 2,160 stores), convenience stores (e.g., 7-Eleven, 2,500 stores), and supermarkets (e.g., Kroger, 2,288 stores). Conwood products are in 81 percent of all retails stores; USSTC's distribution rate is 87 percent; Swedish Match and Swisher are also widely distributed. There are no agreements between retailers and moist snuff manufacturers that force retailers to deal in the products of only one manufacturer.

In offering new products, each manufacturer must justify the retailers' allocation of space to them. About 70 to 90 percent of retailers still used separate racks provided by each moist snuff manufacturer for its own products. In the 1995–1996 period, Wal-Mart asked all manufacturers to compete in designing a single customized cabinet for the display of moist snuff products in order to provide greater uniformity, aid inventory management, and maximize shelf space efficiency. USSTC's design won. Swedish won similar competitions for exclusive rack systems in Kmart and Tom Thumb stores. Due to restrictions on self-service and theft problems, products are no longer displayed on open shelves, but they are increasingly restricted to locked cabinets and secure behind-the-counter areas.

Manufacturers offer retailer's incentive programs and rebates for providing sales data, for participating in promotional programs, or for giving a manufacturer the best placement of racks and displays. Manufacturers have sales personnel in the field, and each one visits 8 to 10 retail stores per day to routinely check racks, to check that stock is current, and to introduce new products and promotions.

COMPETITORS AND MARKET SHARE

The Federal Trade Commission Report to Congress for the years 1998 and 1999 (issued in 2001) indicates that of the five major domestic manufacturers of smokeless tobacco, UST continued to lead the industry in 1999 in terms of pounds sold; it has a 40.5 percent share of the total smokeless tobacco industry altogether. Published reports also indicate that Conwood's 1999 industry share was 23.8 percent, Swedish Match's was 20.5 percent, National's was 7.5 percent, and Swisher's was 6.5 percent. UST reportedly controlled 75 percent of the moist snuff market in 1999 in term of pounds sold, compared to its closest competitor, Conwood, which reportedly had 13 percent of that market. Swedish Match reportedly controlled 39 percent of the loose leaf market in 1999; Conwood controlled 35 percent, National controlled 19 percent, and Swisher controlled 8 percent. Top-selling moist snuff and fine cut tobacco brands are shown in Exhibit 4 and top-selling loose leaf chewing tobacco brands are shown in Exhibit 5.

Conwood has been privately held since the Pritzker family took the firm private in a $400 million buyout in 1985. Conwood makes Kodiak and Cougar snuff and has some 13 percent of the moist snuff market, with UST hovering between 76 and 77 percent of the market. Conwood's market share has risen steadily, from 0.0 percent to 7.6 percent during the 1979–1982 period; from 7.6 percent to 10.6 percent during the 1982–1990 period; and from 10.6 percent to 13.5 percent during the 1990–1998 period. Based in Memphis, Tennessee, Conwood is controlled through a complicated ownership scheme by Chicago's powerhouse Pritzker family.

Conwood's major brand of chewing tobacco is Levi Garrett. Taylor's Pride and Levi Garrett Plug are its moist plug brands. Kodiak and Hawken were moist snuff brands introduced in 1981. Conwood is urging Gen X males not to let peer pressure dictate their chewing preferences with regard to its newest Extreme brand, which was introduced in August 2001. It is a longer cut tobacco and features a big X stamped into a steellike background. Conwood execs chose to launch a new trademark rather than to steer its 20-year-old Kodiak brand toward young adults and in the process turn off its mature audiences.

Headquartered in Jacksonville, Florida, Swisher International, Inc. produces large cigars for the mass-market, such as Swisher Sweets, King Edward, and Optimo. It also produces BeRing, La Primadora, and Siglo 21, all of which are in the premium cigars category. These products are additions to its smokeless tobacco products line, both moist and dry snuff, under the brands Silver Creek, Redwood, and Kayak moist snuff, and the loose-leaf brands of Mail Pouch, Lancaster-Limited-Reserve, and Chattanooga Chew. This company has captured a 5 percent market share, in 1998, it experienced a 3.1 percent growth in sales and a 19.8 percent growth in net income. In 1999, this company, controlled by William Ziegler III, went private. Swisher International is in its 140th year of operations and offers smokers around the globe a full range of quality cigars and smokeless items in all price categories.

Swedish Match, formerly Pinkerton Tobacco Co. (NASDAQ: SWMAY), is owned by the car company Volvo and produces cigars, smokeless tobacco products, and pipe tobacco as well as smoking accessories such as matches and lighters. Swedish is the world's largest maker of matches and the number three producer of disposable lighters (Cricket) behind BIC and the Itochu subsidiary Tokai. Its Red Man chewing tobacco brand leads the U.S. market. Swedish Match's other tobacco offerings include pipe tobacco, snuff, and an array of cigars (it ranks number two in the world behind Altidas), including well known brands such as El Credito, Garcia y Vega, La Paz, Montague, and Tiparillo. It owns 64 percent of U.S. cigar maker General Cigar Holdings. The company makes rolling papers and filters, but it sold its cigarette division to Austria Tabak in 1999. Swedish Match's products are made in 15 countries and sold in 140 countries. The firm was founded in 1915 and is organized in five divisions—North Europe, Continental Europe, North America, Overseas, and Matches. The headquarters' offices are located in Stockholm. Its goal is to strengthen its position as a leading global player in the area of niche tobacco products, particularly in the European and North American markets, and to continue developing its position in certain selected markets in other parts of the world.

Lennart Sunden, chief executive of Swedish Match, Europe's largest producer of moist oral snuff, believes that trends appear to justify the company's decision to divest itself of its cigarette operations in 1998 and to focus on oral snuff. Although in volume terms, sales of cigarettes are declining in most developed countries due to the increased awareness of health risks and public smoking bans, London's *Financial Times* reports that sales of oral snuff are increasing in the markets where it is allowed (May 2, 2001, p. 32). Swedish Match's sales of snuff are increasing. Operating profit margins on the product were above 45 percent. With growth rates of around 20 percent and no exposure to cigarettes, the company is seen as a growth stock rather than a tobacco company.

In Sweden, where snuff consumption has been growing by around 5 percent a year, smoking has declined to less than 20 percent of the adult population. More than one in ten Swedes is a user, including the country's health minister, and Swedish Match has a market share above 90 percent in the country. Internationally, taxes on tobacco products have been hiked sharply in countries throughout the EU in recent years. Advertising prohibitions barring tobacco from British media, for example, were recently broadened to include the Internet, and a bill banning tobacco companies from maintaining databases for direct mail was making its way through Parliament before its dissolution.

However, in the United States, the company feels that it has the largest potential. Here, the market is growing by 3 percent a year, while Swedish Match's sales grew 19 percent in volume last year. Mainly through its popular Timber Wolfbrand, it now has a market share of 8 percent in volume in a market that is worth about $1.8 billion. Timberwolf was introduced in 1995, and the low-priced snuff is grossing some $115 million annually.

Outside the United States, Swedish Match is introducing its snuff products in South Africa and India, yet inside the EU, with the exception of Sweden, its sale has been banned since 1992 on health grounds. Sunden believes this ban will be lifted within a few years. On top of its extensive line of cigars and cigarillos (small cigars the size of cigarettes), the company also acquired two U.S. cigar companies, General Cigars and El Credito, which manufacture mass-market cigars and handmade premium cigars, respectively.

Like Conwood, Swedish Match has rolled out lower-priced cans of snuff that quickly make a splash in the marketplace. These low-price brands are said to be the reason UST's total share of the market during the past 10 years has fallen to 78 percent from about 90 percent. UST may face a crossroads since it has based its reputation on premium brands. Its discounted brand, Red Seal, was a costly introduction in 1999 for UST. Swedish Match also introduced Sequoia, its first premium moist snuff product which featured Cinnamon Ice and Mountain Cider flavors and a unique twist-off can. June 2001 found Swedish Match ads for the new product in *Playboy, Maxim, Hot Rod, Field & Stream, American Hunter,* and on ESPN.

MARKETING, ETHICAL, AND HEALTH ISSUES

As with other tobacco products, there is concern over health hazards associated with chewing tobacco, the major issue being mouth cancer, which includes cancer of the cheeks and gums. As early as 1761, awareness of smokeless tobacco's harmful effects was known as English physician John Hill warned consumers of the dangers of tobacco's use. Today, the American Cancer Society and the American Dental Association oppose tobacco chewing because it stains teeth and causes gum disease and mouth infections, which can lead to cancer.

Spit tobacco poses health hazards to users, contrary to popular notions that it is a safe alternative to smoking. The various forms of spit tobacco have been found to cause mouth cancer, a disease responsible for more than 8,000 deaths annually. Aside from causing oral cancer, spit tobacco also leads to bad breath, teeth stains, gum inflammation, or periodontal disease with bone loss. The concentrated nicotine absorbed orally also accelerates the heart rate, increases blood pressure, and can heighten the risk of coronary artery problems; heart disease, period occlusive vascular and cerebrovascular diseases, as well as stroke.

Also, dry snuff sniffed through the nostrils is considered harmful since it irritates the nerves that control the sense of smell, thus diminishing one's ability to distinguish odors. Specifically, smokeless tobacco use increases the risk of oral cancer by 300 percent. In addition, elevated cholesterol levels and blood pressure are other harmful side effects. The elevated levels of blood pressure appear to result from tobacco's high sodium and sugar contents. According to the American Cancer Society, some of the major ingredients in dip and chewing tobacco are nicotine (an addictive drug), polonium 210 (nuclear waste), formaldehyde (embalming fluid), cancer-causing chemicals, and radioactive elements.

Other health problems associated with smokeless tobacco use include sickness for first-time users, cancer of the mouth and throat, leukoplakia, potential cardiovascular problems, and peptic ulcers. With the use of this variety of tobacco continuing to increase, these health problems will also increase.

Tooth staining periodontal disease, nicotine stomatitis (mouth sores), local gingival (gum) recession, leukoplakia (white patches), or other mucosal conditions are tobacco-related complications. Systematic effects such as nicotine dependence, transient hypertension (high blood pressure), and cardiovascular disease may also result from smokeless tobacco use.

CUSTOMER DEMOGRAPHICS AND MARKETING

Chewing tobacco still remains predominantly a blue-collar, rural/suburban activity, but there has been some penetration into new urban, inner-city markets as a result of the country-western craze. The average annual income of adult consumers of moist snuff is $37,520. A study by the Department of Health and Human Services found that 19 percent of high school males use smokeless tobacco. Usage by the under-19 sector is highest in the South and the Midwest—and, in particular, in the states of Tennessee and Montana. Of student-athletes who used smokeless tobacco products, 57 percent played baseball and 40 percent played football.

Over the last 20 years, consumers have generally been attracted to lighter products in all consumption areas. It is this lighter, milder, sweeter-tasting appeal that smokeless tobacco producers are selling to customers, at least for growth products like loose-leaf and moist snuff. Consumers can enjoy a mild tobacco taste without ever lighting-up. Nationally, states have laws limiting smoking in public areas, according to Health and Human Services. Additionally, many companies have banned smoking on their premises. All of these reasons are conducive to the purchase and use of smokeless tobacco products. In addition, smokeless tobacco manufacturers have promoted their products as the most economical form of tobacco use.

Smokeless tobacco producers are now expanding their customer base into other consumer segments, including active outdoor people, sports enthusiasts, business executives, and professional people. New younger consumers, many of whom have never used any form of tobacco before, are being attracted to smokeless tobacco products, especially to moist snuff. These younger consumers like moist snuff because using this product is more socially acceptable than chewing tobacco and because snuff can be used indoors as well as outdoors insofar as one does not have to spit. Internationally, most find the practice of dipping and spitting to be gross. It is not a social custom taken up by many people.

Typical consumers are fourteen-to-eighteen-year-old boys, and most are white. Nationwide, white students are six times more likely than African Americans and three times more likely than Hispanics to use snuff. The *Courier-Journal* of Louisville, Kentucky (August 5, 2001) reported that in Kentucky, use of smokeless tobacco exceeded the overall state rate of 27.8 percent. According to former Surgeon General David Kessler, Kentucky boys are really buying a "drug-delivery system." A single 1-gram pinch of popular brands like Copenhagen and Kodiak can deliver six milligrams of nicotine—the equivalent of five Marlboro King cigarettes.

The ban on radio and television advertising of smokeless tobacco products was instituted in 1987. Additionally, manufacturers were also required to put warning labels on product packages. Furthermore, the Federal Trade Commission has proposed an amendment to the Comprehensive Smokeless Tobacco Health Education Act of 1986 to include the placement of warning labels on advertising at car races. Targets for additional labeling include cars and uniforms.

Smokeless tobacco producers use various ways to promote their products. Free-product sampling is widely used by manufacturers for new and existing products. Samples are distributed to consumers at sporting events, such as car races, concerts, gun and boat shows, and at the establishments of tobacco retailers. UST has been very successful at promoting the two largest-selling brands of moist snuff in the industry, Skoal and Copenhagen. Branded merchandise is offered by UST through its Country Western Store and concert catalog, where items are sold for a combination of cash and proofs of purchase from Skoal products. T-shirts, knives, watches, key chains, radios, Skoal silver lids, and belt buckles are a few of the branded articles available through the store. UST's sales representatives capitalize on product awareness with one-on-one product sampling to put products directly into the hands of customers. Some analysts feel that premium smokeless tobacco's hold is eroding due to value brands, which grabbed a 14.9 percent share during the second quarter of 2001 according to analyst Bonnie Herzog at Credit Suisse/First Boston. UST had avoided value lines but joined in the competition because the Red Seal brand had cut into its margins. Skoal maintained a 21.8 market share for the year ending June 10, 2001, according to ACNielsen, while Copenhagen and Kodiak slipped slightly to 34.6 percent and 11.3 percent, respectively.

CONCLUSION

While smokeless tobacco users remain loyal to their brands and to the product category, several substitutes are entering the market that compete with nicotine-based products (rather than gum or sugared candy). Ariva is a new product that offers nicotine in a snuff-based product marketed to smokers to urge them to quit. The minty-tasting Ariva, which dissolves completely, could provide an attractive alternative to abstinence, however, as many point out. It provides a jolt of nicotine when smokers can't smoke—on airplanes, in movie theaters, or in smoke-free offices. It contains eucalyptus and mint flavorings. Star Scientific, Inc. of Chester, Virginia, makes Ariva, and it has no intention of marketing Ariva as a smoking-cessation aid due to FDA regulations.

Other substitutes include nicotine gum, nicotine patches, nasal sprays, or nicotine inhalers that deliver nicotine; there are also other tobacco-free alternatives. Although highly profitable, UST's future is uncertain. Some special concerns to consider in strategic planning are listed below:

- Will health claims and litigation against smokeless tobacco users increase?
- Should UST continue to base its reputation and fortunes on premium brands, or should it create lower-priced brands? Would lower-priced brands steal business away from Skoal and Copenhagen? Should the company abandon the lower end of the market?
- Will UST win the appeal against Conwood's antitrust case?
- Will the industry's growth be adversely affected by skyrocketing taxes and the growing stigma surrounding snuff and chewing tobacco sales in the United States?
- How can the firm attract new users and capture current and former cigarette smokers?
- Is diversification beyond wine and smokeless tobacco a key to survival? What products should be added?
- Should the company launch new brands and improve its packaging? Can snuff be made more socially acceptable? Should the company develop a nonspit product?
- Is the 10 percent EPS goal realistic?
- Should UST try to acquire a smaller competitor?

REFERENCES

www.aap.org/advocacy/chmsmles.

www.ada.org.

The Charleston Daily Mail (March 31, 2001).

Courier-Journal (August 5, 2001).

http://democracynow.org/companies/
ust.html.

*The Federal Trade Commission Report to Congress
for the Years 1998 and 1999* (2001).

Financial Times (May 2, 2001): 32.

Hoover's Handbook of American Business (2001).

Journal of the American Dental Association
(September 2000).

Standard & Poor's Industry Surveys (2000).

www.swedishmatch.ch.

COORS—2002

Stephanie Wilhelm
Francis Marion University

RKY

www.coors.com

Coors—It's a name that conjures up an image of cool mountain streams, clear blue skies and all that is inspiring about the Rocky Mountain West. It is a name associated with an uncompromising commitment to quality—a reputation that began more than 100 years ago and thrives to this day.

It is the name of an ambitious 19th-century pioneer whose humble dream grew into the world's largest single-site brewery. But more than anything else, the name Coors is one held dear in the hearts of beer lovers across the country and, increasingly, around the globe. This is the story behind the name. (www.coors.com)

Founded in 1872 in the foothills of the Rocky Mountains, Adolph Coors Company is ranked among the 700 largest publicly traded corporations in the United States. Coors' principal subsidiary is Coors Brewing Company, the nation's third-largest brewer. Coors' corporate headquarters and primary brewery are located in the foothills of the Rocky Mountains in Golden, Colorado, which is the world's largest brewery on a single site. Coors also has another major brewing facility in Memphis, Tennessee, as well as packaging facilities in Virginia's Shenandoah Valley near the town of Elkton, Virginia. In addition, Coors owns major aluminum can and end-manufacturing facilities near Golden and is a partner in the joint venture that operates these plants. Coors is also a partner in a joint venture that owns and operates a glass bottle manufacturing plant in Colorado. More than 90 percent of Coors U.S. production is in Golden, CO.

Throughout its history, Coors has provided consumers with high-quality malt beverages produced through an all-natural brewing process and containing the finest ingredients available. Coors produces, markets, and sells high-quality malt-based beverages. Its portfolio of brands is designed to appeal to a wide range of consumer taste, style, and price preferences. Today, the Coors portfolio consists of Coors Light—the fourth-largest-selling beer in the country—Original Coors, and more than a dozen other malt-based beverages, primarily premium and super-premium beers. Coors' beverages are sold throughout the United States and in select international markets. Coors Light has accounted for more than 70 percent of the company's sales volume in the past three years. Premium and above-premium products accounted for more than 85 percent of its total sales volume in the last three years.

Under the direction of a fourth-generation Coors, Peter Coors, the company began the 1990s by having the fastest volume growth rate in the industry and by reaching its long time goal of becoming the nation's third-largest brewer. In addition, the company started expanding internationally, eventually making its products available to consumers in Japan, Canada, Ireland, the United Kingdom, and other countries. Coors products are now sold in about 30 international markets in North America, Latin America, the Caribbean, Europe, and Asia.

451

Coors developed special strains of barley that it malts itself. Coors adds nothing artificial to its beers. Coors beer, on average, takes about 55 days to brew, age, finish, and package its lagers—about twice as long as its major competitors. The result is a naturally aged, stable, and smooth product. Coors beers are packaged in dark amber bottles and protective cartons to guard against light damage. Most of its beer products are kept cold throughout the brewing, packaging, and distribution process. They are then shipped cold in either insulated or refrigerated railcars and trucks. Coors gives free brewery tours in both Golden (daily except Sundays and holidays) and Memphis (Thursday through Saturday). More than 250,000 visitors tour Coors' breweries each year. Coors' net sales for 2001 were $2.43 billion, down slightly from 2000. Coors' operating income in 2001 was $151 million, up just $1.0 million from 2000. Net income for 2001 increased 12.2 percent to $123 million.

HISTORY

Born in Barmen, Prussia, in 1847, Adolph Coors was the young German immigrant who founded Coors Brewing Company. Adolph began an apprenticeship at age fourteen at the Henry Wenker Brewery in Dortmund, Germany. Soon after he had become an apprentice at the brewing company, both of Adolph's parents died, leaving him to take care of his younger brother and sister. As an apprentice, he received clothing, food, and a place to live. It is also believed that Adolph was the brewery's nighttime bookkeeper, a job that enabled him to earn extra money.

Adolph continued to work at the Henry Wenker Brewery until the war in Germany caused him to stow away on a U.S.-bound ship at the age of 21. He arrived in Baltimore with no job and penniless, but he had a dream, like most immigrants did. Adolph's dream was to own his own brewery. Adolph traveled west through America and wound up in Naperville, Illinois; there, he was hired as a foreman at the Stenger Brewery. Apparently, the owner of the brewery, who had three daughters, saw son-in-law potential in his new foreman, but in order to avoid being pushed into marriage, Adolph continued his journey westward after two and half years.

Adolph arrived in Denver, Colorado, in 1872, and within a month, he had purchased a partnership in a Denver bottling company. Within a year, Adolph was sole owner of the company. It is said that on Sundays, Adolph roamed the foothills until he ran across an old abandoned tannery on the banks of Clear Creek.

In 1873, Adolph and Jacob Schueler, one of Adolph's bottling customers, opened "The Golden Brewery" with $18,000 from Schueler and Adolph's life savings of $2,000. Adolph died in 1929 before Prohibition ended, but one of his sons, Adolph Jr., assumed control of the brewery. In the year after Prohibition ended, the brewery produced more than 136,000 barrels of beer. Although Coors had only distributed its beer in a few isolated markets before Prohibition, the company began to expand its market to include eleven Western states once it had ended.

Since beer was viewed as important to the morale of the troops in World War II, the government allowed breweries to buy enough barley and other materials to continue brewing beer. However, the beer produced was different from the product produced before the war. The alcohol content was reduced from 4.6 percent to only 3.2 percent. Coors set aside one-half of all the beer it produced and sold it to the military. When the war finally ended, demand continued to grow, thus allowing Coors to double the amount of barrels of beer produced before the war. By 1955, Coors was producing a little more than 1 million per year barrels of beer.

Coors, along with other breweries, began to experiment with beer production by tinkering the packaging, with the sizes, and even with the types of beer produced. Before

1959, kegs and bottles were the primary means of selling beer. Then Coors introduced the first all-aluminum two-piece beverage can, along with a recycling campaign that offered one penny for every can returned to the brewery. Since the introduction of the can helped increase demand for Coors' beer, Bill Coors (a third-generation Coors) decided to develop more new technologies to use in the brewing industry. Coors also made the decision to go international in the 1970s.

Coors introduced the Coors Light brand, also known as the Silver Bullet, in 1978. In response to a national increase in the demand for beer, Coors broke ground on a new packaging facility in Virginia's Shenandoah Valley in 1985. Coors expanded again in 1990 with the purchase of a brewery in Memphis, Tennessee. Both of these locations for expansion were selected after an extensive search for water that held the same high quality characteristics as the water in Golden's Clear Creek.

In the 1990s, under the direction of Peter Coors (a fourth-generation Coors), the company became the third largest brewer in the United States and experienced the fastest volume growth rate in the industry. In addition, Coors began expanding internationally and made its products available to consumers in Canada, Ireland, Japan, the United Kingdom, as well as other smaller countries. Today, Coors' products are available in about thirty international markets.

INTERNAL ISSUES

The Coors approach to growth at the field level is two-pronged: First, to build its big brands in locations where it has a high market share; and second, to go into high-potential markets with strong, committed local wholesaler partners. In both cases, it brings proven market-building expertise and works closely with its distributors to identify opportunities, develop clear strategies, and then execute them.

At the retail level, Coors' unique category management approach is based upon bringing value rather than just gaining shelf space. The company uses a sophisticated, objective process to help retailers sell more beer, not just its own beer. That approach builds relationships, loyalty, and, over time, sales for Coors. In 2000, Coors outpaced the U.S. industry volume growth rate for the fourth consecutive year, posted its fifth consecutive year of double-digit earnings growth, and for the sixth straight year grew Coors Light at a strong single-digit rate.

Coors experienced positive growth momentum in Puerto Rico during the second half of 2000 as a result of a new marketing strategy: It placed a stronger emphasis on Coors Light's attributes across print, outdoor, and point-of-sale media. Today, more than half the beer sold in Puerto Rico is Coors Light. Coors develops new international markets in much the same way it develops domestic ones—with highly focused strategies and strong, committed local distributor partners. Coors Light scored a win in the Canadian province of Quebec, nearly doubling its market share in 2000. Coors is constantly getting stronger through alliances and smart spending.

Responsibility in Advertising

Coors has established its own guidelines to ensure that responsible decisions about drinking are promoted. In fact, Coors was the first brewer to incorporate alcohol awareness messages into national product advertising. Coors places advertising only where the clear majority of the audience is 21 years old or over. Coors regularly monitors all advertising placements for compliance with industry and company standards, and it publicly discloses independent audits of its television placements. To ensure compliance, when applicable, it targets television commercials to select programs: At least 60 percent of the audience must have been 21 or older in the prior reporting period. Strict internal reviews are also conducted on all advertising and marketing materials to avoid any advertising that may be misconstrued as targeted to those under 21. Coors even has a series of television ads featuring Peter Coors, Coors' CEO, which ask underage consumers not to drink and which caution adults to be responsible when they drink. As a result, Coors' advertising in the United States meets or exceeds the advertising and marketing codes of the Beer Institute and Inter-Association Task Force, thus ensuring that the company targets only adult consumers and never promotes product abuse.

Operations

Coors' brewing facilities operate at an estimated annual average of approximately 87 percent of capacity. Annual production capacity varies due to product and packaging mix, product sourcing, and seasonality.

Coors' major facilities are shown below.

Facility	Location	Product
Brewery/packaging	Golden, CO	Malt beverages/packaged malt beverages
Packaging	Elkton, VA (Shenandoah)	Packaged malt beverages
Brewery/packaging	Memphis, TN	Malt beverages/packaged malt beverages
Can and end plants	Golden, CO	Aluminum cans and ends
Bottle plant	Wheat Ridge, CO	Glass bottles
Distribution warehouse	Anaheim, CA	Wholesale beer
Distribution	Meridian, ID	
	Denver, CO	
	Oklahoma City, OK	
	San Bernardino, CA	
	Glenwood Springs, CO	

Source: Coor's 2001 *Annual Report.*

Sales and Distribution

Beer in the United States must be distributed through a three-tier system consisting of manufacturers, distributors, and retailers. A national network of 517 distributors currently delivers Coors' products to U.S. retail markets. Of these distributors, 511 are independent businesses and the other six are owned and operated by one of Coors' subsidiaries. Some distributors operate multiple branches, bringing the total number of U.S. distributor and branch locations to 571 for the year ended December 31, 2000. As a result of Coors' new joint venture with Molson, Coors has an additional 350 to 400 domestic distributors that distribute Molson brands within the United States. Additional independent distributors deliver Coors products to some international markets under licensing and distribution agreements. Coors establishes standards and monitors distributors' methods of handling their products to ensure the highest product quality and freshness. Coors monitors the methods to ensure adherence to proper refrigeration and rotation guidelines for its products at both wholesale and retail locations. Distributors are required to remove Coors products from retailer outlets if they have not sold within a certain period of time.

Coors' highest volume states are California, New Jersey, New York, Pennsylvania, and Texas, which together accounted for 44 percent of the firm's total domestic volume in 2001. Coors has approximately 350 full-time salespeople throughout the United States who work closely with its distributors to assist them in implementing the industry's highest-quality practices to improve efficiency and performance. Coors' sales function is organized into two regions that manage a total of six geographic field business areas responsible for overseeing domestic sales. The company believes that this structure enables its salespeople to better anticipate wholesaler and consumer needs and to respond to those needs locally with greater speed. In addition, Coors has a team of category managers responsible for assisting leading U.S. retailers, such as large supermarket chains, in the management of their beer offerings. Coors' category managers work with retailers to enhance overall beer sales by optimizing space allocation, merchandising displays, promotional campaigns, and product distribution throughout the retailer's chain. Coors believes that its success in category management enhances its competitive position. Coors operates under a functional structure with no divisions. Only about 8 percent of Coors' 5,500 employees in the U.S. are unionized, compared with 31 percent of its 3,150 employees in the U.K.

International Business

Coors' international volume is produced, marketed, and distributed under varying business arrangements, including export, direct investment, joint ventures, and licensing. Coors markets its products to select international markets and to U.S. military bases worldwide. Coors' malt beverages compete with numerous above premium, premium, low-calorie, popular-priced, nonalcoholic, and imported brands. National, regional, local, and international brewers produce these competing brands. Coors competes most directly with Anheuser-Busch, Inc. and the Miller Brewing Company.

Canada

Coors is currently engaged in a partnership with Molson Inc., an alliance that is named Coors Canada and that markets Coors Light in Canada. The partnership contracts with a Molson subsidiary for the brewing, distribution, and sale of products. Coors has a 50.1 percent ownership stake in Coors Canada and Molson has a 49.9 percent ownership stake. The Coors Canada partnership contracts with a Molson subsidiary for the brewing, distribution, and sale of products. Coors Canada manages all marketing activities for Coors products in Canada. Currently, Coors Light has a market share of more than 6 percent and is now the number one light beer—and the fourth-ranked beer brand overall—in Canada.

Puerto Rico and the Caribbean

In Puerto Rico, Coors markets and sells Coors Light to an independent local distributor. A local team of Coors employees manages marketing and promotional efforts in this market. Coors Light is the number-one brand in the Puerto Rico market, with more than a 50 percent market share in 2000. Coors also sells products in several other Caribbean markets, including the U.S. Virgin Islands, through local distributors.

Europe

In Europe, Coors focuses its efforts on Ireland and Northern Ireland, where it markets the Coors Light brand. Additionally, Coors is currently testing Coors Light in Scotland, and it will assess the feasibility of expanding into the United Kingdom. During the fourth quarter of 2000, Coors closed its brewery and commercial operations in Spain. This brewery produced beer for Spain and other European markets. Beginning in late 2000, Coors began sourcing beer for its remaining European markets from its Memphis plant. Thomas Hardy then packages the beer for distribution under contract in the United Kingdom.

Japan

In Japan, Coors Japan Company Ltd., which is located in Tokyo, is the exclusive importer and marketer of Coors products. Currently, the Japanese business is focused on Original Coors and Zima. Coors Japan sells Coors products to independent distributors in Japan.

China

In China, Coors markets Original Coors beer under a licensing arrangement, one focused on select cities, with Carlsberg-Guangdong. Under this arrangement, Coors maintains representative offices that oversee the marketing of its products in China.

Segment and Geographic Information

Coors has one reporting segment relating to the continuing operations of producing, marketing, and selling malt-based beverages. Its operations are conducted in the United States, the country of domicile, and several foreign countries, none of which is individually significant to its overall operations. Exhibit 13 reveals Coors' recent net revenues from external customers, operating income, and pretax income attributable to the United States and all foreign countries.

Environmental Matters

Coors has a tradition of environmental responsibility; it was the company responsible for introducing the aluminum beverage can and aluminum can recycling into the United States in 1959. After facing a number of troubling environmental problems in the early 1990s, Coors responded with aggressive programs that have established comprehensive environmental management systems and that greatly reduced Coors' negative impact on the environment.

Coors, like all breweries, is subject to the requirements of federal, state, local, and foreign environmental and occupational health and safety laws and regulations. Coors continues to promote the efficient use of pollution prevention, resources, and waste reduction. It currently has several programs underway, such as recycling bottles and cans and, where practical, increasing the recycled content of product packaging materials, paper, and other supplies. Each year, Coors diverts thousands of tons of materials from landfills by recycling office paper, corrugated cardboard and paperboard, plastic banding, aluminum, and other scrap metal. Coors conducts regular, comprehensive environmental, health, and safety audits of all of its facilities. Coors is a charter member of the Colorado Pollution Prevention Partnership, a group whose members include companies, environmental organizations, the U.S. Environmental Protection Agency (EPA), and the Colorado Department of Public Health and Environment. The postconsumer recycled content of glass bottles manufactured by Coors grew from 9 percent in 1989 to about 35 percent today. The recycled content of both aluminum and corrugated materials used by Coors is about 70 percent. Most of Coors' paper packaging, which a few years ago could not be recycled, is now 90 percent recyclable.

Coors was one of the several parties named by the EPA as a "potentially responsible party" at the Rocky Flats Industrial Park site. In September 2000, the EPA entered into an Administrative Order on Consent with certain parties, including Coors, requiring implementation of a removal action. Coors' projected costs to construct and monitor the removal action are approximately $300,000. The EPA will also seek to recover its oversight costs associated with the project, costs that cannot be estimated at this time, although Coors believes it would be immaterial to its financial position.

In August 2000, an accidental spill into Clear Creek at the Golden, Colorado, facility caused damage to some of the fish population in the creek. As a result, Coors is required to pay certain fines or other costs by implementing a supplemental environmental project. Coors settled with the Colorado Department of Public Health and Environment regarding violations of its permit in the amount of $98,000 on February 22, 2001. This money was paid to the Clear Creek Watershed Foundation to construct a waste rock repository in Clear Creek County. The company has not yet settled with the Division of Wildlife for damage to the fish population, but it has proposed funding the remaining costs for construction of the waste rock repository. While Coors cannot predict its eventual aggregate cost for environmental and other related matters in which it is currently involved, Coors does believe that any payments, if required, for these matters would be made over a period of time in amounts that would not be material in any one year to its operating results or its financial or competitive position. Coors also believes that adequate reserves have been provided for losses that are probable.

EXTERNAL ISSUES

Competition

Coors' malt beverages compete with numerous above-premium, premium, low-calorie, popular-priced, nonalcoholic, and imported brands. National, regional, local, and international brewers produce these competing brands. Approximately 80 percent of U.S. beer shipments are attributable to the top three domestic brewers: Anheuser-Busch, Inc.; Philip Morris, Inc., through its subsidiary, The Miller Brewing Company; and Coors Brewing Company. Coors competes most directly with Anheuser and Miller, the dominant companies in the U.S. industry. Coors is currently the nation's third-largest brewer and, according to Beer Marketer's Insights estimates, it represented approximately 11.1 percent of the total 2000 U.S. brewing industry shipments of malt beverages (including exports and U.S. shipments of imports). This compares to Anheuser's 48.3 percent share and Miller's 20.6 percent share. Coors beer shipments to wholesalers increased 4.7 percent in 2000, representing the fourth consecutive year in which its shipments have outpaced industry growth by 2 percentage points or more. By comparison, Anheuser's shipments increased 2.7 percent in 2000 and Miller's declined 2.6 percent, due in part to reductions in distributor inventories. More than 85 percent of Coors unit volume was in the premium and above-premium price categories, the highest proportion among the largest domestic brewers. This product mix compares to 77 percent premium-and-above volume for Anheuser and 61 percent for Miller.

Coors continues to face significant competitive disadvantages that relate to economies of scale. Besides lower transportation costs achieved by competitors with multiple breweries, the larger brewers also benefit from economies of scale in advertising spending because of their greater unit sales volumes. In an effort to achieve and maintain national advertising exposure and grow its U.S. market share, Coors generally spends substantially more to market its beer, per barrel, than its major competitors. Although the Coors results are primarily driven by U.S. sales, international operations have increased in importance in recent years, including those in Canada, where Coors Light is the number one light beer.

Today, in 2001, the beer industry in the United States is extremely competitive. Industry volume growth has averaged less than 1 percent annually since 1991. Therefore, growing and even maintaining market share requires substantial and consistent investments in marketing and sales. In 2000, a very competitive year, domestic beer shipments increased less than 1 percent after growing 1.2 percent in 1999. In recent years, brewers have focused less on price discounting strategies and more on marketing, promotions, and innovative packaging in an effort to gain market share.

The industry's pricing environment continued to be positive in 2000, with the announcement of modest price increases on specific packages in select markets. As a result, revenue per barrel increased for major U.S. brewers during the year. However, consumer demand continued to shift away from short bottles and toward long-neck bottles, which cost significantly more to make and ship than short bottles. In addition, many raw material prices increased in 2000, including aluminum, glass, and fuel. In 2000, a significant portion of Coors incremental gross profit generated by volume growth and price increases was reinvested in packaging materials, as well as in additional marketing and sales activities.

A number of important trends continue in the U.S. beer market. The first is a trend toward lighter, more refreshing beers. The largest beer brands that grew in the U.S. market are again American-style light lagers, such as Coors Light. More than 80 percent of Coors' annual unit volume is in light beers. The second trend is toward "trading up," as consumers continued to move away from lower-priced brands to higher-priced brands, including imports. Import beer shipments rose more than 10 percent in 2000. The industry sales trends toward lighter, more upscale beers play to Coors' strengths.

The U.S. brewing industry has experienced significant consolidation in the past several years, which has removed excess capacity. Several competitors have exited the beer business, sold brands, or closed inefficient, outdated brewing facilities. The beer industry is also consolidating at the wholesaler level, a trend that continued in 2000 and generally leads to improved economics for the combining wholesalers and their suppliers. U.S. demographics continued to improve for the beer industry, with the number of consumers reaching legal drinking age continuing to increase in 2000, according to U.S. Census Bureau assessments and projections. These same projections anticipate that the 21-to-24 age group will continue to grow for virtually this entire decade. This trend is important to the beer industry because young adult males tend to consume more beer per capita than other demographic groups.

CONCLUSION

Responsible drinking is an issue of great importance to Coors and the rest of the brewing industry. As a result, Coors is responsible for numerous policies and alcohol programs that encourage responsible drinking. Over the years, Coors has become a leader in the creation and support of initiatives aimed at preventing drunk driving, underage drinking, and other forms of alcohol abuse. Coors does not want its products to be consumed by anyone under the legal drinking age. One of Pete Coors' infamous sayings is "If you're under the legal drinking age, we'll wait for your business"—hence, the company's "21 Means 21" campaign.

Coors needs to continue growing its business and increasing profitability both domestically and internationally. Within the next three years, Coors should open new brewing facilities. By opening one facility per year in high-growth, high-margin segments, Coors should be able to increase its market share and remain at the top.

REFERENCES

Anheuser-Busch *Annual Report* (2000).

Coors Brewing Company, *Annual Report* (2000).

CAULFIELD, KEVIN. "Coors and Ball Corporation Sign Letter of Intent For Aluminum Joint Venture" (September 6, 2001). www.coors.com/newsRelease/2001_sep6.asp.

CAULFIELD, KEVIN. "Peter H. Coors, Chairman, Coors Brewing Company, Urges Support for Tougher Drunk Driving Laws in Colorado" (March 13, 2001). Available at www.coors.com/newsReleases/2001_mar13.asp.

HEALEY, PAT. "Coors Finalizes U.S. Joint Venture with Molson" (January 2, 2001).

Available at www.coors.com/newsReleases/2001_jan2.asp.

MOOZAKIS, CHUCK. "Coors Looks For A Silver Bullet" (July 24, 2001). Available at www.internetwk.com/story/INW20010724S0005.

MURPHY, TARA. "Whassup At Anheuser-Busch" (September 27, 2001). Available at www.biz.yahoo.com.

REUTERS. "Consumers Reaching for Sweets" (November 24, 2001). Available at www.dailynews.yahoo.com.

"Which Brew For You?" *Consumer Reports* (August, 2001): 10–16.

EXHIBIT 1   Coors' Segment Financial Data (in thousands)

	2001	2000	1999
United States and its territories			
Net revenues	$2,353,843	$2,331,693	$2,177,407
Operating income	$ 133,361	$ 163,563	$ 148,823
Pretax income	$ 182,317	$ 185,082	$ 161,281
Other foreign countries			
Net revenues	$ 75,619	$ 82,722	$ 159,077
Operating income (loss)	$ 18,244	$ (12,937)	$ (8,288)
Pretax income (loss)	$ 15,696	$ (15,557)	$ (10,614)

Source: Coors' 2001 *Annual Report,* p. 53.

EXHIBIT 2   Coors' Consolidated Statements of Income
(in thousands, except per-share data, for the years ended)

	December 30, 2001	December 31, 2000	December 26, 1999
Sales – domestic and international	$2,842,752	$2,841,738	$2,642,712
Beer excise taxes	(413,290)	(427,323)	(406,228)
Net sales	2,429,462	2,414,415	2,236,484
Cost of goods sold	(1,537,623)	(1,525,829)	(1,397,251)
Gross profit	891,839	888,586	839,233
Other operating expenses			
Marketing, general and administrative	(717,060)	(722,745)	(692,993)
Special charges	(23,174)	(15,215)	(5,705)
Total other operating expenses	(740,234)	(737,960)	(698,698)
Operating Income	151,605	150,626	140,535
Other Income (expenses)			
Gain on sales of distributorships	27,667	1,000	—
Interest income	16,409	21,325	11,286
Interest expense	(2,006)	(6,414)	(4,357)
Miscellaneous – net	4,338	2,988	3,203
Total	46,408	18,899	10,132
Income before income taxes	198,013	169,525	150,667
Income tax expense	(75,049)	(59,908)	(58,383)
Net income	$ 122,964	$ 109,617	$ 92,284
Other comprehensive income (expense), net of tax			
Foreign currency translation adjustments	14	2,632	(3,519)
Unrealized (loss) gain on available-for-sale securities	3,718	1,268	(397)
Unrealized (loss) gain on derivative instruments	(6,200)	(1,997)	6,835
Minimum pension liability adjustment	(8,487)	—	—
Reclassification adjustments	(4,498)	366	—
Comprehensive income	$ 107,111	$ 111,886	$ 95,203
Net income per share – basic	$ 3.33	$ 2.98	$ 2.51
Net income per share – diluted	$ 3.31	$ 2.93	$ 2.46
Weighted-average shares – basic	36,902	36,785	36,729
Weighted-average shares – diluted	37,177	37,450	37,457

Source: Coors' 2001 *Annual Report,* p. 33.

EXHIBIT 3   Coors' Consolidated Balance Sheets (in thousands)

	December 30, 2001	December 31, 2000
ASSETS		
Current assets		
Cash and cash equivalents	$ 77,133	$ 119,761
Short-term marketable securities	232,572	72,759
Accounts and notes receivable		
Trade, less allowance for doubtful accounts of $91 in 2001 and $139 in 2000	94,985	104,484
Affiliates	223	7,209
Other, less allowance for certain claims of $111 in 2001 and $104 in 2000	13,524	15,385
Inventories		
Finished	32,438	40,039
In process	23,363	23,735
Raw materials	41,534	37,570
Packaging materials, less allowance for obsolete inventories of $2,188 in 2001 and $1,993 in 2000	17,788	8,580
Total inventories	115,123	109,924
Maintenance and operating supplies, less allowance for obsolete supplies of $2,182 in 2001 and $1,621 in 2000	23,454	23,703
Prepaid expenses and other assets	21,722	19,847
Deferred tax asset	27,793	24,679
Total current assets	606,529	497,751
Properties, at cost and net	869,710	735,793
Goodwill and other intangibles, less accumulated amortization of $9,049 in 2001 and $12,981 in 2000	86,289	54,795
Investments in joint ventures, less accumulated amortization of $1,625 in 2001	94,785	56,342
Long-term marketable securities	—	193,675
Other assets	82,379	90,948
Total assets	$1,739,692	$1,629,304

(continued)

EXHIBIT 3   Coors' Consolidated Balance Sheets (in thousands)   **(continued)**

	December 30, 2001	December 31, 2000
LIABILITIES AND SHAREHOLDERS' EQUITY		
Current liabilities		
Accounts payable		
Trade	$ 219,381	$ 186,105
Affiliates	3,112	11,621
Accrued salaries and vacations	56,767	57,041
Taxes, other than income taxes	31,271	32,469
Accrued expenses and other liabilities	122,014	92,100
Current portion of long-term debt	85,000	—
Total current liabilities	517,545	379,336
Long-term debt	20,000	105,000
Deferred tax liability	61,635	89,986
Deferred pension and postretirement benefits	141,720	77,147
Other long-term liabilities	47,480	45,446
Total liabilities	788,380	696,915
Commitments and contingencies		
Shareholders' equity		
Capital stock		
Preferred stock, non-voting, no par value (authorized: 25,000,000 shares, issued and outstanding: none)	—	—
Class A common stock, voting, no par value (authorized, issued and outstanding: 1,260,000 shares)	1,260	1,260
Class B common stock, non-voting, no par value, $0.24 stated value (authorized: 200,000,000 shares; issued and outstanding: 34,689,410 in 2001 and 35,871,121 in 2000)	8,259	8,541
Total capital stock	9,519	9,801
Paid-in capital	—	11,332
Unvested restricted stock	(597)	(129)
Retained earnings	954,981	908,123
Accumulated other comprehensive income	(12,591)	3,262
Total shareholders' equity	951,312	932,389
Total liabilities and shareholders' equity	$1,739,692	$1,629,304

Source: Coors' 2001 *Annual Report,* p. 34.